Forensic Science

Forensic Science

Volume 1

Accelerants—DNA database controversies

Edited by

Ayn Embar-Seddon
Capella University

Allan D. Pass
National Behavioral Science Consultants

Salem Press, Inc.
Pasadena, California   Hackensack, New Jersey

Editorial Director: Christina J. Moose

Development Editor: R. Kent Rasmussen   *Layout:* Mary Overell

Project Editor: Judy Selhorst   *Graphics and Design:* James Hutson

Acquisitions Editor: Mark Rehn   *Photo Editor:* Cynthia Breslin Beres

Production Editor: Joyce I. Buchea   *Editorial Assistant:* Dana Garey

Cover photo: Scott Rubins/Forensic Futures Education Group/www.forensicfutures.com

Library of Congress Cataloging-in-Publication Data

Forensic science / edited by Ayn Embar-Seddon, Allan D. Pass.
   p. cm.
Includes bibliographical references and index.
   ISBN 978-1-58765-423-7 (set : alk. paper) — ISBN 978-1-58765-424-4 (vol. 1 : alk. paper) — ISBN 978-1-58765-425-1 (vol. 2 : alk. paper) — ISBN 978-1-58765-426-8 (vol. 3 : alk. paper) 1. Forensic sciences. I. Embar-Seddon, Ayn. II. Pass, Allan D.

HV8073.F5837 2009
363.25—dc22

2008030674

Contents

Contents

Publisher's Note

This entirely new and comprehensive reference work, *Forensic Science*, addresses the rapidly growing academic and public interest in the application of the sciences to criminal investigations. The extent of this interest can be measured by the expansion of academic courses on forensics and criminal justice in schools and colleges and by the proliferation of popular television programs, both dramatic and documentary, on crime scene investigations. Articles in *Forensic Science*'s three volumes cover many topics that figure prominently in the media; however, the set's basic approach to forensic science is factual, and it lays great stress on offering up-to-date material on hard topics in this rapidly advancing field.

Often called simply "forensics" within the legal world, forensic science is essentially the application of the natural sciences to the analyzing and interpreting of legal evidence, particularly in criminal cases. Since the beginning of the twenty-first century—and especially since the terrorist attacks on the United States of September 11, 2001—there has been an explosion of both public and academic interest in the use of forensic techniques to investigate criminal acts. American television audiences have developed a seemingly insatiable appetite for shows such as *CSI: Crime Scene Investigation* and *Bones* that go into the minutiae of forensic techniques. During the spring of 2008, as many as five such shows ranked among the fifteen top-rated television programs during any given week. However, while these shows tend to emphasize crimes of violence, particularly murder, the real-world applications of forensic science are far broader.

It is clear that the forensic sciences play a major role in investigations of murder and other violent crimes. However, they also play equally important roles in investigations into many other types of criminal and civil cases, ranging from arson fires and contract disputes to forgery, paternity suits, and war crimes. Forensic techniques are also often central to efforts to identify victims of major accidents and natural disasters. All these subjects are covered in detail within these volumes.

Scope of This Set

Forensic Science contains 460 articles arranged in alphabetical order that range in length from 500 to 3,000 words. The set approaches the forensic sciences from several different perspectives. The primary perspective is that of investigators in the diverse subspecialties that make up the forensic sciences. The impressive variety of these fields can be seen at a glance in the titles of articles such as Forensic accounting, Forensic anthropology, Forensic archaeology, Forensic botany, Forensic entomology, Forensic geoscience, Forensic nursing, Forensic odontology, Forensic palynology, Forensic pathology, Forensic photography, Forensic psychiatry, Forensic psychology, Forensic sculpture, and Forensic toxicology. Those topics are joined by Ballistics, Computer forensics, Cryptology and number theory, Living forensics, Parasitology, Physiology, Serology, Structural analysis, Taphonomy, Thanatology, Viral biology, and Wildlife forensics.

Attention is also given to the many professional organizations in forensic science fields, such as the American Academy of Forensic Sciences, the American Society of Crime Laboratory Directors, and the International Association of Forensic Toxicologists. In addition to the core articles on subspecialties and allied fields, the set has articles on 30 specific types of investigations, ranging from Alcohol-related offenses, Arson, and Art forgery to Ritual killing, Sports memorabilia fraud, and Suicide.

More than 100 articles focus on investigative techniques and procedures. These include overviews of general subjects such as accident investigation and reconstruction, crime scene investigation, and quantitative and qualitative analysis of chemicals, along with more specialized techniques and procedures, such as autopsies, chromatography, crime scene photography, fingerprint analysis, and polygraph analysis. More than 35 articles examine specialized equipment, such as biodetectors and other detection devices, protective gear, and chemical reagents.

A second broad perspective in *Forensic Science* might be called the scene of the crime. Particularly important within this category are articles on types of evidence, such as fire debris, fibers and filaments, glass, soil, and bloodstains. Other articles cover both general and specific aspects of chemical and biological agents, such as biotoxins, carbon monoxide, illicit drugs, and a variety of poisons. At the center of crime scenes are the participants—the offenders, victims, and witnesses. More than 40 articles cover diverse diseases, medical conditions, and injuries, including various kinds of wounds.

A third broad perspective in *Forensic Science* is the role of the forensic sciences in the American legal system. The set includes brief articles on some of the most important federal laws applying to controlled substances, such as the Harrison Narcotic Drug Act of 1914, the Controlled Substances Act of 1970, and the Anabolic Steroid Control Act of 2004, as well as such international agreements as the Chemical Weapons Convention of 1993. Articles on selected U.S. Supreme Court decisions, including *Miranda v. Arizona*, and a variety of important legal principles, such as habeas corpus and *mens rea*, also help to illuminate the legal dimensions of the forensic sciences. Law-enforcement bodies and government investigative units covered in the set include the U.S. Drug Enforcement Administration, the Federal Bureau of Investigation, and the U.S. Secret Service as well as the Environmental Measurements Laboratory and the National Transportation Safety Board.

A fourth perspective of *Forensic Science*—and one that should have wide appeal to many readers—is its extensive coverage of specific historical subjects. These range from overviews of ancient criminal cases and crime mysteries and ancient science to examinations of such high-profile modern criminal cases as the O. J. Simpson murder trial, the Unabomber case, and criminal cases involving celebrities. The set also includes articles on such subjects as the Lindbergh baby kidnapping case, the exhumations of the remains of U.S. presidents Zachary Taylor and Abraham Lincoln, and mysteries surrounding the deaths of the French emperor Napoleon I and composer Ludwig van Beethoven. These historical topics serve as fascinating case studies in the practical application of forensic science.

Finally, *Forensic Science* makes a special effort to address depictions of forensics in the media. Long overview articles examine misconceptions fostered by the media and the treatment of forensic science in television, literature, and journalism. Briefer articles cover such iconic individual television programs as *CSI*, *Cold Case*, and *Forensic Files*. A special appendix offers brief descriptions of many other television programs.

Organization and Format

The set's alphabetical arrangement—which includes headnote cross-references of alternative terms (such as "Lie detectors. *See* Polygraph analysis")—makes topics easy to find. As in Salem's other encyclopedic reference works, articles in *Forensic Science* contain helpful top matter that defines the topics and offers compact summaries of their relevance to forensic science. Every article also contains a "Further Reading" section, followed by a generous list of cross-references to related topics within the set. The text of the articles is supplemented by more than 250 photographs and more than 180 maps, charts, graphs, and illustrative sidebars.

The appendixes in volume 3 include a guide to Internet resources, a directory of television shows in which forensic science figures prominently, a biographical directory of key figures in the history of the field, a time line of major events, an annotated bibliography of general works, and a glossary. Additional finding aids include a general subject index at the end of volume 3, the complete list of the set's contents at the beginning of each volume, and a list of topics by category at the end of each volume.

Acknowledgments

Salem Press would like to thank the 172 scholars who contributed original articles to *Forensic Science*. Their names and affiliations are listed in the pages that follow here. This publication is especially indebted to its editors, Dr. Ayn Embar-Seddon of Capella University and Dr. Allan D. Pass of National Behavioral Science Consultants.

Contributors

Richard Adler
*University of Michigan,
    Dearborn*

Catherine G. Bailey
*Stetson University College
    of Law*

Thomas E. Baker
University of Scranton

Carl L. Bankston III
Tulane University

Amy L. Barber
Michigan State University

Charlene F. Barroga
*University of California,
    San Diego*

Eric J. Bartelink
*California State University,
    Chico*

Kevin M. Beaver
Florida State University

Raymond D. Benge, Jr.
Tarrant County College

Alvin K. Benson
Utah Valley State University

R. L. Bernstein
New Mexico State University

Robert Bockstiegel
Portland, Oregon

Vivian Bodey
Southwestern Law School

Megan N. Bottegal
*Florida International
    University*

Cliff Boyd
Radford University

Donna C. Boyd
Radford University

Jocelyn M. Brineman
*University of North Carolina
    at Charlotte*

Michael P. Brown
Ball State University

Kevin G. Buckler
*University of Texas at
    Brownsville and Texas
    Southmost College*

Amy Webb Bull
Tennessee State University

Michael A. Buratovich
Spring Arbor University

Mary Car-Blanchard
iHealthSpot.com

Russell N. Carney
Missouri State University

Dennis W. Cheek
*Ewing Marion Kauffman
    Foundation*

Michael W. Cheek
American University

Jennifer L. Christian
Indiana University

Douglas Clouatre
*Mid-Plains Community
    College*

Susan Coleman
West Texas A&M University

Sally A. Coulson
*Institute of Environmental
    Science and Research*

Anne Coxon
*Institute of Environmental
    Science and Research*

Helen Davidson
Portland, Oregon

Martiscia Davidson
Fremont, California

Jennifer Davis
University of Dayton

Seth G. Dewey
Canisius College

Thomas E. DeWolfe
Hampden-Sydney College

Shawkat Dhanani
*Veterans Administration
    Greater Los Angeles
    Healthcare System*

Jackie Dial
*American Medical Writers
    Association*

Joseph Di Rienzi
*College of Notre Dame of
    Maryland*

Kimberly D. Dodson
Lincoln Memorial University

Douglas Elliot
*Institute of Environmental
    Science and Research*

Stephanie K. Ellis
Marymount University

Ayn Embar-Seddon
Capella University

Patricia E. Erickson
Canisius College

Elisabeth Faase
*Athens Regional Medical
Center*

Erin J. Farley
*University of North Carolina
at Wilmington*

Ronald P. Fisher
*Florida International
University*

Dale L. Flesher
University of Mississippi

David R. Foran
Michigan State University

Carl Franklin
Southern Utah University

Dante B. Gatmaytan
University of the Philippines

Gilbert Geis
*University of California,
Irvine*

Phyllis B. Gerstenfeld
*California State University,
Stanislaus*

James S. Godde
Monmouth College

Timothy L. Hall
University of Mississippi

David T. Hardy
Tucson, Arizona

Elizabeth K. Hayden
Northeastern University

Peter B. Heller
Manhattan College

Taiping Ho
Ball State University

Jerry W. Hollingsworth
McMurry University

Kimberley M. Holloway
King College

Mary Hurd
*East Tennessee State
University*

Domingo Jariel
*Louisiana State University
at Eunice*

Edward Johnson
University of New Orleans

Helen Jones
*Manchester Metropolitan
University*

Phill Jones
Spokane, Washington

Susan J. Karcher
Purdue University

Ryan Kelly
Monmouth University

Kelvin Keraga
*New York State Energy
Research and
Development Authority*

M. A. Q. Khan
*University of Illinois at
Chicago*

S. F. Khan
*University of Illinois at
Chicago*

Brianne M. Kiley
Michigan State University

Paul M. Klenowski
Thiel College

Robert Klose
University College of Bangor

David B. Kopel
Independence Institute

Steven A. Kuhl
V and R Consulting

David J. Ladouceur
University of Notre Dame

Lisa LaGoo
Michigan State University

Kristin E. Landfield
Emory University

Abraham D. Lavender
*Florida International
University*

Justyna Lenik
Loyola University Chicago

Erin J. Lenz
Michigan State University

Thomas T. Lewis
St. Cloud State University

Scott O. Lilienfeld
Emory University

Keith G. Logan
Kutztown University

Arthur J. Lurigio
Loyola University Chicago

Richard D. McAnulty
*University of North Carolina
at Charlotte*

Kimberley A. McClure
Western Illinois University

Richard L. McWhorter
*Prairie View A&M
University*

Eric Madfis
Northeastern University

Marianne M. Madsen
*ARUP Laboratories,
University of Utah*

Sergei A. Markov
Austin Peay State University

Lucas J. Marshall
Michigan State University

Eric Metchik
Salem State College

Ralph R. Meyer
University of Cincinnati

Randall L. Milstein
Oregon State University

Damon Mitchell
*Central Connecticut State
University*

Robin Kamienny Montvilo
Rhode Island College

Mario Morelli
Western Illinois University

Lilliana I. Moreno
*Florida International
University*

R. K. Morgan-Smith
*Institute of Environmental
Science and Research*

Turhon A. Murad
*California State University,
Chico*

Michael J. Mutolo
Michigan State University

Edward C. Nwanegbo
*Siouxland Medical
Education Foundation*

Douglas A. Orr
Spokane, Washington

Robert J. Paradowski
*Rochester Institute of
Technology*

Allan D. Pass
*National Behavioral Science
Consultants*

Cheryl Pawlowski
*University of Northern
Colorado*

John R. Phillips
Purdue University Calumet

Nickie D. Phillips
St. Francis College

Nancy A. Piotrowski
*University of California,
Berkeley*

Daniel Pontzer
University of North Florida

Judy L. Porter
*Rochester Institute of
Technology*

Frank J. Prerost
Midwestern University

Maureen Puffer-Rothenberg
Valdosta State University

Cynthia Racer
American Chemical Society

Robert J. Ramsey
Indiana University East

Lillian M. Range
*Our Lady of Holy Cross
College*

Shamir Ratansi
*Central Connecticut State
University*

Margaret C. Reardon
*Florida International
University*

Betty Richardson
*Southern Illinois University
at Edwardsville*

Alice C. Richer
*Spaulding Rehabilitation
Center*

Gina M. Robertiello
Felician College

James C. Roberts
University of Scranton

James L. Robinson
*University of Illinois at
Urbana-Champaign*

Charles W. Rogers
*Southwestern Oklahoma
State University*

Stephen F. Rohde
Rohde & Victoroff

Carol A. Rolf
Rivier College

Kelly Rothenberg
Valdosta, Georgia

David A. Rusak
University of Scranton

Lawrence M. Salinger
Arkansas State University

Neva E. J. Sanders-Dewey
Canisius College

Lisa M. Sardinia
Pacific University

Elizabeth D. Schafer
Loachapoka, Alabama

Heidi V. Schumacher
University of Colorado at Boulder

Jason J. Schwartz
Los Angeles, California

Miriam E. Schwartz
University of California, Los Angeles

Julia E. Selman-Ayetey
King's College London

Brion Sever
Monmouth University

Manoj Sharma
University of Cincinnati

Elizabeth Algren Shaw
Ziegler, Metzger & Miller

Taylor Shaw
ADVANCE Education and Development Center

Martha Sherwood
Kent Anderson Law Associates

Lisa J. Shientag
New York University School of Medicine

R. Baird Shuman
University of Illinois at Urbana-Champaign

Dwight G. Smith
Southern Connecticut State University

Ruth Waddell Smith
Michigan State University

Richard S. Spira
American Veterinary Medical Association

Steven Stack
Wayne State University

Sharon W. Stark
Monmouth University

Rick M. Steinmann
Clarion University-Venango Campus

Joan C. Stevenson
Western Washington University

Russell S. Strasser
George Washington University

David R. Struckhoff
Loyola University Chicago

Patrick Sylvers
Emory University

Rena Christina Tabata
University of British Columbia

Lawrence C. Trostle
University of Alaska Anchorage

Dwight Tshudy
Gordon College

Ruth N. Udey
Michigan State University

Oluseyi A. Vanderpuye
Albany State University

Alana Van Gundy-Yoder
Miami University Hamilton

Sheryl L. Van Horne
Pennsylvania State University

Linda Volonino
Canisius College

C. J. Walsh
Mote Marine Laboratory

Donald A. Watt
Dakota Wesleyan University

James Watterson
Laurentian University

Marcia J. Weiss
Point Park University

George M. Whitson III
University of Texas at Tyler

LaVerne McQuiller Williams
Rochester Institute of Technology

Bradley R. A. Wilson
University of Cincinnati

Richard L. Wilson
University of Tennessee at Chattanooga

Michael Windelspecht
Ricochet Creative Productions

Ming Y. Zheng
Gordon College

Complete List of Contents

Volume 1

Volume 2

Volume 3

Forensic Science

Accelerants

Definition: Any substances, most commonly ignitable liquids, used intentionally to increase the rate and spread of fires.

Significance: In a fire investigation, the primary goal is to identify whether the fire was accidental or intentional. The presence of an accelerant at a fire scene is often indicative of an intentional fire, or arson. Accelerants can be identified from fire debris through conventional forensic analysis.

Accelerants are commonly used in arson fires because they provide additional fuel in areas where the items present may not burn easily. Arsonists often pour accelerants over the areas they want to burn to ensure that their fires spread as much as possible to maximize damage and destruction. Common accelerants are commercially available ignitable liquids—such as gasoline, lighter fluid, and kerosene—that are readily accessible to the arsonist. The identification of an accelerant is significant evidence in a fire investigation because it suggests that the fire was set intentionally.

Identification at the Fire Scene

The identification of accelerants at fire scenes is often a challenge for investigators. Examination of the fire debris by various techniques can be useful in identifying the origin of a fire and any areas of potential accelerant use. After the preliminary identification of a potential accelerant source, samples can be collected and taken back to the forensics laboratory for further analysis.

The types of fire debris most likely to contain sufficient accelerant residue for analysis are porous materials, such as wood and carpet, which can trap residual liquid. Accelerant residue can also pool in the cracks in floors, where it is somewhat protected from the fire. Investigators should collect and store any debris suspected to contain accelerant residue in airtight containers, preferably metal paint cans with friction lids, to eliminate the possibility of the loss of the volatile components within the samples.

Extraction Techniques

Gas chromatography coupled with mass spectrometry is the most common technique used for the analysis of accelerants from fire debris. Before fire debris evidence can be analyzed using the dual instrument known as the gas chromatograph-mass spectrometer (GC-MS), however, the accelerant residue must first be extracted from the debris that was collected. Several techniques can be used to perform this extraction, and each has its own advantages and disadvantages.

In a solvent extraction, the fire debris is washed with a solvent that will dissolve the accelerant residue but not the debris, such as carbon disulfide. The extract can then be injected directly into the GC-MS. A drawback of solvent extraction is that large amounts of potentially hazardous solvents are required to perform an efficient extraction; in addition, this method does not concentrate the accelerant residue effectively. Although solvent extraction was at one time a popular method, it has generally been replaced by quicker, more efficient preconcentration techniques.

In passive headspace extraction, the metal paint can used to collect the debris is heated so that any accelerant present is vaporized and becomes saturated within the area above the debris in the can, which is known as the headspace. A small hole is made in the top of the can and a gastight syringe is used to draw up a sample of the vapor in the headspace, which can then be injected into the GC-MS. Passive headspace extraction is biased toward the more volatile components, but it minimizes the capacity for cross-contamination of the evidence because the accelerant residue is extracted from the same container in which the debris was collected.

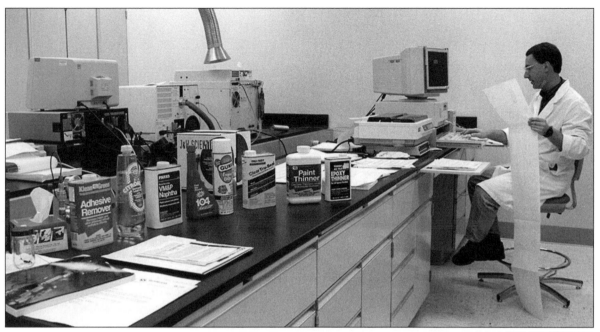

A forensic scientist who specializes in arson study analyzes data from an arson scene in the Kentucky State Police Crime Lab in Franklin County. Arrayed on the counter to his left are several substances that are used as accelerants in arson fires. *(AP/Wide World Photos)*

A variation of the passive headspace extraction technique is adsorption/elution, in which the debris is heated in the can with a strip of activated charcoal suspended in the headspace. The accelerant vapor is trapped on the strip, from which it is dissolved by a solvent for injection into the GC-MS. Adsorption/elution is affected by the same volatility bias as the passive headspace method, but because the vapor is concentrated onto the charcoal strip, adsorption/elution greatly decreases the potential loss of low-volatility compounds.

The solid-phase microextraction (SPME) technique employs a coated fiber that is housed in a retractable apparatus. The can containing the debris is heated, and this fiber is subjected to the headspace of the can, where the accelerant vapor adsorbs onto the fiber. One advantage of SPME is that the fiber apparatus can be placed directly into the injection port of the GC-MS. The heat of the injection port causes the accelerant trapped on the fiber to desorb from the fiber so that it can be carried into the instrument for analysis. Another advantage of SPME is its potential use for on-site accelerant collection. An investigator can use the SPME fiber apparatus to adsorb accelerant vapor at the fire scene; with the fiber retracted into the apparatus, it is protected from the environment and can be transported directly to the laboratory for analysis.

Instrumental Analysis

Although many techniques have proven useful in accelerant identification, gas chromatography (GC) is by far the most commonly used technique in the forensics laboratory for fire debris analysis. GC is a separation technique that is capable of isolating the numerous individual compounds present in typically complex accelerants. The result of a GC analysis is a chromatogram, which is essentially a chart in which all the components are represented as individual peaks. The pattern of these peaks does not change for a substance and thus is characteristic of that substance. Therefore, when an accelerant residue is examined by GC, its peak pattern can be matched to the peak pattern of a known sample of the same accelerant analyzed for comparison.

When GC is coupled with mass spectrometry (MS), the chemical composition of a sample can be identified conclusively. The pairing of GC and MS allows the identification of individual peaks within the peak pattern and thus is the standard convention for accelerant identification. It should be noted that accelerant identification is considered class evidence because it cannot be individualized to one source. For example, if an accelerant is identified to be gasoline, the pump or even the service station from which it was purchased cannot be determined because of the inherent variation in the process of refining crude oil.

The American Society for Testing and Materials (ASTM), an organization that generates and maintains standards for procedures and materials in a wide array of fields, has developed standard accelerant classes for the identification of accelerants in court. The ASTM classification system for ignitable liquids provides a standardized method of accelerant description for forensic scientists. In this system, nine classes of ignitable liquids are subdivided into three boiling point ranges (light, medium, and heavy). The nine classes—gasoline, petroleum distillates, isoparaffinic products, aromatic products, naphthenic-paraffinic products, normal alkane products, dearomatized distillates, oxygenated solvents, and a final miscellaneous grouping—and their subdivisions provide standard guidelines for the identification of ignitable liquids based on chemical composition.

Difficulties in Identification

Although chromatographic pattern matching is the convention for the identification of accelerants in a forensics laboratory, some factors can alter chromatographic patterns and make it difficult for investigators to identify conclusively any accelerant that may be present. Most common accelerants contain refined petroleum products, which are mixtures of hydrocarbons, and several of these hydrocarbons are found in everyday household products. For example, basic carpeting such as that found in many homes contains compounds similar to those found in common accelerants. This overlap presents a problem for a scientist attempting to identify an accelerant that soaked into a carpet before it was burned.

An efficient extraction technique, such as adsorption/elution or SPME, can separate an accelerant from the fire debris itself. Investigators can also use a data-processing technique called extracted ion chromatography (EIC)—in which specific characteristic peaks can be isolated from other peaks—to understand the data more fully. Because of the potential problem of interference, fire investigators should collect several debris samples, including samples in which no accelerant is expected to be found, in order to understand which chromatographic peaks correspond to the debris and which peaks correspond to an actual accelerant.

Lucas J. Marshall

Further Reading

Almirall, José R., and Kenneth G. Furton, eds. *Analysis and Interpretation of Fire Scene Evidence.* Boca Raton, Fla.: CRC Press, 2004. Presents comprehensive information about fire scene investigation and the chemical analysis of fire debris.

DeHaan, John D. *Kirk's Fire Investigation.* 6th ed. Upper Saddle River, N.J.: Pearson Prentice Hall, 2007. Detailed volume covers the physical nature and chemistry of fire and also discusses the various types of fires.

Nic Daéid, Niamh, ed. *Fire Investigation.* Boca Raton, Fla.: CRC Press, 2004. Compilation provides material on the basics of fire investigation with emphasis on laboratory reconstruction and analytical techniques.

Redsicker, David R., and John J. O'Connor. *Practical Fire and Arson Investigation.* 2d ed. Boca Raton, Fla.: CRC Press, 1997. Presents extensive information on the various undertakings of the fire investigator, from scene investigation to courtroom testimony.

Saferstein, Richard. *Criminalistics: An Introduction to Forensic Science.* 9th ed. Upper Saddle River, N.J.: Pearson Prentice Hall, 2007. Textbook discusses the different forensic science fields, including arson investigation.

Tilstone, William J., Kathleen A. Savage, and Leigh A. Clark. *Forensic Science: An Encyclopedia of History, Methods, and Techniques.* Santa Barbara, Calif.: ABC-CLIO, 2006. General reference work covers a broad range of topics in forensic science.

See also: Arson; Bureau of Alcohol, Tobacco, Firearms and Explosives; Burn pattern analysis; Column chromatography; Fire debris; Gas chromatography; Mass spectrometry; National Church Arson Task Force.

Accident investigation and reconstruction

Definition: Collection and analysis of evidence at the scenes of transportation accidents to create models explaining what happened.

Significance: In determining responsibility for motor vehicle and other kinds of transportation accidents, forensic scientists attempt to reconstruct what happened during these events by analyzing the available evidence. The testimony of accident investigators often plays a role in criminal and civil proceedings that stem from accidents.

In the United States, transportation accident investigation and reconstruction are usually carried out by police departments. Some accident investigations, however, fall under federal jurisdiction. The National Transportation Safety Board (NTSB), formed in 1967 as part of the U.S. Department of Transportation, replaced the Civil Aeronautics Board and expanded the role of the federal government in accident investigation and reconstruction. The NTSB became an independent agency in 1975; its duties include the investigation of all civil aviation accidents in the United States as well as all major railroad, highway, marine, and pipeline accidents and any transportation accidents that involve the release of hazardous materials. Private companies also offer accident investigation and reconstruction services.

Accident Investigators

When transportation accidents occur, law-enforcement agencies, insurance companies, manufacturers of the vehicles involved, and the persons involved, including those injured, all have interests in understanding the causes of the accidents and in assigning responsibility. Police officers normally are the first individuals to investigate traffic accidents. Typically, when a serious accident has taken place, the police deal first with any injured people and any hazardous situations created by the accident; they then record information that will allow them to assess how the accident occurred. Most police officers in the United States receive at least brief training in accident investigation; some receive additional specialist training. The accuracy and completeness of the evidence collected by the police at an accident scene affects the degree of accuracy of the accident reconstruction.

In accidents that fall under the jurisdiction of the NTSB, the NTSB becomes the lead investigative agency. In such a case, the role of the local police department initially is to handle any casualties and hazards caused by the accident and then to preserve the scene to the greatest degree possible. NTSB specialists are experienced investigators with strong academic backgrounds in forensic science, physics, structural engineering, aeronautical engineering, and similar fields. NTSB investigators are qualified to serve as expert witnesses in court.

Insurance companies often have their own accident investigators. These investigators, as well as independent investigators hired by attorneys and other interested parties, often enter the accident and reconstruction process after much of the debris from the accident has been cleared away. They may have the opportunity to examine the damaged vehicles, but in attempting to reconstruct the accident they usually must depend on other evidence collected by the police at the accident scene.

Some disagreement exists among experts in accident reconstruction concerning the degree of training and education necessary to qualify an individual as an accident and reconstruction specialist and as an expert witness. Since 1991, the Accreditation Commission for Traffic Accident Reconstruction (ACTAR) has promoted voluntary standards for traffic accident investigators in order to encourage accuracy, consistency, and professionalism in accident investigation and reconstruction. These standards have not been universally adopted, however.

At the highest level, accident reconstruction specialists hold university degrees in engineering, mathematics, physics, or similar fields and have years of experience related to crash analysis and reconstruction. In the United States, the National Academy of Forensic Engineers is empowered by the Council of Engineering and Scientific Specialty Boards to certify accident investigation and reconstruction specialists as "diplomate forensic engineers." This is the highest level of certification, the engineering equivalent of being a board-certified medical specialist. The International Institute of Forensic Engineering Sciences also awards diplomate status to qualified forensic engineers and forensic science professionals.

At the other end of the spectrum, individuals who do not even have high school diplomas can enroll in vocational training programs that focus on accident investigation and reconstruction. These programs call their graduates "certified accident reconstructionists," although many lack the background to do necessary mathematical analyses of accident scenes. Some courts in the United States have begun to reject certified accident reconstructionists as expert witnesses, requiring those who provide expert testimony on accidents to have higher levels of education and expertise.

The Investigation Phase

After immediate needs involving injuries and hazards have been attended to at the scene of an accident, the investigation phase begins. In collecting evidence at an accident scene, the investigators perform some or all of the following tasks: taking witness statements, photographing damage to vehicles and property, measuring and recording tire (skid) marks, recording paint

Crime novelist Patricia Cornwell examines the remains of a small plane dropped from a helicopter during an accident investigation exercise for crime scene investigator trainees at the University of Tennessee's National Forensic Academy in 2005. A best-selling author, Cornwell writes mostly about cases involving a fictional medical examiner, Dr. Kay Scarpetta. (AP/Wide World Photos)

and gouge marks, recording the postcrash locations of all vehicles involved, and recording the positions of all pieces of debris from the accident with photographs and measurements. Using this information, the investigators create a grid map of the crash scene that shows, with measurements, where each skid mark, vehicle, and piece of collision debris and damaged property is located in relation to all others.

Primary accident investigators also use a Haddon matrix to record situational evidence relative to the accident. This tool, developed around 1970 by Dr. William Haddon, the first head of what later became the National Highway Traffic Safety Administration, is a grid on which investigators record information about various conditions before, during, and after the accident at the accident scene. The most common Haddon matrix used for traffic accidents has three rows and three columns, creating nine cells. The rows represent events occurring before the crash, during the crash, and after the crash, respectively, and the columns identify the following factors that could have affected the accident in each time period: human factors (for example, impaired vision, precrash alcohol consumption, speeding, failure to wear a seat belt), vehicle and equipment factors (for example, failed brakes, nonfunctioning lights, mal-functioning air bags, poorly designed fuel tanks that leaked or exploded), and physical, social, and economic factors (for example, missing road signs, nonfunctioning traffic signals, absence of or poorly designed guardrails, cultural attitudes toward alcohol consumption or speeding, interference with or delayed emergency services response).

The Reconstruction Phase

During the reconstruction phase, accident investigators apply their knowledge of the laws of physics to the evidence to determine such elements as the speeds of the vehicles involved, the angle of initial impact, the occurrence of secondary impacts, mechanical failures that may have caused the accident, and environmental factors that may affect responsibility for the accident. Damage-based reconstruction is one of the oldest and simplest forms of accident reconstruction. In this approach, the reconstructionist looks at the damage done by and to vehicles and property.

By using information from vehicle manufacturers and applying knowledge of the laws of physics and structural analysis, the reconstructionist is able to determine the approximate rates of speed of the vehicles and their angle of impact. Damage-based reconstruction requires many assumptions and simplifications. For example, car manufacturers provide the results of crash tests for reconstruction engineers, but in using such results, a reconstructionist must assume that the vehicle involved in the accident had the same structural properties as a new vehicle of the same model that was used in the crash tests.

Ideally, damage-based reconstruction should be done in conjunction with trajectory-based reconstruction, which is based on the principle that momentum (speed multiplied by mass) is conserved in a crash. Starting

Electronic Evidence Improves Precision and Confidence

Many new automobiles are equipped with event data recorders, also known as black boxes. These boxes store data about cars' speed and handling that can provide crucial evidence in accident cases. In November, 2004, Danny Hopkins was convicted of second-degree manslaughter for causing the death of Lindsay Kyle in a car accident. The event data recorder in Hopkins's car had shown that the vehicle was traveling at 106 miles per hour just four seconds before it crashed into the back of Kyle's car, which was stopped at a red light. If Hopkins's car had not been equipped with an event data recorder, a forensic investigation of the physical evidence, such as skid marks and crash damage, could have been used to estimate the speed of the car. The recorder's data evidence, however, provided better precision, increasing the investigators' confidence that the driver's speed was 106 miles per hour at the time of impact.

Linda Volonino

with where the vehicles and debris ended up after a crash, reconstructionists work backward to determine the speed of each vehicle at impact. This method must also take into account forces such as friction of tires on the road, which reduces momentum, and whether the road was wet or dry. The mathematics required to perform trajectory-based reconstruction can be complex, and software programs are available to help with these calculations.

Ultimately, the reconstruction of an accident is only as good as the original information provided by those who measured and recorded the accident scene. All reconstructions involve assumptions, simplifications, and interpretations. Good reconstruction engineers are able to explain their analyses and provide scientific justifications for their conclusions that will stand up to expert examination in a court of law.

Martiscia Davidson

Further Reading

Andrews, Dennis R. "Accident Reconstruction from the Outside in." *Claims* 54 (June, 2006): 18-22. Presents a nontechnical explanation of the information that can be gained from traffic accident reconstruction.

Hermance, Richard. *Snowmobile and ATV Accident Investigation and Reconstruction.* 2d ed. Tucson, Ariz.: Lawyers & Judges Publishing, 2006. Focuses on the investigation of accidents involving off-road vehicles.

Palmer, Scott. "Fighting Fraud with Forensic Intelligence." *Claims* 55 (September, 2007): 54-59. Explains how accident reconstruction can be useful in the investigation of insurance claims.

Rivers, R. W. *Evidence in Traffic Crash Investigation and Reconstruction: Identification, Interpretation, and Analysis of Evidence, and the Traffic Crash Investigation and Reconstruction Process.* Springfield, Ill.: Charles C Thomas, 2006. Comprehensive volume addresses all aspects of the investigation of traffic accidents, including preservation of evidence and accident reconstruction.

Wheat, Arnold G. *Accident Investigation Training Manual.* Clifton Park, N.Y.: Thomson/Delmar Learning, 2005. Provides an extensive introduction to accident investigation, including reconstruction techniques.

See also: Crime scene measurement; Crime scene reconstruction and staging; Cross-contamination of evidence; Direct versus circumstantial evidence; Flight data recorders; Hit-and-run vehicle offenses; ValuJet Flight 592 crash investigation.

Acid-base indicators

Definition: Substances that show the acidity or alkalinity of solutions within a narrow range.

Significance: Among the tools forensic scientists use to identify unknown substances are acid-base indicators, also known as pH indicators. Such indicators can also enable scientists to detect the presence of contaminating chemicals in solutions, and their use in the analysis of human tissues can provide clues to cause of death.

The acidity or alkalinity of a substance is indicated by its pH, which is a measure of the concentration of hydrogen ions (H^+) in a solution. The pH scale is logarithmic and ranges from 0 to 14. The lower the pH, the more acidic the solution, and the higher the pH, the more alkaline, or basic, the solution; pH 7.0 is neutral and is the pH of pure water.

Acid-base indicators are organic dyes that change color depending on the concentration of hydrogen ions present in a solution. The change does not become visible at a precise point; rather, it happens within a fairly narrow pH range. Many different acid-base indicators are available, and they change colors within different pH ranges. For example, phenolphthalein is colorless at a pH of 8.2 but turns red at a pH of 10. Methyl orange is red at a pH of 3.2 but turns yellow at a pH of 4.4.

The most common acid-base indicator is litmus paper. It comes in two forms, red and blue. When dipped into a solution, blue litmus paper turns red if the pH of the solution is 4.5 or below, indicating the solution is acidic. If the pH of the solution is 8.2 or above, blue litmus paper remains its original blue color. Conversely, red litmus paper remains red when dipped into an acidic solution but turns blue when dipped into a basic solution.

Most often, acid-base indicators are used with a technique called titration. Titration allows analytical chemists to make quantitative determinations of how much acid or alkaline material is in a solution. In the titration of an acid solution, a known quantity of base is added until the correct acid-base indicator changes color. The chemist then measures how much base was used and can calculate how much acid is in the solution. The procedure is reversed with a basic solution.

When investigating an unknown substance such as a confiscated drug, a forensic technician may dissolve a small amount of the substance in water and then test its pH. Conversely, if the substance has been identified and the pH of that substance in pure form is known, the technician may dissolve a small amount of the substance in water to see if the pH varies from the known pH. If it does, this suggests that the substance is contaminated with another chemical.

Acid-base indicators are useful but crude analytical tools. To complete most chemical analyses, forensic scientists usually need to employ more precise analytical tools.

Martiscia Davidson

Further Reading

Blei, Ira. and George Odian. *General, Organic, and Biochemistry: Connecting Chemistry to Your Life*. 2d ed. New York: W. H. Freeman, 2006.

James, Stuart H., and Jon J. Nordby, eds. *Forensic Science: An Introduction to Scientific and Investigative Techniques*. 2d ed. Boca Raton, Fla.: CRC Press, 2005.

Oxlade, Chris. *Acids and Bases*. Chicago: Heinemann Library, 2007.

See also: Crime scene screening tests; Quantitative and qualitative analysis of chemicals; Reagents.

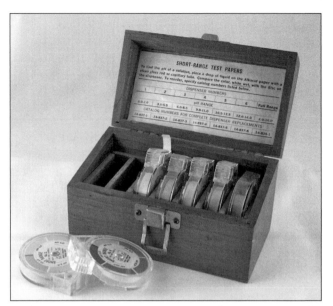

Old-fashioned chemist's kit containing a series of litmus papers capable of measuring different pH ranges. (© iStockphoto.com/Oliver Bogler)

Actuarial risk assessment

Definition: Formation of judgments and predictions regarding dangerous behavior through the application of formulas to particular variables and statistics in preparation for the adoption of necessary preventive measures.

Significance: Forensic psychologists use numerous factors to evaluate the likelihood that particular persons will be involved in violent and dangerous behavior. Predictions based on actuarial risk assessment influence many decisions made in the criminal justice system.

Actuarial risk assessment is one of the many tools that forensic psychologists use to evaluate the likelihood of future violent and dangerous behavior on the part of certain persons. Other methods include clinical predictions, which are based on evidence derived from counseling and experience, and anamnestic predictions, in which psychologists analyze the behavior of specific persons in the past in similar situations. The scientific community has demanded greater reliability in predictions than either clinical or anamnestic methods can provide, and an outcome of this demand has been the use of mathematical formulas to make predictions of risk. Actuarial risk assessment thus employs many of the tools of statistical analysis.

Uses of Risk Assessment

Many people and organizations rely on forensic psychologists and similar experts to make predictions of human behavior. For example, officials in the U.S. criminal justice system rely on risk assessment in making decisions concerning sentencing—for example, in deciding whether to impose probation as a sentence instead of incarceration or whether to sentence a violent offender to death rather than life in prison. A psychologist's prediction concerning a given individual's risk of violent or inappropriate behavior could support the issuance of a restraining order in a domestic dispute or abuse case. Risk assessment may also be used in child-custody decision making and in decisions concerning whether child visitation by a parent should be supervised. Some companies use risk assessment to evaluate the potential for violent behavior in the workplace by terminated employees, and some educational institutions use risk assessment to predict the likelihood of school violence.

Experts also use actuarial risk assessment to predict the potential for recidivism in determining whether to parole prisoners from correctional facilities and in considering the release of offenders who have been confined to mental health facilities. One area of risk assessment that has seen substantial growth concerns the prediction of sexual offending. Predictions in this area may influence whether particular released prisoners must register as sex offenders with their local communities.

Forensic psychologists may also be called upon to predict the likelihood that certain persons will attempt suicide. In addition, psychologists may have a legal obligation to warn others of any potential danger of harm from any persons they are treating. In some cases, the goal of risk assessment is to determine whether to commit persons to mental health facilities involun-

tarily because of the likelihood that they may cause serious harm to themselves or others. Risk assessment is also used to decide whether persons who have been involuntarily confined to mental health facilities have become stable enough in their behavior that they are no longer dangerous and can be released.

Risk Assessment Factors

Actuarial risk assessment involves looking at statistical relationships between variables to make judgments and predictions about future behavior. Risk assessment involves a delicate balance between protecting society from physical harm and ensuring that the rights and liberties of the persons subjected to risk assessment are not unduly restricted. Forensic psychologists look at various behavioral characteristics and other factors to increase the accuracy of their scientific approaches to risk assessment. These factors are derived from research involving large groups of people who have exhibited risky or violent behavior in the past and from data gathered by professional clinicians. Some of the factors or variables considered in risk assessment are specifically associated with one behavior, whereas others are predictive across the entire array of potentially risky or dangerous behaviors.

One of the most significant factors considered in risk assessment is the presence or absence of a history of violent behavior. Other risk factors include static predictors such as psychological and physiological characteristics of the person and the person's personal and family history. Higher risk is associated with relationship and employment instability, education maladjustment, a history of drug and alcohol abuse, and being young. Dynamic characteristics—that is, characteristics that change over time—that are associated with higher risk include a lack of insight about personal behavior, the inability to control hostile and impulsive behavior, negative emotions in response to treatment, and ongoing psychotic symptoms such as hallucinations. Finally, in assessing risk, the person's potential living environments and social networks must be considered, as well as the person's ability to harm others in the future.

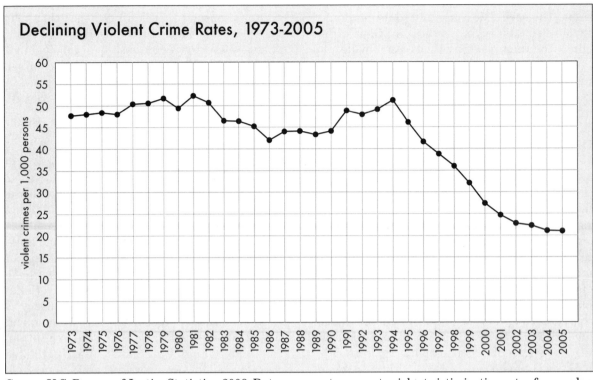

Declining Violent Crime Rates, 1973-2005

Source: U.S. Bureau of Justice Statistics, 2008. Data represent aggregate violent victimization rates for murder, rape, robbery, and assault.

Research has found that actuarial risk assessment is more accurate than clinical assessment. Jurors, however, tend to believe the testimony of clinicians over that of actuarial experts, as jurors perceive that clinicians have stronger relationships with and thus more knowledge of the persons being assessed. Despite the scientific basis of actuarial risk assessment by forensic scientists, the prediction of human behavior is very difficult, and significant criticism has been directed toward actuarial risk assessment. Research has shown that a person's behavior changes over time and that actuarial prediction has an accuracy rate of little more than 50 percent.

Actuarial risk assessment continues to gain acceptance among members of the scientific and legal communities, however, and as risk factors and formulas are enhanced through research, the accuracy rates of this technique should also improve in the future.

Carol A. Rolf

Further Reading

Freeman, Naomi J. "Predictors of Rearrest for Rapists and Child Molesters on Probation." *Criminal Justice and Behavior* 34, no. 6 (2007): 752-768. Compares the recidivism rates of former prisoners who were convicted of rape with those of former prisoners who were convicted of child molestation.

Gran, Martin, and Niklas Langstrom. "Actuarial Assessment of Violence Risk: To Weigh or Not to Weigh?" *Criminal Justice and Behavior* 34, no. 1 (2007): 22-36. Addresses the validity of using risk factors in actuarial formulas for the purpose of predicting violent criminal behavior.

Prins, Her. *Will They Do it Again? Risk Assessment and Management in Criminal Justice and Psychiatry.* New York: Routledge, 1999. Using statistics and discussion of real cases, compares and contrasts the low risk of public harm posed by the mentally ill with society's perception of a high risk of harm. Provides recommendations for managing risky behavior on the part of mentally ill persons.

Webster, Christopher D., and Stephen J. Hucker. *Violence Risk: Assessment and Management*. Hoboken, N.J.: John Wiley & Sons, 2007. Focuses on violent offenders and provides suggestions for protecting the rights of these offenders when they are released from mental health facilities and prisons while also protecting the public from harm. Includes a list of variables that should be considered in the process of risk assessment.

See also: Alcohol-related offenses; Child abduction and kidnapping; Child abuse; *Daubert v. Merrell Dow Pharmaceuticals*; Forensic psychology; Psychological autopsy; Sexual predation characteristics; Suicide; *Tarasoff* rule.

Adipocere

Definition: Naturally occurring substance produced by dead bodies under certain conditions from the hydrolysis of body fat and a sufficient amount of water or moisture.

Significance: Also called grave wax, corpse wax, and mortuary wax, adipocere is commonly formed by the bodies of human beings or animals with sufficient body fat when they lie under wet or moist conditions. The presence of this substance on a human body may help or hinder forensic scientists in estimating the postmortem interval.

The production of adipocere by a body generally requires an anaerobic surrounding (that is, one without free oxygen), a sufficient quantity of body fat (that is, adipose containing connective tissue with lipids present), and any of a variety of bacteria that take oxygen away from other compounds and thus assist in the hydrolysis of the fats. The material was first recognized and described in the seventeenth century, when Sir Thomas Browne wrote in *Hydriotaphia, Urne Buriall* (1658) of encountering the substance while relocating previously buried individuals from an English cemetery. The process of adipocere formation is called saponification, which literally means "soap making" (in times past, soap was made with a combination of animal fat, water, and lye, which produced a grayish-white material that was similar to adipocere in appearance and texture). Because adipose, or body fat, can be either white or brown, adipocere may appear grayish-white or tan in color. It was not until the use of microscopes became widespread during the seventeenth century that scientists began to understand the chemical process of saponification.

Adipocere is an artifact of the decomposition process, and because its formation requires that lipids (fats) be present, it is more commonly seen among animal remains containing comparatively high levels of fat. Among humans, this means that adipocere is found most frequently on the bodies of women, infants, and obese individuals of either sex. In addition, fatter individuals contain more moisture, and fats contain fatty acids that have an affinity to attach to sodium or potassium from the environment. Water assists in this process, and, indeed, adipocere is most often found among tissues that have been kept damp or moist, or even submerged.

It has been suggested that the formation of adipocere on a body may be useful as a guide for forensic scientists in estimating the length of time since death (the postmortem interval, or PMI), much like the appearance of algor, rigor, and livor mortis. However, because adipocere results from a chemical process, the speed with which the substance is formed is temperature-dependent, and, as is true for all other PMI indicators, the rate of formation varies. It appears that the formation of adipocere is speeded up by warmth, but temperature extremes, whether too warm or too cold, impede formation. In addition, because saponification produces a more durable substance than do other processes associated with decomposition, the formation of adipocere can result in a body's retaining facial and other anatomic features well after death.

Turhon A. Murad

Further Reading

Gill-King, Herrell. "Chemical and Ultrastructural Aspects of Decomposition." In *Forensic Taphonomy: The Postmortem Fate of Human Remains*, edited by William D. Haglund and Marcella H. Sorg. Boca Raton, Fla.: CRC Press, 1997.

O'Brien, Tyler G., and Amy C. Kuehner. "Waxing Grave About Adipocere: Soft Tissue Change in an Aquatic Context." *Journal of Forensic Sciences* 52, no. 2 (2007): 294-301.

Spitz, Werner U., ed. *Spitz and Fisher's Medicolegal Investigation of Death: Guidelines for the Application of Pathology to Crime Investigation*. 4th ed. Springfield, Ill.: Charles C Thomas, 2006.

See also: Algor mortis; Decomposition of bodies; Forensic entomology; Livor mortis; Mummification; Rigor mortis; Taphonomy.

Air and water purity

Definition: Extent to which natural water and air supplies are free of harmful forms of contamination.

Significance: Various forms of chemical and biological contaminants that pollute air and water supplies are responsible for death, disease, climate shifts, and the alteration of fragile ecosystems around the world. Techniques used to investigate the nature and causes of pollution are allied with forensic toxicology.

Although challenges to air and water purity have always existed, the assault has taken on forbidding aspects since the advent of the industrial age. So ubiquitous are the sources of air and water pollution that they have become woven into the fabric of everyday modern life. However, it is important to note that although much pollution comes from the processes of industry and commerce, pollution is also a product of natural biological and geographic processes. It should also be kept in mind that purity and pollution are relative. For example, although oxygen is necessary to animal life, it is highly toxic to certain organisms that flourish in an atmosphere of methane, which would be lethal to human beings.

Human-made pollutants come from the combustion of fuels that power ships, aircraft, motor vehicles, factories, and power-generating plants. Natural pollutants come from the discharges of wildfires and volcanoes. Pollutants also come from chemical discharges and landfill outgassing as well as military operations that generate nuclear fallout, pathogens, and toxic gases. Pollutants even ride the wind in the form of dust.

A notorious example of the damage inflicted when human activities alter the air's chemistry comes in the form of chlorofluorocarbons (CFCs), which find wide applications as refrigerants, insulating foams, and solvents. CFCs eventually make their way into the stratosphere, where the ultraviolet (UV) rays of sunlight break the CFCs' chemical bonds and release their chlorine atoms. As one chlorine atom is capable of breaking apart 100,000 ozone molecules, damage to Earth's ozone layer is great. The ozone layer protects Earth's surface from the damaging UV rays of the sun; without its protection, human beings are vulnerable to immune disorders, skin cancer, and cataracts. Additionally, increased UV radiation can reduce crop yields and cause serious dislocations in the marine food chain.

Water Quality

The quality of naturally occurring freshwater may be degraded through natural sources such as bedrock salts or sediment containing organic material. Additional degradation of water quality may be caused by human manipulation, such as fertilizers and petroleum products. When water pollution comes from a single source such as a sewage-outflow pipe, it is called point-source pollution; when the exact source of pollution is not as clear, as in agricultural or urban runoff, it is called non-point-source pollution.

The principal water polluters are industry and agriculture. Rain helps to cleanse air of pollutant emissions from motor vehicles, factories, and heating boilers, but the pollutants ultimately find their way into groundwater and streams. More direct forms of water pollution come from industrial discharges, construction detritus, and agricultural runoff. All these forms of pollution change the chemistry of water, changing its acidity, conductivity, and temperature. Nitrogen runoff fertilizes water, causing it to be choked with new vegetation.

The consequences to human society of impure water are alarming. Intractable diarrhea is a leading cause of death around the world among children under five, and its main cause is degraded drinking water. Cholera, a potentially deadly bacterial infection that plagues much of the underdeveloped world, requires only clean drinking water and proper sanitation to be eliminated as a problem. Contaminated drinking water is responsible for up to fourteen thousand deaths every day in developing countries.

Sources of water pollution include sewage, industrial discharges, surface runoff from farms and construction sites, underground storage tank leakage, and acid rain. It is convenient to categorize water contaminants into subgroups: microorganisms, disinfectants, disinfection by-products, inorganic chemicals, organic chemicals, and radionuclides. The U.S. government's Environmental Protection Agency (EPA) lists eighty-six specific water contaminants, along with their sources and potential health effects.

Examples of specific pollutants include alachlor, an herbicide used in row crops that increases human risks of cancer and can also cause eye, liver, and kidney disease. Cadmium, which reaches water supplies from corroded galvanized pipes and discharges from metal refineries, can cause kidney damage. Dioxin is a

Health Effects of Contaminated Drinking Water

The U.S. Environmental Protection Agency (EPA) provides this information on acute and chronic health effects related to contaminants in drinking water.

EPA has set standards for more than 80 contaminants that may occur in drinking water and pose a risk to human health. EPA sets these standards to protect the health of everybody, including vulnerable groups like children. The contaminants fall into two groups according to the health effects that they cause. . . .

Acute effects occur within hours or days of the time that a person consumes a contaminant. People can suffer acute health effects from almost any contaminant if they are exposed to extraordinarily high levels (as in the case of a spill). In drinking water, microbes, such as bacteria and viruses, are the contaminants with the greatest chance of reaching levels high enough to cause acute health effects. Most people's bodies can fight off these microbial contaminants the way they fight off germs, and these acute contaminants typically don't have permanent effects. Nonetheless, when high enough levels occur, they can make people ill, and can be dangerous or deadly for a person whose immune system is already weak due to HIV/AIDS, chemotherapy, steroid use, or another reason.

Chronic effects occur after people consume a contaminant at levels over EPA's safety standards for many years. The drinking water contaminants that can have chronic effects are chemicals (such as disinfection by-products, solvents, and pesticides), radionuclides (such as radium), and minerals (such as arsenic). Examples of the chronic effects of drinking water contaminants are cancer, liver or kidney problems, or reproductive difficulties.

chemical discharge from factories that causes cancer and reproductive disorders. *Giardia lamblia* is a protozoan parasite found in human and animal waste that often causes gastrointestinal disturbances. Toxaphene, an active ingredient in insecticides used in cotton farming and cattle production, increases cancer risk and can cause kidney, liver, and thyroid problems. Vinyl chlorides from plastics manufacturing discharges and leaching from polyvinyl chloride pipes also increase cancer risks.

Air Quality

Air pollution not only threatens the health of human beings but also compromises the well-being of animal and plant life. It degrades bodies of freshwater, thins the atmosphere's protective ozone layer, and creates haze that shrouds the beauty of nature. The EPA attempts to sus-

A sign at a Sturgeon Bay, Wisconsin, park warns beachgoers of a possible *Escherichia coli* contamination in the water. The local county government by this inlet of Lake Michigan routinely tests the water for possible contaminants and posts warnings when hazards reach certain levels. When health hazards are especially great, the county closes down the beaches. *(AP/Wide World Photos)*

compounds. The EPA is armed with government regulations. Through a cooperative effort that involves private industry and state and local governments, the agency calls for the discontinuation of ozone-depleting substances, the elimination of specified toxic chemicals, and the treatment of polluted areas.

To assess air quality, the EPA's Office of Air Quality Planning and Standards (OAQPS) monitors specific pollutants that can harm human health, the environment, and property. All common throughout the United States, these pollutants include sulfur dioxide, particulate matter, nitrogen dioxide, lead, and carbon monoxide. Based on national ambient air quality standards, geographic areas are designated as attainment or nonattainment areas. OAQPS gives the standards more meaning by subdividing them into primary and secondary standards. Primary standards are about issues of health, whereas secondary standards consider damage to crops, vegetation, or buildings. Further, they assess the health effects for their potential long- or short-term damage.

Richard S. Spira

Further Reading

Friedlander, Sheldon K. *Smoke, Dust, and Haze: Fundamentals of Aerosol Dynamics.* 2d ed. New York: Oxford University Press, 2000. Written by a prominent authority on aerosols, this textbook designed for advanced undergraduates and graduate students covers basic concepts, lab techniques, and many practical applications.

Godish, Thad. *Air Quality.* 4th ed. Boca Raton, Fla.: Lewis, 2004. Up-to-date and comprehensive overview, appropriate for both undergraduate and graduate students, covers a wide variety of issues affecting air quality, with attention to atmospheric chemistry and the impact of polluted air on human health and the environment. Also covers public policy issues and risk assessment.

Heinsohn, R. J., and R. L. Kabel. *Sources and Control of Air Pollution.* Upper Saddle River, N.J.: Prentice Hall, 1998. Engineering textbook offers broad coverage of both natural and human-made sources of air pollution and methods for preventing or reducing pollution.

tain reasonable levels of air purity through regulatory enforcement and voluntary programs, such as Energy Star and Commuter Choice. Through the federal Clean Air Act of 1990, the EPA restricts the amounts of specific pollutants allowed into the atmosphere to help protect public health.

Under the surveillance of the EPA are these broad categories of atmospheric pollutants: aerosols, asbestos, carbon monoxide, chlorofluorocarbons, ground-level ozone, hazardous air pollutants, hydrochlorofluorocarbon refrigerants, lead, mercury, methane gas, nitrogen oxides, particulate matter, propellants, radon, refrigerants, sulfur oxides, and volatile organic

Nathanson, Jerry A. *Basic Environmental Technology: Water Supply, Waste Management, and Pollution Control*. 5th ed. Upper Saddle River, N.J.: Prentice Hall, 2007. Provides a clearly written introduction to water supply, waste management, and pollution control that is ideal for students with limited background in the hard sciences and engineering.

Novotny, Vladimir. *Water Quality: Diffuse Pollution and Watershed Management*. 2d ed. Hoboken, N.J.: John Wiley & Sons, 2003. Useful textbook focuses on all types of water-pollution problems. Especially strong on regulatory laws and judicial decisions.

Viessman, Warren, and Mark J. Hammer. *Water Supply and Pollution Control*. 7th ed. Upper Saddle River, N.J.: Prentice Hall, 2004. Authoritative standard textbook on modern water management issues stresses applications of scientific methods to problems that include pollution.

See also: Biodetectors; Biological Weapons Convention of 1972; Biosensors; Chemical Weapons Convention of 1993; Choking; Decontamination methods; Environmental Measurements Laboratory; Food and Drug Administration, U.S.; Forensic toxicology; International Association of Forensic Toxicologists; Lead; Mercury; Mycotoxins; Pathogen transmission.

Airport security

Definition: All legal measures, law-enforcement activities, regulations, and forensic science applications needed to maintain the safety and security of passengers and operational facilities—including aircraft, terminals, and transportation facilities—associated with airline commerce.

Significance: As rates of world travel have increased and the threat of international terrorism has grown, airport security measures have evolved to keep pace. Forensic science has contributed a number of technologies and methodologies to the effort to keep airports safe.

Airport security measures have been operative since commercial airline traffic began during the 1920's. Initial measures included the establishment of rules for luggage, boarding, and other aspects of air travel intended to provide safe passage. As the volume and complexity of air traffic increased, so did the emphasis on rules and regulations governing air passengers, aircraft, and airport security. The most basic of these took the form of regulations regarding movement of passengers and their baggage within airports and their access to airport facilities, the airplanes, and the flight tarmac.

As airports grew larger and volumes of freight and passenger traffic increased during and following World War II, the movements of passengers within airport terminals and their access to operational infrastructure of air terminals were further restricted. Luggage restrictions and weight restrictions became routine, as did requirements concerning passenger identification and boarding passes, but these rules were established to protect passengers from harm and to ensure airport efficiency rather than as deterrents to perceived threats.

The first important changes in airport security followed several incidents in the 1950's in which bombs were planted on aircraft to destroy them in flight for insurance purposes. These were followed with additional security measures taken in the 1960's in response to a number of high-profile hijackings, some of which led to the destruction of aircraft and crews as well as to passenger injuries and deaths. Airlines, agencies, and various governments around the world, including that of the United States, took the (at that time) extraordinary measure of instituting a program of sky marshals to fly on board aircraft. Sky marshals were armed and were charged with identifying and arresting potential menaces as well as with preventing incidents during flight.

Although the sky marshal program was well conceived and well designed for that time, it never received adequate funding to place marshals on every airplane. Hijackings continued to occur, necessitating additional airport security programs. In response, the U.S. Federal Aviation Administration (FAA) required that all passengers and their luggage be thoroughly screened beginning in January, 1973. The airlines contracted this work to private security companies that supplied equipment and trained personnel. The airlines maintained operational control over their airport and aircraft facilities, and the private security companies controlled the screening of carry-on baggage at designated checkpoints prior to passenger entry to the airport waiting rooms, all under the general oversight of FAA officials.

The terrorist attacks on the World Trade Center in New York City and on the Pentagon on September 11, 2001, precipitated immediate and drastic changes in airport security matters that have remained in place. Immediately following the attacks, the federal government mandated that the highest-priority emphasis be placed on the safety and security of passengers, airport facilities, and aircraft at all airports in the United States and most around the world as well. Dramatically increased levels of security were initially reflected in the presence of armed security guards, uniformed local police officers, and even National Guard and active-duty military personnel in some terminals. The military presence was discontinued after a few months; although some passengers were comforted by the open display of weapons, others had expressed alarm.

Post-9/11 Airport Security

Long-term airport security measures that remain in place since the changes brought about after 9/11 include dramatically increased scrutiny of passengers and their carry-on luggage. This has led to the implementation of a number of measures aimed at passenger behavior. First, people are no longer permitted to leave cars unoccupied at terminals or to leave luggage unattended. Passengers must wait in long lines in which they and their luggage are checked with scanners, metal detectors, and, in some cases, substance-detection dogs. Each individual must present some form of personal identification with a photograph, such as a driver's license or passport, and must agree to extensive searching of luggage. These strictures sometimes lead to long waiting times and travel delays, all of which have been sanctioned by federal authorities; most such measures have met with general passenger approval.

Behind-the-scenes changes in airport security have been equally dramatic. Each airport, similar to a small town, now has a dedicated police force hired specifically to maintain airport security. Depending on locality, the airport force may be a private policing agency or a part of the local police force with a police station maintained at the airport. Most airport police forces also include dogs that have been trained to detect explosives and drugs.

Airports have tested and purchased a number of technologically advanced and very expensive apparatuses that permit rapid scanning of baggage and passengers. These include X-ray backscatter scanners that can detect hidden weapons and explosives on passengers as well as automated explosive detection system (EDS) machines that are able to scan hundreds of pieces of luggage per hour. New and improved

Baggage-Screening Technology

The Transportation Security Administration (TSA), a component of the U.S. Department of Homeland Security, is responsible for the security of the nation's transportation systems, including highways, railroads, buses, mass-transit systems, ports, and airports. The TSA provides this description of one of the security measures in place at American airports.

Ever wonder what happens to your bag once you check it with your airline? We screen every bag—100% of all bags—placed on an airplane, whether taken as carry-on or checked with an airline. With nearly 2 million people flying each day, it's a Herculean task.

We are able to meet this requirement by relying on Explosive Detection System (EDS) machines, which work like the MRI machines in your doctor's office. Through a sophisticated analysis of each checked bag, the EDS machines can quickly determine if a bag contains a potential threat or not. If a weapon or explosive is detected, the machines alert our security officers so they can manage the bag appropriately. In some cases, the alarm is quickly resolved and in others law enforcement and the bomb squad may be called in.

computed axial tomography (CAT) scanners have been developed that provide three-dimensional images, thereby more effectively detailing luggage contents; this advancement promotes rapid and accurate identification of hidden weapons, bombs, and packets of chemicals.

Forensic Applications in Airport Security

Airlines and airline facilities must be protected from all forms of terrorism, including bombs planted in luggage, airplane hijackers, and attacks using chemical or biological weapons. Since September 11, 2001, the U.S. government has poured millions of dollars per year into improving airport security, but security breaches still occur. For the most part, these involve identity fraud, drug trafficking, possession of explosives or weapons, or possession of international contraband, harmful chemicals, or biotoxins. Forensic science plays an important role in the prevention and investigation of such security breaches.

The first line of defense against terrorist threats to airport security involves a system of enclosure and screening that prevents access to aircraft and tarmacs. All airports in the United States are surrounded by tall fences or walls, making it nearly impossible for anyone to sneak in. In addition to constant video surveillance throughout airports, security personnel watch every checkpoint, entry, and exit. Upon entrance, both persons and luggage pass through metal detectors. Luggage is also exposed to X rays and may be searched. Individuals are also required to agree to noninvasive searches if asked to do so. Any person who is deemed a threat is subject to more intensive searches.

Modern airport security measures also involve more clandestine operations, such as profiling and the comparison of passenger names and identifications against lists of known terrorists. Airport security profiling involves gen-

A Transportation Security Administration agent at George Bush Intercontinental Airport in Houston, Texas, screens checked baggage for dangerous or suspicious contents using an X-ray machine. *(AP/Wide World Photos)*

eralizations about the personality types and physical characteristics of persons who may pose threats to other passengers. Security personnel are urged to be on the lookout for particular "types." Therefore, while random baggage and clothing checks are conducted, owing to the nature of many international terrorist attacks, ethnic profiling may also occur. Passengers on flights into the United States from overseas are also subject to profiling and comparison against terrorist "watch lists." If it is discovered that the passenger list of an inbound aircraft includes a known or suspected terrorist, the plane may be turned back, diverted to land at a designated high-security airport, or refused landing permission anywhere in the United States.

Anyone found to be carrying a weapon in an airport is immediately apprehended and the weapon removed. Forensic scientists then confirm and attest in court that the object was cause for the subject's arrest. In the case of gun possession, firearms analyses are performed in a laboratory to determine the model of the weapon and to recover the serial numbers if removed.

Hidden explosives may be detected using modern explosive detectors that use chromatography to detect volatile gases given off by explosive mixtures. Drug-detection and bomb-sniffing dogs are led by specialized teams at customs checkpoints and often can be seen roaming common rooms in airports as well. If a suitcase or other device is suspected of containing harmful material, it is often further tested with a mechanical "chemical sniffer." If hazardous material is found, be it illegal drugs, explosive material, chemicals, or other toxins, the individual is apprehended and held until forensic scientists can conduct toxicological and chemical composition tests to determine the identity of the substance. If the substance is determined to be an illicit one, the individual is further detained to face charges of possession of an illegal substance.

The detection of possible biological weapons is much more difficult than detection of other kinds of harmful substances. However, if airport security authorities are concerned, they can seize any suspicious substance and submit it for forensic analysis to determine what it is. Unfortunately, no standard procedure yet exists among airline or FAA officials for dealing with possible biological weapons.

A valid driver's license is sufficient identification for a person flying within the United States; a passport is needed to fly internationally. Both these forms of identification, however, provide merely photographs and some additional personal information about the appearance, age, and residence of the individual. The future of individual identification in respect to airport security is likely to involve screening systems based in biometrics—that is, human recognition based on physical traits, such as fingerprints. Biometric identification systems include fingerprint scanning, iris and retina scanning, and facial recognition technologies. In some cases, handwriting and voice recognition are also used to confirm identities.

Among the airport security measures that have been put in place in the United States since September 11, 2001, those involving biometric technologies have become particularly controversial. Some feel comforted by the prospect of being identified by their own fingerprints or retinal images, whereas others feel that these methods of identification are invasive and violate personal privacy. Also, many fear the damage that could be done if hackers or identity thieves gain access to the databases in which biometric data are stored.

Above all other matters related to airport security, Americans are often frustrated with the long lines, personal questions, baggage and clothing searches, and other time-consuming measures they are subject to when they fly. Many believe, however, that these inconveniences are a small price to pay for increased passenger safety. With increasing technological capabilities, the U.S. Department of Homeland Security and Department of Defense are working on measures to expedite the security process while ensuring efficiency, effectiveness, and accurate personal identification. The next decision that Americans who fly commercially will probably have to make is whether they would rather put up with the waiting and frustration or have their fingerprints and retinal scans stored in government databases.

Dwight G. Smith

Further Reading

Bullock, Jane, and George Haddow. *Introduction to Homeland Security*. 2d ed. Boston: Butterworth-Heinemann, 2006. Provides a basic introduction to the operations of the U.S. Department of Homeland Security. Outlines certain types of threats and their prevention, addresses responses to threats, discusses the uses of communication and other technologies in security measures, and speculates on the future evolution of such measures in the United States. Appendixes include a number of related legal documents.

Sweet, Kathleen M. *Aviation and Airport Security: Terrorism and Safety Concerns*. Upper Saddle River, N.J.: Pearson Prentice Hall, 2004. Provides a historical overview of aviation terrorism and discusses the changes in security measures through the years, particularly after September 11, 2001.

Thomas, Andrew R. *Aviation Insecurity: The New Challenges of Air Travel*. Amherst, N.Y.: Prometheus Books: 2003. An aviation security expert details the shortcomings of airport security systems from the days preceding September 11, 2001, through the implementation of changes following that terrorist attack.

Wilkinson, Paul, and Brian M. Jenkins, eds. *Aviation Terrorism and Security*. Portland, Oreg.: Frank Cass, 1999. Collection of essays includes a review of past incidents of aviation terrorism and discussion of the trends seen in security responses. Other chapters address the politics of aviation terrorism and security in the United States and the probable directions of global air security in the future.

See also: Biological terrorism; Biological weapon identification; Biometric eye scanners; Canine substance detection; Closed-circuit television surveillance; Facial recognition technology; Improvised explosive devices; Metal detectors; Racial profiling; September 11, 2001, victim identification.

Alcohol-related offenses

Definition: Violations of the law in which consumption of alcohol is a fundamental component.

Significance: Alcohol is a legally available drug that has significant impairing effects on a number of aspects of human cognition and performance. Given that alcohol is used pervasively among the general population, alcohol consumption is a significant element in a wide range of criminal cases. Alcohol may play a contributory role in a variety of offenses, even when the presence of alcohol at concentrations associated with significant intoxication does not form the basis of the offenses.

Ethanol, commonly referred to as alcohol, is a drug whose effects include depression of the function of the central nervous system (CNS).

As is true for other CNS depressants, the severity of alcohol's effects increases with dose, potentially causing significant impairment of psychomotor skills (such as those required for safe driving) and, ultimately, fatal respiratory depression or circulatory collapse.

Effects of Alcohol

At low blood alcohol concentrations (BACs), the effects of alcohol consumption include euphoria, talkativeness, and reductions in anxiety and inhibitions. At progressively greater BACs, speech may become slurred, and dizziness or a significant loss of coordination may be observed. Further increases to BAC may be accompanied by drowsiness, emotional lability, confusion, and loss of consciousness. Uncontrolled overdose can result in fatal respiratory depression.

In addition to these relatively obvious symptoms, alcohol causes BAC-dependent impairment to a number of faculties related to psychomotor performance, including the ability to divide attention over multiple tasks, reaction time, risk or hazard perception, and motor coor-

In an innovative program designed to deter drunk driving by publicly humiliating drivers convicted of driving under the influence of alcohol, Arizona's Maricopa County created special chain gangs. Convicted offenders are required to do roadwork while wearing bright pink shirts and black-and-white striped pants. Chain gang members are also required to perform burials of people who die of alcohol abuse. *(AP/Wide World Photos)*

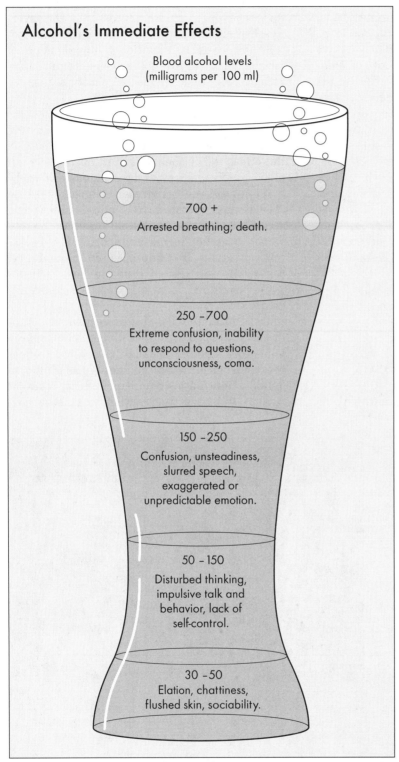

Alcohol's Immediate Effects

Blood alcohol levels
(milligrams per 100 ml)

700 +
Arrested breathing; death.

250 –700
Extreme confusion, inability
to respond to questions,
unconsciousness, coma.

150 –250
Confusion, unsteadiness,
slurred speech,
exaggerated or
unpredictable emotion.

50 – 150
Disturbed thinking,
impulsive talk and
behavior, lack of
self-control.

30 –50
Elation, chattiness,
flushed skin, sociability.

The presence of 30-50 milligrams of alcohol per every 100 milliliters of blood, which represents the effects of an average drink (a glass of beer or wine or an ounce of hard liquor), has immediate effects; as the amount increases, the effects progress toward death.

dination. All these faculties are essential for the safe operation of a motor vehicle. Consequently, one of the most obvious offenses directly related to alcohol consumption is impaired driving, or operation of a motor vehicle with a BAC in excess of the legal limit. Despite the fact that the impairing effects of alcohol on the ability to drive safely have been studied extensively and publicized widely through various public education programs, the incidence of impaired driving offenses remains high in many jurisdictions.

Driving under the influence of alcohol is an example of an offense for which the consumption of alcohol and the associated intoxication form the basis of the offense. In some jurisdictions, other legal offenses are also premised specifically on alcohol consumption; these include public intoxication and the consumption of alcohol by minors.

The consumption of alcohol may also be associated with an increased probability of occurrence of a number of other kinds of offenses. One such offense is sexual assault. A significant amount of research has examined the incidence of the use of drugs and alcohol in cases of sexual assault, especially those in which surreptitious drug administration (so-called drink spiking) is suspected. Over a significant number of jurisdictions worldwide, the most common finding in such studies has been the presence of significant amounts of alcohol in the complainants. In cases of sexual assault, the consumption of alcohol by both complainant and assailant may be important. From the perspective of the complainant, alcohol suppresses behavioral inhibitions, possibly influencing decision-making skills or risk perception. Furthermore, excessive alcohol consumption often leads to substantial impairment and perhaps even unconsciousness, which can place an individual under considerable risk for attack. From the perspective of the assailant, alcohol's suppression of behavioral inhibitions may also be dangerous, but further complications may take the form of alcohol's interference with the perception of social cues.

Forensic Analysis and Interpretation of Evidence

Forensic analysis of the role of alcohol in a particular case typically requires an understanding of the extent of intoxication or impairment, which, in turn, is reflected by the BAC at the time of the incident. In practice, measurement of BAC involves the collection of blood samples or breath measurements, depending on the type of offense (for example, breath analysis is typically done in driving-related offenses, whereas blood sampling is generally done in the course of the examination of victims of sexual assault). Breath alcohol analysis uses instrumentation specifically designed for that particular purpose; analysis of blood samples is generally done by enzymatic methods or gas chromatography. Once a BAC measurement is made, a correction is usually applied to account for the amount of alcohol eliminated from the blood through metabolism and other processes between the time of the incident and the time of sample collection. This provides an estimated BAC range at the time of the incident from which the likely extent of intoxication or impairment may be interpreted.

CNS function is enhanced when other depressant drugs are used in combination with alcohol, with potentially fatal consequences. Additionally, the combination of alcohol with other drugs not associated with CNS depression (such as cocaine or cannabis) may lead to significantly enhanced impairment or unexpected symptoms

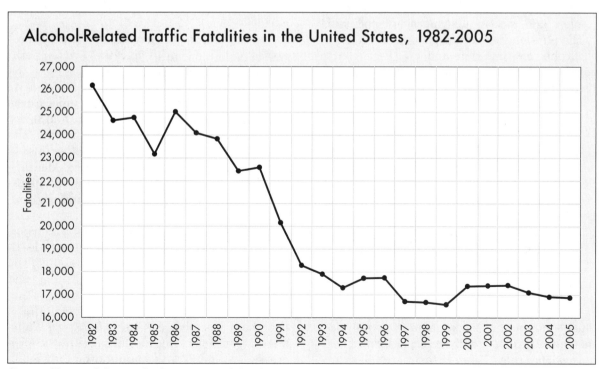

Source: National Center for Statistics and Analysis. Fatality Analysis Reporting System, 2008.

that may nonetheless contribute to some kinds of offenses. Consequently, more comprehensive forensic toxicological analysis may be warranted in some cases.

James Watterson

Further Reading

Baselt, Randall C. *Drug Effects on Psychomotor Performance.* Foster City, Calif.: Biomedical Publications, 2001. Comprehensive reference work presents information on the impairing effects of a wide range of therapeutic and illicit drugs.

Brunton, Laurence L., John S. Lazo, and Keith L. Parker, eds. *Goodman and Gilman's The Pharmacological Basis of Therapeutics.* 11th ed. New York: McGraw-Hill, 2006. Authoritative advanced textbook explains basic pharmacological principles and the specific pharmacological features of therapeutic agents. Includes some discussion of illicit agents.

Garriott, James C., ed. *Medical-Legal Aspects of Alcohol.* 4th ed. Tucson, Ariz.: Lawyers & Judges Publishing, 2003. Comprehensive work covers all aspects of forensic alcohol toxicology, including analysis of biological samples, and alcohol pharmacology, including the physiological and psychomotor effects of alcohol consumption and the time course (pharmacokinetics) of alcohol within the body.

Karch, Steven B., ed. *Drug Abuse Handbook.* 2d ed. Boca Raton, Fla.: CRC Press, 2007. Describes the pharmacological, physiological, and pathological aspects of drug abuse in general, and individual chapters address specific compounds, such as alcohol, as well as specific issues related to drug abuse, such as workplace drug testing.

Levine, Barry, ed. *Principles of Forensic Toxicology.* 2d ed., rev. Washington, D.C.: American Association for Clinical Chemistry, 2006. Introductory textbook describes the analytical, chemical, and pharmacological aspects of a variety of drugs of forensic relevance.

See also: Actuarial risk assessment; Analytical instrumentation; Breathalyzer; Drug and alcohol evidence rules; Forensic toxicology; Gas chromatography; Halcion; Toxicological analysis.

Algor mortis

Definition: Cooling of the body after death.
Significance: Because the temperature of the human body begins to cool at the moment of death, observation of algor mortis is one of the ways in which forensic scientists attempt to estimate the postmortem interval.

Investigators of homicides use various techniques to estimate the length of time since death, or the postmortem interval (PMI). It is likely that before the techniques employed by modern investigators gained wide acceptance, early hunters and gatherers distinguished the same stages of decomposition following death. Such stages include the fresh, bloat, active, and advanced decay stages versus the stage at which remains become dry or skeletonized. However, the indicators that modern forensic investigators consider classic for suggesting PMI are those of algor mortis (cooling of the body), rigor mortis (stiffening of the body), and livor mortis (discoloration of the body from gravitational blood seepage).

Because decomposition reflects chemical processes and all chemical processes are temperature-dependent, the acquisition of many of the conditions noticed after death is affected by temperature. That is, higher temperatures generally speed chemical reactions, and lower temperatures slow them. In algor mortis (the term derives from the Latin words *algor*, meaning "coolness," and *mortis*, meaning "death"), the body is expected to cool until its temperature matches that of the surrounding environment.

If a body cools at a uniform rate, the measure of its temperature decrease following death can assist in the accurate determination of the elapsed time since death. The formula used for making such an estimate, known as the Glaister equation, is based on the notion that a dead body is expected to lose 1.5 degrees Fahrenheit per hour. Because the metabolic processes associated with maintaining life among humans generates a normal body temperature of nearly 98.4 degrees Fahrenheit, the Glaister equation estimates the approximate postmortem interval in hours by subtracting the body temperature (measured in degrees Fahrenheit at the rectum or deep within the liver) from 98.4 degrees and dividing the result by 1.5. Thus, if a decedent's temperature is found to be 90.2 degrees Fahrenheit at the time of the body's discovery, the decedent would be suggested to have died approximately 5.5 hours earlier.

After death, a body cools by radiation, conduction, and convection, so many physical factors can influence algor mortis. One of these is ambient temperature, or, more precisely, the difference between ambient and body temperatures. If, for example, a body were to be discovered in a warm sauna, it might not have cooled at all. Furthermore, the body temperature of the decedent might not have been normal at the time of death owing to the effects of exercise, illness, or infection. Additionally, the amount of subcutaneous fat present, the lightness or heaviness of any clothing worn at the time of death, and any number of insulating coverings can alter the rate at which a body might be expected to cool. Any such variables can alter the effectiveness of employing the Glaister equation to estimate the postmortem interval.

Turhon A. Murad

Further Reading

Randall, Brad. *Death Investigation: The Basics.* Tucson, Ariz.: Galen Press, 1997.

Saferstein, Richard. *Criminalistics: An Introduction to Forensic Science.* 9th ed. Upper Saddle River, N.J.: Pearson Prentice Hall, 2007.

Spitz, Werner U., ed. *Spitz and Fisher's Medicolegal Investigation of Death: Guidelines for the Application of Pathology to Crime Investigation.* 4th ed. Springfield, Ill.: Charles C Thomas, 2006.

See also: Adipocere; Body farms; Decomposition of bodies; Forensic pathology; Livor mortis; Rigor mortis; Taphonomy.

ALI standard

Definition: Statement of the insanity defense that has become widely accepted in federal and state jurisdictions throughout the United States.

Significance: The American Law Institute's carefully formulated insanity defense standard was created to overcome the shortcomings of earlier tests of insanity, such as the M'Naghten rule and the irresistible impulse rule.

During the 1950's and early 1960's, the American Law Institute (ALI) developed the Model Penal Code, the 1962 draft of which contained a statement of the insanity defense composed by a panel of judges, legal scholars, and behavioral scientists. It stated:

> A person is not responsible for criminal conduct if at the time of such conduct as a result of mental disease or defect he lacks substantial capacity either to appreciate the criminality (wrongfulness) of his conduct or to conform his conduct to the requirements of law. . . . the terms "mental disease or defect" do not include an abnormality manifested only by repeated criminal or otherwise antisocial conduct.

In the 1972 case of *United States v. Brawner*, the U.S. Court of Appeals for the District of Columbia adopted the ALI rule, and it became the standard used in almost all federal courts and in twenty-two U.S. state jurisdictions.

The ALI standard is considered a more precisely worded amalgam of two earlier insanity tests, namely, the M'Naghten rule and the irresistible impulse rule. The M'Naghten rule, developed in Great Britain in 1843, was the first formal test of legal insanity. As a test of legal insanity, it focused on whether the defendant's insanity deprived the defendant of a certain kind of cognitive ability, that of knowing what he or she was doing or knowing the difference between right and wrong. The ALI standard uses the broader term "appreciate" instead of "know" yet still retains the key idea of cognitive impairment.

Many jurisdictions had augmented the

M'Naghten test with the irresistible impulse rule to allow for cases in which mental disease or defect impedes a person's power to choose. The ALI standard replaces the somewhat narrow and misleading phrase "irresistible impulse" with the person's not being able "to conform" his or her "conduct to the requirements of law," thus capturing the underlying idea of volitional impairment. In the federal Insanity Defense Reform Act of 1984, the volitional impairment part of the ALI standard was eliminated as part of the definition of the insanity defense.

The ALI rule was also drawn in such a way as to avoid the looseness of two similar legal insanity tests, the New Hampshire rule and the Durham rule. Both tests framed the issue of legal insanity in terms of whether the criminal act was a product of mental disease. They were criticized on the grounds that in practice they resulted in "undue dominance of experts" in the courtroom, specifically, that the testimony of forensic psychiatrists carried too much weight and encroached on the proper role of the jury.

Mario Morelli

Further Reading

Moore, Michael. *Law and Psychiatry: Rethinking the Relationship*. New York: Cambridge University Press, 1984.

Rogers, Richard, and Daniel W. Shuman. *Fundamentals of Forensic Practice: Mental Health and Criminal Law*. New York: Springer, 2005.

See also: Forensic psychiatry; Guilty but mentally ill plea; Insanity defense; Irresistible impulse rule; Legal competency; *Mens rea*.

American Academy of Forensic Sciences

Date: Formed in 1948

Identification: Nonprofit professional organization created to improve, administer, and achieve justice through the application of science to the legal system.

Significance: With a membership made up of forensic scientists from all the field's major specialties, the American Academy of Forensic Sciences represents forensic science and its professionals to the public, offers credibility for their expert court testimony through board certification, and promotes educational and research opportunities for members.

In 1948, a small group of pathologists, psychiatrists, criminalists, and lawyers formed the American Academy of Forensic Sciences (AAFS) to apply science to the law. The AAFS has become the primary organization for professional forensic scientists, representing some six thousand members from across the United States, Canada, and more than fifty other countries. The society represents all the major forensic science disciplines, with sections including Criminalistics, Digital Forensics, Engineering Sciences, General, Odontology, Pathology/Biology, Physical Anthropology, Psychiatry and Behavioral Science, Questioned Documents, and Toxicology. AAFS members include physicians, pathologists, dentists, toxicologists, physicists, engineers, physical anthropologists, attorneys, and other forensic science specialists.

Functions of the society (in association with the Forensic Sciences Foundation) include the promotion of forensic science education through the publication of newsletters, symposia, and the flagship peer-reviewed journal the *Journal of Forensic Sciences*, which was launched in 1956, and through sponsorship of an annual meeting each February. The AAFS also administers board certification exams, continuing education credit (for physicians, dentists, chemists, nurses, and attorneys), and training seminars for members to advance their scientific accuracy and credibility. The AAFS offers job placement, scholarship, and grant opportunities for its members as well as career information for all persons interested in forensic science; the academy also supports research in the forensic science fields and provides ethical oversight in the practice of forensic science.

The AAFS oversees the Forensic Science Education Programs Accreditation Commission, known as FEPAC, which is dedicated to enhancing the quality of college-level academic forensic science education through a formal evaluation and recognition process. FEPAC sets quality standards for undergraduate and graduate forensic science programs and administers their accreditation.

Categories of membership in the AAFS are student affiliate, trainee affiliate, associate member, member, and fellow. The academy's stringent membership requirements include (for associate member and higher) proof of active engagement in and significant contributions to the field of forensic science as well as a minimum education of a baccalaureate degree from an accredited college or university. Each section within the AAFS also has its own additional requirements for membership. Applications for membership are approved only at the annual meeting each February.

Donna C. Boyd

Further Reading

Gaensslen, R. E., Howard A. Harris, and Henry C. Lee. *Introduction to Forensic Science and Criminalistics*. New York: McGraw-Hill, 2008.

Houck, Max M., and Jay A. Siegel. *Fundamentals of Forensic Science*. Burlington, Mass.: Elsevier Academic Press, 2006.

See also: American Society of Crime Laboratory Directors; Ethics; European Network of Forensic Science Institutes; Expert witnesses; Federal Bureau of Investigation Forensic Science Research and Training Center; Forensic Science Service; International Association for Identification; International Association of Forensic Nurses; International Association of Forensic Sciences; Training and licensing of forensic professionals.

American Law Institute standard. *See* ALI standard

American Society of Crime Laboratory Directors

Date: Founded in 1974

Identification: Organization of forensic laboratory professionals that provides a forum for the discussion of laboratory management issues and promotes improvements in forensic techniques and services.

Significance: Through their interaction in the American Society of Crime Laboratory Directors, forensic laboratory managers advanced the standards of labs in North America and internationally and also secured public recognition for the need to require accredited laboratory analysis of forensic evidence.

Dr. Briggs Johnston White (1911-1994), a chemist who served as director of the Laboratory Division of the Federal Bureau of Investigation (FBI), envisioned forming the American Society of Crime Laboratory Directors (ASCLD) to encourage local, state, and federal managers of U.S. forensic laboratories and forensic science programs to share their experiences and suggestions for reinforcing the professionalism of forensic laboratories. In December, 1973, approximately thirty crime laboratory directors participated in a symposium at the FBI Academy in Quantico, Virginia, to discuss White's ideas. In fall, 1974, the laboratory directors returned to Quantico to organize ASCLD, designating White as chairman.

Officers and a board of directors oversee ASCLD administration, with committees addressing specific needs. North American and international forensic professionals who oversee crime laboratories or associated scientific, educational, or legal work qualify for ASCLD membership categories. The ASCLD code of ethics outlines members' accountability to their profession and the public, and the organization's "Guidelines for Forensic Laboratory Management Practices" lists lab managers' duties, including the evaluation of employees and procedures.

ASCLD hosts meetings every year at which members and other forensic professionals can participate in workshops and discussions on topics relevant to the management of crime laboratories, such as personnel and accreditation. Also addressed are scientific and technological advances in forensic tests and techniques used to evaluate evidence in laboratories. Since 1994, ASCLD has presented the Briggs White Award annually to recognize notable forensic science laboratory leaders.

The association also distributes several publications, including *ASCLD News*, *Crime Laboratory Digest*, and *Crime Lab Minute*, which is posted on the ASCLD Web site. ASCLD guides outline forensic laboratory management practices for individual topics such as arson, and the association's laboratory accreditation manuals specify current standards. ASCLD established the National Forensic Science Technology Center (NFSTC) to improve laboratories by aiding crime laboratory directors and personnel to gain proficiency in forensics work.

In 1981, the association's Committee on Laboratory Evaluation and Standards became the ASCLD Committee on Laboratory Accreditation and began evaluating U.S. state police laboratories. By 1993, the autonomous American Society of Crime Laboratory Directors/Laboratory Accreditation Board (ASCLD/LAB) was focused on examining North American and foreign laboratories because of complaints concerning inferior forensic work. The FBI Laboratory Division received accreditation from ASCLD/LAB in September, 1998. Approximately 350 laboratories, including other U.S. federal forensic laboratories, had secured accreditation by late 2006. Several states have passed legislation making the accreditation of government forensic laboratories a requirement for representatives of those labs to present evidence in courts.

As members of the Coalition of Forensic Science Organizations, ASCLD and ASCLD/LAB supported the National Forensic Science Improvement Act, which was enacted in December, 2000. This federal law provides for the distribution of federal funds to state and local crime laboratories.

Elizabeth D. Schafer

Further Reading

Dao, James. "Lab's Errors in '82 Killing Force Review of Virginia DNA Cases." *The New York Times*, May 7, 2005, p. A1.

Lueck, Thomas J. "Sloppy Police Lab Work Leads to Retesting of Drug Evidence." *The New York Times*, December 4, 2007, p. B1.

St. Clair, Jami J. *Crime Laboratory Management*. San Diego, Calif.: Academic Press, 2002.

See also: American Academy of Forensic Sciences; Courts and forensic evidence; Crime laboratories; DNA fingerprinting; Ethics; European Network of Forensic Science Institutes; Federal Bureau of Investigation Laboratory; Forensic Science Service; Quality control of evidence; Training and licensing of forensic professionals.

Amphetamines

Definition: Members of a class of drugs that contain an amphetamine base. These drugs are classified as stimulants, meaning they increase energy levels, reduce fatigue, and cause psychological exhilaration.

Significance: Despite intense effort on the part of both legislative and law-enforcement personnel, the number of users of amphetamines continues to rise. The popularity of these drugs is an ongoing concern because chronic use of amphetamines can produce severe mental and physical problems. These drugs are of particular interest to law enforcement because clandestine methamphetamine laboratories pose a threat to neighborhoods, the environment, and investigating officials.

In the United States, the use of controlled substances is governed at the federal level by the Controlled Substances Act of 1970. The most strongly controlled substances are listed in Schedule I of the act, and those under the least control are listed in Schedule V. Amphetamines,

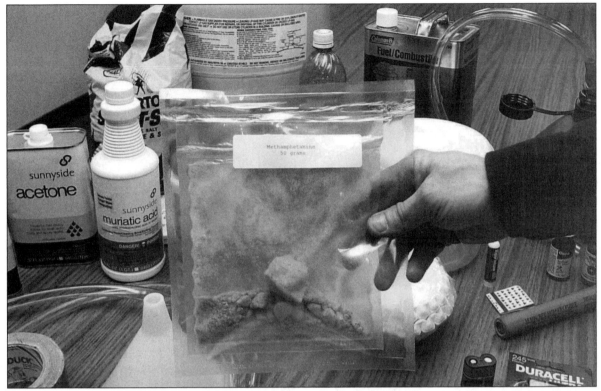

An agent for the North Dakota Bureau of Criminal Investigations holds a bag containing about 50 grams of methamphetamine. Behind the bag are some common household ingredients used to make methamphetamine. *(AP/Wide World Photos)*

along with cocaine, morphine, and phencyclidine (PCP), are listed in Schedule II. Drugs in this class have a high potential for abuse and also have accepted medical uses within the United States (with severe restrictions). Abuse of Schedule II drugs may lead to severe psychological dependence, physical dependence, or both.

Amphetamines are easy to produce, cheap to buy, and cause effects in the body similar to those of cocaine. Most illicit, or "street," amphetamines are actually methamphetamine, which is particularly potent and has long-lasting effects. Street names for amphetamines and methamphetamine include meth, crank, krank, crystal, glass, ice, pep pills, speed, uppers, peanut brittle, and tweak. These names often reflect particular ways the drugs appear; for example, ice is a very pure form, whereas peanut brittle is less so. The street price for one gram of methamphetamine ranges from twenty to three hundred dollars.

Manufacture

The high demand for methamphetamine, along with significant profit potential, has resulted in the production of the drug in thousands of clandestine laboratories, or "clan labs." "Super labs" are clan labs that are capable of producing seventy-five to one hundred pounds of methamphetamine in each production cycle. In comparison, "stove-top labs" typically produce only one to four ounces per batch. Production of one pound of the drug can result in from five to seven pounds of hazardous waste. Most of this waste ends up dumped on the ground or flushed into streams or sewage systems.

The synthetic route by which methamphetamine is prepared is widely known, and the required chemicals are readily available. The three most common production routes are the P2P (phenyl-2-propanone) amalgam method, the hydroiodic acid and red phosphorus reduction method, and the Birch reduction method. Ephedrine and pseudoephedrine, which can be found in many over-the-counter cold remedies, are key starting materials in the production of methamphetamine. Depending on the synthetic pathway, other important materials include iodine, red phosphorus, hydrogen chloride gas, and anhydrous ammonia. The U.S. government has regulated the sale and use of some of these chemicals in an effort to curb production of methamphetamine.

Routes of Ingestion

Amphetamines may be smoked, snorted, injected, or taken orally in pill form. Methamphetamine is often smoked; the drug is placed in a glass pipe, heat is applied to the bowl, and the vapors are inhaled through the stem. Snorting the drug tends to cause irritation to the nasal lining. Heavy, long-term users generally prefer to inject the drug. Like cocaine, amphetamine can be dissolved in water and cooked to prepare it for injection.

The route of ingestion determines the onset of the drug's effects. Effects from oral ingestion are felt within thirty to sixty minutes. When snorted, the drug produces effects within five to twenty minutes. Injecting and smoking the drug both result in an intense "rush" within seconds of ingestion. The intensity of the effects, which can last from six to twelve hours, is related to both the dose of the drug and its purity. Regardless of the route of ingestion, tolerance to the drug may develop quickly, so that the user requires larger and larger doses of amphetamines to produce the desired effect. Whereas medical doses of amphetamines rarely exceed 100 milligrams per day, a super user on a binge may ingest more than 15,000 milligrams every twenty-four hours.

Forms

The appearance of amphetamine and methamphetamine depends on the synthetic process and quality control used in their production. High-quality street meth is generally a white crystalline powder. The color of lower-quality meth may range from dark yellow to brown. The drug may be crystalline, granular, or solid block, and it may have a sticky consistency. It may be packaged in plastic bags, paper bindles, or glass vials.

Ice is a very pure form of methamphetamine with an appearance similar to that of broken glass. It is usually in-

---

Scope of Methamphetamine Abuse

A 2006 research report from the National Institute on Drug Abuse provides this information on methamphetamine use in the United States.

According to the 2005 National Survey on Drug Use and Health, an estimated 10.4 million people age twelve or older (4.3 percent of the population) have tried methamphetamine at some time in their lives. Approximately 1.3 million reported past-year methamphetamine use, and 512,000 reported current (past-month) use. Moreover, the 2005 Monitoring the Future survey of student drug use and attitudes reported 4.5 percent of high school seniors had used methamphetamine within their lifetimes, while eighth-graders and tenth-graders reported lifetime use at 3.1 and 4.1 percent, respectively. However, neither of these surveys has documented an overall increase in the abuse of methamphetamine over the past few years. In fact, both surveys showed recent declines in methamphetamine abuse among the nation's youth.

In contrast, evidence from emergency departments and treatment programs attests to the growing impact of methamphetamine abuse in the country. The Drug Abuse Warning Network, which collects information on drug-related episodes from hospital emergency departments (EDs) throughout the nation, reported a greater than 50 percent increase in the number of ED visits related to methamphetamine abuse between 1995 and 2002, reaching approximately 73,000 ED visits, or 4 percent of all drug-related visits, in 2004.

Treatment admissions for methamphetamine abuse have also increased substantially. In 1992, there were approximately 21,000 treatment admissions in which methamphetamine/amphetamine was identified as the primary drug of abuse, representing more than 1 percent of all treatment admissions during the year. By 2004, the number of methamphetamine treatment admissions increased to greater than 150,000, representing 8 percent of all admissions.

gested by smoking, and the effects can last up to fourteen hours. The price of one gram of ice ranges from two hundred to four hundred dollars.

Effects

As stimulants that act on the central nervous system, amphetamines reduce fatigue and the need to sleep, increase confidence and energy levels, and in general cause psychological and physical exhilaration. These effects are identical to those of cocaine, but the effects of cocaine last from twenty to eighty minutes, whereas those of amphetamines last for four to twelve hours. New users can rapidly develop psychological dependence on amphetamines.

Common effects displayed by people under the influence of amphetamines include alertness, anxiety, euphoria, reduced appetite, talkativeness, and teeth grinding. Chronic abuse of the drug can produce severe mental and physical problems, including delusions, visual and auditory hallucinations, and violent behavior. Long-term high-dose users of amphetamines may experience formication, which is the feeling that bugs are crawling under the skin. People in this state can severely injure themselves while trying to dig or cut the imagined bugs from their skin.

Megan N. Bottegal

Further Reading

Gano, Lila. *Hazardous Waste*. San Diego, Calif.: Lucent Books, 1991. Provides a good discussion of the health risks of the hazardous wastes generated by clandestine labs in the production of methamphetamine.

Hicks, John. *Drug Addiction: "No Way I'm an Addict."* Brookfield, Conn.: Millbrook Press, 1997. Focuses on drug-abuse treatment strategies, with an emphasis on amphetamine addiction.

Laci, Miklos. *Illegal Drugs: America's Anguish*. Detroit: Thomson/Gale, 2004. Comprehensive guide to illegal drugs in the United States includes discussion of the origins, uses, and effects of drug abuse. Of particular interest is the section on drug trafficking.

Menhard, Francha Roffé. *Drugs: Facts About Amphetamines*. Tarrytown, N.J.: Marshall Cavendish, 2006. Provides information on the characteristics, legal status, history, abuse, and treatment of addiction to amphetamines and methamphetamine.

Pellowski, Michael. *Amphetamine Drug Dangers*. Berkeley Heights, N.J.: Enslow, 2000. Discusses stimulant drugs in general and amphetamines in particular. Topics of interest include the signs and symptoms of amphetamine abuse.

See also: Club drugs; Controlled Substances Act of 1970; Drug abuse and dependence; Drug classification; Drug confirmation tests; Drug Enforcement Administration, U.S.; Drug paraphernalia; Meth labs; Stimulants.

Anabolic Steroid Control Act of 2004

Date: Enacted on October 22, 2004
The Law: Federal legislation designed to clarify definitions of anabolic steroids, to provide for research and education activities relating to steroids and steroid precursors, and to expand regulatory and enforcement authority.
Significance: The Anabolic Steroid Control Act of 2004 represented an attempt by the U.S. government to address the growing problem of the use of anabolic steroids, particularly by young people. The law strengthened legal penalties for distribution and possession of these drugs while also encouraging increased education about their dangers for children and adolescents.

Anabolic steroids are synthetic chemicals that mimic the action of the hormone testosterone in the body. They originally found a valued use in maintaining tissue integrity in sufferers of chronic disease. Athletes, however, soon discovered that the muscle-promoting activity of anabolic steroids could enhance performance and give them decided advantages over other athletes in competition, and the use of these drugs became pervasive throughout the sporting world. When they found a place among American male teenagers craving larger muscles and better athletic performance, the U.S. Congress took note.

Congress first criminalized the nonmedical use of anabolic steroids by passing the Anabolic Steroid Control Act of 1990, which made it clear that anyone illegally possessing these drugs was subject to arrest and prosecution. Under the 1990 act, a first offense of simple possession was punishable by up to one year in prison, a minimum fine of $1,000, or both. The penalties increased for those with previous convictions related to narcotics crimes. The act reserved the most severe penalties for individuals who distributed or dispensed steroids. These activities carried a penalty of up to five years in prison, a fine of $250,000, or both. Penalties were higher for repeat offenders, and fines could rise to $1,000,000 for defendants that were other than individuals.

Although the 1990 act was an improvement over previous legislation, it did not go far enough. For example, the 1990 act listed only twenty-seven controlled substances; the Anabolic Steroid Control Act of 2004 act more than doubled that number in addition to stiffening penalties and providing for research and education regarding anabolic steroids. The 2004 act significantly increased the maximum term of imprisonment, fine, and length of supervised release for the manufacture or distribution of anabolic steroids. It also broadened the definition of an anabolic steroid to encompass any drug or hormonal substance chemically related to testosterone. The act specifically excluded estrogens, progestins, corticosteroids, and dehydroepiandrosterone from that list while designating fifty-nine specific drugs as anabolic steroids. Finally, the act encouraged the use of federal grants to carry out science-based education programs in elementary and secondary schools to highlight the harmful effects of anabolic steroids.

Although a great deal of debate continues regarding the negative effects of anabolic steroids, proponents of the 2004 legislation took their lead from studies that had found that these drugs may damage the liver, kidney, heart, and sexual organs. In addition, research has indicated that the use of anabolic steroids by children could prevent them from reaching their full height, and use of the drugs has been associated with outbursts of anger and violence (often referred to as "roid rage"). In recognition of anabolic steroids' potential for damage, U.S. president George W. Bush called for a "get-tough approach" to steroid abuse in his 2004 state of the union address. The Anabolic Steroid Control Act of 2004 was a step in that direction.

Richard S. Spira

Further Reading

Aretha, David. *Steroids and Other Performance-Enhancing Drugs*. Berkeley Heights, N.J.: Enslow, 2005.

Gray, James. *Why Our Drug Laws Have Failed and What We Can Do About It: A Judicial Indictment of the War on Drugs*. Philadelphia: Temple University Press, 2001.

Monroe, Judy. *Steroids, Sports, and Body Image: The Risks of Performance-Enhancing Drugs*. Berkeley Heights, N.J.: Enslow, 2004.

Yesalis, Charles E. *Anabolic Steroids in Sport and Exercise*. Champaign, Ill.: Human Kinetics, 2000.

See also: Athlete drug testing; Drug confirmation tests; Drug Enforcement Administration, U.S.; Forensic toxicology; Performance-enhancing drugs; Toxicological analysis.

Analytical instrumentation

Definition: Tools used during the chemical and physical investigation of physical evidence to identify components and their associated concentrations.

Significance: The scientific evaluation of forensic samples provides information that can be useful to law-enforcement investigators. The instruments employed by forensic scientists are designed to detect and measure small quantities and fine details, thus enabling comparisons of samples that can link suspects to crime scenes or eliminate persons from suspicion.

Advances in analytical instrumentation have significantly changed how forensic investigations are completed. Forensic scientists use many different types of analytical instruments, but all these tools serve the purpose of enabling the scientists to obtain more information on forensic samples. Analytical techniques have the ability to change a sample from one that was thought to have only class characteristics to one that has individual characteristics, making it more valuable in an investigation. This ability to detect individual characteristics is one reason analytical instrumentation has become an important part of forensic investigations.

Analytical instruments can be grouped according to the types of chemical and physical properties they measure. The analytical techniques most commonly used by forensic scientists are microscopy, chromatography, electrophoresis, spectrometry, and spectroscopy.

Microscopy

Light microscopy, or the use of light microscopes, allows forensic analysts to magnify samples so the fine details can be viewed and evaluated. Light microscopes have the ability to magnify up to around 1,500× (that is, 1,500 times normal size). Light microscopy is useful for comparisons of samples and in the evaluation of specimens for similarities and differences. Common light microscopes used in forensic science include the compound microscope, the stereo microscope, and the comparison microscope. A comparison microscope allows an analyst to view two samples side by side, so they can easily be compared; fiber samples and bullets are among the kinds of forensic evidence often compared in this way.

An electron microscope uses a beam of electrons to probe a sample and allows a forensic scientist to view a sample at a greater magnification than is possible with a light microscope. A common type of electron microscope used in forensic applications is the scanning electron microscope (SEM), which can reach a magnification of 100,000× or greater. Another advan-

tage of the SEM is that it enables the scientist to probe the elemental composition and elemental distribution of specimens using the X-ray fluorescence property of the microscope.

Chromatography and Electrophoresis

Forensic scientists use chromatography and electrophoresis to analyze complex mixtures of chemicals. The term "chromatography" is used to refer to a range of techniques that allow the separation of the individual components of chemical mixtures through the use of either a gas or a liquid moving phase. Chromatographic analysis can be used to determine all the different chemical components that make up a sample and how much of each component is present.

The main types of chromatography used in forensic investigations are gas chromatography (GC) and high-performance liquid chromatography (HPLC). GC separates, detects, and quantifies volatile species (atoms, molecules, or ions) or chemical compounds that can be converted to the gas phase by heating. Once in a gas phase, species move at different rates through a column, which results in a physical separation between components. This technique is very useful for arson investigations, in which fire accelerants often need to be evaluated. HPLC involves the analysis of mostly organic samples (molecules containing carbon) in a liquid state. The samples are dissolved in a suitable liquid solvent, such as water or an alcohol. This technique can be used to identify and determine the amounts of different drugs in samples collected at crime scenes.

Capillary electrophoresis is a technique used by forensic scientists to separate charged chemical species such as proteins and peptides. It uses an electric potential to cause positive and negative charged species to migrate and separate into components. The main forensic application of this technique is in DNA (deoxyribonucleic acid) analysis.

Spectrometry and Spectroscopy

Forensic scientists use molecular spectrometry and spectrophotometry to look at the molecular or organic structure of chemical compounds. Techniques such as Fourier transform infrared (FTIR) spectrometry, ultraviolet and visible spectrometry (UV-Vis), and mass spectrometry (MS) allow analysts to classify and identify chemicals by their molecular spectra. FTIR spectrometry uses infrared light, and UV-Vis uses visible and ultraviolet light. A forensic scientist might compare an FTIR spectra of a forensic sample such as a white powder found at a crime scene with a spectral library of known compounds in order to identify the powder. FTIR can also be attached to a microscope to create a microspectrophotometer, which enables examination of the molecular structure of a sample. MS is often carried out in conjunction with gas or liquid chromatography to provide more detailed identification of components in a forensic sample.

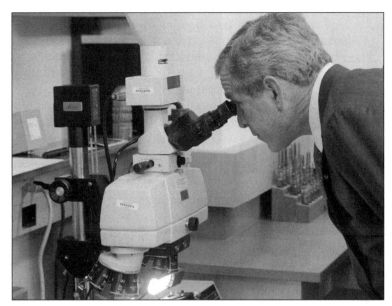

President George W. Bush looks through a comparison microscope in the ballistics room of the Federal Bureau of Investigation Laboratory in Quantico, Virginia. *(AP/Wide World Photos)*

Elemental spectroscopy is accomplished by techniques that measure the elemental composition and concentration in a sample. Atomic absorption (AA), inductively coupled plasma (ICP), X-ray fluorescence (XRF), X-ray diffraction (XRD), and neutron activation analysis (NAA) are typical instruments used in inorganic analysis. XRF can be used to determine the presence of lead and barium in gunshot residue. ICP can be used in finding out what elements are in a metal sample, such as a bullet; this allows the scientist to determine the alloy type, which then may be traced to a manufacturer.

Dwight Tshudy

Further Reading

Bell, Suzanne. *Forensic Chemistry*. Upper Saddle River, N.J.: Pearson Prentice Hall, 2006. Chemistry-focused text presents discussion of the use of analytical instrumentation.

Girard, James E. *Criminalistics: Forensic Science and Crime*. Sudbury, Mass.: Jones & Bartlett, 2008. Textbook includes sections in which instruments and their uses are described.

Houck, Max M., and Jay A. Siegel. *Fundamentals of Forensic Science*. Burlington, Mass.: Elsevier Academic Press, 2006. Good general textbook includes a well-presented section on analytical tools.

James, Stuart H., and Jon J. Nordby, eds. *Forensic Science: An Introduction to Scientific and Investigative Techniques*. 2d ed. Boca Raton, Fla.: CRC Press, 2005. Covers analytical instrumentation in a section on forensic science in the laboratory.

Johll, Matthew. *Investigating Chemistry: A Forensic Science Approach*. New York: W. H. Freeman, 2007. Textbook designed for non-science majors presents simple explanations of analytical instruments and their uses.

Saferstein, Richard. *Criminalistics: An Introduction to Forensic Science*. 9th ed. Upper Saddle River, N.J.: Pearson Prentice Hall, 2007. Introductory text describes and explains the uses of various analytical instruments and techniques.

See also: Atomic absorption spectrophotometry; Chromatography; Column chromatography; Crime laboratories; Electrophoresis; Fourier transform infrared spectrophotometer; Gas chromatography; High-performance liquid chromatography; Homogeneous enzyme immunoassay; Mass spectrometry; Microspectrophotometry; Scanning electron microscopy; Spectroscopy.

Anastasia remains identification

Date: Began in July, 1991

The Event: After Bolshevik revolutionaries executed the members of the Russian imperial family in 1918, rumors persisted—and the notion was popularized in books and films—that two of the czar's children, Anastasia and Alexei, survived. Numerous pretenders came forward claiming to be the missing Princess Anastasia. Beginning in 1991, forensic science was put to use in attempts to clarify which members of the family were in fact executed.

Significance: The forensic investigation undertaken to identify the remains of the Russian royal family, the Romanovs, was the first to employ both short tandem repeats and mitochondrial DNA for the identification of historical figures, portending the application of the same techniques in the identification of the remains of both well-known and obscure persons in future investigations.

On July 17, 1918, Czar Nicholas II of Russia, his family members (Czarina Alexandra, their four daughters—Olga, Tatiana, Maria, and Anastasia—and only son, Alexei), the family physician, and three servants were herded into a basement and executed by firing squad or by stab wounds from bayonets. Eyewitness accounts stated that most of the bodies were then placed in a shallow pit, and sulfuric acid was added to impede identification; the remains of Alexei and an unidentified daughter were burned separately.

In 1991, the Russian government authorized an investigation at the burial site. The July, 1991, exhumation of the grave near Yekaterinburg revealed that it contained nine corpses. A Russian forensic team did extensive work in determining the sexes of the bodies, in estimating ages, and in employing odontology and computer-assisted facial reconstruction to attempt identification, although the latter tests were limited because the facial areas of the skulls were destroyed. The scientists determined that the grave contained the remains of the czar, the czarina, three of the daughters, the physician, and the servants. However, a disagreement about the identification of the daughters developed between the Russian scientists and an American team of forensic anthropologists who had been hired by the city of Yekaterinburg. Relying on the same evidence, the Russian researchers argued that the missing daughter was Maria, whereas the Americans thought her to be Anastasia. No evidence of the allegedly burned children's bodies was found at the site or nearby.

To bolster the authenticity of the identification, a joint team of British and Russian scientists evaluated the remains using three DNA (deoxyribonucleic acid) tests. The first confirmed that the mass grave contained five female and four male bodies. The second test was a short tandem repeat (STR) analysis; this type of test can establish whether individuals are closely related to one another. The second test showed that the remains included parents and three children. The third test was mitochondrial DNA (mtDNA) sequencing, which can be employed for identification even when the related persons are separated by many generations; mtDNA is passed directly from mothers to their children. DNA from the body believed to be that of the czar was compared with DNA samples from two of the czar's maternal grandmother's descendants; DNA from the czarina and the children was compared with DNA from Prince Philip, duke of Edinburgh, whose maternal grandmother was the czarina's sister. In both instances, matches were positive.

The researchers reported a 98.5 percent probability that the remains were those of the imperial family based on the anthropological, historical, and scientific evidence. They de-

The children of the last czar of Russia (from left): Tatiana, Maria, Anastasia, Olga, and Alexei. This photograph was taken sometime around 1916, approximately two years before the members of the Romanov family were executed. *(Library of Congress)*

clined, however, to confirm the individual identities of the daughters. Both American and German authorities tested the DNA of Anna Anderson, the best known of the Anastasia pretenders, using STR analysis, and the DNA was not a match to the royal family.

In 2007, Russian archaeologists announced that they believed they had found the remains of the two missing children of the imperial family near the site where Nicholas, Alexandra, and the other three daughters were found. In April, 2008, Russian forensic scientists who had performed analyses on DNA extracted from teeth, bones, and other fragments of those remains announced their findings: The last two of the Romanov children, Alexei and Maria, had been identified. The remains found in the mass burial site examined beginning in 1991 thus included those of Anastasia.

Susan Coleman

Further Reading

Gill, Peter, et al. "Identification of the Remains of the Romanov Family by DNA Analysis." *Nature Genetics* 6 (February, 1994): 130-135.

Jobling, Mark A., and Peter Gill. "Encoded Evidence: DNA in Forensic Analysis." *Nature Reviews Genetics* 5 (October, 2004): 739-751.

Klier, John, and Helen Mingay. *Quest for Anastasia: Solving the Mystery of the Lost Romanovs.* Secaucus, N.J.: Carol, 1997.

Rudin, Norah, and Keith Inman. *An Introduction to Forensic DNA Analysis.* 2d ed. Boca Raton, Fla.: CRC Press, 2002.

See also: Anthropometry; DNA analysis; Forensic odontology; Louis XVII remains identification; Mass graves; Mitochondrial DNA analysis and typing; Nicholas II remains identification; Short tandem repeat analysis; Skeletal analysis.

Ancient criminal cases and mysteries

Significance: Many ancient humans engaged in illegal behaviors, ranging from theft to murder, that share elements with crimes that have been encountered by centuries of law-enforcement personnel, who in turn developed effective forensic investigation techniques. Intrigued by certain unsolved ancient crimes, some modern investigators have applied the latest forensic methods and tools to the evaluation of the available evidence in those cases, and their work has sometimes led to improvements in modern forensic analysis.

In ancient times, legal systems and procedures were not standardized; they functioned distinctly in diverse locales and during various periods. Biblical accounts, particularly in the Old Testament, depict many crimes, beginning with Cain's killing of Abel. Ancient historians, including Herodotus (c. 484-425 B.C.E.) and Tacitus (c. 56-120 C.E.), recorded incidents of crime based on anecdotes they heard from contemporaries. The historical veracity of many of these accounts is questionable, however. Information regarding ancient crimes is often inconsistent, vague, and greatly distanced from eyewitnesses. Biased chroniclers often excluded information that countered their own beliefs or those of their patrons or incorporated incorrect details. In addition, wars and other disasters led to the loss of records that described crimes.

Ancient Laws

The crimes committed in the ancient world were similar to the malicious actions humans have pursued in all eras. Ancient people robbed, raped, abducted, and murdered much as modern people do, prompted by greed, revenge, and other motives. Rulers shaped most early laws to define crimes and establish punishments. The first known law code was issued by Hammurabi during his reign as king of Babylon, from approximately 1792 to 1750 B.C.E. The behaviors defined as crimes in ancient times were those that violated the moral and social beliefs valued by the leaders who made the laws; these behaviors were often directed against royalty, governments, or temples, and they had negative impacts on communities. People were often considered criminal for disobeying rules and customs, especially those related to religious practices, as ancient theology and politics were often linked. Many ancient people perceived blasphemy to be a criminal activity.

Laws in particular areas changed as the ruling powers changed with invasions and wars, and the laws that were enforced varied depending on rulers' agendas, attitudes, and tolerance for criminality. Ancient philosophers, including Aristotle (384-322 B.C.E.) and Plato (c. 427-347 B.C.E.), contemplated the role of crime and punishment in societies and the need for justice. The punishments for criminal behavior in ancient times included seizure of property, imprisonment, forced labor, mutilation, exile, and execution. Individuals usually dealt with personal crimes, such as embezzlement and extortion, by seeking compensation.

Just as the laws varied, the courts of the ancient world operated differently in different places and times. Most of the courts of ancient Rome were conducted by praetors, or magistrates, who chose the cases that would be heard. Juries came to decisions of acquittal, condemnation, or not proven after hearing cases in which alleged criminals were pitted against their accusers; in these courts, oratorical evidence was offered and witnesses testified. In ancient Greek courts, citizen juries, often consisting of several hundred men, ruled on the cases presented; both prosecutors and defenders in these cases used oratory rather than evidence to sway jurors' decisions.

Murder

Ancient people committed homicide for many of the same reasons modern people do. Some murders were intentional, committed out of jealousy, rage, or vengeance; others were the unintentional result of other crimes, such as theft or assault. Assassinations of rulers occurred frequently throughout ancient history. Although most of the homicides that took place in ancient times remain anonymous, at least one is widely known in the modern world: the assassination of the Roman ruler Julius Caesar (100-44 B.C.E.), whose political actions provoked his rivals to conspire to kill him.

After he attained power in 49 B.C.E., Caesar instituted reforms that outraged his enemies, who feared losing the power and prestige that had been accorded their families for generations. On March 15, 44 B.C.E., Caesar went to the Theatre of Pompey, where the Roman senate was meeting. A group of senators led by Marcus Junius Brutus swarmed around Caesar and slashed him with knives. A physician who later examined Caesar's corpse noted that he had twenty-three stab wounds. Roman officials ordered that Caesar's assassins be apprehended and slain.

Other notorious ancient assassinations targeted Roman and Egyptian leaders. On September 18, 96 C.E., Roman emperor Domitian was assassinated. Tired of Domitian's oppression, his chamberlain had devised a plot against him, involving Domitian's guards as accomplices. A steward named Stephanus fatally stabbed Domitian, whose supporters avenged his death by killing the assassins. In ancient Egypt, women living in the pharaoh's harem plotted to remove Ramses III from power in 1153 B.C.E. A judicial papyrus dating from that time indicates that numerous people were arrested for actions related to the crime, of whom twenty-four were declared guilty and probably executed.

Poisoning

During ancient times, scientific techniques to detect poisons in bodies were nonexistent. This inability to trace toxins to fatalities benefited many people who relied on poisoning as the most effective method of eliminating enemies and rivals. Ancient poisoners derived toxins from organic sources, both plants and animal venoms, to contaminate food and drink or create deadly lotions. Arsenic, which was used to season foods and was incorporated in pharmaceuticals, proved lethal when concentrated in bodily tissues.

Among the notorious poisoners in ancient Rome (around 74 B.C.E.) was a man named Oppianicus, whose criminal acts included poisoning but failing to kill Cluentius, whose stepfather Oppianicus had killed so he could marry Cluentius's mother, Sassia. Oppianicus schemed to acquire Cluentius's belongings, which his mother would inherit after his death. At Oppianicus's trial for attempting to kill Cluentius, his defense tried to discredit Cluentius by claiming that Cluentius had bribed judges. The tactic did not work, and Oppianicus was exiled. Sassia and Cluentius's sister later sought prosecution of Cluentius for allegedly attempting to poison Oppianicus, and Cluentius was acquitted. When Oppianicus was subsequently murdered, Cluentius, who was accused of the crime, benefited from the defense oratory of Roman statesman and philosopher Cicero. Cicero's strategy was not to stress Cluentius's innocence but to focus on the crimes Oppianicus had committed to suggest that his death was justified. Cicero's persuasive statements resulted in Cluentius's exoneration.

Another ancient Roman poisoner, Locusta, was so well-known for her herbal expertise that prominent Romans sought her out for her poisoning services. Her influential clients included the wife of Emperor Claudius (10 B.C.E.-54 C.E.), Agrippina the Younger, who schemed for her son from an earlier marriage, Nero, to succeed Claudius as emperor rather than Britannicus, Claudius's son by a previous wife. Deciding to kill Claudius first, Agrippina contacted Locusta, who served Claudius a meal containing poisonous mushrooms. The physician who attended Claudius when he became ill was allied with Agrippina; he gave the emperor a poisonous enema, ensuring his death. Although Locusta was incarcerated for that murder, Nero, the new emperor, released her so that she could kill Britannicus with tainted wine.

Theft and Civic Crimes

Theft was a common crime in ancient communities. Thieves picked pockets, stole goods from markets and homes, and embezzled. Papyrus records from ancient Egypt describe such notable heists as the Great Tomb Robbery. Royal tombs at Thebes were particularly vulnerable to robbery. Some corrupt officials aided thieves or stole from religious and royal sites. Records describe the plundering of the Karnak temple complex by a guard.

An example of the view of some ideas as criminal according to ancient law is found in the trial of the philosopher Socrates (470-399 B.C.E.) in Athens. Many ancient communities deemed behavior that ignored or denounced tradition as criminal. Trials contemplated whether people should be punished for such sacrilegious acts as vandalizing statues related to gods. In 399 B.C.E., three prominent citizens of Athens—a poet, an artisan, and a politician—initiated prosecution against Socrates, asserting that his crime was suggesting that people reject the city's gods. Also, Socrates had prompted Athenians, particularly young men, to examine their leaders' rules and conduct critically.

Because of his views, Socrates had alienated many Athenians who considered his behavior criminal and sought his conviction. Some people despised Socrates for criticizing their professions and demeaning them personally. A group of 280 jurors, out of a jury of approximately 500 men, declared Socrates guilty and sentenced him to death. They stressed that Socrates had endangered Athenians with his erratic religious views and his arguments that citizens should scrutinize their leaders. Socrates carried out his own execution by consuming hemlock.

Death of Tutankhamen

The mysterious death of Eighteenth Dynasty Egyptian pharaoh Tutankhamen has intrigued people since Howard Carter and his archaeological team located the tomb of the "boy king" in 1922. The objects in the tomb, including the pharaoh's mummy, provoked speculation regarding why and how Tutankhamen died in 1323 B.C.E. at the age of eighteen. The tomb's small size and arrangement were inconsistent with the stature accorded to other royal figures, suggesting that Tutankhamen's death was unexpected and required expeditious arrangements. In addition to suggesting that Tutankhamen may have succumbed to illness, archaeologists and historians have speculated that he may have been the victim of assassination by a rival.

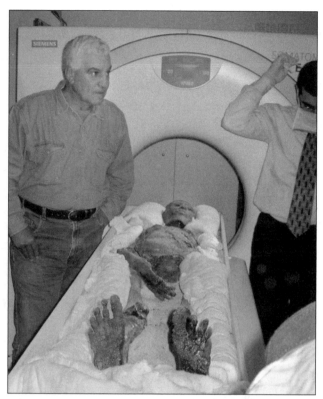

Zahi Hawass, head of the Egyptian Supreme Council for Antiquities, oversees a computed tomography (CT) scan of the mummy of King Tutankhamen in an attempt to learn more about how the young pharaoh died. (AP/Wide World Photos)

For several decades, scientists lacked sufficiently effective forensic methods and tools to evaluate hypotheses regarding Tutankhamen's premature demise. In 1968, Ronald Harrison, head of the Anatomy Department at the University of Liverpool, X-rayed Tutankhamen's mummy. He noted damage to the skull that suggested the pharaoh may have sustained a violent blow to the head. Harrison also observed that some of Tutankhamen's ribs and his breastbone were absent. Murder theorists identified four people who might have slain Tutankhamen to seize power: his adviser Ay, who became the next pharaoh; army commander Horemheb, who succeeded Ay and purged monuments of Tutankhamen references; his treasurer, Maya; or his wife, Ankhesenamun.

Investigation and speculation regarding Tutankhamen's death continued, and in January, 2005, Zahi Hawass, Egypt's chief archaeol-

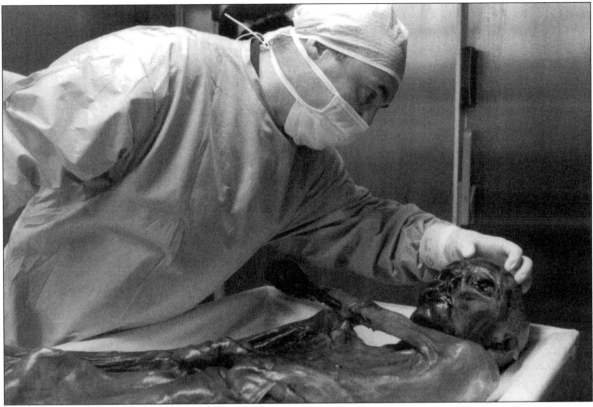

A researcher at the South Tyrol Museum of Archaeology prepares to take samples from the corpse known as Ötzi the Iceman. Scientists have determined that the body is more than five thousand years old. *(AP/Wide World Photos)*

ogist, oversaw a full digital evaluation of Tutankhamen's mummy through the use of a computed tomography (CT) scan. The approximately seventeen hundred images generated in the scan indicated that the pharaoh had been healthy and probably had not suffered fatal trauma, intensifying the mystery regarding his death. The scan revealed a fractured left femur (thighbone), causing scientists to ponder whether the bone had been broken before or after the pharaoh died. Many forensic experts interpreted the evidence provided by the CT scan as proof that Tutankhamen was probably not murdered, but many scientists have continued to seek definitive information that can point to the exact cause of his death.

Unresolved Cases

Several ancient murders have intrigued modern forensic investigators, some of whom have applied their techniques, tools, and knowl-

edge to efforts to understand what happened. Discoveries of the preserved corpses of ancient persons, such as Kennewick man, discovered in the Pacific Northwest in 1996, and related artifacts have allowed scientists to gain insights into ancient lifestyles and communities. Although forensic methods have helped scientists to develop plausible interpretations regarding specific ancient bodies, in cases where they have suspected murder they have been unable to learn conclusively why particular individuals died or who might have killed them. Those crimes remain mysteries, although each advancement in forensic science offers continuing hope for resolution.

In September, 1991, mountain climbers found a frozen male corpse on a glacier in the Ötztal Alps near the border between Austria and Italy. When the clothing on the body and items adjacent to it were examined, the authorities realized the remains were ancient. The corpse, which later became known as Ötzi the Iceman, and the objects found with it were shipped to Innsbruck, Austria, where they were evaluated at the Forensic Medical Institute by Konrad Spindler, an archaeologist. Radiocarbon dating indicated that the remains were approximately 5,300 years old.

Scientists employed numerous methods, including CT scans, in attempting to solve the mystery of Ötzi's demise and whether it was criminal or accidental. In 1998, Ötzi was transported to Bolzano, Italy, where forensic pathologist Peter Vanezis studied the skull and performed a facial reconstruction. During June, 2001, Paul Gostner, a radiologist at Bolzano General Hospital, X-rayed the body and found that an arrowhead was lodged in Ötzi's shoulder. Stating that Ötzi had been murdered, forensic experts suggested various ways in which the death might have taken place. Some speculated that Ötzi may have been killed during warfare, that he may have been the victim of rival hunters, or that he may have been a human sacrifice.

Similarly preserved ancient bodies found in northern Europe have also stimulated forensic analysis. Bodies immersed in peat bogs for centuries have retained evidence useful for forensic examination. Investigators have hypothesized that the so-called bog bodies were those of ancient murder victims, people whose lives were sacrificed to gods, or executed criminals. Radiometric dating has shown that some of those found in the bogs lived during the British Iron Age (seventh century B.C.E. to fifth century B.C.E.). Forensic scientists have evaluated their garments, wounds, and physical characteristics using techniques similar to those employed in the assessment of Ötzi. The evidence they have found, including fingerprints and preserved injuries, indicates that many of these ancient people met violent deaths—strangled with ropes, drowned, stabbed, or decapitated.

Profiting from Ancient Crimes

The appeal of enigmatic ancient crimes, particularly mysteries associated with royalty, has abetted criminal activity in later centuries. Obscure information regarding historic individuals has often enabled criminals to carry out fraudulent schemes involving the deception of antiquities collectors.

In October, 2000, for example, information accompanying a mummy that was seized from the dwelling of a Karachi, Pakistan, chieftain stated that the remains were those of Rhodugune, young daughter of Persian king Xerxes I, who had lived in the fifth century B.C.E. Investigators noted the sloppy mummification procedures evidenced by the body and the odd usage of the Greek version of the princess's Persian name, Wardegauna. Scientists conducted X-ray and CT scans of the mummy at Pakistan's National Museum, and the results, along with further forensic examination, revealed that the mummy, although unusually short, was that of an adult woman in her twenties, not a child, and radiocarbon dating revealed she had died in 1996. Given that the woman's spine was fractured, authorities feared she had been murdered by people engaged in the marketing of counterfeit ancient mummies.

Elizabeth D. Schafer

Further Reading

Emsley, John. *The Elements of Murder: A History of Poison.* New York: Oxford University Press, 2005. Presents details about how killers have used poisons throughout history. Features chapters on arsenic, lead, and other toxins.

Hawass, Zahi. *Tutankhamun: The Mystery of the Boy King.* Washington, D.C.: National Geographic Society, 2005. Egyptian archaeologist describes his experiences with forensic investigations regarding Tutankhamen's death. Features CT images.

Redford, Susan. *The Harem Conspiracy: The Murder of Ramesses III.* De Kalb: Northern Illinois University Press, 2002. Archaeologist describes the women who plotted to kill the Egyptian king and their motivations based on temple and papyri resources.

Wilson, Emily. *The Death of Socrates.* Cambridge, Mass.: Harvard University Press, 2007. Examines how Socrates' ideas were considered criminal in ancient Athens and how the philosopher's trial and execution influenced thought and culture.

Woolf, Greg. *Et Tu, Brute? The Murder of*

Caesar and Political Assassination. Cambridge, Mass.: Harvard University Press, 2007. Presents comprehensive discussion of Caesar's death and the role of assassins in ancient history. Includes photographs of artifacts and artworks that portray the crime and its participants.

See also: Ancient science and forensics; Arsenic; Art forgery; Assassination; Food poisoning; Forensic archaeology; Homicide; Kennewick man; Knife wounds; Mummification; Peruvian Ice Maiden.

Ancient science and forensics

Significance: Although ancient scientific techniques lacked the sophistication of modern forensic methods, individual examples of people applying science and technology to legal issues foreshadowed some of the basic concepts that forensic scientists recognized and developed centuries later.

The introduction of scientifically collected and examined evidence in legal proceedings is a relatively modern development. In ancient times, evidence presented in legal proceedings was generally limited to the oral arguments that prosecutors and defenders presented in courts. No concept of "forensic science" existed. Prosecutors and defenders relied primarily on words to convince officials and juries of the correctness of their cases. Most ancient legal personnel did not consider seeking such evidence as fibers, fingerprints, and hair or have techniques to evaluate them.

The levels to which the hard sciences were developed varied among different ancient civilizations. Scientists typically shaped their pursuits to please patrons and rulers. Many people associated science with superstitions and magic, especially with the ancient world's fascination with the pseudoscience of alchemy, which sought to transform other elements into gold. Religious beliefs frequently influenced ancient science. Nevertheless, some people did pursue science for practical reasons, such as measuring land.

Before Forensic Science

The absence of standardized forensic science practices throughout the ancient world aided criminals in escaping punishment. Without the input of scientifically collected and examined evidence, criminal investigations typically relied on force to secure confessions from suspects. In court trials, the only evidence that was usually considered was the testimonies of witnesses and the arguments of prosecutors and defenders. In rare instances, descriptions of the symptoms displayed by victims of poisoning or the physical damage inflicted by assaults might be presented.

As scientific knowledge expanded, some people began applying common sense to evident connections between physical evidence and crimes. Some records of ancient legal proceedings include records of practices that resemble modern forensic techniques. However, many people were probably unaware of the scientific bases behind their methods. They tended to rely on common sense and practical approaches to solving problems related to problems they considered criminal or threatening. For example, a passage in the Bible's book of Judges describes a technique foreshadowing modern voice identification. Jephthah insisted people say the word *shibboleth* so he could identify his allies and detect enemy Ephraimites who pronounced the word differently. Originating in this passage in the Bible, the ancient Hebrew word for stream, *shibboleth*, came to be used in English as a word or saying that might be used as a kind of password for a group while lacking any true meaning.

Forensic Foreshadowing

Some early forensic scientific methods were based on accidental discoveries, or epiphanies, achieved while pursuing solutions to other problems. For example, the third century B.C.E. Greek mathematician and inventor Archimedes was challenged to prove that a goldsmith had cheated King Hieron II of Syracuse by mixing inferior metals with the pure gold he had been given to make a crown for the king. Archimedes' investigation was constrained by the requirement that he not damage the royal crown in any way. According to legend, while Archimedes was taking a bath, he noticed that his body displaced an amount of water equal to his own weight. Drawing on that observation, he submerged both King Hieron's crown and an amount of gold equivalent to what the goldsmith was supposed to have used for the crown in water. When he determined than the crown displaced less water than the control sample, he proved that the goldsmith had committed fraud.

Poisons had a special fascination for ancient scientists. However, physicians had a difficult time proving that apparent victims of poisoning crimes were actually poisoned, as the symptoms of poisoning and natural seizures were similar. Their attempts to devise methods to prove victims had been poisoned were simplistic compared to later toxicology developments. Around 200 B.C.E., the Middle Eastern physician and poet Nicander of Colophon studied poisons and their antidotes and wrote two books on the subject. *Alexipharmaca* describes many types of poisonings by animals, plants, and inanimate agents and suggests antidotes and other treatments. *Theriaca* deals more narrowly with poisonings caused by animal bites, stings, and scratches. Nicander had a strong reputation during his time, but his books were not published in print until 1499, when a joint edition appeared in Venice.

The modern forensic science of odontology, which is used to identify bodies of victims by their teeth, has at least one ancient precursor. In 49 C.E., the Roman emperor Nero's mother, Agrippina, sent for the head of her enemy Lollia Paulina after the woman reportedly committed suicide so that Agrippina could verify her death. The dead woman's face was distorted beyond easy recognition, but when Agrippina looked at the teeth in the head, she recognized a distinctively colored front tooth that she had previously noticed in Lollia Paulina's mouth.

Detecting Fraud

Documents were frequently forged in ancient times, when most people were illiterate, so gov-

---

Voice Identification in the Bible

These verses from the Bible's book of Judges describe a technique that might be viewed as foreshadowing modern voice identification:

12:4 Then Jephthah gathered together all the men of Gilead, and fought with Ephraim: and the men of Gilead smote Ephraim, because they said, Ye Gileadites are fugitives of Ephraim among the Ephraimites, and among the Manassites.

12:5 And the Gileadites took the passages of Jordan before the Ephraimites: and it was so that when those Ephraimites which were escaped said, Let me go over; that the men of Gilead said unto him, Art thou an Ephraimite? If he said, Nay;

12:6 Then said they unto him, Say now Shibboleth: and he said Sibboleth: for he could not frame to pronounce it right. Then they took him, and slew him at the passages of Jordan: and there fell at that time of the Ephraimites forty and two thousand.

---

ernment officials sought effective methods to detect fraudulent wills, deeds, and contracts. In ancient Rome, legal officials used people considered to be experts in handwriting analysis to evaluate documents by comparing writing styles of known and suspect scribes

Seeking ways to detect lies, some ancients created primitive polygraph techniques. In contrast to modern polygraphs, which measure physiological responses, the techniques of the ancients were based solely on observations of the suspects' behavior, even though psychology was not yet an established scientific field. For example, around 500 B.C.E., priests in India tested people accused of thievery by placing them in darkened tents with donkeys whose tails were coated in soot. The priests would tell the suspected thieves to tug the animals' tails because the donkeys would bray when touched by thieves. Suspects who left the tents with their hands unsoiled by soot were considered guilty. Ancient Arabs conducted similar tests using grease instead of soot on the animals' tails.

Ancient Chinese officials devised a different kind of lie-detecting test. They placed dried rice in the mouths of criminal suspects, whom they told to spit out the grains. Suspects with rice still sticking on their tongues were exposed as liars. This test actually had some scientific validity, as human bodies often respond to stress by being unable to produce the saliva necessary to spit. Because guilty suspects were more likely than the innocent to feel stress, they were less likely to be able to spit the rice out of their mouths.

Prints

Throughout human history, every individual person has had fingerprints, palm prints, and footprints that are unique. These prints have always offered the potential for identifying criminal suspects but had to wait for a time when

Portrait of the ancient Greek mathematician Archimedes by the early seventeenth century Spanish painter Jusepe de Ribera. All depictions of Archimedes are fanciful, as no contemporary pictures or sculptures of him are known to exist. *(Library of Congress)*

their forensic value was understood. The ancients were aware that the lines on their palms and fingertips formed distinct patterns and may have even recognized that those patterns were unique. However, they did not comprehend how prints left on objects could be used to identify criminal who touched things such as murder weapons and stolen items. They used fingerprints primarily to identify objects and documents, not for criminal investigations. Various hand and fingerprints were used for signatures that were recognized in courts and business dealings. In Babylonia, for example, fingerprints were used to mark tablets related to business activities at least as early as 2000 B.C.E. In East Asia, ancient Chinese and Japanese officials and traders used thumbprints to distinguish legal seals and documents, and handprints were often used to sign divorce documents.

A court case in which print evidence did prove significant occurred in Rome during the first century C.E., when a Roman attorney named Quintilian defended a man accused of killing his mother. A talented speaker, Quintilian combined his oratorical skills with some scientific knowledge to build his legal strategy. He showed that a bloody palm print that had dried at the site of the murder was not compatible in size with the hand of his client. He went on to argue that the print had been placed at the crime scene by someone who wished to frame the murdered woman's son. Thanks to his comparison of handprints, he won his client's acquittal; however, the true murderer was never identified.

Medical Evidence

Many ancient rulers and physicians recognized the importance of medical knowledge to legal systems. The eighteenth century B.C.E. Babylonian king Hammurabi included laws relevant to medicine in the famous law code that he formulated. The early fourth century B.C.E. Greek physician Hippocrates recommended that medical practitioners learn how to recognize injuries and poisonings inflicted by criminal assailants.

Ancient physicians were often involved in investigations of crimes because of their specialized knowledge and their connections with rulers and officials. Medical autopsies go back at least as far as the early third millennium B.C.E. As in modern times, they were performed to determine causes of deaths. However, members of many ancient societies opposed invasive examinations of dead people because they believed that bodies had to be intact for their transition to the afterlife.

The word "autopsy" itself comes from ancient Greek, in which it means seeing with one's own eyes, even though the ancient Greeks seldom performed autopsies. During the third century B.C.E., the Greek physicians Erasistratus and Herophilus of Chalcedon performed autopsies in Alexandria, Egypt, and may have explored how evidence of poisoning and injuries were linked to crimes.

Perhaps the most notable autopsy in ancient history was that of the Roman ruler Julius Caesar, who was stabbed to death by assassins on March 15, 44 B.C.E., at the Forum of Rome. The physician who afterward examined Caesar's body reported to Roman officials that the second stab wound Caesar received was the fatal one. The word "forensic" comes from the Latin word *forum*. Some historians believe that the connection between the two words goes back to the autopsy performed after Caesar was killed at the Roman Forum.

Elizabeth D. Schafer

Further Reading

Evans, Colin. *Murder Two: The Second Casebook of Forensic Detection*. New York: John Wiley & Sons, 2004. Discusses ancient efforts to detect liars, identify corpses, and determine cause of death through methods with scientific elements.

Gagarin, Michael. *Antiphon the Athenian: Oratory, Law, and Justice in the Age of the Sophists*. Austin: University of Texas Press, 2002. Provides examples of the forensic speeches, not scientific evidence, that ancient Greeks used strategically to win in court.

Ramsland, Katherine. *Beating the Devil's Game: A History of Forensic Science and Criminal Investigation*. New York: Berkley Books, 2007. Discusses several significant uses of science in ancient Greek and Roman legal settings.

Ricciuti, Edward. *Science 101: Forensics*. New York: HarperCollins, 2007. Illustrations and text highlight early forensic precursors by ancient peoples, placing those achievements in context with later developments.

Riggsby, Andrew M. *Crime and Community in Ciceronian Rome*. Austin: University of Texas Press, 1999. Describes court procedures and verdict options for various ancient crimes. Explains that oratory was the primary evidence utilized.

See also: Ancient criminal cases and mysteries; Autopsies; Crime scene investigation; Document examination; Epidemiology; Forensic odontology; Forgery; Handwriting analysis; Knife wounds; Medicine; Poisons and antidotes; Ritual killing.

Animal evidence

Definition: Organic materials from nonhumans, excluding insects, analyzed by forensic scientists for use in legal cases.

Significance: With advancements in DNA fingerprinting of dogs, cats, and other domesticated and wild animals, animal evidence has become much more useful in criminal and civil court cases than it was in the past, when individual animals, breeds or even species could not be identified.

The animal evidence involved in cases of crimes against humans most often consists of shed hairs and traces of blood, other body fluids (including saliva and urine), and excrement from either dogs or cats. Given that in the United States about 40 percent of households include at least one dog and 30 percent include at least one cat, crime scene investigators frequently encounter this kind of evidence.

Animal Hair

In relation to crimes against humans, the most commonly analyzed type of animal evidence is shed hair. Research has shown that it is almost impossible for a person to enter a house where a dog or cat lives and not have some of the animal's hair transferred to his or her skin, shoes, or clothing. Criminal perpetrators who live with dogs or cats can thus transfer the hair of their animals to victims or crime scenes. Perpetrators can also pick up animal hairs from crime scenes, from victims' clothing, from household items, or directly from victims' pets.

In 1994, white hairs from a cat named Snowball were used to help convict a Canadian man of murdering his wife. Police investigators found the hairs on the husband's black leather jacket. This was the first evidentiary use of nonhuman DNA (deoxyribonucleic acid) to help solve a crime. In this case, the DNA analysis used feline microsatellite markers mapped by English geneticist Alec Jeffreys. Scientists have concluded that both feline and canine microsatellite markers are almost as discriminating as their human counterparts, not very much diminished by the inbreeding often seen in canines.

Because shed hair lacks a viable root, it usually does not contain enough nuclear DNA to allow short tandem repeat (STR, or microsatellite) fingerprinting of individuals. Instead, criminalists extract and amplify mitochondrial DNA (mtDNA) from the hair shaft, which contains thousands of mitochondria. This type of DNA identification of dogs and cats is most often used to add a layer of evidence rather than to provide a strong association to a particular animal, given that only a single locus is used for mtDNA profiling. In 2002, however, canine mtDNA was admitted into court during the prosecution of David Westerfield in the abduction and murder of seven-year-old Danielle van Dam, whose family owned a pet Weimaraner. This was the first trial in the U.S. to admit canine mtDNA analysis as evidence.

Forensic scientists also analyze the morphological (structural) characteristics of animal hair using compound light microscopy. Characteristic patterns of scales on the cuticle covering the shaft, for example, can be used to determine a particular species. Also, the medulla inside the shaft is informative for the identification of different species; for instance, the medullae of feline hairs show a typical "string of pearls" pattern. These features, among others, are usually used in conjunction with DNA profiling to identify particular animals.

Other Types of Animal Evidence

Animal blood found at crime scenes usually contains enough viable nuclear DNA for STR analysis, which can be used to identify an individual animal. As early as 1998, STRs obtained from dried canine blood linked a suspect to the murder of a Seattle couple and the killing of their dog. Although the suspect was convicted, the canine DNA evidence was not admitted at trial because canine DNA typing was not considered reliable at the time. Since then, the reliability of canine and feline STR profiling has been well established in the scientific literature, and dog and cat DNA evidence is regularly admitted in legal proceedings.

Both urine and excrement from dogs have also provided nuclear DNA to help solve crimes and convict criminals. One example of using DNA from animal fecal matter outside the legal justice system is the identification of the Canadian lynx from scat found near the large cat's paw prints in snow. This technique is being investigated as a way to track the health, distribution, and population densities of certain endangered animal species.

The National Fish and Wildlife Forensics Laboratory in Ashland, Oregon, is dedicated to the collection and analysis of evidence of crimes against wildlife. Law-enforcement agencies submit to the lab the types of animal evidence discussed above in addition to more unusual samples, such as hunting trophies (antlers), carved ivory, hides, furs, bones, teeth, leather goods, feathers, claws, talons, whole carcasses, stomach contents, and Asian medicinals, among other organic and inorganic materials usually investigated in criminal cases. Forensic experts at the facility extract and profile DNA from many of these items; they also employ other methodologies such as morphological and chemical analysis to determine whether samples come from particular species. Much of this work is concerned with supporting law-enforcement efforts to address crimes involving endangered species.

The emerging field of veterinary forensics is

involved in identifying cases of animal abuse against domestic pets. In situations where abuse is suspected, veterinarians or veterinary pathologists most often obtain evidence from deceased whole animals, which are worked up in a manner similar to that employed during autopsies in homicide cases. These professionals look for specific patterns of injuries, telltale wounds, bullet holes, ballistic material, evidence of malnutrition or starvation, signs of torture, and incriminating human evidence (such as blood or hairs). Sometimes insects and maggots found on or in proximity to an animal carcass can be employed to determine the time of death or crime scene location.

Lisa J. Shientag

Further Reading

Cassidy, Brandt G., and Robert A. Gonzales. "DNA Testing in Animal Forensics." *Journal of Wildlife Management* 69 (October, 2005): 1454-1462. Discusses how animal DNA is being used to solve human crimes. Gives examples from specific legal cases and notes the potential pitfalls related to DNA processing and collection methods.

Cooper, John E., and Margaret E. Cooper. *Introduction to Veterinary and Comparative Forensic Medicine*. Ames, Iowa: Blackwell, 2007. Includes discussion of wildlife conservation and links between cruelty to animals and violence toward humans. Intended for veterinarians and law-enforcement officials but written at a level understandable by interested laypersons.

Dorion, Robert B. J., ed. *Bitemark Evidence*. New York: Marcel Dekker, 2005. Comprehensive collection of essays on all aspects of the study of human and animal bite marks. Well illustrated.

Merck, Melinda D. *Veterinary Forensics: Animal Cruelty Investigations*. Ames, Iowa: Blackwell, 2007. Readable work discusses the handling of suspected animal cruelty cases.

Saferstein, Richard. *Criminalistics: An Introduction to Forensic Science*. 9th ed. Upper Saddle River, N.J.: Pearson Prentice Hall, 2007. Classic introductory text includes discussion of animal-related evidence.

See also: Biological terrorism; Bite-mark analysis; Canine substance detection; Crime scene investigation; DNA analysis; DNA banks for endangered animals; Evidence processing; Forensic entomology; Hair analysis; Mad cow disease investigation; Trace and transfer evidence; Wildlife forensics.

Antemortem injuries

Definition: Injuries received before death.
Significance: In a death investigation, it is important to determine which injuries the person sustained before death as opposed to any injuries that occurred to the body postmortem (after death) because antemortem injuries may indicate the cause of death or factors that contributed to the death.

To determine cause of death accurately, a pathologist must distinguish between the injuries to a body that were received before death and those that were received after death. The pathologist must also determine whether the body shows evidence of any injuries that occurred well before death. The most difficult determination to make involves which injuries were received immediately prior to death and which occurred immediately after death.

One significant difference between antemortem and postmortem injuries is in the ways in which the wounds have bled or bruised. It is possible for bleeding to occur after death, and, depending on the type of death, it is possible for bruising or pooling of the blood to occur postmortem, but a pathologist can generally tell by the way a wound has bled or bruised whether it is an antemortem injury.

A pathologist also looks at the type of tissue damage associated with injuries to determine when the injuries occurred. Tissues from antemortem injuries contain leukotriene B4, which living tissues produce in a chemical response to inflammation. Tissues that have been damaged by postmortem injuries do not contain this chemical. This information provides another way for the pathologist to determine exactly when injuries occurred.

In a case in which the body has been in water, the pathologist examines lung tissue to determine whether the person drowned or the body was put into the water after death. This tissue can show signs of whether the person struggled to breathe and began coughing before death or whether the lungs simply filled with water after death had already occurred.

The pathologist must also determine which antemortem injuries were the cause of the death as opposed to injuries that may have been received days, months, or even years before the death occurred. To do this, the pathologist looks for evidence of healing, such as wounds that have begun to close or bones that have begun to knit together, to eliminate those injuries as factors contributing to the death. Such older injuries can be significant clues in the determination of cause of death. For example, in cases of deaths resulting from child abuse or domestic violence, bodies may evidence many injuries in various states of the healing process, showing a pattern that can help investigators establish the history of abuse. This pattern may also occur in victims who were tortured before death.

Marianne M. Madsen

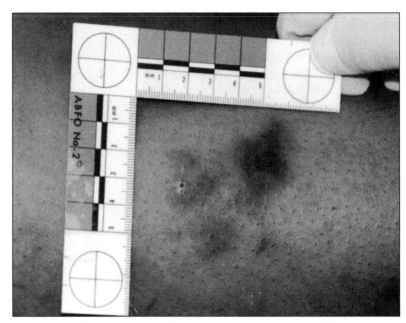

Measurement of bruises on a corpse during an autopsy examination. *(Custom Medical Stock Photo)*

See also: Autopsies; Blunt force trauma; Body farms; Defensive wounds; Forensic anthropology; Forensic pathology; Forensic sculpture; Living forensics; Oral autopsy; Osteology and skeletal radiology.

Further Reading

James, Stuart H., and Jon J. Nordby, eds. *Forensic Science: An Introduction to Scientific and Investigative Techniques*. 2d ed. Boca Raton, Fla.: CRC Press, 2005.

Shkrum, Michael J., and David A. Ramsay. *Forensic Pathology of Trauma: Common Problems for the Pathologist*. Totowa, N.J.: Humana Press, 2007.

Timmermans, Stefan. *Postmortem: How Medical Examiners Explain Suspicious Deaths*. Chicago: University of Chicago Press, 2006.

Anthrax

Definition: Deadly disease caused by the soil bacterium *Bacillus anthracis*.

Significance: Because anthrax is capable of debilitating and killing people and animals quickly, it is an attractive agent for use in biological warfare. The abilities to detect, treat, and neutralize anthrax efficiently are thus necessary to ensure public safety.

The bacterium *Bacillus anthracis* resides in soil, and, like other members of the bacterial genus *Bacillus*, can make a highly resistant resting cell known as an endospore. Endospores can withstand heat, desiccation, harsh chemicals, and ultraviolet radiation and can last in soils for centuries. Anthrax, the disease caused by *B. anthracis*, afflicts herbivorous animals, but human anthrax infections result from contact with infected animals or animal products.

Types of Anthrax Infections

Anthrax is caused by the inhalation or ingestion of *B. anthracis* endospores or, in the case of cutaneous anthrax, by contact between damaged skin and *B. anthracis*. Inhalation of endospores causes inhalation anthrax, which typically occurs among workers in textile or tanning industries who handle contaminated animal products such as wool, hair, and hides. The incubation period of inhalation anthrax ranges from one to six days, and the disease follows a two-stage progression. After infection, the patient develops a dry cough, muscle weakness, tiredness, fever, and pressure in the middle of the chest. The second stage begins with the onset of respiratory distress and typically culminates in death within twenty-four hours. Inhalation anthrax has a mortality rate of 95 percent if untreated.

Gastrointestinal anthrax results from the ingestion of undercooked, contaminated meat. Two to seven days after ingestion, abdominal pain and fever occur, followed by vomiting, nausea, and diarrhea. Gastrointestinal bleeding is observed in some severe cases, and dissemination of the disease throughout the body also results. Fluid loss can result in shock and kidney failure. Approximately 50 percent of cases of gastrointestinal anthrax are lethal.

Cutaneous anthrax results from invasion of the skin by *B. anthracis*. If the skin is damaged by scrapes, cuts, or insect bites, endospores can breach the outer layers of the skin and infect it. After an incubation period of two to five days, small solid and conical elevations of the skin devoid of pus called papules form; these papules then swell, rupture, and blacken. Without treatment, anthrax skin infections can disseminate to other systems, and death occurs about 20 percent of the time.

Detection of Anthrax

Growing *B. anthracis* from a blood sample is the best way to demonstrate an anthrax infection in patients who have not yet been given antibiotics. In patients who have begun antibiotic therapy, serological methods that detect antibodies made by the immune system against the bacterium are efficacious. Blood samples from a person who has died from anthrax should yield copious quantities of relatively large, rod-shaped bacteria that are encapsulated and easily visualized with polychrome methylene blue stains.

Automated detection systems (ADS's) can determine whether *B. anthracis* endospores have been released into a setting. The BSM-2000 (Universal Detection Technology), for example, continuously samples the air and heats it. Captured, heated spores release dipicolinic acid (DPA), a compound unique to bacterial endospores. DPA binds to terbium ions (Tb^{3+}), which, together, fluoresce green under ultraviolet light. Other ADS's use polymerase chain reaction (PCR) to test the air for DNA (deoxyribonucleic acid) sequences specific to *B. anthracis*.

Treatment and Prevention of Anthrax

Several antibiotics are effective in the treatment of anthrax infections. High-dose intravenous penicillin G, ciprofloxacin, and doxycycline are typically quite effective. Preventive treatments with oral ciprofloxacin or doxycycline for six weeks are also effective. Anyone exposed to anthrax should begin treatment immediately because the disease can become untreatable with the passage of time.

BioThrax (made by Bioport Corporation) is a vaccine against anthrax. It consists of an extract prepared from a non-disease-causing strain of *B. anthracis*. It is administered as three inoculations given under the skin at two-week intervals, followed by booster injections at six, twelve, and eighteen months, after which yearly boosters are necessary to maintain immunity. BioThrax vaccinations are 93 percent effective in preventing anthrax infections.

When bodies or clothes are contaminated with *B. anthracis* endospores, personal contact can spread the disease. Washing with antibacterial soap and water and treating the wastewater with bleach can rid contaminated bodies of all endospores. Burning contaminated clothing and the corpses of those who have died from anthrax is an effective means of liquidating anthrax from the environment. Burial does not kill endospores. Endospores of *B. anthracis* released into the air are easily removed by means of high-efficiency particulate air (HEPA) or P100 filters.

Decontamination of areas that have been exposed to *B. anthracis* presents several challenges because the bacterial endospores are rather difficult to destroy. Ethylene oxide, chlorine dioxide, liquid bleach, and a decontamination foam created by Sandia National Laboratories kill *B. anthracis* endospores slowly. A cleanup method approved by the Environmental Protection Agency (EPA) that utilizes liquid bleach, water, and vinegar requires contact with a surface for at least sixty minutes. If chlorine dioxide is used in combination with an iron-based catalyst, sodium carbonate, and bicarbonate, disinfection requires only thirty minutes.

Risks of Anthrax Contamination in the Workplace

After the deaths of postal workers contaminated by anthrax bacteria sent through the mail by terrorists in late 2001, the U.S. Department of Labor's Office of Safety and Health Administration (OSHA) developed a matrix to help employers and workers understand the risks of anthrax exposure and to offer suggestions for preventive measures to avoid contamination. OSHA's matrix identified three levels of risk:

- **Green Zone:** Workplaces in which the risk of anthrax contamination is unlikely. This category encompasses the vast majority of workplaces in the United States.
- **Yellow Zone:** Workplaces in which anthrax contamination is considered possible. This category includes places that handle bulk mail, places handling mail from facilities known to be contaminated or that are close to such facilities, and places likely to be targeted by bioterrorists.
- **Red Zone:** Workplaces that authorities know or suspect to be contaminated.

Anthrax as a Biological Weapon

Many nations have examined the potential of *B. anthracis* as a biological weapon. Growing *B. anthracis* is extremely easy, but processing the endospores into a form that is easily disseminated is extremely difficult. The first attempts to use anthrax as a biological weapon utilized rather crude methods. During World War II (1942), the British military experimented with anthrax on Gruinard Island. This experiment so thoroughly contaminated the site that it was quarantined for the next fifty years. Britain then manufactured some five million "N-bombs," which were anthrax-laced explosive devices, to attack German livestock, but the bombs were never used. In 1986, the British government hired a private company to disinfect the soil of Gruinard Island. The company first carted away the island's topsoil in sealed containers and then used 280 tons of formaldehyde mixed with 2,000 tons of seawater to disinfect the soil that remained. In 1990, the British defense minister declared the island safe.

At Fort Detrick in Frederick, Maryland, the U.S. Army developed a special form of anthrax endospores for use as a biological weapon. Such weaponized endospores lack the ionic charges that ordinarily cause them to stick together. Consequently, the spores are easily dispersed as a fine powder that can float for miles on the wind. On November 25, 1969, an executive order from President Richard M. Nixon outlawed offensive biological weapons research in the United States. All existing U.S. stockpiles of biological weapons were subsequently destroyed.

Despite the fact that it was a signatory to the international Biological Weapons Convention of 1972, which was intended to end the production of biological weapons, the Soviet Union produced extensive quantities of weapons-grade anthrax endospores. On April 2, 1979, more than one million people in Sverdlovsk (now Yekaterinburg), Russia, were exposed to an accidental release of anthrax organisms from the local biological weapons plant. More than sixty people died from inhalation anthrax. An extensive KGB-sponsored cover-up from 1979 to 1992 prevented the international community from learning the truth of what happened until Russian president Boris Yeltsin admitted Soviet involvement in this incident. In Africa, South African intelligence services helped the Rhodesian government of Ian Smith use anthrax against humans and the cattle of the black nationalists who were fighting against his government during the late 1970's.

Weaponized endospores were used in the United States during the final four months of 2001, when spores of *B. anthracis* were mailed within the continental United States. Eleven cases of inhalation anthrax and eleven cases of cutaneous anthrax resulted from these attacks, and five people died.

Anthrax and Microbial Forensics

Microbial forensics is concerned with the isolation and identification of any microbes used during bioterrorist attacks. Upon arrival at the site of an attack, the microbial forensics team must remove all persons from the site and decontaminate them. Sample collections taken from the air, vents, countertops, sinks, floors, and other surfaces can help the scientists to determine the source of the infection. All samples collected must be properly identified and stored in tamper-proof containers to preserve the chain of custody.

By identifying the exact strain of *B. anthracis* involved in an anthrax outbreak, experts can determine whether the disease has occurred as the result of a bioterrorism attack or as a naturally acquired infection. Various strains of *B. anthracis* show very little DNA sequence variation, but because the entire genome of this organism has been completely sequenced, scientists are able to use PCR to detect single base differences between strains, called single nucleotide polymorphisms (SNPs), and thus provide a fingerprint for each *B. anthracis* strain. If the strains found at the scene of an attack and in the infected individuals are the same, then the agent used in the bioterrorism attack is confirmed. This information can be used in determining both the source of the biological weapon employed and the best treatment options. Molecular forensics identified the strain used in the 2001 postal attacks on American soil as the Ames strain of *B. anthracis*, which was, ironically, developed at Fort Detrick.

Michael A. Buratovich

During the middle years of World War II, the British military experimented with explosive munitions containing anthrax spores on Scotland's Guinard Island. The island was so thoroughly contaminated that the government sealed it off from the public after the war. During the 1980's, decontamination work was begun, and in 1990 the quarantine was lifted. *(AP/Wide World Photos)*

Further Reading

Alibek, Ken, with Stephen Handelman. *Biohazard: The Chilling True Story of the Largest Covert Biological Weapons Program in the World—Told from Inside by the Man Who Ran It*. London: Hutchinson, 1999. Provides an insider's view of the extensive Soviet biological weapons program. Includes map and photographs.

Decker, Janet. *Anthrax*. New York: Chelsea House, 2003. Presents a detailed examination of the dynamics of anthrax epidemics and the influence that medical responses can have on them.

Guillemin, Jeanne. *Anthrax: The Investigation of a Deadly Outbreak*. Berkeley: University of California Press, 2001. Noted medical anthropologist discusses the Sverdlovsk anthrax tragedy in depth, including information on the Soviet Union's subsequent cover-up.

Holmes, Chris. *Spores, Plague, and History: The Story of Anthrax*. Dallas: Durban House, 2003. A medical epidemiologist surveys the historical effects of anthrax on human society.

Miller, Judith, Stephen Engelberg, and William Broad. *Germs: Biological Weapons and America's Secret War*. New York: Simon & Schuster, 2001. Three investigative journalists from *The New York Times* relate the deeply disturbing findings of their research into the history of biological weapons and the status of such weapons as of 2001.

Wheelis, Mark, Lajos Rózsa, and Malcolm Dando, eds. *Deadly Cultures: Biological Weapons Since 1945*. Cambridge, Mass.: Harvard University Press, 2006. Offers frank technical descriptions of the biological weapons programs of all the world's major countries.

See also: Anthrax letter attacks; Antibiotics; Bacteria; Bacterial biology; Bacterial resistance and response to antibacterial agents; Biological terrorism; Biological Weapons Convention of 1972; Centers for Disease Control and Prevention; Chemical Biological Incident Response Force, U.S.; Pathogen transmission; Polymerase chain reaction; U.S. Army Medical Research Institute of Infectious Diseases; Viral biology.

Anthrax letter attacks

Date: September-November, 2001

The Event: One week after the terrorist attacks on New York City and the Pentagon of September 11, 2001, the discovery of the bacterium that causes the deadly disease anthrax in letters mailed to various parties in New York, Florida, and Washington, D.C., triggered a forensic investigation.

Significance: Beyond their human toll, infecting twenty-two people overall and killing five, the anthrax attacks that took place in September, 2001, caused heightened panic at a time when the United States was reeling from the tragedy of the terrorist attacks on the World Trade Center and the Pentagon. The 2001 anthrax attacks led to a number of policy changes surrounding preparations to combat biological terrorism in the United States.

On September 11, 2001, the United States endured the largest act of terrorism it had ever experienced when highjackers flew commercial airliners into the towers of the World Trade Center in New York City and into the Pentagon in Arlington, Virginia. These attacks led to a change in ideology within the country that was just getting under way when the United States was attacked again, this time by an unknown assailant using the naturally existing bioterrorism source known as anthrax.

Anthrax

Anthrax is a life-threatening disease caused by the bacterium *Bacillus anthracis*. This bacterium is assiduous in that it turns dormant and into a spore stage when it does not have a host or is threatened by extreme temperatures, and it can survive in this state until it comes into contact with a new host. Then, even if it has been dormant for decades, it can spread very quickly.

Anthrax is most commonly found in agricultural areas, where it often infects cattle, sheep, goats, and other animals, but it can also occur among humans. Humans typically contract the disease through handling products from infected animals (cutaneous anthrax), by inhaling spores from contaminated products or animals (inhalation anthrax), or by eating the meat of infected animals (gastrointestinal anthrax). Anthrax is not known to spread from one person to another as do cold viruses; the large majority of people who become infected with anthrax experience cutaneous exposure. Anthrax outbreaks are rare in the United States, although they were more common in the eighteenth and nineteenth centuries; from the early twentieth

Recognizing and Handling Suspicious Packages

After the anthrax letter attacks in 2001, the Centers for Disease Control and Prevention developed the following guidelines for recognizing and handling suspicious packages.

Identifying Suspicious Packages and Envelopes

Some characteristics of suspicious packages and envelopes include the following:

Inappropriate or unusual labeling

- Excessive postage
- Handwritten or poorly typed addresses
- Misspellings of common words
- Strange return address or no return address
- Incorrect titles or title without a name
- Not addressed to a specific person
- Marked with restrictions, such as "Personal," "Confidential," or "Do not X-ray"
- Marked with any threatening language
- Postmarked from a city or state that does not match the return address

Appearance

- Powdery substance felt through or appearing on the package or envelope
- Oily stains, discolorations, or odor
- Lopsided or uneven envelope
- Excessive packaging material such as masking tape, string, etc.

Other suspicious signs

- Excessive weight
- Ticking sound
- Protruding wires or aluminum foil

If a package or envelope appears suspicious, DO NOT OPEN IT.

Handling of Suspicious Packages or Envelopes

- Do not shake or empty the contents of any suspicious package or envelope.
- Do not carry the package or envelope, show it to others or allow others to examine it.
- Put the package or envelope down on a stable surface; do not sniff, touch, taste, or look closely at it or at any contents which may have spilled.
- Alert others in the area about the suspicious package or envelope. Leave the area, close any doors, and take actions to prevent others from entering the area. If possible, shut off the ventilation system.
- WASH hands with soap and water to prevent spreading potentially infectious material to face or skin. Seek additional instructions for exposed or potentially exposed persons.
- If at work, notify a supervisor, a security officer, or a law enforcement official. If at home, contact the local law enforcement agency.
- If possible, create a list of persons who were in the room or area when this suspicious letter or package was recognized and a list of persons who also may have handled this package or letter. Give this list to both the local public health authorities and law enforcement officials.

century onward, anthrax has been most commonly encountered in developing countries.

Because anthrax kills humans through the multiplication of the *B. anthracis* bacterium within the body, it is most deadly when it reaches the lungs or the bloodstream. Cutaneous anthrax, the least dangerous form of the disease, typically results in blisters or ulcers on the skin. Indeed, more than three-fourths of people who contract cutaneous anthrax survive without medicinal treatment. Inhalation anthrax is the most dangerous of the three forms of the disease; more than half of those infected do not survive despite treatment. Treatment success is greatly influenced by how early the infection is uncovered and treated. People who come into contact with *B. anthracis* generally become sick within a week or ten days, but symptoms can take up to two months to appear.

Anthrax has been used in warfare since World War II, and a number of nations have developed biological weapons that include *B. anthracis*. Although some countries have destroyed their biological weapons facilities, others continue to test new strains of anthrax and conduct research seeking new antidotes for this disease.

The Attacks

On October 1, 2001, Claire Fletcher, an employee at the Columbia Broadcasting System

On October 16, 2001, during the height of concerns regarding anthrax spores sent through the U.S. mail to addresses in New York City, Florida, and Washington, D.C., a New York City Emergency Service police officer inspects a mailbox on Fifth Avenue for evidence of contamination. *(AP/Wide World Photos)*

(CBS) news division in New York City began to develop facial swelling and nausea. Her symptoms were confirmed as cutaneous anthrax, and she was provided antibiotics and later recovered. On October 4, Robert Stevens, an employee at the tabloid newspaper *Sun*, contracted inhalation anthrax and died the next day. *Sun* was published by American Media, Incorporated, located in Boca Raton, Florida

Although the first victim of the anthrax attacks was not identified until October 1, the attacks arguably began when the letters that contained the anthrax were first sent. Five such letters were postmarked in Trenton, New Jersey, on September 18, 2001, and sent to locations in New York City and Florida. Specifically, letters were sent to the news divisions of the American Broadcasting Company (ABC), the National Broadcasting Company (NBC), and CBS as well as the *New York Post* in New

York City and to the *National Enquirer* and American Media in Boca Raton, Florida.

Two more letters containing anthrax were also postmarked in Trenton on October 9, 2001; these were addressed to the Washington, D.C., offices of Senator Tom Daschle of South Dakota and Senator Patrick Leahy of Vermont. After an aide at Daschle's office opened the letter, it was found to contain a more potent form of anthrax than had been used in the earlier mailings; initial news media reports referred to it as "weapons grade" anthrax. The U.S. government mail service was temporarily shut down in response to the attacks, and the letter addressed to Leahy was found a month later, on November 16, after it had been routed to the wrong ZIP Code and placed in an impounded mail bag.

In all, five people died as a result of the anthrax attacks and another seventeen were injured. Many of those who were injured continued to experience ill effects, including fatigue and memory loss, years later. Moreover, a few postal inspectors became ill during the massive cleanup effort that followed the attacks, which continued for two and one-half years. Including the costs of cleanup and replacement of equipment, as well as the investment of human resources, some estimates put the monetary figure for the total damage caused by the attacks at more than one billion dollars.

The Investigation

After 2001, the anthrax attacks became known as Amerithrax, the case name given to them by the Federal Bureau of Investigation (FBI). The investigation that ensued relied on a combination of investigative police work and forensic testing. Investigators from the FBI, U.S. Postal Service, and other governmental agencies worked on the case, but through the seven ensuing years, no suspects were arrested.

Investigators observed that the anthrax used in the attacks was not all of the same grade. That mailed to television networks and the newspaper was of a brown granular form that caused only cutaneous anthrax, while that mailed to the senators and to Florida was a higher grade that caused inhalation anthrax. However, both types came from the same Ames strain that had been distributed to biological research labs across the United States and overseas.

Investigators narrowed the origin of the letters to Princeton, New Jersey, after anthrax spores were found in a mailbox near Princeton University. Hundreds of mailboxes in the area were tested, and no others tested positive. After further testing of the anthrax used in the attacks, investigators backed away from referring to the higher-grade anthrax as "weapons grade." However, several scientists still thought that the anthrax spores had been combined with additives that rendered the material more easily inhaled. They argued that only someone with advanced expertise could have created such a mixture.

DNA (deoxyribonucleic acid) tests of the anthrax inhaled by the first victim, Robert Stevens, ruled out laboratories in England as the source of the anthrax. Later testing found a DNA match with the original Ames strain of an-

thrax produced at Fort Detrick in Frederick, Maryland. Testing also indicated that the anthrax had been made within the two years preceding the attack, using a water source in the northeastern United States.

The person most closely scrutinized by investigators was Dr. Steven Hatfill, an American virologist and bioweapons expert who consistently denied any involvement. U.S. attorney general John Ashcroft labeled Hatfill a "person of interest," and significant amounts of government time and resources were invested in looking into possible connections between him and the anthrax attacks. Hatfill later sued several newspapers and magazines for libel and the FBI and U.S. Justice Department for violating his constitutional rights. In June, 2008, he was exonerated when he won a large settlement from the U.S. government.

Meanwhile, the investigation was moving in a different direction, as the government built a case against Bruce Ivins, a veteran biological-weapon researcher for the U.S. Army who had worked on the type of anthrax used in the attacks. Ivins had a history of suspicious behavior around the time of the attacks. In July, 2008, as the Justice Department was preparing to present its case against him to a grand jury, Ivins committed suicide. In early August, a federal prosecutor announced that Ivins was the sole culprit behind the 2001 anthrax attacks. Ivins clearly had the means and opportunity to perpetrate the attacks. Less certain was the question of what his motive may have been. One theory was the possibility that he stood to profit from his patents for a powerful anthrax vaccine.

Brion Sever and Ryan Kelly

Further Reading

Cole, Leonard A. *The Anthrax Letters: A Medical Detective Story*. Washington, D.C.: Joseph Henry Press, 2003. Presents an in-depth examination of the anthrax attacks and the media frenzy they created as well as the government's response to the attacks. Emphasizes the difficulties that investigators and scientists faced in reacting to the attacks and discusses the continuing threat posed by anthrax.

Graysmith, Robert. *Amerithrax: The Hunt for*

the Anthrax Killer. New York: Berkley Books, 2003. Uses evidence from the official FBI investigation to guide an analysis of the anthrax case. Contends that the anthrax-contaminated letter opened at American Media in Florida on September 19, 2001, is the key to solving the case.

Hasan, Tahara. *Anthrax Attacks Around the World*. New York: Rosen, 2003. Brief volume presents details on the various anthrax attacks that have occurred around the world. Provides useful context for the 2001 attacks in the United States.

Thompson, Marilyn W. *The Killer Strain: Anthrax and the Government Exposed*. New York: HarperCollins, 2003. Focuses primarily on the U.S. government's reactions to the 2001 anthrax attacks. Analyzes the responses of doctors, politicians, scientists, and law-enforcement personnel in responding to the threat in the immediate days and weeks following the attacks.

See also: Anthrax; Bacteria; Bacterial resistance and response to antibacterial agents; Biological terrorism; Biological warfare diagnosis; Biological weapon identification; Biological Weapons Convention of 1972; Chemical Biological Incident Response Force, U.S.; Viral biology.

Anthropometry

Definition: Systematic study of the dimensions of the human body and skeleton.

Significance: Anthropometry has a long history of use in criminalistics and medical sciences. Forensic anthropometry uses the methods and techniques of physical anthropology in a legal context to help law-enforcement agencies identify human remains specifically.

Anthropometry is the application of a quantified series of measures to the study of the human body with respect to origins, relationships, and individual identity. Forensic anthropometry is the application of anthropometrics to human re-

mains—whether victims of accidents, catastrophes, or criminal acts—to identify characteristics and thus help establish personal identities. Anthropometry can be both objective and rigorous when conducted by trained scientists who are familiar with measurement techniques and their subsequent statistical interpretations.

Scientific Basis

The science of anthropometry is based on several premises. First, the body dimensions of each individual represent a subset of unique features that can be used, like fingerprints, for identification purposes. Second, body dimensions provide information regarding additional characteristics such as gender, stature, and, in some cases, ethnicity. Third, body dimensions shed light on health, size, and morphology of internal tissues and organs. Fourth, certain body dimensions and skeletal remains can provide a record of health, accidents, and diseases and permit determination of health at time of death. All of these elements may aid the identification process.

Anthropometry is divided into two subfields: somatometry and osteometry. Somatometry is the measurement of dimensions of the living body, the cadaver, or body fragments. The measurement of the head and face constitutes a special field within somatometry termed cephalometry. Osteometry is the measurement of the bones and distinctive features of bones such as heads of ball joints, protuberances, condyles, articulations, and bone density of the human skeleton. Systematic measurement of the skull is sometimes termed craniometry. Both somatometry and osteometry have been proven useful in the comparison and identification of geographic variation and patterns among human populations in different areas of the world. Anthropometry is especially useful in the sciences of physical anthropology and the paleontological study of human ancestors and hominid relationships.

Collectively, anthropometric analysis of somatometry and osteometry can provide important information about an individual. Depending on the extent of remains collected, anthropometrists can determine age, sex, stature, body shape, diet, work habits, and sometimes ancestry of an individual. Forensic

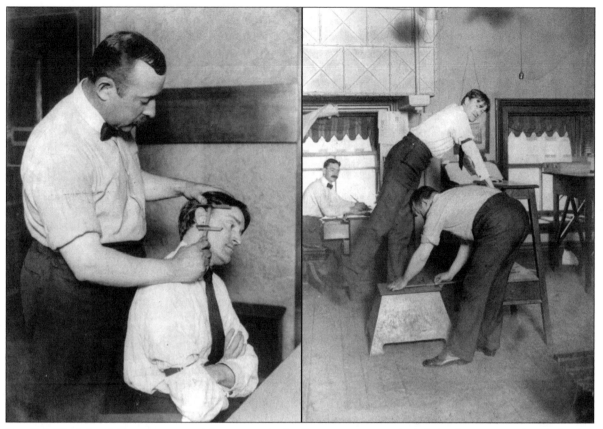

New York City Police Department personnel demonstrate the Bertillon measurement method of identification, an early use of anthropometry. These photographs, taken around 1908, show how measures were taken of two of the many body dimensions used in the Bertillon system, ears and feet. *(Library of Congress)*

anthropometry has proven especially useful in missing persons cases; the anthropometrics of discovered remains can be compared with information obtained from physicians, photographs, and other materials to determine the likelihood of a match between the remains and the missing person or persons. Anthropometric data on remains that do not match the missing persons of immediate interest are archived in an electronic database for future possible comparisons.

History

Anthropometry traces its roots to French criminologist Alphonse Bertillon (1853-1914), who reasoned that because no two persons are exactly alike, an individual could be identified on the basis of his or her body dimensions. Beginning in 1882, Bertillon systematically measured various dimensions on the bodies of criminals in Paris jails, including height, length of ear, and length of foot. He laboriously compiled a vast archive of measurements that was successfully used as a guide to identify repeat criminal offenders. The Bertillon system, or *bertillonage*, as it came to be called, was widely adopted in France and several other European countries.

English scientist Francis Galton (1822-1911) simplified the process originated by Bertillon by reducing the number of body dimensions measured. Galton also introduced the use of fingerprints to identify criminals. The reliability of fingerprints as a means of identification and the ease of fingerprinting were quickly recognized, and fingerprint analysis soon replaced Bertillon's laborious system of measuring body dimensions as a tool of the criminal justice system.

In the later years of the nineteenth century

and well into the early years of the twentieth century, however, anthropologists adopted anthropometrics to compare human races. Although the method was useful at first, anthropometry took a darker turn as some used anthropometric data to suggest that morphological differences among groups of peoples implied superiority of some human groups over others. For example, anthropometry became a political tool in the eugenics policies of the Nazis, who used cranial measurements to distinguish Aryans from Jews. In a similar vein, social anthropologist William Herbert Sheldon contended that one could predict the mental, emotional, and social characteristics of a person, as well as personality and potential criminality, on the basis of the individual's body measurements alone. After the Holocaust, these schools of anthropometry went into decline, and the use of anthropometry to imply racial differences, personality traits, or criminal predisposition was largely discontinued.

Forensic Applications

Although the use of anthropometry in forensic science has been somewhat superseded by the use of DNA (deoxyribonucleic acid) analysis, anthropometry is still widely used to provide initial identification of human remains in cases of natural disasters, automobile accidents, and catastrophes such as airplane crashes or terrorist attacks. Anthropometry is also helpful in identifying remains that have been deliberately destroyed in an effort to make identification impossible.

Forensic anthropologists must be familiar with both field and laboratory techniques, as they are often among the first to arrive at a site to recover and gather remains for identification. These scientists combine expertise in comparative osteology, human osteology, craniometry, osteometry, and racial morphology as well as skeletal anatomy and function and skeletal proportions characteristic of different geographic areas. Forensic anthropologists work with other crime scene investigators, such as forensic pathologists, to reconstruct the biological nature of individuals at the time of postmortem examinations; they also provide expertise in criminal cases.

Depending on the amount and nature of remains, forensic anthropometry continues to be useful in providing such information as age, gender, health, past injuries, and injuries that may have caused death. Forensic anthropometry has proven especially useful in cases in which only partial remains have been recovered. Examples of successful uses of forensic anthropometry include the identification of remains from the Vietnam War and other past conflicts, identification of the remains of victims of the 2001 terrorist attack on the World Trade Center, and identification of the skeletal fragments of the last two members of the family of Russian czar Nicholas II, who were murdered nearly one hundred years ago in a field in Siberia.

Dwight G. Smith

Further Reading

Krogman, Wilton Marion, and Mehmet Yasar Iscan. *The Human Skeleton in Forensic Medicine.* 2d ed. Springfield, Ill.: Charles C Thomas, 1986. Updated and expanded version of Krogman's classic work, which was first published in 1962.

Pheasant, Stephen, and Christine M. Haslegrave. *Bodyspace: Anthropometry, Ergonomics, and the Design of Work.* 3d ed. Boca Raton, Fla.: CRC Press, 2005. Details the many different applications of anthropometrics.

Reichs, Kathleen, ed. *Forensic Osteology: Advances in the Identification of Human Remains.* 2d ed. Springfield, Ill.: Charles C Thomas, 1998. Collection of essays includes discussions of the history, scope, and specialized methodologies of forensic anthropology, including anthropometry.

Ulijaszek, S. J., and C. G. N. Mascie-Taylor, eds. *Anthropometry: The Individual and the Population.* New York: Cambridge University Press, 1994. Collection of essays by anthropologists, biologists, clinical scientists, and other experts describes the many ways in which anthropometry is used.

White, Tim D., and Pieter A. Folkens. *The Human Bone Manual.* Burlington, Mass.: Elsevier Academic Press, 2005. Compact volume offers critical information about skeletal identifications and hundreds of illustrations and photographs. Intended for use by professional anthropologists, forensic scientists, and researchers.

See also: Autopsies; Biometric identification systems; Composite drawing; Crime scene investigation; Forensic anthropology; Forensic sculpture; Osteology and skeletal radiology; Sex determination of remains; Skeletal analysis.

Antianxiety agents

Definition: Group of medications that relieve tension, reduce activity, induce relaxation, and produce drowsiness.

Significance: The use of antianxiety agents is routinely associated with high risk for dependence and abuse that can be associated with criminal activity, drug-seeking behaviors, and suicide. In addition, sexual predators are increasingly using antianxiety agents to reduce the capacity of their victims to react against assault.

The drugs classified as antianxiety agents are frequently prescribed for patients complaining of tension, muscle strain, sleep problems, panic attacks, and phobias. Among the drugs' effects are drowsiness, impaired social or occupational functioning, slurred speech, rapid mood changes, and impaired judgment; these effects become more pronounced with increased dosage. Because of the negative impact on occupational functioning that abuse of antianxiety agents can produce, many employment settings have implemented urine testing of employees to screen for these drugs.

Benzodiazepines

The most commonly prescribed antianxiety agents are the benzodiazepines, which are classified as controlled substances by the U.S. Drug Enforcement Administration (DEA). These include such drugs as chlordiazepoxide (Librium), diazepam (Valium), alprazolam (Xanax), clonazepam (Klonopin), clorazepate (Tranxene), and lorazepam (Ativan). The benzodiazepines act on the central nervous system and produce intoxication and withdrawal symptoms. These drugs can produce physical and psychological dependence within two to four weeks of usage. The symptoms of withdrawal from antianxiety drugs can range form mild discomfort to severe reactions, including seizures. Some of the common symptoms include weakness, rapid pulse, tremor, insomnia, restlessness, nausea, hallucinations, and irritability. Sudden withdrawal from benzodiazepine dependence can lead to seizures and even death. Detoxification involves a gradual decrease of the drug over a period of weeks. Persons who are addicted to antianxiety medications often respond best to detoxification in residential treatment programs.

In medical practice, the benzodiazepines have replaced the usage of barbiturates for control of anxiety. Barbiturates were commonly used throughout the early to mid-twentieth century to induce relaxation, promote sleep, and quell tension, but they had a high abuse potential. Common barbiturates include amobarbital (Amytal), phenobarbital (Luminal), pentobarbital (Nembutal), seconbarbital (Seconal), and thiopental (Pentothal). Barbiturate drugs are still common among the chemical substances sold illegally. Colloquially they are frequently referred to as reds, red devils, yellow jackets, rainbows, downers, phennies, and nembies.

Abuse and Negative Impacts

Although antianxiety agents are legitimately prescribed for the treatment of psychiatric disorders associated with anxiety, a large number of individuals use the drugs illicitly for their mood-altering relaxation effects. Some use only benzodiazepines, but others often use them in conjunction with other controlled substances, including stimulants and hallucinogens, to diminish anxious feelings; some use benzodiazepines with cocaine to reduce withdrawal symptoms or with heroin as a way to enhance the euphoric feelings heroin causes. Benzodiazepine abusers, the majority of whom are under forty years of age, account for approximately one-third of all substance-abuse-related hospital emergency room visits in the United States.

Benzodiazepine intoxication is associated with behavioral disinhibition that can result in heightened physical and sexual aggressiveness, especially when combined with alcohol use. The effects of benzodiazepines are additive to those of alcohol, and in combination the two can lead to respiratory depression that can result in death. In general, when the additive central nervous system depressant effects of alcohol are combined with a benzodiazepine, the results can include excessive sedation, cognitive impairment, and psychomotor slowing. The diagnosis of benzodiazepine intoxication is best confirmed through toxicological analysis of blood or urine samples.

Because of the disinhibition effects of the benzodiazepines, some sexual predators use these drugs to dose intended victims, often by surreptitiously introducing the drugs into liquids the victims are drinking. The drugs can reduce the potential victims' capacity to react strongly against sexual assault or may even render them unconscious. In order to prove a charge of a drug-facilitated criminal offense, law-enforcement officials must be able to prove detection of the substance in the victim during commission of the act. Research has shown that the antianxiety agents are detectable in oral fluid, blood, urine, and hair samples of those who ingest the drugs over the course of hours and days. The evidence of benzodiazepine ingestion in hair samples is significant in cases where long delays separate the time of the alleged crimes and the collection of blood and urine samples, which may be of little value after a certain period of time.

State and federal agencies in the United States have carried out a continuing effort to restrict the distribution of benzodiazepines through strict multiple-form reporting of prescriptions for these medications. Some U.S. states have created databases of the names of physicians who prescribe benzodiazepines, as well as the patients who receive the prescriptions, to monitor the distribution of these medications. Requirements for triplicate-form re-porting of prescriptions have been found to reduce the use of the benzodiazepines for other than legitimate medical purposes.

Frank J. Prerost

Further Reading

Galanter, Marc, and Herbert D. Kleber, eds. *Textbook of Substance Abuse Treatment.* Washington, D.C.: American Psychiatric Publishing, 2004. Extensive volume provides information concerning the effects of substance abuse in the workplace and describes strategies to overcome the problems.

Meyer, Robert G., and Christopher M. Weaver. *Law and Mental Health: A Case-Based Approach.* New York: Guilford Press, 2006. Focuses on the various legal issues surrounding drug abuse. Includes discussion of drug screening and informed consent.

Sales, Bruce, D., Michael Owen Miller, and Susan R. Hall. *Laws Affecting Clinical Practice.* Washington, D.C.: American Psychological Association, 2005. Describes the issues associated with mental health professionals' bringing evidence to trial in criminal and civil litigation.

Simon, Robert I. *Concise Guide to Psychiatry and Law for Clinicians.* 3d ed. Washington, D.C.: American Psychiatric Publishing, 2001. Brief volume aimed at mental health care professionals provides a good overview of the legal issues surrounding substance abuse.

Stern, Theodore A., et al., eds. *Massachusetts General Hospital Handbook of General Hospital Psychiatry.* 5th ed. St. Louis: C. V. Mosby, 2004. Handbook intended for health care professionals includes an extensive discussion of the screening process for abuse of controlled substances in health care settings that is relevant for investigators who gather forensic evidence in criminal cases.

See also: Amphetamines; Club drugs; Crack cocaine; Drug abuse and dependence; Halcion; Hallucinogens; Illicit substances; Opioids; Psychotropic drugs; Stimulants.

Antibiotics

Definition: Therapeutic agents that kill infectious microorganisms.

Significance: Antibiotics kill certain types of bacteria that cause diseases without severely hurting the patients; they can thus abate the progression of some diseases and extensively reduce the effects of those diseases on human populations. Because of increasing threats of terrorism in the modern world, law-enforcement agencies are interested in the effective use of antibiotics for blunting the potential threat of microorganisms as biological weapons.

Microbial infections cause illnesses that diminish the quality of life and productivity and can eventually cause death. Effective early treatment can reverse the progression of some diseases, decrease the convalescence time, and potentially prevent the spread of infection from one person to another. Treatment can also check the onset of particular undesirable aftereffects caused by some diseases. Antibiotics are the first-line treatments against infectious diseases.

Classification

Most antibiotics are derived from compounds made by various microorganisms to kill competing bacteria. Many antibiotics, however, are completely synthetic in their composition, even though their chemical structures are variations of naturally produced antibiotics.

Antibiotics are classified according to their chemical structures, and drugs with similar chemical structures are classified in a common group. The largest group of antibiotics, the beta-lactams, consists of the penicillins (such as ampicillin, amoxicillin, and carbenicillin), cephalosporins (such as cephalexin, ceflaclor, and ceftizoxime), monobactams (aztreonam), and carbapenems (such as imipenem and meropenem). Other antibiotic groups include the macrolide antibiotics (such as erythromycin, clarithromycin, and azithromycin), tetracyclines (such as doxycycline and minocycline), amino-glycosides (such as streptomycin, kanamycin, tobramycin, and neomycin), sulfanilamides (such as sulfadiazine, sulfamethoxazole, and sulfamethizole), trimethoprim (similar to sulfanilamides but does not contain sulfur atoms), fluoroquinolones (such as ciprofloxacin, levofloxacin, moxifloxacin, and norfloxacin), and glycopeptide antibiotics (vancomycin).

Several antibiotic groups consist of only one drug; these include bacitracin, clindamycin, chloramphenicol, cycloserine, and fosfomycin. Streptogramin A and dalfopristin are given as a combination, and these drugs are the only members of the streptogramin group. The oxazolidinones group contains only one member, linezolid. A handful of antibiotics called antimycobacterials are specifically used to treat tuberculosis: isoniazid, ethambutol, pyrazinamide, and rifampin.

Mode of Action

Several chemically unrelated groups of antibiotics can target similar biochemical processes in bacterial cells. The abilities of distinct antibiotics to kill particular bacterial species vary extensively. Some antibiotics can kill only a few bacterial species (narrow-range antibiotics), whereas others can eradicate many different types of bacteria (broad-spectrum antibiotics).

Several antibiotics inhibit bacterial protein synthesis, which quickly kills bacterial cells. The protein synthesis-inhibiting antibiotics include the macrolides, tetracyclines, aminoglycosides, clindamycin, streptogramins, oxazolidinones, and chloramphenicol. Clindamycin is used to treat infections with anaerobic bacteria, and streptogramins and oxazolidinones are used for infections that resist other antibiotic treatments.

Many antibiotics inhibit the synthesis of the bacterial cell wall, which surrounds the bacterium and protects it. Without their cell wall, bacterial cells succumb to the host's immune system. Antibiotics that inhibit bacterial cell wall synthesis include the beta-lactams, glycopeptides, bacitracin, cycloserine, and fosfomycin.

Some antibiotics interfere with the synthesis of essential molecules. Folic acid is an exceedingly vital cofactor for bacterial metabolism, and without it, bacteria die. The sulfanilamides, trimethoprim, and the drug dapsone (used to fight Hansen's disease, or leprosy) obstruct the synthesis of folic acid. The fluoroquinolones inhibit bacterial DNA (deoxyribonucleic acid) replication.

Of the antituberculosis drugs, rifampin inhibits gene expression, and isoniazid and ethanbutol hamper the synthesis of the waxy cell wall of *Mycobacterium tuberculosis*, the bacterial agent that causes tuberculosis. Pyrazinamide inhibits the synthesis of fatty acids, which are used for the construction of biological membranes.

Clinical Use

Antibiotic treatment can have great benefits even when the exact causative agent of a disease is unknown. Antibiotics thus are usually used before the microorganism responsible for the illness is defined. However, because continuous exposure of bacteria to antibiotics allows the evolution of bacteria that are resistant to antibiotics, the overuse of these drugs is ill-advised, and judicious use of antibiotics is the rule. For example, given that more than 90 percent of sinus and upper-respiratory infections are caused by viruses rather than by bacteria, immediate prescription of antibiotics for such conditions is unwarranted.

Dr. Selman Abraham Waksman (left), the discoverer of streptomycin and neomycin, with Sir Alexander Fleming, the discoverer of penicillin, examining cultures in a Rutgers University laboratory in 1949. Waksman donated his profits from streptomycin to help build a new institute of microbiology at Rutgers. *(AP/Wide World Photos)*

Prescribing heath care professionals use a protocol known as empirical antimicrobial therapy (EAT) to guide their choices of antibiotics. Using EAT, the prescribing professional attempts to identify the bacterium most likely responsible for the illness through collection of a medical history, physical examination, and laboratory analyses of infected tissues. Because certain bacterial species have a tendency to infect certain organs, specific antibiotics are typically recommended for particular infections. Typically, certain drugs are considered to be the first choice for particular infections, and alternative drugs are used if the first-choice drugs fail to achieve the desired results. For example, the bacterial organisms *Streptococcus pneumoniae*, *Moraxella catarrhalis*, and *Haemophilus influenzae* cause the vast majority of middle-ear infections (otitis media), so the first-choice treatment for these infections is amoxicillin or a combination of trimethoprin and sulfamethoxazole (in a one-to-five ratio); the second-choice treatment is amoxicillin in combination with clavulanate or cefurxime axetil.

Antibiotics and Forensics

The presence of antibiotics in bodily fluids or tissue samples obtained after death usually indicates the presence of an infection in the deceased. The techniques for detecting antibiotics or their breakdown products in postmortem tissues exploit the unique chemical structure of each antibiotic. Cephalosporins, for example, are detected in postmortem tissues by means of high-performance liquid chromatography (HPLC), which separates compounds according to their differing rates of movement through a porous support material.

The prescription of antibiotics to prevent an impending infection is called antibiotic prophylaxis. In one example of the use of antibioticprophylaxis, ciprofloxacin was given to approximately ten thousand people who had potentially been exposed to *Bacillus anthracis*, the causative agent of anthrax, as the result of bioterrorism attacks in New York City, Washington, D.C., and Boca Raton, Florida, in the fall of 2001. This step probably saved many lives. The aggressive prophylactic use of antibiotics has the potential to thwart a bioterrorism attack.

Michael A. Buratovich

Further Reading

Gilbert, David N. *Sanford Guide to Antimicrobial Therapy 2007.* 37th ed. Sperryville, Va.: Antimicrobial Therapy, 2007. Simple but elegantly written reference guide provides thorough information on antibiotic prescribing.

Sachs, Jessica Snyder. *Good Germs, Bad Germs: Health and Survival in a Bacterial World.* New York: Hill & Wang, 2007. Presents interesting discussion of the interrelationships between bacteria and our bodies and how antibiotic treatments can affect those relationships.

Scholar, Eric M., and William B. Pratt, eds. *The Antimicrobial Drugs.* New York: Oxford University Press, 2000. Detailed reference book on antibiotics offers wonderfully clear explanations.

Smith, Frederick P., ed. *Handbook of Forensic Drug Analysis.* Burlington, Mass.: Elsevier Academic Press, 2005. Provides precise, detailed discussions of the laboratory techniques used to detect substances in postmortem tissue samples, including antibiotics.

Walsh, Christopher. *Antibiotics: Actions, Origins, Resistance.* Washington, D.C.: ASM Press, 2003. Offers encyclopedic treatment of the activities, structures, modes of resistance, and appropriate uses of antibiotics.

See also: Anthrax; Bacteria; Bacterial biology; Bacterial resistance and response to antibacterial agents; Biodetectors; Biological terrorism; Centers for Disease Control and Prevention; *Escherichia coli*; Parasitology; Pathogen transmission; Tularemia.

Antidotes. *See* Poisons and antidotes

Antipsychotics

Definition: Group of drugs used to treat psychotic disorders such as schizophrenia and mania.

Significance: Antipsychotic drugs have the ability to reduce psychotic symptoms without necessarily producing drowsiness and sedation. Forensic psychiatrists as well as law-enforcement personnel are familiar with antipsychotics because many criminals with mental illnesses use such drugs.

Antipsychotic drugs, also known as neuroleptic drugs or neuroleptics, were first discovered in the late 1940's by Henri Laborit, a French surgeon. Laborit found that when phenothiazines were used in conjunction with surgical anesthesia, the patients became less concerned about their surgery, and he thought that these drugs might be useful for reducing the emotionality of psychiatric patients. Since that time, the use of antipsychotics has become common in psychiatry. Initially, these drugs were called tranquilizers, but as that term seemed to imply sedation, its use was dropped.

All antipsychotic drugs tend to block dopamine receptors in the mesolimbic pathway of the brain; this accounts for their antipsychotic action. The drugs range in potency based on their ability to bind with dopamine receptors. High-potency antipsychotics such as haloperidol require lower dosage (usually a few milligrams) than do low-potency antipsychotics such as chlorpromazine (usually several hundred milligrams). Persons who are prescribed antipsychotics need to be monitored for regular intake, as compliance with drug therapy is an important aspect of treatment for psychotic disorders.

Typical Antipsychotics

Antipsychotics are classified as typical or atypical. Typical, or conventional, antipsychotics (and some of the trade names under which they are sold) include chlorpromazine (Thorazine), thioridazine (Mellaril), mesoridazine (Serentil), loxapine (Loxitane), perphenazine (Trilafon), molindone (Moban), thiothixene (Navane), trifluoperazine (Stelazine), fluphenazine (Prolixin), haloperidol (Haldol), and pimozide (Orap). These kinds of drugs were the first antipsychotics to be developed. The efficacy of typical and atypical antipsychotics is comparable, but typical antipsychotics have the drawback of possibly severe side effects. The main side effects of typical antipsychotics are known as extrapyramidal symptoms—a name arising out of the part of the brain that is stimulated by the drugs. Akathisia, a syndrome involving a subjective desire to be in constant motion and an inability to sit still or stand still, with consequent pacing, is the most common side effect.

Side effects of typical antipsychotics may also take the form of facial tics. Sometimes Parkinson's disease (which is marked by tremors of the hands while they are at rest, muscular rigidity, a masklike face, and a shuffling walk) may be precipitated by antipsychotic drugs. Tardive dyskinesia—the term means "late-appearing abnormal movements"—is among the most serious complications of antipsychotic treatment. It involves repetitive sucking and smacking movements of the lips, thrusting in and out of the tongue, and movements of the arms, toes, or fingers.

Typical antipsychotics can also have several anticholinergic side effects, such as dry mouth, blurred near vision, urinary retention, delayed emptying of the stomach, esophageal reflux, and precipitation of glaucoma. Often these drugs have metabolic and endocrine effects as well, such as weight gain, high blood glucose, temperature irregularities, and menstrual irregularities. Some allergic reactions may also occur, such as jaundice or skin rashes. Rarely, agranulocytosis, or low white blood cell count, can develop in the early stages of treatment.

Atypical Antipsychotics

Atypical antipsychotic medications (and some of the trade names under which they are sold) include clozapine (Clozaril, Fazaclo), risperidone (Risperdal), olanzepine (Zyprexa), quetiapine (Seroquel), ziprasidone (Geodon), and aripiprazole (Abilify). These drugs have an advantage over typical antipsychotics in that they have no extrapyramidal side effects (such as Parkinsonism, akathisia, and tardive dyskinesia). Atypical antipsychotics are at least as effective as conventional or typical agents in inducing positive symptoms, and they also help to improve cognition and enhance mood.

Atypical antipsychotics are not completely free of side effects, however, and the side effects differ from drug to drug. Risperidone, for example, causes an increase in prolactin levels—a hormone that can lead to breast enlargement, production of breast milk, and irregular menses. In high doses, this drug can also cause extrapyramidal side effects. Olanzepine can cause weight gain and may produce modest prolactin elevation. Ziprasidone can cause drowsiness, dry mouth, runny nose, symptoms of high blood sugar, and allergic reactions. Quetiapine can cause drowsiness, dizziness, agitation, pain, and weakness. Clozapine can cause weight gain and sedation.

Manoj Sharma

Further Reading

De Oliveira, Irismar R., and M. F. Juruena. "Treatment of Psychosis: Thirty Years of Progress." *Journal of Clinical Pharmacy and Therapeutics* 31, no. 6 (2006): 523-534. Discusses the evolution of antipsychotics, particularly the general replacement of typical antipsychotics with atypical antipsychotics, largely because the latter lack extrapyramidal side effects.

Parker, John, Jana De Villiers, and Samantha Churchward. "High-Dose Antipsychotic Drug Use in a Forensic Setting." *Journal of Forensic Psychiatry and Psychology* 13, no. 2 (2002): 407-415. Presents the results of a study of the application of antipsychotics in a forensic psychiatric setting.

Pinals, D. A., and P. F. Buckley. "Novel Antipsychotic Agents and Their Implications for Forensic Psychiatry." *Journal of the American Academy of Psychiatry and the Law* 27, no. 1 (1999): 7-22. Review of the literature on the clinical efficacy and mechanisms of action of atypical antipsychotics focuses on their use in forensic psychiatry. Concludes that use of these medications may reduce the risk of civil litigation.

Scherk, Harald, and Peter Falkai. "Effects of Antipsychotics on Brain Structure." *Current Opinion in Psychiatry* 19, no. 2 (2006): 145-150. Discusses the different effects of typical and atypical antipsychotics on brain structure and presents evidence that atypical antipsychotics might ameliorate structural changes caused by the disease process underlying schizophrenia.

Silverstone, Trevor, and Paul Turner. *Drug Treatment in Psychiatry*. 5th ed. New York: Routledge, 1995. Examines both general principles of psychiatric drug treatment and specific clinical applications of antipsychotic drugs.

Sinacola, Richard S., and Timothy Peters-Strickland. *Basic Psychopharmacology for Counselors and Psychotherapists*. Boston: Pearson, 2006. Basic text includes a chapter devoted to the treatment of psychotic disorders and the use of antipsychotics.

Stahl, Stephen M. *Essential Psychopharmacology: The Prescriber's Guide*. Rev ed. New York: Cambridge University Press, 2006. Guidebook for practitioners covers the most important and common drugs used for mood stabilization and treatment of psychosis. Includes information on the advantages and disadvantages of each drug, presented in easy-to-read and user-friendly style.

See also: Drug classification; Halcion; Hallucinogens; Nervous system; Psychopathic personality disorder; Psychotropic drugs; Stimulants.

Argentine disappeared children

Date: Disappearances occurred between 1976 and 1983

The Event: From 1976 to 1983, a military dictatorship was in power in Argentina, and about thirty thousand people whom the government considered to be political dissidents or active opponents of the military were taken from their homes by force, interrogated, tortured, and killed. The "disappeared" included young children captured with their parents and pregnant women who were imprisoned until they gave birth. Many of these children were adopted by families associated with the military. Later, relatives of the disappeared filed inquiries with the courts to try to determine the fates of their children and grandchildren. An organization founded by grandmothers of disappeared children successfully lobbied for changes in Argentine laws to allow grandpaternity testing and to establish a national genetic database to aid in identifying children who had been taken from their families.

Significance: The efforts of the Asociación Civil Abuelas de Plaza de Mayo (known in English as the Grandmothers of the Plaza de Mayo) were essential in the recruitment of the help of international scientists in identifying children who had been separated from their families. The scientists established an Argentine national genetic database and confirmed the validity of tests for grandpaternity. By conducting genetic testing, scientists were able to reunite a number of families.

In 1977, the women of the Asociación Madres de Plaza de Mayo (Mothers of the Plaza de Mayo) began to gather weekly in the main public square of Argentina's capital city, Buenos Aires, to protest the military government's practice of "disappearing" opponents. These women, mothers of missing sons and daughters taken by the government, succeeded in bringing international attention to Argentina's "dirty war."

Also in 1977, twelve grandmothers of children who had disappeared because of government actions formed the Grandmothers of the Plaza de Mayo. Although the military dictatorship was still in power, the Grandmothers began to protest and to gather information about the disappearances of their children and grandchildren. Their focus was on locating the missing children; they launched an international campaign to gather support and met with human rights organizations from around the world. By 1982, the Grandmothers had collected information on some three hundred grandchildren whose parents had disappeared.

They knew of the possible whereabouts of fifty grandchildren. After his election to the presidency ended military rule in Argentina in December, 1983, Raúl Alfonsín appointed the Comisión Nacional Sobre la Desaparición de Personas (National Commission on the Disappearance of Persons) to investigate what had happened to the disappeared.

Application of Forensic Science

The Grandmothers sought help from international scientists. Among those who worked on the problem of identifying the missing children were Dr. Fred Allen, an expert on blood groups; Dr. Luigi Luca Cavalli-Sforza, a population geneticist; Dr. Mary-Claire King, a geneticist; and Pierre Darlu, a mathematician. The scientists took an approach that had never been taken before when they applied the idea of grandpaternity testing—that is, they used the same methods used for standard paternity testing to determine the genetic relationships between children and their grandparents.

For the identification of related individuals, genetic markers that are passed from parent to child and that are highly variable in the population are needed. Initially, the scientists used immunological techniques to identify the grandchildren; they examined blood samples from suspected stolen children, their possible grandparents, and other living relatives. No samples were available from the parents of the children because they had been murdered by the military. The genetic markers examined were blood group antigens from red blood cells, such as ABO, Rh, and Kelley, and from white blood cells, such as human leukocyte antigens (HLAs).

King and other scientists also worked to determine what additional genetic markers could be used to identify the children. Mitochondrial DNA (deoxyribonucleic acid) is isolated from blood. The sequence of mitochondrial DNA is an excellent genetic marker for tracking grandpaternity because mitochondrial DNA is maternally inherited—that is, it is passed from a mother to all of her children. Fathers do not pass mitochondrial DNA to their children. Also, one part of the mitochondrial genome that does not contain any genes is the most variable sequence of the human genome.

Members of Argentina's Mothers of the Plaza de Mayo gather in the plaza in April, 1995, to protest the still-unresolved disappearances of thousands of their relatives during Argentina's so-called dirty war of 1976-1983. *(AP/Wide World Photos)*

The mitochondrial genome is a 16,569-base-pair circle that is present in many copies in each mitochondrion, and there are many mitochondria per cell. Because many copies of mitochondrial DNA exist in each cell, it is easier to obtain mitochondrial DNA than it is to obtain nuclear DNA in many cases. In the use of mitochondrial DNA to identify individuals, the highly variable region of mitochondrial DNA is sequenced, and the sequence is compared with the sequences of known persons in a database. Some mitochondrial sequences are unique to particular maternal lineages and can be used to identify grandchildren in these lineages even if the parents cannot be tested.

When the scientists found genetic matches for suspected stolen children, the Grandmothers, the courts, and psychologists worked together to try to ensure that the children were not subjected to further trauma. According to Argentine law, a child could not be considered matched to a family unless circumstantial evidence pointing to the relationship existed in addition to findings from genetic testing indicating a greater than 95 percent probability of a relationship. By 2002, information about more than two hundred grandchildren had been gathered, and more than sixty grandchildren had been identified and returned to their relatives.

Susan J. Karcher

Further Reading

Arditti, Rita. *Searching for Life: The Grandmothers of the Plaza de Mayo and the Disappeared Children of Argentina*. Berkeley: University of California Press, 1999. Describes the work of the grandmothers to identify the disappeared children and return them to their remaining families.

Budowle, Bruce, Marc W. Allard, Mark R. Wilson, and Ranajit Chakraborty. "Forensics and Mitochondrial DNA: Applications, Debates, and Foundations." *Annual Review of Genomics and Human Genetics* 4 (September, 2003): 119-141. Describes the forensic applications of mitochondrial DNA analysis.

Erlich, Henry A., and Cassandra D. Calloway. "Using HLA and Mitochondrial DNA Polymorphisms to Identify Geographic/Ethnic Origins: The Mammoth Lakes Case." *Forensic Magazine*, June/July, 2007, 32, 34-35, 37. Uses a specific murder case to explain the use of mitochondrial DNA in the identification of the remains of unknown persons.

Owens, Kelly N., Michelle Harvey-Blankenship, and Mary-Claire King. "Genomic Sequencing in the Service of Human Rights." *International Journal of Epidemiology* 31 (2002): 53-58. Describes the use of genomic analysis in the identification of victims of human rights abuses, specifically a case in Argentina and one in the Balkans.

Penchaszadeh, V. B. "Abduction of Children of Political Dissidents in Argentina and the Role of Human Genetics in Their Restitution." *Journal of Public Health Policy* 13 (Autumn, 1992): 291-305. Describes the history of the abductions and the actions of the Grandmothers of the Plaza de Mayo as well as the genetic identity testing that was conducted.

_____. "Genetic Identification of Children of the Disappeared in Argentina." *Journal of the American Medical Women's Association* 52 (Winter, 1997): 16-22. Provides an overview of the historical events and the search for the children along with discussion of the genetic research used to identify the missing children.

Scheffler, Immo E. *Mitochondria*. 2d ed. Hoboken, N.J.: John Wiley & Sons, 2008. Presents extensive technical discussion of mitochondrial DNA analysis.

See also: Child abduction and kidnapping; Croatian and Bosnian war victim identification; DNA analysis; DNA database controversies; DNA fingerprinting; DNA profiling; DNA typing; International Association for Identification; Mitochondrial DNA analysis and typing.

Army Medical Research Institute of Infectious Diseases. *See* U.S. Army Medical Research Institute of Infectious Diseases

Arsenic

Definition: Toxic chemical element used industrially in the manufacture of glass, semiconductors, and wood preservatives as well as in insecticides and herbicides.

Significance: Because arsenic is widespread in soil and water and has a number of industrial uses, many opportunities exist for human exposure to this element, which can lead to toxic effects. Both the effects and the mechanisms of exposure to arsenic can be subtle, and the symptoms of intoxication can be confused with those of other conditions.

Life- or health-threatening exposure to the toxic chemical arsenic can result from industrial contact, from deliberate poisoning, or from naturally contaminated food or drinking water. Arsenic poisoning may be acute or chronic, depending on whether a large dose is ingested at one time or smaller doses are taken over a lengthy period.

Acute arsenic poisoning is often associated with attempted murder of the victim. Ingestion of as little as two-tenths of a gram of arsenic trioxide (the arsenic compound most commonly used by poisoners, found in insecticides and weed killers) is followed by intense pain in the stomach and esophagus, followed by vomiting and diarrhea. Chronic poisoning by low levels of arsenic such as may be found in contaminated drinking water produces thickening of the skin (hyperkeratosis) of the hands and feet as well as white lines on the fingernails. Cancer of the bladder or other organs can result with long exposure. Neurological effects are also observed, including weakness in the hands and feet (peripheral neuropathy). These symptoms are not always recognized as arsenic-related unless suitable forensic tests are done.

Arsenic binds to proteins and exerts its toxic effects on the body by interfering with vital enzymes. The presence of arsenic in blood or urine can be confirmed through atomic absorption spectrophotometry, a method developed in the second half of the twentieth century. Previously, the primary method of detecting arsenic was a test developed in 1836 by James Marsh. The Marsh test was first used in Tulle, France, in the 1840 trial of Marie Lafarge, who was accused of murdering her husband.

Occasionally, arsenic poisoning may be suspected as the cause of death long after the person in question has died. In such a case, an expert can analyze a hair sample using neutron activation. In this process, the sample is subjected to a flux of neutrons in a nuclear reactor; the induced radioactivity can reveal arsenic, if it is present. This type of procedure has been used on samples from Napoleon I of France and U.S. president Zachary Taylor, both of whom died in the nineteenth century. Many other long-ago deaths have also been revisited in this way, but a complicating element in such cases is the fact that arsenic was sometimes used in embalming procedures in the past.

Quantitative determination of the arsenic

Clare Boothe Luce in her embassy office one week after arriving in Rome as U.S. ambassador to Italy in April, 1953. Sickened by arsenic-tainted paint chips flaking from her bedroom ceiling, she resigned her post three years later. In 1987, she died from brain cancer at the age of eighty-four. *(AP/Wide World Photos)*

Difficulty of Proving Arsenic Poisoning

The case of Marie Besnard of Loudun, France, provides some perspective on the difficulties that can arise in a trial for murder by arsenic. Besnard was arrested in 1949 on suspicion of having murdered two husbands, her mother, and several other individuals who had died suddenly. Several of the corpses were exhumed and were found to contain high levels of arsenic.

Besnard was brought to trial in 1952 but was not convicted. Her lawyer was able to use the fact that police had mislabeled some of the exhumed remains to impugn all of the forensic evidence, and the trial came to an end with no verdict. Besnard was tried again in 1954, and this time her attorney argued that the arsenic found in the corpses had in fact been carried there from the soil in the graveyard, perhaps by microbial action. Again, the jury could not reach a verdict. In a third trial in 1961, Besnard was acquitted for lack of proof. According to expert testimony, the neutron activation analysis of hair samples taken from the dead had involved too short a period of neutron irradiation, and therefore the results were unreliable. Testimony was also presented that arsenic could be lost from a long-buried body, raising doubt about the significance of the arsenic levels found.

level present in a given person's body is important because a certain amount of arsenic is to be expected from the naturally occurring traces of arsenic that appear in food and water. Elevation of a person's arsenic level above this threshold may indicate accidental or deliberate poisoning. It is estimated that, in the United States, the average person's diet contains 25-30 micrograms of arsenic per day. Excretion of more than 50 micrograms per day is cause for concern. Given that arsenic can exist in many forms of chemical combination, any urine analysis aimed at determining the body's level of arsenic should distinguish between organic arsenic compounds and inorganic ones. The latter are more dangerous.

Arsenic Exposure

In the past, the dangers of arsenic were often treated casually, with the result that many people experienced unnecessary, sometimes dangerous, levels of exposure to the chemical. The use of arsenates as pesticides, now minimal in the United States, once was widespread. Fruit, vegetable, and tobacco crops were often sprayed with such pesticides, and high levels of arsenic were left in the soil and on the crops themselves. When humans suffered ill health as a result, forensic scientists needed to find the source of the trouble. In France, arsenate pesticide residues on grapes found their way into wine that poisoned hundreds of French sailors in 1932. Plants grown on contaminated soil can pick up enough arsenic content to be toxic for human or animal consumption, and residues on tobacco are eventually inhaled by smokers.

Chromated copper arsenate is still used as a wood preservative, but many products that formerly contained arsenic no longer do so. Arsenical pigments were long used in wallpaper and in paint, and this led to many poisonings. Research over many years revealed that wallpaper with pigments such as Paris green or Scheele's green (both arsenicals) could generate arsenic-containing vapors (known as Gosio gas, for Italian physician Bartolomeo Gosio, who published his research on the topic in 1893) if moisture and certain microorganisms were present. This type of vapor, which caused some mysterious deaths in the 1890's, was eventually identified as trimethylarsine during the 1930's. In the 1950's, the U.S. ambassador to Italy, Clare Boothe Luce, became the victim of arsenic poisoning when she absorbed a toxic dose from arsenic-contaminated chips of paint that fell from the ceiling of her bedroom in her embassy quarters. Her resulting health problems forced her to resign her post in 1956 and return to the United States.

Medicines based on arsenic are mostly of historical importance, with some exceptions. Arsenic trioxide has been approved for treatment of leukemia, and arsenicals continue to be used against some tropical parasitic diseases. All these remedies present some danger of arsenic poisoning, as do cosmetic preparations that contain arsenic.

Arsenic is probably an essential trace element in human nutrition in very small amounts. People in the Austrian state of Styria have been known to consume arsenic purposely for its supposed tonic effects. By habituating themselves to ever-increasing doses, they are eventually able to tolerate amounts that would normally be fatal.

Murder by Arsenic

Foul play may be suspected in the death of an otherwise healthy person who develops the symptoms of arsenic poisoning. When such a person dies, forensic testing done postmortem can substantiate toxic levels of arsenic in the liver and other organs, in the stomach contents, and in the blood. If high levels are found, investigators must try to find the source of the poison and its mode of delivery. Accidental or environmental sources must be considered; for example, the victim may have used medicines containing arsenic or taken herbal supplements with arsenic content. If malicious intent is suspected, the dietary habits of the victim may suggest how the poison could have been administered. Any remnants of food or drink known to be ingested by the victim should be tested for arsenic, and anyone who has had access to the victim or the victim's food need should be investigated to see if they have obtained poison or are currently in possession of some.

John R. Phillips

Further Reading

Emsley, John. *The Elements of Murder: A History of Poison*. New York: Oxford University Press, 2005. Discusses the use of arsenic and other poisons in murder. Describes a number of cases in detail, many of which involve one spouse poisoning the other.

Gerber, Samuel M., and Richard Saferstein, eds. *More Chemistry and Crime: From Marsh Arsenic Test to DNA Profile*. Washington, D.C.: American Chemical Society, 1997. Collection of chapters covers the history of forensic science as well as developments in the field through the 1990's. Includes chapters that focus on forensic toxicology, on the search for arsenic, and on the depiction of forensic science in detective fiction.

Jones, David. "The Singular Case of Napoleon's Wallpaper." *New Scientist*, October 14, 1982, 101-104. Discusses the case of Napoleon I, who, in exile on the island of Saint Helena, stayed in a house where the wallpaper contained toxic levels of arsenic. Modern scientists have found elevated arsenic levels in samples of Napoleon's hair, which could have been caused by the wallpaper through Gosio gas.

Meharg, Andrew A. *Venomous Earth: How Arsenic Caused the World's Worst Mass Poisoning*. New York: Macmillan, 2005. Focuses on the health consequences of the arsenic contamination of drinking water (from minerals near the water table) in Bangladesh. Also notes other areas of the world where the problem exists and includes examples of the dangers of arsenic-containing pigments, wallpaper, and other products.

Vilensky, Joel A. *Dew of Death: The Story of Lewisite, America's World War I Weapon of Mass Destruction*. Bloomington: Indiana University Press, 2005. Presents the history of the chemical weapon lewisite, an arsenical poison gas developed by the United States for use as a weapon of war. Notes that stockpiles of the compound still exist and may be hazardous.

White, Peter, ed. *Crime Scene to Court: The Essentials of Forensic Science*. 2d ed. Cambridge, England: Royal Society of Chemistry, 2004. General treatment of forensic science includes chapters on analysis of body fluids, forensic toxicology, and courtroom presentation of expert evidence.

See also: Analytical instrumentation; Ancient criminal cases and mysteries; Atomic absorption spectrophotometry; Blood agents; Chemical agents; Marsh test; Napoleon's death; Spectroscopy; Taylor exhumation.

Arson

Definition: Deliberate setting of a fire with the intent to cause damage to a structure or other piece of property.

Significance: Arson is a destructive crime that often results in significant property and monetary losses. Investigations to determine whether fires were set intentionally or caused accidentally are notoriously difficult because of the high level of damage at most fire scenes. The forensic science of fire debris analysis, however, provides significant information that can help arson investigators make such determinations.

Arson has been committed throughout human history. Its definition as a crime originated in old English common law, where the term "arson" referred specifically to a fire set by one person against the dwelling of another. Since then, the definition of arson has developed to encompass fires deliberately set against any structure, inhabited or not, as well as vehicles or any other personal property. The penal consequences for the commission of arson have also progressed over time. In the United States, arson crimes are prosecuted based on the degree of damage inflicted, with the worst offense being first-degree felony arson—that is, the setting of a fire that results in the injury or death of one or more persons, whether purposely or accidentally.

Prevalence and Perpetrators

Although the occurrence of and monetary damages caused by arson fires in the United States decreased steadily in the decade before, the U.S. Fire Administration (USFA) reported that more than thirty thousand structural fires were intentionally set across the nation in 2006. These cases of arson resulted in more than three hundred deaths and caused approximately $755 million in property damage. An estimated twenty thousand vehicle fires were also set in 2006, causing an additional $134 million in damages.

Based on the demographic patterns among those arrested for arson, most perpetrators are Caucasian males, the majority of whom are juveniles or young adults. The Federal Bureau of Investigation (FBI) reports that almost half of the people arrested for arson are under the age of eighteen, and up to two-thirds are younger than twenty-five. General trends show that between 80 and 90 percent of arson offenders are males, although the number of female arsonists has begun to increase. The FBI also reports that only a small percentage (15 to 20 percent) of arson cases, which are notoriously difficult to prosecute, result in an arrests or convictions. This meager success rate can be attributed to the loss of evidence caused not only by the intense heat of fires but also by firefighting efforts. By attempting to put out fires with pressurized water or fire suppression foam, firefighters often wash away any evidence that may point to arson.

Arson Fires in the United States, 1997-2006

Year	Fires	Deaths	Direct Losses (millions)
1997	78,500	445	$1,309
1998	76,000	470	$1,249
1999	72,000	370	$1,281
2000	75,000	505	$1,340
2001	45,500	330	$1,013
		2,451	$33,440
2002	44,500	350	$919
2003	37,500	305	$692
2004	36,500	320	$714
2005	31,500	315	$664
2006	31,000	305	$755

Source: U.S. Fire Administration, Federal Emergency Management Agency. Note that the first line for 2001 excludes the losses sustained in the terrorist attacks of September 11, 2001; the second line for that year includes those losses.

Motives

The people who set fires intentionally do so for many different reasons. Typically, arsonists are motivated by past events. For example, revenge is frequently a primary motive for arson—the arsonist believes that the damage caused by the fire is tantamount to whatever damage has been inflicted on the arsonist by the person targeted. Revenge arson is commonly committed by angry former spouses or significant others; some are committed by outraged students against their schools or by employees against their workplaces. Along similar lines, some arsonists commit their crimes to demonstrate their opposition to practices they deem offensive or immoral. These fires, usually initiated by radical activist groups, may target such organizations as companies that test their products on animals or genetic engineering research laboratories.

Other arsonists act with no prior instigation whatsoever. These people are considered pyromaniacs; they simply enjoy watching anything burn and set fires to satisfy their addiction. Fires set by juvenile offenders are frequently motivated by nothing more than the exciting sensation of pyromania. This infatuation with fire is classified as an impulse control disorder, but its causes and mechanisms of action are not well understood.

Another motive for arson is the wish to conceal the evidence of other crimes. For example, a murderer may set fire to the homicide crime scene in an attempt to obliterate any incriminating evidence, including the victim's body, or even to make the death seem accidental. Both the Bureau of Alcohol, Tobacco, Firearms and Explosives (ATF) and the Drug Enforcement Administration (DEA) estimate that 30 percent of all arson fires in the United States are set in efforts to hide the effects of other crimes.

Insurance fraud is an increasingly common motive for arson. In old English common law, it was not considered arson for people to burn down their own houses or businesses, as they were allowed to destroy their own personal property as they saw fit. With the inception of property insurance, however, it became prudent for the law to define even the burning of one's own house or business as arson, to discour-

Fire in Fiction

Don Winslow's *California Fire and Life* (1999) is a skillfully constructed novel about an insurance claims adjuster whose uncovering of an arson fire draws him into ever-deepening intrigue. Taking its title from the name of a fictional insurance company, the story provides a fascinating inside look at arson investigation that draws on Winslow's own long real-life experience in that field.

Another novel by an experienced arson investigator is John L. Orr's *Points of Origin . . . Playing with Fire* (1991). This story about a serial arsonist was written by a city fire captain and arson investigator who was himself convicted of three counts of arson soon after his book was published.

age the attempted fraudulent collection of insurance money. Arsonists who attempt to commit insurance fraud hope that the fires they set to destroy their homes or businesses will be ruled accidental, given that the determination of arson voids coverage by fire insurance policies.

Methods

Arsonists use several different methods to set fires, although some are more common than others. The most common method involves the pouring of an accelerant—an ignitable liquid such as gasoline, kerosene, or lighter fluid—throughout the structure. The accelerant allows for easy ignition and also increases the rate and spread of the fire, which will follow the pour pattern of the accelerant. Many kinds of accelerants are readily available to arsonists; some are particularly dangerous because of their tendency to explode rather than just burn.

Some arsonists start fires by using incendiary devices, which can range from simple to very complex in their construction. Simple incendiary devices include lighted candles and flares, which can ignite their surroundings. Another frequently seen incendiary device is the Molotov cocktail: an ignitable liquid contained in a glass bottle along with a cloth soaked in the liquid that acts as a fuse. The cloth is ignited and the bottle is thrown at or into the structure, where, on impact, it shatters and the cloud of ignitable liquid vapor ignites a fireball that spreads to the surrounding areas.

A deputy fire marshal for Snohomish County, Washington, climbs a fire ladder to photograph the damage done to one of three newly constructed homes that were the targets of arson in 2004. The press office for the Earth Liberation Front, a group that uses radical means to stop what members consider to be the destruction of the natural environment, stated that members of the group were probably responsible for the fires. *(AP/Wide World Photos)*

Other chemical incendiary devices, such as those that utilize napalm, thermite, or white phosphorus, are rarely seen in civilian arson cases, although they are frequently used in military attacks. More complicated incendiary devices that operate on timers or other signals are seen occasionally in civilian arson cases. Fire investigators are careful to collect any evidence of incendiary devices found at fire scenes; such evidence may include shattered glass, burned cloth, wires, batteries, and other items that may have been used in timing mechanisms.

Investigations

Arson investigators face difficult, and sometimes dangerous, work at scenes where intensive fires have taken place. At such scenes buildings are often reduced to ruins, making them dangerous to enter and also often making it difficult for investigators to discern the features of the structures themselves. The main job of an arson investigation team is to sift through the soot and charred debris at the fire scene and determine the point of origin of the fire. The origin, along with the evidence around it, plays a significant role in identifying whether the fire was accidental or intentional.

The origin of a fire is determined from the direction and intensity of the burn patterns that are observed along the remaining parts of the structure or in the charred debris itself. A fire tends to burn up and out from its point of origin, which results in the commonly observed V-shaped pattern in which the V typically points back to the source of ignition. Trailers, or pour patterns, are also commonly observed at arson scenes. Arsonists often pour accelerants throughout structures in order to maximize the spread of the fire, and areas of intense burning follow the pouring patterns.

After determining a fire's point of origin, the investigators can begin to hypothesize exactly what caused the fire. Evidence suggesting the presence of faulty wiring or a gas leak around the origin point may indicate that the fire was accidental in nature. If the area around the origin appears to have burned more significantly than it should have for the fuel load present, however, the fire may be determined to have been set intentionally. Other signs that point to arson include multiple sources of origin, accelerant pour patterns, and evidence of an incendiary device.

The area around the origin of a fire contains the most significant evidence about the cause of the fire. Arson investigators must collect and package as much debris from the scene as possible to be sent to the forensic laboratory so that more detailed analyses can be performed to corroborate the initial findings at the fire scene. If accelerant use is suspected, the investigators will usually focus on several types of debris around the origin, as well as any debris showing potential pour patterns, in collecting evidence. Control samples are also be taken for reference. For example, if burned carpet samples are collected because they are suspected to contain accelerant residue, samples of carpet that are not burned, if available, are collected also so that forensic analysts can determine whether any potential accelerant identified in the burned carpet is actually inherent to the carpet itself. The debris collected is stored in airtight containers, typically unused metal paint cans, for transport to the lab; such containers prevent any loss of the volatile components that are present in most commonly used accelerants.

Forensic Analysis of Fire Debris Evidence

After the packaged evidence is received at the crime laboratory, it is analyzed for the presence of accelerants. Gas chromatography cou-

pled with mass spectrometry (GC-MS) is the conventional analytical technique used to identify unknown liquids that are potential ignitable liquids, as well as ignitable liquid residues in fire debris. Before GC-MS analysis can be conducted, the ignitable liquid residue must be extracted from the fire debris. A variety of methods can be used to perform this extraction, the most popular of which is passive headspace adsorption/elution with activated charcoal strips.

Accelerants are identified from fire debris through chromatographic comparison of the pattern of the peaks present in the questioned sample to the pattern of peaks present in a known standard. Accelerants are classified according to a standard system developed and maintained by the American Society for Testing and Materials (ASTM). This classification scheme separates ignitable liquids based on chemical composition as well as boiling-point range.

Accelerant identification is subjective, and the experience of the analyst plays an important role. Identifying accelerants can be problematic because several materials commonly found in American homes contain ignitable liquid residues or compounds that are chemically very similar to such residues. Analysts must take these interferences into account when interpreting analytical results. Researchers who are examining methods of fire debris analysis are working on developing more objective methods for the identification of accelerants that are capable of placing a statistical confidence level on such identification.

Lucas J. Marshall

Further Reading

Almirall, José R., and Kenneth G. Furton, eds. *Analysis and Interpretation of Fire Scene Evidence*. Boca Raton, Fla.: CRC Press, 2004. Comprehensive collection addresses many aspects of fire scene investigation and the chemical analysis of fire debris.

DeHaan, John D. *Kirk's Fire Investigation*. 6th ed. Upper Saddle River, N.J.: Pearson Prentice Hall, 2007. Detailed volume covers the physical nature and chemistry of fire. Includes extensive discussion of arson fires.

Faith, Nicholas. *Blaze: The Forensics of Fire*. New York: St. Martin's Press, 2000. Describes how fire investigators work and the methods that forensic scientists use to contribute to solving the crime of arson.

Nic Daéid, Niamh, ed. *Fire Investigation*. Boca Raton, Fla.: CRC Press, 2004. Compilation provides material on the basics of fire investigation as well as informative discussion of laboratory reconstruction and analytical techniques.

Redsicker, David R., and John J. O'Connor. *Practical Fire and Arson Investigation*. 2d ed. Boca Raton, Fla.: CRC Press, 1997. Describes in detail the various steps involved in fire investigation, from scene investigation to courtroom testimony.

Saferstein, Richard. *Criminalistics: An Introduction to Forensic Science*. 9th ed. Upper Saddle River, N.J.: Pearson Prentice Hall, 2007. Textbook discusses all areas of the forensic sciences, including arson investigation.

See also: Accelerants; Bureau of Alcohol, Tobacco, Firearms and Explosives; Burn pattern analysis; Carbon monoxide poisoning; Fire debris; Gas chromatography; Mass spectrometry; National Church Arson Task Force; Smoke inhalation; Spectroscopy; Structural analysis.

Art forgery

Definition: Deliberate manufacture and sale of misattributed works of art with intent to defraud.

Significance: With individual works of art by acknowledged masters selling for millions of dollars, art forgery is a high-stakes business involving finances, academic reputations, and national pride. Despite great advances in scientific methods of analysis, identification of the most meticulously crafted forgeries still depends on the subjective aesthetic judgment of experts. The authenticity of some works remains uncertain despite exhaustive study, and many fakes undoubtedly escape detection altogether. Forensic analysis can also prove an artwork genuine.

The crime of art forgery is nearly as old as art. Archaeologists have unearthed objects with faked inscriptions from the ruins of ancient Babylon and Egypt. A passion for Greek statuary led the Romans to produce numerous works in the style of classical Greek artists. During the Middle Ages, artists embellished religious relics to reinforce the impression that the objects had biblical origins. The Renaissance produced another flurry of reproductions of Greek and Roman statuary. Commercial art forgery, however, really blossomed in the eighteenth century. With the rise of private collectors and public collections of works of art, demand for examples of choice antiquities and works by popular artists greatly exceeded supply, prices skyrocketed, and unknown artists discovered the monetary advantages of passing off copies of the works of the masters as the real thing.

Scope and Limits of Art Forgery

In general, a reproduction or modern work in historic style is not considered to be a forgery unless it would deceive a knowledgeable buyer. A search of any flea market or low-end antique shop will turn up numerous small art objects, purportedly old, that bear obvious signs, through materials and workmanship, of their recent origin in Asian factories. Sometimes the deception is more elaborate, as in the case of one scheme in which an importer commissioned not only bronze "Tiffany" belt buckles but also a forged catalog, dated 1950, advising collectors of the scarcity and value of an item the Tiffany company never made.

Folk art is another gray area. An item newly handmade in a traditional manner assumes aspects of a forgery if it is deliberately altered to simulate age and traditional use. The countries or regions of origin of such items may also be misrepresented, as with "African" carvings from Indonesia or "Amish" quilts from India. The inauthenticity of fake antiques and folk art can usually be detected readily through analysis of materials (such as wood species) and telltale traces of artificial aging.

Some forgeries involve overzealous restoration of or addition of spurious elements to otherwise authentic pieces. A fad for collecting fifteenth and sixteenth century majolica ware

Special Agent John Stevens of the Florida Department of Law Enforcement stands with two forgeries of sculptures purportedly created by artist Frederic Remington. The art dealer arrested for selling the fakes had duped art buyers out of hundreds of thousands of dollars. *(AP/Wide World Photos)*

during the late nineteenth century spawned a whole industry, first of re-creating missing parts for damaged excavated pottery and then of fabricating entire pieces. Two brothers apprenticed to this trade, the Riccardis, used their skill at faking antique ceramics to perpetrate one of the most notorious art frauds in history, the monumental Etruscan warriors displayed for three decades in New York City's Metropolitan Museum of Art. Analysis of the glazing and construction techniques used on the pieces raised suspicions, and thermoluminescence testing confirmed the pieces as modern.

The most spectacular examples of art forgery have been those in which forgers have created completely new pieces that have passed as the works of famous artists. Successfully carrying off such a forgery requires a high degree of technical skill in the medium used by the artist being imitated, knowledge of the materials and techniques appropriate to that artist's period, careful study of comparable pieces by the artist, and the creation of a plausible chain of provenance (history of ownership) that explains how a previously unknown work by an acknowledged master came to be on the market.

Most nations have enacted laws against exporting national art treasures and archaeological artifacts, and many also have internal laws regulating traffic in such items, such as the regulations prohibiting private excavation and sale of pre-Columbian ceramics within the United States. These laws aid art forgers by making the origins of artworks difficult to trace and by creating reluctance on the part of collectors to publicize their holdings or to consult experts.

Wars and civil upheaval create windows of opportunity for both art thieves and art forgers. Multiple copies of authentic artifacts stolen from museums or private collections often appear on the black market during such chaotic periods. Later, when experts attempt to return these items to the original owners, they must distinguish originals from replicas; they may even conclude that all of the recovered works are fakes, raising the possibility that the original exhibited works were forgeries all along.

Detecting Art Forgery

The question of forgery usually arises when works of art are sold or transferred. Collectors and museums are understandably reluctant to amass evidence that tends to show that their existing holdings, especially showpiece items, are fakes. If they engage experts to examine controversial pieces, it is usually their hope that the findings will support the works' authenticity.

To determine whether a work of art is genuine, the dealer or buyer first has it examined by an expert in the artist, the art form, or the period; the expert compares it with known authentic works and looks for telltale signs of the forger's art, such as lines painted on canvas to simulate the cracking that occurs in old paintings. A labored and hesitant technique indicates a copy, but not necessarily a deliberate forgery. A specialist can detect anachronisms in the clothing and furnishings depicted in an artwork.

Judgments concerning conformity of a particular work to a known artist's style are highly subjective. The same expert who praised the style and artistic quality of a piece while believing it to be genuine may as vociferously point to its artistic worthlessness when it is exposed as the work of an impostor. Experts who work for dealers may have a vested interest in overlooking subtle indications that something is not right, and a few are actually in league with forgers. Experts also examine ownership and sales records to determine whether the provenance of a work has been falsified.

Some researchers have begun using computers to compare complex visual images in an attempt to detect art forgery, but this technology is still in its infancy. A team at Dartmouth University has developed a program for analyzing the frequency and density of brushstrokes in digitized images of paintings. Use of this program to compare different portions of a large painting attributed to the late fifteenth and early sixteenth century Italian painter Perugino (Pietro Vannucci) reinforced expert opinion that several artists contributed to the work. One advantage of this kind of analysis is that the analyst does not need to have the actual work of art in hand.

Most scientific detection of art forgeries relies on techniques that determine the age, chemical makeup, and probable source of the materials used as well as on various means of determining the works' internal structure. For wooden sculptures and paintings on wood or canvas, radiocarbon dating of minute fragments places the substrate within a century but cannot distinguish an old copy or a modern fake executed with antique materials. The notorious Dutch forger Han van Meegeren, working in the 1930's, used seventeenth century canvases from which he had scraped originals by obscure artists. Eric Hebborn, in the 1950's and 1960's, used blank pages removed from antique books to forge drawings in the style of the old masters. Both men mixed their own paints and inks from materials available in the seventeenth century; Hebborn also carefully reproduced period pens and brushes to ensure the right quality of line. Suspicion fell on Manhattan art dealer Ely Sakhai when he purchased large numbers of inexpensive late nineteenth century paintings not intended for resale. Sakhai, who was convicted of fraud in U.S. federal court in 2004, purchased genuine Impressionist paintings from auction houses, commissioned forgeries of the works from an artist, probably in China, whose name remains unknown, and sold the fakes to Japanese collectors. The fraud came to light when Sakhai and one of his victims simultaneously tried to sell the "same" painting.

Dendrochronology, or tree-ring dating, can be used to date some wooden objects. The pattern of rings in the wood indicates the years in which the tree was alive; for example, a violin with a spruce sounding board from a tree felled after 1890 obviously cannot be an authentic Stradivarius, as the last Stradivarius violin was made in the early part of the eighteenth century.

Penetrating X rays can be used to reveal images covered by a final coat of paint, including the artist's preliminary sketches, portions of a painting that have been reworked, and entirely different pictures. Using X-ray technology, an expert can detect such telltale signs of forgery as an under-image of obviously later date than the surface image and retouching intended to introduce the characteristic stylistic peculiarities of a known artist into a mediocre painting by an unknown hand.

Thermoluminescence dating is a useful technique for determining when pottery was fired. Crystalline minerals stored at room temperature accumulate electrons in elevated energy states; when subjected to high heat, the minerals release this energy in the form of light, the intensity of which is proportional to the amount of time since the object was last heated.

Tests involving X-ray emission and X-ray fluorescence are two recently developed techniques used to determine the chemical composition of objects without destructive sampling. When subjected to a high-energy beam of radiation, compounds reemit radiation at a lower frequency in bands diagnostic of the elements and molecules present. Because the presence of certain compounds narrows the time frame in which a work could have been created, this method is helpful in identifying restorations and additions.

Analyses of trace elements and stable isotopes are used to identify the sources, and sometimes the ages, of materials used in artworks. Modern smelting methods generally produce much purer metals than were available in earlier times. Competent art forgers know that lead carbonate, rather than titanium oxide or zinc oxide, was the white pigment used by painters before 1920, but unless they have access to the same natural sources of lead carbonate used by Europeans in the seventeenth century, they will not be able to duplicate the profile of trace elements. Trace impurities help distinguish old silver items from modern reproductions. Elements with more than one stable (nonradioactive) isotope can pinpoint the quarry or mine from which raw materials came; thus, for example, analysis of stable isotopes can distinguish whether a white marble sculpture in classical Greek style is Greek, Roman, Renaissance Italian, or modern in origin.

Sometimes scientific analysis vindicates a dealer's or collector's claim that an artwork is genuine. In one case, a Roman marble bust that was believed to be a nineteenth century forgery on stylistic grounds proved to be genuinely ancient. Analysis showed that a nineteenth century dealer in antiquities had "improved" on the work by sculpting away some of the original drapery. In the early twentieth century, the financier J. P. Morgan purchased a collection of silver plates depicting religious scenes that were supposedly excavated in Cyprus and dated to the third to fourth centuries C.E. Experts labeled the plates modern forgeries on stylistic grounds. When they were later reassessed us-

Art Forgery as Defense

One of history's most notorious art forgers used his craft as a successful defense against treason. Han van Meegeren, a mediocre Dutch painter who adopted an archaic style in his own work, began turning out forgeries of works by seventeenth century Dutch painter Jan Vermeer during the 1930's, using antique canvases, period paints, and an aging process that was undetectable at the time. The outbreak of World War II helped Van Meegeren in that it made it more difficult for art buyers to gain access to experts and added plausibility to stories of the discovery of previously unknown art treasures.

Nazi *Reichsmarschall* Hermann Göring was one of Van Meegeren's customers, and after the war, Van Meegeren was accused of collaboration with the Nazis and selling national treasures. He confessed to having painted the picture himself, and, to prove that he was telling the truth, he produced another fake Vermeer in his prison cell.

Any admiration attached to Van Meegeren for having swindled Göring must be tempered by the fact that he also swindled a number of his fellow Dutch, was motivated entirely by greed, and produced clumsy forgeries that, in retrospect, should not have fooled anyone. When listing his other forgeries for the court, Van Meegeren included paintings for which he was almost certainly not responsible, the authenticity of which is still disputed.

ing trace element analysis as well as analysis of production techniques and manufacturer's marks, however, they proved to be seventh century eastern Roman artifacts made in a deliberately archaic style.

Art Forgery as a Criminal Defense

Art forgers themselves are rarely successfully prosecuted for creating fake art. Because the crime lies not in creating something indistinguishable from a valuable original but rather in marketing it as such, forgers can argue that buyers were deceived by the dealers who sold their works. Frank Kelley, a prolific forger of Impressionist paintings, protected himself by signing his forgeries in white lead, which was readily detectable in X rays. Because of the high level of skill required to forge fine art and a lack of public sympathy for wealthy collectors, successful art forgers may attain the status of public heroes.

Creating and marketing bogus art treasures is simple commercial fraud, typically a much less serious charge than theft, trafficking in stolen goods, conducting clandestine archaeological excavations, or smuggling. Consequently, art forgery operations may be exposed when a party accused on one of these crimes confesses that the goods are fake.

Martha Sherwood

Further Reading

Chervenka, Marc. *Antique Trader Guide to Fakes and Reproductions*. 3d ed. Iola, Wis.: Krause, 2003. Contains much useful advice for the private collector on how to detect mass-produced copies of lower-end nineteenth and early twentieth century art objects.

Hebborn, Eric. *Drawn to Trouble: Confessions of a Master Forger*. New York: Random House, 1991. An experienced forger offers an insider's view, describing how the drawings of the old masters are forged and marketed. Compelling reading.

Hoving, Thomas. *False Impressions: The Hunt for Big-Time Art Fakes*. New York: Simon & Schuster, 1996. A former director of New York City's Metropolitan Museum of Art provides a work that is part history and part vivid firsthand account.

Jones, Mark, ed. *Fake? The Art of Deception*. Berkeley: University of California Press, 1990. Published as a companion to an exhibit of notorious forged art pieces, this copiously illustrated volume examines forgeries and their unmasking on a case-by-case basis.

Spencer, Ronald D. *The Expert Versus the Object: Judging Fakes and False Attributions in the Visual Arts*. New York: Oxford University Press, 2004. Describes scientific methods for authentication of artworks and analyzes the psychological factors that facilitate successful art forgery.

See also: Counterfeiting; Forgery; Handwriting analysis; Paint; Paper; Questioned document analysis; Sports memorabilia fraud; X-ray diffraction.

Asian tsunami victim identification

Date: Tsunamis struck on December 26, 2004

The Event: An earthquake measuring 9.3 on the Richter scale triggered tsunamis that devastated the coastlines of several Asian countries. One of the worst mass-casualty disasters in history, the tsunamis killed as many as 250,000 people, including Asians living in coastal communities and many tourists from Western nations.

Significance: The Asian tsunamis of 2004 presented one of the biggest challenges ever faced by forensic teams in identifying the bodies of massive numbers of victims of a natural disaster. The identification effort drew experts from thirty different nations and produced successful collaboration among them.

On December 26, 2004, a massive earthquake struck in the ocean near the west coast of Sumatra, Indonesia, and triggered a series of deadly tsunamis. It has been estimated that up to 250,000 people became tsunami victims along the coasts of many countries bordering the Indian Ocean; victims included the citizens of eleven countries, many of them tourists who were spending time at Asian resorts. An estimated two million people lost their homes, and thousands were reported missing. The magnitude of the tragedy was unprecedented, and it created an unprecedented challenge for the forensic teams that came together to identify the dead.

The Disaster Victim Identification Center

Following the tsunamis, many bereaved families sought assistance in identifying the dead. Despite their pleas for help, the rate at which the bodies were decomposing caused concerns about epidemics and forced local communities and national authorities to sanction mass burials without identification of the bodies. Many Western states, however, exerted every effort to ensure that their citizens who had died were identified before their remains were interred or cremated.

The challenges of identifying victims after the tsunami were daunting. High temperatures accelerated the rate of decomposition of the bodies, and the bloating and discoloration of faces made visual identification almost impossible after two days. Refrigeration was not immediately available to preserve the remains. In addition, no single country among those affected had sufficient forensic capacity to identify thousands of victims. Lack of national and local plans for mass fatalities further limited the quality and timeliness of the response, as did the absence of practical field guidelines or an international agency to provide technical support.

To respond to the problem of victim identification, Thai authorities set up a multinational disaster victim identification (DVI) center in Phuket, Thailand. The center drew the participation of three hundred investigators from thirty countries. Many of these investigators had expertise in DVI, having worked on teams that had identified mass fatalities from wars, natural disasters, and terrorist attacks.

The global effort to identify the victims of the tsunamis involved the participation of private corporations as well as individuals. Kenyon International Emergency Services, for example,

A volunteer takes fingerprints from the body of a victim of the Asian tsunamis of December, 2004, as part of the identification process. Forensic teams from around the world contributed to the effort to identify thousands of victims of the catastrophe. *(AP/Wide World Photos)*

conducted operations and eventually handed over a state-of-the-art identification tool kit worth ten million dollars to the Royal Thai Police's Thai Tsunami Victim Identification (TTVI) unit. Kenyon fielded more than one hundred employees to help create and run a comprehensive forensics database for use by analysts and Interpol experts who worked at the TTVI center in Phuket.

Identification of the tsunami victims was extremely difficult because many bodies recovered from the sea were badly decomposed. The scientists made positive identifications by analyzing dental records, fingerprints, or DNA (deoxyribonucleic acid); relatives of the deceased provided DNA samples and information that helped identify the bodies.

The Information Management Center at the DVI center processed several types of data, including postmortem data collected during victim examinations conducted in temporary morgues and antemortem data on possible victims gathered from the numerous countries involved. These data were entered into the PlassData system under standard operating procedures laid out by the Interpol Disaster Identification Manual. When the scientists were able to match dental, fingerprint, or DNA records with a body, they presented their findings to the Thai Reconciliation Commission, which, if satisfied, authorized the issuance of a Thai death certificate.

Dental Records

The identification of tsunami victims through the use of dental information (forensic odontology) proved to be highly efficient, reliable, and fast. This method of victim identification, however, favored nationals of Western states, who typically had dental records that helped in the identification process. Dental data were generally unavailable for the Thai population, so this method led to the identification of only a small number of Thai victims. In contrast, for non-Thai victims the successful identification rate using dental data was about 80 percent.

Antemortem dental treatment data include X rays and treatment records as well as plaster models. In most cases, reliable identification of bodies using dental data depends on the availability of recent, high-quality data. If the dental data are scarce or old, investigators must utilize all available methods of identification and the assistance of experienced forensic odontologists to achieve reliable results. In the case of the tsunami victims, this was the case especially for children and adolescents, who had had no or very little dental treatment.

The reliability of dental records as a means of identi-

fication became evident early in the work with tsunami victims. After the first three months, 88 percent of the successful identifications of victims had been accomplished with the help of dental data. The large majority of those successfully identified were non-Thai victims.

Unidentified Bodies

One year after the tsunamis struck, the TTVI center had identified all but 805 of the 3,750 bodies it had received for analysis. About 45 percent of the identifications had been made through dental records, 35 percent through fingerprint analysis, and the remaining 20 percent through DNA analysis. The remaining unidentified bodies were kept in refrigerated containers as efforts to identify them continued. Many of the unidentified were believed to be illegal immigrants, which could explain why their relatives were reluctant to claim them. One year after the tragedy, 160 non-Thais and 548 Thais remained missing.

Two years after the tsunamis, Thailand opened a cemetery for the last of the unidenti-

Controversy in the Identification Process

Despite the progress made in victim identification following the Asian tsunamis, some complaints surfaced, particularly in regard to the use of funds in carrying out the identifications. In a joint letter sent to the Thai authorities in December, 2006, some Western countries demanded an audit, alleging that funds donated for the purpose of completing the identifications had been misused. The letter was signed by the ambassadors to Thailand from Finland, Germany, the Netherlands, Sweden, the United Kingdom, the United States, and France.

The letter noted that more than four hundred recovered bodies remained unidentified and that more than four hundred persons were still missing two years after the tsunamis. The diplomats stated their belief that among the two thousand bodies released to relatives shortly after the tsunamis struck (before the formal disaster victim identification center was established), some bodies had likely been misidentified. They urged the Thai authorities to complete the allegedly much-delayed analysis of the DNA samples taken from those bodies, to correct misidentifications and help identify the remaining bodies. The letter also raised the issue of suspected misuse of funds donated to support the identification work and requested a professional audit by a reputable private accountancy company to clear up the suspicions.

fied victims, about 400 bodies. The remains, mostly those of Burmese migrants, were buried in identical aluminum coffins. The graves are marked with concrete headstones that include registration numbers that will allow authorities to exhume the correct bodies if identifications are made in the future through the use of DNA samples taken from the bodies before burial.

Dante B. Gatmaytan

Further Reading

Alonso, Antonio, et al. "Challenges of DNA Profiling in Mass Disaster Investigations." *Croatian Medical Journal* 46, no. 4 (2005): 540-548. Examines the different steps of DNA identification analysis and reviews the lessons learned and the scientific progress made in some mass-disaster cases described in the scientific literature.

Kieser, Jules A., et al., "Lessons Learned from Large-Scale Comparative Dental Analysis Following the South Asian Tsunami of 2004." *Journal of Forensic Sciences* 51, no. 1 (2006): 109-112. Examines the quality of the antemortem and postmortem dental data that were submitted for entry into the PlassData system in Thailand following the tsunami of December 26, 2004.

Knoppers, Bartha Maria, Madelaine Saginur, and Howard Cash. "Ethical Issues in Secondary Uses of Human Biological Materials from Mass Disasters." *Journal of Law, Medicine and Ethics* 34 (Summer, 2006): 352-365. Addresses the ethical issues of secondary uses of samples collected for identification purposes following mass disasters. Examines whether research is ethically permissible on these samples and, if so, what kind of research.

Schuller-Götzburg, P., and J. Suchanek. "Forensic Odontologists Successfully Identify Tsunami Victims in Phuket, Thailand." *Forensic Science International* 171, nos. 2/3 (2007): 204-207. Analyzes the success rates in the use of dental records in victim identification after this mass disaster.

Sumathipala, A., S. Siribaddana, and C. Perera. "Management of Dead Bodies as a Component of Psychosocial Interventions After the Tsunami: A View from Sri Lanka." *International Review of Psychiatry* 18, no. 3 (2006): 249-257. Discusses the need for the development of a comprehensive and efficient psychosocial intervention at the community level after a disaster. Focuses on the management of the bodies of the dead as an integral part of such an intervention.

See also: Beslan hostage crisis victim identification; Croatian and Bosnian war victim identification; DNA fingerprinting; Fingerprints; First responders; Forensic odontology; Mass graves; National Transportation Safety Board; September 11, 2001, victim identification; Tattoo identification.

Asphyxiation

Definition: Act of causing death or unconsciousness by impairing normal breathing.

Significance: Immediately before death, the body enters a low-oxygen state as respiration slows. Forensically speaking, a death by asphyxiation is one in which the low-oxygen state happened in an unnatural manner, such as by suffocation or smothering.

Death by asphyxiation can occur in a number of ways: through airway obstruction, through displacement of oxygen, or through neck or chest compression. Forensic pathologists determine the types of asphyxiation in particular deaths by looking for certain signs.

In some cases, asphyxiation occurs when oxygen cannot get into the lungs because something is obstructing the airway. This could be a foreign object, such as food, that fills the throat or something from the body itself, such as the tongue or vomit. When oxygen cannot reach the lungs because the airway is swollen, whether as the result of an allergic reaction or heat, this is also classified as airway-obstruction asphyxiation. Hanging or garroting, in which the airway is physically pinched off by a rope or something else wrapped around the neck, is another type of airway-obstruction asphyxiation. This may occur during the practice of autoerotic asphyxiation, in which individuals enhance sexual pleasure by depriving the body of oxygen; this practice sometimes results in accidental death that may be mistaken for suicide.

Asphyxiation by displacement of oxygen is more commonly known as suffocation. It occurs when the oxygen in the air a person is breathing is replaced by something else, such as smoke, toxic fumes, or chemicals. Drowning also qualifies as this type of asphyxiation, as water replaces air in the lungs. In this type of death, pathologists generally observe no external signs of asphyxiation.

Compressing the chest or neck so that no air is able to enter the lungs is another type of asphyxiation. Neck compression, or strangling, also causes asphyxiation because the arteries leading to the brain are not able to provide oxygen to the brain.

A forensic pathologist looks for particular signs to determine whether asphyxiation was the cause of death and, if so, what type of asphyxiation occurred. One of these signs is cyanosis, or a bluish tinge to the skin caused by a decreased amount of oxygen in the blood at the time of death. Facial congestion or edema may occur in a strangling asphyxiation. Because blood is not able to return through the veins to the rest of the body, the face may be swollen. Petechial hemorrhages, which are small broken blood vessels, usually in the eyes, eyelids, or lining of the mouth and throat, may occur during a strangling or hanging type of death, when blood is not allowed to return to the body and the blood pressure causes the veins to rupture.

Marianne M. Madsen

Further Reading

Dix, Jay, Michael Graham, and Randy Hanzlick. *Asphyxia and Drowning: An Atlas.* Boca Raton, Fla.: CRC Press, 2000.

Sheleg, Sergey, and Edwin Ehrlich. *Autoerotic Asphyxiation: Forensic, Medical, and Social Aspects.* Tucson, Ariz.: Wheatmark, 2006.

See also: Autoerotic and erotic asphyxiation; Choking; Drowning; Hanging; Inhalant abuse; Petechial hemorrhage; Smoke inhalation; Suffocation.

Assassination

Definition: Intentional killing of a human being for political, moral, or ideological reasons.

Significance: The consequences of assassinations can often be greater than the consequences related to other murders because of the kinds of positions held by many of the targets of assassination; in cases of political assassination, for instance, wars or civil unrest may result. It is therefore critical that forensic investigations into such deaths determine the objective facts of these events.

Even a brief look at the history of assassination suggests the important role forensic science could have played in providing objective information as to cause of death in various assassinations. In ancient times, many assassinations were committed at very short range, as were many other murders. Victims were stabbed, strangled, or clubbed to death, and often the assassins, like other murderers, were quickly identified and apprehended. Philip II of Macedonia (382-336 B.C.E.) and Julius Caesar (100-44 B.C.E.) are only two of a long list of political leaders assassinated in ancient times.

Given the likely apprehension of assassins who used such short-range killing techniques as stabbing or strangling, poisoning became a widely used alternative. Although it required that the assassin gain immediate access to the target, poisoning constituted a much less obvious attack, and proving that someone had been poisoned was difficult after the fact. In the cases of such assassinations, better forensic science would have been helpful in the apprehension of the perpetrators. In modern times, the facts revealed through forensic science in the poisoning deaths of Bulgarian dissident Georgi Markov (poisoned with ricin) in 1978 and Russian dissident Alexander Litvinenko (poisoned with polonium 210) in 2006 pointed to the killers, implicating, in both cases, the secret police forces in Russia (under communist rule in 1978 and under the more "democratic" regime of Vladimir Putin in 2006). The motivation for both killings was presumably a desire to silence the victims' criticisms of the regimes under which they lived.

American Assassinations

The importance and the limitations of forensic science in the investigation of assassinations are clear in the modern era and in the United States, where law-enforcement resources make exhaustive investigations possible. In the cases of the assassinations of U.S. presidents James A. Garfield and William McKinley, in 1881 and 1901, respectively, the role of forensic science was small, as both were shot at close range by individuals who were captured immediately. The fact that the assassins of both presidents were obviously deranged obscured the political aspects of these events, but the questions raised by these assassinations later motivated attempts to use forensic psychology to construct profiles of persons who become assassins.

In the case of President Abraham Lincoln, dozens of spectators saw John Wilkes Booth, a well-known actor, leap from the president's box at Ford's Theatre after Booth fired the fatal shot. Better forensic science than was available in 1865 could have been helpful in resolving another aspect of the case, however. Booth escaped from the theater and from Washington, D.C., despite having injured his leg when he jumped from the president's box. Law-enforcement officials pursued Booth and eventually cornered him—or at least a person they believed to be him—in a barn in Virginia. Before they could take Booth into custody, the barn burned down, presumably with Booth inside. Although a corpse with an injured leg was recovered from the ashes, the body was too badly burned to be readily identified, and ever since that time, some commentators have raised the possibility that Booth may have escaped. If the techniques used by modern forensic scientists had been available then, the question of the burned man's identity would have been resolved.

Modern forensic science has sometimes been used in novel ways with regard to deaths of the past, including possible assassinations. For example, U.S. president Zachary Taylor was hated by certain political opponents, and his death in 1850, reputedly from food poisoning, was a boon to them. Although some suspicions were raised at the time, the primitive nature of forensic science precluded an effective analysis. In 1991, given the advances that had been made in forensic science, some researchers thought it might be possible to determine whether Taylor was in fact poisoned. His body was exhumed and examined by a team of experts who concluded that he had died of natural causes, most likely food poisoning.

Uses and Limitations of Forensic Science

Three major assassinations in recent American history provide ample examples of the uses of a wide variety of forensic scientific techniques in attempts to find objective evidence about these crimes. In the 1968 assassinations of the Reverend Martin Luther King, Jr., and Senator Robert F. Kennedy, the purported assassins (James Earl Ray and Sirhan Sirhan, respectively) were apprehended, convicted of the crimes, and sentenced to imprisonment for life. A preponderance of the forensic evidence in each case clearly supports the conclusion that the accused man was involved in the assassination—probably by actually pulling the trigger. However, the forensic evidence available so far cannot reveal whether anyone else might have been involved in either case. Both Ray and Sirhan denied their guilt and sought new trials. Ray died in 1998 without achieving his goal of a new trial, and Sirhan has had no success in gaining a retrial.

In the case of James Earl Ray, the heart of the issue turned on Ray's contention that he was set up as a fall guy by other conspirators who have never been found. Ray was the principal witness to the existence of any conspirators. Sirhan's case is more complicated, as he clearly fired a gun in the direction of Senator Kennedy and was seized at the scene. Some conspiracy theorists, however, question whether any of the shots Sirhan fired at Kennedy actually struck him. They argue that there was a second gunman who fired two shots—one of which was the fatal shot to the head.

The conspiracy theorists gained a major piece of supporting forensic evidence for their theory when a tape recording of the shooting was found. Three acoustical experts have concluded that the tape reveals that at least ten shots were fired at the scene. Given that Sirhan was apprehended with a single gun with only eight shells in it and that he had no time to reload, this points to the existence of a second gunman. The recording further reveals that some of the shots came too close together to have been fired by Sirhan's weapon. Whatever one makes of this evidence, the basic problem is that forensic science often cannot eliminate the possibility that persons other than the person who pulls the trigger may have been involved in an assassination.

Nowhere is this clearer than in the case of the assassination of President John F. Kennedy in 1963. The first major report on the assassination by the government investigative panel known as the Warren Commission claimed to provide a thorough review of the available forensic evidence, but subsequent research has shown a great deal of sloppiness in the commission's work—inadequacies that have fueled a plethora of conspiracy theories. The proponents of these theories advance different forensic evidence or arrive at strikingly different conclusions based on the same evidence. The greatest problem with the use of forensic science in the case of the Kennedy assassination has been the failure of various government agencies to maintain control of the evidence on which the forensic science relies. For example, if—as some contend—Kennedy's body was altered to make it appear that he was shot from the back when he was in fact shot from the front, then any subsequent autopsy would obviously be faulty.

Despite the advances that have been made in forensic science, forensic evidence often cannot answer every question related to a case of political assassination, including the question of whether anyone other than the direct assassin is involved.

Richard L. Wilson

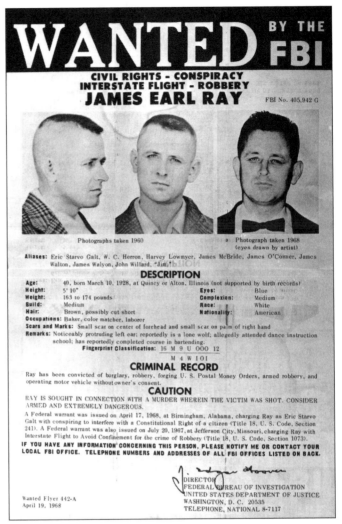

Wanted poster for James Earl Ray, the suspected assassin of Martin Luther King, Jr. Ray was apprehended in London, England, slightly more than two months after King was shot in June, 1968. *(AP/Wide World Photos)*

Further Reading

Ayton, Mel. *The Forgotten Terrorist: Sirhan Sirhan and the Assassination of Robert F. Kennedy*. Washington, D.C.: Potomac Books, 2007. Comprehensive review of the Robert F. Kennedy assassination supports the view that Sirhan, a Palestinian, was the assassin, motivated by his hatred of Kennedy's support of Israel.

Bugliosi, Vincent. *Reclaiming History: The Assassination of President John F. Kennedy*. New York: W. W. Norton, 2007. A major supporter of the Warren Commission's conclusion that Oswald was the lone assassin offers an exhaustive reexamination of the evidence from his point of view.

James, Stuart H., and Jon J. Nordby, eds. *Forensic Science: An Introduction to Scientific and Forensic Techniques*. 2d ed. Boca Raton, Fla.: CRC Press, 2005. Provides an excellent overview of forensic science for the general reader.

Kurtz, Michael L. *The JFK Assassination Debates: Lone Gunman Versus Conspiracy*. Lawrence: University Press of Kansas, 2006. Weighs the forensic evidence supporting the views of both sides of the main debate concerning the Kennedy assassination. One of the best sources available on the topic.

Lifton, David S. *Best Evidence: Disguise and Deception in the Assassination of John F. Kennedy*. New York: Signet, 1992. Argues that much of the forensic evidence used to prove Oswald was the lone assassin is faulty because Kennedy's body was altered before the official autopsy to prove that Kennedy was shot only from behind, whereas he was really shot from the front.

Posner, Gerald. *Case Closed: Lee Harvey Oswald and the Assassination of JFK*. New York: Random House, 1993. Carefully reviews the forensic evidence and concludes that Oswald—and Oswald alone—killed Kennedy.

_____. *Killing the Dream: James Earl Ray and the Assassination of Martin Luther King, Jr*. San Diego, Calif.: Harcourt Brace, 1999. Exhaustive account marshals all the forensic evidence to support the argument that James Earl Ray killed Martin Luther King while holding out the possibility that Ray may not have acted alone.

Sturdivan, Larry M. *The JFK Myths: A Scientific Investigation of the Kennedy Assassination*. St. Paul, Minn.: Paragon House, 2005. Comprehensive account of the forensic evidence disposes of several myths about the assassination without conclusively resolving all potential conspiracies.

See also: Ancient criminal cases and mysteries; Ballistics; Eyewitness testimony; Federal Bureau of Investigation Laboratory; Fingerprints; Forensic psychology; Gunshot residue; Kennedy assassination; Markov murder; Silkwood/Kerr-McGee case; Taylor exhumation.

ATF. *See* Bureau of Alcohol, Tobacco, Firearms and Explosives

Athlete drug testing

Definition: Analyses conducted on athletes to determine if they have taken banned substances.

Significance: Athletes competing at high levels seek to gain advantages over their opponents. Some do so by using substances that they believe can improve athletic performance or the body's physical work capacity. Many of these substances are drugs and many are banned by various organizations that regulate sports, such as the National Collegiate Athletic Association and the International Olympic Committee. Despite such bans, some athletes still use these substances, making drug testing necessary to keep competition fair. Athletes who fail drug tests may be ruled ineligible for competition or may have their previously awarded medals or titles revoked.

The use of particular substances to improve athletic performance dates back to the ancient Greeks. It was not until 1928 that the International Amateur Athletic Federation became the first sports organization to ban athletes' use of certain substances. The federation, however, had no way to detect whether athletes were breaking the rules, and the use of performance-enhancing substances continued to increase. Drug testing of athletes for banned substances was first used in 1966 by the international federations governing the sports of soccer and cycling. They were soon followed by the International Olympic Committee (IOC), which began drug testing in 1968 with the Grenoble Winter Olympic Games and the Mexico City Summer Olympic Games. The first athlete in Olympics history to be disqualified based on the results of drug testing was a Swedish modern pentathlon participant who tested positive for excessive alcohol in Mexico City.

By the 1970's, the widespread use of anabolic steroids among athletes forced the introduction of drug testing by most international sports organizations. The National Collegiate Athletic Association (NCAA) implemented a drug-testing program in the fall of 1986 for all athletes participating in NCAA bowl games and national championships. By 1990, the NCAA had adopted year-round testing of athletes on teams within the association.

Drug-Testing Techniques

Common methods used to detect illicit drug use include the testing of blood, urine, hair, and saliva samples. The method chosen for a particular purpose must take into consideration the accuracy level provided by the test, the ease of

U.S. major league sports executives and player representatives appear before the Senate Commerce, Science, and Transportation Committee in September, 2005, to discuss drug-testing policy. From left: Antonio Davis, president of the National Basketball Association (NBA) Players Association; David Stern, NBA commissioner; Gene Upshaw, executive director of the National Football League (NFL) Players Association; Paul Tagliabue, NFL commissioner; Donald Fehr, executive director of the Major League Baseball Players Association; Ted Saskin, executive director of the National Hockey League (NHL) Players Association; and Gary Bettman, NHL commissioner. *(AP/Wide World Photos)*

obtaining the sample, and the period of time for which the test can detect drugs in the sample. Urine testing is most commonly used for athletes because it is accurate, no cutting or piercing of the skin is involved, and it can detect drug use for the previous seven days or longer.

To complete a urine test, an athlete must provide a fresh sample of urine collected in a clean vessel under supervision. Although this may be awkward for some, it is important that the tester be certain that the vessel contains that particular athlete's actual urine. After the vessel is appropriately labeled, it is sent to a laboratory for analysis.

The techniques used to examine urine for the presence of drugs include gas chromatography, mass spectrometry, and immunoassay. In gas chromatography, the urine sample is vaporized in the presence of a gaseous solvent as it travels through a machine called a gas chromatograph. Because the various substances in the urine dissolve in the solvent at different rates, they come out of the solvent at different times, leaving a pattern on a liquid or solid material. The pattern is analyzed by a detector, and a chromatogram is produced. Because different drugs produce different chromatograms, the analyst can compare the urine sample output with known drug outputs to identify the presence of specific drugs in the urine.

A mass spectrometer is a machine with a long magnetic tube with a detector on the end. An electron beam blasts the urine sample and sends it down the tube to the detector. Every substance has a unique mass spectrometer output, so by comparing the outputs of known drugs with the urine output, the analyst can identify any specific drugs present in the urine.

Immunoassay tests are used to detect the presence of hormonelike drugs in urine. A specific antibody (a protein that binds to particular substances) is tagged with a fluorescent dye or a radioactive marker and then mixed with the urine sample. The antibody binds to the drug (hormone), and the analyst measures the amount of fluorescent light or radioactivity in the sample to determine the amount of the drug or hormone present. Because this test also measures naturally occurring hormones in the urine, the analyst must know the athlete's nat-

ural hormone level to determine whether the athlete has taken a hormonelike drug.

Challenges to Drug Testing

In 1987, one year after the NCAA adopted its drug-testing program, a member of Stanford University's women's diving team filed a lawsuit in which she claimed that the program violated her right to privacy. As the case made its way through the courts, the drug testing continued, and in 1994 the California Supreme Court ruled that the NCAA was "well within its legal rights" to conduct drug testing. This ruling cleared the way for other athletic organizations to establish drug-testing programs.

The ongoing challenge of athletic drug testing is the constant development of new drugs that existing methods and technologies are unable to detect. Athletes are continually looking for new advantages, and manufacturers are developing new drugs to improve athletic performance. After a new performance-enhancing substance becomes available, it often takes months or years for it to become popular enough to warrant the attention of sports officials. Then months or even years may elapse before scientists can develop new tests to determine whether athletes have used these drugs. During this lag of up to several years before a given drug is detectable, even more drugs are developed and the process begins again. This cycle creates a perpetual challenge to those who seek to keep sports competitions free from the use of banned performance-enhancing substances.

Bradley R. A. Wilson

Further Reading

Bahrke, Michael S., and Charles E. Yesalis, eds. *Performance-Enhancing Substances in Sport and Exercise*. Champaign, Ill.: Human Kinetics, 2002. Text includes information on the history of athletes' use and abuse of performance-enhancing drugs. Chapters 27 and 28 address the topic of drug testing in sports.

Cotten, Doyice J., and John T. Wolohan. *Law for Recreation and Sport Managers*. 3d ed. Dubuque, Iowa: Kendall/Hunt, 2003. Comprehensive text on sports law includes information on drug testing of athletes in chapter 7.

Gardiner, Simon, Mark James, John O'Leary, and Roger Welch. *Sports Law*. 3d ed. Portland, Oreg.: Cavendish, 2006. Discusses the legal issues related to governing sports. Chapter 7 is devoted to the topic of illegal doping and includes discussion of drug testing.

Ray, Richard. *Management Strategies in Athletic Training*. 3d ed. Champaign, Ill.: Human Kinetics, 2005. Chapter 10 provides an overview of existing programs concerned with athlete drug testing.

Yesalis, Charles E., and Virginia S. Cowart. *The Steroids Game*. Champaign, Ill.: Human Kinetics, 1998. Provides interesting historical information about how drug testing has been used in sports and how athletes have tried to beat the tests.

See also: Anabolic Steroid Control Act of 2004; Analytical instrumentation; Drug abuse and dependence; Drug classification; Drug confirmation tests; Gas chromatography; Mandatory drug testing; Mass spectrometry; Performance-enhancing drugs; Sports memorabilia fraud.

Atomic absorption spectrophotometry

Definition: Technique used to determine the concentrations of metal elements in a sample based on the absorption of light energy by atoms.

Significance: By using atomic absorption spectrophotometry, forensic scientists can determine the concentrations of the elements that are present in evidence samples collected at crime scenes. Using this information, they may be able to match evidence samples with materials linked to suspects or found at other crime scenes.

The phenomenon of atomic absorption was discovered as the result of the observation of the dark absorption lines in the spectrum of the sun, which are caused by the absorption of light by elements existing as gaseous atoms being promoted from "ground" state to "excited" state in the sun's atmosphere. These dark lines were first observed by William Hyde Wollaston in 1802, then rediscovered by Joseph von Fraunhofer in 1814; they are now known as Fraunhofer lines. In 1953, Alan Walsh developed the first chemical analysis using atomic absorption.

Atom-Light Relationship

Atoms absorb light energy based on electrons surrounding the atomic nuclei. Every atom of a specific element has a specific number of electrons in orbital positions. The most stable orbital configuration for an atom, called the "ground" state, possesses the lowest energy. The light energy resonates, or travels in space, like waves with specific wavelength. If light energy strikes an atom, the light is absorbed by the atom, and the electron in the outer orbital position is promoted to an unstable higher energy configuration, called the "excited" state. The excitation from ground to excited state is called atomic absorption; this absorption can be measured by the instrument known as the atomic absorption spectrophotometer. Because of the instability of the excited state, the electron decays and returns to the ground state; in doing so, it emits energy equivalent to the energy absorbed during the excitation process. The energy emitted during the decay process is not measured by the instrument.

Instrumentation and Sample Analysis

The atomic absorption spectrophotometer has five basic features: a light source that emits a spectrum specific to the element of interest, an absorption cell in which gaseous atoms are produced during excitation, a monochromator that disperses light, a detector that measures absorption, and a readout system (printer or computer) that shows the results of the analysis. The spectrum emitted by the light source (for example, a hollow cathode lamp) is focused through the absorption cell leading to the monochromator. The lamp contains a specific metal element that emits a specific wavelength of light for the same element to be determined in the sample. For example, to determine the concentration of iron in the sample, the lamp used

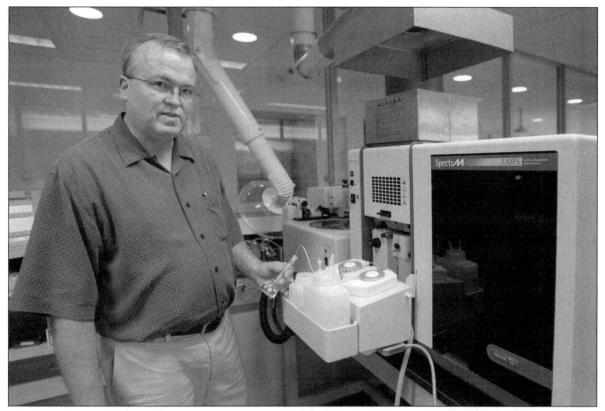

Chemistry professor Jeffrey Weidenhamer poses next to an atomic absorption spectrophotometer in the laboratory at Ashland University in Ashland, Ohio, where, in 2006, researchers using this technology found high levels of toxic lead in toy jewelry imported from China. (AP/Wide World Photos)

must contain iron. The light source must be modulated, or chopped, so that it is possible to distinguish between the emission from the lamp and the emission from the absorption cell. The monochromator disperses the modulated signal emitted from the lamp (not from the absorption cell) and isolates the specific wavelength of light that passes to the detector, which processes the light absorbed by the atoms. The absorption, which is proportional to the concentration of the element in a sample, is then displayed in the readout system.

A sample is introduced and atomized in the absorption cell in liquid or solid form (depending on atomizers) to accomplish the excitation process. If a liquid solution is required, elements are extracted by liquid reagents from solid materials. The liquid sample in the absorption cell is atomized, with thermal means (flame or graphite furnace) or chemical means

(hydride or mercury vapor generator) used to excite the atoms. Flame produced by an air-acetylene mixture (2,100-2,400 degrees Celsius) is used for most metal elements (such as calcium or zinc) that do not form refractory compounds, which cannot be ionized or atomized at this temperature range. A hotter nitrous oxide-acetylene flame (2,600-2,800 degrees Celsius) is used for elements (such as silicon or aluminum) forming refractory compounds (silicon dioxide or aluminum dioxide). A graphite furnace atomizer provides a wider range of temperatures (2,100-2,900 degrees Celsius) and handles liquid or solid samples.

A hydride or mercury vapor generator converts certain elements into gas. Elements that chemically react with sodium tetrahydridoborate (such as arsenic and selenium) are reduced to form hydride vapor. Mercury is reduced to mercury vapor. The vapors in the absorption cell are excited to absorb energy from the light source.

Not all elements are detected by atomic absorption. Elements with wavelengths of resonance lines below 190 nanometers, nonmetals (such as hydrogen, carbon, nitrogen, and oxygen), and noble gases are volatile, easily absorbed by air, immediately lost at temperatures greater than 2,100 degrees Celsius, and disappear before excitation. Elements that form very strong refractory compounds have extremely high melting points (greater than 2,900 degrees Celsius). Because these compounds cannot be atomized by flame or furnace, no atoms can be excited.

Use in Forensics

In a criminal investigation, atomic absorption spectrophotometry can be used to discover the presence and the concentration of the elements in sample evidence. When explosives or poisons are used to kill, for example, they leave evidence that can be examined through chemical analysis. Some explosives contain platinum; others contain nickel, silver, cadmium, or mercury. The elements that are found in the residues of signature explosive products can be used to find the sources, manufacturers, and buyers of such explosives.

Atomic absorption spectrophotometry can also be used to detect concentrations of elements from poisons found in human victims. Poisoning is confirmed to have occurred (whether accidentally or intentionally) if concentrations of toxic elements—such as arsenic or mercury—exceed safe levels in the body. The atomic absorption spectrophotometer enables analysts to determine whether poisoning has occurred by examining the levels of toxic elements appearing in a victim's blood, urine, and hair.

Domingo Jariel

Further Reading

Caroli, Sergio. *The Determination of Chemical Elements in Food: Applications for Atomic and Mass Spectrometry.* Hoboken, N.J.: Wiley-Interscience, 2007. Covers the quantification of beneficial and toxic elements in food products.

Emsley, John. *Elements of Murder: A History of Poison.* New York: Oxford University Press, 2005. Describes the properties of five toxic elements (arsenic, antimony, lead, mercury, and thallium) and how they were used in some of the most famous murder cases in history.

Tsalev, Dimiter L. *Atomic Absorption Spectrometry in Occupational and Environmental Health Practice.* Boca Raton, Fla.: CRC Press, 1995. Covers fifty-five elements and provides almost eight hundred atomic absorption procedures for analysis of blood and other biological specimens.

Vandecasteele, C., and C. B. Block. *Modern Methods for Trace Element Determination.* New York: John Wiley & Sons, 1993. Describes the theory and usage of atomic absorption and other spectroscopy for element determination.

Welz, Bernhard, Helmut Becker-Ross, Stefan Florek, and Uwe Heitmann. *High-Resolution Continuum Source AAS: The Better Way to Do Atomic Absorption Spectrometry.* New York: John Wiley & Sons, 2005. Discusses both instrumentation and measurements of elements.

See also: Analytical instrumentation; Arsenic; Crime laboratories; Forensic toxicology; Quantitative and qualitative analysis of chemicals; Spectroscopy.

Attention-deficit/hyperactivity disorder medications

Definition: Pharmacologically produced agents used in the treatment of the syndrome of disruptive behavior known as attention-deficit/hyperactivity disorder.

Significance: Medication management of attention-deficit/hyperactivity disorder targets the areas of the disorder that contribute to the patient's impairment: inattention, hyperactivity, and impulsivity.

These conditions can, at times, lead persons with the disorder to involvement with legal authorities. Researchers who have studied attention-deficit/hyperactivity disorder in prison populations have estimated its prevalence from as low as 20 percent to as high as 70 percent.

Most medications used in the treatment of attention-deficit/hyperactivity disorder (ADHD) are rudimentarily separated into stimulant and nonstimulant categories; further distinctions are made between those that are approved for treatment of the disorder by the U.S. Food and Drug Administration (FDA) and those that are nonapproved or used "off-label" by prescribing physicians. FDA-approved medications in the stimulant category comprise amphetamine preparations (brand names include Adderall and Dexedrine) and methylphenidate preparations (brand names include Ritalin, Metadate, Concerta, and Focalin). Although many nonstimulant medications are used to treat ADHD, only one, atomoxetine (brand name Strattera), has been approved by the FDA for use in children, adolescents, and adults.

Stimulants

Although it may seem counterintuitive to treat a hyperactive patient with a stimulant, a simple explanation regarding the theory of ADHD is as follows: In the ADHD patient, the frontal lobe of the brain, which is responsible for executive functions (such as planning, organizing, and focusing attention) and other tasks (including controlling impulses, motivation, and movement), is deficient in the neurotransmitters that are restored to a more normative state with the use of stimulant medications. The main catecholamine neurotransmitters that are affected by the use of stimulants are dopamine and norepinephrine. These transmitters are involved in focusing attention, motivation, learning, and other cognitive functions that are adversely affected in patients with ADHD.

In general, the use of methylphenidate and amphetamine medications with patients who have ADHD leads to an approximation of a normal neurochemical state, both by blocking the reuptake of dopamine into and promoting the release of dopamine out of the nerve cells in the brain wherein dopamine is produced, stored, and released. The net effect is an increase in the amount of dopamine available to communicate between nerve cells. This area of communication between the cells is termed the synapse. Amphetamine preparations have the added effect of promoting release and blocking reuptake of norepinephrine.

When treatment is optimized, between 77 and 90 percent of patients with ADHD will have a favorable response to stimulant medications. This may be reflected in improvements in academic accuracy and grades, parent-child relations, and social functioning. However, although the stimulant medications have well-documented usefulness in the treatment of ADHD and are generally well tolerated, they may also be associated with side effects. These side effects include, but are not limited to, insomnia, weight loss, headaches, irritability, loss of appetite, stomach upset, and increases in blood pressure and heart rate. Other less common but potentially serious side effects include the development of undesired movements called tics, slowing of growth, the possibility of seizures, and the risk of developing psychotic symptoms such as hallucinations and paranoia. Often, side effects can be minimized or eliminated through the reduction of the medication dosage or through a change to a different type of stimulant that may be better tolerated.

Atomoxetine

Atomoxetine is a selective norepinephrine reuptake inhibitor that is approved by the FDA for treatment of ADHD in children and adults. It is thought that atomoxetine blocks the norepinephrine transporter in nerve cells in the brain, thereby increasing the amount of norepinephrine in the synapse between nerve cells. It is further hypothesized that in the brain's frontal lobe, norepinephrine transporters may, to some extent, also be responsible for the reuptake of dopamine, not just norepinephrine. Research indicates that atomoxetine may be as effective in the treatment of ADHD as the stimulant methylphenidate, but atomoxetine may take a longer period of time to reach its full benefit.

Atomoxetine's side effects may include stomach upset, constipation, decreased appetite, headache, fatigue, irritability, and an inability to empty the bladder completely when urinating. More serious side effects include rare cases of liver toxicity and the concern, given that the chemical structure of atomoxetine is similar to that of certain antidepressants, that it could promote suicidal thinking and behavior in children and adolescents such as that seen clinically in 3-4 percent of patients in the population taking traditional antidepressants.

Other Treatments

Typically, alternative medications have been used as second- or third-line options to treat ADHD. Although these approaches are not approved by the FDA, they still have usefulness for those patients who cannot tolerate or do not benefit from more traditional treatments. Further, these medications may be used in conjunction with other treatments to augment or boost a patient's response.

Tricyclic antidepressants, such as imipramine (brand names include Tofranil and Antideprin) and nortriptyline (brand names include Aventyl and Pamelor), have been used in the treatment of ADHD with some success. It is theorized that the beneficial effects of these antidepressants on ADHD symptoms are related to the blockade of norepinephrine reuptake into nerve cells. Use of these medications, however, has fallen out of favor with most treatment providers because of the limiting side effects associated with the drugs, the most concerning of which is the risk of sudden cardiac death if the medications are taken in overdose or if the blood levels of the medications get too high. Concerns also exist regarding an increase in suicidal thoughts and behaviors in child and adolescent patient populations. Nevertheless, in experienced hands and with proper monitoring, these medications can be prescribed safely and effectively for treatment of ADHD.

An alternative and structurally chemically different antidepressant with usefulness in treating ADHD is bupropion (brand names include Wellbutrin and Zyban). It is thought that bupropion helps patients with ADHD through its effects on norepinephrine and dopamine.

This medication does not have the cardiac concerns that are present with tricyclic antidepressants, but, in high doses, it may make patients more prone to seizures. The suicide risk warnings with children and adolescents are the same as those applied to tricyclic antidepressants.

Alpha-2 Adrenergic Agonists

The medications known as alpha-2 adrenergic agonists include clonidine (brand names Catapres and Disarit) and guanfacine (brand names Tenex and Intuniv). These drugs are used to treat high blood pressure and, through their effects on the central nervous system mediated by norepinephrine-containing nerve cells, are helpful in diminishing impulsivity, hyperactivity, and even aggression in patients with ADHD. They may also help with sleep disturbance and motor (movement) tics that are seen in some patients. The main side effects are dry mouth, headache, sedation, constipation, slowing of heart rate, and lowering of blood pressure.
Neva E. J. Sanders-Dewey and Seth G. Dewey

Further Reading

Sadock, Benjamin James, and Virginia Alcott Sadock. *Kaplan and Sadock's Synopsis of Psychiatry: Behavioral Sciences/Clinical Psychiatry*. 10th ed. Philadelphia: Lippincott, Williams & Wilkins, 2007. General text aimed at mental health practitioners provides an overview of the entire field of psychiatry.

Schatzberg, Alan F., Jonathan O. Cole, and Charles DeBattista. *Manual of Clinical Psychopharmacology*. 6th ed. New York: American Psychiatric Publishing, 2007. Practical manual addresses the psychotropic management of psychiatric conditions.

Stahl, Stephen M. *Essential Psychopharmacology: Neuroscientific Basis and Practical Applications*. 3d ed. New York: Cambridge University Press, 2008. Good resource for readers seeking an understanding of the fundamentals of psychotropic interventions.

_____. *Essential Psychopharmacology: The Prescriber's Guide*. Rev. ed. New York: Cambridge University Press, 2006. Guidebook for practitioners provides information regarding the advantages and disadvantages of the various psychotropic medications.

See also: Bacterial resistance and response to antibacterial agents; Forensic psychiatry; Psychotropic drugs; Stimulants.

Autoerotic and erotic asphyxiation

Definition: Potentially deadly practice of increasing sexual pleasure by restricting oxygen to the brain through hanging or suffocation during sex acts.

Significance: Deaths resulting from autoerotic and erotic asphyxiation are often mistaken for suicide (especially among teenagers) or homicide because many health care workers, emergency personnel, and police personnel are unfamiliar with the signs of these sexual practices. More widespread education about the dangers of these practices could save lives.

Erotic asphyxiation (EA) is the practice of depriving the brain of oxygen during sexual stimulation with a sex partner for purposes of increasing sexual pleasure and heightening orgasm. Autoerotic asphyxiation (AEA) is the same practice carried out by one person, without a sex partner; that is, autoerotic asphyxiators masturbate while voluntarily strangling themselves. Neck compression (strangulation), exclusion of oxygen (suffocation), airway obstruction (blocking the airway with a foreign object), and chest compression (restricting the movement of the chest) are all methods of depriving oxygen used during erotic asphyxiation.

During a normal breath, carbon dioxide is exhaled and oxygen is inhaled, keeping the brain's oxygen at an adequate level. In AEA and EA, oxygen deprivation is achieved in a variety of ways, including the use of a plastic bag over the head and self-strangulation using a ligature. When a person's supply of oxygen to the brain is too low and carbon dioxide is too high, some resulting effects may be a sense of euphoria, dizziness, lowered inhibitions, and even hallucinations.

Statistics

Research indicates that some 70 percent of those who practice autoerotic or erotic asphyxiation are under the age of thirty. In the United States, AEA and EA are most common among single, white, middle-class, male teenagers and young adults (thirteen to twenty years of age). Teenagers are also the practitioners who most often die as the result of these practices. The most common reasons teenagers take part in AEA and EA are sexual experimentation, thrill seeking, and fantasies of masochistic bondage. No research has linked gender confusion, homosexuality, or transvestism with the practice of AEA or EA. Some psychologists believe that a history of child sexual abuse may influence later participation in these sexual practices.

Teenage girls and women also participate in AEA and EA, but to a much lesser extent than do young men. The techniques of AEA that women use tend to be less obvious than those used by men. Often a female practitioner will use a single neck ligature and only limited sexual props, such as a vibrator or a dildo. The small amount of evidence available when a woman dies as the result of AEA may be a cause of underreporting of AEA practices among women.

One study of autoerotic asphyxiation found that adult practitioners, in contrast with teenagers who participate in these acts, were often lonely and depressed. Other experts disputed this finding, however, noting that anecdotal reports indicate that adults who have died as a result of AEA have often been happily married men who were not deprived of sex or companionship.

Suicide is one of the leading causes of death among teenagers in the United States, and some researchers believe that many of the teen deaths labeled as suicide are actually accidental deaths from AEA or EA. According to estimates of the Federal Bureau of Investigation (FBI), some five hundred to one thousand deaths result from the practice of AEA and EA each year in the United States, but they are often misreported as suicide or homicide. Some experts theorize that in many cases embarrassed or shocked relatives of the deceased clean up AEA and EA death scenes before the police arrive.

Additionally, emergency personnel and police are not always educated about the signs of AEA and so may easily misinterpret deaths resulting from this practice as suicide.

AEA Syndrome

Although release mechanisms are often built into devices intended for use in autoerotic asphyxiation, the practice remains extremely dangerous. Death or permanent brain damage can result if a practitioner loses consciousness before removing the device used to deprive oxygen or if a release mechanism malfunctions.

The paraphernalia and practices of sexual bondage are common to both AEA and EA. Sometimes practitioners insert foreign bodies in the rectum for anal stimulation, and many place mirrors strategically to view themselves during the act of sexual asphyxiation. Some other signs of AEA and EA that may appear at death scenes, and of which investigators should be aware, include the presence of lubricants, sex toys, and pornographic pictures or literature and the binding of the body and genitals with chains, leather strips, or ropes. Items that may be found at such scenes include belts, cords, ropes, scarves, and neckties. Practitioners of AEA and EA also sometimes cover their heads with plastic bags to deprive their brains of oxygen.

Evidence of asphyxia by strangulation, protective padding around the neck, and evidence of trying to prevent marks on the body are all common elements of a death scene involving AEA. In addition, the presence of devices with self-release mechanisms, sexual aids and props, and pornography is associated with an AEA death. Body position—with feet touching the floor, sitting in a chair or lying in bed, partially or totally nude, with arms and legs bound in chains or ropes—and evidence that masturbation occurred are also indicators of an AEA death. Another feature of the AEA death scene is what it lacks—no suicide letter or other evidence that the death resulted from a suicide attempt is found.

Some warning signs that a person may be participating in autoerotic asphyxiation include unexplained marks on the neck, bloodshot eyes, complaints of frequent headaches, and possession of knotted short ropes and neckties. Teen-age boys who engage in AEA may install locks on their bedroom doors, keep women's clothing hidden in their rooms, and show a strong interest in sexual bondage and sadomasochism. Parents, teachers, and counselors of young people should be aware of all these signs. Each sign by itself is not necessarily indicative of AEA, but in combination these indicators should not be ignored. When parents and others involved with teenagers suspect the practice of autoerotic or erotic asphyxiation, they should investigate and communicate with these young people to inform them about the risks of such activities. Accidental deaths can be prevented when young people involved in these practices receive prompt counseling by professionals who are familiar with AEA and EA.

Sharon W. Stark

Further Reading

Boglioli, Lauren R., and Mark L. Taff. "The Medicolegal Investigation of Autoerotic Asphyxial Deaths." In *The Handbook of Forensic Sexology: Biological and Criminological Perspectives*, edited by James J. Krivacska and John Money. Amherst, N.Y.: Prometheus Books, 1994. Provides an overview of autoerotic asphyxiation, statistics, and description of the biological events that occur during AEA. Also discusses individual victims and death scenes.

Brody, Jane E. "'Autoerotic Death' of Youths Causes Widening Concern." *The New York Times*, March 27, 1984. Discusses growing concerns among members of the public about adolescents' experimentation with autoerotic asphyxiation. Offers information on the warning signs of AEA in young people.

Jenkins, A. "When Self-Pleasure Becomes Self-Destruction: Autoerotic Asphyxiation Paraphilia." *International Electronic Journal of Health Education* 3, no. 3 (2000): 208-216. Presents statistics and describes the characteristics of AEA participants.

Sheleg, Sergey, and Edwin Ehrlich. *Autoerotic Asphyxiation: Forensic, Medical, and Social Aspects.* Tucson, Ariz.: Wheatmark, 2006. Reviews the research regarding AEA and discusses the practice from the perspectives of both professionals and society.

Tournel, Gilles, et al. "Complete Autoerotic Asphyxiation: Suicide or Accident?" *American Journal of Forensic Medicine and Pathology* 22 (June, 2001): 180-183. Focuses on the topic of deaths associated with AEA.

See also: Asphyxiation; Choking; Hanging; Psychological autopsy; Strangulation; Suffocation; Suicide.

Automated fingerprint identification systems. *See* Integrated Automated Fingerprint Identification System

Autopsies

Definition: External and internal medical examinations of dead bodies to determine cause of death, identify decedents or their body parts, or study changes caused by disease.

Significance: An autopsy is a very important part of many forensic investigations, given that the body is usually the center of any death case. In a death investigation, the body is just as much a crime scene as the geographic area in which it was found. During the autopsy, evidence is collected from the body "scene." This evidence, along with the determination of the cause and manner of death, contributes greatly to the resolution of the investigation. It can also positively identify an otherwise visually unidentifiable person, making it possible for authorities to release the remains to the appropriate family.

Autopsies may be divided into two primary types: the clinical autopsies done at hospitals and the forensic autopsies executed by medical examiners or coroners. The aim of the clinical, or academic, autopsy is to determine, clarify, or confirm diagnoses that remained unknown or did not become sufficiently clear during the stay of a patient in a hospital or other health care facility. The forensic, or medicolegal, autopsy focuses primarily on violent death (death by accident, suicide, or homicide), suspicious and sudden death, death without medical assistance, or death that could result in a lawsuit, such as a death related to surgical or anesthetic procedures. The purposes of the forensic autopsy are to find the cause and manner of death and to identify the decedent.

Cause, Manner, and Mechanism of Death

The term "cause of death" refers to the situation or illness that resulted in the loss of life. Examples of causes of death include heart disease, stroke, knife wound to the wrist, gunshot wound to the chest, and hanging. In assigning the cause of death, some medical examiners use the "but for" test, as in "But for the gunshot wound, the victim would still be alive." The cause of death is what brought about the person's death.

Manner of death is determined according to a classification system that coroners and medical examiners use to certify a death. Only five manners of death are possible: natural, accidental, homicide, suicide, and undetermined. Any doctor can pronounce death, but only a coroner or a medical examiner can certify a death as a manner other than natural. A natural death is one that results from the normal course of life. Death from heart disease would be a type of natural death. An accidental death is one that results from a mishap, such as a death resulting from a fall off a ladder.

Homicide, in this context, is a death that results from the actions of another person. This is a medical declaration only; it does not imply anything about the guilt or motives of the other person. A manner of death of homicide on a death certificate is not a legal assertion. The determination of the other party's culpability is made by the legal system, independent of the autopsy. Deaths that result from vehicle accidents that involve other vehicles are often clas-

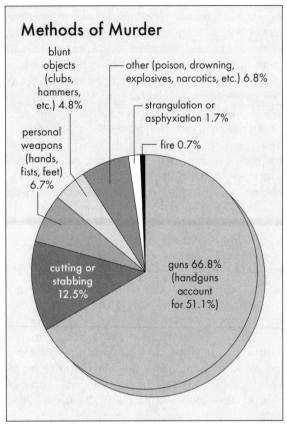

Methods of Murder

blunt objects (clubs, hammers, etc.) 4.8%

other (poison, drowning, explosives, narcotics, etc.) 6.8%

strangulation or asphyxiation 1.7%

personal weapons (hands, fists, feet) 6.7%

fire 0.7%

cutting or stabbing 12.5%

guns 66.8% (handguns account for 51.1%)

Source: Federal Bureau of Investigation, *Crime in the United States.* Figures are based on 14,274 murders in the United States in 2002.

sified as homicides. Accidental shootings also are often classified as homicides, although they do not warrant a verdict of murder. Aside from such exceptions, however, many cases with a manner of death of homicide are indeed the result of malicious actions that would constitute the legal determination of murder.

Suicide is the manner of death used to describe a death that resulted from the victim's own determined actions. Hangings and self-cuttings are both classified as suicide manners of death. A finding of undetermined manner of death simply means that enough evidence was not available for the pathologist to distinguish between two or more of the other manners of death. As an example, without proper investigative information, a medical examiner may have problems ruling between accidental death and suicide if the deceased took a few too many pills

or mixed medications. The attending coroner or medical examiner makes every effort to gain as much information as possible to avoid the need to use the undetermined manner of death classification.

Laypersons often confuse the concept of mechanism of death with cause of death. Mechanism of death is much more specific than cause of death, however; it is the actual specific biological reason the person died. In a case where the cause of death is a gunshot wound to the chest, the mechanism of death might be exsanguination, meaning that the victim bled out; death was the result of the loss of blood caused by the gunshot wound. Chronic alcoholism and cirrhosis are causes of death, whereas hepatic encephalopathy (the impairment of the brain cells caused by the release of liver toxins into the body) would be the actual mechanism of death in such cases. Cardiac arrest is often a stated mechanism of death, but many coroners and medical examiners disapprove of this determination, as heart failure (meaning the heart stopped) is a result of every death and may not be the true mechanism of death.

Identification of the Deceased

In addition to establishing cause and manner of death, the forensic autopsy positively identifies the deceased. Visual identification is not considered sufficiently accurate to be counted as positive identification. The body goes through many physical changes during decomposition that can make recognizing an individual difficult. Also, the person who is asked to identify the deceased visually is often in a highly emotional state, which can lead to mistakes and misidentification.

The clothing on the body, likewise, is not a positive identifier. For example, members of the U.S. military have their last names on every uniform they are required to wear, and they also must wear dog tags that bear their names, but even these precautions do not guarantee that a dead soldier will be correctly identified by these items. Sometimes people do not wear their own clothes, and, in some documented cases, good friends in the military have exchanged dog tags in particularly dire situations as a means of encouraging each other or lifting morale. Reliance on clothing and dog tags has occasionally resulted in the misidentification of deceased military personnel.

To make a positive identification of a deceased person, investigators use one of three main recognized methods. The first is fingerprint examination. If the decedent was part of the military, ever served time in prison, worked for the government, or participated in a local "Protect Our Children" or similar drive, he or she likely had fingerprints taken. These antemortem (prior to death) records can be compared with fingerprints taken from the body at autopsy to identify the decedent with certainty.

Another positive identification technique is forensic odontology, in which the decedent's teeth are compared with antemortem dental records. To carry out the comparison, a forensic odontologist takes X rays and castings of the decedent's teeth and then compares tooth positions, shapes of fillings, root lengths, and other factors with those found in the dental records of the person suspected to be the deceased.

The third method used for positive identification of a body involves the examination of DNA (deoxyribonucleic acid). DNA comparison methods are of two types. One uses nuclear DNA, which is in the blood and tissue; this DNA is somewhat fragile and can be damaged by decomposition. Identification using this DNA involves strict comparison of the DNA found in the blood and tissue of the deceased to antemortem material. If the nuclear DNA cannot be used, it is possible to use mitochondrial DNA, which is much sturdier and can withstand decomposition changes. Mitochondrial DNA is a bit trickier in its comparison because this type of DNA is

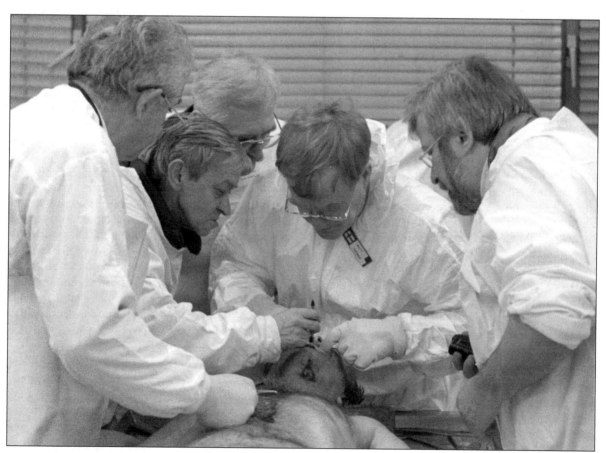

A team of Yugoslav and Finnish forensic specialists perform an autopsy in a Kosovo morgue on one of forty-five ethnic Albanians killed by Serbian security forces in early 1999. (AP/Wide World Photos)

passed on only from the mother to the child, so a family member from the mother's side of the family is needed for comparison.

Other methods of positive victim identification are also available. A radiologist can compare X rays of the body to X rays from any previous injuries in the medical records of the person believed to be the deceased. If evidence of previously documented injuries can be found on the postmortem (after death) X rays, the pathologist can identify the victim. If antemortem facial X rays exist, a radiologist can compare how the sinuses line up, as well as their sizes and shapes. Evidence of some type of extreme medical procedure, such as the attachment of a metal plate to a bone to aid in the healing of a serious injury, can also be an identifier. These methods, however, are used relatively rarely because they rely on the presence of previous X rays in the suspected victim's medical records and on the uniqueness of those X rays.

Initial External Examination

Significant examination of the body occurs during an autopsy prior to any cutting. This initial procedure may vary a bit from practitioner to practitioner, but the same basic principles are always followed. The first and most important step in any autopsy is photography. Pictures of the body are taken before the body is removed from the body bag, to document exactly how the remains appeared when they came into the care of the coroner or medical examiner. Typically, a few shots of the body bag are taken, with any identifying tags visible, and then the bag is opened and the first shots of the body are taken, still in the body bag. In cases of mass disasters and severe commingling of bodies, these initial shots are very important to show what exactly was received and then later put together as related remains.

In another external stage of the autopsy, full-body X rays are taken of the remains so that when the body is ready for postmortem examination, the pathologist can get an idea of what is inside prior to cutting. Broken bones and other injuries are documented, as these may help to guide the pathologist in determining the cause of death. X rays are essential in shooting cases because they allow the pathologist to document

and count the bullets that remain in the body before cutting and provide information on where the bullets will be when the cutting begins, thereby saving a search that could otherwise take hours.

The coroner or medical examiner also typically allows any law-enforcement personnel attending the autopsy to take the fingerprints of the deceased at this time. Some medical examiner offices have their own investigators who work as liaisons between the medical examiners and law-enforcement agents. These inhouse investigators may be the ones who routinely take decedents' fingerprints.

Forensic odontology may be done before the pathologist cuts or after, depending on the procedures set up for that office. The forensic odontologist makes a thorough postmortem dental examination and compares the findings to antemortem dental records. Dental X rays are taken, casts are made, and, if necessary, sometimes the jaw is removed from the body for examination. (The jaw is removed only in specialized cases, however, and only when it has already been determined with certainty that there will be no open-casket funeral.)

After all of the steps described above have taken place, the pathologist does an external examination as well. The body is taken out of the body bag, and pictures are once again taken. The doctor then carefully removes the clothing and jewelry from the body while noting any cuts, tears, or other indicators of injury or struggle shown by these items. These personal effects are then set aside and photographed separately for documentation. The doctor may refer back to the clothes if they have any cuts in them to marry up the cuts with injuries on the body or perhaps to find marks on the body that are not readily visible. If there are other marks on the body, the doctor may also refer to the clothing to see if the marks may have been made by it.

All salvageable personal effects that are not going to be kept as evidence are set aside for return to the family of the deceased. The doctor tries not to add further damage to any salvageable effects; for example, if possible, the clothes are unbuttoned or unzipped as opposed to cut away from the body. If the clothes are not salvageable, whether because they are saturated

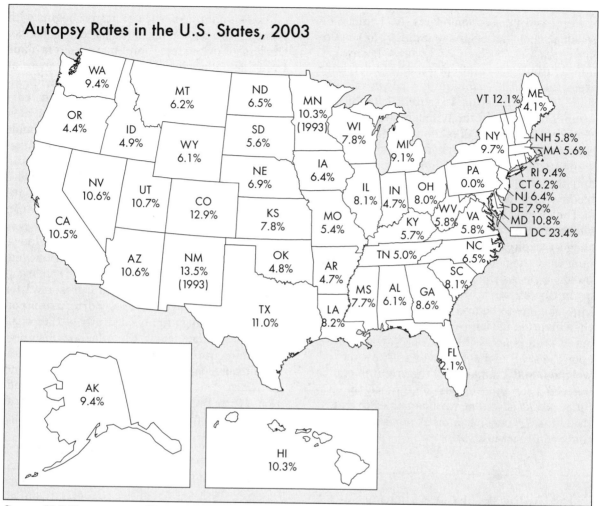

Autopsy Rates in the U.S. States, 2003

WA 9.4%
OR 4.4%
ID 4.9%
MT 6.2%
ND 6.5%
MN 10.3% (1993)
WI 7.8%
MI 9.1%
VT 12.1%
ME 4.1%
NY 9.7%
NH 5.8%
MA 5.6%
NV 10.6%
UT 10.7%
WY 6.1%
SD 5.6%
NE 6.9%
IA 6.4%
IL 8.1%
IN 4.7%
OH 8.0%
PA 0.0%
RI 9.4%
CT 6.2%
NJ 6.4%
DE 7.9%
MD 10.8%
DC 23.4%
CA 10.5%
CO 12.9%
KS 7.8%
MO 5.4%
KY 5.7%
WV 5.8%
VA 5.8%
NC 6.5%
AZ 10.6%
NM 13.5% (1993)
OK 4.8%
AR 4.7%
TN 5.0%
SC 8.1%
MS 7.7%
AL 6.1%
GA 8.6%
TX 11.0%
LA 8.2%
FL 2.1%
AK 9.4%
HI 10.3%

Source: U.S. Department of Health and Human Services, Centers for Disease Control and Prevention, 2007. Figures indicate percentages of deaths for which autopsies were reported in 2003, except in Minnesota and New Mexico, whose figures are from 1993.

in blood or somehow destroyed, they are usually cut off. If a garment is covered with body fluid, it is dried prior to packaging to prevent spoilage from bacteria activity.

The doctor then examines the body itself, documenting any and all injuries as well as any unusual markings (birthmarks or tattoos), noting their placement on the body, their shapes, and their measurements. References to placement on the body are always made from the decedent's perspective. That is, an injury on the right side of the body's chest is described as such, although the injury appears on the left as the doctor views the body from above.

Sometimes, depending on the type of case, the pathologist will also take fingernail scrapings or clippings from the body for evidence; materials of interest to investigators may include soil samples and blood or skin that may have been left on the body by a suspect. The naked body is then washed, and the wounds are cleaned. The corpse is photographed once again, with separate shots taken of all identified injuries.

Internal Examination

After all the external evidence is recorded and set aside for possible further examination, the process of dissection begins. As a rule, a forensic pathologist begins an autopsy at the upper portion of the body and works downward. Some pathologists may open the head at a later step, but initial examination always starts there. First, the scalp is searched for hidden wounds or artifacts, and hair samples are taken if needed. The mouth is examined for tooth damage, tongue lacerations, chemicals or toxic substances, and cuts on the lip and inner mouth, and the nose and ears are examined for any blood accumulations.

The inner eyelids are examined for petechiae, which are tiny pinpoint blood specks that may suggest asphyxiation. Whether at the beginning or at the end of the autopsy, when the pathologist opens the head to gain access to the brain, an incision is made that reaches from behind one ear to behind the other. The scalp is then inverted until it rests over the face and the outer skull is accessible. A bone saw is used to open the skull so that the brain can be removed, weighed, and sampled and the cranium can be inspected for injuries. In some cases the cranium is also sawed at various angles to expose the sinuses, jawbone, or other parts of the skull that require scrutiny.

The standard American autopsy begins with a cut known as a Y incision (the cut looks like the letter Y when it is completed). A cut is made from each shoulder, and the two cuts meet at the lower part of the sternum (breastbone), although some pathologists intersect these cuts as low as the stomach. A straight cut is then made from the intersection down to the pubic bone. The skin and muscle are then cut back, revealing the rib cage beneath. The ribs are examined for any breaks or healing injuries before each rib is cut so that the breastplate—beneath which many of the body's organs are housed—can be removed.

Each organ (the heart, lungs, liver, kidneys, spleen, stomach, and testicles) is removed, weighed, and examined for injury. Each organ is then sliced, and samples are preserved for toxicology screens (tests for any drug use or poison) and histology analysis (study of the organ on a microscopic level). Samples are also preserved in case they are needed for reexamination at some point in the future. Blood, bile, and urine are also taken, examined, and preserved, along with fluids from the lungs and pleural cavity. The contents of the stomach are also inspected.

The autopsy ends in the pelvic cavity. The external and internal anus and genitalia are inspected, the bladder is removed and studied, and, in cases of suspected sexual assault, vaginal and anal swabs are made.

Upon completion of the examination, all organs (including the brain) are placed in a bag that is put into the chest cavity. The piece of the skull that has been removed is put back into place, and the scalp is pulled back down to hold it in place. The scalp and chest incisions are sewn shut, so that when the body is dressed for viewing, no cuts are visible and open-casket viewing is possible.

After all else is completed,

The Autopsy Through History

The term "autopsy" comes from *autopsia*, a Greek word meaning "to see with one's own eyes." Around 3000 B.C.E., the Egyptians practiced mummification—removing organs through tiny slits in the body so that the body itself remained whole—and the Greek Herophilus broke religious taboos by dissecting bodies to learn how the inner organs worked. By around 150 B.C.E., autopsy results had legal parameters in the Roman Empire. In 1761, the Italian anatomist Giovanni Battista Morgagni published *De Sedibus et Causis Morborum per Anatomen Indagatis* (*The Seats and Causes of Diseases Investigated by Anatomy*, 1769), the first exhaustive written work on pathology.

The nineteenth century Austrian anatomy professor Karl Rokitansky is regarded as the founder of the modern autopsy. Rokitansky personally performed or supervised more than one hundred thousand autopsies and was also one of the world's first pathologists. Under his leadership, all autopsies were carried out equally so that every part of the body in question could be studied exactly the same way.

Kelly Rothenberg

including any toxicology, DNA, and histology analyses, the pathologist writes a full report that describes the autopsy procedures and findings in detail. Included in the report is a brief history of the case; a death scene description; a list of all persons present at the scene; an X-ray description of the body; descriptions of the clothing found on the body, of the naked body prior to dissection, of the condition of the organs at autopsy, and of the wounds; the toxicological findings; and the cause and manner of death.

Russell S. Strasser

Further Reading

DiMaio, Vincent J., and Dominick DiMaio. *Forensic Pathology*. 2d ed. Boca Raton, Fla.: CRC Press, 2001. One of the best reference sources available in the field of forensic pathology. Covers autopsies in detail as well as certain techniques for specific kinds of deaths.

Mann, Robert, William Bass, and Lee Meadows. "Time Since Death and Decomposition of the Human Body: Variables and Observations in Case and Experimental Field Studies." *Journal of Forensic Sciences* 35, no. 1 (1990): 103-111. Excellent comprehensive study focuses primarily on the decomposition of a body but gives a good idea of what to expect at autopsy from certain types of cases. Discusses the difficulty of determining time of death.

Sheaff, Michael T., and Deborah J. Hopster. *Post Mortem Technique Handbook*. London: Springer, 2001. Provides a very good in-depth look at postmortem examinations. Thorough discussion covers every step of an autopsy extensively.

Shkrum, Michael J., and David A. Ramsay. *Forensic Pathology of Trauma: Common Problems for the Pathologist*. Totowa, N.J.: Humana Press, 2007. Excellent technical reference work discusses how trauma affects a body and the problems that forensic pathologists face in conducting trauma autopsies.

Spitz, Werner U., ed. *Spitz and Fisher's Medicolegal Investigation of Death: Guidelines for the Application of Pathology to Crime Investigation*. 4th ed. Springfield, Ill.: Charles C Thomas, 2006. Indispensable volume for those conducting forensic investigations and forensic pathology. Includes comprehensive sections on specific cases along with their pathological findings.

Timmermans, Stefan. *Postmortem: How Medical Examiners Explain Suspicious Deaths*. Chicago: University of Chicago Press, 2006. Outstanding work on forensic pathology explains the autopsy process and gives case study examples.

Zugibe, Frederick, and David L. Carroll. *Dissecting Death: Secrets of a Medical Examiner*. New York: Broadway Books, 2005. A forensic pathologist discusses some of his cases and how he performed the autopsies. Interesting book aimed at readers who like the popular *CSI* television shows.

See also: Antemortem injuries; Coroners; DNA analysis; Fingerprints; Forensic odontology; Forensic pathology; Forensic toxicology; Gunshot wounds; Oral autopsy; Petechial hemorrhage; Psychological autopsy; Puncture wounds; Suicide; Thanatology; Toxicological analysis.

B

Bacteria

Definition: Single-celled organisms lacking a nucleus, found in and on humans and widespread in the environment.

Significance: Bacteria are ubiquitous on Earth, and some species can cause disease in humans. An understanding of the classification of bacteria as well as the ways in which bacterial populations grow and reproduce is useful to the identification, diagnosis, and treatment of bacterial diseases.

The tiny unicellular organisms known as bacteria define the biosphere on Earth—that is, if bacteria do not inhabit a particular environment, no living things reside there. Bacteria are extremely adaptable and have managed to exploit a wide variety of habitats successfully. One niche exploited by bacteria is the human body. Humans support a population of more than two hundred species of bacteria in numbers greater than the cells that make up an individual human host. These members of the normal flora are found on the skin and in the digestive, urinary, reproductive, and upper respiratory tracts of humans.

Although some species of bacteria can cause disease in humans, other animals, and plants, the majority of bacterial species are not pathogenic (disease-causing). Bacteria are key players in the ecology of the Earth, functioning in important roles in global chemical cycles. Perhaps most important, bacteria are the only organisms on Earth that possess the ability to fix nitrogen—that is, to convert the nitrogen gas in the atmosphere to a form that is usable by other organisms.

Disease-causing bacteria have attracted the most interest and study since the confirmation of the germ theory of disease by Louis Pasteur and Robert Koch in the 1870's. It is interesting to note that Koch's proof that germs cause disease involved the bacterium *Bacillus anthracis*, which causes anthrax, an organism that has been used as a biological weapon.

The first sixty years of the study of medical bacteriology focused on identification and diagnosis, with little attention to the basic biology of bacteria. The discovery and development of antibiotics led to an overly optimistic view that infectious disease had been conquered. The emergence of antibiotic-resistant strains of bacteria as well as outbreaks of previously unknown pathogens stimulated a renewed interest in bacteriology.

Classification and Taxonomy

Bacteria are classified as prokaryotic cells—that is, the genetic material of a bacterium is not enclosed in a nucleus. This lack of a nucleus distinguishes bacterial cells from the cells that make up plants and animals, which are classified as eukaryotic. Additional differences between bacterial cells and eukaryotic cells include the types of molecules found in the cell walls, organization and expression of genes, and sensitivity to certain antibiotics.

Bacteria themselves have been classified in several ways. In 1923, the first edition of *Bergey's Manual of Determinative Bacteriology* offered descriptions of all the species of bacteria then identified, an outline of the taxonomic relationships among bacteria, and keys for diagnosis of diseases caused by bacteria. The ninth edition of *Bergey's Manual*, published in 1994, focuses primarily on identification of bacteria and uses taxonomic divisions that do not necessarily reflect evolutionary relationships.

During the 1980's, *Bergey's Manual of Systematic Bacteriology* was published in an attempt to organize bacterial species into the type of hierarchical classification schemes that have been applied to eukaryotic organisms. This manual later underwent revision to include new species and to cover the progress that had been made in molecular classification methods.

The International Committee on Systematics of Prokaryotes (ICSP) is the organization that oversees the nomenclature of prokaryotes and issues opinions concerning related taxonomic matters. When a researcher discovers a previously undescribed bacterium, the ICSP must approve the researcher's proposed name for the newly described species as well as the taxonomic classification of the species.

Clinically, classification of bacteria is performed primarily to diagnose particular diseases. Identification of bacteria in a clinical specimen can be accomplished through direct microscopic examination, isolation and culture of the responsible bacteria, and biochemical and immunological tests. Researchers have developed and marketed a number of automated microbial diagnosis systems that allow rapid diagnosis without the need to isolate the organisms of interest.

Cell and Population Growth

In discussing the growth of living organisms, one can focus on the growth of an individual or the growth of a population. Because bacteria are single-celled organisms, growth of an individual bacterium does not include development of organs or other body parts, but rather just enlargement of the cell itself.

Discussion of the growth of bacterial species is usually concerned with the growth of a population of cells. Because almost all bacteria reproduce through the division of one cell into two, the growth of a population of bacterial cells is geometric—that is, the population doubles in size with each round of cell division. The length of time required for a population of bacterial cells to double varies depending on the species and strain of bacteria as well

as on the environmental conditions, including temperature, pH, nutrient availability, and waste accumulation.

Some bacteria, such as *Escherichia coli*, have a maximum doubling rate of less than thirty minutes. At this rate, a single cell could generate a population of one million cells in less than ten hours. In fact, if the environmental conditions remained optimal, with ready nutrients and regular waste removal, a culture of maximally reproducing *E. coli* bacteria would equal the mass of the planet Earth within one week. Other bacteria, such as *Mycobacterium tuberculosis*, divide much more slowly, taking twelve to eighteen hours under optimal conditions for one

Dr. Robert Koch with his wife in 1908, three years after he won the Nobel Prize in Physiology or Medicine for his work on tuberculosis. During the 1870's, Koch and French biologist Louis Pasteur proved the germ theory of disease that laid the foundation for modern bacteriology. *(Library of Congress)*

round of binary fission. The optimal growth rates estimated for many bacteria are merely speculative because the majority of species have not yet been cultured on defined or artificial media.

Even slowly dividing bacteria can reproduce in far less time than nearly every other type of organism. Because of their rapid reproductive rates and omnipresence in the living world, bacteria can rapidly overwhelm any unpreserved biological sample. Unrefrigerated food, blood and tissue samples, and other biological specimens can quickly become host to a diverse, rapidly growing population of bacteria.

Reproduction

Most bacteria reproduce by binary fission. One cell grows by manufacturing more cellular components. The genome is replicated, and the single cell divides into two essentially identical cells. This type of reproduction is termed asexual because it does not involve the recombination of genetic material from two parents. Because the cells that result from binary fission are virtually identical genetically, the individual cells in a group or colony of bacteria all descended from a single ancestral cell could well be clones of the original cell.

The cellular machinery involved in replicating the genetic material does not perform this replication with perfect fidelity. At each round of replication, there is a finite probability of errors occurring. These errors lead to changes in the genetic material known as mutations. These mutations may result in cells with characteristics that are different from those of the other cells in the population. These altered characteristics may lead to cells that are better adapted to a particular environment—perhaps the ability to metabolize a new nutrient or survive in the presence of an antibiotic. Because bacterial cells reproduce by simple cell division, altered characteristics are transmitted to all offspring of the altered cell (barring further mutation).

Although bacteria do not reproduce sexually by recombination of genetic material from two parents, many bacteria are capable of obtaining genetic material from other cells through various methods. Some bacteria can take up DNA

(deoxyribonucleic acid) from the environment (probably released from decomposing cells), can receive DNA through viral infections, and can transfer DNA directly from one living cell to another. These genetic recombination processes allow genes (such as those that confer antibiotic resistance) to be spread throughout a bacterial population rapidly.

Lisa M. Sardinia

Further Reading

Betsy, Tom, and James Keogh. *Microbiology Demystified*. New York: McGraw-Hill, 2005. This alternative to hefty textbooks is intended as a review for allied health students having difficulty understanding concepts in microbiology. Clearly written.

Madigan, Michael T., John M. Martinko, Paul V. Dunlap, and David P. Clark. *Brock Biology of Microorganisms*. 12th ed. Upper Saddle River, N.J.: Pearson Prentice Hall, 2008. The industry standard for introductory microbiology textbooks. Contains extensive information on bacterial classification and diversity.

Nester, Eugene W., Denise G. Anderson, Jr., C. Evans Roberts, and Martha T. Nester. *Microbiology: A Human Perspective*. 5th ed. New York: McGraw-Hill, 2007. Introductory textbook intended for nonscience majors and allied health students includes frequent discussion of real-world applications of concepts.

Pommerville, Jeffrey C. *Alcamo's Fundamentals of Microbiology*. 8th ed. Sudbury, Mass.: Jones & Bartlett, 2007. Accessible textbook is designed for introductory college students, particularly those in the health sciences. Includes numerous sidebars and case studies.

Willey, Joanne, Linda Sherwood, and Chris Woolverton. *Prescott, Harley, and Klein's Microbiology*. 7th ed. New York: McGraw-Hill, 2007. Comprehensive textbook has sections on bacterial growth (including techniques) and diversity (several chapters describe various categories of bacteria). The organization is clear and logical; introductory discussions of topics are accessible to readers with little scientific background.

See also: Anthrax; Anthrax letter attacks; Antibiotics; Bacterial biology; Bacterial resistance and response to antibacterial agents; Biological terrorism; Biological warfare diagnosis; Biotoxins; Bubonic plague; Centers for Disease Control and Prevention; Decomposition of bodies; *Escherichia coli*; Food and Drug Administration, U.S.; Parasitology; Pathogen genomic sequencing; Pathogen transmission; Tularemia.

Bacterial biology

Definition: Study of prokaryotic organisms that lack membrane-bound organelles and nuclei—simple, single-celled microscopic organisms that grow by cell division to produce identical daughter cells.

Significance: Forensic scientists are sometimes called upon to identify the bacterial strains that caused such problems as hospital-acquired infections, food-borne infections, or microbial diseases; they may also need to identify the biological agents used in acts of bioterrorism. Bacteria have different DNA polymorphisms (variations in DNA sequence between individual bacteria or bacterial strains) that serve as markers for typing different bacteria.

Several types of polymorphisms are used for DNA (deoxyribonucleic acid) profiling. One type is single nucleotide polymorphisms (SNPs), in which only a single nucleotide in a sequence varies. A second type is variable number of tandem repeats (VNTRs). A sequence of DNA is tandemly (end-to-end) repeated, with the number of repeats differing between individual bacteria. An example is a sequence of thirty nucleotides that is repeated between twenty to one hundred times in different bacterial cells. To identify VNTRs in bacteria, polymerase chain reaction (PCR) primers are designed for both sides of the VNTR locus. With PCR, the sequence between the two primers is amplified, giving a large amount of this specific DNA, which is then separated by gel electrophoresis to determine the size (number of repeats) of the region amplified. The different numbers of tandem repeats are thought to arise from mistakes in DNA replication that generate INDEL (insertion or deletion of DNA) mutations.

An additional polymorphism is short tandem repeats (STRs), which are short sequence elements that repeat themselves within the DNA molecule. The repeating sequence is usually three to seven bases in length, and the entire length of an STR is fewer than five hundred bases in length.

Other types of markers used to identify bacteria are the sequences of 16S rRNA (ribosomal ribonucleic acid) and the spacer between the 16 and 23S rRNAs. Ribosomal RNA is part of the ribosome that translates messenger RNA into proteins. By comparing rRNA sequences, scientists can identify types of bacteria. PCR is used to amplify the specific DNA coding for the 16S rRNA. For example, 16S rRNA can be used to identify the bacterial pathogen causing disease in different persons.

Forensic Applications

The ability to identify bacteria is important in many kinds of cases. For example, when patients develop infections while in the hospital, this can pose a particular problem because of the extensive use of antibiotics and the development of antibiotic-resistant bacterial strains such as methicillin-resistant *Staphylococcus aureus*, which is seen in hospital-acquired infections. The different strains of *Staphylococcus* can be identified through DNA typing. The identification of an antibiotic-resistant strain of a bacterium leads to a more effective type of antibiotic treatment for the patient. Also, in some cases infections may be caused by inadequate hygienic precautions taken during surgery or in postoperative care. DNA analysis is important to identify the source of such infection-causing bacterial strains.

In cases of food-borne infections, it is important to be able to trace the microbes that caused them to the sources—whether companies, farms, or persons—to determine the origin of the microbes. Scientists use DNA analysis to track food-borne infections caused by *Salmonella* or the *Esherichia coli* strain O157:H7 to identify the types of bacteria causing the problems.

Molecular techniques are used to follow outbreaks of microbial diseases. The U.S. Centers for Disease Control and Prevention (CDC) maintains a database of microbial DNA fingerprints (PulseNet). Scientists have examined some thirty-one VNTR loci to compare strains of *Mycobacterium tuberculosis*, the bacterium that causes tuberculosis.

It is also important to be able to identify bacteria in cases of biological terrorism. For example, in 2001, letters containing *Bacillus anthracis*, the bacterium that causes anthrax, were sent through the mail in the eastern United States, and five people died of inhalation anthrax. Because *B. anthracis* spores are commonly found in soil, it was essential that prosecutors prove that spores found in a suspect's home or laboratory were the same strain that was found on the material mailed to the victims. In 2002, the American Academy of Microbiology met to formulate standards for evidence collection and analysis of molecular tests for microbial forensics.

Bacteria can also be used to estimate time of death. After death, the action of bacteria destroys the soft tissues of the body. The bacteria generally found are those normally present in the respiratory and intestinal tracts, such as bacilli, coliform, and clostridiuim. The temperature of the environment surrounding the body determines the rate of bacterial growth.

Susan J. Karcher

Further Reading

Breeze, Roger G., Bruce Budowle, and Steven E. Schutzer, eds. *Microbial Forensics*. Burlington, Mass.: Elsevier Academic Press, 2005. Details the importance of forensic microbiology and discusses its uses.

Butler, John M. *Forensic DNA Typing: Biology, Technology, and Genetics of STR Markers*. 2d ed. Burlington, Mass.: Elsevier Academic Press, 2005. Accessible textbook provides a detailed overview of DNA methodologies used by forensic scientists.

Cho, Mildred K., and Pamela Sankar. "Forensic Genetics and Ethical, Legal, and Social Implications Beyond the Clinic." *Nature Genetics* 36 (2004): S8-S12. Discusses the ethical considerations related to DNA profiling and genetic analysis.

Jobling, Mark A., and Peter Gill. "Encoded Evidence: DNA in Forensic Analysis." *Nature Reviews Genetics* 5 (October, 2004): 739-751. Provides an informative summary of DNA forensics.

Kobilinsky, Lawrence F., Thomas F. Liotti, and Jamel Oeser-Sweat. *DNA: Forensic and Legal Applications*. Hoboken, N.J.: Wiley-Interscience, 2005. Presents a general overview of the uses of DNA analysis and profiling.

Madigan, Michael T., John M. Martinko, Paul V. Dunlap, and David P. Clark. *Brock Biology of Microorganisms*. 12th ed. Upper Saddle River, N.J.: Pearson Prentice Hall, 2008. Widely respected basic microbiology textbook includes information about biological weapons and methods of microbial identification.

See also: Antibiotics; Bacteria; Bacterial resistance and response to antibacterial agents; Biological terrorism; Biological warfare diagnosis; Biological weapon identification; Biotoxins; Centers for Disease Control and Prevention; *Escherichia coli*; Food poisoning; Pathogen genomic sequencing; Pathogen transmission.

Bacterial resistance and response to antibacterial agents

Definition: Ability of some bacteria to resist or entirely withstand the effects of antimicrobial agents.

Significance: Although most bacteria are benign, a small percentage are pathogenic, or disease-causing. Bacteria rank among the most important of all disease-causing organisms in humans, and bacterial infections are countered by a wide variety of antibiotic and antibacterial agents. Repeated use of such agents results in bacterial resistance, necessitating the development of stronger antibacterial agents.

Increasing fears that antibiotic-resistant strains of bacteria may be used as bioweapons add urgency to efforts to develop new antibacterial agents.

Less than 10 percent of all bacteria threaten human health. These disease-causing species are notorious for such diseases as cholera, typhus, and syphilis. The most common and some of the most deadly forms of bacterial diseases are respiratory infections, such as tuberculosis, which kill millions of people every year. Countries around the world have used antibiotic drugs to treat bacterial infections for more than fifty years. The initial introduction of antibiotics was markedly successful, but continued and widespread use has resulted in a phenomenon in which microbial adaptation is making targeted bacteria increasingly difficult to control. This bacterial resistance to antibiotics is of special concern, as ever more powerful antibiotics must be developed.

Antibiotics and Antibacterials

In its broadest definition, an antibacterial is an agent that interferes with the growth and reproduction of bacteria. Although antibiotics and antibacterials both attack bacteria, these terms have evolved over the years to mean two different things. The term "antibacterials" is most commonly applied to agents that are used to disinfect surfaces and eliminate potentially harmful bacteria. The term "antibiotics" is commonly reserved for medicines given to humans or animals to treat infections or diseases.

Bacteria become resistant to antibacterial agents in one of three ways: natural resistance, vertical evolution, and horizontal evolution. Therefore, bacteria exhibit either inherited or acquired resistance to antibacterial agents. Natural resistance occurs when bacteria are inherently resistant to an antibacterial. For example, a gram-negative bacterium has an outer membrane that establishes an impermeability barrier against the antibiotic it manufactures, so it does not self-destruct.

Acquired resistance occurs when bacteria develop resistance to an antibacterial agent to which the population has been exposed. This may occur through mutation and selection (ver-

tical evolution) or exchange of genes between strains and species (horizontal evolution) of the bacteria exposed to the antibacterial agent.

Vertical evolution represents an example of Darwinian evolution driven by principles of natural selection. Genetic mutations in the bacteria population create new genes or combinations of genes that are resistant to the antibacterial agent. While the nonmutant, sensitive bacteria are killed, bacteria containing the mutated genes survive, and their progeny populate the increasingly resistant colony.

Another form of acquired resistance, horizontal evolution, is the transfer of resistant genes from one bacterium to another in the population. For example, *Escherichia coli* or *Shigella* may acquire a gene from a streptomycete that is resistant to the antibiotic streptomycin. Following this transfer, the population contains a mutant *E. coli* bacterium now resistant to streptomycin. Then, through the process of selection, it donates these genes to further generations, creating a resistant strain.

Transfer of genes in bacteria occurs in one of three ways: conjugation, transduction, or transformation. In conjugation, the gene-containing DNA (deoxyribonucleic acid) crosses a connecting structure, called a pilus, from a donor bacterium to recipient bacteria. In transduction, a virus may transfer genes between bacteria. In transformation, DNA is acquired directly from the environment, having been released from another bacterium. Following transfer, the combination of the newly acquired gene or genes results in a process called genetic recombination that may lead to the emergence of a new genotype. The combination of transfers and genetic recombination promotes rapid spread of antibacterial resistance through a species population and also between strains and other bacterial species.

The combined effects of fast growth rates, high concentrations of cells, genetic processes of mutation and selection, and genetic recombination account for the extraordinary rates of adaptation and evolution observed in bacteria populations. For these reasons, bacterial resistance to antibacterials is a common occurrence and one that promises to be of increasing concern in the future.

Facts About Antibiotic Resistance

The Centers for Disease Control and Prevention provides the following information about the growing problem of antibiotic resistance.

- Antibiotic resistance has been called one of the world's most pressing public health problems.
- The number of bacteria resistant to antibiotics has increased in the last decade. Nearly all significant bacterial infections in the world are becoming resistant to the most commonly prescribed antibiotic treatments.
- Every time a person takes antibiotics, sensitive bacteria are killed, but resistant germs may be left to grow and multiply. Repeated and improper uses of antibiotics are primary causes of the increase in drug-resistant bacteria.
- Misuse of antibiotics jeopardizes the usefulness of essential drugs. Decreasing inappropriate antibiotic use is the best way to control resistance.
- Children are of particular concern because they have the highest rates of antibiotic use. They also have the highest rate of infections caused by antibiotic-resistant pathogens.
- Parent pressure makes a difference. For pediatric care, a recent study showed that doctors prescribe antibiotics 65% of the time if they perceive parents expect them, and 12% of the time if they feel parents do not expect them.
- Antibiotic resistance can cause significant danger and suffering for people who have common infections that once were easily treatable with antibiotics. When antibiotics fail to work, the consequences are longer-lasting illnesses; more doctor visits or extended hospital stays; and the need for more expensive and toxic medications. Some resistant infections can cause death.

health threats of enormous proportions at both local and global levels.

Some research has suggested that bacterial infections can lead to criminal behavior. For example, *Streptococcus* infections have been linked to hyperactivity, and hyperactivity has been linked to criminal behavior. Some defense lawyers have used such research findings in attempts to explain their clients' actions, connecting criminal behavior with infection-caused states of delirium.

In some cases, the bacteria present at the site of a crime can give important clues about the crime itself. For instance, bacteria can reveal how long a person has been dead or the temperature the body was subjected to after death. Heart and spleen blood cultures may be taken at autopsy to identify any possible infections or diseases the deceased may have had.

Dwight G. Smith

Bacterial Resistance and Forensic Science

The importance of bacteriology in forensic science is recognized in diverse areas, including DNA profiling, toxicology studies, fingerprinting, and the tracing of violence stemming from or potentially relating to murders. Bacteria have been used as weapons and can be the causes of violence, but they may also serve as tools in the investigation of crimes.

The most serious threat posed by bacteria is their possible use in biological warfare, especially in acts of bioterrorism. For example, *Bacillus anthracis*, which causes anthrax, has become a preferred bacterial strain used by terrorists. Strains of deadly bacteria selected especially for their antibody resistance can pose

Further Reading

Bartelt, Margaret A. *Diagnostic Bacteriology. A Study Guide.* Philadelphia: F. A. Davis, 2000. Provides a comprehensive, user-friendly introduction to bacteriology for general readers.

Breeze, Roger G., Bruce Budowle, and Steven E. Schutzer, eds. *Microbial Forensics.* Burlington, Mass.: Elsevier Academic Press, 2005. Details the importance of forensic microbiology and discusses its uses.

Cummings, Craig A., and David A. Relman. "Microbial Forensics: When Pathogens Are 'Cross-Examined.'" *Science* 296 (2002): 1976-1979. Discusses the science involved in inferring the origin and transmission route of a microbial strain that has caused an infectious disease outbreak.

Larkin, Marilynn. "Microbial Forensics Aims to Link Pathogen, Crime, and Perpetrator." *The Lancet Infectious Diseases* 3, no. 4 (April, 2003): 180-181. Brief discussion of microbial forensics covers basic information on the field.

Tsokos, Michael, ed. *Forensic Pathology Reviews.* Vol. 4. Totowa, N.J.: Humana Press, 2006. Collection of articles by forensic pathologists includes valuable information on advances in forensic work concerned with bacteria.

See also: Anthrax; Antibiotics; Bacteria; Bacterial biology; Biological warfare diagnosis; Biotoxins; Bubonic plague; Pathogen genomic sequencing.

Ballistic fingerprints

Definition: Marks that are etched on a rifle or handgun bullet as it is pushed through the gun's barrel.

Significance: The analysis of ballistic fingerprints is used in criminal investigations to gain information about the models of guns as well as the individual guns that fired bullets recovered from crime scenes. By comparing the marks that guns leave on bullets, experts can often identify the weapons used in crimes.

The examination of ballistic fingerprints is part of the field of internal ballistics, which is the study of events that begin when the firing pin of a rifle or handgun strikes the cartridge and end when the bullet exits the barrel. Ballistic fingerprinting is not a new science. In June, 1900, Dr. Albert Llewellyn Hall published an article titled "The Missile and the Weapon" in the *Buffalo Medical Journal*, in which he presented the first analysis of bullet marks imparted by rifling in a gun barrel.

The interior of the barrel of a rifle or handgun has raised and lowered spirals, called rifling, that impart spin to the bullets as they are fired, making them more aerodynamically stable. As a bullet is pushed down a gun's barrel by the gas that is generated by burning gunpowder, it is etched with fine lines, or striations, from the rifling. Under microscopic examination, these striations look something like the parallel lines of a universal product code. In addition, "skid marks" may be left on a bullet in the short period after it leaves the firing chamber and before it is fully engaged by the rifling.

The striations common to all guns of a particular model are known as class characteristics. Individual characteristics are the striations unique to a particular gun; these result from tiny imperfections in the rifling process and in the rifling tools used as well as from the wear

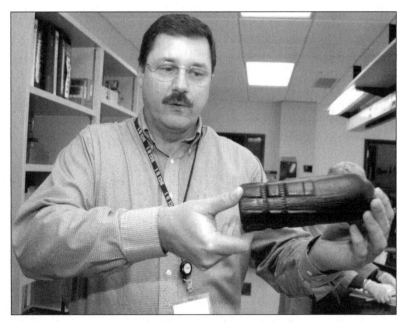

A forensic firearms examiner at the Ohio Bureau of Criminal Identification and Investigation uses a model of an enlarged bullet to explain how bullet comparisons are made using unique barrel marks. *(AP/Wide World Photos)*

and tear caused by the particular usage of that gun. Individual characteristics change over time. Criminals sometimes deliberately change a gun's individual characteristics; common techniques include shortening the barrel and rubbing the interior of the barrel with a steel brush.

Different types of ammunition fired through the same gun will produce very different striations. Even the small natural variations from one cartridge to another in the same box of commercial ammunition can produce some differences in patterns.

The analysis of ballistic fingerprints produces its most accurate results when the cartridge case (which holds the bullet, gunpowder, and primer before firing) as well as the bullet has been recovered; the firing pin, extractor, magazine, and other parts of the gun often leave distinctive marks on the case. Ballistic fingerprinting cannot be used on shotgun pellets because shotgun bores are smooth rather than rifled. However, shotgun cases can still be examined for firing pin marks and the like.

Several databases of digitized ballistic fingerprints of bullets recovered from crime scenes are available to criminal investigators. Forensic experts who conduct ballistic fingerprinting can use these databases to narrow their selection of bullets for microscopic examination. Binocular microscopic comparison of two bullets can take many hours.

A few jurisdictions require that ballistic fingerprint samples from new, lawfully sold handguns be put into a digitized database, but the efficacy of such efforts is the source of ongoing debate.

David B. Kopel

Further Reading

Burnett, Sterling, and David B. Kopel. *Ballistic Imaging: Not Ready for Prime Time*. Dallas: National Center for Policy Analysis, 2003.

Heard, Brian J. *Handbook of Firearms and Ballistics: Examining and Interpreting Forensic Evidence*. New York: John Wiley & Sons, 1997.

Warlow, Tom. *Firearms, the Law, and Forensic Ballistics*. 2d ed. Boca Raton, Fla.: CRC Press, 2005.

See also: Ballistics; Bullet-lead analysis; Class versus individual evidence; Firearms analysis; Gunshot residue; Integrated Ballistics Identification System; Microscopes.

Ballistics

Definition: Study of the motion, behaviors, effects, and impact signatures of projectiles.

Significance: When projectiles—whether bullets, bombs, or missiles—are involved in crimes, ballistics experts play a vital role in the investigations. Forensic scientists trained in ballistics can identify the specific types of firearms used in crimes based on bullets, shell casings, and other evidence found at crime scenes. By comparing this information with weapons belonging to possible suspects, they can confirm individual weapons as those used in the crimes.

A ballistic body is any object used to exert force to make another object move or change in form, state, or direction. A bullet, for example, is a ballistic body when it is propelled by the sudden increase of pressure that takes place within a handgun or other firearm when the trigger is pulled and a discharge of explosive powder propels the bullet forward in a direction dictated by the barrel of the weapon. When the bullet exits the weapon, it is subject to the laws of ballistics. As the projectile reaches its target, its velocity and trajectory cause distinctive entry and exit wounds.

The science of firearms ballistics is divided into four components: internal ballistics, transition ballistics, external ballistics, and terminal ballistics. Internal ballistics is the study of the forces that cause the acceleration of ballistic bodies; in the case of a bullet fired from a gun, internal ballistics is concerned with the detonation of the bullet, its discharge from the chamber, and its pathway through the barrel. Transition, or intermediate, ballistics is the study of the immediate effects on ballistic bodies as they leave the barrels of weapons; this area of ballistics focuses on forces such as air pressure, gravity, and air density, which act collectively on projectiles as their initial acceleratory force is reduced.

External ballistics is the study of projectiles' flight through the air. This includes the examination of changes in velocity and trajectory of ballistic bodies during the time they are in flight from weapons to targets. The last component of basic ballistics, terminal ballistics, is concerned with the impacts of projectiles on the objects with which they come in contact. This includes the effects of impacts on projectiles themselves and the ways in which bullets penetrate various surfaces (including human flesh).

Criminal Cases

Because the barrels of firearms are rifled (that is, they have raised and lowered spiral surfaces) to impart spin to bullets, distinctive marks (striations) are left on bullets as they swirl down the shafts of barrels after firing. The first recorded use of such marks as evidence in a criminal case took place in 1835. It was found that bullets fired from a weapon taken from the home of the primary suspect had a distinctive ridge that was identical to the ridge seen on a bullet recovered from the scene of the crime. When confronted with this evidence during questioning, the suspect confessed to the crime. Nearly seventy years later, in 1902, attorney Oliver Wendell Holmes, Jr., introduced ballistics evidence in a court of law. In a murder case, Holmes had a local gunsmith test fire a weapon belonging to the suspect into a wad of cotton stuffing. Under magnification, the marks on the test-fired bullet were seen to match those on the bullet retrieved from the crime scene, and this evidence was presented to the jury.

Shortly thereafter, two ballistics experts of that time, Calvin Goddard and Charles Waite, began compiling a database of information on all known gun manufacturers and on specific types of handguns as well as the marks made on bullets fired from them. Waite later invented the comparison microscope, which forensic scientists use to make side-by-side comparisons of the marks on two bullets at a time.

In the twenty-first century, forensic ballistics

examinations are undertaken in virtually every criminal case involving firearms in the United States. The two basic types of weapons involved in forensic ballistics cases are handheld weapons (handguns or pistols) and shoulder weapons (rifles). The two types of firearms produce unique marks on bullets and shell casings when fired. Even after a weapon has fired hundreds of rounds, a bullet from that weapon will still match the first bullet from its barrel. For experts in forensic ballistics, bullet marks are like fingerprints; each firearm leaves marks that are unique to that weapon.

Forensic Techniques

Experts in forensic ballistics perform many different kinds of analyses, including making bullet comparisons, matching projectiles to weapons, and estimating the lengths of projectile flights, which enables them to determine the types of weapons used and the locations of the operators of weapons when they were fired. During investigations of crime scenes involving shootings, ballistics experts analyze the impacts of bullets on victims, whether wounded or dead, to determine the types and sizes of projectiles fired and the types of weapons used, the distances from the shooters to the victims, and the angles at which the shots were fired.

If bullets, cartridges, or cartridge cases are not found at the scene of a fatal shooting, a forensic pathologist will usually analyze the victim's wounds to determine information about the type of weapon used. Entry wounds are generally smaller than exit wounds and have dark rings around the injured surfaces, and by examining these, experts can often determine the width and thus the likely caliber of the bullets that made the wounds. This technique is referred to as wound ballistics.

When bullets are recovered from crime scenes, ballistics experts compare the striations on the bullets to those on other bullets from known sources. If the firearm suspected to have been used in a given crime is available, a test bullet is shot from that weapon and then the marks on that bullet are compared with the marks on the bullets found at the crime scene. The bullets found at crime scenes are also often

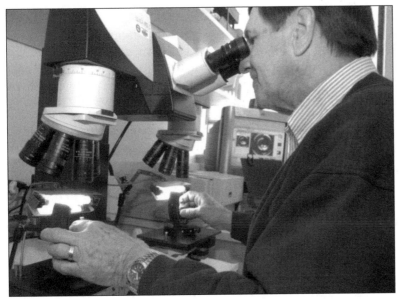

A forensic scientist and arms examiner at the Ohio Bureau of Criminal Identification and Investigation uses a comparison microscope to conduct a side-by-side comparison of two fired bullets. *(AP/Wide World Photos)*

compared with thousands of images of bullets stored in law-enforcement databases. Matches to bullets in such databases can give investigators important information about the histories of the weapons that fired the bullets.

The identification of specific weapons is another important aspect of the forensic investigation of crimes involving firearms. Many criminals remove the serial numbers from the guns they use—by filing the numbers off or using acid washes—because they believe this will make the weapons untraceable. Forensic scientists, however, are able to reclaim obliterated serial numbers using sophisticated techniques. To recover a gun's missing serial number, the examiner files down the metal that carried the serial number to retrieve a strip of highly polished and hardened metal located beneath where the original serial number was stamped. By adding a solution of copper salts and hydrochloric acid to the area, the scientist can dissolve the weaker metal below where the numbers were stamped to reveal an imprint of the original serial number. This imprint is then photographed before the metal dissolves completely, and the photograph serves as documentation of the weapon's serial number.

Related to the work of ballistics experts is the detection and evaluation of gunshot residue, which figures importantly in forensic investigations. The amount and scatter of gunshot residue provides information about the proximity of a victim to a weapon as it was fired. In addition, gunshot residue on the hands, skin, hair, and clothing of persons who were present at the time of a crime can reveal how close those individuals were to the weapon. Firearms give off a back-spray of gunpowder when discharged, and this hot and sticky substance adheres to most items of clothing and skin with which it comes in contact. It may remain embedded in objects during subsequent and sometimes repeated washings or cleanings. Forensic scientists sometimes use electron scanning techniques to detect minute particles of gunshot residue on watches and other jewelry worn by people suspected of having used guns in crimes.

Dwight G. Smith

Further Reading

Carlucci, Donald E., and Sidney S. Jacobson. *Ballistics: Theory and Design of Guns and Ammunition*. Boca Raton, Fla.: CRC Press, 2008. Comprehensive work covers all aspects of the topic, including the theory and fundamental physics of ballistics, design techniques for firearms and ammunition, and the tools used to investigate firearms-related crimes.

Heard, Brian J. *Handbook of Firearms and Ballistics: Examining and Interpreting Forensic Evidence*. New York: John Wiley & Sons, 1997. Thorough volume focuses on the science of forensic firearms analysis.

Rinker, Robert A. *Understanding Firearm Ballistics: Basic to Advanced Ballistics, Simplified, Illustrated, and Explained*. 6th ed.

Clarksville, Ind.: Mulberry House, 2005. Provides an easy-to-understand general introduction to theory of weapons ballistics.

Zukas, Jonas A., and William P. Walters, eds. *Explosive Effects and Applications*. New York: Springer, 1998. Collection of essays by experts focuses on the component of ballistics concerned with the explosive impacts of bullets.

See also: Ballistic fingerprints; Bullet-lead analysis; Bureau of Alcohol, Tobacco, Firearms and Explosives; Firearms analysis; Gunshot residue; Improvised explosive devices; Integrated Ballistics Identification System; Sacco and Vanzetti case.

Barbiturates

Definition: Family of chemically related drugs belonging to the sedative-hypnotic class.

Significance: The habit-forming drugs known as barbiturates have a variety of therapeutic applications and have been used as drugs of abuse. Barbiturates depress the central nervous system and can cause significant psychomotor performance impairment as well as fatal toxicity. The potential for toxic interactions with other drugs, including alcohol, is significant. Forensic toxicologists are often called upon to measure barbiturate concentrations in biological samples.

The barbiturates are a family of drugs with related chemical structures derived from barbituric acid. In the past, barbiturates were used extensively as sedative-hypnotics—that is, drugs that reduce anxiety and induce sleep. Barbiturates are also used as anticonvulsants and in anesthesia. Because of barbiturates' significant potential for toxicity, their use has been largely replaced by the safer benzodiazepines, but selected barbiturates are still used in specific applications.

Effects

Barbiturates depress central nervous system (CNS) function in general rather than specific CNS functions. The severity of CNS depression increases with dose, potentially causing significant impairment of psychomotor skills (such as those required for safe driving) and, ultimately, fatal respiratory depression. Dose-dependent effects also extend to the peripheral nervous system, where they manifest primarily as reductions in blood pressure and heart rate. However, at appropriate sedative-hypnotic doses, these latter effects are not hazardous.

At subanesthetic doses, barbiturate effects may include euphoria, reduced anxiety and inhibitions, slurred speech, loss of coordination, and dizziness. CNS depression intensifies with increasing dose; sedation becomes more pronounced, and significant stupor, drowsiness, and loss of coordination may ensue. Anesthetic doses produce coma as well as depressed respiration and blood pressure. Uncontrolled overdose can result in fatal respiratory depression. These effects are intensified in combination with other CNS depressants (such as alcohol or benzodiazepines), and significant impairment or death may occur at lower barbiturate doses (or blood concentrations) when such drugs are coadministered.

Chronic barbiturate use results in the development of tolerance—that is, progressively larger doses are required to achieve a given effect. Repeated administration of and tolerance to the effects of one barbiturate confers tolerance to the effects of the others as well as to other depressant compounds with similar mechanisms of action (for example, alcohol and benzodiazepines). Chronic use can lead to physical dependence and corresponding withdrawal symptoms upon cessation of use. Symptoms of barbiturate withdrawal range from minor symptoms—nausea, vomiting, agitation, and confusion—to more severe symptoms including seizures, hallucinations, delirium tremens, very high fevers (hyperpyrexia), and death.

Other Chemical and Pharmacological Properties

Barbiturates are weakly acidic and are often prepared as the sodium salts. Their weakly acidic nature becomes important in the design of analytical methods requiring extraction of the drug from a complex forensic sample (for example, blood or tissue). Alteration of the chemical structure results in variation in drug potency (the magnitude of effect at a given dose) and time course of action.

Even in cases where the drug effects last a short time, barbiturates have a relatively long time course within the body. One indicator of this is the half-life of the drug, or the time required for the reduction of drug concentration to 50 percent of its original value. Half-life values for the various barbiturates range from approximately 3 hours to 80 hours. Any drug with a long half-life poses the risk of accumulation in the blood if dosing regimens are not carefully

One of the most famous victims of barbiturate poisoning was film star Marilyn Monroe, seen here on the set of *The Misfits* (1961), the last film in which she appeared, flanked by Montgomery Clift (left) and Clark Gable. Two years after this picture was taken, Monroe was found dead from an overdose of drugs that included the barbiturate Nembutal. Los Angeles County coroner Dr. Thomas Noguchi attributed her death to "acute barbiturate poisoning." *(AP/Wide World Photos)*

monitored, creating the potential for toxicity. Half-life is also related to the duration of drug action: Typically, a drug with a shorter half-life has a shorter duration of action. This is relevant to forensic investigation, as the half-life is indicative of the time window over which a drug may be detected in the blood; generally, a drug is essentially completely eliminated from the blood within five elimination half-lives.

Duration of action and half-life are important considerations in the choice of a barbiturate for a particular therapeutic action. For example, thiopental is an ultrafast-acting barbiturate, typically used in induction of anesthesia. Due to its high lipid solubility, it is rapidly and extensively distributed into the central nervous system, wherein it exerts its anesthetic effect through depression of various functions. The elimination half-life for thiopental is 8 to 10 hours, although its ability to diffuse into and out of the CNS results in anesthetic action lasting only minutes following a single intravenous dose. Conversely, phenobarbital, a barbiturate used as an anticonvulsant and as a sedative-hypnotic, is significantly longer acting, with a half-life of 80 to 120 hours.

The route of administration of the drug is also dependent on the desired therapeutic action. Barbiturates used as sedative-hypnotics or anticonvulsants may be administered orally and have a slower onset of action than those given by parenteral (for example, intravenous) administration, where the onset of drug action is very rapid. Accordingly, parenteral administration is typically used in the treatment of status epilepticus (a condition in which the brain is in a state of persistent seizure) and for general anesthesia. The route of administration is ultimately related to the maximum blood drug concentration achieved, and therefore the magnitude of drug effect, at a given dose. Consequently, knowledge of the route of administration is valuable to toxicological interpretation. It should be noted, however, that some drugs intended for oral administration—in tablet form—are illicitly administered by parenteral routes, potentially leading to greater toxic effects.

The metabolism of most barbiturates occurs primarily in the liver, where the drugs undergo various biotransformation reactions (such as oxidation) that reduce or eliminate pharmacological activity. In a few cases (for example, aprobarbital, phenobarbital), renal elimination of unchanged drug into the urine also occurs to a significant extent. Consequently, barbiturate metabolism may be affected by processes that affect hepatic metabolism (for example, liver disease or drug interactions). Inhibited barbiturate metabolism may result in the development of significant toxicity.

Forensic Analysis and Interpretation of Evidence

Law-enforcement personnel may encounter barbiturates in the form of suspicious materials (for example, tablets) requiring identification or quantitative analysis. Forensic scientists may analyze biological samples (such as blood, tissues, urine, or stomach contents) to establish exposure to barbiturates. Correlation of toxic symptoms with measured barbiturate concentration is done in both clinical and forensic settings and in attempts to establish a toxicological cause of death.

Methods used for forensic barbiturate analysis include immunoassay, spectrophotometry, gas or liquid chromatography, and mass spectrometry. Usually, the analysis of biological samples for barbiturates requires preparatory steps to extract the drug from the complex matrix and minimize or eliminate other compounds (such as lipids or proteins) that may be present in those samples that may interfere with analysis, leading to spurious results. The exact nature of the sample preparation steps taken is determined by the nature of the sample being analyzed. Solid samples typically require dissolution or digestion as a first step.

Extraction of drugs from complex samples may be accomplished through the manipulation of chemical conditions (such as pH adjustment) and subsequent partition into a suitable organic solvent system or into a solid phase with subsequent recovery. Following extraction, analysis is typically done using gas chromatography or liquid chromatography to separate extracted constituents for accurate quantitative analysis.

The interpretation of measurements requires consideration of the nature of the sample

analyzed as well as the measured drug concentration. Drug concentrations in blood may allow estimation of toxic effect, with consideration given to the potential for tolerance to drug action. Conversely, detection of a barbiturate in hair under properly controlled conditions is indicative of drug exposure only, but it may be useful in establishing an approximate time line of drug exposure.

The forensic detection of a particular barbiturate must be considered in the context of the case under investigation. The tolerance of the individual must be considered in the interpretation of measured barbiturate concentrations as well. For example, in toxicological analysis of blood samples from a known epileptic, the detection of phenobarbital may be consistent with a therapeutic regimen, and some degree of tolerance may often be assumed. In routine forensic practice, tolerance is difficult or impossible to quantify, so interpretation is difficult. Correlation of a measured blood concentration with toxicity or fatality requires comparison of the result to other similar cases that have been previously reported, giving due consideration to the history of use of barbiturates and other drugs by the subject, the detection of other relevant drugs in the sample (such as CNS depressants), and any observed symptoms (such as shallow breathing, impaired coordination, or slurred speech).

James Watterson

Further Reading

Baselt, Randall C. *Disposition of Drugs and Chemicals in Man*. 7th ed. Foster City, Calif.: Biomedical Publications, 2004. Describes the properties and associated tissue concentrations of a wide range of toxic compounds and discusses the techniques used to analyze these chemicals.

_____. *Drug Effects on Psychomotor Performance*. Foster City, Calif.: Biomedical Publications, 2001. Comprehensive reference work presents information on the impairing effects of a wide range of therapeutic and illicit drugs, including barbiturates.

Brunton, Laurence L., John S. Lazo, and Keith L. Parker, eds. *Goodman and Gilman's the Pharmacological Basis of Therapeutics*. 11th ed. New York: McGraw-Hill, 2006. Authoritative advanced textbook explains basic pharmacological principles and the specific pharmacological features of therapeutic agents. Includes some discussion of barbiturates.

Karch, Steven B., ed. *Drug Abuse Handbook*. 2d ed. Boca Raton, Fla.: CRC Press, 2007. Describes the pharmacological, physiological, and pathological aspects of drug abuse in general, and individual chapters address specific compounds, such as alcohol, as well as specific issues related to drug abuse, such as workplace drug testing.

Levine, Barry, ed. *Principles of Forensic Toxicology*. 2d ed., rev. Washington, D.C.: American Association for Clinical Chemistry, 2006. Introductory textbook describes the analytical, chemical, and pharmacological aspects of a variety of drugs of forensic relevance.

See also: Analytical instrumentation; Antianxiety agents; Controlled Substances Act of 1970; Drug abuse and dependence; Forensic toxicology; Gas chromatography; High-performance liquid chromatography; Homogeneous enzyme immunoassay; Illicit substances; Mass spectrometry; Nervous system; Pseudoscience in forensic practice; Truth serum; Ultraviolet spectrophotometry.

BATFE. *See* Bureau of Alcohol, Tobacco, Firearms and Explosives

---

Beethoven's death

Date: March 26, 1827

The Event: Ludwig van Beethoven suffered from many chronic ailments during his life, and the precise cause of his death has long been a topic of debate. Dr. William Walsh, director of the Beethoven Research Project, announced at a press conference on October 17, 2000, that samples of Beethoven's hair revealed extremely heavy lead deposits, indicating that lead poisoning may have caused the great composer's many illnesses and death.

Significance: The forensic investigation into the death of Beethoven proves both the achievements of forensic technology in historical investigation and the limitations of such technology. Analyses of hair and bone fragments have shed light on Beethoven's many illnesses, but researchers still question whether lead poisoning or lead poisoning alone caused Beethoven's problems.

Born in Bonn, Germany, in mid-December, 1770, Ludwig van Beethoven died on March 26, 1827, in Vienna, Austria, where he had lived since 1792. Ferdinand V. Hiller, a German admirer who visited the composer's deathbed, received a lock of Beethoven's hair that was later enclosed in a locket inscribed with names and date. This keepsake remained in the Hiller family until the 1930's, when the family, which was Jewish, was forced to flee Adolf Hitler's Nazi regime. The lock of hair then became the property of a Danish physician who aided Jewish refugees; the physician's family had possession of the hair until 1994, when it was offered for auction.

The hair was purchased by a consortium of members of the American Beethoven Society. Arizona urological surgeon Dr. Alfredo Guevara, the principal purchaser, retained 27 percent of the hair (160 individual hairs), and the remaining 422 strands were donated to the Ira F. Brilliant Center for Beethoven Studies at San Jose State University in Northern California. Guevara wanted to know if forensic technology could show the cause of Beethoven's poor health and death. In addition to becoming totally deaf, Beethoven suffered from eye disorders, liver disease, and a broad range of gastrointestinal and respiratory symptoms. When an autopsy was performed on his body on March 27, 1827, visual inspection showed abnormalities of the liver, gallbladder, spleen, pancreas, and kidneys.

Forensic Analysis

Dr. Werner Baumgartner of Psychemedics Corporation's laboratories in Los Angeles examined twenty hairs to determine whether Beethoven received relief from opiates during his final illness. A radioimmunoassay found no evidence of opiates. William Walsh speculated that Beethoven, who continued to compose music until very near the time of his death, rejected substances that would dull his mind.

McCrone Research Center in Chicago performed side-by-side analyses of two hairs from Beethoven and three samples from living subjects, using a scanning electron microscope, energy-dispersive spectroscopy, and scanning ion microscope-mass spectrometry. Using nondestructive synchrotron X-ray beams, the U.S. Department of Energy's Argonne National Laboratory tested six Beethoven hair strands in a side-by-side comparison with hair from a control group and a glass film of known lead composition. Both facilities found heavy lead concentrations. Beethoven's hair revealed an average lead content of 60 parts per million; living Americans, in comparison, average 0.6 parts per million. Researchers concluded that Beethoven suffered from lead poisoning, or plumbism.

In Beethoven's time, lead was used in pewter cups and dinnerware as well as in paint, cosmetics, medical preparations, and food coloring. Wine bottles were sealed (plumbed) with lead to keep the contents from turning sour. In an online interview on December 6, 2005, on *Online NewsHour*, Walsh offered an explanation for Beethoven's exceptionally poor health, speculating that the composer may have been among the 5 percent of people who are extremely sensitive to heavy metals and cannot excrete lead.

Scientists who examined Beethoven's hair found no traces of mercury, which led them to conclude that Beethoven had not been treated for syphilis, given that mercury was the most common treatment for the disease in Beethoven's time.

Because some of the hairs in the Beethoven sample included partial bulbs, DNA (deoxyribonucleic acid) examination was possible. In 2005, researchers at the Argonne National Labora-

William Walsh, director of the Beethoven Research Project, holds a vial containing a sample of Ludwig van Beethoven's hair at the press conference held to announce scientists' findings that lead poisoning may have caused the composer's many illnesses and death. *(AP/Wide World Photos)*

tory's Advanced Photon Source facilities conducted additional testing using elemental X-ray fluorescence analysis on hair and fragments of Beethoven's skull made available after the original research was completed. DNA testing positively identified the bone and hair as Beethoven's. Researchers used microimaging to calculate the distribution of lead in the bone and hair fragments and again found substantial lead deposits. Mitochondrial DNA testing was also performed at the University of Münster in Germany.

Controversy

A number of researchers have noted that not all questions concerning Beethoven's death can be answered through hair and bone analysis. They question whether lead poisoning or any single problem explains Beethoven's ill health, which was markedly worse than that of most of his contemporaries, or could be conclusively named as the sole, primary, or immediate cause of the composer's death. Concerns about the relatively simple explanation of lead poisoning begin with Beethoven's family history. In his early years, Beethoven was exposed to the tuberculosis that killed his mother and one brother. His father and his paternal grandmother were incapacitated by alcohol abuse, suggesting inherited alcohol intolerance. Some have speculated that Beethoven may have overused alcohol; observers at the time were divided, but consumption of alcoholic beverages was high in his lifetime, a period when urban water supplies, including Vienna's Danube River, were badly contaminated with human and animal waste. (No connection had yet been made between contaminated water and disease.)

Peter J. Davies has raised the possibility that Beethoven suffered from adult-onset diabetes mellitus, which was then uncontrollable. Deborah Hayden has noted that if Beethoven had been treated for syphilis in early manhood, the treatment would leave no evidence at his death decades later. In 1796, Beethoven contracted typhus, and this illness may have undermined his general health; his hearing loss began soon afterward.

The medical treatment that Beethoven received may have been immediately responsible for his death. He consulted at least a dozen physicians, usually insisting on receiving unknown medications and altering dosages. Four times in a period of three months, Dr. Johann Seibert, chief surgeon of the Vienna General Hospital, tapped Beethoven's abdomen to drain fluid. Neither anesthesia, other than opiates, nor the need for sterile conditions was known at that time, and physicians did not wash their hands between patients, as the possibilities of contagion and fatal infection were not recognized. Surgery was conducted hastily for the patient's sake, but, as Davies has noted, rapid fluid drainage may cause shock or acute renal failure. Effective diuretics were unknown during Beethoven's lifetime.

Betty Richardson

Further Reading

Davies, Peter J. *Beethoven in Person: His Deafness, Illnesses, and Death*. Westport, Conn.: Greenwood Press, 2001. Includes a time line of the composer's symptoms, information on the credentials of his physicians, critiques of the various suggested possible causes for his many symptoms, and a glossary of medical terms.

Emsley, John. *Elements of Murder: A History of Poison*. New York: Oxford University Press, 2005. Volume devoted to the use of poisons in murder includes a brief account of the Beethoven findings. Also discusses the historical use of lead in common substances and the effects of lead exposure on the human body.

Hayden, Deborah. *Pox: Genius, Madness, and*

A Finding of Lead Poisoning

In a press release dated December 6, 2005, the U.S. Department of Energy's Argonne National Laboratory announced the findings of research conducted on fragments of bone from Ludwig van Beethoven's skull:

The bone fragments, confirmed by DNA testing to have come from Beethoven's body, were scanned by X-rays from the Advanced Photon Source at Argonne, which provides the most brilliant X-rays in the Western Hemisphere. A control bone fragment sample from the same historic period was also examined. Both bone fragments were from the parietal section—the top—of the skull.

"The testing indicated large amounts of lead in the Beethoven bone sample, compared to the control," said Bill Walsh, chief scientist at the Pfeiffer Treatment Center in Warrenville, Ill., and director of the Beethoven Research Project. . . .

"The finding of elevated lead in Beethoven's skull, along with DNA results indicating authenticity of the bone/hair relics, provides solid evidence that Beethoven suffered from a toxic overload of lead," Walsh said. "In addition, the presence of lead in the skull suggests that his exposure to lead was not a recent event, but may have been present for many years."

the Mysteries of Syphilis. New York: Basic Books, 2003. Argues that Beethoven may have had both lead poisoning and syphilis.

Mai, François Martin. *Diagnosing Genius: The Life and Death of Beethoven.* Montreal: McGill-Queen's University Press, 2007. Includes information about Beethoven's physicians and treatment and a timetable of his symptoms. Suggests the possibility that the conductor suffered from liver cirrhosis or infectious hepatitis and bacterial peritonitis, among other disorders.

Martin, Russell. *Beethoven's Hair: An Extraordinary Historical Odyssey and a Scientific Mystery Solved.* New York: Broadway Books, 2000. Describes the history of the famous lock of hair, from Beethoven's deathbed through the research results announced in 2000.

See also: DNA analysis; Exhumation; Hair analysis; Lead; Mitochondrial DNA analysis and typing; Napoleon's death; Opioids; Scanning electron microscopy; Taylor exhumation.

Benzidine

Definition: Chemical formerly used in the standard presumptive test for blood at crime scenes.

Significance: A positive reaction to benzidine or tetramethylbenzidine of a stain found at a crime scene suggests that the stain is probably blood; such information can facilitate an initial reconstruction of a crime and prompt follow-up.

For most of the twentieth century, benzidine was the standard chemical used in presumptive testing for blood at crime scenes. In the presence of heme iron and hydrogen peroxide, benzidine, which is clear in the reduced state, is converted to the oxidized state, which is deep blue. Because heme iron is present in hemoglobin, the protein that carries oxygen in the blood, a positive test can indicate the presence of

blood. This test does not distinguish between human blood and animal blood, however; further testing is necessary to make that distinction and, if the blood is human, to determine whose blood it is. In addition, constituents of some plants, such as potatoes and horseradish, as well as oxidizing agents found in some cleansers, can catalyze the reaction. Accordingly, a benzidine test is only presumptive of blood; a positive result must be confirmed by laboratory test.

Developed in 1904, the benzidine test became the most popular presumptive test for blood because of its high sensitivity, specificity, and reliability. Benzidine, however, which was also used for the synthesis of dyes in the textile industry, proved to be highly carcinogenic, and its use and manufacture in the United States was banned by the Environmental Protection Agency in 1974. At that time, 3,3′,5,5′ tetramethylbenzidine (TMB) was developed as a presumptive test for blood. It is not as sensitive as benzidine, but it is much safer to use, although it is a probable carcinogen.

Typically, a forensic investigator performs the TMB test by moistening a cotton swab with deionized water and rubbing the swab on the suspect stain, adding a drop of TMB solution to the swab, waiting thirty seconds, and then adding a drop of 3 percent hydrogen peroxide to the swab. A positive reaction will turn the swab a blue-green color within fifteen seconds. Often a swab taken from near the stain is used as a control. If the swab turns blue-green before the hydrogen peroxide is added, the test is invalid. Validation of the reagents using a known blood standard is usually conducted.

The TMB reagent in a colloidal mixture can also be used to spray an area in order to raise faint bloodstains, such as might be left by handprints or shoe prints. Like luminol, this substance can allow investigators to see evidence of attempts to clean up blood from crime scenes. The standard TMB test does not destroy the sample, which can be subsequently tested for blood type and DNA, but the spray reagent, like luminol, fixes a stain so that it cannot be tested further; investigators must thus take care to limit the use of the reagent.

James L. Robinson

Further Reading

Lee, Henry C., Timothy Palmbach, and Marilyn T. Miller. *Henry Lee's Crime Scene Handbook*. San Diego, Calif.: Academic Press, 2001.

Nickell, Joe, and John F. Fischer. *Crime Science: Methods of Forensic Detection*. Lexington: University Press of Kentucky, 1999.

See also: DNA recognition instruments; DNA typing; Luminol; Orthotolidine; Phenolphthalein; Presumptive tests for blood; Reagents; Serology.

Beslan hostage crisis victim identification

Date: Hostage siege occurred between September 1 and 3, 2004

The Event: On September 1, 2004, a group of about thirty men and women, who were reportedly Muslim Chechen separatists, took over School Number One in the town of Beslan in the Russian Federation republic of North Ossetia-Alania, and held nine hundred students and fifty-nine teachers hostage. A three-day siege ended when Russian special forces and civilian volunteers attacked the school. This resulted in a violent confrontation in which the hostages were caught in the middle of gunfire and explosions; when it was over, nearly four hundred people were dead. The incident contributed to a growth in the power of the Russian government, which instituted new security measures, at the same time it heightened public mistrust of Russian authorities, who were suspected of covering up official incompetence in the handling of the incident and of censoring press coverage about it.

Significance: Forensic scientists played an important role in the aftermath of the tragedy in efforts to identify the dead as well as in the investigation of the motivations and the actions of the terrorists.

Since the dissolution of the Soviet Union in 1991, the region of Chechnya, located between the Black Sea and the Caspian Sea on part of the northern border of Georgia, has fought for independence from the Russian Federation. The Chechens are Muslim, and the separatist struggle has given rise to radicalism that is based both in nationalism and in Islamic extremism. The terrorists who took over School Number One in Beslan identified themselves as Chechen separatists, and most were indeed later found to be Chechens.

The hostage takers seized the school on the traditional first day of the Russian school year. After a brief exchange of gunfire with the police, the terrorists forced their hostages to crowd into the school's gymnasium. The terrorists then shot a number of men who appeared to be most capable of resistance and forced other hostages to throw out the bodies and clean up the blood.

The perpetrators may have hidden weapons and explosives in the school before their attack, but this point is denied by official reports and remains open to question. As security forces surrounded the school, the terrorists mined the gym and set up wires that, if tripped, would cause the explosives to go off. They also announced that if anyone attempted to intervene forcefully, they would kill fifty hostages for every one of their own number killed and twenty hostages for every one of their group injured.

The Tragedy

On the afternoon of the second day of the siege, the hostage takers allowed Ruslan Aushev, the president of the Russian republic of Ingushetia, to enter the school. Several of the hostage takers were later revealed to be Ingushetians, an ethnic group closely related to the Chechens. Aushev was allowed to bring twenty-six hostages out of the school with him. The terrorists also gave Aushev a list of demands, apparently authored by Chechen rebel leader Shamil Basayev, who reportedly had ordered the seizure of the school but was not present. One of the demands was that Russia recognize the independence of Chechnya.

The events that took place on September 3 are still not entirely clear. Some members of the

In the aftermath of the Beslan school hostage siege, authorities were faced with the task of identifying the dead, many of whom had been badly burned. *(AP/Wide World Photos)*

Russian military were allowed to approach the school to take away bodies, and as they did so, bombs went off in the gymnasium and the hostage takers began firing, killing two of the servicemen. About thirty hostages were able to escape in the chaos. Then Russian special forces, along with civilian volunteers, began to attack the school, and a pitched battle ensued. Explosions and gunfire continued for the rest of the night, and when the fighting was over, 334 hostages, 31 hostage takers, and more than 20 other people were dead.

The Application of Forensic Science

The primary use of forensic science in relation to the Beslan incident was in the identification of the dead, both victims and hostage takers. After the tragedy, family members initially attempted to identify children and other victims from their clothing or by looking for distinguishing physical features. Many of those who died had been badly burned, however, so investigators had to use more sophisticated approaches.

More than one hundred of the corpses were so badly damaged that DNA (deoxyribonucleic acid) analysis was necessary to establish positive identification. This involved comparison of the DNA of the victims with the DNA of existing family members; investigators took blood samples from the bodies of the dead and from relatives of those lost in the event and sent the samples to Moscow for matching. In many cases, the bodies were so badly damaged that the extraction of DNA for testing was very difficult. Researchers used the technique of polymerase chain reaction (PCR) to amplify pieces of DNA to provide sufficient material for testing.

Forensic investigators also helped to examine the motivations and behavior of the terrorists. Along with identification of the thirty-one attackers who died in the incident, the investigation revealed that drug use appeared to be an element in the Beslan tragedy. Moscow researchers reported that toxicological analyses of the hostage takers' bodies showed that the blood of several of them showed high levels of the narcotics heroin and morphine, and several showed signs of other drugs in their systems. Moreover, the hostage takers who had been drug users had apparently not taken in these substances in several days, and so they were likely in states of drug withdrawal. Some observers have suggested that the experience of withdrawal may have accounted for the remarkable brutality and callousness with which the hostage takers treated children and other innocent victims at the school.

Carl L. Bankston III

Further Reading

Giduck, John. *Terror at Beslan: A Russian Tragedy with Lessons for America's Schools.* Golden, Colo.: Archangel Group, 2005. Describes the background, events, and aftermath of the Beslan incident and provides a good description of the investigation. Asserts that similar events could happen in the United States and draws on the Beslan example to suggest how American schools should prepare for this possibility.

Kornienko I. V., V. V. Kolkutin, and A. V. Volkov. "Molecular-Genetic Identification of the Hostages Killed in the Terror Act on September 1-3, 2004, in Beslan." *Forensic Medical Examination* 5 (2006): 31-35. Examines the technical forensic issues involved in the identification of the Beslan victims and notes the importance of the precise staging of the investigation.

Lansford, Lynn Milburn. *Beslan: Shattered Innocence.* Charleston, S.C.: Booksurge, 2006. Addresses the needs of the Beslan survivors for support and assistance following the tragedy. Lansford has worked with children's relief programs and was involved in helping the Beslan survivors.

Phillips, Timothy. *Beslan: The Tragedy of School No. 1.* London: Granta Books, 2007. Account of the ordeal at Beslan includes testimony by the people of the town and a critique of the Russian government's response.

See also: Asian tsunami victim identification; Autopsies; Croatian and Bosnian war victim identification; DNA extraction from hair, bodily fluids, and tissues; DNA fingerprinting; Forensic toxicology; Hostage negotiations; Mass graves; Osteology and skeletal radiology; Police psychology; September 11, 2001, victim identification.

Biodetectors

Definition: Devices comprising highly specific sensing components—such as biolayers of DNA, proteins, or enzymes—immobilized on surfaces that serve as transducers that measure electrical signals produced by interactions between the biomolecules of interest and the biolayers.

Significance: Combining the ability to process data with the selectivity of biological systems, biodetectors are powerful analytical tools employed in forensic science. They can be used to counter the growing threat of biocrimes or acts of bioterrorism because of their ability to detect even minute levels of colorless and odorless harmful agents (such as pathogenic viruses, fungi, bacteria, and other noxious substances) days before concentrations of the agents are high enough to cause medical symptoms.

Following a biocrime, responses based on data obtained from biodetection may include forensic investigation, medical diagnoses, and crisis management. In 2001, the importance of timely forensic investigation of surface contamination was demonstrated following identification of the anthrax bacterium found in letters sent to the Hart Senate Office Building in Washington, D.C.; early detection allowed for prophylactic treatment with antibiotics, thus saving the lives of those exposed to the pathogen. For highly contagious diseases such as smallpox, it may be crucial to institute immediate measures such as vaccination or quarantine to halt the spread of the disease.

The significance of early detection of harmful biological agents cannot be overemphasized. At first, medical symptoms may seem mild, and outbreaks may be mistaken for ordinary influenza; this can delay necessary remedial actions that could lessen, or even prevent, morbidity and mortality. The greatest benefit of biodetectors may be to protect against highly lethal pathogens such as Ebola and Marburg viruses, for which no vaccines, treatments, or cures have been developed.

In the mid-1960's, Leland C. Clark, considered the "father of biosensors," developed the first enzyme electrodes, which eventually led to creation of more advanced versions for applications in biotechnology and forensic science, especially as the latter pertains to countering acts of bioterrorism. Biosensors of this type, employed to detect DNA and related biomolecules, are also known as biodetectors; they are key players in the investigation of events leading up to and following exposure to such pathogenic agents as ricin (a highly toxic protein derived from the castor bean) and *Bacillus anthracis*, the bacterium that causes anthrax. Biodetectors may also be employed for continuous monitoring of the environment, surveillance of medical symptoms, and ancillary intelligence activities that may be put in place to mitigate or prevent the aftereffects associated with biocrimes and acts of bioterrorism.

Ideally, biodetectors should be networked— that is, decentralized—during an attack involving biological weapons so that they can be used to define the perimeter of the assault. Portability is another desirable characteristic for biodetectors; such devices could be moved quickly to the locations of biocrimes to perform evaluation and monitoring. Although the task of building a system of networked biodetectors is fraught with complexity, the future of emerging biosensor technology lies in scientists' ability to develop networks of sophisticated alarmbearing biodetectors that can differentiate between harmful and benign entities and can be used anywhere, with wireless and remote capabilities.

Cynthia Racer

Further Reading

Behnisch, Peter A. "Biodetectors in Environmental Chemistry. Are We at a Turning Point?" *Environment International* 27 (December, 2001): 441-442.

Cooper, Jon, and Tony Cass, eds. *Biosensors: A Practical Approach*. 2d ed. New York: Oxford University Press, 2004.

Malhotra, Bansi D., et al. "Recent Trends in Biosensors." *Current Applied Physics* 5 (February, 2005): 92-97.

See also: Air and water purity; Biological terrorism; Biological warfare diagnosis; Biological weapon identification; Biosensors; Breathalyzer; Cadaver dogs; Canine substance detection; Chemical Biological Incident Response Force, U.S.; DNA recognition instruments.

Biohazard bags

Definition: Containers used by laboratories for the safe disposal of blood and other potentially infectious wastes.

Significance: Forensic, clinical, and research laboratories, as well as publicly and privately owned health care establishments such as hospitals, medical clinics, longterm care facilities, dental clinics, and blood banks, are required to use safety containers known as biohazard bags when disposing of blood or other potentially infectious materials. Forensic laboratories often analyze such materials when they are obtained as evidence in various crimes.

The use of biohazard bags, as an element of hazard communication, is one of the key provisions in the Standard on Occupational Exposure to Bloodborne Pathogens issued by the U.S. Occupational Safety and Health Administration (OSHA) on December 6, 1991. Biohazard bags are used to communicate the presence of blood or other potentially infectious materials (OPIM). Such bags serve to warn workers who may be exposed to potentially hazardous and infectious materials; facilities that use biohazard bags must train their workers to use universal precautions in handling the bags and their contents.

According to OSHA, OPIM include human body fluids (semen, vaginal secretions, saliva, any body fluid visibly contaminated with blood, and all body fluids that are difficult or impossible to differentiate) and any unfixed tissue or organ from a human being (dead or alive). OSHA also considers as OPIM any materials containing human immunodeficiency virus (HIV) or hepatitis B virus (HBV), such as blood, liquids, solutions, and cell, tissue, and organ cultures used in clinical, research, and forensic laboratories. Forensic laboratories often conduct evidence analyses on blood and OPIM.

The Bloodborne Pathogens Standard also uses the term "regulated waste," which refers to blood, OPIM, and materials or wastes contaminated with either one. Regulated waste requires special handling, including placement in containers with biohazard warnings (that is, biohazard bags) and safe disposal in keeping with federal, state, and local regulations.

Biohazard bags are color coded red (sometimes red-orange) and generally display the universal biohazard symbol to warn individuals that the materials contained are potentially infectious. As part of the special handling of regulated waste, before disposal biohazard bags are often sterilized in an autoclave, a device that uses high pressure and high-temperature steam to eradicate bacteria, viruses, and other microbes. OSHA thus requires that biohazard bags be made of substances—such as thick blended polymers—that are resistant to leakage and can withstand high pressure and high temperature. Biohazard bags also have indicators that change color after exposure to steam and thus indicate that the materials contained inside have been subjected to sterilization or decontamination.

Miriam E. Schwartz and Charlene F. Barroga

Biohazard bags are clearly marked with the blaze-orange biohazard symbol. The symbol itself has no intrinsic meaning; it was chosen because it is distinct and easily recognized. *(© iStockphoto.com/Mark Evans)*

Further Reading

Acello, Barbara. *The OSHA Handbook: Guidelines for Compliance in Health Care Facilities and Interpretive Guidelines for the Bloodborne Pathogens Standard*. Clifton Park, N.Y.: Thomson/Delmar Learning, 2002.

Barker, Kathy. *At the Bench: A Laboratory Navigator*. Cold Spring Harbor, N.Y.: Cold Spring Harbor Laboratory Press, 2004.

O'Neal, Jon T. *The Bloodborne Pathogens Standard: A Pragmatic Approach*. New York: Van Nostrand Reinhold, 1996.

World Health Organization. *Laboratory Biosafety Manual*. Geneva: Author, 2005.

See also: Blood residue and bloodstains; Blood spatter analysis; Crime laboratories; Crime scene cleaning; Decontamination methods; Forensic pathology; Saliva; Semen and sperm; U.S. Army Medical Research Institute of Infectious Diseases.

Biological terrorism

Definition: Spread of dangerous biological agents within civilian populations or agricultural areas with the intent of causing disorder and intense fear.

Significance: A bioterrorist attack is perhaps one of the events most feared by emergency responders and government officials in the field of counterterrorism, in large part because, although the probability of a wide-scale attack is rather low, in the event of such an attack, the potential for catastrophic results is high.

Ever since the influenza pandemic of 1918-1919 (a natural event), which killed some forty million people around the world, a heightened awareness has existed of the potential for the spread of harmful, even lethal, biological cultures among human populations. Among the purposeful biological attacks that have been perpetrated, perhaps the one with which the most Americans are familiar is the case in which letters containing the bacterium that causes anthrax were sent to addresses in New York City, Washington, D.C., and Boca Raton, Florida, in October and November of 2001, shortly following the September 11 terrorist attacks on the World Trade Center and the Pentagon. This case, which remains unsolved, greatly increased awareness of the need for government agencies (including the U.S. Postal Service) to learn how to identify and respond effectively to any biological crisis. The outbreak of severe acute respiratory syndrome (SARS) in Canada in 2002-2003, which quickly spread from one to more than two hundred persons in Toronto-area hospitals and resulted in thirty-three deaths among patients and health workers, also demonstrated the need for improvements in government and health care responses to epidemic and pandemic disease outbreaks. The investigation and prevention of biological terrorism have become foremost components of nations' efforts to improve their homeland security.

Bioterrorist attacks can target human populations directly or indirectly, through food and water supplies. Agroterrorism—biological terrorism that targets agricultural food sources—is a very real threat to national security in some countries because modern agricultural systems are tightly integrated, and many points in the harvesting, processing, and distribution systems represent potentially "soft" targets for terrorists and difficult targets to defend from terrorist acts. The routine transport and commingling of production and processing systems greatly aid the dissemination of any biological pathogens. It is estimated that 75 percent of the value production in U.S. agriculture occurs on just 6.7 percent (143,500) of U.S. farms, so a successful attack on any of these locations would be catastrophic.

History

The use of biological weapons can be easily traced back to ancient times. Soldiers used to dip their weapons in animal excrement or known plant toxins before battle so as to cause infection in whomever they stabbed or shot with arrows. In both ancient and medieval times, poisoning water supplies with dead animals was a favorite tactic, as was slinging or firing dead animal or human carcasses over defender walls in the hopes of spreading disease. Although few records exist to prove that European settlers in the New World purposely spread disease among Native Americans, sufficient evidence is found in the form of a letter from Colonel Henry Bouquet to Lord Jeffrey Amherst in 1763 to suggest that the British attempted to spread smallpox to their Native American opponents during the French and Indian War. Emperor Napoleon I drew on the expertise of French scientists to visit swamp fever on his opponents in the eighteenth century, and Confederate soldiers were known to poison ponds as they retreated from the advancing Union Army during the American Civil War.

By the time World War I began in 1914, science was sufficiently advanced that the mechanisms of the spread of disease were understood, and serious consideration was given to making use of biological agents during this global conflict. The German government formally and repeatedly refused to deploy biological agents against humans during the war, however, and the Allied Powers followed Germany's lead in

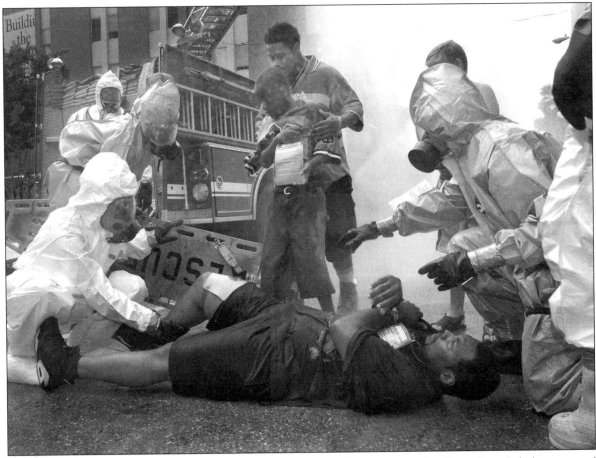

Emergency personnel in chemical and biological protective suits respond to the simulated injuries of a volunteer "victim" who has just passed through a decontamination shower. This emergency training exercise, which simulated a terrorist attack on Baltimore Ravens Stadium, was held by the University of Maryland Medical Center and the U.S. Air Force. *(AP/Wide World Photos)*

this regard. Nevertheless, German saboteurs deployed anthrax against horses and mules that were to be sent to Allied soldiers on the front lines. During World War II, as ample surviving film footage and written evidence shows, the Japanese tested biological agents extensively on Chinese prisoners and Chinese civilians. Whether the Japanese employed these agents as weapons of war, as some scholars allege, has not been proved. The Geneva Protocol, signed by various nations in 1925, outlaws the use of biological weapons, but such prohibitions are only as good as the resolve of nations to follow the protocol.

A number of terrorist organizations have at least discussed the use of biological weapons, including the Italian Brigate Rosse (Red Bri-

gades) and the German Rote Armee Fraktion (Red Army Faction), earlier known as the Baader-Meinhof Gang. Members of cults in the United States have poisoned restaurants with agents such as salmonella to cause sickness. The Japanese group Aum Shinrikyo (known as Aleph since 2000) actively acquired and cultured *Bacillus anthracis* (the bacterium that causes anthrax) and Ebola virus, both of which were found in significant quantities when police raided the group's headquarters in 1995 following its sarin gas attack on the Tokyo subway. The group purportedly released botulinum toxin as well as anthrax in the same period, but these attempts were not successful. Experts are not sure why these attacks failed; possible reasons include the method of delivery, manufacturing problems, and that the group may have released an anthrax vaccine and a slowly reproducing botulinum toxin rather than more potent varieties of these pathogens.

Since 1996, the Federal Bureau of Investigation (FBI) has opened numerous cases involving the potential use of biological agents. Many have amounted to mere threats, but some have included attempts to produce such pathogens as botulinum toxin, anthrax, and ricin.

Types of Agents

Because the variety of biological agents available for use in terrorist acts is quite extensive, stockpiling vaccines that may be needed in the event of biological attacks is extremely difficult; it is virtually impossible to have safeguards in place against every potential type of biological agent. Some of the most dangerous pathogens that may potentially be used by bioterrorists, as categorized by the Centers for Disease Control and Prevention, are anthrax, pneumonic plague, botulinum toxin, smallpox, and ricin.

Anthrax is perhaps the biological pathogen most likely to be used in a bioterrorist attack. It is relatively easy to cultivate the spores of *B. anthracis*, and the spores are fairly stable under a variety of conditions, so dissemination of the pathogen is not particularly difficult. When inhaled, the agent works into the lungs and causes fever, shock, and, ultimately, death. Anthrax can also cause sores on the skin of people working with infected livestock, which can result in other bodily infections. Approximately ten thousand spores of *B. anthracis* must be inhaled to prove deadly, but a mere gram of the bacterium contains millions of lethal doses.

The possibility of the use of pneumonic plague in a biological attack is high on the list of such threats maintained by first responders because this disease is incredibly virulent. Its killing potential in an uninoculated population is extremely high, close to 90 percent, and lethal exposure requires far fewer spores (around three thousand) than does anthrax. Pneumonic plague first appears as a fever accompanied by coughing, which progresses into hemorrhaging in the lungs. If left untreated for a relatively short period, the disease is almost always fatal.

Botulinum toxin is also fairly easy to cultivate. The potential of this toxin for use in aerosol form makes it very attractive as a biological weapon because the pathogen can be spread rapidly over a wide area. Botulinum toxin attacks the muscle nerves, paralyzing the nerve endings and preventing the muscles from responding to the brain. The paralysis begins near the head and works its way down through the body.

Smallpox is considered to be high on the list of potential bioterrorism pathogens because many people in the United States and around

The Danger of Developing Biological Weapons

In April of 1979, Sverdlovsk, Russia, was afflicted by an outbreak of anthrax during which at least sixty people died. At the time, the government of the Soviet Union claimed that the deaths and illness were caused by tainted meat, thoroughly denying any connection between the outbreak and the development of biological weapons.

In 1992, after the dissolution of the Soviet Union, a team of experts in pathology, biology, anthropology, and veterinary science traveled to Sverdlovsk, now known as Yekaterinburg, to ascertain what had happened there in 1979. In the course of the team's investigation, anthropologist Jeanne Guillemin discovered, through interviews with victims' families, a pattern regarding those who became infected with the anthrax virus. Guillemin ascertained where each victim had been on April 2, 1979, when the outbreak began, and subsequently compared this information with data on wind direction for that day. She found that the wind was blowing only from the northwest and that the victims' positions on that day placed them in the path of the wind. A biological weapons factory operated by the Soviet government was also directly in line with the wind, northwest of the city. Given this information, Guillemin concluded that the anthrax deaths did not result from tainted meat; the specific pattern of illness in Sverdlovsk pointed to the biological weapons factory as the source of the anthrax outbreak.

the world are no longer immunized against the disease, ever since aggressive vaccination programs let to its global eradication, which was verified and announced in December, 1979. The *Variola major* virus, which causes the most deadly form of smallpox, is relatively easy to cultivate and is easily spread using aerosols. Smallpox is contracted through inhalation, and after it incubates, the infected person normally experiences headache, fever, and other common signs of the flu. Next a rash develops, followed by pus-filled bumps on the skin. The mortality rate is approximately 30 percent for victims who have not been inoculated.

Ricin is a toxic protein found in castor beans; it is extracted from the waste produced in the manufacture of castor oil. Ricin is relatively easy to acquire and also much easier to stockpile than most other biological pathogens. A large dose is required to kill, but the toxin can be either ingested or inhaled. When employed in conjunction with other pathogens, ricin can enable other pathogens to attack an already afflicted body. Ricin can cause respiratory problems, fever, cough, abdominal pain, and, when ingested, damage to organs such as the liver and kidneys. Ricin prevents cells in the body from making protein, which causes the cells to die off.

Methods of Investigation

Perhaps the greatest difficulty in the investigation of biological attacks is the fact that many of the initial symptoms caused by intentionally introduced agents are very similar to the symptoms of common diseases, such as influenza. Most often, the only way first responders are even aware that a biological attack has potentially taken place is the presence of a massive influx of people with the same symptoms. Such attacks are not usually discovered until after the pathogens have been widely disseminated and have infected large numbers of people.

The teams that investigate biological attacks need to include persons with knowledge of both biology and chemistry, who can understand the interplay between the body and the pathogen. Other areas of knowledge that are extremely important in the investigation of such attacks include the disciplines of anthropology and geography. An understanding of human living, interaction, and moving patterns, combined with meteorological data, can help investigators to track a disease back to where it may have originated, particularly in the case of aerosol dissemination.

Much of the investigative strategy used in determining whether biological agents have been intentionally spread involves the review of medical diagnoses and the employment of effective vaccines against the various agents. Investigators usually trace such agents back to their sources by comparing strains of genetic material with a database that catalogs various strains and the laboratories or environments in which the strains originated. Many materials used in the manufacture of biological agents are sold commercially, and investigators try to track where such materials may have been purchased and by whom. Scientists have been working on developing a system of biological agent detection that will be able to identify pathogens through size, nucleic acid sequence, and antigen recognition.

It is clear that the modern world has seen neither the end of bioterrorist activities nor the full range of bioterrorism possibilities yet displayed. It is equally certain that just as formal counterterrorism measures evolve and successfully propagate, so will the methods, means, and modes of bioterrorism.

Michael W. Cheek and Dennis W. Cheek

Further Reading

Anderson, Burt, Herman Freedman, and Mauro Bendinelli, eds. *Microorganisms and Bioterrorism.* New York: Springer, 2006. Provides comprehensive coverage of infectious diseases, including smallpox, anthrax, tularemia, brucellosis, pneumonic plague, Q fever (caused by *Coxiella bernetii*), and rickets.

Cordesman, Anthony H. *Terrorism, Asymmetric Warfare, and Weapons of Mass Destruction: Defending the U.S. Homeland.* Westport, Conn.: Praeger, 2002. Extremely comprehensive work addresses potential terrorist attacks. Includes sections on specific biological weapons as well as extensive suggestions for improvements in the area of homeland security. Provides a good overview of the difficulties in responding to biological attacks.

Foster, George T., ed. *Focus on Bioterrorism.* New York: Nova Science, 2006. Presents a well-written overview of the topic with discussion of attention to vaccine stockpiles, the U.S. Postal Service, responses to bioterrorism, and existing laws on proliferation sanctions in the United States and internationally.

Katz, Linda B., ed. *Agroterrorism: Another Domino?* New York: Novinka Books, 2005. Surveys threats, preparedness, and continuing challenges of biological actions against American agriculture. Topics include the specific challenges that the tightly interlocking system of modern agriculture presents to counterterrorism efforts and the ease with which various aspects of the food supply could be assaulted with biological weapons.

Pilch, Richard F., and Raymond A. Zilinskas, eds. *Encyclopedia of Bioterrorism Defense.* Hoboken, N.J.: Wiley-Liss, 2005. Large reference work includes essays by noted experts on the many dimensions of bioterrorism and how various strategies, organizations, and individuals are used to counter the many different types of bioterrorist threats in the modern world.

Ursano, Robert J., Anne E. Norwood, and Carol S. Fullerton, eds. *Bioterrorism: Psychological and Public Health Intervention.* New York: Cambridge University Press, 2004. Provides an excellent overview of the psychological and public health dimensions of bioterrorism. Includes an extensive case study of the 1918 influenza pandemic as well as chapters that discuss the psychological effects of bioterrorism on individuals and communities and the role of public health in communication, prevention, and management response.

Wagner, Viqi, ed. *Do Infectious Diseases Pose a Serious Threat?* New Haven, Conn.: Greenhaven Press, 2005. Collection of essays addresses the potential use of infectious diseases in terrorism and which agents are the most serious threat to the United States.

Wheelis, Mark, Lajos Rózsa, and Malcolm Dando, eds. *Deadly Cultures: Biological Weapons Since 1945.* Cambridge, Mass.: Harvard University Press, 2006. Discusses developments in biological warfare since World War II and addresses the issue of why states acquire biological weapons.

See also: Airport security; Anthrax; Anthrax letter attacks; Bacterial biology; Biodetectors; Biological warfare diagnosis; Biological Weapons Convention of 1972; Biosensors; Bubonic plague; Centers for Disease Control and Prevention; Chemical Biological Incident Response Force, U.S.; Chemical terrorism; Decontamination methods; Pathogen transmission; U.S. Army Medical Research Institute of Infectious Diseases; Viral biology.

Biological warfare diagnosis

Definition: Determination of the specific nature of disease-producing agents used as weapons.

Significance: The use of deadly organisms as weapons is perhaps more feared than chemical warfare because biotoxins have the potential of wreaking havoc on plants, animals, and humans. Detailed genomic determinations of these agents are critical parts of forensic analyses for the detection, diagnosis, and prosecution of biocrimes, bioterrorism, and biological warfare.

A large number of infectious organisms exist in nature, and many of them can be pathogenic (disease-causing) to humans. Microbiologists have developed bioengineering tools to increase the numbers and virulence of these organisms. Because biological weapons could cause catastrophic harm to a nation's population and economy, some political and military leaders have confessed that they fear the use of biological weapons more than the use of nuclear weapons. This anxiety has led several countries to develop techniques for detecting the use and diagnosing the nature of biological weapons in order to assist in the medical treatment of victims as well as in the prosecution of those who use these weapons.

The ideal agent of biological warfare is easy and cheap to produce, aerosolizable for effective delivery, and highly infectious for rapid person-to-person transmission. Although microbiologists have not yet developed the perfect biological weapon, they have discovered ways of manufacturing microorganisms that have the potential for creating mass casualties. For example, the following microbes have been developed into biological weapons: *Bacillus anthracis*, the bacterium that causes anthrax; *Variola major*, the virus that causes smallpox; *Yersinia pestis*, the bacterium that causes pneumonic (or bubonic) plague; *Francisella tularensis*, the bacterium that causes tularemia; and viruses that cause hemorrhagic fevers. Because of the secrecy surrounding research on potential biological weapons, specific examples of new, highly virulent strains of naturally occurring organisms or artificial pathogens are hard to come by.

Detection and Diagnosis

By the early twenty-first century, more than 140 nations had signed and ratified the 1972 Biological Weapons Convention, which prohibits the development, manufacture, and stockpiling of bacteriological weapons. Although this treaty did lead some countries to destroy their stockpiles of biological weapons, the advent of modern bioengineering made several of the convention's provisions obsolete.

After an exercise simulating a germ attack on Denver in 2000 revealed weaknesses in state and federal responses to such a threat, and particularly after the terrorist attacks against the United States on September 11, 2001, the U.S. government developed new organizations to deal with the assessment of and reaction to threats of biological warfare. The Department of Homeland Security established the National Biodefense Analysis and Countermeasures Center to help Americans anticipate, prevent, respond to, and recover from biological attack (previous countermeasures had been erroneously based on models for chemical warfare).

Because of the necessity of medical involvement in diagnostics and forensics, the National Response Plan developed in 2004 focused on the U.S. Department of Health and Human Services as the primary agency to deal with bioterrorist events. The Centers for Disease Control and Prevention developed the Labora-

---

The Laboratory Response Network

The Centers for Disease Control and Prevention provides the following information about the Laboratory Response Network (LRN).

The LRN's purpose is to run a network of labs that can respond to biological and chemical terrorism, and other public health emergencies. The LRN has grown since its inception. It now includes state and local public health, veterinary, military, and international labs. . . .

The LRN Structure for Bioterrorism

LRN labs are designated as either national, reference, or sentinel. Designation depends on the types of tests a laboratory can perform and how it handles infectious agents to protect workers and the public.

National labs have unique resources to handle highly infectious agents and the ability to identify specific agent strains.

Reference labs, sometimes referred to as "confirmatory reference," can perform tests to detect and confirm the presence of a threat agent. These labs ensure a timely local response in the event of a terrorist incident. Rather than having to rely on confirmation from labs at CDC, reference labs are capable of producing conclusive results. This allows local authorities to respond quickly to emergencies.

Sentinel labs represent the thousands of hospital-based labs that are on the front lines. Sentinel labs have direct contact with patients. In an unannounced or covert terrorist attack, patients provide specimens during routine patient care. A sentinel lab could be the first facility to spot a suspicious specimen. A sentinel laboratory's responsibility is to refer a suspicious sample to the right reference lab.

tory Response Network to detect and diagnose biological agents. Also, because biological attacks cause more fatalities the longer they remain undetected, the U.S. government established BioWatch, a network of air samplers around metropolitan areas, and BioShield, a program designed to accelerate medical countermeasures against biological hazards. The information gathered from these and other organizations and programs is also intended to be used by experts at the National Bioforensic Analysis Center to discover the sources of any biological agents used in attacks.

Forensic Analysis

A bioterrorist attack creates problems not only for early and rapid detection and diagnosis but also for forensic analysis. To deal with such problems, the Federal Bureau of Investigation (FBI) established the Scientific Working Group for Microbial Genetics and Forensics in 2002 to facilitate the identification of any organism used in a biocrime or bioterrorist attack.

Because the diagnostic requirements of microbial forensics are much more stringent than those of public health, experts at the location of a biological attack and in laboratories have to document sample collection with great care and perform detailed genomic analyses of the biological agent while maintaining a clear chain of custody for all evidence to be used in future legal proceedings. Advanced technologies, such as miniaturized immunoassay devices that can collect data in the area of an attack, have improved the chances for convictions of the attackers, but the cooperation of medical professionals, military personnel, law-enforcement officials, and forensic scientists is necessary to minimize deaths immediately after an attack as well as in the later identification and conviction of those responsible for it.

Robert J. Paradowski

Further Reading

Clinics in Laboratory Medicine 26 (June, 2006). Special issue titled "Biological Weapons and Bioterrorism" includes articles that examine the laboratory and forensic aspects of deadly biological agents.

Croddy, Eric A., with Clarisa Perez-Armendariz and John Hart. *Chemical and Biological Warfare: A Comprehensive Survey for the Concerned Citizen*. New York: Copernicus Books, 2002. Detailed overview for the layperson includes sections on the nature, history, detection, and control of biological weapons.

Dudley, William, ed. *Biological Warfare: Opposing Viewpoints*. Farmington Hills, Miss.: Greenhaven Press, 2004. Collection discusses differences of opinion among scientists and other experts on how to understand, prepare for, and prevent biological warfare.

Lederberg, Joshua, ed. *Biological Weapons: Limiting the Threat*. Cambridge, Mass.: MIT Press, 1999. Compendium of historical and technical essays includes information on the detection of biological agents and responses to biological attack. Intended for both doctors and students.

Mauroni, Al. *Chemical and Biological Warfare: A Reference Handbook*. 2d ed. Santa Barbara, Calif.: ABC-CLIO, 2007. Addresses the history of chemical and biological weaponry and presents information on experts and related organizations as well as case studies.

See also: Anthrax; Anthrax letter attacks; Bacteria; Biodetectors; Biological terrorism; Biological weapon identification; Biological Weapons Convention of 1972; Biotoxins; Blood agents; Chemical warfare.

Biological weapon identification

Definition: Identification of weapons of mass destruction that are based on bacteria, viruses, fungi, and toxins produced by these microorganisms.

Significance: Heightened concerns regarding the possibility of bioterrorist attacks have led to increased emphasis on microbial forensic science. Microbial forensic data may be presented in court as evidence in cases of terrorist attacks.

Virtually all disease-causing microorganisms are potentially useful as biological weapons. The most important candidates for biological weapons are microorganisms that cause diseases with high human mortality rates, such as anthrax, smallpox, plague, encephalitis, and hemorrhagic fever. In addition, biological weapons that are designed to wipe out crops or kill livestock could cause mass starvation and devastating economic losses.

In 2001, the general public in the United States became aware of biological weapons as a result of a series of attacks involving mail containing *Bacillus anthracis* (the bacterium that causes anthrax). Since that time, the possibility that terrorists might employ biological weapons, many of which are easily produced and spread, has been a growing concern. In response to the threat of terrorist attacks, the U.S. government has led efforts to develop quick and efficient methods of biological weapon identification, ultimately leading to the establishment of the new scientific discipline of microbial forensics. In general, the identification of microorganisms is based on techniques that rely on microscopic examination, analysis of the growth and metabolic functions of the microbes (growth-dependent and biochemical tests), and immunological and genetic tests.

Growth-Dependent and Biochemical Tests

Classic methods of microbial identification involve preliminary examination of stained specimens under a microscope, followed by growth-dependent tests. Growth-dependent tests are based on the growth patterns of microorganisms on artificial food sources (media). Particular media can be selected that will produce microbial populations—known as colonies—that have distinctive appearance and color. By comparing the reactions on these media with the known characteristics of different species of microorganisms, scientists can usually identify which microbe is present. However, most growth-dependent tests do not provide results that are extremely specific; that is, they may not distinguish among closely related microorganisms.

To aid in definitive microorganism identification, scientists have developed a series of biochemical tests that can be used to differentiate even the most closely related microbes. These tests are based on the identification of various metabolic reactions and products of different microbes. Microbial species can often be identified on the basis of fermentation patterns and the production of different chemical compounds, such as indole or hydrogen sulfide. Microorganisms are not easily identified by a single biochemical test, so it is usually necessary to perform several tests. A number of rapid identification systems are available that allow several (approximately twenty) biochemical tests to be performed quickly on a particular microorganism.

Immunological Tests

Immunological tests utilize antibodies that are produced in response to the presence of a specific microorganism; actually, they respond to the presence of specific molecules, called antigens, on the microorganism cell surfaces. Antibodies are proteins produced by the body that recognize and bind to those antigens. Specific antibodies for many known disease-causing microorganisms are commercially available. Immunological tests vary in the ways they make the antigen-antibody reaction visible; some show obvious clumps and precipitates, whereas others show color changes or the release of fluorescence.

An example of an immunological test is the agglutination test, which is performed routinely in hospitals to determine blood types. In an agglutination test, antibody-antigen complexes form visible clumps on a test glass slide. Extremely sensitive immunological tests called immunoassays permit rapid and accurate measurement of trace bioweapon agents. These methods are being used increasingly in criminology. A good example of such an immunoassay is the enzyme-linked immunosorbent assay (ELISA). A positive result in this immunoassay is the appearance of a colored product. ELISA is a common screening test for the antibodies to toxins and bacteria that may be used as bioweapons. In radioimmunoassays, antibodies are labeled with radioactive isotopes and traced. Immunological methods are especially important for the identification of viruses, as other identification methods are not suitable to them, and growth times are long.

Genetic Tests

Genetic tests of microorganisms are based on the detection of the unique DNA (deoxyribonucleic acid) sequences of potential weapon microorganisms. Certain viruses maintain their genetic material in the form of RNA (ribonucleic acid), which can be converted into corresponding DNA for detection purposes. One particular technique has been widely used for identifying microorganisms based on their DNA sequences: polymerase chain reaction (PCR).

Two variations of the PCR technique have been adopted for identification: PCR and real-time PCR. Both utilize specific sets of primers (short DNA sequences) to amplify and detect DNA sequences unique to a particular microorganism. In PCR, amplified DNA sequences are subjected to separation by electrophoresis, where negatively charged DNA fragments move toward the positive pole. Separated DNA fragments can be classified by the distance they traveled depending on their molecular size. Each microorganism exhibits a characteristic DNA moving pattern by which it can be identified. In real-time PCR, detection of a microorganism's amplified DNA and confirmation of that microorganism's presence are sensed by activation of a fluorescent dye. Officials of the United Nations used portable PCR detectors when they conducted their 2002-2003 inspections of Iraqi facilities for weapons of mass destruction. These detectors can identify a single *B. anthracis* bacterium in an average kitchen-sized room.

Ongoing Challenges

Although, in most cases, agents used as biological weapons could be identified easily within twenty-four hours, prosecutors may have difficulty proving that microorganisms identified in the homes or laboratories of suspects are in fact the same microorganisms used as weapons or intended for such use. One problem with making legal arguments based on weapon microbe identification is that some potentially danger-ous microorganisms, such as *B. anthracis*, are found widely in soil. A prosecutor thus must prove that the microbes submitted as evidence in a given case are the same microbes used in the attack in question, and not simply microorganisms that have been transported into the suspect's home or lab accidentally.

Sergei A. Markov

Further Reading

Cowan, Marjorie Kelly, and Kathleen Park Talaro. *Microbiology: A Systems Approach.* 2d ed. Boston: McGraw-Hill, 2008. General microbiology text focuses on the health sciences. Includes a chapter devoted to description of microbial identification techniques.

Fritz, Sandy, comp. *Understanding Germ Warfare.* New York: Warner Books, 2002. Collection of materials describes twenty-first century bioterrorism and germ weapons, including anthrax, smallpox, plague, viral fevers, and toxins. Also discusses methods of delivery of biological agents and their identification, symptoms, and treatment.

Lindler, Luther E., Frank J. Lebeda, and George W. Korch, eds. *Biological Weapons Defense: Infectious Diseases and Counterbioterrorism.* Totowa, N.J.: Humana Press, 2005. Prominent experts in biodefense research—many from the U.S. Army Medical Research Institute of Infectious Diseases—describe how to identify the presence of biological weapons through proteomic and genomic analysis.

Madigan, Michael T., John M. Martinko, Paul V. Dunlap, and David P. Clark. *Brock Biology of Microorganisms.* 12th ed. Upper Saddle River, N.J.: Pearson Prentice Hall, 2008. Widely respected basic microbiology textbook includes information about biological weapons and methods of microbial identification.

Peruski, Anne Harwood, and Leonard F. Peruski, Jr. "Immunological Methods for Detection and Identification of Infectious Disease and Biological Warfare Agents." *Clinical and Diagnostic Laboratory Immunology* 10 (July, 2003): 506-513. Technical article describes immunological methods of biological weapon identification.

See also: Anthrax; Bacterial biology; Biological terrorism; Biological warfare diagnosis; Biosensors; Biotoxins; Bubonic plague; DNA analysis; Ebola virus; Polymerase chain reaction; Smallpox; Tularemia; Viral biology.

Biological Weapons Convention of 1972

Dates: Opened for signature April 10, 1972; entered into force March 26, 1975

The Convention: International agreement designed to ban the development, production, and stockpiling of a variety of biological weapons.

Significance: Seeking to increase international security, the Biological Weapons Convention of 1972 outlawed all biological weapons and delivery systems for such weapons. The openness required by this treaty can assist forensic scientists who investigate crimes that involve such organisms.

Early in human history, people in certain hunting societies learned how to use plant or animal poisons to make their weapons more deadly. As human beings gained more detailed knowledge of diseases and biological processes, they developed other, more efficient, means of using biological agents to infect or kill their enemies. After more than one million casualties in World War I, mainly from chemical weapons, the international community adopted the Geneva Protocol in 1925; this agreement limited the first use of chemical or biological weapons in future wars. The method of conducting warfare was thus recognized as being subject to international law.

The United States researched and developed biological weapons on a large scale until 1969, when President Richard M. Nixon ordered a halt to these programs and instructed the Department of Defense to design a plan to dispose of the weapons. Around the same time, the British govenment proposed international negotiations on banning biological weapons. In 1971,

an agreement was reached, and in 1972, the process of signing and ratification of the Convention on the Prohibition of the Development, Production and Stockpiling of Bacteriological (Biological) and Toxin Weapons and on Their Destruction began. According to the convention, also known as the Biological and Toxin Weapons Convention or simply the Biological Weapons Convention, biological weapons were supposed to be destroyed beginning in 1975. This was at the height of the Cold War, however, and verification procedures that required countries to allow international observers into their military facilities were not acceptable to many signatories. Enforcement of the provisions of the convention was impossible because no system existed for verifying that countries were adhering to those provisions.

Adding to the enforcement problem since the convention entered into force in March, 1975, has been the fact that virtually everything that is needed to develop biological weapons also has a peaceful use. The existence of sealed biological research facilities, for instance, does not necessarily indicate that biological weapons research is being conducted. Sealing such a facility is a common procedure to keep contamination, in either direction, from affecting a biology experiment. Those who seek to enforce the terms of the treaty must use indirect means to verify that nations are following those terms. A series of Review Conferences have been held to clarify certain aspects of the treaty and generally assist with its implementation in an ever-changing world. The Fourth Review Conference directed a working group to develop a protocol for a mandatory multinational verification process. In 2002, at the last meeting prior to the protocol's going to the Fifth Review Conference for adoption, the United States effectively vetoed the proposed protocol as not being strong enough to guarantee that it would be completely effective.

Posttreaty Incidents

Although the Biological Weapons Convention allows countries to keep small quantities of biological agents for medical or defensive purposes, the treaty prohibits active work on the development of such agents. Many people were surprised when, in April, 1979, an outbreak of anthrax killed more than sixty people in the Soviet city of Sverdlovsk (now Yekaterinburg, Russia). Soviet authorities denied any relationship of the outbreak to biological weapons, but given that anthrax is a commonly produced biological agent and the disease has been virtually wiped out, the rest of the world was certain that the anthrax deaths had resulted from an accident at a biological research facility. Without a mandatory inspection process in place, however, international observers were unable to investigate the situation fully and determine the cause of the outbreak with complete certainty.

The possible use of biological agents by terrorists was dramatically demonstrated in September and October, 2001, when letters containing anthrax spores were mailed to five news media operations in New York City and Boca Raton, Florida, and later to two U.S. senators. As a result of these attacks, twenty-two people became ill, five of whom died. Although law-enforcement investigators were eventually able to track the letters to a specific mailbox in New Jersey, the case remains unsolved. Forensic scientists have spent countless hours trying to determine the source of the anthrax, focusing on the slight differences that distinguish the various samples of anthrax spores stored at different locations. One early analysis indicated that the anthrax used in the attacks came from a U.S. military base, although this was never officially confirmed, and dozens of sites have been searched.

As a result of the possible contamination of multiple sites owing to the method the terrorist used, sending the anthrax spores through the mail, the U.S. government has spent hundreds of millions of dollars cleaning up various locations, especially postal facilities. The fact that even after years of intensive investigation the perpetrator of the crime has not been found indicates how difficult it is to track weapons of this type. If the signatories of the Biological

---

First Four Articles of the Biological Weapons Convention

Article I

Each State Party to this Convention undertakes never in any circumstances to develop, produce, stockpile or otherwise acquire or retain:

1. Microbial or other biological agents, or toxins whatever their origin or method of production, of types and in quantities that have no justification for prophylactic, protective or other peaceful purposes;
2. Weapons, equipment or means of delivery designed to use such agents or toxins for hostile purposes or in armed conflict.

Article II

Each State Party to this Convention undertakes to destroy, or to divert to peaceful purposes, as soon as possible but not later than nine months after entry into force of the Convention, all agents, toxins, weapons, equipment and means of delivery specified in article I of the Convention, which are in its possession or under its jurisdiction or control. In implementing the provisions of this article all necessary safety precautions shall be observed to protect populations and the environment.

Article III

Each State Party to this Convention undertakes not to transfer to any recipient whatsoever, directly or indirectly, and not in any way to assist, encourage, or induce any State, group of States or international organizations to manufacture or otherwise acquire any of the agents, toxins, weapons, equipment or means of delivery specified in article I of this Convention.

Article IV

Each State Party to this Convention shall, in accordance with its constitutional processes, take any necessary measures to prohibit and prevent the development, production, stockpiling, acquisition, or retention of the agents, toxins, weapons, equipment and means of delivery specified in article I of the Convention, within the territory of such State, under its jurisdiction or under its control anywhere.

President Richard M. Nixon at his first inauguration in January, 1969. Later that same year, Nixon ordered the discontinuation of biological weapon development in the United States. As other world powers followed suit, a movement began that led to an international ban on such weapons. *(NARA)*

Weapons Convention follow the intent of the treaty and reduce the amount of stored biological materials available for misuse by terrorists and closely guard what remains, incidents such as the 2001 anthrax attacks may not happen in the future.

Donald A. Watt

Further Reading

Cirincione, Joseph, Jon B. Wolfsthal, and Miriam Rajkumar. *Deadly Arsenals: Nuclear, Biological, and Chemical Threats*. Rev. ed. Washington, D.C.: Carnegie Endowment for International Peace, 2005. Provides an overview of the range of chemical weapon threats facing the United States.

Gillemin, Jeanne. *Biological Weapons: From the Invention of State-Sponsored Programs to Contemporary Bioterrorism*. New York: Columbia University Press, 2006. Discusses biological weapon programs from before World War II through the 1990's, with special attention to the remnants of those programs that later became "available" to terrorists.

Hoover Institution on War. *The New Terror: Facing the Threat of Biological and Chemical Weapons*. Palo Alto, Calif.: Hoover Institution Press, 1999. Covers a wide range of issues, including the constitutional constraints on U.S. law enforcement in combating chemical weapons and suggestions for reducing the damage from such weapons.

Lederberg, Joshua, ed. *Biological Weapons: Limiting the Threat*. Cambridge, Mass.: MIT Press, 1999. Examines the dangers posed by biological weapons as well as the ways in which the United States has tried to decrease those dangers.

Tucker, Jonathan B., ed. *Toxic Terror: Assessing Terrorist Use of Chemical and Biological Weapons*. Cambridge, Mass.: MIT Press, 2000. Presents twelve case studies of the use of chemical and biological agents by terrorist groups. Identifies terrorists' patterns of behavior and discusses strategies to combat them.

See also: Anthrax; Anthrax letter attacks; Biological terrorism; Biological warfare diagnosis; Biological weapon identification; Biotoxins; Chemical Weapons Convention of 1993; Pathogen genomic sequencing; Smallpox; U.S. Army Medical Research Institute of Infectious Diseases.

Biometric eye scanners

Definition: Imaging technologies that use the iris or retina of the eye to identify individuals.

Significance: Biometric eye scanning can facilitate the automated control of access to areas where high levels of security must be maintained, such as correctional institutions and military and government installations that house sensitive materials.

The goal of biometric identification systems is to provide automated identity assurance—that is, the capability to recognize individuals accurately—with reliability, speed, and convenience. The complex nature of the human eye provides two of the most accurate biometric measures available. The iris and the retina, located on the front and back of the eye, respectively, are individually distinguishing structures. Retinal recognition became commercially available in the early 1980's, preceding iris recognition systems by about five years.

The iris is the round, pigmented membrane that surrounds the pupil of the eye. The intricate pattern of furrows and ridges in the iris is randomly formed prior to birth and remains stable from early childhood until death. In a typical iris scan, the person being identified aligns one eye close to a wall-mounted scanner for a few seconds. The scanner uses a near-infrared light to scan an image of the eye, and computer software then isolates the iris in the image and performs size and contrast corrections. Computer software then compares the final digital image with other iris images stored in a database; when a match is made, the person is identified.

Prisons throughout the United States use iris-scanning technology to verify the identities of convicts before release. Correctional facilities also enroll visitors in their iris image databases and scan the irises of people leaving the facilities to be certain they are visitors, not inmates. Some organizations use small, semiportable iris scanners to control access to sensitive computer files and information.

Retina biometric identification is based on the individually distinguishing characteristics of blood vessel patterns on the back of the eye. These patterns are thought to be created by a random biological process and remain unchanged throughout life in a healthy individual. During retina scanning, the person being identified aligns one eye with a wall-mounted scanner for several seconds. The scanner illuminates the retina with a low-intensity infrared light and creates an image of the patterns formed by the major blood vessels. The image is then digitally encoded, stored, and compared using computer software.

Because the retina is located on the back of the eye, this type of scan requires a high degree of cooperation from the user to ensure proper illumination and alignment. Given that retina scanning is more complex than the iris-scanning process, retina-scanning technology is best deployed in high-security, controlled-access environments where user convenience is not a priority. Employees in military weapons facilities, power plants, and sensitive laboratory environments are commonly required to undergo retina scanning to gain access.

Ruth N. Udey

Further Reading

Coats, William Sloan, et al. *The Practitioner's Guide to Biometrics*. Chicago: American Bar Association Publishing, 2007.

Nanavati, Samir, Michael Thieme, and Raj Nanavati. *Biometrics: Identity Verification in a Networked World*. New York: John Wiley & Sons, 2002.

Woodward, John D., Jr., Nicholas M. Orlans, and Peter T. Higgins. *Biometrics*. New York: McGraw-Hill, 2003.

See also: Airport security; Biometric identification systems; Facial recognition technology; Imaging; Iris recognition systems.

Biometric identification systems

Definition: Technologies that use automated measurements and database comparisons of physiological and behavioral characteristics to identify target individuals.

Significance: Biometric identification systems are becoming increasingly important given heightened concerns with security in many contexts. Compared with many other means of authorization and authentication, including password recognition, biometric technologies represent a significant advance in terms of ease of use, reliability, and validity.

The constantly evolving science of biometrics has produced a wide variety of systems capable of comparing hand, facial, eye, signature, vocal, and brain measures of given individuals against profiles of such measures stored in large databases. The applications of this technology for law-enforcement purposes are extensive. Biometric systems have been used to identify offenders who are using aliases, to fight illegal immigration, and to identify inmates as they are moved through various phases of the correctional system. Biometric data can be used to verify identity claims or to screen for persons who have been identified as potential security risks.

Accuracy

Biometric identification systems represent a huge improvement over the traditional "token"

(credit card or document) and password systems. Credit cards can be lost or stolen and then used as false identification. Similarly, passwords can be "cracked," forgotten, or stolen. Biometric characteristics, on the other hand, are much more stable and permanent. Their inherent complexity renders them difficult or impossible to replicate, and the person being identified usually needs to be physically present at the time of the verification attempt. In addition, biometric systems can couple identifying information with other important background data, such as health or employment records (a fact that has led some to criticize the use of these systems as infringing on civil liberties).

The components of the typical biometric system are relatively straightforward; they consist of a sensor and a computer. The sensor is the device that gathers the biometric data from the individual being evaluated. The computer then processes the data collected; in some cases, the computer may refine the data by removing irrelevant information and background "noise" that may interfere with the interpretation of the results. The computer captures the biometric features being measured and creates a template, which it then compares to a database of biometric information on known individuals, looking for an identification match, or "hit." The consequences of a successful identification are as varied as the systems themselves. At the point of identification, an individual might be allowed into a restricted area, picked up for further questioning in a specific investigation, or observed further for any suspicious behavior.

The accuracy of a biometric system is typically assessed using one or more of the following measures: the failure-to-acquire rate (a measure of the percentage of unsuccessful attempts by the system to obtain specific biometric information from subjects), the false accept rate (also known as the false positive rate, a measure of the percentage of incorrect matches of subjects' biometric profiles to profiles already included in the database), and the false reject rate (also known as the false negative rate, the percentage of failures to match subjects' biometric profiles with identical profiles already included in the database). Minimization of all these kinds of error rates reduces the numbers of suspects who

Mark Twain and Fingerprints

Although Mark Twain never knew the word "biometrics," he might fairly be credited with introducing that science to fiction in *Pudd'nhead Wilson* (1894)—the first novel to use fingerprint evidence as a plot device. During the mid-nineteenth century, the novel's title character, attorney David Wilson, mystifies and amuses the simple people of Dawson's Landing, Missouri, by collecting their fingerprints on glass slides.

For years, the villagers dismiss him as a "pudding-headed" fool—until the final chapter, when he displays his legal brilliance in a murder trial. Wilson creates a sensation by using his slides to prove the innocence of the murder suspect whom he is defending. That revelation is minor, however, compared to his second use of fingerprint evidence at the trial. Drawing on glass slides he has collected over more than two decades, he proves that the culprit in the murder case is a man who was born a slave and somehow got switched with the infant son of his master in infancy. The theme of switched identities that are sorted out by fingerprint evidence gives the novel a strong claim to being called the first application of biometrics in fiction.

David Wilson examining his fingerprint collection in the first edition of *Pudd'nhead Wilson.*

are needlessly detained, restricted from air travel, or otherwise affected by law-enforcement "false alarms" while maximizing the appropriate identification of true security threats.

Applications

Law-enforcement agencies employ biometric technologies in many ways, including for facial recognition, fingerprint identification, iris recognition, and voice recognition. Facial recognition systems use specific aspects of facial features from scanned photographs to make identifications. The features analyzed may include the physical distance between specific features, skin color, thermal patterns of blood flow, and facial lines. One application of facial recognition technology is the establishment by police departments of archives containing many thousands of offender photographs. These are matched with suspects' pictures or used to produce photo lineups that can be shown to crime victims or witnesses.

Numerous evaluations of facial recognition technology have produced mixed results. One Australian system, for example, tested in the Sydney airport, was found to have a false reject rate of 2 percent. This rate was confirmed by tests sponsored by the U.S. government. Although this error rate seems low, major world airports typically service several million passengers annually, which means that the systems could potentially falsely reject many thousands of people. A meta-analysis of facial recognition systems produced accuracy rates ranging from 51 percent to 94 percent. Factors affecting the rates included lighting, the quality of the photographs taken, movements of the subjects, the angles of the poses in the photographs, and the presence of eyeglasses on subjects. In general, male subjects and older persons were more easily recognized than were female and younger subjects. An inverse relationship was also found between accuracy and the size of the database against which the subjects' facial features were compared.

Fingerprint identification is the oldest form of biometric identification, having been in use for more than one hundred years. The Federal Bureau of Investigation (FBI) established a central database of fingerprints in 1924 against which law-enforcement agencies can seek to match the prints of crime suspects and victims.

With modern electronic and laser technology, fingerprint images are often taken and transmitted "live" to the database. Efforts to automate the analysis and identification of fingerprints began in the 1960's.

Fingerprint identification systems use electronic fingerprint readers to locate where the ridges of fingerprints start, end, or split up. These areas, known as minutiae points, form the basis for the identification. Each fingerprint typically contains thirty to forty minutiae points, and no two people's prints will match on more than eight such points.

In terms of accuracy, the false accept rates of fingerprint identification systems have generally been less than one in one million, and false reject rates have been 2 percent or less. The accuracy of the analysis of fingerprints taken from crime scenes, however, is often reduced because of the poor quality of the prints themselves. In addition, although it is often assumed that fingerprints are stable over a lifetime, research has shown that they in fact can change in re-

Recognition by this electronic fingerprint reader is required for entry into a secure room at the Alpharetta, Georgia, Disaster Preparedness Center. *(AP/Wide World Photos)*

sponse to physiological growth, activity, or intentional alteration; it has also been shown that many fingerprint matching systems can be "spoofed." Despite some limitations, fingerprinting is less controversial and more highly developed than any other type of biometric identification system. This is reflected in court acceptance of fingerprinting evidence.

In iris recognition identification systems, an image of the iris of the eye (the colored ring surrounding the pupil) of the person to be identified is recorded by a digital camera and then converted into a template, which is checked for matches against an existing database. False positive rates for such systems have averaged 0.1 percent, and false negative rates have averaged 1.5 percent. An advantage of using this biometric technique is that, unlike fingerprints, the structure of the iris is permanent by the age of one and is unique for each person (this includes comparisons between identical twins and even between the left and right eyes of the same person). Unlike with fingerprint identification, however, no large databases yet exist for iris templates, and iris evidence is not left at crime scenes. In addition, failure rates as high as 15 percent have been found when iris-scanning technology is used in brightly lit settings. This technology has many potential applications, including security screening at airports and borders, passport and immigration control, and identification for banking and issuance of drivers' licenses.

Voice recognition systems use physical and behavioral aspects of the voice to identify individuals; the voice features measured are based on the physiology of the windpipe, nasal cavity, and vocal cords. A digital "voice signature" is recorded, and a computer measures the features and compares them against known samples for identification and verification. One drawback to the use of voice biometrics is that voice patterns can vary with age, and they can also be affected by medical problems (including even a cold) and the emotional state of the examinee. Background noise can also be a problem with the use of this identification technology.

Another biometric identification technology that has been investigated is hand geometry scanning, which involves more than ninety measurements of different parts of the hand. To detect forgery, dynamic signature identification has been developed; in this system, the specific dimensions of the pen strokes a person makes while writing his or her signature (including pressure, speed, and direction) are recorded and stored for later matching. This technology is prone to high false negative rates, however, because even though signatures are ubiquitous in daily transactions, only specific parts of a person's signature remain constant across every signing. Gait analysis, which focuses on people's unique walking patterns, is another type of biometric technique. Limitations to gait analysis include the fact that making gait measurements may be invasive; also, gait can be affected by injury or by a change in shoes.

Eric Metchik

Further Reading

Crompton, Malcolm. "Biometrics and Privacy: The End of the World as We Know It or the White Knight of Privacy?" In *Biometrics: Security and Authentication*. Sydney: Biometrics Institute, 2003. Presents psychological and sociological perspectives on the civil rights implications of increased use of biometrics.

Jain, Anil K., Arun Russ, and Sharath Pankanti. "Biometrics: A Tool for Information Security." *IEEE Transactions on Information Forensics and Security* 1, no. 2 (2006): 125-143. Provides a comprehensive technical analysis of several of the major biometric approaches.

Krishnan, K. N., with D. R. Berwick. *Developing a Police Perspective and Exploring the Use of Biometrics and Other Emerging Technologies as an Investigative Tool in Identity Crimes*. Payneham, S.Aust.: Australasian Centre for Policing Research, 2004. International review of basic biometric technology use includes recommendations for law-enforcement applications.

Mansfield, A. J., and J. L. Wayman. *Best Practices in Testing and Reporting Performance of Biometric Devices: Version 2.01*. Teddington, Middlesex, England: National Physical Laboratory, 2002. Emphasizes comparison of evaluation methodologies and data for the leading biometric instruments.

Mills, Kelly. "University Opts for Biometric Security." *Computerworld*, January 25, 2002, 3-4. Describes the adaptation of biometric technology to ensure the security of institutions of higher education.

Vacca, John R. *Biometric Technologies and Verification Systems*. Burlington, Mass.: Elsevier, 2007. Comprehensive, well-organized text includes discussion of how biometrics works, analysis of biometric data, and uses of biometric data.

See also: Airport security; Anthropometry; Biometric eye scanners; Biosensors; Brain-wave scanners; Ear prints; Electronic voice alteration; Facial recognition technology; Fingerprints; Integrated Automated Fingerprint Identification System; Iris recognition systems; National Institute of Justice; Voiceprints.

Biosensors

Definition: Devices that use biological molecules or cells to detect and measure chemicals, biological agents, or physical conditions and then use nonbiological components to convert the data into signals or readouts.

Significance: Biosensors have attracted a lot of interest for their potential in countering the use of chemical and biological weapons by terrorists and for their applications as on-site forensic analytical devices at crime scenes. Biosensors potentially offer sensitive and rapid detection of harmful organisms and substances in food and water supplies. Such instruments have demonstrated usefulness for measuring many substances that are of interest to forensic science, such as toxins, drugs of abuse, poisonous chemicals, and DNA.

Biosensor devices differ in the biological components they use for sensing chemicals. Examples are enzymes, antibodies, receptors, and whole

Research scientist Daniel P. Campbell holds a portable biosensor that he and his team developed at Georgia Tech in 2003 using parts from a CD player and a Webcam, among other items. The inexpensive device can be used to detect harmful chemical and biological agents in the field. *(AP/Wide World Photos)*

cells. The most common biological components used in biosensors are enzymes and antibodies. Different types of biological components result in different types of signals that must be converted into readouts.

Biosensors can be classified according to the ways in which the detection that is mediated by their biological components is converted into measurable signals. After the initial recognition of a chemical species by the biological component, a biosensor generates a readout signal in a process called transduction. At least five different kinds of transducers are used in biosensors: Amperometric transducers involve the movement of electrons resulting from a biorecognition event among three electrodes; potentiometric transducers exploit biological sensor-induced changes in the movement of ions, which results in the generation of an electric potential; thermal transducers utilize heat from biorecognition events that are endothermic reactions; optical transducers make use of the production or absorption of light resulting from biological recognition of detected chemicals or biological molecules; and piezoelectric transducers react to changes in mass produced by biological recognition of target chemicals or biological molecules.

The physical component of a biosensor's transducer, which is in contact with the biological sensor, may comprise electrodes, semiconductors, and optical constructions such as fiber optics and nanoparticles. Most biosensors use electrochemical types of transduction, such as amperometric and potentiometric methods, and enzymatic, antibody, or DNA biological recognition components.

Working and Organization

A biosensor contains an external and an internal interface. In the first step, at the external interface of the device, the substance being measured (analyte) binds with the biological recognition component of the biosensor. In the second step, at the internal interface, the biological recognition system interacts with the transducer component, and this produces a physical or chemical response. This response may involve the production of hydrogen ions, other ions, or electrons for amperometric, potentiometric, and conductimetric biosensors. A second type of transducer response may involve the biologically coupled production or absorption of light (fluorescence, chemiluminescence, or visible wavelength). A third type of transducer response would be a change in mass at the transducer such as occurs in piezoelectric (or microelectromechanical) systems. A fourth type of transducer response involves changes in temperature for thermal or calorimetric systems. The physical or chemical response produced by the transducer is processed and amplified to produce a readout signal that serves to indicate the presence and amount of a substance of interest.

Applications

Nanotechnology—that is, the application and study of the structuring and behavior of materials at nanometer scale—has also been used in making biosensors. Gold, cadmium selenide, and zinc selenide nanoparticles and single-walled carbon nanotubes are among the nanoscale substances that are being used to make biosensors to detect metal ions, biological molecules, and even viruses such as those responsible for strains of influenza (such as influenza A and the avian flu virus H5N1).

Challenges in the uses of biosensors arise from the need for small, portable devices, the inherent instability of most biological molecules and cells, and the need for highly sensitive devices that can measure a wide range of substances simultaneously. Biosensors used at crime scenes by forensic investigators and in national defense applications must perform reliably and produce quick results under field conditions. In the United States, in addition to their uses by law-enforcement personnel and by national security agencies for the detection and prevention of bioterrorist attacks, biosensors are used for environmental monitoring, for quality control during food processing and the processing of pharmaceuticals, and for monitoring of agriculture.

Oluseyi A. Vanderpuye

Further Reading

Cooper, Jon, and Tony Cass, eds. *Biosensors: A Practical Approach*. 2d ed. New York: Oxford University Press, 2004. Provides multidisciplinary coverage of biosensor research, construction, and operation, with descriptions of practical methods in the field.

Eggins, Brian R. *Biosensors: An Introduction*. New York: John Wiley & Sons, 1996. Offers an overview of the various classes of biosensors and describes the methods used in their manufacture.

Hall, Elizabeth A.H. *Biosensors*. Englewood Cliffs, N.J.: Prentice Hall, 1991. Provides an approachable introduction to the concepts behind biosensors as well as information on their construction and applications.

Kress-Rogers, Erika, ed. *Handbook of Biosensors and Electronic Noses: Medicine, Food, and the Environment*. Boca Raton, Fla.: CRC Press, 1997. Discusses both the design and the practical uses of biosensors. Includes informative figures and tables.

See also: Air and water purity; Biodetectors; Biological terrorism; Biological warfare diagnosis; Biological weapon identification; Immune system; Pathogen genomic sequencing; Toxicological analysis; Tularemia.

Bioterrorism. *See* Biological terrorism

Biotoxins

Definition: Toxic substances that originate from biological sources, including viruses, bacteria, fungi, algae, and plants.

Significance: Biocrimes present law-enforcement agencies with serious challenges, as the perpetrators of such crimes can use numerous pathogens that exist naturally and do not require sophisticated expertise or technology to prepare. Further, because the effects of biotoxins are as diverse as the substances' multiple origins, it can be difficult for investigators to ascertain the types of biotoxins employed in particular crimes or terrorist attacks.

The use of biological agents and their toxins in criminal acts and as weapons of war has a long history. In the Far East, opium was the poison used for murder and suicide for several centuries. In the fourteenth century, Mongol warriors used plague-infected bodies as weapons of war, triggering an outbreak that killed thousands. During the French and Indian War (1754-1763), the British approved a plan to distribute to Native American tribes blankets contaminated with smallpox. These examples, however, pale in comparison with the chilling prospects of modern bioterrorism aided by a rapidly expanding knowledge of biological agents, biotoxins, and their potential to wreak havoc in complex, interdependent societies.

Common Microbial Agents

Various microbes can be the sources of biotoxins, including viruses, bacteria, and fungi. It is relatively easy to propagate bacteria and fungi with small samples, but the propagation of viruses for use in biocrimes requires certain training and access to specific technologies. Some of the common viruses that produce devastating effects include smallpox, Ebola, and Marburg. Smallpox, a highly contagious virus, is transmitted easily and carries a high mortality rate. By the 1970's, a worldwide vaccination program had eradicated smallpox. Three decades later, only two places in the world still officially maintained live cultures of the virus: a laboratory of the Centers for Disease Control and Prevention (CDC) in the United States and a lab in Russia. The Ebola and Marburg viruses are also extremely lethal; both cause hemorrhagic fever and profuse bleeding from bodily orifices. No cure or effective treatments for either virus have yet been found.

Bacterial biotoxins include anthrax, botulism, plague, and tularemia. *Bacillus anthracis*, the bacterium that causes anthrax, produces spores that are extremely resistant to the environment and are highly infectious when inhaled. Botulism is caused by a potent neurotoxin produced by the bacterium *Clostridium botulinum*. Once inhaled or ingested, the toxin causes respiratory failure and paralysis. Plague is also highly contagious; it causes a type of pneumonia and can be fatal if not treated early. *Francisella tularensis* causes tularemia, a generally nonlethal disease that is extremely incapacitating; symptoms include weight loss, fever, and headaches.

Many fungi produce remarkable amounts of toxic secondary metabolites, some of which are toxins. Fungal toxins are grouped into two categories: mycotoxins, which are produced by common molds, and mushroom toxins, which are formed in the fleshy fruiting bodies of sac or club fungi. Mycotoxins are major contributing factors to many cases of food poisoning. Some mycotoxins, such as aflatoxins, are believed to be among the most potent known carcinogens. Ingestion of even minute amounts of aflatoxins over long periods of time through contaminated food can cause liver cancer. In 1974, hundreds of people were poisoned by aflatoxin-contaminated corn in India; more than one hundred died. Several members of the mushroom genus *Amanita* contain amanitin, one of the deadliest poisons found in nature. The poison contained in false morels, monomethyl hydrazine (MMH), can cause diarrhea, vomiting, and severe headaches; ingestion of this poison occasionally results in death.

Marine and Plant Biotoxins

Many plants produce poisonous secondary metabolites that induce toxic effects when the plants or their extracts are consumed. Although sensitivity to plant toxins may vary among individuals, a good correlation generally exists between the amount of poison ingested and the severity of the clinical symptoms. Some highly toxic substances derived from plants include ricin (derived from castor beans), aconitine (from monkshood), strychnine (from the vomit nut), and huratoxin (from jimsonweed, also known as thorn apple). Ricin has been employed as a murder weapon in many cultures. In South America, native tribes have long used various plants to prepare curare, a common name for a deadly poison used on the tips of arrows or darts.

Harmful algal blooms represent a real threat to virtually all U.S. coastal and fresh waters.

Potential impacts range from devastating economic effects to public health risks to ecosystem alterations. The phenomena commonly known as "red tides" produce extremely potent biotoxins. When such toxins accumulate in marine food chains, they cause mass mortalities of birds, fish, and marine mammals and often lead to closures of commercial and recreational fisheries. When humans accidentally consume seafood contaminated with algal toxins, illness develops and even death occurs in extreme cases. Two classes of algal toxins have been well studied: the paralytic shellfish poisoning (PSP) toxins and domoic acid, both of which act on nerve systems.

The Cow-Pock — or — the Wonderful Effects of the New Inoculation! — Vide. the Publications of ⅄ Anti-Vaccine Society.

Although smallpox is one of the most virulent and most easily transmitted viruses known to humankind, it was also one of the first biotoxins to be eradicated. During the 1790's, the British physician Edward Jenner developed a vaccine from material taken from infected cows that effectively protected people against smallpox. Despite the early success of Jenner's procedure, it was slow to win public acceptance. This British cartoon from 1802 caricatures a scene at a public hospital in which Jenner is vaccinating a frightened woman as cows emerge from the bodies of people already vaccinated. *(Library of Congress)*

Microbial Forensics

Criminal investigations involving biotoxins rely on forensic scientists who work in the cross-discipline known as microbial forensics. It can be challenging at times to distinguish symptoms and signs that may be caused by toxins from those that are just variants of normal health. Physicians and forensic scientists may not be able to recognize early symptoms associated with particular pathogens or biotoxins. Often, the identification of particular biotoxins requires the careful study of highly skilled professionals using sophisticated analytical instruments. Furthermore, confirmation of the presence of biological agents or toxins in evidence samples is generally not enough to guarantee conviction of a suspect without other supporting evidence.

Ming Y. Zheng

Further Reading

Beasley, Val Richard, et al. "Diagnostic and Clinically Important Aspects of Cyanobacterial (Blue-Green Algae) Toxicoses." *Journal of Veterinary Diagnostic Investigation* 1 (October, 1989): 359-365. Scholarly article focuses on the diagnosis of biotoxins in animals.

Breeze, Roger G., Bruce Budowle, and Steven E. Schutzer, eds. *Microbial Forensics.* Burlington, Mass.: Elsevier Academic Press, 2005. Reviews the relationships between microbe physiology and forensics.

Cooper, Marion R., Anthony W. Johnson, and Elizabeth A. Dauncey. *Poisonous Plants and Fungi: An Illustrated Guide.* 2d ed. London: TSO, 2003. Comprehensive volume describes the many varieties of poisonous plants and fungi.

Garrett, Laurie. *The Coming Plague: Newly Emerging Diseases in a World Out of Balance.* New York: Farrar, Straus and Giroux, 1994. Discusses the increase in outbreaks of infectious diseases in the late twentieth century as well as ways to prevent such outbreaks.

Nelson, Lewis S., Richard D. Shih, and Michael J. Balick. *Handbook of Poisonous and Injurious Plants.* 2d ed. New York: Springer, 2007. Provides useful information on many different plant biotoxins.

See also: Bacterial resistance and response to antibacterial agents; Biological terrorism; Biological warfare diagnosis; Biological weapon identification; Biological Weapons Convention of 1972; Botulinum toxin; Centers for Disease Control and Prevention; Chemical agents; Mycotoxins; Poisons and antidotes; Ricin; Smallpox; Toxicological analysis; Viral biology.

Bite-mark analysis

Definition: Examination and comparison of wounds caused by biting during physical attacks.

Significance: The bite marks analyzed by forensic scientists may include marks made by attackers on victims and marks made by victims on attackers. Also, in some cases, crime victims and the perpetrators of crimes leave bite marks on objects found at crime scenes. Bite-mark analysis can sometimes provide important physical evidence linking an offender to a victim or crime scene.

The reliability of the evidence resulting from bite-mark analysis depends greatly on the skill and experience of the forensic odontologist who conducts the analysis. The occurrence of bite marks in criminal cases is not common; when bite marks are found, they are seen most often in cases of violent sexual crimes or child abuse.

Procedures

When investigators suspect that a particular wound is a bite mark, they record every detail about it, including its appearance, color, location on the body, and size, and whether the bite seems to be human or animal. They also photograph the mark from all possible angles, laying a ruler alongside the mark in each photo to show both the mark's length and its width. If a ruler is not available, another object of known size, such as a coin, is included in the photographs to clarify the size of the mark.

If the indentation of the bite mark is suffi-

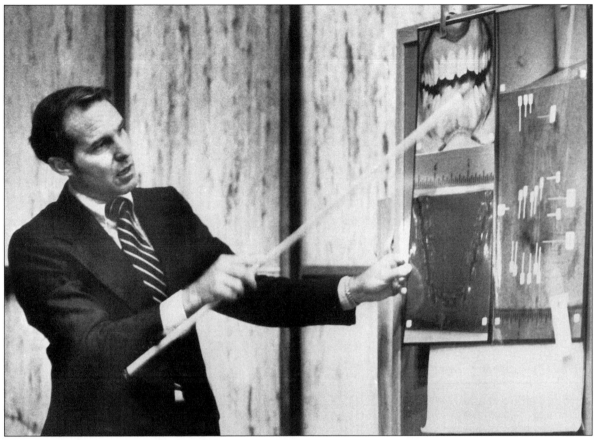

Forensic odontologist Dr. Richard Souviron points to an enlarged photograph of the teeth of accused murderer Ted Bundy during Bundy's murder trial in Miami, Florida. Souviron testified that only Bundy's teeth could have made the bite marks discovered on the body of one of the victims in the Chi Omega murder case. *(AP/Wide World Photos)*

cient, an impression is made of the mark before the skin is able to smooth over or change shape. Obtaining a good impression of a bite mark can be difficult, particularly if the skin was distorted before being bitten or the teeth slid across the skin while biting. The suspected bite-mark area is also wiped with sterile cotton swabs to collect any saliva or other evidence left behind by the biter that might yield DNA (deoxyribonucleic acid) for analysis; the swabs are placed in sterile tubes to preserve the evidence.

If a suspect has been identified, a dentist or forensic odontologist then makes an impression of the suspect's teeth. From this impression, a transparency or computer image of the bite mark that would be left by that suspect's teeth is created. The dentist also examines the suspect's

bone and muscle structure to determine if any unusual factors are present that would affect the suspect's bite. Also taken into account in the analysis of a suspect's bite are factors such as fillings, lost teeth, the curve of the teeth, and any spaces between teeth.

The American Board of Forensic Odontology has set specific guidelines regarding the presentation of bite-mark evidence in court. In testifying as expert witnesses regarding such evidence, forensic odontologists are held to the standard of "reasonable medical certainty," which means that they must be confident in their conclusions.

Questionable Evidence?

In a study conducted in 1999, a member of the American Board of Forensic Odontology found that bite-mark analyses wrongly identified the persons who made the bite marks about 63 percent of the time. This study concluded that bite-mark analysis is always subjective and that no standards are accepted across the forensic odontology field.

Some widely publicized cases of men wrongly convicted based at least in part on bite-mark evidence include those of Ray Krone, Roy Brown, and Ricky Amolsch. Krone was convicted of murdering a woman based on a bite mark on the victim's breast; he was later released when DNA evidence showed another man had left the bite mark. Brown was also convicted of murder but was freed after serving fifteen years in prison when DNA analysis of the saliva left in the bite marks on the murder victim showed that the saliva was not his. Based on the flawed testimony of a forensic dentist, Amolsch spent ten months in jail, during which time he lost his life savings, his home, and his children. He was freed when the work of the same dentist was called into question in another case involving bite-mark evidence.

Marianne M. Madsen

Ted Bundy and Bite Marks

When the infamous serial rapist and murderer Ted Bundy was finally convicted, his conviction owed a great deal to bite-mark analysis. During the attack and murder of two young women at Florida State University, distinctive bite marks were left on the breast and buttocks of one of the women. After Bundy was arrested and charged with the murders, investigators asked Bundy to submit to the making of a dental impression for a forensic odontologist to use for comparison with the bite marks. Bundy refused, but the investigators were given a search warrant to get Bundy's dental impression in any way possible, as he was suspected of attempting to grind his teeth in a way that would eventually make a match impossible. Dr. Richard Souviron, a dentist, took photos of Bundy's teeth and gums, noting that he had an unusually uneven bite pattern that could improve the likelihood of matching his teeth to bite marks.

At Bundy's trial, Souviron was able to show how the bite marks matched Bundy's unusual teeth. During his testimony, Souviron placed a transparent overlay showing an impression of Bundy's bite mark on top of an enlarged photograph of the bite mark left on the victim's buttock, leaving no doubt in the minds of the jurors that Bundy had left the mark. Souviron had an unusual amount of evidence with which to work: The attacker had bit, turned sideways, and bit again. These two bite marks left plenty of evidence to match with Bundy's teeth, and he was convicted and sentenced to death.

Further Reading

Bowers, C. Michael. *Forensic Dental Evidence: An Investigator's Handbook*. San Diego, Calif.: Elsevier Academic Press, 2004. Discusses the management of dental evidence, including the collection and documentation of bite-mark evidence.

Dorion, Robert B. J., ed. *Bitemark Evidence*. New York: Marcel Dekker, 2005. Focuses on the anatomy and physiology of bite marks and on the process of bite-mark analysis. Includes information on landmark cases involving bite-mark evidence.

Johansen, Raymond J., and C. Michael Bowers. *Digital Analysis of Bite Mark Evidence*. Santa Barbara, Calif.: Forensic Imaging Institute, 2000. Hands-on reference book for forensic scientists discusses how to use and understand digital photography and computer imaging in bite-mark analysis.

Libal, Angela. *Fingerprints, Bite Marks, Ear Prints: Human Signposts*. Philadelphia: Mason Crest, 2006. Brief work discusses bite marks along with other types of evidence that may be found at crime scenes and used to identify suspects.

See also: Animal evidence; Child abuse; Crime scene documentation; Crime scene measurement; DNA analysis; DNA fingerprinting; Evidence processing; Forensic odontology; Innocence Project; Rape kit; Saliva; Tool marks.

Blast seat

Definition: Point of detonation of an explosive device.

Significance: The blast seat is generally the area that suffers the most damage when an explosion takes place. It is very important that the investigators at an explosion scene locate the blast seat, because that area provides many clues about the nature of the explosion.

After an explosion, prompt identification of the blast seat (also known as the seat of explosion, blast hole, or epicenter) makes it possible for investigators to locate evidence quickly and to determine the type of explosion that occurred. The type of crater formed at the blast seat depends on the type and quantity of explosives used, how the device was placed, and whether the explosives were in a container, such as in a pipe. Depending on the magnitude of the explosion and the amount of explosives used, the process of finding the crater can be easy or difficult.

Blast seats are characterized as either point source, such as when a large crater is produced, or diffuse. This characterization is one of the most important determinations for investigators to make when a major explosion occurs, because it can provide information about what caused the blast, such as whether the explosive materials were concentrated or dispersed. A concentrated explosive will typically excavate

An agent of the U.S. Bureau of Alcohol, Tobacco and Firearms measures the crater at the blast seat of a pipe-bomb explosion that took place at Centennial Olympic Park in Atlanta, Georgia, on July 27, 1996, while Atlanta was hosting the Summer Olympic Games. *(AP/ Wide World Photos)*

the blast seat and form a crater. In fact, a distinct crater is usually a very good indication that an explosive device was used. In such a case, thermal imaging cameras can detect a thermal effect surrounding the blast seat. Other types of explosions, such as those that are caused by fuel gas, vapors, or dust explosives, do not produce craters or have definite blast seats. With dispersed explosives, a thermal effect near the immediate blast seat is also absent.

The type of surface on which an explosion takes place can affect the blast seat that forms. When an explosion occurs on the ground, dirt, rock, and other debris are blasted out to form a crater. These materials land near the top of the crater, with some rock and debris falling back into the crater. When a blast is caused by large amounts of explosives, the debris that falls back into the crater can cover it completely, making it difficult for investigators to find the blast seat. Explosions that take place on hard surfaces such as concrete also produce craters, but these are generally not as deep as the craters formed by explosions on open ground.

C. J. Walsh

Further Reading

Beveridge, Alexander, ed. *Forensic Investigation of Explosions*. New York: Taylor & Francis, 1998.

Ellis, John W. *Police Analysis and Planning for Homicide Bombings: Prevention, Defense, and Response*. Springfield, Ill.: Charles C Thomas, 2007.

Horswell, John, ed. *The Practice of Crime Scene Investigation*. Boca Raton, Fla.: CRC Press, 2004.

National Institute of Justice. *A Guide for Explosion and Bombing Scene Investigation*. Washington, D.C.: Author, 2000.

Thurman, James T. *Practical Bomb Scene Investigation*. Boca Raton, Fla.: CRC Press, 2006.

See also: Bomb damage assessment; Bombings; Bureau of Alcohol, Tobacco, Firearms and Explosives; Crime scene investigation; National Church Arson Task Force; Oklahoma City bombing; Structural analysis; World Trade Center bombing.

Blood agents

Definition: Chemical agents that affect the body by being absorbed into the blood.

Significance: Forensic investigators must be aware of the signs and symptoms of the presence of blood agents when these chemical substances are involved in homicides or other deaths. The possibility that such agents may be used in terrorist attacks is also of concern to law-enforcement agencies.

Chemical agents are toxic substances that are classified by their primary sites of effect; blood agents are thus chemical agents that exert their primary effects in the blood. Known blood agents are either cyanide- or arsenic-based. Examples of cyanide-based blood agents include hydrogen cyanide and cyanogen chloride. Arsine is an example of an arsenic-based blood agent.

Characteristics

Blood agents are fast-acting, potentially deadly chemicals. Cyanide can be a highly volatile colorless gas, such as hydrogen cyanide or cyanogen chloride, or can exist in crystal forms, such as sodium or potassium cyanide. Cyanogen chloride is slightly less volatile than hydrogen cyanide. Arsine exists as a colorless gas. As gases, blood agents are lighter than air and quickly dissipate. Consequently, these agents are more toxic in confined areas than in open areas.

Blood agents typically have a slight odor detectable at higher concentrations. Cyanide gas, for example, may have a smell of peach kernels or bitter almonds, but the odor can be faint and many people cannot detect it—only about half of all persons have the ability to smell cyanide gas. Arsine has a mild garlic odor that can be detected only at concentrations greater than those that are fatal.

Exposure Routes

Blood agents are difficult to detect, volatile, and fast-acting, features that render such compounds potentially useful in chemical warfare. When these agents are used as chemical weapons, they are typically disseminated as aerosols, and inhalation is one of the deadliest exposure routes.

Cyanide occurs naturally in the environment, and small amounts are present in certain foods and in cigarette smoke. Both cyanide and arsine are used in various manufacturing processes, so some people may be exposed at their workplaces. Cyanide is present in the chemicals used to make paper, textiles, and plastics and to develop photographs; it is also used in metallurgy, electroplating, and mining. Because cyanide gas can be released when synthetic fabrics and polyurethane burn, cyanide poisoning may contribute to fire-related deaths.

Cyanide gas has been used to exterminate pests. Arsine, which was developed initially as an insecticide, is used in the manufacture of computer chips. Arsine gas forms when arsenic encounters an acid, and most common reports of arsine exposure have resulted from accidental formation of arsine in the workplace.

Effects

Blood agents poison the blood quickly and can result in very rapid death. Often, powerful gasping for breath occurs, followed by violent convulsions. Death from cyanide poisoning is painful, and it takes a few minutes to die from blood agent poisoning.

Blood agents are taken into the body either by ingestion or by inhalation. Cyanide-based blood agents irritate the eyes and respiratory tract. Arsine, in contrast, is nonirritating. Respiratory failure is usually the cause of death. Blood agents interfere with oxygen utilization at the cellular level by preventing exchange of oxygen and carbon dioxide between blood and tissues, causing cells to suffocate from lack of oxygen. Arsine works by damaging red blood cells, which also impairs the ability of cells to deliver oxygen throughout the body. The lack of oxygen to tissues and cells can quickly lead to death unless the victim is immediately removed from the toxic atmosphere.

Symptoms of blood agent exposure depend on concentration and duration. Breathing in or ingesting very small amounts of cyanide may have no effects, whereas exposure to somewhat higher concentrations may result in dizziness, weakness, and nausea. If removed from exposure, the person generally will begin to feel better. Over time, exposure to low concentrations can produce mild symptoms followed by permanent brain damage and muscle paralysis. Moderate exposure can result in headache, dizziness, and nausea, symptoms that can last for several hours, and may be followed by convulsions and possible coma. Higher concentrations or longer exposure may also result in convulsions and coma. With very high concentrations, severe toxic effects begin in seconds, and death occurs rapidly.

Detecting Blood Agents as Causes of Death

Because blood agents prevent adequate utilization of oxygen, the blood of persons exposed to these chemicals is a rich red rather than blue-red. Cyanogen chloride injures the respiratory tract, which results in severe congestion and inflammation in the lung. A smell of bitter almonds may be detected. The presence of thiocyanate or cyanide in the blood can also be used to detect cyanide poisoning. Arsine may leave a garlic smell on the victim's breath, but no specific tests have been developed to determine arsine poisoning.

C. J. Walsh

Blood Agents in Chemical Warfare

The cyanide-based blood agents hydrogen cyanide and cyanogen chloride were studied extensively as potential chemical weapons and used sporadically during World War I. In practice, these compounds were rarely used in military situations because their effectiveness was limited by quick dispersion. Arsine was considered as a potential warfare agent during World War I, but because of the substance's high volatility and chemical instability, weaponization of arsine was abandoned, and arsine has never been used in chemical warfare. During World War II, Nazi Germany used hydrogen cyanide, under the name Zyklon B, as a genocidal agent. Hydrogen cyanide gas, along with other chemical agents, may also have been used during the Iran-Iraq War (1980-1988).

Further Reading

Crippen, James B. *Explosives and Chemical Weapons Identification*. Boca Raton, Fla.: CRC Press, 2005. Provides useful information for first responders on identifying chemical weapons.

Ellison, D. Hank. *Handbook of Chemical and Biological Warfare Agents*. 2d ed. Boca Raton, Fla.: CRC Press, 2007. Excellent reference source for information on agents used in chemical and biological warfare, including blood agents.

Hoenig, Steven L. *Compendium of Chemical Warfare Agents*. New York: Springer, 2007. Describes and discusses the use of various agents that may be employed in chemical warfare, including how they can be identified at scenes of release and in the laboratory.

Wecht, Cyril H., ed. *Forensic Aspects of Chemical and Biological Terrorism*. Tucson, Ariz.: Lawyers & Judges Publishing, 2004. Resource designed for personnel involved in public health and safety includes discussion of the symptoms of chemical exposure.

See also: Blood residue and bloodstains; Chemical agents; Chemical terrorism; Chemical warfare; Chemical Weapons Convention of 1993; Crime scene cleaning; Nerve agents; Presumptive tests for blood.

Blood residue and bloodstains

Definition: Wet or dry remnants and areas of discoloration on surfaces resulting from the shedding of blood.

Significance: Analysis of bloodstains and other blood residue found at a crime scene can help investigators identify objects used as weapons, reconstruct the events that took place at the scene, and link suspects to the crime.

Blood consists principally of plasma and blood cells. Plasma is the yellowish fluid that carries suspended blood cells called erythrocytes and leukocytes. Erythrocytes, commonly known as red blood cells, get their color from the hemoglobin that carries oxygen from the lungs to the organs and periphery of the body. Mammalian red blood cells do not have nuclei and do not contain DNA (deoxyribonucleic acid), but they do have antigens on their outer membranes that can be used to type the blood. Leukocytes, commonly known as white blood cells, do contain nuclei and do contain DNA that is unique to an individual (with the exception of identical twins, who carry identical DNA); this DNA can be isolated and characterized to identify the source of the blood.

Because blood accounts for 8 percent of a healthy person's weight, typically 5 liters (a little more than 5 quarts), and it circulates near the surface of the skin, almost all kinds of trauma to the body result in the loss of blood. At crime scenes, blood's red color generally makes it readily apparent; in cases where attempts have been made to remove it, residues are difficult to eliminate completely. Blood residue has been identified on 100,000-year-old stone tools, and bloodstains left by Confederate soldiers wounded at the Battle of Gettysburg in 1863 have been recovered from between the floorboards of an attic where the soldiers had been hiding.

Examining a Crime Scene

A dried, but relatively fresh, bloodstain is generally reddish-brown in color and glossy. The gloss eventually disappears under the action of sunlight, wet weather, or attempts to remove the stain, and the color turns gray. The color and gloss of blood may also be affected by the surface on which it is found.

At a crime scene, investigators' search for bloodstains is facilitated by the use of flashlights, which are held so that the light falls at an angle to the surfaces being examined. Presumptive tests for blood are sometimes used when small quantities of fluids suspected to be blood are present, especially if it appears that an attempt has been made to clean the area; these tests are also used to differentiate blood from other stains, such as rust, ketchup, or chocolate syrup.

A crime scene search for blood extends beyond the immediate area of the crime, because bloody fingerprints may have been left in other areas, such as on doorknobs, drawers, or sinks. Towels, draperies, or other fabrics may have been used to wipe blood off hands. If a floor has been cleaned, blood may be found in the cracks or joints in the floor or under the edges of carpets or linoleum. Investigators must search clothing at the scene carefully; even clothes that have been cleaned can contain blood residue in seams or linings, or inside sleeves or pockets. Persons who were present at the scene during the crime may also have bloodstains on their bodies.

Compared with indoor crime scenes, crime scenes that are open to the elements pose many more difficulties for the search for blood. Blood residues may have been obliterated by the weather or may have changed color in contact with soil. At outdoor crime scenes, investigators need to pay special attention to damp areas on the ground and to surfaces such as blades of grass, leaves, and tree branches.

Description and Recording of Bloodstains

Crime scene investigators record descriptions of all bloodstains found, including information on their forms, colors, sizes, and positions. Information on the physical appearance of bloodstains is best preserved through photography; photographs are usually taken at wide range, medium range, and close up. A scale is included in all close-up shots to show the sizes of the bloodstains or drops pictured.

A rough sketch of the crime scene is also often created to show the relationship of the bloodstains and other blood residue to other elements of the scene. At violent crime scenes, blood spatter evidence is often present, and its analysis can be invaluable in reconstructing how the crime occurred.

Collection and Preservation

After crime scene bloodstain patterns and distribution have been well documented, the collection and preservation of blood residue and stains may proceed. Because these substances present the possibility of blood-borne disease, such as hepatitis or human immunodeficiency

virus (HIV), investigators must be careful to protect themselves from infection. Also, they must take proper care to avoid contaminating the scene or cross-contaminating the samples collected. For collecting blood and other biological samples, investigators wear multiple layers of latex gloves, which they change frequently. Clean equipment is also essential to prevent contamination.

Blood is fragile, and to maintain its properties, investigators must ensure that blood evidence samples are properly preserved. If wet or damp bloodstains are stored in airtight containers, the blood will putrefy and be useless for forensic examination in a matter of days. In contrast, air-dried samples stored at room temperature or, better, under refrigeration will retain their usefulness for a much longer period.

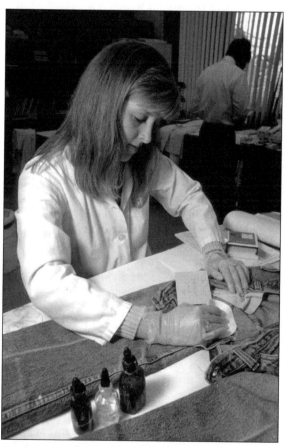

A technician performs a bloodstain analysis in the New Jersey State Police crime laboratory in Totowa. (*Custom Medical Stock Photo*)

Ideally, biological samples should be stored in a frozen state, especially if they cannot be analyzed immediately.

Wet blood may be collected with a sterile disposable pipette or syringe and placed in a tube containing an anticoagulant to keep it from clotting any further. Alternatively, wet blood may be collected from pools of liquid blood with pieces of absorbent material such as filter paper, cotton fabric, or cotton-tipped applicators. Each swab with absorbed blood is placed inside a clean, unstoppered tube to permit it to air-dry. With large bloodstained items, such as carpets or mattresses, investigators may cut out bloodstained areas to transport them to the lab for analysis. As with all evidence collected at a crime scene, each sample must be clearly labeled with information on who collected it and when.

An investigator may collect dried blood by scraping the surface on which it is found with a clean razor blade, scalpel, or pocketknife, placing the scrapings in a clean tube. If dried blood cannot be scraped, it may be collected with a fabric swab or cotton-tipped applicator moistened with distilled water (or saline solution). The area of interest is swabbed, and the sample is placed in a clean tube that is left unstoppered to allow the swab to air-dry. The investigator swabs an unaffected area nearby as well, to provide a control sample for analysis. Bloodstains may also be "lifted" using gel lifter or fingerprint tape if it is determined that the gel or tape will not interfere with subsequent tests.

Bloodstained clothing and other items, such as possible weapons, that can be transported from the scene are often best submitted to the laboratory whole for analysis. Investigators generally air-dry such objects and pack them in wrapping paper or paper bags for transport. They should never be tightly rolled or stored in plastic bags, as this may result in cross-contamination.

Blood Typing

If presumptive tests indicate the presence of blood at a crime scene, further tests are performed to establish whether it is of human or animal origin. Reaction to appropriate antibody serum definitely establishes the species of origin. In addition, the blood group to which a hu-

man blood sample belongs can be established. Although more than twenty-nine human blood group systems are known, the ABO and Rh (or rhesus) groups are commonly used. With respect to the former, blood may be typed as A, B, AB, or O, characterized by the presence of antigen A, antigen B, both antigens, or neither antigen on the surface of red blood cells, respectively. With respect to the Rh group, a sample is either positive or negative for Rh antigen. A person's blood type is inherited and hence unchangeable. Although ABO and Rh blood group analysis does not link a sample to a particular person, it can enable investigators to include or exclude a person of interest as a suspect or victim. Because blood group antigens deteriorate with age or improper storage, samples that have not been collected and stored with care often cannot be typed.

Blood also contains DNA, however, which is less subject to deterioration. Given that DNA testing of bloodstains and other blood residues can provide positive identification of the source of the blood, law-enforcement agencies around the world rely on DNA analysis of any blood and other biological samples recovered from crime scenes.

James L. Robinson

Further Reading

Fisher, Barry A. J. *Techniques of Crime Scene Investigation.* 7th ed. Boca Raton, Fla.: CRC Press, 2004. Standard text in the field includes a chapter on blood and other biological evidence.

Geberth, Vernon J. *Practical Homicide Investigation: Tactics, Procedures, and Forensic Techniques.* 4th ed. Boca Raton, Fla.: CRC Press, 2006. Text used in many U.S. police academies provides full coverage of all aspects of homicide investigations, including the collection of blood evidence.

Lee, Henry C., Timothy Palmbach, and Marilyn T. Miller. *Henry Lee's Crime Scene Handbook.* San Diego, Calif.: Academic Press, 2001. Practical guide to crime scene procedures includes a section on the collection, preservation, and analysis of blood.

Tilstone, William J., Kathleen A. Savage, and Leigh A. Clark. *Forensic Science: An Encyclo-*

pedia of History, Methods, and Techniques. Santa Barbara, Calif.: ABC-CLIO, 2006. Comprehensive work covers the role of blood analysis in forensic investigations, including blood groups, bloodstain identification, blood spatter analysis, and presumptive tests for blood.

See also: Biohazard bags; Blood agents; Blood spatter analysis; Blood volume testing; Control samples; Crime scene cleaning; Crime scene investigation; Crime scene protective gear; Crime scene search patterns; DNA typing; Luminol; Multisystem method; Petechial hemorrhage; Presumptive tests for blood; Trace and transfer evidence.

Blood spatter analysis

Definition: Application of the principles of projectile motion to the examination of patterns of human bloodstains.

Significance: By analyzing bloodstain patterns (blood spatter) found at crime scenes, forensic scientists can determine such details of crimes as where victims were located when they received the wounds that produced the blood spatter, whether victims were standing or seated when the wounds were inflicted, and even sometimes whether the assailants wielded the weapons in their right or left hands.

Blood spatter analysis is a valuable tool of forensic investigators in the determination of the events that transpired during crimes in which victims received wounds that resulted in bloodstains. Investigators can apply the physical principles of the motion of blood through the air to the patterns of blood droplets found at crime scenes, as well as the droplets' overall shapes, to ascertain the exact locations where victims' wounds were received.

Blood Spatter Ballistics

Blood is a fluid of constant density that is not affected by temperature, pressure, or other at-

mospheric conditions when it is in flight. The large surface tension of blood drops holds them together during their time of flight, and as they move through the air, the drops assume a spherical shape. Blood spatter patterns are influenced by the distance the blood travels through the air and the material with which it comes in contact.

A blood drop that falls straight down from its ejection point will project a circular stain on the material that absorbs it. In contrast, a blood drop that travels an extended distance from the source of the wound will follow a parabolic path, striking any surface it meets at an angle. When this angle of impact is not 90 degrees measured with respect to the horizontal surface (which would be a straight-down motion), the blood drop will leave an elongated (elliptical-shape) stain on the surface that it strikes. The more pointed end of the stain will be in the direction the blood drop was traveling.

Analysis of Blood Spatter

The patterns of bloodstains observed on surfaces provide evidence of the points of impact of wounds and the force of the punctures. Crime scene investigators can use the directionality of bloodstain patterns to work backward toward the two-dimensional point on the surface level with the blood spatter to identify the point of ejection and distance from the wound. (Given that the pointed ends of blood drops indicate the direction of travel, the more rounded ends converge toward the point of origin.) In the early days of blood spatter analysis, crime scene investigators laid out series of strings or wooden rods in the diverging direction of a blood spatter pattern to determine the convergent point. Modern forensic tools include computer software packages that use the data of the coordinates of blood spatter to determine the point of emergence of the blood drops.

In addition to the two-dimensional determination of the victim's position when the injury occurred, the blood spatter analyst can estimate the vertical position of the wound from the angle of impact of the blood spatter. This can provide evidence in terms of whether the victim was standing, sitting, or lying down at the time of the injury. In examining a bloodstain, a forensic

North Carolina State Bureau of Investigation agent Duane Deaver, a blood spatter expert, testifies during the murder trial of author Michael Peterson, explaining how tests of blood spatters found inside Peterson's home strengthened his opinion that Peterson's wife was beaten to death and did not die as the result of a fall, as Peterson claimed. In October, 2003, Peterson was found guilty and was sentenced to life in prison without the possibility of parole. *(AP/Wide World Photos)*

investigator measures its length and width. The angle of impact is then determined by the trigonometric relation involving the sine of the angle:

$$Sin(a) = w/l,$$

where w is the width of the bloodstain, l is its length, and a is the angle of impact. Solving this equation for the angle a (inverse sine) can determine where above the surface level the wound was inflicted. Using the results from the two-dimensional analysis that identifies how far away the victim was from the blood spatter pattern, the analyst can use this equation to solve for the height (third coordinate) where the point of puncture occurred. (In actuality, this can determine only the maximum height the victim was at the moment the wound occurred, because the action of gravity tends to change the shape of the blood's trajectory from straight-line motion.)

Analysis of bloodstains that are determined to have come from the tip of a weapon, such as a knife, can provide another kind of evidence. Passive bloodstains are drops caused only by the action of gravity, with no external force projecting the droplets forward. Such blood spatter appears as small circular drops. If these drops show a rotational sense (that is, if they curve either right or left), this directionality can indicate which of the assailant's hands the weapon was in at the time of the assault, providing information on whether the attacker was right-handed or left-handed.

Obstacles to Useful Analysis

The major problem faced by forensic scientists attempting to conduct blood spatter analysis is that many crime scenes lack well-defined blood spatter patterns even when blood is present. Difficulties may arise because of the effects of blood on different surfaces, because smaller blood droplets have broken off from larger droplets, because the victim moved after the injury and disturbed the initial spatter pattern, or simply because of the overall chaos of an environment where a violent crime has been committed. In such cases, often the only substantive evidence that can be gained from bloodstains involves identification of victims and possibly assailants through the blood types found at the crime scene and through analysis of DNA (deoxyribonucleic acid) extracted from the blood found.

Joseph Di Rienzi

Further Reading

Adams, Thomas F., Alan G. Caddell, and Jeffery L. Krutsinger. *Crime Scene Investigation.* 2d ed. Upper Saddle River, N.J.: Prentice Hall, 2004. Handbook for law-enforcement professionals includes a chapter titled "Evidence Collection" that has an informative section on blood and blood analysis.

Bennett, Wayne W., and Kären M. Hess. *Criminal Investigation.* 8th ed. Belmont, Calif.: Wadsworth/Thomson Learning, 2007. Comprehensive textbook provides in-depth discussion of forensic techniques and procedures. Includes checklists and questions at the ends of chapters to highlight the most important ideas presented.

Camenson, Blythe. *Opportunities in Forensic Science Careers.* Chicago: VGM Career Books, 2001. Presents accounts of professionals working in forensic science and identifies the education needed and the job responsibilities related to various disciplines within forensics.

James, Stuart H., and Jon J. Nordby, eds. *Forensic Science: An Introduction to Scientific and Investigative Techniques.* 2d ed. Boca Raton, Fla.: CRC Press, 2005. Comprehensive introductory textbook uses many case studies to illustrate crime investigation methodologies. Includes a section on recognition of bloodstain patterns.

Nickell, Joe, and John F. Fischer. *Crime Science: Methods of Forensic Detection.* Lexington: University Press of Kentucky, 1999. Very thorough examination of forensic investigative work includes discussion of blood spatter analysis.

See also: Ballistics; Biohazard bags; Blood residue and bloodstains; Blood volume testing; Crime scene investigation; Crime scene sketching and diagramming; Defensive wounds; Gunshot wounds; Knife wounds; Luminol; Presumptive tests for blood; Puncture wounds; Serology; Simpson murder trial.

Blood volume testing

Definition: Technique used to determine how much blood has been shed at crime scenes and accident scenes.

Significance: Forensic examiners can learn much about the wounds inflicted on victims of crimes from the volume of blood found at crime scenes. Blood volume testing may also be used to determine whether wounds were inflicted on victims at locations other than where the victims were ultimately found.

When blood is present at a crime or accident scene, a forensic team attempts to collect the blood or at least to determine how much blood was spilled at the scene. The human body generally contains about 5 liters (a little more than 5 quarts) of blood, but this amount is affected by factors such as body size and amount of fat tissue. The volume of blood present at a crime scene—and, sometimes, the blood spatter pattern—can inform investigators as to the types, depths, and seriousness of the wounds that caused the blood loss. Blood volume testing may also help to determine whether a victim has been moved—that is, if the amount of blood found at the scene is not consistent with the victim's loss of blood, it is likely the victim was moved after the wounds were inflicted.

Any blood present at a crime scene is collected (or collection is at least attempted) and sent to a forensic laboratory for typing and identification. Fresh blood is collected in plastic containers. Dried blood may be collected in various ways: Fabrics with dried bloodstains may be transported to the lab, and sticky tape, such as fingerprint tape, may be used to peel spots of dried blood away from hard surfaces. Dried blood may also be collected with swabs or pieces of sterile cloth that have been moistened with distilled water or saline solution.

At the laboratory, a forensic scientist can estimate the blood volume found at the crime scene by determining how many red blood cells are present in the collected blood and then calculating how much whole blood would contain that many red blood cells. Alternatively, the scientist can determine how much plasma was left behind and calculate a blood volume from that figure.

When no body or victim is found at a crime scene where blood is present, knowing the volume of blood shed at the scene can help investigators determine what kind of wound was inflicted; for example, a minor cut produces only a small volume of blood, whereas a deep stab wound or an arterial puncture is likely to produce copious amounts of blood. A blood volume test can also help determine how much time was necessary for the amount of blood present to be left behind.

Marianne M. Madsen

Further Reading

Geberth, Vernon J. *Practical Homicide Investigation: Tactics, Procedures, and Forensic Techniques*. 4th ed. Boca Raton, Fla.: CRC Press, 2006.

Genge, N. E. *The Forensic Casebook: The Science of Crime Scene Investigation*. New York: Ballantine, 2002.

Platt, Richard. *Crime Scene: The Ultimate Guide to Forensic Science*. New York: Dorling Kindersley, 2003.

See also: Blood residue and bloodstains; Blood spatter analysis; Crime scene investigation; Crime scene search patterns; Crime scene sketching and diagramming; Presumptive tests for blood.

Bloody Sunday

Date: January 30, 1972

The Event: During a civil rights march in the Roman Catholic section of Londonderry, Northern Ireland, British army troops shot twenty-six marchers, thirteen of whom died immediately. A fourteenth shooting victim died several months later.

Significance: One of the most significant episodes in the long, violent conflict between the Catholic and Protestant factions in Northern Ireland, Bloody Sunday was met with outrage in both local and international communities and led to a dramatic increase in support for the Irish Republican Army (IRA) in Northern Ireland. Meanwhile, in response to charges that the British soldiers had fired without provocation, the British government quickly launched an investigation to determine who had fired the first shots. The official report that came from the investigation exonerated the soldiers, but its findings were criticized because of the commission's questionable handling of forensic evidence.

Two days after the Bloody Sunday shootings, the British parliament ordered an investigation under Baron Widgery, the lord chief justice of England and Wales. The report of the Widgery Tribunal supported the account of the event given by the army, which claimed that marchers began the incident by firing weapons and hurling explosives at the soldiers. The evidence considered by the tribunal included the results of paraffin tests used to identify bullet-lead residues from the weapons that fired the fatal shots, along with nail bombs that had been recovered from one of the bodies. Preliminary tests for traces of explosives on the clothes of all but one of the victims of the shootings proved negative. The clothes of the remaining victim could not be tested as they had already been compromised by careless handling. The report offered no analyses of the individual shots fired by the soldiers.

The Bloody Sunday massacre intensified the campaign of the Provisional Irish Republican

Army (PIRA) against British occupation of Northern Ireland and helped to win more public support for PIRA among Roman Catholics. The massacre helped to aggravate two decades of anti-British rioting in Northern Ireland and attacks on British economic targets and social institutions.

The findings of the Widgery Tribunal remained controversial in the 1990's. In 1998, British prime minister Tony Blair ordered the formation of a second commission of inquiry to reevaluate evidence from Bloody Sunday. Assembled under the chairmanship of Lord Saville, the new commission completed its hearings in November, 2004. Although the full report of the Saville Inquiry was not published as late as mid-2008, it is considered to be a more comprehensive study than that of the Widgery Tribunal. Its evidence, which included witness testimonies from local residents, soldiers, journalists, and politicians, appears to call into question the credibility of the Widgery Tribunal's report. At the center of the controversy is the new report's finding that forensic evidence collected from shooting victims' bodies may have been contaminated when bodies of shooting victims were placed alongside weapons and explosives. That finding appears to contradict the original report's conclusion that trace evidence found on the bodies indicated that the shooting victims had themselves used firearms or explosives.

Investigations

The march that ended in the Bloody Sunday shootings began as a protest rally organized in Londonderry by the Northern Ireland Civil Rights Association to demand an end to the internment without trial of suspected IRA terrorists. Reports of the number of participants in the march are conflicting. Some observers estimated there were twenty thousand marchers; however, the Widgery Report estimated there were only three to five thousand marchers.

The marchers initially walked toward the Bogside area of Londonderry (which is also known as Derry). There, local residents joined the protest, and the marchers were redirected to another street to avoid army blockades. A planned highlight of the march was to have been a speech by the Irish nationalist Bernadette Devlin, who then held a Northern Ireland seat in Great Britain's Parliament. Around 3:30 P.M., however, a small number of young men began throwing stones and hurling insults at troops manning the army barricades that had been erected to contain the march. The troops initially responded with tear gas grenades, fire hoses, and rubber bullets. When the paratroopers began crossing the barricades to arrest demonstrators, they met such strong resistance that they feared for their own safety and began firing real bullets into the crowd. Within twenty minutes, thirteen young, unarmed men were dead. At least eighteen other people were seriously injured. The paratroopers later justified their actions by claiming that they had been fired on, but evidence in support of their claim was controversial.

Pallbearers carry one of thirteen coffins of Bloody Sunday victims during a funeral in Derry, Northern Ireland, on February 2, 1972. About ten thousand people shared in the funeral services for those killed by British army troops. *(AP/Wide World Photos)*

Forensic Issues

The central question in the Bloody Sunday massacre that remains to be resolved is whether the solders who shot the marchers were attacked by firearms and nail bombs before they began shooting into the marchers. The weight of known evidence says no. Eyewitness accounts by civilians do not support that finding; no soldiers were injured during the confrontation, and no civilian firearms were found. Additionally, the initial investigation into the shootings found no conclusive proof that the marchers who were shot had even handled firearms. Moreover, there was no evidence that the Irish Republican Army was then planning to provoke the British military. Nevertheless, the initial investigation did not call eyewitnesses and did not take testimony from survivors. The investigation's interpretation of forensic evidence was believed to be inaccurate and incomplete. Nonetheless, Lord Widgery concluded from the traces of firearm residue found on the bodies of the men who had been shot to death that some of them, at least, had been in close contact with firearms or explosives.

Elizabeth K. Hayden

Further Reading

Coates, Tim. *Bloody Sunday: Lord Widgery's Report 1972.* London: Stationary Office Books, 2001. Reprints the report of the first government commission to investigate the shootings.

Dunn, Seamus, ed. *Facets of the Conflict in Northern Ireland.* New York: St. Martin's Press, 1995. Collection of scholarly articles highlights fundamentals of politics in Northern Ireland. Selected authors—funded by the Centre for the Study of Conflict, University of Ulster—address the social, legal, political, and economic ramifications of the events that have shaped Irish history.

Hayes, Patrick Joseph, and Jim Campbell. *Bloody Sunday: Trauma, Pain, and Politics.* Ann Arbor, Mich.: Pluto Press, 2005. Covers the political and psychological aspects of the incident. Based on interviews with families of those killed by British soldiers.

Holland, Jack. *Hope Against History: The Course of Conflict in Northern Ireland.* New York: Henry Holt, 1999. Engaging narrative covers the origins of IRA and loyalist paramilitary groups, the events of Bloody Sunday, the Northern Ireland civil rights movement, and attempts to settle the conflict. Illuminates the experiences of both Protestant and Catholic communities in Northern Ireland.

McClean, Raymond. *The Road to Bloody Sunday.* 2d ed. Londonderry, Northern Ireland: Guildhall Press, 1997. Presents the eyewitness account of a medical doctor who treated shooting victims on Bloody Sunday.

Mullan, Don, and John Scally, eds. *Eyewitness: Bloody Sunday.* Rev. ed. Dublin, Ireland: Merlin, 2002. Contains testimonies by both soldiers and marchers at the incident. Many of the eyewitness accounts in this collection dispute the conclusions of the Widgery Report. Includes a foreword written by film director Paul Greengrass, whose 2002 film *Bloody Sunday* is based on this work.

See also: Ballistic fingerprints; Ballistics; Bombings; Bullet-lead analysis; Firearms analysis; Gunshot residue; Improvised explosive devices; Interrogation.

Blunt force trauma

Definition: Trauma caused to a body part by a blunt instrument or surface through physical impact, injury, or attack.

Significance: By examining the types of injuries incurred by a victim of blunt force trauma, forensic scientists may be able to determine the cause of the accident or crime that resulted in the injuries as well as what type of instrument caused the injuries.

"Blunt force trauma" is a general term that covers trauma to the body from a variety of sources. Blunt force trauma, also known as blunt trauma, results when the body is struck by an object or when the body strikes an object. When a forensic scientist is asked to investigate blunt force trauma, it is usually to determine what instrument or event caused the injuries—for example, to determine whether the injuries resulted from a beating as opposed to a fall. Blunt force trauma to the body is not always life-threatening (unless organs or blood vessels rupture), but blunt force trauma to the head may cause death. Injuries that indicate blunt force trauma include lacerated blood vessels (including major vessels such as the aorta), lacerated or crushed organs, hematomas, contusions, crushed or fractured bones, and severed spinal cord.

Causes

Blunt force trauma is often caused by motor vehicle accidents in which the body is slammed into a steering wheel or dashboard. This slamming action, caused by the rapid deceleration of the vehicle, may cause contusions or rupturing of internal organs. Another common type of blunt force trauma is an accidental fall. The many other possible causes of blunt force trauma include assault by another person (through clubbing with an object, hitting, kicking, or punching) and sporting accidents.

When blunt force trauma is caused by a beating or clubbing, the type of weapon used by the assailant can often be identified by the characteristics of the wound. If the wound shows characteristics that can identify only a class of instrument (as opposed to the specific type of instrument) as the weapon, such as a bone fracture showing smooth, curved lines that could have been made by any smooth weapon, these are called "class characteristics" of the weapon. At times, however, a specific weapon can be identified by the distinctive marks it has left on skin, bone, or other tissues. For instance, a hammer that had individualized marks of wear on it before it was used to inflict wounds could leave those specific marks on the victim. These are called "individual characteristics" of the weapon.

A single weapon can also cause a variety of wounds. For example, if a shovel is used as a weapon, it may cause a large flat wound if the back of the shovel is used. The same shovel wielded so that its side or blade struck the victim would produce a sharp, linear wound.

In addition to examination of the victim's injuries, blood spatter analysis can provide clues as to the type of weapon used in a situation involving blunt force trauma, the strength of the person wielding the weapon, and the relative spacing of the victim and the attacker.

Injuries

Abdominal trauma is the most common type of blunt force trauma, and the liver, spleen, and small intestine can be affected. This often happens during a car accident, which may cause organ rupture.

Abrasions, or scrapes, are also often seen in cases of blunt force trauma. These injuries result when the skin is forcefully rubbed away by a rough surface, such as asphalt. Abrasions are usually only surface injuries. Lacerations may also occur; these can be either external or internal injuries, damaging the skin and penetrating into other tissues deeper within the body, such as muscles or organs.

In addition to other head injuries, such as skull fracture, that can result from blunt force trauma, the brain can also be damaged by the force of the blow. This can cause damage to the nerve cells deep inside the brain, even when there is no breaking of the skin.

Contusions, or bruises, from blunt force trauma can be either internal or external injuries. Bruises happen when blood vessels are damaged and begin to leak blood into surrounding tissues. Bruising on the skin surface shows up as swelling of the tissues and dark shades of color (blue, red, or purple). The amount of discoloration can vary with a person's age and weight: Older people and those who are heavier may show more bruising than younger and less heavy people. Deep bruising caused by extreme blunt force can occur so far inside the body that nothing shows on the surface; such injuries can be seen only with the aid of technologies such as magnetic resonance imaging (MRI). Contusions of the brain may not be noticeable at all from surface injuries; they may manifest themselves only through neurological symptoms such as confusion and weakness.

Marianne M. Madsen

Further Reading
DiMaio, Vincent J. M., and Suzanna E. Dana. *Handbook of Forensic Pathology.* 2d ed. Boca

Raton, Fla.: CRC Press, 2007. Comprehensive volume discusses common issues in forensic pathology, including determination of instruments in blunt force trauma situations.

Ferllini, Roxana, ed. *Forensic Archaeology and Human Rights Violations.* Springfield, Ill.: Charles C Thomas, 2007. Collection of essays by experts in various disciplines includes discussion of the forensic examination of bodies subjected to blunt force trauma and other deadly injuries in human rights violation cases.

Moore, Ernest E., Kenneth L. Mattox, and David V. Feliciano. *Trauma Manual.* 4th ed. New York: McGraw-Hill, 2003. Focuses mostly on trauma surgery, but discusses blunt force trauma in surgical situations.

Shkrum, Michael J., and David A. Ramsay. *Forensic Pathology of Trauma: Common Problems for the Pathologist.* Totowa, N.J.: Humana Press, 2007. Addresses common trauma patterns, including determination of blunt force trauma, in forensic settings.

Wilson, William C., Christopher M. Grande, and David B. Hoyt, eds. *Trauma: Critical Care.* Vol. 2. New York: Informa Healthcare, 2007. Discusses the determination of types of blunt force trauma and wound analysis.

See also: Antemortem injuries; Blood residue and bloodstains; Blood spatter analysis; Child abuse; Crime scene investigation; Defensive wounds; Driving injuries; Forensic anthropology; Osteology and skeletal radiology; Peruvian Ice Maiden; Physical evidence; Skeletal analysis.

Body farms

Definition: Outdoor facilities that allow forensic anthropologists to study postmortem decomposition of human remains.

Significance: Research conducted at body farms helps the practitioners of a number of forensic disciplines—including medical examiners, crime scene investigators, and law-enforcement personnel—with the identification of human remains.

The first body farm was established in 1972 by Dr. William M. Bass at the University of Tennessee in Knoxville. Shortly after he moved to Tennessee, Bass was asked to join the staff of the state's medical examiner's office as state forensic anthropologist. Part of Bass's duties in this position included consulting on death investigations being conducted by federal, state, and local law-enforcement agencies. Although Bass had extensive training in forensic anthropology, he did not have a lot of knowledge about or experience with the decomposition of human remains. In addition, research in this area was nearly nonexistent. This need led Bass and his colleagues to open the University of Tennessee Anthropological Research Facility, which came to be known as the Body Farm.

Purpose of Body Farms

The research conducted on body farms allows forensic anthropologists to study the postmortem decomposition of human remains. This work is important for a number of reasons. First, it helps scientists to gain a more comprehensive understanding of what occurs to the body after death and thus to develop better methods of determining the "time since death" in specific cases. Time since death, or the postmortem interval, is a critical element in homicide investigations, as law-enforcement officers or crime scene investigators must often confirm or disprove the alibis of potential suspects.

Second, the research on body farms provides information that is useful to forensic anthropologists and medical examiners who must identify bodies from skeletal remains. By examining a set of skeletal remains, a forensic anthropologist or medical examiner can determine a great deal about the decedent, including age, sex, stature, ancestry, and the presence of unique features. Body farm research also provides information that can help examiners to determine the cause of death in individual cases. In homicide investigations, law-enforcement officers or crime scene investigators need to know whether the decedents have died of natural causes or whether they have been the victims of foul play.

When the University of Tennessee's Anthropological Research Facility first began its work, almost no research had been done documenting

Author Patricia Cornwell, whose best-selling crime novels feature forensic pathology, shakes hands with Dr. William M. Bass, founder of the first body farm in the United States, the University of Tennessee Anthropological Research Facility. Cornwell is wearing a special outfit because of her participation in a mock airplane crash event staged for a crime scene investigation training exercise in July, 2005. *(AP/Wide World Photos)*

what happens to the human body after death. Even the most rudimentary questions—for example, When do blowflies show up on a body? How long does it take for a corpse to become a skeleton?—could not be answered. As the Body Farm's studies progressed, the questions became more sophisticated: How do decomposition rates differ between sunshine and shade? How do climate differences (cool versus hot) affect decomposition rates? How is decomposition affected when bodies are buried in shallow graves as opposed to left on top of the ground? Do bodies decompose faster in water than they do on land? How do bodies decompose in vehicles? What effects do other variables—such as clothing, body weight, and condition of the body—have on rates of decomposition?

What Happens to Bodies

The University of Tennessee's body farm occupies a three-acre tract of land situated near the University of Tennessee Medical Center; it is surrounded by razor wire and a wooden privacy fence. When a corpse arrives at the facility, it is assigned an identification number to ensure the confidentiality of the donor. The body is then examined and its condition is thoroughly documented. Bodies are placed in various environmental conditions across the property. For example, some bodies are placed in car trunks, some are left lying in the sun or shade, some are buried in shallow graves, some are covered with brush, and some are submerged in water.

Two things happen when a body decays. At death, enzymes in the digestive system, having no more nutrition, begin to eat on the body and the tissues liquefy. This process is known as putrefaction. Insects gather on the body, and maggots consume the rotting flesh. At the University of Tennessee, forensic anthropologists Dr. Richard Jantz and his wife, Dr. Lee Meadow Jantz, document such insect activity and how long it takes the insects to do their work. Most of the characteristics used to determine time since death are related to insect activity.

After the bodies at the Tennessee facility have completed the decomposition process, the bones are cleaned and measured, and the data are entered into the University of Tennessee's Forensic Anthropology Data Bank, which was created by Dr. Richard Jantz. This database is the primary tool that forensic anthropologists use to determine age, sex, stature, ancestry, and other unique characteristics from skeletal remains. The database is the central component of a computer program called FORDISC (for Forensic Discrimination). The FORDISC software is used all over the world as a tool to assist in the identification of bodies. For example, a medical examiner or anthropologist can enter a few skeletal measurements and the program can predict with a fairly high degree of accuracy the age, race, sex, height, and ancestry of the decedent. The bones are then cataloged and added to the William M. Bass Donated Skeletal Collection, which is the largest modern bone collection in the United States.

Sources of Bodies

The bodies studied at body farms come from three primary sources. First, bodies are often donated through state medical examiners' offices. For instance, if a body comes through a county medical examiner's office and it ends up unclaimed—either because the decedent is never identified or because the decedent had no friends or relatives to claim the body— the medical examiner may choose to send it to a body farm for decomposition re-

search or for addition to the facility's skeletal collection. Second, family members who are aware of the valuable research conducted at body farms and who are genuinely interested in furthering the cause of science may choose to donate the bodies of loved ones. Third, some people make the decision before their deaths to donate their bodies to body farms; by completing donor consent forms, they ensure that their wishes are carried out.

Body farms do not accept the corpses of persons who were infected with the human immunodeficiency virus (HIV), with hepatitis, or with antibiotic-resistant bacteria. These facilities will accept the donation of anyone's bones, however.

Impact of the University of Tennessee's Body Farm

The success of the research conducted at the Body Farm in Tennessee inspired the opening of other body farms in the United States and abroad. Western Carolina University in Cullowhee, North Carolina, created a body farm in 2006 as part of the Western Carolina Human Identification Laboratory. The facility is run by the university's forensic anthropology program on several acres of land near the campus. Like the original Body Farm, the North Carolina facility studies the decomposition of human remains. Researchers at the facility hope to learn more about the decomposition of bodies in the

The Body Farm in Popular Culture

The University of Tennessee's Anthropological Research Facility came to widespread public attention, and gained its nickname, with the 1994 publication of Patricia Cornwell's novel *The Body Farm*. In 2003, the nonfiction book *Death's Acre: Inside the Legendary Forensic Lab the Body Farm Where the Dead Do Tell Tales*, by Bill Bass and Jon Jefferson, increased the public's knowledge of the work done on body farms. In addition, author Mary Roach visited the Tennessee facility and included discussion of its work in a chapter of her 2003 nonfiction book *Stiff: The Curious Lives of Human Cadavers*. Since coming to the attention of television writers, body farms have figured as settings in several episodes of crime and suspense shows, including *CSI: Crime Scene Investigation*, *Law & Order: Special Victims Unit*, and *The Dead Zone*.

western Carolina mountain terrain, which is very different from the terrain of eastern Tennessee. They are interested in discovering whether these differences may affect rates of decomposition and suggest that it is important to study postmortem decomposition in a variety of geographic locations.

Texas State University planned to have a body farm operational by the fall of 2007, but completion of the facility, which will be run by the San Marcos Department of Anthropology, part of the Forensic Anthropology Center at Texas State, was delayed by objections from residents in the area and concerns about the presence of buzzards, which might interfere with flight operations at a nearby airport. Researchers at Texas State are interested in learning about rates of decomposition in Texas, where both geography and climate are significantly different from those of western Carolina and eastern Tennessee. Differences in climates may well be found to affect the rates of decomposition in human remains.

Other body farms are in various stages of planning and development across the United States, including in California, Florida, Kansas, and Iowa. In India, a student, Roma Kahn, who received a master's degree in forensic archaeology from Bournemouth University in England, has been conducting preliminary work on the decomposition of cattle. She hopes to open a facility to study human decomposition in India, modeled along the lines of the body farms operating in the United States.

Dr. Bass and the faculty of the University of Tennessee's Department of Anthropology have played a key role in shaping the field of forensic anthropology. It has been estimated that as of 2007, the University of Tennessee was responsible for the education of some 25 percent of the board-certified forensic anthropologists in the United States. Entry into the forensic anthropology program at the University of Tennessee is highly competitive, with roughly sixty students applying for the fewer than ten doctoral positions available annually.

The University of Tennessee's Forensic Anthropology Center also inspired the formation of the National Forensic Academy (NFA), one of the leading law-enforcement investigation

training centers in the United States. The NFA offers an intensive ten-week training program designed to educate law-enforcement agents in evidence identification, collection, and preservation. The primary goal of the NFA is to prepare law-enforcement officers to recognize crucial components of crime scenes and improve the process of evidence recovery and submission.

Opposition to Body Farms

Although the research conducted at body farms has undoubtedly contributed a great deal to the field of forensic anthropology, some people are disturbed by the idea of such facilities in their neighborhoods. At the heart of many debates is the placement of body farms. Residents who live near proposed sites often protest the opening of these facilities for a variety of reasons, including fears that insects will be attracted to the area or that scavenging animals will carry off body parts, perhaps dropping them in residents' backyards. When Texas State University proposed placing its body farm about two miles from the San Marcos Outlet Mall, one of the biggest tourist attractions in the area, local government officials objected, saying that the mall's businesses would likely be hurt by their proximity to such a facility.

The University of Tennessee's Body Farm was subject to similar opposition in its early days. Members of a local health care advocacy group called Solutions to Issues of Concern to Knoxvillians (SICK) protested at the research facility, holding up signs proclaiming, "This makes us SICK." A number of local residents also complained about the odor emitted from the Body Farm. The primary point of contention, however, was that the facility was not completely fenced in, and some people could see the decaying bodies from their homes. The university solved this problem by agreeing to install a privacy fence.

Kimberly D. Dodson

Further Reading

Bass, Bill, and Jon Jefferson. *Beyond the Body Farm: A Legendary Bone Detective Explores Murders, Mysteries, and the Revolution in Forensic Science.* New York: William Morrow, 2007. Examines the forensic science employed in a number of cases and discusses advances in forensic anthropology.

_____. *Death's Acre: Inside the Legendary Forensic Lab the Body Farm Where the Dead Do Tell Tales*. New York: G. P. Putnam's Sons, 2003. Traces the development of the University of Tennessee's body farm and presents real-life accounts of forensic cases.

Hallcox, Jarrett, and Amy Welch. *Bodies We've Buried: Inside the National Forensic Academy, the World's Top CSI Training School*. New York: Berkley Books, 2006. Describes the National Forensic Academy's ten-week training course for law-enforcement agents. Topics of the training include the identification, collection, and preservation of evidence.

Roach, Mary. *Stiff: The Curious Lives of Human Cadavers*. New York: W. W. Norton, 2003. Discusses the evolution of the study of human decomposition as well as the use and handling of corpses. Profiles the University of Tennessee's Anthropological Research Facility.

See also: Adipocere; Autopsies; Crime scene investigation; *CSI: Crime Scene Investigation*; Decomposition of bodies; Evidence processing; Forensic anthropology; Forensic entomology; Forensic pathology; Osteology and skeletal radiology; Skeletal analysis; Taphonomy; University of Tennessee Anthropological Research Facility.

Bomb damage assessment

Definition: Assessment of the severity of blast effects caused by explosions.

Significance: By conducting bomb damage assessment, investigators can aid in the identification of explosive devices or explosive propellants. Such analysis can also provide information on bomb delivery systems and their targeting accuracy.

An explosive device is designed to release large amounts of energy quickly from a concentrated source. The explosion results from the reaction of a solid or liquid chemical or vapor that forms highly pressurized gases, propagating an outward-moving pressure wave. In a high-explosive detonation, the speed of the reaction is faster than the speed of sound, 5,000 to 8,000 meters (about 16,000 to 26,000 feet) per second. Such an explosion produces an intense shock wave that expands within milliseconds of detonation. The effects of explosions vary, but the initial destructive effects on targets are directly related to stress-wave propagation, pressure-driven phenomena resulting in the impact and penetration of propelled objects, ground-transmitted shock, and explosion-generated effects such as fire, smoke, dust, and pressure damage to organs and tissue.

A bomb detonation can have catastrophic effects, destroying or severely damaging its intended human or material targets. The amount of damage done by a detonated bomb depends on the nature and size of the explosive device and its location relative to its target. Additional factors relate to specifics of the target, such as materials and construction, surroundings, and the proximity of potential victims. Bomb damage to targets is the direct result of explosive detonation involving shock-wave blast pressure and high-speed impact from ejected target materials, shrapnel, and debris. The postdetonation distribution of these materials reflects physical processes and properties that can be measured and correlated directly to the initiating explosive device.

The physical and chemical characteristics of explosions and their structural by-products are well defined by known scaling laws and equations of state, and any explosion can ultimately be referenced by its geometry, density, and temperature. As the result of more than one hundred years of testing, a large cross-referenced database has been compiled regarding the major and minor damage potential of shock waves generated by explosions. Most blast data come from unclassified war documentation, industrial records, scientific and engineering research, and forensic analyses. These data correlate explosive type and quantity to blast pressure, detonation velocity, target strata, ground shock, atmospheric conditions, target distance, target materials, above- or below-ground penetration, and confined or unconfined conditions. Blast injuries from explosive shock waves include body displacement, dismemberment, ruptured eardrums and internal organs, and tissue destruction from propelled objects; the extent of such injuries has been well documented, cataloged, and correlated according to detonation proximity.

As explosions involve predictable quantitative chemical and physical signatures, after a bombing forensic scientists can determine the size and type of device detonated and its effectiveness. In addition to conducting trace chemical analyses to identify the explosives used, the scientists examine such elements as the dimensions of the blast area and crater, the target's materials, weather conditions at the time of the explosion, the fallout distance of blast-propelled objects, and the extent of bodily harm caused by the blast.

Randall L. Milstein

Further Reading

Cooper, Paul W. *Explosives Engineering*. New York: Wiley-VCH, 1996.

Fannelöp, Torstein K. *Fluid Mechanics for Industrial Safety and Environmental Protection*. New York: Elsevier, 1994.

Thurman, James T. *Practical Bomb Scene Investigation*. Boca Raton, Fla.: CRC Press, 2006.

Zukas, Jonas A., and William P. Walters, eds. *Explosive Effects and Applications*. New York: Springer, 1998.

See also: Ballistics; Blast seat; Bombings; Bureau of Alcohol, Tobacco, Firearms and Explosives; Crime scene reconstruction and staging; Improvised explosive devices; Oklahoma City bombing; Structural analysis; World Trade Center bombing.

Bombings

Definition: Incidents involving weapons that explode and release destructive shock waves and shrapnel that damage buildings and other property and injure and kill people.

Significance: In modern society, law-enforcement agencies are increasingly faced with the investigation of crimes involving explosives. Forensic scientists and law-enforcement officers use a number of different techniques to detect explosives before they can be used in bombs, and, after bombings have taken place, they examine the resulting debris for evidence that can link the explosions to the perpetrators.

Bombs create destructive shock waves, flying shrapnel, and intense heat and flame capable of destroying objects and killing people. As the materials needed for bomb making (especially such dual-use products as fertilizer) and the technical information needed to construct and detonate bombs have become more readily available than in the past, in large part because of the advent of the Internet, bombings have increased in frequency. The availability of potentially explosive chemicals, dynamite, and, in some countries, military explosives has provided the criminally disposed with the ability to wield very destructive and deadly weapons. Furthermore, the news coverage that inevitably follows bombing incidents may inadvertently embolden those so inclined to carry out additional bombing attacks.

Types of Explosives

Every bomb has an igniter, a primer or detonator, and a main charge. Most kinds of bombs are confined within some sort of shell, such as a pipe or a box. The igniter may be either a fuse or a primer. A primer is a small explosive charge that may be ignited by flame, electrical spark, or friction. When the primer is ignited, it explodes, causing the bomb's main charge to detonate. A firearm cartridge, for example, is an explosive that is set off when a shock-sensitive primer located at one end of the cartridge is struck by a pin. When a gun's firing pin strikes the primer on a firearm cartridge, the primer explodes and ignites the main charge, the smokeless black powder located behind the bullet. The explosion of the main charge is what forces the bullet to travel through the barrel of the gun and downrange.

The speed at which an explosive detonates

determines whether it is classified as a low or high explosive. Low explosives, such as black and smokeless powder, are typically used as propellants for ammunition and rockets because they burn relatively slowly. Most homemade bombs tend to be low explosives because they are often constructed with black powder, which is easy to obtain from gun stores. High explosives such as dynamite and C-4, in contrast, produce more of a smashing, shattering effect.

High explosives may be divided into two types, primary and secondary. Primary high explosives tend to be sensitive to heat, shock, and friction and detonate very easily. Because of this, they are generally used in primer devices to set off larger, secondary explosives. Secondary high explosives tend to be relatively insensitive to heat, shock, and friction and usually require a primary charge explosion to detonate. In most cases, this involves the use of a blasting cap, initiated by a burning fuse or by an electrical current. Homemade bombs are usually initiated by an electronic blasting cap wired to a battery that is switched on by a device such as a clock, mercury switch, vehicle ignition switch, or cell phone ring.

Dynamite is a high explosive known for producing a quick shattering effect. It is mainly used for construction, mining, and demolition. When it was first developed in 1866, it was made from nitroglycerin, diatomaceous earth (soft, chalklike sedimentary rock), and sodium carbonate wrapped in distinctive red paper. The "kick" that is produced by dynamite is derived from the nitroglycerin it contains. Nitroglycerin is a very powerful shock-sensitive explosive, meaning that vibrations may cause it to explode. This makes it very dangerous to handle. However, when diatomaceous earth and sodium carbonate are combined with nitroglycerin to create dynamite, the nitroglycerin becomes more stable and safe to handle.

The explosive strength of a stick of dynamite is designated by the percentage of nitroglycerin it contains; for example, in a 60 percent grade stick of dynamite, 60 percent of the stick consists of nitroglycerin. The actual blasting power of a stick of dynamite, however, is not in proportion to its grade percentage markings. That is, a 60 percent grade stick of dynamite is not three times as powerful as a 20 percent grade stick; it is only about one and one-half times as strong.

By the early years of the twenty-first century, the use of nitroglycerin-based dynamite had all but disappeared. Dynamite was replaced by ammonium nitrate-based explosives, which are more stable and useful in wet conditions. Ammonium nitrate/fuel oil (ANFO) explosives are high explosives that are often used in the mining and construction industries. They consist of ammonium nitrate soaked in fuel oil and require a primer explosive to detonate. About 80 percent of the explosives used in North America are ANFO explosives. The availability of ammonium nitrate in the form of fertilizer makes it a readily obtainable ingredient for homemade explosives, and its use in bombs has become a trademark of various criminal and terrorist groups around the globe. Timothy McVeigh used a variation of an ANFO bomb when he attacked the Alfred P. Murrah Federal Building in Oklahoma City in 1995, killing 168 people and injuring hundreds more.

The explosive known as RDX is currently the high explosive most commonly used by the U.S. military. It is second in strength only to nitroglycerin. RDX is widely used in plastic explosives, detonators, artillery rounds, Claymore mines, and demolition kits. It is combined with plasticizers to make C-4, which is a pliable, puttylike explosive that can be molded into a variety of shapes and has a long shelf life. It is believed that al-Qaeda used C-4 in 1996 to blow up the Khobar Towers (a military housing complex) in Saudi Arabia and again in 2000 in its attack on the military destroyer the USS *Cole*. In the Khobar Towers bombing, nineteen U.S. service personnel were killed. In the bombing of the *Cole*, seventeen sailors were killed and thirty-nine others were injured.

Triacetone triperoxide (TATP) is an explosive created through the combination of the common ingredients of acetone and hydrogen peroxide with a catalyst such as hydrochloric acid. Persons who are so inclined can purchase its base ingredients (drain cleaner, bleach, and acetone) easily and without attracting suspicion, and instructions for making TATP can be found on the Internet. In its finished form, this explosive is almost undetectable by substance-detection dogs or by conventional bomb-detection systems. Because of this, the Palestinian militant organization Hamas has favored TATP for use by suicide bombers sent into Israel. Al-Qaeda has also used it when conducting terror missions abroad. TATP was included as a trigger in the shoe bomb that Richard Reid intended to detonate on a flight from Paris, France, to Miami, Florida, in 2001. It is also the type of explosive that was used in the 2005 public transit bombings in London, England, which killed fifty-two commuters and injured seven hundred people. The drawback of TATP, from a criminal or terrorist's point of view, is that it is highly unstable and sensitive to heat and friction.

Detecting Explosives at Airports

Terrorists around the globe have successfully used explosives to end lives and undermine public confidence in air travel. In response to such threats, airports and their cargo terminals employ a number of different techniques and technologies to aid in the identification and interdiction of explosives.

X-ray machines are used to scan large numbers of people and items to identify hidden suspicious shapes that could indicate the presence of bombs. Because it is possible that such explosive devices could be hidden inside electronic equipment, such as laptop computers, security measures often include chemical analyses. In such a test, a swab is wiped across a piece of electronic equipment, such as a laptop, and is then placed into a device that heats it up and performs a spectrographic analysis of the resulting vapors. The machine searches for traces of nitrogen, which is found in the majority of explosives.

Trace-detection machines (sniffers), which look like metal detectors, search for explosives

Investigators carefully sift for evidence in rubble on the ground at the site of the Alfred P. Murrah Federal Building bombing in Oklahoma City in April, 1995. *(AP/Wide World Photos)*

by blowing air over persons or their luggage. The blowing air releases particles from the surface of the person or object of interest, and the machine then processes the air and analyzes it for traces of known explosives. Airport security measures also include the use of dogs that have been trained to alert their handlers by sitting near any objects or persons that give off the telltale odors of explosives.

Responding to Bomb Threats

Most bomb threats turn out to be nothing more than prank phone calls from misguided individuals who take pleasure in causing others fear and inconvenience. Unfortunately, those whose true intent is to kill, maim, and destroy are unlikely to notify their intended victims prior to the detonation of their bombs. When a bombing does occur, individuals who have specialized training in bomb disposal, bomb-site investigation, forensic analysis, and criminal investigation work together to determine what happened so that those who are responsible may be apprehended.

When a bomb threat is called in, the authorities who are given the task of responding to the scene (the first responders) need to enlist the assistance of people who are familiar with the area, such as building managers and employees, because such persons may be more adept at determining whether something is out of place than someone who is not as familiar with the surroundings. Those participating in a search for a bomb must turn off all their radios and transmitters before they begin the search, because the signals

these devices emit may set off an explosion. When searchers first enter a room in a location where a bomb may have been planted, they pay special attention to items such as unattended bags, boxes, baby carriers, briefcases, trash cans, flowerpots, incoming mail, and panels in the ceiling that may be easily pushed up. Experts also recommend that when searchers enter a room, they should stand quietly in the room's center, close their eyes for several seconds, and listen. Unusual noises may indicate the location of a bomb.

If a bomb is found, the searchers are careful

Bomb Scene Equipment

Because first responders and investigators may not know the details of a situation involving explosives until they arrive at the scene, prior preparation is vital. The following is a list of the kinds of tools and other equipment frequently used by investigative teams at bombing scenes. This list is not exhaustive, and all of the items listed may be not applicable to every situation.

- First-aid kit
- Biohazard materials (bags, tags, labels)
- Respiratory equipment
- Hard hats, safety glasses, protective safety boots, and kneepads
- Protective outerwear (disposable suits, shoe covers)
- Heavy, disposable cotton gloves
- Barrier tape
- Flashlights, flares, and auxiliary lighting
- Hand tools (rakes, shovels, trowels, screwdrivers, crowbars, hammers)
- Brushes and brooms
- Ladders
- Sifters/screens
- Swabbing kits
- Vacuum
- Evidence collection kits
- Writing equipment (notebooks, pens, permanent markers)
- Drawing equipment (sketchbooks, pencils)
- Measuring equipment (tape measure, tape wheel)
- Photography and video equipment
- Computer and computer-aided design program
- Consent-to-search forms
- Audio recorders
- Evidence flags or cones, placards, and tags
- Bags and corrugated or fiberboard boxes
- Chemical test kits and vapor detectors
- Trace explosives detectors (sniffers) and detection canines

not to touch it, because contact may cause it to explode. Only bomb disposal personnel are tasked with handling any suspected devices that are located. Bomb squads in larger police departments use robots to approach and detonate certain bombs. After a bomb is found, the area is cleared and the crime scene is secured to prevent further contamination. Emergency services are requested from bomb technicians, firefighters, emergency medical personnel, and law-enforcement officers, and a search for secondary explosive devices is then conducted.

Investigating Bomb Explosions

When an explosion occurs, law-enforcement personnel must identify scene hazards such as the possibility of building collapse, hazardous chemicals, and secondary explosives. Bombing scenes may contain secondary explosive devices specifically designed to kill or maim public safety responders. If a suspected secondary device is located, the area must be evacuated immediately and bomb disposal personnel must be contacted. As soon as conditions permit, investigators need to establish a security perimeter that restricts access into and out of the scene; they also begin documenting the scene (taking notes, identifying witnesses, and videotaping bystanders).

During an initial scene walk-through, investigators pay special attention to various safety concerns, such as structural damage, the possibility of the presence of secondary devices and unconsumed explosive materials, failed utilities, and hazardous materials. Following this walk-through, the investigators meet with available emergency responders and investigative personnel to determine what resources, equipment, and additional personnel may be needed.

The search for evidence typically starts at the seat of the blast, which is usually indicated by a crater, and spirals out in ever-increasing circles. The scene is documented with both written and photographic records before anything is removed or disturbed. The material at the scene is then sorted in an attempt to recover the materials that were used to construct the bomb. All of the personnel involved in the search must wear disposable gloves, shoe covers, and overalls so

that they do not contaminate evidence and compromise the investigation.

To uncover clues to the construction and thus the origin of a bomb, investigators usually sift material from the blast scene through a series of increasingly finer mesh screens to collect portions of the explosive device for analysis. For instance, if a pipe bomb was used, a forensic investigator may find the bomb's end cap; in many cases, this part of a pipe bomb will retain small specks of unexploded material that becomes trapped in the threading. These small specks of explosive may then be used to trace the origins of the materials used to construct the bomb. Investigative leads may also develop from tool marks left on a pipe from a vise used in cutting and threading. Other clues that may aid an investigation include the type of wire that was used, the type of timing device used, the particular type of wrapper paper (indicating the origin of a piece of dynamite), or a unique method of bomb construction.

The materials from the scene that are collected for laboratory examination are placed in sealed containers and labeled. Soil and other soft materials are placed in metal containers or plastic bags. Evidence samples that are packaged in plastic bags must not be kept next to each other, because it has been demonstrated that some explosives can diffuse through plastic and contaminate nearby containers.

Bombing victims should also be examined for evidence, as bomb component fragments may be found on or in their clothing or bodies. Autopsies should include full-body X rays.

When the debris evidence from a bomb scene arrives at the laboratory, it is examined microscopically, and an acetone wash is often used to extract explosives from the debris. Chromatographic techniques (which can separate and identify the components in chemical mixtures) may then be used to determine the types of explosives that were used.

Explosive residues are often collected at bomb scenes with a portable machine called an ion mobility spectrometer (IMS). The IMS uses a vacuum to suck in explosive residues from surfaces. Depending on the types of surfaces found at a bomb scene, however, investigators may collect explosive residues more efficiently by

Explosive Incidents Investigated by ATF, 2000-2003

	2000	2001	2002	2003
Incidents	807	763	711	386
Persons injured	81	98	80	55
Persons killed	19	12	13	7
Damage	$5,634,681	$7,279,023	$5,153,448	$267,000

Source: Bureau of Alcohol, Tobacco, Firearms and Explosives.

wiping the surfaces down with paper disks and then using the IMS to collect the residues off the disks. Once the residues are in the IMS, they are vaporized into electronically charged molecules or ions. Identification of the size and structure of the molecules and ions enables investigators to determine the types of explosives that were detonated at the bomb scene.

Investigators often examine bomb blast craters using an ultraviolet light and magnetic probe in the hope of finding small particles, called taggants, that are sometimes put into explosives by manufacturers. Taggants are tiny color-coded magnetic fluorescent chips the size of sand grains. The color of the fluorescent chips indicates where an explosive was made and when it was produced. Switzerland requires all explosives manufacturers in that nation to add taggants to their products. The U.S. government has not taken such a step, but increasing concerns about terrorism may eventually result in a similar requirement for American manufacturers.

Daniel Pontzer

Further Reading

Bennett, Wayne W., and Kären M. Hess. *Criminal Investigation*. 8th ed. Belmont, Calif.: Wadsworth/Thomson Learning, 2007. Introduces the challenges encountered by criminal investigators and discusses investigators' basic responsibilities. Details the work involved in the investigation of violent crimes such as death, assault, rape, and robbery as well as property offenses such as burglary, arson, and crimes using explosives.

Gaensslen, R. E., Howard A. Harris, and Henry C. Lee. *Introduction to Forensic Science and Criminalistics*. New York: McGraw-Hill, 2008. Addresses the types of forensic science techniques used in crime laboratories in criminal cases and by private examiners in civil cases. Discusses various crime scene procedures and analyses, physical pattern evidence, biological evidence, and chemical and materials evidence.

Martin, Gus. *Essentials of Terrorism: Concepts and Controversies*. Thousand Oaks, Calif.: Sage, 2008. Addresses the topic of modern-day terrorism by reviewing different types of terrorism and the nations, movements, and individuals who have engaged in terrorist violence.

National Institute of Justice. *A Guide for Explosion and Bombing Scene Investigation*. Washington, D.C.: Author, 2000. Outlines the tasks that investigators should consider at every explosion scene and provides guidance on the procurement of equipment and tools, prioritization of initial response efforts, evaluation of the scene, documentation of the scene, and processing of evidence at the scene.

Saferstein, Richard. *Criminalistics: An Introduction to Forensic Science*. 9th ed. Upper Saddle River, N.J.: Pearson Prentice Hall, 2007. Comprehensive introductory textbook addresses the role of science in the criminal justice system. Includes in-depth discussion of the technologies that law-enforcement agencies use to apprehend criminals and the use of trace evidence to link perpetrators to crime scenes.

Simonsen, Clifford E., and Jeremy R. Spindlove. *Terrorism Today: The Past, the Players, the Future*. 3d ed. Upper Saddle River, N.J.: Pearson Prentice Hall, 2007. Provides background on the history and legal issues associated with terrorism and discusses the types of terrorism and terrorist groups found around the world. Includes suggestions regarding counterterrorism tactics and speculation on the directions terrorism may take in the future.

Trimm, Harold H. *Forensics the Easy Way.* Hauppauge, N.Y.: Barron's, 2005. Presents information on the applications of physics and chemistry in the criminal justice system by focusing on forensics, including discussion of physical evidence, body fluids, explosives and incendiaries, firearms, fingerprints, and DNA evidence.

See also: Atomic absorption spectrophotometry; Blast seat; Bomb damage assessment; Bureau of Alcohol, Tobacco, Firearms and Explosives; Canine substance detection; Chromatography; Driving injuries; Illicit substances; Improvised explosive devices; Mass spectrometry; National Church Arson Task Force; Oklahoma City bombing; Unabomber case; World Trade Center bombing.

Borderline personality disorder

Definition: Disorder in which personality characteristics are maladaptive in nature, including chronic difficulties in maintaining stable interpersonal relationships, severe mood swings that are reactive in nature, impulsivity, hostility, feelings of emptiness, and propensity to engage in self-harm behaviors.

Significance: Persons with borderline personality disorder are at high risk for engaging in criminal and antisocial behavior and tend to be overrepresented in prison populations. Because of their often violent and aggressive demeanor, such individuals are extremely disruptive to forensic settings and tend to pose additional risks to themselves and others when placed within these environments.

It has been estimated that from 1 to 2 percent of the world's population qualify for a diagnosis of borderline personality disorder (BPD) based on the guidelines in the fourth edition, text revision, of the American Psychiatric Association's *Diagnostic and Statistical Manual of Mental Disorders* (*DSM-IV-TR*). A disproportionate number of the people diagnosed with BPD found in psychiatric inpatient, psychiatric outpatient, and forensic settings are female.

Individuals with BPD exhibit enduring patterns of emotional and behavioral instability. The pervasive and often inflexible nature of their behavior can result in actions that are harmful and, sometimes, criminal in nature. These erratic behaviors are believed to result from a dangerous combination of extreme affective instability and high levels of impulsivity. Although self-destructive in nature, these behaviors—including reckless driving, sexual promiscuity, substance abuse, and aggressive acts—may result in legal repercussions. People with BPD are highly likely to exhibit symptoms of additional psychopathology and often warrant additional comorbid diagnoses of depression, anxiety, and other Axis II personality disorders (disorders classified in the *DSM-IV-TR* as underlying pervasive or personality conditions), most predominantly of the histrionic or antisocial types.

An intense fear of abandonment, often stemming from psychosocial factors during development (such as sexual abuse, neglect, separation or loss, or parental psychopathology), is believed to contribute to the manipulative behaviors exhibited by persons with BPD. To avoid either real or imagined abandonment, persons with BPD put forth significant effort to thwart others' attempts to leave them. In these situations, they may engage in flagrantly manipulative behaviors, including significant threats of self-harm or attempts at suicide. These behaviors, although intended to keep others from departing, can result in life-threatening or lethal injuries. In addition to such self-harm behaviors, persons with BPD often engage in self-mutilating acts such as repetitive cutting or burning; most often, they perform these acts on their forearms or legs, but sometimes they may mutilate their faces, chests, or genitals.

In addition to exhibiting unstable behavior, individuals with BPD tend to have extreme difficulty with interpersonal relationships, self-image, and moods. They often report histories of intense but stormy relationships, typically involving severe fluctuations between overidealization of friends or lovers and bitter disappointment, frustration, and disillusionment with these persons, which, at times, may lead to violence. These drastic mood shifts and difficulties modulating and controlling anger can lead individuals with BPD to display intense behavioral and emotional outbursts with little provocation.

Neva E. J. Sanders-Dewey and Seth G. Dewey

Further Reading

Friedel, Robert O. *Borderline Personality Disorder Demystified: An Essential Guide for Understanding and Living with BPD*. New York: Marlowe, 2004.

Kreisman, Jerold J., and Hal Straus. *Sometimes I Act Crazy: Living with Borderline Personality Disorder*. Hoboken, N.J.: John Wiley & Sons, 2004.

Mason, Paul T., and Randi Kreger. *Stop Walking on Eggshells: Taking Your Life Back When Someone You Care About Has Borderline Personality Disorder*. Oakland, Calif.: New Harbinger, 1998.

See also: ALI standard; Child abuse; *Diagnostic and Statistical Manual of Mental Disorders*; Forensic psychiatry; Guilty but mentally ill plea; Insanity defense; Irresistible impulse rule; Minnesota Multiphasic Personality Inventory; Psychopathic personality disorder; Suicide.

Bosnian war victim identification. *See* Croatian and Bosnian war victim identification

Botulinum toxin

Definition: Highly toxic substance produced by the *Clostridium botulinum* bacterium that targets nerve tissue and blocks neuromuscular transmission of impulses in the body, causing the paralytic disease botulism.

Significance: Botulinum toxin is one of the most lethal known toxic substances; a few grams of the toxin introduced into the food supply could kill millions of people, making it an attractive agent for potential use as a biological weapon. In addition to that possibility, nonintentional poisonings sometimes occur through the consumption of food containing the toxin or through contamination of wounds with the toxin. Whenever botulinum toxin is suspected in cases of poisoning, law-enforcement agencies are concerned with identifying the toxin and its source.

Although the possibility that botulinum toxin could be used in biological warfare has been acknowledged for many years, no uses of the poison as a weapon have been reported in any major wars. Despite the Biological Weapons Convention of 1972, however, it is generally believed that many countries have stockpiles of the *Clostridium botulinum* bacterium and toxin as part of their biological warfare programs.

The most common form of botulinum poisoning occurs through the ingestion of foods containing the toxin. Food products contaminated with *C. botulinum* spores that are stored at room temperature can cause poisoning if they are consumed without first being adequately heated. Canned cheeses, ham, and sausage are common sources of the toxin. In a typical incident that took place in Italy in 1996, eight people contracted the poison by eating commercial cream cheese. One died, and the others had prolonged medical recoveries. In a 1995 incident in Canada, a sixteen-year-old girl was poisoned when she ate smoked fish. She died a few months later despite having received intensive medical treatment. In September, 2006, four cases of botulism in the United States and two cases in Canada were traced to the consumption of contaminated carrot juice.

Mechanism of Toxicity

The toxin, which was first isolated from *C. botulinum* in 1944 by Edward Schantz, must come into contact with nerve tissue to cause damage. The toxin attaches to the axon terminal of nerve endings, where it blocks the release of the principal neurotransmitter in the body, acetylcholine. This blockage prevents transmission of nerve impulses, resulting in loss of muscle contractility and flaccid paralysis.

In food-related poisoning, symptoms occur six to thirty-six hours after ingestion of food containing the toxin. Symptoms include excessive dry mouth, diarrhea, and vomiting. These may be followed by blurred vision, droopy eyelids, generalized muscle weakness, and progressive difficulty in breathing. Death may occur as a result of paralysis of the respiratory muscles. Symptoms of botulinum poisoning may occur more rapidly if the toxin is inhaled rather than ingested.

Medical and Cosmetic Uses

Some medical treatments have been developed that take advantage of the botulinum toxin's neuromuscular blocking action; tiny concentrations of the toxin are used, for example, in the treatment of involuntary eye muscle contractions (blepharospasm). The toxin is also used in the treatment of migraine headaches and cervical dystonia, a neuromuscular condition involving the head and neck. Another important medical use of the toxin is in the treatment of excessive underarm perspiration (severe primary axillary hyperhidrosis). The toxin has also been employed at times in the treatment of the following ailments and symptoms, although it is not approved by the U.S. Food and Drug Administration (FDA) for these uses: overactive bladder, anal fissure, stroke, multiple sclerosis, Parkinson's disease, excessive salivation, neurological complications of diabetes mellitus, and muscle problems affecting the limbs, face, jaw, and vocal cords.

Commercial botulinum toxins, marketed under the names Botox and Dysport, among others, are used cosmetically to remove facial wrinkles and improve facial appearance. The toxin works on wrinkle lines that have been formed in the upper part of the face, particularly the forehead and around the eyes. Because very low concentrations of the toxin are used in these cosmetic preparations, treatment is usually safe. However, occasional adverse effects—such as allergic reactions and paralysis of the wrong muscles—have been reported. Four cases of poisoning caused by cosmetic use of a type of botulinum toxin that had not been approved by the FDA were reported in Florida in 2004.

Investigation of Botulinum Poisoning

When deaths or illnesses are suspected to be attributable to botulinum toxin poisoning, both forensic scientists and public health experts are usually involved in investigating the incidents. The immediate goal in any case is to identify the source of the toxin as quickly as possible to prevent any further harm. In the United States, law-enforcement agencies are required to re-

---

Diagnosing Botulism

The U.S. Centers for Disease Control and Prevention (CDC) provides this information on the diagnosis of botulinum poisoning.

Physicians may consider the diagnosis if the patient's history and physical examination suggest botulism. However, these clues are usually not enough to allow a diagnosis of botulism. Other diseases such as Guillain-Barré syndrome, stroke, and myasthenia gravis can appear similar to botulism, and special tests may be needed to exclude these other conditions. These tests may include a brain scan, spinal fluid examination, nerve conduction test (electromyography, or EMG), and a tensilon test for myasthenia gravis. The most direct way to confirm the diagnosis is to demonstrate the botulinum toxin in the patient's serum or stool by injecting serum or stool into mice and looking for signs of botulism. The bacteria can also be isolated from the stool of persons with foodborne and infant botulism. These tests can be performed at some state health department laboratories and at CDC.

A lab technician with the Centers for Disease Control and Prevention grinds food with a mortar and pestle to enable the extraction of botulinum toxin. The CDC treats every case of food-borne botulism as a public health emergency. (Centers for Disease Control and Prevention)

port all cases of such poisoning to the Centers for Disease Control and Prevention (CDC).

Evidence at the suspected poisoning site must be preserved so that it can be analyzed for clues that may point to the source of the toxin. Apart from food, botulinum toxin and the toxin-producing *C. botulinum* bacterium may be found in the blood and feces of patients suffering from botulinum poisoning. In some fatal cases, forensic examination of tissue samples and suspensions of body fluids have been used to demonstrate the presence of the toxin even after advanced putrefaction.

Edward C. Nwanegbo

Further Reading

Balkin, Karen F., ed. *Food-Borne Illnesses*. San Diego, Calif.: Greenhaven Press, 2004. Collection of essays offers a variety of perspectives on issues of food safety.
Breeze, Roger G., Bruce Budowle, and Steven E. Schutzer, eds. *Microbial Forensics*. Burlington, Mass.: Elsevier Academic Press, 2005. Details the importance of forensic microbiology and discusses its uses. Includes discussion of botulism.
Scott, Elizabeth, and Paul Sockett. *How to Prevent Food Poisoning: A Practical Guide to Safe Cooking, Eating, and Food Handling*. Hoboken, N.J.: John Wiley & Sons, 1998. Provides thorough information on the causes and symptoms of food poisoning, including botulism.
Smith, Louis D. S., and Hiroshi Sugiyama. *Botulism: The Organism, Its Toxins, the Disease*. 2d ed. Springfield, Ill.: Charles C Thomas, 1988. Textbook covers virtually every aspect of botulism.
Tucker, Jonathan B., ed. *Toxic Terror: Assessing Terrorist Use of Chemical and Biological Weapons*. Cambridge, Mass.: MIT Press, 2000. Collection of case studies discusses var-

ious uses of chemical and biological agents by terrorist groups. Identifies terrorists' patterns of behavior and discusses strategies to combat them.

See also: Biological terrorism; Biological Weapons Convention of 1972; Chemical agents; Chemical terrorism; Food poisoning; Food supply protection; Forensic toxicology; Poisons and antidotes.

Bovine spongiform encephalopathy. *See* Mad cow disease investigation

---

Brain-wave scanners

Definition: Instruments used to map regions of the brain or to measure brain responses to stimuli.

Significance: Brain-wave scanners can be used to monitor brain activity to determine whether or not a person is telling the truth and to perform postmortem mapping of the brain to determine whether death may have resulted from trauma to the head.

Brain-wave scanners are used to map activity in the brain. The patterns seen in the three-dimensional images produced by brain-wave scanning are indicative of whether or not a person is lying. The images are formed using magnetic resonance imaging (MRI). When experts examine the images to determine which areas of a person's brain become active in response to questions, pictures, or other stimuli, this method is referred to as functional magnetic resonance imaging (fMRI). The subject is placed inside the scanning machine and allowed to interact with a computer screen to answer specific questions related to a crime. The MRI machine is interfaced with special computer software that recognizes specific brain patterns. When a person is telling a lie, the brain has to expend more energy than it does when the person is telling the truth. Even when a lie has been rehearsed in the mind of the subject, the subject uses more brain energy to think beyond the truth and access the lie. The extra brain activity shows up as a "bright" region on the brain-scanned image. In tested case studies, the fMRI method has shown an accuracy of more than 90 percent in detecting lies.

Although still undergoing development and refinement, the fMRI technique has many possible forensic applications. These include situations that involve libel, slander, fraud, or terrorist activities; the technology may also be useful in the security screening of potential employees for important government positions. The technique might be used in the interrogation of criminal suspects or in the assessment of the intentions of prisoners before they are released. Because individuals involved in terrorist plots have detailed knowledge of plans and activities that innocent persons do not have, brain scans might be used to identify persons who have terrorist training and knowledge of terrorist activities.

The primary ethical issue that needs to be addressed in regard to the use of brain-wave scanners as lie detectors is that of the invasion of personal privacy. This problem may be resolved by safeguards that ensure that subjects are fully informed about brain-wave scanning and agree to be examined in this way.

For examination of the brain after death, postmortem multislice computed tomography (PMSCT) provides detailed in situ images of the brain. These are useful for screening corpses for foreign matter in the brain or for identifying whether head trauma resulting in skull fractures or cerebral hemorrhaging was the cause of death. Both two-dimensional cross-sectional images and postprocessed three-dimensional images of the skull can be made. Postmortem computed tomographic (PMCT) scans of an infant's brain can reveal signs that are indicative of shaken baby syndrome. This type of child abuse is accompanied by subdural hemorrhage of ruptured cerebral bridging veins, which can be identified in PMCT images but is difficult, if not impossible, to detect in a typical autopsy.

Alvin K. Benson

Further Reading

Saferstein, Richard. *Criminalistics: An Introduction to Forensic Science*. 9th ed. Upper Saddle River, N.J.: Pearson Prentice Hall, 2007.

Tilstone, William J., Kathleen A. Savage, and Leigh A. Clark. *Forensic Science: An Encyclopedia of History, Methods, and Techniques*. Santa Barbara, Calif.: ABC-CLIO, 2006.

White, Peter, ed. *Crime Scene to Court: The Essentials of Forensic Science*. 2d ed. Cambridge, England: Royal Society of Chemistry, 2004.

See also: Biometric identification systems; Forensic psychiatry; Forensic psychology; Interrogation; Nervous system; Polygraph analysis; Psychological autopsy.

Breathalyzer

Definition: Device used to measure ethanol in the breath of a subject as an indication of blood alcohol concentration. Breathalyzer is also the trade name of a series of instruments designed to analyze breath alcohol.

Significance: Police officers commonly conduct analyses of the breath of drivers suspected of driving under the influence of alcohol, and Breathalyzer results are often used as grounds for arrest in cases of impaired driving. Such analyses are increasingly used also in workplace drug-testing and research applications. The accuracy and precision of the measurements produced by Breathalyzer testing, which are related to physiological and instrumental variables, are often debated in court.

Police officers often ask drivers whom they suspect are under the influence of alcohol to provide samples of their breath by blowing into

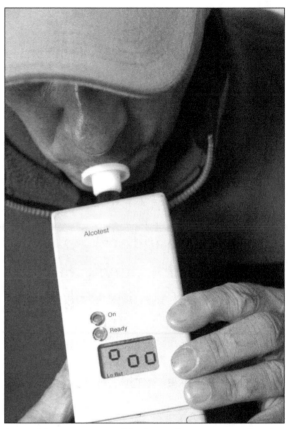

A man blows into a portable device that measures ethanol in the breath to indicate blood alcohol concentration. *(© iStockphoto.com/Marjan Laznik)*

instruments—at the roadside or at police detachments—that can determine the concentration of alcohol in their breath. Such breath analysis is valuable because the sample collection is minimally invasive, especially in comparison with direct analysis of blood. Breath samples are analyzed upon collection, which establishes sample continuity. When the results are properly documented, and when the instrument is properly calibrated and in good working order, the measurements are typically used as evidence in court.

The instruments used in breath alcohol analysis are based on a variety of designs. The Breathalyzer 900/900A uses oxidation of ethyl alcohol (ethanol) in a fixed volume of breath by potassium dichromate in a standard solution to cause a shift in the solution absorbance spectrum (that is, a color change); the change in absorbance is correlated with the alcohol concentration in the breath sample. Newer instrument designs typically rely on ethanol detection based on absorbance of infrared radiation at selected wavelengths or on electrochemical reaction of the ethanol in the breath sample. Some instruments are portable, and small, handheld units are often used as screening devices; that is, law-enforcement personnel use them to determine whether alcohol is present in subjects within a concentration range that warrants further evidentiary breath testing. Different designs often vary in terms of accuracy and in their susceptibility to other interfering compounds in the breath.

Breath alcohol concentration (BrAC) is correlated with blood alcohol concentration (BAC). Henry's law states that, at a given temperature, the ratio of the concentration of a volatile substance in solution to that of the substance in the vapor above the solution is fixed. Physiologically, such a system exists in the capillaries within the alveoli (air sacs) of the lungs. Volatile compounds, including alcohol, are exchanged between the alveolar air and the blood within these capillaries. BAC is thus determined by multiplication of the measured BrAC by this ratio, termed the blood/breath ratio (BBR). Reported BBR averages typically fall within the range 2,200-2,500.

To be detected in the breath, a compound must be sufficiently volatile, present at sufficient blood concentrations, and measurable by the detection scheme of the instrument. To characterize potential interferences, the response of evidentiary instruments to volatile compounds (such as acetone, isopropanol, methanol, and toluene) should be measured in vitro at toxicologically relevant fluid concentrations (that is, those associated with occupational or environmental exposure, a disease state such as diabetes mellitus, or nonfatal substance abuse). The influence of such compounds on BrAC measurements depends on their chemical properties and the detection scheme of the instrument. Further safeguards against falsely elevated results are provided by careful observation of the subject by the test administrator and by the collection of a detailed history of the subject being tested.

James Watterson

Further Reading

Garriott, James C., ed. *Medical-Legal Aspects of Alcohol*. 4th ed. Tucson, Ariz.: Lawyers & Judges Publishing, 2003.

Karch, Steven B., ed. *Forensic Issues in Alcohol Testing*. Boca Raton, Fla.: CRC Press, 2007.

Levine, Barry, ed. *Principles of Forensic Toxicology*. 2d ed., rev. Washington, D.C.: American Association for Clinical Chemistry, 2006.

See also: Alcohol-related offenses; Analytical instrumentation; Chain of custody; Drug and alcohol evidence rules; Forensic toxicology; Infrared detection devices; Sobriety testing; Toxicological analysis.

Brockovich-PG&E case

Date: Settled out of court in 1996

The Event: A law firm filing clerk instigated an investigation into the contamination of a small California town's water supply with a chemical toxin known as chromium 6 by the Pacific Gas and Electric Company (PG&E) that led to the largest settlement ever paid in a lawsuit in the United States up to that time.

Significance: Because the terms of the PG&E settlement have never been made public, details of the forensic investigation leading to that settlement are mostly unknown. Nevertheless, the commercial and critical success of the motion picture *Erin Brockovich* (2000) helped elevate public awareness of the importance of forensic science in identifying toxic pollutants in the environment. The case itself was regarded as a precedent for future litigation for similar cases.

Thanks to a major Hollywood film using her name for its title, Erin Brockovich is indelibly associated with one of the biggest water-contamination cases in U.S. history. While working as a filing clerk in a Southern California law firm, she investigated medical records connected with a real estate case and found evidence that a PG&E facility connected with a natural gas pipeline had contaminated the drinking water of the tiny Mojave Desert community of Hinkley, California, from the 1960's through the 1980's. Brockovich's investigation helped trigger the class-action suit brought against PG&E, and she received a significant share of the money that came out of the case's settlement. However, much of the impetus for the case was provided by residents of Hinkley themselves. Brockovich's name is closely tied to the case largely because of the unusual circumstances of her personal involvement, which was magnified by the film made about the case.

Erin Brockovich during an appearance at California's De Anza College, where she spoke on behalf of the Silicon Valley Toxics Coalition in late 2000. *(AP/Wide World Photos)*

Brockovich's interest in environment cases began after she had been seriously injured in a traffic accident in Nevada. To represent her interests in the legal suit emerging from that accident, she engaged the Thousand Oaks, California, law firm of Masry & Vititoe. Soon afterward, the firm hired her to work as a file clerk, although she was not a college graduate and had no legal training.

While filing papers for a real estate case concerning the community of Hinkley during the early 1990's, Brockovich found information in medical records of Hinkley residents that piqued her curiosity. With her employer's permission, she began researching the matter. Her investigation found that the health of many people who lived in and around Hinkley during the three preceding decades had been damaged by exposure to hexavalent chromium, also known as chromium 6, a suspected carcinogen that had leaked into the groundwater from PG&E's nearby repressurization station. Brockovich's investigation eventually led to a class-action lawsuit against PG&E, which settled most of the cases out of court by paying $333 million in damages to more than six hundred Hinkley residents.

Background

Hinkley, California, is the site of a repressurization, or compressor, station built by PG&E in 1952 to help push natural gas through a long pipeline that connects Texas with Northern California. As gas moves through pipelines, friction causes it to lose the pressure it requires to keep it moving. Compressor stations like that of Hinkley raise the pressure within pipelines to facilitate the transmission of the gas. The gas compressors themselves require cooling, which is done with oil and water. To prevent rust from corroding the cooling system PG&E, PG&E put chromium 6 in the water. Chromium 6 is one of the cheapest and most efficient corrosion inhibitors but is also a highly toxic chemical that many scientists believe is a carcinogen. Between 1952 and 1966 alone, the runoff of fluids from Hinkley's pumping station's cooling system poured about 370 million gallons of chromium-tainted water into the open and unlined ponds near the community.

The Complex Geography of PG&E

The Brockovich-PG&E case revolved around the Southern California community of Hinkley, a tiny, unincorporated town about fourteen miles west of Barstow, on the fringes of the Mojave Desert. One of the largest energy utilities in the United States, PG&E services Northern California and supplies no energy to the southern part of the state. However, much of the natural gas that the company supplies to its Northern California customers comes to it from the Texas Panhandle, through long pipelines that pass through Southern California. To move the gas the great distances it must travel, PG&E maintains repressurization, or pumping, stations every several hundred miles. Leakage of water mixed with chromium 6, a rust inhibitor, from the station near Hinkley contaminated the town's underground water supplies.

During an environmental assessment in 1987, PG&E discovered that chromium 6 had entered Hinkley's groundwater supply and contaminated ten private drinking wells with concentrations of the chemical that exceeded the safety standard set by the state. In December, 1987, PG&E notified the Lahontan Regional Water Quality Board (LRWQB), which managed local water sources, about the contamination. The LRWQB quickly ordered PG&E to clean up the contaminated groundwater. PG&E began to comply, but, after spending $12.5 million on the effort, it approached the owners of three farms and ten houses drawing on the groundwater to inquire about buying their property. When the company offered to pay ten times fair market value for one property, other Hinkley residents became suspicious and took measures to file suit against PG&E.

For the first time, Hinkley residents began to believe that PG&E's use of chromium 6 was causing severe health problems within their town. Many residents cited such health problems as cancer, tumors, and birth defects. PG&E countered by arguing that the incident rates of the health problems the residents cited were not statistically significant in a population the size of Hinkley, even though residents were drinking, bathing in, and inhaling vapor from water contaminated with chromium 6 every day.

Eventually, with the help of Brockovich and the firm for which she worked, approximately 650 plaintiffs claimed that PG&E had failed to warn them adequately of the potential health risks associated with the chromium 6 exuded by the company's compressor plant. Their lawyers also alleged that two PG&E employees who had become whistle-blowers had been instructed by PG&E to dispose of all records from the Hinkley compressor station. The lawsuit the residents filed in 1993 was eventually settled for a $333 million payment in an undisclosed arbitration agreement. Other cash settlements were made over the ensuing decade.

PG&E's out-of-court settlement may have allowed the company to escape a finding of liability by a court, as settlement offers cannot be used in court as evidence of one party's wrongdoing. Because the arbitration was closed to the public, it remains unclear exactly what scientific proof of harm plaintiffs in the case presented or whether PG&E's actions actually damaged the health of Hinkley residents. However, in the public's perception, PG&E's $333 million settlement was equivalent to a conviction. PG&E's alleged cover-up of its activities and the sheer size of the settlement dramatically increased the intrigue of the story and helped to focus public attention on the potential dangers of chromium 6. Despite the size of the settlement, the Hinkley case and the dangers of chromium 6 might have been quietly forgotten, had the story not become the subject of a major Hollywood film.

The *Erin Brockovich* Film

Erin Brockovich's role in the PG&E case inspired a film in the year 2000 that used her name for its title and starred Julia Roberts as Brockovich. The film was an instant box-office hit and eventually grossed almost as much money as PG&E had paid out in its 1996 settlement. The film also received many major awards, including five Academy Award nominations, and won Roberts the Oscar for Best Actress in a Leading Role. More important, the film did a great deal to raise public awareness of the dangers of chromium 6 but did not do so without controversy. PG&E downplayed the film's message, claiming that the story had been highly dramatized for entertainment value, and it sent a memo to its employees warning them that not everything in the film was true. Regardless of the film's historical accuracy, however, it clearly increased public awareness of the importance of water quality and the role that forensic scientists play in uncovering environmental crimes. It also opened up discussion for proponents of more stringent water regulation by creating a media forum in which broader issues of water quality were addressed.

Erin Brockovich led to several concrete changes in government policies regarding environmental health. For example, the state of California passed two bills requiring assessment of chromium 6 levels in drinking water in its San Fernando Basin aquifer and setting limits for chromium 6 in drinking water sources. The federal government allocated $3 million for a treatment plant and technology to remove chromium 6 from drinking water.

Despite the critical acclaim and commercial success enjoyed by the film *Erin Brockovich*, the Brockovich-PG&E case has continued to generate controversy. Some scientists have concluded that chromium 6 is not, after all, a carcinogen. In 2001, the Chromate Toxicity Review Committee, a panel made up of university scientists that had been formed at the request of the California Environmental Protection Agency's Office of Environmental Health Hazard Assessment (OEHHA) concluded that there was no basis for concluding that chromium could cause cancer when ingested through water. Although the panel's report posed a serious challenge to future lawsuits concerning water contamination, some critics suggested that the panel's composition was suspect and its report had been skewed to protect the utility industry's interests.

Dante B. Gatmaytan

Further Reading

Banks, Sedina. "The 'Erin Brockovich Effect': How Media Shapes Toxics Policy." *Environs: Environmental Law and Policy Journal* 26 (2003): 219-251. Presents an interesting exploration of the impact of the film *Erin Brockovich* on public policy decisions.

Brockovich, Erin, and Marc Eliot. *Take It from Me: Life's a Struggle but You Can Win*. New York: McGraw-Hill, 2002. Motivational autobiography in which Brockovich recounts the events in her life that led to her involvement in the PG&E case.

Egilman, David. "Corporate Corruption of Science: The Case of Chromium (VI)." *International Journal of Occupational Environmental Health* 12 (2006): 169-176. Scholarly discussion addresses the controversy over the suspected health hazards of chromium 6.

Ellis, Erin Brockovich, and Dan Levine. "*Erin Brockovich*." *Conservation Matters* 8 (June 22, 2001): 12. Views the film *Erin Brockovich* in the broader context of the impacts on the environment of PG&E's practices.

Grant, Samantha. "*Erin Brockovich*": *The Shooting Script*. New York: Newmarket Press, 2001. Complete script of the Hollywood film based on the Brockovich-PG&E case; edited, with notes, by the original screenwriter, Samantha Grant.

Martens, Daniel L. "Chromium, Cancer, and Causation: Has a Death-Blow Been Dealt Chromium Cases in California?" *Natural Resources and Environment* 16 (2002): 264-266. Focuses on the possible legal impacts of the Brockovich case.

Pellerin, Cheryl, and Susan M. Booker. "Reflections on Hexavalent Chromium: Health Hazards of an Industrial Heavyweight." *Environmental Health Perspectives* 108 (2000): A402-A407. Discusses the potential hazard posed to the environment by chromium 6.

See also: Air and water purity; Chemical terrorism; Decontamination methods; Nuclear detection devices; Nuclear spectroscopy; Toxicological analysis.

Bubonic plague

Definition: Highly contagious human bacterial disease with a very high rate of mortality.

Significance: Natural outbreaks of bubonic plague still occur periodically, with an average of 18 cases in the United States and 1,666 cases worldwide per year. A larger cause for concern, however, is the possibility that weaponized plague bacteria could be used in biological terrorism.

Bubonic plague is caused by a gram-negative, facultative anaerobe bacterial species, *Yersinia pestis*, acting as an intracellular parasite. The disease is transmitted primarily by fleas from infected hosts, including more than two hundred species of rodents as well as domestic cats, dogs, rabbits, and even sheep or camels. Transmission may also occur through contact with infected bodily fluids or tissues as well as through aerosol exposure from a coughing patient. The bubonic plague is also known as the Black Death because it results in buboes, infected and inflamed lymph nodes that turn black as they become necrotic and hemorrhagic.

Three forms of plague are known. The skin form of the disease, bubonic plague, has a mortality rate of 50-90 percent if untreated and up to 15 percent if treated. A second form, pneumonic plague, results when the bacteria invade the lungs. Pneumonic plague is especially virulent, with mortality of 100 percent if not treated within twenty-four hours. Moreover, it causes bronchial pneumonia, which leads to coughing of highly infective aerosols of bacteria. The third form of plague is septicemic plague, in which blood-borne bacteria are widespread throughout the body, invading almost all organs. Septicemic plague is 100 percent fatal if untreated, and some 40 percent of those who contract it die even with treatment. Incubation time for plague before symptoms appear is one to six days.

Symptoms of bubonic plague include fever (as high at 105 degrees Fahrenheit), chills, mus-

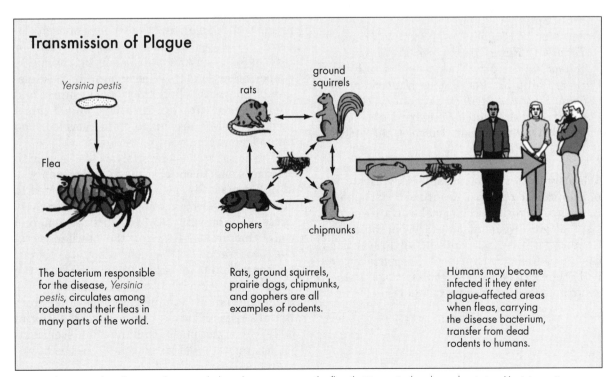

Transmission of Plague

Yersinia pestis

Flea

rats

ground squirrels

gophers

chipmunks

The bacterium responsible for the disease, *Yersinia pestis*, circulates among rodents and their fleas in many parts of the world.

Rats, ground squirrels, prairie dogs, chipmunks, and gophers are all examples of rodents.

Humans may become infected if they enter plague-affected areas when fleas, carrying the disease bacterium, transfer from dead rodents to humans.

A variety of small mammals, particularly rodents, may carry the flea that transmits the plague bacterium *Yersinia pestis*.

cular pain, sore throat, headache, severe weakness, extreme malaise, and enlarged, painful lymph nodes especially in the groin, armpits, and neck. In later stages, accelerated heart rate, accelerated breathing, and low blood pressure ensue. The normal course of treatment is antibiotics of the tetracycline or sulfonamide families. A vaccine does exist, but it is no longer available in the United States; it is used to contain local outbreaks in other parts of the world.

Because of the highly contagious nature of *Y. pestis*, this organism poses a grave danger as an agent in a biological terrorism attack. Aerosolized plague organisms as well as antibiotic-resistant strains of plague have been developed in former biological weapons facilities in Russia and the United States. Rapid identification of the agent is essential in any bioterrorism event.

Ralph R. Meyer

Further Reading

Brubaker, Bob. "*Yersinia pestis* and the Bubonic Plague." In *The Prokaryotes*, edited by Martin Dworkin et al. 3d ed. Vol. 6. New York: Springer, 2006.

Orent, Wendy. *Plague: The Mysterious Past and Terrifying Future of the World's Most Dangerous Disease*. New York: Free Press, 2004.

Parker, Philip M., and James N. Parker. *Bubonic Plague: A Medical Dictionary, Bibliography, and Annotated Research Guide to Internet References*. San Diego, Calif.: ICON Health Publications, 2003.

See also: Bacteria; Bacterial biology; Bacterial resistance and response to antibacterial agents; Biological terrorism; Biological warfare diagnosis; Biological weapon identification; Biotoxins; Centers for Disease Control and Prevention; Chemical Biological Incident Response Force, U.S.; Hemorrhagic fevers; Parasitology; Pathogen transmission; Smallpox; Tularemia.

Bugs. *See* Electronic bugs

Bullet-lead analysis

Definition: Examination of the amounts of trace elements in lead bullets to enable comparison of bullets and determination of their sources.

Significance: Analysis of the trace elements present in bullets can be conducted on bullet fragments found at a shooting scene and on any bullets found in the possession of suspects; comparison of the findings can link a suspect to a crime.

Bullets found at crime scenes may be compared with test bullets fired from weapons suspected to have been used in the crimes, but such analysis is not possible when only bullet fragments are recovered or no weapons are found. To address such situations, the technique of bullet-lead analysis was developed during the 1960's. In this process, a fragment of a bullet is dissolved, the solution is vaporized, and the vapor is heated until it glows. By examining the spectrum of light from the glowing vapor, the analyst can determine what trace elements are present in the lead and the amount of each element. Lead typically has traces (1 percent or less) of antimony, arsenic, bismuth, cadmium, copper, silver, and tin. The amounts of these elements vary with where the lead was mined and what kinds of scrap lead have been added. (Most modern bullets are made from recycled lead taken from automobile batteries.)

The use of bullet-lead analysis has been criticized by some. In one case involving the analysis of bullet lead, Michael Behm was convicted in 1997 of murdering a man in South River, New Jersey. The only physical evidence presented in court that linked Behm to the murder was a chemical match between the amounts of trace elements found in bullet fragments from the crime scene and the amounts of those elements found in ammunition recovered from Behm's home. The prosecution led the jury to believe that this meant that the crime scene bullet fragments must have come from the box of ammunition in Behm's possession. This was a serious misuse of bullet-lead analysis because such a match does not necessarily pinpoint a bullet's source. A large batch (or melt) of lead might produce millions of bullets, so hundreds of people in each of dozens of towns might have had bullets matching the crime scene fragments.

Another serious problem with bullet-lead analysis is the question of how the level of experimental error should be calculated. For example, the amount of antimony in a sample might be reported as 0.85 percent ± 0.15 percent, meaning that the amount of antimony is between 0.70 percent and 1.0 percent. If the level of experimental error (in this instance ±0.15 percent) is estimated from too few measurements, confusion can result. Suppose that the antimony content of a different lead sample is reported as 0.51 percent ± 0.20 percent, so that it lies between 0.31 percent and 0.71 percent. Because this range overlaps with the antimony range given for the first lead sample, it appears that the antimony contents in the two lead samples "match" or are "analytically indistinguishable." Had the second measurement been reported as 0.51 percent ± 0.10 percent, no overlap, and thus no match, would have resulted.

A questionable practice sometimes used in the presentation of evidence involving bullet-lead analysis is called chaining: Because bullet A is found to be a chemical match to bullet B, which in turn matches bullet C, the claim is made that bullet C matches bullet A, regardless of whether A and C are chemical matches. Chaining was used in convicting Behm. On March 7, 2005, an appellate judge ruled this interpretation of the bullet-lead analysis results invalid and overturned Behm's conviction. On September 1, 2005, after extensive review, the Federal Bureau of Investigation (FBI) announced that it would discontinue the use of bullet-lead analysis.

Charles W. Rogers

Further Reading

Boyce, Nell. "Do Bullets Tell Tales?" *U.S. News & World Report*, November 24, 2003, 60-61.

Goho, Alexandra. "Forensics on Trial: Chemical Matching of Bullets Comes Under Fire." *Science News*, March 27, 2004, 202.

See also: Atomic absorption spectrophotometry; Ballistic fingerprints; Ballistics; Firearms analysis; Gunshot residue; Gunshot wounds; Integrated Ballistics Identification System; Lead; Nuclear spectroscopy.

Bureau of Alcohol, Tobacco, Firearms and Explosives

Date: Established in 1972 as the Bureau of Alcohol, Tobacco and Firearms, an independent division of the U.S. Department of the Treasury

Identification: Regulatory and law-enforcement unit of the U.S. Department of Justice.

Significance: The lead agency for much of the U.S. government's forensic work involving firearms, explosives, and arson.

The bulk of the work of the Bureau of Alcohol, Tobacco, Firearms and Explosives (ATF, also sometimes known as BATFE) involves the regulation of lawful firearms and explosives businesses in the United States as well as some regulation of alcohol (for example, labeling laws) and tobacco. The bureau also enforces federal criminal laws related to these products and, accordingly, conducts forensic investigations involving firearms and explosives as well as illegal sales of alcohol and tobacco.

Firearms

Pursuant to U.S. law, all firearms must have serial numbers, and persons who sell firearms (whether as manufacturers, wholesalers, or retailers) must keep written records of the sales. Starting in the 1990's, many manufacturers and wholesalers of firearms began providing ATF's National Tracing Center with computerized records of all their sales. In conjunction with local law-enforcement agencies, ATF frequently uses serial numbers to trace the histories of recovered crime guns. In some cases, ATF agents conduct fieldwork to attempt to find out what happened to particular guns after their retail sale.

ATF's National Integrated Ballistic Information Network (NIBIN) uses the Integrated Ballistics Identification System (IBIS) to supply 182 federal, state, and local law-enforcement agencies with ditigized images of bullets and cartridge cases recovered from crime scenes. These images can be used in ballistic fingerprinting—for example, to investigate whether the same gun might have been used in crimes in two different states.

Arson and Explosives

Federal law regulates the manufacture, sale, and possession of explosives in the United States and provides penalties for the misuse of explosive materials. Under the theory that some fires are started with accelerants that might legally be considered explosives, ATF has become the leading federal agency involved in arson investigation. In 1978, the bureau created its National Response Team (NRT), which assists local authorities in investigating significant arson fires. The NRT comprises four units, each assigned to a different region of the United States. Each NRT unit includes ATF agents with expertise in arson or bombing investigation, forensic chemists, dogs trained in the detection of explosives or accelerants, and various support personnel.

The main purpose of the NRT is to assist in local investigations of major commercial arson fires, but the NRT also provides help to local law-enforcement agencies that must investigate bombings. The NRT was involved with the investigations of the 1993 World Trade Center bombing, the 1995 Oklahoma City bombing, and the 1996 Atlanta Summer Olympics bombing. The NRT also supports ATF's regulatory role by participating in investigations of illegal explosives manufacturing and by responding to explosions at lawful ammunition and fireworks factories.

ATF's International Response Team (IRT) assists in arson and explosives investigations in foreign countries, with the approval of the U.S. ambassadors to the particular nations. The IRT has participated in the investigation of Islamist terrorist bombings in Argentina as well as in investigations involving improvised explosive devices (IEDs) in other nations.

In 1996, many news media outlets in the United States reported on what some observers described as a massive wave of racist arson attacks on black churches in the South. Although no actual increase in church arson attacks had occurred, in response to the perceived need

---

ATF's Stated Mission, Vision, and Values

Mission
The Bureau of Alcohol, Tobacco, Firearms and Explosives (ATF) is a principal law enforcement agency within the United States Department of Justice dedicated to preventing terrorism, reducing violent crime, and protecting our Nation. The men and women of ATF perform the dual responsibilities of enforcing Federal criminal laws and regulating the firearms and explosives industries. We are committed to working directly, and through partnerships, to investigate and reduce crime involving firearms and explosives, acts of arson, and illegal trafficking of alcohol and tobacco products.

Vision
The Bureau of Alcohol, Tobacco, Firearms and Explosives must protect the public against crime, violence, and other threats to public safety. Our vision will help us chart the course to improve the way we serve and protect the public, provide leadership and expertise, and achieve new levels of effectiveness and teamwork.

Values
We value each other and those we serve. We will:
- Uphold the highest standards of excellence and integrity;
- Provide high quality service and promote strong external partnerships;
- Develop a diverse, innovative, and well-trained work force to achieve our goals; and
- Embrace learning and change in order to meet the challenges of the future.

Agents of the Bureau of Alcohol, Tobacco, Firearms and Explosives search through the ashes for evidence after an arson fire destroyed the Mount Pleasant Missionary Baptist Church in Kossuth, Mississippi. This fire was one of numerous arson attacks on African American churches in the South in 1996. *(AP/Wide World Photos)*

the U.S. Congress and President Bill Clinton created the National Church Arson Task Force (NCATF), a multiagency federal organization in which ATF assisted with church-related arson and bombing investigations.

Research and Training

In its database known as the Arson and Explosives National Repository, ATF compiles information about arson and explosives crimes and suspected crimes. The bureau uses the Advanced Serial Case Management (ASCMe) system to manage the collection and organization of data from arson scenes.

In 1986, ATF and the Federal Bureau of Investigation (FBI) began a joint program to profile at-large criminals who are perpetrating arson or bombings. The Arson and Bombing Investigative Services (ABIS) subunit is part of

the FBI's National Center for the Analysis of Violent Crime (NCAVC) in Quantico, Virginia.

The U.S. Bomb Data Center was created by Congress in 1996. Led by ATF, the center compiles data about arson and explosives crimes from various agencies and makes those data available for statistical research by scholars and law-enforcement personnel.

ATF also operates three laboratories (in Atlanta, San Francisco, and suburban Maryland) that work on cases involving alcohol, tobacco, firearms, explosives, and fire debris. The ATF National Laboratory Center in Maryland has a facility where scientists researching arson can re-create the circumstances of particular fires under controlled conditions. Each of the three ATF labs has a Rapid Response Laboratory that can join on-scene investigations.

ATF conducts many training programs for

other law-enforcement agencies, covering topics such as arson investigation, recovery of defaced serial numbers on firearms, and postblast explosives investigation.

David B. Kopel

Further Reading

Kopel, David B., and Paul H. Blackman. *No More Wacos: What's Wrong with Federal Law Enforcement and How to Fix It*. Amherst, N.Y.: Prometheus Books, 1997. Offers a close analysis of the disastrous 1993 raid on the Branch Davidians compound in Waco in the context of broader problems with the Bureau of Alcohol, Tobacco and Firearms.

Moore, James. *Very Special Agents: The Inside Story of America's Most Controversial Law Enforcement Agency—The Bureau of Alcohol, Tobacco, and Firearms*. Champaign: University of Illinois Press, 2001. Presents a fervent and heartfelt defense of the bureau. Includes several informative appendixes.

National Learning Corporation. *Alcohol, Tobacco and Firearms (ATF) Inspector: Test Preparation Study Guide—Questions and Answers*. Syosset, N.Y.: Author, 2005. Volume designed to prepare students to pass a qualifying test to become an ATF inspector. Focuses on the bureau's regulatory side.

U.S. Bureau of Alcohol, Tobacco, Firearms and Explosives. *2008 Essential Guide to the ATF: Complete Coverage of Firearms Publications, Laws, Forms*. Washington, D.C.: Author, 2007. This guide on CD-ROM, published annually, provides all the material available on the ATF Web site as well as many other public documents related to the bureau.

Vizzard, William J. *In the Cross Fire: A Political History of the Bureau of Alcohol, Tobacco, and Firearms*. Boulder, Colo.: Lynne Rienner, 1997. A retired ATF supervisor criticizes the bureau's institutional weaknesses.

See also: Accelerants; Arson; Ballistic fingerprints; Body farms; Bombings; Canine substance detection; Exhumation; Federal Bureau of Investigation; Firearms analysis; Improvised explosive devices; Integrated Ballistics Identification System; National Church Arson Task Force; World Trade Center bombing.

Buried body locating

Definition: Determination of the placement of human remains that are obscured from view—whether by water, soil, or other intervening materials—for the purpose of their recovery.

Significance: Law-enforcement authorities are concerned with the systematic and efficient location of human remains in cases of crimes, accidents, and natural disasters, as location of the remains is the vital first stage in the recovery and identification of the victims, the investigation of the manner of their death, and the return of the remains to surviving relatives.

Human remains may be obscured from view, or buried, as the result of intentional human acts, accidents, or natural events. Bodies can be buried in a variety of settings, depending on the circumstances preceding death and at the time of death. In cases of crimes, accidents, and natural disasters, bodies may be obscured by water, soil, building debris, or other materials. Different burial environments require different methods of body location.

Possible Locations of Bodies

Human remains in bodies of water may be trapped in sunken ships, automobiles, or aircraft, or they may be entangled in or obscured by trees, logs, or brush floating in the water or along the banks of rivers or lakes. In the case of a disaster such as the collapse of a bridge over water, bodies may be further obscured by debris from the fallen structure.

Bodies buried in soil may be found at various depths, depending on the circumstances of the deaths. Perpetrators of homicides might bury victims covertly only a few inches below the surface. Bodies buried by mudslides might be found several feet under the surface, and those of the victims of an airplane crash might be interred deeply (along with associated debris) as a result of the impact of the aircraft. Victims of a building collapse might not be buried in the soil but may be obscured from view under construction debris. Victims of floods or tornados might also be hidden under debris, whether that of buildings or natural materials.

Methods

The method of body location applied is specific to the particular case at hand. When bodies are believed to be in a body of water, physical searches may be conducted by certified divers, although in some circumstances floating sediment or algae can obscure visibility. Small, localized bodies of water, such as ponds, may be dredged or drained to enhance exposure of any human remains. Side-scan sonar, which produces sound pulses that reflect off submerged objects and are recorded, is a remote-sensing technology that has been used with success to identify sunken vessels, crashed airplanes, and even individual drowning victims submerged in water. Computer simulations may also be conducted to predict the locations of drowning victims, given known hydrological data for a body of water.

For bodies buried under soil, a variety of location methods may be used. A walkover line survey, wherein several searchers are aligned and move in unison across the search area, is effec-

Employees of a commercial locating service stand near their ground-penetrating radar equipment while awaiting permission to enter an Indianapolis home to assist in a homicide investigation in early 2005. With the aid of their equipment, the bodies of three recent murder victims were found buried under freshly laid concrete. Although used primarily for locating underground utility conduits at construction sites, ground-penetrating radar is also invaluable to homicide investigations and archaeologists, as this technology often enables the quick location of human remains without damaging structures or other property. *(AP/Wide World Photos)*

tive in identifying the disturbed soil or vegetation indicative of a covert (hidden) burial, usually fairly close to the surface. Even though this method works best in open areas, some modified form of walkover survey is a useful first step even in urban mass-disaster settings (such as the aftermath of a tornado). In such a setting, individual remains may be partially covered or intermingled with debris on or near the surface of the soil.

Remote-sensing techniques such as infrared aerial photography and electromagnetic devices such as ground-penetrating radar (GPR), soil resistivity or conductivity meters, and metal detectors are also useful. Infrared aerial photography is most useful for identifying large buried features, such as mass graves. GPR is considered the best ground survey tool for identifying graves, although it works best in well-drained soil. Resistivity or conductivity meters and metal detectors can find buried metallic objects that may be associated with buried bodies. These remote-sensing devices identify anomalies (unusual patterns) in the electromagnetic signals coming from the ground. Forensic investigators can then narrow their focus on these anomalies as potential locations of buried remains. Actual controlled excavation of these anomalies is necessary to confirm their forensic significance.

When bodies are obscured by vegetation debris or by debris from destroyed structures following natural or human-made disasters, such as Hurricane Katrina or the September 11, 2001, terrorist attacks on the World Trade Center in New York City, special measures may be needed to locate them. In localized events, cadaver dogs can help to locate bodies under debris by scent. When large mass disasters occur, local authorities may be overwhelmed and may require outside assistance. In 1993, the U.S. government established ten regional Disaster Mortuary Operational Response Teams (DMORTs) to provide local agencies with added expertise in the location, recovery, and identification of deceased individuals after such disasters. These teams, under the direction of the U.S. Department of Health and Human Services (National Disaster Medical System), are made up of pathologists, forensic anthropolo-

gists, forensic odontologists, medical technicians, medical examiners, nurses, medical technologists, counselors, and funeral home directors. Team members are skilled private citizens who, when deployed, have the initial goal of location and recovery of remains in complex, debris-filled settings.

Cliff Boyd

Further Reading

Buck, Sabrina. "Searching for Graves Using Geophysical Technology: Field Tests with Ground Penetrating Radar, Magnetometry, and Electrical Resistivity." *Journal of Forensic Sciences* 48 (2003): 5-11. Reports on the results of tests of the efficiency of three geophysical remote-sensing techniques in a variety of settings, including cemeteries and in a murder investigation. Discusses the limitations of each method in detail.

Dupras, Tosha L., John J. Schultz, Sandra M. Wheeler, and Lana J. Williams. *Forensic Recovery of Human Remains: Archaeological Approaches.* Boca Raton, Fla.: CRC Press, 2006. Provides detailed descriptions of search-and-recovery methods and the equipment used for such purposes in forensic scene investigations. Includes standardized recording forms and conversion tables in appendixes.

Haglund, William D., and Marcella H. Sorg, eds. *Advances in Forensic Taphonomy: Method, Theory, and Archaeological Perspectives.* Boca Raton, Fla.: CRC Press, 2002. Extensive edited volume presents several case studies of the recovery of human remains in a variety of settings, including remains found in water, in burned structures, and in mass graves.

Killam, Edward W. *The Detection of Human Remains.* 2d ed. Springfield, Ill.: Charles C Thomas, 2004. Presents thorough descriptions of intrusive and nonintrusive forensic search methods, including various forms of remote sensing.

Owsley, Douglas. "Techniques for Locating Burials, with Emphasis on the Probe." *Journal of Forensic Sciences* 40 (1995): 735-740. Discusses the effectiveness of intrusive methods of locating graves.

Burn pattern analysis

Definition: Analysis of the spread of a fire from its site of origin, along with the type of burn damage and extent of destruction, to determine the cause of the fire.

Significance: Burn pattern analysis helps investigators to determine whether fires were started by natural events (such as lightning strikes) or by human activity and, if the latter, whether they were caused accidentally (for example, by cooking fires or welding sparks) or intentionally. Determining the causes of fires is important to both law-enforcement and insurance investigators because arson is the most common cause of major structure fires (houses, schools, warehouses) and accounts for greater monetary losses than any other category of fires.

Every twenty seconds, a fire department somewhere in the United States responds to a fire. According to the National Fire Protection Association, in 2006 more than 1.6 million fires caused 3,245 civilian and 89 firefighter deaths and $11.3 billion in property damage. More than 31,000 structure fires and 20,500 vehicle fires were intentionally set, about half of them by juveniles. Nevertheless, despite the high rate of arson fires, few arsonists are successfully prosecuted.

In the past, much of the information investigators had about how different types of fires behave and the burn patterns they leave behind was gleaned from firefighter observation. In the twenty-first century, however, the desire to improve the rates of arson convictions has combined with advances in technology to create a movement to develop a better and more scien-

tific understanding of how fires behave under specific conditions. Researchers at educational agencies such as the Maryland Fire and Rescue Institute at the University of Maryland use controlled experiments to demonstrate that different types of fires create different burn patterns and to validate what burn pattern analysis reveals about the origin, type of fuel, and other factors that characterize a fire.

Point of Origin and Ignition

Every fire starts somewhere. Burn pattern analysis begins with an attempt to determine the site or origin of the fire. When a fire ignites simultaneously in several locations within a building, for example, this pattern suggests that the fire was intentionally set. A single point of origin does not by itself rule out arson, however. Investigators also consider whether the fire started inside or outside the structure or vehicle, if it started in a location where one might normally expect to find an ignition source (such as in a kitchen or workshop), and what type of fuel was likely to be available. In determining the point of origin, investigators may not only examine the physical remains of the structure or vehicle but may also request a chemical analysis of the remains and interview witnesses for information about the early stages of the fire.

Spread and Intensity

Once a fire has ignited, how it behaves is determined by three factors: availability of fuel, availability of oxygen, and the heat these produce. These factors are in turn influenced by such elements as the type of fuel available, weather conditions, ventilation systems, drafts from open windows and doors, functioning of installed fire suppression equipment within a building, and firefighter intervention. Although most fires follow a characteristic pattern of development, the constellation of conditions surrounding each fire is unique, and a burn pattern analysis must consider all these factors.

Investigators know that certain materials burn in predictable ways and leave particular telltale signs. Burn pattern analysis involves putting all these signs together to explain the behavior of the fire. Examples of signs that fire investigators might look for that can become part of their burn pattern analyses include the following:

- V-shaped charring patterns on walls, which can give clues to the intensity of fires
- Spalling, or flaking, patterns on concrete or stone floors, which may indicate that accelerant liquids were dribbled across the floors and ignited
- Large, shiny char blisters, which are more likely to form when accelerant liquids are present (small, dull blisters are more characteristic of slow-igniting accidental fires)
- Atypical burn rates for specific materials, which may suggest that accelerants were used
- Abnormal or atypical continuity of burn patterns

Because of the many factors that influence the behavior of any given fire, burn pattern analysis evidence is often successfully challenged in court. Only 2 percent of arson cases result in conviction. Since the late 1990's, the federal Building and Fire Research Laboratory (BFRL) has conducted research to gather scientific documentation on specific burn patterns. For example, researchers have started experimental fires under precisely the same conditions but using different types of accelerants; they have also started fires in rooms that are identical except for having different types of flooring. The burn

patterns and other data from these experiments are documented and made available to fire investigators. In addition, the BFRL has developed computer simulations of fire scenarios to assist in training fire investigators and to help explain the results of burn pattern analyses to jurors.

Martiscia Davidson

College students in a class on arson investigation observe the burn patterns in several staged fires. *(AP/Wide World Photos)*

Further Reading

Almirall, José R., and Kenneth G. Furton, eds. *Analysis and Interpretation of Fire Scene Evidence*. Boca Raton, Fla.: CRC Press, 2004. Examines the technical aspects of fire scene investigation with emphasis on what burn patterns can tell investigators.

Faith, Nicholas. *Blaze: The Forensics of Fire*. New York: St. Martin's Press, 2000. Describes how fire investigators work and the methods that forensic scientists use in examining evidence from fire scenes.

Icove, David J., and John D. DeHaan. *Forensic Fire Scene Reconstruction*. 2d ed. Upper Saddle River, N.J.: Pearson Prentice Hall, 2008. Shows how investigators trace the history of a fire by using physical evidence of human activity and knowledge of burn patterns.

MacDonald, Jake. "After the Inferno: Winnipeg's Arson Squad Can Tell How a Fire Started and Often Who Started It, by Sifting Through the Ashes and Reading Scorch Marks on the Wall." *Saturday Night*, May 20, 2000, 24-32. Explains how fire investigators use burn pattern analysis to determine how a fire started.

Redsicker, David R., and John J. O'Connor. *Practical Fire and Arson Investigation*. 2d ed. Boca Raton, Fla.: CRC Press, 1997. Provides comprehensive coverage of all aspects of fire investigations, with emphasis on fires that cause death.

See also: Accelerants; American Academy of Forensic Sciences; Arson; Bureau of Alcohol, Tobacco, Firearms and Explosives; Crime scene documentation; Electrical injuries and deaths; Fire debris; National Church Arson Task Force; Physical evidence; Structural analysis.

Cadaver dogs

Definition: Dogs that are specially trained to find the scents associated with decomposing human remains.

Significance: Although dogs have been used for many years to aid in crime detection, their use in more highly specialized investigative techniques is a relatively recent development. During the last two decades of the twentieth century, law-enforcement agencies and dog trainers increasingly focused on training dogs to search out human remains in addition to the already established use of dogs to track living humans.

Cadaver dogs constitute a subcategory of search-and-rescue dogs, which are used to help law-enforcement officials find missing people. Cadaver dogs differ from other kinds of search-and-rescue dogs in that cadaver dogs search only for human remains; they are not used to find living humans or other kinds of evidence. Training dogs for the purpose of finding human remains is a fairly recent development in law enforcement's use of dogs. In addition to their use by law enforcement at crime scenes, cadaver dogs are used to find bodies following natural and human-caused disasters.

Cadaver dogs receive specialized training in which they are cross-trained for use both in trailing living humans and in detecting the scents of decomposing human remains. These dogs are trained to differentiate among a variety of scents and to recognize the difference between decomposing human flesh and other scents. In addition to identifying the locations of recent human remains, cadaver dogs can detect the presence of bones and blood as well as other residual scents.

Most cadaver dogs are first trained as trailing and air-scenting dogs, which are used in tracking lost and injured people. After their initial training in tracking general scents, they begin their training as cadaver dogs. In this stage, trainers use special chemicals that mimic the smells of decomposing human flesh to familiarize the dogs with the scents associated with human remains. Careful screening is necessary to identify those dogs that are likely to become good cadaver dogs; trainers must attempt to determine the dogs' abilities to track the necessary scents and whether the dogs are attracted to those scents.

The Institute for Canine Forensics and other organizations draw distinctions among different kinds of search-and-rescue dogs. Subcategories of dogs used by law enforcement, in addi-

A cadaver dog and his handler from Rhode Island Urban Search and Rescue search for human bodies near Waveland, Mississippi, in September, 2005, after Hurricane Katrina destroyed homes and property there. *(AP/Wide World Photos)*

tion to cadaver dogs, include search dogs, area search dogs, trailing dogs, forensic evidence dogs, water search dogs, and human remains detection dogs. The last of these are similar to cadaver dogs but more specialized, in that human remains detection dogs are trained only to scent decomposing human flesh; they have never been trained to track living humans. The training of human remains detection dogs includes training in the ability to rule out the scent of live human flesh and other animal scents.

The science of canine forensics is a fairly new discipline in law enforcement. As more dogs are used successfully in new capacities, the idea of using dogs for many law-enforcement purposes is gaining popularity. Highly trained dogs such as cadaver dogs are becoming an indispensable part of many law-enforcement agencies.

Kimberley M. Holloway

Further Reading

Bulanda, Susan. *Ready! The Training of the Search and Rescue Dog.* Irvine, Calif.: Doral Publishing, 1994.

Rebmann, Andrew, and Edward David. *Cadaver Dog Handbook: Forensic Training and Tactics for the Recovery of Human Remains.* Boca Raton, Fla.: CRC Press, 2000.

Snovak, Angela Eaton. *Guide to Search and Rescue Dogs.* New York: Barron's Educational Series, 2004.

See also: Animal evidence; Buried body locating; Canine substance detection; Crime scene investigation; Decomposition of bodies; Fire debris; Forensic archaeology; Scent identification.

Canine substance detection

Definition: Work carried out by trained dog and handler teams to discover contraband items and hazardous materials associated with criminal activities or security threats.

Significance: Well-trained dogs, with their natural scent abilities, are able to locate illegal narcotics and explosive and flammable chemicals expeditiously, whereas humans and technological search devices might overlook these materials or discover them only slowly. Canine substance detection has proven useful in the apprehension and prosecution of lawbreakers.

For several centuries, dogs have assisted humans in seeking forensic evidence related to crimes, including tracking missing people and finding human remains. Law-enforcement agencies' use of canines to detect illegal drugs, explosives, and accelerants intensified during the late twentieth century. Although other animals, such as rats, also have keen smelling abilities, law-enforcement personnel prefer dogs because of their appeal to many people, their ability to work in congested areas and shift quickly to additional sites, and their willingness to obey commands.

The scent capabilities of canines significantly exceed those of humans. A dog's sense of smell is enhanced by the presence of approximately 220 olfactory receptors in the nose. Mucus covers these receptors, enabling them to capture molecules released by chemicals when the dog sniffs nearby. Information from these molecules reaches the dog's brain through a nerve, alerting it to the presence of specific substances. These qualities make dogs ideal for law-enforcement use in detecting various illegal and dangerous substances.

Training and Certification

Law-enforcement personnel procure detection dogs from various sources. The Australian Customs Service Detector Dog Breeding Program provides stock for U.S. detection dog breeders, particularly the Transportation Security Administration (TSA) Explosive Detection Dog Program and Auburn University's Canine Detection Training Center (CDTC) at McClellan, Alabama, which supply detection dogs for governments at various levels. As the sole training program of its kind affiliated with a veterinary school, the CDTC benefits from studies conducted by veterinarians and scientists at the Canine and Detection Research Institute. The government and university programs focus on refining detection qualities in Labrador retrievers, Belgian Malinois, and shepherd breeds considered to be behaviorally reliable and physically sturdy.

Detector dog selection and training are rigorous, and only the most competent canines are approved for deployment to law-enforcement agencies. Several government facilities, the CDTC, and private businesses train canines and handlers for substance-detection duties. The Bureau of Alcohol, Tobacco, Firearms and Explosives (ATF) Canine Training Center at Front Royal, Virginia, where the U.S. Customs and Border Protection (CBP) also has a canine training site, certifies dogs that complete successfully national odor recognition testing. The U.S. Drug Enforcement Administration (DEA) licenses the use of drugs at government and approved private training facilities. ATF also trains canines to detect explosives, working with forensic chemists to choose appropriate explosives for effective training.

According to their individual intended purposes, the dogs are trained to detect and distinguish the scents of many substances, ranging from chemicals found in heroin, cocaine, marijuana, and methamphetamine to explosive nitroglycerin, trinitrotoluene (TNT), and smokeless powders. In ATF training for arson dogs, the dogs learn to detect specified odors of gasoline, kerosene, and other accelerants.

Detection and Effectiveness

Many law-enforcement officials consider the use of canines to be the most efficient and effective method of detecting narcotic substances, resulting in arrests of suspects. Substance-detection dogs are taken to public and private locations, including schools, businesses, prisons, stadiums, and motor vehicles, where they seek the scents they are directed to detect; they alert their handlers to any substance finds by scratching, barking, or sitting.

At border checkpoints, CBP and U.S. Department of Agriculture detection dogs search for illegal substances, including harmful agricultural products. For example, in 2004, U.S. customs authorities using substance-detection dogs conducted 11,600 narcotics seizures totaling approximately 1.8 million pounds of narcotics as well as 6,500 pounds of illegal plant and animal products.

Substance-detection dogs that locate explosives effectively defuse potentially hazardous situations. The U.S. Department of Homeland Security oversees canine substance detection in its antiterrorism work; this work is conducted by CBP and TSA dogs that are trained to locate dangerous chemicals and bombs. Because such substances are often hidden in sealed containers and in concealed areas, dogs can swiftly find them where humans might not easily detect them. Explosives experts provide information on the chemicals that have previously been used by terrorists, and the dogs are trained to detect those substances.

As part of enhanced security measures in the United States and elsewhere, canines sniff luggage, packages, mail, and cargo for illegal substances, explosives, and bombs at airports, train stations, ports, and crowded areas that could be terrorist targets. Dogs are used to examine industrial sites for potential sabotage. The ability of dogs to detect explosive chemicals has also led to their use in arson investigations to find accelerants at sites of suspicious fires. As new chemical threats emerge, researchers and trainers are constantly refining their training procedures to expand the abilities of substance-detection dogs to detect chemical and narcotic substances.

Despite detector dogs' high accuracy rates, many courts disregard evidence located by dogs through scent detection because this method lacks a sufficient scientific basis. Some judges, however, have ruled that search warrants can be issued based on detection dogs' alerts, as in the finding in *United States v. Trayer* (1990), a

An officer with the Maryland Transportation Authority works with a substance-detecting dog to check luggage for the presence of explosives or other hazardous materials at Baltimore-Washington International Airport. *(AP/Wide World Photos)*

case that involved a dog alerting to drugs at the door of a train compartment.

To reinforce legal acceptance of the forensic contributions of detector dogs, researchers are attempting to gain a better scientific understanding of canine scent-detection capabilities. Scientists study handler-canine interactions, canine behavior, and environmental factors to try to find ways to improve dogs' scent-detection training and performance. Law-enforcement agencies consistently evaluate and recertify substance-detection canines and their handlers, removing from service those that do not perform adequately and might discredit canine substance detection as a forensic tool.

Elizabeth D. Schafer

Further Reading

Bidner, Jen. *Dog Heroes: Saving Lives and Protecting America.* Guilford, Conn.: Lyons Press/Globe Pequot Press, 2002. Presents examples of canines performing police and customs work, including ATF detection dogs that search for drugs and bombs.

Bryson, Sandy. *Police Dog Tactics.* New York: McGraw-Hill, 1996. Comprehensive text written by a police dog trainer and handler. Includes sections on drug searches and the detection of explosives and accelerants.

Derr, Mark. "With Dog Detectives, Mistakes Can Happen." *The New York Times*, December 24, 2002, p. F1. Relates some incidents in which detection canines falsely alerted to locating substances and examines the reasons for dogs' scenting errors.

Needles, Colleen, and Kit Carlson. *Working Dogs: Tales from Animal Planet's K-9 to 5 World.* Photographs by Kim Levin. New York: Discovery Books, 2000. Profiles several drug enforcement, arson, police, and customs inspector dogs.

U.S. Congress. House. Committee on Homeland Security. *Sniffing Out Terrorism: The Use of Dogs in Homeland Security.* Washington, D.C.: Government Printing Office, 2007. Transcript of statements made by canine detection trainers, handlers, scientists, and law-enforcement representatives at a congressional hearing held on September 28, 2005.

See also: Airport security; Bombings; Bureau of Alcohol, Tobacco, Firearms and Explosives; Cadaver dogs; Courts and forensic evidence; Drug Enforcement Administration, U.S.; Fire debris; Narcotics; Scent identification; Training and licensing of forensic professionals.

Carbon monoxide poisoning

Definition: Poisoning caused by exposure to toxic levels of carbon monoxide, a colorless, odorless, and tasteless gas derived from incomplete burning of carbon-containing organic materials, such as gasoline, natural gas, oil, propane, coal, and wood.

Significance: Carbon monoxide (CO) poisoning is the most common type of accidental poisoning that occurs in the United States. Undetected, unsuspected, or undiagnosed, carbon monoxide poisoning can result in death. Hospital emergency departments treat thousands of patients with confirmed and probable CO poisoning yearly, and hundreds of fatalities occur as the result of unintentional, non-fire-related CO exposure. It is estimated that the incidence of intentional CO poisoning, such as suicide and homicide, is even higher.

Carbon monoxide is known as the "silent cold-weather killer" and as "the Great Imitator" because the manifestations of its toxicity are nonspecific. If CO is not considered as a cause when CO poisoning occurs, health care personnel can easily misdiagnose the victim. CO is a ubiquitous gas that is present in workplaces, recreational areas, and homes. The most common sources of carbon monoxide include motor vehicle exhaust, smoke from fires, portable kerosene heaters, charcoal grills, propane stoves, and tobacco smoke. Chemical sources include spray paints, solvents, degreasers, and paint removers containing methylene chloride, which is processed in the liver and changed into CO.

The annual incidence of fatal and nonfatal toxic exposure to carbon monoxide is highest during the winter months, when many homes are closed up against cold weather; cases of CO poisoning are fewest during the summer months. More than two hundred CO poisoning fatalities are caused annually in the United States by fuel-burning appliances such as furnaces, gas ranges, water heaters, and kerosene space heaters. CO poisoning occurs at low levels in susceptible individuals, such as young infants, pregnant women, the elderly, and those with anemia or heart and lung diseases.

The symptoms of CO poisoning are vague; in many ways they are similar to those of viral illnesses, and victims may be misdiagnosed. The most common symptoms are headache, dizziness, nausea, and fatigue. More severe symptoms include loss of consciousness, shortness of breath, confusion, and loss of muscle control. Some patients develop delayed symptoms of the nervous system, such as memory loss, personality changes, and movement disorders. All of these symptoms arise because CO binds tightly to hemoglobin, a protein found in red blood cells, and this binding causes a decrease in oxygen supply, especially in the heart and brain. Medical personnel should be suspicious if anyone displaying such symptoms reports circumstances of the illness that could relate to possible CO exposure.

The diagnosis of CO poisoning is made through the measurement of the CO bound to hemoglobin. Treatment consists of providing supplemental oxygen to dissociate the CO-hemoglobin binding. Oxygen may be delivered through a face mask, through hyperbaric oxygen therapy, or through mechanical ventilation.

Preventive measures to avoid CO poisoning include having heating and ventilation systems, water heaters, and other similar devices serviced yearly by qualified technicians. Generators, charcoal grills, camp stoves, and other similar appliances should not be used indoors or near buildings, and gas ovens should not be used to heat homes. In addition to these precautions, many experts recommend the installation of home CO detectors, which should be checked regularly. Finally, medical attention should be obtained immediately if CO poisoning is suspected.

Miriam E. Schwartz and Shawkat Dhanani

Further Reading

Occupational Safety and Health Administration. *Carbon Monoxide Poisoning Fact Sheet*. Washington, D.C.: Government Printing Office, 2002.

Penny, David G., ed. *Carbon Monoxide Poisoning*. Boca Raton, Fla.: CRC Press, 2007.

Piantadosi, Claude A. "Perspective: Carbon Monoxide Poisoning." *New England Journal of Medicine* 347, no. 14 (2002): 1054-1055.

See also: Air and water purity; Arson; Centers for Disease Control and Prevention; Chemical agents; Food poisoning; Forensic toxicology; Livor mortis; Nervous system; Poisons and antidotes; Smoke inhalation; Suffocation; Suicide.

Casting

Definition: Production of three-dimensional models of impressions left by footwear, tires, or tools at crime scenes.

Significance: Forensic scientists use casts, permanent physical records of marks left at crime scenes, to compare with the vehicle tires, footwear, or tools found in the possession of possible suspects.

Perpetrators often leave traces of their presence at crime scenes in the form of tire impressions or footprints in dust, soil, mud, or snow. The tools used by perpetrators also leave distinctive impressions, such as the marks left on a door by a crowbar. Casting is a way of making permanent three-dimensional records of these impressions. Because tires, footwear, and tools do not wear evenly, they develop unique use patterns. Using a cast made from an impression found at a crime scene, a forensic scientist can compare the unique wear pattern shown by that impression with the wear patterns on the possessions of any suspects. Casts often show marks with a degree of accuracy that either confirms or eliminates the presence of some persons at the crime scene. In court, casts are used as physical evidence to show a link between the accused and the crime.

Casting in Soil

Castings in mud, dirt, and sand are made with a product known as dental stone. Dental stone creates a crisper, more detailed cast than does plaster of paris or other plasters and is less likely to be damaged during cleaning. Dental stone comes in powder form, and water is added at the crime scene to make a runny, batterlike mixture that is used to fill the impression. Photographs are taken to locate the impression within the scene, and a plastic frame is placed around the impression before the cast is made.

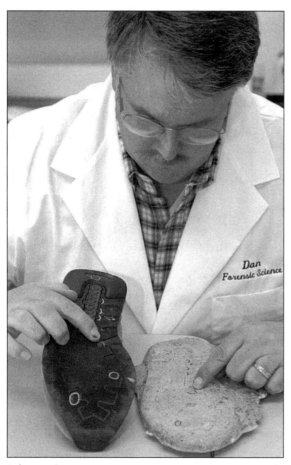

A forensic latent impressions examiner compares a cast made from a shoe print at a crime scene with the sole of the shoe that may have made the print. (AP/Wide World Photos)

In loose soil or sand, the impression may be sprayed with a chemical that hardens the surface before casting.

To prevent distortion of the impression, the technician fills it with dental stone gently. After the impression is filled, the dental stone is allowed to harden for at least half an hour in warm weather and longer in cold or very humid conditions. Before hardening is complete, the technician inscribes the cast with identifying information. Once the cast has solidified, it is removed from the soil and is allowed to air-dry for several days, after which it is cleaned of clinging soil and examined.

Casting in Snow

Casting in snow creates special problems because of the fragility of the impression. This is especially true when the impression has been made in very dry, nonpacking, or windblown snow, or in snow that has begun to melt. Two techniques can be used to cast in snow. In one, before the dental stone cast is made, several layers of a product called Snow Print Wax are sprayed over the snow to stabilize the impression. The impression is then cast in the same way as an impression in soil. Cold conditions substantially slow the hardening of the cast, and it may be several hours before the cast can be removed from the snow.

Another way of casting in snow involves the use of Snow Print Wax and prill sulfur, a pellet form of sulfur that is a by-product of natural gas refining. The pellets are melted and then cooled so that the sulfur will not melt the snow. The impression is first sprayed with Snow Print Wax and then filled with the melted sulfur. Pouring the sulfur when it is at the correct temperature—not hot enough to melt the snow yet not so cold that it starts to form crystals before it is poured—is a critical step in creating a good prill sulfur cast. After about twenty minutes, the cast is hard enough to remove. Because prill sulfur casts are brittle and easily broken, they are often embedded in a protective layer of dental stone. In 2003, the Royal Canadian Mounted Police tested both methods of casting in snow and found that prill sulfur casting produced sharper, more detailed casts than did Snow Print Wax casting alone.

Casting Tool Marks

Tools that are used to pry, scrape, cut, or drill hard surfaces leave marks that can be cast. For example, a hammer hitting a nail leaves a reproducible and distinctive mark. When tool marks found at a crime scene are on objects too large to move to the laboratory (such as on a safe or a door frame), photographs are taken to locate the marks within the scene and casts are then made with sprayable silicone rubber or a similar silicone resin. This material dries quickly and accurately reproduces the unique indentations and ridges made by tools. Tool marks are more difficult to match than are tire or footwear marks, and the marks made by a tool may change over time if the tool is heavily used.

Martiscia Davidson

Further Reading

Bodziak, William J. *Footwear Impression Evidence: Detection, Recovery, and Examination.* 2d ed. Boca Raton, Fla.: CRC Press, 2000. Comprehensive guide to handling footwear evidence includes information on casting both footwear and barefoot impressions.

Du Pasquier, E., J. Hebrard, P. Margot, and M. Ineichen. "Evaluation and Comparison of Casting Materials in Forensic Sciences: Applications to Tool Marks And Foot/Shoe Impressions." *Forensic Science International* 82, no. 1 (1996): 33-43. Presents a review of various casting materials and their appropriate uses.

Hilderbrand, Dwane S. *Footwear, the Missed Evidence: A Field Guide to the Collection and Preservation of Forensic Footwear Impression Evidence.* 2d ed. Wildomar, Calif.: Staggs, 2005. Provides information about all aspects of preserving, collecting, and interpreting footwear impressions, including detailed information on how to cast impressions under a variety of conditions.

James, Stuart H., and Jon J. Nordby, eds. *Forensic Science: An Introduction to Scientific and Investigative Techniques.* 2d ed. Boca Raton, Fla.: CRC Press, 2005. Easy-to-read introductory textbook covers all aspects of forensics, including the casting of footwear and tire impressions.

McDonald, Peter. *Tire Imprint Evidence.* Boca Raton, Fla.: CRC Press, 1993. Classic work in the field of tire imprint collection and interpretation.

See also: Autopsies; Bite-mark analysis; Disturbed evidence; Evidence processing; Footprints and shoe prints; Oral autopsy; Prints; Tire tracks; Tool marks.

Celebrity cases

Definition: Forensic investigations of accidents and alleged crimes involving well-known persons.

Significance: Whenever a celebrity is involved in an incident requiring law-enforcement investigation, the event receives widespread coverage in the news media. The in-depth reporting on these cases by some media outlets brings public attention to the uses of forensic science and demonstrates the need for investigators to follow correct procedures in the collection of evidence.

Tragedies among the rich and famous typically garner significant attention from the general public. Among others, the cases described below involving entertainment industry celebrities have drawn public attention to the use of forensic techniques in law-enforcement investigations.

Robert Blake

Best known for his role as the star of the television series *Baretta* (1975-1978), Robert Blake, who had also been a member of the cast of the Our Gang series of comedy shorts in the 1930's and 1940's, gained renewed notoriety in 2001 as the prime suspect in the murder of his wife, Bonny Lee Bakley.

Bakley was shot and killed as she sat in a car outside a Los Angeles restaurant, and Blake was charged with one count of murder, two counts of solicitation of murder, and one count of murder conspiracy. He was accused of trying to hire two Hollywood stuntmen to kill his wife. Blake was tried for and acquitted of the murder charge and of one count of solicitation of murder; the other charges against him were dropped. In 2005, however, Blake was found liable for Bakley's wrongful death by a jury in a civil suit filed by Bakley's four children and was ordered to pay the family thirty million dollars.

Among the forensic evidence introduced during Blake's criminal trial was the finding from an analysis of the amount of gunshot residue (GSR)—particles emitted when a gun is fired—

found on Blake's hands after Bakley was shot. An independent scientist testified that she found only five particles of GSR on the actor's hands and that the killer would likely have had ninety-seven to ninety-eight particles; the GSR found on Blake could have been a result of Blake's handling his own gun, which was not the murder weapon. Other experts testified that the source of the GSR on Blake's hands could not be confirmed. Additionally, no latent fingerprints could be found on the murder weapon.

Another area of suspicion for both the prose-

Robert Blake (left), with his attorney Thomas Mesereau, Jr., during a hearing in a Los Angeles Superior Court in February, 2004. Blake was charged in the shooting death of his wife, Bonny Lee Bakley. *(AP/Wide World Photos)*

cution and the defense was the fact that Blake had no blood on his clothes immediately after the shooting. A forensics expert who analyzed the blood-spray patterns in the car where Bakley was killed said that the killer would not necessarily have been sprayed by blood because of the angle of the shooting. Other forensic testimony was presented in the case by a psychopharmacologist, who testified that frequent methamphetamine and cocaine use could cause delusions, paranoia, and hallucinations; this testimony was used to discredit the claims of the two stuntmen Blake was alleged to have tried to hire to kill his wife.

Christian Brando

Known for having a bad temper fueled by frequent drug and alcohol abuse, Christian Brando, the son of actor Marlon Brando, had an especially close relationship with his sister, Cheyenne, who also had drug and alcohol problems. In 1990, Christian Brando was accused of murdering his sister's longtime boyfriend, Dag Drollet, whom Cheyenne had accused abusing her. After a night of drinking, Christian, carrying a handgun, confronted Drollet in a bungalow on the Brando estate. Drollet was shot and killed; Brando claimed that the gun had gone off accidentally.

Evidence reports, as well as two autopsies, called into question Brando's story that the two men were struggling for the gun when it went off. Forensic analyses indicated that Drollet had died from a bullet to the back of the head, not in the face, as Brando originally reported. Further, investigators found that the scene of the death did not indicate that a struggle had taken place.

Forensic psychologists who testified for the prosecution characterized Christian Brando as a violence-prone threat to society, whereas defense experts described him as chronically depressed with diminished capacity as the result of long-term drug abuse. Key witnesses were not available to testify at the trial, and the court ruled that Brando's Miranda warning was inadequately administered, rendering his earlier confession inadmissible. Eventually, Brando pleaded guilty to voluntary manslaughter and was sentenced to ten years in prison.

Bob Crane

The 1978 murder of Bob Crane, who is best known as the star of the television series *Hogan's Heroes* (1965-1971), remains a mystery. After Crane was found brutally beaten to death in a Scottsdale, Arizona, apartment, investigators determined that he had been bludgeoned while he slept. The murder weapon was never found, but it was believed to be a camera tripod. The prime suspect was a video expert, John Henry Carpenter, who frequently participated in group sex parties that Crane organized. Criminologists found blood in Carpenter's car that matched Crane's relatively rare blood type, but at the time, the source of the blood could not be confirmed; DNA (deoxyribonucleic acid) typing did not yet exist. The case was closed for lack of evidence. When it was reopened in 1992, it was discovered that improper storage of the evidence made DNA analysis of the blood impossible. Nonetheless, Carpenter was indicted, and forensic photography experts were called to testify as to the authenticity of photos of an unknown material found in Carpenter's car. Despite these attempts, Carpenter was acquitted.

John Holmes

Dubbed the "Sultan of Smut," John Holmes starred in more than two thousand pornographic movies and was the template for one of the characters in the 1997 film *Boogie Nights*. By the 1980's, he had become debilitated by drug use, and his career had collapsed. Holmes came under suspicion of being one of the three masked thugs who committed the brutal 1981 quadruple homicide that became known as the "Wonderland murders," named for the street on which the killings occurred. The murders were later confirmed to be drug-related retaliation killings.

From a forensic standpoint, the Wonderland murders marked a turning point in courtroom evidence. The first law-enforcement investigators at the crime scene were so appalled by the amount of blood they found—the victims had all been beaten to death—that they videotaped the scene, and the prosecutors used the tape at trial. This marked the first time video evidence was admitted in court. Despite significant evidence pointing to Holmes's involvement in the killings, he was acquitted in 1982.

Manson Family

In August, 1969, starlet Sharon Tate was eight months pregnant by her husband, film director Roman Polanski. On a warm Saturday evening, Tate gathered with friends at her home near Beverly Hills. Early the next morning, Tate's housekeeper discovered a gruesome scene: five bodies, including Tate's. Investigators found that the victims had been shot, beaten, strangled, and mutilated. The word "PIG" had been scribbled in blood on a door, and the broken grip of a .22 caliber revolver was discovered at the scene.

The next day, in another part of town, Leno and Rosemary LaBianca were discovered stabbed and strangled. The word "WAR" had been carved into Leno's body, and "DEATH TO PIGS," "RISE," and "HEALTHER SKELTER" (misspelled this way) had been scrawled in blood. A few days

Charles Manson (left), leader of the so-called Manson Family, confers with his public defender attorney on December 4, 1969, soon after his arrest for eight murders. *(AP/Wide World Photos)*

earlier, music teacher Gary Hinman had been stabbed to death, and "POLITICAL PIGGY" had been written on his wall in his own blood.

Initially, the Los Angeles Police Department (LAPD) refused to draw connections among the three crimes, claiming that the Tate murders were a result of a drug deal gone bad. Two weeks after the murders, a .22 revolver with a broken grip was found in another Los Angeles suburb, but police failed to connect it to the earlier crimes. The Los Angeles County Sheriff's Department and the LAPD continued to pursue the cases separately for three months. In October, 1969, the two departments began to work together on the cases, and investigations led to a commune run by Charles Manson; Manson and his followers were known as the Manson Family.

A key piece of evidence in the Tate case was a fingerprint found in Tate's home that belonged to one of Manson's followers. In addition, bullets matching those found at the crime scene were discovered in the Manson compound. The .22 revolver in LAPD custody was finally rediscovered and matched to the bullets. In March, 1971, Manson was found guilty of first-degree murder. Several of his followers were later convicted.

In the years since the Manson murders, forensic historians have frequently referred to these cases in terms of "what not to do" for crime scene investigators. For example, the bodies found at the scenes were initially covered with household sheets, which could have contaminated evidence with unrelated fibers. Blood that had been left by the killers on the security gate button at the Tate estate was smeared by police officers who used the button. Police also smeared possible fingerprints on the .22 revolver when they received it, and pieces of the broken gun grip were inadvertently kicked under a chair. In addition, investigators tracked blood throughout the Tate house, and insufficient blood samples were taken from the crime scene and from the victims.

Marilyn Monroe

Officially, Marilyn Monroe died of an accidental overdose of sleeping pills, but some experts have suggested that Monroe was actually murdered, speculating that her death may have been related to her involvement with President John F. Kennedy and his brother, Robert F. Kennedy. Several elements of the August 5, 1962, death have raised questions. For example, Monroe's housekeeper found her unconscious at about 3:30 A.M. and called Monroe's psychiatrist and her physician. Despite confirming the death upon their arrival, the two doctors then waited at least a half hour to call the police. Further, although toxicologists found Nembutal (a barbiturate) in her system (the drug had been prescribed for Monroe as a sleep aid), they also found high levels of chloral hydrate of unknown origin.

The initial autopsy was performed by Dr. Thomas Noguchi of the Los Angeles County Coroner's Office, who would go on to become somewhat famous as the "coroner to the stars." Although later investigation would deem his autopsy to have been thorough, Noguchi wanted to investigate further. Shortly after his initial autopsy, he tried to reexamine the tissue samples, but they were missing. In addition, one of the nation's top forensic pathologists deemed the toxicology report incomplete.

Other evidence suggested that Robert Kennedy had visited Monroe in the evening before her death; it has been asserted that he went there to break off contact between Monroe and the Kennedy brothers. Additionally, it has been alleged by some that actor Peter Lawford, who was the brother-in-law of John and Robert Kennedy, may have removed from Monroe's house any evidence suggesting her involvement with the Kennedys. The Los Angeles District Attorney's Office reopened the case in 1982, but after a lengthy examination of the evidence, investigators again concluded that Monroe's death was a probable suicide.

George Reeves

George Reeves, star of the 1950's television show *Adventures of Superman*, died of a gunshot wound to the head in his California home on June 16, 1959. The death was ruled a suicide; it was believed to have been the result of Reeves's despondency over the cancellation of his television series and his waning career. Much later, unofficial investigations into Reeves's death raised questions about this ruling, citing forensic evidence that appears to contradict a finding of suicide. For example, no fingerprints were found on the gun, no gunpowder burns were present around the entry wound, and no record exists of any test for gunshot residue on Reeves's hands. Forensics experts have noted, however, that the gun was too well oiled to retain fingerprints, that gunpowder stippling frequently does not occur when a gun is held directly against the skin, and that tests for gunshot residue were not commonly performed in the 1950's.

Elizabeth Short

The case of the "Black Dahlia" is still considered one of the most notorious Hollywood murders. Nicknamed perhaps for her penchant for black clothes, Elizabeth Short was an aspiring starlet. On January 15, 1947, her nude body was found in a weed-covered lot by a pedestrian. Her remains had been slashed and stabbed, and the body was neatly cut in half. Further, the young woman had been posed spread-eagle with the two halves set a foot apart, and the letters "BD" were carved into her thigh. Perhaps most disturbing, her face had been slashed to resemble a clownish death grin. The body appeared to be washed clean and there was little blood at the scene, leading investigators to surmise that Short had been killed elsewhere.

Forensic technicians working for the Federal Bureau of Investigation (FBI) used fingerprint analysis to identify the body as Short's. The Los Angeles Coroner's Office reported that Short had died of massive internal hemorrhaging caused by blows to the head, and no traces of sexual activity were found. The clean bisection of her body led some investigators to believe the murder might have been the work of a medical student or butcher. The young woman's shoes and purse were found in a trash receptacle several miles away from the scene where her body was discovered.

Although "confessions" began pouring in to the LAPD and the FBI, and investigators eventually interviewed more than one thousand people, it was all to no avail. Nine days after Short's body was found, the *Los Angeles Examiner* newspaper office received a package containing Short's belongings, including photos, her birth certificate and Social Security card, and an address book containing the names of seventy-five men—none of whom could be connected to the murder. The sender had soaked the package in gasoline, apparently to remove any fingerprints or other identifying materials.

One key suspect, Robert Manley, had been the last to see Short alive, but the police released him after he passed a polygraph test. Later, he was committed to a mental institution; he was questioned again there after being dosed with sodium thiopental—a so-called truth serum—and he still denied the murder. Over a period of years following Short's death, police and various news media outlets received thirteen letters thought to be written by the murderer, but they produced no identifying evidence. The case remains unsolved.

O. J. Simpson

O. J. Simpson's murder trial became one of the most highly publicized trials in American history and brought DNA evidence to the forefront of public awareness. Nicole Brown Simpson, the former wife of sometime actor and retired professional football star O. J. Simpson, was stabbed to death outside her home on the night of June 12, 1994, along with an acquaintance, Ronald Goldman.

After police responded to the crime scene, detectives immediately went to Simpson's home, where they found a bloodstain on the door of his Ford Bronco along with a trail of blood leading up to his house. As they questioned Simpson, the investigators noticed a cut on his left hand. Crime scene investigators had already concluded that the killer also had been cut on his left hand. In addition, analysis of drops of blood found at the crime scene indicated that they had DNA factors that pointed toward Simpson. In-

vestigators also found footprints in Simpson's size at the crime scene and determined that they had been left by an exotic brand of shoe that Simpson owned. They also discovered a bloodstained glove on his property that matched one taken from the crime scene. Finally, investigators found traces of Nicole Brown Simpson's blood in Simpson's car and house, intermingled with Simpson's blood.

During the trial, Simpson's defense attorneys called forensic witnesses who asserted that the blood samples used as evidence by the prosecution had been mishandled, raising the possibility that they were contaminated or too degraded to produce accurate DNA analysis results. The prosecution produced other criminologists to refute these claims, but Simpson was eventually acquitted on all counts. In 1997, the jury in a civil suit brought by Ronald Goldman's father found Simpson responsible for the deaths of Brown Simpson and Goldman.

Phil Spector

Phil Spector, a well-known music producer who had worked with the Righteous Brothers, the Beatles, and many other famous recording artists, was arrested on February 3, 2005, when police discovered the body of actress Lana Clarkson in the foyer of Spector's home in Alhambra, California. Although Spector initially told police, "I think I killed someone," he later claimed the shooting was an "accidental suicide."

Spector's 2007 murder trial was surrounded by controversy. Famed forensic expert Henry C. Lee was accused by the district attorney of hiding evidence that proved Spector's guilt. In addition, a coroner concluded that bruises on Clarkson's tongue indicated that the gun had been forced into her mouth. The defense got a break when a DNA expert testified that only Clarkson's DNA was found on the murder weapon and that none of Spector's DNA was found under Clarkson's fingernails. In addition, a forensic pathologist testified for the defense that Clarkson had mental problems that could have led to suicide.

During the trial, forensic witnesses for the defense used a sophisticated three-dimensional plexiglass bust of the victim to demonstrate how

Defense witness Dr. Vincent DiMaio, testifying in Phil Spector's murder trial in June, 2007, introduces a rod into the mouth of a plastic model of a human head to demonstrate the damage caused by a self-inflicted intraoral gunshot wound. Spector was charged with killing actor Lana Clarkson, but the defense argued that the latter's death was an "accidental suicide." *(AP/Wide World Photos)*

the bullet went through her head and into her spine. The defense ended its arguments by presenting a computer-animated demonstration of the shooting as Spector asserted it took place. The trial ended in a hung jury, resulting in a mistrial, and the Los Angeles District Attorney's Office began preparing for a new trial.

Cheryl Turner

Cheryl Turner, daughter of movie queen Lana Turner, was fourteen years old when police investigated her role in the 1958 death of her mother's boyfriend, Johnny Stompanato. Lana and Johnny had a tempestuous relationship, and Cheryl had witnessed several incidents in which Stompanato had been violent toward her mother. During one of these episodes, Cheryl apparently intervened and stabbed Stompanato with a knife.

At a grand jury inquest during which Lana Turner gave what was described as a stunning performance, the Los Angeles coroner introduced an autopsy report outlining the extent of Stompanato's injuries. Further testimony indicated some confusion over details such as the lack of fingerprints on the knife, strange fibers in the blood on the knife, and a lack of blood on Lana Turner's clothes. Nonetheless, the jurors deemed the death justifiable homicide, and the prosecutor decided not to file charges. Stompanato's family subsequently brought a wrongful-death suit against Lana Turner; it was eventually settled out of court.

Cheryl Pawlowski

Further Reading

Bugliosi, Vincent. *Outrage: The Five Reasons Why O. J. Simpson Got Away with Murder.* New York: W. W. Norton, 1996. Famous former Los Angeles prosecutor presents a compendium of alleged mistakes by the legal system that resulted in the acquittal of O. J. Simpson.

Bugliosi, Vincent, with Curt Gentry. *Helter Skelter: The True Story of the Manson Murders.* 25th anniversary ed. New York: W. W. Norton, 1994. Best-selling book by the chief prosecutor in the case tells in graphic detail the story of the investigation and prosecution of Charles Manson and his followers.

Gilmore, John. *Severed: The True Story of the Black Dahlia Murder.* Los Angeles: Amok Books, 1994. Luridly detailed account of the investigation into the death of aspiring starlet Elizabeth Short, written by the son of a Los Angeles police officer who helped investigate the case.

Graysmith, Robert. *Auto Focus: The Murder of Bob Crane.* New York: Berkley Books, 2002. Examines Crane's life and discusses how the investigation into his murder was marred by conflicts and the inexperience of the investigators.

Noguchi, Thomas T., with Joseph DiMona. *Coroner.* New York: Simon & Schuster, 1983. Los Angeles coroner Noguchi explores some of the more famous cases in which he was involved, including the deaths of Robert Kennedy, Sharon Tate, and Marilyn Monroe.

See also: *Cold Case*; *CSI: Crime Scene Investigation*; DNA extraction from hair, bodily fluids, and tissues; Fingerprints; *Forensic Files*; Forensic photography; Homicide; Journalism; Misconceptions fostered by media; Prints; Pseudoscience in forensic practice; Simpson murder trial; Sports memorabilia fraud.

Centers for Disease Control and Prevention

Date: Founded in 1946 as the Communicable Disease Center

Identification: Agency of the U.S. Department of Health and Human Services that promotes a higher quality of human life through the prevention and control of disease, injury, and disability in the United States and globally.

Significance: The Centers for Disease Control and Prevention, the highest-level governmental health organization in the United States, employs forensic and public health experts who can efficiently investigate outbreaks of disease, mass-casualty events, and biological, chemical, nuclear, and radiological terrorist attacks domestically and elsewhere. Because of the organization's vast resources and expertise, all public health institutions in the United States as well as institutions in many other countries look to the Centers for Disease Control for training and investigation of mysterious diseases and deaths.

The agency now known as the Centers for Disease Control and Prevention (CDC) was called the Communicable Disease Center when it was organized in Atlanta, Georgia, during World War II. At that time, its major mission was to assist in the prevention and control of malaria in the southeastern United States and in war zones with endemic malaria. The agency was organized by Dr. Joseph W. Mountin, a visionary public health official. Within a few years, the center eradicated malaria in the southeastern United States. The success of this project was confirmed through the disease surveillance programs that the agency established in 1949. With the outbreak of the Korean War in 1950 and the threat of biological warfare, the CDC launched the Epidemic Intelligence Service (EIS) to carry out biological warfare surveillance. This program trained "disease detectives" to be deployed throughout the world to monitor outbreaks of diseases and to investigate suspected biological warfare-induced conditions.

Late Twentieth Century Achievements

The credibility of the CDC in disease investigation was bolstered after the successful control of poliomyelitis outbreaks among recipients of the new Salk polio vaccine in 1955. This success was followed by the successful tracing of the course of an influenza epidemic that led to the CDC's development of a flu vaccine in 1957. During the early 1960's, the CDC expanded its mission to work involving surveillance of chronic diseases, nutrition, occupational safety, quarantine services, and immunizations against measles, rubella, and smallpox. The agency also joined international efforts to control malaria and expanded its disease control programs globally.

To combat the menace of smallpox, the CDC developed and tested the jet-gun immunization device, which was used successfully in immunizing people in South America and Central and West Africa in 1966. Following increasing involvement in international projects, in 1970 the agency's name was changed to the Center for Disease Control; it was renamed the Centers for Disease Control in 1980.

In collaboration with the World Health Organization, the CDC assisted in the global eradication of smallpox, which was declared accomplished in 1977. The CDC was also involved in the identification of Ebola virus, isolation of hepatitis C, and the first description of the sexual transmission of hepatitis B. In another investigation, the agency successfully described the association between Reye's syndrome and aspirin. The agency also helped to explain the relationship between occupational exposure to vinyl chloride and liver cancer, and, after a thorough investigation, the agency reported the harmful effects of a popular liquid protein diet.

From 1970 through early 1980, the CDC investigated mysterious deaths that occurred in the United States and found their causes in toxic shock syndrome and Legionnaires' disease; the agency both de-

scribed health hazards and applied appropriate preventive measures to combat them. The CDC also described the first case of acquired immunodeficiency syndrome (AIDS) in 1981 and published information on the disease's associated risk factors and control measures. In collaboration with the National Center for Health Statistics, the CDC identified the dangers to human health of lead, which was subsequently removed from gasoline.

During the 1980's the CDC also investigated the use of estrogen replacement therapy and oral contraceptives and the relationship of such use to risks of breast, cervical, and ovarian cancers. At the request of the U.S. Congress, the agency investigated the effects of service in Vietnam on the health of Vietnam War veterans and their offspring. This led to the development of a serum test for a toxin called dioxin, which

Dr. Jonas Salk speaks to the press during a visit to the Centers for Disease Control in 1988. The credibility of the CDC in disease investigation was bolstered by the successful control of poliomyelitis outbreaks among recipients of the polio vaccine created by Salk in 1955. *(Centers for Disease Control and Prevention)*

was identified as a potential cancer-inducing chemical. In the 1990's, the CDC participated in the investigation of an outbreak of hantavirus pulmonary syndrome in the United States. In addition, the agency played major roles in global efforts to eradicate polio and to prevent neural tube defects among unborn babies. In recognition of the CDC's diverse roles in both disease control and prevention, the U.S. Congress changed the agency's official name to the Centers for Disease Control and Prevention in 1992.

Twenty-first Century Missions

The CDC's role in monitoring the use of biological and chemical weapons intensified in the twenty-first century. Following the September 11, 2001, terrorist attacks on Washington, D.C., and New York City and the anthrax bioterror mail attacks that occurred shortly thereafter, the agency embarked on policies that would improve its ability to respond to similar events in the future. In addition, the Emergency Operation Center (EOC) of the CDC collaborated with law-enforcement agencies and state and local health departments in an investigation of the source of the anthrax used in the 2001 attacks and the hunt for victims of the attacks.

When Hurricane Katrina struck the U.S. Gulf coast in August, 2005, the CDC's disaster response team was involved in attempting to help manage the crisis. The agency also provided support to the National Disaster Medical System and the Federal Emergency Management Agency (FEMA). The CDC played similar roles during the Hurricane Rita disaster of September, 2005.

As part of its ongoing work, the CDC maintains constant surveillance for new infectious diseases and signs of biological and chemical terrorist attacks. The agency also coordinates training aimed at enhancing its responses to future attacks through its strategic plan for bioterrorism preparedness and response, which was developed in conjunction with other federal agencies responsible for public health and safety.

CDC Partners and Investigations

The CDC works with many other domestic agencies, as well as agencies of foreign govern-

ments, to carry out disease surveillance around the world. It is also involved in the detection and investigation of health problems and the management of disaster events involving mass casualties. Furthermore, the CDC conducts research to determine the best ways to enhance efforts to prevent such problems. In addition, the center fosters the training of public health leaders while assisting in the development of sound public health policies and the implementation of prevention strategies.

Among the CDC's notable external partners is the World Health Organization, with which it works to control and prevent infectious diseases. In addition to collaborating with public health institutions and laboratories in other countries, the CDC maintains its own laboratories in other parts of the world. Through these networks, the CDC plays a crucial role in world health. Because it operates the finest health laboratories in the world, the agency serves as an international center for training and disease investigation. Law-enforcement agencies employ its services in investigations of homicides, terrorist attacks, and unusual deaths.

CDC investigations focus on identifying the causes, current victims, and potential victims of major public health problems, including both natural and human-made disasters. The agency's experts collaborate with officials of local and national law-enforcement agencies in conducting investigations of particular events.

Chronic and Infectious Diseases

Investigations of health problems involve isolating the agents or risk factors responsible. For example, in cases of chronic disease, investigators seek to establish the association between agents and diseases, such as in the CDC's work that connected aspirin consumption by young children with Reye's syndrome. The CDC frequently carries out investigations of suspected relationships between toxic agents and exposure to special occupational and environmental conditions. Forensic toxicologists are often involved in such investigations.

When it began during World War II, the CDC was concerned primarily with the control of malaria. It gradually evolved to become one of the most important institutions in the world in the investigation of infectious diseases. Apart from employing a large number of highly trained public health experts, the agency maintains one of the best laboratories devoted to the study of infectious diseases in the world. CDC investigators examine outbreaks of infectious diseases by isolating the infectious agents responsible, characterizing those agents, identifying possible vectors and reservoirs of the organisms, and mapping transmission patterns.

In some cases involving fatalities, the CDC uses forensic samples to identify or isolate the infective agents. Samples from body fluids and suspected harbingers of infectious agents may also be used in CDC investigations. The CDC has identified, isolated, and characterized a number of infectious agents in this way. The agency's Special Pathogens Branch studies highly infectious viruses that cause human diseases. This group's laboratory studies such dangerous microorganisms as hantaviruses and Ebola, Lassa, and Nipah viruses. All outbreaks of infectious disease in the United States are reported to the CDC, and many foreign governments engage the CDC to investigate disease outbreaks in their countries.

Bioterrorism

The investigation of biological attacks has become an increasingly important part of the CDC's work, as the U.S. government has recognized the potential for such attacks to produce mass casualties. Organisms used in biological attacks may be dispersed through the atmosphere or introduced into domestic food and water supplies.

In late 2001, the CDC was involved in the investigation of attacks in several American cities in which the bacterium that causes anthrax was sent through the U.S. mails. The investigation identified eleven cases of inhalation anthrax and eleven cases of cutaneous anthrax. Organisms were isolated from samples of blood, cerebrospinal fluids, and wound and skin biopsies taken from victims of the attacks. In seeking to identify the sources of the organisms, investigators recovered four letters that had been sprayed with powder containing the anthrax bacterium and were able to trace the paths of the envelopes. Further investigation revealed

the presence of the organism in facilities where U.S. mail was sorted. Although the perpetrator of the attacks was not identified, this investigation was helpful in identifying the attack agents and the victims. Because the potential sources of the anthrax were identified, people who were exposed to anthrax were promptly treated, and others were protected from potential infection.

Among the many other infectious agents that bioterrorists may disseminate are smallpox virus, plague bacteria, and the Ebola, Marbug, and Lassa viruses. The CDC classifies such viruses, which can cause high mortality and can be disseminated relatively easily, as Category A agents. The CDC has also recognized the dangers posed by agents causing lower mortality rates that may be used by terrorists. Category B agents include *Coxiella burnetii* (the bacterium that causes Q fever), alphaviruses, ricin (a toxin derived from castor beans), *Clostridium perfringens* (a bacterium involved in food-borne illnesses), and bacteria such as *Salmonella*, *Shigella*, and *Escherichia coli*.

Category C organisms include emerging infectious agents and other pathogens that are readily available and may be engineered for mass dissemination. Members of this group include hantaviruses, Nipah virus, tick-borne hemorrhagic fevers and encephalitis viruses, and multidrug-resistant tuberculosis.

Chemical Agents

The CDC maintains a nationwide surveillance system for the detection of possible terrorist attacks with a wide range of dangerous chemical agents. These include nerve agents such as tabun, sarin, soman, cyclosarin (GF), and VX; blood agents such as hydrogen cyanide; blister agents such as lewisite and mustard gas; volatile toxins such as benzene, chloroform, and trihalomethanes; pulmonary agents such as phosgene, vinyl chloride, and chlorine; poisonous industrial gases such as cyanides and nitriles; and incapacitating agents such as BZ. The CDC provides guidelines for local health authorities to help them manage possible chemical attacks. As poisons are often used as murder weapons, all cases of suspected poisoning in the United States are reported to both local health authorities and the CDC, which has helped solve many cases of murder by poison.

Edward C. Nwanegbo

Further Reading

Fong, I. W., and Ken Alibek, eds. *Bioterrorism and Infectious Agents: A New Dilemma for the Twenty-first Century.* New York: Springer, 2005. Provides information on bioterror agents and emerging infectious diseases that will foster understanding, treatment, and protection against these agents.

Hogan, David E., and Jonathan L. Burstein. *Disaster Medicine.* 2d ed. Philadelphia: Lippincott, Williams & Wilkins, 2007. Presents excellent coverage of human-made and natural disasters in different parts of the world and steps to be taken in managing medical emergency situations. Discusses the allocation of resources during disasters as well as treatment of the individuals affected.

Landesman, Linda Young. *Public Health Management of Disasters: The Practice Guide.* 2d ed. Washington, D.C.: American Public Health Association, 2005. Comprehensive discussion of natural and human-made disasters in the United States takes a practical approach to disaster response and management.

Lashley, Felissa R., and Jerry D. Durham, eds. *Emerging Infectious Diseases: Trends and Issues.* 2d ed. New York: Springer, 2007. Collection of essays provides information on the epidemiologies and clinical manifestations of various infectious diseases and discusses prevention and treatment of those diseases. Includes chapters on bioterror agents and avian influenza.

McQueen, David V., and Pekka Puska, eds. *Global Behavioral Risk Factor Surveillance.* New York: Kluwer Academic/Plenum, 2003. Excellent collection presents information on lifestyle behaviors in different parts of the world that foster development of chronic diseases such as diabetes, cancer, cardiovascular disease, and chronic obstructive airway diseases. An important resource for readers interested in understanding the roles of alcohol, tobacco, unhealthy diet, and inactivity in the development of chronic diseases.

Roy, Michael J. *Physician's Guide to Terrorist Attack.* Totowa, N.J.: Humana Press, 2003. Provides an informative review of the infectious and chemical agents that potentially can be used in terrorist attacks. Includes diagnostic and therapeutic guides to assist physicians in recognizing and managing the problems caused by such agents as well as information on the treatment of blast injuries.

Tucker, Jonathan B., ed. *Toxic Terror: Assessing the Terrorist Use of Chemical and Biological Weapons.* Cambridge, Mass.: MIT Press, 2000. Presents twelve case studies of the use of chemical and biological agents by terrorist groups. Identifies terrorists' patterns of behavior and discusses strategies to combat them.

Veenema, Tener Goodwin, ed. *Disaster Nursing and Emergency Preparedness: For Chemical, Biological, and Radiological Terrorism and Other Hazards.* 2d ed. New York: Springer, 2007. Nursing management guide addresses emergency needs for different categories of terrorist attacks as well as postdisaster care and psychological support for victims and their families.

See also: Autopsies; Bacterial biology; Biological terrorism; Biological warfare diagnosis; Biotoxins; Chemical Biological Incident Response Force, U.S.; Chemical terrorism; Chemical warfare; Food poisoning; Food supply protection; Forensic toxicology; Mustard gas; September 11, 2001, victim identification; U.S. Army Medical Research Institute of Infectious Diseases; Viral biology.

Chain of custody

Definition: Documentation of the location of physical evidence from the time it is collected until the time it is introduced at trial.

Significance: The establishment of chain of custody is important for all physical evidence collected in criminal investigations, but it is particularly crucial when items of evidence might become confused with other evidence or when there is a possibility that someone could have tampered with the evidence.

In criminal investigations, the identification of an object as one found at a certain place involves the establishment of a proper chain of custody, or paper trail. Each piece of physical evidence must be authenticated or identified by a witness or through other means.

Authentication

Authentication involves proof that the evidence is what it purports to be. Rule 901 of the Federal Rules of Evidence sets out methods of authenticating or identifying evidence. According to the rule, authentication or identification may be established by any of the following means: testimony of a witness with knowledge that a matter is what it is claimed to be, a nonexpert opinion as to the genuineness of handwriting based on familiarity, comparison by the trier of fact (jury) or expert witness with specimens that have been authenticated, distinctive characteristics, voice identification, telephone conversations showing that a call was made to a certain number and the identification of the person who answered the phone individually or on behalf of a business, ancient document or data compilation in existence twenty years or more at the time it is offered, evidence describing a process or system used to produce a particular result, or a method provided by act of Congress or by other rules pursuant to statutory authority.

Proper Chain of Custody

The first clause of Rule 901 addresses proper chain of custody. A weapon found next to a victim and then taken by the police and put into a bag that is sealed and marked with identification can later be identified by an officer on the stand at trial as the one found next to the victim. If more than one person had access to the bag, however, the role of each must be accounted for to ensure that the evidence is truly the object it is claimed to be. Similarly, when a powder is put into an evidence bag that is then sealed and checked in to the evidence room, the bag may later be checked out and sent to a laboratory for analysis of the contents. The laboratory technician has the responsibility of keeping track of the substance while testing it. The technician can then take the stand and testify about the identity of the substance.

It should be noted that minor gaps in the chain of custody are permissible and do not destroy the chain of custody. The evidence can be considered by the jury, which will determine its reliability and its probative value, if any, given the missing links in the chain. If, however, the evidence is not what the proponent claims it to be because of tampering in the chain of custody, the judge may prevent the jury from seeing or considering the evidence.

Chain of Custody in Court

It is important that law-enforcement personnel document the seizure, custody, control, trans-

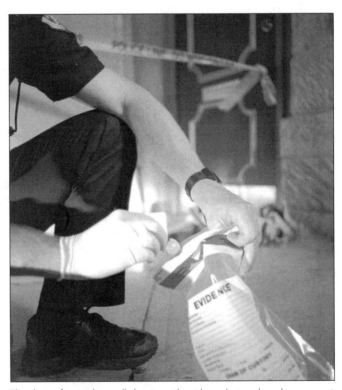

The chain of custody usually begins with evidence being placed in appropriate packaging at the scene of a crime. *(Brand-X Pictures)*

fer, analysis, and disposition of physical and electronic evidence. Because evidence can be used in court to convict persons of crimes, it must be handled carefully to avoid later allegations of tampering or misconduct that can compromise cases. Establishing a chain of custody is especially significant when the evidence takes the form of fungible goods—that is, goods that can easily be substituted for other items in the same category. This applies to illegal drugs seized by law enforcement.

An identifiable person must always have custody of the evidence. Therefore, when a police officer or detective takes charge of a piece of evidence, the officer or detective must document the item and give it to an evidence clerk for secure storage. This transaction and every succeeding transaction affecting that evidence, from its collection to its appearance in court, should be completely documented so that the evidence can withstand any challenges to its authenticity. Properly detailed documentation includes the conditions under which the evidence was gathered, the identities of all those who handled the evidence and how long they had it in their possession, the security conditions that existed during handling and storing of the evidence, and the manners in which the evidence was transferred to subsequent custodians.

In the case of the recovery of a bloody weapon at a murder scene, for example, every transfer of the weapon from person to person must be documented, from the time the weapon is picked up at the scene to the time it is presented in court. Law-enforcement personnel must be able to prove that only persons with legitimate reasons to inspect, test, or otherwise examine the weapon have had access to it. In cases involving chemical sampling, proper chain of custody ensures maintenance of the condition of samples by providing documentation of their control, transfer, and analysis.

Marcia J. Weiss

Further Reading

Broun, Kenneth S., ed. *McCormick on Evidence.* 6th ed. St. Paul, Minn.: Thomson/West, 2006. Considered to be the ultimate standard reference on the law of evidence. Contains detailed explanations and case references.

Mauet, Thomas A. *Trial Techniques*. 7th ed. New York: Aspen, 2007. Handbook covering all aspects of the trial process includes extensive examples of patterns of questions that attorneys use in examining expert witnesses.

Rothstein, Paul F., Myrna S. Raeder, and David Crump. *Evidence in a Nutshell*. 5th ed. St. Paul, Minn.: West, 2007. Provides a succinct summary of the law of evidence. Useful for both students and practitioners.

Stopp, Margaret T. *Evidence Law in the Trial Process*. Albany, N.Y.: West/Delmar, 1999. Undergraduate textbook intended primarily for paralegals discusses the principles of the law of evidence. A chapter on lay and expert witnesses includes cases and examples.

See also: Biological warfare diagnosis; Crime scene documentation; Disturbed evidence; Drug and alcohol evidence rules; Drug confirmation tests; Evidence processing; Handwriting analysis; Locard's exchange principle; Quality control of evidence; Rape kit; Toxicological analysis.

Challenger and *Columbia* accident investigations

Dates: *Challenger* accident took place January 28, 1986; *Columbia* accident took place February 1, 2003

The Event: After the accidents that destroyed the *Challenger* and *Columbia* space shuttles, investigators began the difficult tasks of finding and identifying evidence that would allow scientists to understand what had happened and allow the families of the dead crew members to bury their loved ones.

Significance: High-profile, widely publicized, multiple-casualty disasters create particular complexities in the search, collection, and identification portions of the investigation process. The investigations of the *Challenger* and *Columbia* tragedies required the use of many forensic tools.

The National Aeronautics and Space Administration (NASA) began the space shuttle program with *Columbia*, which launched for the first time in April, 1981. *Challenger* was the next shuttle to be launched, after *Columbia* had completed five missions. *Challenger* made its maiden flight in April, 1983.

On January 28, 1986, seventy-three seconds after it lifted off for its tenth mission, the space shuttle *Challenger* disintegrated. Investigators would later determine that the disaster was caused by the failure of an O-ring seal in the craft's right solid rocket booster. This failure caused a flame leak that engulfed the fuel tank and resulted in structural breakdown. With the structure compromised, aerodynamic forces broke the shuttle apart.

On January 16, 2003, as it was lifting off for its twenty-eighth mission, the space shuttle *Columbia* sustained damage when a piece of foam insulation broke off the main propellant tank and struck the shuttle's left wing, damaging the thermal protection system. The crew continued and completed their mission, but the damage was enough to compromise the wing's structure, and the shuttle began to fall apart during reentry into Earth's atmosphere on February 1. Eyewitnesses on the ground reported seeing debris break off the shuttle prior to its disintegration above Texas and Louisiana.

Government-appointed review boards were commissioned to look into the two shuttle disasters, and both found that the accidents were caused by malfunctions of which NASA officials were already aware. Both boards cited NASA administrators' insensitivity to the true potential risks posed by these documented issues as the main contribution to the tragedies.

Forensically speaking, every investigative scene analysis is intended to answer the same basic questions: How does the scene fit into what really happened, and what evidence within the scene supports the conclusions about what happened? Forensic scene searches are concerned with the identification, collection, and preservation of evidence. Scenes of the magnitude of the two shuttle destructions are no different from smaller scenes; they are simply amplified. When everything from the number of people involved to the amount of evidence available is on a grand scale, it becomes essential for investigators to establish a system to keep track of every detail.

Jurisdiction

The first thing that must be established in any type of law-enforcement investigation is which agency has the proper jurisdiction to investigate the case—that is, which agency is going to take charge of the investigation based on its legal authority over the crime or event, the geographic area, or the laws of the area. Sometimes jurisdictions can overlap, such as when both state and federal agencies have interests in particular cases. In these cases, agencies can share authority; this known as concurrent jurisdiction. It is always better, however, for one agency to take the lead in an investigation so that the work is not hampered by any competing goals and agendas the different agencies may have.

The investigators of both the space shuttle accidents had to contend immediately with jurisdictional issues. The agencies and other entities involved in the *Challenger* investigation included NASA, the Federal Bureau of Investigation (FBI), a specially appointed presidential commission chaired by former U.S. secretary of state William P. Rogers (known as the Rogers Commission), and the U.S. Air Force, Navy, and Coast Guard. The *Columbia* investigation included personnel from NASA, the FBI, the National Transportation Safety Board, the Secret Service, the U.S. Marshals Service, the Air Force, the Office of the Armed Forces Medical Examiner (OAFME), many Texas and Louisiana state and local agencies, and, later, the North American Aerospace Defense Command (NORAD). The *Columbia* incident was also reviewed by a presidential commission known as the *Columbia* Accident Investigation Board.

NASA took the lead in the *Challenger* investigation, confiscating tapes and pictures of the incident and making decisions to release little information to the news media. The FBI conducted an investigation to determine whether sabotage was involved, but eventually the Rogers Commission took jurisdiction to direct the investigation. In the *Columbia* incident, the FBI initially guided the search for shuttle parts and human remains on the ground, but NASA and the OAFME soon became the two main agencies involved. All recovered parts of the shuttle were sent to NASA for technical analysis, and the astronauts' remains and uniforms were sent to the OAFME for identification and examination.

Searching the Scenes

When *Challenger* broke apart, it was about 10 miles above the Atlantic Ocean, approximately 18 miles offshore. Pieces of the shuttle continued to fall for an hour, making it dangerous for search crews to enter the area immediately. *Challenger*'s nose section, with the crew

cabin inside, was blown free from the rest of craft. NASA later learned from flight-deck intercom recordings and the apparent use of some emergency oxygen packs that at least three of the astronauts were alive during *Challenger*'s fall. The nose section shattered upon hitting the ocean at what is estimated to be about 200 miles per hour. The wreckage scene covered approximately 93,000 square miles of ocean that included depths of up to 1,200 feet.

An hour after the incident, search-and-recovery planes and ships began the search for survivors and wreckage. Although some pieces of the shuttle floated on the surface of the ocean, most of the debris had sunk to the bottom. The bodies

Two days after the space shuttle *Columbia* broke up on reentry on February 1, 2003, contractors for the National Aeronautics and Space Administration record the location and description of a piece of debris that fell from the craft. Hundreds of experts in engineering, aircraft accidents, and forensic science joined in the search for debris over an area nearly 60 miles wide by 250 miles long over East Texas and Louisiana. *(AP/Wide World Photos)*

of the crew were not found right away, despite a search effort that included twenty-two ships, six submersibles, and thirty-three aircraft. Over the next few months, pieces amounting to about 50 percent of the shuttle were recovered, including parts of the external tank, both solid rocket boosters, and the orbiter. About 45 percent of the orbiter itself was found, including all three main engines, which were recovered intact, leading investigators to believe the engines were not involved in the incident.

On March 8, 1986, thirty-nine days after the search began, search teams found the crew cabin, which had not been destroyed. The bodies of all seven crew members were found inside, still strapped into their seats. The bodies were transported to the OAFME mortuary at Dover Air Force Base in Delaware for autopsy.

On the morning of February 1, 2003, NASA officials lost contact with the crew of the space shuttle *Columbia* about fifteen minutes prior to its scheduled landing. Video evidence depicts the shuttle breaking apart over Texas, approximately 39 miles above the ground. It has been estimated that the shuttle was traveling at approximately 12,500 miles per hour. The debris covered a rectangular area nearly 60 miles wide by 250 miles long over East Texas and Louisiana, in terrain that ranged from arid ground to bogs.

In contrast with the *Challenger* scene, which, as it was in the ocean, was relatively isolated from the public, the *Columbia* scene was accessible to anyone within the vicinity. Control of the scene became an immediate concern for investigators, and they found such control nearly impossible to achieve. Within the first few hours after the accident, materials alleged to be parts of the shuttle were being offered for sale on the auction Web site eBay. Authorities quickly shut down the auctions, and the posters were charged with tampering with an investigative scene and evidence.

The *Columbia* scene was so large that no single investigative agency could handle the search independently. All local law-enforcement agencies were contacted and asked to help within their areas of responsibility. If searchers came across anything they thought could possibly be related to the *Columbia* or its crew, they were told to collect it, note the appropriate location and time, and send it to NASA officials. NASA held all the recovered mechanical debris at Barksdale Air Force Base in Louisiana, and all organic materials found were sent to the OAFME mortuary at Dover Air Force Base for identification.

Autopsies and Victim Identification

A question often arises concerning autopsies conducted on persons who died as the result of a known disaster: What can such autopsies prove beyond what is already known? In both of the space shuttle tragedies, the deaths of all fourteen crew members were obviously the result of the shuttles' disintegration. Forensic pathology, however, can shed light on other important aspects of cases in addition to cause and manner of death, including incident analysis and victim identification. Remains may be identified through the analysis of DNA (deoxyribonucleic acid), fingerprints, or dental records. It is important to identify remains positively for the sakes of the families of the deceased.

In the case of *Challenger*, all seven crew members were found in their uniforms and strapped into their seats, so presumptive identification was easily accomplished. The news media and the crew members' families, however, also wanted to know when the crew died and whether they had suffered before their deaths. The autopsy findings in this case were inconclusive, largely because the remains had been submerged in the ocean for more than a month, and severe decomposition had set in. NASA officials found evidence that some of the crew may have survived the initial breakup of the craft, but then the crew cabin fell more than 50,000 feet and hit the water at approximately 200 miles per hour—no one could have survived such an impact.

Victim identification was an extremely important element of the investigation of the *Columbia* incident. The remains of the *Columbia* crew were found in parts, scattered with the shuttle debris over a very large search area. Identification of every body part was essential, so that the family of each crew member could be presented with as complete a body as possible for burial.

Findings

The Rogers Commission concluded that the space shuttle *Challenger* did not explode; rather, it was torn apart by aerodynamic stress after the structural failure of an external tank. The condition of the shuttle's three main engines showed no signs that they contributed in any way to the incident. An assessment of the external tank debris suggested that the tank itself was not responsible for the accident; rather, the failure of an O-ring used to seal joints in the solid rocket booster compromised the structure.

The *Columbia* Accident Investigation Board concluded that a puncture in the leading edge of the shuttle's left wing was caused by a piece of insulation foam that peeled off the external tank at launch. The hot gases formed during reentry into Earth's atmosphere expanded inside the wing, causing the shuttle to break apart on its final approach.

Russell S. Strasser

Further Reading

Cabbage, Michael, and William Harwood. *Comm Check . . . : The Final Flight of Shuttle Columbia*. New York: Free Press, 2004. Offers a good summary of the ethics of *Columbia*'s mission and the debate among engineers on the ground concerning whether it was safe for the shuttle to return. Notes that opportunities to learn the extent of the spacecraft's problems were missed and that repeated warning signs were ignored.

Feynman, Richard P. "Richard P. Feynman's Minority Report to the Space Shuttle *Challenger* Inquiry." In *The Pleasure of Finding Things Out: The Best Short Works of Richard P. Feynman*, edited by Jeffrey Robbins. Cambridge, Mass.: Perseus, 1999. One presidential commission member—a Nobel laureate in physics and widely renowned scientist and teacher—presents his explanation of what caused the *Challenger* accident.

Kubey, Robert W., and Thea Peluso. "Emotional Response as a Cause of Interpersonal News Diffusion: The Case of the Space Shuttle Tragedy." *Journal of Broadcasting and Electronic Media* 34, no. 1 (1990): 69-76. Good post-*Challenger* look at how NASA dealt with the media and the visual depictions of the *Challenger* incident. Discusses how these factors may have affected the investigation.

Langewiesche, William. "*Columbia*'s Last Flight." *The Atlantic Monthly*, November, 2003, 58-87. Excellent overview of the investigation that followed the *Columbia* tragedy, with good explanations of the findings of the *Columbia* Accident Investigation Board.

Lighthall, F. F. "Launching the Space Shuttle *Challenger*: Disciplinary Deficiencies in the Analysis of Engineering Data." *IEEE Transactions on Engineering Management* 38 (February, 1991): 63-74. Analyzes the field data acquired before the launch and compares them with the results of the investigation. Somewhat technical, but very informative.

McDanels, S. J. "Space Shuttle *Columbia* Postaccident Analysis and Investigation." *Strain: An International Journal for Experimental Mechanics* 42 (August, 2006): 159-163. Presents a thourough, technical review of the *Columbia* incident and investigation.

Report of the Presidential Commission on the Space Shuttle Challenger Accident. Springfield, Va.: National Aeronautics and Space Administration, 1986. Provides a comprehensive view of what caused the *Challenger* accident and the tragedy's repercussions.

Vaughan, Diane. "Autonomy, Interdependence, and Social Control: NASA and the Space Shuttle *Challenger*." *Administrative Science Quarterly* 35 (June, 1990): 225-257. Provides informative discussion of NASA's failure to identify legitimate risks, which resulted in the *Challenger* tragedy.

See also: Accident investigation and reconstruction; Crime scene search patterns; Evidence processing; Flight data recorders; Mitochondrial DNA analysis and typing; Oral autopsy; ValuJet Flight 592 crash investigation.

Check alteration and washing

Definition: Process of changing checks intended for others, by simple alteration or exposure to chemical substances, to collect funds from bank accounts fraudulently.

Significance: The fraudulent cashing of stolen checks costs individuals and businesses in the United States hundreds of millions of dollars each year. Unfortunately, many altered checks are not detected until funds have already been transferred and the criminals are long gone. Security features are constantly evolving to combat this problem.

Check alteration is a very common problem in the United States, causing losses to victims of many millions of dollars each year. A common scenario is as follows: Someone writes a check to pay a bill and places the envelope containing the check in a residential mailbox, raising the box's red flag so that the letter carrier will pick up the outgoing mail. Unfortunately, the red flag also alerts a criminal that outgoing mail is in the box, and when no one is around the criminal rifles through the mail and takes anything that looks like it might contain a check. After collecting checks from a number of different mailboxes in the neighborhood, the criminal alters them, either by washing and rewriting them or by using simpler methods, so that he or she can cash them using a false identity. By the time the victims discover the withdrawal of funds from their accounts, the criminal has moved on to another identity or another town.

How Checks Are Changed

In the most basic type of check alteration, the perpetrator simply makes small changes to a check using a pen or other writing instrument similar enough to the one that was used to write the check to avoid detection. Examples of this include an individual changing a check for five dollars to a check for five thousand dollars by adding extra zeros and the word "thousand." Another example involves checks made out to the IRS (Internal Revenue Service). A criminal can take these checks and by adding two pen strokes change "IRS" to read "MRS." The criminal can then add a last name, making the check payable to "MRS. SMITH" or something similar, and then uses false identification to cash the check.

More complex check alteration involves actually removing the writing on the "payable to" line of the check, along with the amount. When this is done through the submersion of the check in a bath of fluid to dissolve the ink, it is known as check washing. Practiced criminals, and even some amateurs, can use a variety of household products to remove the inks of many commonly used pens from handwritten checks.

Common substances such as acetone (found in many products, including nail polish remover), bleach, and isopropyl alcohol can be used to wash checks. Different chemicals are often effective at removing different types of ink, and seasoned check washers can recognize many inks and choose just the right solutions to accomplish their goal. Check washers protect the signatures on the checks during the washing process, either by covering them with tape or by holding them out of the wash solution, so that after the chemicals have done their work, they have blank, signed checks that they can rewrite for any amount. Check washers often have many false identities supported by false driver's licenses, identification cards, and other documentation to help them cash checks without raising suspicion. After the checks are cashed, the victims often remain ignorant of the fraud for days or weeks, and by the time they report the crimes, the criminals have usually moved on.

Detection and Prevention

The most basic types of check alteration, those involving the simple addition or modification of writing on the payee line or in the amount of the check, can often be detected through close visual inspection or examination of the check with a magnifying glass or microscope. Very rarely is it possible for a criminal to find exactly the same type of pen used to write the check originally or to match the handwriting of the original check writer perfectly. Unfortunately, bank tellers, store clerks, and others in the first line of defense against check fraud rarely have the training, or the time, to do significant examination of each check that is presented for cashing. Because of this, most of even the most basic types of check alteration can slip through undetected; they are not caught until it is too late, when the victims whose accounts were charged receive their bank statements.

It can be difficult to detect check washing, but careful examination of a check can often reveal clues. In some cases, especially when the check washer is an amateur, some traces of the original ink markings may be visible. One problem with detecting check washing is that when the process does not work well, the criminal usually will simply not attempt to pass that particular check. This is good for the person whose check was stolen; instead of losing hundreds or even thousands of dollars, the individual is simply inconvenienced by the apparent disappearance of a check that never made it to where it was intended to go. Checks that seem to have been lost in the mail may have been stolen by individuals who planned to wash them; thus persons who realize that checks they have written are missing should be extremely vigilant.

Increasingly, security measures are being built into checks, especially high-security checks, that make it more difficult for criminals to copy or wash the checks and also make it easier for professionals to detect check alteration. Features of checks that can deter attempts to pass photocopied versions include watermarks, thermal verification seals, and the use of colored fibers woven into the paper. These features do not necessarily protect against washing, however. The best protection against check washing that is offered by check manufacturers involves the treatment of checks with chemicals that cause the paper to change color if it is submerged in any of the solutions commonly used by check washers.

Some simpler means of protecting against check alteration and washing are also available. One of these is the use of gel pens, instead of ballpoints or other pens, to write and sign checks. Gel inks are much more difficult to wash successfully because these inks enter the paper fibers of checks and become trapped. Another

way to prevent check washing is to prevent the stealing of mail containing checks. People can help to protect themselves from check fraud by mailing bill payments only at post offices or by handing such mail directly to letter carriers. If they must place mail containing checks in home or business mailboxes for pickup, they should be careful to put the mail out as close to the pickup time as possible.

Helen Davidson

Further Reading

Abagnale, Frank W. *The Art of the Steal: How to Protect Yourself and Your Business from Fraud—America's Number One Crime*. New York: Broadway Books, 2001. Explains the various ways in which most common types of fraud, including check alteration, are committed and offers advice regarding how individuals can avoid becoming fraud victims.

Abagnale, Frank W., with Stan Redding. *Catch Me If You Can*. New York: Grosset & Dunlap, 1980. True story of a master of check alteration and washing, who passed more than $2.5 million in fraudulent checks in only five years.

Koppenhaver, Katherine M. *Forensic Document Examination: Principles and Practice*. Totowa, N.J.: Humana Press, 2007. Overview of document examination includes a chapter dedicated to check fraud and information on the presentation of evidence of document alteration in the legal process.

Wells, Joseph T. *Principles of Fraud Examination*. Hoboken, N.J.: John Wiley & Sons, 2005. Covers many different aspects of fraud, including check tampering, and discusses red flags that may indicate fraud. Provides many real-world examples.

_____, ed. *Fraud Casebook: Lessons from the Bad Side of Business*. Hoboken, N.J.: John Wiley & Sons, 2007. Collection of more than sixty real cases written by the fraud experts who investigated them. Includes information about the practices and investigative techniques used.

See also: Document examination; Fax machine, copier, and printer analysis; Forensic accounting; Handwriting analysis; Hughes will hoax;

Identity theft; Microscopes; Paper; Questioned document analysis; Secret Service, U.S.; Sports memorabilia fraud; Typewriter analysis; Writing instrument analysis.

Chemical agents

Definition: Chemical compounds with toxic properties that can be used to cause harm to humans, plants, and animals.

Significance: Chemical agents are classified as weapons of mass destruction and have the capability of inflicting massive amounts of damage and death. Given that some domestic terrorist groups have attempted to deploy chemical agents within the United States, it is important that forensic investigators have a thorough understanding of these compounds, their effects on the human body, and effective ways to combat chemical attacks.

Since their first use as weapons during World War I, chemical agents have been deployed numerous times. Large stockpiles of these agents are maintained in different parts of the world, largely because of nations' needs to develop chemical programs for research purposes.

The U.S. Department of Homeland Security lists six main categories of chemical agents: biotoxins, blister agents, blood agents, choking agents, nerve agents, and incapacitating agents. Biotoxins are agents that come from plants or animals; these include compounds such as ricin and nicotine. Blister agents, also known as vesicants, are among the agents most commonly associated with the term "chemical weapons"; these cause blistering to the skin, eyes, and respiratory system on contact. Mustard gas, perhaps the most widely known blister agent, was first employed by Germany in 1917, during World War I. Blood agents, which include cyanide and carbon monoxide, enter the body through the bloodstream.

Choking agents, when inhaled, damage the membrane of the respiratory tract and cause asphyxiation from pulmonary edema. Chlorine and phosgene are both choking agents. Nerve agents are some of the most recently used chemical weapons (during the Iran-Iraq War, 1980-1988); these compounds are designed to disrupt the nervous system and keep it from functioning properly. The nerve agent sarin was employed in the Tokyo subway attack perpetrated by the religious cult Aum Shinrikyo in 1995. Nerve agents can kill within minutes of exposure to a lethal dosage. Incapacitating agents, in contrast with other chemical agents, are not generally lethal; they produce mental or physiological effects that inhibit normal functioning. Law-enforcement agencies sometimes use such highly irritating agents for purposes of crowd control; tear gas is the most widely known example.

Numerous chemical detection devices are in common use by law-enforcement and emergency medical personnel who respond to scenes where chemical contamination may be suspected. One type consists of a glass tube that contains reagents (substances designed to foster a reaction with another substance) that will react chemically with a suspected agent in a predetermined volume of air. By measuring the stain produced, the user can determine which agent was detected. Among the least effective methods of detecting chemical agents is the use of pH test strips. When chemicals come into contact with such strips, they indicate the alkalinity or acidity of the chemicals through a change of color. A gas chromatograph-mass spectrometer (GC-MS) is a device made of two separate tools that are most effective in combination. A GC-MS separates the various elements that make up compounds and measures their quantity to identify the compounds. Many of the devices that first responders use to detect chemical agents are most reliable when they are employed in conjunction with other tools of forensic science.

Michael W. Cheek

Further Reading

Bevelacqua, Armando, and Richard Stilp. *Terrorism Handbook for Operational Responders.* 2d ed. Albany, N.Y.: Delmar, 2004.
Croddy, Eric A., with Clarisa Perez-Armendariz and John Hart. *Chemical and Biological*

Warfare: A Comprehensive Survey for the Concerned Citizen. New York: Copernicus Books, 2002.

Hoenig, Steven L. *Handbook of Chemical Warfare and Terrorism*. Westport, Conn.: Greenwood Press, 2002.

See also: Blood agents; Centers for Disease Control and Prevention; Chemical Biological Incident Response Force, U.S.; Chemical terrorism; Chemical warfare; Chemical Weapons Convention of 1993; Decontamination methods; Mustard gas; Nerve agents; Sarin; Soman; Tabun.

Chemical Biological Incident Response Force, U.S.

Date: Activated on April 4, 1996

Identification: Branch of the U.S. Marine Corps designed to respond rapidly to terrorist-initiated chemical and biological threats against the United States.

Significance: Developed in response to growing threats of terrorist attacks during the mid-1990's, the U.S. Chemical Biological Incident Response Force is designed to work with other federal, local, and state emergency response agencies. The force's services include chemical and biological agent detection, emergency medical care, casualty search and rescue, and personnel decontamination.

A self-sustaining unit under the command of the U.S. Marine Corps, the Chemical Biological Incident Response Force, or CBIRF, is part of the Fourth Marine Expeditionary Brigade. It is headquartered at Indian Head, Maryland, twenty-seven miles from Washington, D.C. Its personnel represent a variety of military occupational specialties. The CBIRF owns and maintains commercially available radiological, biological, and chemical defense equipment; general support equipment; and medical equip-

ment used in support of its quick-response mandate to terrorist incidents occurring throughout the world.

Although the CBIRF is not directly involved in counterterrorist operations, its personnel are trained to deal with the consequences of chemical and biological attacks. Other government agencies have expertise and responsibilities that overlap those of the CBIRF. What makes the CBIRF exceptional is that it is a completely self-contained unit capable of handling all its mandated responsibilities on its own.

Background

Creation of the CBIRF was a response to such terrorist events as the bombing of Oklahoma City's federal office building and the Aum Shinrikyo cult's nerve gas attack on a Tokyo subway station—both of which occurred in 1995. In the aftermath of those events, U.S. president Bill Clinton issued a directive on counterterrorism policy calling for specific efforts to deter deadly terrorist attacks in both the United States and allied nations. The most tangible outcome of that presidential directive was the establishment of the CBIRF within the U.S. Marine Corps in April, 1996.

Shortly after its creation, the CBIRF was deployed to assist in a series of high-profile events. One of the first of these was the Summer Olympic Games in Atlanta, Georgia, during 1996. Less than ten minutes after a pipe bomb exploded in the Olympic Village, a CBIRF unit on standby only one mile away went into action. Since that time, CBIRF units have been deployed to serve at presidential inauguration ceremonies, subsequent presidential state of the union addresses in Congress, papal visits to the United States, and the 1999 summit meeting of the North Atlantic Treaty Organization (NATO).

Since the terrorist attacks on the United States of September 11, 2001, CBIRF units have been active in collecting biological samples and screening congressional mail and office equipment. In December of 2001, the CBIRF sent a one-hundred-member initial-response team into the Dirksen Senate Office Building in Washington, D.C., to detect and remove anthrax. CBIRF units have also supported overseas exercises in such countries as Bahrain, France, Iceland, Italy, Jordan, the Philippines, and Japan.

The Five CBIRF Elements

The CBIRF is organized to operate through five areas of responsibility called "elements": reconnaissance, decontamination, medical, security, and service support. After the nuclear, biological, and chemical (NBC) reconnaissance element defines the locations of incident sites, the decontamination element decontaminates personnel and equipment exposed to chemical or biological agents. Meanwhile, the medical element provides triage support to casualties, the security element provides security for the contaminated site, and the service support element provides shelter, food, and water.

Members of the reconnaissance elements are always the first to enter affected areas. They are trained and equipped to detect, classify, and identify all known chemical and biological agents. This element has two reconnaissance vehicles equipped to detect vapor and liquid contamination. The unit's twenty Marines, ten corpsmen, and one medical officer also provide emergency casualty evacuation teams capable of stabilizing and extracting casualties from the affected area.

Decontamination elements made up of twenty-seven Marines and sailors are responsible for the decontamination of personnel and casualties, and they stabilize casualties waiting for further treatment. Decontamination elements establish themselves at the edges of contaminated areas, near the medical elements' triage stations. There, personnel and casualties, both ambulatory and nonambulatory, are pro-

cessed through a series of stations derived from NBC decontamination standards.

As contaminated individuals enter the areas, their personal effects and equipment are collected, and clothing items are removed. The individuals themselves are then sprayed and sponged with a 0.5 percent bleach solution and led through showers that rinse off the decontaminating liquid. The personal effects and equipment of the contaminated individuals are also processed through the cycle.

Individuals are then monitored with handheld chemical agent monitors (CAMs) to determine whether traces of contamination are still present. Those found still to be contaminated are again sent through the full decontamination cycle. After all casualties are decontaminated, element members change their bandages and dressings as needed and transport the individu-

---

CBIRF Teams in Action

At any given moment, CBIRF units are ready for rapid deployment in large diesel vans. These vans are specially equipped with onboard analytical systems designed to provide early detection and identification of chemical and biological agents used in terrorist attacks. When the units must be deployed rapidly to remote locations, the vans are loaded into C-130 aircraft.

During suspected terrorist attacks, the personnel of the CBIRF recon and rapid intervention group are typically first on the scene. There, they provide security, area isolation, and assistance to local medical authorities and service support. They assess the types of chemical agents present and determine the levels of protective clothing required for greatest safety:

- **Level C clothing:** full suits and gas masks
- **Level B clothing:** biological suits with air tanks
- **Level A clothing:** sealed, domelike environments

After donning the requisite clothing, casualty search teams enter the scene to locate and assess victims. They are soon followed by extract teams, which remove the casualties to decontamination tents, where up to thirty victims may receive attention. In assembly-line fashion, victims are placed on rollers that facilitate their movement from station to station within the tents as they progress through levels of assessment and treatment.

Meanwhile, Marines in full decontamination suits work to remove all clothing material for proper disposal. Victims are then sponged with decon solutions, rinsed with water, and sent to the final stations, where medical corpsmen tag them for appropriate medical attention.

New York City firefighters participate in a training exercise conducted by Marines of the U.S. Chemical Biological Incident Response Force in late 2003. Playing victims in a simulated biochemical incident, the trainees are lying on stretchers designed for rapid evacuation. *(AP/ Wide World Photos)*

als to waiting medical personnel. Although the decontamination element's personnel includes Marines with a variety of occupational specialties, more than half of the Marines are NBC defense specialists who have undergone nine-week training courses at Fort McClellan, Alabama.

Equipment

When the CBIRF was first organized, it used "off-the-shelf" equipment, such as chemical-protective overgarments and gas masks. Other items included NBC reconnaissance vehicles capable of detecting both vapor and liquid con-

tamination, chemical agent monitors, vapor and liquid agent detection kits, remote chemical agent sensing alarms, and decontamination kits. As the CBIRF has developed, it has played an increasing role in testing innovative concepts in equipment, techniques, and procedures used in its mandated tasks.

During the fall of 2004, CBIRF personnel began conducting exercises with a naval hovercraft on the Potomac and Anacostia rivers. Thanks to its air-cushion technology, the hovercraft is able to land on more than 70 percent of the world's coastlines. This is a huge increase over the approximately 15 percent of coastlines accessible by conventional landing craft. Capable of carrying payloads of up to seventy-five tons, the hovercraft significantly increases the CBIRF's ability to move quickly and efficiently into future emergency situations.

Richard S. Spira

Further Reading

Bolz, Frank, Jr., Kenneth J. Dudonis, and David P. Schulz. *The Counterterrorism Handbook: Tactics, Procedures, and Techniques.* 3d ed. Boca Raton, Fla.: CRC Press, 2005. Practical handbook describes the procedures that should be followed during and after terrorist attacks. Includes many of the procedures used by the CBIRF.

Boss, Martha J., and Dennis W. Day, eds. *Biological Risk Engineering Handbook: Infection Control and Decontamination.* Boca Raton, Fla.: CRC Press, 2003. Provides extensive coverage of the kinds of biological contaminants with which the CBIRF deals.

Cirincione, Joseph, Jon B. Wolfsthal, and Miriam Rajkumar. *Deadly Arsenals: Nuclear, Biological, and Chemical Threats.* Rev. ed. Washington, D.C.: Carnegie Endowment for International Peace, 2005. Presents an authoritative overview of the range of biological, chemical, and nuclear threats that the United States faces from terrorist attacks.

Environmental Protection Agency. *Compilation of Available Data on Building Decontamination Alternatives.* Washington, D.C.: Author, 2005. Provides information on the various technologies employed to decontaminate buildings affected by chemical and biological attacks.

Sauter, Mark A., and James Jay Carafano. *Homeland Security: A Complete Guide to Understanding, Preventing, and Surviving Terrorism.* New York: McGraw-Hill, 2005. Comprehensive textbook discusses the nature, methods, and dangers of terrorism and offers practical advice on dealing with terrorist threats at both national and individual levels.

Tucker, Jonathan B., ed. *Toxic Terror: Assessing the Terrorist Use of Chemical and Biological Weapons.* Cambridge, Mass.: MIT Press, 2000. Presents twelve case studies of the use of chemical and biological agents by

terrorist groups. Identifies terrorists' patterns of behavior and discusses strategies to combat them.

See also: Anthrax; Anthrax letter attacks; Biodetectors; Biological terrorism; Biological warfare diagnosis; Biological weapon identification; Centers for Disease Control and Prevention; Chemical agents; Chemical terrorism; Environmental Measurements Laboratory; Quantitative and qualitative analysis of chemicals.

Chemical microscopy. *See* Polarized light microscopy

Chemical terrorism

Definition: Use of dangerous toxic chemicals that cause mass casualties and economic damage to achieve the objectives of terrorist groups.

Significance: The dangers posed to public health by attacks with lethal toxic chemicals are potentially catastrophic. When such attacks occur or are threatened, forensic toxicologists, public health officials, and law-enforcement agencies work together closely to identify the toxins involved, treat victims, decontaminate affected areas, bring perpetrators to justice, and provide protection to the public against future attacks.

Chemical agents capable of causing life-threatening injuries and death present serious threats to human communities. Many agents can be easily produced and disseminated in the atmosphere or public water and food supplies. When they make contact with human skin, mucous membranes, eyes, and respiratory and digestive systems, they can have harmful and even lethal effects. The dangers posed by chemical weapons are made greater by the ready availability of information on how to produce them in printed publications and on the Internet. Would-be terrorists with little or no chemistry training can produce dangerous chemicals easily and cheaply.

Chemical Toxins in History

Although potential uses of chemicals as poison weapons have been known for several centuries, they were not used as important weapons until World War I (1914-1918). In that European conflict, Germany, which then had the world's largest chemical industry, introduced poison gases into combat against Allied ground troops. The numbers of casualties from gas attacks were small in comparison with the overall casualty rates that troops suffered in that war. Nevertheless, the disruptions caused by fear of gas attacks and the need for troops to adopt protective equipment and procedures made poison gas an effective weapon. New lethal chemicals were produced during World War II but were not used as extensively in that conflict as in the earlier war, partly because of conventions against their use that the combatants honored.

After World War II, research and development on chemical weapons accelerated. By the late twentieth century, chemical weapons remained integral parts of many countries' secret military programs. Proliferation of these weapons gave many nations reason for concern that some of them might fall into the hands of terrorist organizations and be used in attacks that would over-whelm public health care delivery systems and cause high fatality rates and general chaos. By the early twenty-first century, no terrorist group had yet successfully mounted a large-scale chemical attack, but numerous small-scale attacks had occurred, and evidence that some groups have planned larger attacks has been found.

During the 1970's, a radical political group known as the Weather Underground Organization, or Weathermen, threatened to use chemical toxins during its series of terrorist attacks on institutions of the U.S. government. In 1984,

---

Classification of Chemical Toxins

The Centers for Disease Control and Prevention defines the following basic categories of chemical toxins.

- **Biotoxins:** Poisons derived from plants and animals, such as ricin, a poisonous protein extracted from castor beans.
- **Blister agents:** Also known as vesicants, chemicals that cause severe blisters on contact with eyes, the respiratory tract, and skin. An important member of this group is mustard gas.
- **Blood agents:** Chemical agents that cause pathological changes when absorbed into the bloodstream. Important members of this group include arsine and cyanide.
- **Caustics:** Chemicals that cause severe burns or corrosion on contact with the skin, eyes, and mucous membranes. Hydrogen fluoride is an important example.
- **Choking and pulmonary agents:** Chemicals that attack the respiratory tract, causing severe irritation and swelling of the tract and the lungs. Examples include ammonia, chlorine, methyl isocyanate, phosgene, and phosphine.
- **Incapacitating agents:** Chemicals that alter the consciousness of victims, such as BZ and opioids, which include natural and synthetic derivatives of opium.
- **Long-acting anticoagulants:** Toxins that prevent blood clotting, such as warfarin, which was originally developed as a medication for heart patients.
- **Metallic poisons:** Naturally occurring substances such as the chemical compound arsenic and the element mercury.
- **Nerve agents:** Powerful toxins that inhibit nerve functions, such as sarin and VX.
- **Toxic alcohols:** Poisonous alcohols that attack the heart, the kidneys, and the nervous system. An important member of this group is ethylene glycol, which is chemically similar to the ethyl alcohol consumed in liquor, wine, and beer products. Ethyl alcohol itself can also be toxic when consumed in large quantities.

---

an animal liberation group claimed it had laced candy bars manufactured by Mars, Incorporated, with rat poison. That claim moved the company to recall millions of chocolate bars and sustain a hefty economic loss. In 1985, federal agents found large quantities of potassium cyanide when they raided the Arkansas headquarters of an extremist organization called The Covenant, the Sword and the Arm of the Lord. That organization's apparent intention was to poison the water supply of several large cities. In 1989, Israeli forces found a stockpile of toxic chemicals in a Tel Aviv hideout of the Palestinian Liberation Organization. Three years later, a German neo-Nazi group attempted to pump hydrogen cyanide gas into a synagogue.

Two widely publicized atrocities involving chemical toxins occurred in Iraq and Japan. During the 1990's, the Iraqi government used chemical weapons against its own Kurdish citizens. In Japan, members of the Aum Shinrikyo religious cult attacked civilians in the Tokyo subway system with the nerve gas sarin in 1995. When police afterward raided the headquarters of the cult, which was later renamed Aleph, they found significant quantities of dangerous biological agents.

Combating Chemical Terrorism

The success of chemical terrorist attacks depends on the types of agent used, the ports of introduction of those agents, the methods of disseminating the agents, and the weather conditions. Nerve gas agents such as sarin and VX are strongly toxic and associated with high fatality rates. When such agents are disseminated in the open air, high humidity, high air temperatures, and strong winds can affect their potency and diminish their effectiveness. By contrast, when such agents are disseminated within enclosed buildings, fatality rates are likely to be high. Similarly, the dissemination of such agents with rockets or explosive ammunition in any almost environment can cause massive casualties. Poisoning an entire city's water supply is unlikely to be a practical method of chemical attack because of the massive amounts of toxic chemicals needed to make them effective in a large water system. Chemicals such as cyanide are most dangerous when

they are used to target patrons of individual eating places or they are introduced into commercially sold beverages or foods.

Collaboration among the forensic experts and security agents of law-enforcement agencies, such as the Federal Bureau of Investigation (FBI) in the United States, and public health agencies is especially important in investigations of suspected chemical agent attacks. The first task of any investigation is to determine exactly what has happened and whether, in fact, chemical or biological agents have been used. The investigators then work to identify the toxic agents and their source.

Forensic scientists are assisted by security agents in collecting samples from crime scenes. The identification of any chemical agents that are collected assists health care professionals to provide treatment for survivors of the attacks. Public health officials also use forensic investigators' findings to plan and execute environmental decontamination of such crime scenes. Public health officials also work to identify everyone who has been exposed to the toxic agents, provide needed treatment, and monitor their health in case complications later emerge.

Terrorist Incidents in Japan

Immediately after a chemical attack in the Japanese city of Matsumoto in 1994, local police were alerted to a strange illness that claimed the lives of 7 victims and hospitalized 274 others. An initial investigation of the area that had been attacked found dead animals and abnormal changes in vegetation of the area. Autopsies found similarly unusual pathologies in the organs of human victims. Finally, a forensic analysis of the water in a pond within the area found traces of sarin nerve gas, conclusive proof of a deliberate chemical attack.

Japan suffered another, similar attack in March, 1995, during the midst of rush-hour commuter traffic in a Tokyo subway station. This attack exposed more than five thousand people to the dangerous sarin gas. The survivors of this attack who were checked by medical teams demonstrated symptoms similar to those of victims in the previous year's incident. Likewise, forensic pathological examinations of the dead revealed pathologies similar to those of the previous year's victims. Evidence collected from the subway attack confirmed the presence of sarin.

These events demonstrated the importance of close collaboration between security agencies and forensic experts in the investigation of suspected chemical terrorist attacks. The role of security agents is crucial in secluding the area affected by an attack, both to preserve evidence and to prevent more people from becoming exposed to any noxious agents. Security agents also serve important functions during rescue efforts, particularly in the management of mass-casualty disasters such as the Tokyo subway chemical terrorist attack.

Edward C. Nwanegbo

Further Reading

Charles, Daniel. *Master Mind: The Rise and Fall of Fritz Haber, the Nobel Laureate Who Launched the Age of Chemical Warfare*. New York: HarperCollins, 2005. Biography of the scientist who led the German chemical weapons effort during World War I places Haber's work in the context of his times. Includes bibliography and index.

Coleman, Kim. *A History of Chemical Warfare*. New York: Palgrave Macmillan, 2005. Describes the development and use of chemical weapons from 700 B.C.E. to the beginning of the twenty-first century, with extensive discussion of World War I. Also assesses current attempts to control the use and proliferation of such weapons and analyzes their potential use by terrorist groups.

Keyes, Daniel C., ed. *Medical Response to Terrorism: Preparedness and Clinical Practice*. Philadelphia: Lippincott Williams & Wilkins, 2005. Provides a review of clinical treatments for exposure to biological and chemical agents. Also discusses health care organizations' readiness for responding to terrorist attacks.

Roy, Michael J. *Physician's Guide to Terrorist Attack*. Totowa, N.J.: Humana Press, 2003. Provides an informative review of the infectious and chemical agents that potentially can be used in terrorist attacks.

Tucker, Jonathan B., ed. *Toxic Terror: Assessing the Terrorist Use of Chemical and Biological Weapons*. Cambridge, Mass.: MIT Press, 2000. Presents twelve case studies of the use of chemical and biological agents by terrorist groups. Identifies terrorists' patterns of behavior and discusses strategies to combat them.

Veenema, Tener Goodwin, ed. *Disaster Nursing and Emergency Preparedness: For Chemical, Biological, and Radiological Terrorism and Other Hazards*. 2d ed. New York: Springer, 2007. Nursing management guide addresses emergency needs for different categories of terrorist attacks as well as postdisaster care and psychological support for victims and their families.

Von Lubitz, Dag K. J. E. *Bioterrorism: Field Guide to Disease Identification and Initial Patient Management*. Boca Raton, Fla.: CRC Press, 2004. Volume aimed at medical professionals focuses on rapid recognition of the symptoms of exposure to biological or chemical weapons and on first steps in treatment for such exposure.

See also: Biological terrorism; Biosensors; Biotoxins; Botulinum toxin; Centers for Disease Control and Prevention; Chemical agents; Chemical Biological Incident Response Force, U.S.; Chemical warfare; Chemical Weapons Convention of 1993; Decontamination methods; Forensic toxicology; Mustard gas.

Chemical warfare

Definition: Use of toxic chemical substances to increase military and civilian casualties or to make habitat conditions unsuitable for military use by opponents during war.

Significance: Following the widespread use of chemical weapons during World War I, a number of countries tested and maintained stocks of such weapons as supplements to their stockpiles of more traditional military weapons. This work produced new chemical warfare agents as well as increasingly sophisticated ways to deliver and disseminate them, which led in turn to the development of better means of early detection of these agents and prevention of their spread. Forensic science is concerned with detecting and tracing specific chemicals used in the manufacture of chemical weapons, locating facilities that manufacture and store chemical weapons, and identifying nations with military programs that include chemical weapons in their arsenals.

Rudimentary forms of chemical warfare have been employed for millennia. Poisons of different kinds have been used to destroy livestock and armies' food supplies, with varying degrees of success, through the centuries. New World versions of chemical warfare measures include the arming of arrows, darts, and spears with batrachotoxins extracted from the poison dart frog in the tropics of Latin America. Modern chemical warfare was introduced during the early years of World War I, when French chemists loaded tear gas into small, hand-thrown bombs to be used by French troops to drive German soldiers out of their trenches. In response, German chemists manufactured chlorine gas, which was released from canisters downwind of the Russian army on the eastern front, marking the first time that lethal chemical weapons were used on a massive scale by any army. France responded with phosgene gas loaded in artillery shells, and before the end of the war all the major combatants were using chemical weapons. Gas masks became standard issue for soldiers of all sides on all fronts.

Since World War I, many countries have experimented with and stockpiled chemical weapons, and some have promoted chemical warfare, either openly or secretly. Modern chemical warfare involves the production of several types of chemical weapons, which may be classified according to their form (fluids, vapors, gases, or powders) or their persistence (that is, the length of time they maintain their toxic properties after dissemination). Chemical weapons can be further categorized based on how they affect human beings. Some recognized classes include lachrymatory (tear-causing) agents, such as chlorine gas and tear gas; nerve gases, such as sarin, which disrupt the nervous system; cyanides, which poison the digestive system; and agents containing acids that damage the skin or respiratory system.

When chemical substances are the cause of military and civilian casualties in war, specially trained forensic scientists are often called upon to collect and test evidence to determine the substances involved. Such scientists are trained in the detection of the chemicals used in weapons and in locating the sites where such weapons are manufactured. Their first objective is to collect chemical samples from corpses and from the scenes where the chemicals were deployed so that they can conduct tests to determine precisely what chemicals are present. Most substances used in chemical weapons have origin signatures or contain toxins that must be manufactured using specific types of equipment and techniques. By pinpointing the chemicals used, investigators may be able track the weapons from the chemicals' points of origin to the sites where the weapons were manufactured and to any storage locations. The evidence collected in this manner may aid in the investigation of war crimes and may be presented in national and international courts of law when accused perpetrators face trial.

Dwight G. Smith

Further Reading

Harris, Robert, and Jeremy Paxman. *A Higher Form of Killing: The Secret History of Chemical and Biological Warfare*. New York: Random House, 2002.

Marrs, Timothy C., Robert L. Maynard, and Frederick R. Sidell, eds. *Chemical Warfare Agents: Toxicology and Treatment*. 2d ed. Hoboken, N.J.: John Wiley & Sons, 2007.

Romano, James A., Jr., Brian J. Lukey, and Harry Salem. *Chemical Warfare Agents: Chemistry, Pharmacology, Toxicology, and Therapeutics*. 2d ed. Boca Raton, Fla.: CRC Press, 2008.

Somani, Satu M., and James A. Romano, Jr., eds. *Chemical Warfare Agents: Toxicity at Low Levels*. Boca Raton, Fla.: CRC Press, 2001.

Sun, Yin, and Kwok Y. Ong. *Detection Technologies for Chemical Warfare Agents and Toxic Vapors*. Boca Raton, Fla.: CRC Press, 2004.

Tucker, Jonathan B. *War of Nerves: Chemical Warfare from World War I to al-Qaeda*. New York: Pantheon Books, 2006.

See also: Blood agents; Chemical agents; Chemical Biological Incident Response Force, U.S.; Chemical terrorism; Chemical Weapons Convention of 1993; Decontamination methods; Mustard gas; Nerve agents; Poisons and antidotes; Sarin; Soman; Tabun.

Chemical Weapons Convention of 1993

Dates: Opened for signature January 13, 1993; entered into force April 29, 1997

The Convention: International agreement designed to outlaw the production, stockpiling, and use of chemical weapons.

Significance: In addition to contributing to international security, the Chemical Weapons Convention mandated that signatory nations declare all chemical agents they had developed for possible military use and all production facilities for such agents. This information was made publicly available, assisting forensic scientists in their efforts to investigate crimes involving these or similar compounds.

Although crude types of poisonous and other chemical weapons have been known since the Spartans burned sulfur and pitch to create toxic fumes during the Peloponnesian War, it was not until the industrial age that massive quantities of chemical weapons could be produced. The use of substances such as mustard gas and chlorine gas in World War I caused massive deaths and brought chemical weapons to the attention of the world. The 1925 Geneva Protocol sought to limit the use of such weapons, but it did not outlaw the possession of chemical substances that might become weapons. Given that the violation of international law is most likely to happen during wars, at which time the enforcement of the law is least likely, chemical weapons continued to be used at various times throughout the twentieth century, although on a lesser scale than in World War I and often more hidden from public view.

Terms of the Agreement

During the early 1980's, negotiators representing various national governments began seeking to reach an agreement to go beyond the Geneva Protocol and outlaw the possession of chemical weapons. Finally, in 1992, a formal agreement was reached, and the Convention on the Prohibition of the Development, Production, Stockpiling and Use of Chemical Weapons and on Their Destruction, also known simply as the Chemical Weapons Convention, was signed in January of the following year. As the name indicates, the convention broadened international law to prohibit not just the use but also the possession of virtually all chemical substances used as weapons.

The agreement mandated that all countries that signed the new law had to declare all their chemical weapons and production facilities publicly. The convention also included a long-term schedule for the destruction of stocks of weapons. An independent entity, the Organization for the Prohibition of Chemical Weapons, was created to oversee the provisions of the treaty. Of the 71,300 metric tons of chemical weapons declared by the more than 180 nations that have signed the treaty, more than 23,000 tons were destroyed during the first decade after the treaty entered into force. All the sixty-five production facilities declared were either destroyed or converted to peaceful purposes.

The international law has thus been upheld, which should have decreased the possibility that illegal groups can obtain chemical weapons, but this has not necessarily been the result. After the technology to create a chemical weapon has been developed, others can copy what had previously been done only in government laboratories.

Sarin Attack and Its Aftermath

Although rare, attempts to use chemical substances as weapons on a large scale have been made by individuals and nongovernmental groups. One of the most widely publicized attempts to use a chemical weapon as a tool of terrorism took place in 1995, when members of the Japanese religious cult Aum Shinrikyo released sarin gas, a nerve agent, in the Tokyo subway system. Owing to the relatively small amount of the gas released in the subway cars and an inefficient system of circulating the gas, the death toll was very low in this case, with only twelve people killed. Some fifty-five hundred others were injured by the gas, however. It was later found that the sect had legally purchased tons of materials capable of being used in the production of chemical weapons. The laws in Japan concerning such materials have since changed, as this incident brought vividly into focus the scope of the potential dangers posed by chemical weapons.

The fact that one group had used a chemical agent to push its agenda of destruction made law-enforcement agencies much more vigilant around the world. When the Chemical Weapons Convention had been ratified by enough countries to go into force in 1997, law-enforcement officials gained significant knowledge regarding chemical weapons. As nations declared their weapons stockpiles and production facilities, it became clearer what types of chemical agents might be available and from what sources. After the secrecy surrounding chemical weapons was removed, law-enforcment agencies could make better plans for responding to the threats that did exist. This also facilitated investigation into the possible use of these agents, as law-enforcement personnel could be better prepared to watch for activities that might indicate that criminal groups were trying to create such weapons.

One other aspect of the treaty that affected law-enforcement practices in some countries is

Article I of the Chemical Weapons Convention
General Obligations

1. Each State Party to this Convention undertakes never under any circumstances:
   a. To develop, produce, otherwise acquire, stockpile or retain chemical weapons, or transfer, directly or indirectly, chemical weapons to anyone;
   b. To use chemical weapons;
   c. To engage in any military preparations to use chemical weapons;
   d. To assist, encourage or induce, in any way, anyone to engage in any activity prohibited to a State Party under this Convention.
2. Each State Party undertakes to destroy chemical weapons it owns or possesses, or that are located in any place under its jurisdiction or control, in accordance with the provisions of this Convention.
3. Each State Party undertakes to destroy all chemical weapons it abandoned on the territory of another State Party, in accordance with the provisions of this Convention.
4. Each State Party undertakes to destroy any chemical weapons production facilities it owns or possesses, or that are located in any place under its jurisdiction or control, in accordance with the provisions of this Convention.
5. Each State Party undertakes not to use riot control agents as a method of warfare.

the provision limiting the types of chemical agents that can be used for crowd control and other domestic concerns. Unlike some other international treaties, the Chemical Weapons Convention includes provisions that are binding on domestic law-enforcement agencies in signatory nations. Police are not allowed to use chemicals that are on the convention's list of prohibited agents and "have irritation or disabling physical effects which disappear within a short time following termination of exposure."

Donald A. Watt

Further Reading

Cirincione, Joseph, Jon B. Wolfsthal, and Miriam Rajkumar. *Deadly Arsenals: Nuclear, Biological, and Chemical Threats.* 2d ed. Washington, D.C.: Carnegie Endowment for International Peace, 2005. Provides an overview of the range of chemical weapon threats facing the United States.

Drell, Sidney D., Abraham D. Sofaer, and George D. Wilson, eds. *The New Terror: Fac-*

ing the Threat of Biological and Chemical Weapons. Palo Alto, Calif.: Hoover Institution Press, 1999. Collection of essays with commentary covers a wide range of issues, including the constitutional constraints on U.S. law-enforcement agencies combating chemical weapons and methods for minimizing the damage caused by such weapons.

Kirby, Reid D., and U.S. Army Chemical School. *Potential Military Chemical/Biological Agents and Compounds.* Wentzeville, Mo.: Eximdyne, 2005. U.S. military field manual identifies various chemical agents and their properties. Includes additional information on industrial chemicals.

Sun, Yin, and Kwok Y. Ong. *Detection Technologies for Chemical Warfare Agents and Toxic Vapors.* Boca Raton, Fla.: CRC Press, 2004. Covers the means for detecting both military and industrial chemicals that might be used by terrorists and discusses steps that should be taken to prepare for such attacks or for accidents.

Tucker, Jonathan B., ed. *Toxic Terror: Assessing the Terrorist Use of Chemical and Biological Weapons.* Cambridge, Mass.: MIT Press, 2000. Presents twelve case studies of the use of chemical and biological agents by terrorist groups, identifying terrorists' patterns of behavior and strategies to combat them.

See also: Blood agents; Chemical agents; Chemical terrorism; Chemical warfare; Mustard gas; Nerve agents; Quantitative and qualitative analysis of chemicals; Sarin; Soman; Tabun.

Chicago nightclub stampede

Date: February 17, 2003

The Event: Twelve women and nine men, ages twenty-one to forty-three, were killed and more than fifty other persons were injured when they were trampled or crushed as a

panicked crowd attempted to flee Chicago's E2 nightclub through a single exit after pepper spray was used inside the club to break up a fight.

Significance: Situations in which surging crowds of people cause injuries and deaths are of great concern to law-enforcement officials and public safety authorities. When such events occur, coroners and medical examiners must perform autopsies to determine the specific causes of any deaths.

The E2 nightclub occupied the second floor of a building above the Epitome restaurant on South Michigan Avenue in Chicago, Illinois. E2 was frequented by celebrity figures and was considered by many in the local African American community to be the place to be seen. On the night of Monday, February 17, 2003, a party promoted by Envy Entertainment was in progress in the nightclub. The promoter had hired ten security guards to maintain order and assist patrons. When one of the security guards used pepper spray to attempt to stop a fight among some patrons, some people in the crowd began choking on the chemicals and then some began to shout, "Poison gas!" It was later reported also that someone said, "I bet it's Bin Laden."

The panicked crowd scrambled to get to the club's only open staircase leading outside. In the stampede, some smaller people were pushed and trampled by others as they tried to get to the door. The crowd got stuck on the restricted stairway, but people continued to pile on top of those already trapped. Some were literally squeezed to death or asphyxiated by crushing; many sustained broken bones. By the time police and fire officers arrived, even though security guards had been trying to remove fallen victims from below, the crush was so tight that significant exertion was required to begin to disentangle individuals from the pile of patrons.

Following the incident, the Cook County medical examiner's office performed routine after-death activities. The office certified the causes of death and held bodies at the morgue, where, even after several days, families and

Two attorneys watch an expert witness take measurements in the stairwell leading from the E2 nightclub in Chicago. Early the previous morning, February 17, 2003, twenty-one people died in a panic-driven stampede down the narrow stairwell after pepper spray was used in an attempt to break up a fight inside the nightclub. *(AP/Wide World Photos)*

friends came looking for loved ones. Much of the investigation into the incident itself was assigned to the Chicago Fire Department. A deputy medical examiner eventually testified at a hearing that "all E2 victims were crushed."

The deaths triggered a series of investigations and disputes involving licensing of the club and permits issued by the city of Chicago. Prominent African Americans spoke out in support of the club owners, and the owners of the club and their attorneys maneuvered to avoid criminal charges by attempting to discredit Chicago city officials. Significant civil damages were eventually paid.

David R. Struckhoff

Further Reading

Horan, Deborah, and Sean Hamill. "It Was People on Top of People." *Chicago Tribune*, February 18, 2003.

Sadovi, Carlos. "All E2 Victims Were Crushed." *Chicago Tribune*, January 26, 2007.

"Stampede at Chicago Nightclub Leaves Twenty-one Dead." *USA Today*, February 19, 2003.

See also: Asphyxiation; Autopsies; Choking; Fire debris; Forensic pathology; Smoke inhalation; Suffocation.

Child abduction and kidnapping

Definition: Unlawful seizing and detaining of children, through force or enticement, with the intent of keeping the children permanently or with the intent of harming the children or concealing them from their legal parents or guardians until ransoms are paid.

Significance: State and federal law-enforcement agencies working to solve child abduction and kidnapping cases often draw upon the tools of forensic science to locate missing children and to identify children when they are recovered or when their bodies are found.

Distinctions between "child abduction" and "child kidnapping" are not always clear-cut, as the terms are not always used consistently in the news media, the sociological literature, and statutory law. Generally, however, "child abduction" is the more inclusive term and is almost always the term applied to the unlawful seizing or detaining of children by their own close relatives. Abductions by family members are also the most common form of child abduction. The word "kidnapping" tends to be applied more to abductions by nonrelatives, particularly people who are strangers to their youthful victims. That term is generally applied to cases in which perpetrators abduct children with the intention of demanding ransoms for their return, physically abusing or harming the children, or keeping them permanently separated from their legal guardians for other reasons.

In the popular public perception, many if not most abductions of children are perpetrated by strangers or by little-known acquaintances of the victims. However, most nonrelative abductions are actually perpetrated by people with whom the victims' families are well acquainted. Nevertheless, fear of kidnapping by strangers is behind public campaigns to alert families to what is called "stranger danger" and efforts to have children carry identification cards, to collect fingerprints and DNA (deoxyribonucleic acid) samples of children for possible future need, and to have current photos available. Public awareness of the danger of child abduction has been kept alive by such practices as advertising missing children on milk cartons and the broadcasting of AMBER Alerts. Taking their name from "America's Missing: Broadcast Emergency Response," AMBER Alerts are designed to disseminate information on missing children as widely and quickly as possible. In many regions, the alerts interrupt television programs and are broadcast on electronic traffic signs over freeways. These and other practices help to dramatize the dangers of child abduction and foster the perception that most abductions are perpetrated by dangerous criminals.

Abduction and the Law

The abduction of children is everywhere regarded as a horrendous crime against society and has prompted legislation and law-enforcement efforts to prevent its occurrence. Highly publicized kidnapping cases typically prompt fresh legislation and new antikidnapping campaigns. One of the most famous child kidnapping cases in American history was the 1932 abduction and murder of the infant son of Charles A. Lindbergh, a famous aviator who was regarded as a national hero. The widespread public revulsion against that crime prompted the U.S. Congress to pass legislation, the Federal Kidnapping Act, popularly known as the Lindbergh Law. This law was significant because it authorized the investigation of kidnapping cases by the Federal Bureau of Investigation (FBI), which draws on the largest databases and most advanced forensic tools available to law enforcement.

In 1980, Congress enacted the Federal Parental Kidnapping Prevention Act to address the lack of uniformity in state laws regarding kidnapping. Disparities in the laws among different states encouraged some noncustodial parents forcibly to take their children to states with less stringent requirements or to refuse to return their children to the custodial parents' states so they could retain custody themselves. The new federal law gave the home states of abducted children priority in the resolution of custody disputes.

Several federal agencies provide assistance to local law-enforcement agencies that are investigating abducted children. In addition to the FBI, these agencies include the National Center for Missing and Exploited Children and the Forensic Services Division of the U.S. Secret Service. The services the agencies provide include on-site investigators, access to handwriting and fingerprint databases, and laboratory analyses of evidence and written reports. In addition, they make available consultations with forensic experts in such fields as computer forensics, forensic photography, graphic arts, video production, imaging, voice analysis, and computer modeling, and they provide experts to testify in court proceedings.

Prevalence

Among the various violent crimes perpetrated against children and juveniles in the United States, abduction is comparatively rare. In a study published in 2000, David Finkelhor and Richard K. Ormrod found that child abduction was responsible for less than 2 percent of all violent crimes against juveniles that were reported to law enforcement. Although large numbers of children are annually abducted, most abductees are returned to their families within short periods of time. However, parents and other family members are themselves responsible for most child abductions. In the year 1999, for example, roughly 78 percent of the approximately 262,100 children abducted throughout the United States were taken by relatives. Slightly fewer than 1,000 of the abductions were perpetrated by parents who were citizens of other countries.

Kidnapping and abductions by nonrelatives, both family acquaintances and strangers, accounted for about 22 percent of child abductions in 1999. In contrast to popular belief, the most frequent victims of nonfamily kidnapping—about 80 percent—are not young children but youths age twelve and older. Children from fifteen to seventeen years old make up nearly 60 percent of acquaintance and stranger kidnapping.

Family and Acquaintance Abductions

"Parental abduction" is generally defined as taking and not returning a child in violation of the custodial rights of the child's parent or guardian by another member of the family or someone acting on behalf of a family member. Indeed, any form of concealment of a child to prevent return, contact, or visitation is consid-

Megan's and Jessica's Laws

In 1994, a seven-year-old girl named Megan Kanka was kidnapped, raped, and brutally killed by a man who lived across the street from her family home in New Jersey. Unbeknownst to her parents up until that time, her murderer and his two housemates were all convicted sexual predators. After Megan's death, her parents created the Megan Nicole Kanka Foundation to put pressure on New Jersey's government to enact legislation requiring public notification of the residences of known sex offenders. The state legislature responded quickly, making New Jersey the first state to pass such legislation. Most other states soon followed New Jersey's lead. Details of legislation requiring community notification regarding persons convicted of sex crimes against children vary widely among the states, but all such legislation has become popularly known as "Megan's Law." The federal government also enacted similar legislation. The Jacob Wetterling Crimes Against Children and Sexually Violent Offender Registration Act of 1994 requires convicted sex offenders to notify local law enforcement of any changes in their addresses or employment.

Another horrific case of kidnapping occurred in Florida in 1995, when a nine-year-old named Jessica Lunsford was kidnapped, raped, and murdered by a forty-seven-year-old man. Public outrage against this crime led Florida's legislature to pass a law setting mandatory minimum prison sentences on adults convicted of sex crimes against children under thirteen years of age. Florida's law and those of the many other states that passed similar legislation are popularly known as "Jessica's Law."

ered be unlawful abduction. Likewise, transporting a child out of a state or country with the intent to deprive the caretaker of custodial rights or contact is also unlawful abduct in order for the act to be considered abduction. In cases involving children who are fifteen years of age or older and considered mentally competent, unlawful abduction occurs only when the perpetrators use physical force or threats of bodily harm to the children who are hidden or are taken from the state. Most parental abductions involve children six years or younger, with two-year-olds being the most frequently abducted. Such abductions typically occur at the children's homes.

Gender appears to have little bearing on parental child abduction. Statistics show that girls and boys are equally at risk of being abducted by their parents. Moreover, both mothers and fathers abduct children. However, although some studies find that noncustodial mothers and fathers are equally likely to abduct their children, others find that noncustodial fathers are more likely than mothers to be perpetrators.

Statistics for other types of abduction do show patterns that are more clearly gender-related. For example, almost three-quarters of acquaintance abductions of teenagers involve female victims. In general, teenage girls are more likely to be abducted by acquaintances than by strangers. Almost one-third of perpetrators are teenage boys. Moreover, boyfriends and former boyfriends account for nearly one-fifth of teenage girl abductions.

Stranger Abductions

Although the media often publicize stranger kidnapping, Finkelhor and Ormrod's study of juvenile kidnapping found that stranger and nonfamily child kidnapping is rare. A comparatively small percentage of juvenile abductions conform to the stereotypical model of kidnapping—that is, the taking of children and holding them for extended periods of time, whether to attempt to extort ransom or to subject the children to sexual assault and murder. The majority of perpetrators of that kind of abduction are strangers to their victims. Most stranger kidnappings occur in outdoor settings. Nearly 60 percent of the crimes occur in such outdoor public places as parks, streets, and parking lots. Kidnappings rarely occur on school grounds.

Some gender and age patterns can be seen in stranger abductions. For example, girls are twice as likely as boys to be victims of nonfamily kidnapping. Teenagers account for more than half the victims, elementary school-age children account for just over one-third of the victims, and preschoolers are rarely targeted. About 95 percent of perpetrators of stranger kidnapping are male. About 20 percent of the abductions are connected with other violent crimes, such as sexual assault, which is most commonly inflicted on girls. When kidnapping is connected with robberies, boys are more likely to be victims, and firearms are often involved in the kidnapping.

Among infants between six and twelve months old, boys and girls are equally at risk of being abducted by strangers, and most perpetrators kidnap infants of the same race. Infants who are kidnapped tend to be in good health, and their risk of being physically injured during

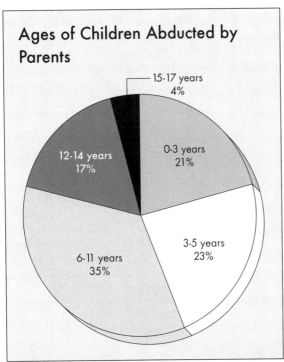

Ages of Children Abducted by Parents

- 15-17 years 4%
- 0-3 years 21%
- 3-5 years 23%
- 6-11 years 35%
- 12-14 years 17%

Source: Office of Justice Programs, Office of Juvenile Justice and Delinquency Prevention, 2002. Figures are based on 203,900 incidents of child abduction in the United States in 1999.

their abductions is low. However, the risk of harm to the parents—especially mothers—during kidnapping is high when infants are taken from their homes. Mothers are occasionally killed by kidnappers; in some instances, unborn babies are taken from their mothers' wombs.

Forensic Techniques Used in Investigations

As with investigations into any specialized field of crime, child abduction and kidnapping investigations draw on specialized forensic tools and procedures. One of the most important aspects of many child kidnapping investigations is identifying recovered children who have not been seen by their families for many years. The method most frequently used to identify kidnap victims is simple visual recognition by their parents. However, that method may not work in cases involving children who have been away from their parents so long that their physical appearance and voices have changed and their memories have faded. Such cases generally call for advanced forensic techniques. For example, photographic manipulation and age regression techniques may be used. These techniques entail manipulating old photographs artificially to age the faces of children so they will appear to match the current ages of the kidnapped children.

Some of the methods used to identify abducted infants after they are returned employ evidence that may have been collected when the children were born. For example, matching footprints to prints recorded on birth documents is the second-most-frequently used method of identification. Other evidence that is used includes blood tests, photographs, birthmarks, hospital wristbands, and DNA samples.

In kidnapping cases, it is vital that the initial investigators collect as much evidence as possible from the crime scenes, especially when children are abducted by nonfamily members and there is a possibility of their being held for ransom or becoming targets of sexual or violent crimes. Blood samples, hair samples, fibers, and other forensic evidence must be collected as soon as possible and properly stored. Such evidence often proves crucial in tracking victims' movements and identifying young victims after they are recovered.

Characteristics of Strangers Who Kidnap Children

- Most are male.
- Most are white.
- Most are under thirty years of age.
- Most are single.
- About half are employed.
- Employed male kidnappers typically work in unskilled and blue-collar occupations.
- About two-thirds of male kidnappers have prior arrest records, mostly for violent crimes, especially sexual assault against children.
- Female kidnappers are less violent than their male counterparts and rarely murder their victims.
- Female kidnappers are often motivated by revenge, the desire to have a child, or other emotional reasons.

Analysis of latent fingerprints is frequently an important tool in investigations of child abductions and missing children. Fingerprints often reveal the specific locations where children have been or the vehicles in which they have been transported. Latent prints also can be used to identify the child. A special problem in using fingerprint evidence in child abduction cases is that the latent prints of children may not last as long as those of adults, possibly because children's fingers secrete less oily residue.

DNA samples taken at birth from an infant or provided by the guardians of the missing child can be very helpful in identifying a missing child. Also, DNA can place a child at a scene or in an area or in a vehicle, and this information can help authorities to track the child's movements.

Identifying Dead Kidnap Victims

In the unfortunate cases in which kidnapping victims die, a primary task of forensic investigators is to identify the remains of whatever bodies have been recovered. The basic techniques used to identify children's remains are the same as those used to identify remains of adults. However, the remains of juveniles do

In 2004, the Internal Revenue Service joined in the effort to raise public awareness of child abductions in the United States by printing pictures of missing children on income tax preparation materials. *(AP/Wide World Photos)*

present some special problems. For example, juvenile skulls are not as fully developed as skulls of adult human beings. The shapes of skulls change considerably as individuals grow older, making it more difficult to identify the remains of children who have been missing for long periods. Changes in skull shape are particularly great during the first few years of children's lives. The length of an infant skull is about one-quarter the full height of the body. Adult skulls are only about one-eighth of full body height. As children grow older, their skulls and bodies gradually assume adult proportions. Meanwhile, the proportions of their facial features to their heads change. For example, the nasal and dental areas become larger relative to the rest of their faces. Other physical changes occur in the pigmentation and elasticity of their skin and the distribution of fatty tissue in their faces. The forensic reconstruction of juvenile faces

must take into account these and other differences between juvenile and adult faces.

Some changes in skulls of children may actually assist in estimating the children's ages. For example, there is a consistent and predictable sequence for the formation, eruption, and loss of a child's first teeth—or baby teeth—and their replacement with permanent teeth. Thus, the age of a preadolescent child can be estimated by examining how many of its teeth have emerged, the extent of calcification of the first molars, and the calcification of the dentition in its entirety.

Judy L. Porter

Further Reading

Bartol, Curt R., and Anne M. Bartol. *Introduction to Forensic Psychology*. Thousand Oaks, Calif.: Sage, 2004. Comprehensive work provides an easily understood guide to forensic psychology.

Beyer, Kristen R., and James O. Beasley. "Non-family Child Abductors Who Murder Their Victims: Offender Demographics from Interviews with Incarcerated Offenders." *Journal of Interpersonal Violence* 18 (October, 2003): 1167-1188. Presents the results of an analysis of data gleaned from personal interviews with offenders who have kidnapped and murdered children.

Blasdell, Raleigh. "The Longevity of the Latent Fingerprints of Children Versus Adults." *Policing: An International Journal of Police Strategies and Management* 24, no. 3 (2001): 363-370. Presents evidence from a study that found that children's latent fingerprints do not last as long as those of adults and discusses the implications of this finding for forensic science and law enforcement.

Burgess, Ann Wolbert, and Kenneth V. Lanning. *An Analysis of Infant Abductions*. Washington, D.C.: National Center for Missing and Exploited Children, 2003. Discusses in depth the national data on infant abductions.

Finkelhor, David, and Richard K. Ormrod. *Kidnaping of Juveniles: Patterns from NIBRS*. OJJDP Bulletin NCJ 181161. Washington, D.C.: U.S. Department of Justice, 2000. Brief work presents an analysis of the patterns found in the data concerning child abductions collected by the National Incident-Based Reporting System.

Hammer, Heather, David Finkelhor, and Andrea J. Sedlak. *Children Abducted by Family Members: National Estimates and Characteristics*. Washington, D.C.: U.S. Department of Justice, 2002. Brief work reports on data collected on family abductions by the National Incidence Studies of Missing, Abducted, Runaway, and Thrownaway Children.

James, Stuart H., and Jon J. Nordby, eds. *Forensic Science: An Introduction to Scientific and Investigative Techniques*. 2d ed. Boca Raton, Fla.: CRC Press, 2005. Provides an overview of forensic science procedures, including those involved in the investigation of cases of kidnapping. Informative for both practitioners and students.

Steadman, Dawnie Wolfe. *Hard Evidence: Case Studies in Forensic Anthropology*. Upper Saddle River, N.J.: Prentice Hall, 2003. Pre-sents constructive case studies that demonstrate the scientific foundations of forensic anthropology as well the broad scope of its modern applications.

Wilkinson, Caroline. *Forensic Facial Reconstruction*. New York: Cambridge University Press, 2004. Provides detailed description of the procedures involved in reconstructing faces and addresses the problems related to the determination of age, sex, and race using only the skull. Notes the particular problems of reconstructing the faces of children.

See also: Argentine disappeared children; Child abuse; DNA fingerprinting; Federal Bureau of Investigation Laboratory; Fingerprints; Forensic anthropology; Hostage negotiations; Lindbergh baby kidnapping; Megan's Law; Ritual killing.

Child abuse

Definition: Mistreatment of children that encompasses sexual molestation, infliction of physical injuries, emotional and psychological maltreatment, neglect, forced isolation, and threats of inflicting harm and other forms of intimidation.

Significance: Child abuse, long one of the most underreported and underinvestigated forms of violent crime, is among the most difficult crimes to uncover and prosecute. In the past, investigations were typically relegated to child protective workers who were untrained in crime scene investigation and evidence collection and processing. With increasing frequency, however, child abuse investigations are being conducted by trained law-enforcement officers and by technicians who draw heavily on the tools of forensic science.

Child abuse is a serious crime whose victims' psychological and physical scars often last for years. Child abuse cases are typically difficult to investigate and prosecute, but the tools of modern forensic science are making important contributions in identifying and convicting offenders. Teamwork plays a special role in these investigations, which typically involve not only law-enforcement professionals but also social workers, mental health providers, physicians, and others.

Forms of Abuse

Both sociological and legal definitions of child abuse and molestation have varied over time. "Child abuse" and "child molestation" can be subsumed under the more inclusive phrase "child maltreatment," which encompasses neglect, child endangerment, emotional and psychological abuse, physical abuse, and sexual abuse. Perhaps the most common form of child maltreatment is neglect—the failure to provide minor children with the most basic needs of food, shelter, clothing, education, and medical care.

Legal definitions of child abuse and subtypes of abuse are codified in state statutes and vary among jurisdictions. In contrast to sociological definitions, which may be vague and open to different interpretations, legal definitions and individual statutes spell out exactly what behaviors are illegal. For example, when adults who are legally responsible for the care of children expose those children to dangerous conditions, the adults are guilty of child endangerment. Examples of endangerment range from leaving young children unattended in parked cars while running errands to leaving minors completely alone in their homes for extended periods.

Physical abuse takes many forms that are easy to define—hitting, slapping, punching, kicking, beating, striking with objects, stabbing, cutting, burning, and choking. Somewhat less obviously abusive but equally serious is the violent shaking of infants or toddlers, which often manifests itself in shaken baby syndrome. Severe instances of physical abuse can lead to death.

Physical abuse may be one of the most underreported crimes against children. Part of the reason is that very young children lack the ability to communicate the abuse. Also, some abused children may regard what their parents do to them as normal behavior. They may even think that they deserve to be hit because of their own misbehavior. Forms of emotional and psychological abuse are less easy to define legally. They include verbally abusing or deriding children and threatening or terrorizing them.

Laws against the sexual abuse of children generally provide precise definitions of illegal behavior. Such abuse encompasses any or all forms of sexual contact between minors and adults, from improper touching and fondling to forced vaginal, oral, or anal intercourse. Consensual sexual contact between two minors can be considered sexual abuse when a significant age difference exists between them. In some jurisdictions, a difference of only three or four years in the ages of sexual partners may be regarded as significant. Sexual abuse also includes involving minors in the making of pornography.

Criminal Investigations

The gathering and preservation of evidence in child abuse investigations can be a daunting job. Police investigators must find out what has happened, how it happened, and other information in order to make arrests and bring offenders to justice. The forensic sciences provide important tools for collecting evidence in these crimes.

The first step in collecting evidence of abuse in cases that are reported is to determine when the crimes occurred and how much time has elapsed since the crimes took place. When child abuse is reported immediately after incidents occur, police can usually collect more physical evidence than in cases in which longer periods of time have elapsed.

The clothing worn by victims during times when they have been abused often provides valuable physical evidence. Hairs and traces of tears, dirt, blood, and semen found on clothing can be used as direct evidence of crimes. Investigators also comb the crime scenes, which often contain such physical evidence as bloodstains, hair samples, semen stains, and fragments of damaged clothing. All items that are collected must be carefully packaged, labeled, analyzed, and protected for use in court.

Medical Evidence of Abuse

Most injury evidence can be documented through medical procedures. Ideally, victims of child abuse should receive physical examinations by qualified physicians as quickly as possible. Indeed, in most cases of physical abuse of children, physicians discover evidence that maltreatment has occurred in the injuries themselves. For example, spiral arm fractures provide almost conclusive evidence of abuse, as such fractures are caused by arm twisting and can occur in almost no other way.

Another almost conclusive sign of child abuse that may be detected by physicians is traumatic alopecia—the forceful pulling of hair or breaking of hair shafts by friction, traction, or other forms of physical trauma. Traumatic alopecia occurs when abusers deliberately pull the hair

of their child victims. Hair pulling can cause hemorrhaging under the scalp, which has a rich supply of blood vessels. Accumulations of blood under the scalp are often important clues in differentiating between abusive and nonabusive hair loss.

Medical evaluations can discover evidence of shaken baby syndrome, which is responsible for at least half the deaths of victims of child abuse. Vigorous shaking of an infant or toddler causes a number of medical conditions that physicians can read as signs of the syndrome. These include closed-head injuries that are evidenced by altered levels of consciousness, coma, convulsions, or death; central nervous system injuries

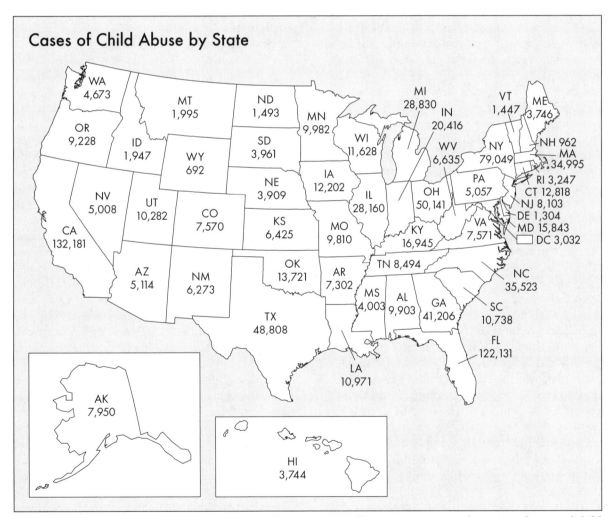

Cases of Child Abuse by State

WA 4,673
OR 9,228
ID 1,947
MT 1,995
ND 1,493
MN 9,982
MI 28,830
IN 20,416
VT 1,447
ME 3,746
NV 5,008
UT 10,282
WY 692
SD 3,961
WI 11,628
WV 6,635
NY 79,049
NH 962
MA 34,995
CA 132,181
CO 7,570
NE 3,909
IA 12,202
IL 28,160
OH 50,141
PA 5,057
RI 3,247
CT 12,818
NJ 8,103
DE 1,304
MD 15,843
DC 3,032
AZ 5,114
NM 6,273
KS 6,425
MO 9,810
KY 16,945
VA 7,571
TX 48,808
OK 13,721
AR 7,302
TN 8,494
NC 35,523
MS 4,003
AL 9,903
GA 41,206
SC 10,738
LA 10,971
FL 122,131
AK 7,950
HI 3,744

Source: U.S. Department of Health and Human Services, 2004. Figures represent substantiated cases of child maltreatment in 2002. Total number of cases for the entire United States in 2002 was 897,168.

that are evidenced by central nervous system hemorrhaging, lacerations, contusions, and concussions; and retinal hemorrhages.

Central nervous system injuries can be identified through magnetic resonance imaging (MRI) and computed tomography (CT) scans. Both of these techniques are used to discover a variety of injuries that reveal abuse, such as intracranial and intra-abdominal abnormalities. Ultrasound, a technique that creates two-dimensional images and is used for examining internal body structures, can be used to detect physical abnormalities. It is especially useful for detecting intracranial hemorrhaging in children under the age of two.

Techniques for determining the age of skeletal injuries are also valuable in abuse investigations because they can help differentiate between accidental and intentionally inflicted injuries. For example, radiology studies that determine the ages of bone injuries make it possible to identify patterns of physical abuse over long periods of time.

Among all types of cases involving physical injuries, human bites are the most common and easily recognized form of physical maltreatment. The ability to recognize injuries as human bite marks is thus particularly important, and forensic dentistry (also known as forensic odontology) contributes a great deal to the investigation of such injuries. By analyzing bite marks, forensic dentists can often help to identify the individuals who made them.

DNA Evidence

Although many proven forensic science techniques are helpful in the investigation of child abuse, perhaps nothing has helped solve more crimes in this area than DNA (deoxyribonucleic acid) testing. DNA carries coded genetic information that determines individual traits. Analyses of DNA samples can be used to identify the persons from whom the samples come. DNA testing was first used in criminal investigations during the early 1980's and almost immediately became one of the most valuable tools available to forensic science.

Many parts of human DNA are the same in different persons; however, the parts found in nonfunctioning sequences vary greatly. The variable parts can be matched to single individuals. In criminal child abuse cases, investigators often collect samples of fluids, hairs, and tissues left behind on victims by their abusers. These samples are then compared with samples taken from suspected perpetrators. When samples are found to match, the possibilities of misidentification are remote. DNA testing requires only small amounts of sample material. Bloodstains the size of a dime and semen samples the size of a quarter are usually sufficient. Results of analyses are usually obtained within four to six weeks. DNA evidence has been used successfully in the prosecution of many perpetrators of child abuse.

Jerry W. Hollingsworth and the Editors

Further Reading

Barkan, Steven E. *Criminology: A Sociological Understanding*. 3d ed. Upper Saddle River, N.J.: Pearson Prentice Hall, 2006. Examines criminal justice issues from a sociological perspective. Includes discussion of child abuse.

Buzawa, Eve S., and Carl G. Buzawa. *Domestic Violence: The Criminal Justice Response*. 3d ed. Thousand Oaks, Calif.: Sage, 2003. Presents information on how law-enforcement agencies and the courts approach cases of child and spousal abuse.

Fontes, Lisa Aronson, ed. *Sexual Abuse in Nine North American Cultures: Treatment and Prevention*. Thousand Oaks, Calif.: Sage, 1995. Collection of essays discusses the characteristics of child sexual abuse in various cultural communities in North America.

Monteleone, James A. *A Parent's and Teacher's Handbook on Identifying and Preventing Child Abuse*. St. Louis: G. W. Medical Publishing, 1998. Provides valuable information on the signs and symptoms of child abuse for lay readers.

_____, ed. *Child Abuse: Quick Reference for Healthcare Professionals, Social Services, and Law Enforcement*. St. Louis: G. W. Medical Publishing, 1998. Illustrated guide is designed to help those who might come into contact with abused children in their professional capacities.

Walker, Lenore E. A., and David L. Shapiro. *In-*

troduction to Forensic Psychology: Clinical and Social Psychological Perspectives. New York: Kluwer Academic/Plenum, 2003. Presents an overview of the applications of psychology to the law. Includes case examples.

See also: Bite-mark analysis; Blunt force trauma; Child abduction and kidnapping; DNA extraction from hair, bodily fluids, and tissues; False memories; Parental alienation syndrome; Rape; Rape kit; Semen and sperm; Shaken baby syndrome; Strangulation.

Choking

Definition: Medical emergency that occurs when partial or complete obstruction of the airway interferes with breathing, depriving the body of the oxygen necessary to maintain life.

Significance: Appropriate actions may be taken to prevent death in choking victims if others present recognize the signs of choking. Choking deaths may be mistaken for other types of deaths, such as suffocation, strangulation, or asphyxia, which may be intentional or accidental.

Choking is almost always accidental and preventable. The signs of active choking vary depending on the age of the person and the type of choking (partial or complete) involved. In adults, choking on food is most commonly found in situations of alcohol intoxication. Children often choke as the result of putting small objects, such as coins or small toys, into their mouths and then unintentionally inhaling them into the trachea (airway). Children also sometimes choke because they have put large amounts of food into their mouths and have not chewed the food properly before swallowing; the objects enter the airway rather than the esophagus.

A choking victim who is able to cough or speak is receiving adequate oxygenation to sustain life; the only action needed in such a situation is observation. The person should be al-lowed to cough in an attempt to dislodge the object. A partial airway blockage, however, may progress to a complete blockage. When the airway is completely blocked, the victim is not taking in adequate oxygen and is unable to speak or cough. A blue discoloration of the mouth and fingernails may become apparent.

A person who is choking may panic because of the lack of oxygen and fear of death. An adult may avoid seeking help in public owing to embarrassment, whereas a child may run from help out of fear. If the blockage is not quickly resolved, the individual will lose consciousness because of the lack of oxygen to the brain. At that point, the muscles in the airway will relax, but the object will remain in the airway unless the victim receives assistance from another person. If choking continues, the victim's heart will eventually stop beating and death will occur.

Medical and police personnel need to be aware of the signs of choking that may be present at the scene of a death. By thoroughly examining the scene and interviewing witnesses, emergency responders and police officers may aid the medical examiner in determination of the cause and manner of death. Bruising of the neck should not be seen in a choking victim. A person who has died from choking may have scratch marks at the neck from grabbing at the throat; if any skin is found under the fingernails, it will be the victim's own. The eyes of a choking victim may be bloodshot from vigorous coughing or from straining to relieve the blockage. As death occurs, the muscles relax. The bladder also relaxes, and urine may be present at the scene.

Amy Webb Bull

Further Reading

American Red Cross. *American Red Cross First Aid: Responding to Emergencies.* 5th ed. Yardley, Pa.: StayWell, 2006.

Lynch, Virginia A. *Forensic Nursing.* St. Louis: C. V. Mosby, 2006.

See also: Air and water purity; Asphyxiation; Autoerotic and erotic asphyxiation; Chemical agents; Epilepsy; Hanging; Petechial hemorrhage; Smoke inhalation; Strangulation; Suffocation.

Chromatography

Definition: Laboratory techniques used to separate chemical mixtures into their individual components and to quantify and identify the isolated components.

Significance: Chromatography techniques are useful for a variety of purposes in the forensic sciences, including determining causes of death, linking individuals to specific crime scenes, and analyzing the residues from explosives to identify possible suspects.

Chromatography was invented in 1903 by the Russian botanist Mikhail Semyonovich Tsvet, who used it to separate plant pigments, the various colored components of plants. It has been suggested that Tsvet arrived at the name "chromatography" for this process by combining the Greek words *chroma* and *graphein*, literally meaning "color writing." The uses of chromatography are not limited to colored substances, however.

The various forms of chromatography all share certain characteristics. For example, the sample to be analyzed is dissolved in a mobile phase, typically a liquid or a gas, which then comes into contact with a stationary phase, typically a solid or a liquid. As the mobile phase flows over the stationary phase, the various components of the sample are attracted to each phase to different extents, based on their physical characteristics. Those components that are attracted more to the stationary phase will move less quickly than those that are attracted more to the mobile phase, so the components separate from each other.

Chromatographic techniques may be categorized based on the nature of the mobile phase. In liquid chromatography, the mobile phase is a liquid. In gas chromatography, the mobile phase is a gas. Additionally, many of these techniques use columns containing the stationary phase; the mobile phase flows through the column after the sample has been dissolved in the mobile phase and applied to the column. When the components of the chemical mixture have been separated, they may be identified through the use of a detector attached to the chromatographic system. The detector, which may include one of several instruments used in chemical analysis, records various physical properties of the components. When a column is used, the detector is attached to the end of the column where the components are released.

Chromatography is used in the forensic sciences whenever it is necessary to separate the chemical components of a sample to determine the identity or the quantity of one or more of those components. The uses of chromatography include detecting the presence of explosives in airport baggage, analyzing explosives residues to identify the sources as well as possible suspects, and determining cause of death in autopsies through the screening of biological samples (such as blood, hair, and skin) for drugs or poisons. Chromatography is also used to identify the chemical makeup of seized illicit drugs and to determine blood alcohol levels in persons accused of driving under the influence of alcohol. Using chromatography techniques, analysts can determine the composition and quantity of the dyes in textile fibers left at a crime scene and thus help identify the potential source of the fibers, examine the ink on legal documents to determine whether any information has been fraudulently inserted, compare small amounts of soil to link suspects to a crime scene, determine the likely factory source of automobile paint left at the scene of a hit-and-run accident, detect the presence of accelerants at the scene of an arson investigation, and screen foods to determine whether they have been contaminated with dangerous chemicals.

Jason J. Schwartz

Further Reading

Bogusz, M. J., ed. *Handbook of Analytical Separations*. Vol. 6 in *Forensic Science*, edited by Roger M. Smith. 2d ed. New York: Elsevier, 2007.

Miller, James M. *Chromatography: Concepts and Contrasts*. 2d ed. Hoboken, N.J.: John Wiley & Sons, 2005.

See also: Analytical instrumentation; Column chromatography; Forensic toxicology; Gas chromatography; High-performance liquid chromatography; Homogeneous enzyme immunoassay; Mass spectrometry; Quantitative and qualitative analysis of chemicals; Separation tests; Spectroscopy; Thin-layer chromatography; Toxicological analysis.

Class versus individual evidence

Definitions: Class evidence is evidence that can be linked to a type (or class) of items; individual evidence is evidence that can be linked to a specific individual or item.

Significance: Because the majority of evidence at crime scenes is class evidence and not individual evidence, it would be difficult to link objects at crime scenes to specific suspects were it not for the fact that many objects pick up individual characteristics.

Class evidence makes up the vast majority of all evidence in forensic cases. For example, a glass fragment can be analyzed to determine its refractive index and chemical makeup. The resultant laboratory report can tell investigators that the fragment's properties are consistent with a certain type of glass, such as that from windowpanes or car headlights. What the analysis usually cannot reveal is from which particular window or which particular car headlight the fragment comes.

By contrast, individual evidence can be linked to specific objects, such as fingerprints, no two of which have ever been found to be exactly alike. For this reason, any fingerprint that is found must have been made by one, and only one, person. Other examples of individual evidence include human lip prints, ear prints, and sole prints. Researchers have also found through X-ray analyses of skulls that sinus prints—the unique patterns of bone and space in sinus cavities—are also individual. Forensic anthropologists can use this information to identify bodies of long-dead people. Surprisingly, DNA (deoxyribonucleic acid) evidence is not individual, as identical twins have identical DNA.

Many objects that would otherwise fall under the heading of class evidence pick up individual characteristics. For example, the soles of all shoes of a specific model and size come out of their factories looking exactly the same. After they have undergone some substantial wear, however, they develop distinctive wear patterns. The ways in which different users distribute their weight, the feet that they favor, and many other factors, including chemical and biological materials on which they step, contribute to making the soles of their shoes take on individual characteristics.

The individuation of characteristics can be seen in many different types of evidence. For example, tools can develop distinctive wear patterns and leave distinctive marks when they are used. Vehicle tires develop distinctive wear patterns over time, just as shoes do. Firearms can leave distinctive marks on the bullets they discharge. Glass may fracture in ways that make it possible for investigators to reassemble the broken pieces, much like a jigsaw puzzle. In forensic investigations, considerable time is devoted to looking at how class evidence becomes individualized.

Ayn Embar-Seddon and Allan D. Pass

Further Reading

Beavan, Colin. *Fingerprints: The Origins of Crime Detection and the Murder Case That Launched Forensic Science*. New York: Hyperion, 2001.

Platt, Richard. *Crime Scene: The Ultimate Guide to Forensic Science*. New York: Dorling Kindersley, 2003.

See also: Ballistic fingerprints; Chain of custody; Courts and forensic evidence; Crime scene reconstruction and staging; Cross-contamination of evidence; Direct versus circumstantial evidence; Disturbed evidence; DNA fingerprinting; Ear prints; Evidence processing; Federal Rules of Evidence; Fingerprints; Footprints and shoe prints; Physical evidence; Prints; Sinus prints; Trace and transfer evidence; Voiceprints.

Closed-circuit television surveillance

Definition: Monitoring of activities in public or private spaces conducted through the use of video cameras that transmit to limited sets of monitors.

Significance: As a tool of crime deterrence and detection, closed-circuit television technology is used extensively to monitor movement in public areas, despite the serious questions this form of surveillance raises regarding civil liberties. With improvements in video technology and growing fears of terrorism around the world, increasing numbers of law-enforcement agencies are employing closed-circuit television surveillance.

Combating crime committed in public locations has long been an important law-enforcement priority, and closed-circuit television (CCTV) has become an integral part of the technologies used in this effort. CCTV surveillance of public movements is especially pervasive in England, where hundreds of thousands of video cameras are already mounted and the numbers continue to grow, requiring an enormous expenditure of public funds. Other European countries that are heavily involved in CCTV monitoring include Ireland, France, Belgium, Finland, and Scotland. The use of CCTV surveillance in England has attracted widespread attention in high-publicity cases, such as the 2005 London subway bombings, when several of the suspects were caught after they appeared on CCTV cameras.

Methods and Results

Logistically, the monitoring of the images captured by CCTV cameras is conducted remotely. In England, monitoring is conducted from central stations, which are frequently found in police headquarters. The personnel who monitor CCTV feeds may be police or civilians. Across departments, variations are found in terms of the staff time allotted to live monitoring or post hoc monitoring of surveillance tapes and in terms of the periods of time for which the tapes are kept.

The empirical results of the implementation of CCTV surveillance have been mixed, ranging from reports of crime reduction as large as 90 percent to reports of crime increases up to 20 percent. Any interpretation of crime expansion must be made in terms of two basic goals of CCTV use: crime deterrence and crime detection/clearance. An increase in crime might actually be viewed as a success if the presence of CCTV enhanced crime detection.

In terms of property crime, the studies that have found the most positive results have reported long-term reductions in burglary, car theft, and general theft in CCTV areas, with concomitant increases in non-CCTV zones. CCTV may have a displacement effect, whereby the total volume of crime remains fairly constant but much of it is shifted to areas that lack video monitoring. Other studies have found that reported crime reductions in areas with CCTV surveillance could not be isolated from reductions that might have come about because of the large amount of publicity given to the CCTV program itself. Some property crime studies have reported no substantial crime reductions as the result of CCTV surveillance, but it is possible that the monitoring had an impact by holding down projected crime increases.

In studies of elderly populations, CCTV tapes were found to provide records useful for identifying suspects (a task in which elderly persons are typically weak). In another group of studies, CCTV reduced the volume of some crimes, particularly those the commission of which took long enough to be recorded by cameras, such as auto theft. However, the frequency of relatively "quick" crimes, such as burglary and shoplifting, increased. Studies have also found a "fading effect" associated with the implementation of CCTV surveillance—that is, crime rates decline initially but then begin to rise again, after the novelty of the monitoring wears off and its deterrent impact on would-be offenders recedes. Researchers have also found it difficult at times to separate the effects of CCTV monitoring from other simultaneous changes in the areas being studied, such as better lighting or overall security.

Little research has addressed the effects of CCTV implementation on crime trends for violent offenses such as robbery and assault. Because violent offenses are generally more impulsive than property offenses, violent crime is less amenable to preventive measures, but CCTV surveillance could allow police to intervene faster when violent offenses take place.

Public Responses

Researchers have also looked at the effects of CCTV surveillance on fear of crime. In some studies, the majority of the people who were surveyed thought that the use of CCTV would reduce crime in their jurisdictions, but actual fear levels did not decline. Results of such studies have varied depending on the populations involved and the exact crimes and camera locations. In a survey of elderly persons residing in sheltered housing, for example, reduced levels of fear of burglary were found, as the respondents widely believed that the cameras made stranger entry into their homes more difficult.

Studies have found that fears of crime are reduced more by CCTV cameras located in parking lots than by the presence of cameras in shopping centers or on the streets. A sex effect has also been noted regarding fear of crime, with some studies indicating that women are particularly fearful at night in bus and train stations even with CCTV monitoring. Subjects in one study felt that CCTV surveillance was superior to other police crime detection strategies, but they also said that they preferred retaining police foot patrols in order to feel safer, because this facilitated quicker law-enforcement response if needed in any given situation.

CCTV surveillance is appealing in terms of its potential to deter and detect crime. It may also have beneficial effects in terms of reviving businesses located in high-crime areas and increasing

the numbers of guilty pleas made by defendants who know their crimes were caught on tape. The use of CCTV surveillance raises several concerns regarding civil rights, however. Some critics have asserted that members of minority groups are disproportionately targeted for observation and that the police or others may use the monitoring videotapes for purposes that exceed the original scope of the surveillance. Members of the public may not always know when they are being monitored, and the actions seen on the tapes (which include images of varying clarity and lack auditory information) may sometimes be misinterpreted. Nevertheless, the use of CCTV surveillance is growing steadily, and the refinement of video technology is expected to become increasingly important in helping law-enforcement authorities meet their crime deterrence and investigatory goals.

Eric Metchik

Further Reading

Gill, Martin, ed. *CCTV*. Leicester, England: Perpetuity Press, 2003. Wide-ranging collection of articles by leading European academics discusses various social and legal aspects of CCTV surveillance.

A closed-circuit television surveillance system operator for the Baltimore Police Department monitors activity on a street where a possible drug deal was taking place in late 2006. *(AP/Wide World Photos)*

Gill, Martin, Anthea Rose, Kate Collins, and Martin Hemming. "Redeployable CCTV and Drug-Related Crime: A Case of Implementation Failure." *Drugs: Education, Prevention, and Policy* 13, no. 5 (2006): 451-460. Presents an analysis of the practical and logistical issues involved in the use of portable CCTV systems to fight drug crimes in three English police precincts.

Goold, Benjamin. "Open to All? Regulating Open Street CCTV and the Case for 'Symmetrical Surveillance.'" *Criminal Justice Ethics* 25, no. 1 (2006): 3-17. Provides a legally oriented analysis of the increasing use of CCTV surveillance of public spaces in the United States.

Newburn, Tim, and Stephanie Hayman. *Policing, Surveillance, and Social Control. CCTV and Police Monitoring of Suspects.* Portland, Oreg.: Willan, 2002. Comprehensive work reviews the English empirical research on the impact of CCTV surveillance.

Norris, Clive, and Michael McCahill. "CCTV: Beyond Penal Modernism?" *British Journal of Criminology* 46 (2006): 97-118. Integrates discussion of the theoretical literature and empirical research findings, emphasizing the experience of four different applications of CCTV technology in the United Kingdom.

See also: Airport security; Electronic bugs; Facial recognition technology; Forensic photography; Night vision devices; Racial profiling; Satellite surveillance technology.

Club drugs

Definition: Variety of illicit hallucinogenic substances that share the general traits of being used in social situations and exciting or sedating users.

Significance: The use of so-called club drugs is known to be widespread in the United States, even though these unregulated substances may put users in dangerous situations and have been linked to risky sexual behavior and sudden death. Law-

enforcement agencies expend significant resources in efforts to reduce the illegal manufacture, sale, and use of such drugs.

The group of substances that can be categorized as club drugs includes those that have historically been known as psychedelic drugs (that is, substances that alter perception and thinking) as well as so-called designer drugs, which are typically made by people who seek to profit from manufacturing drugs or are interested in finding substances that patrons of nightclubs or dance clubs can use legally to enhance their enjoyment. The creators of designer drugs often modify unregulated or illegal chemical substances to make them technically legal and thus suitable for such purposes. After problems emerge in connection with these substances, however, the legal system moves in to identify and classify them and assign legal consequences for their inappropriate use.

Types of Club Drugs and Their Effects

Club drugs comprise a large number of different substances, and new drugs emerge every day as various ingredients are designed or redesigned. One of the most popular club drugs is methylenedioxymethamphetamine, or MDMA, which is also known as ecstasy, X, or Adam. MDMA is different from so-called herbal ecstasy (other names include cloud nine, herbal bliss, and herbal X), which is also used as a club drug. MDMA is a derivative of methamphetamine, whereas herbal ecstasy is made from ephedrine or pseudoephedrine and caffeine. Other club drugs include ketamine hydrochloride (known as ketamine or special K), gamma-hydroxybutyrate (GHB, also known as Georgia home boy or liquid X), and rohypnol (known as roach, roche, or roofies). One long-established substance often used as a club drug is lysergic acid diethylamide (LSD), which is also known as acid or blotter.

The effects of these drugs vary from substance to substance. Club drugs generally have no medical uses, although researchers have examined the usefulness of some of them in the treatment of problems such as trauma and antisocial personality disorder. As a group, these substances are known for eliciting positive feel-

Street Names for Club Drugs

GHB (gamma-hydroxybutyrate)
- G
- Georgia home boy
- grievous bodily harm
- liquid ecstasy

Ketamine
- bump
- cat Valium
- green
- honey oil
- jet
- K
- purple
- Special K
- special la coke
- super acid
- super C
- vitamin K

LSD (lysergic acid diethylamide)
- acid
- blotter
- blotter acid
- boomers
- dots
- microdot
- pane
- paper acid
- sugar
- sugar cubes
- trip
- window glass
- windowpane
- yellow sunshine
- Zen

Methamphetamine
- chalk
- crank
- crystal
- fire
- glass
- ice
- meth
- speed

Methylenedioxy-methamphetamine (MDMA)
- Adam
- Clarity
- ecstasy
- Lover's Speed
- X
- XTC

Rohypnol
- forget-me pill
- roche
- roofies
- rophies

ings, such as happiness, euphoria, and a general sense of well-being. Users may also experience feelings of emotional clarity, a decreased sense of personal boundaries, and feelings of empathy with and increased closeness to others. They may also experience pleasant psychedelic effects in the form of other changes in their way of perceiving themselves, others, and their surroundings.

Negative effects of club drugs include physical symptoms such as chills, high blood pressure, rapid heartbeat, respiratory distress, sweating, tremors, and impaired motor control. In some cases, convulsions may occur. The drugs can also have negative psychological effects: Users may experience impaired judgment, memory loss, and unpleasant hallucinations. Club drugs can trigger irrational (sometimes violent) behavior, panic, and paranoia. In addition, as a result of using these substances, some individuals may suffer blackouts and drug flashbacks. In users who are compromised by

physical or mental health problems, reactions to club drugs may be magnified.

Risks of Use

These substances can be very dangerous when mixed with alcohol, energy drinks, herbal remedies, prescription medications, or other drugs, even over-the-counter drugs. The synergistic effects—that is, effects from drug interactions—may be multiplicative rather than simply additive, so that any of the drugs consumed together with other substances becomes much more pronounced in its effects. Because club drugs are not manufactured by regulated pharmaceuticals laboratories, their quality varies widely. Some may contain contaminants, and some may simply look like the drugs they are purported to be and thus may deliver unknown drug effects.

How and where these substances are used can mitigate or increase the risks involved. In a medical or laboratory setting, or in a private home under observation, relatively few risks may be present. In contrast, in situations involving crowds, heightened emotions, and the company of strangers, the risks of club drugs may be pronounced. At raves, for instance, users of club drugs may not realize they are becoming seriously dehydrated from continual dancing and other physical activity; this is one reason users often end up in emergency rooms.

The proximity of strangers may add to the risks involved in the use of club drugs in part because users may be easy targets for physical or sexual assault or property crimes. In addition, driving under the influence of these substances may result in accidents, criminal charges, or both.

Beyond the short-term risks associated with use, club drugs may also expose users to risks related to substance abuse and dependence. Habitual use of club drugs may result in problems with functioning at work, home, or school, and may bring users into frequent contact with law-enforcement authorities. Some users may find that they repeatedly use club drugs in dangerous situations or that they are in constant conflict with their significant others over their substance use.

Substance-dependence problems related to the use of club drugs may include issues of tolerance, withdrawal, the use of greater quantities or more frequent use than intended, and persistent desire to quit or unsuccessful efforts to quit. Those who become dependent on these substances are likely to spend increasing amounts of time in obtaining and using the drugs and recovering from their effects, giving up other activities to do so. Both the drug abuse and the abandonment of other activities may cause or exacerbate other psychological or physical problems. For some users, club drugs may interact with other states of mind or conditions, such as anxiety or depression, and trigger more lasting problems with anxiety or mood.

Legal Issues

The legal issues related to club drugs may be seen as a microcosm of the legal issues related to substance use in general, from the drugs' creation to how they are used and their impacts. Manufacturing and distribution issues are rele-

vant in that these drugs are unregulated substances that form the basis for an unregulated economy. Issues of drug identification and classification are also relevant in that the drugs often are designed around the law, challenging the process of identification as well as the issue of enforcement of laws concerning their use and sale. Harmful use related to impaired personal judgment and behavior is also important in terms of the accidents and related crimes it may cause, such as driving under the influence, assault, and property damage. Of additional interest to law-enforcement authorities is the potential for the use of these drugs by individuals wishing to harm others, as in the use of rohypnol and similar substances in sexual crimes.

Nancy A. Piotrowski

Further Reading

Holland, Julie. *Ecstasy: The Complete Guide— A Comprehensive Look at the Risks and Benefits of MDMA*. Rochester, Vt.: Inner Traditions International, 2001. Presents data and arguments pertaining to the typical risks that may be expected from ecstasy and other club drugs. Includes discussion of research perspectives on the potential benefits of these drugs.

Jansen, Karl. *Ketamine: Dreams and Realities*. Ben Lomond, Calif.: Multidisciplinary Association for Psychedelic Studies, 2004. Provides a historical perspective on the uses of ketamine and addresses the risks and benefits related to the drug.

Julien, Robert M. *A Primer of Drug Action: A Comprehensive Guide to the Actions, Uses, and Side Effects of Psychoactive Drugs*. 10th ed. New York: Worth, 2005. Reliable text provides full coverage of the topic, including information about how these drugs affect people from youth to old age.

Stafford, Peter. *Psychedelics*. Oakland, Calif.: Ronin, 2003. Provides broad descriptions of drugs that affect perception, focusing on what these substances may look like and how they may affect users. Also discusses the drugs' individual and societal impacts.

Weil, Andrew, and Winifred Rosen. *From Chocolate to Morphine: Everything You Need to Know About Mind-Altering Drugs*. Rev. ed.

Boston: Houghton Mifflin, 2004. Presents a down-to-earth discussion of drugs that affect the mind. Easy to read.

See also: Amphetamines; Antianxiety agents; *Diagnostic and Statistical Manual of Mental Disorders*; Drug abuse and dependence; Drug confirmation tests; Drug paraphernalia; Hallucinogens; Illicit substances; Inhalant abuse; Psychotropic drugs; Stimulants.

CODIS

Date: Established in 1990
Identification: Database maintained by the Federal Bureau of Investigation that stores DNA profiles for comparison purposes, used by federal, state, and local crime laboratories.
Significance: CODIS allows forensic laboratories to compare DNA profiles related to crimes (forensic profiles) to those obtained from other crimes or from individuals previously convicted of felonies. Through such comparisons, links may be found between crime scenes and repeat offenders may be identified.

The Combined DNA Index System, better known as CODIS, was established as the result of a suggestion from the Technical Working Group on DNA Analysis Methods; the intent was to create a national database of DNA (deoxyribonucleic acid) profiles collected from convicted criminals. When CODIS was initiated in 1990 as a pilot project of the Federal Bureau of Investigation (FBI), it included fourteen state and local laboratories.

The DNA Identification Act of 1994 allowed the formation of a national DNA database and clarified which types of DNA evidence could be stored in it. DNA profiles from persons convicted of crimes, evidentiary items obtained from crime scenes, and unidentified human remains were to be included, as well as profiles voluntarily submitted by relatives of missing persons. In 1998, the national database became

operational, and by 2003 it was accepted by all fifty states. Qualified city, county, regional, state, and federal crime laboratories, as well as labs in several in other countries, now contribute to this powerful crime-solving tool.

Structure of the Database

CODIS is operational at three tiers: the National DNA Index System (NDIS), the State DNA Index System (SDIS), and the Local DNA Index System (LDIS) levels. A DNA profile originates locally and then migrates to the state and national levels. This approach allows each state access to a database that is concurrent with its individual legislation, including what crimes will result in submission of a DNA profile (for example, sexual assault, any violent crime, all felonies).

CODIS consists of two main databases: the forensic index and the convicted offender index. The forensic index contains data on DNA profiles obtained from victims or crime scenes, whereas the convicted offender index includes the profiles of those convicted of offenses. Using the two indexing systems, it is possible to link crimes together for the purpose of identifying a repeat perpetrator or to link a crime to a person

Indexes Within CODIS

- **Convicted offender index:** Contains profiles of individuals who have been convicted of crimes
- **Forensic index:** Contains DNA profiles developed from crime scene evidence, such as semen stains or blood
- **Arrestees index:** Contains profiles of arrested persons (from those states in which laws permit the collection of arrestee samples)
- **Missing persons index:** Contains DNA reference profiles from missing persons
- **Unidentified human remains index:** Contains DNA profiles developed from unidentified human remains
- **Biological relatives of missing persons index:** Contains DNA profiles voluntarily contributed by relatives of missing persons

who is or was in prison. Other databases existing in CODIS include the arrestees index, the missing persons index, the unidentified human remains index, and the biological relatives of missing persons index. Whether an individual state participates in these at the national level depends on state policy or law. In order for a state to be eligible to participate in CODIS, the appropriate state authority must sign a memorandum indicating that the state's laboratory (or laboratories) adheres to FBI quality assurance standards; the laboratory must also pass a series of inspections and subsequent reviews.

A DNA profile found in CODIS contains only the following: an identification code for the submitting agency, an identification number for the specimen, the DNA profile itself, and the name of the person who submitted the information. Only the submitting laboratory can place a name on a DNA profile. The limited data ensure that the DNA profiles are not exploited and that the identities of those whose profiles are submitted to the database are protected. It is also important to note that the profiles do not contain any information about medical conditions. CODIS is accessible only to those working within the field of law enforcement. Participating laboratories submit their information through a secure intranet called CJIS WAN, which is located in Clarksburg, West Virginia.

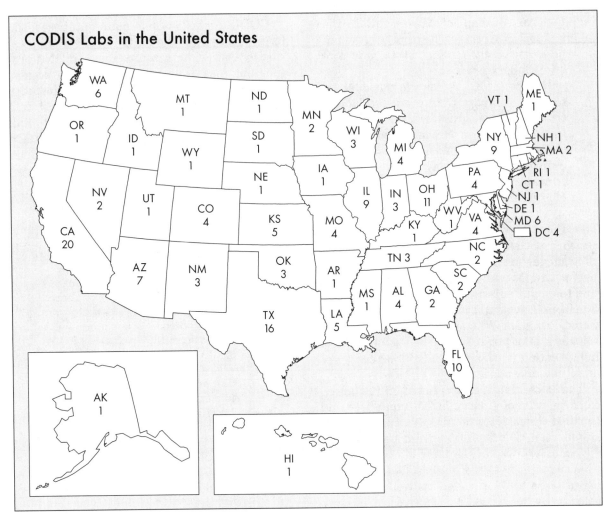

CODIS Labs in the United States

Source: Federal Bureau of Investigation, 2008.

An FBI unit chief holds a chart outlining the Combined DNA Index System during a 1998 news conference, when the system's national database became operational. *(AP/Wide World Photos)*

Putting a DNA Sample Through CODIS

DNA samples can be taken from convicted persons in several different ways. Blood or buccal swabs (swabs of the inside of the cheek) are generally collected, although in theory almost any tissue could be used. Forensic samples come from a huge variety of sources, the most common being semen from sexual assault cases, but blood, hair, saliva, bone, or virtually any other tissue or body fluid can be tested. New developments have allowed for touch samples—samples extracted from items that have come into direct contact with the persons of interest (such as held objects)—to be used also as potential sources of profiles.

DNA profile information is submitted to CODIS in the form of short tandem repeats (STRs). Thirteen core STR loci were chosen for use with CODIS; the profiles of convicted of-

fenders must contain all thirteen of these loci to be uploaded to CODIS, whereas forensic profiles, which often originate from less-than-ideal sources, are required to have at least ten loci.

At the local level, analysts have some leeway when searching the database. For instance, a laboratory may require that a complete match be made at a locus for that locus to be considered, whereas another laboratory, recognizing that degraded DNA from a crime scene can result in the loss of part of a profile, might find a partial profile probative. Likewise, the minimum number of loci needed to be considered informative can vary from case to case.

After a potential match has been found by CODIS, the laboratories responsible for the corresponding profiles must contact each other to authenticate the results. The samples are often then retested to ensure the validity of the

253

match. Upon confirmation that the two profiles are consistent with each other, the laboratories exchange any additional information they need.

Erin J. Lenz and David R. Foran

Further Reading

Balding, D. J., and P. J. Donnelly. "Evaluating DNA Profile Evidence When the Suspect Is Identified Through a Database Search." *Journal of Forensic Sciences* 41 (1996): 603-607. Leads the reader through the process of entering a DNA profile into a database and discusses the population genetics associated with such a profile.

Butler, John M. *Forensic DNA Typing: Biology, Technology, and Genetics of STR Markers.* 2d ed. Burlington, Mass.: Elsevier Academic Press, 2005. Provides a detailed overview of short tandem repeats and their applicability to forensic science.

Houck, Max M., and Jay A. Siegel. *Fundamentals of Forensic Science.* Burlington, Mass.: Elsevier Academic Press, 2006. Good general textbook includes discussion of DNA analysis.

National Research Council. *The Evaluation of Forensic DNA Evidence.* Washington, D.C.: National Academy Press, 1996. Spells out the guidelines on methods of DNA analysis that are accepted in the courtroom.

Walton, Richard H. *Cold Case Homicides: Practical Investigative Techniques.* Boca Raton, Fla.: CRC Press, 2006. Examination of cold cases includes a section on applying CODIS to the investigation of old, unsolved crimes.

See also: DNA analysis; DNA database controversies; DNA fingerprinting; DNA profiling; DNA typing; Ethics of DNA analysis; Federal Bureau of Investigation DNA Analysis Units; Federal Bureau of Investigation Laboratory; Integrated Automated Fingerprint Identification System; National Crime Information Center; National DNA Index System; Rape; Restriction fragment length polymorphisms; Short tandem repeat analysis.

Coffin birth

Definition: Spontaneous delivery of a fetus from the uterus of a dead woman.

Significance: When a fetus is found outside the dead body of the mother, it may be necessary for forensic scientists to determine whether the mother died while the fetus was still in the uterus, the fetus later expelled by the buildup of decomposing gases in the mother's body, or whether the fetus was delivered before the mother's death and died separately. The distinction may be important when charges are brought against a suspect for the murder of a pregnant woman.

Although it has always been rare, the phenomenon of coffin birth, or postmortem birth, has occurred throughout history. Paleopathologists have discovered evidence of coffin birth (or *Sarggeburt* in German, the language in which it was first described) in archaeological digs in ancient graveyards. With modern embalming techniques, it has become even more unusual, although it still may occur in cases of accidental death, murder, or incorrect embalming practices.

Coffin birth is truly the birth of a fetus, not a case of the fetus being expelled through the body through the abdomen, such as with a wound mimicking a birth by cesarean section. The buildup of gases in the decomposing body of a pregnant woman may put pressure on the uterus to the point of expelling an unborn fetus through the birth canal. Scientists believe that this buildup could take weeks or months to happen, and the possibility of a coffin birth occurring depends on many outside factors, such as the air temperature and whether the woman's body is in water or buried in the ground.

Coffin birth is so rare that it does not often appear in the medical literature. The topic came into the news spotlight in 2003, however, in the case of Laci Peterson. Peterson was about seven and one-half months pregnant when she disappeared in December, 2002, leading to speculation that her husband, Scott Peterson, had murdered her. Later, when her body and the body of

Missing-person broadside posted near the police command center in Modesto, California, while the pregnant Laci Peterson was still being sought in early 2003. *(AP/Wide World Photos)*

her late-term fetus were found separately on the shores of the San Francisco Bay, coffin birth was raised as the possible reason that the fetus was no longer in her uterus. Coffin birth was only one possibility of many, but it was thought a strong possibility, partly because Laci Peterson had no external wounds consistent with the fetus's exiting her body other than through the birth canal. Despite the confusion over whether she was still pregnant when she was killed or whether the baby was born before her death, charges were filed against Scott Peterson for the murder of both his wife and son. He was convicted in March, 2005, and sentenced to death for the murders.

Marianne M. Madsen

Further Reading

Fleeman, Michael. *Laci: Inside the Laci Peterson Murder*. New York: St. Martin's Press, 2003.

Lyle, D. P. *Forensics and Fiction: Clever, Intriguing, and Downright Odd Questions from Crime Writers*. New York: St. Martin's Press, 2007.

See also: Autopsies; Decomposition of bodies; Forensic archaeology; Paternity evidence.

Cognitive interview techniques

Definition: Interviewing protocols based on the science of cognitive psychology.

Significance: Because eyewitness evidence is critical to solving many crimes, it is important that law-enforcement personnel employ interviewing techniques that elicit extensive and accurate information from witnesses. The use of cognitive interview techniques can maximize the effectiveness of witness interviews.

Evidence collected from cooperative witnesses is critical for solving many crimes and for determining what happened at accident scenes. Nevertheless, many police and accident investigators receive only minimal or no training in techniques to use when interviewing cooperative witnesses. Often the only training they get comes from on-the-job experience or from watching more senior investigators conduct interviews—whether well or poorly. Police and other investigative interviewers therefore often make avoidable errors and collect less information than is potentially available. Even worse, through poor questioning techniques, interviewers may entice witnesses to recall or describe critical events incorrectly.

The most common interviewing mistakes include asking suggestive or leading questions, asking too many short-answer questions and too few open-ended questions, interrupting witnesses during their answers, and asking questions that are unrelated to the witness's thoughts and mental images. To remedy this problem, two research psychologists, Ronald P. Fisher and R. Edward Geiselman, began work during the 1980's to develop an improved interviewing technique, the cognitive interview (CI), to increase the amount of accurate information collected from cooperative witnesses. CI techniques incorporate the theoretical principles of cognitive and social psychology and borrow elements and techniques from other investigative domains, including journalism, medicine, and social work. Part of the training in CI techniques involves the modeling of the differences between effective and ineffective police interviewers.

Principles of the Cognitive Interview

Cognitive interview techniques were developed to improve three psychological processes: the social dynamics between the witness and the interviewer, the thought processes of both the witness and the interviewer, and the communication between the witness and the interviewer. Interviewers can create more favorable social dynamics for interviews by developing personal rapport with respondents. This is especially true when they are interviewing victims and suspects. Interviewers should also instruct witnesses to take an active role within the interview and not merely answer questions with brief responses. Interviewers can accomplish this by instructing witnesses to generate detailed narrative descriptions without waiting for more questions, by asking mainly open-ended questions, and by not interrupting witnesses during their narrative responses.

Witnesses sometimes cannot recall critical details even though they have the information stored in their memories. Interviewers can help witnesses search through their memories more efficiently by instructing them to re-create the context of the original event (asking, for example, What were you thinking about at the time?), to search through their memories repeatedly, and to use all of their senses. Interviewers

Cognitive Interview Versus Hypnosis

The use of cognitive interview techniques with crime witnesses has been criticized as similar to the use of hypnosis, which can raise legal issues. CI techniques and hypnosis do have some elements in common; for instance, in both, interviewers need to develop rapport with witnesses, witnesses are instructed to close their eyes, and witnesses are asked to re-create in their minds the contexts of the original events. Scientific research shows, however, that the cognitive interview and hypnosis function differently: The cognitive interview enhances recall more reliably than does hypnosis; the accuracy of the information collected during cognitive interviews is relatively high, whereas hypnosis may promote fabrication; the cognitive interview does not influence witness confidence, whereas hypnosis elevates confidence; and the cognitive interview reduces witness suggestibility to leading and suggestive questions, whereas hypnosis increases suggestibility. The legal problems associated with hypnosis thus do not plague the cognitive interview.

also make cognitive errors, as they have to do many mental tasks at the same time, including listening to and notating the witness's answers, formulating hypotheses about the critical event, and asking questions. Interviewers can improve their own thought processes by encouraging witnesses to generate information without waiting for questions and by developing more efficient methods to record witnesses' answers.

Interviewers often fail to communicate to witnesses their investigative needs for detailed and extensive information. As a result, witnesses do not report all of their available knowledge. Interviewers should inform witnesses explicitly that they need to provide detailed and informative answers. In addition, interviewers should understand that witnesses may have much information that is stored nonverbally (for example, a mental picture of the crime scene) and should facilitate witnesses' communicating such information by encouraging nonverbal responses (such as making a sketch).

The sequence of the cognitive interview is based on two principles. First, the interviewer should try to develop a general understanding of the witness's cognitive map of the event—that is, how the witness mentally represents the event—and then ask questions that are compatible with the witness's cognitive map. Second, questioning should generally proceed in a funnel-like fashion, from more global, open-ended questions to more specific, closed-ended questions.

The cognitive interview is not a set of specific questions that are posed in the same fashion to all witnesses. Rather, CI techniques comprise a collection of many tools that should be used flexibly, depending on the specific factors of the case, such as the amount of time that has passed since the event and the witness's state of anxiety and verbal skills.

Scientific Testing of the Cognitive Interview

CI techniques have been tested repeatedly in laboratory and field studies. In a typical laboratory study, volunteer witnesses—often college students—see a videotape of a simulated crime or accident or a live, innocuous event. Shortly thereafter, each witness is interviewed by some-

one trained to use CI techniques or by someone using a more conventional technique (as in, for example, a typical police interview). Researchers have introduced many variations in the basic laboratory study by testing different types of witnesses (children, elderly, learning disabled, autistic), types of events (crimes, vehicular and industrial accidents, medical procedures), and time intervals (immediately after the event, hours later, weeks later, and up to thirty-five years later). Two field studies have also been conducted with victims and witnesses of real crimes.

Approximately one hundred such validation studies have been conducted in the United States, England, Germany, Spain, Australia, and elsewhere. Generally, CI techniques have been found to elicit between 25 percent and 75 percent more correct statements than the conventional technique and at comparable or slightly higher accuracy rates. Only one kind of witness task has not shown the cognitive interview to be superior to conventional interview techniques: identifying a perpetrator from a lineup.

Practical and Legal Concerns

CI techniques are taught and used in some police departments and investigative agencies, but such techniques are not employed universally. Within the United States, CI techniques are more likely to be taught at major investigative agencies (such as the Federal Bureau of Investigation and the National Transportation Safety Board) than at smaller police departments. Internationally, CI techniques are taught and used extensively in England, Australia, Canada, Sweden, and Israel, but less so in other countries. More time is required to conduct a cognitive interview than a conventional police interview, so CI techniques are most likely to be used in relation to major crimes and accident investigations and by follow-up detectives (rather than first responders).

Although CI techniques were developed for interviews with cooperative witnesses, some component techniques are also valuable for interviewing suspects (such as establishing rapport and reporting events in different orders). The cognitive interview has been credited with generating extensive witness information to solve several high-profile cases, ranging from kidnapping to terrorist bombings and accidents at sea.

CI techniques have been challenged unsuccessfully in a few court cases. In England, an appeals court overturned an earlier decision on the basis of information obtained with CI techniques. Although the court did not explicitly mention the cognitive interview in its ruling, the ultimate decision was consistent with the information elicited by the interview. In a California case, the prosecutor used evidence that had been elicited by a police officer trained in CI techniques. The defense attorney claimed that the cognitive interview was similar to hypnosis and that it promoted inaccurate eyewitness testimony. The judge, however, ruled against the defense's argument and allowed the CI-elicited testimony to stand. A Nebraska court evaluated CI techniques for their reliability according to the *Daubert* standard (a standard set by the U.S. Supreme Court concerning expert witness testimony) and found that these techniques met the standards of scientific testing, peer review and publication, known (and acceptably low) error rates, and general acceptance.

Ronald P. Fisher and Margaret C. Reardon

Further Reading

Fisher, Ronald P., and R. Edward Geiselman. *Memory-Enhancing Techniques in Investigative Interviewing: The Cognitive Interview*. Springfield, Ill.: Charles C Thomas, 1992. Written for investigative interviewers; describes in detail how to conduct the CI. Also includes chapters on training and learning the CI technique as well as sample interviews to illustrate good and poor interviewing techniques.

Fisher, Ronald P., R. Edward Geiselman, and Michael Amador. "Field Test of the Cognitive Interview: Enhancing the Recollection of Actual Victims and Witnesses of Crime." *Journal of Applied Psychology* 74 (1989): 722-727. Describes a scientific field study comparing the effectiveness of CI-trained police interviewers with other untrained (but experienced) interviewers. Aimed at forensic researchers.

Kebbell, Mark R., and Graham F. Wagstaff. "Hypnotic Interviewing: The Best Way to Interview Eyewitnesses?" *Behavioral Sciences and the Law* 16 (1998): 115-129. Compares the effectiveness of hypnosis and the CI as methods for eliciting information from witnesses.

Köhnken, Günter, Rebecca Milne, Amina Memon, and Ray Bull. "The Cognitive Interview: Meta-Analysis." *Psychology, Crime, and Law* 5 (1999): 3-27. Applies the statistical technique of meta-analysis to examine the data on the effectiveness of the CI gathered in more than fifty laboratory and field studies.

See also: Accident investigation and reconstruction; Composite drawing; *Daubert v. Merrell Dow Pharmaceuticals*; Eyewitness testimony; Forensic psychology; Interrogation; National Institute of Justice; *People v. Lee*; Police psychology.

Cold Case

Date: First aired on September 28, 2003
Identification: Television series that focuses on Philadelphia detectives who solve cold cases in part through the examination of forensic evidence.
Significance: By immersing viewers in the scientific context of each case it depicts, *Cold Case* demonstrates the relevance and application of forensic science within the criminal justice system.

Cold Case focuses on a fictional special investigative team located in Philadelphia, with particular emphasis on the lead investigator, Detective Lilly Rush (played by Kathryn Morris). Rush and her coworkers investigate cold cases—that is, cases that have gone unsolved, often for long periods, and on which active investigation has ceased because the leads or evidence trails have gone cold—that are brought to their attention for various reasons. Sometimes new evidence is found that relates to an old case

Cold Case police detectives (from left) John Stillman (John Finn), Lilly Rush (Kathryn Morris), and Scotty Valens (Danny Pino) in a scene from the television program. *(Cliff Lipson/CBS/Landov)*

or a witness presents new information; sometimes a body is discovered that has a connection to an unsolved case.

The show's format revisits each unsolved case through the utilization of flashbacks that feature music specific to the year of the case. Cases on the show have ranged from a murder that took place in 1919 to current cases that have no leads. Although the resolutions of some cases rely on witness recall, the majority of the cases are solved through the introduction of new forensic evidence or the reanalysis of evidence that was tainted or misused when it was examined previously. The types of forensic evidence that have figured into the program's plots have included fingerprint analysis, DNA (deoxyribonucleic acid) analysis, ballistics, and blood evidence. *Cold Case* often showcases new forensic technologies that are used to solve criminal cases.

Examples of *Cold Case* episodes in which forensic evidence played an important role include one in which blood evidence on a policeman's nightstick linked the officer to the murder of a college baseball player. In another episode, a skull with a bullet in it was found beneath the remains of an old nightclub, and subsequent ballistics analysis and examination of arson evidence showed that a murder at the scene had been covered up by arson; this information also led to the discovery of twenty-three new murder cases. An episode about the drowning of a military academy's swim coach featured the use of DNA evidence and handwriting analysis, which indicated that children at the academy whom the coach had molested were responsible for his death. DNA evidence was important in an episode in which the detectives found that an innocent man had been convicted of the murder of a fifteen-year-old girl; DNA evidence also identified the correct killer. Skeletal analysis and DNA evidence were featured in an episode that involved the misidentification of some human remains left outside a prison, and in an episode in which the detectives investigated a drive-by shooting, ballistics evidence and fingerprint analysis were important elements.

Alana Van Gundy-Yoder

Further Reading

Ramsland, Katherine. *The Science of "Cold Case Files."* New York: Berkley Books, 2004.

Walton, Richard H. *Cold Case Homicides: Practical Investigative Techniques.* Boca Raton, Fla.: CRC Press, 2006.

See also: Blood spatter analysis; Bullet-lead analysis; Celebrity cases; *CSI: Crime Scene Investigation*; DNA analysis; DNA fingerprinting; Fingerprints; *Forensic Files*; Handwriting analysis; Literature and forensic science; Misconceptions fostered by media.

Columbus remains identification

Date: Began in 2002

The Event: The cities of Seville, Spain, and Santo Domingo, Dominican Republic, have long debated which of them is the resting place of the authentic remains of Christopher Columbus. Modern DNA analysis techniques have been put to use in the examination of the remains in Seville, but efforts to settle the issue conclusively have not been successful because the Dominican Republic has refused to allow the remains in its possession to be tested.

Significance: The use of DNA analysis to test the remains held in Seville that were reputed to be those of Columbus brought international attention to the use of such techniques for the positive identification

of individuals. For the countries involved in the debate over Columbus's burial site, national and regional pride are at stake, but tourism and other financial benefits are also major factors.

Christopher Columbus was born in 1451 and died on May 20, 1506, at age fifty-five. He died, from a variety of ailments and exhaustion, in Valladolid, Spain, while pursuing a successful effort to secure financial benefits for his heirs from King Ferdinand II. He was buried in Valladolid, his temporary residence. Although Columbus died surrounded by his close loved ones, the death of the great explorer went almost unnoticed in Spain.

A few years after Columbus died, one of his sons, Diego, had his body transferred to the Carthusian monastery of Santa María de las Cuevas, near Seville, more than three hundred miles from Valladolid, where Columbus had rested for months after returning from his fourth voyage in 1504. In 1526, the bones of his son Diego were also buried there. Christopher Columbus had asked to be buried in Santo Domingo, his favorite island, and in 1537, his and Diego's remains were transferred to Santo Domingo, to a temporary location and then to the cathedral. In 1796, to avoid French control when Hispaniola was ceded to France, the Spanish government had Columbus's body moved again, this time to Havana, Cuba. When Spain lost Cuba to independence in 1898, Columbus's body was again transferred, this time to the Cathedral of Seville.

Meanwhile, in 1877, during renovation of the cathedral in Santo Domingo, a lead box had been found that was inscribed with Columbus's name; the box contained thirteen large and twenty-eight small bone fragments. Despite questions about the location of the lead box, Santo Domingo claimed that the wrong remains (perhaps those of Columbus's son Diego) had been sent to Havana, and that it had the true remains of Columbus.

In 2002, Marcial Castro, a historian and teacher from the Seville area, began a project that would perform DNA (deoxyribonucleic acid) analysis on the reputed Columbus remains held at the Cathedral of Seville. José

Antonio Lorente, a forensic geneticist who had worked on criminal cases and had helped to identify the bodies of victims of brutal Latin American regimes of the 1970's, was enlisted as the leader of a team of genetic experts. By June, 2003, the researchers had obtained fragments of the remains believed to be those of Christopher Columbus as well as fragments from known relatives of Columbus: his son Hernando and his brother Diego, both of whom had been buried in Seville. Comparison of the Y (male) chromosomes of the remains attributed to Columbus and those of Hernando proved impossible because of deteriorated conditions.

Tourists walk past the tomb of explorer Christopher Columbus in the Cathedral of Seville, Spain. The remains tested by researchers are housed in the casket held high by figures representing the Kingdoms of Spain. *(AP/Wide World Photos)*

In January, 2005, the researchers gained permission to view the purported Columbus remains in Santo Domingo, but Dominican authorities then withdrew permission and refused to allow any attempt to extract DNA from the bones, citing religious objections. In May, 2006, the researchers announced that they had matched the mitochondrial (maternally inherited) DNA of the remains in Seville claimed to be those of Columbus with the mitochondrial DNA of Columbus's brother Diego, proving that the two sets of remains were those of brothers. Despite this evidence, controversy about the true burial site of Christopher Columbus remains because of Santo Domingo's refusal to allow testing on the remains in its possession.

Abraham D. Lavender

Further Reading

Dugard, Martin. *The Last Voyage of Columbus.* New York: Little, Brown, 2005.

Wilford, John Noble. *The Mysterious History of Columbus: An Exploration of the Man, the Myth, the Legacy.* New York: Alfred A. Knopf, 1991.

See also: Anastasia remains identification; Anthropometry; Buried body locating; DNA analysis; DNA extraction from hair, bodily fluids, and tissues; DNA typing; Exhumation; Louis XVII remains identification; Mitochondrial DNA analysis and typing; Nicholas II remains identification; Y chromosome analysis.

Column chromatography

Definition: Technique used to analyze complex samples by separating the mixture of chemical species into individual components so their identities and concentrations can be determined.

Significance: Forensic samples can be complex mixtures of components, and determination of the individual components in a sample may provide investigators with valuable information. The components, once separated, are normally evaluated by a detector that is able to determine specific chemical or physical information about each component. The similarity between samples or the likelihood that samples have a common origin may be determined after individual components are evaluated.

The term "column chromatography" is applied to variety of techniques that can be classified by the phase of the material that is moving through the column. When this mobile phase is a gas, the technique is called gas chromatography (GC); when the phase is a liquid, it is called liquid chromatography. The column can be filled with particles, which is called a stationary phase, that allow a separation of individual components to take place. Instrumentation is often used to push the mobile phase through the column at higher pressures, allowing faster and improved separation of components.

Capillary GC is a common technique that requires that chemical components be analyzed in their gas state. It uses narrow glass columns that can be as long as 100 meters (roughly 330 feet). The insides of the columns can be coated with different chemical polymers so different types of chemical species can be separated. These columns are coiled for easy placement in an oven so the temperature can be controlled accurately. By changing the temperature, the scientist can analyze different chemical species. GC is commonly used to analyze samples taken from fire scenes in arson investigations.

High-performance liquid chromatography (HPLC) is a widely used analysis technique that employs high-pressure pumps to force a liquid phase through columns packed with small particles. Columns come in a variety of sizes, with inside dimensions smaller than 0.10 millimeters (0.004 inches) to as large as a few centimeters. To handle the high pressure, the columns are commonly made of stainless steel, but they may be made out of plastic for specific applications such as ion chromatography. Solvents such as methanol and water are commonly used as mobile phases. HPLC can be used to separate and analyze a range of forensically important samples; it is commonly used to de-

termine the presence of illegal drugs and to determine what substances were used in suspected poisonings.

Solid phase extraction (SPE) is a specific type of column chromatography designed for sample preparation. It uses plastic columns filled with particles specifically designed to either attract or ignore different chemical compounds that would be found in a sample. For example, it can be used to concentrate drugs of abuse from urine.

Dwight Tshudy

Further Reading

Dong, Michael. *Modern HPLC for Practicing Scientists*. Hoboken, N.J.: Wiley-Interscience, 2006.

Grob, Robert L., and Eugene F. Barry, eds. *Modern Practice of Gas Chromatography*. 4th ed. Hoboken, N.J.: Wiley-Interscience; 2004.

Telepchak, Michael. *Forensic and Clinical Applications of Solid Phase Extraction*. Totowa, N.J.: Humana Press, 2004.

See also: Accelerants; Analytical instrumentation; Chromatography; Fax machine, copier, and printer analysis; Forensic toxicology; Gas chromatography; High-performance liquid chromatography; Micro-Fourier transform infrared spectrometry; Quantitative and qualitative analysis of chemicals; Questioned document analysis; Separation tests; Thin-layer chromatography.

Combined DNA Index System. *See* CODIS

Competency. *See* Legal competency

Competency evaluation and assessment instruments

Definition: Psychological evaluation instruments that assess the ability of persons to function meaningfully and knowingly, without serious deficiencies, in understanding legal proceedings, communicating with attorneys, understanding their roles in proceedings, and making legally relevant decisions.

Significance: Legal competency is the capacity to understand the nature and purposes of legal rights, obligations, and proceedings. Forensic psychiatrists are often involved in conducting competency evaluations, which assist in protecting the rights of those being evaluated by determining the subjects' competency to stand trial.

In 1960, the U.S. Supreme Court established a law based on an appeal filed by a man named Milton Dusky, who was diagnosed with schizophrenia, after he received a forty-five-year jail sentence for kidnapping and assisting two teenagers in carrying out the rape of a sixteen-year-old girl. In its decision in *Dusky v. United States*, the Court ruled that to be deemed competent to stand trial, individuals must have a minimum level of understanding of the legal proceedings and the ability to assist their attorneys in their own defense. As a result, Dusky's sentence was reduced to twenty years.

The perception of competency is related to a defendant's ability to understand charges, relevant facts, legal issues and procedures, potential legal defenses, and possible dispositions, pleas, and penalties as well as the roles of the lawyers, judge, jury, witnesses, and defendant. Also important are the individual's abilities to identify witnesses, to communicate rationally with counsel, to comprehend instructions and advice, to make decisions, to help plan legal strategy, to follow testimony for contradictions or errors, to testify and be cross-examined, to challenge prosecution witnesses, to tolerate stress at trial and while awaiting trial, to refrain from irrational behavior during trial, to disclose pertinent facts surrounding alleged offenses, and to use available legal safeguards.

Aside from competency, two other areas of defense are related to mental capacity: diminished capacity and mitigating circumstances. Diminished capacity evaluations focus on the ability of defendants to intend to commit the crimes of which they are accused. Evaluations of mitigating circumstances focus on defendants' ability to understand that their behavior was wrong.

Evaluation Process

An evaluation of a defendant's competency to stand trial can be ordered by the defense, the prosecution, or the judge. Competency to stand trial involves the defendant's ability to understand the legal proceedings, the charges, the roles of court personnel, the difference between pleas of guilty and not guilty, and the meaning of a plea bargain. It also encompasses the defendant's ability to assist in his or her defense, to work with the attorney, and to take an active part in the defense.

A psychological evaluation of an individual's competency to stand trial includes a review of the person's medical and psychological histories as provided by the individual being evaluated as well as by that person's family members. Assessment for brain damage caused by head injuries, dementias, and acute or chronic alcohol and drug abuse may also be included. A clinical interview follows and includes assessments regarding orientation, short-term memory, and ability to reason. After the clinical interview, psychological testing is performed based on the results of the interview.

In criminal court, a defendant must be competent to waive Miranda rights if a confession is being used, to stand trial, to be sentenced, and to serve a sentence if found guilty. Additionally, the defendant must have been competent at the time of the offense and must be competent to be executed if a death penalty is ruled. Individual competency determinations do not automatically lead to determinations of competency in other areas. For example, competency at the time of the offense does not guarantee that the defendant will be competent to stand trial later. The courts can dismiss charges against individuals if there is no indication that competency will return following treatment.

Competencies to waive constitutional rights and to waive the right to counsel are addressed in the evaluator's report on competency to stand trial. Such a report includes the following elements: information regarding the source of the referral; date, place, and time of evaluation; nonconfidentiality statement; references and interviews used to prepare the report; criteria for competency to stand trial; background information on the defendant; information on the defendant's history of psychiatric and medical treatment and substance abuse; results of the mental status exam; the evaluator's findings on the defendant's level of mental function and ability to understand the proceedings; and statements from the defendant that demonstrate the defendant's understanding of the issues of the case (charges, legal situation, roles of courtroom personnel, differences between pleas, and range of possible verdicts). The report also assesses the defendant's ability to assist in the defense (based on the defendant's ability to recount his or her whereabouts and activities at the time of the offense) and to interact with the defense attorney and behave in an acceptable manner in the courtroom. Some reasons that defendants are deemed incompetent to stand trial are low intelligence, dementia, depression, mania, and paranoid delusions.

Assessment Instruments

Many psychological tests have been developed for use in evaluating mental competency. Among those most frequently employed by forensic psychiatrists are the Competency Screening Test, the Competency Assessment Instrument, the Interdisciplinary Fitness Interview, and the Georgia Court Competency Test.

The long form of the Competency Screening Test (CST), developed by a group of Harvard psychologists, comprises twenty-two sentence stems concerning hypothetical legal situations; the person being evaluated is asked to complete each sentence. An example item is "When I go to court, the lawyer will _____." The evaluator scores each answer as indicating competency, questionable competency, or incompetency. A short form of the CST is also sometimes used; the short form comprises just five sentence stems.

The Competency Assessment Instrument (CAI), developed by the same group of psychologists who created the CST, requires a one-hour structured clinical interview that explores the thoughts and feelings of the person being evaluated in thirteen topic areas, including coping with stress and sense of optimism as well as an understanding of legal proceedings. The CAI provides sample questions for each topic area, and the evaluator scores the responses of the person being evaluated using a five-point scale of competency.

The Interdisciplinary Fitness Interview (IFI) is administered jointly by a mental health professional and an attorney. The IFI, which takes thirty minutes, addresses both legal and mental health issues, with greater focus on mental illness than some other instruments.

The Georgia Court Competency Test (GCCT) consists of twenty-one questions related to the client's general legal knowledge and knowledge of such specifics as the judge's job and the lawyers' job. This tool is particularly useful for measuring behavioral aspects of competency.

Other competency tests that have shown promise but have not yet been determined to be both reliable and valid include the MacArthur Competence Assessment Tool-Criminal Adjudication, the Computer-Assisted Determination of Competence to Proceed, and the Competence Assessment for Standing Trial for Defendants with Mental Retardation.

Sharon W. Stark

Further Reading

Bardwell, Mark C., and Bruce A. Arrigo. *Criminal Competency on Trial: The Case of Colin Ferguson*. Durham, N.C.: Carolina Academic Press, 2002. Case study of a notorious mass murderer examines the legal and psychological issues associated with his competency to stand trial.

Dagher-Margosian, Jeanice. "Representing the Cognitively Disabled Client in a Criminal Case." *Disabilities Project Newsletter* (State Bar of Michigan) 2 (March, 2006). Presents an overview of the types of mental incapacities that may be reviewed in considering a person's competency to stand trial.

Grisso, Thomas. *Evaluating Competencies: Forensic Assessments and Instruments.* 2d ed. New York: Springer. 2002. Offers useful tools for evaluating legal competency in both criminal and civil cases.

Resnick, Phillip J., and Stephen Noffsinger. "Competency to Stand Trial and the Insanity Defense." In *Textbook of Forensic Psychiatry*, edited by Robert I. Simon and Liza H. Gold. Arlington, Va.: American Psychiatric Publishing, 2003. Uses case vignettes to illustrate various aspects of the determination of competency to stand trial.

Rogers, Richard, and Daniel W. Shuman. *Fundamentals of Criminal Practice: Mental Health and Criminal Law.* New York: Springer, 2005. Textbook covers all aspects of criminal law as it applies to issues of mental health, including competency to stand trial.

Swerdlow-Freed, Daniel H. "Assessment of Competency to Stand Trial and Criminal Responsibility." *Michigan Criminal Law Annual Journal* (2003). Discusses the protocols and procedures involved in legal proceedings concerning the evaluation of a defendant's mental competency to stand trial.

See also: *Diagnostic and Statistical Manual of Mental Disorders*; Forensic linguistics and stylistics; Forensic psychiatry; Forensic psychology; Innocence Project; Insanity defense; Legal competency; Living forensics; Trial consultants.

Composite drawing

Definition: Artistic rendering of the facial features of unknown persons, often crime suspects, based on eyewitness information for use in narrowing law-enforcement searches.

Significance: The ability of law-enforcement officials to solve a crime depends largely on the cooperation and participation of private citizens in the investigatory process. Without eyewitness identification, many offenders remain at large and are never brought to justice for their crimes. Police sketch artists often contribute to investigations by creating composite drawings of the perpetrators of crimes based on descriptions provided by victims or other eyewitnesses. The productions of sketch artists have been instrumental in the capture of many notorious criminals, including the serial killer Ted Bundy and Richard Allen Davis, the kidnapper and murderer of twelve-year-old Polly Klaas.

Forensic artists, also known as police artists or sketch artists, are specially trained professionals whose work assists law-enforcement investigators in the identification, apprehension, and conviction of unknown suspects in unsolved criminal cases. Certified by the Forensic Art Certification Board of the International Association for Identification, forensic artists contribute to the investigatory process primarily through their creation of composite drawings or sketches, called composite imagery.

Forensic artists create composite drawings of unknown suspects on the basis of reports from victims or other witnesses (informants) about the perpetrators of unsolved crimes. From memory, an informant provides a sketch artist with a description of a suspect, and the artist creates a composite drawing that emerges as the artist obtains increasingly specific information about the suspect's facial features. With the exception of the largest police departments in the United States, few American law-enforcement agencies employ full-time sketch artists. Most share the services of police artists with other agencies or hire local professional artists on an ad hoc basis to create composite imagery.

Beginnings of Forensic Art

The field of forensic art has a long history. In the United States, the earliest practitioners were the artists of the Old West who created the posters depicting wanted criminals that were displayed in a wide range of public settings, including in churches, schools, saloons, and post offices. During the late nineteenth century, French criminologist Alphonse Bertillon created the first formal system of criminal identification, which included techniques that became the forerunners of forensic art. Bertillon's book on anthropometry (the study of the dimensions of the human body), *Identification anthropométrique; instructions signalétiques* (1893; *Signaletic Instructions Including the Theory and Practice of Anthropometrical Identification*, 1896), laid the groundwork for the basic procedures of composite drawing that continue to influence practitioners of the art.

During the 1950's, a kit designed to aid in the creation of composite imagery, the Identi-Kit, became a huge commercial success. Use of the Identi-Kit became standard practice among U.S. law-enforcement agencies, especially in

A police sketch artist refers to a catalog of facial features in creating a composite drawing of a crime suspect. *(AP/Wide World Photos)*

cases involving multiple victims or other witnesses. The kit contained a large collection of hand-drawn facial features (hairlines, mouths, cheekbones, eyes, noses, ears, and so on) from which informants could choose in building composite faces. By the 1970's, police sketch artists had replaced the use of the Identi-Kit with composite drawings, which produced richer and less contrived portraits of unknown suspects.

Uses of Composite Imagery

Composite drawings can be used in several ways. In most cases, a composite drawing is created to capture the facial appearance of an unknown suspect so that law-enforcement investigators can begin to narrow the pool of viable suspects and better target their search for the unknown offender. Although composite drawings are usually of faces, forensic artists also sometimes provide useful visual depictions of evidence in criminal cases, such as stolen property or automobiles, or of actions that transpired at crime scenes. All of these kinds of images can be submitted as demonstrative evidence in the trial process.

Composite drawings can be modified to simulate how suspects might appear as they naturally change or age or as they might attempt to alter their appearance by adopting various disguises. For example, a sketch artist can modify the original image of a suspect by adding or subtracting weight or by adding signs of aging. Other image modifications might include the addition of various types of facial hair (mustaches, beards, sideburns) and different types of glasses, hats, or piercings.

Creating the Drawings

Forensic artists can create two-dimensional depictions of suspects by hand or with the aid of computer-imaging software. The success of either technique depends largely on the ability of the informant to describe the suspect accurately and on the talent of the police artist in translating the informant's description into a precise recreation of the suspect's facial features.

Police sketch artists must possess not only artistic ability but also effective interviewing, listening, and intuitive skills. The creation of a composite drawing necessitates close communication between the informant and the sketch artist. To jog the informant's memory, the artist asks the informant a series of questions covering all aspects of the crime incident, including questions about the length of time the perpetrator was observed, the lighting conditions at the crime scene, the distance between the perpetrator and the informant during the incident, and any obstacles that obstructed the informant's view of the perpetrator.

Helping the informant return to the crime scene in his or her mind's eye is a critical first step in the composite-drawing process. A well-executed rendering based on inaccurate information about a suspect's appearance can be costly to a criminal investigation, wasting police time and resources and allowing an offender to remain at large to commit subsequent crimes. The sketch artist must take care to elicit precise details from the informant that will enable the creation of a successful drawing.

The process of creating the composite image continues with the sketch artist showing the informant a series of photographs that depict various face shapes as well as various types of eyes, noses, hair, ears, and so on. The informant selects from those choices the characteristics that most closely resemble those of the perpetrator, and the police artist assembles the selected features to create the first draft of the composite. The artist then carefully refines the drawing through several iterations until the informant decides that the artist has achieved a match.

The most common type of composite image is a freehand drawing that represents the artist's attempt to reproduce the informant's reports as closely as possible. The drawing's approximation of the suspect's actual appearance might be close enough to generate productive leads for police investigation, and it might also be close enough to jog the memories of other possible witnesses among the general public.

Some law-enforcement agencies employ computer-based assemblages of features in creating composite drawings, instead of or in tandem with the renderings of sketch artists. Although such software packages are useful, they do have shortcomings. For example, basic packages are restricted in the variations they can generate in terms of human features, which in reality are virtually limitless in their shapes, sizes, and shades of color. Stocking such programs with greater numbers of features is costly and makes the programs more challenging to operate; in addition, it takes more time to find the correct feature when the pool is large. Even with an abundant stock of features, an image program might lack a particular feature or combination of features that fits a given unknown suspect, especially one with an uncommon profile (for example, a middle-aged Asian woman).

Identifying the Dead

In addition to creating images of suspects for use in criminal investigations, police sketch artists are sometimes called upon to lend their skills to the identification of unknown deceased persons whose faces are unrecognizable because of suicide-related trauma, homicide, or accident, or as a result of decay, decomposition, or skeletonization. In such facial reconstruction or approximation, tissue depth markers and special drawing techniques are used to produce three-dimensional images.

A thorough examination of the human skull by a forensic anthropologist can reveal a great deal of information about the deceased, including the unknown person's gender, approximate age, race, and overall size. A forensic artist can then use existing knowledge about the likely depths of tissue covering various parts of the face to fill in missing areas or to correct facial distortions in front- and profile-angle portraits or models so that the decedent's re-created face can be used for postmortem identification. In some cases, forensic artists use clay to build three-dimensional faces on casts of the skulls of unidentified deceased persons. Facial reconstruction is usually employed only after other avenues of identifying an individual—such as by matching fingerprints, DNA (deoxyribonucleic acid), or dental records—have failed.

Arthur J. Lurigio

Further Reading

Boylan, Jeanne. *Portraits of Guilt: The Woman Who Profiles the Faces of America's Deadliest Criminals.* New York: Pocket Books, 2001. Provides a behind-the-scenes look at the career of Boylan, a nationally renowned police sketch artist. Dramatic narrative relates the author's participation in several high-profile cases, including the searches for the Unabomber and for the perpetrators of the bombing of the Alfred P. Murrah Federal Building in Oklahoma City. Enables readers with no law-enforcement background to understand the painstaking work of criminal investigations.

Clement, John G., and Murray K. Marks. *Computer-Graphic Facial Reconstruction*. New York: Academic Press, 2005. Focuses on a variety of approaches to computer-aided identification of deceased persons based on skull structure.

Fridell, Ron. *Forensic Science*. Minneapolis: Lerner, 2007. Brief volume intended for young readers includes an outstanding chapter on identification that describes methods of forensic facial reconstruction.

Gibson, Lois, and Deanie Francis Mills. *Faces of Evil: Kidnappers, Murderers, Rapists, and the Forensic Artist Who Puts Them Behind Bars*. Liberty Corner, N.J.: New Horizon Press, 2005. Interesting volume intended for a general audience discusses the work of Gibson, a forensic artist, on thirteen individual cases.

Taylor, Karen T. *Forensic Art and Illustration*. Boca Raton, Fla.: CRC Press, 2001. Definitive compendium on the subject by an internationally recognized forensic artist and in-demand instructor in law-enforcement agencies and universities. Highly illustrated work covers all aspects of the field, including chapters on the history of forensic art, lessons in human anatomy, and step-by-step descriptions of the practical methods and techniques that are used by top practitioners in the investigatory process. Features numerous interesting case studies that show how forensic artistry is used in solving crimes and identifying dead persons.

See also: Anthropometry; Biometric identification systems; Child abduction and kidnapping; Cognitive interview techniques; *Cold Case*; Crime scene investigation; Crime scene sketching and diagramming; Facial recognition technology; Forensic anthropology; Forensic sculpture; Tattoo identification.

Computer crimes

Definition: Crimes in which computers, computer networks or databases, digital devices, or the Internet have been attacked or infiltrated as well as crimes that are facilitated by computers, wireless Web devices, or the Internet.

Significance: The investigation and prosecution of computer crimes are concerns for the private, public, and government sectors responsible for information security. Computer crime, also called cybercrime, is ranked third in priority by the Federal Bureau of Investigation, behind terrorism and espionage.

Computer-based crimes caused an estimated $14.2 billion in damages to businesses throughout the world in 2005, including the cost of repairing systems and lost business. Costs to individuals who were victims of identity theft were also tremendous. Criminals are committing traditional and high-tech crimes using their own computers, hijacked computers, cellular telephones, personal digital assistants (PDAs), credit card readers, iPods, and BlackBerry devices.

Because computer crime can be committed anonymously from anywhere in the world, and because it is difficult to prove who was at the keyboard in any given case, the number of computer criminals successfully captured and prosecuted remains very low. The people who carry out such crimes are difficult to identify or locate in part because they work hard to hide the electronic tracks left by their activities. They can disguise or hide their identities by hacking into and taking control of Internet-connected computers anywhere in the world and routing their activities through them.

With few effective deterrents in place, traditional criminals such as con artists, extortionists, child pornographers, money launderers, industrial spies, and drug dealers have been able to increase the scope and frequency of their crimes by using computer and communication technologies. In addition, with increasing numbers of users connected to the Internet, particularly in developing countries, geographic barriers to entry into criminal activity have been eliminated. One of the greatest financial threats in computer crime comes from spyware programs sent from developing countries that secretly record passwords, banking information, or other keystrokes. These confidential data are then sent to data thieves who sell them to money launderers or other criminals.

Serious crimes involving the exploitation of children have moved online. Pedophiles cultivate relationships with children using social network Web sites and then arrange to meet them in public places. Child pornographers use file servers, chat rooms, and e-mail to distribute images.

Computer crimes do leave electronic evidence on individual computers, on computer networks, and in log files. The downloading, storage, and distribution of images or files leave electronic evidence. Because spyware programs get installed on victims' computers, evidence of their existence can be found in the receiving computers' registries. Although different types of computer crimes are investigated differently, a number of generally accepted policies and procedures, if strictly followed, can help investigators to locate, acquire, and recover electronic evidence that is admissible in court.

History

In its earliest forms, cybercrime was carried out with hacker tools that required computer expertise to use. During the 1970's, most computer criminals were hackers who were highly motivated people with technical knowledge; some worked at universities or computer centers. In 1988, Robert Morris, Jr., a graduate student at Cornell University and son of a chief scientist at the U.S. National Security Agency, developed an Internet worm that infected thousands of computers and cost an estimated $100 million in cleanup.

In 1992, the Federal Bureau of Investigation (FBI) proposed expanding federal wiretapping laws to require all public and private networks in the United States to be capable of intercepting an intruder's or suspect's activities. The FBI wanted real-time remote access to all data, fax, voice, and video traffic in the United States.

Civil liberties groups contested this proposal, however, and were able to defeat it.

The first federal computer crime statute was the Computer Fraud and Abuse Act of 1984 (CFAA). Only one indictment was made under the CFAA before it was amended in 1986. By the mid-1990's, almost every U.S. state had enacted a computer crime statute. These statutes criminalize any wrongful access into a computer, regardless of whether any damage occurs as a result. Other statutes under which the FBI investigates computer-related crimes include the Economic Espionage Act and the Trade Secrets Act.

Many countries have adopted similar statutes designed to protect electronic commerce, the financial industry, and information stored on computers. An ongoing challenge for those investigating computer crime is keeping up with hardware and software advances that can affect forensic analysis.

Computer Crime and Physical Investigations

Because considerable overlap exists between computer crimes and traditional physical and financial crimes, traditional criminal personality profiling is valuable in computer forensic investigations, where computers and the Internet are the electronic crime scenes. For example, fraud and extortion are age-old crimes that are more easily committed using computer technol-

---

The FBI and Cybercrime

The Federal Bureau of Investigation's stated fourfold "cyber mission" is as follows:

First and foremost, to stop those behind the most serious computer intrusions and the spread of malicious code; second, to identify and thwart online sexual predators who use the Internet to meet and exploit children and to produce, possess, or share child pornography; third, to counteract operations that target U.S. intellectual property, endangering our national security and competitiveness; and fourth, to dismantle national and transnational organized criminal enterprises engaging in Internet fraud.

ogy. Cyberterrorists have extorted millions of British pounds by threatening to knock out computer-dependent financial systems, and extortionists have hacked into corporate databases and demanded huge payoffs in exchange for not destroying or publishing the data stored there. Investigators should assess how they would investigate particular crimes or criminals in the physical world and then apply that knowledge to the digital world. By examining the similarities between crimes committed through physical methods and those committed using electronic methods, investigators can better understand the perpetrators and where to search for evidence.

Given the dramatic increase in the incidence of computer crimes, prosecutors and law-enforcement agents must be knowledgeable concerning how to go about obtaining the electronic evidence stored in computers. Electronic records such as computer network logs, e-mails,

word-processing files, and electronic picture files increasingly provide authorities with essential evidence in criminal cases. Computer hard drives and other storage media are the digital equivalents of filing cabinets holding information that investigators can turn into proof of a variety of crimes, including the distribution of child pornography, embezzlement, drug trafficking, money laundering, identity theft, sexual harassment, theft of trade secrets, cyberterrorism, and cyberstalking.

Computer investigations, like other forensic investigations, require specialized knowledge to acquire, preserve, analyze, and interpret the evidence. Incriminating evidence may be found in e-mail and logs of Internet activity on a single computer or may reside on many computers that cannot be physically located. Complicating computer investigations are criminals' attempts to avoid detection by deleting electronic files or formatting hard drives to hide the evi-

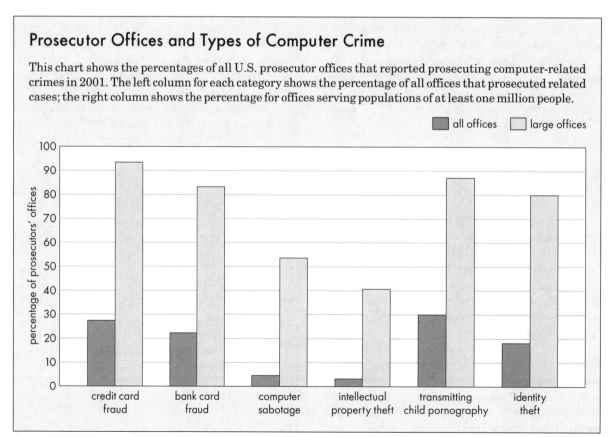

Prosecutor Offices and Types of Computer Crime

This chart shows the percentages of all U.S. prosecutor offices that reported prosecuting computer-related crimes in 2001. The left column for each category shows the percentage of all offices that prosecuted related cases; the right column shows the percentage for offices serving populations of at least one million people.

Source: U.S. Bureau of Justice Statistics.

dence, but even in such cases, trained computer forensic examiners can almost always find electronic evidence of crimes as well as evidence of the efforts made to hide or delete incriminating material. In some ways, computer forensic examiners must take even greater care than investigators of traditional crime scenes because of the extremely fragile and easily altered nature of electronic evidence.

Because electronic evidence has become increasingly crucial to many civil and criminal cases, the field of computer forensics has gained national recognition. In the United States, the FBI has established fourteen state-of-the-art Regional Computer Forensics Laboratories (RCFLs). In these labs, computer forensics techniques are increasingly applied to the investigation of a variety of crimes, not just those involving computers, as Internet and mobile phone technologies become a pervasive part of everyday life and criminal activity. The U.S. Secret Service has established a national computer forensics lab in Alabama with partial funding by the Department of Homeland Security's National Cyber Security Division. The facility serves as a national cybercrimes training center for prosecutors and judges as well as law-enforcement investigators.

Preserving Electronic Evidence

Computers can be the instruments used to commit crimes as well as the targets of crimes. These crimes leave electronic evidence, but that evidence is rarely readily apparent. To obtain and protect potential legal evidence for use in criminal prosecutions, investigators must search computers, computer networks, and data storage devices using generally accepted computer forensics methods and tools. Experts use established investigative and analysis techniques to uncover information and system data, including damaged, deleted, hidden, or encrypted files. They seize and collect digital evidence at crime scenes, conduct impartial examination of the computer evidence, and then testify as required.

In matters of evidence, it is mandatory that law-enforcement personnel observe strict procedures regarding chain of custody, and all items must be preserved for independent analy-

sis. The successful prosecution of computer criminals depends on the presentation of evidence that shows the connections between the suspects and the crimes. All records concerning the illegal intrusions or incidents of interest must be preserved; nothing should be deleted, tampered with, or altered.

To ensure the preservation of electronic evidence, an investigator needs to be prepared with a forensic kit that includes the following: tools such as screwdrivers, pliers, and scissors; duct tape; watertight and static-resistant plastic bags to store collected evidence; labels to use in marking items such as cables, connections, and evidence bags; bootable media such as DOS start-up diskettes, bootable CDs, and bootable USB drives; power, USB, printer, and FireWire cables; logbook to record the investigator's actions; and external USB hard drive to transfer large amounts of data or images.

Steps in the Forensic Examination

When the evidence arrives at the computer forensic lab, the investigator must document the time and date and complete the appropriate chain-of-custody forms. The evidence must be stored in a secure area, where access to it is limited and controlled.

The acquisition phase of a computer investigation can take place either on-site or in the forensic lab. In either case, steps must be taken to ensure the integrity of the evidence. The preferred method is to conduct this phase in the trusted environment of the laboratory whenever circumstances permit. The acquisition of electronic evidence is a crucial step in the investigation because this is where the potential for alteration of the original evidence is greatest. It is vitally important that the investigator follow standard procedures and document all actions in order to ensure the integrity of the evidence beyond a reasonable doubt.

At the start of the acquisition process, the investigator must document the computer hardware and software that will be used to conduct the acquisition and analysis. After this documentation is complete, the next step is to disassemble the suspect computer. The main purpose of this is to allow the investigator access to the storage device on the suspect computer. The investigator must have access to the storage device to get data off the label of the device and to identify all storage devices, both internal and external, that are part of the computer.

The acquisition of evidence then proceeds with the copying of the suspect computer's hard drive; this process is called imaging or mirroring. The acquired forensic image must be verified to be an exact copy of the original. Specialized computer forensics software, such as EnCase or Forensic Toolkit (FTK), is typically used to create and verify the image. After a forensic image has been created, the investigator makes a duplicate to have a working copy of the image to analyze, so that if one image is destroyed or damaged or becomes corrupted, another copy is available without having to involve the original evidence.

The next phase is examination of the forensic image. Although computer forensic examiners should always follow certain basic procedures and start the examination phase in particular areas, an experienced examiner will also try to understand how the suspect thinks and works and then use that information to steer the examination method. For example, if the suspect is a novice computer user, the examination will usually cover only the basics. In contrast, examining the machine of an expert user who can hide or manipulate data forces the examiner to look for stealth activities when searching for evidence. Usually, this work is done with an image of the suspect's drive, and a separate hard drive is used to save evidence and tools for the case.

In the extraction phase, the examiner extracts data files for further analysis. It is during this step of the investigation that the data are searched for proof of crimes. The files are searched using key words, names, dates, and other file properties. One challenge faced by computer forensic examiners is data hiding—that is, the files to be examined may be password protected, encrypted, disguised, compressed, deleted, or corrupted. To crack a password, an examiner needs password-cracking software for the specific data file type. The difficulty of cracking a password is usually in direct correlation to the sophistication of the computer user.

One form of data hiding is the disguising of files by changing their file extensions. This is easily detected by most forensic software packages that do an analysis of file headers and compare them to established file extensions. Passwords on files usually yield clues in and of themselves, in that some passwords are very personal in nature and connect users to particular files. Another reason passwords are evidentiary in nature is that they help to prove that suspects intended to hide the contents of their files.

For file compression, forensic examiners use utilities that simply let the software reverse the compression process and specify where the uncompressed versions are to be saved. Dealing with encrypted files is much more difficult, as the encryption of a file itself may be so strong it can literally take years to decrypt.

Another method of data hiding is steganography, in which data are hidden within another file, such as a picture or music file. The technologies used in steganography vary, but the basic premise is that a small portion of an existing file is replaced by an embedded or hidden file. If a suspect has used "stego," it is very hard for an investigator to find the hidden file unless "before-and-after" versions of the file in which it is hidden are available. If the user has kept the original file on the computer's storage device and embedded data in a copy, the investigator can literally compare the two files bit by bit to determine whether they are different. The investigator must then find out which stego program was used to embed the file, because only the software used can realistically reverse the process.

In the final step of a computer forensic examination, the examiner completes the necessary documentation and writes a report of the processing, analysis, and interpretation of the evidence. Most organizations have standard sets of forms that forensic examiners must use in documenting their cases; these forms also provide examiners with guidelines to follow.

Tracking Criminals in Internet Relay Chat

Investigators sometimes track criminals through their use of Internet chat rooms. Pedophiles and other criminals often meet in such chat rooms to find victims, advertise, learn new skills, or teach others. They may also dis-

A special agent of the Federal Bureau of Investigation explains how the bureau tracked down and arrested thirty-nine suspects on child pornography charges in early 2005. Its "Operation Guardian" benefited from major advances in the technologies used to detect child pornography files shared over the Internet. The rapid expansion of the Internet since the early 1990's has enabled an explosion in online child pornography that has required federal and local law-enforcement agencies to devote ever-greater resources to combating the crime. *(AP/Wide World Photos)*

cuss their personal lives, allowing law-enforcement personnel to learn more about the social cultures of these criminals. System logs can enable investigators to track down criminals because such logs hold evidence that crimes have been committed and where the intrusions occurred. These logs cannot identify intruders, however—that is, they cannot indicate who was physically using given keyboards at any particular times. In Internet Relay Chat (IRC), however, individuals can be identified.

Hackers often do not connect to IRC directly. By using a variety of servers or hosts, hackers can subvert bans or trick others into thinking they are other people. Usually, hackers seek to hide their real IP addresses so that no one can find them and monitor their activities. They do so by using bounce programs (such as BNC and

WinGate), which read from one port and write to another. These programs allow users to make a connection, connect to a destination, and then relay anything from the original connection to the destination. Hackers who have access to such programs can "bounce" through proxy servers to hide their tracks. Even if a complete audit trail shows that an intruder came from a specific account on a specific ISP, the only evidence will be billing information for the account, which does not prove identity.

Linda Volonino

Further Reading

Casey, Eoghan. *Digital Evidence and Computer Crime: Forensic Science, Computers, and the Internet.* 2d ed. New York: Elsevier, 2003. Explains how computers and networks function, how they can be involved in crimes, and how they can be used as sources of evidence. Includes a CD-ROM that provides valuable hands-on training.

_____, ed. *Handbook of Computer Crime Investigation: Forensic Tools and Technology*. San Diego, Calif.: Academic Press, 2002. Collection of fourteen chapters directed toward law-enforcement personnel and forensic examiners. Numerous case studies make this a good reference manual for both new and experienced investigators. Describes how to search hard drives for remnants of illicit images, illegal software, and harassing e-mails.

Kipper, Gregory. *Wireless Crime and Forensic Investigation*. New York: Auerbach, 2007. Presents an overview of the various types of wireless crimes and the computer forensic investigation techniques used with wireless devices and wireless networks. Explores a wide range of wireless technologies, including short text messaging and war driving.

Thomas, Douglas, and Brian D. Loader, eds. *Cybercrime: Law Enforcement, Security, and Surveillance in the Information Age*. New York: Routledge, 2000. Collection of articles covers topics such as criminality on the electronic frontier, hackers, cyberpunks, and international attitudes toward hackers. Points out mistakes that law-enforcement personnel and prosecutors sometimes make during the investigation of computer crimes.

U.S. Department of Justice. Criminal Division. *Federal Guidelines for Searching and Seizing Computers and Obtaining Electronic Evidence in Criminal Investigations*. Washington, D.C.: Government Printing Office, 2002. Explains the guidelines developed by the Justice Department's Computer Crime and Intellectual Property Section in conjunction with an informal group of federal agencies known as the Computer Search and Seizure Working Group.

Volonino, Linda, Reynaldo Anzaldua, and Jana Godwin. *Computer Forensics: Principles and Practice*. Upper Saddle River, N.J.: Prentice Hall, 2007. Explains the use of investigative tools and procedures to maximize the effectiveness of evidence gathering. Also covers

the legal foundations for handling electronic evidence, how to keep evidence in pristine condition so it will be admissible in a legal action, and how to investigate large-scale attacks such as identity theft, fraud, extortion, and malware infections.

See also: Computer forensics; Computer Fraud and Abuse Act of 1984; Computer hacking; Computer viruses and worms; Cryptology and number theory; Cyberstalking; Identity theft; Internet tracking and tracing; Steganography.

Computer forensics

Definition: Forensic specialty that applies science to the acquisition and analysis of electronic data from computers, other digital devices, and the Internet to assist in civil and criminal investigations.

Significance: Every use of a computer or other digital device is recorded, leaving a digital trail of evidence. Because computer crimes as well as physical crimes—and the criminals who commit them—often leave trails of electronic evidence, computer forensics has come to play an increasingly prominent role in law enforcement, crime investigations, civil cases, and homeland security.

Since 1991, when the World Wide Web was developed, rapid growth has been seen in personal, professional, and criminal uses of the Internet—through e-mail, instant messaging, online chat rooms, social networking Web sites, Web logs, and more—and of networked computers and cellular devices. Computers and digital communication devices create and store huge amounts of details in their memory or log files. When computer files are saved, sent, or downloaded, the computer's operating system and other software automatically record and store this information. The records and files stored on computers and other digital devices can be used as evidence to support or defend against allegations of wrongdoing.

Rarely are users aware that their activities have left multiple trails of evidence, and many may not even attempt to purge those trails regardless of how incriminating they are. Even technology-savvy users who want their activities to go undetected may not be able to delete or disguise all their trails of evidence completely. Often it is impossible to delete all traces of electronic evidence. The work of computer forensic investigators involves finding, analyzing, and preserving relevant digital files or data for use as electronic evidence.

The three primary types of evidence presented in legal proceedings are the testimony of witnesses, physical evidence, and electronic evidence. The newest of these is electronic evidence. Common types of electronic evidence are the contents of e-mail and instant messages and chat-room conversations, records of Web sites visited, downloaded and uploaded files, word-processing documents, spreadsheets, digital pictures, Global Positioning System (GPS) records, and data from personal digital assistants (PDAs). Investigations of computer crimes, identity theft, computer hacking and viruses, electronic espionage, and cyberterrorism require computer forensic technical and investigative skills and tools because of the digital or electronic nature of the evidence.

The thorough investigation and unbiased analysis of electronic evidence requires specialized computer forensics tools used by experts who understand both computer technologies and legal procedures. It may seem that because electronic evidence falls into the category of hearsay evidence, which is secondhand evidence, it would not be admissible in court, but electronic evidence is one of the exceptions to the hearsay rule. It is considered reliable provided that it is handled properly.

Rule 34 of the Federal Rules of Civil Procedure

In 1970, Rule 34 of the Federal Rules of Civil Procedure was amended to address changing technology and communication methods. The amended Rule 34 made electronically stored information subject to subpoena and discovery. Therefore, any communication or file storage device is subject to computer forensic searches to identify, examine, and preserve potential electronic evidence—the electronic equivalent of a "smoking gun."

This rule has had far-reaching implications for electronic records and communications—gateways to evidence of a person's or organization's activities and conduct. Every computer-based activity—whether it is using the Internet for money laundering or identity theft or sending e-mail containing incriminating or threatening messages—leaves an electronic trace that computer forensics may recover. Thus a good probability exists that, deleted or not, electronic mail, histories of Web site visits, drafts and revisions of documents, spreadsheets, and other materials can be retrieved. Computer forensics is playing a growing and major role in legal cases, as new legislation is passed to combat cybercrimes, traditional crimes, and terrorism.

Principles of Computer Forensics

A computer forensics investigation uses science and technology to acquire and examine electronic data in order to develop and test theories that can be entered into a court of law to answer questions about events that have occurred. Generally accepted computer forensics principles have been established to ensure that the chain of custody of the evidence can be verified later in court or other legal proceedings. Like physical evidence, electronic evidence can be easily contaminated if investigators ignore the forensic science principle of "do no harm." The crime scene, which is the state of the computer, must be preserved to protect the integrity of the evidence; simply turning on a computer and searching through the files can alter those files and the computer's records.

Forensic investigators are aware that they will need to defend their findings. Their electronic evidence-processing methods, tools, and techniques may be challenged rigorously by the opposing side in a court case. Documentation is important so that investigators can refresh their memories about the steps taken and duplicate the results of processing if necessary. Investigators must thus follow rigorous processes and procedures in the acquisition, authentication, analysis, and interpretation of electronic evidence.

The first step in any computer forensics investigation is acquisition of the evidence through the careful collection and preservation of the original files on a hard drive (or other storage device); this is accomplished through the creation of an exact bit-stream duplicate copy of the entire hard drive using computer forensics software, such as Forensic Toolkit (FTK) or EnCase, that is recognized by the courts as acceptable for verifying evidence. This duplicate, which is referred to as the mirror image or drive image, is used for the analysis; the original evidence is used only in extreme situations. Making a mirror image of a hard drive is simple in theory, but the accuracy of the image must meet evidence standards. To guarantee accuracy, imaging programs rely on mathematical cyclic redundancy check (CRC) computations to validate that the copies made are exactly the same as the originals. CRC validation processes compare the bit stream of the original source data with the bit stream of the acquired data.

The second step in the computer forensics investigation is authentication of the mirror image, or verification that the copy is identical to the original or source. Evidence verification depends not only on the use of the proper software and hardware tools but also on the equipment, environment, and documentation of the steps taken during evidence processing. At a minimum, preservation of the chain of custody for electronic evidence requires proving that no information was added, deleted, or altered in the copying process or during analysis, that a complete mirror image copy was made and verified, that a reliable copying process was used, and that all data that should have been copied were copied. This is accomplished when the mirror image is "fingerprinted" using an encryption technique called hashing. Hashing ensures the integrity of the file because it makes any modification of the data detectable.

The third and often most extensive step in the investigation is the technical analysis and evaluation of the evidence, which must be done is a manner that is fair and impartial to the person or persons being investigated. Investigators evaluate what could have happened as well as what could not have happened. The key to effective electronic evidence searches is careful preparation. Poor preparation during the early stages of an investigation can lead to failures in prosecution, as information can be ignored, destroyed, or compromised. Experienced computer forensics examiners are skilled in formulating search strategies that are likely to find relevant revealing data. Analyses are more productive when examiners have some sense of what they are seeking before they begin their searches. For example, if the focus is on documents, the investigators need to know names, key words, or parts of words that are likely to be found within

A computer forensic specialist of the Virginia State Police holds a hard drive from a computer seized during an investigation in late 2007. The growing demand for expert analysis of digital evidence has forced an increasing number of law-enforcement agencies to create special cybercrime investigation units. (AP/Wide World Photos)

those documents. If the issue is trade secrets, it is helpful for the examiners to know which search terms are uniquely associated with the proprietary data. If the focus is child pornography, Web site addresses uniquely associated with prohibited content are valuable.

The final steps are the interpretation and reporting of the results. Examiners' conclusions must be accurate, complete, and usable in legal proceedings. Explaining the findings of computer forensic investigations in court can be difficult, especially when the evidence must be presented to persons with little technical knowledge. The value of the evidence ultimately depends on the way it is presented and defended in court. Because of the complexity of many of the tools involved in computer forensics, investigators must be trained and certified in their use. General training and certifications are also available for computer forensics investigators.

Regional Computer Forensics Labs

In 1999, the Federal Bureau of Investigation (FBI) launched an innovative pilot program in San Diego, California. The Regional Computer Forensics Laboratory (RCFL) program was designed to help state, local, and other federal law enforcement gather electronic evidence from computers, PDAs, cell phones, digital cameras, and other digital devices. The FBI undertook the project because computer forensics was one of the fastest-growing disciplines within law enforcement, and the RCFL program quickly became a dynamic tool for fighting crime and terrorism. By 2007, the RCFL program had evolved into a network of cutting-edge electronic evidence labs created to meet a rapidly increasing need. The RFCLs have supported high-profile investigations such as the Enron case, the bribery case against former California congressman Randy "Duke" Cunningham, the public corruption case against former Illinois governor George Ryan, and the dissolution of an international child pornography ring.

Each RCFL is a full-service forensics laboratory and training center devoted to the examination of electronic evidence in support of criminal investigations, including terrorism, child pornography, crimes of violence, the theft or destruction of intellectual property, Internet crimes, and fraud. In 2006, the RCFLs, which are staffed by trained computer analysts from the FBI and more than one hundred other agencies, collectively analyzed almost sixty thousand media items, including CDs, cell phones, hard drives, and PDAs. During 2006, requests for assistance on computer crimes, which included child pornography and other violent acts against children, were the most frequent kinds of requests in eleven of fourteen RCFLs, followed by violent crimes, major thefts, and white-collar crimes.

Linda Volonino

Further Reading

Carrier, Brian. *File System Forensic Analysis*. Boston: Addison-Wesley, 2005. Good reference source for anyone who wants to understand file systems; aimed at professionals who need to be able to testify about how file system analysis is performed.

Kipper, Gregory. *Wireless Crime and Forensic Investigation*. New York: Auerbach, 2007. Presents an overview of the various types of wireless crimes and the computer forensic investigation techniques used with wireless devices and wireless networks.

Sheetz, Michael. *Computer Forensics: An Essential Guide for Accountants, Lawyers, and Managers*. Hoboken, N.J.: John Wiley & Sons, 2007. Provides a useful introduction to the essentials of preserving evidence on a computer, understanding how computer crime occurs, and what to do when it is found and suspected.

Steel, Chad. *Windows Forensics: The Field Guide for Corporate Computer Investigations*. Hoboken, N.J.: John Wiley & Sons, 2006. Presents a primer on how Windows file systems work and how to perform forensic analysis on these systems.

Volonino, Linda, Reynaldo Anzaldua, and Jana Godwin. *Computer Forensics: Principles and Practice*. Upper Saddle River, N.J.: Prentice Hall, 2007. Comprehensive work addresses how investigators use forensically sound methodologies and software to acquire admissible electronic evidence. Includes discussion of computer and e-mail forensics, cell phone forensics, and PDA and BlackBerry forensics.

See also: Chain of custody; Computer crimes; Computer hacking; Computer viruses and worms; Crime scene documentation; Crime scene investigation; Cyberstalking; Evidence processing; Forensic accounting; Internet tracking and tracing.

Computer Fraud and Abuse Act of 1984

Date: Enacted on October 12, 1984, and amended in 1986, 1996, and 2001

The Law: First comprehensive federal legislation in the United States designed to address concerns about the growth of computer fraud and other computer-related crimes.

Significance: The enactment of the Computer Fraud and Abuse Act of 1984 generated computer-specific criminal laws and sentencing guidelines for computer criminals.

Prior to the passage of the Counterfeit Access Device and Computer Fraud and Abuse Act of 1984 (commonly referred to as the Computer Fraud and Abuse Act, or CFAA), computer crimes in the United States were prosecuted under a number of statutes generally dealing with interstate communications, wire fraud, and attacks against government property. Little legislation had been passed to deal specifically with computer crimes. Federal statutes addressed crimes against federal institutions, interstate crimes, and acts against the country's security, such as terrorism. Because of the nature of computer networks, hackers were often prosecuted under interstate commerce and federal telecommunications laws originally written to address telephone fraud.

Content

Technological advances during the mid-1980's brought computers into mainstream American homes as well as into high schools, colleges, and businesses. The rapid growth of interconnectivity of computers by telephone lines and modems and the storage of vast numbers of confidential documents on computers compelled the passage of legislation to protect computer users. Existing laws were no longer sufficient to handle the kinds of theft and trespass that were possible using the new technology.

Originally limited in scope to interstate crime and instances involving government computers or those of financial institutions, the purpose of the 1984 Computer Fraud and Abuse Act was to protect classified, financial, and credit information that was maintained on federal government computers. The act made it a crime to knowingly access a federal-interest computer without authorization to obtain certain defense, foreign relations, or financial information or atomic secrets. A federal-interest computer was defined as a computer used by a financial institution, a computer used by the U.S. government, or one of two or more computers used in committing the offense, not all of which were located in the same state. The act also made it a criminal offense to use a computer to commit fraud, to "trespass" on a computer, and to traffic in unauthorized computer passwords.

Amendments

The Computer Fraud and Abuse Act of 1986 was designed to strengthen, expand, and clarify the intentionally narrow 1984 act. It safeguarded sensitive data harbored by government agencies and related organizations, nuclear systems, financial institutions, and medical records. The 1986 act forbade interference with any federal-interest computer system or any system that crossed state lines. It also prohibited the unauthorized access of any computer system containing classified government information. It specified three categories of classified information: information belonging to a financial institution, credit card issuer, or consumer reporting agency; information from a department or agency of the United States; and information from any computer deemed "protected" or used exclusively by a financial institution, by the U.S. government, or in interstate or foreign commerce or communication.

The 1986 act aimed to safeguard the integrity of computer systems with specific prohibitions against computer vandalism, including transmission of a virus or similar code intended to cause damage to a computer or system, unauthorized access that caused damage recklessly, or unauthorized access of a computer without malicious intent. The law established punishments of prison sentences up to twenty years and fines up to $250,000 for the perpetration of knowing and reckless damage to any computer system. Establishing criminal intent at time of trial, however, can prove difficult.

As computing evolved, the CFAA was further amended in 1996 by the National Information Infrastructure Protection Act, which broadened the law's scope to include conduct committed by or through the use of the Internet, World Wide Web, or other computer networks. It also removed the wording "federal-interest computer" and replaced it with "protected computer." In so doing, Congress broadened the scope of the act's protection from federal computers to include all computers involved in interstate and foreign commerce.

The Patriot Act of 2001 amended the CFAA again, raising the maximum penalties for some violations to ten years for a first offense and twenty years for a second offense, ensuring that violators who cause damage generally can be punished, and enhancing punishments for violations involving any damage to government computers involved in criminal justice or the military, including damage to foreign computers involved in interstate commerce. In addition, the 2001 amendments expanded the act's definition of "loss" to include the time spent by authorities in investigating and responding to damage assessment and restitution.

In its decision in the 2003 case *Theofel v. Farey Jones*, the U.S. Court of Appeals for the Ninth Circuit referred to the Computer Fraud and Abuse Act, holding that disclosure by the plaintiff's Internet service provider of e-mail messages pursuant to the defendant's invalid and overly broad subpoena did not constitute an "authorized" disclosure. This decision has potentially serious implications for law-enforcement authorities because of the limitations it places on their ability to obtain information from Internet service providers without having to obtain search warrants.

Marcia J. Weiss

Further Reading

Cantos, Lisa, Chad Chambers, Lorin Fine, and Randi Singer. "Internet Security Legislation Introduced in the Senate." *Journal of Proprietary Rights* 12 (May, 2000): 15-16. Provides a concise summary of the Computer Fraud and Abuse Act.

Conley, John M., and Robert M. Bryan. "A Survey of Computer Crime Legislation in the United States." *Information and Communications Technology Law* 8 (March, 1999): 35-58. Presents information on the various laws passed by local, state, and federal governments to attempt to address the issue of computer crime.

Montana, John C. "Viruses and the Law: Why the Law Is Ineffective." *Information Management Journal* 34 (October, 2000): 57-60. Addresses the difficulty of creating laws that can have any impact on the global problem of computer crime.

Toren, Peter J. *Intellectual Property and Computer Crimes*. New York: Law Journal Press, 2003. Treatise intended for attorneys and computer security professionals includes useful references to sources of information on intellectual property issues.

See also: Computer crimes; Computer hacking; Computer viruses and worms; Cyberstalking; Forensic accounting; Legal competency.

Computer hacking

Definition: Intrusions, unauthorized access, or attempts to circumvent or bypass the security mechanisms of a computer, computer network, computer program, or information system. Unauthorized access includes approaching, trespassing within, communicating with, storing data in, retrieving data from, or otherwise intercepting and changing computer resources without authorized consent.

Significance: The financial damage, destruction, and disruption caused by computer hackers worldwide have been tremendous. The incidence and severity of computer hacking have severely worsened since the 1980's, when hackers' primary aims were to steal bandwidth or gain fame in the hacker community. Since 2001, computer hacking has expanded into a global form of white-collar crime motivated by profit, with hackers engaging in data theft, identity theft, computer hijacking, sabotage, extortion, and money laundering for personal financial gain or to fund illegal activities.

The term "hacking" has various meanings, but it is commonly used to refer to forms of intrusion into a computer, computer database, or computer network without authority or in excess of authority. Hackers are criminals who exploit vulnerabilities in computers, information systems, e-mail systems, and digital devices. Hackers routinely break into computer networks through the Internet by "spoofing" the identities of computers that the networks expect to be present.

Hackers may be thieves, corporate spies, or disgruntled individuals; they may work for organized crime organizations or for nations or political groups. Hackers motivated by personal grievances who attack individuals they know or their own companies are the easiest to track down. In contrast, the investigation of hacking and Web-based illegal activities used to finance terrorism is complex, requiring the cooperation of national intelligence agencies. Common to all computer hacking investigations is the use of computer and network forensic tools and techniques to follow digital trails back to the computers used for hacking, to determine the identities of the hackers, or to learn how and why hackers' attacks were successful.

Computer hacking is one type of computer crime that might violate several federal laws in the United States as well as laws in many individual U.S. states. The federal laws under which hacking might be prosecuted include the Computer Fraud and Abuse Act of 1984, the Electronic Communications Privacy Act of 1986, and, depending on whether copies of materials have been made, the Copyright Act.

Electronic Evidence Left by Hackers

Although hackers vary in their intentions, all tend to use similar techniques, all of which require expertise in computers and computer networks; those who investigate hacking must have this expertise as well. The first step in hacking is usually to gain access to a networked computer and install an unauthorized hacker program, such as a Trojan horse or backdoor. All computer networks create logs that record the exact times of all attempts to log in, the IP (Internet protocol) addresses of the source computers, the commands that were used, and the programs that were installed. Those logs are valuable sources of information in the investigation of hack attacks unless the hackers covered their tracks by deleting entries from log files. Investigators can examine a computer's registry for stored information on installed software.

Not all hacking involves great technical skill. A hacker can sometimes gain access to a corporate system by calling an employee and pretending to be a coworker who needs help logging in. Because hackers can gain access through authorized accounts, investigators must consider the possibility that a person whose account was used to hack was not the hacker.

Tracing Hackers' Locations

Software programs such as Netstat are available that enable investigators to trace hackers' IP addresses to geographic locations. Hackers often use computers owned by other parties, however, such as those in public libraries or in public Internet cafés. This complicates investigations because such hackers must be prosecuted using evidence they leave on other people's computers. The longer hackers are allowed to compromise particular computers or networks, the more evidence can be collected against them to build solid cases. It is important that law-enforcement investigators are aware of this fact, but in some cases it may be neces-

Teenagers use computers at an Internet "café" in Beijing, China. A major problem in tracking the locations of computer hackers is that many of them operate from computers in public places such as libraries and commercial cafés. In late 2001, the Chinese government responded to the problem of Internet crime by closing down more than eight thousand Internet cafés across the country. *(AP/Wide World Photos)*

sary to shut down networks immediately to protect them.

In addition to needing an IP address, investigators need to identify the Internet service provider (ISP) from which an attack originated. Software is available that can reveal this information.

Hackers may try to hide their locations and identities by using software that routes Internet communications through untraceable IP addresses. Determining the IP address of the computer used to launch an attack is an important first step in discovering a hacker's identity. Most often, the IP address will be traceable back to a particular ISP. ISPs usually own "blocks" of IP addresses, in which only the last few digits differ, through which their customers connect to the Internet. These IP addresses are either stat-

ically or dynamically assigned, depending on the configuration of the ISP. An IP address of a static cable modem user constitutes a constant, traceable "fingerprint" of both the ISP provider and the specific user's computer terminal.

Linda Volonino

Further Reading

Casey, Eoghan. *Digital Evidence and Computer Crime: Forensic Science, Computers, and the Internet.* 2d ed. New York: Elsevier, 2003. Explains how computers and networks function, how they can be involved in crimes, and how they can be used as sources of evidence.

Kipper, Gregory. *Wireless Crime and Forensic Investigation.* New York: Auerbach, 2007. Presents an overview of the various types of wireless crimes and the computer forensic investigation techniques used with wireless devices and wireless networks.

Thomas, Douglas, and Brian D. Loader, eds. *Cybercrime: Law Enforcement, Security, and Surveillance in the Information Age.* New York: Routledge, 2000. Collection of articles covers topics such as criminality on the electronic frontier, hackers, cyberpunks, and international attitudes toward hackers. Points out mistakes that law-enforcement personnel and prosecutors sometimes make during the investigation of computer crimes.

Thomas, Timothy L. "Al Qaeda and the Internet: The Danger of 'Cyberplanning.'" *Parameters: U.S. Army War College Quarterly* 33 (Spring, 2003): 112-119. Discusses how the Internet is used to support and fund terrorism.

U.S. Department of Justice. Criminal Division. *Federal Guidelines for Searching and Seizing Computers and Obtaining Electronic Evidence in Criminal Investigations.* Washington, D.C.: Government Printing Office, 2002. Explains the guidelines developed by the Justice Department's Computer Crime and Intellectual Property Section in conjunction with an informal group of federal agencies known as the Computer Search and Seizure Working Group.

Volonino, Linda, Reynaldo Anzaldua, and Jana Godwin. *Computer Forensics: Principles and Practice.* Upper Saddle River, N.J.: Prentice Hall, 2007. Explains the use of investigative tools and procedures to maximize the effectiveness of evidence gathering. Chapter 10 discusses how investigators track down hackers and conduct large-scale investigations.

See also: Computer crimes; Computer forensics; Computer Fraud and Abuse Act of 1984; Cyberstalking; Steganography.

Computer viruses and worms

Definition: Malicious computer programs, also known as malware, that use embedded instructions to carry out destructive behavior on computers, computer networks, and digital devices.

Significance: Computer viruses and worms have the potential to disrupt computer networks and thus to cause great damage to a nation's economy. The U.S. Department of Justice has devoted significant resources to investigating and prosecuting persons who release viruses or worms on the Internet. In addition, government agencies investigate connections between malware and organized crime, identity theft, and terrorism.

Given the capacity of computer viruses and worms to spread to millions of computers within minutes and cause billions of dollars in damage, the distribution of malware is a criminal act. In the United States, causing damage to a computer connected to the Internet is a federal crime that carries substan-

tial penalties for those convicted. The principal U.S. law-enforcement weapon against malware is the Computer Fraud and Abuse Act of 1984.

Many dangerous computer viruses have been spread through e-mail attachments and files downloaded from Web sites, and a rise has been seen in the numbers of professional virus writers—that is, people who are paid to infect computers with malware. Tracking down and catching virus authors is extremely difficult. The investigative methods used in this work include analyzing virus code for clues about the authors; searching online bulletin boards, where virus authors may boast of their accomplishments; and reviewing network log files for originating IP (Internet protocol) addresses of viruses. Even when law-enforcement agencies make concerted efforts in applying these techniques, it is still near impossible to track down virus and worm authors.

Some malware authors have been apprehended, however. When the Melissa virus overwhelmed commercial, government, and military computer systems in 1999, the Federal Bureau of Investigation (FBI) launched the largest Internet manhunt ever. Investigators

Members of the Computer Emergency Response Team who battled the outbreak of the Melissa computer virus in 1999 from the Software Engineering Institute at Carnegie Mellon University in Pittsburgh, Pennsylvania (from left): Jeff Carpenter, Shawn Hernan, and Tom Longstaff. *(AP/Wide World Photos)*

succeeded in tracking down the virus creator by following several evidence trails. They identified David L. Smith of Aberdeen, New Jersey, as the suspect by analyzing the virus and the e-mail account used to send it, by searching America Online (AOL) log files that showed whose phone line had been used to send the virus, and by searching online bulletin boards intended for people interested in learning how to write viruses. Smith tried to hide the electronic evidence related to Melissa by deleting files from his computer and then disposing of it. The FBI found the computer, however, and used computer forensics techniques to recover incriminating evidence. Smith was caught within two weeks. He was the first person prosecuted for spreading a computer virus.

In August, 2005, Turkish and Moroccan hackers released an Internet worm, named Zotob, to steal credit card numbers and other financial information from infected computers. Zotob crashed innumerable computer systems worldwide. Investigators gathered data, including IP addresses, e-mail addresses, names linked to those addresses, hacker nicknames, and other clues uncovered in the computer code. Less than eight days after the malicious code hit the Internet, two suspects were arrested. Computer forensic experts on the FBI's Cyber Action Team (CAT) verified that the code found on seized computers matched what was released into cyberspace.

Linda Volonino

Further Reading

Dwight, Ken. *Bug-Free Computing: Stop Viruses, Squash Worms, and Smash Trojan Horses.* Houston: TeleProcessors, 2006.

Erbschloe, Michael. *Trojans, Worms, and Spyware: A Computer Security Professional's Guide to Malicious Code.* Boston: Butterworth-Heinemann, 2005.

See also: Computer crimes; Computer forensics; Computer hacking; Cryptology and number theory; Steganography.

Confocal microscopy

Definition: Optical imaging technique often used when a high degree of contrast or reconstruction of a three-dimensional image is desired.

Significance: Confocal microscopy has rapidly gained popularity in forensic science as a method of choice for imaging evidence samples because confocal microscopes produce images of a quality superior to what can be achieved with conventional fluorescence microscopes.

Forensic scientists can use various microscopic methods to examine samples obtained from accident or crime scenes. The choice of technique is determined in part by the size of the target. Confocal microscopy utilizes point illumination and a pinhole in an optically conjugate plane to eliminate light flare, producing high-quality images.

Three types of confocal microscopes are available: confocal laser scanning microscopes (CLSMs), spinning-disk (Nipkow disk) confocal microscopes, and programmable array microscopes (PAMs). Modern instruments are highly evolved compared with the earliest versions, but the principles of confocal imaging established by Marvin Minsky in 1957 are shared by all confocal microscopes. The method of image formation in confocal microscopes is fundamentally different from that of wide-field microscopes, which light entire specimens. Confocal microscopes produce in-focus images of thick specimens through a process called optical sectioning using focused beams of light. Through the use of digital image-processing technology, serial (consecutive) images can be reassembled to construct three-dimensional representations of the sample or structures being studied.

Prior to imaging with confocal microscopy, specimens are usually fixed and stained. The preparatory protocols (that is, cutting, fixing, and staining of specimens) are largely derived from those used in conventional microscopy. During the staining stage, specific regions of specimens (such as specific organelles) can be labeled with antibodies conjugated with fluo-

A scientist with the Centers for Disease Control and Prevention uses a confocal microscope to examine a sample in three dimensions. *(Centers for Disease Control and Prevention)*

rescent probes. By examining the relative distribution of epitopes of interest, investigators can ascertain many details about a sample, including the type of specimen, pathological condition, and phase in the cell cycle.

Live-cell imaging and time-lapse imaging can be achieved with confocal microscopy, and inert and nonbiological specimens can also be examined using this technique. Forensic scientists can use confocal microscopes to examine evidence samples that are not easily visualized with conventional microscopes, such as the marks on bullets and cartridge cases as well as gunshot residue that is expelled when a firearm is discharged.

Another application of confocal microscopes in forensic science is in the analysis of paper documents. Specifically, confocal microscopy can enable an analyst to determine the se-quence of two crossing strokes in different colors or different types of inks. Because confocal microscopes are able to capture serial images in various depths, with computer reconstruction imaging techniques, scientists can identify the sequence in which marks were made on a given document.

Rena Christina Tabata

Further Reading

Matsumoto, Brian, ed. *Cell Biological Applications of Confocal Microscopy.* 2d ed. San Diego, Calif.: Academic Press, 2002.

Paddock, Stephen W., ed. *Confocal Microscopy Methods and Protocols.* Totowa, N.J.: Humana Press, 1999.

Pawley, James B., ed. *Handbook of Biological Confocal Microscopy.* 3d ed. New York: Springer, 2006.

See also: Analytical instrumentation; Fibers and filaments; Imaging; Micro-Fourier transform infrared spectrometry; Microscopes; Microspectrophotometry; Paper; Polarized light microscopy; Quantitative and qualitative analysis of chemicals; Scanning electron microscopy.

Control samples

Definition: Samples of known substances used to ensure that laboratory analyses produce reliable results.

Significance: Quality control is an important part of eliminating inaccuracy in laboratory results. Control samples ensure that laboratory results are reliable and can be duplicated in other laboratories following the same quality-control standards.

Control samples (also called controls, known samples, or knowns) provide a level of quality control that can verify laboratory test results. When a control sample is not used, it is possible for a laboratory result to be a false positive (a result that indicates something is true when, in fact, it is false) or a false negative (a result that indicates something is false when, in fact, it is true).

Forensic laboratories may use a variety of control samples to ensure accurate results. For example, they may use known combustibles to verify that particular combustibles are present in arson cases and known drug samples to verify that particular drugs are present in drug cases. Known DNA (deoxyribonucleic acid) samples are used to compare with unknown DNA samples (for example, in the comparison of a suspect's DNA with DNA found at a crime scene).

In many cases, forensic laboratories acquire the known samples they use as controls from reliable outside sources. For example, the Forensic Science Service in England, an internationally recognized leader in applied forensic technology, is a widely respected source of reliable control samples for fibers and paints. Crime labs around the world use control samples from such sources to ensure that they are meeting the quality standards necessary for their results to be accepted in courts of law.

Another type of control sample is a blank, or a control sample that is known to contain nothing. In this type of control, the sample is known to not contain the substance for which an investigator is testing. For example, if a known blank and a substance suspected of being an illegal drug are tested and both tests produce positive results, indicating the presence of the drug, something is wrong with the quality control in the laboratory. It is possible that the equipment is contaminated by previous drug testing and needs to be sterilized, that there is some problem with the questioned sample, or that the control sample has been contaminated in some way.

Marianne M. Madsen

Strategies for Obtaining DNA Samples Legally

DNA samples collected in the course of criminal investigations are of limited value unless they can be matched with control samples taken from known individuals. Four basic strategies provide law enforcement with legal means of collecting DNA samples from suspects:

- **Noncompulsory compliance:** Asking suspects to provide samples voluntarily by permitting their blood to be drawn or, more commonly, by submitting to the swabbing of the insides of their cheeks.
- **Court orders:** Obtaining court orders by showing reasonable cause to compel suspects to submit DNA samples.
- **Statutory law:** Taking advantage of the fact that certain defined groups, such as convicted offenders or arrestees, are required by law to submit samples for inclusion in state DNA databases.
- **Abandonment:** Collecting items containing suspects' DNA, such as cigarette butts and gum, that suspects have clearly intended to discard and abandon.

Further Reading

Evans, Colin. *The Casebook of Forensic Detection: How Science Solved One Hundred of the World's Most Baffling Crimes*. Updated ed. New York: Berkley Books, 2007.

Fisher, Barry A. J. *Techniques of Crime Scene Investigation*. 7th ed. Boca Raton, Fla.: CRC Press, 2004.

Genge, N. E. *The Forensic Casebook: The Science of Crime Scene Investigation*. New York: Ballantine, 2002.

James, Stuart H., and Jon J. Nordby, eds. *Forensic Science: An Introduction to Scientific and Investigative Techniques*. 2d ed. Boca Raton, Fla.: CRC Press, 2005.

See also: Blood residue and bloodstains; DNA extraction from hair, bodily fluids, and tissues; Drug confirmation tests; Ethics of DNA analysis; Evidence processing; Fire debris; Forensic Science Service; Mitochondrial DNA analysis and typing; National DNA Index System; Quality control of evidence; Trace and transfer evidence.

Controlled Substances Act of 1970

Date: Enacted on October 27, 1970

The Law: Legislation that established rules and regulations for the federal control of drugs in the United States in terms of drug classifications and punishments for violations of the legislation's provisions.

Significance: Law-enforcement agencies in the United States are frequently concerned with crimes related to trafficking in drugs that are classified as illegal under the Controlled Substances Act.

Part of the Comprehensive Drug Abuse Prevention and Control Act of 1970, the Controlled Substances Act replaced the Harrison Narcotic Drug Act of 1914 by creating five schedules, or classifications, of controlled substances. Drugs fall into different schedules based on three main factors: their potential for abuse, whether or not (or to what extent) they have medical uses, and their potential to lead to psychological or physical dependence. Schedule I drugs, which include lysergic acid diethylamide (LSD) and marijuana, are defined as drugs with the highest potential for abuse and dependence, without any accepted medical use in the United States; these drugs are believed to be unsafe to administer and may not be prescribed. Schedule II drugs, which include amphetamines and morphine, are classified as drugs with high abuse potential, some accepted medical use, and potential to lead to significant psychological or physical dependence.

Schedule III drugs have less potential for abuse than Schedule I or II drugs, have some accepted medical uses, and present moderate to low potential for physical dependence or high potential for psychological dependence. Schedule III and IV drugs are available only by prescription with limitations (only five refills within six months). Schedule IV drugs, which include benzodiazapines, are defined as drugs that have a lower potential for abuse compared with Schedule III drugs. They also have some accepted medical uses and may lead to limited physical or psychological dependence. Schedule V drugs are sometimes available without a prescription and can include medications with small amounts of codeine. Drugs in the Schedule V classification are considered to have the lowest potential for abuse compared with those in all the other schedules, and they have accepted medical uses. These drugs may lead to limited physical or psychological dependence, but the likelihood of dependence is lower than with drugs in the other schedules.

The processes laid out in the act for changing the classification of a drug from one schedule to another or adding a newly developed drug to a schedule are complex, but ultimately the Department of Justice and the Department of Health and Human Services determine the schedules into which drugs are classified. A number of interested parties may petition for changes in drug classifications, including the Drug Enforcement Administration, the Department of Health and Human Services, medical associations, public interest groups, drug manufacturers, state or local government agencies, and individual citizens. The Drug Enforcement Administration investigates all such petitions.

The Controlled Substances Act also requires that any individual or agency authorized by the Drug Enforcement Administration to handle controlled substances must be registered, must securely store the controlled substances, and must keep accurate inventories and records of all transactions involving those substances.

Sheryl L. Van Horne

Further Reading

Califano, Joseph A., Jr. *High Society: How Substance Abuse Ravages America and What to Do About It*. New York: PublicAffairs, 2007.

Smith, Frederick P., ed. *Handbook of Forensic Drug Analysis*. Burlington, Mass.: Elsevier Academic Press, 2005.

See also: Amphetamines; Anabolic Steroid Control Act of 2004; Barbiturates; Drug classification; Drug Enforcement Administration, U.S.; Harrison Narcotic Drug Act of 1914; Illicit substances; Narcotics; Opioids; Psychotropic drugs; Stimulants.

Copier analysis. *See* Fax machine, copier, and printer analysis

---

Coroners

Definition: Presiding officers of special courts, medical officers, or officers of the law responsible for investigating deaths, particularly those that have taken place under unusual circumstances.

Significance: The work of coroners ensures that wrongful deaths are noted as such and are investigated, so that the interests of both government and the families of the deceased are served.

The office of coroner seems to have been established in Western culture after the Norman invasion of England in 1066. The term "coroner" is derived from the Latin word *corona*, which means crown, because the original coroners were servants of the crown appointed at the local level to protect the financial interests of the monarch. Although coroners' duties overlapped with the emerging duties of sheriffs, eventually coroners focused primarily on protecting the crown's financial interests, particularly in matters of the property of deceased persons that might be claimed by the crown. Coroners are thus part of the common-law tradition and appear in most of the nations colonized by England, including Australia and the United States. Elsewhere in the world, functions similar to those of coroners are often performed by medical practitioners.

Coroners may be either elected or appointed, depending on jurisdiction (a jurisdiction is usually a county). As the investigator of cause of death, the coroner generally has power to subpoena testimony concerning given deaths and to conduct inquests (reviews of the facts of deaths by panels of jurors). Coroners are not judicial officers; rather, they are considered to be part of the executive branch of government.

Qualifications

The qualifications required of coroners vary across jurisdictions. In many jurisdictions coroners must have medical degrees, but this is not always a requirement. A general trend has been seen in recent years toward increasing demand for professionalism in the office of coroner. Some U.S. jurisdictions have replaced the office of coroner with that of medical examiner, which differs from coroner in several ways. For example, coroners are generally placed in office through countywide elections (usually serving terms of four years), whereas medical examiners are typically appointed by the chairs of county boards or by county executives. Most jurisdictions with medical examiners require that these officials be qualified medical doctors licensed to practice in the states in which they serve and that they be certified as licensed pathologists in anatomic and forensic pathology.

After coroners or medical examiners are installed in office, they are usually required to attend specialized training programs. In Illinois, for example, new coroners must apply for admittance to the coroners' training program run by the Illinois Law Enforcement Training Standards Board and must then complete the program within six months. In addition, all coroners are required to send their deputy coroners to the same training program.

Responsibilities

The responsibilities of coroners include, but are not limited to, responding or dispatching deputy coroners to death scenes, collection of toxicological samples and their analysis, making death notifications to next of kin, and coordination and facilitation of organ donation. Coroners also determine the necessity for autopsy in individual deaths, facilitate the autopsy process, coordinate transport of deceased persons from death scenes, conduct death investigations when necessary, schedule and conduct inquests, summon juries for inquests, and issue temporary and permanent death certificates. Coroners are responsible for establishing the autopsy protocols used in their jurisdictions—that is, they determine what must be identified in autopsies and in the toxicology reports that list foreign substances found in the bodies of deceased persons.

Coroners in many jurisdictions are responsible for facilitating the burial of indigent persons, issuing cremation permits, maintaining records of all deaths reported, maintaining permanent records of all inquested cases, and

Coroners remove the body of a homicide victim from an Indianapolis motel room in 2004. The specific duties of coroners vary greatly from jurisdiction to jurisdiction, but in most jurisdictions they have primary responsibility for transporting bodies from suspected homicide scenes and for determining whether autopsies are necessary. *(AP/Wide World Photos)*

maintaining vital statistics related to all cases reported. Coroners also generally take charge of the personal property of deceased persons until the property can be released. In addition to these duties, coroners are expected to be generally prepared for all possible disaster situations, during which they may need to hire and supervise "disaster deputy coroners."

In some states, coroners have duties beyond those related to death investigations. In Illinois, for example, coroners have the same powers as county sheriffs with regard to conservation of the peace; in the absence of a jurisdiction's sheriff, the coroner is empowered to act as sheriff. In Louisiana, coroners assist in determining the nature and extent of mental illness in living people.

Coroners and medical examiners are called upon to investigate many different types of deaths, including those resulting from criminal violence, suicide, and accident. Coroners become involved when persons who were apparently in good condition die suddenly, when deaths are unattended by practicing licensed physicians, and when deaths take place under suspicious or unusual circumstances. Coroners often investigate cases of death attributable to criminal abortion, poisoning, adverse reaction to drugs or alcohol, disease constituting a threat to public health, or injury or toxic agent resulting from employment. They also investigate deaths that have taken place during medical diagnostic or therapeutic procedures and deaths that have occurred to those confined in penal institutions or in police custody. In addition, coroners are generally involved when dead bodies are transported into medicolegal jurisdictions without proper medical certification and whenever any human body is to be cremated, dissected, or buried at sea.

David R. Struckhoff

Further Reading

Gerber, Samuel M., and Richard Saferstein, eds. *More Chemistry and Crime: From Marsh Arsenic Test to DNA Profile*. Washington, D.C.: American Chemical Society, 1997. Collection of chapters covers the history of forensic science as well as developments in the field through the 1990's.

Hendrix, Robert C. *Investigation of Violent and Sudden Death: A Manual for Medical Examiners*. Springfield, Ill.: Charles C Thomas, 1972. Classic work in the field describes the duties of coroners.

National Medicolegal Review Panel. *Death Investigation: A Guide for the Scene Investigator*. Washington, D.C.: U.S. Department of Justice, 1999. Brief work provides guidelines for coroners and medical examiners working at crime scenes.

Spitz, Werner U., ed. *Spitz and Fisher's Medicolegal Investigation of Death: Guidelines for the Application of Pathology to Crime Investigation*. 4th ed. Springfield, Ill.: Charles C Thomas, 2006. Indispensable volume for those conducting forensic investigations and forensic pathology. Includes comprehensive sections on specific cases along with their pathological findings.

Timmermans, Stefan. *Postmortem: How Medical Examiners Explain Suspicious Deaths*. Chicago: University of Chicago Press, 2006. Outstanding work on forensic pathology explains the autopsy process and gives case study examples.

See also: Autopsies; DNA typing; Drug confirmation tests; Exhumation; Forensic pathology; Forensic toxicology; Homicide; Medicine; Oral autopsy; Poisons and antidotes; Psychological autopsy; Quantitative and qualitative analysis of chemicals.

Counterfeit-detection pens

Definition: Devices that use a chemical reaction to detect some types of counterfeit money.

Significance: Counterfeit-detection pens allow users with no significant training to check paper money for genuineness quickly and cheaply. These tools offer an effective way of combating counterfeiting that is done using computers, copiers, and printers instead of high-technology counterfeiting equipment.

A store clerk uses a counterfeit-detection pen to check the authenticity of a fifty-dollar bill. Counterfeit-detection pens contain solutions of iodine that react with the starch in common photocopier or computer printer paper, leaving easily recognizable dark marks on counterfeit bills printed on such paper. *(AP/Wide World Photos)*

The growing use and availability of technologically advanced devices for reproducing images on paper since the 1990's has created a new breed of counterfeiters, many of whom are amateurs. According to the U.S. Secret Service, the federal agency responsible for fighting attempts to counterfeit American currency, in 1995 less than 1 percent of the money that was confiscated as counterfeit in the United States was created using devices such as commonly available copiers and printers. By the year 2000, however, nearly half of all counterfeited U.S. bills that were confiscated had been created using such relatively simple methods. This large increase in the use of widely available technology such as color copiers and laser printers in counterfeiting meant that new methods of detection and prevention were needed.

The paper on which real currency is printed contains cotton and other fibers and does not contain significant amounts of starch. The types of paper used for photocopying and computer printing, in contrast, contain large amounts of starch. The chemical element iodine reacts in a predictable way when combined with starch, and this reaction was the basis for the pens that were developed to help detect counterfeit bills. The first such pen received a patent from the U.S. Patent Office on November 5, 1991.

The user of a counterfeit-detection pen swipes the point of the pen across the surface of a piece of paper currency. Instead of ink, the pen contains a solution of iodine that will react with starch, turning dark brown or black. When such a pen is swiped on a bill that was counterfeited using copier or printer paper, an easily recognizable dark mark appears. If the bill has no starch present, the mark made by the iodine solution remains clear or turns a light amber color. Some counterfeit-detection pens have colored dyes added to the iodine solution, so that users can easily tell which bills they have already verified. The color usually fades after a day or so, so that no permanent marks are left on the bills.

Counterfeit-detection pens are important tools in the ongoing battle against counterfeiting. They are inexpensive, usually less than five dollars each, and cashiers and other users need no significant training to be able to use them effectively. They are not, however, generally useful for detecting bills made by relatively sophisticated counterfeiting operations, which are more likely to use paper that is somewhat similar to that used in the printing of legitimate currency. The lack of a significant amount of starch in such bills makes them unlikely to be detected with the iodine solution used in counterfeit-detection pens.

Helen Davidson

Further Reading

Van Renesse, Rudolf L., ed. *Optical Security and Counterfeit Deterrence Techniques.* Bellingham, Wash.: SPIE, 2006.
Williams, Marcela M. *Handicapping Currency*

Design: Counterfeit Deterrence and Visual Accessibility in the United States and Abroad. St. Louis: Federal Reserve Bank of St. Louis, 2007.

See also: Counterfeiting; Fax machine, copier, and printer analysis; Forgery; Identity theft; Paper; Questioned document analysis; Secret Service, U.S.

Counterfeiting

Definition: Creation of false currency or other items that are intended to be used, sold, or passed off as original or real.
Significance: Counterfeiting, both of currency and of objects such as clothing, accessories, antiques, and pharmaceuticals, costs consumers, governments, and businesses millions of dollars annually. Counterfeiters range from amateurs trying their luck to international rings of professional criminals organized solely for the purpose of manufacturing and selling counterfeit merchandise.

The counterfeiting of coins, currency, and artifacts for profit has been a problem for as long as such items have existed. Counterfeiting operations cost honest individuals and businesses millions of dollars every year, and governments spend millions more in attempts to prevent and detect counterfeiting and on enforcement of laws against the practice. Methods for detecting counterfeiting and for gathering evidence to use in the prosecution of counterfeiters are constantly evolving as counterfeiters find new ways around them.

History of Counterfeiting

The first currency ever produced is believed to have originated around 600 B.C.E. in Lydia, a Greek province located in what is today known as Turkey. The first attempts at counterfeiting soon followed. Ancient coins were generally made of precious metals, such as gold, silver, and copper, and were minted by local rulers or national governments. The process of making the coins usually involved heating small pieces of metal and then stamping them with likenesses of rulers, animals, or objects or with inscriptions. Because precious metals were valued by weight, each coin was supposed to weigh a certain amount, corresponding with the prescribed amount of metal. The first attempts to alter or counterfeit coins were often made by individuals who removed small amounts of metal from the edges of legitimate coins and then melted the removed bits of metal together to make more coins. Some counterfeiters melted legitimate coins, mixed in other, less valuable, metals, and stamped the mixtures into larger numbers of coins.

The introduction of paper currency presented new opportunities for counterfeiters as well as new challenges for the groups charged with protecting the integrity of the currency. In the early United States, paper currency was not issued by the federal government; rather, more than sixteen hundred different banks printed their own currency. Each of these banks used a different design for each different denomination of bill, resulting in a total of more than seven thousand designs of bills that were valid currency. It is not hard to imagine how difficult it must have been to determine real bills from counterfeit ones, as people were constantly presented with bills that looked different from any other bills they had encountered before. During the Revolutionary War, the British capitalized on this situation by counterfeiting American currency at a very high rate.

The problem of widespread counterfeiting that was encouraged by varying bill designs was a concern of many early American government leaders, but it was not until 1862 that the U.S. government adopted a national currency and took over responsibility for printing that currency. Counterfeiting was reduced by this action, but it did not stop, and in 1865 the U.S. Secret Service was created to protect American currency and to investigate and combat counterfeiting.

Although the designs used in modern U.S. currency are much more complex than those used in the mid-nineteenth century, counterfeiting is still a significant problem. The Department of the Treasury is constantly seeking new ways to prevent and detect counterfeiting; frequent changes to the designs of bills are part of the department's efforts to make counterfeiting more difficult. The invention and widespread availability of computerized scanning devices and laser printers has allowed increasing numbers of amateur counterfeiters to experiment cheaply with producing false bills. The counterfeiting of items other than currency, such as clothing, accessories, antiques, and medicines, has also emerged as a widespread problem.

Counterfeiting Currency

At one time, the counterfeiting of American currency was a labor-, time-, and equipment-intensive process. Many counterfeiters used hand-carved metal printing plates, special presses, and carefully created dyes to imitate the printing on legitimate bills. Although the end of the twentieth century saw a surge in counterfeiters' use of materials and technologies available to many people in their homes, the counterfeiting of U.S. currency remains a difficult process, as many complicated security measures have been introduced into modern bills.

Counterfeiters often use high-quality scanners with very high resolutions to create pictures of the bills they want to counterfeit. Such high-resolution images contain many of the features of the original bills, even many of the features intended to prevent counterfeiting. Such bills usually do not look exactly right, but many people do not examine the bills they receive very closely, especially in crowded, busy shopping areas or in dark places such as bars or nightclubs.

Security Features in U.S. Currency

The U.S. Department of the Treasury's Bureau of Engraving and Printing provides the following description of the anticounterfeiting security features added to several U.S. currency denominations since 2003.

There are two distinct security features on the $5, $10, $20 and $50 bills the public can use to check the authenticity of their bills. Hold the bill up to the light and check for:

- **Watermark:** Each redesigned bill includes a watermark, which is a faint image within the paper itself. There are now two watermarks on the redesigned $5 bill. A large number "5" watermark is located to the right of the portrait, replacing the watermark portrait of President Lincoln found on the older design $5 bill. Its location is highlighted by a blank window incorporated into the background design. A second watermark—a column of three smaller "5"s—has been added to the new $5 bill design and is positioned to the left of the portrait. The watermarks for the $10, $20 and $50 bills are images of portraits located to the right of the larger portrait found on each denomination. On the $20

bill, the watermark is similar to the large portrait of President Jackson; on the $50 bill, there is a watermark portrait of President Grant; and on the $10 bill, there is a watermark portrait of Treasury Secretary Hamilton.

- **Security thread:** Each redesigned bill includes an embedded security thread in the paper, which is a plastic strip that runs vertically through each bill. If you look closely, you can see the letters "USA" followed by the number "5" printed in an alternating pattern along the thread on the new $5 bill, "USA TEN" printed on the $10 bill thread, "USA TWENTY" on the $20 bill thread, and "USA 50" on the $50 bill thread. The security thread is visible from both sides of the bill.

The higher-denomination $10, $20 and $50 bills have a third easy-to-check security feature:

- **Color-shifting ink:** Look at the number in the lower right-hand corner on the front of the new $10, $20 and $50 bills, depicting each bill's denomination. The color-shifting ink changes from copper to green when you tilt the bill up and down.

One difficulty encountered by counterfeiters who use computer scanners is in printing bills from even excellent digitized images. High-quality printers can print very small lines, but the lines on modern currency have been designed to be small enough to foil most computer printers. In addition, computer printers cannot reproduce the effects of the special inks used in legitimate currency, which change color depending on the way light hits them. Bills printed by laser printer also do not contain the small blue fibers present in real bills, nor can such bills contain the metallic strip that has been added to U.S. currency as a security device.

Even with all of these shortcomings, the bills that counterfeiters can create using many widely available laser printers can look very much like real bills, and many could survive the quick glance that bills generally receive during a transaction, except for one important feature: the paper. The kinds of paper used by photocopiers and computer printers is not the same as the paper on which the U.S. Treasury prints money. U.S. currency is printed on paper made of linen and cotton fibers; it is thinner than copier and printer paper, and it has a distinctive feel to the touch. The types of paper normally used in copiers and printers are made out of tree fibers that contain cellulose, a starch; the paper on which real currency is printed does not contain starch.

Although some counterfeiters may be able to obtain paper made of linen and cotton fibers, it is highly unlikely that any can obtain the same paper as that used by the Treasury Department, as possession of such paper is very tightly controlled. In many cases, however, similar types of paper may suffice.

Although many modern counterfeiters use widely available means to produce moderate- to low-quality imitation currency, some use other techniques to make counterfeit bills. Some counterfeiters bleach the parts of small-denomination bills that show the denomination and then print the resulting blank areas with images from larger-denomination bills. In this way, they use real Treasury paper, so the counterfeited bill has the feel of a real bill, because in a way it is a real bill. In this technique, the original bill's serial number can be left on, so each counterfeited bill has a distinct serial number, making the counterfeiting somewhat more difficult to detect. Large-scale counterfeiting operations may use metal printing plates, special inks, and other devices in their attempts to imitate actual currency.

Detection of Counterfeit Currency

Some types of counterfeiting can be detected through the visual and tactile examination of the currency in question. Counterfeit bills created using printers and photocopiers do not feel like real bills, and close visual inspection of such bills often reveals lines that run together and images that appear to be slightly off in color. An important first line of defense against counterfeiting is proper training in recognizing the signs of counterfeit bills; bank tellers, cashiers, clerks, and anyone else who frequently accepts money in exchange for goods, services, or credit should receive such training. Many counterfeiting operations, especially those being run by relative amateurs, have been stopped after their bills were detected by just such individuals.

Not every clerk or cashier is likely to receive thorough training in spotting counterfeit bills, however, and during busy times with many customers making transactions, it is often not reasonable for businesses to expect employees to inspect closely all bills that pass through their hands. For these reasons, devices have been developed that can make counterfeit detection easier and more efficient. Counterfeit-detection pens offer a fast, easy, and inexpensive way for persons with little or no training to check the authenticity of currency. Such pens contain iodine, which reacts with starch; when the iodine comes into contact with a counterfeit bill made on a printer or photocopier, the mark turns a dark color because of the starch in the paper. On genuine bills, these pens' marks do not change color because the paper in the bills does not contain significant amounts of starch. Ultraviolet counterfeit-detection machines are also fast and effective. Cashiers or tellers quickly view bills under the devices' ultraviolet lights to ensure that the bills contain the security threads found in genuine U.S. currency.

Over time, the U.S. Treasury has added many complex features to paper currency to help prevent counterfeiting. Among these is the use of special types of ink. For example, the denomination is printed in the lower left-hand corner of the front of each bill in a special optically variable ink, which appears to be different colors when the bill is viewed from different angles. This aspect of genuine bills is extremely difficult to reproduce. Another special ink used in the printing of genuine bills is magnetic ink, which can be detected by the bill-accepting devices in vending machines. Such machines will automatically reject bills on which they cannot detect the presence of such ink.

Counterfeit bills are almost always detected eventually. Some are detected very quickly by cashiers or tellers who notice telltale signs, such as bills that feel wrong or multiple bills with the same serial number. Others are not detected until long after the individuals who originally passed them are gone. Many businesses, including banks, scan bills regularly using a variety of devices available to detect counterfeits. The U.S. Treasury Department also regularly scans bills that come back to it, using machines that are extremely complex, with more than thirty separate sensors to help evaluate all aspects of a bill.

Cases of possible counterfeiting are investigated by the U.S. Secret Service. Although it is permissible to make copies of American currency for novelty purposes, the copies must differ from real currency in one or more of these ways: printed in black-and-white ink, 50 percent larger than real bills, or 25 percent smaller than real bills. Anything else can be considered counterfeiting, and the Secret Service has a strict zero-tolerance policy for counterfeiters. Counterfeiting is a felony offense in the United States, punishable by up to fifteen years in prison, a fine, or both. Bleaching and reprinting real currency with larger denominations is also considered counterfeiting and is punishable in the same way.

Other Types of Counterfeiting

Noncurrency counterfeiting is also a crime of increasing concern in the United States and throughout the world. In general, in such counterfeiting an imitation of something of high monetary value—produced using lower-quality, inferior materials and workmanship—is sold or passed off as the high-value item. In some cases, the aspects of the imitated items that give them value are their age or their historical significance rather than their strict monetary value.

One of the most common types of counterfeiting that involves noncurrency items is the counterfeiting of clothing and accessories. Brand-name merchandise is often expensive, and many consumers are happy to find low prices on what they believe to be brand-name goods. Designer and brand-name goods are often made of high-quality fabrics, metals, or plastics and bear trademarked names and logos. Such clothing and accessories are often relatively costly to produce, with the cost including the value of the designs themselves.

The counterfeiters of designer and brand-name clothing and accessories often have complex operations, often of a very large scale; they frequently operate outside the United States, where manufacturing and copyright regulations are not stringently enforced. They create very similar products out of inferior-quality components and infringe on trademarks and copyrights by using brand names and logos without permission. They then sell the products to consumers, leading the consumers to believe that the items are genuine. In many cases, counterfeiters attach fake labels and tags to their products to increase their plausibility. Some of these items are easily understood by most consumers to be fakes, such as the "Rolex" watches often sold on urban streets. Others, however, are much harder to identify, and even wary consumers might purchase counterfeit goods occasionally without ever realizing it.

In addition to clothing and accessories, toys, auto parts, and even edible goods such as baby formula have been known to be counterfeited. When goods such as these are counterfeited, they are not produced under the supervision of any regulatory body, so consumers who purchase and use these products are at serious risk of getting inferior, and even possibly dangerous, goods.

The rising prices of prescription drugs in the United States, in conjunction with the fact that large numbers of Americans have no health insurance or inadequate insurance, have led to what is probably the most dangerous of the many kinds of counterfeiting operations: the counterfeiting of medications. This is a problem that presents many different dangers to unaware consumers. Pharmaceutical companies spend millions of dollars developing new drugs and putting them through the extensive testing required before they can be approved for sale by the U.S. Food and Drug Administration. Although this process contributes to the high cost of drugs, it also allows consumers access to many lifesaving medications that have been tested for safety and effectiveness.

> ## If You Receive a Counterfeit
>
> *The U.S. Secret Service provides these instructions for anyone who receives a counterfeit U.S. bill.*
>
> - Do not return it to the passer.
> - Delay the passer if possible.
> - Observe the passer's description, as well as that of any companions, and the license plate numbers of any vehicles used.
> - Contact your local police department or United States Secret Service field office. These numbers can be found on the inside front page of your local telephone directory.
> - Write your initials and the date in the white border areas of the suspect note.
> - Limit the handling of the note. Carefully place it in a protective covering, such as an envelope.
> - Surrender the note or coin only to a properly identified police officer or a U.S. Secret Service special agent.

Counterfeit drugs, in contrast, may be manufactured under unsanitary conditions, as the factories that produce them are not regulated. Some counterfeit drugs are not even produced in factories at all; rather, they are made in home "laboratories" or warehouses. These products may not contain the ingredients that make the genuine drugs they imitate effective (the active ingredients), or they may contain the wrong amount. In some cases, unsanitary manufacturing conditions or the substitution of ingredients may lead to serious side effects and even death. Counterfeit drugs are often sold over the Internet, although they may also be sold in other locations as well. To protect themselves against the dangers of counterfeit drugs, consumers should always have prescriptions filled at state-licensed pharmacies and should be aware of what the medicines they receive should look like.

Helen Davidson

Further Reading

Eban, Katherine. *Dangerous Doses: How Counterfeiters Are Contaminating America's Drug Supply*. Orlando, Fla.: Harcourt, 2005. An experienced investigative reporter uncovers the truth about counterfeit pharmaceuticals and their effects on U.S. society. Includes an account of law-enforcement investigators' pursuit of a national criminal group involved in the counterfeit drug trade.

Mihm, Stephen. *A Nation of Counterfeiters: Capitalists, Con Men, and the Making of the United States*. Cambridge, Mass.: Harvard University Press, 2007. Provides historical perspective, presenting true stories of counterfeiting before the Civil War and discussion of the impact counterfeiting had on the economy and growth of the nation.

Phillips, Tim. *Knockoff: The Deadly Trade in Counterfeit Goods—The True Story of the World's Fastest Growing Crime Wave*. Sterling, Va.: Kogan Page, 2005. Discusses the economic consequences of the worldwide trade in counterfeits and introduces some of the people who have been its victims. Argues that the violence associated with the counterfeit trade warrants greater attention.

Sayles, Wayne G. *Classical Deception: Counterfeits, Forgeries, and Reproductions of Ancient Coins*. Iola, Wis.: Krause, 2001. Provides a vast array of information about the creation and detection of counterfeit ancient coins. Discusses the history of coin counterfeiting and presents interesting accounts of the careers of some people who have successfully created counterfeit ancient coins.

Travers, Scott A., ed. *Official Guide to Coin Grading and Counterfeit Detection*. 2d ed. New York: Random House, 2004. Comprehensive volume contains all the information anyone needs to know to determine whether or not a coin is legitimate as well as detailed information on coin grading. Features numerous high-detail photographs.

Tremmel, George B. *Counterfeit Currency of the Confederate States of America*. Jefferson, N.C.: McFarland, 2003. Provides an exciting look at the counterfeiting of Confederate currency, which was common during the commotion of the Civil War, and how the Treasury of the Confederacy acted to try to stop the counterfeiters. Includes illustrations of the counterfeit currency and information on the methods used to produce it.

Williams, Marcela M., and Richard G. Anderson. *Handicapping Currency Design: Counterfeit Deterrence and Visual Accessibility in the United States and Abroad*. St. Louis: Federal Reserve Bank of St. Louis, 2007. Discusses the various trade-offs that governments make when deciding how best to design currency and the necessity of periodic design changes to help protect currency against counterfeiting. Pays special attention to currency design in relation to the needs of persons who are visually impaired.

See also: Art forgery; Counterfeit-detection pens; Fax machine, copier, and printer analysis; Forgery; Identity theft; Microscopes; Paper; Photograph alteration detection; Questioned document analysis; Secret Service, U.S.

Courts and forensic evidence

Significance: One of the most important reasons law-enforcement investigators gather evidence is to prove guilt in a court of law. The techniques used by forensic scientists must be acceptable to courts in order for the evidence obtained through those tech-

niques to be admissible. Forensic scientists must thus be familiar with the types of evidence and the techniques used to gather and examine evidence that are most likely to be admissible in court.

Any evidence that has been gained through the application of scientific means can be considered forensic evidence. However, not all forensic evidence is considered legitimate; in the United States, federal, state, and military courts have had varied histories in regard to different types of forensic evidence. Many types of forensic techniques have not always been accepted, and the legitimacy of many continues to be debated.

Before evidence gathered through the use of a particular forensic technique can be considered admissible in a court of law, the technique must first be proven reliable. Most often, forensic techniques become accepted through common law, which is the practice of following prior decisions made in court. Any new forensic technique must be vetted by a judge; usually, this means that an attorney presents the technique in court and argues that the evidence produced using the technique should be admitted in a case.

For example, one of the first courts in the United States to accept the use of DNA (deoxyribonucleic acid) evidence was the Circuit Court in Orange County, Florida. In 1987, Assistant State Attorney Tim Berry successfully argued that the DNA from semen found on a murder victim matched DNA from a blood sample taken from the defendant, Tommy Lee Andrews, and that DNA comparison was a reliable method of establishing identity. To support his argument, Berry presented testimony by David Houseman, a research biologist from the Massachusetts Institute of Technology, and Michael Baird, a scientist at the laboratory where the samples where analyzed. Berry also compared the use of DNA matching to fingerprint identification, an already commonly accepted forensic method. In 1989, in the case of *People v. Castro*, the use of DNA for identification was seriously challenged in the New York Supreme Court. Over twelve weeks of testimony and arguments, the cases for and against DNA evidence were presented. In the end, the court found that DNA evidence is accepted by the scientific community and that DNA comparison is an accepted forensic technique. Since then, cases that use DNA evidence usually cite the case of *People v. Castro* to establish the admissibility of DNA evidence.

Admissibility of New Forensic Techniques

Before judges will accept evidence produced by new types of techniques, the evidence must first pass several tests. The first of these is the traditional relevance test. To pass this test, evidence must bring some fact to light and must not tend to confuse jurors more often than it enlightens them. Beyond that test, differences exist between the federal admissibility standard and the standard used by many state courts, the *Frye* standard, established in the case of *Frye v. United States* in 1923. The *Frye* standard's "general acceptance" test requires merely that the techniques used to obtain or produce evidence must be generally accepted by the scientific community.

Federal courts, in contrast, as well as many state courts, now follow a standard established by the U.S. Supreme Court case of *Daubert v. Merrell Dow Pharmaceuticals* in 1993. The so-called *Daubert* standard has multiple parts: For evidence to be admissible, the technique used to obtain or produce it must be tested and peer-reviewed, the technique's margin of error must be known and controlled, and the technique must be accepted within a relevant scientific community. The determination of whether these tests have been met is the responsibility of the trial judge. Since the *Daubert* decision, a great deal of debate has taken place concerning the role of judges as the "gatekeepers" of evidence. Many experts have lauded the decision as a way to keep pseudoscience out of the courtroom, whereas others have argued that *Daubert* gives judges too much individual discretion over what constitutes acceptable expert testimony.

Unlike fingerprint identification and DNA identification, some forensic techniques have not been accepted by U.S. courts. In 1999, a Washington appeals court had to address an unusual new identification technique used by investigators in the case of *State of Washington v.*

Kunze. An intruder who had killed two people in a house before robbing the house of most of its valuables had left a full impression of one of his ears on a wall in a hallway at the crime scene. An investigator from the Washington State Crime Laboratory was able to lift the ear print from the wall using a technique normally used for fingerprints. This print was compared with ear prints taken from the suspect, David Wayne Kunze, and a criminologist from the laboratory, Michael Grubb, concluded that the print from the wall was a likely match to the suspect. During pretrial hearings, however, Grubb admitted that he had never worked with ear prints for identification before and that he had not seen any studies about how often a particular ear shape might occur in the general population. Even though several other identification experts were called in, the prosecution could not establish that ear-print identification was generally accepted by the scientific community (the court in Washington followed the *Frye* test, not the *Daubert* test), and the court refused to accept ear-print identification as a legitimate forensic technique.

Some types of forensic evidence that were accepted by U.S. courts for years have later been found to be unreliable. One forensic technique that has been discredited, comparative bullet-lead analysis (CBLA), was long practiced by the Federal Bureau of Investigation (FBI) and had been accepted by U.S. courts since the 1960s. The technique involves comparing the composition of the metal in a bullet that was used in a crime with the composition of the metal in other bullets to establish the origins of the crime scene bullet. The technique is based on the idea that if the composition of two bullets is the same, then the bullets must have been made by the same manufacturer on the same day, using the same batch of material. This technique was used to produce the key evidence in a 1986 case against a man in North Carolina named Lee Wayne Hunt. He was convicted of two counts of murder and has been in prison for more than twenty years. However, in a 2004 report on a study requested by the FBI, the National Research Council of the National Academy of Sciences stated that CBLA is unreliable and can produce misleading results. Because of this, many cases like the one against Hunt are under review, and it is probable that some verdicts may be overturned.

Even forensic techniques that have come to be thoroughly accepted have not always been viewed as so reliable. In 1873, in the case of *Tome v. Parkersburg Railroad Company*, the court rejected photographic evidence because it said that photographs produced only "secondary impressions of the original" and that they were susceptible to changes in lighting. Only one year later, in the case of *Udderzook v. Commonwealth*, the Supreme Court of Pennsylvania found that photographs taken by an insurance company should be admitted as evidence. These photographs were used to prove that a body found in the woods was that of a particular man whom the insurance company had photographed when he took out his policy. The court wrote, "The [photographic] process has become one in general use, so common that we cannot refuse to take judicial cognizance of it as a proper means of producing correct likeness." Since that day, attorneys have cited the case of *Udderzook v. Commonwealth* when presenting photographic evidence in court.

Federal, State, and Military Standards

Case law, also known as common law, is not the only source of determination for admissibility of evidence in court. In 1934, the U.S. Congress passed the Rules Enabling Act, which gave the U.S. Supreme Court the power to prescribe rules of practice and procedure and rules of evidence for the federal courts. Following this mandate, in 1965 Chief Justice Earl Warren appointed an advisory committee to write a comprehensive federal code of evidence. Over a ten-year period the committee debated, researched, drafted, heard public commentary, rewrote, and finally issued its code, the Federal Rules of Evidence (FRE). This code was debated in both houses of Congress and signed into law on January 2, 1975. The advisory committee was then disbanded and the rules were left unreviewed until 1992, when the Evidence Advisory Committee was re-created to oversee revisions to the FRE. Since that time, the committee has made few substantive changes to the code. The FRE is the codification of decades of precedence, and it is the core of admissibility standards in federal courts.

The FRE applies to all federal courts throughout the United States, but cases tried in state courts are subject to the states' own individual standards of evidence. For the most part, states have followed the federal standards, but some, such as California, have entirely separate sets of rules. Even in states that follow the federal standards, some important differences exist. For example, some states (including Connecticut, Massachusetts, and Texas) follow the federal *Daubert* test, whereas others (including California, Florida, and New York) continue to apply the *Frye* test; still others (such as Delaware, Oregon, and Vermont) follow their own standards regarding the admissibility of forensic evidence. It is important for forensic scientists to understand the evidence standards that apply to their particular states.

In September of 1980, the U.S. military established its own separate rules of evidence to apply to courts-martial and other military courts. Although these rules were designed to follow the FRE closely, there are some noteworthy differences. One such difference stems from the 2005 Detainee Treatment Act, which says that military judges must, for statements made after the act was passed, determine whether the statements were obtained through cruel, inhuman, or degrading treatment before the statements can be considered as evidence. Some significant differences also exist between the FRE and military rules regarding hearsay, because witnesses in military trials are likely to be foreign nationals who are not amenable to the process.

The American legal system has had a difficult relationship with new forensic techniques because of the important role that forensic evidence can play. A case can turn on a single piece of evidence, such as the composition of the metal in a bullet, and the justice system must be careful in the decisions it makes about allowing particular evidence-gathering practices and the admissibility of specific kinds of expert testimony. If a process is not carefully vetted and established, then injustices are likely to occur.

Robert Bockstiegel

Further Reading

Best, Arthur. *Evidence: Examples and Explanations*. 6th ed. New York: Aspen, 2007. Uses the Federal Rules of Evidence to organize examples and explanations of types of evidence, relevance requirements, and exclusionary rules.

Genge, N. E. *The Forensic Casebook: The Science of Crime Scene Investigation*. New York: Ballantine, 2002. Provides examples of court cases in which forensic science was able to provide critical evidence.

Karagiozis, Michael Fitting, and Richard Sgaglio. *Forensic Investigation Handbook: An Introduction to the Collection, Preservation, Analysis, and Presentation of Evidence*. Springfield, Ill.: Charles C Thomas, 2005. Provides a thorough overview of the forensic investigation process, from the gathering of evidence to its use in the courtroom.

Kiely, Terrence F. *Forensic Evidence: Science and the Criminal Law*. 2d ed. Boca Raton, Fla.: CRC Press, 2006. Introductory textbook discusses the acceptance of different types of forensic evidence by U.S. state and federal courts. Presents examples from actual court decisions.

Lissitzyn, Christine Beck. *Forensic Evidence in Court: A Case Study Approach*. Durham, N.C.: Carolina Academic Press, 2008. Uses the case of a 1973 murder that took place in New Haven, Connecticut, to address the various aspects of the admissibility of forensic evidence.

Sapse, Danielle S. *Legal Aspects of Forensics*. New York: Chelsea House, 2006. Discusses the legal issues relating to forensic science techniques and the presentation of forensic findings in the courtroom.

See also: ALI standard; *Daubert v. Merrell Dow Pharmaceuticals*; Direct versus circumstantial evidence; Drug and alcohol evidence rules; Evidence processing; Expert witnesses; Eyewitness testimony; Federal Rules of Evidence; *Frye v. United States*; *Holland v. United States*; Legal competency; *Miranda v. Arizona*; *People v. Lee*; Quality control of evidence; *Tarasoff* rule; Trial consultants.

Crack cocaine

Definition: Form of cocaine that transforms into rocklike chips during its creation and is believed to produce a more intense high than powder cocaine.

Significance: Crack cocaine emerged during the early 1980's, and a seeming epidemic of use of the drug led to an intense media frenzy in the United States. Powder cocaine had been in use in the United States for many years, but crack cocaine quickly became the more popular of the two because of its cheap price and intense high. The hysteria surrounding the drug was in part a reaction to the amount of systemic violence created by crack cocaine dealers establishing territories within the black market.

Crack cocaine remains one of the most problematic drugs in the United States because of its impacts on users and their communities. Significant resources are spent on attempts to decrease the supply of crack cocaine within the United States through law-enforcement efforts, to decrease demand for the drug through education and prevention programs, and to decrease the number of those addicted to it through drug treatment. Cocaine is listed as a Schedule II drug under the Controlled Substances Act of 1970, meaning that it has a high potential for abuse, is used medically with restrictions, and can lead to severe physical and psychological dependence.

Production of Crack

Crack cocaine is a pure form of cocaine that is manufactured by a simpler method than that used to create freebase cocaine. In making freebase cocaine, which was popular in the 1970's, powder cocaine is dissolved in water with ammonia and ether added; a solid cocaine base is then separated from the solution and used for smoking. Freebase cocaine was overshadowed by crack during the 1980's.

Unlike other forms of cocaine, crack does not include hydrochloride salt. In the manufacture of crack, cocaine is mixed with water and baking soda; this mixture is then heated, and when it cools, cocaine "rocks" are formed. The rocks can be smoked in pipes, heated and then inhaled, or even injected. One reason for crack cocaine's popularity is that, unlike powder cocaine, it can be produced in small quantities; thus users at all income levels can buy the drug.

Effects of the Drug

Most crack users typically place the drug in a glass pipe with a steel wool filter and heat the pipe from below. When smoked, crack cocaine passes into a user's bloodstream much faster than cocaine that is snorted. The drug is then transported to the brain, where it interferes with a neurotransmitter, or chemical messenger, called dopamine. Dopamine sends signals of pleasure from neuron to neuron during pleasant activities. It does so by attaching to the synapse of the neuron, sending a message, and then being reabsorbed back into the neuron. Crack cocaine disrupts this process and slows the absorption of dopamine, creating longer-lasting feelings of pleasure. Crack is thus considered to be a stimulant drug because it causes dopamine to build up and send exaggerated feelings of exhilaration. Users generally begin to feel the effects of crack cocaine in fifteen seconds, compared with fifteen to twenty minutes for cocaine that is snorted.

Cocaine is a highly addictive drug, and there seems to be a higher correlation between addiction and cocaine in its crack form as opposed to its powder form. Researchers have not been able to rule out extraneous factors that may affect this correlation, however, such as the income levels of the users of crack cocaine. In other words, it has not been determined conclusively whether crack cocaine is more highly addictive than powder cocaine or whether its users, who are generally poor, may be more susceptible to drug addiction than users of other forms of cocaine.

The use of crack cocaine is associated with many of the same physical problems found in users of powder cocaine: constricted blood vessels, increased blood pressure, and risk of heart attack and stroke. Crack cocaine users may also experience extreme respiratory problems, including lung trauma and coughing. Crack use can also affect the digestive tract, causing users to lose their appetites or to feel nauseated. In large amounts, crack can make users feel restless, anxious, or even paranoid.

Unlike heroin addiction, for which treatment with methadone maintenance is available, addiction to crack cocaine has no proven effective medical treatment, although a number of medications have begun to be investigated for this purpose. Other treatment strategies are used to counteract crack addiction, including cognitive therapy, psychotherapy, and twelve-step programs.

Brion Sever and Ryan Kelly

Further Reading

Brownstein, Henry. *The Rise and Fall of a Violent Crime Wave: Crack Cocaine and the Social Construction of a Crime Problem*. Guilderland, N.Y.: Harrow & Heston, 1996. Examines the crack cocaine crime wave of the 1980's as well as the responses of the mass media and governments. Discusses the crime problem posed by crack cocaine as a social construction and analyzes the reasons behind the phenomenon.

Cooper, Edith. *The Emergence of Crack Cocaine Abuse*. New York: Novinka Books, 2002. Discusses the evolution of crack cocaine, its emergence in the black market during the early 1980's, and the factors that led to the drug epidemic that surrounded crack cocaine during the mid- to late 1980's. Also reviews the process by which crack cocaine is made and the effects the drug has on users' health.

Smith, Frederick P., ed. *Handbook of Forensic Drug Analysis*. Burlington, Mass.: Elsevier Academic Press, 2005. Focuses on methods used to detect drugs in the human body. Presents analyses of a number of drugs, including cocaine, and discusses their chemical properties and the ways they are identified in tests.

Washton, Arnold. *Cocaine Addiction: Treatment, Recovery, and Relapse Prevention*. New York: W. W. Norton, 1991. Focuses on some of the causes of crack addiction, including the psychological state of the cocaine addict. Discusses the various stages of addiction as well as addiction treatment.

See also: Amphetamines; Antianxiety agents; Drug abuse and dependence; Drug classification; Drug confirmation tests; Drug Enforcement Administration, U.S.; Drug paraphernalia; Harrison Narcotic Drug Act of 1914; Illicit substances; Psychotropic drugs; Stimulants.

Crime laboratories

Definition: Public and private facilities at which forensic specialists analyze materials collected from crime scenes for purposes of identification and interpretation.

Significance: Since the founding of the first such facility in France in 1910, crime laboratories have employed a scientific approach to dealing with evidence collected by crime scene investigators. The work conducted by crime labs provides invaluable assistance to criminal investigators and legal professionals around the world.

Forensic scientists, also known as criminalists, apply scientific methods to the analysis, identification, and interpretation of evidence gathered at crime scenes. They conduct much of their work at crime laboratories, facilities that are specially equipped with the technological and other tools they need to carry out the careful examination of evidence.

Sherlock Holmes and Early Crime Laboratories

A direct connection can be drawn between the detective novels of Sir Arthur Conan Doyle and the establishment of the first crime laboratory. Renowned for the creation of the fictional detective Sherlock Holmes, Doyle was well trained in science. He was a practicing physician with a strongly held conviction that scientific method can be applied logically and effectively to solving crimes. In 1887, Doyle introduced the world to Sherlock Holmes and his sidekick, Dr. Watson. He continued to write about them for the next thirty-five years.

Among Doyle's most ardent fans was Edmond Locard, a Frenchman who devoured the Sherlock Holmes stories. Convinced of the efficacy of applying scientific method to solving crimes, Locard established the world's first forensic crime laboratory, the Institute of Criminalistics for the Rhone Prefecture of the University of Lyon in France. This early laboratory occupied modest quarters in the Lyon courthouse. Locard, whose laboratory equipment consisted of a microscope and a spectroscope, gained credibility by using scientific means to solve a puzzle surrounding the counterfeiting of coins in the Lyon area. Obtaining some clothes belonging to a suspect, he extracted from them samples of dirt in which he found traces of metal that matched the metal in the counterfeit coins. This discovery caused the suspect to confess and gave people confidence in Locard's methods.

The first crime laboratory in the United States was established in Los Angeles by August Vollmer in 1923. It was not until 1932 that the Federal Bureau of Investigation (FBI), under the leadership of J. Edgar Hoover, established its first crime laboratory. From modest beginnings, equipped with only a microscope and minimal ultraviolet light equipment, the FBI Laboratory grew to become the most extensive and sophisticated crime laboratory in the world.

Discovering and Preserving Evidence

One of the most important elements in gathering evidence from the scene of a crime or accident is the preservation of that evidence so that it is not contaminated following its discovery. For each piece of evidence, a record (referred to as the chain of custody) is kept of every single person who deals with the evidence from the time it is discovered to the day the evidence is used in court or in some other official venue.

Evidence must be gathered by people trained in forensic science techniques. Before evidence samples are collected for transportation to a crime laboratory, investigators examine the evidence as they find it at the crime or accident scene, which the police preserve as nearly as they can, making it inaccessible to unauthorized or untrained people. In the early stages of an investigation, the scene is photographed from a variety of angles and careful measure-

A crime scene analyst works on identifying unknown substances in Arizona's Western Region Crime Lab in Lake Havasu City. Not all crime laboratories are equipped to provide all possible services. This small lab, which serves a lightly populated region, specializes in analyzing latent prints, dangerous drugs, and blood alcohol. Evidence requiring more advanced types of analyses is sent to Arizona's Central Lab in Phoenix, the state's capital and largest city. *(AP/Wide World Photos)*

ments are taken; a forensic artist also sketches the scene.

Among the kinds of evidence that criminalists gather are fingerprints. Surfaces that may hold prints are carefully dusted with a powder that creates strong contrasts in the ridges and valleys of such prints. Fingerprints that are uncovered in this way are first photographed and then are lifted from the surface with a sterile adhesive tape and transferred to a fingerprint card. Visible prints, such as those found on surfaces in blood or grease, are photographed and transferred to fingerprint cards.

Criminalists also collect tire-track and footprint evidence, measuring and photographing such impressions and often making plaster casts of them to preserve them for analysis. Trace evidence—substances such as hairs, fibers, and fragments of glass or paint—is col-lected with vacuum cleaners specially designed for this purpose. Items such as knives, shell casings, and instruments that may have been used as weapons are carefully collected so that any fingerprints or traces of blood, hair, or flesh on them are preserved. Each piece of evidence collected is properly packaged and carefully labeled before it is transported to the laboratory for analysis.

Laboratory Equipment and Techniques

Crime laboratories are equipped with a variety of specialized microscopes that are used to examine closely the materials found at crime scenes. Stereoscopic binocular microscopes are essential for the examination of trace elements detected at the scenes of crimes and are also used to examine and classify handwriting and text created by typewriters and computer printers.

Polarizing microscopes enable forensic scientists to examine and identify minerals, narcotics, and other elements by enlarging their crystal forms. Essential to those engaged in ballistic examinations, comparison microscopes enable forensic scientists to compare the markings on shells and casings found at crime scenes with other samples, possibly linking them to particular weapons.

Using spectrophotometry, investigators can uncover light and heat rays that the human eye cannot see. The spectrophotometer shows the patterns of such rays, and by examining these patterns criminalists can detect alterations on documents, such as erasures, that may indicate fraud or forgery. The gas chromatograph, a sophisticated instrument that identifies the constituent components of substances and measures each component, is used to identify many different unknown substances. It is also the instrument that forensic scientists employ to determine the blood alcohol levels of persons suspected of driving under the influence.

The analysis of DNA (deoxyribonucleic acid) evidence has become an increasingly important part of the work of crime laboratories. By comparing DNA profiles derived from the DNA extracted from biological materials—such as blood, semen, saliva, and hair—found at crime scenes with the DNA profiles of known persons, forensic scientists can identify victims, link suspects to crimes, and exclude innocent persons from suspicion.

Training of Crime Lab Personnel

Nearly all law-enforcement officers receive some training in identifying and handling the evidence with which they come into contact at crime scenes. Because of the growing level of sophistication of the work done in crime laboratories, many colleges and universities in the United States have established special programs designed to train forensic scientists.

Generally, one requirement for employment in a crime laboratory in the United States is an undergraduate degree in chemistry or in some aspect of criminology. The undergraduate preparation of forensic scientists usually includes extensive course work in a variety of chemistry subdisciplines as well as courses in anatomy, physics, biology, geology, and psychology.

Some major American universities offer training in forensic science that leads to a master of science degree; some offer doctorates in criminalistics or forensic science. Many institutions of higher learning provide short training courses in forensic science for law-enforcement personnel and for practicing attorneys; these are helpful for persons within the criminal justice system who lack the typical undergraduate background in forensics or who seek to update their training.

Most forensic scientists in the United States work for local, state, or federal public agencies, although some are private consultants for businesses, industry groups, or other private organizations. The American Academy of Forensic Sciences encourages training and research in the field. Its quarterly publication, the *Journal of Forensic Sciences*, informs readers about current research in all branches of the forensic sciences. The American Society of Crime Laboratory Direc-

Media Perceptions Versus Real-Life Caseloads

As crime labs have become increasingly important in the investigation of crime, they have faced a growing number of challenges. One of these is overwhelming caseloads and limited personnel and budgets. In 2002, for example, the fifty largest crime labs in the United States received more than 1.2 million requests for services. Although these labs had 4,300 full-time employees, they had a backlog of 270,000 requests by the end of that year. As a result of such backlogs, and contrary to what is often depicted in popular television shows such as *CSI: Crime Scene Investigation*, real-life law-enforcement agencies must often wait more than a month to obtain the results of scientific analyses. This situation contributes to slowing down the criminal justice system's response to crimes. The delays allow some guilty people to escape justice, and suspects who are in fact innocent are detained for longer periods than they would be if forensic analyses could be performed more quickly.

Phyllis B. Gerstenfeld

tors, a professional society open to past and current laboratory directors and forensic science educators, was established in 1974 to grant accreditation to crime laboratories that voluntarily invite examiners to evaluate their programs.

R. Baird Shuman

Further Reading

Baden, Michael, and Marion Roach. *Dead Reckoning: The New Science of Catching Killers*. New York: Simon & Schuster, 2001. Provides detailed information on how law-enforcement agencies track down criminals through the use of modern forensic techniques. Shows how Sherlock Holmes stories led to the founding of the first crime laboratory in 1910.

Bass, Bill, and Jon Jefferson. *Death's Acre: Inside the Legendary Forensic Lab the Body Farm Where the Dead Do Tell Tales*. New York: G. P. Putnam's Sons, 2003. Presents a fascinating account of the University of Tennessee's Body Farm, the facility that Bass established to study the process of decomposition of the human body.

Bell, Suzanne. *Encyclopedia of Forensic Science*. New York: Facts On File, 2004. Provides a brief and incisive account of the development of crime laboratories in France, the United States, and other countries.

Campbell, Andrea. *Forensic Science: Evidence, Clues, and Investigation*. Philadelphia: Chelsea House, 2000. Overview of the forensic sciences intended for young adult readers includes information about the genesis and importance of crime laboratories.

Conklin, Barbara Gardner, Robert Gardner, and Dennis Shortelle. *Encyclopedia of Forensic Science: A Compendium of Detective Fact and Fiction*. Westport, Conn.: Oryx Press, 2002. Includes an overall account of crime laboratories and also deals separately with the FBI Laboratory.

Innes, Brian. *Bodies of Evidence*. Pleasantville, N.Y.: Reader's Digest Association, 2000. Presents extensive forensic case studies and devotes a section to the establishment of crime labs in England.

James, Stuart H., and Jon J. Nordby, eds. *Forensic Science: An Introduction to Scientific and Investigative Techniques*. 2d ed. Boca Raton, Fla.: CRC Press, 2005. Section III contains eleven chapters that focus on the functions of crime laboratories.

See also: American Academy of Forensic Sciences; American Society of Crime Laboratory Directors; Analytical instrumentation; CODIS; Control samples; Environmental Measurements Laboratory; European Network of Forensic Science Institutes; Federal Bureau of Investigation Forensic Science Research and Training Center; Federal Bureau of Investigation Laboratory; Forensic Science Service; National Crime Information Center; Quality control of evidence; University of Tennessee Anthropological Research Facility.

Crime scene cleaning

Definition: Professional cleaning and decontamination of a crime scene, including disposing of biologically or chemically hazardous materials and restoring the site to habitable condition.

Significance: Crime scene cleaners restore a site after forensic investigators have documented the event, collected evidence, and released the scene. Sometimes, in the course of complete restoration of a crime scene, professional cleaners uncover forensic evidence previously overlooked by investigators.

Police and forensic investigators officially release a crime scene after it has been documented and all victims and evidence have been physically removed. Such a scene, particularly if it was the site of a violent crime or drug-related activity, may then be uninhabitable and unusable until it has been cleaned by specialists. The owners of crime scene locations may hire professional cleaning services to avoid the psychological and emotional impact of cleaning these sites themselves. In addition, crime scenes often pose a hazard of contamination by blood-borne

Two employees of a crime scene cleaning business pose in the protective suits they wear to avoid contact with possible biological hazards in their work. Their company specializes in erasing evidence of violent crimes, such as bloodstains, from scenes after law-enforcement investigators have completed their evidence collection. *(AP/Wide World Photos)*

pathogens, microscopic organisms that can cause disease, including hepatitis B, hepatitis C, and human immunodeficiency virus (HIV). In the United States, federal law prohibits employers from exposing workers to blood-borne pathogens unless they have been trained to handle blood; thus commercial enterprises, landlords, and business owners usually hire specialists rather than have their janitorial staff restore crime scenes where blood has been spilled.

Crime scene cleaning is sometimes referred to as biohazard remediation, bioremediation, crime and trauma scene decontamination, or biorecovery. Crime scene cleaners are also called biorecovery technicians or trauma scene practitioners. Technicians in the United States can be trained and certified by occupational groups according to standards set by the U.S. Occupational Safety and Health Administration (OSHA).

Crime scene cleaning involves complete disinfection of floors, walls, ceilings, plumbing, and furniture, where possible, and safe disposition of irretrievably damaged furniture and personal items. Potentially infectious substances—such as bone fragments, blood and other bodily fluids, human tissue, and insects—are isolated, packaged, and disposed of in accordance with state and federal regulations for handling biohazardous material. Chemicals left behind by emergency medical personnel or investigators are completely removed.

Biohazard technicians also clean areas where suicides have occurred or where bodies have decomposed over time, accident scenes, and places damaged by animal waste or remains, mold, water or fire, odors, and chemicals left behind by illegal drug manufacturing (typically the poisonous substances used to make methamphetamine). Some are prepared to respond to bioterrorism, decontaminating areas where disease-bearing bacteria have been deployed.

Beyond surface cleaning, professional crime scene cleaners search for bodily fluids and other materials hidden under floors, in plumbing, and underneath or behind installed furnishings. They may therefore find evidence relevant to an investigation that was not immediately apparent to police or forensic investigators. Crime scene cleaners should be trained to identify and report such findings; otherwise, their thorough cleaning and remediation of a scene will completely destroy any evidence left behind.

Maureen Puffer-Rothenberg

Further Reading

Cooperman, Stephanie. *Biohazard Technicians: Life on a Trauma Scene Cleanup Crew*. New York: Rosen, 2004.

Jacobs, Andrew. "Cleaning Needed, in the Worst Way." *The New York Times*, November 22, 2005, pp. B1-B6.

Reavill, Gil. *Aftermath, Inc.: Cleaning up After CSI Goes Home*. New York: Gotham Books, 2007.

See also: Bacterial biology; Blood agents; Blood residue and bloodstains; Chemical Biological

Incident Response Force, U.S.; Crime scene protective gear; Decomposition of bodies; Decontamination methods; Illicit substances; Pathogen transmission.

Crime scene documentation

Definition: All documents, notes, sketches, and photographs generated in the processing and recording of a crime scene.

Significance: The very act of processing a crime scene alters the scene. The purpose of crime scene documentation is to create as accurate a record as possible of all information about the scene that may be relevant to the investigation. This documentation subsequently provides the only permanent record of the scene and is the only way of conveying information about the scene to investigators, scientists, lawyers, and the court.

Any type of environment or location has the potential to become a crime scene. Crimes can occur in urban, suburban, or rural areas, indoors or outdoors, in commercial or residential buildings, in public or private areas, in sparse, clean, tidy locations or hideously filthy and cluttered locations. Each crime scene, and each crime event, is in some way unique, and, correspondingly, each scene has unique aspects that are relevant to the investigation.

One of the primary purposes of the crime scene examination is to produce accurate and comprehensive records of everything at the crime scene that has the potential to be relevant to the current criminal investigation and any subsequent prosecution. The information in the records must be sufficient to support any expert interpretations, conclusions, or opinions.

At the early stages of an investigation, the information available to the scene examiner may be very limited. It may be that the only thing known is that a body is in an alley. It is often difficult, sometimes impossible, to predict how an investigation will progress and develop over time. Some item, fact, or detail that does not appear to be particularly significant during the scene examination may turn out to be crucial. Because poor documentation of a crime scene can greatly affect the investigation's progress and outcome and, ultimately, any trial that may eventuate, crime scene examinations and their resulting documentation have become increasingly comprehensive.

Background Scene Information

The first law-enforcement officer to arrive at a crime scene may be one of the few individuals to see the scene in a pristine condition. The observations of that first officer often direct the actions or the focus of any investigators subsequently involved with examination of the scene. For example, the first officer on the scene could observe a trail of shoe prints leading away from the scene on grass wet with early-morning dew, whereas scene examiners attending later in the day would not be able to see those prints. If such observations are not documented appropriately and conveyed to the scene examiners, important aspects of the scene exam may be missed.

From the moment a crime scene is made secure, it is important that investigators are able to demonstrate that control of any items within the scene has been maintained. Scene logs are used to record information regarding who has had access to the scene and therefore access to items within it. The chain of custody of scene items begins at the scene and is recorded in exhibit registers, or evidence logs.

Types of Documentation

Crime scene documentation can encompass a huge range of documents or records. In principle, records should be kept of all observations made and any actions taken by all persons involved in securing and processing the crime scene. This includes any handwritten notes and notes transcribed from audio recordings, any photographs taken, and any sketches made by investigators. Depending on the case circumstances, it may also include any notebook entries, or daily job sheets, from the first attending law-enforcement officers or paramedics, scene guard logs, and records from others who have had some contact or involvement with the scene that was peripheral to the actual scene examination.

Photography is a significant part of recording the crime scene, and comprehensive photographing of the scene prior to and during the scene examination is essential. The use of video recording of scenes can also be of value.

Where it was once considered sufficient for crime scene examiners to make notes regarding their observations and the various things they found at a crime scene, it has become increasingly common for examiners to make notes also regarding things they do not find. That is, absences of some kinds of items are often recorded, particularly where those absences allow conclusions to be drawn about actions or events that could subsequently be claimed or suggested.

End Users

In many cases, criminal trials take place months, or even years, after the crimes occurred. It is not realistic to expect anyone to remember accurately the minute details of a crime scene that he or she processed long ago when presenting evidence in court. Consequently, crime scene examiners are allowed the use their notes to aid their recall when they appear as witnesses. In fact, such notes are often deemed more accurate than an individual's recall if significant time has passed.

For many years, investigators' notes were precisely that—their own notes. Gradually, however, it has become accepted that crime scene notes are made to be reviewed, or scrutinized, by others. In many crime laboratories, peer review of notes is a standard quality-assurance practice. Correspondingly, it is expected that notes should be clear and comprehensive enough not only to support any findings, interpretations, and conclusions but also to allow other suitably qualified colleagues to reach those same findings, interpretations, and conclusions independently. Defense analysts may also request copies of scene notes for review. They rely solely on the information, or lack thereof, contained in the scene documentation.

Reviews of older unsolved crimes, or "cold cases," are becoming increasingly common-place. These case reviews, many of which are driven by advances in technology, have revealed that gradual alterations and improvements have occurred over time in the practices of crime scene documentation. As is true of many things, some of the practices deemed acceptable as recently as ten years ago have come to be seen as lacking by more current standards. Crime scene examiners can make an effort to "future-proof" their scene examination notes by documenting every scene as thoroughly as possible.

R. K. Morgan-Smith

Further Reading

Elliot, Douglas. "Crime Scene Examination." In *Expert Evidence: Law, Practice, Procedure, and Advocacy*, edited by Ian Freckelton and Hugh Selby. 3d ed. Pyrmont, N.S.W.: Lawbook, 2005. Covers broad aspects of crime scene examination, including scene processing and recording.

O'Hara, Charles E., and Gregory L. O'Hara. *Fundamentals of Criminal Investigation*. 7th ed. Springfield, Ill.: Charles C Thomas, 2003. Detailed work devotes significant discussion to the processes of crime scene documentation.

Saferstein, Richard. *Criminalistics: An Introduction to Forensic Science*. 9th ed. Upper Saddle River, N.J.: Pearson Prentice Hall, 2007. Good general text covers a broad range of topics, including crime scene examination and documentation.

Walton, Richard H. *Cold Case Homicides: Practical Investigative Techniques*. Boca Raton, Fla.: CRC Press, 2006. Comprehensive volume on cold-case investigation includes discussion of the use of original crime scene documentation when old, unsolved cases are examined.

See also: Chain of custody; Crime scene investigation; Crime scene measurement; Crime scene reconstruction and staging; Crime scene sketching and diagramming; Evidence processing; Forensic photography; Quality control of evidence.

Crime scene investigation

Definition: Process of recognizing, preserving, collecting, analyzing, and reconstructing evidence located at a crime scene

Significance: By using proven principles and procedures to ensure that all physical evidence at a crime scene is discovered and analyzed, crime scene investigators help to clarify exactly what happened there. The information they gather can link possible suspects to the scene or eliminate them from suspicion.

"Crime scene investigation" is an umbrella term often used to refer to a range of methods and techniques applied during a criminal investigation. Focused on the discovery, recovery, and processing of evidence, crime scene investigation applies reasoned principles in the pursuit of truth. From the moment a crime is discovered until the final appeal in court, the methods and techniques employed during crime scene investigation are under scrutiny.

Modern crime scene investigators combine the logic of fictional detective Sherlock Holmes with advanced scientific techniques in identifying and processing evidence. The basic crime scene procedures used by forensic scientists focus on physical evidence recognition, documentation, collection, packaging, preservation, and analysis. A systematic approach to the investigative task reduces the likelihood of error and improves the investigators' chances of attaining the ultimate goal of justice.

Crime Scene Classification

Crime scenes are traditionally classified based on location, complexity, and relation to the crime in question. The first step in classifying a crime scene is to define the outer boundaries of the physical location. These boundaries establish the geographic limits within which the initial crime will be investigated; this area is known as the primary scene.

The nature of some crimes may involve more than one physical scene, and these are often identified as the secondary, tertiary, and subsequent scenes. For example, in a murder case the death may occur in one location and the body of the victim may be found in another. The primary scene is where the killing took place; the secondary scene is the location where the body was discovered. Both scenes may reveal relevant evidence, and the processing of both constitutes an important part of the criminal investigation.

Crime scenes are also classified as macroscopic or microscopic. A macroscopic crime scene is one that can be viewed and analyzed with the naked eye. Such a scene also includes the potential for several levels of the investigation. Each macroscopic scene is a part of the larger crime. For instance, the scene of a robbery at a convenience store may involve the doorway where the culprit entered, the cash register from which money was stolen, and the back room of the store where the offender placed the clerk before leaving. Each of these scenes is a part of the larger crime scene, but each also constitutes an individual scene for processing. The methods and techniques employed by crime scene investigators depend on both the larger scene and the individual portions within it.

A microscopic crime scene is one in which trace evidence, residues, and similar evidence may be found. Microscopic scenes are often parts of larger macroscopic scenes and therefore require individual processing as well. In processing these scenes, investigators usually require the aid of mechanical or other tools for examination and analysis. A microscopic scene may also be a secondary or higher-level scene that is independent of the primary macroscopic scene. An example is hair or fiber samples from a victim that may be found in a suspect's car. Such samples create a secondary scene that requires microscopic examination. Other examples of microscopic scenes include the clothing of a murder victim, the tire tread left by a getaway car, and the genetic material used in DNA (deoxyribonucleic acid) identification.

A third method of classifying crime scenes is based on the type of crime committed, as different kinds of evidence may be found at the scenes of homicides, robberies, sexual assaults, and other crimes. The methods for processing crime scenes are often determined by the types of crimes and the expected evidence. For example, the scene of a sexual assault is likely to involve evidence very different from the evidence found at the scene of a robbery.

The type of criminal behavior associated with particular crimes may also be used in classifying crime scenes. This is especially important when investigators are attempting to establish the perpetrator's modus operandi, or method of operation (MO), and to recognize potential "signatures" of the perpetrator. The MO used by the perpetrator of a particular crime can often help to define potential suspects, and forensic investigators can help identify and analyze elements of the crime scene that point to the perpetrator's MO.

Crime Scene Objectives

Each crime scene requires a specific systematic investigative approach that is adapted to the needs of that particular crime or scene. The objectives of any crime scene investigation are to identify, preserve, collect, and interpret each piece of evidence. In processing a scene and analyzing evidence, crime scene investigators typically follow a pattern aimed at meeting specific objectives.

The first objective is to determine the essential facts of the case as they relate to the establishment of a crime and its corpus delicti (Latin for "body of the crime"—commonly defined as the substantive nature of the crime). The corpus delicti makes up the essence of a crime, including the legal elements and proof arising from evidence. By first defining the essential facts, investigators can best determine the types of evidence likely to be found and the appropriate processes for recovery of that evidence.

The second objective of the crime scene investigator is to determine the perpetrator's MO. Each crime type requires that the perpetrator perform specific actions to achieve the criminal goal, but perpetrators use many different means for achieving their goals. Individual perpetrators may have specific methods they tend to use in carrying out given crimes. By establishing the MO, investigators can help to define the type of evidence as well as its application to the criminal conduct.

The third objective of the crime scene investigator is to identify witnesses and secure sufficient statements from them. This task includes verifying witness statements, corroborating the statements with other evidence, and, in some instances, disproving the statements as related to physical evidence. The identification of witnesses often helps define other processes and objectives for the crime scene investigation.

The next objective is the identification of suspects. Often a culmination of the earlier objectives, the identi-

---

A Crime Scene Example

Officers respond to a homicide call at a residence and discover the body of a young woman in the bedroom. After securing the scene, they set up the crime scene log, which controls all people having the right of access to the crime scene. The preliminary survey requires written notes, sketches, and identification of fragile evidence. Officers identify footprints outside the bedroom window. They alert investigators and crime scene specialists to the locations of fragile evidence.

Officers establish a pathway for medical personnel; this pathway prevents destruction of physical evidence. If emergency medical responders request assistance from the pathologist, the pathway allows such follow-up investigators opportunities to locate obvious physical evidence—for example, a weapon, blood, and footprints. The initial point-to-point search turns up additional evidence to be photographed.

Special attention to points of entry and exits assists in identifying the offender's travel pattern. Officers locate broken glass near a damaged window and notice a bloody fingerprint below the putty line. This is a strong indicator that the offender pulled the broken glass from the window frame.

The corpse represents a secondary crime scene. The autopsy examination provides essential information on the manner of death, which in this case is determined to be homicide (as opposed to the other four possible findings: natural, accidental, suicide, or undetermined). The autopsy report links trace evidence from the victim to the scene and the offender.

fication of suspects brings together physical evidence, witness statements, and evidentiary conclusions and allows the investigators to move to their final objective: reconstruction of the crime and the potential evidence related to it. Crime scene investigation focuses on the how and why of the criminal act. In crime scene reconstruction, investigators put together the pieces of evidence, including witness statements, to create a picture of the crime in question.

Methods of Crime Scene Investigation

Crime scene investigation often involves two distinct processes. The first, known as linear progression, focuses on the systematic identification of evidence. Often performed by technicians, this process follows specific guidelines

and patterns for identification and management of evidence. In this process, proper procedure is crucial to guarantee the high quality of the evidence and thus support an effective investigation.

Linear progression focuses first on a system of recognition. Initial steps in this part of the crime scene investigation include scene survey and documentation. The investigators describe the crime scene in narrative reports that are often supplemented by diagrams, sketches, photographs, and related material.

The next step in linear progression is identification, which may include comparison and testing. In this step, the investigators identify potential evidence to separate it from irrelevant items found at the crime scene and to help in the collection, preservation, and processing of the evidence. For example, fingerprints discovered in the initial phase of identification of evidence may be lifted at the scene and later identified through a logical system of comparison. The testing of evidence may include chemical, biological, physical, and other methods.

Together, the collection and preservation of evidence constitute an important step in linear progression. Specific collection and preservation methods must be used for particular evidence types, so that the evidence is best protected for later use. In some instances, evidence may be collected and preserved for archival purposes, whereas in others it may be secured for later analysis. Investigators must follow a specific set of procedures for processing each type of evidence.

The final step of linear progression is known as individualization. This involves

A crime scene investigator places an evidence marker next to a handgun outside a bank in Philadelphia where a robber shot and killed two armored car guards who were servicing an automated teller machine on October 4, 2007. (AP/Wide World Photos)

the evaluation of evidence and interpretation of the findings as related to the crime. For example, although many fingerprints may be found at a given crime scene, only select prints will be usable for helping to determine the suspect. The individualization of each set of prints allows investigators to identify persons on the scene, which in turn helps to build a better understanding of the crime itself.

The second process in crime scene investigation is known as nonlinear progression. This process focuses on patterns of recognition and reasonable inference. Also known as a dynamic process, in this step investigators search for patterns and links between evidence and the elements of the crime. This step focuses on critical scene analysis and specified definition techniques. During this process, which is less systematic than linear progression, investigators use inferences and logic to draw connections that lead to reasonable conclusions.

Processing the Crime Scene

The first step in processing a crime scene is to secure it. This begins when the first responding officer arrives at the scene. Initial concerns are for the safety of any victims, witnesses, and others who may be on the scene, but as soon as the responding officer is sure that no persons are in danger, the focus turns to the protection of potential evidence. In many instances, responding officers work to address these two concerns simultaneously.

Securing the crime scene allows investigators to control the potential for loss or destruction of evidence. It also provides an opportunity for investigators to begin the chain of custody— that is, the documentation of the location of all the evidence recovered during the investigation and its eventual use in the courts.

In large police departments, and especially on major crime scenes, the tasks associated with crime scene investigation may be assigned to different individuals. In some instances a lead investigator takes a proactive and supervisory role, controlling and monitoring all activities at the crime scene. In other agencies, a crime scene supervisor takes that role; in still others, various crime scene duties are assumed by individual units.

Small crime scenes and relatively low-level crimes may involve limited numbers of investigators. For example, a classic case of burglary may initially involve only the responding officer, who then has the duty to evaluate the scene and make recommendations concerning additional investigative needs. A crime scene technician may be called to the scene to process physical evidence, but in smaller departments this task may actually fall on the responding officer.

Forensic Science and Crime Scene Investigation

The tools, methods, and techniques used in modern crime scene investigation have made tremendous advances in the past fifty years. The role of forensic science in law-enforcement investigations has increased steadily as methods have improved. Scientific testing that was once prohibitively expensive is now readily available, and new technologies have increasingly improved the accuracy of the findings of criminal investigations.

These advances have come at some cost, however. For instance, jurors in general may have high expectations regarding what investigators can do at crime scenes, in part because of the fictional portrayals of forensic investigators that have become common on television and in films. This means that investigators must be particularly careful to follow standard operating procedures as well as the accepted techniques related to individual kinds of crimes.

Crime scene investigation has also changed dramatically because of changes in the investigative approach taken by many law-enforcement agencies. The trend toward community-oriented policing, among other developments, has led to more accommodating approaches to interagency investigation. The nature of criminal activity, especially when similar crimes take place across multiple jurisdictions, demands that agencies cooperate with each other in the investigation process.

The foundations of science change slowly, but the application of scientific methods to criminal investigations has changed very quickly. Forensic science has seen great improvements in technologies that enable the identification of trace or microscopic evidence, and crime scene investigators in the field have increasing access to devices that were once reserved for the laboratory.

Carl Franklin

Further Reading

Adams, Thomas F., Alan G. Caddell, and Jeffrey L. Krutsinger. *Crime Scene Investigation*. 2d ed. Upper Saddle River, N.J.: Prentice Hall, 2004. Handbook for law-enforcement professionals focuses on excellence in the conduct of crime scene procedures.

Bennett, Wayne W., and Kären M. Hess. *Criminal Investigation*. 8th ed. Belmont, Calif.: Wadsworth/Thomson Learning, 2007. Provides in-depth discussion of forensic techniques and procedures.

Fisher, Barry A. J. *Techniques of Crime Scene Investigation*. 7th ed. Boca Raton, Fla.: CRC Press, 2004. Provides a broad overview of many areas of forensics, including the specific methods used by investigators at crime scenes.

Gilbert, James N. *Criminal Investigation*. 6th ed. Upper Saddle River, N.J.: Pearson Prentice Hall, 2004. Comprehensive text includes discussion of the procedures forensic scientists follow at crime scenes.

Ogle, Robert R., Jr. *Crime Scene Investigation and Reconstruction*. 2d ed. Upper Saddle River, N.J.: Prentice Hall, 2007. Well-organized text covers all aspects of the work of forensic scientists during criminal investigations.

See also: Chain of custody; Crime laboratories; Crime scene cleaning; Crime scene documentation; Crime scene measurement; Crime scene protective gear; Crime scene reconstruction and staging; Crime scene screening tests; Crime scene search patterns; Crime scene sketching and diagramming; Criminalistics; *CSI: Crime Scene Investigation*; Evidence processing; First responders; Forensic photography; Quality control of evidence.

Crime scene measurement

Definition: Precise recording of the exact locations of all elements of a crime scene, including all items found there and all evidence collected.

Significance: The accurate recording of all measurements of a crime scene, particularly the locations of the various items found there, enables investigators to reproduce the scene at a later date, so that they can examine each item in relationship to the others and to the overall scene.

After a crime scene has been identified and the evidence found there has been located, numbered, tagged, and photographed, the scene must be measured in detail. This procedure allows investigators to reproduce the scene later, with all items of evidence and other important items depicted. This reproduction, made to scale, may take the form of a detailed sketch; it may be used for investigative purposes, for courtroom presentation, or both. A three-dimensional reproduction of the crime scene may also be made to assist jurors in visualizing the scene as it was found. Photographs are helpful, but they are limited because they are two-dimensional and do not indicate the exact locations of all the items present and the relationships among the items.

When a crime scene is measured, it is critical that each item be measured from a fixed point, so that it can be repositioned in its exact location at a later date. It would not be helpful, for example, to position an item found in the street by measuring its position in relation to a car parked next to the curb, because the car will be moved at some point. The position of an item in the street should be measured from something that will not move, such as a piece of curb or a point on a building. For a crime scene in a house, a measurement could be made from a specific point on a given wall.

Using the example of a crime scene in the street, a measurement could be made from curb prolongations (usually employed in traffic accident investigations) or other fixed objects, such as buildings or power poles. For example, at the scene of a shooting in which investigators find an expended twelve-gauge shotgun shell in the street, a triangulation method of positioning the shell could be used. The notes on such a measurement might read as follows:

Evidence item 1: One 12-gauge shotgun shell, Remington Express, 3″ mag, red, expended. Found in the center of First Street, south of Los Osos Blvd. Shell was 22′ southeast of ConEd Power Pole #3216, located on the southwest corner of First St. and Los Osos Blvd. and 29′8″ southwest of the northwest corner of Bean's Café located at 1608 First St., Big City.

The items noted can be cross-referenced with crime scene photographs.

Using the example of a gun found on the floor of a room, the measurements could be made from the walls of the room:

Evidence item 6: Gun, S&W blue steel revolver, 4″ barrel, Mod 28, serial number unknown. Found 6′3″ south of the north wall of bedroom number 3 and 18″ from the west wall of said bedroom.

In this example, two right angles are employed to fix the exact position of the gun on the floor of the bedroom; this is frequently referred to as the rectangle method.

In crime scene measurement, the most critical issue is precision. All measurements must be exact, so that the crime scene can later be reproduced accurately, with all items placed where they were found. Many law-enforcement agencies have begun to employ computer programs designed to assist in this endeavor.

Lawrence C. Trostle

Further Reading

Gilbert, James N. *Criminal Investigation.* 6th ed. Upper Saddle River, N.J.: Pearson Prentice Hall, 2004.

O'Hara, Charles E., and Gregory L. O'Hara. *Fundamentals of Criminal Investigation.* 7th ed. Springfield, Ill.: Charles C Thomas, 2003.

Weston, Paul B., and Charles A. Lushbaugh. *Criminal Investigation: Basic Perspectives.* 9th ed. Upper Saddle River, N.J.: Prentice Hall, 2003.

See also: Accident investigation and reconstruction; Crime laboratories; Crime scene documentation; Crime scene investigation; Crime scene reconstruction and staging; Crime scene search patterns; Crime scene sketching and diagramming; Forensic photography.

New York City police officers take measurements at a crime scene where a shooting took place. The numbered tags mark the places where spent shell casings were found. *(AP/Wide World Photos)*

Crime scene protective gear

Definition: Clothing worn by forensic scientists at crime scenes to minimize their direct contact with materials at the scenes.

Significance: It is important that forensic scientists, as well as other professionals who attend crime scenes, take precautions to prevent the inadvertent transfer of potential evidence between them and the scenes. These precautions include the wearing of protective gear, which serves both to protect crime scenes from contamination and to protect forensic scientists from coming into direct contact with possibly dangerous substances.

The examination of a crime scene is essentially like the examination of any exhibit in a forensic laboratory, in that a main function of the crime scene examiner is to collect evidence from the scene, just as a laboratory scientist collects evidence from an exhibit. Both types of investigators should wear protective clothing during their respective examinations.

The wearing of protective gear at a crime scene serves three primary purposes. First, it minimizes the chances that a forensic scientist will leave trace evidence at the scene or on samples collected, which could result in contamination of the evidence and thus affect the interpretation of any results. Second, it minimizes that chances that a scientist will carry trace evidence from the scene to the laboratory or to other collected samples relating to the case being investigated or to other cases. Third, it helps protect the scientist from any biological, physical, or chemical hazards at the scene, which may or may not be directly related to the case being investigated.

Protecting the Scene

Simply wearing protective clothing is not enough. Forensic scientists must follow established procedures that specify the kinds of protective gear they must wear, when they must wear it, and when they must change it. They must also follow appropriate crime scene management procedures.

Protocols for the use of protective gear need to consider all the types of evidence that forensic scientists can leave at a scene or collect from a scene. Scientists may shed hairs from their heads or facial hairs. They could shed fibers from their clothing. They could leave fingerprints on any items they touch. In walking through the scene, they could leave shoe prints.

Increasingly, forensic scientists have come to realize that DNA (deoxyribonucleic acid) should

be regarded as a form of trace evidence, especially given the steadily increasing sensitivity of DNA analysis. A bloodstain or semen stain is not a fixed deposit of potential DNA evidence. Rather, just as fibers can be shed from an item of clothing, DNA-containing cells can be shed from a biological stain onto other items or stains. Scientists who attend crime scenes need to be aware of this potential for contamination and must dress accordingly.

Scientists also need to be aware that they may shed DNA from themselves to crime scenes and thus contaminate items. By touching an item, a person can transfer skin cells that could give a DNA profile. Coughing, sneezing, or breathing on objects may also transfer cells. The analysis of this sort of DNA sample, often called trace DNA, is an important part of the work of forensic scientists.

Essential Gear

A minimum standard of protective gear for a forensic scientist generally involves gloves, appropriate footwear, and something that covers the scientist's clothing, such as overalls or a lab coat. Many crime laboratories are moving to the use of disposable overalls, eliminating the need to have overalls laundered. Disposable overalls make it easy for scientists to change their protective outerwear if it becomes stained or contaminated during crime scene examination, or when they must collect evidence from several areas of a crime scene that need to be kept separate or from multiple scenes associated with the same incident. In addition, because such overalls are disposed of according to protocols established for biohazardous waste, their use minimizes potential contamination from the scene to the laboratory.

Gloves are an essential part of crime scene examiners' gear because no matter how well-intentioned examiners are, they might accidentally touch important surfaces. Generally, disposable gloves made from vinyl or latex are worn. Some scientists wear two pairs of gloves at a time (a practice called double-gloving), especially when the samples collected are likely to be subjected to particularly sensitive DNA analysis techniques.

Forensic scientists have two options for footwear at crime scenes. Some prefer to keep dedicated pairs of scene boots or shoes, which they clean between scenes with 70 percent ethanol or a surface disinfectant such as TriGene. The other option is the use of disposable overshoes. Both approaches minimize the inadvertent transfer of trace or biological evidence from examiners to crime scenes.

Head coverings and face masks provide an extra level of protection at crime scenes. Forensic scientists may cover their heads with the hoods attached to most disposable overalls or with separate disposable caps. If trace DNA analysis is considered as a possible technique in a case, head coverings and masks should be regarded as essential. Low levels of DNA from persons examining the scene could contaminate

these sample types if precautions are not taken, and such contamination could render the DNA results difficult or impossible to interpret. Some scientists consider head coverings and face masks to be essential for all scene examinations, whereas others prefer to address the level of protective gear needed based on individual case circumstances, which may change during their examinations.

Health and Safety Issues

At many crime scenes, forensic scientists can expect to encounter biological fluids. The standard protective gear discussed above should help scientists to avoid possible infection, but some may wish to consider additional precautions if particularly heavy dried or wet blood is present.

Crime scene investigators put on protective overalls, shoe coverings, and gloves as they prepare to enter a home in Deltona, Florida, where six people were found dead a few hours earlier. *(AP/Wide World Photos)*

Some scene types present particular physical and chemical hazards. For example, examiners collecting evidence at clandestine drug laboratories may encounter volatile chemicals, and they may need to protect themselves with body coverings and breathing apparatuses suitable for such exposure. Because they must often must move through unstable debris, arson investigators protect themselves with heavy footwear and hard hats or helmets.

In testing substances at crime scenes, scientists may need to use reagents that can present health hazards. For example, the reactive dyes used in presumptive testing for blood and semen can be carcinogenic. Also, crime scene examination techniques involving the use of luminol and leuco crystal violet (for the enhancement of bloodstains and bloodied shoe prints or other impressions) require the spraying of scenes with chemicals. In such cases, some kind of breathing apparatus may be needed, particularly if the area being examined is enclosed or not well ventilated.

Douglas Elliot

Further Reading

Elliot, Douglas. "Crime Scene Examination." In *Expert Evidence: Law, Practice, Procedure, and Advocacy*, edited by Ian Freckelton and Hugh Selby. 3d ed. Pyrmont, N.S.W.: Lawbook, 2005. Takes a multijuridictional point of view in discussing all aspects of crime scene examination.

Fisher, Barry A. J. *Techniques of Crime Scene Investigation*. 7th ed. Boca Raton, Fla.: CRC Press, 2004. Provides a broad overview of many areas of the forensic sciences. Includes discussion of the health and safety issues related to crime scene examination.

Geberth, Vernon J. *Practical Homicide Investigation: Tactics, Procedures, and Forensic Techniques*. 4th ed. Boca Raton, Fla.: CRC Press, 2006. Text used in many U.S. police academies includes discussion of the protective gear required for those involved in the collection and handling of evidence.

Houck, Max M., and Jay A. Siegel. *Fundamentals of Forensic Science*. Burlington, Mass.: Elsevier Academic Press, 2006. Good general textbook devotes a thorough section to the safety aspects of the work done by crime scene investigators.

See also: Blood residue and bloodstains; Chemical Biological Incident Response Force, U.S.; Crime scene cleaning; Crime scene investigation; Cross-contamination of evidence; Decontamination methods; DNA extraction from hair, bodily fluids, and tissues; Food supply protection; Footprints and shoe prints; Trace and transfer evidence.

Crime scene reconstruction and staging

Definitions: Crime scene reconstruction is an investigatory technique in which evidence is gathered, organized, and analyzed to recreate the precise sequence of events that occurred during the course of a crime. Crime scene staging is a stratagem sometimes used by criminal offenders in which a crime scene is rearranged or fabricated to disguise the true nature of the offense and suggest other causes or perpetrators of the crime.

Significance: Crime scene reconstruction is the process of piecing together the evidence in a criminal case to determine what, when, where, and how criminal actions occurred. This process is fundamental to the successful apprehension and conviction of criminals. Without painstaking examination of the crime scene, investigators can easily overlook crucial evidence; if the evidence is not then assembled to tell a coherent story of what happened, the perpetrator of the crime might never be apprehended or convicted. Law-enforcement investigators must also be alert to the possibility that the perpetrator has manipulated elements of the crime scene to mislead them. Crime scene reconstruction and staging are related in that both help answer important questions that can lead to the apprehension of perpetrators.

Criminal investigation is a systematic fact-finding endeavor that involves numerous professionals with special expertise and training. Law-enforcement officers arrive at the scene in response to a report that a crime has been committed. Their job is to preserve and protect the crime scene. Criminalists collect physical evidence at the crime scene and deliver that evidence to the laboratory. Crime scene investigators or detectives scour the scene for evidence, ask witnesses questions, and track leads concerning possible suspects. Laboratory scientists analyze and test physical evidence from the scene. In homicide cases, forensic pathologists perform autopsies to ascertain the manner and cause of death. The work of all of these professionals lays the groundwork for crime scene reconstruction.

Criminal investigations must adhere to a deliberate process. Physical evidence is carefully collected, handled, transported, and preserved for the purpose of solving a crime and bringing the offender to justice. Failure to protect the integrity of the evidence can render it inadmissible in court. Notwithstanding its importance, physical evidence, by itself, might not be enough to close a criminal case. Discrete bits of evidence must be properly collated and placed in a context to be useful in the arrest, prosecution, and conviction of offenders.

Reconstructing Crime Scenes

Crime scenes are locations where illegal acts have been committed and physical evidence is found. Crime scenes can be categorized as primary, secondary, or tertiary. For example, an offender may kidnap a victim from her home (a primary crime scene) and transport her by car (a secondary crime scene) to another location (a tertiary crime scene), where the offender murders her. The place where the offender disposes of the victim's body is yet another tertiary crime scene. Crime scenes thus include any indoor or outdoor locations that afford opportunities for the recovery of direct physical evidence of crimes. Connecting the activities and establishing the nature and sequence of events within and among those scenes is the essence of crime scene reconstruction.

Crime scene reconstruction is a methodology that is used to re-create the events of a crime, including the course of actions that unfolded immediately before, during, and after the incident. Forensic scientists reconstruct a crime scene by examining and interpreting physical evidence as well as the physical layout of the location. Reconstruction begins with the gathering of data from the scene; in the case of homicide, these may include data on blood spatter, gunshot residue, bullet trajectories, and objects from which DNA (deoxyribonucleic acid) evidence can be collected. In a homicide case, the positioning and condition of the victim's body can also yield valuable details about the specific unfolding and timing of the criminal act.

A thorough reconstruction includes photographs from the crime scene, results of laboratory analyses of physical evidence, and autopsy findings. Measurements and sketches of the scene are also carefully done and integrated to form a logical and evidence-based re-creation of the criminal act. Information from the crime scene is synthesized so that investigators can make educated guesses about what happened during the crime, where it happened, when it happened, and how it happened. Witness statements are compared with the physical evidence to determine whether the hypothesized sequence of actions is refuted or supported by witness recollections.

During the crime scene reconstruction process, investigators typically walk through the crime scene while attempting to apply the mind-set of an offender. They formulate realistic scenarios that might match the actual events of the crime. Investigators must be able to interpret the crime scene from every visual perspective in order to discover, interpret, and collate pertinent facts. One primary focus of investigation involves the determination of the offender's modus operandi, or method of operation, which consists of the actions that an offender employs to complete the crime (choice of target, method of entry, use of weapon, means to control the victim, and so on).

Crime Scene Staging

The possibility that a crime scene has been staged is another important consideration in crime scene reconstruction and analysis.

Staging is a deliberate attempt to thwart or confuse crime scene investigators by rearranging the crime scene. In one type of staging, the offender modifies the elements of the crime scene to make the offense appear as a suicide or an accident. Crime scene investigators must be careful in accepting evidence at face value. For example, a man found in his apartment with a fatal bullet wound in his head and gun in his right hand might not be a suicide victim. Detailed investigation may lead to the conclusion that the case is, in fact, a homicide, as evidenced by the angle of the exit wound, the gunshot residue on the victim's hand, the nature of the wound, the distance of the shell casings from the gun and the body, and the type of gun used in the crime. Crime investigators must be skeptical and methodical in their efforts to explore all possible aspects of a crime scene in order to differentiate between the actual events of the crime and any likely staging of the scene.

In another type of staging, serial killers position physical evidence and victims' bodies to humiliate, punish, and degrade victims and taunt the police. Some serial killers compulsively leave psychological markers, known as signatures, at their crime scenes. These can include posing the victims' bodies or concealing or inserting objects in the victims' bodies after death. A serial killer's signature is unnecessary for the completion of the crime but critical to the killer's psychological and sexual gratification.

Arthur J. Lurigio and Justyna Lenik

Further Reading

Clemens, Daryl W. "Introduction to Crime Scene Reconstruction." *MAFS Newsletter* 27 (April, 1998). Discusses the differences between crime scene reconstruction and criminal profiling. Also describes different types of reconstruction techniques, the steps in the reconstruction process, and how criminal profiling and crime scene reconstruction complement each other in helping investigators understand how and why crimes are committed.

Gardner, Ross M. *Practical Crime Scene Processing and Investigation*. Boca Raton, Fla.: CRC Press, 2005. Thoroughly illustrates and explains the importance of each step in a criminal investigation. Outstanding chapter titled "The Role of Crime Scene Analysis and Reconstruction" explicates the methodology of crime scene investigation and enumerates the steps in event analysis. Includes vivid photographs and sketches from crime scenes to illustrate the various stages of the reconstruction process.

Geberth, Vernon J. "The Homicide Crime Scene." In *Practical Homicide Investigation: Tactics, Procedures, and Forensic Techniques*. 4th ed. Boca Raton, Fla.: CRC Press, 2006. Describes the different types of crime scene staging and presents examples of actual crimes in which the scenes were staged in a section headed "The Staged Crime Scene." Written by a former commander for the Bronx Homicide Division of the New York City Police Department.

Gibson, Dirk. *Clues from Killers: Serial Murder and Crime Scene Messages*. Westport, Conn.: Praeger, 2004. Presents the details of the crimes committed by some of history's most notorious serial killers, including the Unabomber, Jack the Ripper, and the BTK Killer, and analyzes the messages and other forms of communication each of the perpetrators used. Opens with an excellent introduction that discusses the nature of serial killers' signatures and how these idiosyncratic and often cryptic expressions vary depending on what the killers are trying to accomplish.

Ogle, Robert R., Jr. *Crime Scene Investigation and Reconstruction*. 2d ed. Upper Saddle River, N.J.: Prentice Hall, 2007. Provides a good overview of all procedures used in crime scene investigation and discusses the steps taken and the kinds of physical evidence used in reconstructing the events that took place at a given scene.

See also: Accident investigation and reconstruction; Bomb damage assessment; Crime scene documentation; Crime scene investigation; Crime scene measurement; Crime scene sketching and diagramming; Criminal personality profiling; Criminalistics; DNA analysis; DNA fingerprinting; Forensic anthropology; Forensic photography; Forensic sculpture; Structural analysis.

Crime scene screening tests

Definition: Color tests that provide rapid information regarding the presence or absence of given classes of drugs or compounds.

Significance: At crime scenes, forensic scientists need to provide information to law-enforcement personnel on any possible illicit drugs or other compounds that may be present. They must also make decisions on the most appropriate samples to be collected. The use of crime scene screening tests, generally in the form of chemical reagents that show positive results with distinct color changes, can assist in these decision-making processes by providing initial indications of what questioned substances or compounds may or may not be.

Although crime scene screening tests, commonly known as spot tests, can be used to identify a wide range of compounds, forensic scientists most commonly use these tests at crime scenes related to the use and manufacture of illicit drugs. Spot tests are used to exclude or potentially identify given classes of drugs or compounds as being present in samples. Spot testing may be used to determine whether a large single package seized by police, such as a bulk powder, is homogeneous or to determine whether numerous packages or other items seized at a single scene are all the same. At crime scenes, spot tests can provide forensic scientists with information as to whether particular items should be sampled or whether they should be taken whole to the laboratory for further analysis.

Properties of a Spot Test

The ideal spot test would be specific for a given drug or compound, would be sensitive (so that only a small amount of sample need be subjected to analysis), and would provide an unambiguous result, allowing no misinterpretation. In the interests of efficiency and safety, the test reagents would be cheap and harmless, and the test itself would be quick and easy to carry out.

In reality, most spot tests sacrifice specificity in favor of fulfilling the other desired criteria; they do not individually identify specific drugs or compounds, but rather given classes. For example, Marquis reagent turns a positive purple color with an opiate alkaloid, whether it be morphine, diacetylmorphine, or one of the many other compounds in the same class.

As most spot tests are relatively sensitive, a negative result provides a good indication of the absence of the class of drug or compound that would normally provide a positive result. A positive result may develop with a compound outside the class of compound being screened for; such a result is commonly referred to as a false positive. Other compounds present in the sample may prevent an unambiguous identification of a drug. Sugars are often used as diluting agents in powered drug samples, and these can turn brown when combined with sulfuric acid (present in Marquis reagent). This brown color may obscure any color change resulting from a drug present

Spot Tests at Clandestine Drug Laboratories

The use of spot tests at clandestine laboratories manufacturing drugs can help forensic scientists to determine whether powdered materials found there are final products or precursors, in which case the whole items will need to be seized, or less important compounds that need only be sampled. Spot tests may also be used to determine the presence of other chemicals at such crime scenes. For example, the identities of common acids found at clandestine drug laboratories may be tentatively distinguished through the use of spot tests employing a silver nitrate solution. Hypophosphorous acid, commonly used in the manufacture of methamphetamine, will produce a black precipitate, although further testing is required to distinguish it from phosphorous acid. Hydrochloric acid will produce a white precipitate, and sulfuric acid will produce no reaction. Forensic scientists need to combine the results of spot tests with other observations to determine the nature of the acids at drug lab crime scenes, and, in all cases, further testing is required to confirm the identities of the acids.

in the sample, such as an amphetamine, which would produce a positive orange color.

Spot tests require no sophisticated equipment and can easily be carried out away from the laboratory at crime scenes. A forensic scientist generally carries out a spot test by adding the test reagent to a small amount of the sample material in a small glass tube or on the well of a spotting tile.

Spot tests tend to be destructive, but each test requires only a small amount of the sample material, leaving the bulk of the sample for further testing if required. The reagents are not necessarily harmless; they often contain strong acids or chemicals with undesirable properties. They are required only in small amounts, however, and can be safely transported to scenes in suitable containers.

Quality Control

The age of spot test reagents and the conditions under which they have been stored may affect the colors produced during use. Forensic scientists need to run positive and negative controls with spot test reagents on a regular basis to ensure that they are working correctly.

Little training or expertise is required in the use of spot tests, and such tests may be readily carried out by nonscientific staff, such as police or customs officers. Because it is unlikely that a positive control will be able to be carried out at every scene where a sample is tested, persons using spot tests should carry out their own positive and negative controls with the test reagents to ensure that they are familiar with the color changes expected. In addition, tests should be carried out on compounds known to produce "false positive" results. This will prevent misinterpretation of results owing to subjectivity when describing colors.

Anne Coxon

Further Reading

Camilleri, Andrew M., and David Caldicott. "Underground Pill Testing, Down Under." *Forensic Science International* 151 (2005): 53-58. Evaluates the use of spot tests for identification of the drugs contained in so-called party pills.

Cole, Michael D. *The Analysis of Controlled Substances*. New York: John Wiley & Sons, 2003. Describes the major classes of drugs of abuse in a clear manner and addresses the use of spot testing, thin-layer chromatography, and instrumental analysis.

Horswell, John, ed. *The Practice of Crime Scene Investigation*. Boca Raton, Fla.: CRC Press, 2004. Collection of essays covering all aspects of scene investigations includes a chapter on drug operations that provides a good explanation of the use of spot tests and discusses how their use coincides with other important forensic aspects of such investigations.

Moffat, Anthony C., M. David Osselton, and Brian Widdop, eds. *Clarke's Analysis of Drugs and Poisons*. 3d ed. 2 vols. Chicago: Pharmaceutical Press, 2004. Comprehensive work provides data and describes methods relating to the detection, identification, and quantification of drugs and poisons.

O'Neal, Carol L., Dennis J. Crouch, and Alim A. Fatah. "Validation of Twelve Chemical Spot Tests for the Detection of Drugs of Abuse." *Forensic Science International* 109 (2000): 189-201. Presents the results of research that assessed the specificity and sensitivity of twelve spot tests commonly used in drug analysis.

United Nations. *Rapid Testing Methods of Drugs of Abuse*. New York: Author, 1995. Manual intended for forensic laboratories and law-enforcement personnel provides technical detail but is easy to read and includes clear information relating to the practical use of spot tests for drugs.

See also: Acid-base indicators; Crime scene investigation; Crime scene measurement; Drug classification; Evidence processing; Illicit substances; Meth labs; Presumptive tests for blood.

Crime scene search patterns

Definition: Geometric template method used to search for evidence at a crime scene.

Significance: The orderly approach of following a geometric pattern in the search for and gathering of evidence at a crime scene maximizes discovery efforts and minimizes the disturbance of evidence prior to discovery.

Law-enforcement investigators organize their searches of crime scenes to maximize the likelihood of finding evidence and to minimize the likelihood that they will fail to discover existing evidence. The discovery process itself should not cause undue disturbance of the scene, as this could cause evidence to be damaged or overlooked. To organize their searches, investigators choose from various geometric templates, which are then imposed on the scenes to be searched; four commonly used templates are the spiral, the strip, the wheel, and the zone pattern. Evidence discovery points at a crime scene can be diagrammed at corresponding points on a paper or digital record that serves as a blueprint of the crime scene.

A spiral search emanates from a center point and travels in widening curves from that point like a coiled snake. The search path may begin from either end of the spiral. For example, a bloody knife found on the street would most likely generate a spiral search path starting at the location of the knife (center of the spiral) and working outward. A crime scene with a victim inside a room having a single doorway would probably generate a spiral search pattern that starts from the doorway (outer end of the spiral) and works inward, toward the center.

A strip (or linear) search pattern divides a crime scene into long, narrow sections. Investi-

Law-enforcement investigators search for human remains within areas staked off into a grid pattern at a Cass County, Missouri, residence where bone fragments from at least two people had been found. *(AP/Wide World Photos)*

gators may begin an evidence search at either end of the strip. This sort of search is often used across large land areas to look for evidence such as the presence of a person in that vicinity. In a typical strip pattern search, searchers walk shoulder to shoulder or separated by an arm's length in a line that moves simultaneously across an area.

The wheel pattern search has a center point from which spokes radiate outward to connect to a circle enclosing the search area. The sections of the wheel pattern search thus are shaped like slices of a pie. Searchers can investigate sections simultaneously from the outer perimeter toward the center without crossing or disturbing possible evidence in other sections. The wheel pattern search may be used when time for searching is limited, such as when adverse weather conditions make it likely that the crime scene will soon be disturbed.

The zone (or grid) search pattern uses perpendicular lines that form square search areas (quadrants); each quadrant can be further divided into smaller quadrants pertinent to the search. Crime scene investigators who need to search buildings often do so by dividing each floor into zones. Zoned investigations may quickly rule out particular zones that are not pertinent to the crime, thus freeing investigators to concentrate on the zones that do contain evidence.

Taylor Shaw

Further Reading

Genge, N. E. *The Forensic Casebook: The Science of Crime Scene Investigation*. New York: Ballantine, 2002.

Pentland, Peter, and Pennie Stoyles. *Forensic Science*. Philadelphia: Chelsea House, 2003.

Platt, Richard. *Crime Scene: The Ultimate Guide to Forensic Science*. New York: Dorling Kindersley, 2003.

See also: Blood residue and bloodstains; Buried body locating; Crime scene documentation; Crime scene investigation; Crime scene measurement; Crime scene sketching and diagramming; Disturbed evidence; Evidence processing; Forensic archaeology; Locard's exchange principle; Metal detectors; Physical evidence.

Crime scene sketching and diagramming

Definition: Creation of representative depictions of locations and appearances of important and relevant features and objects found at crime scenes.

Significance: In creating sketches and diagrams of crime scenes, examiners extract from the abundance of background visual information at such scenes only those features that are relevant and portray them in visual form. Such sketches are complementary to the scene notes and photographs that also document crime scenes.

Crime scenes are often very cluttered, jumbled, and confusing. Crime scene photographs can contain vast amounts of visual information, much of which may not relate to the particular incident being investigated. By making a sketch or diagram, a crime scene examiner can create a document that visually highlights only those aspects of the scene that are considered to be relevant to the crime. Like all crime scene documentation, sketches can be made to aid the recollection of the investigators who make them, but ultimately they serve to convey information to other investigators, attorneys, and courts.

An annotated sketch or diagram, with appropriate measurements marked, can provide a format for focusing the attention on one aspect, or a small number of aspects, of the crime scene that may be particularly relevant. For example, a single sketch of a light switch showing the general appearance and location of a bloodstain and indicating where a sample of the stain was taken from provides a clear, easily understood visual representation of one aspect of the scene examination. Another, more typical, example would be a sketch of the floor plan of a room indicating the location of a body relative to items of furniture and other significant objects, such as the murder weapon.

Rather than attempting to include a lot of information in a single sketch, which can lead to confusion, a crime scene examiner may create multiple sketches of the same area of interest.

A crime scene investigator for the Florida Department of Law Enforcement testifies in court, using a crime scene diagram to indicate the locations where six bodies were found inside a Deltona, Florida, home in August, 2004. *(AP/Wide World Photos)*

One such sketch might indicate the location of a body and other physical items relative to each other, a second might depict the locations of bloodstains, and a third might show the locations of shoe prints. This kind of separation of layers of information allows viewers of the sketches to comprehend the individual points of interest more easily.

Most crime scene sketches are not intended to be perfectly accurate scale re-creations of the scenes. Rather, they are nearly always companions to detailed scene photographs. Sketches are valuable because they are simple to create and can readily convey specific information. Increasingly, however, crime scene examiners are making use of modern surveying equipment and associated computer software to create accurate visual depictions of crime scenes and the locations of items within them.

R. K. Morgan-Smith

Further Reading

Elliot, Douglas. "Crime Scene Examination." In *Expert Evidence: Law, Practice, Procedure, and Advocacy*, edited by Ian Freckelton and Hugh Selby. 3d ed. Pyrmont, N.S.W.: Lawbook, 2005.

Horswell, John, ed. *The Practice of Crime Scene Investigation*. Boca Raton, Fla.: CRC Press, 2004.

Saferstein, Richard. *Criminalistics: An Introduction to Forensic Science*. 9th ed. Upper Saddle River, N.J.: Pearson Prentice Hall, 2007.

See also: Composite drawing; Crime scene documentation; Crime scene investigation; Crime scene measurement; Crime scene reconstruction and staging; Crime scene search patterns; Evidence processing.

Criminal personality profiling

Definition: Investigatory technique in which a detailed composite description of an unknown perpetrator is constructed on the basis of crime scene evidence.

Significance: By providing police officers with descriptive information about what type of individual probably committed an offense, including demographic and psychological characteristics, profiling narrows the range of likely offenders and helps investigators concentrate their limited resources and time in search of suspects.

Criminal personality profiling is based on the notion that serial offenders engage in similar patterns of behavior and that each serial offender leaves a unique trail of evidence with each crime. Profilers believe that the actions of serial offenders are deeply motivated, however bizarre, random, or senseless those actions might appear to untrained observers. The criminal activities in which these offenders engage are windows into their hidden desires, tendencies, and psychological traits. Conversely, these offenders' thoughts as well as their emotional and sexual needs drive their criminal behaviors.

Serial Criminals

Profiling is most often employed in cases of serial homicides or rapes. These crimes, which tend to receive widespread media coverage, often involve female victims with common physical characteristics. The general profile of serial murderers, which matches the actual characteristics of most of the persons apprehended for such crimes, is as follows: They are white men with average or above-average intelligence, in their mid-twenties to mid-thirties, who have an interest in criminal law and police work. Serial killers also tend to be interpersonally adept; they are typically friendly, charming, and engaging, which explains their success at attracting and luring victims to horrific deaths. Other types of serial criminals have also been the subjects of criminal personality profiling, including arsonists, bank robbers, kidnappers, and child molesters.

Profilers assume that perpetrators leave telltale signs of their psychopathology at their crime scenes (in the case of serial murderers, the locations where they kill, torture, and mutilate their victims) and in the areas where they conceal their victims' bodies—so-called dump sites. Profilers examine these clues to characterize an unknown suspect (that is, an individual who is likely to have committed the crime given the evidence at the scene). However, they rarely provide police investigators with the specific identity of an actual perpetrator.

Major Profiling Tasks

The three primary tasks of a criminal personality profiler are to generate details about an unknown perpetrator's personality and sociodemographic characteristics, to predict the items that are likely to be discovered in a suspected offender's possession, and to recommend various interrogation strategies for suspects in custody. In accomplishing the first of these tasks, the profiler provides police investigators with leads that narrow the pool of unknown suspects with respect to age, race, ethnicity, employment, education, and marital status. Profiling unfolds a biographical sketch of an at-large killer or rapist as the number of that person's crimes increases and more information becomes available to the profiler. Profiling can also give investigators insights into where a perpetrator might live relative to the locations of the crimes.

The most important aspect of the profiler's first task is to arrive at an educated guess about a likely offender on the basis of police and autopsy reports as well as the consistent elements found at different crime scenes, such as how the victims were killed (for example, stabbing, bludgeoning, strangling, suffocating) and how the bodies were positioned or displayed (for example, naked, partially clothed, posed). Based on these data, the profiler can help police officers to focus their attention on a certain type of suspect. The profiler can also provide police with information on where the offender is likely to live as well as when and where the offender is likely to strike again.

The defining aspects of a criminal's behaviors are the individual's modus operandi (MO) and signature. The modus operandi consists of the steps the offender follows and the techniques and tools the offender uses when engaging in criminal activities. An offender's MO can evolve. In other words, an individual's criminal skills are honed and practices are modified with experience. As criminals become more seasoned, their MOs becomes more effective and efficient; they also become less likely to leave clues that will lead to their capture. An example of an MO is that of the serial rapist who uses burglary tools to pry open the bedroom windows of women sleeping in basement apartments. He wears gloves and thus never leaves fingerprints, and he enters and exits the apartment through the same window.

This serial rapist might also display a signature—an action taken not to accomplish the crime but to satisfy the perpetrator's distinctive and perverse psychological needs. For example, the bedroom rapist might force his victims to assume degrading poses while he photographs them following the act of sexual violence. Signatures are unique to specific offenders because they emerge from the offenders' idiosyncrasies and personal tendencies. MOs can be replicated by other offenders, but signatures cannot. Offenders who appropriate the MOs of fellow criminals are committing so-called copycat crimes. Signatures are often tied to the pathological sexual satisfaction that serial killers obtain from their offenses.

The second profiling task occurs after a prime suspect or person of interest has been identified. Knowledge about the alleged offender's belongings can reinforce other evidence that ties that person to the crimes. For example, some serial killers collect crime scene souvenirs, newspaper clippings, photographs, fetish items, pornography, or other materials that help them remember, relive, and re-create their crimes, providing them with prolonged sexual or other types of gratification. The items taken from crime scenes for these purposes are sometimes referred to as "trophies." Jeffrey Dahmer, for example, showcased the macerated skulls and bones of his victims in his apartment and consumed pieces of his victims' flesh to re-create the pleasure he received from sexually violating their corpses.

The third profiling task follows the arrest of the suspect. Based on inferences about the suspect's personality traits and psychological disturbances, the profiler guides the police in the selection of interrogation techniques that will best elicit incriminating information from the suspected offender. Different strategies must be implemented with consideration of each suspect's personality and psychological disorders. For example, with some offenders, unrelenting and aggressive questioning is most productive, whereas with others, a more relaxed and conversational tone is most likely to elicit confession. Still other serial offenders respond best in interrogation situations in which they perceive themselves, rather than the police investigators, as being in full control.

Pioneers in Profiling

Cesare Lombroso (1836-1909) was among the first criminal profilers. He and many of his contemporaries believed that criminals, unlike noncriminals, could be identified by physical characteristics such as bushy eyebrows or a receding chin. Early profilers also noted criminals' tendency to wear shabby clothes and to be tattooed. Dr. James Brussel, a New York-based psychiatrist and the first renowned profiler in the United States, was influenced by these theories in his work with the New York Police Department. From the late 1950's to the early 1970's, Brussel helped investigators track suspects in cases of serial bombing, arson, and murder. His most famous criminal personality profile, of the "Mad Bomber," was uncanny in its accuracy.

From 1940 to 1956, New York City was terrorized by a series of bombs planted randomly in crowded public places, such as busy streets, stores, and movie theaters. These actions were attributed to the ever-mysterious, paranoid, and elusive character the city's newspapers called the "Mad Bomber." Over the years, the bombs became deadlier, and the Mad Bomber's letters to the police and the news media, signed "F.P." for "Fair Play," became increasingly hostile and grandiloquent.

Profiling Serial and Mass Murderers

Given that every serial and mass murderer is unique, it can be dangerous to generalize about "typical" offenders. Nevertheless, multiple-murder offenders have many characteristics in common.

Trait	Patterns
Gender	Most offenders are male. Female serial killers occur, but they are much less common than male killers. Female mass murderers are extremely rare.
Race	Most offenders are white, but there are exceptions to this rule. For example, Wayne Williams, the Atlanta child killer of 1979-1981, was African American.
Age	Serial killers usually begin killing when they are in their twenties. Mass murderers are typically ten to twenty years older than that when they begin killing.
Intelligence	Serial killers are typically intelligent but often have experienced severe failures in their careers and personal lives. Mass murderers are often unemployed, sometimes losing their jobs only shortly before they begin killing.
Personal histories	Serial killers often display patterns of sociopathic behavior and may have histories of deviant sexual or violent behavior, including animal abuse. Mass murderers usually do not display such patterns.
Fantasy lives	Serial killers often fantasize about their crimes.
Alcohol and drugs	Serial killers sometimes use drugs or alcohol before or while committing their crimes. Mass murderers rarely do so.
Childhoods	Serial killers often have had miserable childhoods and have suffered physical or mental abuse. They may also have histories of serious head trauma and neurological disorders.
Military	Mass murderers often have served in the military.

Despite the diligent efforts of seasoned police officers and investigators, no viable clues brought authorities any closer to identifying a suspect and ending the terror. Frustrated with traditional police measures to catch the Mad Bomber, Inspector Howard Finney of the New York City Crime Lab suggested a radical approach. After one of the Mad Bomber's devices injured six patrons in a movie theater on December 2, 1956, Finney summoned Brussel and posed basic questions that the police had failed to answer in their work on the case: "What kind of demented person would hurt innocent people in such a horrific manner?" "What is motivating the Mad Bomber?" "Who is he and what is the best way to catch him?" With his impressive background as assistant commissioner of mental hygiene for the state of New York and head of the U.S. Army's Neuropsychiatry Unit during

the Korean War as well as his training as a psychoanalyst, Brussel was dubbed by the press the "Sherlock Holmes of the couch."

Brussel pored over the police records of the bombings and developed the following criminal personality profile. The bomber was a man—historically, most bombers had been male. His letters suggested that he was a former employee of Consolidated Edison, the city's electric power company, and that he harbored a deep-seated grudge against the company for real or imagined injuries. The bomber was paranoid and believed that the electric company and the public were "out to get him." Brussel surmised that the bomber was approximately fifty years old because paranoid ideation peaks at the age of thirty-five and the bombings had been occurring for sixteen years. He also surmised from the bomber's carefully crafted letters and explosive devices that the bomber was a deliberate person who dressed fastidiously and was highly sensitive to criticism.

Brussel concluded from his analysis of the Mad Bomber's letters that the bomber was from Eastern Europe (a part of the world where bombs were weapons of choice) and self-educated. The postmarks on the letters suggested to Brussel that the bomber lived in Connecticut and commuted to New York City for the purpose of planting his bombs. Brussel guessed that the unknown suspect was unmarried and that he lived with his brothers or sisters; he further conjectured that the bomber had been unable to form mature relationships with women because he suffered from an "Oedipus complex."

Brussel told the detectives that they should publicize his criminal personality profile of the Mad Bomber in order to antagonize the perpetrator and force him out into the open. He also instructed them to search the records of Consolidated Edison carefully for disgruntled former employees. Brussel's strategy worked. Soon after his profile was published in the newspapers, the Mad Bomber revealed his motive in a letter to the press: He had been injured on the job and believed the company was cheating him out of his worker's compensation payments. This revelation confirmed the bomber's identity and led to his capture.

The Mad Bomber was George Metesky. He lived in Connecticut with his two sisters. He was middle-aged, Slavic, and very well groomed. Before the detectives went to Metesky's home to place him under arrest, Brussel told them to expect Metesky to be wearing a double-breasted suit, buttoned. When the police took him into custody, he was indeed wearing a double-breasted suit—carefully buttoned. Metesky was found insane by the courts and was committed to the Matteawan Hospital for the Criminally Insane. In 1973, he was released and returned to his family home in Connecticut. In 1994, he died there quietly, and in obscurity, at the age of ninety.

Brussel attempted to systematize and standardize his profiling techniques, working with two agents of the Federal Bureau of Investigation (FBI), Howard Teten and Patrick J. Mullany. In the 1970's, they created a seminal course in applied criminology that helped to spawn the FBI's Behavioral Science Unit, later renamed the Behavioral Analysis Unit, which is now a part of the National Center for the Analysis of Violent Crime in Quantico, Virginia.

Types of Serial Criminals

Expert criminal personality profilers trained by the FBI have created several typologies or groupings of serial murderers. One scheme for categorizing these offenders focuses on their mobility. Geographically stable serial killers (examples include Ed Gein, Wayne Williams, and John Wayne Gacy) live in the same areas where they hunt for, kill, and bury their victims.

John Douglas in his office at the Federal Bureau of Investigation Training Facility in 1991. As an FBI agent, Douglas, along with agent Robert K. Ressler, developed one of the most widely known methods of criminal personality profiling. Douglas served as a consultant on the 1991 film *The Silence of the Lambs*, a thriller featuring an FBI profiler. *(Hulton Archive/Getty Images)*

Geographically transient serial killers (examples include Ted Bundy and Henry Lee Lucas), in contrast, move from place to place in search of victims and bury the bodies in areas that are distant from the killing sites. These killers travel to confuse law-enforcement authorities, and they are much less vulnerable to capture than geographically stable serial killers. Another categorization scheme differentiates among four types: visionary serial killers, who have serious mental illnesses and select victims by listening to auditory command hallucinations; mission serial killers, who are driven to murder certain types of people; hedonistic serial killers, who murder for sexual gratification; and power/control serial killers, who achieve sexual pleasure from dominating and controlling their victims.

One of the most widely known criminal profiling methods was developed by FBI agents John Douglas and Robert K. Ressler; their system categorizes serial killers on the basis of whether their crime scenes are organized or disorganized. Organized offenders are likely to be average or above average in intelligence, engaged in skilled occupations, married or living with partners, and interested in the media's coverage of their crimes. In contrast, disorganized offenders are likely to be below average in intelligence, socially awkward, living alone, and uninterested in the media's coverage of their crimes.

Caveats and Ethical Issues

Criminal personality profiling is more an art than a science. Profilers use a few general approaches that can be readily adapted to fit specific types of crimes, but no tried-and-true profiling techniques have been developed that work in every case. Instead, the formulas that profilers use are based largely on the particular circumstances of each case and the evidence at hand; these yield educated guesses derived from knowledge, practical experience, and clinical acumen.

Despite the fact that profiling has often been glamorized or sensationalized in novels, films, and television programs, it is only one component in a wide range of strategies used by law-enforcement agencies to apprehend serial of-fenders. Profiling is an adjunctive tool that supplements and complements the investigatory activities of experienced law-enforcement officers. Profilers are consultants to the police; they are generally summoned after officers have failed in their attempts to identify or question suspects. Profilers must be careful not to oversell their capabilities.

Many experienced homicide investigators regard criminal personality profiling with skepticism and disdain. The field is without a sound scientific basis and relies on weak standards of proof, although psychologists have begun to conduct more research on the validity of profiling techniques. The field of profiling is also lacking in professional standards and minimal educational requirements, and no credentialing bodies exist to govern and oversee the conduct of practitioners. Profilers have an ethical obligation to be unbiased and impartial in their collection and interpretation of evidence, to restrict their opinions to the specific facts of the case, to present their qualifications honestly and openly, and never to use a profile to assert the guilt or innocence of any suspect.

Arthur J. Lurigio

Further Reading

Brussel, James. *Casebook of a Crime Psychiatrist*. New York: Bernard Geis, 1968. Classic volume presents case studies drawn directly from Brussel's files. A must-read for profiling enthusiasts.

Hickey, Eric. *Serial Murderers and Their Victims*. Belmont, Calif.: Wadsworth, 2002. Offers an extensive account of serial murder that is grounded in social science research. Examines the lives of four hundred serial murderers and attempts to explain their behaviors from biological, psychological, and sociological perspectives.

Holmes, Ronald, and Stephen Holmes. *Profiling Violent Crime: An Investigative Tool*. Thousand Oaks, Calif.: Sage, 1996. Solid introductory text on profiling presents the principles and techniques that investigators employ in developing the profiles of violent criminals.

Petherick, Wayne. *Serial Crime: Theoretical and Practical Issues in Behavioral Profiling*. Burlington, Mass.: Academic Press, 2006.

Text designed for advanced students is divided into two sections, one on behavioral profiling—including its theoretical foundations and history as well as discussion of media depictions—and one on specific serial crimes, including arson, murder, rape, and stalking.

Turvey, Brent E. *Criminal Profiling: An Introduction to Behavioral Evidence Analysis*. San Diego, Calif.: Academic Press, 2002. A definitive source of information on deductive profiling methods. Describes crime scene reconstruction techniques as well as procedures for the collection and analysis of evidence.

See also: Bite-mark analysis; Crime scene investigation; Criminology; *Diagnostic and Statistical Manual of Mental Disorders*; Federal Bureau of Investigation Forensic Science Research and Training Center; Forensic psychiatry; Forensic psychology; Geographic profiling; Minnesota Multiphasic Personality Inventory; Police psychology; Psychopathic personality disorder; Questioned document analysis; *Silence of the Lambs, The*; Unabomber case.

Criminalistics

Definition: Use of scientific principles in the evaluation of physical evidence to detect, analyze, and solve crimes.

Significance: Criminalists work in various professional settings, but they have a common goal: To use the evidence from crime scenes to tell the stories of what happened there in order to link offenders with crime victims and scenes. Criminalists analyze and interpret various forms of physical evidence and then disseminate their findings in reports that can be used by law-enforcement officers, lawyers, judges, and juries.

The term "criminalistics" is often used interchangeably with "forensic science," and criminalistics may be broadly interpreted as the science of policing or the profession of forensic science. A narrower definition of criminalistics, however, focuses on the use of scientific principles in the evaluation of physical evidence of crimes. Science has an important role to play in the criminal justice system, and this role continues to develop and change as technology advances and improves the techniques available for investigating crimes. Criminalistics is a broad field that incorporates the use of the scientific method in the processing of evidence and the investigation of crimes.

The practitioners of criminalistics, known as criminalists, work in many different settings and in a variety of professions. Some work in crime labs as medical professionals, dentists (forensic odontologists), chemists, toxicologists, biologists, geneticists, physicists, geologists, or anthropologists, whereas others work as researchers in university settings. Generally, criminalists have some specialized training in science as it is applied to the recognition, collection, analysis, and preservation of physical evidence from crime scenes. Criminalists may also be found in courtrooms as expert witnesses, providing testimony to help juries understand the science behind particular findings concerning evidence.

Work of Criminalists and Criminologists

The discipline of criminalistics is often confused with the discipline of criminology, but the two differ in several ways. Although both criminalists and criminologists seek to understand the patterns and truth behind criminal activities, they use different approaches and ultimately have different goals. Criminalists seek to examine evidence in order to detect class and individual characteristics. The ultimate goal of a criminalist is to link three things: a victim, a crime scene, and an offender. The physical evidence that may be found at a crime scene may be invisible to the naked eye, such as fingerprints; it may be minute trace evidence, such as fibers from the clothing or the environment of the offender; or it may be as obvious as a body and a pool of blood. The job of the criminalist is to uncover the story that the evidence has to tell.

The investigative tasks in which criminalists are involved are widely varied. For example, a criminalist in a crime lab may examine the chemistry of inks in a threatening letter to identify the types of materials used in an effort to determine the origin of the letter. Another criminalist may apply techniques of forensic chemistry to understand the use of drugs in a homicide investigation. Yet another may examine fragments of a broken taillight from a hit-and-run accident, with the goal of identifying class characteristics that can be used to identify the type of vehicle from which the taillight came. In such a case, the criminalist's next job may be to look for individual characteristics in the evidence that could link it to a specific vehicle.

Criminologists are also interested in understanding why and how crime occurs, but they do not usually examine and evaluate the physical evidence left at crime scenes to try to link crimes to specific persons or specific groups. Rather, criminologists examine psychological and sociological causes of crime, such as mental illness, low cognitive abilities, certain personality traits, socioeconomic disadvantage, poor neighborhood conditions, and dysfunctional families. Criminologists often try to understand why crime occurs and attempt to predict who is at risk to engage in criminal endeavors by finding patterns in offending. They use various methods to achieve these ends, including survey research methods and statistical analyses.

Criminalists ask questions, examine patterns, and analyze evidence to answer legal questions. In other words, the starting point for the criminalist is to translate legal questions into scientific research questions. The goal is to use the evidence to formulate hypotheses and test the research questions. The evidence and the questions vary depending on the crime scene, but the goal remains the same: to disseminate the findings in reports that can be used by law-enforcement officers, lawyers, judges, and juries.

Stephanie K. Ellis

Further Reading

Barnett, Peter D. *Ethics in Forensic Science: Professional Standards for the Practice of Criminalistics.* Boca Raton, Fla.: CRC Press, 2001. Examines various ethical scenarios in light of the codes of ethics of the most prominent professional organizations for criminalists in the United States.

Eckert, William G., ed. *Introduction to Forensic Sciences.* 2d ed. Boca Raton, Fla.: CRC Press, 1997. Textbook intended for students considering careers in the forensic sciences includes discussion of all aspects of criminalistics.

Fisher, Barry A. J. *Techniques of Crime Scene Investigation.* 7th ed. Boca Raton, Fla.: CRC Press, 2004. Comprehensive work provides an overview of the uses of the forensic sciences, particularly in criminal investigations.

Gaensslen, R. E., Howard A. Harris, and Henry C. Lee. *Introduction to Forensic Science and Criminalistics.* New York: McGraw-Hill, 2008. Covers the types of forensic science techniques used in crime laboratories as well as those employed by private examiners in civil cases. Discusses various crime scene procedures and analyses.

Girard, James E. *Criminalistics: Forensic Science and Crime.* Sudbury, Mass.: Jones & Bartlett, 2008. Examines the procedures that criminalists undertake at crime scenes and in laboratories. Explains scientific concepts clearly for readers with no background in chemistry or biology.

Inman, Keith, and Norah Rudin. *Principles and Practice of Criminalistics: The Profession of Forensic Science.* Boca Raton, Fla.: CRC Press, 2001. Addresses the interpretation of various kinds of evidence, with a focus on best practices in the forensic science profession.

Saferstein, Richard. *Criminalistics: An Introduction to Forensic Science.* 9th ed. Upper Saddle River, N.J.: Pearson Prentice Hall, 2007. Comprehensive introductory textbook provides in-depth discussion of the activities carried out by criminalists.

See also: American Academy of Forensic Sciences; Crime laboratories; Crime scene investigation; Criminology; Forensic anthropology; Forensic entomology; Forensic geoscience; Forensic nursing; Forensic odontology; Forensic pathology; Forensic photography; Forensic toxicology; Living forensics; Locard's exchange principle; Medicine.

Criminology

Definition: Scientific study of crime and criminal behavior.

Significance: Criminologists examine how people interact with the criminal justice system. They also study crime victims to understand why offenders target them and what risk factors increase the likelihood of victimization. The research that criminologists conduct into the causes of crime and social deviance assists with the classification and treatment of offenders as well as the identification of forensic evidence in relation to crime.

More than two hundred years ago, two utilitarian philosophers, Cesare Beccaria (1738-1794) and Jeremy Bentham (1748-1832), studied human behavior. They asserted that human beings conduct cost-benefit analyses regarding their future behavior and then act out of greed and personal need. The theory now known as classical criminology is based on these premises: Potential criminal offenders have the free will to choose to act, and in making their decisions they compare risks to possible gains.

Although this theory lost popularity to newer theories over time, it has seen a resurgence in recent decades. Routine activities theory, for example, is a perspective in criminology that attempts to use deterrence theory to explain crime (and the treatment of criminal behavior). According to routine activities theory, in order for a crime to occur, three elements must be in place at the same time: someone who is motivated to commit that crime, a target worthy of victimizing, and the lack of a capable person to protect that target.

A potential criminal is less likely to victimize someone who has no money or material goods, or to victimize a person who is walking with a group of other people. Such circumstances should deter someone from committing a crime because they decrease the offender's chances of financial gain and increase the offender's chances of being caught, hurt, or identified. To design successful punishments based on deterrence theory, however, criminologists would

need to prove that all criminals are rational human beings, that they think about the consequences of their actions, and that they actually believe they could be caught.

Challenges to Classical Criminology

Several criticisms have been directed toward classical criminology and deterrence theory. First, many offenders commit crimes under conditions that make it likely for them to be caught (that is, witnesses or victims can identify them). Second, most offenders know the risks involved (arrest, jail time, loss of the respect of friends and family) when they commit crimes. Further, some criminals do know the difference between right and wrong, but they nevertheless cannot stop themselves from committing crimes; mental illness or very low IQ, for example, might prevent some from understanding the consequences of certain behaviors.

Given the shortcomings of classical criminology and deterrence theory, some criminologists have suggested other explanations for criminality. For example, some theorists believe that the behavior of offenders is not something that can be controlled. Instead, factors beyond these individuals explain why they would commit crimes under less-than-ideal circumstances. These theories are part of the positivist school of criminology.

Positivist Criminology and Other Theories

In the nineteenth century, Cesare Lombroso (1836-1909), known as the father of positivist criminology, developed a theory of criminal behavior related to his medical research. As a doctor, he had noted similar physical characteristics among delinquents. He asserted that criminals exhibited apelike physical traits and that they were biologically and physiologically similar to the primitive ancestors of humans. Some criminologists and other theorists postulated that psychological problems (such as personality disorders) caused criminal behavior. Sigmund Freud (1856-1939), the founder of psychoanalysis, believed that human behavior was controlled by unconscious processes.

Criminologists have also examined how environmental factors play a role in predicting criminality. Sociological explanations of crime focus on social structure, culture, poverty rates, racial disparities, and neighborhood instability in relation to criminal behavior. They also examine community changes, the strength and weakness of social controls, and the role of the family, school, peers, and religion in explaining behavior. All of these theories blame criminality on factors outside of offenders' control.

Criminologists have developed many competing theories that attempt to explain why crime happens and what the relationships are among offenders, victims, and the criminal justice system. Each theory has merit, yet a single explanation is insufficient, in part because each criminal is unique—an individual with a particular past and a person who may or may not have a conscience. Just as experts continue to debate the role of nature versus nurture in shaping human behavior, arguments continue between classical and positivist theorists in criminology. At the same time, some criminologists are at-

tempting to develop integrated theories that combine some of the characteristics of both to explain criminal behavior.

Gina M. Robertiello

Further Reading

Cohen, Albert K. *Delinquent Boys: The Culture of the Gang*. New York: Free Press, 1955. Early study explains class differences in expectations of boys and asserts that lower-class boys have less ability to defer gratification than do middle-class boys.

Cohen, Lawrence E., and Marcus Felson. "Social Change and Crime Rate Trends: A Routine Activity Approach." *American Sociological Review* 44 (1979): 588-608. Explains how people's everyday behaviors can increase their likelihood of becoming crime victims.

Cullen, Francis T., and Robert Agnew, eds. *Criminological Theory: Past to Present— Essential Readings*. 3d ed. Los Angeles: Roxbury, 2006. Collection of writings brings together past theories on crime and criminology and reports of more recent research in this field.

Merton, Robert K. "Social Structure and Anomie." *American Sociological Review* 3 (1938): 672-682. Classic article on strain theory as an explanation of criminal behavior provides a sociological viewpoint. Asserts that criminal offenders develop adaptations to the strain of their lack of opportunity to reach universal norms.

Shaw, Clifford R., and Henry D. McKay. *Juvenile Delinquency and Urban Areas: A Study of Rates of Delinquency in Relation to Differential Characteristics of Local Communities in American Cities*. Rev. ed. Chicago: University of Chicago Press, 1969. Addresses the ecology of crime, specifically focusing on the geographic locations of cities' central business districts in relation to where crime occurs.

Vito, Gennaro F., Jeffrey R. Maahs, and Ronald M. Holmes. *Criminology: Theory, Research, and Policy*. 2d ed. Sudbury, Mass.: Jones & Bartlett, 2007. Comprehensive text discusses the criminological theories of the past as well as modern theories and reviews the research conducted on these theories.

Winslow, Robert W., and Sheldon X. Zhang.

Cesare Lombroso, known as the father of positivist criminology, developed a theory that related criminal behavior to physical traits. (The Granger Collection, New York)

Criminology: A Global Perspective. Upper Saddle River, N.J.: Pearson Prentice Hall, 2008. Provides in-depth information on the field of criminology across the United States and internationally.

See also: Criminal personality profiling; Criminalistics; Drug abuse and dependence; Federal Bureau of Investigation; Forensic psychiatry; Forensic psychology; Geographic profiling; Insanity defense; Irresistible impulse rule; *Mens rea*; Police psychology; Psychopathic personality disorder; Racial profiling; Victimology.

Croatian and Bosnian war victim identification

Date: Began in 1996

The Event: Forensic scientists have been involved in ongoing efforts to identify the bodies of victims of genocide recovered from mass graves in Croatia and Bosnia and Herzegovina.

Significance: The deaths of thousands of individuals in the former Yugoslavia during the 1990's presented a daunting victim identification task for forensic scientists. Despite a number of factors hindering identification efforts, progress has been made, in large part owing to the work of the International Commission on Missing Persons, which established a program to collect DNA samples from living relatives of the missing.

The wars that took place in the former Yugoslavia in the period 1991-1995 resulted in the disappearance of an estimated forty thousand individuals from Croatia and Bosnia and Herzegovina alone. Many of those who disappeared were executed in acts of genocide and buried in mass graves throughout the countryside. In 1996, forensic scientists began the task of locating these clandestine grave sites and identifying the victims. Since that time, thousands of individuals have been excavated from

Forensic experts work on the collection of human remains at the site of a mass grave in a Bosnian village in July, 2006. This site is considered to be a secondary grave in which more than two hundred bodies that had been initially buried elsewhere were later dumped. *(AP/Wide World Photos)*

mass graves and their remains have been examined for purposes of identification and determination of the cause and manner of death. Law-enforcement investigators, pathologists, anthropologists, archaeologists, odontologists, radiologists, and database technicians have worked collaboratively in the identification process.

Identification

A number of agencies have played important roles in the efforts to identify genocide victims from Bosnia and Herzegovina and Croatia, including Physicians for Human Rights (PHR), the United Nations International Criminal Tribunal for the former Yugoslavia (UN-ICTY), the Bosnia State Commission on Missing Persons, and the International Commission on Missing Persons (ICMP). Much of the effort of the UN-ICTY has involved the documentation of genocide and has focused on the use of forensic evidence from mass graves in the prosecution of war criminals. Other agencies have placed greater emphasis on identification of remains and the return of those remains to living relatives.

A number of factors have hindered efforts to identify the bodies found in the mass graves of the former Yugoslavia. For one thing, antemortem (before death) medical and dental records for comparison to the bodies are nonexistent or difficult to find for most of the missing, unlike in the United States and Western Europe, where such records, along with fingerprints, are commonly used in the positive identification of remains. The unidentified population is also relatively homogeneous—the majority of the victims are young to middle-aged adult males. Further, methods for estimating age at death and stature from skeletal remains are often based on North American standards, which are inappropriate for Balkan populations; forensic anthropological assessments are thus limited.

For some time, the teams working on identifying the genocide victims relied heavily on clothing and personal effects (such as identification cards and religious items) found with the bodies in making presumptive identifications. It became increasingly apparent, however, that this method could lead to misidentifications, as the clothing and personal effects associated with remains may not have belonged to the deceased. Another hindrance to identification of remains has been the fact that many mass graves have been disturbed by human scavengers; as these grave robbers attempted to hide some remains in secondary locations, they created large-scale commingling of remains of individuals and also separated some intact bodies into multiple body parts.

International Commission on Missing Persons

In 1996, the ICMP was established to develop an antemortem database of missing persons that could be compared against postmortem records of unidentified remains. This effort, which is ongoing, requires that the ICMP develop close working relationships with the families of the missing; since 1999, this has included the widespread collection of DNA (deoxyribonucleic acid) samples from living relatives of missing persons. Because nuclear DNA is often degraded in the decomposed remains taken from mass graves, mitochondrial DNA (mtDNA), which is more abundant in the cell and less susceptible to degradation, is often used for identification. This type of DNA is inherited along the maternal line, so samples taken from unidentified remains can be matched only to relatives who share the same maternal mtDNA as the victim. DNA analysis has been essential in the identification of victims of the massacre that took place in the Bosnia and Herzegovina town of Srebrenica in July of 1995, in which approximately eight thousand Bosniak (Bosnian Muslim) men died.

The ICMP considers DNA testing the gold standard for positive identification; over time, the organization has placed decreasing emphasis on presumptive methods of identification. After the ICMP began its DNA program, the numbers of persons identified increased dramatically; in 2002 alone, approximately twelve hundred individuals were identified, more than a tenfold increase over the numbers identified in all the previous years combined. New developments in DNA technology continue to provide the best avenue for identification of remains in Bosnia and Herzegovina and Croatia, where traditional methods have had limited success. However, forensic archaeologists, anthropologists, and pathologists continue to play pivotal roles in the meticulous excavation of remains recovered from mass graves, in the sorting of commingled remains from primary and secondary grave sites, and in the assessment of the circumstances surrounding death.

Eric J. Bartelink

Further Reading

Haglund, William D. "Recent Mass Graves: An Introduction." In *Advances in Forensic Taphonomy: Method, Theory, and Archaeological Perspectives*, edited by William D. Haglund and Marcella H. Sorg. Boca Raton, Fla.: CRC Press, 2002. Comprehensive overview for forensic professionals addresses the issues involved in body identification in cases of mass graves and war crimes investigations; focuses on the former Yugoslavia.

Komar, Debra A. "Lessons from Srebrenica: The Contributions and Limitations of Physical Anthropology in Identifying Victims of War Crimes." *Journal of Forensic Sciences* 48, no. 4 (2003): 1-4. Offers an illuminating discussion of the prospects and challenges of the use of anthropological methods in the identification of victims from Srebrenica, Bosnia.

Simmons, Tal. "Taphonomy of a Karstic Cave Execution Site at Hrgar, Bosnia-Herzegovina." In *Advances in Forensic Taphonomy: Method, Theory, and Archaeological Perspectives*, edited by William D. Haglund and Marcella H. Sorg. Boca Raton, Fla.: CRC Press, 2002. Penetrating discussion for forensic professionals addresses the investigation of execution and disposal sites of genocide victims in Bosnia-Herzegovina.

Skinner, Mark F., and Jon Sterenberg. "Turf Wars: Authority and Responsibility for the Investigation of Mass Graves." *Forensic Science International* 151 (2005): 221-232. Discusses the ethics, professionalism, and responsibility of forensic scientists in relation to human rights investigations. Also addresses the challenges faced by forensic teams composed of individuals from a wide variety of backgrounds.

Skinner, Mark F., Heather P. York, and Melissa A. Connor. "Postburial Disturbance of Graves in Bosnia-Herzegovina." In *Advances in Forensic Taphonomy: Method, Theory, and Archaeological Perspectives*, edited by William D. Haglund and Marcella H. Sorg. Boca Raton, Fla.: CRC Press, 2002. Discussion aimed at forensic professionals focuses on the challenges associated with the investigation of primary and secondary mass graves in Bosnia-Herzegovina.

Williams, Erin D., and John D. Crews. "From Dust to Dust: Ethical and Practical Issues Involved in the Location, Exhumation, and Identification of Bodies from Mass Graves." *Croatian Medical Journal* 44, no. 3 (2003): 251-258. Discusses the ethics and responsibility of forensic professionals working on human rights investigations. Addresses forensic, cultural, and psychological aspects related to genocide investigations.

See also: Argentine disappeared children; Asian tsunami victim identification; Beslan hostage crisis victim identification; Buried body locating; Ethics; Expert witnesses; Forensic anthropology; Forensic archaeology; Genocide; Mass graves; Skeletal analysis; Taphonomy.

Cross-contamination of evidence

Definition: Failure to preserve the purity or exclusivity of physical evidence related to a crime scene through the introduction of transferred materials from other sections of the crime scene, various related crime scenes, or other sources.

Significance: Crime scenes yield evidence that can link suspects, victims, and the actions of persons present when the crimes occurred. The collection and preservation of evidential materials without cross-contamination is thus crucial, as incorrect conclusions may be drawn from contaminated evidence.

Forensic investigation of a crime scene relies on Locard's exchange principle, which states that when two objects come in contact, they exchange trace evidence. A crime scene thus contains evidence that may place a suspect at the scene, and analysis of that evidence may reveal the associations between perpetrator and crime that are necessary for a prosecutor to obtain a conviction in a court of law. Evidence may also refute theories that link a suspect to a crime and thus may exonerate the innocent.

The methods used in the collection and preservation of evidence are intended to ensure that the preserved materials did originate from the crime scene, that the materials are pertinent to the crime, and that the materials can be analyzed in a comparable state to the way they were found at the scene. Cross-contamination of evidence results from the failure to protect an evidence sample from the transfer of other material onto or into it. Evidence may become cross-contaminated at the crime scene during collection and packaging of evidential materials, during transportation to laboratories or other facilities, during storage, or while it is undergoing analysis.

At the crime scene, cross-contamination of evidence is most likely to occur when the actions of first responders and others moves materials such as hairs, fibers, and fluids around the scene. Evidence may also be compromised by cross-contamination when investigators do not use crime scene protective gear or use such gear improperly, resulting in their leaving their own fingerprints, hair, and fluids at the scene. Also, when investigators leave the crime scene to search related areas (such as a suspect's car), evidence may be transferred from one scene to the other, resulting in cross-contamination.

Materials other than the evidential materials gathered at the crime scene may cause cross-contamination if the evidence samples are not properly packaged and safeguarded during transportation to labs or other locations. In addition, evidence must be stored properly and protected while it is being analyzed or tested to prevent cross-contamination.

Taylor Shaw

Further Reading

Genge, N. E. *The Forensic Casebook: The Science of Crime Scene Investigation*. New York: Ballantine, 2002.

Pentland, Peter, and Pennie Stoyles. *Forensic Science*. Philadelphia: Chelsea House, 2003.

Platt, Richard. *Crime Scene: The Ultimate Guide to Forensic Science*. New York: Dorling Kindersley, 2003.

See also: Accident investigation and reconstruction; Crime scene investigation; Crime scene protective gear; Disturbed evidence; DNA extraction from hair, bodily fluids, and tissues; Evidence processing; First responders; Locard's exchange principle; Physical evidence; Quality control of evidence; Trace and transfer evidence.

Cryptology and number theory

Definitions: Cryptology is the scientific study of the hiding, disguising, or encryption of messages. Number theory is the branch of mathematics that is concerned with the properties of the positive integers.

Significance: Computer security experts use public-key cryptography to ensure the confidentiality of electronically transmitted messages through encryption and the integrity of messages with digital signatures. Cryptology is an important part of investigations regarding attempts by computer hackers to decrypt messages or modify digital signatures. Hackers sometimes use public-key encryption to hide attacks, such as Trojan horses, and forensic analysis techniques have been developed to detect such attempts.

Cryptology encompasses both cryptography, the hiding of messages, and cryptanalysis, the revealing of hidden messages. Number theory is involved in cryptography in many ways, but its most important use is in public-key encryption.

A number of computationally intensive algorithms exist in number theory, one of which is factoring the product of two large prime numbers. In 1978, Ron Rivest, Adi Shamir, and Leonard Adleman published a public-key encryption algorithm named RSA (from the initials of the inventors' last names) that uses the difficulty of factoring large numbers to protect the value of a private key. RSA has been used to encrypt electronic files to ensure their confidentiality and to create digital signatures for e-mail to ensure its integrity.

When computer hackers want to see encrypted files, they often devise attacks to steal the receivers' private keys, which will allow them to decrypt the files. When such attacks occur, forensic experts can use tools designed to detect the attacks; similar tools are available to defend against such attacks. Hackers recognize that digital signatures can be used to guarantee the integrity of e-mail. They often intercept e-mail messages, modify the contents, and then attach invalid signatures. The hackers then have to ensure that the receivers use fake public keys to check the signatures. One way hackers could do this would be by replacing certificate authorities' public keys in the recipients' e-mails. Antivirus software can protect against this kind of attack by performing its usual checks of e-mail.

Encryption and Number Theory

Encryption is the process of using a key to transform a readable plaintext message into an unreadable ciphertext message. Decryption reverses encryption to recover the plaintext message. When the encryption and decryption key are the same, the encryption is described as algorithm-symmetric. Although symmetric algorithms are complex, they do not use much number theory.

Public-key encryption algorithms, which are often based on number theory, use different keys for encryption and decryption. The most famous public-key encryption algorithm, RSA, selects two large prime numbers (a prime number is divisible only by one and by itself) and forms a modulus, n, as their product. The modulus n is too large to be factored. The ciphertext message, C, is created by raising the integer value of the plaintext message, M, to the power e modulo n, and the plaintext message is recovered from C by raising C to the power d modulo n. The public key is the pair (e, n) and the private key is the pair (d, n).

RSA is widely used for encrypting files and signing messages. It has proven to be very resistant to brute-force attacks on the private keys. A major part of the RSA scheme involves creation of the private keys and the safe distribution of the corresponding public keys. Usually, the private key is safely transmitted to its owner by a trusted public-key infrastructure (PKI) vendor who then uses digital certificates, which contain the owner's public key and are signed by the PKI vendor, to distribute the public key.

Computer Hacking and Encryption

In 1976, Whitfield Diffie and Martin Hellman developed an algorithm that allowed two people to create a shared symmetric key. The algorithm is similar to the RSA public-key algorithm and makes considerable use of modular exponential arithmetic. To create the shared symmetric key, each person involved uses a secret number that never leaves his or her computer but generates the shared secret key as the result of several data exchanges. If a hacker knows that a purchaser and an online store are generating a symmetric key with the Diffie-Hillman key exchange, the hacker could drop a Trojan horse into the purchaser's computer, capture the secret information, and then masquerade as the purchaser to buy items for personal gain. In investigating such an attack, a forensic expert could log into the purchaser's computer and check to see if the Trojan horse is still there; if it is, it might provide information on the location of the hacker.

Hackers can gain access to other people's computers in a number of ways, not the least of which is through Web browsers. When they gain access, they often try to leave files that con-

Early Cryptographers

Julius Caesar is generally recognized as the earliest military leader to utilize ciphers to encrypt and decode messages. His ciphering system became the basis for many more advanced ciphers in later centuries. Eventually, mechanical devices were invented to make encryption and decryption faster and easier. In the late eighteenth century, Thomas Jefferson invented a drumlike device that was used to encode and decode messages. During World War II, the Enigma machine, a brilliant conception of the German military, was used to add complexity to codes. Enigma's scheme was eventually broken, first by Polish mathematicians suspicious of the intentions of Germany's Nazi rulers. The Polish then shared their knowledge with the French and British. None of these early pioneers in cryptology could have envisioned the impacts that computers would have on the necessity for systems of covert communication to be used not only in wars and by spies but also by average people in daily life.

Heidi V. Schumacher

tain worms, Trojan horses, or viruses. Given these threats, computers have become increasingly well equipped with antivirus software that is designed to protect users from such attacks. One of the most important techniques used by antivirus software is to check all files and quarantine any files that look suspicious. A clever trick used by modern hackers is to encrypt attack files with private RSA keys so that the files are not detected by antivirus software. This allows the hackers to return later, decrypt the files, and carry out their intended attacks. Web browser helper objects are especially susceptible to this kind of delayed attack. Increasingly sophisticated forensic software has been developed to catch multilevel attacks of this type.

George M. Whitson III

Further Reading

Hellman, Martin. "An Overview of Public Key Cryptography." *IEEE Communications Magazine*, May, 2002, 42-49. Very good survey article provides basic information. Written by one of the founders of the field of public key encryption.

Mandia, Kevin, Chris Prosise, and Matt Pepe. *Incident Response and Computer Forensics.* 2d ed. Emeryville, Calif.: McGraw-Hill/Osborne, 2003. Includes several chapters on incident response to cryptology attacks.

Shieneier, Bruce. "Inside Risks: The Uses and Abuses of Biometrics." *Communications of the ACM* 42 (November, 1999): 136. Brief but informative article describes methods of defeating encryption by subversion.

Shinder, Debra Littlejohn. *Scene of the Cybercrime: Computer Forensics Handbook.* Rockland, Mass.: Syngress, 2002. Bridges the gap between the computer professionals who provide the technology for cybercrime investigations and the law-enforcement professionals who investigate the crimes.

Vacca, John R. *Computer Forensics: Computer Crime Scene Investigation.* 2d ed. Hingham, Mass.: Charles River Media, 2005. Provides a good introduction to computer forensics. Devotes several chapters to cryptology forensics.

Yan, Song Y. *Cryptanalytic Attacks on RSA.* New York: Springer, 2008. Covers most of the known cryptanalytic attacks and defenses of the RSA cryptographic system. Also provides a good introduction to the use of number theory in the RSA encryption algorithm.

See also: Computer crimes; Computer forensics; Computer hacking; Computer viruses and worms; Crime scene search patterns; Electronic voice alteration; Internet tracking and tracing; Steganography.

CSI: Crime Scene Investigation

Date: First aired on October 6, 2000

Identification: Popular television series involving a team of crime scene investigators who solve unusual crimes through the collection of physical evidence and analysis of this evidence using technologically advanced forensic procedures.

Significance: The original *CSI: Crime Scene Investigation* television series and its two spin-offs (*CSI: Miami* and *CSI: NY*) are very popular both within and outside the United States. Some criminal justice authorities and legal scholars have voiced concern that exposure to these shows has generated unrealistic expectations in the general public about the collection and forensic analysis of crime-related evidence. This phenomenon is commonly referred to as the "*CSI* effect." Although the existence of such an effect has not been confirmed by systematic research, anecdotal evidence of the *CSI* effect has been widely shared among legal authorities, and concerns regarding the television programs' negative impact continue to be a topic for discussion and debate.

CSI: Crime Scene Investigation is a television crime drama that depicts how a team of crimi-

Crime scene investigators Catherine Willows (Marg Helgenberger) and Gil Grissom (William Petersen) examine evidence in an episode of *CSI: Crime Scene Investigation.* (Ron Jaffe/CBS/Landov)

nal investigators solve crimes by gathering and examining forensic evidence using technically advanced methods and tools. Created by Anthony E. Zuiker, the original *CSI* debuted in 2000 and soon became one of the most-watched crime dramas on television. The show's popularity can be attributed to its fresh and modern portrayal of criminal investigation. What made *CSI* different from traditional police shows of the past was its story lines, which focus more on the "how" of crime than on the "who." The popularity of *CSI* eventually led to two spin-off series, *CSI: Miami* began airing in 2002 and *CSI: NY* in 2004. Both of these programs follow the same premise: a team of crime scene investigators solve crimes through the collection and ex-

amination of forensic evidence. By 2007, the original *CSI* was being aired in two hundred countries and was watched by an estimated two billion viewers. In addition to the two spin-off television series, *CSI* spawned comic books, novels, and computer games.

Examples of Forensic Evidence

CSI episodes depict many different types of physical evidence that can be collected at crime scenes as well as the various tools and procedures that can be used to analyze such evidence. The types of physical evidence that can be collected from crime scenes vary greatly and depend heavily on location and type of crime. For example, the physical evidence available for collection at the scene of a robbery is quite different from that available at a murder scene. Physical evidence might include marks on a victim's body, such as abrasions or bite marks. Fingerprints on a door or a window frame also constitute physical evidence, as does blood left behind by a likely perpetrator. Trace evidence is a type of physical evidence that can be collected and forensically examined; this kind of evidence is commonly depicted in *CSI* episodes. Trace evidence is found when a small amount of material has transferred from either one location or person to another location or person. Examples of trace evidence include gunshot residue and fibers from clothing or carpeting.

Just as many types of physical evidence can be found at crime scenes, forensic scientists use many different tools and procedures to examine and test physical evidence. The tools of crime scene investigators may range from the brushes used to apply powder to fingerprint areas to the zNose, an "electronic nose" that has the ability to detect and identify different types of gases and vapors. Crime scene investigators use a number of different tools to collect blood samples, fiber samples, tire impressions, shoe impressions, and bite marks. These and many other types of tools allow for the identification and collection of potentially important samples of physical evidence. By collecting and testing samples from crime scenes, forensic scientists help to piece together the events that took place there, which can lead to the identification of the perpetrators.

The Impact of CSI

In the television world, crime scene investigators have a variety of responsibilities in addition to the collection and analysis of the physical evidence found at crime scenes. On *CSI* they also interview witnesses, victims, and suspects. If the forensic evidence reveals an individual's guilt, the crime scene investigators are involved in tracking down, confronting, and arresting the perpetrator. These dramatic embellishments of the role of crime scene investigators and their use of forensic evidence have generated a great deal of concern and debate among legal authorities. This concern is directed at the possibility that *CSI* and similar shows have created unre-

alistic expectations among viewers and the general public regarding how forensic evidence is used in the criminal justice system, and these expectations may have repercussions in the courts. For example, when *CSI* viewers serve on juries, they may expect all types of forensic evidence, specifically DNA evidence, to be presented during trial, and they may expect this evidence to be conclusive in revealing the guilt or innocence of defendants. This potential problem is popularly referred to as the *CSI* effect.

Although this topic has received a great deal of attention, the existence of the *CSI* effect has yet to be confirmed. Despite many anecdotal reports from prosecuting attorneys and other legal authorities, no systematic empirical research has proven that the *CSI* effect has had any real impact on legal proceedings. In another way, however, *CSI* and similar television programs have had a clear impact: After they began to air, forensic science programs across the United States experienced noticeable increases in applications.

Erin J. Farley

Further Reading

Cather, Karin H. "The *CSI* Effect: Fake TV and Its Impact on Jurors in Criminal Cases." *The Prosecutor* (National District Attorneys Association), March/April, 2004, 9-15. Presents interviews with attorneys to show support for the seriousness of the concept of the *CSI* effect.

Genge, N. E. *The Forensic Casebook: The Science of Crime Scene Investigation*. New York: Ballantine, 2002. Good source for an overall description of different kinds of crime scene investigators and their job responsibilities.

Marrinan, Corinne, and Steve Parker. *Ultimate "CSI: Crime Scene Investigation."* New York: Dorling Kindersley, 2006. Discussion of *CSI* focuses on how forensic evidence and techniques have been used on the program.

Podlas, Kimberlianne. "'The *CSI* Effect': Exposing the Media Myth." *Fordham Intellectual Property, Media, and Entertainment Law Journal* 16 (Winter, 2006): 429-465. Presents findings of a research study that call into question the existence of the *CSI* effect.

Ramsland, Katherine. *The "C.S.I." Effect*. New

York: Berkley Books, 2006. Not a critical discussion of the so-called *CSI* effect but rather a discussion of how various types of forensic evidence are used in real criminal investigations, with a focus on demystifying forensic processes and technologies. Features examples from the *CSI* program throughout.

_____. *The Forensic Science of "C.S.I."* New York: Berkley Books, 2001. Uses the television show to discuss how various types of forensic evidence are employed in real-world cases. Attempts to demystify the process of forensic investigation.

Tyler, Tom R. "Viewing *CSI* and the Threshold of Guilt: Managing Truth and Justice in Reality and Fiction." *Yale Law Journal* 115, no. 5 (2006): 1050-1085. Offers a relatively complex discussion of the *CSI* effect, with a review of prior research findings that support or refute the existence of the effect.

See also: Celebrity cases; *Cold Case*; Composite drawing; Crime laboratories; Crime scene documentation; Crime scene investigation; Crime scene measurement; Crime scene reconstruction and staging; *Forensic Files*; Journalism; Literature and forensic science; Misconceptions fostered by media.

Cyanoacrylate fuming. *See* Superglue fuming

Cybercrime. *See* Computer crimes

Cyberstalking

Definition: Electronic communication in which perpetrators repeatedly contact victims with the intent of abusing, exploiting, annoying, threatening, slandering, terrifying, or embarrassing them.

Significance: Cyberstalkers use the anonymity allowed by electronic communications technologies to disguise their true identities while they harass and threaten their victims. Depending on its severity, cyberstalking can be a misdemeanor or a crime punishable by jail time. Investigating cyberstalking is difficult for several reasons, not least of which is the lack of physical evidence in many cases. To find and prosecute cyberstalkers and authenticate the electronic evidence in these cases, law-enforcement personnel must typically use computer forensics investigative methods.

Rather than engaging in physical confrontation, cyberstalkers take advantage of the impersonal, nonconfrontational, and anonymous nature of the Internet and e-mail to harass or threaten their victims. This makes it difficult for authorities to measure the full extent of the crime of cyberstalking. Perpetrators can use various Internet-based technologies from any location; they may live next door to their victims or on the other side of the world.

In cases where cyberstalkers know their victims, the most common motive is revenge. Cyberstalking frequently occurs in workplace settings, perpetrated by employees who are angry with management or fellow workers. Pedophiles also sometime engage in cyberstalking, using social network Web sites, such as MySpace, to find potential victims. Law-enforcement investigations of cyberstalking may be valuable to defend against child sexual exploitation and other physical crimes, as many cyberstalking attacks have the potential to escalate to violent criminal acts. Some law-enforcement agencies are able to respond aggressively to cases of cyberstalking by following trails of digital evidence and seizing computers of suspects, but others lack the expertise and resources to pursue such cases.

Legal Defenses Against Cyberstalking

The incidence of cyberstalking has increased over the years as growing numbers of people around the world have gained access to the Internet. In response to this trend, nations have enacted increasingly strict legislation to deal with cyberstalking. The first antistalking legislation in the United States went into effect in 1990. Since 1999, federal and state jurisdictions have amended existing general antistalking and antiharassment statutes to include instances of cyberstalking or have enacted new statues to protect victims of cyberstalking.

By mid-2007, forty-five U.S. states had laws against cyberstalking. The federal antistalking law prohibits anonymous Internet communications "with intent to annoy, abuse, threaten or harass." Laws to combat cyberstalking include federal statute 18 U.S.C. 875(c), which makes it a federal crime, "punishable by up to five years in prison and a fine of up to $250,000, to transmit any communication in interstate or foreign commerce containing a threat to injure the person or another." Because most states have also enacted their own specific legislation, investigators as well as victims of cyberstalking in the United States may face complicated sets of laws offering varying definitions, protections, and penalties.

A growing number of law-enforcement agencies have recognized the serious nature and extent of cyberstalking and have responded by providing training in computer forensic techniques and software. In large cities, such as New York and Los Angeles, police departments and district attorneys' offices have developed specialized units to investigate cyberstalking cases. The Federal Bureau of Investigation (FBI) has established Computer Crime Squads throughout the country; these units investigate all kinds of computer crime, including cyberstalking.

Nature of Cyberstalking

Cyberstalking is similar to traditional forms of stalking in several ways. Many stalkers, both online and off, are motivated by a desire to control their victims, and both kinds of stalkers engage in behaviors aimed at gaining control. Online forums such as chat rooms, blogs, and social network sites make it easy for cyberstalkers to trick third parties into harassing or threatening the cyberstalkers' intended victims. To carry out such ruses, cyberstalkers post inflammatory or salacious messages in online forums while impersonating their victims, causing viewers of the messages to send unwelcome or threatening messages to the victims. Cyberstalkers with knowledge of their victims' screen names may use software that advises them when their victims are online; the stalkers then send their victims lewd or threatening instant messages.

Cyberstalking is different from other types of stalking in that it may not involve any physical contact at all. As with other types of stalking, the majority of perpetrators are men and the majority of victims are women, although cases of women cyberstalking men and same-sex cyberstalking have been reported.

Tracking Down Cyberstalkers

In cyberstalking cases, computers and the Internet are the weapons. Experienced cyberstalkers often use anonymous remailers, which can make it impossible for investigators to determine the true sources of e-mail and instant

---

Contentious Legislation Versus Legal Recourse

In the United States, laws concerning cyberstalking have generated controversy because many civil libertarians maintain that prohibiting anonymous communication that merely annoys others is a restraint on free speech online. They assert that the right of free speech extends to the Internet and even includes anonymous free speech. In contrast, many of the victims of cyberstalking have argued that legislation is necessary to provide victims of this behavior with legal recourse.

messages, Internet Relay Chat (IRC), or other electronic communication. Anonymity gives cyberstalkers an advantage over investigators. Anonymous services on the Internet allow individuals to create free Web-based e-mail accounts, and most Internet service providers (ISPs) provide their services without authenticating or confirming users' identities. The investigation of cyberstalking thus requires the use of sophisticated computer and e-mail forensics methods to trace cyberstalkers' activities through their phone records. Investigators usually need subpoenas to obtain such records, whether from telephone companies or ISPs.

After investigators have identified suspects in cyberstalking cases, or the addresses of suspects' computers, they generally obtain search warrants that allow them to seize the computers, any electronic storage equipment, and digital devices. Because of the fragile nature of such equipment, these are usually transported to computer forensics labs, where experts make copies of the electronic evidence to investigate further.

Law-enforcement officers are sometimes frustrated by jurisdictional limitations in cyberstalking cases, as when they find that stalkers are located in other cities or states, making further investigation difficult or impossible. Officers who travel to other legal jurisdictions to continue their investigations may have trouble obtaining assistance from other agencies. It is likely that such limitations on law enforcement will diminish in the future, as cybercrimes, including cyberstalking, become increasingly widespread.

Statutes that require a showing of a "credible threat" may hinder prosecution in some cyberstalking cases. Cyberstalkers often do not threaten their victims overtly or in person, although they engage in conduct that would cause reasonable persons to fear violence. In the context of cyberstalking, the legal requirement of the existence of a credible threat is especially problematic because cyberstalkers may in fact be located far away from their victims (although their victims do not know that), and so the threats they pose might not be considered credible.

Preserving Evidence

Connecting suspects to the crime of cyberstalking is a challenge without some evidence in addition to the electronic evidence, such as a former romantic or work-related link between the stalker and victim. With or without such other evidence, the key to successful prosecution in cyberstalking cases is the preservation of the full electronic trail of evidence. Tracking down cyberstalkers and convicting them depends a great deal on the cooperation of the victims. Victims of cyberstalking should save all communications from their harassers as evidence; these should not be altered or edited in any way. Victims should also keep logs of the times and dates of their Internet activity and when they received communications from the stalkers.

The requirements for the preservation of electronic evidence for legal purposes differ from the requirements for other types of evidence. The admissibility of electronic evidence in court depends on the existence of a reliable record of chain of custody for that evidence. Investigators must be able to demonstrate that they have not added to or otherwise altered the data or communications presented as evidence. They can help to satisfy this requirement by write protecting and virus checking all the media used. Investigators must be able to demonstrate to the court that what is purported to be a complete forensics copy of a suspect's hard drive or storage medium is indeed such a copy.

Linda Volonino

Further Reading

Bocij, Paul. *Cyberstalking: Harassment in the Internet Age and How to Protect Your Family*. Westport, Conn.: Praeger, 2004. Discusses how Internet and communication technologies are used to harass and what individuals can do to prevent technological harassment.

D'Ovidio, Robert, and James Doyle. "A Study on Cyberstalking: Understanding Investigative Hurdles." *FBI Law Enforcement Bulletin* 72 (March, 2003): 10-17. Bulletin for law-enforcement personnel focuses on the challenges of tracking the digital trails of cyberstalkers.

Proctor, Mike. *How to Stop a Stalker*. Amherst, N.Y.: Prometheus Books, 2003. Provides information on various types of stalkers and their methods of stalking and discusses the courses of action people can take when they are being stalked. Presents many examples taken from actual cases.

Smith, Russell G., Peter Grabosky, and Gregor Urbas. *Cyber Criminals on Trial*. New York: Cambridge University Press, 2004. Discusses the results of an international study of the ways in which cybercriminals are handled by different nations' judicial systems.

Willard, Nancy E. *Cyberbullying and Cyberthreats: Responding to the Challenge of Online Social Aggression, Threats, and Distress*. 2d ed. Champaign, Ill.: Research Press. 2007. Discusses cyberstalking and other cyberbullying against students and offers advice regarding how victims can prevent and respond to those threats.

See also: Computer crimes; Computer forensics; Computer Fraud and Abuse Act of 1984; Computer hacking; Electronic voice alteration; Internet tracking and tracing; Rape.

Daubert v. Merrell Dow Pharmaceuticals

Date: Ruling issued on June 28, 1993
Court: U.S. Supreme Court
Significance: In *Daubert v. Merrell Dow Pharmaceuticals*, the U.S. Supreme Court held that under the Federal Rules of Evidence, a judge is required to make an independent reliability and relevance determination before allowing expert testimony to be admissible.

Daubert v. Merrell Dow Pharmaceuticals was a suit brought by two minor children who were born with serious birth defects, which they alleged were the result of their mothers' ingestion during pregnancy of Benedectin, a prescription antinausea drug marketed by Merrell Dow Pharmaceuticals. A U.S. district court granted summary judgment in favor of Merrell Dow because a great deal of scientific evidence demonstrated that Benedectin did not cause birth defects and because the scientific evidence offered by the plaintiffs was found to be inadmissible, as the evidence lacked general acceptance in the scientific community. The court of appeals agreed, stating that expert opinion is inadmissible unless the scientific technique on which the opinion is based is generally accepted by the relevant scientific community.

The U.S. Supreme Court disagreed and remanded the case for a new determination of the admissibility of the scientific evidence in question. The Court explained that the Federal Rules of Evidence (FRE) govern the admissibility of evidence in federal court, thus the rule stated in *Frye v. United States* (1923) requiring general acceptance of a scientific technique is no longer an absolute requirement and has been superseded by Federal Rule of Evidence 702. Under the governing rule of FRE 702, judges should examine the reliability and relevance of proffered expert scientific evidence in determining the admissibility of that evidence.

Specific Requirements of *Daubert* and FRE 702

To determine the reliability of scientific evidence, judges should assess whether the methodology is scientifically valid and whether the methodology offers scientific knowledge that will assist the trier of fact (the jury in a jury trial, the judge in a bench trial) in determining the outcome of the case. Specifically, the four factors that judges should consider are whether the methodology and scientific evidence being offered can be and has been tested for validity, whether the scientific theory or technique has been peer-reviewed and published, what the known or potential rate of error is of the technique and the existence and maintenance of standards that control the technique's operation and use, and whether the methodology is generally accepted by the relevant scientific community.

In using the consideration of these four factors as a guide for evaluating scientific evidence, trial judges have great latitude in determining the reliability of evidence. The Supreme Court thus concluded in *Daubert v. Merrell Dow* that general acceptance of scientific evidence is no longer a precondition of admissibility under the Federal Rules of Evidence, but that factor may still have some bearing. In *Kumho Tire Company v. Carmichael* (1999), the Supreme Court later extended the requirements of *Daubert* in a loosened form to all experts, regardless of whether or not the experts are testifying as to scientific evidence.

Applications of the *Daubert* Standard

Because forensic scientific evidence is often presented in the courtroom through the use of expert testimony, the *Daubert* standard greatly affects the admissibility of such evidence. For example, evidence that was previously rejected under *Frye* as not being generally accepted has been reexamined by courts to see if the evidence does embody good science. Polygraph results were viewed as inadmissible under *Frye*, but under *Daubert*, this form of evidence is no longer subject to a per se ban. Although polygraph evidence is still rarely admitted, judges at least give its admissibility minimal consideration.

In some cases, courts have reevaluated the validity and applicability of evidence that many would previously have accepted automatically as being valid under *Frye*. For instance, court decisions allowing handwriting comparisons and fingerprint identification date back to before the 1920's, but no empirical studies were conducted on the validity of handwriting comparisons or fingerprint identification because empirical scientific foundations for these methods were not required under *Frye*.

Some commentators have questioned the tacit acceptance by courts of forensic fingerprint

identification evidence because they believe that such evidence is not as reliable as previously assumed, as indicated by erroneous convictions and inconsistencies in protocols. It is extremely difficult to make accurate comparisons of poor-quality latent fingerprints left at a crime scene with rolled fingerprints taken directly from a defendant, and such comparisons often require fingerprint analysts to make subjective assessments. The scientific bases underlying fingerprint identification have yet to be tested fully under *Daubert*, but this form of evidence may one day be found to be unreliable and inadmissible. No appellate court has held that such evidence is definitively inadmissible, but in 2003 the U.S. Court of Appeals for the Fourth Circuit, in *United States v. Crisp*, became the first appellate court to hold that expert testimony on handwriting comparisons and fingerprint identification is admissible under *Daubert*.

The *Daubert* decision thus created a gatekeeper role for judges, who became responsible for assessing the reliability of the opinions of expert witnesses. This new role might result in previously accepted expert testimony being found inadmissible at the same time modern techniques of forensic science may have greater opportunities to alter the outcomes of cases as they are deemed admissible by more courts.

Vivian Bodey

From the Court's Decision in *Daubert v. Merrell Dow*

Respondent expresses apprehension that abandonment of "general acceptance" as the exclusive requirement for admission will result in a "free-for-all" in which befuddled juries are confounded by absurd and irrational pseudoscientific assertions. In this regard, respondent seems to us to be overly pessimistic about the capabilities of the jury and of the adversary system generally. Vigorous cross-examination, presentation of contrary evidence, and careful instruction on the burden of proof are the traditional and appropriate means of attacking shaky but admissible evidence.... Additionally, in the event the trial court concludes that the scintilla of evidence presented supporting a position is insufficient to allow a reasonable juror to conclude that the position more likely than not is true, the court remains free to direct a judgment, . . . and likewise to grant summary judgment. . . . These conventional devices, rather than wholesale exclusion under an uncompromising "general acceptance" test, are the appropriate safeguards where the basis of scientific testimony meets the standards of Rule 702.

Further Reading

Benedict, Nathan. "Fingerprints and the *Daubert* Standard for Admission of Scientific Evidence: Why Fingerprints Fails and a Proposed Remedy." *Arizona Law Review* 46 (Fall, 2004): 519-549. Explores the history behind the *Daubert* standard and its possible application to fingerprint identification evidence.

Judicial Gatekeeping Project, ed. *The Judge's Role as Gatekeeper: Responsibilities and Power*. Cambridge, Mass.: Berkman Center for Internet and Society, Harvard Law School, 1999. Collection of essays, written for a general audience, provides detailed discussion of *Daubert* and the case's ramifications.

Klein, Daniel A. "Reliability of Scientific Technique and Its Acceptance Within Scientific Community as Affecting Admissibility, at

Federal Trial, of Expert Testimony as to Result of Test or Study Based on Such Technique: Modern Cases." In *American Law Reports, Federal*. St. Paul, Minn.: Thomson/West, 2007. Offers analysis of court cases dealing with the admissibility of expert testimony involving a wide range of scientific and technical areas and techniques.

National Research Council. *The Polygraph and Lie Detection*. Washington, D.C.: National Academies Press, 2003. Provides interesting discussion of the polygraph and concludes that use of the polygraph for legal purposes is not likely to increase.

Rothstein, Paul F., Myrna S. Raeder, and David Crump. *Evidence*. St. Paul, Minn.: Thomson/West, 2003. Presents a broad discussion of the Federal Rules of Evidence as well as a detailed description of the history and current analysis of the admissibility of expert testimony and scientific evidence.

See also: Cognitive interview techniques; Courts and forensic evidence; DNA fingerprinting; Drug and alcohol evidence rules; Ethics; Expert witnesses; Federal Rules of Evidence; *Frye v. United States*; Polygraph analysis; Pseudoscience in forensic practice; Toxic torts.

Decomposition of bodies

Definition: Process by which cadavers become skeletons through the destruction of the body's soft tissue.

Significance: Understanding the processes that take place during decomposition of a human body can help investigators determine a number of important pieces of information, including approximate time of death and whether the body was moved after death. Sometimes, the decomposition of remains can contribute to the determination of cause and manner of death. Investigators need to remember that because of the number of variables involved in decomposition, it is rare to find two instances that share identical processes.

Decomposition begins at the moment of death, when all of the internal functions that work together to maintain the body's homeostasis cease. At this stage, decomposition manifests as the result of two processes: autolysis, which is the breaking down of tissues by the body's own internal chemicals and enzymes; and putrefaction, which is the breaking down of tissues by bacteria. These processes release gases that are the chief source of the distinctive odor of dead bodies. A great many factors affect the progression of decomposition, accelerating, hampering, or otherwise changing the process; these factors vary from body to body .

Knowledge of the decomposition process can help investigators and forensic pathologists to estimate time of death and to determine whether the body has been moved. Although often on popular television shows and in movies, characters portraying forensic experts make impressive specific statements about time of death, estimating using intervals of thirty or sixty minutes, in reality, forensic investigators are grateful if the time of death can be narrowed to a twelve-hour window. In contrast, analyis of decomposition manifestations makes the determination that a body has been moved more clear-cut. The fact that a body has been repositioned provides investigators with a very important piece of information—someone was on the scene before their arrival.

Initial Body Changes

Immediately upon the discovery of a body, investigators look for four initial body changes. All of these changes begin at the moment of death; thus the presence or absence of manifestations of these changes can be used in the determination of an estimate of time of death. The four all have Latin names ending in *mortis*, the Latin word for death: pallor (paleness, fading) mortis, algor (cold or cooling) mortis, rigor (stiffening) mortis, and livor (black and blue mark, bruise) mortis.

Pallor mortis is the paleness that is associated with death; it results from the fact that the blood is no longer at the skin's surface because circulation has ceased. Full paleness happens in the first three hours after death. It is difficult to quantify the progression of this process, however, so this change generally is of little value in determining the time of death.

Algor mortis is the cooling of the body's temperature following death as it falls from the static 98.6 degrees to the ambient temperature. A body's temperature—usually measured using a rectal thermometer—provides some information that is useful in estimating the time of death, but bodies do not all cool at a consistent rate, so a somewhat complex equation must be used. Many factors can influence the rate of a body's cooling, including the presence of excessive humidity, lack of humidity, and the body's position near a heat source (such as a radiator), so any estimation has a wide margin of error.

Rigor mortis is the stiffening of the body's muscles after death. The muscles become so stiff that they are nearly impossible to move or manipulate. If the entire body is moved from its position at death while rigor mortis is fully es-

tablished, the body's limbs will maintain their original pose, appearing to defy gravity. The cause of rigor mortis is a chemical reaction in which water reacts with the body's adenosine triphosphate (commonly referred to as ATP) and converts it to another compound. ATP is the chemical energy source required for movement in living tissue.

Rigor mortis follows what is typically referred to as the "rule of twelves." It normally takes the first twelve hours after death for rigor mortis to set fully and the body to become completely rigid. The body stays in full rigor for the next twelve hours (twelve to twenty-four hours after death), and then rigor begins to release during the third twelve hours (twenty-four to thirty-six hours after death). After thirty-six hours, the rigor mortis is fully released and the body is once again limp. Knowing what stage of rigor mortis a body is in can help in the determi-

Employees of the District of Columbia medical examiner's office remove one of four decomposing bodies of youths found in a house in early 2008. The ability of forensic scientists to estimate how long bodies have been decomposing plays an important role in the determination of what took place at crime scenes. *(AP/Wide World Photos)*

nation of time of death, but many factors—such as ambient temperature, antemortem physical condition, and humidity—can vary the rigor schedule by hours.

A body's stage of rigor mortis can be very helpful in the determination of whether the body has been moved. If a body's limbs appear to be defying gravity or the body is in a position that does not make sense given the circumstances (leaning against a wall instead of crumpled on the floor, for example), investigators can conclude with certainty that the body was moved several hours after death.

Livor mortis occurs when the blood, no longer in circulation, passes through the capillaries to settle in the gravity-dependent areas of the body. The blood stains the skin a dark red color in those areas. Lividity, as this process is also called, begins within the first hour of death and continues until full staining occurs at approximately twelve hours after death. An estimation of time of death can be made based on how deeply the skin is stained, but such an estimation is not specific and cannot be made until after full lividity is reached.

If the body is moved before full lividity is reached, the blood will shift and settle in the new gravity-dependent areas of the body. Partial staining may have already occurred in the original position, meaning the body has dual lividity. The only way dual lividity can occur is if the body is moved after death and prior to full livor mortis. Another sure indication that a body was moved after death is that it has reached full livor mortis, but the staining is not in the gravity-dependent areas of the body. In other words, if a body has full lividity of the chest but is found found lying on the back, the body must have been flipped over after full lividity was reached while the body was facedown.

Autolysis and Putrefaction

Autolysis is the destruction of a cell after its death by the action of its own enzymes, which break down its structural molecules. Human cells have an organelle known as the lysosome, which is a membrane containing up to forty digestive enzymes that are made by the endoplasmic reticulum and Golgi apparatus (sometimes called the Golgi complex). The lysosomes are responsible for digesting nucleic acids, polysaccharides, fats, and proteins within the cell. They are active in recycling the cell's organic material and in the intracellular digestion of macromolecules. At the point of a person's death, the digestive enzymes are released from the lysosomes' membranes and begin destroying the cell.

Putrefaction usually begins concurrent with autolysis in the first stages of decomposition. Putrefaction is the breaking down of flesh and tissue caused by bacteria, which creates the strong, unpleasant odor associated with decomposition. The stages of putrefaction vary, as do the times within each stage, depending on environmental conditions. Some of the factors that influence the speed of putrefaction include the atmospheric temperature and humidity level, the movement of air, the state of hydration of the tissues and the nutritional state of the body before death, the age of the deceased, and the cause of death. Low temperatures, which inhibit the growth of bacteria, retard the process considerably.

One of the earliest signs of putrefaction in human decomposition is the discoloration of the lower abdominal wall near the right hip bone because of the proximity of the cecum and large intestine to the skin's surface there. Human bodies house many bacteria that assist in the digestion process. After death, as intestinal bacteria begin the putrefaction process, the lower-right abdomen turns a greenish to black color. The gases produced by the bacteria are also responsible for swelling of the face and neck. This swelling may cause the eyes and tongue to protrude and may make visual identification of the decedent difficult. Other effects produced by the gases include a marked increase in the volume of the abdomen, which is under tension, and of the scrotum and penis, which may become larger than normal.

The intestinal bacteria begin colonizing the entire body, utilizing the venous system as pathways. The discoloration of the abdomen eventually spreads as the bacteria migrate, changing the veins and arteries of the rest of the abdomen, the thighs, the chest, and the shoulders to the same green and black. The discolored venous system makes visible lines across the body; this is referred to as marbling.

A few days to a week after death, as the bacteria continue to devour tissue, the skin begins to blister in the sloping regions of the body. Eventually the blisters, which contain a thick reddish liquid, erupt, making the epidermis (the outer layer of skin) fragile. Ultimately, the epidermis becomes so delicate that it tears easily and may come off in large areas, leaving the red dermis below visible. This phenomenon is referred to as skin slippage. At times, the epidermis of an entire hand may detach, creating a glove of skin. If the skin of the fingertips detaches, identification of the body through fingerprints may be difficult, but as long as the fingertip skin is still available, fingerprints may be retrievable; forensic scientists have had success in placing such skin over their own latex-gloved fingers to retrieve the fingerprints.

As the body enters the second week following death, the increased pressure on the abdomen produced by putrefactive gases leads to the ejection of feces and urine. This pressure also leads to the expulsion of liquids from other body orifices, particularly from the mouth and nostrils. Because this liquid is often bloody, its presence sometimes leads to a misdiagnosis of injury. At this stage, the orifices as well as the organs may take on a foamy appearance as the gases mix with liquids internally.

In the following weeks, the skin begins to darken to black, making identification even more difficult. The face becomes even more bloated and blackens as well, so that racial characteristics may be masked. The cadaver continues to bloat with internal gases, giving the impression that the deceased was a very heavy individual.

Internal decomposition of the organs tends to occur at a slower pace than that of the rest of the body. The capsules of the kidney, spleen, and liver resist putrefaction more than do other tissues, but eventually they become sacs containing a thick reddish liquid. These sacs will ultimately burst. The viscera and soft tissues disintegrate, whereas organs such as the uterus, heart, and prostate last longer, as do tendon tissues and ligaments attached to the bones. These different rates of decay of the organs may be proportional to the amounts of muscular and conjunctive tissue they contain.

Saponification

Decomposition tends to be slower in water than in air because of the usually lower temperature of water, which retards bacterial growth. Water also protects the body from insects and predatory animals, with certain birds and fish as notable exceptions. A body typically floats head down, because the head does not develop gas formation as easily as the abdomen; this causes fluids to gravitate to the head. Putrefaction of a body that has been decomposing in water is thus more visible on the face and front of the neck, making visual identification particularly difficult. Identification is further hampered by saponification, which is a chemical process in which water converts the body's fatty acids into a different compound called adipocere. A grayish-white or tan spongy substance that adheres to the body, adipocere can act as a preservative, counteracting the effects of decomposition.

Saponification requires at least partial immersion of the body in an aquatic environment with warm temperatures. It normally presents as peeling, blanched skin. Adipocere has been found on bodies in bathtubs, ponds, lakes, and oceans. It has also been discovered on bodies inside caskets, on bodies found in caves, and on remains wrapped in plastic.

Mummification

Mummification is the process of drying out the tissues of a body. It is characterized by dryness and brittle, torn skin, especially on the protruding areas of the body, which is generally brown in color. It is possible for slight adipocere to form in mummified bodies, as the hydration needed to create the fats contributes to the drying of the body. Mummification is found in dry, ventilated environments and generally in warm places where bodies lose fluids through evaporation. Mummification is often found in desert environments, but it can also occur in dry, closed spaces, such as attics and closets. Dehydration before death may contribute to the process of mummification.

Mummified bodies are often found in a state of preservation, so that it is usually much easier to investigate the identities of the deceased than it is in cases of saponification. Performing autopsies on mummified remains is very difficult because the skin is extremely brittle and disintegrates easily. A variety of methods have been developed to rehydrate mummified bodies for better autopsy results. This rehydration is often referred to as tissue building.

Skeletonization

Skeletonization, or the removal of all soft tissue from the bone, is generally considered the last stage of decomposition. Skeletonization may be complete, meaning the entire body has no flesh, or partial, with areas of the body in different stages of decomposition.

Under normal conditions, skeletonization occurs only after a considerable amount of time has passed. An unembalmed adult body buried six feet deep in ordinary soil without a coffin normally takes ten to twelve years to decompose fully to a skeleton, given a temperate climate. Immerse the body in water, and skeletonization occurs approximately four times faster; expose it to air, and it occurs eight times faster. The intervention of predatory insects or animals can greatly speed up this timetable, however.

Insect and Predator Activity

Predatory insects and animals can accelerate decomposition by eating the flesh of a cadaver, separating the body into parts, or using the body as a repository for their eggs. The involvement of insect predators in particular can be beneficial to investigators in that it can help in the determination of an estimate of time of death. Insects are the first organisms to arrive on a body after death. They colonize the remains in a predictable sequence, as each stage of decomposition, from fresh body to skeletonization, is attractive to a different group of insects.

When remains are found weeks or months after death, the examination of insect evidence is often the only method available that can help investigators to determine an approximate time of death. Forensic entomologists study what insects are present in and on the body and pinpoint the development stages of those insects. They also take note of the species that are not present. Every group of insects that has inhabited the body will have left evidence of having been there, even the groups that have moved on as the body progressed through successive decomposition stages. Blowflies, which can detect death from great distances, are the first to colonize a body.

Russell S. Strasser

Further Reading

Catanese, Gerard, and Tamara Bloom. "Recovery of a Mummified Pregnant Woman from a Fifty-five-Gallon Drum More Than Thirty Years After Her Death." *American Journal of Forensic Medicine and Pathology* 23, no. 3 (2002): 245-247. Interesting article on mummification discusses the case of a twenty-eight-year-old woman whose mummified remains were found in steel drum in a crawl space under a house.

DiMaio, Vincent J., and Dominick DiMaio. *Forensic Pathology.* 2d ed. Boca Raton, Fla.: CRC Press, 2001. One of the best reference sources available in the field of forensic pathology. Includes a very informative section on human decomposition.

Mann, Robert, William Bass, and Lee Meadows. "Time Since Death and Decomposition of the Human Body: Variables and Observations in Case and Experimental Field Studies." *Journal of Forensic Sciences* 35, no. 1 (1990): 103-111. Excellent comprehensive study of the decomposition of a body includes discussion of determination of time of death.

O'Brien, Tyler G., and Amy C. Kuehner. "Waxing Grave About Adipocere: Soft Tissue Change in an Aquatic Context." *Journal of Forensic Sciences* 52, no. 2 (2007): 294-301. Presents the results of a study of the saponification process on submerged bodies. Excellent source for further information on this phenomenon.

Rodriguez, William, and William Bass. "Decomposition of Buried Bodies and Methods That May Aid in Their Location." *Journal of Forensic Sciences* 30, no. 3 (1985): 836-852. Interesting article coauthored by one of the foremost forensic anthropologists in the United States; Rodriguez has conducted extensive research on the decomposition of human bodies.

Spennemann, Dirk H. R., and Bernd Franke. "Decomposition of Buried Human Bodies and

Associated Death Scene Materials on Coral Atolls in the Tropical Pacific." *Journal of Forensic Sciences* 40, no. 3 (1995): 356-367. Informative, penetrating study of decomposition focuses on the effects of tropical conditions.

Spitz, Werner U., ed. *Spitz and Fisher's Medicolegal Investigation of Death: Guidelines for the Application of Pathology to Crime Investigation.* 4th ed. Springfield, Ill.: Charles C Thomas, 2006. Indispensable volume for those conducting forensic investigations and forensic pathology. Includes comprehensive sections on specific cases along with their pathological findings.

See also: Adipocere; Algor mortis; Autopsies; Bacteria; Body farms; Coffin birth; Forensic anthropology; Forensic archaeology; Forensic entomology; Livor mortis; Mummification; Rigor mortis; Taphonomy; University of Tennessee Anthropological Research Facility.

Decontamination methods

Definition: Chemical and physical methods of eradicating, inactivating, or cleaning potentially dangerous biological, chemical, or radiological agents that are present on persons or objects, including surfaces and building structures.

Significance: Exposure to certain kinds of biological, chemical, and radiological agents can be detrimental to human beings. Forensic scientists as well as members of the general public may find themselves in situations where they may be exposed to such agents, thus decontamination procedures need to be in place. Such procedures include removal of contaminants, prevention of infectious transmission from biological hazards, reduction of contaminant levels to ensure protection from harm, and provision of decontaminated objects or surfaces that are safe for use, handling, storage, or disposal.

Exposure to various hazardous agents can take place in the home, in the workplace, or in other environments. For example, workers in health care institutions and in laboratories of many kinds (forensic, clinical and research) are often exposed to bloodborne pathogens and other potentially infectious materials. Individuals who work in manufacturing industries are also often exposed to potentially toxic chemicals specific to their work environments. In addition to such everyday exposure, public concern has risen regarding the prospect of the use of chemical and biological agents as weapons. A radiological (nuclear) agent was last used as a weapon in World War II, but such agents are also present in nuclear power plants, in some weapons manufacturing plants, and in small quantities in forensic, clinical, and research laboratories when particular experiments require them. Forensic scientists may be exposed to biological, chemical, or radiological agents in the course of their work.

Because of the dangers of exposure to hazardous agents, the issue of decontamination is increasingly important. Decontamination methods include two broad categories: chemical and physical. Specific cleaning and decontamination procedures apply to different situations. For example, different methods of cleaning and decontamination would be used for a crime scene, for an operating room in a hospital, for a patient examination room in an outpatient clinic, for a blood bank, for a research laboratory, and for a facility exposed to a biological or chemical war agent, such as the anthrax-laden letters that contaminated the Hart Senate Office Building and the associated U.S. Postal Service mail-handling and -sorting centers in the fall of 2001. Moreover, specific protocols are in place in the United States for decontaminating civilians as opposed to military personnel in military settings, where quick and efficient strategies need to be employed. The choice of decontamination methods depends also on the severity and consequences of the exposure and on the nature of the item that will be decontaminated, including the material of which it is made.

General Methods

The U.S. Occupational Safety and Health Administration (OSHA) recommends several gen-

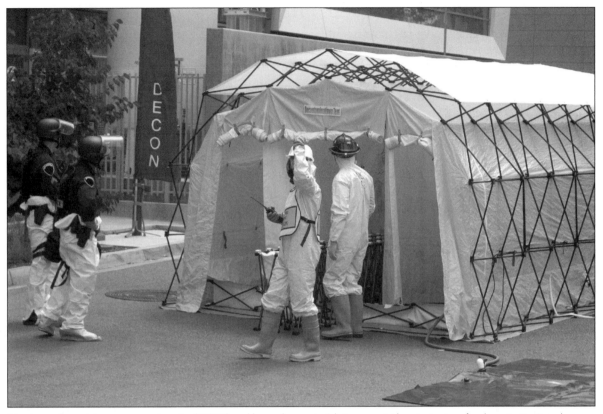

Members of special weapons and tactics (SWAT) and hazardous-materials teams outside a tent set up for decontamination showers. (© iStockphoto.com/Loren Rodgers)

eral measures of decontamination. Hand decontamination by completely washing hands with soap and water, rinsing, and drying with a clean towel or air-drying can help prevent transmission of disease. This method is useful in many different settings, including food-related industries, health care institutions, and forensic laboratories.

Clothing, tools, and appropriate equipment should be washed completely using soap and clean water. A solution of chlorine bleach (sodium hypochlorite) and water (one-fourth cup of bleach per gallon of water) should be used to wipe down surfaces; gloves, eye protection, and appropriate clothing should be worn by those using bleach solutions for decontamination.

Chemical Methods

Chemical disinfectants that are often used in medical, surgical, and research facilities include alcohols (isopropyl and ethyl alcohol, usu-ally 70 percent solutions, are used to inactivate biological hazards, including adenoviruses, murine retroviruses, and human immunodeficiency virus, or HIV); halogen-containing compounds such as iodophors (iodine combined with an organic substance); oxidizing chlorine solutions such as bleach (a 10 percent chlorine solution made fresh daily is recommended); phenolic compounds such as chlorhexidine; strong bases such as calcium, sodium, and potassium hydroxides; mild acids such as vinegar; surface-active compounds such as soaps and detergents (quaternary ammonium compounds commonly known as quats); and aldehyde compounds such as glutaraldehyde and formaldehyde.

The necessary length of exposure to these chemical decontaminating agents depends on the level of disinfection required (low, medium, or high) as well as the limitations of each situation (for example, the nature of the item being disinfected is a factor, whether it is a sample containing bloodborne pathogens or other potentially infectious materials, the surface of a laboratory workbench, or a soft surface such as a carpeted area). One type of chemical decontamination used in forensic science involves dichloromethane. Forensic investigators often obtain samples of DNA (deoxyribonucleic acid) from hair, teeth, body fluids, and fingernails. Hair is usually decontaminated with dichloromethane for two minutes before extraction of DNA. In addition to the chemical decontamination, most of these objects are placed in specially designed biohazard bags or containers for disposal; these are then sterilized using an autoclave, a device that employs heat, steam, and pressure to destroy biological pathogens.

Chemical disinfectants that may be used for decontamination of building structures in cases of toxic industrial events or biological or chemical attacks include three broad categories: liquid-based topical agents (such as bleach and aqueous chlorine dioxide), foams and gels (such as the L-Gel System and a decontamination foam created by Sandia National Laboratories), and gaseous and vapor technologies, or fumigants (such as chlorine dioxide gas, vapor-phase hydrogen peroxide, and paraformaldehyde).

The L-Gel System is an innovative decontaminant of biological hazards as well as of chemical and biological warfare agents, such as the spores of *Bacillus anthracis*, the bacterium that causes anthrax. L-Gel, which was developed at the Lawrence Livermore National Laboratory in California, is based on a Du Pont Corporation product called Oxone, a commercial oxidizer that uses potassium peroxymonosulfate as its active ingredient. L-Gel incorporates Oxone solution and a silica gelling agent, which allows it to cling to walls, ceilings, and other surfaces.

The decontamination foam developed at the Sandia National Laboratories in New Mexico, known as Sandia foam, uses aqueous-based hydrogen peroxide as its active ingredient. Sandia foam can also eradicate bacterial spores through its surfactant and oxidizer properties.

Radioactive material contaminants, especially from water-cooled nuclear reactors, are decontaminated with chemical reagents. For example, alkaline permanganate is used for pretreatment, citrate-oxalate solution for treatment, acidified hydrogen peroxide solution for posttreatment, and demineralized water for rinsing in between steps.

Radioactive contamination from spills that occur in laboratories is usually minor and easily contained. Exposed personnel are decontaminated using the protocols in place for such events. Chemical decontamination methods include using soaps or detergents with chelating compounds and special decontaminants for radioactivity, such as Decon90, Count-Off, and Radiacwash. For personnel decontamination, hydrogen peroxide, potassium permanganate, and sodium metabisulfite can be used for decontamination of exposed skin, provided there are no wounds and the skin does not become inflamed or irritated. If radioactive material is ingested, vomiting is induced and copious amounts of water are given to dilute the radioactivity. Most institutions where radioactive materials are present have environmental health and safety officers and radiation safety officers who are responsible for reporting radioactive contamination incidents and for more extensive decontamination per institutional protocols.

Most of the decontamination technologies developed in the United States for use in case of biological, chemical, and radiological attacks have been developed for military purposes, but these technologies and their potential uses have been expanded to include civilian purposes since the events of fall, 2001, when the United States experienced terrorism on a scale that it had never before seen.

Physical Methods

Physical methods of decontamination range from simply scrubbing off microbes with an antimicrobial chemical agent to more sophisticated methods, such as the use of ultraviolet (UV) light, ionizing radiation, microwave irradiation, absorbents, filtration, dry heat, and moist heat (steam). UV light is often used to cause mutation experimentally; its main application as a decontaminant is in laboratories that use hazardous microbes and in irradiation of air near important surgical sites. Ionizing radiation includes electron beams, X rays, cathode rays, and gamma rays; these have greater energy than UV light. Ionizing radiation is often used in industrial processes such as the sterilization of disposable medical and surgical supplies. Microwave irradiation has been used to sterilize items such as sponges and scrub pads.

Absorbents are natural materials, such as fuller's earth, that can take up liquid contaminants or impurities. An absorbent used by the military is M291, a dried resin used for rapid decontamination of the skin. Filtration is a method of sterilizing large volumes of liquid to remove contaminants by passing the liquid through one or more filters. Dry-heat sterilizers are often used to disinfect instruments that can withstand high temperatures. Moist heat (steam) is used in autoclaves to sterilize equipment, liquids, and other objects. Some bacteria that form spores (such as those that belong to the genera *Bacillus* and *Clostridium*), however, cannot be completely eradicated by autoclaving because the spores can survive extremely high pressures and temperatures.

Miriam E. Schwartz and Charlene F. Barroga

Further Reading

Boss, Martha J., and Dennis W. Day, eds. *Biological Risk Engineering Handbook: Infection Control and Decontamination*. Boca Raton, Fla.: CRC Press, 2003. Provides extensive coverage of biological contaminants in relation to industrial hygiene, including methods for measuring, controlling, and containing human exposure.

Environmental Protection Agency. *Compilation of Available Data on Building Decontamination Alternatives*. Washington, D.C.: Author, 2005. Presents information on the technologies that could be used for decontaminating buildings in the event of chemical or biological attacks in the United States.

Johansson, I., and P. Somasundaran, eds. *Handbook for Cleaning/Decontamination of Surfaces*. 2 vols. New York: Elsevier, 2007. Comprehensive reference resource includes up-to-date discussion of the physicochemical features of the cleaning process, different materials used for decontamination, effects of cleaning on the environment, and other related matters.

Occupational Safety and Health Administration. *Bloodborne Pathogens Fact Sheet*. Washington, D.C.: Government Printing Office, 2002. One of a series of brief informational publications that highlight OSHA standards.

O'Neal, Jon T. *The Bloodborne Pathogens Standard: A Pragmatic Approach*. New York: Van Nostrand Reinhold, 1996. Provides practical information to help employers interpret and implement the OSHA standard and discusses what to do if exposure to pathogens occurs.

Raber, E., et al. *Universal Oxidation for CBW Decontamination: L-Gel System Development and Deployment*. Springfield, Va.: National Technical Information Service, 2000. Presents a comprehensive discussion of the L-Gel System, which is used for decontamination of chemical and biological agents.

Ryan, Kenneth J., and C. George Ray. *Sherris Medical Microbiology: An Introduction to Infectious Diseases*. New York: McGraw-Hill Medical, 2003. Textbook on microorganisms includes discussion of the spread and control of infections.

See also: Air and water purity; Anthrax; Biohazard bags; Biological terrorism; Brockovich-PG&E case; Chemical agents; Chemical Biological Incident Response Force, U.S.; Chemical terrorism; Chemical warfare; Crime scene cleaning; Crime scene protective gear; Radiation damage to tissues; U.S. Army Medical Research Institute of Infectious Diseases.

Defensive wounds

Definition: Injuries received by victims as the result of trying to defend themselves during physical attacks.

Significance: Defensive wounds can provide key pieces of evidence during investigations of criminal acts. Because they are inflicted on victims while the crimes are being committed, they can reveal a great deal about the crimes themselves.

Defensive wounds often occur during crimes of violence, such as homicides, rapes, and other assaults. Most such wounds are found on victims' forearms and palms of hands, but they can also be found on other parts, such as the lower legs and feet of victims who attempt to kick their attackers. Defensive wounds are typically inflicted by knives or other sharp instruments or result from blunt force trauma from objects such as baseball bats and hammers. Less commonly, defensive wounds are inflicted by firearms.

Defensive wounds can reveal where perpetrators were in relation to their victims, what types of weapons they used, and the amount of force they used. Such wounds can also be important in reconstructing the time lines of crime scenes, and they may produce other kinds of evidence. For example, blood from wounds may leave smears or spatters. When victims scratch their attackers—as they often do in physical struggles—traces of the attackers' skin cells can almost always be found under the victims' fingernails. These traces can be scraped, and the DNA (deoxyribonucleic acid) they contain can be analyzed. At the same time, considerable amounts of trace and transfer evidence can be transferred between victims and their attackers.

A popular misconception about defensive wounds is that if they are not found on victims' bodies, the victims must not have chosen to fight back or were compliant. This is often untrue, especially in cases of sexual assault. An absence of defensive injuries may indicate several possible sequences of events. For example, victims may fight back without sustaining any injuries. More frequently, however, victims simply cannot fight back, usually because they are quickly overpowered or are incapacitated during the attacks. Victims may be asleep or rendered unconscious through the use of drugs or alcohol during their attacks. Victims might also be caught unaware by their attackers and thus not have time to fight back. When the body of a victim has many fresh wounds, none of which seems to be defensive in nature, it may mean that the victim was already dead or unconscious when the wounds were inflicted. The victim may also have been restrained to prevent defensive movements.

Ayn Embar-Seddon and Allan D. Pass

Further Reading

Hopping, Lorraine Jean. *The Body as Evidence.* Milwaukee: Gareth Stevens, 2007.

Houck, Max M. *Forensic Science: Modern Methods of Solving Crime.* Westport, Conn.: Praeger, 2007.

_____, ed. *Mute Witnesses: Trace Evidence Analysis.* San Diego, Calif.: Academic Press, 2001.

See also: Antemortem injuries; Bite-mark analysis; Blood residue and bloodstains; Blood spatter analysis; Blood volume testing; Blunt force trauma; DNA extraction from hair, bodily fluids, and tissues; Gunshot wounds; Hesitation wounds and suicide; Homicide; Knife wounds; Puncture wounds; Rape; Strangulation; Trace and transfer evidence.

Deoxyribonucleic acid. *See* DNA

Diagnostic and Statistical Manual of Mental Disorders

Date: First published in 1952; fourth edition, text revision (*DSM-IV-TR*), published 2000

Identification: The text-revised fourth edition of the *Diagnostic and Statistical Manual of Mental Disorders*, commonly called the *DSM-IV-TR*, provides an authoritative scheme that mental health professionals use to classify psychological disorders.

Significance: The *Diagnostic and Statistical Manual of Mental Disorders*, published by the American Psychiatric Association, provides detailed information about mental disorders for mental health professionals, including, for each disorder, key diagnostic features, associated features and disorders, specific age and gender features, familial pattern, and differential diagnosis. Mental health professionals use the *DSM-IV-TR* in treatment and when serving as forensic experts, such as when they must determine defendants' competency to stand trial.

In the United States, the *DSM-IV-TR* provides the most widely used classification system for mental disorders. This comprehensive manual lists approximately four hundred psychological disorders, including mental retardation, simple phobia, and paranoid schizophrenia. The manual was developed in coordination with the tenth edition of the World Health Organization's *International Classification of Diseases* (*ICD-10*), which covers both medical and psychological disorders.

Structure

The *DSM-IV-TR* is structured to require the diagnostician to evaluate a person's condition along five axes, or separate branches, of information. First, the diagnostician must determine whether the person displays one or more clinical disorders from an extensive list. These include disorders usually first diagnosed in infancy, childhood, and adolescence, such as enuresis (bedwetting); delirium, dementia, amnesia, and other cognitive disorders; mental disorders due to a general medical condition; substance-related disorders; schizophrenia and other psychotic disorders; mood disorders; anxiety disorders; somatoform disorders; factitious (intentionally feigned) disorders; dissociative disorders (such as what was formerly called multiple personality disorder); eating disorders (such as bulimia); sexual disorders and gender identity disorder; sleep disorders; impulse-control disorders; and adjustment disorders. Some of the most frequently diagnosed disorders are anxiety disorders and mood disorders (depression).

Second, the diagnostician must decide whether the person is displaying long-standing problems including retardation and personality disorders, which can be overlooked because of the first set of clinical disorders. Mental retardation involves significantly below-average intellectual functioning plus impairments in present adaptive functioning and usually occurs before age eighteen. Personality disorders are rigid, maladaptive patterns that deviate markedly from cultural expectations, are pervasive and inflexible, start in adolescence or early adulthood, are stable over time, and lead to distress or impairment. For example, antisocial personality disorder involves persistent disregard for and violation of the rights of others, and narcissistic personality disorder involves a pattern of grandiosity, need for admiration, and lack of empathy.

Third, the diagnostician must ascertain whether the person has any relevant general medical conditions. For example, many people who have recently experienced open heart surgery report clinical depression afterward, and people with diabetes may experience problems with sexual functioning. Fourth, the diagnostician must determine whether the person faces any special psychosocial or environmental problems, such as school or housing problems. Fifth, the diagnostician must rate the person's overall functioning on a scale from zero to one hundred.

It is possible for a person to have more than one diagnosis. For example, a person could have anorexia, an eating disorder that involves self-starvation, and bipolar disorder, a mood disorder that involves periods of depression that last at least two weeks and periods of mania that last at least a week.

Strengths and Weaknesses

Two issues with any kind of diagnostic system are reliability (that is, different people agree on the diagnosis) and validity (that is, the diagnosis is accurate). The people who developed the *DSM-IV-TR* conducted extensive reviews of research to pinpoint which categories in past versions of the *DSM* had been too vague. They next developed some new diagnostic criteria and categories and conducted field trials in which many professionals and researchers used the new criteria in their work. It was found that, most of the time, the same clients or kinds of clients were receiving the same diagnoses, although some problems occurred. One problem was that practitioners had some trouble distinguishing one kind of anxiety disorder from another. Thus, although not totally reliable or valid, the most recently published version of the manual represents the best information available about diagnosis.

The *DSM-IV-TR* is designed to be primarily descriptive, so it avoids suggesting underlying causes for a person's behavior. Instead, it paints a picture of the behavior itself. Also, it provides precise information so that researchers can explore causes of a problem, and two persons diagnosing the same person will arrive at the same diagnosis. This emphasis on behavior could be considered a strength or a weakness of the manual's approach.

A potential problem with the *DSM-IV-TR* is that it compartmentalizes people into inflexible, all-or-nothing categories rather than considering the degree to which individuals display disordered behavior. In addition, some mental health professionals have expressed concern that attaching the label of "abnormal" to a person imparts a dehumanizing, lifelong stigma. Further, a particular diagnosis might cause professionals who deal with that person to concentrate on the problem diagnosed and neglect others. Despite such drawbacks, which are inherent in any labeling system, the *DSM-IV-TR* offers a logical way to organize the major types of mental disturbance.

Lillian M. Range

Further Reading

American Psychiatric Association. *Desk Reference to the Diagnostic Criteria from DSM-IV-TR*. Washington, D.C.: Author, 2000. Abridged version of the *DSM-IV-TR* is designed to be more portable and easier to use than the full 943-page edition. Includes the *DSM-IV-TR* classification chart, a differential diagnosis decision tree, and a list of the appendixes that appear in the unabridged edition.

Durand, V. Mark, and David H. Barlow. *Essentials of Abnormal Psychology*. 4th ed. Belmont, Calif.: Wadsworth, 2006. Presents thorough descriptions of the different diagnostic groups and includes examples of interviews with individuals who have specific disorders.

First, Michael B., and Allan Tasman. *Clinical Guide to the Diagnosis and Treatment of Mental Disorders*. Hoboken, N.J.: John Wiley & Sons, 2006. Provides clear, concise, and practical diagnostic and therapeutic advice to all practitioners involved in the treatment of mental disorders, covering all *DSM-IV-TR* diagnostic categories in a reader-friendly way.

Klott, Jack, and Arthur E. Jongsma, Jr. *The Co-occurring Disorders Treatment Planner*. Hoboken, N.J.: John Wiley & Sons, 2006. Contains the elements practitioners need to develop formal treatment plans quickly and easily, with a focus on treating adults and adolescents with alcohol, drug, or nicotine addictions and co-occurring disorders such as depression, post-traumatic stress disorder, eating disorders, and attention-deficit/hyperactivity disorder.

Kupfer, David J., Michael B. First, and Darrel A. Regier, eds. *A Research Agenda for "DSM-V."* Washington, D.C.: American Psychiatric Association, 2002. Presents attempts to stimulate research and discussion in the field in preparation for the eventual start of the revision process for the fifth edition of the *DSM*.

See also: Borderline personality disorder; Competency evaluation and assessment instruments; Drug abuse and dependence; Forensic psychiatry; Guilty but mentally ill plea; Hallucinogens; Minnesota Multiphasic Personality Inventory; Psychopathic personality disorder; Victimology.

Dial tone decoder

Definition: Device that deciphers all numbers dialed from a particular telephone and sends the information to an external recorder.

Significance: During criminal and foreign intelligence investigations, information about what telephone numbers have been called from specific telephones can be important for establishing connections among individuals.

When a number key is pressed on a touch-tone telephone, two tones are generated. Each vertical column on the keypad generates a high-frequency tone, and each horizontal row produces a low-frequency tone. When the high- and low-frequency tones of any key are mixed, they produce a tone of unique frequency associated with that specific keypad number. A dial tone recorder deciphers these unique frequencies on an outgoing telephone line and uses the information to route the call to the correct receiving telephone.

When a dial tone decoder is connected to an external device, information about the number called can be recorded, so that a third party can tell what number has been dialed. This is called a pen register tap. The telephone conversation is not accessible to the third party, only the number called. A modern pen register tap usually sends the information to a computer with an infrared port (an infrared data association, or IRDA) that can communicate wirelessly with the dial tone decoder in the same way a remote control turns on a television. The presence of a pen register tap on a telephone line is difficult to detect.

Historically, wiretap laws in the United States were designed to protect the content of telephone conversations. Initiating a telephone wiretap required a court order and a high level of proof that the wiretap was essential to an investigation. Because pen register taps (or the reverse, trap and trace taps, which decipher the numbers of the telephones that originate incoming calls) do not allow access to the contents of calls, it has historically been much easier for investigators to obtain court orders for these types of taps. The Patriot Act, which was passed following the 2001 terrorist attacks on the Pentagon and the World Trade Center in New York City, made it even easier for law-enforcement agencies to place pen register taps. All the act requires is that the requesting agency certify that information likely to be obtained from the tap is relevant to an investigation.

In the twenty-first century, telecommunication companies routinely record originating and receiving telephone numbers of all calls for billing purposes, so pen register taps are not as useful as they once were. Law-enforcement agencies can get the same information by obtaining court orders that require telecommunication companies to release the calling information for particular individuals or telephones.

Martiscia Davidson

Further Reading

Diffie, Whitfield, and Susan Landau. *Privacy on the Line: The Politics of Wiretapping and Encryption.* Cambridge, Mass.: MIT Press, 2007.

Olejniczak, Stephen P. *Telecom for Dummies.* Indianapolis, Ind.: Wiley, 2006.

See also: Computer crimes; Crime laboratories; Electronic voice alteration; Internet tracking and tracing; Telephone tap detector.

Direct versus circumstantial evidence

Definitions: Evidence that links directly to material facts is direct evidence; evidence that requires inferences to link it to material facts is circumstantial evidence.

Significance: Most forensic evidence collected from crime scenes is circumstantial evidence in its relationship to the material issue of whether suspects are guilty of the crimes charged, although such evidence may be direct evidence of lesser material facts of the crimes.

Direct and circumstantial evidence of a series of material facts related to a crime builds the case and leads to an outcome of guilt or innocence. In obtaining evidence, forensic scientists rely on Locard's exchange principle, which states that every contact of an individual with another person, place, or object results in an exchange of materials. The work of forensic science applies scientific disciplines to the law and encompasses the discovery, gathering, investigation, preservation, examination, comparison, documentation, and quality control of materials found at the scenes of crimes. The work of forensic science enables investigators to use the physical evidence or the absence of particular physical evidence at crime scenes to develop associations that prove or disprove material facts as those facts relate to the crimes.

Direct evidence is evidence that links directly to material issues in a case; it may take the form of witness testimony, video or audio recordings of the events that took place, or confession of the suspect. Fingerprints also may be direct evidence of material facts. The fact finder (judge or jury) does not have to infer anything from this evidence, as the evidence is considered to speak for itself. For example, a witness testifies that he saw the suspect strike the victim. The eyewitness testimony relates directly to the material fact that the suspect struck the victim. A video surveillance tape showing that the suspect struck the victim would also be direct evidence relating to the material issue of the suspect's guilt or innocence.

Direct evidence may link directly to a lesser material fact but not directly to the material issue of guilt or innocence. For example, a fingerprint found at a crime scene is direct evidence that a particular person was at the crime scene at some point in time. However, it is not direct evidence that the person was at the crime scene at the time the crime was committed or that the person committed the crime. The fingerprint evidence does not directly prove guilt or innocence. A photograph taken by a passenger on a passing tourist bus that shows a suspect entering a bank that was robbed may be direct evidence that the suspect was at the crime scene, but the same evidence would be circumstantial evidence that the suspect robbed the bank.

Circumstantial evidence does not establish proof in a direct sense. It requires the drawing of inferences between the evidence and a material issue before a conclusion is reached. For example, the material issue may be that the suspect struck the victim with a baseball bat. A date-stamped credit card receipt for the purchase of a baseball bat may be direct evidence that the suspect bought the bat, but it is indirect, or circumstantial, evidence that the suspect struck the victim with the bat. The receipt directly proves one fact (the purchase), but it does not directly prove the other fact (the suspect struck

the victim with a baseball bat). With circumstantial evidence, the fact finder must infer any number of things to link the suspect to the material issue of guilt or innocence. The majority of forensic evidence found at crime scenes is circumstantial evidence as it relates to the material issue of suspect guilt or innocence because inferences must be made to link the evidence to guilt or innocence.

Direct and circumstantial evidence may also be found at secondary scenes of crimes—other locations where evidence connected to crimes are discovered. For example, a piece of jewelry found on a body in a shallow grave may contain a fingerprint that can be direct evidence that a suspect handled the jewelry of the deceased, but it is circumstantial evidence that the suspect had involvement with the victim's death. A fiber from a victim's clothing found in the home of a suspect may be direct evidence that the suspect had contact with the victim's clothing, but it would be circumstantial evidence that the suspect killed the victim. In each of these examples,

---

Case Example: Direct and Circumstantial Evidence

If valuable assets have been stolen from a company safe that was opened without the use of force at a time when no company employees had any business on the premises, evidence for the crime would fall into two categories. Direct evidence might include fingerprints on the safe, trace evidence inside the safe, a video surveillance camera tape showing the thief opening the safe, an eyewitness sighting of the thief entering or leaving the premises, or discovery of the stolen assets in someone's possession.

If no such evidence is available, investigators would turn their attention more closely to circumstantial evidence. Suspicion might then fall on a company employee who knows the combination to the safe, who shortly after the robbery quit his job and left the area, and who cannot account for his whereabouts at the time of the theft. None of these facts would directly link the employee to the crime, but in combination such circumstantial evidence could be used to build a case against him.

one must infer other actions from the indirect evidence to reach a conclusion of guilt or innocence.

Courts in the United States make no distinction between direct and circumstantial evidence in terms of importance toward proving guilt or innocence. In most of the fifty states, evidence in court cases falls under the guidelines of the Federal Rules of Evidence, which specify all instances in which evidence is relevant (pertaining to the case at hand), probative (likely to aid a fact finder in determining truth), and admissible (obtained under proper legal sanctions) to establish the facts of a case. Relevance is important in terms of whether or not a piece of evidence will be seen or heard by the court and in terms of how the evidence relates to the material issues of the case, but a determination of whether evidence is direct or circumstantial is not pertinent to the determination that the evidence is relevant and admissible at trial.

Direct evidence and circumstantial evidence hold equal weight in a court of law. Likewise, from a forensics point of view, evidence is evidence. Each piece of evidence serves to build the associations that prove or disprove material facts related to a crime.

Taylor Shaw

Further Reading

Best, Arthur. *Evidence: Examples and Explanations.* 6th ed. New York: Aspen, 2007. Uses the Federal Rules of Evidence to organize examples and explanations of types of evidence, relevance requirements, and exclusionary rules.

Genge, N. E. *The Forensic Casebook: The Science of Crime Scene Investigation.* New York: Ballantine, 2002. Presents examples of evidence sleuthing from real cases to illustrate the work involved in forensics.

Giannelli, Paul C., Albert J. Weatherhead III, and Richard W. Weatherhead. *Understanding Evidence.* 2d ed. Albany, N.Y.: LexisNexis/Mathew Bender, 2006. Provides an informative summary of the basic concepts of evidence law.

Pentland, Peter, and Pennie Stoyles. *Forensic Science.* Philadelphia: Chelsea House, 2003. Discusses the scientific methods used to investigate crime scenes. Intended for young adult readers.

Platt, Richard. *Crime Scene: The Ultimate Guide to Forensic Science.* New York: Dorling Kindersley, 2003. Explains concepts in forensic science using well-known cases and easy-to-understand examples.

Sapse, Danielle S. *Legal Aspects of Forensics.* New York: Chelsea House, 2006. Provides an overview of the legal issues relating to forensic science techniques and their uses in trials.

See also: Accident investigation and reconstruction; Class versus individual evidence; Courts and forensic evidence; Crime scene documentation; Crime scene investigation; Criminal personality profiling; Evidence processing; Eyewitness testimony; Federal Rules of Evidence; Locard's exchange principle; Physical evidence; Quality control of evidence.

Disturbed evidence

Definition: Materials that have been altered, moved, or destroyed at the scene of a crime after the crime has occurred.

Significance: An undisturbed crime scene yields the most reliable physical evidence to support the investigative process. When evidence is disturbed, the truth of what happened at the crime scene may be compromised or impossible to determine and may be impossible to prove in a court of law.

The objective of crime scene investigation is to gather evidence that supports or refutes theories surrounding the crime. Toward this end, investigators carefully choose and employ procedures that will maximize the likelihood of the discovery of pertinent evidence and minimize actions that could disturb that evidence. Taking into account Locard's exchange principle (which states that every contact of an individual with another person, place, or object results in an exchange of materials), it is implausible that all evidence at a crime scene will remain undisturbed throughout the duration of the investigation.

Although investigators may make every effort to maintain evidence in an undisturbed state, it is not unusual for evidence to be disturbed in many different ways. Frequently, evidence is disturbed in the period between discovery of the crime and securing of the scene, when numerous individuals may be present. Evidence such as blood trails, footprints, fingerprints, and pertinent biological fluids may be smeared or inadvertently erased by first responders, and materials not pertinent to the crime (such as fibers from blankets) may be introduced to the scene. Moving a living person or a dead body from the scene without taking precautionary steps to preserve surrounding evidence may result in disturbed evidence.

Evidence may be disturbed when individuals at the scene move objects, break objects, spill liquids, wipe up spills, remove clothing, cover victims, or otherwise introduce materials onto the scene that are not pertinent to the crime. Natural occurrences can also disturb evidence, such as when a crime victim dies in an outdoor setting and is exposed to weather conditions that alter or wash away materials. Evidence may also be disturbed by inappropriate or careless investigative techniques, such as when a technician pours casting material into a depression on a surface before checking the surface for fingerprints.

Investigators minimize or prevent the disturbance of evidence by securing the crime scene, by choosing an appropriate crime scene search pattern, and by following an effective sequence of evidence collection. Securing the crime scene entails controlling who is allowed onto the crime scene, designating the entrance and exit paths for responders administering to any victims, and establishing the search methods that will be used. An appropriate crime scene search pattern guides a methodical search that maximizes evidence discovery efforts while minimizing disturbance of the scene. In an effective sequence of evidence collection, pertinent materials are gathered before other investigative actions are taken that could disturb those materials. Through these actions and methods, investigators attempt to ensure that crime scene evi-

dence is not disturbed; when these methods are followed and evidence is nevertheless somehow disturbed, investigators make note of any reasonable explanation for the disturbance so that it does not jeopardize the utilization of pertinent evidence in a court of law.

Taylor Shaw

Further Reading

Genge, N. E. *The Forensic Casebook: The Science of Crime Scene Investigation.* New York: Ballantine, 2002.

Pentland, Peter, and Pennie Stoyles. *Forensic Science.* Philadelphia: Chelsea House, 2003.

Platt, Richard. *Crime Scene: The Ultimate Guide to Forensic Science.* New York: Dorling Kindersley, 2003.

See also: Chain of custody; Crime scene investigation; Crime scene search patterns; Cross-contamination of evidence; Evidence processing; First responders; Locard's exchange principle; Physical evidence; Quality control of evidence.

DNA analysis

Definition: Process in which DNA is obtained from biological materials—such as saliva, blood, semen, sweat, urine, hair, tissue, or bone—for use in typing that can reveal information on individual identities or genetic relationships between individuals.

Significance: After crime scene investigators identify and collect evidence samples consisting of biological materials, forensic scientists extract DNA from the samples so that the sources of the samples can be determined. This work allows further analysis that can link suspects to crimes and exclude innocent persons as suspects.

DNA (deoxyribonucleic acid) is a small biological molecule that contains the genetic material that dictates individual traits. It is contained in every cell in the human body except mature red blood cells. Because DNA is the basic unit of all life, the cells of nonhuman living organisms, such as plants, microbes, and animals, also contain it.

In addition to identifying potential suspects, the results of DNA analysis have been used to exonerate innocent persons who have been wrongly convicted, to establish paternity, and to identify the victims of mass murder and natural catastrophes. In some cases, DNA analysis of canine samples has been used when dogs have been involved in crimes or to establish the presence of persons at crime scenes through the matching of canine hairs on their clothing or other personal belongings. DNA analysis has also been performed on microbial samples, to trace the origins of deadly pathogens, and on botanical samples, to gather information about the origins of certain plants (such as marijuana) and about plant specimens found at crime scenes.

Biological evidence obtained at crime scenes can provide investigators with little or no information unless the DNA contained within the evidence samples is analyzed. A forensic scientist cannot compare a sample of saliva, for example, with a sample of a suspect's blood or a sample of the suspect's saliva just by looking at the swab on which the saliva was collected, nor can the scientist compare such samples simply by looking at them under a microscope. To compare and contrast samples of biological evidence and determine whether two samples could have originated from a particular individual, the scientist needs to extract the DNA from the evidence samples. The process of DNA analysis consists of a series of steps that lead to samples that can be separated into distinct DNA fragments, or sequenced, to obtain profiles for comparison to the DNA profiles of known persons, thereby establishing individual identities.

DNA Extraction

After biological evidence samples are submitted to the laboratory, DNA analysts carefully obtain subsamples from the original samples and then use one of the available extraction (also known as isolation) methods to isolate the DNA in the subsamples. Just as there are different biological sources from which scientists

Ohio's Cuyahoga County coroner examines the remains of a body found buried in Cleveland in 1938. During the late 1930's, bones from five women and seven men believed to be the victims of a serial-killing spree known as the Torso Murders were uncovered in and around Cleveland. Using the forensic techniques available at that time, investigators could identify only three of the victims. In 2003, a documentary filmmaker proposed using DNA analysis to identify the remaining victims. However, investigators still faced the monumental problem of finding control samples with which to match DNA samples from the bodies. (AP/Wide World Photos)

must obtain DNA samples, different methods have been developed for this purpose. The methods vary in complexity and the amounts of time they take as well as in quality and sample throughput, but the same principles underlie all of these extraction technologies.

The sample is first subjected to a lysis (dissolution) step, which can be mechanical, chemical, or a combination of both, depending on the material. During this step, the cells are broken open to allow their contents to be released. Following this, the DNA in solution is bound to a membrane or magnetic beads and the remaining of the cell's contents are subsequently subjected to a series of washes that usually contain ethanol. Because DNA is insoluble in ethanol, it remains attached to the membrane or it is pelleted during centrifugation while the remaining components are either dislodged from the membrane or stay in solution (the supernatant) and are discarded. In the last step of the extraction, the DNA is resuspended in distilled water or an elution buffer.

The process of obtaining high-molecular-weight DNA from known mixed samples, as is often necessary in cases of rape, or from degraded samples or samples that have been exposed to harsh environmental conditions is usually more complicated, as the forensic scientist must take special care either to separate the fractions corresponding to the potential mixture or to remove environmental contaminants. When potential DNA inhibitors (such as dyes, humic acids, or heme) are present, a DNA purification step must be performed before the analysis can proceed.

DNA Quantification

After the DNA has been isolated, the analyst needs to quantify the DNA and dilute it to a predetermined amount in order to amplify it. An analyst can estimate DNA concentrations using agarose gels, fluorometry, or spectrophotometry, but the most accurate means of determining the DNA concentration of a particular sample is through real-time polymerase chain reaction (qPCR). This process follows the same principle as the traditional PCR, but it quantifies the sample as it is amplified using fluorescence. Specific primers are added so that only the type of DNA of interest is quantified.

The technology of qPCR works with fluorescent dyes that are introduced into the double strands of the DNA and emit a signal or with gene-specific probes that fluoresce when they find a complementary DNA strand with which to bind. The emitted signals are recorded and transferred to a computer, which provides the output and transforms it into a numerical value. After the DNA is quantified, it is diluted to the required concentration for that type of sample and the corresponding PCR amplification "recipe."

DNA Amplification

The final step of the analysis is the amplification of the DNA sample. Amplification is the exponential copying of a gene fragment or fragments of interest. The sample is subjected to cyclic increases and decreases in temperature while in a mixture of (fluorescent) primers that demarcate the fragments of interest, an enzyme that extends the newly created fragments, and other reagents that provide the optimal conditions for in vitro replication of the specific genetic marker or markers of interest.

The steps described above are only the first portion of a series of procedures performed on a biological evidence sample. When DNA analysis is complete, the forensic scientist can begin the task of DNA typing, which allows the comparison of an evidence DNA sample to a known DNA standard.

Lilliana I. Moreno

Further Reading

Budowle, Bruce. "Genetics and Attribution Issues That Confront the Microbial Forensics Field." *Forensic Science International* 146 (Fall, 2004): S185-S188. Discusses the potential for using microbial DNA as a means of attribution in forensic scenarios.

Gehrig, Christian, and Anne Teyssier. "Forensic DNA Analysis." *CHIMIA International Journal for Chemistry* 56 (March, 2002): 71-73. Describes the various techniques available for DNA analysis of human samples.

Hunter, William. *DNA Analysis*. Philadelphia: Mason Crest, 2006. Presents an interesting discussion of the different applications of DNA analysis in crime scene investigations.

Miller, Heather. *Nonhuman DNA Typing*. Boca Raton, Fla.: CRC Press, 2007. Introduces the field of nonhuman DNA typing and its applications to forensics. Includes interesting case examples with information on legal decisions.

Rudin, Norah, and Keith Inman. *An Introduction to Forensic DNA Analysis*. 2d ed. Boca Raton, Fla.: CRC Press, 2002. Uses very simple language to describe all the basic principles of DNA analysis in the forensic sciences. Includes a useful glossary.

See also: CODIS; DNA extraction from hair, bodily fluids, and tissues; DNA fingerprinting; DNA isolation methods; DNA profiling; DNA sequencing; DNA typing; Ethics of DNA analysis; Federal Bureau of Investigation DNA Analysis Units; Mitochondrial DNA analysis and typing; National DNA Index System; Polymerase chain reaction; Postconviction DNA analysis; Y chromosome analysis.

DNA banks for endangered animals

Definition: Facilities that preserve genetic materials from and information about endangered animal species.

Significance: Building on the advances being made in DNA-related technologies in forensic science and the knowledge being accumulated in the related field of wildlife forensics, some organizations have undertaken to collect and store the genetic materials of endangered animal species in the hope that someday technological advancements will enable scientists to use these materials to restore the species.

Organizations that are concerned with the loss of animal species to extinction have established banks to preserve the DNA (deoxyribonucleic acid) of endangered animals. In addition to collecting and storing biological samples from endangered species (sperm, embryos, and body tissues), preserving them in liquid nitrogen at nearly −400 degrees Fahrenheit, these organizations store information on the species' natural habitats and maintain databases to keep track of the materials that have been collected. Organizations devoted to preserving animal DNA have been established in the United States, Great Britain, China, India, and Australia; among the most widely known animal DNA banks are those maintained by the Frozen Ark Project in England and the Frozen Zoo Project in San Diego, California.

Several factors have come together to fuel the animal DNA bank movement, including advances in DNA technology and growing environmental activism. The banking of animal DNA is a conscience-driven effort by people who also want to increase awareness of the threats posed to existing species by human advancement. Estimates of potential extinctions in the twenty-first century are ominous, with some researchers asserting that the world is in the midst of a mass extinction period. Many species considered to be endangered or threatened in the early twenty-first century may someday benefit from DNA banks, including the California condor, the Florida panther, the polar bear, the killer whale, the black rhino, the panda, and the yellow seahorse.

Critics of the organizations that maintain DNA banks for endangered animals have asserted that these organizations may inadver-

The keeper of zoology at the Natural History Museum in London, England, holds a test tube on which rests a Polynesian tree snail, one of the endangered species whose DNA is stored at the museum. The museum is part of the Frozen Ark Consortium. *(AP/Wide World Photos)*

tently create an underground market for the animals they mean to protect; the stored genetic materials could potentially have high monetary value. Moreover, many scientists believe that species extinction is a natural part of the planet's life cycle, one that humans should not tamper with, at least until they have had much more time to observe the interactions between species and Earth's environment. The animal DNA banks, however, enjoy widespread support among scientists, if only for the value they provide as historical databases.

Brion Sever

Further Reading

McGavin, George. *Endangered: Wildlife on the Brink of Extinction.* Richmond Hill, Ont.: Firefly Books, 2006.

Stone, Richard. *Mammoth: The Resurrection of an Ice Age Giant.* New York: Basic Books, 2002.

See also: Animal evidence; DNA extraction from hair, bodily fluids, and tissues; DNA isolation methods; DNA typing; Forensic botany; Polymerase chain reaction; Wildlife forensics.

DNA database controversies

Definition: Debates on social, ethical, and legal issues that surround the existence of databases containing the individual DNA profiles of large numbers of persons.

Significance: DNA databases constitute extremely important tools for law enforcement, but the existence of such repositories raises social, ethical, and legal issues, particularly concerning privacy rights and confidentiality. Because of the potential for misuse of the information stored in DNA databases, issues of public safety need to be balanced with the protection of civil liberties.

Each person has a unique DNA (deoxyribonucleic acid) profile that may be used to identify that individual. DNA samples, however, may also be used for other purposes; a person's DNA can reveal susceptibility to certain diseases, for example, or predisposition to certain behaviors. The establishment of DNA databases has helped law-enforcement agencies greatly in identifying suspects, but many observers have expressed concerns regarding the potential for misuse of the information stored in these databases.

DNA Dragnets and Fourth Amendment Issues

After serious crimes have been committed, law-enforcement agencies sometimes conduct so-called DNA dragnets to attempt to identify suspects; that is, they obtain DNA samples from all persons in selected groups of individuals to compare with DNA found at the crime scenes. In these cases, the people involved are generally pressured to "volunteer" DNA samples or the samples are taken without due process. In one case, all men in Truro, Massachusetts (a town with a population of approximately eighteen hundred), were requested to volunteer DNA samples after a murder. In Baton Rouge, Louisiana, samples were collected from about twelve hundred men during a hunt for a serial killer. The Fourth Amendment to the U.S. Constitution protects against unreasonable searches and seizures, and it has been argued that such collection of DNA samples without probable cause (a reasonable belief that the individuals have some involvement with the crimes) may constitute "unreasonable search"

Fourth Amendment to the U.S. Constitution

The right of the people to be secure in their persons, houses, papers, and effects, against unreasonable searches and seizures, shall not be violated, and no Warrants shall issue, but upon probable cause, supported by Oath or affirmation, and particularly describing the place to be searched, and the persons or things to be seized.

under the Fourth Amendment. It is likely that this issue will ultimately be decided by the U.S. Supreme Court.

The DNA profiles produced as a result of DNA dragnets are usually entered into state criminal databases. In most cases, removal of a profile from such a database requires a court order. In some states, including Virginia and Louisiana, the DNA profiles of any individuals who are arrested, even if they are not convicted, are also retained in databases. Some critics have argued that the inclusion of unconvicted individuals in DNA databases may be viewed as a violation of the concept of presumption of innocence.

The national DNA database maintained by the Federal Bureau of Investigation (FBI), known as CODIS (Combined DNA Index System), does not permit the entering of "volunteer" DNA profiles. The U.S. Congress, however, has made it legal for federal agencies to collect DNA samples from suspected illegal immigrants, and those profiles are entered into CODIS.

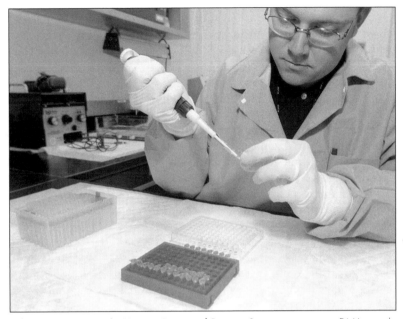

A forensic scientist at the Virginia Division of Forensic Science prepares a DNA sample found at a crime scene for testing. As of 2001, the state's database of DNA from felons was averaging one "cold hit" per day, where DNA found at a crime scene was matched to DNA on file in the database. The American Civil Liberties Union has expressed opposition to this use of the technology, saying that it violates the rights of felons, who, by law, must give blood samples to the state for inclusion in the database. (AP/Wide World Photos)

Familial Issues

People who are related by blood have similar, but not identical, DNA profiles. Given this fact, law-enforcement agencies sometimes search DNA databases for less-than-perfect matches to their suspects' DNA profiles; this is known as familial searching. By finding first-degree relatives, the police may identify suspects. Such searches have been criticized as violating the privacy rights of the parties involved; they have yet to be tested in the courts. Familial searching has also been criticized as racially discriminatory. For instance, because African Americans are disproportionately represented in CODIS, they are approximately four times more likely

than Caucasians to be "findable" through familial searching.

In addition to the use of DNA databases by law-enforcement agencies, the storage of DNA profiles in such repositories raises many other issues, particularly in the areas of privacy and confidentiality. Information on adoption and sperm and egg donation, for example, can be very sensitive, with many parties wishing to remain anonymous. Such anonymity is threatened by the placement of DNA profiles in searchable databases.

Universal Databases and Discrimination

By 2007, nine countries had established population-based DNA databases as resources for the study of genealogy and gene-disease relationships. In some nations, initiatives have been undertaken to include DNA profiles of all newborns in these databases. The storage of this information may be useful to scientists who seek to understand the genetic components of disease, but it raises issues of privacy and confidentiality. Of particular importance is the question of who has the right to access the data. In the United States, the courts have yet to decide whether DNA database information falls under the security and privacy provisions of the Health Insurance Portability and Accountability Act (HIPAA) of 1996.

It has been argued that universal DNA databases and disease gene databases have great potential for abuse. Disease genes are being identified at an increasing rate, and screening for many such genes is becoming easier and cheaper. In addition to government databases, private DNA databases are being established, and these pose additional issues of confidentiality because they contain more detailed information than that found in the government databases and so will be less likely to protect individuals' anonymity. As critics have pointed out, the availability of information on individuals' genetic characteristics has the potential to lead to discrimination by insurance carriers, employers, educational institutions, and government agencies.

Retention of DNA samples

A DNA profile only identifies the individual. The genetic markers used are short tandem repeat (STR) regions of the genome where there are variable numbers of certain DNA segments. These regions do not encode functional genes, so a person's DNA profile does not contain information on the individual's genetic makeup. In contrast, the DNA sample from which the profile was created contains all of that person's genetic information. Most U.S. states do not have laws that require the destruction of DNA samples after DNA profiling is complete.

Moreover, hospitals, clinics, and doctors' offices store tissue samples taken for biopsies or retained for research from which DNA may be extracted and analyzed. No set policy exists among forensic laboratories regarding destruction of DNA samples, and many preserve such samples in case additional testing is deemed necessary or the results of previous tests need to be confirmed. It has been argued that govern-

ment agencies have not adequately regulated the retention and future potential uses of such DNA samples.

Ralph R. Meyer

Further Reading

Greeley, Henry T. "The Uneasy Ethical and Legal Underpinnings of Large-Scale Genomic Biobanks." *Annual Review of Genomics and Human Genetics* 7 (2007): 343-364. Discusses the various issues related to the existence of private databases that contain genetic information on individuals.

Lazer, David, ed. *DNA and the Criminal Justice System: The Technology of Justice.* Cambridge, Mass.: MIT Press, 2004. Collection of essays explores the ethical and procedural issues related to DNA evidence. Includes a chapter by Associate Justice Stephen G. Breyer of the U.S. Supreme Court.

Moulton, Benjamin W. "DNA Fingerprinting and Civil Liberties." *Journal of Law, Medicine and Ethics* 34 (Summer, 2006): 147-148. Presents an overview of the issues addressed at a symposium on the topic of DNA fingerprinting and civil liberties. Contributions to the symposium appear as articles in the same issue of the journal.

Swede, Helen, Carol L. Stone, and Alyssa R. Norwood. "National Population-Based Biobanks for Genetic Research." *Genetics in Medicine* 9, no. 3 (2007): 141-149. Focuses on the ethics issues related to the establishment of national genetic databases.

Weiss, Marcia J. "Beware! Uncle Sam Has Your DNA: Legal Fallout from Its Use and Misuse in the U.S." *Ethics and Information Technology* 6, no. 1 (2004): 55-63. Discusses the constitutionality of DNA profiling.

See also: Argentine disappeared children; CODIS; DNA analysis; DNA fingerprinting; DNA typing; Ethics of DNA analysis; Federal Bureau of Investigation DNA Analysis Units; Jefferson paternity dispute; National DNA Index System; Paternity testing; Short tandem repeat analysis.

Category Index

Category Index

ACCIDENT RECONSTRUCTION

Accident investigation and reconstruction, 4
Challenger and *Columbia* accident
    investigations, 214
Driving injuries, 386
Flight data recorders, 478
National Transportation Safety Board, 759
Silkwood/Kerr-McGee case, 926
ValuJet Flight 592 crash investigation, 1010

BIOLOGICAL AGENTS. *See* CHEMICAL AND BIOLOGICAL AGENTS

CHEMICAL AND BIOLOGICAL AGENTS

Accelerants, 1
Air and water purity, 12
Amphetamines, 26
Anthrax, 46
Antianxiety agents, 57
Antibiotics, 59
Antipsychotics, 62
Arsenic, 66
Attention-deficit/hyperactivity disorder
    medications, 90
Bacteria, 102
Bacterial biology, 105
Bacterial resistance and response to
    antibacterial agents, 106
Barbiturates, 113

Biological terrorism, 125
Biological warfare diagnosis, 129
Biological weapon identification, 131
Biological Weapons Convention of 1972, 134
Biotoxins, 144
Blood agents, 150
Botulinum toxin, 174
Brockovich-PG&E case, 179
Bubonic plague, 183
Carbon monoxide poisoning, 198
Chemical agents, 221
Chemical Biological Incident Response Force,
    U.S., 222
Chemical terrorism, 225
Chemical warfare, 228
Chemical Weapons Convention of 1993, 230
Club drugs, 248
Crack cocaine, 299
Decontamination methods, 352
Ebola virus, 404
Escherichia coli, 418
Food poisoning, 481
Halcion, 576
Hallucinogens, 578
Hantavirus, 585
Hemorrhagic fevers, 588
Illicit substances, 616
Lead, 674
Mercury, 722

INVESTIGATIVE TECHNIQUES

SURVEILLANCE

D0686980

James I

James I

SCOTLAND'S
KING *of* ENGLAND

JOHN MATUSIAK

WITHDRAWN

Look not to find the softness of a down pillow in a crown,
but remember that it is a thorny piece of stuff and full of continual cares.

James I, Meditations of Matthew 27

For my father

First published 2015

The History Press
The Mill, Brimscombe Port
Stroud, Gloucestershire, GL5 2QG
www.thehistorypress.co.uk

British Library Cataloguing in Publication Data.
A catalogue record for this book is available from the British Library.

ISBN 978 0 7509 5562 1

Typesetting and origination by The History Press
Printed in Malta by Melita Press

Contents

1 ✦ Heir to Scotland's Woe

No more tears now. I will think upon revenge.

Words attributed to Mary Queen of Scots by Claude Nau de la Boiselliere,
her confidential secretary from 1575–86

In the mid-morning of 19 June 1566, Mary Queen of Scots was gratefully delivered of her first and only live-born child in a tiny closet tightly lodged in the south-east wing of Edinburgh's ancient castle. Her labour had, it seems, been long and arduous, and ten days earlier, plainly fearing the worst, she had written her will. At that time, too, she had sent to Dunfermline Abbey for a sacred reliquary containing the skull of St Margaret, set in silver-gilt and 'enriched with several pearls and precious stones', which she intended to sustain her throughout the ordeal to come. Accordingly, as Mary endured the torment within her chamber's sombre panelled walls, the remains of the saint – a Catholic queen of Scotland like herself – duly loomed above her, along with the arms of the House of Stuart and a series of embossed crowns and thistles adorning the ceiling overhead. Beside her all the while stood Margaret Asteane, her midwife, specially garbed for the occasion in a brand new gown of black velvet, not far from the royal cradle, which was likewise draped in finest fabric.

By 11 a.m., however, the midwife's task was ended. For the queen was 'lighter of a bonny son' whom, she promptly predicted, 'shall first unite the two kingdoms of Scotland and England'. The boy had entered the world, like Napoleon after him, with a fine 'caul', or birth membrane, covering his head – an augury, it was said, of future greatness – and his mother's lofty hopes seemed far from fanciful, since her royal cousin across the Border was, of her own admission, 'but a barren stock'. If, therefore, Elizabeth I should now die childless, or if any plot against her life were to run its fatal course, Scotland's queen was not only the obvious female successor in her own right, but, much more importantly still, the bearer of a healthy male heir. And the blood of Mary's son, directly drawn from Henry VII through both his parents, was of plainly purer stock than any other rival.

All, then, was swiftly set for outward rejoicing throughout the northern kingdom, though not before Mary's secret messenger, Sir James Melville, was safely past the Border at Berwick on route hotfoot to London. Thereafter, nobles, officers of state and common folk alike gave solemn thanks in Edinburgh's Great Kirk, as the castle's mighty guns – long a stirring symbol of national pride – boomed their glad approval. Deputations and messages of goodwill arrived from far and wide, further couriers were dispatched to France and Savoy, and loyal toasts were heartily raised to Scotland's fledgling 'Solomon'. Later that night, 500 bonfires would blaze on Scottish hillsides, as all the due and proper customs associated with any royal birth were studiously observed.

But the mask and show of celebration was mainly sham, since Mary Queen of Scots was also Scotland's woe. It was not for nothing that she had shunned the comfort of Holyroodhouse as her birthing place and made instead for Edinburgh and the security it afforded. Nor were all the salutations she now received by any means sincere. Indeed, for most of the vested interests in her restless kingdom, the newborn child represented little more than a fresh and unwelcome complication of a political and religious situation already critically dangerous. Powerful sections of the nobility had hoped, for their own self-interested motives, that he might never be born, and the stilted congratulations of John Spottiswoode, the Lothian superintendent of the Protestant Kirk of Scotland's General Assembly, could not conceal his misgivings that the new heir would inevitably be baptised a Roman Catholic, with all that this entailed for the reformed religion that had made such rapid strides since its apparent triumph only six years earlier. Even the child's father, Henry, Lord Darnley, had already done his feckless yet malignant best to prevent the birth of the son who shattered his best chance of seizing the throne for himself.

It was Darnley, moreover, who had sedulously propagated the rumour that his wife's new son was merely the bastard offspring of David Riccio, her Italian secretary and musician, whom he had helped to murder in her very presence just four months previous. Jaundiced, jealous, vain and volatile – resembling 'more a woman than a man' and stricken by inner demons of his own devising, which he could neither tame by infidelity nor dowse with drink – the queen's husband was now a pox-ridden parody of the dashing blonde-haired lover who had first dazzled his bride only two years earlier 'as the properest and best proportioned long man that she had ever seen'. Both Mary and Darnley knew, furthermore, that she too had been 'struck with great dread' and in 'extreme fear' for her life when Riccio met his end, even though, within hours of the new birth, the queen's abject husband was once again reminding his wife of her subsequent promise to 'forgive and forget all'.

But while the queen might dutifully forgive, forgetting was another matter. 'What if Fawsdonsyd's pistol had shot?' she had asked her husband, recalling that fateful night when a gun, which had allegedly 'refused to give fyr', had been pressed to her own breast by one of Darnley's accomplices. 'What wold have become of him [the child] and me both?' Nor could she ever entirely quash those spiteful rumours propagated by her husband that would continue to shadow her son's legitimacy. It was vital to Mary, of course, that Darnley should swiftly undo as much of the harm he had already wrought with his loose and ill-intentioned tongue, and he was soon compelled to acknowledge the child in the presence of the queen's half-brother, the Earl of Moray, as well as the earls of Mar, Atholl and Argyll, and her Privy Council. Yet the queen's caustic quip to her husband that 'he is so much your son that I fear for him hereafter' would never entirely convince the world at large or spare her heir the barbs of ne'er-do-wells in years to come. As a child, indeed, the boy would weep in mortification at the slander, and the occasional taunts of the Scottish mob did nothing to ease his misery. 'Come down, thou son of Seigneur Davy', a baying Perth rabble would jeer in 1600 as he stood at the window of Ruthven House, and much later still, the King of France would chuckle at the boy who had by then become both James VI of Scotland and James I of England, dismissing his fellow ruler as 'Solomon the son of David who played upon the harp'. There were even creeping whispers that Mary's child had died at birth, to be replaced by a child of John Erskine, Earl of Mar – empty legends which were nonetheless given a further lease of life in the eighteenth century when the skeleton of a newborn child, 'wrapped in a rich silken cloth ... belonging to Mary Stuart, Queen of Scots', was uncovered in a wall of Edinburgh Castle's banqueting hall next to the castle courtyard.

9

Yet, aside from hurtful jibes and murky tales, there was never serious doubt about the legitimacy of the child who presently occupied the royal cradle. At the time of his conception, after all, the boy's mother was still wildly infatuated with her lawful husband – so much so, indeed, that she appeared to have sacrificed all judgement on his behalf. 'The queen,' wrote the English diplomat Thomas Randolph, 'is so altered with affection towards Lord Darnley that she has brought her honour in question, her estate in hazard, her country to be torn in pieces.' And the child's resemblance to his father in an early portrait depicting him with a sparrowhawk on his arm remains striking. His flaxen hair, finely contoured features and, above all, his distinctive widely spaced eyes left little doubt about his parentage. Nor, in any case, was Darnley, for all his twisted bitterness, the new heir's greatest liability. Instead, it was the very mother who had borne him, for though she was bold, courageous and gracious, with a charm and allure that still captivates across the centuries, she was also headstrong, careless and ambitious – a passionate, high-spirited and ultimately self-centred creature who yearned for adulation but could neither bridle her emotions nor curb her whims. It was she, above all, who barred the way to long-term peace within her realm and she too, who, in spite of initial successes, menaced the fortunes and security of her longed-for son.

Sent away to France in 1548 at the age of 6, after a planned betrothal to young King Edward VI of England finally proved intolerable to her countrymen, Mary had spent nearly the whole of her life abroad. In her absence, English bullying would increase Scotland's traditional reliance on the French Crown, as the Queen Mother, Mary of Guise, herself a Frenchwoman and staunch Catholic, served as regent, holding Scotland somewhat precariously to the old religion and alliance with her homeland until her death in 1560. As part of this alliance, the absent queen had been betrothed and finally married to the dauphin, and from 1559 to 1560, the absorption of the Scottish Crown, which had eluded the English, consequently became a reality for their enemies across the Channel. By 1560, moreover, Mary Queen of Scots was not only Queen Consort of France, but rightful Queen of England in the eyes of every loyal Catholic in Europe by virtue of her paternal grandmother, Margaret Tudor, elder sister of Henry VIII.

But the early death of her husband, Francis II, and the animosity of her mother-in-law, Catherine de Medici, confirmed the fickleness of Mary's fortunes as a 19-year-old widow and drove her back to Scotland in 1561 after an absence of thirteen years, which had seen the overthrow of the Roman Catholic Church and growing division at the very heart of the Scottish political nation. For reasons of policy and for the sake of a more secure future she now moderated her direct claim to the English throne, in the hope that Elizabeth might recognise her as heiress without duress. And she remained uncommitted, likewise, to any specific party or policy in Scotland when she landed at Leith on 19 August 1561, to reclaim her realm. Indeed, Mary had announced in advance to the Scottish Parliament, the so-called 'Estates', that its members were free to establish whatever religious settlement they chose, though her own faith was to remain non-negotiable. She, personally, would adhere to the Church of Rome come what may – and hope, in doing so, to straddle the coming storm unruffled.

In this, however, Mary had not counted upon the influence and bitter hostility of John Knox, the most formidable of all the Calvinist missionaries from Geneva, whom Queen Elizabeth had just transferred from England under safe conduct with the deliberate intention of undermining the Catholic 'party' among the Scottish nobility. A thundering Scots Elijah, who had served as a French galley slave in payment for his Protestant faith, Knox now called upon his countrymen to forsake the false prophets of Baal and, in doing so, declared a single Catholic Mass more awful than the landing of 10,000 foes. Nor, above all, would he spare the sensibilities of Scotland's newly arrived ruler. On the contrary, he would blast her as an idolatrous Jezebel and bewail her very coming. Upon her return, which was marked by a curiously ill-omened mist lasting some five days, 'the very face of heaven', wrote Knox, '… did manifestly speak what comfort was brought into this country with her: to wit, sorrow, dolour, darkness and all impiety.' And sure enough, on the very first Sunday after Mary's landing, a riotous demonstration broke out at Holyrood when Mass was said within the royal chapel for the queen and her predominantly French household.

Yet, for the first four years of her reign, it seemed that Mary might prevail. Though she was no stateswoman and her intelligence was often at the mercy of her passions, she was nevertheless dogged and determined and could often more than hold her own in the tangled world of shifting alliances and affrays that were such a notable feature of Scottish politics. And though there were restive murmurings among 'the godly', her secretary, William Maitland of Lethington, himself a Protestant, was able to argue convincingly that she might well be brought round to 'sweet reasonableness'. Not least of all, there were early signs of common sense and tolerance. Other members of her council, for instance, were also staunchly Protestant and she was prepared, to her credit, to countenance the funding of the reformed church. Moreover, on the occasion of her arrival in Edinburgh, she not only accepted the gift of a vernacular bible and prayer book, but witnessed the burning of a priestly effigy unmoved. Accordingly, a calmer atmosphere soon descended. As one ardent Protestant declared, 'At first I heard men say, "Let us hang the priest", but after that they had been twice or thrice in the Abbey [of Holyrood, at the Queen's Court], all that fervency was past. I think there be some enchantment whereby men are bewitched.' And that enchantment was undoubtedly the queen herself.

Nor was Mary's early success confined to religious affairs, for, in spite of the undoubted glamour of her court, she avoided taxation and largely paid for the regular cost of her household from the income of her French lands. She was visible, too, covering a distance of some 1,200 miles in various progresses across her realm from August 1562 to September 1563: something which demonstrated not only her vitality but also her determination to unite the nobility, the mainstay of her government. Until the very end of her reign, indeed, the backbone of her noble support, for whom John Knox remained a largely marginal figure, would hold steady. And though she was a female, she gained considerable authority from her status as both dowager Queen of France and prospective heir to the throne of England. Almost as important, she was an adult after a prolonged and troubled period of Scottish history in which the throne had been bedevilled by minority government. If, therefore, she married prudently, gained loyal and competent counsel from the men on whom she now relied, and duly circumvented the intrigues of her wily royal cousin south of the Border, the prospects were far from bleak. But her head was proud, her spirit restless and ambition welled within her. The result was the crowning disaster of her marriage to her first cousin, Henry, Lord Darnley.

The son of Matthew Stewart, 4th Earl of Lennox, whose family was closely related to the Scottish royal line, and Margaret Douglas, daughter of Margaret Tudor by her second marriage, Darnley appeared an ideal candidate for Mary's hand in terms of his lineage, boasting a direct claim to the throne of England in his own right. Furthermore, though a Catholic by upbringing, he had toyed with Protestantism and was not associated initially with any dangerous cause either at home or abroad. But, although he was 'accomplished in all courtly exercises' and a gifted lutenist who penned elegant Scottish verses, he was also stupid and treacherous – 'a man of insolent temper' who swiftly alienated most of his potential allies in Scotland, though not, it seems, the queen, who had soon fallen madly in love with the 'fayre, yollye yonge man' and married him on 24 July 1564. Accordingly, when Mary chose the day before the wedding to declare her husband 'King of Scots' – a title which she could not legitimately bestow without the consent of the Scottish Estates – her proclamation was received in stony silence at Mercat Cross by all save the bridegroom's father who offered up a sturdy cry of 'God save his Grace!'

Thereafter, the elements of the final tragedy, which created such an unfavourable start to the life of the future James I, unfolded with a remorseless momentum. Within three weeks of her marriage, Mary's scheming half-brother, the bastard Earl of Moray, whose considerable influence had been threatened by the queen's marriage, came out in open rebellion in the name of the Protestant Kirk, backed by £3,000 from England's Queen Elizabeth. And though he was eventually defeated and driven into exile south of the Border after a chaotic engagement known as the 'Chaseabout Raid', in which a pistol-toting Mary rode in armour and plated cap, 'ever with the foremost' of her troops until 'the most part waxed weary', the price was heavy. For the Queen of Scotland was now placed in a position of open hostility to both Scottish Protestants and her English cousin. Edinburgh, it is true, had ignored Knox's fervent appeals and remained loyal when Moray entered the city in August, but Mary had survived rather than solved her underlying problems, and both her husband's and her own indiscretions would multiply uncontrollably with the mutual antipathy that now exploded between them.

'No woman of spirit', wrote Sir James Melville, 'would make choice of such a man', and whether it was she who first spurned Darnley or he who rejected her remains unknown. But what began as an overwhelming infatuation on Mary's part degenerated within six months into outright and irremediable repulsion, as Darnley cavorted with loose women and, on occasion, behaved with great brutality towards his wife. Refusing absolutely to grant him the Crown Matrimonial, which would have allowed him to rule co-equally and keep the throne in the event of her death, Mary turned increasingly for counsel and consolation to her 'evil-favoured' Italian minion, 'a man of no beauty or shape', and the altogether more dangerous James Hepburn, Earl of Bothwell. While Riccio – 'that great abuser of the commonwealth, that poltroon and vile knave Davie', as Knox graciously dubbed him – flaunted the queen's good offices more and more injudiciously; he courted, of course, the kind of mortal disaster which duly befell him on the night of 9 March 1566. Dragged from the queen's apartments while at supper with her at Holyroodhouse, the helpless secretary was stabbed some fifty-six times within earshot of his horrified mistress. The men responsible included Darnley himself and a motley crew of disgruntled Protestant lords, which numbered the Earl of Morton and his Douglas cronies, the old and dying Lord Ruthven and the exiled Moray, who had been loitering darkly in Newcastle with his fellow rebels awaiting the first available opportunity to conjure trouble.

Whether the intention was also to kill the queen herself or at least encourage her to miscarry from the trauma involved remains uncertain, though some accounts suggest as much. Certainly, Mary appeared to be in danger of miscarrying soon afterwards and the whole event may well have prompted what appears to have been her mental collapse the following year. But if her child was nearly lost and her judgement was to disintegrate catastrophically not long afterwards, for the time being she would show remarkable resources of inner strength and resourcefulness. With the power of Huntly in the Highlands and of Bothwell on the Borders still intact, she could, after all, fight back with every chance of victory and before the bloody night was done her cringing husband, whose very own blade had been left in Riccio's shredded corpse, became so terrified by the possible consequences of his actions that he swiftly deserted his fellow assassins and agreed to take her the 25 miles to the safety of Bothwell's castle at Dunbar. 'Come on! In God's name,' Darnley urged along the way. 'By God's blood, they will murder both you and me if they can catch us … If this baby dies, we can have more.' And when Mary's double-dealing brother, Moray, rode in prudently late next morning, he too was graciously detached from an ill-conceived plot that had so clearly failed to achieve its purposes. A pardon and a cynical guarantee of reinstatement were all that was required.

So there had occurred, even before he was born, the first mortal threat to the future James I of England. Within a week, however, his mother was back in her capital and apparently secure. Already Riccio's murderers were scattered in hiding or in exile and the queen's outward reconciliation with both her husband and Moray was complete. Moreover, for the six months that elapsed from baby James's birth to his christening at Stirling, the surface calm remained intact. Much, if not all, depended upon the child's security, of course, for if he should fall into the hands of the queen's enemies, the pretence of protecting the child would lend a sheen of respectability to any would-be rebel. With this in mind, therefore, James was duly whisked into the guardianship of the Earl of Mar at Stirling Castle when two months old and would remain there for the next twelve years. Mar's family had, in fact, been frequently trusted with similar charges in the past and could claim with some justification to be the hereditary guardians of Scotland's infant royalty, though in this case the boy was largely entrusted to the less than capable hands of a wet nurse named Helena Little. While his father detested him and his mother fought for her political life, Lady Mar, it is true, exercised a genuine, if superficial, tenderness for the child. But Little would remain both everyday overseer of his welfare and a drinker, too, it seems, who is sometimes alleged to have either dropped the prince or neglected an attack of rickets which left him with weakened legs – his right foot 'permanently turned out' – and a shambling, much-mocked walk for the rest of his life.

Yet, at the time of his birth, James's health and appearance left nothing to be desired. Sir Henry Killigrew, the new English ambassador, saw the infant when he was only five days old, and described him as 'a very goodly child'. First, he watched him 'sucking of his nurse' and afterwards saw him 'as good as naked ... his head, feet and hands, all to my judgement well proportioned and like to prove a goodly prince'. The new heir could, moreover, even charm his mother's religious rivals, for on the day following his birth, John Spottiswoode was given the privilege by Mary of holding the child, whereupon he fell to his knees, utterly disarmed, and proceeded to play with him, attempting to teach the infant to utter the word 'Amen'.

And while Spottiswoode's request for a Protestant christening was met with resolute silence, there was nothing coy or even remotely restrained about the ceremony that did eventually follow. The child, after all, was of critical national importance and the lingering slur upon his legitimacy made it doubly necessary that his baptism at Stirling Castle, in December 1566, should be suitably splendid. For the few days involved, therefore, and in spite of the fearful strain upon the Crown's meagre resources, the Scottish court would give free vent to its mistress's extravagance and rival the standards of its French counterpart. Though the child's godparents – the King of France, the Queen of England and the Duke of Savoy

– were unable to appear in person, the embassies and gifts they sent with their proxies were nevertheless suitably impressive. The Comte de Brienne arrived with an entourage of thirty gentlemen and a necklace of pearls and rubies, the Earl of Bedford presented a golden font on Queen Elizabeth's behalf, and the Duke of Savoy, represented by Philibert du Croc, the resident French ambassador, delivered a jewelled fan, trimmed with peacock feathers.

At the service itself, which was to prove the last great Catholic ceremony in sixteenth-century Scotland, the prince was borne from his chamber to the chapel by Brienne, who walked between two rows of barons and gentlemen and was followed by a number of Scottish nobles – all Catholics – proudly bearing the baptismal emblems of their religion: the great 'cierge', or ceremonial candle, the salt, the rood, the basin and the laver. Waiting at the font to officiate was another strident symbol of the old religion, Archbishop Hamilton of St Andrews, attended by the Bishops of Dunkeld, Dunblane and Ross in full episcopal regalia – 'such as had not been seen in Scotland these seven years' – and the entire college of the Chapel Royal. At the font, meanwhile, it was the Countess of Argyll, Elizabeth I's representative as godmother, who held the baby while Hamilton christened him 'Charles James' – 'Charles' after Charles IX, the current King of France, and 'James' in recognition of his five Scottish predecessors of that name. In one respect only did the ceremony vary from ancient Catholic practice, since Hamilton was widely known to be stricken by venereal disease and the queen herself refused to have a 'pocky priest' smear his saliva on her son's mouth, as time-honoured custom normally dictated.

Thereafter, the Lord Lyon King of Arms proclaimed the prince's name and titles – Charles James, Prince and Steward of Scotland, Duke of Rothesay, Earl of Carrick, Lord of the Isles and Baron of Renfrew – and the celebrations ensued. There was triumphant music and dancing, a masque devised by the prince's tutor-to-be, George Buchanan, Latin verses, a torchlight procession, two magnificent banquets and spectacular pyrotechnics of 'fire balls, fire spears and all other things pleasant for the sight of man'. For three whole days, in fact, Mary Queen of Scots allowed herself the illusion that the gentility, carefree excitement – and security – of her Gallic past was still intact, as she danced and charmed with her old familiar energy and aplomb, speaking French at every opportunity, while studiously ignoring the rising tide against her.

And much, indeed, was far from well behind the scenes. The fact that the Earl of Bothwell – dressed in shoes of cloth and silver, and a new suit of 'taffetie' provided at the queen's expense – would not venture beyond the door of the Chapel Royal was proof in its own right of Scotland's religious divisions. But the fact that the Countess of Argyll was subsequently forced to do penance by the Protestant Kirk for her participation in the papist ritual spoke no less eloquently of the simmering discord. Even at the junketing which followed, there was ill feeling. According to Sir James Melville, his fellow ambassadors were affronted, because they believed that the English had been treated 'more friendly and familiarly used than they'. But Melville would claim that the English, too, were no less offended when several men dressed as satyrs, 'running before the meat' at one of the banquets, had 'put their hands behind them to their tails, which they wagged with their hands, in such sort as the Englishmen supposed it had been done and devised in derision of them'. Ultimately, it seems, only the Earl of Bedford's timely intervention prevented an ugly incident.

Much more ominous, however, was Darnley's conspicuous absence from all proceedings, for although he was present at Stirling, 'neither was he required nor permitted to come openly' – or so, at least, it seemed. In fact, he had been furnished by his wife with a splendid suit of cloth of gold and had made his own decision to boycott a ceremony at which none were prepared to accept him as king. Indeed, although his father, the Earl of Lennox, continued to scheme on his behalf for the Crown Matrimonial and a genuine share in government, the queen's husband was now treated with open contempt. The Earl of Bedford, for example, was under strict orders to show Darnley 'no more respect in any way than to the simplest gentlemen present' and when one of the Englishman's assistants happened to encounter Darnley by chance, he was severely reprimanded for referring to him as king. Brienne was under similar instructions and, after three attempts had been made to summon du Croc to Darnley's chamber, the ambassador admitted that he had been told 'to have no conference with him', since he 'was in no good correspondence with queen'.

Mary, moreover, did indeed remain at deepest odds with her husband. Soon after the prince's birth, she had taken herself to the pleasant, airy retreat of Craigmillar Castle and lamented to Maitland, Moray, the Earl of Bothwell and others that she could see no 'outgait' from her marriage, since she dared not consider divorce for fear of affecting her son's legitimacy. And now, perhaps, she was more vulnerable to her husband's bitterness, not to mention the suspicions of her nobles and the venomous denunciations of the Kirk. When summoned to the queen's presence on 22 December, for example, du Croc found her 'laid on the bed weeping sore', complaining of 'a grievous pain in her side' and the effects of a riding accident, in which she had 'hurt one of her breasts'. She was, it is true, as resolved as ever to consolidate her power, particularly against her husband, and du Croc recognised as much. 'The injury she received is exceeding great,' he commented, 'and her majesty will never forget it.' But, as Sir James Melville, one of her few entirely faithful servants, observed, 'there were overfew to comfort her'. And it was in these circumstances that Mary turned to the Earl of Bothwell – 'a man', according to Lord John Herries, 'high in his own conceit, proud, vicious and vainglorious above measure, one who would attempt anything out of ambition'.

A reckless and acquisitive adventurer who was widely thought to be 'of no religion' and who attracted women as effortlessly as he discarded them, Bothwell had at first won Mary's trust and swiftly ascended to become the controlling passion of her life, though he possessed none of the good looks or superficial graces which had first made Darnley so attractive to the queen. On the contrary, he was a short, broad man, whom George Buchanan saw fit to describe as a 'purple ape'. He did, however, exhibit a rugged strength, which had burnished his reputation as a fighting Border magnate and which, to an embattled and infatuated female ruler, might well pass for reliability at a time of flux and crisis. Likewise, though he was no courtier or man of letters, he was nevertheless well educated. Indeed, he had acquired an impressive veneer of French culture during his time on the continent as commander of the King of France's Scottish Guards and was known to be widely read. Had he not had these qualities, it is doubtful whether even the impulsive Queen of Scots might have become such a slave to her own passions and determined to 'go with him to the end of the world in a white petticoat'.

Yet it was undoubtedly as a man of action – the bold, rock-like, canny and decisive manipulator of men and events – that Bothwell made his mark upon Mary. He was, it is true, without scruple, but he was also without fear – 'a rash and hazardous young man' in the words of Sir Nicholas Throckmorton, who scorned both the spiteful effeminacy of her husband and slippery double-dealing of a Maitland or a Moray. And he had proven his mettle already when his quick thinking and notorious private army had plucked the queen from disaster in the aftermath of Riccio's assassination. That Bothwell, who was so dismissive of all convention, should have had so many enemies was something that Mary might certainly have considered before rashly throwing in her lot with him. But that such a character would manage to exercise so overpowering an influence over so vulnerable and notoriously impressionable a ruler is not nearly as surprising as is often assumed.

With or without Bothwell, however, the noose was tightening rapidly for Darnley. On 24 December, only a week after his son's christening, Mary's panic-stricken husband learned that his wife had pardoned the survivors of Riccio's murderers, whom he had blatantly betrayed. At least half the nobility of Scotland were now slavering for his blood, and by this time, too, the queen had certainly been shown at least one of the 'bands' that Darnley had signed with the assassins. Knowing now that his feeble pretence of acting against his wife's Italian favourite on a blind and passionate impulse could no longer be sustained, Darnley made at once for his father's house in Glasgow, then a small village on the River Clyde, and the hoped-for safety of Lennox territory, while the atmosphere all around thickened with plots and ugly whispers.

Back at Craigmillar Castle before Christmas, Maitland of Lethington had already assured Mary that a 'mean', not involving divorce, might be devised to rid her of her husband both neatly and without prejudice to her son's legitimacy and that Moray, who was a 'little less scrupulous for a Protestant than your Grace is for ane Papist', would 'look through his fingers thereto'. No specific decision, it seems, was actually taken at that time, but in that same month Mary managed to restore Archbishop Hamilton's authority to pronounce decrees of divorce by nullity, whether for her own marriage or perhaps Bothwell's. At the same time, there were unsettling reports – originating with William Hiegait, town clerk of Glasgow – of a counterplot by Darnley and his father to kidnap the baby prince from Stirling.

By now, as matters reached a climax, Darnley was convalescing at Glasgow after an attack of either syphilis or smallpox, which had overtaken him during his flight. Blue blisters had broken out upon him and he was said to be 'in very great pain and dolour in every part of his body'. Then, at his father's home, Lord Herries tells us, 'his hair fell off'. But this did not, it seems, impair either his gall or his libido. On 14 January, Mary's request to visit him had been met by a rude verbal answer and when Mary arrived nonetheless a week later, her husband's main concern appears to have been that she should restore his conjugal rights as soon as he was fit once more. Already, more than a year earlier, according to the records of Catherine Maxwell Stuart, 21st Lady of Traquair, Darnley had disgraced himself when Mary excused herself from accompanying him on a hunting expedition for fear that she might again be pregnant. 'What,' retorted Darnley, 'ought we not to work a mare well when she is in foal?' And now, with his disfigured face still covered by a taffeta mask, the husband's prurience remained as undiminished as his bile.

Once more, however, Mary was quick to re-establish her ascendancy and Darnley – notwithstanding the sensible forebodings of his father – swiftly conceded to be brought to Edinburgh in a litter that his wife had brought with her, so that he should not be 'far from her son'. Upon his arrival, he was eventually lodged outside the walls, not only 'in a solitaire place at the outmost part of ye town' but in a squalid, ruined neighbourhood approached by a street known as 'Thieves' Row', where there lay a small and wholly unsuitable four-roomed house known as the Kirk o' Field, in which the queen had nonetheless established a magnificent bedroom for herself on the ground floor. It was there on the night of Sunday, 9 February that Mary visited her husband, by torchlight, for what would prove to be the last time. Leaving shortly before midnight to attend a masque in honour of the wedding of her French servant, Bastien Pagès, she may well have done so in full knowledge of what would shortly ensue. For Bothwell and his most trusted retainers had secretly packed the basement of Kirk o' Field with gunpowder, which was duly ignited two hours later. Though Darnley's naked corpse showed no marks of the explosion when it was later discovered in the garden, along with that of one of his pages, there was no doubting that the 'deid was foully done', and there was no doubt either of the gravity of what followed. If, wrote one contemporary, Darnley 'had not been cruelly vyrriet [strangled], after he fell out of the aire, with his own garters, he had leived'. And in subsequently flaunting all serious pretence at justice, Mary duly incurred outright moral disgrace, not only in Scotland but throughout Catholic and Protestant Europe alike.

Though Bothwell underwent a spurious form of trial before fifteen hand-picked peers and lairds, which conveniently foundered for lack of evidence, since Darnley's father dare not enter Edinburgh while 6,000 of Bothwell's armed Borderers remained in firm control, Mary herself made no effort to clear her name, and then, to crown all, carelessly embarked upon her ultimate folly. With the capital awash with denunciations of her lover and the abuse of Protestant preachers ringing in every kirk, the queen remained impervious. She remained equally unmoved, too, by Moray's final warning in early April that she was courting disaster 'because of the great trouble seeming to come to the realm'. Moray himself had already cannily distanced himself from Darnley's murder by removing to Fife on the actual night of the deed and now he carefully avoided any involvement in what he clearly perceived to be his half-sister's imminent ruin, leaving for England on ostensibly amicable terms with Bothwell, to wait as he had before for events to turn decisively in his favour.

Nor was Moray's reasoning anything other than sound. On 17 April, as the ultimate insult to the whole of Scotland, Bothwell was selected to carry the crown and sceptre before the queen at the opening of Parliament. And upon the very evening that the Estates dissolved, he finally revealed the full scale of his ambitions for the first time. Appropriately, perhaps, it was at Ainslie's Tavern, which had been thoroughly surrounded by his armed retainers, that Bothwell brazenly forced his noble guests to pledge their belief in his innocence and commit their support to a 'marriage betwixt her Highness and the said noble lord'. The pledge, of course, was as empty as the dreams of the man who imposed it, but the die had now been irretrievably cast – both for him and for the queen who had given herself over to him so entirely.

Around this time, Mary would pen for Bothwell a series of sonnets and appallingly indiscreet love letters, but even now, it seems, her passion for the frenzied earl had not entirely blinded her to the interests of her infant son. Accordingly, on 21 April, she rode to Stirling to pay what was to prove her last visit to the prince. Such, however, was the general collapse of her credibility that not even that most loyal of servants, the Earl of Mar, would surrender the child to her. On the contrary, knowing full well that the whole future of the realm was inextricably tied to the boy's well-being, Mar would only allow the queen to bring two of her ladies with her into the castle, and her two-day sojourn brought little consolation to all concerned. It was even rumoured, albeit wholly improbably, that, at one point during her stay, Mary had attempted to coax the child to stop screaming by the offer of an apple, which he brusquely rejected. Whereupon the apple was subsequently eaten by a greyhound bitch that promptly swelled and died.

Certainly, Mary left Stirling without the prince and swiftly succumbed to the final episode in her disgrace and downfall, for at Linlithgow – with almost farcically suspicious ease – she was duly 'kidnapped' by Bothwell and carried off to Dunbar. Deluded by the pledges delivered at Ainslie's Tavern, the earl seems to have fondly imagined that the majority of Scots nobles would actually condone his action, while Mary, if her subsequent behaviour is any guide, was apparently too besotted to care. If, moreover, her claim that she had been raped carried no conviction, her decision to marry the perpetrator on the grounds that she had been irretrievably compromised by her violation, was the ultimate act of political madness. Nevertheless, during the three weeks that Mary remained at Dunbar, Archbishop Hamilton rushed through an annulment of Bothwell's marriage to his current wife, Janet Gordon, and the new union of queen and earl was formally sanctioned. Though even Mary would not dare to grant her husband the title of king, he was nevertheless created Duke of Orkney and Shetland, which caused sufficient scandal it its own right. And as if to seal the scale of Mary's current derangement, the wedding itself was duly performed according to Protestant rites.

Soon, moreover, it was patently clear that Mary had not only abandoned her son but placed his life in dire peril, since Bothwell determined at once to gain possession of the prince, and the mother was ready to comply. 'She intends,' wrote one Scots lord, 'to take the prince out of Mar's hands and put him in Bothwell's keeping, who murdered his father.' In the meantime, for the next three weeks the couple honeymooned unhappily at Borthwick Castle in a state of near siege, while the earl continued to ply Janet Gordon with letters and steadily honed his plans for ultimate mastery. If the prince should fall into his new stepfather's hands, it was generally acknowledged that the earl would 'make him away … as well to advance his own succession, as to cut off the innocent child, who in all probability would one day revenge his father's death' – all of which seems to have escaped Mary herself. Likewise, as the remnants of her supporters, including Lethington, deserted the rapidly sinking ship and the situation in the capital grew steadily more menacing, the queen continued to hope against hope that events might yet turn decisively in her favour. Accordingly, by the time that she and Bothwell slipped away once more to Dunbar, everything already depended upon a final trial of arms, which would not be long in coming.

The Protestant 'Lords of the Congregation', who had all been implicated more or less in Bothwell's assassination of Darnley, had already committed themselves by bond to protect Prince James. And now these 'True Lords' had the brazen effrontery to march against the mastermind of the murder under a banner depicting the victim's naked body. Yet Mary remained undaunted and on 15 June, both she and Bothwell moved out to confront their enemies at Carberry Hill. For most of the day, in fact, the two armies faced each other, very reluctant to fight, and while the uneasy posturing continued, there were last minute attempts at mediation by the French ambassador, du Croc. Mary, however, refused to accept the condition that she leave Bothwell and refused, too, to concede to her husband's outlandish request that matters be resolved by single combat with any one of the opposition lords. In the event, as Bothwell frothed and she in her turn clutched at any straw to hand, the royal army slowly disintegrated.

Surrendering herself, therefore, in return for an agreement that her hated spouse be permitted to escape with his life, Mary now encountered at first hand the full wrath and resentment that her actions had stirred. Kirkaldy of Grange, a brave and chivalrous soldier who negotiated the queen's final surrender, had guaranteed her respectful treatment, but he had not counted upon the venom and violence of the Edinburgh mob. Indeed, such was Mary's reception that Kirkaldy did well to keep her alive and eventually joined her cause in disgust at her enemies' hysteria. Surrounded by the victorious Protestant lords, whom she continually cursed and threatened, she rode into the capital for the last time to cries that she be lynched or drowned as an 'adulteress' and 'murderess', and further howls that 'the whore' be burnt. Utterly distraught at the full, brutal shock of her new condition, she was ultimately detained at the provost's lodging in the High Street, where she made a fleeting appearance at a window to issue a final appeal for aid. With her hair loosened and her clothes indecently torn and disordered, she appeared for the moment to have lost her reason.

Even at this critical pitch of despair, however, Mary nevertheless represented an ongoing threat to her captors. With Huntly in arms in the north and the Hamiltons secure in the west, the future was still uncertain, and the queen, for all her faults and wretchedness, was queen nonetheless. At 26, moreover, she was likely to be a danger for many years to come. Nor was this all, for open rebellion by the Protestant lords against the anointed queen could still be guaranteed to raise a majority of Scots against them. Elizabeth, too – though she wrote privately to her cousin sharply condemning both the murder of Darnley and subsequent marriage to

Bothwell – left no doubt that she would declare war, if there was any attempt to stage a deposition. The lords' ostensible target had therefore always been Bothwell, and when Mary was now closely confined among the Fifeshire bogs surrounding the island castle of Loch Leven, it was firmly emphasised that she was undergoing 'seclusion' rather than imprisonment.

Yet her treatment, predictably, left much to be desired. A month or so after her arrival, she capped her misfortunes by miscarrying Bothwell's twins, though this, it must be said, did nothing to soften her captors. Her gaoler, for instance, was Sir William Douglas – a 'depender' of the Earl of Morton, one of Riccio's assassins, and her disaffected half-brother, Moray – who did little to protect her from the insults and ill-treatment, which were blatantly intended to break her spirit. Lord Ruthven, on the other hand, the son of the corpse-like old murderer whose appearance had so alarmed the queen on the night of Riccio's murder, oppressed her with his lust, while Moray's mother, Lady Margaret Erskine, also took every opportunity to insult her. Worse still, perhaps, Lord Lindsay, a brutal and unscrupulous bully, subjected her to outright threats of physical force. Sick, imperilled and wholly beyond the reach of any 'friends', Mary was therefore hardly equipped to withstand these ultimate assaults upon her fast-waning reserves of resilience and utterly shredded integrity.

Ironically, however, the Queen of Scots was once more undone by her own indiscretions. Only one week after her capture, in fact, the silver casket in which Bothwell had kept her secret sonnets and letters to him, as well as her pledge to marry him, was duly discovered. The earl, it seems, had left them behind for safekeeping in Edinburgh, only to furnish his enemies with the most explosive of weapons. Indeed, irrespective of any tampering that may have occurred, the 'Casket Letters' not only stirred John Knox and his fellow pulpiteers to new heights of invective by their 'coarseness' but also placed Mary in alarmingly real danger for her life, for according to an ancient Scottish statute, which had been recently revived, adultery was not only a capital offence but punishable in the case of females by burning.

All sober, moderate opinion now accepted, in any case, that 'a Queen hath no more liberty or privilege to commit adultery or murder than any other private person, either by God's laws, or the laws of the realm', and even Elizabeth's heartfelt appeals on Mary's behalf had already lost much of their force. In these circumstances, therefore, the only remaining option, as the queen grudgingly accepted, was abdication and a subsequent minority government on behalf of her son. Finally broken by her captors' naked intimidation and threats that she would be brought to trial and execution, Mary duly provided the lords and, above all, her half-brother with the documents they required. Though Moray was not present at the final disgraceful scene, where threats of throat-cutting, drowning in the loch and even marooning on a desert island were aimed at his half-sister, he was duly authorised to assume the regency, with the assistance of a commission of seven noblemen, 'in caisse', it was almost laughably claimed, 'he should refuse to exercise ye same alone'. No such refusal was, of course, forthcoming and on 24 July, Mary duly acquiesced. 'When God shall set me at liberty again,' she declared through bitter damned-up tears, 'I shall not abide these, for it is done against my will.' But her reign as Queen of Scots was over forever.

2 ⚶ King and Pawn

'I was alone, without father or mother, brother or sister, King of this realm, and heir apparent of England.'

James VI, 1589

On 29 July 1567, in the church of the Holy Rude at Stirling, on a craggy hillside rising to the castle, Prince James was crowned King of Scots, the sixth ruler of his kingdom to have governed with that name. With its commanding view over the River Forth and the Ochils, no fortress in Scotland boasted a more dramatic setting. A few miles to the north, rising sharply from the plain, lay the 'Highland Line', one of the great geological faults to which Scotland owed not only its shape but its history, while to the north-west spread the expanse of bog land, across which meagre, sluggish streams ambled off to supply the river Forth. To the south, on the other hand, spread the humbler ridge of the Campsies, though these, too, reflected the wall of the Highlands and the more imposing peaks of Ben Ledi, Ben Vorlich and Ben Lomond. All in all, no spot resonated more with Scottish prowess, Scottish pride and Scottish royalty. Bannockburn, the most decisive battle in Scottish history had been fought for the castle and the vital bridge below it, and both James IV and James V had left their indelible mark upon the place, improving its buildings and rendering the six main apartments of its royal palace comparable to any in Northern Europe. Plainly, then, Stirling was the benchmark for high Scottish culture and the clearest possible statement of Stuart legitimacy and permanence – the traditional home of the current dynasty, and the right and natural starting-point, by any standards, for the reign of the 13-month-old James VI.

Yet the new king's inauguration was a mean and meagre affair, tainted by circumstance and shrouded in fears for the future. Staged only five days after the deposition of the former queen, it was the worst-attended coronation in Scottish history. In the opinion of one of her spokesmen, indeed, only seven lords, no more than a tenth of the Scots nobility, were present, and even the English ambassador – a fervent Protestant – was obliged to boycott the ceremony, since it was the act of an illegal regime that had challenged the sovereignty of the Crown and threatened the established order of things. As such, the Elizabethan government, which was still engaged in establishing its own respectability, could not afford to become entangled with it. This was not the only oddity, since the ceremony also involved a change of name for the monarch – something that had occurred only once before in the whole of Scotland's past. For, as a result of its association with the French king, the king's baptismal name of 'Charles James' was suitably clipped and the new monarch would henceforth be known only as James VI.

Crowned, then, not in the castle's Chapel Royal, where his mother had been enthroned in 1542, but in the altogether humbler setting of the burgh's parish church, the infant king found himself at the centre of a ritual which fully reflected the tensions existing in his realm. Though anointed in the style of previous Scottish monarchs, there were neither candles nor copes nor incense on hand. Nor were there fanfares or heralds to proclaim the new king in what was consciously presented as an aggressively Protestant reaction against the former regime. Latin, too, was carefully avoided; instead, all prayers were 'in the English tongue'. It was not without irony either, of course, that the infant ruler's crown was placed upon his head by Robert Stewart, the former Catholic Bishop of Orkney, who had last appeared in public to marry the child's mother to Bothwell. And it was an equally curious footnote to Queen Mary's reign that the subsequent sermon should have been preached by none other than John Knox. Taking his text from 2 Chronicles 23: 20–21, he declaimed with characteristic candour and at typical length upon the coronation of the child king Joash, whose mother, Queen Athaliah, had rent her clothes and cried 'treason, treason', before being taken out and slain by the sword.

To seal the transformation at the heart of government, however, it was none other than James Douglas, 4th Earl of Morton, who read aloud the new king's coronation oath. Arguably the most crooked and treacherous of the whole shifty crew that had brought Mary Stuart to her ruin, it was red-headed Douglas who had held Holyrood for Riccio's murderers and signed Bothwell's bond against Darnley. And now it was he who pledged the king not only to maintain the 'lovable laws and constitutions received in this realm' and 'to rule in the faith, fear and love of God', but also to 'root out all heretics and enemies to the true worship of God that shall be convicted by the true Kirk of God of the aforesaid crimes'. For his efforts on the new government's behalf, Morton was duly nominated as chancellor in the Regency Council that now assumed power.

It was composed, said George Buchanan, the king's future tutor, 'of nourishers of theft and raisers of rebellion', who were characterised by 'insatiable greediness' and 'intolerable arrogance'. 'For the most part', it seems, its members were men 'without faith in promises, pity to the inferior, or obedience to the superior'. 'In peace', moreover, they were 'desirous of trouble, in war thirsty of blood'. But the power of Buchanan's beloved Kirk depended on these men. Like him, his fellow preachers desired that the whole government of Scotland, civil and ecclesiastical, be subordinated to their charge, while the nobles were determined merely to maintain power and wealth for themselves. To say, therefore, that both parties were uneasy allies is an understatement of some magnitude, though their mutual dependence was unavoidable, and both were also driven to an equally distasteful dependence upon England, which most thinking Scotsmen had long been struggling to avoid. It was English intrigues and often English subsidies, after all, which had assisted the present clique of Protestant lords into power and now, as conservative and moderate opinion alike recoiled from the implications of this dependence, it was English influence that would hold their opponents at bay.

In the meantime, the infant boy who might one day serve to guarantee good order and government was entrusted once more, at Regent Moray's behest, to the Earl and Countess of Mar. Formally appointed on 22 August, Moray had chosen the obvious candidates, since the earl in particular was a nobleman of the highest order, respected by both his own party and its opponents. And until his death in 1572, when his role was assumed by his brother, Sir Alexander Erskine, his conduct was exemplary. Like the earl himself, moreover, Erskine was another genuinely benign influence – 'a nobleman', observed Sir James Melville, 'of a true, gentle nature, well-loved and liked of every man for his good qualities and great discretion, in no wise factious or envious' – though in the countess, King James was not perhaps so fortunate. For while, as we have seen, she played his foster-mother with due conviction initially, referring to him always as 'the Lord's Annointed' and occasionally objecting when he was beaten, she was nevertheless a stern enough governess in her own right – especially after her husband's death when she continued in her post and held the king in 'great awe' of her. Rather more worryingly, she also continued to delegate too much of the child's everyday care to Little, his tippling wet nurse. Though hardly the fount of all objectivity, Knox described Lady Mar as 'a very Jesabell' and a 'sweet titbit for the Devil's mouth', and if his intention on this occasion was to highlight her connection to the former queen, it was true, nevertheless, that the king's own feelings about the countess were always likely to have been mixed.

Certainly, the provision of the royal household, though less than extravagant, was adequate to its purposes. Four young women, for example, were employed to rock the king in his cradle – perhaps the wooden cradle of Traquair which is traditionally supposed to have been his – and there were also three gentlemen of the bedchamber, two women to tend the king's clothes and two musicians, Thomas and Robert Hudson, though James himself exhibited no ear for music in later life. And while the Master of the Household, Cunningham of Drumwhassel, was not only Moray's cousin but in Melville's view an ambitious and greedy man, even he appears to have devoted himself effectively enough to the day-to-day management of the king's domestic arrangements, which changed little throughout his early childhood. Food and drink were ample, with an allowance for the 'King's own mouth daily' of two and a half loaves of bread, three pints of ale and two capons. And though most of the former queen's furniture lay idle at Holyrood, three fine tapestries were nevertheless brought to Stirling for her son's comfort, notwithstanding the fact that his bed in the Prince's Tower was a gloomy contrivance of black damask, with ruff, head-piece and pillows also fringed in the same colour.

In the king's bedchamber too, fittingly enough, hung a portrait of his ill-fated grandfather, James V, who, along with boy's great-grandfather, James IV, had played such a key role in fashioning Stirling Castle. The latter, arguably the most heroic of all Scotland's kings, had been killed in battle by the English at Flodden Field in 1513, and although the boy would show no such prowess whatsoever, his great-grandfather's legacy was all around him – not only in stirring tales of his martial deeds and tragedy, but in the very walls of the castle itself. Known as 'James of the Iron Belt', the fallen hero of Flodden had, for instance, erected the great defensive bulwark across the main approach to the fortress around 1500 and had probably completed the royal courtyard, now dubbed the Upper Square, about the same date. James V, meanwhile, influenced by two marriages to French princesses and his own sojourn in France, imported French masons and built the palace on the south side of the square and the Great Hall. In particular, the sculpted figures of the Devil and King James himself on the south walls displayed the same French influence that had characterised the whole reign, so that while the new monarch would be reared in expectation of the English Crown, he was left in no doubt either that his roots were plainly Scottish and that the realm across the Border was both foreign and fierce.

Before he could unify his God-given kingdoms, however, James would have to grow and learn – two tasks that, in his case, were far from carefree. Before he had reached his fourth birthday, in fact, two scholars were appointed by the government to supervise the king's education: the formidable George Buchanan, poet, humanist, historian and unyielding taskmaster, and the altogether more temperate Peter Young, a young man fresh from his studies under Theodore Beza at Geneva. Learned, gifted, and widely lauded for his accomplishments, Buchanan, on the one hand, had lengthy experience as a tutor to some of the best families in both Scotland and France, and had once been the instructor of none other than the great French essayist, Michel de Montaigne. But he was ill-suited to deal with a child scarcely out of the nursery – and especially one as nervous, excitable and overstrung as James would prove to be. Melville, for his part, described the elderly master aptly enough as a 'stoic philosopher' and fully acknowledged the 'notable qualities' of his learning and knowledge which were 'much made account of in other nations'. There was ample recognition, too, that Buchanan was 'pleasant in company, rehearsing on all occasions moralities, short and forceful', 'of good religion for a poet' and a man of commendable frankness and honesty – someone who, as Melville put it, 'looked not far before the hand'. Yet Buchanan was also, we are told, 'easily abused', 'factious in his old days' and, worse still, 'extremely vengeable against any man that offended him which was his greatest fault'.

Nor, it seems, was Buchanan especially inclined to forgiveness of his royal pupil. More than sixty years older than the king and in declining health, he found his new role, at times, an irritating distraction from his own more serious studies – even though he had lobbied for the post before it became available – and in consequence occasionally vented his frustrations upon both the boy and reputation of his mother. Curiously enough, the old man had once taught Mary herself and at that time commended 'the excellency of her mien, the delicacy of her beauty, the vigour of her blooming years, all joined in her recommendation'. But he had become Protestant in 1563 and thenceforth the schoolmaster's antipathy to that 'bludy woman and poisoning witch' knew no bounds. Indeed, his scornful *Detectio Mariae Regina Scotorum* not only rivalled Knox's vitriol but possibly surpassed it, ranking perhaps as one of the most powerful pieces of rhetorical invective of its day. She, who had formerly been the object of Buchanan's elegiacs, a woman 'of nobility rarer than all her kindred', now suddenly degenerated, into the caricature reviled in every Edinburgh gutter – the personification of 'intemperate authority' whose 'immeasurable but mad love' for Bothwell had brought her to shame. In due course, indeed, it would be Buchanan who confirmed Mary's handwriting in the Casket Letters before both the Scottish Parliament and Elizabeth I's court at Westminster.

And now James would be exposed to the full blast of Buchanan's sulphurous wrath. On one particularly notorious occasion, a boyish tussle had, it seems, broken out between the king and his playmate, John Erskine, son of the Earl of Mar, over possession of a sparrow, in the course of which the unfortunate bird met its end. When Buchanan heard of the incident, he went to work with characteristic gusto, slapping the king's ear and adding, with all his usual venom for the former queen, that the boy himself was 'a true bird of that bludy nest'. On another occasion, when James and Mar were somewhat noisy at their play and the master was at his books, he warned the king that 'if he did not hold his peace, he would whip his breach'. The result was a not altogether unprecedented attempt at cheek from the king and the due delivery – 'in a passion' – of a thorough thrashing by Buchanan. When, moreover, the Countess of Mar came to the boy's rescue, rebuking the old man for laying hands upon 'the Lord's Annointed', Buchanan responded in style. 'Madam,' he replied with the kind of cudgel subtlety that could be guaranteed to thwart his protagonist in mid-flight, 'I have whipped his arse, you may kiss it if you please.'

It is small wonder, then, that James should have recalled his tutor in considerable awe, if not outright fear. Years later, at the age of 53, he would tell one of his officials 'that he trembled at his approach, it minded him so of his pedagogue'. Nor, perhaps, is it altogether surprising that the king should have gone on to challenge so roundly some of the political lessons that his tutor had been at such pains to instil. In 1579, when James was 13, not far from the time of his personal rule in Scotland, Buchanan wrote *De Jure Regni apud Scotis* (*The Rights of the Crown in Scotland*). Dedicated to James, the book emphasised that kings should be lovers and models of piety, bringing dread to the bad and delight to the good. But though, in Buchanan's view, a king was the father of his people, he was also accountable to them, existing for their benefit rather than vice versa. Kings, he asserted, were bound by the power which first made them kings, which was not God, but the people. More radically still, Buchanan also taught that it was desirable not only to resist tyrants, but to punish them. Clearly, James's later claims that kings were God's lieutenants on earth would have appalled his former teacher. And it was not insignificant, of course, that, years later in 1584, when James had achieved his majority, Buchanan's work was duly condemned at the king's behest by Scotland's Parliament.

Yet James would also boast, with full justification, of his training under a teacher of such renown. In 1603, for instance, he told Nicolo Molin, the Venetian ambassador, how his tutor had instructed him in the excellence of Venice's constitution, and when, as King of England, an English scholar praised the elegance of his Latin, James was quick to acknowledge his debt: 'All the world knows that my master, Mr George Buchanan, was a great master in that faculty,' he observed. 'I follow his pronunciation both of the Latin and the Greek, and am sorry that my people of England do not the like; for certainly their pronunciation utterly spoils the grace of these two learned languages.' Nor, surprisingly enough, was James entirely unforgiving of his former tutor's temperament. 'If the man hath burst out here and there into excess or speech of bad temper, that must be imputed to the violence of his humour and heat of his spirit, not in any wise to the rules of true religion rightly by him conceived.' Buchanan's character was, after all, a curious mixture of opposing qualities, as James's backchat prior to his most notorious beating and the master's subsequent encounter with Lady Mar clearly confirm. Like other men of intellect before and after, in fact, George Buchanan was both humane and vindictive, mirthful and morose, cultured and coarse, full of prejudice, but above all fond of truth.

And there was in any case, of course, the mollifying influence of the king's other tutor to compensate for the older man's more pitiless approach. Born in 1544, the gentle, lovable, 'wise and sharp' Peter Young believed in praise and encouragement rather than the rod as the foundation of learning, and was probably James's first real friend, bringing a note of genuine humanity to his childhood that the pupil would not, it seems, forget. Young, indeed, would remain about the king's person to the end of the reign, by which time he had served as chief almoner, performed ambassadorial roles in Denmark, and been endowed with a long string of ecclesiastical preferments which eventually left him the Master of the Hospital of St Cross in Winchester. Whether, of course, Buchanan consciously encouraged the contrast in teaching styles with his younger protégé is unknown but, as Young's superior, he made no effort to discourage it and spoke of his colleague in the highest terms in his *Epistolae*. Given Buchanan's advancing years, moreover, Young may well in any case have undertaken the major share of teaching duties.

There were, it is true, notable gaps in the king's upbringing. Not least of all, James ate and drank carelessly, making slovenliness almost a virtue at a time when courtly graces were widely considered the hallmark of true nobility. Doubtless, Buchanan regarded such refinements as largely unimportant and, from some perspectives, even reprobate. A king's main business, after all, was simply to rule and to rule simply at that. Dour democrat that he was, the old man frequently reminded his pupil how affectation as well as flattery were loathsome vices, in much the same way that titles – 'majesties', 'lordships' and 'excellencies' – served only to erect an artificial barrier between rulers and ruled. More worryingly, however, the very rigour of the king's education propagated at least two long-term side effects, for while the iron self-discipline of scholarship and the equally rigid spiritual constraints of Calvinism were intended to fashion a careful and conscientious ruler, the adult James was only truly diligent under compulsion and never consistently so. Nor, for that matter, could his tutors eliminate the devious secret side that became compounded by the broader circumstances of a childhood beset by political insecurity and physical threats.

Of considerable significance, too, was the fact that Buchanan's own particular brand of pedantry and intellectual intolerance seems to have left another lasting imprint. Certainly, the young king was not without wit – albeit of the more sardonic kind often characteristic of the highly educated. Indeed, under Buchanan's guidance, the exercise of a quicksilver, caustic tongue may well have taken the form of an ancillary education in its own right. But what might have developed into an accomplishment of sorts became in this particular case a clear-cut vice. On one occasion, the tedium and imperfection of the young Earl of Mar's French became too much for James, who detonated with all the vigour worthy of his tutor.

'I have not understood a single word you have said,' declared James, adding, 'what the Lord Regent has said of you seems to be true, that your French is nothing and your Scots little better.' And when Peter Young reminded the king that he should never lose his temper, he was met with more irritation still. 'Then,' came the response, 'I should not wear the lion on my arms but rather a sheep.'

Equally regrettable, in some respects, were the effects of James's comparative isolation from women. Apart from the Countess of Mar, whom he affectionately dubbed his 'Lady Ninny', there was little female company on hand to leaven his childhood – something, it is sometimes said, that may partly explain his later, almost tragic, yearning for affection. On one occasion we hear of him thanking the countess for a gift of fruit, but apart from Lady Mar herself, who was also capable of a distinct hardness in her own right, the influence of female society was little in evidence. Significantly or otherwise, Young mentions a game of *trou-madame* in which the king made a small wager with several young ladies but, upon losing, brusquely displayed his irritation at having to pay the forfeit. It is tempting to speculate, too, that Buchanan's own influence as a hard-bitten bachelor and outright misogynist may well have reinforced the strength of James's opinions in later life about the role and station of women.

Meanwhile, the distance – both physical and emotional – between the king and his mother remained considerable. It was not only Buchanan, for instance, who impressed upon James that his sole surviving parent was a murderer and adulteress, and it was not long either before the boy realised that this alone was why he was king. More disconcertingly still, perhaps, he soon appreciated that from her exile in England, Mary remained a threat to his status, since she had never accepted her enforced abdication and had therefore never recognised her son's assumption of the Crown. And while she hoped for reconciliation with the child she still considered her heir, the gulf between them would be carefully maintained by those controlling James's destiny. After Mary attempted, for instance, 'to remind him of his afflicted mother', she explained to Queen Elizabeth in England how her efforts had been ruthlessly suppressed. She had sent him when he was 2 years old an ABC and a pony complete with saddle and bridle, but because the affectionate letter that went with them was addressed to 'my dear son, James Charles, Prince of Scotland' rather than to the king, they were never given to him. Two years later, moreover, the Scottish Parliament formally decreed at Stirling that there should be no contact between James and his mother, except through the Council. No feeling of tenderness or pity was therefore ever forthcoming from the boy until Mary's head was finally severed from her shoulders, at which point he would denounce the Casket Letters as forgeries and bemoan the fate of 'that poor lady, my mother'.

In the meantime, however, the king would continue to persevere in his studies, which, in spite of any shortcomings and for all their rigours, were not without considerable virtues. 'First in the morning', Young tells us, 'he sought guidance in prayer, since God Almighty bestows favour and success upon all studies', and having been 'cleansed through prayer and having propitiated the Deity', James then devoted himself to Greek, practising the rules of grammar and reading either from the New Testament or Isocrates, or from the apophthegms of Plutarch. But this, in fact, was still only the start of his daily programme, since breakfast was followed by readings in Latin, either from Livy, Justin, Cicero, or from Scottish or foreign history. After which, with dinner over, he devoted himself to composition, before spending the remainder of the afternoon, if time permitted, upon arithmetic or cosmography – which included geography or astronomy – or dialectics or rhetoric. As a result, the young king was soon able not only to compose both competent verse and accurate pithy prose in English, French and Latin, but to hold his own in argument against many much older men – especially when discourse in Latin was involved.

In the process, however, James acquired a love for rigorous logic and incontrovertible argument that would later smack of dogmatism and pedantry – and nowhere more so, perhaps, than in the field of religion where his familiarity with Calvinist theology and methods of reasoning left an indelible mark upon his general outlook. Calvin's whole system, in fact, was based upon the notion of absolute truths derived by remorseless reasoning from infallible premises. This narrow, rigid and dialectical method, with its cast-iron approach to divinity, leaving no room for compromise, appealed to James strongly, for though he was fully versed in the humanism of the Renaissance, he was also immersed in the thinking of the medieval schoolmen and, above all, the power of the syllogism. Having thereby derived his thoughts on any matter, whether theological or secular, James could be guaranteed to hold firm against all comers, especially upon the subject of Catholicism.

At the age of 11, indeed, the king was declaiming against the Catholic controversialist Archibald Hamilton with all the vigour that one would expect from a pupil of both Buchanan and Young. The king 'marvelled', it seems, that Hamilton's most well-known book 'should be put forth by a Scotsman'. 'I love him not so evil because he is a Hamilton,' he concluded, 'as that I do because he is an apostate.' On another occasion, in speaking of the papal claim to the keys of heaven and hell, James readily quoted St Luke (6:52): 'Woe unto you lawyers: for ye have taken away the key of knowledge: ye enter not in yourselves, and them that are entering ye hindered.' He was more than capable, too, of exercising his learning at the expense of the younger of his tutors. When Peter Young punished a small fault by forbidding the king to read the lesson for the day, which was the 119th Psalm, James quoted the text very aptly: 'Wherewith shall a young man cleanse his way?' It was this kind of 'smartness' and yen for having the last word, too, which may well have encouraged some of Buchanan's more brutal responses to his precocious young charge.

Yet James's supreme confidence in his own opinions was by no means entirely vacuous, for rarely has a youthful royal mind been so successfully filled by his tutors, and his 'great towardness in learning' was widely and rightly acknowledged by those well placed to judge. 'At this early age,' Buchanan told the king when he was 16, 'you have pursued the history of almost every nation and have committed many of them to memory.' And a passing comment scribbled in one of James's copy-books – possibly a flash of penetrating protest or at least exasperation – bears ample testimony to the intensity of his education. 'They gar me speik Latin,' he observed, 'ar I could speik Scotis'. Furthermore, the Protestant minister James Melville tells in his autobiography how he encountered the king at Stirling in 1574 when he was only 8 and found him 'the sweetest sight in Europe that day for strange and extraordinary gifts of wit, judgement, memory and language'. 'I heard him discourse,' said Melville, 'walking up and down in the old Lady Mar's hand, of knowledge and ignorance, to my great marvel and astonishment.' Nor did Sir Henry Killigrew, who observed the king regularly, harbour any doubt whatsoever about the boy's considerable ability. Writing to Queen Elizabeth in the same year that Melville recorded his observations, the ambassador informed the queen how the boy 'was able extempore ... to read a chapter of the Bible out of Latin into French, and out of French after into English, so well as few men could have added anything to his translation.' The boy was, concluded Killigrew, 'a Prince sure of great hope, if God give him life'. And in 1588 the Jesuit James Gordon would also highlight James's intimate knowledge of biblical texts – something which both Buchanan and Young, wholly predictably, had placed at the top of their educational agenda. A chapter of the Bible was read and discussed at every meal and the effects were notable. James, said Gordon, 'is naturally eloquent, has a keen intelligence, and a very powerful memory, for he knows a great part of the bible by heart'. 'He cites not only chapters,' Gordon added, 'but even the verses in a perfectly marvellous way.'

Buchanan in particular, however, was determined to fashion a king as well as a scholar – an individual endowed with self-knowledge as well as book learning, and a grasp of the ways of the world as well as the narrower realm of the classroom. In an attempt, for instance, to halt James's tendency to grant favour too freely and to neglect the content of requests, the master implemented a test, which involved presenting the boy with two stacks of papers that he subsequently signed without reading. As a result, Buchanan then spent the next few weeks declaring that he rather than James was actually King of Scotland. When questioned by James about his behaviour, the old scholar duly produced one of the documents previously signed by his pupil. 'Well,' declared Buchanan, 'here is the letter signed in your hand in which you have handed the kingdom to me.'

Nor did the intensity of the king's education entirely stifle his broader development. Though his childhood was comparatively solitary, he was not, for example, without companions of his own age, the closest of whom was John Erskine – the young Earl of Mar – whom he nicknamed Jockie o' Sclaittis (pronounced slates) in recognition of his knack for mathematics. There was also John Murray, a nephew of the Countess of Mar, Walter Stewart (a distant relative) and Lord Inverhyle. And though the rough and tumble of normal boyhood games was off-putting to James, it is not insignificant, perhaps, that so many of his early portraits depict him with a hawk on his wrist or that a beautiful hawking glove was gifted to him. There were many presents of bows and arrows, too, as well as two golfing gloves. But in spite of his undoubted physical awkwardness, it was his love of horses and hunting that came to dominate his leisure. Two relations of the Earl of Mar, David and Adam Erskine (lay Abbots of Cambuskenneth) were employed to train him, and in early life he acquired a passion for stag hunting, which would never desert him, notwithstanding a loose seat in the saddle and poor hands that may have caused his near death in the summer of 1580 when his mount fell upon him. Last but not least (and somewhat surprisingly, perhaps, in light of his reputation for ungainliness), he was also a competent dancer in childhood. 'They also made his Highness dance before me,' observed Killigrew, 'which he likewise did with a very good grace.' And the encouraging hand behind this particular aptitude was, it seems, none other than the redoubtable old Buchanan himself.

But if James's everyday circumstances were not, then, quite so pathetic and bleak as is frequently suggested, the political circumstances of his early childhood were altogether a different matter. The upheavals of Queen Mary's reign, which had awoken old feuds and created new ones among the Scots nobility, and finally forced her into flight in 1568, were followed not by peace but by five years of civil war. Both she and her supporters refused to recognise her deposition or the legality of her son's government, and though these wars left him untouched physically, they created nevertheless an insidious atmosphere of mistrust and insecurity, as the Earl of Moray and the three regents who followed him attempted to protect the Protestant settlement and alliance with England over twelve troubled years. One of those regents – James's own grandfather, the Earl of Lennox – would become the victim of a sudden raid on Stirling by Marian lords, and James would recall years later how the earl was borne into the castle and died the same day. It was not for nothing, perhaps, that James was said to have been 'nourished in fear', beset, in his own words, by 'daily tempests of innumerable dangers', or that in 1605, in the aftermath of the Gunpowder Plot, he would explain that his 'fearful nature' had been with him 'not only ever since my birth, but even as I may justly say, before my birth: and while I was in my mother's belly'.

In August 1567 Moray had made a characteristically well-timed return from England to exploit the growing chaos in his homeland. Already invited to become regent by the rebel lords, this cold, calculating and double-dealing individual would not accept the role until he had visited his half-sister at Loch Leven, where he fuelled her fears and posed as her only saviour from trial and the subsequent 'fiery death', which she believed was bound to follow from the publication of her letters to Bothwell. In this way, he was able to assume the regency at nothing less than the urgent request of both sides, while also retaining the support of his patron, Elizabeth, south of the Border. 'That bastard', as King James called him later, 'who unnaturally rebelled and procured the ruin of his owne sovran and sister', then proceeded to sell the English queen the majority of those very pearls that Mary had delivered into his hands for safe-keeping, while giving most of the remainder to his wife. To complete his betrayal, moreover, one of his first acts as regent was to order that the Casket Letters be read aloud to the Scottish Parliament and their handwriting authenticated to preclude any likelihood of the former queen's restoration.

Even so, Moray's problems were far from over. In particular, he was forced to contend with the bitter enmity of the powerful Hamilton and Gordon families who, with their great following of warlike dependants, continued to support the queen. And when Mary finally escaped from Loch Leven in May 1568, it was they who not only welcomed her, but endorsed her revocation of the abdication and prepared to do battle with Moray and the 'True Lords Maintainers of the King's Majesty's action and authority'. But notwithstanding the queen's apparently inexhaustible supply of personal magnetism, Moray moved swiftly to corner her in the south-west before her forces could gather in overwhelming force. The result was victory for the regent at Langside, and a disastrous decision by his sister – taken against the advice of her closest advisers – to abandon the fight and cross the Border at Workington to seek sanctuary within England, where she would remain a constant, overwhelming threat to her royal cousin Elizabeth and, in consequence, face various forms of house arrest, humiliation and harsh imprisonment for the rest of her life.

In Scotland, thereafter, the queen's cause encountered a slow death over five more years, which merely perpetuated the rancour and insecurity of the new reign. In 1573 Huntly and the Hamiltons surrendered at last, and only Edinburgh Castle held out under Kirkcaldy of Grange and Maitland of Lethington who had been forced at last to come down on Mary's side, since she possessed the only absolute proof that he had been 'art and part of Darnley's murder'. That same year the walls of the castle were at last breached with guns borrowed from England and the remnants of the former queen's support finally mopped up. Grange, one of the few truly honourable men around, was hanged, while Lethington, already a very sickly man, may well have killed himself rather than face trial.

Before that time, however, the Earl of Moray was already cold in the grave, along with two more of his successors. For all his mendacity, perhaps in part because of it, the earl remained a more than capable statesman who bolstered the king's authority, consolidated the progress of Protestantism and sought to cement relations with Scotland's southern neighbour by looking ultimately towards the union of the two Crowns. At the time of his coronation, James had been unacknowledged by a sizeable proportion of his subjects, but by the end of Moray's regency, he was appreciably nearer to acceptance – not least of all because it was Moray who guaranteed that the Queen of Scots was firmly imprisoned once and for all in England. And in the meantime, the earl's desire for peace and good government had actually won him the respect and even the love of the majority of Scottish people who dubbed him, it seems, 'the Good Regent'. Even in the lawless Borders, for that matter, 'there was', wrote one contemporary observer, 'such obedience made by the said thieves to the said regent, as the like was never done to no king in no man's day before'.

Yet if harsh times necessitated harsh government, they also spawned the kind of grudges and gangsterism that eventually brought Moray to his doom. And almost inevitably, therefore, he was assassinated at Linlithgow on 23 January 1570, by his enemy James Hamilton of Bothwellhaugh who had already stalked him from Glasgow to Stirling and finally 'pierced him with one ball, under the navel, quitt through'. Though Moray had 'leapt from his horse and walked to his lodging on foot', the initial optimism of the surgeons proved ill founded and he 'gave up the ghost', we are told, 'that same night', mourned as the 'defender of the widow and the fatherless' and revered by John Knox who preached his funeral sermon on the text 'Blessed are the dead which die in the Lord'. And while James himself would never accept such glowing judgements of his uncle, there was still no doubt that the king's interests had been desperately compromised by the death.

There followed, indeed, six months of civil war and large-scale Border raids, which culminated ultimately in a muddy compromise that pleased no one. For no good reason beyond lack of alternatives, therefore, it was the king's grandfather – the elderly, treacherous and nominally Catholic Duke of Lennox – who assumed the role of regent. Widely believed to have ordered a massacre of children many years previously, which had left him unable to endure his own conscience, the former exile and father of Darnley was thoroughly mistrusted by Protestants for his religious views, and vilified, too, by Catholics for his present opposition to Mary, which had finally earned him the assistance of England in securing his new role. Only James himself, in fact, seems to have harboured any real affection for the duke who was now widely dismissed as the 'sillie Regent'. And in 1572 he too paid the ultimate price for Scotland's present divisions – fatally wounded during a wild raid on Stirling, conceived by Kirkcaldy of Grange and led by the Earl of Huntly and Lord Claud Hamilton.

Leaving Edinburgh just after sunset on 3 September, the raiders reached Stirling with the first grey light of dawn, when the town was still in the silence of sleep, 'so quiet as not a dog was heard to open his mouth and bark'. Whether their intention was to kidnap the king remains uncertain, but the violence, clamour and general disorder that followed would certainly leave their own indelible imprint upon both the boy and the man he would later become. In the initial onslaught, a dozen of the king's lords, rudely awoken by the war cries, the clattering of horses' hooves and the clash of weapons quickly submitted to demands that they should 'render themselves'. Among them was Lennox. But the tide was eventually turned, first by the Earl of Morton's resistance, who defended his burning residence until 'two of his men were slain and the lodging filled with smoke', and then by the Earl of Mar who sallied forth from the castle with a handful of harquebusiers and 'set upon the attackers, who then realised that all was lost'.

Lennox, in fact, had first surrendered to David Spence, Laird of Wormeston, on condition that he be spared, but the laird's guarantee, honestly given, proved worthless in the noisy chaos that now prevailed. 'So afraitt that they took the flight, and going out at the port trod upon others for throng', the raiders were attempting to make off with their captives, when a certain Captain Calder discharged his gun into Lennox's back, leaving the valiant Wormeston, who was 'shott through also' with the same bullet, to be dragged from his horse and hacked to pieces, while the dying regent 'cryed continually' that the man 'who had done what he could for his preservation' should not be killed. His only other concern, it seems, was the safety of the king. 'If the bairn be well, all is well,' he is said to have muttered after he had been returned to the castle, slumped in his saddle, for the last time.

The king was, indeed, unharmed, though not unmoved. For the clash of naked steel, the clatter of firearms, the acrid smell of burning timber, the frenzied cries of anguish and fury, and the general buzz of danger that accompanied them had not eluded him. On the contrary, the memories of that night of gunfire and confusion would remain with him – and none more so than the image of his wounded grandfather carried directly past him to the bed where he died later that afternoon. When Lennox 'called for a physician, one for his soul and another for his body', it marked the end not only of his brief regency but of his grandson's innocence, as bars now went up over the windows of his apartments and elaborate measures were devised to surround him whenever he rode out. Henceforth, more than ever, he was brought up under a blanket of suspicion and unease, for fear of what 'the lords of the Queen, his mother' might do at any moment. For a studious, sensitive and imaginative child, who lacked the physical resources to outface the savage, unruly men whom God had called him to govern, the prospect was truly daunting.

Within the year, moreover, the duke's successor John Erskine, Earl of Mar was also dead. An honourable, grave and mainly peaceable man, Mar may well have died of simple exhaustion, outright desperation or a mixture of both. One contemporary suggested that the main cause of his 'vehement sickness' was that 'he loved peace and could not have it'. But there were whispers, too, of poison, administered by the very man who replaced him: James Douglas, Earl of Morton – in some respects the most blackguardly of all the former queen's enemies, but a strong ruler nevertheless who, for all his ruthlessness and lack of scruples, would eventually gain the king's respect. Often intimidated by the fourth and last of his regents, James still acknowledged that 'no nobleman's service in Scotland was to be compared to Morton's'. There may even have been a shred of affection on the king's part for the fearsome earl, for on one occasion when Morton bemoaned his advancing years, James's response was as kindly as it was sincere. 'Would to God you were as young as the Earl of Angus [Morton's nephew] and yet were as wise as you.'

For six years of Morton's regency, moreover, James remained unmolested – at liberty to pursue his studies under Buchanan's guidance while regaining some modicum of inner peace after the murder of his grandfather. Even his enemy, Sir James Melville, who rightly regarded Morton as avaricious and much too fond of the English, acknowledged that 'he held the country under great obedience in an established state'. And if tyranny rather than pity or remorse was his trademark, it was only by tyranny, after all, that Scotland could for the moment be governed. Yet by the spring of 1578 a formidable coalition had formed against him, led by the Highland earls of Atholl and Argyll, and the quiet routine of the king's schoolroom was once more rudely interrupted. Appearing at Stirling on 4 March, the two earls explained to James that they wished him to summon the nobility to judge a dispute between them and the regent, who was presently in Edinburgh. When, however, Morton responded by demanding that the king must either punish the earls or accept his resignation, his boldness backfired, since a formidable body of lords at Stirling, supported by the king's guardian, Alexander Erskine, quickly advised the young monarch to adopt the latter course. 'The king,' it was said, 'liking best the persuasions that were given to him to reign (a thing natural to princes), resolution was taken to discharge the regent of authority and to publish the King's acceptance of government.'

But while Morton temporarily retired to Loch Leven to tend his gardens and on 8 March the 12-year-old monarch was formally installed at the head of his council table, the counter-revolution was not long in coming. Cleverly exploiting family tensions to persuade James's former playmate, the young Earl of Mar, that his uncle, Erskine, should be supplanted, Morton had stirred an ingenious *coup de main* even before April was out. As Mar took control of the castle, the king was once more woken in the small hours by the clash of arms in the castle courtyard and filled with uncontrollable terror when word reached him that Erskine, whom he loved, had been killed. In fact, the news was false, though his son was trampled to death in the confusion and the king remained inconsolable. 'He was in great fear,' wrote Sir Robert Bowes, the English ambassador, 'and teared his hair, saying that the Master [Erskine] was slain.' And his distress was soon compounded by the realisation that Morton had swiftly ridden to the scene to assume control of government once more.

There followed a brief flurry of threatened civil war as Morton began to raise an army and the people of Edinburgh turned out under a banner depicting a boy behind bars, with the motto 'Liberty I crave and cannot have it'. The king's mother, too, was eager to interfere from her confinement in England as she intrigued with her uncle, the Duke of Guise, to remove her son to France, yet English influence remained dominant and foiled not only Mary's madcap schemes but the prospect, too, of civil war in Scotland. Even George Buchanan featured, to the tune of £100, on Elizabeth's list of prominent Scottish nobles and gentlemen to be bribed in her kingdom's interest, though Peter Young alone chose to reject the £30 earmarked for him. When, therefore, the English ambassador intervened with the offer of a patched-up compromise whereby Morton gave up the regency in return for 'first roome and place' in the Privy Council, with Atholl next in dignity, even Argyll complied with the arrangement. Nor was there any appreciable resistance from Erskine whose earlier flash of resistance had been broken by grief at the death of his son.

On 16 April, however, there was one more dastardly footnote when Morton delivered a great banquet at Stirling to which all his current allies and erstwhile enemies were invited, among them Atholl, who left the celebration 'very sick and ill at ease', in much the same way that Regent Mar had left a previous banquet of Morton's at Dalkeith. Just like Mar before him, moreover, Atholl was soon to die amid rampant rumours of poisoning. When subjected to persistent 'rhyming libells' that he was the culprit, the earl's initial response was merely to hang the unlucky authors. But such was the persistence of the Countess of Atholl that he was obliged to sanction a post mortem, which proved a drama in its own right. Conducted by several eminent doctors, only one physician, a certain Dr Preston, saw fit to dismiss the charge of poisoning, though in doing so he opted for a method of proof that would cost him dear. For, as a masterful expression of scorn at his colleagues' conclusions, he decided to lick the contents of the corpse's stomach 'and having tasted a little of it with his tongue, almost had died, and was after, so long as he lived, sicklie'.

Such, then, was the flavour of Scottish politics as James VI neared adolescence. Nevertheless, Morton's rivals remained temporarily hamstrung, though the king himself had already fluttered his fledgling wings and failed to fly. Now, therefore, for one more year at least, he would have to shelter in his classroom refuge and brood upon the violence that had once more broken his slumbers. He was silent and outwardly compliant, but anxious nonetheless for change and troubled by his prospects. For, as Bowes noted in the aftermath of Morton's coup, 'his Grace by night hath been by this means so discouraged as in his sleep he is therefore greatly disquieted'.

3 ❧ Love and Liberation

'His Majesty, having conceived an inward affection to the Lord d'Aubigny, entered in great familiarity and quiet purposes with him.'

David Moysie, Memoirs of the Affairs of Scotland, 1577–1603

Though James's first attempt at independence had been roundly frustrated, it preceded nonetheless the onset of a marked alteration in his status – a subtle but decisive sea change in his role and influence, which saw him transformed by turns from a regent's plaything into the outright guide and instigator of his kingdom's affairs. By the time of his thirteenth birthday in June 1579 – within only fourteen months of Morton's 'triumph' – the lords of Scotland, and in particular the former regent himself, were having to accept the inevitable: that the helpless child of yesteryear was growing older and that, for all his previous frailty, he was plainly king by God's decree. To confirm the point officially, on 17 October James made formal entry into the capital, where he was greeted at the West Port by a pageant depicting King Solomon rendering judgement. It was his first visit in more than a decade, and provosts, baillies and councillors turned out in force to greet him, along with 300 prominent citizens clad in silks and velvet. At the port of the Strait Bow, a boy descended from a great globe to present the king with a set of massive silver keys to the city worth 6,000 marks, while Latin orations, stirring sermons and music from viols flowed as freely as the puncheons of wine at the Mercat Cross. From Canongate to

Holyrood, the front of every house was draped with fine tapestries and, to cap all, further pageants celebrated the genealogy of Scotland's kings and the favourable conjunction of the planets at James's nativity. It was, in short, a spectacle fit for any ruler – not only a heartfelt statement of civic pride, but, much more important still, a clear-cut sign of changing times and an equally emphatic rite of passage for a freshly empowered king.

James, it is true, remained separated from most of those who had originally set him against Morton. But by no means all Morton's enemies were gone, for the council was still an uneasy coalition which contained some, like Argyll, who were reconciled only in appearance to the present status quo. These dissenters were keen, moreover, to find a suitable replacement for Atholl – a figure acceptable to both the king and those who still favoured his mother. And across the Channel in Esmé Stuart, Seigneur d'Aubigny, they found not only someone to alter the entire situation in Scotland radically, but a figure who was to exercise a profound influence upon the king's whole life. Any alternative to Morton was by now, after all, infinitely attractive and d'Aubigny's nearness in blood to the king was a distinct recommendation, as was his right to the earldom of Lennox which made his arrival in Scotland inevitable sooner or later. The fact that he was more French than Scottish, Catholic and something of a moral reprobate into the bargain was neatly overlooked. 'The King has written to summon his cousin the Lord d'Aubigny from France,' the Bishop of Ross noted in a letter dated 15 May, before adding in all apparent innocence that he was 'a man of sound judgement and marked prudence, a constant upholder of the Catholic religion, and one whom the king is anxious to have at his side'.

For nearly two centuries, in fact, the Lennox Stuarts had held lands and titles on either side of the Channel, rendering distinguished service as soldiers and diplomats to the kings of both France and Scotland, but especially the latter. As the son of John Stuart, brother of James's grandfather and former regent, the Earl of Lennox, Esmé Stuart was therefore first cousin to Lord Darnley. And although his ostensible aim upon his arrival in September 1579 was the re-establishment of his family's Scottish position as the last male representative of his line, his real intent was altogether more sinister. As the secret agent of the Guises, he would win, he hoped, the confidence of the king, promote the cause of France and Mary Stuart – by whom he had been given 'fourtie thousand pieces of gold, in crowns, pistolets [coins] and angels' for use at the Scottish court – and save the Catholic faith before it was too late. Such was his gift for deception and intrigue that before long he would declare himself a convert to Protestantism and play an astonishing series of double games, not only with Guise, Mary and the Catholic powers, but with Elizabeth of England and the Scottish Kirk as well. Yet one consistent thread ran through the machinations of this fascinating but sinister figure all the while: the pursuit of personal ambition. And once established, though not unmindful of his original mission, he soon discovered that his control over the king's affections had infinitely more to offer than the favour of France or Spain, the interests of the old religion, or, even more obviously, the vanishing hopes of the former queen.

For more than a decade the ministers of the Scottish Kirk, propped up by a body of powerful and unscrupulous nobles, had maintained a deceptive dominance in Scotland, which poorly reflected the wishes of even most Protestants. Catholicism, in fact, had collapsed largely by default under the strain of a series of weaknesses, structural and circumstantial, which had left it easy prey to its enemies. The remoteness of the centres of Catholic power in the north and west, on the one hand, coupled to the calamity of Mary Stuart's example, the collapse of France into religious civil war and, perhaps most of all, English interference, had all taken a mighty toll, and the lands of the old Church had been readily seized, along with four-fifths of her revenues, by the ever-watchful Lords of the Congregation. But the subsequent Presbyterian settlement, pushed through by Knox and his fellow zealots, was far from universally welcome. Nor did the English alliance it entailed or its dependence upon ruffians like Morton enhance the new Kirk's moral authority. Starved of funds and short of educated recruits, it could actually find no more than 289 ministers for Scotland's 1,000 parishes, and in such circumstances, it was far from inconceivable that the Counter-Reformation might yet gain a foothold or that the 'auld alliance' with France might still be revived – especially if the king himself could first be won to d'Aubigny and then to Rome.

The dashing French courtier's arrival could not therefore have been better timed, since James, at the age of 13, was maturing both politically and physically, if not emotionally. At that moment, as Morton's stifling authority waned, any influence exerted over the king might indeed prove decisive, and none more so than the easy-going, affectionate glamour which Esmé Stuart exhibited in such abundance. A man of great personal magnetism around 37 years old – 'of comely proportion', 'civil behaviour' and 'honest' conversation – this elegant, red-bearded visitor, whose piercing black eyes spoke eloquently of his Italian ancestry, brought colour, amusement and gaiety to the dour Scottish court. He delivered civilisation and learning, too, of the kind that contrasted starkly with Buchanan's bleak instruction and was bound to appeal to the scholarly young king. The cultural amenities at Stirling were, after all, limited to say the least. As a concession to gentility, the Scottish Parliament had funded the employment of four fiddlers at the castle and this, in effect, was the limit of James's exposure to the frills of high refinement. D'Aubigny and his train of twenty gentlemen, however, brought with them not only grace and elegance, but respect and deference in the sharpest possible contrast to Morton's gruff and Spartan realism. Above all, however, as events would prove, they brought intimacy and love.

James's weak physique, shambling gait and slovenly manners left much to be desired, of course. But an earlier attack of smallpox had left him unscarred and his appearance was generally considered 'not uncomely'. According to Sir Henry Killigrew's description of 1574, indeed, he was 'well grown, both in body and spirit'. Even kings, however – especially those as perceptive as James – are sometimes capable of grasping realities and reflecting upon their own limitations. And James was no physical paragon. But the newcomer who now doted upon him was all this and more – so much so that even his potential enemies were at first wholly taken with him. Sir James Melville, for instance, thought him 'upright, just and gentle', and though he spoke only French and made little attempt to learn 'Scottis', even the hard-edged Scottish nobility were soon won over, in the main, to what John Spottiswoode called his 'courteous and modest behaviour'. And if d'Aubigny could allure even ministers of the Scottish Kirk, how much more susceptible to his attention would be the awkward, graceless youth upon whom he had set his sights?

Certainly, the Frenchman's rise to influence was instantaneous. Indeed, by the time that James made his grand 'entrie to his kingdome' at Edinburgh in October, he had already insisted that d'Aubigny accompany him, and honours followed thick and fast. Given first the rich Abbey of Arbroath and a sizeable endowment from the Hamilton lands forfeited after Mary's final downfall, he was then created Earl of Lennox in 1580 after his ineffectual uncle Robert was encouraged to renounce the title in exchange for that of March. He was admitted, too, to the council, awarded custody of Dumbarton Castle – the key to western Scotland and gateway to France – and before long had become both Lord Chamberlain, responsible for the king's safety, and First Gentleman of the Bedchamber. Most important of all, however, on 5 August 1581, he was finally made Duke of Lennox – the only duke in Scotland at that time and the first in Scottish history, apart from Bothwell, not to be a 'prince of the blood'. 'Lennox's greatness is greatly increased,' wrote Robert Bowes, 'and the king so much affected to him that he delights only in his company.' 'Thereby,' Bowes added, 'Lennox carries the sway.'

And as the duke's star ascended, so Morton's, of course, continued to wane, though he remained curiously unmoved at first by the mounting threat. Predictably, the preachers of the Kirk were from the outset deeply suspicious of the 'papistes with great ruffs and side bellows' that Lennox carried in tow with him. But, as the king continually hung on his favourite's shoulder and fiddled with his fine clothes and jewels as they walked together, Morton appears to have dismissed the spectacle as little more than a boyish enthusiasm – a passing fad resulting from 'the flexible nature of the king in these tender years'. In forsaking the regency and pushing the king to the political forefront as the figurehead for his own power and policies, he had in any case burned his bridges. In October 1579, just after his triumphal entry into Edinburgh, James had presided over Parliament and formally presented himself as the governor of his kingdom in his own right. And though Morton continued to pull the strings, the prospect of any return to a regency had gone forever. More ominously, however, by May 1580 the earl had retired in frustration to his estates at Dalkeith gathering his friends about him, while the English ambassador whispered in turn of the king's 'great myslyknge' for his former regent.

Nevertheless, throughout 1580 the holiday atmosphere continued, though events were steadily darkening behind the scenes. While James stayed at Holyrood, Lennox was even prepared to undertake some informal instruction in Calvinism at the king's hands, seeing the plain advantage that such a move might yield with the Kirk's preachers, many of whom were apparently 'much overtaken with the conceytt of his reformation'. By May, indeed, Lennox had officially committed himself to the new faith at St Giles in Edinburgh before returning to Stirling and signing the so-called 'Articles of Religion' in the Chapel Royal. Naturally, his action was dismissed by many as a cynical manoeuvre. 'Those who wish to rule,' Mauvissière, the French ambassador in London commented at the time, 'must learn to conceal themselves.' But Lennox would die a Protestant and his conversion captured the king entirely – so much so that the two travelled together on progress around the kingdom that summer.

In the meantime, the impending showdown between Morton and his supplanter edged ever closer. In England, Elizabeth and Burleigh were increasingly alarmed at the prospect of Franco-Scottish reconciliation, and the queen hinted to James for the first time that he might succeed her as king, while advising him 'rather to fear for his ambition than to comfort and delight his affection'. She encouraged Morton, too, to 'lay violent hands' on Lennox and sent Bowes north once again to galvanise the Protestant lords into some kind of effective action. In a secret midnight meeting with the former regent, the ambassador learned how the king was indeed beginning 'to commend and be contented to hear the praises of France'. And as rumours of kidnapping mounted once more, James also revealed a new and curious turn of mind. When Argyll spread word that Morton was bent on abducting him to Dalkeith, the king swiftly abandoned his hunting and returned to Stirling. Lacking the resources to fund a permanent armed guard, he was, after all, sorely exposed – especially as his councillors' attendance was irregular, since they too lacked funds and had to pay their own charges while they remained at court. But now, as Bowes noted, the king was more convinced of his ability to frustrate his enemies, since 'into whose hands soever he should fall, they should note in him such inconstancy, perjury and falsehood' that they would swiftly regret their action. Plainly, the king had learnt an important lesson from past experience, but in doing so he had also drawn a suspect moral conclusion for the future.

The opportunity for kidnap or any other decisive act of self-preservation on Morton's part had, however, already passed, for he was, it seems, 'loved by none and envied and hated by many, so that they all looked through their fingers to see his fall'. When James conducted his leisurely royal progress that summer, with Lennox and a bevy of loyal lords in attendance, Morton was left behind, laid up with a leg injury after a horse had kicked him. And when the embattled earl, 'indifferently well recovered', finally joined the king at St Andrews, where a convention of the Scottish Estates was due to assemble, he received a harrowing warning from the most unlikely of quarters. At a play performed before the king at the New Inns of the Abbey, a mad seaman – 'a known phrenetick man' who, Morton was convinced, could not have been put up to it – warned him that a plot was afoot and his 'doom in dressing'. Always susceptible to superstitious fears, the earl remembered, no doubt, how 'a lady who was his whore' had already shown him 'the answers of the oracles' and told him 'that the king would be his ruin'. And both the sailor and the whore would now be proven right.

Weary of his self-interest, even the Kirk had grown disillusioned with its former champion, and the English, too, who had previously seen the earl as such a worthwhile asset, now hesitated, relying on threats and intrigue when only armed assistance would do. When Bowes warned James of the dangers involved in preferring 'any Earl of Lennox before a Queen of England', however, and demanded that his favourite be removed from the Privy Council, the Scottish king's alarm was nevertheless palpable, whereupon the only remaining question was how the blow to Morton might be delivered most conveniently – and profitably. For Lennox, with typical Gallic finesse, now devised a masterstroke not only to remove his enemy, but to do so in a way that suited both his French patrons and the former queen more admirably than even they might have hoped. The method would involve raising the ghost of Darnley from its sordid resting place, while the instrument for the dirty work in hand was to be not Lennox himself, but a bold, ambitious opportunist who had been hovering watchfully about the court for some years past.

The murder of the king's father at Kirk o' Field more than a decade earlier was, of course, fertile ground for any ill-intentioned intriguer. Still mired with mystery and wrapped in rumour, any number of candidates might plausibly be connected with the deed and countless 'witnesses' found to attest to order. In the event, it was Sir James Balfour, brother of the owner of Kirk o' Field, and himself a suspect, who now came forward to furnish the evidence that finally did for Morton. Claiming to possess the bond signed by the conspirators, and assuring Lennox that Morton's signature was on it, Balfour had provided the duke with a tool that would finally exonerate the former queen from any involvement and, in doing so, both heartily relieve her son and place the English in serious embarrassment at her current treatment. With James Stewart, Captain of the King's Guard – a newly formed body of sixty men at arms, specially commissioned by Lennox – more than willing to undertake the task, all was set for Morton's final erasure.

Gloriously self-assured, splendidly handsome and exuding what might best be described as a coarse variety of magnificence, Stewart, the son of Lord Ochiltree, revelled in his courage and resolution and 'thought no man his equal'. He was, moreover, as capable as he was confident – intelligent, educated and, no less importantly, politically astute. And his connections with John Knox, who at the age of almost 60 had married his sister, also gave Stewart a cachet of sorts with the Kirk. But his swaggering conceit and single-minded brutality had already earned him the suspicion of many and hatred of some. To Sir James Melville, who detested him, he was 'a scorner of all religion, presumptuous, ambitious, covetous, careless of the commonwealth, a despiser of the nobility, and of all honest men'. His confederates, too, were aware of his baser motives. Even Lennox, for that matter, was conscious that his henchman in what now followed was 'eager to win credit by what means soever'.

Nor would the king pass up his own duplicitous part in the tawdry circumstances of Morton's downfall. On 30 December, the former regent was taken hunting by James and treated cordially throughout the day. Upon their return that evening, indeed, the lily was perfectly gilded by the canny youth, who delighted increasingly, it seems, in the finer points of double-dealing. 'Father,' he told his quarry, 'only you have reared me, and I will therefore defend you from your enemies.' Whether Morton had somehow elicited the comment by expressing his concerns is unknown, but soon enough the hollowness of James's assurance was starkly exposed. For only the next day, during a meeting of the Privy Council at which the king was personally present, Captain Stewart burst into the room, fell on his knees before his sovereign, and pointing histrionically at Morton, accused him of being 'art and part for knowledge and concealing' of Darnley's murder. When, moreover, Morton dismissed him as the 'perjured tool' of his enemies, uproar ensued with both men grasping their swords whilst being held apart by Lords Cathcart and Lindsay.

In the meantime, Lennox had feigned incomprehension at the furious exchange conducted in a foreign tongue. But his purposes had been served to perfection. The king, now thoroughly implicated in the whole affair, made no move whatsoever on behalf of Morton, who was duly arrested and eventually removed to Dumbarton, where he became not the first to declare that 'if he had been as upright to his God as he was faithful to his prince, he had not been brought to this pinch'. Thereafter, on 1 June 1581, he was tried and condemned in Edinburgh and executed the next day. In the process, he admitted foreknowledge and concealment, but declared Bothwell to be Darnley's principal murderer. And though the Queen of England had sent 2,000 men to the Border to save him, her young Scottish counterpart, revelling in his newfound confidence, brazenly outfaced her. 'Though he be young,' wrote Thomas Randolph the English emissary, before being sent packing by a pistol shot through his window, 'he wants neither words nor answers to anything said to him.'

Morton's Douglas kinsmen under the Earl of Angus, meanwhile, had plotted only half-heartedly to save him, and though the condemned earl conducted himself bravely throughout his ordeal – claiming as he mounted the scaffold that he was 'entering into the felicity of Almighty God' – only a few members of the Kirk would ever mourn him. Indeed, the night before he was beheaded by the so-called 'Maiden' (an early prototype of the guillotine) that he had earlier brought from Halifax for his own nefarious purposes, he had written letters to James defending his conduct, 'but the king would not look upon them, nor take heed what they said; but ranged up and down the floor of his chamber, clanking with his finger and thumb'.

Not surprisingly, when Elizabeth heard of James's betrayal of his erstwhile regent her fury was undisguised, deriding him as 'that false Scotch urchin' from whom only 'double dealing' could be expected. And while the Scottish king might rightly bridle at the 'urchin' epithet, the second claim in the queen's outburst was hardly deniable. The circumstances of his childhood had, of course, already taught him cunning but, in procuring Morton's ruin, Lennox had also taught him to regard the practice of duplicity as something much more: a necessary skill and intellectual art, if not outright virtue. 'The king's fair speeches and premises,' wrote an English noble, 'will fall out to be plain dissimulation, wherein he is in his tender years better practised than others forty years older than he is.' He 'is holden among the Scots for the greatest dissembler that ever was heard of for his years'. And Lennox was attempting to teach him too, perhaps, that condign justice gave little cause for regret. For though James had commuted the verdict that Morton should be hanged, drawn and quartered, and was absent from the execution, Lennox's supporters showed few such qualms. Indeed, Lord Seton 'stood in a stair' close by, while Ker of Fernihurst, gained the best view of all 'in a shott over against the scaffold, with his large ruffs, delighting in this spectacle ...'

To James's credit, this last lesson was never lasting, if ever learned at all, though there were others delivered up by Lennox that would indeed prove permanent. It was under Lennox's influence, for instance, that the king came to scorn the more radical elements of the Scottish Reformation as anti-monarchical rebels against properly constituted authority, and, more generally, to question the broadly democratic principles that George

Buchanan had been so keen to imbue in him. From this time forth, the Scottish clergy became to James what the Huguenots were to his French counterparts – seditious disturbers of the peace. In that time of confusion, the king would write, 'some fiery-spirited men in the ministry got such a guiding of the people as finding the gust of government sweet they began to fancy a democratic form of government'. He was made to think evil, wrote the minister James Melville, against those who served him best and to regard the Reformation as 'done by a privy faction turbulently'. And in this regard Lennox would also, it seems, frequently discuss the absolutism of the King of France and emphasise its virtues, working along with Captain James Stewart, another driven by his own self-interested purposes, to encourage the king to assert his God-given authority more stridently. Suppressed and disregarded for so long, and treated hitherto like a chattel of the high and mighty – a political talisman to be controlled and brandished at convenience by contending rivals – it is easy to see how an impressionable 15 year old might well have reacted to such advice and adulation.

The Kirk, after all, had been flexing its muscles more and more stridently, and in James's current state of growing confidence, it was hardly surprising that he should listen so readily to more gratifying alternatives. John Knox had set the mould in the first instance by affirming in his own inimitable way that the laws of God, needing no confirmation from any king or parliament, were to guide the state, and that kings who resisted the Kirk's injunctions should be swept from office. Under the pressures of practical politics, however, Andrew Melville, who led the Kirk in James's reign adapted the strongly theocratic emphasis in Knox's thinking into what would become known as the 'doctrine of the two kingdoms', whereby secular authority should be exercised by the reigning monarch, while the clergy assumed sole responsibility for religious affairs. On this view, all spiritual authority flowed from God the Father through Jesus Christ the Mediator directly to his Kirk, by-passing entirely both king and state, since the Kirk had 'no temporal head on earth, but only Christ, the only spiritual king and governor of his Kirk'. The king, therefore, had no higher place within the Kirk itself than any private person and must obey the clergy in all matters of the spirit.

By 1581, moreover, with the publication of the *Second Book of Discipline*, the authority of the secular ruler was being further undermined. For now the king was encouraged to follow the clergy's advice even in matters that had hitherto been deemed his own. 'The ministers,' it was still accepted, 'exercise not the civil jurisdiction.' But the new departure was apparent in the proposal that they should nevertheless 'teach the magistrate' how that jurisdiction should be exercised, and in the further claim that 'all godly princes and magistrates ought to hear and obey'. To compound the king's frustration, the same radical ministers were conducting a steady assault on the authority of his bishops. Calvinism, after all, plainly asserted the equality of all pastors and called for church government through an ascending structure of presbyteries, synods and General Assemblies. Bishops in any form were, from this perspective, symbols of Roman error and instruments of royal tyranny – the king's agents in controlling and perverting the exercise of God's true design for his people. No monarch, however, could lightly accept such an assault upon his prerogative and, under the influence of his new friends, James was therefore quick to seize upon what he eventually termed in 1604 the 'No bishop, no king' principle – a notion that would have such significant long-term consequences.

It was not coincidental either that James's relationship with his mother appeared to warm significantly after Lennox's arrival. As a boy he had always resented Buchanan's spiteful attacks upon her reputation and continued to exhibit a sentimental interest in her story. Now, however, he equated criticism of his mother with the more general assault upon royal authority in progress at that time, and in 1584 he prevailed upon Parliament to condemn his elderly tutor's writings formally. Years later, too, he would advise his son to read history but not 'such infamous invectives as Buchanan's and Knox's chronicles'. Nor, he urged, should his son countenance malicious words against his predecessors, since those who speak ill of a king 'seek craftily to stain the race and to steal the affection of the people from their posterity'. He had found his most loyal servants, he added, among those who had been faithful to his mother – once again combining filial devotion with notions of loyalty to the Crown and hatred of all challenges to the political and religious hierarchy which, in his view, guaranteed order and stability throughout the body politic.

For her part, of course, Mary was still unable to acknowledge the legality of her abdication or the resulting transfer of sovereignty to her son, and Morton's execution had only served to heighten her hopes of rehabilitation. In 1581, therefore, she proposed the so-called 'Association' whereby James, who had not hitherto been recognised by the Catholic powers of Europe, should 'demit' the Crown to her, after which she would immediately bestow it upon him again with her full blessing. As a result, he would be universally acknowledged as King of Scotland and become joint sovereign with her while ruling the country in their joint names. And this was not all, since the former queen also suggested that her abdication be formally annulled, that James be crowned anew and that her supporters be pardoned. Catholics were to be granted liberty of worship and it was clear, too, that no important decision was to be delivered without her approval. Above all, Mary asked that her son be reconciled to Rome. Only by means of the Association, she suggested, could he ever hope to secure the English throne.

It was a scheme shot through with wild improbabilities and, as such, wholly worthy of the woman who fashioned it, but the temptations it offered were not without appeal to the young king. And though the former queen was actually coldly suspicious of Lennox and the plan itself a palpable threat to his own primacy if ever implemented, the favourite had little actual option but to mask his concerns and indulge the queen's machinations. His links to the House of Guise, after all, made it virtually impossible to reject the Association outright, and at his instigation, therefore, James now began to correspond with Mary, writing her brief but affectionate letters, which assured her that he continued to hold her in high honour and would act at all times as her obedient son. Always a lover of animals, he referred in one instance to 'the fidelity of my little monkey, who only moves near me', though the strength of the renewed link between son and mother should not be measured by such disarming comments. On the contrary, the king offered no concrete concessions and though he addressed his mother as Queen of Scots, he never neglected to sign himself as 'James R'. In fact, he seems to have been playing, at Lennox's behest, what was becoming an increasingly familiar game of gracious deception, and in doing so he now slithered into an elaborate ruse, which would allow him (in theory) to retain his options while paying lip service at one and the same time to his obligations as son.

In the meantime, however, the king's everyday behaviour as well as his character and relationships had gradually begun to evolve upon new and questionable lines. Though swearing was something that he severely condemned in his writings, deeming it all the more reprehensible since it was a sin 'clothed with no delight or gain', he nevertheless developed a habit for it and sought to justify the vice in part, so long as it sprang from sudden, unpremeditated anger. Certainly, his conscience does not seem to have troubled him unduly in this respect, for when admonished by the clergy 'to forbear his often swearing and taking the name of God in vain', he merely replied, 'I thank you' – with a little laughter. Nor was this the only vice to trouble the ministers, for now, it seems, he was sometimes remiss in attending the Kirk, no longer called for preaching at dinner and supper, and disliked to hear his shortcomings rehearsed from the pulpit. He indulged too, we are told, in pastimes on the Sabbath. And though James's sports and entertainments were mainly innocent enough, bawdy jests became another facet of his behaviour, which accorded aptly with the declining tone of the company he now kept. Lennox's colourful French associates were as free in their language as they were in their habits, and Captain James Stewart, soon to be rewarded with the stolen title of Earl of Arran, did nothing to moderate their influence. On the contrary, his wife, a daughter of the Catholic Atholl and now the chief lady at the Scottish court, had gained a pungent reputation for licence and immorality. Formerly married to the king's uncle, the Earl of March, she had subsequently divorced him on grounds of impotency – or, as Moysie put it, 'because his instrument was not guid' – though she was pregnant at the time with Stewart's child.

Much more significantly still, however, the king's love for Lennox was widely thought to have contained a sexual element. Indeed, it was Lennox, according to many, who first awakened James's lifelong interest in beautiful young men. Courtiers and ambassadors were fully aware, of course, that the king was 'in such love' with his favourite 'as in the open sight of the people often he will clasp him about the neck with his arms and kiss him'. But the ministers of the Kirk were also ready to suggest that the relationship had passed beyond affection and that Lennox had 'provoked' the king 'to the pleasure of the flesh' and drawn him to 'carnal lust'. And if the indignation of earnest Calvinist clergymen may be treated with due suspicion, there were other voices of the same opinion. 'His Majesty,' wrote the chronicler David Moysie, 'having conceived an inward affection to the Lord d'Aubigny, entered in quiet purposes with him,' a phrase bearing special connotations in the Scots idiom of the time. And the English clergyman John Hacket, writing many years later, reinforced the like conclusion for posterity by observing how James had clasped Lennox 'Gratioso in the embraces of his great love above all others'.

The precise nature of the sexual relationship can never, of course, be known. But in later life, James condemnation of sodomy was certainly unwavering. Whether he accepted the biblical prohibition of this specific act only and regarded other homosexual activity as pardonable remains debatable. However, his book on kingship, *Basilikon Doron*, published in 1599 at a time when he was without a serious attachment to any specific male favourite, would categorise sodomy itself among those 'horrible crimes which ye are bound in conscience never to forgive', and thereafter he followed the same line with total and unembarrassed consistency, using the full force of English law to reinforce his opinions. Writing to Lord Burleigh, for instance, he would give a forthright directive that judges were to interpret the law rigidly and were not to issue any pardons, stating unequivocally that 'no more colour may be left to judges to work upon their wits in that point'. And while Lennox confided to the king that he had given up his wife and children 'to dedicate myself to you entirely', such statements were entirely consistent with the usual conventions of the day – as, indeed, was much of the emotional excess exhibited on James's part. Prematurely old in some respects and painfully naive in others, the king's ability to baffle and mislead modern observers remains palpable, and even allowing for the objectivity of certain contemporary commentators, which is by no means self-evident, the precise extent of the king's sexual involvement with Lennox remains as doubtful as ever.

In any event, the year after Morton's death was probably the happiest of James's life as he basked in the freedom and gaiety of the new status quo. Six pairs of fine horses, a gift from the Duke of Guise, filled him with joy, and he revelled, too, in the company of a leading light in Lennox's entourage, a certain M. Momberneau – 'a merry fellow, very able in body, most meet in all respects for bewitching the youth of a prince'. Not least among Momberneau's winning accomplishments was his skill as a horseman. 'Tuesday last,' wrote Thomas Randolph, capturing the regular routine of James's newly liberated existence, 'the king ran at the ring, and, for a child, did very well. Momberneau challenged all comers. The whole afternoon and great part of the night were passed with many pleasures and great delights. The next day the king came to Edinburgh to the preaching. That afternoon he spent in like pastimes as he had done the day before.' Meanwhile, at Leith, where he dined a few days later, a castle, derisively dubbed the 'pope's palace', had been built on boats to be burnt before him for his entertainment. Horse racing on the sands followed, along with a ludicrous joust between courtiers. All, in fact, was a continual round of jollity and high spirits as James left the business of government, or what he called 'auld men's cummer' to Lennox and Arran.

But such a state of affairs could not, of course, last. Predictably, the first rumours of the proposed Association between James and Mary had caused a fresh wave of anti-Catholic hysteria, in which Lennox was the principal object of suspicion. His signature of the so-called 'Negative Confession', which denounced 'the usurped authority' of the pope, 'that Roman Anti-Christ', had left his enemies unconvinced of the 'frutes of his conversion', while the composition of the pro-Lennox party in government, which contained a number of the former queen's supporters, such as Seton, Maxwell, Fernihurst and Maitland of Lethington, only confirmed existing doubts. Worse still, the arrival of Spanish and Guisard agents during 1581 and 1582 now brought matters to a pitch, placing Lennox in the most intractable of dilemmas. For, despite the implications of the Association for his own personal influence, the mounting tide of opposition at home made the prospect of foreign assistance in a far-ranging Catholic scheme to convert the king and subdue England increasingly irresistible.

From the time of his earliest memories, in fact, James had been encouraged to set his sights upon the English succession, but for good reason Elizabeth had never acknowledged his right to the throne. When his mother, in the days of her good fortune, had pressed her royal cousin to recognise her as successor, Elizabeth had made it clear that to do so would provide a ready focus for the plots of her enemies. 'Think you,' she is said to have responded, 'that I should love my own winding sheet?' And the same reservation applied with equal force, of course, to the claims of Mary's son. During 1581, therefore, as his own position in Scotland became increasingly fragile, Lennox suggested to James that the key to the English throne might lay not so much in Elizabeth's approval as in her removal. If the king was prepared to compromise with his mother and accept the Catholic faith into the bargain, the rewards for both he and Lennox would be considerable. A successful Catholic invasion of England which resulted in the release by force of Mary Stuart and the deposition of Elizabeth would bring Mary and James jointly to the thrones of both Scotland and England, leaving Lennox rescued at last from his Scottish Protestant enemies.

As the plots thickened on all fronts, James meanwhile continued to exhibit both craft and coolness, committing himself to no one but entertaining overtures from, in some cases, the most unlikely of sources. In the summer of 1581, for instance, Bernardino de Mendoza, the Spanish ambassador in London, dispatched two Jesuits to Scotland for a secret interview with the king, who received them cordially and gave his assurances that, though he deemed it advisable to appear pro-French in public, his heart was inclined to Spain. At the same time, however, he showed no inclination to change his religion, for early the next year the same Jesuits were mentioning a plot by Catholic noblemen to secure his conversion by force. Nor it seems, did the arrival of another Jesuit, William Crichton, yield any more progress, as Lennox's position continued to decline steadily. Clearly, the king was prepared to probe a range of possibilities upon his favourite's advice, but only on his own terms. And if the favourite was reduced to fear and frustration as a result, then that would have to be. For, as Mendoza made plain, Lennox's continual troubles and terror at feeling himself in the daily presence of death were reducing him to 'a deplorable condition'.

Even former allies now became threatening, in fact. On 22 April 1581, Captain James Stewart had been created Earl of Arran and was now firmly fixed in the king's affections in his own right. Like Lennox, he too had good looks to recommend him, though in this case the king's attraction was primarily psychological rather than physical, since Arran exhibited a gift for leadership and imperious mastery of events to which James's subservient personality paid natural homage. Where Esmé Stuart offered reverence, James Stewart, by contrast, exuded raw, untempered masculinity. In some respects, the contrast between the two personalities tapped into the contrasting needs of James's own character: on the one hand, the hankering for love and deference; on the other the wish for security and control of events. But it was still to the duke, his 'dearest cousin' and 'nearest heir male', that the king looked first and when Arran quarrelled with his rival in the winter of 1581 he found himself forbidden to attend the Chistmas celebrations at Dalkeith, which James enjoyed with Lennox instead.

Predictably, the reconciliation that occurred soon afterwards was nothing more than a matter of mutual convenience, as Lennox continued to connive with Spain and Mary, and, in doing so, courted disaster ever more freely. His schemes took no account of Franco-Spanish rivalry, and ignored both James's deep-seated Protestantism and innate reluctance to share his throne. They underestimated, too, the very forces that had broken the king's mother and would break him far more easily still: the volatility of the Scottish nobility and, just as important, the vengeful wrath of the Scottish Kirk. His power, after all, was based upon nothing more dependable than the doting favour of a 16-year-old king. And while James had grown in confidence and learnt some kingcraft in rapid time, he remained no match for concerted dissent and, above all, that tried and trusted trump card of Scotland's nobility: abduction.

In attempting to encourage his Catholic allies while feathering his nest financially, therefore, Lennox now made a crucial blunder which would actually pave the way to his downfall. When Robert Montgomery, a minister at Stirling who had publicly denounced episcopal government of the Kirk, was appointed Archbishop of Glasgow under terms that left the revenues of the see in Lennox's hands, the result was general outrage, which demonstrated all too conclusively the practical limits of royal authority. Angry deputations of ministers, threatening to excommunicate Montgomery, descended upon James, whose attempts at resistance proved painfully futile. 'We will not suffer you,' declared James in a forlorn attempt to outface his clergy, but the response was predictable. 'We must obey God rather than men,' retorted the small but fiery John Durie whom Lennox had dubbed 'a little devil'. 'And we pray God,' the minister continued, 'to remove evil company from about you. The welfare of the Kirk is your welfare; the more sharply vice is rebuked the better for you.' Smarting and angry, the king was close to tears. But his only familiar weapons – deceit and subterfuge – were now, of course, useless. The dam had been breached and, in the process, James once again stood exposed as a raw and vulnerable youth. Nor was this the end of his chastening. For, not long afterwards, Andrew Melville preached a famous sermon in which 'he inveighed against the bloody gully [knife] of absolute authority, whereby men intended to pull the crown off Christ's head and to wring the sceptre out of his hand'.

Coming, as it did, at a time when James had been experiencing the first stirrings of genuine pride in his regal status, the whole experience could not have been more significant, and matters reached a harrowing crescendo when a certain 'Seigneur Paul', an emissary of the Duke of Guise arrived on Scottish soil. When Durie encountered the Frenchman, he responded with an act of histrionics that, for all its excess, nevertheless captured the intensity of disgust and sense of betrayal experienced by his clerical colleagues in general. Pulling his bonnet over his eyes, he declared that his eyes should not be polluted by the sight of the Devil's messenger, and then berated James to his face – with no trace of deference or hint of restraint. James should adhere to his religion, refuse a Catholic marriage and, added Durie for good measure, keep his body unpolluted. He had, in short, misbehaved as errant children are wont to do, and now he must amend. It was a put-down of withering proportions. But what made the pill more bitter still – and the memory so indelible – was his own response. Overawed by the white heat of the minister's invective, the king merely conceded on all points – in hushed voice and plainly broken spirits.

By now, too, the anti-Lennox faction among the nobility had grown to critical proportions. Staunch Protestants, such as Lord Lindsay and the Earl of Glencairn, were joined in conspiracy by two of Morton's kinsmen, the Earl of Angus and Douglas of Loch Leven, as well as the new Earl of Gowrie, who had supported Lennox initially, only to balk before long at his selfishness. And when the young Earl of Mar and the 5th Earl of Bothwell lent their support, the 'band' of discontented nobles was complete. Emboldened by English bribes and bolstered by the Kirk's delivery to James in July of a set of articles, denouncing his traffic with France and reliance on 'bloody murtherers and persecutors', the plotters shaped for action.

Nor would they have to await their opportunity long, for in the summer of 1582 James and Lennox were for once apart. The king, in fact, was hunting in Atholl, while Lennox remained in Edinburgh to preside over a court of justice in his judicial capacity as Lord Chamberlain. And on 22 August, as James was riding south once more towards Perth, he was met by Gowrie, who cordially offered him hospitality at his nearby castle of Ruthven. Suspecting that something was afoot, James 'yet dissembled the matter', we are told, 'thinking to free himself the next day when he went abroad with his sports'. Next morning, however, he discovered the full extent of his predicament. For, as his departure neared, Mar and Gowrie accosted him with a list of grievances which he at first attempted to ignore. But when making for the door of the parlour in which the exchange occurred, the Master of Glamis barred his way with a leg. Storms of rage and floods of tears were unavailing. 'Better that bairns should weep than bearded men,' observed Glamis.

Arran, meanwhile, had foolishly chosen to ride on his own to the king's rescue on the false assumption that he would be released on demand, whereupon he too was promptly arrested; and though Lennox 'lurkit' at Dumbarton throughout the autumn, 'waiting upon opportunity' and conceiving hopeless schemes for the king's rescue, his cause was thoroughly lost. James, in fact, was so closely guarded that when a secret message arrived from Lennox, the bedchamber attendant who delivered it, a certain Henry Gibbe, could do so only in the privacy of the king's 'close stool' or toilet. And, even then, all that James dared answer to his favourite was that he should send no more dangerous messages of this kind. In any case, only a few days after his abduction, James had been forced to sign a proclamation declaring himself a free king and wrote to Lennox ordering him to leave the country. He had, it is true, protested bitterly and continued to speak out against his oppressors. 'His Majesty,' wrote Sir James Melville, 'took the matter further to heart than any man would have believed, lamenting his hard estate and mishandling by his own subjects, and how he was thought but a beast by other princes for suffering so many indignities.' It was only with great difficulty, too, that the Ruthven lords obtained the king's consent to a proclamation acknowledging the freedom of the Kirk. 'He spared not to say,' wrote David Calderwood, 'that the ministers were but a pack of knaves, that he had rather lose his kingdom than not be avenged upon them, that the professors of France [the Huguenots] were but seditious traitors, rebels and perturbers of commonwealths.' Yet the intensity of James's bitterness only reflected the hopelessness of his position – a fact which Lennox, too, reluctantly accepted when he finally returned to France on 21 December. 'And sa the King and the Duc was dissivered,' wrote one contemporary laconically, 'and never saw [each] uther againe.'

Before his departure, however, James had been forced to accuse Lennox of 'disloyalty and inconstancy' in not leaving Scotland in accordance with previous orders, and in answer the duke had penned a last message which must have made the most painful reading for the shamed and heartbroken young king. James was, Lennox declared, his 'true master, and he alone in this world whom my heart is resolved to serve'. 'And would to God,' he continued, 'my body should be cut open, so that there should be seen what is written upon my heart; for I am sure there would not be seen there those words "disloyalty and inconstancy" – but rather these, "fidelity and obedience".' The message, moreover, was as gratefully received as one might expect, for in the winter of 1583 James would write a long and poignant lament for his exiled loved one, entitled *Ane Metaphorical Invention of a Tragedie called Phoenix*. As Lennox came from France, James wrote, so the phoenix flew to Scotland from Arabia; as Lennox was converted to Protestantism, so the phoenix was tamed; as Lennox experienced the enmity of the ministers of the Kirk and of Gowrie and his associates, so the phoenix; and as Lennox was exiled to France, so the phoenix flew off to Arabia and sacrificed itself on its own pyre.

By the time the verse was complete, however, Lennox was already dead. According to one report he had been suffering from an 'affection [i.e.

infection] hepatick and dissenterick', and according to Calderwood from 'a dysentery, or excoriation of the inner parts, engendered of melancholy, wherewith was joined gonnorhea'. As he lay on his deathbed on 26 May 1583, he had refused the last rites from the Catholic priest who came to attend him. And though his wife, Catherine, would bury his remains at Aubigny according to full Roman ritual, he had also – perhaps as the supreme compliment to his former royal master – declared his commitment to the Protestant faith. Already, of course, he had provided James with the inviolable memory of his first love and liberation, in return for which the king would exhibit a lifelong concern for his children. And now, last of all, he would bequeath his former royal master his embalmed heart.

4 ❧ Lessons in Life and Kingcraft

'A king will have need to use secrecy in many things.'

James VI, Basilikon Doron, 1599

Though the so-called 'Ruthven Raid' had been conducted with minimal violence, its effect upon the king could not have been more profound. On the one hand, it had dealt a withering blow to his youthful self-esteem and newfound confidence in his own potential as a ruler. But it had also represented the grossest insult to his sovereignty – that God-given authority, as he saw it, marking him out so absolutely from each and every one of his subjects. In October, moreover, the forty-sixth General Assembly of the Kirk had described the raid as 'a good and godly cause', and James's continuing captivity in the months that followed merely compounded both the insult and his fury. On one winter evening at supper, we are told, he had toasted Lennox in his captors' presence amid stony silence, 'wherewith the king moved after he had drunk and hurled the rest over his shoulder'. Like his mother before him, he was clearly not without the stomach for a bold gesture when desperation left him no option. And, like her too, two objectives now consumed him. One, of course, was escape, and he confided to Sir James Melville, the only associate of Lennox allowed to approach him, that he had 'taken up a princely courage either to liberate himself fully, or die in the attempt'. The other was revenge for, as he told Sir Robert Bowes later, he would never forget how 'greatly wounded' his honour had been.

But if James found himself in what Bowes described, with remarkable understatement, as a 'ticklish situation', the quandary facing his enemies was, if anything, even more daunting. On the one hand, the Earl of Gowrie and the other so-called 'Lords Enterprisers', though temporarily in control, were finding, even more than Morton before them, that the king was now too old to be held under compulsion convincingly. The unwritten conventions governing royal abduction required that the act should be conducted for the king's own good and that there should be some degree of co-operation between kidnappers and kidnapped. He would also have to be paid for and even this was not the end of their predicament, for unless the king endorsed their authority, they could make little use of it, and to gain his support in the first place, they would have to grant him the kind of additional freedom that might well lead to his escape. In short, the mouse had cornered the cat and was now faced with the consequences.

The pro-English sentiments of James's captors were also proving of limited value. Indeed, Elizabeth's support for the Ruthven Raid was characteristically equivocal, which was amply demonstrated by her lukewarm response to the embassy that she received in London in April 1583. With typical artfulness, the king had already written to tell her how he wished to follow her counsel in all matters of importance, since ingratitude was the vilest of vices. But without her financial support, the Lords Enterprisers could not hope to remain long in power, and they were subsequently offered only a quarter of the £10,000 they claimed to require for guarding and maintaining the king. Elizabeth was even prepared to guarantee their subservience by threatening to consider Mary's earlier suggestion of establishing joint sovereignty with her son. In reality, of course, the Association that now briefly reappeared on the agenda remained the non-starter it always had been, not least because James was less prepared than ever in Lennox's absence to entertain the notion, but it nevertheless demonstrated England's coolness to the Ruthven conspirators aptly enough, and fuelled the unease which was soon steadily infecting their ranks.

The future, then, was on James's side, and in preparation for his bid for freedom, he now adapted his behaviour accordingly. Dissimulating with all the skill that was now his trademark, he duly probed and prodded for opportunity. In early 1583, he had given his secret assurance to two French ambassadors that 'although he had two eyes, two ears, two hands, he had but one heart, and that was French', and in response the Marquis de Mainville busied himself in harnessing an anti-Gowrie party among the Scottish nobility. Huntly, Atholl, Montrose, Rothes, Eglinton, Seton and Maxwell all readied themselves to support the king's escape, while James himself duly swallowed his pride and set out to exploit his enemies' wishful thinking. Now, therefore, he ceased his ill-tempered outbursts and acts of defiance and progressively convinced the Lords Enterprisers that he was willing to remain in their hands, even conceding on one occasion that Lennox was 'not wise'. Indeed, his stubborn sullenness gave way by degrees to feigned good humour as he exhibited a surprising graciousness even to the Earl of Gowrie himself, whom he considered to be as directly responsible for Lennox's death as if he had murdered him outright. The duke's privations at Dumbarton in the autumn of 1582, coupled to the rigours of the subsequent winter journey back to France, had served, or so James believed, to break his favourite's health irreparably. But even this would not impair the king's performance. And in playing his role to perfection, he duly seized his chance.

It was not without some irony that in allowing James the liberty of a hunting trip in June 1583, his captors made the same mistake as Lennox before them. And James's escape plan was in essence no less straightforward than the one that had led to his capture in the first place. He was to be issued a sudden and apparently innocent invitation by his great-uncle, the Earl of March, to come to St Andrews – where other members of the anti-Gowrie faction would be on hand – and 'make good cheer with him'. In the meantime, the need for hasty attendance was emphasised on the far from compelling grounds that the elderly earl had prepared a feast of 'wild meat and other fleshes that would spoil' in the event of delay. No greater artifice than this was required, it seems, and even the trip from his designated hunting spot at Falkland to St Andrews was conducted in apparently holiday spirits as the exultant king rode towards safety 'passing his time in hawking by the way'. 'His Majesty,' wrote Sir James Melville, already 'thought himself at liberty, with great joy and exultation, like a bird flown out of a cage ... Albeit I thought his estate far surer when he was in Falkland.' And though Gowrie rode hard to catch him, he was indeed too late to stop the king.

There followed a day and night of tension, as St Andrews Castle eventually teemed with armed supporters of both factions – each ready to unleash murderous riot, though neither anxious to take responsibility for doing so – until the Earl of Gowrie's nerve finally broke. Accepting the inevitable and falling to his knees in James's presence, the earl 'in all humility asked pardon of the King's Majesty ... and showed himself penitent in particular in the offences he had made and uttered against the late Duke of Lennox ... and above all, against his Majesty's own person'. Reproaching him first before pardoning him, James duly savoured the occasion, though the sweetest moment of all did not arrive until the morning of 28 June when the king duly announced to his assembled nobles that he was now free from all faction and intended to rule henceforth as a 'universall king' in his own right, drawing them 'to unity and concord' and 'impartial to them all'. Faithful and ever willing to listen to good counsel, he would forgive past offences and surround himself with wise and virtuous advisers, though decisions would be delivered ultimately according to his princely judgement alone.

There was now, wrote Sir Robert Bowes, 'a great alteration both in his mind and also in his face and countenance', and there was indeed no denying that Scotland had, at long last, an independent ruler with a mind of his own, for James was not only free from those who had held him captive physically. Gone, long since, was the first man in whom he had hoped to find a mentor, the Earl of Atholl. Gone too, for the time being, was his childhood companion, the factious Earl of Mar. Gone finally, though long since repudiated by his pupil, was George Buchanan who had died in October 1582 and now, like Morton and Lennox, was forever out of influence. Henceforth, as Bowes also reported resentfully, James would keep the key of the box containing his private papers himself, so that the English ambassador could not 'get any certainty of the contents'. For the time being, too, freedom from faction at home would also free the king from subservience to England. From now on, it seemed, neither pungent letters from England's queen or embassies from her ailing Secretary of State, Sir Francis Walsingham, could alter the fact that Scotland had, in effect, a new king – albeit, as Walsingham observed angrily, 'a dissembling king, both with God and man,' and one who 'with a kind of jollity said that he was an absolute king'.

Yet James still had call for a man of strength about the throne, and that man now would prove to be the Earl of Arran, whose temporary imprisonment in the aftermath of the Ruthven Raid served as no more than a minor setback. Certainly, it had done nothing to temper either his ambition or his ruthlessness. 'Quick, penetrating, subtle, desirous of goods and greatness, arrogant, confident and capable of many things', Arran was ideally suited to become the king's chosen instrument for government at this critical juncture – not only willing to wield the cudgel, but also to lift the broader burden of rule from his royal master's shoulders. For though James was wilful and headstrong – so much so, indeed, that 'he could hardly be withdrawn from the thing that he desired' – and was resolute in his determination to direct policy, the daily routine of government remained repugnant to him.

The Frenchman Fontenay, who came to Scotland in 1584, considered the young king 'too lazy and thoughtless about business, too devoted to his pleasures, especially to hunting, leaving all his affairs to be managed by the Earl of Arran'. But James, it seems, was keen to explain away any hint of indolence. Excessive work was inclined to make him ill, he claimed, but nothing of importance occurred without his knowledge, since he had spies at the chamber doors of his councillors and was told everything they said. And though he lacked endurance, he could, or so he believed, do more work in an hour than others might do in a day when he applied himself. Indeed, it was his boast that he often accomplished more than six men together. He watched, listened and spoke simultaneously and sometimes did five things at once, he said. Besides which, he had advanced only simple soldiers and gentlemen rather than high-ranking nobles, since he could easily ruin them if they proved either inefficient or disloyal. In consequence, the king remained as confident of his application as he was of his ability – and it was this naive faith in his superiority over ordinary mortals that would, of course, explain many of his subsequent miscalculations.

For the while, however, James could indulge his passions while Arran steered the ship of state. Now, for instance, his 'vacant hours' were spent increasingly in the company of the poet Alexander Montgomerie – a hard-drinking, witty man, whose raffish exterior hid a nature of considerable sensitivity and sweetness – and a coterie of other literary 'brethren', consisting of figures like Sir Patrick Hume of Polwarth, Alexander Scott, Thomas Hudson, John Stewart of Baldyneiss, and the poetess Christian Lindsay. To the king, Montgomerie was 'Belovit Sanders, master of our art', and while Lennox may well have been the first to ignite James's love for the muse, it was Montgomerie who seems to have been most influential in guiding his pen. Yet, far from living up to the flattery heaped upon him by his 'bretheren' as the 'royal Apollo', the king's was in fact a 'dull Muse', as he himself admitted, and he was actually at his most inspired only rarely – usually when writing on political themes. His famous sonnet 'God gives not kings the style of gods in vain' was certainly creditable enough but he remained, in general, no more than a competent spinner of verses, to the extent that his first published work, *The Essayes of a Prentice in the Divine Art of Poesie*, was published anonymously in Edinburgh in 1584.

Nevertheless, the king's reliance upon his dutiful earl remained of considerable overall benefit in personal terms. Freed at last from fear and insecurity, he found himself liberated, too, from tiresome obligations and able, in the process, to fly in whatever direction – artistic, social, recreational – his fancy took him. But more generally, his relationship with Arran was at the very best a mixed blessing, for while the latter's drive and efficiency made up for the king's frailties in these areas, he was generally unpopular and widely mistrusted both at home and abroad. Certainly, there could be no charges laid against Arran of the kind made previously against Lennox by the minister Andrew Melville that the king had been kept 'in a misty night of captivity and black darkness of shameful servitude'. On the contrary, James was no puppet and Arran no 'pseudo-regent'. Indeed, the king remained in a position of commanding partnership, employing the earl, who became chancellor in 1584, as both executor and enforcer where his own youth might otherwise have compromised his wishes. But Sir Francis Walsingham and the English as a whole were deeply suspicious of Arran's former link with Lennox's pro-French inclinations, and the execution of the Earl of Gowrie on 3 May 1584, ostensibly for a new act of treason, confirmed the worst fears of many Scottish noblemen. For it was believed in most quarters that Gowrie's death was an act of revenge – a final token of retribution for the Ruthven Raid and Lennox's untimely demise. There were ominous rumours, too, that Arran had tricked his victim into making a full confession of his second plot by a promise to obtain for him the king's clemency, which, if true, was a shabby return for the mercy that Gowrie had earlier extended to him in the aftermath of the king's abduction.

Subsequent to the execution, moreover, the earls of Angus and Mar and the Master of Glamis were all forced to fly to England while others were ruined, it seems, for no better reason than that they were worth ruining; some, it was rumoured, at the prompting of Arran's capable but greedy wife who was roundly hated by the preachers and reviled as a witch. 'These cruel and rigorous proceedings,' wrote Sir James Melville, 'caused such a general fear, as all familiar society and intercourse of humanity was in a manner lost, no man knowing to whom he might safely speak or open his mind.'

And it was not long either, of course, before Arran was delivering the king's revenge upon the Kirk and its ministers, the more outspoken of whom had already fled to Berwick in anticipation.

James's first interview with the Kirk's leaders after his escape from the Ruthven lords had already augured ill. When they entered his presence at Falkland, he glared at them in silence for fully fifteen minutes before rising and leaving the room and eventually calling them to his cabinet. Furthermore, the exchange which followed was hardly less strained. 'No king in Europe,' James informed his audience, 'would have suffered the things that I have suffered,' and in response to complaints about developments at his court, he went on to declare that he alone might choose 'any that I like best to be in company with me'. Equally provocatively, the king justified his stand on the grounds that he was 'Catholic King of Scotland' – a somewhat injudicious choice of terms, to say the least, which finally prompted the intervention of one of the more amenable ministers. 'No brethren,' said David Ferguson, 'he is universal king and may make choice of his company, as David did in the 110th Psalm,' though few of his colleagues were satisfied. 'We will look no more to your words,' James was informed, 'but to your deeds and behaviour; and if they agree not, which God forbid, we must damn sin in whatsoever person.'

Even worse was to follow, however, when John Durie and Andrew Melville refused to recognise the council's jurisdiction after being called before it to answer for their sermons. Appointed moderator of the General Assembly in 1578, Melville had led the Kirk's onslaught against Robert Montgomery and emerged by turns as the leading and most vociferous critic of secular interference in religious affairs. Famed for his unashamed irreverence towards the 'anointed monarch', it was he, who in defending the principle of the 'two kingdoms' dismissively referred to James as 'God's sillie vassal', and now he would prove no less defiant. The king, Melville pointed out, perverted the laws of God and man, and councillors possessed no authority over the messengers of a king and council far more powerful than they. Taking a Hebrew Bible from his belt, Melville then, it was said, 'clanked it down on the board before the king and chancellor'. 'There,' he declared, 'are my instructions and my warrant,' after which he was ordered into confinement at Blackness Castle before fleeing to England.

Under such circumstances, it was hardly surprising, perhaps, that James and Arran would move to subdue the more radical elements within the Kirk, and in May 1584 the Presbyterian system in Scotland was temporarily ended by what would become known as the 'Black Acts'. In a sweeping attempt to bring the Kirk to heel, the king was henceforward declared head of religious affairs and given jurisdiction over ecclesiastical cases. The courts and assemblies of the Kirk were now to convene only with royal permission and, more provocatively still perhaps, the authority of bishops was confirmed in preference to that of 'pretended presbyteries'. From this point forward, moreover, all affairs of state were to be reserved purely for the judgement of the secular ruler without interference or comment from the pulpit. And to drive the message home, Arran added his own inimitable brand of subtlety. To those ministers who persisted in their objections, the chancellor's message was clear. Their heads would be shaven as an example to all who held their sovereign ruler in contempt.

There was, however, altogether less scope for assertiveness abroad, where James and Arran found themselves forced to renew the foreign intrigues begun by Lennox. Estranged from England, menaced by exiled lords and ministers, and threatened by growing rumbles of discontent at home, the appeal of French or Spanish assistance grew increasingly irresistible, and James slithered accordingly into a further bout of diplomatic intrigue. Sir Francis Walsingham, in a fit of pique, had already told the Scottish king that his power was insignificant and that rulers as young as he were apt to lose their thrones, so when James was contacted by the Duke of Guise after his escape from captivity, his response was predictable: thanking the duke warmly for his friendship and offers of protection, James praised him as the first soldier of the age and expressed his willingness to join an enterprise to release his mother and bring vengeance upon her captors. Further appeals for help were also addressed to the Kings of France and Spain, and most surprisingly of all to the pope himself. 'I trust,' wrote James, clearly implying the possibility of his conversion at some later date, 'to be able to satisfy your Holiness on all other points, especially if I am aided in my great need by your Holiness.'

But this, as the king well knew, was playing with fire, and the pitfalls of his dealings were soon painfully exposed with the appearance of a new favourite – the eminently plausible and equally treacherous Patrick, Master of Gray. As with Arran, no portrait of Gray exists. But he was a handsome, urbane and polished nobleman, who had been appointed a gentleman of the privy chamber in October 1584 and made Master of the King's Wardrobe and Menagerie, in charge of James's jewels, clothing and tapestries, and the employment of tailors and shoemakers. He was also fully conversant with the affairs of Queen Mary, especially in France, where he had been her agent. Indeed, he was still in her service – or so she believed at least, for he had lost faith in a Catholic assault upon England and now considered her situation hopeless. Spain, it seemed, was hesitant, the pope niggardly and Guise weighed down by domestic concerns, and if the Spanish king should actually succeed in unseating his English counterpart, he was hardly likely to bestow her throne upon the Protestant King of Scots. Thus, Gray reasoned, James should abandon his mother's interests and ally instead with Elizabeth.

In the meantime, of course, James would continue to court his mother's representatives, though he had already confirmed to Sir Robert Bowes that her entanglements with Catholic powers rendered her unfit to rule either Scotland or England. The Association, he told Bowes, had been offered by Mary only out of self-interest and was 'tickle to his crown'. Yet when M. de Fontenay, the former queen's representative, arrived in the summer of 1584, James protested loudly that he would never abandon her. On one occasion, in fact, he went so far as to summon Arran, before whom he delivered an oath in Fontenay's presence that Scottish policy would support Mary's cause unwaveringly – an astonishing example of James's tendency to overact in his attempts to deceive. In fact, he fooled no one – least of all the canny Frenchman who noted nonetheless that 'he has a remarkable intelligence, as well as lofty and virtuous ideals'. And this was not all that Fontenay said of the king, for in accepting that his mission was a failure, he also went on to present us with one of the most illuminating brief portraits of the king on record.

The envoy's letter to the Queen of Scots was, in effect, a long and rambling report of his mission in which he attempted to offer some assurance of her son's goodwill towards her. But the letter he addressed to his brother-in-law, Claude Nau, Mary's secretary, was altogether more informative and bore the superscription 'My brother, the letter which follows will remain secret between you and me'. From one other observation, too, it is clear that Fontenay was planning to furnish a full and frank account of his judgements that should not be seen by Mary herself. The king, he noted, 'has never asked anything about the Queen, neither of her health, nor of the way she is treated, nor of her servants, nor of what she eats or drinks, nor of her recreation, nor any similar matter, and yet, notwithstanding this, I know that he loves and honours her much in his heart'. Clearly, the intention was to provide the kind of intimate pen portrait not necessarily normal or appropriate to a visit of the kind that Fontenay had just conducted, though the account that resulted was both fair and perceptive.

On the one hand, the young king's merits were listed in full. 'Three qualities of the mind,' Fontenay observed, 'he possesses in perfection: he understands clearly, judges wisely, and has a retentive memory.' His questions were 'keen and penetrating', his replies 'sound' and 'in any argument, be it about religion or any other thing, he maintains the view that appears to him most true and just' – to the extent that 'I have heard him support Catholic against Protestant opinions'. The king was also 'well instructed in languages, science and affairs of state; better, I dare say, than anyone else in his kingdom' … 'In brief,' Fontenay concluded, 'he has a remarkable mind, filled with virtuous grandeur,' though it was also noted that he possessed 'a good opinion of himself' and had a great desire to hide his deficiencies, attempting anything in pursuit of virtue. Though timid, for example, he wished greatly to be considered courageous. Nor could he bear to be surpassed by other men. Upon hearing that a Scottish laird had passed two days without sleep, the king passed three, and if ever a man succeeded in outstripping him, he abhorred them, it seems, forever.

But Fontenay furnishes us, too, with a range of comments on the king's habits and everyday demeanour that not only picture him minutely, but came to shape the standard image of him down the centuries. We hear, for instance, how he disliked 'dancing and music in general', along with 'all the little fopperies of court life', whether they involve 'amorous talk or curiosities of dress'. In particular, he had 'a special aversion to ear-rings'. There is also the earliest reference on record to James's lack of physical grace. 'He never stays still in one place,' commented the Frenchman, 'taking a singular pleasure in walking up and down, though his carriage is ungainly, his steps erratic and wandering, even in his own chamber.' And there is mention, too, of other less savoury characteristics. His manners, it seems, were 'aggressive and very uncivil, both in speaking and eating and in his clothes and sports', as well as in 'conversation in the company of women'. His body, meanwhile, was 'feeble' – though he was not himself 'delicate' – and his voice 'loud'; his words 'grave and sententious'. 'In a word,' concluded Fontenay, 'he is an old young man,' though he loved hunting, of course, above all other pleasures, 'galloping over hill and dale with loosened bridle' for six hours at a time.

Most intriguingly of all, however, Fontenay explored what he considered James's chief deficiencies as a ruler. In all, he noted 'only three defects which may possibly be harmful to the conservation of his estate and government'. The first was his 'failure to appreciate his poverty and lack of strength, overrating himself and despising other princes' – common enough faults in many contemporary rulers, of course, and especially understandable, perhaps, in so young a king, though James's reputation for extravagance would be heavily reinforced by his behaviour in later life. Then Fontenay observed how James 'loves indiscreetly and obstinately despite the disapprobation of his subjects', and criticised him further for being 'too idle and too little concerned about business'. In this latter connection, the king was apparently 'too addicted to pleasure, principally that of the chase, leaving the conduct of business to the Earl of Arran, Montrose [the treasurer] and the Secretary [John Maitland of Thirlestane]'. And here, too, the criticisms levelled against James would be raised repeatedly in years to come. In all, he emerges as a ruler of considerable intellect but one of limited political intuition: cunning but also prone to naivety; thoughtful but of limited self-awareness; proud and determined to lead but lacking in self-control and charisma – in short, a king of many commendable qualities without the hallmarks of genuine majesty.

Above all, perhaps, Fontenay had been shocked by James's carelessness concerning money. 'The king is extremely penurious,' it was noted. 'To his domestic servants – of whom he has but a fraction of the number that served his mother – he owes more than 20,000 marks for wages and for the goods they have provided.' 'He lives,' said Fontenay, 'only by borrowing.' Yet this, we are told, in no way restricted his spending. The confiscated lands and revenues of the Ruthven lords were frittered upon courtiers and when James was quizzed about money his answers were unsatisfactory. Having claimed at first that his finances were sound, he then confessed they were not, only to add that his youth and nature made it difficult for him to fulfil his promises to be less liberal. It was hardly surprising, then, that in his official letter to Mary, Fontenay warned her against sending any money to her son.

Nor was it without irony that one of the major beneficiaries of the king's generosity at this time was none other than the Master of Gray, who had recently received the tidy sum of 6,000 marks that had been gifted to James by the Duke of Guise. More and more influential with each passing day, Gray was now sent to England in August 1584 with the specific intention of forging an Anglo-Scottish alliance that would not only ignore but directly undermine the interests of the former queen, upon whose behalf he had supposedly been working. With the expulsion of the Spanish ambassador from London in January 1584, the English were increasingly anxious to secure their northern border, and the very choice of Gray as emissary to Elizabeth gave the clearest possible proof that James was prepared at last to abandon his mother openly, since his mission was to reveal her secrets and reach an agreement with her English rival in which she had no part. In the process, he would also reveal the existence of his own enmity with Arran, which could be exploited as Elizabeth saw fit.

When, however, Mary discovered the true nature of Gray's dealings, she was both appalled and terrified. Fondly believing that he had been negotiating for her release, it was not until March 1585 that she discovered his treachery. Worse still, the duplicity of her son was soon equally manifest, for, upon receiving an English pension of some £4,000 a year and a gift of fallow deer, James would finally disavow the Association upon which Mary had staked so much. Politically, of course, his decision was a wise one, since the way now stood open not only for a league with England but even, perhaps, the prospect of his nomination as Elizabeth's successor. The English Parliament's Act of Association in 1584 had, after all, explicitly disqualified from the succession any candidate who supported armed action in favour of Mary Stuart. And there was no denying either that Mary's dealings had been equally tainted with self-interest from the outset. When the time came, then, the choice was a clinical one. Though, as John Colville pointed out, James seemed 'not to have lost all affection to his mother … yet (as those about him will speak) hee had rather have hir as shee is, then him self to give hir place'. Coldly informing her in 1586 that he could not 'associate her with himself in the sovereignty of Scotland' and that he could not in future 'treat with her otherwise than as Queen-Mother', James duly delivered his parting thrust. Nor, when Mary condemned her 'ungrateful son' and threatened to disinherit him in favour of Philip of Spain, did he offer any further justification. Instead, he offered only silence and never wrote to her again.

The Queen of England, meanwhile, was fully aware of James's slippery tendencies. 'Who seeketh two strings to one bow,' she told him, 'they may shoot strong, but never straight.' And she knew no less certainly that any alliance with Scotland could never be confidently secured without the departure of Arran who was now increasingly exposed on all fronts. To the long list of his former enemies he had added the Catholic nobles, alienated by the negotiations with Elizabeth, and the insolence of both him and his wife had by now even upset the king. William Davison, the English ambassador 'observed the strangeness of their behaviour towards the poor young prince, who is so distracted and worried by their importunities as it pitied me to see, and, if I be not abused, groweth full of their fashions and behaviours, which he will sometimes discourse of in broad language, showing he is not ignorant of how they use him'. Men of influence like Maitland of Thirlestane, who had initially supported Arran, were also no longer his friends, and with the Master of Gray now bolstered by English approval as well as the king's high favour, the time of crisis was not far off.

With Gray's return from London, his enmity with Chancellor Arran was soon spawning mutual fears of assassination, as the court sank into confusion and uproar and English agents awaited their opportunity. For all his panache and earlier bravado, Arran's heart, in particular, began to fail him as he awaited the inevitable onslaught. Armed at all times as he went about his daily affairs distractedly, he brought armour and supplies into Edinburgh Castle, and strengthened his apartments at Holyrood. On one occasion, too, he showed that even for a soldier of such dashing reputation as he, discretion could yet be the better part of valour. Returning one night through the ill-lit alleys of the capital, he let his wife pass on up the High Street, it seems, while he, with torches extinguished and a cloak about his shoulders, stole into the fortress by a secret route accompanied by a lone servant.

When the time came, however, neither the dark, nor disguises, nor secret passageways could save Arran. Nor, for that matter, could innocence on the one occasion, perhaps, when he had done no real wrong. For when Lord Francis Russell (the son of the Earl of Bedford) was shot and killed by Sir Thomas Kerr of Ferniherst (the Scottish warden of the Middle March) during a 'day of truce on which Scottish and English representatives were meeting to settle Border disputes', the blame was at once ascribed to the chancellor. Since Ferniherst owed his appointment to Arran, it was easy for the latter's enemies to accuse him of instigating the killing as a means of preventing the conclusion of the proposed Anglo-Scottish treaty. And even though Arran had actually been responsible for initiating the discussions with England's representatives, this was conveniently ignored. Indeed, Sir Edward Wotton, the leading English negotiator, later admitted without embarrassment how he had 'aggravated the matter not more than it deserved but as much as he could'.

The Scottish king, moreover, offered comparatively little resistance in abandoning his leading enforcer. Though greatly distressed by the incident, his concerns were at least as much for his pension and prospects for the English succession as they were for the fate of his chancellor. Wotton found him, in fact, alone and melancholy in his chamber, his eyes swollen by weeping. In discussing Russell's murder, the king, wrote Wotton, 'shed tears over it like a newly beaten child, protesting by his honour and crown that he was ignorant of this practice, desiring her Majesty not to condemn him for other men's faults'. The Queen of England, he lamented, would consider him a dissembler, though he would rather lose all the kingdoms of the world than be found untrue to his word. Indeed, for twenty-four hours he neither ate nor drank nor slept before proving his good faith to Elizabeth by ordering Arran's imprisonment in St Andrews Castle. And though the earl was released a week later on James's orders, it was no difficult task for Elizabeth to finish the matter by agreeing to 'let slip' the exiled 'Ruthven Raiders' across the Border, where they could be guaranteed to tip the balance. On 2 November, therefore, the earls of Mar and Angus, the two Hamiltons and the Master of Glamis duly appeared before Stirling Castle with sufficient forces to compel the king to abandon his favourite once and for all.

Inside the castle there followed the usual chaotic scenes of violent recrimination in which Gray and Arran and their rival gangs squared off in the king's presence without actually striking, since both 'suspected falsehood in friendship' and feared to trust his own side. Arran denounced Gray as the instigator of the exiles' return, while Gray protested his innocence – apparently with some success, for in the morning Arran's nerve broke and he opted to save himself by flight, closely followed by the king who, in nervous terror, attempted unsuccessfully to exit through a postern gate previously locked by Gray. In the event, the decisive factor in Arran's submission was probably the powerful threat posed by the new Earl of Bothwell, nephew of Mary's lover and already, with his considerable Border power, one of the key political players in Scotland. With his political career at an end, Arran had no other choice, in fact, than to head west and to settle for the obscurity that must have been so intolerable for such a one as he. In conceding that he should forfeit his earldom and the chancellorship, James did, however, protect him as best he could from the further vengeance of his enemies – until, that is, a nephew of the former regent, Morton, with a long memory and lingering sense of duty finally butchered him in 1595.

5 ❦ The Headsman and the King of Spain

'[We are] in a despair to do any good in the errand we came for, all things disheartening us on every side, and every hour giving us new advertisement that we deal for a dead lady.'

George Young, member of the Scottish embassy to plead for the life of Mary Stuart, 10 January 1587

On 3 November 1585, the King of Scotland was once again obliged to 'make vertue of a need' and receive the returned Ruthven raiders in the Great Hall of Stirling Castle. Though they sank to their knees and professed their loyalty, it was surely a scene to excite mixed emotions in the young man occupying the throne. In Sir James Melville's view, the king spoke pertly and boastfully, as if victorious over the rebels. Yet Calderwood suggests that he addressed them 'with cheerfulness, it seemed', thanking God that they had returned with so little bloodshed. In any event, he pardoned them and proceeded to demonstrate not only his rapidly developing adroitness by the speed with which he turned the new situation to his advantage, but the extent to which he was now – as he had been for some time – the master of policy in his kingdom. By finally accepting the overthrow of Arran and reinstating the exiled lords in Scotland, James had, indeed, freed himself from further compulsion. And the continuance of his recent measures was the firmest possible proof that he rather than his favourite had been the instigator of policy all along. The 'Black Acts', for example, though modified in application, were not rescinded, and when the exiled ministers returned in the wake of the lords, who now distanced themselves from religious radicalism, the king maintained the initiative. Andrew Melville, for his part, found himself ordered north to spend his time looking for Jesuits and to 'travail, so far as in him lies, to reduce them to the true and Christian religion', while others even more vociferous, such as John Gibson, were given short shrift. After denouncing James for maintaining 'the tyranny of bishops and absolute power', Gibson was swiftly dispatched to prison, but not before the king enjoyed the final word. 'I give not a turd for thy preaching,' he had howled in derision at the hapless minister.

Nor, when James pressed forward with the Anglo-Scottish treaty was he succumbing to external pressure. Though the arrival in January 1586 of a resident French ambassador, M. de Courcelles, was consciously designed to assert his independence, alliance with England remained his first best option, and was actually the most assured means of nullifying once and for all any potential threat from the old Gowrie faction. For, by becoming England's ally, James would curb at once the baleful effects of that country's interference in Scottish politics, which had led to his abduction at Ruthven in the first place. He had, moreover, already shown his teeth over Gowrie's execution, so that the earl's former associates were more than grateful to receive their lands anew, in spite of their past misdeeds. And the loss of Arran was never, in any case, the blow to royal prestige – let alone the emotional trauma - that Lennox's departure had represented. Indeed, James had become increasingly concerned in his own right about the chancellor's over-mighty posturing and may even have tacitly encouraged Gray in his machinations. Much more importantly still, Arran's removal left the way clear at last for the promotion of John Maitland of Thirlestane, the gifted and comparatively selfless statesman, who eventually succeeded to the vacant chancellorship in July 1587: a man who was more ready than most to shun the limelight and more able than any to harness the king's talents while masking his weaknesses.

All was set fair, then, for the effective restoration of royal authority with considerable smoothness and in exceptionally quick time. James's former enemies were, after all, not so much a compact party as a coalition drawn from discordant elements, united for a brief space of time only by a common hatred of Arran. While Angus, Mar and Glamis had headed the coup which restored them to power, the returning exiles also included

Lord John Hamilton, an old adherent of Mary though a Protestant, his younger brother, Lord Claud, a Catholic, and the Catholic Border chieftain, Maxwell. Other Catholics joined the council, too, alongside men like Maitland, Gray and Sir Lewis Bellenden, who were all retained from the previous government. In consequence, there was a healthy balance which gave the king, for the time being at least, an unexpected degree of independence – especially when it is remembered that most of his former enemies were heavily preoccupied with restoring their private fortunes. Indeed, to humour the king they even yielded precedence to his new young favourite, Ludovic Stuart, the 10-year-old son of Lennox, whom James had recently brought over from France. No guard was placed about the king as he hunted to his heart's content, and in matters of state, too, he would be crossed more rarely than ever before.

By the summer of 1586, moreover, James even had reason to believe that Scotland's age-old enmity with England, which had hitherto proved so damaging to his kingdom might well be ending. His power to negotiate the most advantageous terms had been limited, in fact, by his keenness for official recognition as heir to the English throne, though the most that Elizabeth would offer was a 'firm promise in the word of a queen' that she would never bar him from 'any right or title that might be due to him in any time present or future', unless 'by manifest ingratitude she should be justly moved and provoked to the contrary'. Plainly, the Queen of England was still intent upon exerting the maximum control over James's actions – and for good reason, too, since any assurances given to James while his mother lived involved tacit acceptance of her own place in the succession. But on 5 July, notwithstanding such snares and limitations, the treaty of alliance was indeed formally signed, and James could congratulate himself, it seemed, at another sign that his earlier difficulties were at long last reaching resolution.

The unforeseen complication which now presented itself therefore left James both stricken and dumbstruck, for at the very moment the alliance was being sealed, the final act of his mother's sad drama was about to begin. Her complicity in the Babington Plot had been painstakingly monitored by Elizabeth's spymaster, Walsingham, and on 3 August her papers were seized and she was duly arrested along with her secretaries. Such was his surprise that James had no idea at first of Mary's full predicament. As late as October he was assuring the French ambassador that she was 'in no danger' and should henceforth meddle with nothing beyond prayer and service to God, though he acknowledged that 'as for the conspiracy, she must be content to drink the ale she has brewed'. From his perspective, this was likely to entail little more than closer confinement. Mary's servants, on the other hand, should be hanged, new ones appointed, while she herself should be 'put in the Tower or some other manse and kept from intelligence'. Even by Christmas, moreover, he seemed unable to comprehend that Mary's execution was a distinct possibility, though she had already been brought to trial at Fotheringay on 11 October and sentenced to death before the month was out. Certainly, the thought that he had signed away his mother's life for a pension of £4,000 only months earlier would never occur to him.

Nor was James much inclined to disturb his personal relations with Elizabeth on his mother's behalf. 'The only thing he craves is her life,' wrote Roger Aston, an Englishman in his service. But reports from Archibald Douglas, the Scottish representative in London, whom James had appointed in spite of his implication in the murder of Darnley, gradually seem to have taken effect. Douglas, along with Sir William Keith, a young member of the royal household who acted as the king's messenger, had been instructed by James to pursue two objectives: 'the one to deal very earnestly both with the Queen and her councillors for our sovereign mother's life', the other to ensure that his title to the English Crown 'be not pre-judged'. On 22 November, however, Douglas informed the Master of Gray that Mary was 'in extreme danger of her life' and Gray's response reveals his master's growing concern – as much for himself as for his mother. 'The king nor no man ever believed that the matter would have gone so far,' wrote Gray, before pointing out James's concern not only for his mother but 'the opinion of all his people' and the implications for his 'honour'. And James was indeed largely hamstrung, for, as Douglas had reminded him, the English Parliament's Bond of Association rendered any interference on his part a most risky undertaking, since it might easily be employed against him if any suspicion arose that he was party to Mary's plottings. In effect, therefore, he was faced with an excruciating choice between his mother's life and his hopes for the English throne.

But the pressure was raining in upon James from other quarters, too. That Elizabeth should threaten violence against a Scottish queen was wholly abhorrent to his nobles who assumed automatically that Mary's death would at once bring war with England and alliance with her enemies.

The Earl of Bothwell, who shared, it seems, his ill-fated uncle's knack for plain speaking, told James that if he countenanced his mother's execution, he would deserve to be hanged next day – at which the king is said to have laughed and suggested that he would prepare for that. Lord Claud Hamilton, on the other hand, swore that he would burn Elizabeth's kingdom as far as Newcastle if Mary was injured, and even an enemy of the former queen, like Angus, declared that Mary would be fully justified in slitting Elizabeth's throat. Clearly, when national pride and the old enemy were involved, even the Scottish elite, famous for their blood feuds and divisions, could unite. And this meant only further trouble for their king, since his other subjects, too, were deeply embittered by the presumption of Mary's captors. 'I never saw all the people so willing to concur in anything as this,' wrote Gray. 'All men drive at him.'

Under the growing pressure, James's temper seems, in fact, to have compromised his judgement and he adopted a curiously provocative tone in the first letter of formal protest that he dispatched for Elizabeth's attention on 27 November. Sovereign princes like his mother, 'descended of all hands of the best blood in Europe' could not, he affirmed, be judged 'by subjects' mouths' and on this basis it was to the Queen of England's discredit that 'the nobility and counsellors of England should take upon them to sentence a Queen of Scotland'. Much more strongly still, he reminded Elizabeth that, while her father had stained his reputation 'by the beheading of his bedfellow', that particular 'tragedy' was 'far inferior' to what she was now contemplating. There were further references, too, to James's personal predicament and an ambivalent suggestion that he wished only to protect the English monarch's name and interests north of the Border. 'I desire you to consider,' he appealed, 'how my honour stands engaged, that is her son and a king, to suffer my mother an absolute princess to be put to an infamous death.' 'Guess ye,' he added, 'in what state my honour will be in, this "unhappe" being perfected; since, before God, I already scarce dare go abroad for crying out of the whole people; and what is spoken by them of the Queen of England it grieves me to hear, and yet dare not find fault with it except I would dethrone myself, so is the whole of Scotland incensed with this matter.'

Far from helping matters, however, the letter succeeded only in infuriating Elizabeth. Above all, the reference to Henry VIII's 'bedfellow', her mother Anne Boleyn, raised an altogether unmentionable subject and, in consequence, she was said to have taken 'such a chafe as ye would wonder'.

Indeed, according to Douglas who delivered the letter on 6 December, she 'conceived such a passion as it was a great deal of work to us all … to appease her'. Nor were the after-effects of her rage in any way to James's advantage. Keith, his messenger, was now informed that if he 'had not delivered unto Her Majesty so strange and unseasonable message as did directly touch her noble father and herself', she would have delayed proceedings against the Queen of Scots, but now would not do so if any emergency should arise. Equally significantly, Elizabeth refused to receive a new delegation of two Scottish noblemen and decided instead that the Queen of Scots' case could only be presented to her by two commoners. In doing so, she ensured that James's final embassy on behalf of his mother would lack the prestige of nobility to lend it weight.

James, then, had clearly miscalculated and, in the meantime, the fact that his baiting of Elizabeth had been framed in a private letter did nothing to convince his subjects of his resolve. Worse still, his determination to defend his mother was, in any case, effectively non-existent. Indeed, on 3 December, the day that James's letter arrived in London, Douglas had conferred informally with the Earl of Leicester in his carriage and left little doubt of the king's real intentions. After offering to support his claim to the English Crown, Leicester had at first made clear the advantages accruing to James in the event of his mother's death. Then, without further ceremony, he had asked Douglas directly whether Mary's execution would put paid to the alliance between the two countries. The response was negative. The treaty, said Douglas, was the king's policy and he would not break it unless the English forced his hand – an implicit but unmistakable reference to his right to succeed Elizabeth.

Meanwhile, the official delegation that James had dispatched in accordance with Elizabeth's conditions was making its way to London, though Douglas's private discussion with Leicester had already largely undermined its mission. The two non-noble ambassadors stipulated by Elizabeth were Gray and Sir Robert Melville of Murdocairney, a steadfast partisan of Queen Mary, assisted by George Young, a member of the king's household and Sir Alexander Stuart, a dubious and fickle character who, along with Douglas, would eventually help to hammer the final nails into the queen's coffin. The plan, in fact, was to present the most cogent plea for Mary's life to date, assuring the Queen of Scots' abstinence from further political intrigue and guaranteeing Elizabeth's deliverance from further conspiracies. This time, moreover, there was to be no risk of offence. 'If neither of the overtures aforesaid be thought sufficient,' wrote James, 'ye shall with all instance press our dearest sister to set down by advice of her wisest and best affected counsellors such form of security as she and they shall think sufficient', making clear that 'we will not only yield for ourselves but also do our best endeavour to obtain the performance thereof'. For good measure, the ambassadors were to 'protest before God' that 'the life of our dearest sister is no less dear unto us in all respects than the life of our dearest mother or our own'.

On 15 December, James had also written to the Earl of Leicester, having learned only the day before of Douglas's dialogue with him. He knew therefore that unless he directly contradicted the impression that Leicester had been left with, his mother would die. But he knew, too, that to break the alliance with England would not only remove all hope of the English succession but throw him into a league with Spain that was potentially more damaging still. The prospect of Spanish victory was, after all, far from guaranteed and if it did indeed occur, dependence on his new Catholic ally was inevitable – with all that this would entail for the religious harmony of his realm. Both alternatives were heavy indeed, but one, as James realised, nevertheless remained preferable. Given that his ambassadors were already, in all likelihood, 'dealing for a dead lady', since Elizabeth's chief ministers had in effect staked their own lives by condemning Mary, he would salvage what he could from a lost cause and look through his fingers at his mother's fate. 'I am honest, no changer of course, altogether in all things as I profess to be', he informed Leicester, before declaring how 'fond and inconstant' he would be 'if I should prefer my mother to the title'.

Whether this last statement was meant to imply that he had no intention of 'preferring', i.e. supporting, his mother's claim to the title or whether he was referring to the choice between his mother's life and his own claim to the succession remains unclear. But such ambivalence is unlikely to have been coincidental and the impression remains that James was content for Leicester to retain the impression given earlier by Douglas. In any case, the letter was not genuinely indicative of the callous indifference of a son to his mother's plight. Instead, it was little more than a resigned footnote to a drawn-out saga that had already all but run its course. The end, if not the ending, had long been sealed in fact. And James was left with little more than empty gestures and hollow professions, concluding his communication with Leicester by pointing out once more how 'my honour constrains me to insist for her life', though 'my religion ever moved me to hate her course'.

There followed another letter to Elizabeth, delivered by Gray and Melville, which was another exercise in dutiful posturing. Employing precisely the kind of bold language that the decorum of abject submission demanded from a monarch in such circumstances, James spoke this time of the divinity of kings, whose sacred diadems were not to be profaned, and suggested once more that rulers were beyond the condemnation of their subjects. Elizabeth should, he said, beware the revenge of his mother's supporters and send her abroad under guarantees of future good behaviour. Alternatively, Mary might be encouraged to sign a bond committing her to a traitor's death if implicated in any further conspiracies. But James, as well he knew, was whistling in the wind and his choice of Gray as ambassador, when the latter had already betrayed the Queen of Scots on a previous mission, did little to hide the fact.

Gray and his partner, Melville, were in any case fighting a losing battle against the very men who were intended to assist them. Sir Alexander Stuart, for instance, lost no time in claiming to possess instructions superior to theirs and, together with Douglas, was soon informing Elizabeth that his royal master would accept Mary's death and 'with tyme digest the worst' – an impertinence which later so infuriated James that, according to Courcelles, he fell into a 'marvellous choler' and vowed to hang Stuart upon his return 'before he put off his boots'. But for all the displays of royal anger and fits of wounded conscience, Stuart's only fault had been to say what the king himself could not, as Elizabeth remained impervious to James's 'earnest suite' and 'friendly advice'. Indeed, when Gray suggested that Mary, in return for her life, should transfer to her son the right to the English Crown, Elizabeth did not hold back. 'By God's passion,' she exclaimed, 'that were to cut my own throat, and, for a duchy or an earldom to yourself, you or such as you would cause some of your desperate knaves to kill me.' When, likewise, the Scottish ambassadors appealed for a reprieve of firstly fifteen days and then eight, the response was unyielding. 'Not for an hour,' declared the queen.

One further letter followed in which James recited the familiar mantra: if Elizabeth knew of his grief and his problems in Scotland, she would spare him this ordeal. Princes, he repeated, were not subject to earthly censure, while Sir Alexander Stuart was to be condemned for exceeding his authority. Elizabeth should consider, too, he added, the 'almost universal hatred' that his mother's execution would evoke among other rulers. Yet such implicit threats were wholly unavailing, and when the Queen of

England hesitated at the last to sign her cousin's death warrant, it was her own private misgivings rather than fear of James that made her do so. When, moreover, the warrant was finally sealed in February she contrived, in any case, to confer the blame for 'that miserable accident' upon her hapless secretary William Davison – irrespective of the fact that she had spent a week attempting to persuade Mary's gaoler Sir Amyas Paulet to arrange the death in secret. 'God forbid that I should make so foul a shipwreck of my conscience or leave so great a blot to my poor posterity to shed blood without law or warrant,' Paulet had responded. But the axe duly fell on 8 February – the very day that Gray and Melville received the official thanks of the king's council for their efforts in England.

Accounts of James's reaction to the news of his mother's death vary markedly, in fact. One contemporary eyewitness, Ogilvie of Powrie, suggested in a letter to Archibald Douglas that the king was apparently indifferent to the report that reached him. 'The king,' we are told, 'moved never his countenance at the rehearsal of his mother's execution, nor leaves not his pastime and hunting more than of before.' David Calderwood, meanwhile, who was a child at the time and therefore not on hand to witness events, suggested that the king could not suppress his delight that his rule in Scotland was now at last unchallenged. 'When the king heard of the execution,' wrote Calderwood, 'he could not conceal his inward joy, howbeit outwardly he seemed sorrowful.' That night, it seems, he expressed his satisfaction at being 'sole king' – a comment which left Maitland so ashamed that he ordered a gaggle of onlooking courtiers from the room. Yet not all descriptions reflect quite so poorly upon James's lack of sensitivity. Moysie, for instance, suggests that he 'was in great displeasure and went to bed without supper' and rode to Dalkeith next morning 'desiring to be solitaire'. And when he was later given a moving description of his mother's final moments by one of her ladies-in-waiting, he was said to have been 'very sad and pensive all that day and would not sup that night'.

An English spy, on the other hand, reported that James reacted 'very grievously and offensively and gave out in secret speeches that he would not digest the same or leave it unavenged'. And the sense of outraged dignity that the king often exhibited certainly seems to have manifested itself in some angry talk about the Queen of England in the period that followed. He suggested in private, for instance, that he would not allow himself to be intimidated by an old woman, who was so unloved by her subjects and in such perpetual fear of assassination that she fled at the approach of strangers. 'He protesteth,' wrote one observer, 'though he be a mean king with small ability, he would not change fortune with her, choosing rather to live securely among his subjects than to seek after the blood of his people of contrary religion as she does.'

As always, however, James's frothy talk gave way to clear-cut deference when dealing with Elizabeth in person, and his response to her letter excusing herself of Mary's death was a further example of the one-sidedness of their actual relationship. In acknowledging her 'long professed goodwill' to his mother, for instance, he also accepted Elizabeth's 'solemn attestations of innocency' and 'unspotted part' in the death of the one whom he merely referred to as 'the defunct'. Not even the slightest veiled hint of disapproval, let alone reprisal, was delivered, and there was no suggestion either that relations between the two rulers would remain anything other than cordial in time to follow. Instead, James merely concluded with the familiar reference to his hopes for the succession: 'And, as for my part, I look that ye will give me at this time such full satisfaction in all respects, as shall be a mean to strengthen and unite this isle, establish and maintain the true religion, and oblige me to be, as before I was, your most loving.'

Overly extravagant professions of grief might well, of course, have opened James to the charge of hypocrisy, but if the king's correspondence with his English counterpart suggested a rational and pragmatic acceptance of political realities, his subjects' response to the death of their former queen was altogether less thin-blooded. The ministers of the Kirk did not, of course, regret her passing. Indeed, when James had exhorted them to pray for her safety, a certain John Cowper needed to be hauled from his pulpit as he railed against him to his face. Inspired, or so he claimed, by the spirit of God, Cowper prophesied trial and tribulation for all who lived in Edinburgh and foretold that the day of calamity when it came would be 'a witness against the king'. When, moreover, the ministers had finally agreed to offer prayers for the former queen, their objective had been not her delivery from death, but only that she 'should become a profitable member of Christ's Kirk'.

Yet there were those, among the nobility especially, who were more inclined to express outrage at Mary's treatment. When James chose, for instance, to follow the custom of wearing a 'dule weid' (mourning garment) of dark purple, he was told by Earl Francis of Bothwell that his only 'dule weid' should be a suit of armour until the Queen of Scots was avenged against a kingdom that had harried Scotland for the last three centuries.

Likewise, at a Parliament in July 1587, Maitland made an impassioned plea for retribution – after which each and every one of the attending nobles swore on bended knee to assist James in military action. And while James the poet remained studiously silent on the subject of his mother's death, other quills were busily at work, one of which – wielded by an outraged Scots versifier, who was wise enough to remain anonymous – promised nothing less than the gift of a noose for the Queen of England:

> To Jesabel that English heure [whore]
> receive this Scottish cheyne,
> As presages of her gret malhoeur
> for murthering of our Quene.

Such, indeed, was the clamour that James had little option other than to countenance some token gestures against his kingdom's time-honoured oppressors. Even when Sir Robert Carey first brought news of the execution, he had been refused passage beyond Berwick, where he was met by Peter Young, and now James was prepared to take the cynical step of consenting to the temporary imprisonment and banishment of Gray who became the scapegoat for the government's failure to save Mary. He also wrote lamely to Henry III of France, to Catherine de Medici and to the Duke of Guise to appeal for aid in avenging his mother, and retained the Archbishop of Glasgow as an ambassador to the French court - while refraining, predictably, from signing or dating his appointment. Nor did his correspondence with Henry III prevent him from cultivating the friendship of the French king's arch-enemy, Henry of Navarre. Though he had promised the king that no Scot would serve in the armies of Navarre, the promise was at once broken when he allowed Sir James Colville of Easter Wemyss to raise a company of soldiers for precisely that purpose. And it was at this time, too, for good measure, that James chose to entertain the Huguenot poet, Guillaume Sallust du Bartas, at the Scottish court with no expense spared, irrespective of the fact that the poet came as an unofficial envoy for Navarre's cause.

Plainly, then, James's gestures were no less hollow in the wake of his mother's death than they had been all along, albeit justifiably, perhaps, in light of his limited resources and equally limited options, though his subsequent quest for the English Crown – not to mention his hungry pursuit of his English pension and the English estates of the Lennox family which Elizabeth had annexed – often seemed less than becoming. To remove all suspicion of evil after the infernal proceedings against his dearest mother, he proposed, for instance, that Elizabeth should give him the requisite lands in northern England, along with the title of duke. But the queen remained coldly dismissive of his desire for material advantage. Though it eventually averaged the stipulated £4,000 per year, James's pension was paid only irregularly and when, on one occasion, he managed to screw the sum of £2,000 from her special envoy, William Ashby, Elizabeth later repudiated the payment on the grounds that Ashby had exceeded his authority in agreeing to it. As such, a quip recorded by a Spanish diplomat was much to the point. For when the Spaniard related to an English counterpart how the wound to James's honour could only be healed by a declaration that he would succeed Elizabeth, the Englishman was said to have replied that 'this was rather a point of profit than of honour'.

But it was not so much repartee as the growing Spanish threat that was soon preoccupying James and diverting his subjects' attention away from the treatment of their erstwhile queen. Although he had initially intended to make Mary Queen of Scots the lawful Catholic ruler of England, King Philip's position had altered fundamentally during the last months of her life as he decided to press Spanish claims to the English throne on the strength of Mary's alleged will, the existence of which was never proven, and his own somewhat tenuous descent from Edward III's son, John of Gaunt. In consequence, the queen's execution had been met with no small relief in Madrid, as Philip now pushed forward with plans to place the crown of England upon the head of his own daughter. In fact, on 11 February 1587, four days before Mary was actually beheaded, he wrote to the Count of Olivares, his ambassador at the papal court, revealing his intentions plainly. 'You will impress upon His Holiness,' he informed Olivares, 'that I cannot undertake a war in England for the purpose merely of placing upon the throne a young heretic like the King of Scotland, who, indeed, is by his heresy incapacitated to succeed. His Holiness must, however, be assured that I have no intention of adding England to my own domains, but to settle the crown upon my daughter, the Infanta.'

Nor was James's prospective loss of the English throne his only fear, for if England were conquered by Spain, Scotland would be bound, as an English envoy had once reminded him, to follow close behind. And there were, of course, powerful interests within the Scottish kingdom that might be ready to assist such a turn of events. The Catholic nobility in the north, led by the Earl of Huntly, head of the great clan of Gordon, and his supporters, Crawford and Montrose, had grown to considerable strength, and by 1588 were hatching plans, along with Lord John Maxwell and Lord Claud Hamilton in the south, to welcome a Spanish army and force James's conversion. Yet the king, in spite of the obvious dangers, would remain loath to tackle Huntly and his associates, for though the earl had been educated in France as a Roman Catholic, he was nevertheless James's kinsman through the marriage of two of his forebears and had signed the Presbyterian confession of faith in 1588. More importantly still, he had helped free James from the Ruthven raiders and become an object of considerable affection to the king, who, with characteristic lack of inhibition, was sometimes seen to kiss him in public – 'to the amazement of many'.

There were considerations of policy, too, firmly underpinning James's indulgence towards the Catholic lords in general, since they enhanced his bargaining power with Elizabeth, formed a counterpoise against the Kirk, and offered hope of survival in the perfectly likely event of Spanish victory. He was even, it seems, prepared to meet with their spies in an attempt to hedge his bets. Robert Bruce, for example, met the king on three occasions and suggested that he was willing to negotiate with Philip. The same was said, for that matter, by a Spanish agent from the Netherlands named Colonel Semple, who was subsequently permitted to move freely around Scotland, plotting at leisure. Nor, of course, would this be the last occasion that James was prepared to flirt with Rome, for, long after the current crisis of imminent invasion had passed, he would pursue a similar approach in the hope that English Catholics would support his quest for their kingdom's Crown.

Early in the same year, however, he published a short meditation on selected verses of the Book of Revelation which confirmed his unwavering commitment to the Protestant faith by 'commenting of the Apocalypse' and setting out 'sermons thereupon against the Papists and Spaniards'. After all, 1588 had been ushered in by an ominous tide of baleful prophecies, and the final book of the New Testament, with its lurid descriptions of the end of times and compelling reflections on the fragility of all earthly power, had, in any case, always been a particular source of fascination to him. 'Excellent astronomers,' observed David Calderwood, foretold that the year would be 'fatal to all estates'. 'And if the world did not perish,' he added, 'yet there should be great alterations in kingdoms and empires, so that thereafter it should be called the year of wonders.' In Spain, too, as preparations for the Armada proceeded apace, 1588 was deemed to be 'pregnant with misfortune'. In such circumstances, nothing, it seems, could have been a more fitting subject for the royal pen than the loosing of Satan and the rise and fall of empires. And the villain throughout is the papal Antichrist – the king of locusts, the beast rising from the sea and the woman in scarlet sitting upon the waters.

If, however, any further proof were required of James's inherent hostility to Rome, he was not long in providing it, for, around the same time, he saw fit to challenge James Gordon, the Jesuit uncle of the Earl of Huntly, to a public disputation at court. Over five long hours, in fact, James held his own with both rigour and the utmost courtesy, leaving his rival to reflect afterwards that no one could 'use his arguments better nor quote the Scriptures and other authorities more effectively' than the king. And while one of his courtiers, flushed with pride at his sovereign's knowledge, suggested that even the most learned papist in Europe would never trip him, Mendoza, too, the Spanish ambassador, acknowledged James's performance. 'I hear,' wrote the Spaniard, 'that after the disputation the king said in his chamber that Gordon did not understand the Scripture, which is a fairly bold thing to say, except that the king has the assurance to translate Revelation and to write upon the subject as if he were Amadis of Gaul.'

When the day of reckoning arrived, moreover, and the Spanish Armada conducted its vain enterprise upon England, James remained faithful to his alliance with Elizabeth throughout. Though he had offered her 'his forces, his person and all that he commanded against yon strangers', his assistance was in fact never more than moral, but he had stirred no coals upon either the Border or in Ireland and could fairly record that Spanish forces 'never entered within any road or haven within his dominion, nor never came within a kenning near to any of his coasts'. Nor, typically, was he stinting in his estimation of the significance of the English victory. Indeed, in a meditation upon the fifteenth chapter of the Book of Kings that he penned soon afterwards, James suggested that the victory over Spain was far greater even the David's victory over the Philistines – though his personal gains were predictably limited, as Elizabeth remained silent on the succession issue and, in August, refused him the payment of further money previously promised by William Ashby. 'I am sorry to know from Scotland,' wrote the exiled Master of Gray, 'that the king our master has, of all the golden mountains offered, received a fiddler's wages.'

Meanwhile, the news for James at home in 1589 was no more pleasing either. In February, the English intercepted letters signed by the Earl of Huntly and his associates, which expressed their regret at the failure of the Armada and promised their assistance to King Philip in the event of any future invasion attempt. The plan, in fact, was to bring the Duke of Parma over from the Netherlands with a force of 6,000 men as a prelude to a joint invasion of England, and Elizabeth's response was predictable. 'Good Lord! Methinks I do but dream,' she protested, in a letter that left her embarrassed counterpart no choice other than to act, though in what would prove to be, under the circumstances, an astonishingly half-hearted manner. For, after removing Huntly from the captaincy of the royal guard and imprisoning him in Edinburgh Castle, the king went on to dine with him only the next day. Rather than serving up condign punishment, James also wrote pathetically to the traitor to the Protestant faith whom he believed he had converted only the year before. 'Are these,' he inquired lamely, 'the fruits of your new conversion?' And within days, Huntly was not only released but restored to his former position – an action which provoked Maitland to threaten resignation until James reversed his decision yet again, dismissing the earl once more and ordering him to his estates in the north.

It was Maitland, indeed, whom Huntly had blamed for his fall in the first place and it was Maitland, too, who, since his appointment as chancellor, had become the butt for the animus of a noble class sensing that the days of its free play with the Crown might well be numbered. He was, wrote Spottiswoode, 'a man of rare parts ... learned, full of courage, and most faithful to his king and master.' 'No man,' Spottiswoode added, 'ever carried himself in his place more wisely, nor sustained it more courageously than he did.' The brother of Sir William Maitland of Lethington, Sir John Maitland of Thirlestane had at first been an adherent of Mary's and had entered the king's service during Lennox's time of influence when the former queen's supporters had been welcome. Thereafter, his rise had been steady, becoming secretary to the king in 1584, vice-chancellor in 1586 and chancellor a year later – an office that he would hold until his death in 1595. And in demonstrating his efficiency and good sense, there was much about him in personal terms that appealed to the king. Not least of all, he wrote English and Latin verse, possessed a sharp Scots tongue, loved raillery and sarcasm, and mingled grave affairs of state with jests and facetiousness. But it was policy and politics that rendered him so invaluable, and his judicious mix of firmness, pragmatism, devotion to duty and loyalty that distinguished him so markedly from his predecessors. Despite his indifference to the religious disputes of the age he urged upon the king the necessity of better relations with the Kirk, and though he bitterly resented Mary's death he saw clearly that moderate friendship with England was essential to Scotland's interests.

More importantly still, perhaps, the chancellor stood for rigorous administration and the firm reassertion of monarchical authority through a series of reforms which, if successful, would modernise and strengthen the whole fabric of government. Tough new measures were intended to purge the kingdom of lawlessness and crime, while James was also encouraged to assume a much more prominent role. At home, too, reforms to the royal chamber and household not only curtailed expense but enhanced the king's dignity – something that was also to be encouraged, albeit with only limited success, by tightening the notoriously lax rules governing access to the royal presence. The Borders, Highlands and Western Isles were to be pacified, and the 'ordinary and daily' council of the king, as well as the Court of Session, were to be shorn of noble influence, even if this meant packing them with his friends and relatives, most of whom were lairds like himself.

And it was for precisely this reason, of course, that Maitland found himself surrounded by such a formidable ring of noble foes. The office of chancellor had long been one that the nobility regarded as their perquisite, so that his comparatively low-born origins only added to the anger caused by his policies. In Bothwell's view, indeed, he was nothing more than a 'puddock stool [toadstool]' in contrast to the ancient cedars of the traditional ruling caste, and James was therefore pressed to govern 'with his nobility in wonted manner, not by private persons hated'. Both Catholic and Protestant lords despised the chancellor, in fact, and in such circumstances it was imperative that the king should have done everything possible to protect him from the individual he had recently offended so grievously. For, though a man of no great ability, Huntly had developed nevertheless into a competent military leader. And quite apart from his ambition and disloyalty, beneath the earl's superficial charm, there lurked an even darker side that the king had so far neatly ignored. It was Huntly, after all, who butchered the Earl of Moray in a foul murder and made a pastime of summary justice. Not content with roasting alive two cooks from an enemy clan as an example to all, the turrets of his castle at Strathbogie were proudly adorned with the severed limbs of those who crossed him.

Yet even after James had deprived Huntly of the captaincy of his guard and dismissed him to his lands in the north in accordance with Maitland's ultimatum, he still found it impossible to break the knot of friendship cleanly. On the contrary, his intention, it seems, was to maintain both Huntly and Maitland in some inexplicable state of balance, and merely by the exercise of his own influence bring them somehow to accept each other. 'The King,' wrote one of the English government's informants, 'hath a strange, extraordinary affection to Huntly, such as is yet unremoveable … The Chancellor is beloved of the king in another sort, for he manages the whole affairs of this country … The king had a special care to make and keep these, his two well-beloved servants, friends, but it never lasted forty days without some suspicion or jar.' And Huntly had surrounded the king with his friends at court, not the least of whom was the king's current 'best-loved minion' and 'only conceit', Alexander Lindsay, younger brother of the Earl of Crawford. Eventually ennobled as Lord Spynie in 1590, 'Sandie', as the king called him, was actually a mediocre figure of few political ambitions in his own right, but he had been made vice-chamberlain and, though the emotional connection between the two was comparatively limited, was known to be James's 'nightly bedfellow'.

With influences such as these at work, it was not entirely surprising therefore that James should cling so doggedly to Huntly and his circle. 'There is not one in the chamber or of the stable,' the English intelligencer Thomas Fowler told Lord Burghley on 28 March 1589, 'which two sorts of persons are nearest attending on the king's person, but are Huntly's […] and the Chancellor cannot mend it, for the king will not change his mind, he loves them so well.' Even before the earl left Edinburgh, therefore, James foolishly insisted upon hunting in his company and only narrowly escaped capture when he awoke in panic the morning after a banquet and left the scene of danger in haste. A few weeks later, moreover, while spending the night in the countryside outside the capital, he was suddenly warned of Huntly's approach in the company of Errol and Crawford. All three, it seems, were marching down from the north with a view to appre-hending him, while Bothwell, who had joined the enterprise in the hope of ruining Maitland, was advancing from the Border. Ultimately, in fact, it was only the chancellor's timely intervention that saved the day. For at midnight the king took flight and by 3 a.m. was safe in Maitland's house in Edinburgh, after which Bothwell retired to Dalkeith and the Catholic earls to Perth.

It would take an outright act of rebellion, therefore, before James could be stirred to some semblance of decisive action. Yet now, faced with absolutely no alternative, he reacted with surprising vigour in what would prove to be the only military action in which he directly participated. Assembling his Protestant nobles and supporters in the south, he mustered his forces in Edinburgh and marched north so rapidly that within two weeks he was approaching Aberdeen where, at the Bridge of Dee, Huntly and his 3,000 or so supporters prepared for battle. Indeed, throughout the brief campaign James's personal involvement was exemplary. When it was rumoured, for example, that the royal army was about to be attacked by night the king responded with commendable resolve. 'That night we watched in arms,' wrote a member of the expedition, 'and his Majesty would not so much lie down on his bed, but went about like a good captain encouraging us.' And in other respects, too, James warmed to the task with surprising energy and commitment, as his officers pressed in upon him with information, advice and requests. 'These people,' wrote Fowler, 'must have free access to the king's presence. If there were no more but the continual disquiet of such a throng from morning to night and their entertainment, it were too much toil for any prince; but he must visit their watches nightly, he must comfort them, be pleased with them passing from place to place, that day or night the good king has little quiet or rest. He hath watched two nights and never put off his clothes.'

James's efforts would ultimately prove needless, however, as Huntly's followers lost heart and melted away into the hills. Nor would James sustain the resolve that had largely carried the day. Instead, the opportunity to follow up a worthy bloodless victory with a long-overdue assertion of his regal authority was sacrificed yet again for sentiment's sake and the fond hope that clemency might heal rather than chafe his kingdom's wounds. It was true, of course, that his position was still less than entirely secure. When James finally entered Aberdeen, for example, his men remained weary from forced marches and the ravages of Highland weather, and supplies were low. Huntly, moreover, was still at large, and without a captive ringleader, the king could hardly return to his capital in triumph. Overreaction on his part would also surely lead to calls for vengeance later.

But the line between moderation and weakness is a thin one and if discretion is always laudable, hesitancy and appeasement are rarely so – especially when the seeds of further disruption remain intact. The king's decision to offer Huntly a secret deal was therefore as unwise as it was typical. So long as he surrendered himself, James told the earl, he would be treated mercifully, and this he did, along with Crawford and Bothwell. In consequence, what might have represented a defining triumph for the king became another lesson that treason was a low-risk enterprise, especially when the culprits were objects of affection for the man they sought to control. Tried for treason and found guilty, the rebels were merely placed in leisurely confinement until, a few months later, they were released – much to the exasperation of the Kirk, the chancellor and the Queen of England, though much to the comfort and pleasure of one particular malcontent who still awaited his moment.

6 ✦ 'Cupide Blinde' and Wyches' Waies

'The king's impatience for his love and lady hath so transported him in mind and body that he is about to commit himself, Leander-like, to the waves of the ocean ...'

William Ashby to Elizabeth I, 23 October 1589

Though 1589 had begun with threats, intrigue and calls to battle, by spring the tide had turned and happier thoughts had scope at last to blossom. With varying degrees of seriousness, the king's marriage had been discussed since 1582, but now, after the merits of various Catholic and Protestant princesses had been duly weighed and pondered, two alone stood out as fitting candidates: the Calvinist Catherine of Navarre and the Lutheran Anne of Denmark. Those who regarded tight-knit community of religion with the Kirk of Scotland as essential to the maintenance of a united front against the Counter-Reformation supported the case for Catherine, while those who were broadly anti-Catholic, yet more pragmatically concerned with preserving commercial links between Scotland and Denmark, naturally backed her Danish rival. Nor was the king prepared to dally further in making his choice, even though it had been generally acknowledged until now that he 'never regards the company of any woman, not so much as in any dalliance'. At first, in fact, it was to be a question of form and duty rather than a matter of a young man's yearning. 'God is my witness,' the king admitted at the time, 'I could have abstained longer than the weal of my country could have permitted, [had not] my long delay bred in the breasts of many a great jealousy of my inability, as if I were a barren stock.' But before long, as fresh horizons opened and new adventure beckoned, all would be headlong love and reckless courtship.

Even so, the choice of bride had not been straightforward. Marriage to a daughter of the Danish king, Frederick II, had been one of the earliest options to be discussed and during the spring of 1587 an embassy headed by the king's former tutor, Peter Young, and the wealthy merchant, Sir Patrick Vaus of Barnbarroch, had been empowered to negotiate the terms, though talks finally faltered over the perennial bugbear of the princess's dowry. A French marriage, on the other hand, was supported by both Chancellor Maitland and a majority of Scottish nobles, and had influential enthusiasts across the Channel too, including the poet du Bartas who had urged the match unofficially during his earlier visit to Scotland. Yet once again there were pitfalls, since Henry of Navarre, Catherine's brother, was initially fighting to become King of France and hoped for Scottish assistance. In the meantime, moreover, he remained relatively penurious and, like Frederick in Denmark, proved reluctant to supply the kind of hefty financial settlement for which James thirsted.

Ultimately, however, a decisive combination of policy, pressure and personal attraction had swung the balance in Princess Anne's favour. Denmark was, after all, an orderly, well-established and Protestant kingdom which had largely escaped the religious tensions engulfing Europe and served as a convenient bridge for Scottish alliance with the Protestant princes of north Germany. Furthermore, Anne seemed to have the edge over her rival in terms of both age and beauty. In September 1587, William Melville of Tongland had been sent to France to inspect Catherine and returned with 'a good report of her rare qualities'. But while Anne was eight years younger than James, Catherine was eight years older, and though prudent, virtuous and capable of offering good counsel, might therefore prove less than perfectly biddable in her dealings with a considerably less experienced husband. Worse still, it was said that 'the sister of Navarre was old and crooked and something worse if all were known'. And when the worthy burgesses of Edinburgh, 'having their most necessary trade with the Easterlings', decided to press the case for a Danish match by rioting in May 1589 and actually breaking in upon Maitland's chambers with threats of death amid fears that he was about to prevail once more with the king and seal a marriage to Catherine, the die was finally cast. James, it seems, had already 'conceived a liking in imagination' for Anne, and now his imagination could be given full vent.

The passion for the 15-year-old princess which presently consumed him had not, however, been apparent from the outset. According to Sir James Melville, the king had agonised at length over his decision, arming himself with portraits of the two princesses and making up his mind only after 'fifteen days' advertisement and devout prayer'. When, moreover, Young and Vaus had opened negotiations in 1585, the king was hoping mainly for the hand of King Frederick's elder daughter, Elizabeth, but when asked what should be done if the princess were betrothed already, James's sound business sense swiftly prevailed. 'Forfend the omen,' he exclaimed, 'but if it happen, ask for the other.' And the fears of James's ambassadors were indeed well founded, for, as they soon found upon arrival, the Duke of Brunswick had already been promised Princess Elizabeth's hand. Only when the Danes had finally convinced the Scots that, though Elizabeth 'was the more beautiful', Anne was nevertheless far from unlovely and for her age taller and more fully developed than her sister, were negotiations allowed to go forward.

Even at this point, however, the deal was far from done. When James's representative, George Keith, the Earl Marischal, sailed for Denmark in mid-June, he went with a series of Scottish demands that remained excessive. In addition to a dowry of £1,000,000 (Scots), he was to ask that the Danes offer naval and military assistance should Scotland be invaded or James had cause to fight for a foreign title due to him by just inheritance. Furthermore, Denmark was to abandon its ancient claim to the Orkneys and join an anti-Catholic league, along with Scotland and other Protestant states. Such, indeed, was the scale of Scottish demands that only the increased influence of the Danish Queen Mother, Sophia, after King Frederick's death the year before, saved the match at all. Five hundred tailors and embroiderers had, it seems, been at work on Princess Anne's trousseau for the best part of three months, and her bridal coach – fashioned throughout from silver rather than iron parts – was already underway. The proud mother refused, therefore, to see her efforts sacrificed at the last, and, as she pushed and the would-be bridegroom pined, Scottish demands not only abated but virtually disappeared.

In succumbing to Cupid's dart, therefore, James finally conceded that he 'would not be a merchant for his bride', and settled in August for a dowry of 75,000 thalers. But his generosity, gracious though it may have been, did not befit his straitened circumstances. The king, remarked Thomas Fowler, 'has neither plate nor stuff to furnish one of his little half-built houses, which are in great decay and ruin. His plate is not worth £100, he has only two or three rich jewels, his saddles are of plain cloth. He is served with six or seven dishes of meat but eats but of two; no bread but of oats, and cares not what apparel.' And Fowler's gloomy observations were echoed by another of his counterparts. 'Surely Scotland was never in worse state to receive a Queen than at present,' commented William Ashby, 'for there is not a house in repair.' A tax of £10,000, raised by the Scottish Parliament for the marriage, had already been spent and fears grew that the Danish princess might arrive before James's wedding garments had been prepared – leaving him no alternative, ultimately, but to scrounge the necessary funds from England. 'It is now time to give proof of affection,' he wrote to Burghley in London. 'No time must be lost, for tempus deals most straitly with me.' The result was a grudging gift of £2,000 worth of plate and £1,000 from the Queen of England, who, for her own good reasons, was already infuriated by his decision to choose the Danish princess over the French.

In the event, James's concerns about his loved one's premature arrival proved unfounded. For although the marriage was celebrated by proxy in Copenhagen on 9 August 1589, and she set sail for Scotland on 1 September, her passage was swiftly halted by raging west winds. Three times, in fact, her ship the *Gideon* was forced to turn back, and at the tempest's height the young princess herself had narrowly escaped death when three cannon broke loose from their housings and careered back and forth across the deck. Two clergymen on board, Drs Knibbe and Kragge, had been urged to pray for calm and safety, and when their prayers went unanswered, Peter Munk, the Danish admiral, assumed that the weather was witches' work. For prior to the journey he had quarrelled with the husband of a woman reputed to be skilled in the black arts, and now felt impelled to seek safe haven in a Norwegian fjord.

James, meanwhile, waited with increasing anxiety as the same storms prevented news of his bride from reaching Scotland. Indeed, as the days lengthened into weeks he became deeply alarmed, ordering public prayers for Anne's safekeeping and retiring to Craigmillar near Edinburgh to ponder her fate in isolation. 'The king, as a true lover, wholly passionate and half out of patience with the wind and weather, is troubled that he hath been so long without intelligence of the fleet and thinketh every day a year till he see his joy and love approach.' By 8 October, moreover, the same lovelorn king had dispatched a messenger of his own to determine her whereabouts, and convey to her a tender note in French – the language that Anne had been learning rather than Scottish to communicate with him. He wrote to his 'only love' of 'the fear which ceaselessly pierces my heart' and ended by 'praying the Creator' to grant her a 'safe, swift and happy arrival upon these shores'. There were verses, too, in which he compared his plight to Leander and lamented the 'full manie causes suire' that now increased his 'woe and caire'.

Ultimately, it was only on 10 October that James finally received word of Anne's safety in Oslo, and it was now, beside himself with a mounting surge of chivalry, romance and raw impatience, that he decided to opt for bold solutions. His Lord High Admiral the Earl of Bothwell would achieve by Scottish seamanship what the Danes had failed to do and bring Anne home with minimum delay. James, moreover, would accompany him, just as his grandfather had braved the Channel to bring home Madeleine de Valois, his first queen. He would 'commit himself and his hopes Leander-like to the waves of the ocean, all for his beloved Hero's sake', and prove his manly credentials at last. The 'nakedness' caused by his lack of parents and siblings, he admitted somewhat extraordinarily in the proclamation announcing his decision, had always left him weak before his enemies. Likewise, 'the want of the hope of the succession breeds disdain'. So he would seize the opportunity to prove once and for all that he was 'a true prince' and no 'irresolute ass who could do nothing of himself'. Nor, he claimed, should Maitland continue to be blamed 'for leading me by the nose, as it were, to all his appetites, as if I were an unreasonable creature or a bairn that could do nothing of myself'.

What the king had not counted upon, however, was the cost of such an expedition, and it was left to Maitland to volunteer to foot the bill as a means, no doubt, of compensating for his earlier opposition to the marriage. Neither was James unduly concerned about the potential political consequences of his adventure. In the aftermath of Huntly's abortive rising that spring and two unsuccessful 'bands' to remove Maitland from office in 1588, Scotland was still hardly at rest, and it was for fear of concerted opposition to his decision to absent himself from his troubled kingdom so needlessly that James kept his planned departure secret from his councillors. By now, after all, his bride's safety had been confirmed, and her arrival was hardly likely to be long delayed with or without his intervention. South of the Border, meanwhile, Elizabeth was immediately anticipating the worst when she heard of James's impending absence – warning her wardens of the Marches to be on the alert for trouble and sending Sir Robert Bowes north again to hold the Protestant interest together against a possible Catholic *coup de main.*

In the event, the queen's worst fears did not materialise, since the arrangements for Scotland's governance while James was away proved surprisingly effective under the circumstances – albeit, perhaps, with a healthy slice of good fortune. To James's credit, administration was left in the hands of a Privy Council in which all interests were represented and in which authority was so delicately shared out among the most dangerous nobles on both sides that they would act as automatic checks upon each other. A number of key roles were also filled by men of proven ability. Melville of Murdocairney was deputed to carry out the routine duties of the chancellor, in the absence of Maitland who was to accompany the king and be thereby spared the hostile attention of both Huntly and Bothwell. Lord John Hamilton, in his turn, was given overall responsibility for military affairs and policing the Borders, while Robert Bruce, a minister of the Kirk whom James actually liked and trusted, was accorded the role of independent watchman and whistle-blower, ensuring where possible that correct behaviour prevailed and guaranteeing that loud protest would follow in the event that it did not.

Assuming, then, that no divisive issue arose during the king's absence and that comparatively little positive action was required, such an arrangement would prove effective. Yet Bruce's ability to calm troubled waters if discord arose remained questionable, and there remained other aspects of the plan that could hardly be justified even in the event of James's incapacity through a genuine crisis, as opposed to the current self-imposed quandary. The president of the council was, after all, to be the 15-year-old Ludovic, son of Esmé Stuart and now Duke of Lennox in his own right. Though he was actually Scotland's 'Second Person' or heir presumptive at this time and his new role was largely nominal, he was far from ideal as a figurehead at a time when the whole tenor of government, particularly in the prevailing Scottish context, was so intensely personal in nature. More problematic still, however, was the decision to install the Earl of Bothwell as his advisory associate. As wild and fractious as ever and, as events would later demonstrate, no less disgruntled, Bothwell's inclusion as de facto conciliar head was purely the result of his arrant unwillingness to settle for anything less.

Yet James, as he now joyfully confessed, had been 'inflam'd and 'pearc'd' by 'Cupide Blinde', so that even the tempestuous autumn seas, let alone considerations of state, would not deter him. Six ships, the largest of which was the king's own at 130 tons, had been well provisioned with food, wine and livestock, and he therefore set sail on 22 October, reaching Flekkefjord on the southern coast of Norway six days later. Fortunately, the prevailing winds had eventually favoured his passage as much as they had hindered his bride's, and he arrived safe and unruffled. 'All in good health,' reported one of the party, 'the king's majesty was never sick.' But he too had at first been driven back upon the coast of Pittenweem by tempests and the last day was so stormy that his flotilla was thought to be in great hazard. Clearly, though James's outright terror of any naked blade was already well established, his willingness to face danger on the high seas would have matched many a hardened sailor's. The cold, moreover, was bitter and the final stage of his journey required a further voyage along the Norwegian coast to Tönsberg, which was not completed until 11 November, followed by a hard cross-country journey of more than 50 miles before he arrived in Oslo.

But in spite of his long and arduous travels, it seems James still managed to cut an impressive figure upon his arrival in Norway's capital. Travelling in considerable pomp, accompanied by Danish, Swedish and Norwegian noblemen and preceded by heralds, he was described by eyewitnesses as tall and thin, with deep-set eyes. He was also splendidly dressed in a red velvet coat decorated with gold and a black velvet cloak lined with sable fur. Nor did he tarry in meeting – and somewhat embarrassing – his bashful bride. According to David Moysie, he made his way at once to the old Bishop's Palace where Anne was lodged and 'passed quietly with boots and all to her Highness', whereupon he 'minded to give the queen a kiss after the Scottish fashion', only to be told by his loved one that such intimacy upon first meeting was not the custom of her own country. The rebuff was not sustained, however, and 'after a few words privately spoken' there did indeed pass 'familiarity and kisses' between them. Next morning, moreover, dressed in blue velvet bespangled with gold and preceded by local nobles and six heralds clad in suits of red velvet, he visited Anne again and spent the day in her company.

Still almost a month short of her fifteenth birthday, the princess was a tall, blue-eyed, slender, graceful girl whose white skin and radiant, golden hair were the subject of much admiration as she grew steadily towards the statuesque beauty of her adult years. Like James, she enjoyed hunting and was also amused by dressing up and acting. And though her intelligence has often been treated dismissively, her ability to speak French and her rapid acquisition of Scottish go some way to countering this view, as indeed does her eventual patronage of Inigo Jones and other artists. If, moreover, she was not politically minded, this was to prove more of a virtue than a vice from her husband's perspective and her subsequent intrigues at the Scottish court were driven more often than not by mainly worthy motives, such as a wish to exercise greater control over the upbringing of her children. Her wish to manipulate behind the scenes declined in any case over time, and she became over the years a shrewd judge of character and a generally discreet influence, who never lapsed from faithfulness herself and was prepared, though not always patiently, to tolerate James's relationships with good-looking young men. Certainly she could not sustain a great passion in her husband, mainly perhaps, because she never became what he most wanted throughout his life – an intellectual peer and genuine confidante with whom he could share his innermost secrets. But there was much early optimism at the match. 'I trust,' wrote David Lindsay, the minister of Leith, who had been brought over from Scotland to officiate at the wedding, 'she shall bring a blessing to the country, like as she giveth great contentment to his Majesty.'

After their earlier proxy marriage, the two were finally wed in person at St Halvard's church in Oslo on 23 November. The ceremony, lasting just over an hour, was conducted in French and included a sermon upon the significance of Christian marriage delivered by the local bishop, after which Anne left and James remained to receive the congratulations of all attending, to whom he replied in Latin. Thereafter, the wedding banquet was held in the imposing hall at Akerbus, a fortress standing in a rocky promontory in Oslo fjord. Almost one month later, moreover, on 21 January 1590, the marriage was solemnised once again in the presence of the Danish royal family in the castle of Kronborg, by which time the winter was so far advanced that James rejected the opportunity to return to his own kingdom and opted instead to accept an invitation to stay with his new relatives. Leaving Scotland to fend for itself, he travelled overland by sledge and arrived at Bohus Castle near the Swedish frontier on New Year's Day, before being finally welcomed in state at Kronborg Castle once again on 21 January amid volleys of cannon fire lasting a whole half hour.

What had begun as an absence from his homeland intended to last some twenty days had therefore already extended to some three months, but this was still by no means the end of James's stay. Indeed, he would remain in Denmark until late April 1590 where his new brother-in-law, the 12-year-old Christian IV, was already impressing by the tremendous pace of his hospitality. Predictably, there was much hunting and hawking, and there was also much drinking. 'Our king made good cheer and drank stoutly till the spring time,' wrote David Lindsay. And James made no secret of his activities, informing his current favourite, Alexander Lindsay, how he was writing to him 'from the castle of Kronborg where we are drinking and drinking over in the old manner'. But there was also entertaining company and more intelligent conversation on offer from his Danish hosts than he had been used to in Scotland and this, too, encouraged James to prolong his stay. He was worried, indeed, that the inadequacy of preparations in his own kingdom for his return might well be an embarrassment. 'For God's sake,' he urged Robert Bruce, 'take all the pains ye can to tune our folks well now against our homecoming lest we be all shamed before strangers. Thus recommending me and my new rib to your daily prayers, I commit you to the only All-sufficient.'

In the meantime, however, James would not only revel to his heart's content, but enjoy every opportunity both to extend the scope of his learning and display his own scholarship to best possible advantage. At Roskilde, for example, he discussed the Calvinist doctrine of predestination with Dr Nils Hemmingsen, and later treated the theological faculty at Copenhagen University to a three-hour oration in Latin, after which he received a silver goblet in honour of the occasion. At the Danish royal academy, meanwhile, he attended lectures on both theology and medicine, and was complimented on his learning by Dr Paulus, Superintendent of Sealand. Nor was James's response anything other than honest. 'From my most tender years,' he replied, 'I have been given to books and letters, which even today I willingly acknowledge.' And finally, most famously of all, there was also an encounter between James and the intensely difficult, but brilliant, astronomer Tycho Brahe, who had lost the bridge of his nose in a duel over the legitimacy of a mathematical formula and now sported an eye-catching brass prosthetic in its place. At his castle and observatory on the island of Hven, Brahe had spent a day with James in learned discourse upon Copernican theory, which so impressed the young king that he subsequently composed a sonnet in his host's honour.

Even the King of Scotland could not, however, remain away from his homeland indefinitely, and once a new round of festivities was concluded after the marriage of Anne's elder sister Elizabeth to the Duke of Brunswick on Easter Day, the time for fond farewells inevitably arrived. On 21 April, therefore, James and his bride sailed from Denmark, and on 1 May they landed at Leith where they lodged in 'the King's Wark', a building which doubled as both a customs house and a royal or ambassadorial lodging, while preparations were laid for the state entry into Edinburgh of a brand new Queen of Scots. In the event, James's worries about the reception proved largely unfounded – not least because Anne had brought with her the coach of silver, drawn by eight white horses, prepared by her mother. It was in this fairytale carriage that she entered the capital on 6 May accompanied by her husband, with the Duke of Lennox, the Earl of Bothwell and Lord John Hamilton riding beside her. All had co-existed in apparent harmony throughout the winter and all now played their parts with due grace and loyal flourishes.

Eleven days later, Anne was duly crowned in the Abbey Kirk of Holyrood, though the ceremony had, it seems, been the cause of not inconsiderable dispute beforehand. There had already been complaints from the Kirk that the queen had made her entry upon the Sabbath, but the main bone of contention now concerned the practice of anointment, which the more radical clergy dismissed as a pagan and Jewish custom and one more objectionable remnant of 'popish' superstition in need of eradication. James, however, had himself been anointed by the Bishop of Orkney and insisted that it confirmed the sacred character of kingship. Nor would the king be thwarted in his plans for the forthcoming coronation of his wife, even if it did involve the kind of impish provocation to which he now resorted. With characteristic adroitness, he selected none other than Robert Bruce to perform the ceremony and when the ministers objected that one of their own brethren should be chosen to conduct such an offensive ritual, the king's response bore all the hallmarks of his familiar wile and wit. Firstly, he pointed out that anointing had been instituted in Old Testament times, and then – no doubt relishing his opportunity to enjoy such an elegant checkmate – he duly added that, if Bruce's involvement was so wholly unacceptable, he would call upon a bishop to act as a replacement.

On 17 May, therefore, after sermons and orations in Latin, French and Scots, the Countess of Mar duly opened the queen's gown and Robert

Bruce poured on her breast and shoulder 'a bonny quantity of oil'. Whereupon the king took the crown in his own hands – one of which was said to be painfully swollen by the pressure of correspondence which had given him scarcely three hours' sleep at night since his return and left him 'much disquieted in mind and spirit' – and honoured his chancellor, Maitland of Thirlestane, by passing it to him to place upon Anne's head. Having received the sceptre from Lord John Hamilton and the sword of state from the Earl of Angus, the young Lutheran queen finally swore an oath 'to procure peace to the Kirk of God within this kingdom,' and, notwithstanding the holy oil on her breast, to 'withstand and despise all papistical superstitions and ceremonies and rites contrary to the word of God'. The oath, however, was little more than a formality from Anne's perspective and carried little real conviction, it seems, for she soon grew to resent the freedom with which ministers of the Kirk deigned to instruct royalty and eventually converted to Catholicism in the 1590s, though never, it must be said, devoutly – rather, perhaps, as a diversion from some of the drearier aspects of her new existence.

Certainly, the Scottish court was not ideally suited to the new queen's high spirits and gaiety. Her childish love for games, masques and pageants earned her an unwelcome reputation for empty-headedness and the ministers were soon condemning her 'want of godly and virtuous exercise among her maids', her 'night-walking and balling' and, most disconcerting of all, her absence from the services of the Kirk. Furthermore, her pastimes were expensive – so much so that the king was appreciating before long that her household cost more than his. And when frustration overwhelmed her, childish tantrums, spiteful words and acts of indiscretion were not always sufficiently resisted. Above all, she nurtured a smouldering resentment towards Maitland of Thirlestane for first opposing her marriage. Yet the queen was also, of course, a vivacious, naive and sometimes innocent figure in a dour and largely colourless setting, where ill-willed courtiers, embroiled in faction and intrigue, often proved more than willing to involve her in the rivalries of the moment and set her, if necessary, against her husband or his councillors.

Even when the heat of James's ardour for his 'Chaste Diana' and 'Cytherea faire' had gradually abated and they had finally ceased to live together, he would continue to treat her with tenderness and affection. And the marriage was undoubtedly a procreative success, for Anne bore her husband seven children. Henry Frederick, a somewhat long-awaited heir was born in 1594, and two daughters followed – Elizabeth in 1596 and Margaret in 1598 – before the future Charles I arrived in 1600. Robert, Mary and Sophia were also born over the next six years, though only Henry, Elizabeth and Charles actually survived childhood, and the promising and greatly loved Prince Henry would eventually die on the cusp of manhood at the age of 18. Nevertheless, when the scale of Anne's task in satisfying a husband of James's complexity and outright oddity is considered, it was no small credit to her that the marriage fared as well as it did. Nor was it any discredit to James either, for his inherent sentimentality and sense of fair play continued to the end of his wife's life. Ultimately, in fact, it was only after the birth and death of his last child that the homosexual preference of his youth seems to have reasserted itself. Until that time, there is every reason to accept Bishop Goodman's later observation that the royal couple managed to 'live together as well as man and wife could' without 'conversing'.

Yet one of the bishop's other contentions – namely, that James was 'never taxed nor tainted with the love of any other lady' – is thrown into doubt by some sparse though tantalising evidence. In a letter written by Sir John Carey to Lord Burghley on 10 May 1595, for instance, there is a reference to 'fair mistress Anne Murray, the king's mistress', and on 3 June Carey also reported a marriage to be solemnised in the near future at Linlithgow 'between young Lord Glamis and the king's mistress'. The lady concerned was once again Anne Murray of Tullibardine who did indeed go on to marry Patrick Lyon, Lord Glamis. Nor are these fleeting comments the only foundation for suspicion, since James composed a narrative poem entitled 'A Dream on his Mistress my Ladie Glammes', in which he dreams that the God Morpheus transports his loved one to him as he lies sleeping and finds it impossible to resist her charms, for 'onlie mot I conquered be'. Beyond this, in fact, the records are silent, but it remains difficult to avoid the impression that the first flush of nuptial bliss may well have carried James forward to at least one extra-marital excursion with a member of the opposite sex.

Soon after his return from Denmark, however, and long before his ardour for his wife had begun to pall, the king was deeply engrossed with women of an altogether different kind. The notorious Scottish witch-hunt throughout the winter of 1590-91 may well have originated in the belief of the Danish admiral Peter Munk that the storms which forced his fleet to abandon the passage of Princess Anne to England had been raised by witchcraft. Doubtless James will have heard this opinion when he arrived to collect her in person, and the unusually stormy weather accompanying the return journey to Scotland the following spring will only have served to reinforce the conviction that malevolent powers were being invoked to harm both him and his wife. For, like other contemporaries across Europe, James displayed an implicit faith in the powers of evil and the efficacy of black magic – along with a cold terror of witches in particular – that would continue to hold even a well-trained, rational mind like his in thrall. Supplied by the devil with enchanted stones, magical powders, poisons and other even more mind-boggling paraphernalia, witches could raise storms, induce insanity, impotence or exaggerated sexual desire, raise spirits to plague mankind and even cause death. They could also (as James recorded in his own book on the subject) fly – so long as they held their breath. Their gender, moreover, made them especially susceptible to diabolical influence, since, in James's view, Satan had seduced Eve in the beginning and been 'the homelier with that sex' ever since.

Towards the end of the king's life, it is true, he was to admit some doubts, though chiefly on the question of the actual prevalence of witchcraft and the nature of confessions wrung under torture from plainly deluded persons. At some time, it seems, he had gone on to read Reginald Scot's *The Discoverie of Witchcraft*, which was brave enough to express scepticism at the efficacy of the black arts. But when his own *Daemonologie* was published in 1597, James left no doubt that his intention was to refute the 'damnable opinion' of Scot, who was 'not ashamed in public print to deny that there was such a thing as witchcraft'. And in his preface to the reader he spoke too of the 'fearful abounding at this time, in this country, of these detestable slaves of the devil, the witches and enchanters'. He wrote that he claimed, 'not in any way (as I protest) to serve for a show of my learning and ingenuity, but only (moved by conscience) to press thereby, so far as I can, to resolve the doubting hearts of many both that such assaults of Satan are most certainly practised, and that the instruments thereof merit most severely to be punished'.

Presenting his book in the form of a dialogue between the uninformed and questioning Philomanthes and the didactic Epistemon, James's discourse encompasses the entire range of supernatural phenomena known to the ancients – ghosts, wizards, spirits, demons, possession, fairies, even werewolves – but it is most concerned with witches and their abilities. Nor had he moderated his opinions significantly by the time he became King of England in 1603. Indeed, although he eventually mitigated the ferocity of some aspects of his new kingdom's witch trials, one of his first priorities upon his succession was to have his book republished and to follow this with a significant stiffening of the old Witchcraft Act in employment under Elizabeth I. Still seeing himself as the white knight of the biblical Book of Revelation, wielding a flaming sword of justice, his personal crusade as the terror of witches and scourge of the devil continued to serve in his view as proud testament to his love of virtue and thirst for justice, so that crimes that had previously been punishable by a prison term now became punishable by death. Furthermore, the explanation James offers in his *Daemonologie* for the contemporary upsurge in the practice of witchcraft is extremely significant. 'The consummation of the world, and our deliverance drawing near,' he wrote, 'make Satan to rage the more in his instruments, knowing his kingdom to be so near an end.' For James, then, as with other contemporaries, the occult was not so much a belief as an ideology in its own right, encompassing the direction of history itself, as well as his own place within it – and in the winter of 1590–91 he would find more than ample scope for indulging his fixations to the full.

The end of the sixteenth century had seen the onset of a tenacious 'witch craze' across Northern Europe and nowhere more so than in Scotland where the Kirk was more or less continually engaged in detecting and combatting dark forces. Deriving in part from ancient Scottish fertility rituals in which devotees worshipped an incarnate deity that appeared before them, the so-called 'Dianic Cult' of James's time was said to be celebrated in midnight orgies by covens of men and women who claimed to have sold their souls to the Devil. It was perceived, moreover, as an organised phenomenon, permeating every class. In Scotland, for instance, the Ruthven family had dabbled in it for generations and their activity had certainly added to James's aversion to them. But it was the exposure of a far-reaching occult conspiracy in East Lothian that now fired the king's interest so keenly that for almost a year he would work at little else than 'the sifting out of them that were guilty' – attending some of the more important examinations in person and, at one point, even making one of the key participants, a maidservant from Tranent called Geilie Duncan, play to him the tunes she had piped for the Kirkyard dances on All Hallows' Night at North Berwick.

It appears, then, to have been the king's trip to Denmark, and conceivably his discussions with the theologian Hemmingsen, author of the well-known treatise on witchcraft *Admonitio de Superstitionibus Magicis Vitandis* that turned James's interest in the occult into something of a more consuming passion culminating in the publication of his own *Daemonologie* in 1597. Though references to Satan are plentiful in his early published works, for instance, he made no direct statements at all on the subject of witchcraft before 1590. But throughout the North Berwick witch trials – and especially from April 1591 when the evidence mounted that James had been the object of a concerted satanic conspiracy involving some 300 individuals of various social ranks – his involvement reached a peak. In all, three or more organised covens were said to have been working against the king and his marriage with all the usual tools and tricks of the craft: toads hanged and roasted to extract their venom 'for his Higness' destruction'; cats bound to the severed joints of dead bodies cast into the sea; magical practices upon the king's bed linen that he and it might waste away together; and finally the fashioning of a waxen image to be melted slowly in a fire to ensure an agonising death.

James listened, it seems, with all the credulity that might have been expected from any contemporary, but also exhibited a particularly acute fascination with some of the more outlandish and curious features of the spectacle. A bewitched man, for example, was said to have capered and shrieked before the king 'to the great admiration of his Majesty', while one of the witches, Agnes Sampson, 'a renowned midwife', whispered things he had said to the queen on their wedding night, at which he 'swore by the living God that he believed all the devils in hell could not have discovered the same'. There were tales, too, of the devil incarnate for James to pore over. According to Sir James Melville, the witches met by night in the kirk of North Berwick, 'where the devil, clad in a black gown, with a black hat upon his head, preached unto a great number of them out of the pulpit, having light like candles round about him'. 'His face,' Melville recorded, 'was terrible' – his nose 'like the beak of an eagle', his eyes 'great' and 'burning' – and his limbs were hairy, 'with claws upon his hands and feet like a griffin'. 'He spoke,' we are told, 'with a hollow voice.'

Certainly, James was prepared on occasion to countenance some of the more notorious excesses associated with witchcraft investigations of the period. When, for example, Agnes Simpson was examined by the king in person at Holyroodhouse, she was fastened to the wall of her cell by a 'witch's bridle', an iron instrument with four sharp prongs forced into the mouth, so that two prongs pressed against the tongue and two others against the cheeks. She was also kept without sleep, and thrown to and fro with a rope around her head before confessing to fifty-three indictments against her and suffering subsequent death at the stake. Likewise, a local schoolmaster at Saltpans by the name of Dr John Fian, who was accused of being a coven leader, was subsequently tortured with both the rack and 'the boot', and by having needles inserted under his fingernails before the fingernails themselves were eventually torn out with pincers.

Above all, though, it was the case of Barbara Napier, widow of Earl Archibald of Angus, that best demonstrates the king's tenacity in rooting out and punishing what he himself considered 'the highest point of idolatry, wherein no exception is admitted by the law of God'. When Napier had the good luck to be acquitted with the help of influential friends like her brother-in-law, the Laird of Cairschoggil, on the pretence that she was pregnant, James was not prepared to let the matter rest. On the contrary, when he learned of her escape from being 'put into a great fire', he insisted that her jurors be arrested and tried for delivering a false verdict. At issue in part, of course, was the credibility of the king's justice, which James correctly emphasised in making his decision. For the practice of corrupting juries and witnesses, and flouting due process on grounds of kinship and friendship was a long-established evil in Scotland – one, said James, that 'here bairns suck at the pap' – and he made clear that it must be dealt with 'not because I am James Stuart and can command so many thousands of men, but because God hath made me a king and judge, to judge righteous judgements'.

Yet the same conviction that witchcraft was a living, potent force also firmly underlay the king's determination that Barbara Napier must pay the ultimate price for her sacrilege. 'We are taught,' James told her jurors, 'by the laws both of God and men that this sin is most odious; called *Maleficium* or *Veneficium*, an ill deed or a poisonable deed, and punishable likewise by death.' 'As for them who think these witchcrafts to be but fantasies,' he continued, 'I remit them to be catechised and instructed in these most evident points.' And although the number of executions resulting from the North Berwick witch trials remains uncertain, Napier was only one among some seventy in all who found themselves prosecuted. She, along with Geillie Duncan, Dr Fian, Agnes Sampson and Euphemia MacCalzean, daughter of Lord Cliftonhall, the well-known judge, were each executed for conspiring to bring about the death of the king, who had only, it seems, survived against all odds. When, according to one confession, the devil inquired of the witches whether their magic was proving effective, he was disappointed 'and because a poor old silly ploughman named Grey Meill chanced to say that nothing ailed the king yet, God be thanked, the Devil gave him a great blow'. When, moreover, the witches sought the devil's explanation for the king's unexpected survival, the Devil could offer only one explanation, which he chose to deliver, curiously enough, in French. '*Il est,*' retorted the Prince of Darkness, '*un homme de Dieu.*'

In the meantime, a sea captain called Robert Grierson, who was also implicated, had died as a result of torture before he could be formally tried. But it was the alleged involvement of none other than Francis Stewart Hepburn, 5th Earl of Bothwell, which gave the entire case a new and altogether more sinister significance. For on the evidence of various suspects it was suggested that Agnes Sampson had proposed the king's destruction at the earl's request, and that a waxen image melted before the devil at Acheson's Haven near Prestonpans had been the result. Indeed, on 5 May 1591, in what seems to be an increasingly manipulated statement to be used for political ends, Bothwell was specifically incriminated by Geillie Duncan and others as the one who commissioned and provided funds for the making of the wax image to be used to destroy the king. As the image was passed from hand to hand, it was said, all present uttered the following words: 'This is King James the Sixth, ordained to be consumed at the instance of a nobleman – Francis, Earl of Bothwell.'

Nor was this the only claim of its kind. The king was to be destroyed, said one defendant, 'that another might rule in his Majesty's place and the government might go to the Devil'. And there was talk, too, of the English queen's involvement with Bothwell's treachery after the unfortunate Grierson had let slip that 'it would be long before the gold came out of England'. When, moreover, the warlock Richard Graham, who had already produced a garbled Latin conjuration invoking syphilis upon the king, agreed to tell all he knew about the earl, so long as he was granted the protection of Edinburgh Castle's walls, the scene was well and truly set for what would prove to be the prelude to a final and decisive reckoning between the King of Scotland and his turbulent nobles.

7 ⚜ The Wrath of Earls and Kirk

'He hath oft told me the wickedness of his nobility and their evil natures, declaring himself weary of his life among them.'

Thomas Fowler, chief agent of Sir Francis Walsingham's intelligence network in Scotland, writing of King James in 1589

In May 1587, more than two years before his marriage, James had made a characteristically eccentric attempt to heal his kingdom's endemic divisions by staging a curious feast of reconciliation at Holyrood. Gathering his nobles together for what was ostensibly a celebration of his twenty-first birthday, he urged them with all the earnestness and naivety that was so typical of his nature to foreswear their feuds and hatreds by drinking three solemn pledges to eternal friendship. Thereafter, in a gesture that smacked more of dark humour than statecraft, the king delighted his capital with a procession of the entire nobility of Scotland walking two by two, each man coupled with his most notorious enemy, to take their place at banquet tables laid out by the Mercat Cross amid fireworks, salvoes of cannon fire and a lavish distribution of free wine for the onlookers who gaped with a mixture of astonishment and cynical amusement at the spectacle before them. It was, in its way, a not unlovable gesture from a king whose good intentions were rarely in overall doubt. But it was symbolic, too, of the same king's impotence in the face of powerful forces that he lacked both the material and personal resources to quell. Within a year, there had been two unsuccessful attempts to lever his chancellor out of office and in the spring of 1589 a major rising was narrowly averted. Now, as a final straw, one of those self-same would-be rebels, who had been treated with such remarkable leniency, was firmly implicated in a sacrilegious murder plot against his sovereign master.

In many respects, the character and career of Francis Stewart Hepburn, 5th Earl of Bothwell and godson to Mary Queen of Scots, mirrored the influence of his two more famous uncles. Born in 1563, the earl was the son of John Stewart, one of the numerous bastard sons of James V – a distinction that he shared with his dead brother, the Earl of Moray. And from his uncle Moray, who had served as regent before his assassination, Bothwell derived a somewhat anomalous alliance with the Kirk, which could not afford to be overly fastidious in its choice of political champions and whose interests he strove to maintain at court, in spite of his own waywardness and his family's stained reputation. For the mother of the current Earl of Bothwell was Jean Hepburn, sister of the Bothwell who had been Queen Mary's notorious lover, and it was this latter uncle, rather than the erstwhile regent, whom the fifth earl most resembled in conduct and character. Fierce, dissolute, profligate and lawless, wedded to feuds and loose living, he lived, in fact, in a world of fantasy, which encompassed a vain hope that the Crown might one day be his, irrespective of the superior claims to the succession of the Lennox-Stuart families.

Not surprisingly, the king had already been greatly incensed by Bothwell's participation in the recent revolt. But largely as a result of blind hopefulness born of weakness and superstitious fear, he had opted for mercy and reconciliation, telling the volatile earl that just as he 'had resolved to be a reformed king, so he would have him to be a reformed lord'. As so often in such instances, however, James was merely postponing the inevitable. Bothwell's companions in his Border district of Liddesdale were, almost to a man, thieves and murderers, and the general lawlessness and disorder that pertained there was a constant source of tension not only for James but for the English, too. In January 1591, for instance, during the trial of one of his cronies, Bothwell abducted a witness from the Tolbooth at Edinburgh, regardless of the fact that the king himself was residing in an adjoining chamber. That same night, moreover, James found himself forced to ride to Kelso in the hope of preventing a brawl in which he knew Bothwell was bound to take part. But when the earl was summoned before him the following day, James issued only threats. He had loved and favoured Bothwell, he said, only to be treated to insults in return. Unless there was a change in behaviour, the law would be enforced with full vigour.

Even so, like his uncle before him, Francis Stewart Hepburn was a man of contradictions. 'There is more wickedness, more valour, and more good parts in him,' wrote Thomas Fowler, 'than in any three of the other noblemen,' and there was no doubting either his brains or his charm, for he was handsome, dashing and eloquent. On one occasion, for example, he found himself the guest for a few nights of the Bishop of Durham, the shrewd and perceptive Tobie Mathew who made no secret of the earl's more admirable qualities. 'This nobleman hath a wonderful wit,' wrote Mathew, 'and as wonderful a volubility of tongue as agility of body on horse and foot; competently learned in the Latin language, well versed in the French and Italian; much delighted in poetry, and of a very disposition, both to do and to suffer; nothing dainty to discover his humour or any good quality he hath.' In the early days, indeed, Bothwell's considerable charm had made him a favourite of the king, who liked to embrace him tenderly and hang about his neck in the familiar fashion. Had he never become a symbol of aristocratic hatred for Chancellor Maitland and of Protestant loathing for the Catholic earls, it is doubtful whether he could ever have created nearly so much trouble. But his support within the Kirk increased his threat and behind the veneer of French culture, which attracted James, there remained a lingering undercurrent of terrifying unpredictability that made his involvement in the black arts wholly plausible and now rendered him an object of the king's deepest fear and hatred.

It had not been until 15 April 1591, however, that Bothwell was finally accused of plotting with Agnes Sampson and Richard Graham against the king's life. And he would prove a difficult man to bring to heal, for on 24 June at two in the morning, according to David Moysie, he succeeded in escaping from Edinburgh Castle, where he was being held pending his trial. Outlawed, he remained in his fortresses along the Border, sometimes spending the nights in the woods. But although the council proclaimed him a traitor, many secretly sympathised with the man who promised to be Maitland's nemesis and who had, in any case, been charged on the evidence of witches. Certainly, the contrast between Bothwell's treatment and the leniency accorded earlier to Huntly was widely acknowledged, while the Kirk, on the other hand, remained willing to apply a remarkable degree of tolerance to its influential ally. Emboldened, therefore, by widespread support, he flouted the king's threats by appearing at Dalkeith, Crichton and Leith, and most blatantly of all at the Canongate in Edinburgh, where he issued a taunting challenge to the chancellor. In response, the king made a token effort to raise troops and capture Bothwell at Kelso, though his own superstitious dread of the nobleman and nagging fear of capture continued to militate against more decisive action. Without a standing army and with few dependable friends of his own, James's position remained, to say the least, precarious. Indeed, such was the earl's power that no appointments were made to the offices he had lost and no one accepted his forfeited estates.

On the dark night of 27 December he made a daring raid upon Holyroodhouse, along with Archibald Douglas, son of William, Earl of Morton, and some forty or fifty 'murderers and broken men'. Forcing their way into a stable, they seized the keys of the porter and succeeded in pursuing Maitland to his chamber, while the king, whose poverty had deprived him of an adequate guard, was left to seek shelter in a remote tower as the intruders careered through the buildings amid cries of justice for their leader. As doors were broken with hammers and set on fire, it seemed yet again, then, that the king's authority was about to be rudely shattered by a show of brute force and daring. And only when the common bell of the City of Edinburgh was rung and the local citizenry, armed with pikes, rallied to the royal cause did the attempted coup finally collapse. In the confusion, Bothwell and four of his associates fled downstairs and after killing John Shaw, master of the stables, and a number of others, made good their escape on horseback. Even then, however, the king's embarrassment was not over, for, although Bothwell had been publicly proclaimed a traitor at the Mercat Cross, the king was reprimanded by the ministers officiating at a thanksgiving service held at St Giles only one day afterwards.

In the process, the self-same ministers had all but justified the raid, notwithstanding the fact that eight of Bothwell's Borderers were now hanging from the palace's walls. And the earl himself, of course, remained at large, while James and his household were forced to move for safety into cramped lodgings at the top of the city, under the shelter of the castle guns. The king's words, it is true, were brave enough, and in a sonnet composed to commemorate the slain John Shaw he wrote of his intention 'with deeds, and not with words to pay'. But it was easier to posture than deliver, and though he pursued Bothwell courageously enough, his bleak

January chase through the Border country, where the canny, hardy earl had so many friends, was unavailing. Indeed, far from apprehending the outlaw, James nearly perished when his own horse fell and plunged him into the icy waters of the Tyne.

While Bothwell was flaunting his liberty quite openly at race meetings and football games and accepting invitations to card parties with the English Border gentry, the king's other tormentors were also making hay. The earls of Huntly, for their part, had long been at odds with the earls of Moray, since Mary Queen of Scots had first bestowed that title upon her half-brother Lord James Stewart, the later regent, thereby depriving the 4th Earl of Moray of an earldom that he considered to be rightfully his. And to compound matters, James Stewart Doune, who had married the elder daughter of the regent and become Earl of Moray in right of his wife, had been contriving to extend his influence in the north-east of Scotland at the expense of Huntly's family, the Gordons, thus continuing the policy followed earlier by the queen's half-brother. Handsome and high-spirited, Doune was the 'Bonny Earl' of the famous ballad, 'comely, gentle, brave and of a great stature and strength of body', beloved by both Kirk and people as the heir and son-in-law of the former 'good' regent.

He too, however, would now fall victim to the kind of bloody retribution in which Huntly specialised so avidly. For when the Queen of England's representative, Lord Worcester, came north in 1590 with a belated wedding present, to confer on James the Order of the Garter, he also brought with him some of Huntly's treasonable correspondence that had been intercepted by English intelligence. It was widely known, too, that Huntly and his confederate, the Earl of Errol, had remained in continuous touch with Spain, even in 1590 when they had not yet been formally pardoned for their last act of defiance which had ended at the Bridge of Dee. In spite of all, though, James had nevertheless pressed ahead with a formal pardon for Huntly in December of that year, and by early 1592 was resolved, or so he claimed, to settle the earl's outstanding feud with Moray. By calling the latter to his mother's castle at Donibristle on the northern bank of the Firth of Forth, the king intended, ostensibly, to reconcile the two contending nobles by little more than the magic of his own personality. The result, however – both sadly and predictably – was one of Scotland's most spectacular and notorious aristocratic murders.

Certainly, there was no shortage of speculation at the time that James himself had duped Moray into attendance at Donibristle and thereby connived in his death. The king's dislike for all connected with 'that bastard', the former regent, remained as intense as ever, of course, and Moray's friendship with Bothwell will have done nothing to soften relations. There were rumours, too, reflected in the ballad that celebrated him, that the earl was 'the Queen's love' and had been privy to the Christmas raid at Holyrood. Add to this the evidence that Maitland was eyeing some of Moray's lands and had procured a warrant for Huntly to arrest him as a Bothwell partisan, and the case suggesting an orchestrated assassination is far from implausible.

If, moreover, James himself was not in fact directly involved, the timing of his invitation could not have been more conducive to Huntly's purposes. For on 7 February 1591, while accompanying the king on a hunting trip with an escort of forty horsemen in the vicinity of Donibristle, Huntly absented himself on the pretext of pursuing a group of Bothwell's accomplices who were known to be close by. In the encounter with Moray that actually followed, however, the earl and his clansmen held the castle all day until it was finally set ablaze and he was left with no option but to flee from the inferno towards the shore – his hair and helmet plume, it was said, in flames. Thereafter, he was finally dispatched among the rocks by Huntly himself who delivered a killing dagger blow to the face. 'You have spoilt a better face than your own', the handsome victim is said to have declared before he expired.

Yet the deed in itself was still not one that appears to have troubled James unduly, for he was capable of a striking indifference to injustice or suffering when his own affections were not directly involved. At the same time, of course, the assassination was wholly in keeping with a long-standing culture of political violence in Scotland, with which James was already all too familiar, and in addition to liking Huntly and despising Moray, he also needed the former's strength in the north of the kingdom to counterbalance both Bothwell and the Kirk. But any wishful thinking on James's part that the martyring of a popular Protestant hero by Scotland's premier papist might somehow pass unmarked was soon disproven, as Moray and his dead friends lay in state in Leith church and the earl's bloodstained shirt was paraded on a spear around the Highlands amid the growing clamour for clan war. In the meantime, for further dramatic effect, his mother made her own demand for vengeance, presenting James with a picture of her murdered son and a musket ball plucked from his body.

The subsequent treatment of Huntly, moreover, only added fuel to the flames that had already consumed Donibristle. Having placed himself voluntarily in the king's custody at Blackness, he was yet again indulged and released almost immediately amid howls of disapproval from both Presbyterian ministers and common people alike. 'Always,' James told Huntly, 'I shall remain constant,' while Maitland rather than the king was left to incur the main blame of the rioting Edinburgh mob. 'Since your passing from here,' James informed Huntly, 'I have been in such danger and peril of my life as since I was born I was never in the like, partly by the grudging and tumults of the people, and partly by the exclamation of the Ministry whereby I was moved to dissemble.' But while such dissembling came naturally to James, on this occasion it counted for little as rumours of his involvement in the murder mounted. Above all, there was talk that when Moray's kinsman, Andrew Stewart, 2nd Lord Ochiltree, attempted assistance, he had found the ferry to Donibristle barred by the king's express order from all but Huntly.

If so, then James had clearly miscalculated grievously. On the one hand, England's Queen Elizabeth was not slow to repeat her familiar warnings that no good could come from clemency to Catholics, and least of all a wholly wild card like Huntly. Balancing rival forces was, of course, a key art of political management, but when Huntly and Bothwell were the counterweights involved, no happy outcome was ever conceivable. And now relations with the kingdom to the south worsened significantly, as James complained to Elizabeth of his English pension and how she was not 'content as freely to pay it as freely ye promised it'. Equally gallingly, the queen showed no inclination to stem the flow of unofficial assistance tendered to Bothwell, who had now been gifted a popular cause to fight for and the wholehearted backing of the Kirk to wage it. Even with his connection to the black arts, he was nevertheless viewed as what one minister, John Davidson, termed a 'sanctified plague' whose divinely ordained mission was to cause the king to 'turn to God' and deliver Scotland from the papist scourge. Far from damaging him, then, the loss of Moray would actually render Bothwell the bane of James's life for at least two more years to come.

Certainly, in June 1592 the turbulent earl was once more snapping at the king's heels – this time with a midnight attack upon Falkland Palace involving 300 men and a battering ram, during which James had to withstand a seven-hour siege before help arrived. Furthermore, when two of Bothwell's accomplices, the Lairds of Logie and Burley, were subsequently arrested in early August, even this would prove a source of vexation to the king. For Logie's escape on the night of his interrogation was apparently achieved with the help of his sweetheart Margaret Vinster, one of the queen's Danish maids. Leading her lover through the royal sleeping-apartments at Holyrood in the dead of night, Vinster, we hear, 'conveyed him out at a window in a pair of sheets'. And such was James's dejection at his betrayal by those so near to him that he not only had his first recorded quarrel with his wife, but, more significantly, entered another of those phases of dejection to which he was always prone, 'lamenting his estate and accounting his fortune to be worse than any prince living'. Indeed, he would spend the rest of that summer and autumn fleeing from place to place in dread of Bothwell, and was further weakened in August when Maitland, finally bowing to the raft of opposition existing at court, retired temporarily to his estates at Lethington.

In the summer of 1593, moreover, Bothwell came again, and this time successfully. By now, he had enlisted almost all the leading Stewarts to his cause – Lennox, Atholl and Ochiltree – and when Lady Atholl allowed a raiding party to slip into Holyroodhouse between eight and nine in the morning of 24 July there followed the familiar royal surrender. Half-dressed and trapped in his bedchamber, James was finally confronted by Bothwell in person, emerging from behind the hangings in the king's ante-room and 'craving mercy and pardon most humbly' but carrying nevertheless a naked sword which he laid at the king's feet. Nor could James's apparent boldness in telling the kneeling earl that he could not, like Satan dealing with a witch, obtain his immortal soul, conceal his actual impotence. For, in spite of his brave words and cries of 'treason', he found himself forced all the same into what was arguably the most humiliating capitulation of his entire life. Compelled on the one hand to dismiss his friends at court, the king was also left to agree a compromise whereby Bothwell himself would withdraw from court in return for an acquittal at his forthcoming witchcraft trial and an additional pardon for all other offences.

When, furthermore, a crowd of armed citizens soon gathered around the palace, they were duly informed by the king, leaning from his window in thoroughly unkingly fashion, that all was well. Pretending that the band of Bothwell's ruffians now escorting him everywhere were being employed at his own request, James then duly acquitted Bothwell of witchcraft on 10 August notwithstanding the fact that the earl's chief accuser, Richard Graham, had already insisted upon his involvement up to the very time that he himself was executed in February. Worse still, the verdict of outlawry previously proclaimed three times against the earl at the Mercat Cross was soon formally revoked. With greater bravado than ever Bothwell then wrote in triumph to Queen Elizabeth, whom he addressed as 'Most Renowned Empress', expressing his hope that he might become Lord Lieutenant of Scotland and assuring her how, with continued help, he could 'manage the estate about the king'.

Yet, like other subverters of royal will before him, Bothwell's sway and swagger concealed weaknesses of his own that would grow increasingly apparent in the longer term. Not least of all, the uneasy confederation of malcontents that he had conjured around him would eventually demonstrate tensions of its own, as hidden rivalries resurfaced, mutual suspicion crept in and the inherent need for stable monarchical authority became apparent once more. Furthermore, Bothwell's agreement to abandon the court in return for his acquittal and pardon proved a costly error, since it allowed James to improvise a middle party to protect him from both the earl himself as well as Huntly's supporters. Lennox and Mar, for example, were easily detached from their temporary ally, and Maitland was now reconciled with a group of his former adversaries, including Glamis, the treasurer, Lord John Hamilton, one of the greatest of all the nobles, and the Catholic Homes and Maxwells, with whom Bothwell was at feud along the Border. Such an alliance could not last for long itself, of course, but it enabled James to slip away from a parliament at Stirling to the security of Loch Leven and subsequently raise an army of sufficient strength to banish Bothwell once again.

The delinquent earl's campaign of force and fury had, in any case, no real substance of policy behind it beyond his own self-aggrandisement and the general contempt for Maitland that would ultimately evaporate with the chancellor's death in 1595. Bothwell's final rebellious fling in 1594 was therefore little more than a swansong – the act of an increasingly frustrated man who had no more imaginative cards in his pack. By now, his usefulness to the Queen of England was largely spent and the paltry subsidy of £400 that she offered to assist his latest adventure was wholly inadequate to the task, though in April he would drive a force of royal cavalry back upon Edinburgh, leaving the king, as David Calderwood observed, to retire into the city 'at full gallop with little honour'. This initial setback was only the prelude, however, to an altogether more decisive rally on James's part as 1,000 Edinburgh citizens, aided by three great cannon from the castle, turned out to resist Bothwell's assault. After a short engagement which cost the king's forces no more than twelve men killed, Bothwell promptly disbanded his army and withdrew to England, where he was this time promptly disavowed by Elizabeth.

The ultimate folly was yet to come, however, as Bothwell now threw in his lot with none other than Huntly, which guaranteed at a single stroke the loss of any residing sympathy from the Kirk. For at this time Huntly was further mired by his involvement in one more Catholic intrigue, dating back to the end of 1592. The conspiracy of the so-called 'Spanish Blanks' had been hatched, it seems, by two Jesuits, James Gordon and William Crichton, and involved a heady project to land a force of 30,000 Spaniards from the Netherlands, of whom 5,000 were to establish Catholic control in Scotland, while the rest marched south to England. Since the plan contained no provision whatsoever for securing the necessary sea lanes, the immediate danger posed by the plan was actually negligible. But the Scottish messenger, George Ker, who was arrested while embarking for Spain, was in possession of mysterious blank papers signed by Huntly, Angus, Errol and Sir Patrick Gordon of Auchindoun committing them to some unspecified, but no doubt dastardly, compact with the enemy. The upshot was another largely futile punitive campaign in the north, in which James got as far as Aberdeen and hanged a few peripheral players, while the main culprits went into hiding in Caithness.

Throughout 1593, in fact, the king continued to treat the conspirators with extraordinary leniency. Plainly despairing of his ability to bridle them, he had admitted to Sir Robert Bowes, the English ambassador, that Huntly, Errol and Angus were three of the most powerful nobles in the kingdom and that 'if he should again pursue them and toot them with the horn he should little prevail'. In summer, the parliament which was expected to pass an act of forfeiture against the conspirators' lands did not do so, and, in November, James obtained from a sparsely attended convention of nobles held at Edinburgh an Act of Oblivion by which the guilty earls were forgiven their involvement in the conspiracy of the Spanish Blanks on condition that they made a formal submission to the Kirk – which was never in fact forthcoming. To obtain the Act, James was, it seems, quite willing to manipulate the convention blatantly and, ultimately, even to tamper with the text of the submission itself. In consequence, the whole clergy raved and the Synod of Fife excommunicated the earls without consulting the king, while Elizabeth added to the chorus of disapproval by dispatching a stinging letter in which she rued the sight of a 'seduced' king and a 'wry-guided' kingdom.

So it was, then, in the summer of 1594, that Bothwell and Huntly finally found themselves consorting in the most consummately unholy alliance of all. On Midsummer Eve, indeed, the Catholic earls, buoyed by common cause with Bothwell and assurances of Spanish help, held a great feast with dancing and drinking to celebrate their impending triumph, notwithstanding the fact that at the time of Bothwell's raid at Leith, James had already issued a solemn pledge to his subjects that could not be easily repudiated. 'If ye will assist me against Bothwell at this time,' he had pleaded, 'I promise to prosecute the excommunicated lords so that they shall not be suffered to remain in any part of Scotland.' And now, faced with Bothwell's escalating defiance, even James could not avoid a more decisive response. Drawing his strength not from the nobility, but from the lairds, the burghs and the Kirk, the king therefore prepared for a punitive expedition, and by sheer good fortune resulting largely from the Crown's inherent advantage as the only potential source of long-term order, it at last proved possible to cut the cancer. For unlike his enemies, James had always been able to rely ultimately upon a feudal army to contain any threat for a month or two at any given moment, and it was this advantage which now rendered him well placed to employ such a contingent for offensive purposes.

In September 1594, therefore, a royal force led by the king himself and accompanied by Andrew Melville, whose presence confirmed the Kirk's determination to deal with Huntly once and for all, duly marched into Aberdeenshire. And though the royal army received an early reverse on 3 October when the young Earl of Argyll's advance detachment was defeated in a minor skirmish, known rather more grandly than it deserved as the 'Battle of Glenlivet', Huntly's men had no stomach for a further encounter with the main force following close behind. Instead, they returned once more to the wilds of Caithness and, at the Kirk's insistence, agreed to the destruction of their dwellings. In the process, Huntly's fortified stronghold was blown up, along with Errol's in Buchan and another half-dozen Catholic fortresses, after which, within only a few months, James duly obtained an agreement whereby Huntly and Errol accepted exile abroad, leaving only Angus to lurk, albeit impotently, among his Highland cronies.

Bothwell, meanwhile, had also escaped to Caithness after Huntly purposely delayed in surrendering him to the king, and a certain Edinburgh merchant named Francis Tennant refused to betray him. Yet it was not long before Bothwell, too, settled for exile in Europe and a later career mirroring, in many respects, that of his more famous uncle. While the last husband of Mary Queen of Scots fell into the hands of Scandinavian enemies and died imprisoned and insane, his deranged young successor would, it is true, manage to retain his freedom. But by April 1595, he was in France without friends or means, since his Scottish estates had been forfeited to powerful neighbours, and before long, like many an unsuccessful rebel unlucky enough to evade the more merciful retribution of the executioner's blade, he faced lingering loneliness, ignominy and penury. Journeying forlornly through Spain and Italy, he would eventually die in poverty in Naples in 1612.

By contrast, Huntly once more returned to Scotland and yet again enjoyed the king's boundless clemency. He remained, of course, a tool of sorts for James to juggle against the Kirk and a grubby diplomatic counter to hold in reserve in his dealings with Elizabeth, but the absence of more decisive punishment remains profoundly puzzling. His return to Scotland in 1596 was, in fact, accompanied the following year by his reception into the Kirk at the king's insistence. Yet even James's further decision to reward him with a marquisate would not ensure his religious compliance in the longer term. For, while he conformed in James's lifetime, he would nevertheless choose to die a Catholic in 1636. And it was only fitting, perhaps, that a man who had both milked and abused royal favour so consistently should have staged this final gesture of defiance upon his deathbed. Insofar as he had ever been defeated in any really meaningful sense of the term, Huntly had, after all, been largely vanquished by default – a victim not so much of the king's strength or political wisdom as of his own latent weakness and eventual lack of options. The king he could shake with ease, the Crown ultimately he could not.

The same, moreover, was true of the nobility in general and James's apparent 'victory' over them, for although his authority would never again be flouted quite so flagrantly, James triumphed over his aristocratic enemies as much by luck and circumstance as by judgement. Bothwell, for his part, had ruined himself by his own outrageous behaviour, while Huntly and his henchmen were chasing a vain Catholic cause that had long since had its day in Scotland. As a result, their peers were largely tired of a stream of disorder, subsidised too often from abroad, which could only harm both Scotland's and their own interests in the longer term. Ultimately, indeed, Bothwell and Huntly had not only demonstrated the futility of politics by kidnapping, but served to underline the central importance of monarchy in a Scottish context. More, in fact, was to be gained from partnership with the Crown than opposition at a time when James's succession to the throne of England appeared to be drawing closer and as James, in any case, employed the lands once held by Rome to coax compliance. Above all, however, it was the growing political leverage of the kingdom's emerging middle classes – the very lairds, burgesses and moderate clergymen who had rescued James on more than one occasion – that persuaded even the most die-hard advocates of noble rule that their interests were best conserved by co-operation rather than conflict.

In the event, it was more radical sections of the clergy who still potentially posed the most fundamental challenge to the king's authority, and at Maitland's instigation every effort had been made to achieve an accommodation between Church and state. Shortly after his return from Denmark, for example, James was encouraged not only to visit the General Assembly to thank God that he had been born into the Scottish Kirk, but to deride its Anglican equivalent, which had already been bitterly attacked by the likes of James Melville for its 'bell-god bishops' who were anxious to advance the cause of episcopacy in Scotland. 'As for our neighbour Kirk in England,' the king declared, 'it is an evil said Mass in English, wanting nothing but the liftings.' Nor did he entirely buckle under Elizabeth's pressure to prevent the Kirk from extending support to English Puritans, three of whom – John Udall, Robert Waldegrave and John Penry – had sought asylum in Scotland. 'There is risen both in your realm and mine,' Elizabeth protested:

> a sect of perilous consequence, such as would have no kings but a presbytery and take our place while they enjoy our privilege. Yea, look well unto them. I pray you stop the mouths or make shorter the tongues of such ministers as dare presume to make orisons in their pulpits for the persecuted in England for the Gospel.

But while prayers for English Puritans were indeed forbidden and Penry was expelled in accordance with Elizabeth's wishes, James moved slowly and retained Waldegrave as his printer. As a further gesture towards the Kirk, he would also continue to intercede on behalf of Thomas Cartwright and other English Puritans during 1591.

In the wake of Huntly's assassination of Moray, Maitland and James seemed especially keen to placate the Kirk, with the result that in May 1592 Parliament had been encouraged to agree a string of concessionary measures. The so-called 'Golden Act', for instance, had fully and clearly established ecclesiastical government by presbyteries, synods and General Assembly, while a law of 1584, which confirmed the status of bishops, was now rescinded.

Nor were James's actions altogether as surprising as they may at first seem. Though he feared and hated any threat to his own primacy in secular affairs and equated incursions on his ecclesiastical authority as the first step on a broader slippery slope, he had been raised and educated nevertheless within the structure of the Kirk, and respected both the institution itself and the Calvinist theology upon which it was based. He was also, by nature, averse to confrontation where compromise might be attainable and, with Maitland's guiding hand, it was still conceivable that the Kirk could itself be finessed into compliance. The process, of course, might well be long and fraught, as was demonstrated later in 1592 when an Act asserting the royal supremacy led to a string of attacks from the pulpit, while the king himself 'chafed and railed' against the ministers after a law to silence them was rejected. But if the Kirk could be bought off ultimately by substituting the term 'presbyter' for 'bishop', might not the Crown's control of secular affairs continue unchallenged?

All depended, in fact, upon a firm stand against Catholicism, and the goodwill of key personnel at the summit of the Kirk's hierarchy: neither of which would be forthcoming. Indeed, James's lame response to the affair of the Spanish Blanks appeared to be one more demonstration of his indecision and ambivalence regarding his treasonous Catholic subjects, and left his Presbyterian ministers demanding condign punishment not only for the Catholic earls involved, but for the entire body of Scottish Catholics who took it for granted that the king himself had been a party to the plot. At the time of George Ker's arrest, after all, a private memorandum drawn up by James had been found among his papers in which the king discussed the scheme's merits as a means of assisting his succession to the English throne. And although the memorandum concluded that any invasion of England was impractical at that time, its inclusion in a portfolio bound for Spain nevertheless offered fertile ground for speculation. Nor did James altogether rule out dealings with the Spanish in his efforts to achieve his dynastic ambitions. 'In the meantime,' he noted:

I will deal with the Queen of England fair and pleasantly for my title to the Crown of England after her decease, which thing, if she grant to (as it is not impossible, howbeit unlikely), we have attained our design without stroke of sword. If by the contrary, then delay makes me to settle my country in the meantime and, when I like hereafter, I may in a month or two (forewarning of the King of Spain) attain to our purpose, she not suspecting such a thing as she does now, which, if it were so done, would be a far greater honour to him and me both.

At this very time, meanwhile, the Kirk was once more firmly under the influence of the man whose fire-breathing capabilities exceeded, by reputation, even those of John Knox. For since March 1586, Andrew Melville had been back at his post at St Andrews where he would continue for the next twenty years. By 1590, indeed, he had become the university's rector. A veteran of Calvin's Geneva, and an expert not only in theology but in Hebrew, Chaldee, Syriac and Rabbinical languages, Melville had already fled to England to escape a treason charge in November 1584, but returned within twenty months to champion the liberties of the Scottish Kirk against all encroachments of the government. And from that time forth his opportunities multiplied. Not least of all, James's Act of Annexation of 1587, which had appropriated episcopal temporalities to the Crown, had contributed significantly to the decline of the very episcopacy upon whose continued existence he staked so much. In principle, the measure had represented a sensible attempt to win the sympathy of the General Assembly, but the subsequent action of the Catholic earls and James's weak-kneed response meant that no such sympathy could ever be sustained.

More worryingly still, James's Act of Oblivion in 1593, which forgave Huntly for his involvement in the affair of the Spanish Blanks, merely reinforced Melville's primacy. Indeed, while James continued to insist upon employing the Catholic earls as a counterweight to his Presbyterian clergy, so Melville's leadership of the Kirk became not only increasingly critical but, if anything, even more radical. The king, it is true, was caught in a vicious circle. Yet it was one at least partly of his own making, since it was dictated not only by politics but by his ongoing personal favouritism for Huntly. Leniency towards Scottish Catholicism resulted too, no doubt, from James's wish to enlist the support of Catholics south of the Border in his quest for the English succession. However, his eventual decision to allow

Huntly and Errol to return from exile in the summer of 1596 would stretch far beyond the bounds of subtle signal-sending to potential sympathisers south of the Border. On the contrary, it would needlessly flout all political common sense, and flagrantly inflame those very forces within the Kirk that he most feared – the self same forces indeed that he would help to entrench in the absence of Maitland's moderating influence after the latter's death in October 1595.

8 ❦ 'King and Sovereign Lord' of Scotland

'Here is a strange country. I would say a most vile people.'

Thomas Fowler, chief agent of Sir Francis Walsingham's intelligence network in Scotland, May, 1589

The birth of James's first child at Stirling on 19 February 1594 was a welcome glint of sunlight amid the storm clouds surrounding him on all sides. According to David Moysie, the news was greeted with joy by 'the whole people', and 'moved them to great triumph, wantonness and play ... as if the people had been daft for mirth'. And though the child's arrival opened up fresh possibilities to every plotter in Scotland seeking another target for kidnap and an alternative power source of exactly the kind that James himself had become during his mother's reign, the king could not be anything but happy overall. For the birth not only strengthened his dynastic position in Scotland, but also improved his eligibility for the Crown of England as the father of a healthy heir. Notwithstanding the continued presence of Bothwell and ongoing preparations for the campaign against Huntly, the baptism, therefore, was to prove a particularly grand and symbolic event. In memory of his two grandfathers and with the founder of the Anglo-Scottish marital alliance, Henry VII, no doubt also in mind, the prince was to be named Henry Frederick, and by the time festivities were staged in August, enough money had been scraped from the meagre Scottish treasury to do full justice to the spectacle – the highlight of which was a masque in which James appeared as a Christian Knight of Malta, alongside the Border lord, Buccleugh, and other nobles in female garb, representing Amazons.

The christening itself, moreover, was no less colourful – and ritualistic – than James's own twenty-eight years earlier, including to the fury of Andrew Melville and his like-minded ministers an anointing with holy oil by the Bishop of Aberdeen. But while the full-bearded clergy fumed, the king could take due satisfaction from other aspects of the event. Certainly, the exotic arrangements for the serving of dessert at the evening banquet left no doubt of James's determination to emulate the opulence of more prestigious courts in Europe. A great chariot, 12ft long and 7ft broad, was drawn, it seems, by a single Moor, while Ceres, Fecundity, Faith, Concord, Liberality and Perseverance, dressed in silver and crimson satin, dispensed fruit from it. Then, to symbolise James's voyage to Denmark to claim 'like a new Jason, his new queen', there followed a great ship 18ft long and with 40ft masts, taffeta sails and silken rigging, which discharged a volley of thirty-six cannon into Stirling Castle's great hall before distributing all kinds of fish and shell fish 'made of sugar and most lively represented in their own shape'. Whereupon, the choir sang a fourteen-part harmonised version of Psalm 128: 'For thou shalt eat the labours of thine hands: O well is thee, and happy shalt thou be'.

In other respects, however, not all was quite so satisfying for the king's ego. It had been wise of James to invite the English queen to be godmother and in spite of her notorious parsimony in present-giving, she had shown her appreciation generously enough with 'a cupboard of silver-over-gilt, cunningly wrought' and some massive gold cups. Much more importantly still, she would soon sharply forbid Bothwell to 'show banner, blow trumpet, or in any way live or breathe in England'. At the baptism itself, however, Elizabeth was represented only by the young and surprisingly unsophisticated Earl of Sussex, while the French ambassador failed to turn up at all. Carried away, moreover, by an overwhelming desire to impress, the king had taken too much responsibility for the subsequent junketing at a time when he was already overstretched, and increased his burden further by attempting grandiose and ultimately fruitless negotiations with a number of his foreign guests – too many of whom had actually been invited in the first place. In consequence, many details of the event went awry, and in the midst of proceedings he was further perplexed by a malicious rumour that the Duke of Lennox was the child's real father. While James was busy commissioning spectacular entertainments involving oversize chariots, mock ships and muscular Moors, another seed of dissatisfaction with his marriage was being vindictively sown. And within a year, in the summer of 1595, this same seed had blossomed into a full-blown quarrel between king and queen over the new prince's custody.

It was not long after she had settled in to her new home and accustomed herself to the astonishing vicissitudes of her husband's kingdom that Queen Anne first developed an occasional taste for political intrigue. Above all, and much to her spouse's irritation, she had become enmeshed in all the recent combinations against Maitland. Now, however, when James decided that his son should be brought up, just as he himself had been, in the comparative seclusion of Stirling Castle, and under the guardianship of his old playfellow, the Earl of Mar, Queen Anne was given a deep grievance with which to underpin her broader misgivings. The king's decision was in fact firmly upheld by long custom, but there was more involved in the decision than the emotional ties between mother and son or the maintenance of tradition, since Anne, as James well knew, perceived the custody of Prince Henry as a source of political leverage and an opportunity to achieve the importance that had so far been denied her. Notwithstanding Mar's own history of wavering loyalty, the king was therefore determined to abide by his decision, irrespective of his wife's rages and entreaties.

When husband and wife were together at Linlithgow in May 1595, she reminded him 'how she had left all her dear friends in Denmark to follow him, and that King Christian her brother, for love of her, had ever been his sure friend'. But when Anne tried to obtain possession of her son while James was on a hunting expedition at Falkland, it was clear that she would not necessarily confine herself to moral blackmail. Returning in a furious temper, James did indeed take her to Stirling and grant her access to her son for several hours, but beyond this the king would not compromise, as a letter he dispatched to the Earl of Mar makes quite clear. 'Because in the surety of my son consisteth my surety,' wrote James, 'and I have concredited unto you the charge of his keeping upon the trust I have of your honesty, this I command you out of my own mouth, being in company of those I like, otherwise for any change or necessity that can come from me, you shall not deliver him. And in case God call me at any time, see that neither for the queen nor estates, their pleasure, you deliver him till he be eighteen years of age, and that he command you himself.'

Finding her protests unavailing, therefore, Anne found her only solace in a largely irrational antipathy for Mar, which lasted for the next eight years and led her, ironically, to heal her old quarrel with Maitland and intrigue at the same time with a string of other nobles who happened to be Mar's enemies. Maitland, meanwhile, was so devoid of friends at court that he was prepared to make common cause with the queen, albeit without benefit ultimately to either himself or her. When she claimed to be ill, moreover, her pleas that James should visit her at Holyrood fell on deaf ears, since the king had become so suspicious, even of his chancellor, that he feared being made captive, and only after her illness was proven to be genuine did James relent. Ultimately, his greeting for her was both tender and admonitory. 'My heart,' he told her, 'I am sorry you should be persuaded to move me to that which will be the destruction of me and my blood.' For Maitland, however, he had only anger and reproof, declaring heatedly that 'if any think I am further subject to my wife than I ought to be, they are but traitors and such as seek to dishonour me'. In the event, the whole affair gradually subsided as the queen's faction departed for their homes and James and Anne headed for Falkland, apparently reconciled.

Yet 1595 marked a watershed of sorts in the royal marriage, as Anne and her husband continued to drift apart. Four years later, in his *Basilikon Doron*, James would make a number of revealing observations on marriage in general and his own in particular. 'For your behaviour to your wife,' he wrote, 'treat her as your own flesh, command her as her lord, cherish her as your helper, rule her as your pupil, and please her in all things reasonable.' But there were hints of the king's experience of his own domestic quarrels: '... Be never angry both at once, but when ye see her in a passion ye should with reason danton [subdue] yours: for when both ye are settled, ye are meeter to judge of her errors; and when she is come to herself, she may be best made to apprehend her offence ...'

True, a good deal of tenderness continued to exist between the two and James urged his heir to have the greatest respect for the woman who would eventually learn to accept even the increasingly overt homosexual dalliances of her husband. 'If it fall out that my wife shall outlive me,' he wrote, 'as ever ye think to purchase my blessing, honour your mother.' Yet, for all James's genuine regard and sympathy, there remained a cultural, temperamental and intellectual gulf, which was bound to grow, on both sides, with long familiarity.

Maitland's days as the king's right-hand man were also numbered in more senses than one, for on 3 October he died – comparatively unlamented by the man whom he had striven so hard to guide and nurture. James did, it is true, compose a graceful sonnet to his former chancellor, which was carved on a marble memorial tablet above his tomb in Haddington church. There was reference to the 'vicious men' who rejoiced at his fall and praise, too, for Maitland's 'wisdom and uprightness of heart' as well as his piety, intelligence and 'practice of our state'. But the king had always found Maitland more inclined to lead than listen and his sorrow at the loss of a gifted servant was tempered by a distinct sense of liberation. 'His Majesty,' one courtier noted, 'took little care for the loss of the Chancellor'. Shortly after Maitland's death, moreover, James went so far as to declare that he would 'no more use chancellor or other great men in those his courses, but such as he might convict and were hangable'. And though the last comment was partly made in jest, it was indeed more than three years before the chancellorship was finally filled.

Now James was determined and able, it seemed, to rule in his own right. Though he refused to acknowledge it, he would build upon the foundations that Maitland had laid over all of eleven years, but he was also to apply an energy and discipline to the task that the chancellor himself would doubtless have admired. Fully aware of his altered status in the wake of his victories of 1594 and 1595, James firstly wasted little time in issuing a proclamation warning all men to obey the law. 'As he is their king and sovereign lord', the proclamation affirmed, so the king's subjects should know 'that he will be obeyed and reverenced as a king, and will execute his power and authority against whatsoever persons' as shall 'contemn his Highness, his authority or laws'. Nor did James settle merely for words and noble sentiments. On the contrary, the registers of the council were filled from this time with rules and orders against common criminals and outlaws and those within the law who nevertheless carried 'pistols and dags'. Feuding lairds were hauled before king and council, while, 'at his own pain and travail', James sought by a mixture of force and persuasion to heal long-standing enmities. It was to be, in fact, nothing less than a political coming of age for the king. And it was a time, too, when James generally succeeded in imposing his stamp upon a country that was at long last finally ready to accept it.

There were even attempts to tackle the wilder regions of the kingdom, though success here was predictably more limited. Three areas above all –

the Highlands, the Isles and the Borders – had always proved resistant to the consistent imposition of law and order, and, as James would find, the geographical isolation and cultural idiosyncrasies of these areas meant that only long-term strategies were likely to be of any effect. Taken together, the Highlands and the Northern and Western Isles lie beyond the meandering 'Highland Line' which bisects Scotland from north-east to south-west. North of the 'Line', the clans pursued a pattern of life that had changed little with the centuries: pastoral, sparse, heroic and warlike. Wringing a meagre existence from primitive agriculture and fishing, the Highlanders' private wars and feuds and raids upon their neighbours' cattle and sheep had made them, at every social level, among the fiercest fighting men in Europe. And though many of their chieftains had acquired feudal titles from the king, the intense closeness of the clan meant that for generation upon generation the power and independence of a Huntly or an Argyll had been effectively unbreakable.

Earlier endeavours to assert some degree of centralised control had even proved counter-productive. By the time of his death in 1286, Alexander III had, for example, come close to uniting his subjects, who then included English, Norman-French and Gaelic speakers, in a common loyalty which might over time have created some degree of homogeneity. But the Wars of Independence against England, which followed Alexander's death, actually entrenched and magnified existing differences, so that when Scotland eventually confirmed its status as a free nation, it had become firmly divided not only on broadly cultural lines, but even linguistically with the Gaelic-speaking Highlands and Isles, and Scots or Anglo-Scots-speaking Lowlands. Even the decision to move the royal court to Perth in the fifteenth century and to make the town a capital for both regions proved unavailing as the political centre of Scotland shifted inexorably towards Edinburgh. It was the narrow belt of the Lowlands, after all, that contained some of the country's richest agricultural land and witnessed the first shoots of commercial and industrial development, largely concentrated in Edinburgh itself.

To compound matters, the later Stewart kings had looked to France, the Low Countries and Scandinavia for their political alliances, and indulged in frequent enmity with England. On Scotland's southern border, therefore, they were forced not only to tolerate but actively encourage the fierce local magnates whose task was to engage in ceaseless conflict with the 'auld enemy'. In the process, the priorities of central government were increasingly directed eastward and southward, while the north-west of the kingdom was largely abandoned to its own devices. As such, it was hardly surprising perhaps that the last Gaelic-speaking Scottish king should have been James IV, who died fighting the English at Flodden Field in 1513, or that George Buchanan had never felt the need to teach the king's great grandson the language. James VI, indeed, was in no doubt regarding the inherent superiority of the agrarian and trading communities of the Lowlands over their Highland cousins. 'As for the Highlands,' he wrote in *Basilikon Doron*, 'I shortly comprehend them all in two sorts of people: the one that dwelleth on our main land, that are barbarous for the most part, and yet mixed with some show of civility: the other, that dwelleth in the Isles, that are utterly barbarous without any sort of show of civility.'

Yet James, flushed with his newfound confidence as Scotland's outright 'King and Sovereign Lord', was determined, as best he could, to make his own efforts to impose the law-abiding culture of the Lowlands across his kingdom. Twice he announced his intention of visiting the Isles and Western Highlands, though lack of provisions aborted his first expedition and on the other occasion he reached no further than Glasgow and Dumbarton. Similarly, when he summoned the western chieftains to Edinburgh to render proof for their titles to land, few attended. And his efforts to tame the Isles 'within short time' by implanting Lowland culture through colonisation was equally unsuccessful. For, far from influencing the Islesmen, whom James scornfully compared to wolves and wild boars, the few settlers who managed to stay put were mostly absorbed into Gaelic ways and habits. Most, in fact, like those planted in Kintyre and Lochaber and on the island of Lewis as a result of an Act of 1597, became victims of botched planning and a smattering of bad luck. On the one hand, the gentleman-adventurers, who established the Lewis settlement on the present site of Stornoway, soon abandoned their project, while a further attempt to revive the project in 1605 resulted in equally dismal failure. Indeed, James's most significant success in pacifying this part of his realm only resulted eventually from the application of 'general bonds', by which chieftains accepted responsibility for the conduct of their clansmen – a policy that had in fact been established even before he became king.

On the Borders, however, there was ultimately better progress, though not before the king's wavering hand had been forced by fierce English protests about the antics of a celebrated Scottish freebooter named William Armstrong of Kinmont – more commonly known as 'Kinmont Willie'.

When Armstrong was finally apprehended by the deputy of the English Warden of the West March on a 'Day of Truce in 1596' and held captive at Carlisle Castle, the blue touchpaper had been lit for a major test of wills between not only the governments of England and Scotland, but between James and his notoriously feisty Border magnates. Swearing that he would avenge English treachery, the Scottish Warden, Sir Walter Scott of Buccleugh, had scaled the castle's walls on a dark and stormy night and with a few others bore 'Kinmont Willie' off in his irons, whereupon the Queen of England herself 'stormed not a little', insisting that Buccleugh should be delivered into her hands. And though his subjects urged him to resist, James nevertheless felt compelled to detain the valiant rescuer at St Andrews before delivering him to Elizabeth as requested. Indeed, so alarmed was James at Elizabeth's anger that in a curious display of anxiety before his council, he produced and formally entered in the register a letter she had written him some years earlier promising not to oppose his lawful right of succession. And when his second child, a daughter, was born at Dunfermline in August, he deferred to England's queen once more by naming the girl Elizabeth.

It was no small irony, therefore, that the queen's eventual meeting with Buccleugh suggested that James's panic was largely unnecessary. When asked how he had dared to storm one of her castles, the Borderer responded with characteristic boldness. 'What is there, Madam,' he inquired 'that a brave man dare not do?' And far from being infuriated by Buccleugh's quip, the queen seems to have been impressed by his courage. 'With a thousand such leaders,' she told her onlooking courtiers, 'I could shake any throne of Christendom.' It was hardly indicative of uncontrollable outrage – any more than the entire affair of 'Kinmont Willie' was the kind of episode that might have seriously compromised James's succession to the English throne. In truth, the King of Scotland's tunnel vision concerning the English Crown had on this occasion merely undermined his already limited credibility as a leader of genuine resolution, and in the immediate aftermath of his climb down, there was a significant increase in lawlessness along the Border.

Yet James was rescued once again by circumstance and good fortune, for in 1597 a joint commission drew up an Anglo-Scottish agreement, which laid the foundation for forty years of comparative tranquillity in the Border territories. With the prospect of a Scottish King of England drawing closer and with firebrands like the Bothwells well and truly spent, the era of raids and culture of military bravado and brooding bitterness seemed increasingly irrelevant, and it was agreed that a treaty should be drawn up to provide means of bringing notorious offenders to justice. With the conditions for disorder thus eradicated, James was subsequently well placed to play a vigorous role in steadily exerting the control of central government, visiting the Borders frequently and hanging large numbers of the dying breed of ruffians who had thrived for so long. And it was in these circumstances, as the turmoil receded, that men came to speak – albeit somewhat simplistically – of 'King James's Peace'.

In the meantime, Maitland's place in government had been taken by a group of eight ministers, known as the 'Octavians': James Elphinstone, Lord Balmerino; Walter Stewart, Lord Blantyre, who had been educated as a boy at Stirling along with the king, and would eventually become Lord Treasurer; Sir David Carnegie of Colluthie; Sir John Skene of Curriehill, the Lord Justice Clerk; Thomas Hamilton, Lord Drumcairn, a shrewd and versatile, though ultimately corruptible individual, who was known by the king as 'Tam o' the Cowgate' as a result of his residence in that street; John Lindsay, Lord Menmuir, who received worthy praise from John Spottiswoode as a man of 'exquisite learning and sound judgement'; Sir Alexander Seton, Lord Urquhart, who was President of the Court of Session, and went on to become Chancellor and Earl of Dunfermline; and Sir Peter Young, the king's former tutor. Though sometimes assumed to be of broadly middle-class origins, the Octavians were all substantial landowners and drawn in certain cases from highly respected noble families - 'Tam o' the Cowgate', for instance, being a kinsman of the royally connected Hamiltons. All, moreover, were capable and experienced servants of the Crown. Some, indeed, had succeeded in helping the queen to become more solvent, and it was in their capacity as financial troubleshooters that the group were initially employed by the king.

The state of the royal treasury had already been brought home to James particularly starkly on New Year's Day 1596, when Queen Anne's advisers had been able to provide her with a purse containing £1,000 in gold. Keen to exploit such an opportunity to tease her husband, Anne therefore approached him, shook the purse in his face, and condescendingly delivered half its contents to him, inquiring in the process when his council would give him as much. For some time, in fact, James had been reduced to increasingly miserable shifts by his financial predicament, and the queen's gesture was, in effect, the final embarrassment. In November 1588, indeed, the English agent, William Ashby had reported to Sir Francis Walsingham that the King of Scots was 'so poor [that] he can neither reward nor punish', and things had not changed since. His household had continued to be maintained from the private means of his officials, and his debts to moneylenders were common knowledge. He had long suspected, too, that that the officers of the Exchequer were making considerable profits at the expense of the Crown, though his only recourse had been to plunder the mint and debase the coinage. And without exception, his lack of personal magnetism had failed to galvanise – and in particular intimidate – those conducting his business. 'I have been Friday, Saturday and this day waiting upon the direction of my affairs, and never man comes,' he told Sir John Skene in an undated letter. 'Them of the Exchequer that were ordained to take accounts, never one. The affairs of the household should have been ended this day, no man comes down ... In short no tryst or meeting is kept. What is spoken this night is forgot the morn ...'

But while James bemoaned the self-interest and inefficiency of those around him, he did little to curb his own extravagance and remained the root cause of his problems. 'He gives to everyone that asks, what they desire,' wrote Thomas Fowler to Walsingham in December 1588, 'even to vain youths and proud fools the very lands of his crown or whatever falls, leaving himself nought to maintain his small, unkingly household. Yea what he gets from England, if it were a million, they would get it from him, so careless is he of any wealth if he may enjoy his pleasure in hunting, the weather serving.' James, moreover, freely acknowledged what amounted to a pathological profligacy on his part. 'I have offended the whole country, I grant, for prodigal giving from me,' he noted to Maitland in 1591. And like many victims of addiction, he vainly professed his determination to amend. In the same letter to Maitland, he noted how 'the two aids of the kitchen ran out yesterday and would not make the supper ready, saying condition was not kept'. The chancellor therefore was to remedy the situation. 'Suppose us be not wealthy, let us be proud poor bodies,' James instructed, though a true measure of his pride had already been furnished by his insistence in 1590 that the laird of Caldwell make the customary gift of a hackney, so that Queen Anne's ladies could be transported in some kind of style, and by his earlier alleged plea to the Earl of Mar for the loan of a 'pair of silken hose' before he received a foreign ambassador.

As a token of the king's new resolve, however, Glamis, the treasurer and other members of the Exchequer were now to be summarily dismissed and replaced by the Octavians in the hope that the king's finances might receive the same much-needed attention as his wife's. The preamble to their commission made clear that the king's income was declining as a result of 'unprofitable dispositions out of the property and collectory', increased pensions, falling customs revenue in spite of increased shipping, decay of the coinage, and general neglect and improper management, 'so that all things are come to such confusion … that there is not wheat nor barley, silver nor other rent, to serve his Highness sufficiently in bread and drink'. Furthermore, the new body was to be granted an unprecedented degree of control to achieve its stated objective of augmenting the king's income by £100,000 – so much, indeed, that the king pledged himself to do nothing in financial matters without the consent of at least five of its members. He agreed, too, to abide by any directives they might draw up, though his zeal to place so much power in his ministers' hands was governed, predictably, at least as much by a wish for self-preservation as by any wholehearted commitment to the kind of financial discipline that they might impose. Knowing full well the kind of general odium that his new watchdogs were bound to incur, it made sound political sense – especially to a ruler of James's disposition – to distance the Crown from the impact of their decisions.

And the Octavians neither shirked their task nor retreated from the hostility that came their way. On 18 January 1596, the English agent Roger Aston was not exaggerating when he observed that 'these new Checker men begin very sharp'. By the end of the month they had discharged seventy people from the king's household and required the Earl of Mar to present a list of Prince Henry's retainers so that his household might also be pruned. Pensions were reduced, appropriate rents were set for Crown lands, and the first general customs duty on imports in Scottish history was successfully imposed. They also tried to obtain financial assistance from the General Assembly of the Kirk, though this would prove a step too far even for their considerable drive and ingenuity. Nonetheless, for the short period that they held the reins, their impact was considerable. During 1596 and 1597, while their reforms were in effect, the expenses of the royal household averaged about £3,650 a month. However, for the half-year period from November 1598 to May 1599, by which time their restraining grip had already been removed, the average was £4,580. Likewise, the comptroller's excess expenditure for the fiscal year 1596–97 had been merely £258 – only to rise to £3,141 during 1597–98. Indeed, during 1598–99, the year of Duke

Ulrick of Denmark's expensive and alcohol-fuelled visit, it would rise to over £26,000. Still needing to pawn his jewels occasionally, by 1598 James was in debt to two Edinburgh merchants to the tune of £160,000. Nor would he be spared the final indignity in 1599 of receiving the resignation of one of his ministers on the grounds that service to the Crown entailed almost certain financial ruin.

In fact, the Octavians would be overcome ultimately by a mixture of religious intolerance and the machinations of a somewhat amorphous opposition group known as the 'Cubiculars', not to mention the king's own short-lived enthusiasm for the rigours of financial austerity. Hostility from holders of Crown land whose tenures were of dubious validity and courtiers whose pensions had shrunk or vanished altogether was of course inevitable, and chief among the disaffected was Sir George Home of Sport, Gentleman of the Bedchamber – a fat and ruthless *faux bonhomme* who wished to be rich and retained the king's ear by mending his quarrels with the queen. 'Where Sir George declares himself either a friend or an enemy,' wrote Samuel Cockburn to Archibald Douglas in June 1596, 'there is none to stand to the contrary.' And though the days of deadly feuds were largely over, Home had little difficulty in exploiting Alexander Seton's sympathy for Catholics for his own ends. Faced with outcries from the Kirk at a time when the return of Huntly and his crew was already causing consternation, James therefore decided to neutralise Seton's moderating influence and place financial control in the hands of Lord Treasurer Blantyre – the most impeccably Protestant and mediocre of all the Octavians – with the result that the body, which had promised so much, swiftly disintegrated.

The battle with the Kirk on the other hand, far from abating, was fast approaching its climax. Even the birth of the king's daughter on 19 August 1596, had served to highlight the growing tension, since the Presbyterian ministers did not on this occasion offer even token congratulations. Nor would the queen herself escape the wrath of indignant clergymen. Once more she lost the custody of her child when Princess Elizabeth was handed over to the excellent guardianship of Lord and Lady Livingstone – both suspected Catholics – who gave the child seven happy years of care and affection in Linlithgow Castle. But the queen could not have anticipated the remorseless assault upon her own religious beliefs, which duly rained down upon her from the pulpit of the Reverend David Black of St Andrews, who had already acquired a dubious celebrity in

1594 by damning the king's councillors as 'atheists of no religion' and declaring the nobility to be 'degenerate, godless dissemblers, enemies to the Kirk'.

At some point, in fact, the queen, who had never taken kindly to Presbyterianism nor to the freedom of the Scottish clergy in instructing her husband, had become a secret, though half-trifling, Roman Catholic under the influence of her intimate friend the Countess of Huntly, the former Lady Henrietta Stuart, sister of Esmé Duke of Lennox. And as a result, on 19 October 1596, she was openly insulted by Black who proclaimed in a sermon that 'the devil was in the court' and professed that though required to pray for the queen, 'we have no cause', since 'she will never do us good'. To add salt to the wound, Black did not hesitate to deny that the king had any right to judge him when called before the council a month later to account for his behaviour. In the pulpit, he declared, he was subject only to Christ's word, and answerable for that solely to 'the prophets', i.e. ministers or 'the ecclesiastick senat'.

The fuel for this high-octane clash had been provided, of course, by the king's decision to seek the return of Huntly and his confederates that summer. 'Papists,' James told his clergy at that time, 'might be honest folks and good friends' to the Crown, since his mother was a Catholic and yet had been 'an honest woman.' And with precisely this kind of specious reasoning, which could be guaranteed to outrage the likes of Andrew Melville, James duly obtained the assent he desired from a convention of the Estates held at Falkland in August – though the victory was not achieved without a price. Melville himself, for instance, had appeared at the convention and, in spite of the king's command that he withdraw, proceeded to accuse the entire assembly of treason against Christ. A month later, moreover, Melville was back at Falkland for a conference, during which he 'broke out upon the king in so zealous, powerful and irresistible manner, that howbeit the king used his authority in most crabbed and choleric manner, yet Mr Andrew bore him down', referring to the ruler as 'but God's sillie [i.e. simple] vassal' and taking him by the sleeve to tell him, 'Sir, you are brought in extreme danger both of your life and crown'. 'There are,' Melville continued, 'two kings and two kingdoms in Scotland. There is Christ Jesus the King and his kingdom the kirk, whose subject King James the Sixth is, and of whose kingdom not a king, nor a lord, nor a head, but a member.'

With a mixture of self-control, incredulity and cold apprehension at the prospect of a face-to-face confrontation with a zealot of Melville's cast-iron will, James nevertheless managed to dismiss the ministers pleasantly, promising that the Catholic earls would receive no favour from him until they had satisfied the Kirk of their good intentions. But the preachers of Edinburgh, far from responding with similar latitude, merely, we are told, 'pressed forward and sounded mightily' – with the result that the capital was soon rocked by mayhem and disorder. On 17 December during the course of violent sermons at St Giles the cry went up for the congregation to defend itself, with the result that rioting broke out, mainly around the Tolbooth, where the king was meeting with his lords of session. In the event, the crowd was beaten back and the rioters swiftly calmed by the provost, who then hastened the king down the Canongate to the security of Holyroodhouse. But it had been another chastening experience for the king, and it was small wonder, perhaps, that he would warn his heir so forcefully about the threat posed by 'Puritans' within the Kirk.

'Take heed therefore, my son,' he wrote in *Basilikon Doron*, 'to such Puritans, very pests in the church and commonweal, whom no deserts can oblige … breathing nothing but sedition and calumnies, aspiring without measure, railing without reason and making their own imaginations the square of their conscience. I protest before the great God that ye shall never find with any Highland or Border thieves greater ingratitude and more lies and vile perjuries than with these fantastic spirits.' Yet by the time that James wrote, the threat of which he spoke was already in full retreat, for the radicals within the Kirk, like the errant nobles before them, had over-stepped the mark and finally detached themselves from their more moderate counterparts – a fact which the king, to his not inconsiderable credit, appears to have at least partially appreciated at the time. For the very next day after a rioting mob had massed outside the Tolbooth, he, his queen and the entire court, along with judges, lawyers and other government officials, removed from the capital to Linlithgow, leaving a herald to proclaim at the Mercat Cross that their departure was to be permanent, since the city was no longer fit to be a royal residence. Nobles, likewise, were ordered to withdraw to their country estates.

Far from staging an ignominious retreat, however, James had literally turned the tables overnight, for if Melville, Black and their counterparts were more than capable of outfacing their monarch in eyeball-to-eyeball confrontation, they lacked his political skill and, in particular, his sense of timing. Faced with certain ruin as a result of the king's departure, the capital abandoned its preachers and within a fortnight James was back on his own terms, accompanied by a daunting troop of Border ruffians who now were more than willing to do his bidding. Not only did Edinburgh's citizens make their peace with the king, moreover, they did so gladly, even accepting a fine of 20,000 marks without demur. Those guilty ministers who were not imprisoned, meanwhile, had no recourse but flight, leaving the Kirk largely purged of its most troublesome elements. Thereafter, a General Assembly of the Kirk called to Perth later in the year formally withdrew the extreme claims made by Melville and, by accepting representation in Parliament, acknowledged their status under the authority of the secular ruler in precisely the way that James desired. Henceforth, a clerical commission set up by the General Assembly would merely advise the king on ecclesiastical affairs rather than dictate policy in the way that had been suggested previously. Kings, it seems, were no longer 'Satan's bairns' and all talk of theocracy was conveniently shelved.

Yet even this was not the limit of James's victory, for he used this heaven-sent conjunction of circumstances to install moderate ministers of the Kirk in Parliament as 'bishops' – a term hitherto anathematised because of its papist connotations. He had long opposed the so-called 'parity' of ministers 'whereby the ignorants are emboldened to challenge their betters', and proposed instead to 'advance the godly, learned and modest men of the ministry to bishoprics and benefices [and thus] not only banish their conceited parity but also re-establish the old institution of three estates, which can no otherwise be done'. 'I mind not,' he said, 'to bring in papistical or Anglican bishoping; but only to have the best and the wisest of ministers to have place in Parliament.' And in October 1600, notwithstanding Andrew Melville's opposition to the king's 'Anglo-piscal, papistical conclusions', James duly appointed three diocesan bishops to the sees of Caithness, Ross and Aberdeen. Though their influence lay only in Parliament and they had no defined function within the government of the Kirk, which remained thoroughly Presbyterian in nature, it was a triumph no less significant in its way than the taming of the earls. Now at last, perhaps, James could genuinely rule as 'king and sovereign lord' in the way that he had always intended. 'Alas,' lamented James Melville, 'where Christ guided before, the court began then to govern all'.

9 ❧ Towards the 'Land of Promise'

'St George surely rides upon a towardly riding horse, while I am bursten in daunting a wild, unruly colt.'

James VI of Scotland, comparing the kingdom of England with his own

Against all expectation, including his own, the King of Scotland had taken only nine months from the time of his son's christening to be rid of all the major torments that had plagued him for so long. And for the next six years, aside from one rogue tremor of noble insolence in 1600, there was comparative peace. In the wake of Maitland's death, moreover, there remained no single, dominating figure at the centre of politics beyond the king himself. Such, indeed, was the king's confidence and sense of liberation that he found himself able to indulge his intellect in a spate of writing that fully reflected his determination to be master of his kingdom and of all estates within it, be they noble or clerical. In September 1598, his *Daemonologie* was quickly followed by a 1,000-word pamphlet entitled *The Trew Law of Free Monarchies: Or The Reciprock and Mutual Dutie Betwixt a Free King and his Natural Subjects*, in which he forcefully expounded what would become known to history as the principle of 'divine right'. Then, one year later, there occurred the publication of *Basilikon Doron* or 'Kingly Gift' – the book dedicated to his infant son, into which he attempted to pack all the wisdom and understanding of kingship that he had accumulated over the previous sixteen years or so. Written exclusively for the prince and falling only accidentally into the hands of a wider readership, it was the least self-conscious, most transparently honest and pleasantest of all James's works to read. Thus diverted, he was able at last to recover and take stock before his last, all-absorbing and defining project as King of Scotland: the acquisition of the Crown of England.

Though *The Trew Law of Free Monarchies* was published anonymously, its regal tone and direct and informal style left little doubt about its authorship. Aside from his *Daemonologie*, James had already published four books: *The Essays of a Prentise in the Divine Art of Poesie* (1584); *Ane Fruitfull Meditatioun on the Seventh, Eighth, Ninth and Tenth Versies of Chapter XX of Revelations* (1588); *Ane Meditatioun upon the First Buke of the Chronicles of Kings* (1589); and *His Majesties Poeticall Exercises* (1591). But now his aim was more directly didactic: to teach his subjects in no uncertain terms the nature of their duty to their king, and in particular the necessity of obedience and the wickedness of revolt. Nor was the simplicity of James's language coincidental, since *The Trew Law* was never intended as an abstract academic treatise. On the contrary, it was meant to be understood in the most lucid, vivid and cogent way, and read in entirety without labour or ambiguity. James's purpose, he said, was 'to instruct and not irritate'.

Yet the tract certainly contained statements that would rightly or wrongly redound to his discredit down the centuries. Though there was nothing novel in the claim, for instance, that it was the duty of subjects to obey even tyrannical kings and to accept that, as God's appointees, anointed rulers were open only to divine judgement, his words, like those of many a well-intentioned pedant, frequently have an unfortunate ring to them. 'Kings are called Gods by the prophetical King David,' he reminded his readers, 'because they sit upon God His throne in the earth, and have the [ac]count of their administration to give unto him'. In Scotland, he argued, kings existed before any Parliaments were held or laws were made and so 'it follows from necessity, that the kings were the authors and makers of the laws, and not the laws of the kings'. Likewise, the coronation oath involves no compact between ruler and ruled. Instead, the good king is a loving father to his people, cherishing their welfare, tempering punishment with pity, and safeguarding order and harmony for the mutual benefit of all concerned by the very inviolability of his authority. As for evil kings, their chastisement will follow in the afterlife. Indeed, they will be punished far above other men, 'for the highest bench is sliddriest to sit upon'.

All such claims were, in fact, standard political fare for any Early Modern ruler and accepted, at least implicitly, by the vast majority of contemporary men and women. But whether James had on this occasion chosen the most judicious time to air such views is more open to question. And although the whole concept of the tract may well have sprung in part from the decidedly quixotic streak in his nature, it continues to carry with it certain uneasy resonances. In practice, James's kingship would often prove eminently pragmatic and flexible – much more so than *The Trew Law* implied was actually necessary. From his own perspective, moreover, James was genuinely committed to the principles of good kingship – establishing good laws, ministering justice, advancing good men and punishing wrongdoers, ensuring peace and security, and guaranteeing sound religion. Yet 'divine right' was a double-edged sword for a king like James. Though it offered order, it sat ill with impatience, timidity and, above all, any lack of genuine 'majesty' on the part of the ruler who attempted to exemplify its virtues. And as a principle founded, or so James claimed, upon the bedrock of ancient biblical precedent, its application would need to be especially subtle at a time of such pronounced social, political and religious change.

Basilikon Doron, meanwhile, further emphasised the patriarchal nature of kingship and the virtues required by the godly ruler. Originating, or so James claimed, from a dream which left him fearing that his life would be short, the book is a moral and didactic work outlining a series of precepts for his son's guidance. And once again the divinely ordained authority of kings features prominently. 'God gives not kings the stile of Gods in vain', runs the well-known sonnet opening the work. But James's primary concern remained the 4-year-old Prince Henry's education, or as he himself put it, 'timeously to provide for his training up in all the points of a king's office'. In this regard, Henry was firstly to attain a knowledge and fear of God by study of the scriptures, by prayer, by preservation of a sensitive conscience, and by learning to distinguish between essentials and non-essentials in matters of faith. It was also essential that he avoid not only pride per se but 'the preposterous humility' of those who demand parity in religious affairs. 'Surely,' James tells his son, 'there is more pride under such a one's black bonnet than under Alexander the Great his diadem.'

There are observations, too, on the Scottish Reformation and predictable sideswipes at the troublesome Scottish nobility. We hear, for instance, how 'some fiery-spirited men of the ministry got such a guiding of the people at that time of confusion, as finding the gust of government sweet, they begouth [began] to fantasy to themselves a democratic form of government … and after usurping the liberty of their time in my long minority, settled themselves so fast upon that imagined democracy as they fed themselves with the hope to become Tribuni plebis: and so in a popular government by leading the people by the nose, to bear the sway of all the rule'. The prince, therefore, was not to tolerate the pretensions of these 'fantastic spirits … except ye would keep them from trying your patience as Socrates did an evil wife'. Nor should he forget the problems associated with over-mighty subjects. For while James accepted that 'virtue followeth oftest noble blood' and urged his son to employ those that are 'obedient to the law among them … in all your greatest affairs', he could not forget the damage that had been done to the kingdom by the arrogance of some and the feuds they had waged. 'The natural sickness that I have perceived this estate subject to in my time,' he observed, 'hath been a feckless arrogant conceit of their own greatness and power.' All too often, it seems, they were prepared to 'bang it out bravely, he and all his kin, against him and all his …'.

Slightly less expected, however, are the passages concerning warfare. The image of James as a man of peace is, of course, firmly established in popular perceptions, and rightly so. Yet when he wrote *Basilikon Doron*, his own expeditions against Huntly and Bothwell had recently demonstrated that, when extremity demanded, he appreciated well enough the need for any prince to wield the sword. And though his advice on warfare was conventional, it did not merely rehearse the advice of others or limit itself to generalities. 'Choose old experimented captains and young able soldiers,' he told his heir. 'Be extremely strait and severe in martial discipline, as well for the keeping of order, which is as requisite as hardiness in the wars, and punishing of sloth, which at a time put the whole army in hazard.' There was praise, too, for the renowned discipline of the Spaniards and especially the Duke of Parma's infantry. Caesar's *Commentaries* were also cited as recommended reading, 'for I have ever been of that opinion that of all … great captains that ever were, he hath farthest excelled, both in his practice and in his precepts in martial affairs'.

The third and final section of the book, meanwhile, dealt with the ruler's public image and everyday behaviour – matters which James considered of no small significance, since 'a king is as one set on a stage whose smallest actions and gestures, all the people gazingly do behold'. Though James appreciated the elegant manners of those who had resided at the French court, he nevertheless considered it preferable for his son to adopt the simpler ways of Scottish practice. Indeed, he spoke of 'the vice of delicacy, which is a degree of gluttony' and recommended that eating, for instance, be conducted 'in a manly, round and honest fashion'. A king should likewise 'keep a proportion' in his dress appropriate to the occasion, and 'look gravely and with a majesty' when sitting in judgement, while remaining 'homely' in the private company of his servants and 'merry' during his pastimes. Perfume, long hair and unclipped nails were to be avoided, along with the idle company of females 'which are no other things else but irritamenta libidinis'. The language of a king should be plain, honest, natural and brief, avoiding crudeness, and he should engage in all types of athletic exercise, especially riding, 'since it becometh a prince, best of any man, to be a fair and good horseman'. Chess, on the other hand, was to be discouraged on the grounds that it was 'over fond and philosophic a folly'.

Taken as a whole, *Basilikon Doron* is rightly considered to contain the best prose ever written by James, for in spite of certain artificialities of style it is generally fresh, natural and spontaneous, abounding in racy phrases and picturesque passages that are tinged with James's characteristic dash of wry humour. Nor does the king's frequent inability to follow his own advice detract from its significance. If anything, indeed, it adds to the book's interest. Certainly, it was an immense success, and reappeared constantly in the publications on courtesy produced for the education of upper-class young men during the seventeenth century – notwithstanding the fact that it had first been printed in a secret edition of seven copies which the king distributed among his most trusted servants. Above all, he had wished to keep it from the knowledge of the clergy and later feared that passages might reach England in garbled form and cause suspicion. Yet within days of Elizabeth's death it was on sale in London, eagerly snapped up by Englishmen and foreigners alike. Ultimately, it would be translated into most of the languages of Western Europe and remains one of the most intriguing windows into the king's attitudes and personality.

Only two years later, moreover, a brief sketch of James and his court, penned by the English diplomat and poet Sir Henry Wotton, would offer us a further series of perspectives on the man and his ways, which are among the most well known of all contemporary descriptions. According to Wotton, he was 'of medium stature, and of robust constitution', 'fond of literary discourse, especially of theology', and 'a great lover of witty conceits'. His speech, we are told, was 'learned and even eloquent' and rather more surprisingly, perhaps, he was also described as 'patient in the work of government' – a claim belied, of course, by his incorrigible tendency to neglect the routine tasks of administration in favour of pastimes, especially hunting. Another of his admirable qualities, it seems, was his chastity which, Wotton suggested, 'he has preserved without blemish, unlike to his predecessors who disturbed the kingdom by leaving many bastards'. Above all, however, though James enjoyed 'listening to banter and to merry jests, in which he takes great delight' and was 'extremely familiar' with the gentlemen of his bedchamber, there was another, less personable side to him. Indeed, he was 'said to be one of the most secret princes of the world', Wotton informs us, and capable of 'bitter hatred, especially against the Earl of Gowrie' – though the king's antipathy to this particular individual was hardly surprising in light of what had transpired only the year before.

The Gowrie conspiracy of August 1600 was, in fact, the only violent episode to disturb the peace that had descended so unexpectedly on the closing years of James's direct rule in Scotland. But it was also, arguably, one of the most impenetrable of all the baffling mysteries associated with James's reign, not least of all because the king alone, of all the principal persons involved, lived to tell the tale, and because his skill at concealment and subterfuge had been honed by this time to little less than an art form. As Wotton correctly realised, of course, James had already consciously drawn a veil of uncertainty over many episodes in his life, and in *Basilikon Doron* he had freely admitted how 'a king will have need to use secrecy in many things'. Even some of his portraits – and none more so than that produced by Adrian Vanson in 1595 – suggest a ruler who, in spite of frequent flashes of bonhomie, possessed a deeper, warier, cannier and more circumspect side. Vanson had, in fact, been patronised by James for all of fourteen years by the time the portrait was produced, and in 1584 had succeeded Arnold von Bronckhorst as official painter to the Scottish court. One year later, he had also produced a portrait of the king for the Danish court as part of the ongoing marriage negotiations. He knew the king intimately over time and he knew the king's circumstances: his insecurities, the indignities to which he had been subjected and the methods by which he survived them. As such, the brooding immobility of the face he painted in 1595 was surely no more of a coincidence than the suspicious watchfulness of the heavy-lidded eyes, conveying a mind full of concealed and private thoughts – a mind more than capable, too, of confounding posterity about the precise nature of what passed at Gowrie House during a summer hunting trip that had begun so routinely.

According to James's account, he was met outside the palace of Falkland in the early morning of 5 August by Alexander, Master of Ruthven, the younger brother of the Earl of Gowrie, who related a strange tale to him. The day before, it seems, a man had been apprehended while attempting to bury a pot of gold coins in a field outside Perth. Since buried gold was forfeit to the Crown as treasure trove and since the man had been about to bury it, the implication was that the king could legitimately claim it for himself. But James, in his version of events, was too preoccupied for the time being with his day's sport and left the matter to the local magistrates. Only later in the day, after the master's story had been running in his mind, did he ride back to Perth, accompanied by ten to fifteen lightly-armed attendants – at which point he was met by Gowrie, who had been informed by his brother of the king's approach, and invited to dinner at Gowrie House. There was, James suggested, a certain uneasiness and lack of cordiality in the earl's invitation, and the poor quality of the meal itself, which consisted of moorfowl, mutton and chicken, suggested that no trouble had been taken to ensure adequate preparation for the royal visit. Even so, the king was apparently ready afterwards to accompany Ruthven to a remote turret chamber, in order to interview the mysterious captive who had been found with the treasure.

What followed from this point becomes more curious still, for as the king made his way to the turret through a series of chambers, Ruthven allegedly locked each door behind him before bringing him to a small apartment where, to the king's horror, there was no pot of gold, but a retainer of Ruthven's, named Henderson, clad in armour and bearing a dagger in his belt. While James's own men were eating cherries in the garden below, awaiting his return, Ruthven, we are told, seized Henderson's dagger, accused the king of murdering his father, and declared that he must die. Whereupon, with Ruthven's dagger at his breast, James entered upon a long discourse on the wickedness of shedding innocent blood and thereby persuaded his assailant to consult his brother before proceeding. While he was gone, James also, it seems, managed to prevail upon Henderson who denied any foreknowledge of an assassination plot and obligingly opened a window – which would prove mightily convenient when Ruthven returned and announced to his captive once more that he would have to die. 'By God, sir,' Ruthven is said to have declared, 'there is no remedy'.

In the struggle that followed, however, James claimed to have got the better of his would-be assassin, dragging him to the open window and crying for help to his attendants below, one of whom, young John Ramsey, made his way to the turret and found Ruthven on his knees before the king, his head under James's arm, and his hand raised over the king's face as though to stifle his cries for help. Striking him from behind, Ramsey wounded the would-be assassin severely and then called for help to Thomas Erskine and Dr Hugh Herries who subsequently finished him with their swords. Gowrie, meanwhile, was also killed after rushing upstairs in wild excitement, sword in hand, to confront his brother's killers. Thus, it seems, were both Ruthvens done to death.

It was, however, a highly improbable story, riddled with inconsistencies and outright falsehoods, which has fed the opinion down the centuries that James himself somehow engineered the episode. Certainly, there was no love lost between the king and the handsome, 22-year-old Gowrie, who had just returned from six years of travel and study on the Continent. The earl's grandfather, Patrick, had of course been Queen Mary's enemy and Riccio's assassin, while his father had been beheaded for treason following the Ruthven Raid of 1582, which had robbed him of his beloved Esmé Stuart. Before his departure abroad, moreover, Gowrie had been not only a supporter of the Kirk but a suspected sympathiser with Bothwell. And to cap the king's resentment, he was also popular, both in Scotland and England. He had been warmly received in London upon his return from his travels, and there was even talk in certain quarters that he might come to rival James as a potential successor to the English throne. His subsequent entry into Edinburgh, meanwhile, attracted such enthusiasm that James was unable at the time to resist a stinging remark. There had been even more people present to mark the earl's return, he quipped, than there had been at the scaffold for the execution of his father. So undisguised, indeed, was the king's hostility that Gowrie was forced to retire briefly to his estates before returning to anger his royal master once more by opposing him at the June parliament. When it is considered, too, that James owed the earl some £80,000 and knew that he had dabbled in magic and astrology during his travels, it is not hard to appreciate why suspicions of subterfuge and skulduggery have been so prevalent down the years.

But there is another side to the story, which continues to render events largely inexplicable. The Master of Ruthven, for instance, was a handsome young man of only 19, who was a known favourite of the king, and whose sister Beatrix was one of Queen Anne's leading ladies. Much more curious still, however, is the fact that James could have brought about Gowrie's downfall at far less personal risk to himself. A decision to put paid to Gowrie in his own house is no more inherently plausible than the unlikely image of James overcoming him in a hand-to-hand brawl while a third party, Henderson, was seemingly close at hand. The king, indeed, explained away any involvement in plots of his own by employing precisely such an argument. 'I see, Mr Robert,' he said to the Edinburgh minister who refused to believe his account, 'that ye would make me a murderer. It is known very well that I was never bloodthirsty. If I would have taken their lives, I had causes enough; I needed not to hazard myself so.' Besides which, though James was actually wholly capable of removing his enemies by violence, he would always do so through due legal process – from the death of Morton in 1581 to the execution of Sir Walter Raleigh in 1618.

Was Gowrie therefore guilty, after all, notwithstanding the question marks beside James's version of events? If so, his blunders and miscalculations remain nothing short of remarkable. Above all, he appears to have made no attempt to enlist the support of other influential nobles, whose consent would have remained so crucial in the unlikely event of his success. The only incriminating evidence to this effect was in fact provided by the discredited lawyer, George Sprot, who confessed on the verge of his own execution in 1608 that he possessed letters confirming Gowrie's plan to spirit James away to Fast Castle, Sir Robert Logan of Restalrick's impregnable cliff-top fortress on the Berwickshire coast. But while the government made every effort to prove the complicity of others in the plot and Logan, a particularly notorious and dissolute conspirator, was eventually convicted posthumously of complicity in the Gowrie conspiracy on Sprot's evidence, the incriminating letters concerned were clear-cut forgeries made in imitation of Logan's handwriting. Whether, as has been claimed subsequently, they were copies of original letters that actually did exist, remains unknown.

With such a dearth of certainties, however, other more imaginative theories have occasionally emerged to exploit the vacuum. One particularly flimsy hypothesis has suggested, for instance, that James may have been responsible for the incident by committing an indecent assault on Alexander Ruthven, which he then attempted to conceal by improvising his strange account of what happened. There has also been play upon the whispers of scandal linking Ruthven's name to Anne of Denmark, though here, too, the king could certainly have dealt with any problems more rationally and conveniently. And then, of course, rather less implausibly, there remains the possibility of a sudden and unpremeditated quarrel which spiralled out of control when the king panicked and called upon his attendants for protection. Significantly, this was the explanation accepted by Sir William Bowes, the English ambassador, who believed that James had referred to Ruthven's father as a traitor when they were alone together 'whereat the youth showing a grieved and expostulatory countenance' caused the king, 'seeing himself alone and without a weapon', to cry 'Treason!' 'The Master,' Bowes continued, 'abashed to see the king to apprehend it so … put his hand to stay the king showing his countenance in that mood, immediately falling upon his knees to entreat the king …', at which point Ramsey entered and 'ran the poor gentleman through'. James, moreover, certainly seems to have called upon Ramsey to deliver the wounding blow. 'Strike him high,' he is said to have cried, 'because he has a chain doublet upon him.'

Whatever the true story, equally interesting in its own way is the speed and astonishing effectiveness with which James turned the incident to his advantage. On 7 August, two days after the deaths, the Privy Council ordered that the corpses of Gowrie and his brother should remain unburied until further investigations had been made, and also that no person of the name of Ruthven should approach within ten miles of the royal court. In the meantime, the bodies of the dead brothers were disembowelled and preserved, and on 30 October sent to Edinburgh to be produced before the bar of Parliament. Thereafter, on 20 November the Ruthven estates were declared forfeit and the family name and honours extinct. For good measure, the corpses of the earl and his brother were then hanged and quartered at the Mercat Cross – their heads being placed on spikes at the Old Tolbooth, their arms and legs likewise placed on spikes at various locations round and about Perth. Ultimately, another Act would be passed which abolished the name of Ruthven forever and laid down that the barony of Ruthven should henceforth be known as the barony of Huntingtower. Gowrie House in its turn was levelled to the ground, while 5 August was henceforth designated a day of solemn thanksgiving. Ramsey, too, was not forgotten, for he was not only knighted upon James's eventual accession to the English throne but became Earl of Holderness.

Nor was propaganda and the skilful application of political leverage neglected. James's account of the episode was published within the year under the title *Gowrie's Conspiracie: A Discourse of the Unnaturall and Vyle Conspiracie, Attempted against the Kings Majesties Person at Sanct-Iohnstoun [Perth], upon Twysday the Fifth of August, 1600* (Edinburgh, printed 1600, *cum privilegio regis*). And James followed this publication by commanding his clergy to offer public thanksgiving for his deliverance from assassination – a gesture which resulted initially in the refusal of five Edinburgh ministers to comply. Their refusal, moreover, was hardly a surprise – and least of all to a shrewd political manipulator like James – since the Ruthvens had, of course, been consistent supporters of the Kirk and the official explanation was, after all, wholly worthy of scepticism. But James was determined to make his account of events both a test of clerical loyalty and a new weapon with which to cow the Kirk. Not only were compliant clergy found to fill the places of the five recalcitrant ministers, but four soon relented, whereupon they were dispatched to various parts of the country to repeat their submissions publicly. The only figure to stand firm, in fact, was Robert Bruce, a man of great dignity and authority, and former confidant of the king, who found himself banished from Scotland on pain of death.

But even after James had obtained approval for his actions from a convention of the clergy, there remained, not altogether surprisingly, a good deal of scepticism, though the conspiracy itself, in its broader historical context, is best perceived as little more than a final, largely meaningless episode, typical of an unfortunate phase of Scottish history that was already effectively at an end. Courtiers continued to whisper of foul play, while the queen, angry at the banishment of Beatrix Ruthven, sulked in her rooms and refused to be dressed, insisting that she required the assistance of her former lady-in-waiting. And though James finally placated his wife by spending considerable sums upon a tightrope walker for her entertainment, the courts of both England and France continued to doubt and sneer. Elizabeth, for instance, upon congratulating James at his escape, remarked nevertheless that since Gowrie had so many familiar spirits she supposed that there were no longer any left in hell. In France, meanwhile, as the diary of James Melville makes clear, the king's account of the Ruthvens' death was met with such ridicule that the Scottish ambassador was forced to suppress it in his reports.

If, then, there really were any doubt before the events of 1600 that James was indeed 'one of the most secret princes of the world', the Gowrie conspiracy had clearly banished it once and for all. Yet even the closeness with which James played his hand at that time pales by comparison with his sustained efforts to ensure that he would succeed to the English throne upon the death of Elizabeth I. Much of his anxiety and subterfuge was, in fact, unnecessary, for although he was a foreigner and therefore technically excluded by the common law, he remained throughout the only really plausible candidate – notwithstanding even the additional problem that Henry VIII's will had excluded his sister Margaret Stuart's descendants. For some time before 1592, it is true, Arbella Stuart, great-great-granddaughter of Henry VII via his daughter Margaret, had been considered one of the natural candidates to succeed Queen Elizabeth, her first cousin twice removed. But, in spite of her inherent advantage of having been born on English soil she, like the other potential candidates on offer, was effectively a non-starter, since her hereditary claim was much inferior to James's and she displayed in any case no appreciable desire for the Crown. Already, then, between the end of 1592 and the spring of 1593, the influential Cecils – Elizabeth's Lord Treasurer, Lord Burghley, and his son and future successor as Secretary of State, Sir Robert Cecil – had turned their attention away from Arbella towards her cousin, the King of Scotland.

The other potential claimants were, moreover, even less worthy of consideration. Certainly, none of the Englishmen whose Plantagenet or Tudor blood gave them some right to consideration – Lord Beauchamp, Lord Derby and the Earl of Huntingdon – had either the prestige, character or ambition to make them acceptable, and continental options were no more inviting. For English Catholics living abroad and nurturing hopeless dreams of an imminent resurrection of the old religion in their homeland, the pretensions of Philip III of Spain, either by descent or as Mary Stuart's nominated heir, seemed to offer some sustenance, though not even Father Robert Persons, the Jesuit responsible for English affairs at Rome and a strong Spanish partisan, seriously believed that another Spanish king could occupy the English throne. Instead, attention focused mainly upon Philip's sister, Infanta Isabella Clara Eugenia, who was married to Archduke Albert and ruled the Netherlands with him. As a descendant of Edward III through John of Gaunt, her claim to the English throne had already served as a pretext for the sailing of the Armada. But even in her case the chances of success were effectively non-existent, for the 150,000 or so Catholics remaining in England were vastly outnumbered and in any case preferred patriotism to the prospect of foreign rule. Nor, for that matter, had the infanta and archduke any real desire to exchange the comfort and security of Brussels for a reckless English gamble at the longest possible odds. And Persons' fond belief that Sir Robert Cecil was more sympathetic to a Spanish claimant than the father whom he had succeeded as Elizabeth's leading minister in 1598 would prove to be wholly mistaken.

James I: Scotland's King of England

Unless King James foolishly alienated both the Queen of England and her leading ministers by some act of major indiscretion, his succession was therefore virtually assured. Even to Elizabeth herself, indeed, James remained the best available option, irrespective of his Scottish background and links with Mary Queen of Scots, and the same was true not only for Elizabeth's ministers but for those of her subjects that especially cared. He was, after all, an experienced ruler who had always appeared amenable to English interests and whose accession would unite the two kingdoms, and thereby achieve, in effect, the subjugation of Scotland that had always been a long-term goal of her southern neighbour. Most important of all, however, James's bloodline underpinned his claim more convincingly than any other alternative, and at a time when the hereditary principle was still paramount, this alone was enough. With or without Elizabeth's direct say-so, then, the King of Scotland would soon be Scotland's King of England, and if he were to behave as bid and promptly discard the Scottish baggage accompanying his succession, he would doubtless suffice.

In the meantime, however, such was James's fever of anxiety and impatience that he buzzed around Elizabeth with continual requests for confirmation of her intentions and far-fetched schemes to force her hand. In 1596, for instance, he had taken offence at certain passages in Spenser's *The Faerie Queen* which reflected upon his mother, and demanded at once from Elizabeth that the poet be tried and punished. He nagged the queen continually, too, to grant him the English estates of his grandparents, the Earl and Countess of Lennox, on the assumption that these would circumvent the English common law's bar to the succession of aliens. And then there was his near obsession with the act passed by Parliament in 1584 debarring plotters against the queen from inheriting her Crown, notwithstanding the fact that he had not been involved in any of his mother's intrigues. When, for instance, Valentine Thomas, a villainous Catholic ruffian to whom James had once unwisely granted an audience, was later arrested in England and claimed that the King of Scotland had encouraged him to assassinate Elizabeth, James's panic far outstripped the bounds of common sense.

Though Elizabeth assured him that she did not believe Thomas's tale and kept him quietly in prison without trial, so that his slander against the King of Scotland would not be broadcast in public, James nevertheless demanded that she erase his name from all records connected with the accusation and issue a declaration of his innocence. When she refused, moreover, James then declared not only that Thomas had been bribed into making a false confession but that he would issue a public challenge to do battle with anyone doubting his own innocence. Rather less eccentrically, he also saw fit to print the letter in which Elizabeth had expressed her disbelief in Thomas's story and to circulate it on the Continent. Once again, however, James's protests fell on deaf ears, since he lacked the cold conviction and depth of respect to make good his wishes. For James, as so often, did not so much threaten as bleat, and, in consequence, Thomas would remain in prison until Elizabeth's death when he was promptly tried and executed at James's command. Furthermore, the queen's imperious and frequently caustic dismissal of the Scottish ruler's protests demonstrates once more that the fundamental flaw in James's kingship was not so much a deficiency of political acumen or even of material resources but a more intangible, though nevertheless crippling, deficiency of vigour and resolve. As long as sheer pluck and backbone remained a crucial ingredient of majesty, therefore, James would always be ultimately lacking.

Nor was pestering the only method employed by James to achieve his longed-for goal. Much more provocatively, embassies were dispatched to various Protestant courts in northern Europe to conjure up armed support for his wish to 'be declared and acknowledged the certain and undoubted successor to the Crown'. Confident of his links with Denmark, Holland and the Protestant princes of Germany, James had been considering a league of Protestant states as early as 1585, although Elizabeth disliked his pretensions and in consequence purposely snubbed him by excluding Scotland from her own alliance with France and the Netherlands in 1596. Even so, in 1598 James dispatched his ambassadors to Denmark and Germany in what would prove to be the vain hope that a new league might be formed both to oppose the Turks and, much more importantly, prevail upon the Queen of England to name him her successor. Worse still, armaments were purchased and the Scottish Parliament of 1600 found itself faced with an apparently earnest request for the funding of an army to enforce his claim – all of which only succeeded in provoking Elizabeth's anger and prompting the English ambassador to wonder whether James was meaning 'not to tarry upon her Majesty's death'. 'He hasteth well,' Elizabeth warned her would-be successor, 'that wisely can abide', before assuring him that she would favour his claim 'as long as he shall give no just cause of exception'. But in spite of his squirming and posturing, she would not nominate him officially and thereby endure the indignity of seeing her courtiers and ministers turning away from her towards the 'sun rising' in the way that she herself had witnessed during the last months of her sister's life.

Such reasoning was, of course, eminently sensible and palpably transparent – to all, it seems, but James. Indeed, it is a measure of the soundness of James's claim to Elizabeth's throne and the needlessness of his behaviour that she chose to countenance his harassment at all. Certainly, his embassies abroad, his dalliances with papal and Spanish agents, and his attempts to fashion a party for himself at the English court all provided the Queen of England with precisely the 'just cause for exception' of which she warned him, had there been any conceivable alternative. James had even, it was believed in some quarters, secretly dispatched John Ogilvy of Powrie to Rome to angle for loans and promise toleration to English Catholics if he became their king. And even if Ogilvy's claims that he was James's accredited mouthpiece cannot be substantiated, there is no such question mark beside Lord Robert Semple's mission to Madrid in 1598, which sought recognition for James's claim. Nor, for that matter, was Elizabeth likely to have been any more reassured by a mysterious letter allegedly sent to Pope Clement VIII in 1599 in which her would-be successor was said to have addressed Clement as 'Most Blessed Father', before signing himself the pontiff's 'Most Obedient Son'.

James, in all fairness, consistently denied responsibility for the letter and eventually obtained a not altogether convincing confession from his secretary, Lord Balmerino, that it had been written without the king's consent and that his signature had been appended only by placing the document among others which had been signed hurriedly as he departed upon a hunting expedition. But it was enough to prompt a reply from Pope Clement in April 1600 in which he implored James to convert, and further fuelled concerns that the king's penchant for double games might well be carrying him into ever deeper waters. 'He practises in Rome, in Spain, and everywhere else, as he does with me,' wrote Henry IV of France, 'without attaching himself to any one, and is easily carried away by the hopes of those about him without regard for truth or merit.' And in the meantime he was equally prepared to offer restricted toleration on his own terms to English Catholics, corresponding with one of their most influential figures, the Earl of Northampton, and in the process nullifying any residual support for the Spanish infanta's candidacy. 'It were a pity,' wrote Northumberland, 'to lose so good a kingdom for not tolerating a Mass in a corner.' And James's reply confirmed his correspondent's high hopes: 'As for the Catholics,' he told Northumberland, 'I will neither persecute any that will be quiet and give but an outward obedience to the law, neither will I spare to advance any of them that will by good service worthily deserve it.'

That such reassurances should be offered at a time when intolerance was everywhere the norm might well seem to confirm the view that James's wish for compromise and moderation placed him ahead of the age in which he lived. But his contradictory signals to English Puritans suggest a ruler who was prepared to offer whatever potential supporters might wish to hear in a way that could only lead to trouble in the longer term when vague hints and outright guarantees would have to be made good. His agent in London, James Hamilton, was instructed in 1600, for instance, to assure all honest men that the king would 'not only maintain and continue the profession of the gospel there, but withal not suffer or permit any other religion to be professed and avowed within the bounds of that kingdom'. This, it should be remembered, was the king who had already set out his stall so firmly against all 'Puritans', dangerously conflating in the process the considerable range of opinion and outlook encompassed by the very term. Now, however, Puritans too, it seems, were to be courted at the very time that Elizabeth was resisting their pressure at every opportunity.

Equally provocative, in any case, was James's failure at this time to assist Elizabeth in her desperate struggle with the Earl of Tyrone's Irish rebels, which had flared up in 1595 and would rage for the next nine years, resulting in the disaster of the Battle of Yellow Ford and the overall loss of some 30,000 of Elizabeth's troops during the course of the whole campaign. As her ally, James sought outwardly to meet his obligation by issuing proclamations which forbade the clansmen of the Western Isles to assist the Irish rebels or trade with them. When Spanish troops landed at Kinsale, moreover, he offered England military aid. But in perceiving Tyrone as a potentially influential figure after Elizabeth's death, James gladly entered into secret correspondence with him and consistently turned a blind eye when his own royal proclamations were ignored. In fact, the towns of south-west Scotland continued to trade with the rebels as Tyrone recruited Scottish soldiers with apparent impunity. When Elizabeth protested, moreover, James merely issued new proclamations, which again went unenforced. In the meantime, he gladly accepted Tyrone's promises of future service when the time of reckoning finally arrived - though even with this, James's taxing of Elizabeth's patience was not over. Indeed, it was during her own crisis with the Earl of Essex that he came closest to breaking her forbearance once and for all.

Tenuously descended from Edward III, Robert Devereux (2nd Earl of Essex) had steadily emerged as the glittering star of the English court since the time of his arrival in 1584 and within three years had become Elizabeth I's unrivalled favourite. Tall, handsome, brave, ardent and flamboyant, possessing a remarkable capacity for self-dramatisation, which he demonstrated as both a flamboyant courtier and impetuous soldier, he was also the stepson of the Earl of Leicester, who perhaps had been the only man that the queen had ever loved until his death in 1588. But the same peacock brilliance, which made Essex so irresistible to the ageing and increasingly careworn and disillusioned queen, also carried with it an unruly spirit. 'The man's soul,' wrote the queen's godson Sir John Harington, 'seemeth tossed to and fro like the waves of a troubled sea.' And surely enough, while he could dazzle as romantic hero, blaze as dashing adventurer and sparkle as generous patron to writers and artists alike, he was nevertheless spoilt, vain and headstrong: a man incapable of moderation in either his behaviour – or his ambitions. Encouraged by his mother Lettice Knollys and his sister Penelope Rich, who had inspired Sir Philip Sidney's sonnet sequence *Astrophel and Stella*, he believed that by charming or sulking as occasion demanded, he could mould the queen to his will and prevail against those who opposed him.

Chief among these was Sir Robert Cecil who had by now succeeded his father, Lord Burghley, as Secretary of State. No man, in fact, could have presented a greater contrast to his adversary than Cecil to Essex. Immensely hardworking like his father, Sir Robert was, however, an altogether more complex and ambiguous figure than the man who both sired and reared him for high office. About 5ft 3in and suffering from a crooked back that may have resulted from being dropped by a nurse in infancy, the younger Cecil's infirmity seems to have made him all the more sensitive to the grace and panache of Elizabeth's courtiers, and left him curiously detached in spirit from the posturing of those around him. But while he was secretive and reserved by nature, he was also brilliantly clever – a perfect foil for Essex in all respects and someone bound, of course, for collision with him sooner rather than later. For not only were the two men so temperamentally at odds, they were also divided over the crucial political issue of the day: Essex, predictably enough, leading the war party at Elizabeth's court, and Cecil their opponents. In consequence, the late 1590s were dominated by their rivalry.

Towards the 'Land of Promise'

And it was into this political maelstrom that James now chose to slither. Already, from 1592 onwards, he had made a habit of dealing with Essex rather than Burghley when he had a cause to further at the English court, for no good reason other than his conviction that the latter had been responsible for delaying the pension promised to him by Elizabeth. In due course, indeed, the association had hardened into a dubious alliance of sorts, as Essex convinced him that only he and his friends would guarantee the English throne for him upon Elizabeth's death. It was, of course, an irresistible offer for one of James's impatience and anxieties. But as the relationship unfolded and Essex's own flaws became increasingly manifest, it was an offer that became more and more of a liability: so much so that before 1599 was out, Essex was hoping to oust his rivals at the English court by force, and indulge, with James's help – 'at a convenient time' – in a version of the old Scottish kidnapping game, involving the Queen of England herself.

As it transpired, the wayward earl had already quarrelled seriously with Elizabeth in 1598 when she unwisely decided to give him command of her army in Ireland. The result had been a mismanaged campaign, a disorderly and unauthorised truce with the Earl of Tyrone, and Essex's uninvited return to England. Early one morning in September 1599, moreover, he had forced an entry into the queen's bedchamber at Nonsuch Palace before she was properly wigged or gowned, ostensibly to justify his conduct, but possibly to force her to retain him in favour – in much the same way, curiously, that Bothwell had once coerced James. Arrested and condemned by the Privy Council for his truce with Tyrone and return to England which amounted, it was said, to a desertion of duty, Essex was nevertheless merely committed at first to the custody of Sir Richard Berkeley in his own York House before being convicted and deprived of public office – largely as a result of relentless pressure from Sir Walter Raleigh and Cecil – by an eighteen-man commission in June 1600.

In the interim, however, the earl was able not only to contact James but to ply him with schemes, misinformation and treacherous promises. On Christmas Day 1600, for example, he wrote concerning Cecil and his supporters. 'Now,' the letter runs, 'doth not only their corrupting of my servants, stealing of my papers, suborning of false witnesses, procuring of many forged letters in my name, and other such like practices against me appear; but their … juggling with our enemies, their practice for the Infanta of Spain, and their devilish plots with your Majesty's own subjects against your person and life ...' The clear implication, then, was that Cecil – to whom James himself referred as 'Mr Secretary, who is king there in effect' – was not only favouring another candidate for the succession but had secretly encouraged the Gowrie Plot. Around the same time, furthermore, James received assurances from an agent named Henry Leigh that Essex would tolerate no successor to the English throne other than the King of Scotland who should demand a public recognition of his right. Refusing to rebuff such dangerous baits outright, James replied cautiously that he 'would think of it and put himself in a readiness to take any good occasion'.

And as James temporised, Essex's allies grew bolder. In February 1600, indeed, Leigh came to Scotland once more – this time with a specific plan. The new commander of England's forces in Ireland, Lord Mountjoy, who was himself an intimate friend of Essex, would return with troops and join him in staging a coup at court, while James would gather an army on the Border and dispatch an ambassador to London to demand confirmation of his rights as heir. But whether James seriously entertained the proposal is, in fact, unclear. He had, it is true, been redoubling his efforts to increase his military strength throughout 1599 and on 1 May had ordered a grand muster or 'wapanschowing' and commanded his subjects to supply themselves with arms. In December, moreover, as well as in June of the following year, he had appealed for funds from the Scottish Parliament, only to be met with open derision at any suggestion that Scotland could pose any significant military threat to her southern neighbour, 'at which the king raged'. But while two confessions at Essex's eventual treason trial did imply that James's tardy response to Leigh's offer amounted to a rejection, even this must be balanced by the claim of Henry Wriothesley, Earl of Southampton, and someone on close terms with Essex, that the King of Scotland 'liked the course well and prepared himself for it'.

In all likelihood, James may well have been characteristically ambivalent – hedging his bets and accumulating as many cards in his hands as possible until they inevitably tumbled from his grasp for all to see. Certainly, the scheme was never realised, for when Essex called upon Mountjoy to deliver in the spring of 1600, the latter was already reversing English fortunes in Ireland with a brilliant campaign against Tyrone and duly refused. But even at this point, James was still not free from Essex's overtures as the earl's irrepressible ambition and declining fortunes led him inexorably to the ultimate and fatal gamble. In August, his freedom had been granted, but the main source of his income – the sweet wines monopoly – was not renewed, and he found himself moved 'from sorrow and repentance to rage and rebellion'. Accordingly, he summoned his followers to London in December, with a view to obtaining access to Elizabeth by force, driving Cecil and his other enemies from office, and summoning a parliament that would both endorse his action and recognise James as heir apparent.

This time, however, the King of Scots was not required to call his subjects to arms, but simply to send an ambassador to London by 1 February. 'You shall,' Essex promised, 'be declared and acknowledged the certain and undoubted successor to this Crown and shall command the services and lives of as many of us as undertake this great work.' For good measure, James was even sent a cypher, to be returned as proof of his acceptance, and so it was that the king's dabbling had finally brought him to the brink. Lacking the self-assurance to reject them outright, he had flirted with Essex's schemes and relied upon his skill at the double game to survive the brush with potential disaster. In consequence, the cypher was indeed returned, though no ambassadors made their way south at the appointed time, leaving Essex to stage his insane raid on 8 February and suffer the consequences. Blocked at Ludgate Hill by Sir John Leveson's barricade and forced to surrender soon afterwards, he was tried for treason eleven days later and executed on 25 February – the last man to be executed in the Tower of London. Thomas Derrick, the headsman, would require three strokes to complete the job, as Sir Walter Raleigh, it was said, watched the spectacle from a window on Tower Green, puffing out tobacco smoke in sight of the condemned man.

James, meanwhile, was said to have been 'in the dumps' when news reached him that Essex's rebellion had indeed gone ahead as planned, and by the time that his ambassadors – the Earl of Mar and Edward Bruce, Abbot of Kinloss – finally left for London in mid-March, their instructions had changed significantly. Now, for instance, while ascertaining whether a general rising against Elizabeth was still a possibility, they were to 'dally with the present guiders of the court' and tread the middle ground 'betwixt these two precipices of the queen and the people who now appear to be in so contrary terms'. They were to request, too, that Elizabeth issue a statement that the King of Scotland had taken no part in any rising – though the ambassadors, unlike James, fully realised that such a statement would not only never be granted, but amounted in any case to an effective acknowledgement of James's guilt. Repeatedly in March, on the other hand, James asked George Nicolson, the English ambassador in Scotland, whether he was being mentioned in the trials taking place in the aftermath of Essex's death, while making it clear to his ambassadors that if Cecil would not assist him, he should expect no favours in the future 'but all the queen's hard usage of me to be hereafter craven at his hands'.

Once again, though, James was tearing his hair needlessly. For in spite of his indiscretions, Elizabeth had little choice but to suppress all mention of the King of Scotland in what transpired. Unable to accuse him of conspiracy without excluding him from the succession and thereby opening wide once more the whole knotty issue of who should follow her, she actually accepted the inevitable in precisely the way that even Sir Robert Cecil now did, too. Summoning the Scottish ambassadors to the most secret of interviews the Secretary of State offered, under the most stringent of conditions, to correspond with their ruler and to promote his interests in England. With Essex cold in the ground and James coolly in his pocket, Cecil had ultimately been more than happy to oblige, and what James may or may not have promised Essex was now, in any case, an irrelevance. Before his defeat, the rebellious earl was said to have worn a letter from James in a black bag around his neck, and to have destroyed it along with his other papers before surrendering for the last time. Ashes were therefore all that remained, and from those ashes James's hopes were now revived and renewed.

There followed a truly remarkable secret dialogue between the King of Scotland and the very man who had appeared for so long to be the frustration of his hopes. At his trial, Essex had retracted his claims that Cecil favoured the succession of the Spanish infanta, and the final obstacle to James's trust was effectively cleared. Elizabeth's Secretary of State was soon offering, moreover, not only to support the King of Scotland's claim to the throne, but to advise and instruct him in preparation for it. Carefully constructing his letters to guarantee that no treasonable content could be found in them, Cecil referred to James's impending succession as 'that natural day ... wherein your feast may be lawfully proclaimed (which I do wish may be long deferred) ...' and went on 'to profess before God that if I could accuse myself to have once imagined a thought which could amount to a grain of error towards my dear and precious sovereign ... I should wish with all my heart, that all I have done, or shall do, might be converted to my own perdition.' But he also spoke of Elizabeth's tacit goodwill and assured him that he could rest secure 'as long as we see our way clear from lively apparitions of anticipation' – or, in other words, precisely the kind of intrigues that James had already been much too inclined to countenance.

Cecil showed his considerable shrewdness too by employing Lord Henry Howard to share with him the task of mentoring the future King of England. Mary Queen of Scots had, after all, been closely and tragically connected with Howard's elder brother, Thomas, Duke of Norfolk, who had been executed in 1572 for plotting to marry her. And although Lord Henry was now an elderly, bombastic and penurious Catholic sycophant who had little influence with Queen Elizabeth, he was nevertheless the most able member of a premier noble family, which, as Cecil rightly judged, made him altogether more appealing to James than the coterie of bellicose malcontents who had congregated around Essex. Henceforward Cecil, James and now Howard, too, would all correspond as numerical ciphers – 10, 30 and 3 respectively – easing the way for James's eventual takeover, while continuing to hide their dealings from the existing queen. 'The subject itself,' wrote Cecil, 'is so perilous to touch amongst us as it setteth a mark upon his head forever that hatcheth such a bird.' And now, of course, the dwarfish Secretary of State, with his long, delicate hands, high white forehead and darkly piercing eyes could do no wrong in James's mind. 'My dearest and trusty Cecil,' wrote James, 'my pen is not able to express how happy I think myself for having chanced upon so worthy, so wise and so provident a friend.'

All was now sweetness and light too in James's relationship with Elizabeth. He had been warned by Cecil 'to secure the heart of the highest' by 'clear and temperate courses' and to avoid for this reason 'either needless expostulations or over much curiosity in her own actions'. Instead of the petulant and jibing tone of his former letters, therefore, he now consulted her as an oracle and commended her in his letters as that 'richt excellent, richt heich and michtie princess, our dearest sister and cousin'. More importantly still, he committed himself to securing the English Crown by patience alone. 'It were very small wisdom,' he told the Earl of Northumberland, 'by climbing of ditches and hedges for pulling of unripe fruit to hazard the breaking of my neck, when by a little patience and by abiding the season I may with far more ease and safety enter at the gate of the garden and enjoy the fruits at my pleasure.' And when a doughty Scottish laird drank in his presence to the speedy union of the Crowns, declaring that he had forty muskets ready for the king's use, he was promptly and roundly reproved.

In the meantime, James's mind was steadily moulded by both Cecil and Howard. But it was the latter, above all, whose darker side now surfaced most sordidly. Howard possessed, in fact, a deeply flawed but brilliant intellect which had already displayed its twists and shortcomings more than conclusively. Quite apart from periods of poverty he had, in fairness, experienced other reverses too that might well have taken their toll on men of altogether worthier fibre – at one point even 'suffering the utmost misery' in the Fleet Prison after publishing in 1583 his *Preservative Against the Poison of Supposed Prophecies*, which in addition to attacking astrology also contained allegedly treasonous passages. But he was nevertheless a paid pensioner of Spain, receiving 1,000 crowns annually from the Spanish ambassador, and now wheedled his way into James's trust by both lies and the grossest and most odious forms of flattery that Elizabeth had never fallen for. Henceforth, for instance, James would readily believe Howard's claim that Sir Walter Raleigh, along with Lord Cobham and the Earl of Northumberland, was one of 'a diabolical triplicity' of wicked plotters, hatching treasons from cockatrice eggs that were 'daily and nightly sitten on'.

By such slanders, then, Raleigh was already hopelessly compromised before James's reign in England began, and by such murky counsels, creeping schemes and fulsome flattery did James's 'long approved and trusty Howard' secure a place of prominence at the new king's table when Elizabeth's reign finally ended. Nor would his wait be a long one. For the queen who James had once complained seemed likely to outlive the sun and moon, was showing every visible sign of her own mortality. 'The tallest of ruffs,' it was said, 'could not conceal it, the most glittering of diamonds could not overpower it; voice, action, attitude all disclosed it ...'

10 ✤ Scotland's King of England

'Forasmuch as it has pleased Almighty God to call to his mercy, out of this transitory life, our Sovereign Lady the high and mighty Princess Elizabeth, late Queen of England, France and Ireland, by whose death and dissolution the Imperial Realms aforesaid are come absolutely, wholly and solely to the high and mighty Prince James the Sixth, King of Scotland …'

Opening lines of a proclamation read by Sir Robert Cecil at the High Cross in Cheapside on the morning of 24 March 1603

It was in January 1603 that Queen Elizabeth had first developed a bad cold and been advised by Dr Dee, her astrologer, to move from Whitehall to Richmond – the warmest of her palaces – on what would prove to be 'a filthy rainy and windy day'. Once there, it seems, she refused all medicine and, as the Earl of Northumberland informed King James in Scotland, her physicians were soon concluding 'that if this continue she must needs fall into a distemper, not a frenzy but rather into dullness and lethargy'. The death on 25 February of her cousin and close confidante the Countess of Nottingham had only served to compound her illness with grief, and while all Scotland stirred in happy anticipation of her demise, the queen merely reclined on floor cushions, refusing Robert Cecil's instructions that she take to her bed. 'Little man,' she had told him, 'the word must is not to be used to princes.' She was 69, plagued with fever, worn by worldly cares and frustrations, and dying – so that even she was forced at last to accede to her secretary's pleas. Then, in the bedraggled early hours of 24 March, as the queen's laboured breathing slackened further, Father Weston – a Catholic priest imprisoned at that time in the Tower – noted how 'a strange silence descended on the whole City of London … not a bell rang out, not a bugle sounded'. Her council was in attendance and, at Cecil's frantic request that she provide a sign of acceptance of James as her successor, she was said to have complied at last.

At Richmond Palace, on the eve of Lady Day, Elizabeth I had therefore finally put paid to her successor's interminable agonising and on that same morning of her death Sir Robert Carey, who had once conveyed her pallid excuses for the demise of Mary Queen of Scots to King James, was now dispatched north with altogether more welcome tidings. Leaving at mid-morning and bearing at his breast a sapphire ring that was the prearranged proof of the queen's demise, Carey had covered 162 miles before he slept that night at Doncaster. Next day, further relays of horses, all carefully prepared in advance, guaranteed that he covered another 136 miles along the ill-kept track known as the Great North Road linking the capitals of the two kingdoms. After a further night at Widdrington in Northumberland, which was his own home, the saddle-weary rider set out on the last leg of his journey, hoping to be with James by supper time, but receiving 'a great fall by the way' which resulted in both his delay and 'a great blow on the head' from one of his horse's hoofs 'that made me shed much blood'. Nevertheless, 'be-blooded and bruised', he was in Edinburgh that evening and though the 'king was newly gone to bed', the messenger was hurriedly conveyed to the royal bedchamber. There, said Carey, 'I kneeled by him, and saluted him by his title of England, Scotland, France and Ireland', in response to which 'he gave me his hand to kiss and bade me welcome'.

James had dwelt upon the potential difficulties of the succession for so long, however, that he could scarcely credit the ease with which it appeared to be taking place and wasted no time in consolidating his position. To the very last, of course, Elizabeth had made no official acknowledgement of the King of Scotland as her heir, and until he had taken physical possession of his new realm, his fear of invasion or insurrection remained tangible. The day after Carey's arrival, therefore, the Abbot of Holyrood was urgently dispatched to take possession of Berwick – the gateway to the south – and within a week, as his English councillors pressed him to make haste, plans for James's transfer to London were complete. Summoning those nobles who could be contacted in the time available, he placed the government in the hands of his Scottish council and confirmed the custody of his children to those already entrusted with them. Likewise, his heir, Prince Henry, was offered words of wisdom upon his new status as successor to the throne of England. 'Let not this news make you proud or insolent,' James informed the boy, 'for a king's son and heir was ye before, and no more are ye yet. The augmentation that is hereby like to fall unto you is but in cares and heavy burdens; be therefore merry but not insolent.' Queen Anne, meanwhile, being pregnant, was to follow the king when convenient, though this would not be long, for she miscarried soon afterwards in the wake of a violent quarrel with the Earl of Mar's mother, once again involving the custody of her eldest son – whereupon James finally relented and allowed the boy to be handed over to her at Holyrood House prior to their joining him in London.

Before his own departure, however, James had certain other snippets of business to attend to. On Sunday 3 April, for instance, he attended the High Kirk of St Giles in Edinburgh to deliver 'a most learned, but more loving oration', in which he exhorted his subjects to continue in 'obedience to him, and agreement amongst themselves'. There was a public promise, too, that he would return to Scotland every three years – though he would ultimately do so only once, in 1617 – and a further suggestion that his subjects should take heart upon his departure, since he had already settled 'both kirk and kingdom'. All that remained thereafter was a plea to the council for money, since he had barely sufficient funds to get him past the Border, and a series of meetings with both English officials on the one hand and a mounting flood of suitors already seeking lavish rewards and promises. In the first category, came Sir Thomas Lake, Cecil's secretary, who was sent north to report the king's first thoughts as he became acquainted with English affairs, and the Dean of Canterbury, who was hastily dispatched to ascertain James's plans for the Church of England. To the second belonged a teeming, self-seeking throng. 'There is much posting that way,' wrote John Chamberlain, an eagle-eyed contemporary reporter of public and private gossip, 'and many run thither of their own errand, as if it were nothing else but come first served, or that preferment were a goal to be got by footmanship'.

In the event, James's progress south might well have dazzled many a more phlegmatic mind than his, since it was one unbroken tale of rejoicing, praise and adulation. Entering Berwick on 6 April in the company of a throng of Border chieftains, he was greeted by the loudest salute of cannon fire in any soldier's memory and presented with a purse of gold by the town's Recorder. His arrival, after all, represented nothing less than the end of an era on the Anglo-Scottish border. In effect, a frontier which had been the source of bitter and continual dispute over five centuries had been finally transformed by nothing more than an accident of birth, and no outcome of James's kingship before or after would be of such long-term significance. That a King of Scotland, attended by the wardens of the Marches from both sides of the Border, should enter Berwick peacefully amid cries of approval was almost inconceivable – and yet it was now a reality for the onlookers whose forebears' lives had been so disrupted and dominated by reprisal raids and outright warfare.

Nor did a sudden rainstorm the following day dampen the king's spirits. The sun before the rain, he declared, represented his happy departure, the rain the grief of Scotland, and the subsequent fair weather the joy of England at his approach. Such, in fact, was his keenness to press forward into his new kingdom that his stop in Northumberland at Sir Robert Carey's Widdrington Castle was deliberately cut short. For he departed, we are told, 'upon the spur, scarce any of his train being able to keep him company', and rode nearly 40 miles in less than four hours. Pausing to slay two fat deer along the way – 'the game being so fair before him, he could not forbear' – he rested over Sunday at Newcastle, and heard a sermon by Tobie Mathew, Bishop of Durham, with whom he joked and jested in high humour. Indeed, the urbane, serene world of the Anglican episcopacy, which so happily combined theological soundness with a proper deference for royal authority could not have been more agreeable to James. Received at the bishop's palace by 100 gentlemen in tawny liveries, he was treated at dinner to a fine diet of delicious food and Mathew's own unique brand of learning, humanity and worldly wisdom, which would bring the bishop considerable rewards three years later when he found himself Archbishop of York and Lord President of the Council of the North. Even before the king left next morning, moreover, Mathew's bishopric had already recovered much alienated property, including Durham House in the Strand, which had been granted previously to Sir Walter Raleigh.

By the time that James entered York on 14 April, however, he had already found much else about his new kingdom to impress him. Above all, he was struck by the apparent richness of a land he was visiting for the first time and knew only by reputation. The abundance of the countryside, the splendour of the great mansions, the extensive parklands through which he travelled, even the quaintness of the villages scattered along his route all proclaimed the contrast with Scotland. Everything, indeed, seemed to lift James into a heady state of expectation after the rigours of his rule in Scotland. According to the eminent lawyer and Master of Requests Sir Roger Wilbraham, the king travelled onwards 'all his way to London entertained with great solemnity and state, all men rejoicing that his lot and their lot had fallen in so good a ground. He was met with great troops of horse and waited on by the sheriff and gentlemen of each shire, in their limits; joyfully received in every city and town; presented with orations and gifts; entertained royally all the way by noblemen and gentlemen at their houses …'. But the same observer's concerns about what might be awaiting England's new king in the longer term were more revealing still. 'I pray unfeignedly,' wrote Wilbraham, 'that his most gracious disposition and heroic mind be not depraved with ill-counsel, and that neither the wealth and peace of England make him forget God, nor the painted flattery of the court cause him to forget himself.'

And the scale of 'painted flattery' on offer to James, both now and later, was greater by far than anything he had experienced before. Elizabeth I, of course, had skilfully nourished the cult of her own personality. Symbolically represented as a virgin goddess – variously named Gloriana, Belphoebe, Astraea, Cynthia, Diana – she had been the object of much poetic worship. But sober statesmen, no less than poets like Edmund Spenser and Ben Jonson, had also observed the convention of addressing James's predecessor as though she were indeed a goddess. In 1592, for instance, Cecil had referred to the 'sacred lines' of a letter written by the queen, before going on to eulogise her 'more than human perfection'. Now, moreover, as the king continued his journey through England, he would hear in a continual series of panegyrics, similar words which seemed to conform so closely to the theories of kingship that he himself had expressed with such conviction in *The Trew Law of Free Monarchies* and *Basilikon Doron*. 'Hail, mortal God, England's true joy!' ran John Savile's poem, written to salute James upon his acquisition of his new realm.

At York, in particular, he experienced the full gust of exultation at his new status. Initially, at least, his English privy councillors had not planned to supply him with the full trappings of royalty until he had passed through the north of the country and reached Burghley in Nottinghamshire where they were due to meet him for the first time. It was true, too, that up to this point when warm and spontaneous welcomes had been the norm, James's lack of natural dignity had actually been an asset of sorts. His talkativeness and familiarity, and above all his easy, impulsive generosity had been enough to create a favourable impression upon his new subjects. But York was a different matter and James had insisted quite correctly that he enter 'our second city' with appropriate solemnity and magnificence, so that by the time of his arrival on 16 April he was suitably equipped with jewels, regalia, heralds, trumpeters and men-at-arms – though at the King's Manor where he was lodging prior to his entry, he had refused a coach. 'I will have no coach,' he declared, 'for the people are desirous to see a king, and so they shall, for they shall see his body and his face.' Nor, it seems, was he prepared to swap his shabby doublet – specially padded for protection against an assassin's dagger – for a more elegant garment, as he appears to have been wearing it at his first meeting with Sir Robert Cecil, who finally greeted him in York on 18 April.

Cecil had made the journey north, full of his usual cares and perplexity, and troubled in particular by financial affairs and rumours that complaints from Ireland had reached the king's ears. Yet James, it seems, was more concerned with the details of his own journey to London than with weightier matters, and after delivering a jovial greeting and confirming Cecil's ongoing role as Secretary of State, proceeded to his main concerns. He was worried, for instance, that his arrival in the capital might coincide with Elizabeth's funeral – an event he otherwise declined to discuss, since he had a horror of all things relating to death and dissolution. And he was equally anxious to ensure that his coronation did not occur before the arrival of his wife. Indeed, like the lucky lottery winner he was, James became wholly absorbed in the here and now, and in the process allowed his excitement, as so often, to spill over into a characteristic display of rough-hewn humour and familiarity that is unlikely to have been wholly to Cecil's taste. Already dubbed by Elizabeth her 'Pygmy', the secretary became known at once to James as his 'Little Beagle'. 'Though you be but a little man,' James told him, 'we shall surely load your shoulders with business.'

Yet by the time he parted from the king to attend Queen Elizabeth's funeral on 28 April, Cecil had been suitably impressed, recording that James's 'virtues were so eminent as by my six days' kneeling at his feet I have made so sufficient a discovery of royal perfections as I contemplate greater felicity to this isle than ever it enjoyed'. The fact that his new master had already made his first requests for money to the council may have escaped Cecil's attention at this stage, as indeed the additional appeal for jewels and ladies-in-waiting for Queen Anne may have done. Certainly, the king had already laid down that new coins were to be minted, one side of which would join the arms of Scotland to those of his other kingdoms and declare the Latin legend, *Exsurgat Deus Dissipentur Inimici* – 'Let God arise and His enemies be scattered'. And this was only to be expected. But whether Cecil had already begun to guess at the extent to which such coins would soon be slipping through his new master's fingers is a matter of conjecture, for even by the time he reached York, the early signs of extravagance were plain for all to see.

James's journey had already been punctuated, as might be expected, by prolonged and princely civic entertainments, as well as hunting and feasting in the great country houses through which he passed. It had been conducted, too, amidst a growing shower of royal gifts and knighthoods. But by the time the royal progress reached York, matters had become almost unmanageable. For while James had set out with a representative selection of Scottish nobles and an appropriate train of English and Scottish courtiers and officials, numbers were soon swelling as north-bound English place-hunters and impoverished Scots hurrying south for rich pickings, converged from all points of the compass to create a disorderly rabble of more than 1,000 greedy souls. Newcastle had shouldered the whole charge of the royal household for three days and York for two more. But now increasingly the burden fell on private estates like that of Sir Edward Stanhope at Grimstone Hall who extended 'most bountiful entertainment' to 'all comers' – 'every man' eating 'without check' and 'drinking at leisure'.

Nor were desultory attempts to stem the hordes effective. Proclamations ordering home all Scots not in immediate attendance upon the king, and restraining 'the concourse of idle and unnecessary posters' were, for instance, largely ineffectual – not least because James's carefree distribution of gifts, grants and favours continued unabated. The bestowal of knighthoods, for example, which had been so carefully restricted by Elizabeth I was now conducted more and more casually, so that by the time he reached London, James had delivered the title to less than 300 individuals. During the entire forty-five years of the former queen's reign, in fact, only 878 men had been knighted, while in the first months alone of James's reign, there were 906 such promotions. The landlord of the Bear Inn at Doncaster, meanwhile, received the lease of a valuable royal manor as reward for one good night's entertainment. And thus the locust horde continued to swell, consuming all that came in its path and placing an intolerable strain even on such great households as the Earl of Shrewsbury's at Worksop and Lord Rutland's at Belvoir, not to mention the equally impressive resources of a certain Sir Oliver Cromwell at Hinchingbrooke in Huntingdonshire.

Cromwell was uncle, ironically enough, to the future Lord Protector that he eventually came to loathe, and had married the widow of the immensely rich Italian-born financier Sir Horatio Bavarino, whose wealth he had subsequently chosen to lavish in an apparently ceaseless quest for popularity. Now, however, he seems to have exceeded all expectation in terms of both the quality and range of entertainment he provided for the king. Certainly, the dinner provided for James's entourage may well have been the best of the whole journey – 'such plenty and variety of meats, such diversity of wines, and those not riffe ruffe, but ever the best of their kind; and the cellars open at any man's pleasure'. But there were other treats, too, to whet the new king's broader appetites. The Vice-Chancellor of Cambridge University, for instance, along with the heads of the colleges, all attended James, bringing a present of books and proferring speeches and poems of welcome. And just beyond Hinchingbrooke, at Godmanchester, seventy ploughing teams were carefully drawn up, not merely to see the king upon his way, but to emphasise once more the prosperity of his new kingdom.

Nor, it seems, were such displays of goodwill anything less that heartfelt. Just before Worksop, for example, 'there appeared a number of huntsmen all in green; the chief of which, with a woodman's speech, did welcome him', leaving the king, we are told, 'very much delighted'. All the way from Sir John Harington's house to Stamford, moreover, 'Sir John's best hounds with good mouths followed the game, the king taking great leisure and pleasure in the same'. And though James blundered at Newark-on-Trent by ordering that a cut-purse be hanged without trial, he generally charmed and responded in kind as only he probably could. He spoke lovingly, for instance, to Sir Henry Leigh, an honourable old knight, who presented himself 'with sixty gallant men' wearing yellow scarves embroidered with the words Constantia et fede. Even a fall from his horse near Burghley, which led Mayerne, his physician, to suggest that he had broken his collarbone, could not stem his enthusiasm or stifle his will to please. Perhaps, indeed,

James would never again feel so entirely and satisfactorily a king as during the three weeks of his journey. With no financial restraints in place and the pressure of state affairs still in front of him, he was able to pose as what he had always wished to be in Scotland – the beneficent, affable, patriarchal dispenser of largesse and justice, responsible only to God for the welfare of a grateful and pliable realm.

And, in the meantime, the fact that James's winning words and lofty promises would one day have to be made good continued, it seems, to elude him. 'Nor shall it ever be blotted out of my mind,' the king would tell his first Parliament, 'how at my first entry into this kingdom the people of all sorts rid and ran, nay rather flew to meet me.' But the resulting effusiveness and spontaneity on his part would come at a price. It was all too tempting, of course, to assure the mayor and aldermen of Hull that they should be 'relieved and succoured against the daily spoils done to them' by Dunkirk pirates, regardless of the naval expenditure involved in properly securing England's lengthy coastline, or to earn popularity cheaply by promising 'their hearts' desire' to Huntingdonshire folk, complaining of the enclosure of their land by a certain Sir John Spencer. Likewise, when 1,000 Puritan brethren presented their so-called 'Millenary Petition', the king could graciously offer to consider and redress their grievances without any real appreciation that English Puritans might prove just as intractable in their own way as their Presbyterian counterparts within the Scottish Kirk.

But when James arrived on the outskirts of London at Theobalds, the home of Sir Robert Cecil, his new kingdom was already dowsed in heady expectation and primed for later disappointment, even if, for the time being, the general euphoria continued. At the border of Middlesex, he had been greeted by 'three score men in fair livery cloaks', before meeting the Lord Mayor and aldermen, accompanied by 500 prominent citizens, all on horseback and clad in velvet cloaks and chains of gold. And by this time the crowds of common people were becoming so dense that when one observer tried to count them, he could not do so, declaring that each blade of grass had become a man. At Stamford Hill, indeed, a humble cart owner was able to charge eight groats for the use of his vehicle as a grandstand for no more than a quarter of an hour. 'The multitude of people in highways, fields, meadows, closes and on trees were such that they covered the beauty of the fields,' wrote John Nichols, 'and so greedy were they to behold the countenance of the king that with much unruliness some even hazarded to the danger of death.' Ultimately, James would have no choice but to avoid the roads on his way to the Charterhouse, where he was entertained for three days by Lord Thomas Howard and saw fit to create a further 130 knights.

But what should have been the climax of the entire trip – James's state entry into the City of London – proved something of an anti-climax, since the death rate from the plague had risen to twenty a day and the king could only skirt the city in a closed coach to Whitehall and inspect the capital from the river on his way to the Tower. There followed, moreover, a further two months of maddening delay while the daily toll of plague victims rose to 700 to 800, and James was left to shuttle uneasily from Greenwich and back to Whitehall, prior to a trip to Windsor, where he presided over a chapter of the Order of the Garter, and a tour of some of the better-stocked deer parks of the home counties. The plague, observed Cecil, 'drives us up and down so round, as I think we shall come to York.' And the king, in the meantime, gave little time to official business. 'Sometimes he comes to council,' wrote Thomas Wilson, an author whom Cecil had been employing as a foreign intelligencer, 'but most time he spends in fields and parks and chases, chasing away idleness by violent exercise and early rising.'

In the end, James's state entry into the City would have to be delayed until the following spring. But the coronation could not wait so long, and the queen was duly summoned from Scotland, causing another northward flood of interested court folk. The 13-year-old Lady Anne Clifford, who was only one of those many noble wayfarers frantically traversing the Great North Road around this time, had already met the king at Theobalds where she, her mother and her aunt had been 'used very graciously' by him, notwithstanding the fact that she had noticed 'a great change between the fashion of the court as it is now and of that in the queen's time, for we were all lousy by sitting in the chamber of Sir Thomas Erskine'. Presently, however, she was in headlong motion once again, recording in her celebrated diary how she and her mother killed three horses in their haste to intercept the queen, and noting that near Windsor, where James eventually met his wife, 'there was such an infinite number of lords and ladies and so great a court as I think I shall never see the like again'.

Even so, the coronation that occurred on 25 July, the feast of St James the Great, was shorn of its usual splendour. By this time, as many as 30,000 Londoners had succumbed to the plague and Prince Henry had been sent to Oatlands near Weybridge in Surrey to avoid infection. 'By reason of God's visitation for our sins,' noted one commentator, 'the plague and pestilence there reigning in the City of London … the king rode not from the Tower through the city in the royal manner …' The pageants in their turn were postponed until the New Year, which was probably for the best as the day was further blighted by pouring rain. And to add the general gloom, the ceremony itself would take place in a sadly empty Abbey, since any concourse of people was forbidden, and nobles and dignitaries were severely limited in the numbers of attendants they brought − an earl, whose rank normally entailed a following of at least 150 for a London visit, being allowed only sixteen, and those of humbler station proportionately less. Among the other more mournful details of the occasion was the queen's refusal to accept Holy Communion according to the Anglican rite from Archbishop Whitgift of Canterbury and James's less than majestic response to Philip Herbert, Earl of Montgomery, who had already established himself as the king's first English favourite. For when the earl flouted tradition by kissing his sovereign as he paid homage, James showed no sign of displeasure but merely tapped him on the cheek indulgently.

By the time that James and his queen set out on a tour of the southern counties shortly afterwards, there were already signs that the brief honeymoon period of the succession was rapidly waning. Royal progresses were, of course, an essential means of popularising the monarchy and maintaining links between king and kingdom. But they were also exceedingly expensive, as James's initial journey from Edinburgh to London had demonstrated, and only the monarchy's ancient right to requisition horses and vehicles and fix low prices for the purchase of local produce made these lavish journeyings feasible at all. Even as he reached the capital in May there were murmurs against the 'general, extreme, unjust and crying oppression' of 'cart takers and purveyors', who, as Parliament was soon to point out, 'have rummaged and ransacked since your Majesty's coming in far more than under your royal progenitors'. The fact was that James had already spent £10,000 on his initial journey south and literally given away another £14,000 in gifts of various kinds at a time when Queen Elizabeth's funeral had already cost £17,000 and the outstanding debt resulting from the Irish campaign stood at £400,000. Before long, in fact, Cecil would be writing anxiously to the Earl of Shrewsbury about his royal master's spending in general. 'Our sovereign,' he observed, 'spends £100,000 yearly on his house, which was wont to be but £50,000. Now think what the country feels, and so much for that.'

Another spate of hunting, banqueting, masques and pageants, however necessary in terms of conventions and expectations, was therefore bound to carry with it political as well as purely financial costs, particularly if the king's extravagance were to continue in the longer term – which, indeed, it did. The habit of idleness formed in those early months when plague had kept him out of London was quick to take root, moreover, for after one month of bickering with his first parliament, he had gone off to hunt and left the management of the rest of the session to Cecil. And when official business followed him, he reacted testily. When, for instance, a swarm of local petitioners troubled him with pleas on behalf of nonconforming clergy and what Chamberlain termed 'foolish prophecies of dangers to ensue', James did not hesitate to summon the council to Northampton, with the result that the shell-shocked petitioners were summarily hauled up and rebuked for opposing the king in a manner that was deemed to be 'little less than treason'.

Nor, it seems, was James so inclined to play to the crowds in public or revel in the limelight of official ceremonies once his coronation was finally over. Upon his entry into London, we are told, he had 'sucked in their gilded oratory, though never so nauseous, but afterwards in his public appearances, especially in his sports, the access of the people made him so impatient that he often dispersed them with frowns, that we may not say with curses'. Henceforth, if Thomas Wilson is to be believed, the people missed the affability of their dead queen, since the new ruler 'naturally did not love to be looked on, and the formalities of State but so many burdens to him'. And Wilson was not the only one to suggest as much, for Sir John Oglander observed that the king would now swear with passion when told by his attendants that the people had come of love to see his royal person. 'Then,' said Oglander, 'he would cry out in Scottish, "God's wounds! I will put down my breeches and they shall also see my arse!"'

Yet if James's improvidence and disaffection with some of the more irksome niceties of kingship were already emerging, other facets of his personality continued to create favourable first impressions with many who served him. 'He is very facile,' wrote Sir Thomas Lake, 'using no great majesty nor solemnity in his accesses, but witty to conceive and very ready of speech.' Sir Roger Wilbraham, meanwhile, observed that 'the king is of sharpest wit and invention, ready and pithy speech and exceeding good memory; of the sweetest, pleasantest and best nature that ever I knew; desiring nor affecting anything but honour'. And even the critical eye of Sir Francis Bacon, while quietly hinting at certain vices and indiscretions, remained generally positive about the new King of England during his first interview with him at Broxbourne. In a letter to the Earl of Northumberland, Bacon found James to be 'a prince farthest from the appearance of vainglory that may be'. 'His speech,' Bacon continued, 'is swift and cursory, and in the full dialect of his country; and in the point of business short; in point of discourse large.' Moreover, while he was considered 'somewhat general in his favours', it was also observed that 'his virtue of access is rather because he is much abroad and in press than that he giveth easy audience about serious things'. On the whole, then, there was much praise for James's nimble mind, his loquacity, his affable and homely manner, his good nature and his apparent virtue.

And equally favourable impressions were recorded in the observations of many foreigners. 'The King of England,' wrote the Venetian ambassador, 'is very prudent, able in negotiation, capable of dissimulating his feelings. He is said to be personally timid and averse from war. I hear on all sides that he is a man of letters and business, fond of the chase and of riding, sometimes indulging in play. These qualities attract men to him and render him acceptable to the aristocracy. Besides English, he speaks Latin and French perfectly and understands Italian quite well. He is capable of governing, being a prince of culture above the common.' Even James's physical appearance had its share of admirers, it seems. 'The king's countenance is handsome, noble and jovial,' wrote another Italian, 'his colour blond, his hair somewhat the same, his beard square and lengthy, his mouth small his eyes blue, his nose curved and clear-cut, a man happily formed, neither fat nor thin, of full vitality, neither too large nor small.'

James's carriage and bearing, meanwhile, were far from universally berated. At his first audience with the king in May 1603, the Venetian ambassador 'found all the council about his chair, and an infinity of other lords almost in an attitude of adoration'. Dressed 'in grey silver satin, quite plain, with a cloak of black tabbinet reaching below his knees and lined with crimson', the ambassador also noted that 'he had his arm in a sling, the result of a fall from his horse'. But no mention was made of any lack of grace or manners, and though 'from his dress he would have been taken for the meanest among his courtiers', we hear, too, that this was only the result of 'a modesty he affects'. Nor, for that matter, was such modesty merely a matter of public posturing. On the contrary, James's ability to relate informally and humanely to lesser mortals would remain in evidence long after his early courting of the crowds had begun to wane. Indeed, one of his most sentimental attachments, it seems, was eventually formed with Robin, an old keeper of Theobalds Park, who would make him presents of thrushes and blackbirds' nests and endeared himself to the king by his 'plain, honest and bold speech'.

There were times, it is true, when James's penchant for the common touch crossed the borders of seemliness and decorum, and detracted from the distance and respect properly associated with genuine majesty. Among many trivial, but nonetheless awkward instances of the king's excessive exuberance and over-familiarity was his tendency to visit newly-wed couples after their first night together, even lying on the bridal bed and quizzing the couple on what had passed. When, for instance, his favourite Sir Philip Herbert, whom he had recently created Earl of Montgomery, married the Lady Susan de Vere in Whitehall during 1604, the king was overcome by boyish high spirits as all fashionable London celebrated the event. Giving the bride away 'in her tresses and trinkets', the king, wrote Sir Dudley Carleton, proudly declared that 'if he were unmarried, he would not give her, but keep her himself'. It was a fatherly and endearing comment wholly in keeping with the joy and light-heartedness of the occasion. But whether James's behaviour was quite so appropriate next morning is rather more debatable, for 'the king', John Chamberlain tells us, 'in his shirt and nightgown gave Philip Herbert and his bride a reveille-matin before they were up and spent a good time in or upon the bed, choose which you will'. The fact that Chamberlain commented upon the event and that, more importantly still, the incident had come to his attention in the first place suggests, at the very least, that James's behaviour had once again been less than apt.

Nevertheless, the classic caricature of James, traditionally attributed to Sir Anthony Weldon, stands in stark – and largely unconvincing – contrast to most contemporary descriptions of the man. Weldon came, in fact, from a family that had long associations with the royal household and had served in his own capacity as Clerk of the Green Cloth, auditing accounts and organising the household's travel arrangements. He had, moreover, clearly prosecuted his role effectively, since he was knighted for his efforts, before losing his job, it has always been suggested, in deeply embarrassing circumstances. According to the usual account, he had written an unpleasantly satirical account of the Scots, which subsequently fell into the king's hands when it became carelessly mixed up with official papers. In consequence, even though the king granted him a small pension after his dismissal, Weldon, we are told, apparently went on to pen his famous portrait, *The Court and Character of James I*, although his responsibility for the work is not as certain as is often assumed, since it was not actually credited to him until after his death in 1648 when anti-Stuart feeling was at its height. Curiously, too, the work which allegedly provoked James to sack Weldon – *A Perfect Description of the People and Country of Scotland* – was actually published six years beforehand.

In any event, the description supplied by *The Court and Character of James I* certainly gained currency across the centuries. The king, it suggests, was 'of middle stature, more corpulent through his clothes than in his body, yet fat enough, his clothes ever being made large and easy, the doublets quilted for stiletto proof, his breeches in pleats and full stuffed'. Thus derives the classic picture of a timorous and suspicious monarch, padding his clothing against assassin's knives and pistol shots, 'his eye large, ever rolling after any stranger come into his presence, in so much as many for shame have left the room, as being out of countenance'. We hear, too, of those physically unprepossessing images of the king that have always been so closely associated with him. His beard, in Weldon's account, was 'very thin' and 'his tongue too large for his mouth, which ever made him drink very uncomely', while his skin was 'as soft as taffeta sarsnet, which fell so, because he never washed his hands, only rubbed his finger ends slightly with the wet-end of a napkin'. The king's legs, in their turn, were very weak, 'having as was thought some foul play in his youth, or rather before he was born', with the result that he was 'ever leaning on other men's shoulders'. And his walk was 'ever circular' – 'his fingers ever in that walk fiddling about his cod-piece'.

According to this account, James was also somewhat intemperate in his use of alcohol – with a particular liking, it seems, for 'Frontiniack, Canary, high country wine, tent wine and Scottish ale' – though he was seldom drunk, since he had a 'very strong brain'. 'He naturally loved not the sight of a soldier, nor of any valiant man', the account continues, 'and was crafty and cunning in petty things', and though he was 'infinitely inclined to peace, it was more out of fear than conscience'. 'Wise in small things, but a fool in weighty affairs', he was, we hear, 'very liberal of what he had not in his own grip, and would rather part with £100 he never had in his keeping than one twenty shilling piece within his own custody'. Yet he was 'constant in all things (his favourites excepted)' and 'had as many ready witty jests as any man living, at which he would not smile himself, but deliver them in a grave and serious manner'. 'In a word,' the account concludes, 'take him altogether and not in pieces, such a king I wish this kingdom have never any worse, on the condition, not any better, for he lived in peace, died in peace, and left all his kingdoms in a peaceable condition, with his own motto: *Beati Pacifici* [Blessed are the Peacemakers].'

Whether all this amounted to a species of character assassination in the way that many later authorities came to accept, is perhaps debatable – not merely in terms of the accuracy of the author's claims, but more importantly still, perhaps, in terms of his work's tone. This, after all, was said to be a king who, apart from being a peacemaker, 'loved good laws and had many made in his time' – hardly the kind of declaration that might be expected from a slighted hatchet-wielder. There is no denying, of course, that Sir William Sanderson in his *Aulicus Coquinariae: or a Vindication in Answer to a Pamphlet entitled the Court and Character of King James* (1650) suggested that the author, whom he considered to be Weldon, had later disowned the work 'which with some regret of what he had maliciously writ', he had 'intended to the fire' before 'it was since stolen to the press out of a ladies closet'. But the eleven-page pamphlet remains, perhaps, more sinned against than sinning – more maligned for its supposed subjectivity than any real malignity it actually directed at James himself. That it is a caricature is beyond dispute, but like all successful caricatures it may well have captured more of the essence of the man than it is often credited for. And even if Weldon was indeed the author and carried the grudge for which he is charged, grounds for grievance need not necessarily entail outright ill will. Nor, in the grand scheme of things, can he be said to have exacted his vengeance especially cruelly.

Certainly, some of James's most telling flaws are left unexplored – one of which was his susceptibility to the very 'painted flattery' of which Sir Roger Wilbraham had spoken. Upon his succession, he had passed at once from the brusque and often insolent frankness of his Scottish homeland to the altogether more obsequious conventions of a highly sophisticated court. And unlike the chisel-tongued nobles and ministers of his other kingdom, Cecil was only one among many who now addressed him in terms of the deepest deference, while the likes of Henry Howard grovelled unashamedly. For Howard, in particular, the king was 'your resplendent Majesty', the sun itself – sacred, peerless, wise and learned – and with such a flow of adulation to confirm the king's opinion of his exalted status, it was not long before ceremonies discarded by the former queen now began to reappear once more. An early medal struck in his honour had already borne the title *Caesar Caesorum* ['Caesar of Caesars'], but before long the Venetian ambassador was observing how 'they are introducing the ancient splendours of the English court and almost adoring his majesty, who day by day adopts the practices suitable to his greatness'. State dinners at which the nobility served the king on bended knee – 'a splendid and unwonted sight' – now became increasingly common, while a flood of eulogistic verses flowed with regularity from the pens of Henry Petowe, Samuel Rowlands and Anthony Nixon. 'The very poets with their idle pamphlets,' wrote John Chamberlain, 'promise themselves great favour.'

Even more unfamiliar to James – and equally intoxicating – was the lavish praise heaped upon him by the English clergy. Bullied and derided by the most vocal elements of the Kirk, he now found a halo of holiness placed around his head by bishops who were more than prepared to accede to his claims as God's direct representative on Earth. 'God hath given us a Solomon,' declared Bishop James Montagu, 'and God above all things gave Solomon wisdom; wisdom brought him peace; peace brought him riches; riches gave him glory.' Indeed, Montagu continued, the king surpassed Solomon, since he had been steadfast in the true religion longer than Solomon had reigned, nor had he been immoderate in his dealings with women. And to gild the lily further, there were frequent comparisons with the Roman Emperors Constantine and Theodosius, not to mention Israel's very own sweet singer, David. In the same way that David had united the laws of Judah and Israel, it was proclaimed, so James had bonded the rival kingdoms of England and Scotland.

All in all, then, it was small wonder that James basked in the veneration that now came his way and gave full vent to the inherent sense of his own celebrity that had hitherto been so roughly and so frequently challenged north of the Border. When Roger Aston, a Scottish envoy who had been sent ahead to England upon Elizabeth's death was asked how his master felt about his succession, the answer could not have been more clear-cut or apt. 'Even, my lords,' came the reply, 'like a poor man wandering about forty years in a wilderness and barren soil and now arrived at the land of promise'. Not long afterwards, moreover, James himself would be remarking how little he could find to alter in the state of England, 'which state, as it seemed, so affected his royal heart that it pleased him to enter into a gratulation to Almighty God for bringing him into the promised land where religion was purely professed, where he sat among grave, learned and reverend men, not as before, elsewhere, a king without a state, without honour, without order, where beardless boys would brave him to his face'.

James, of course, could smile at some of the excessive adulation heaped upon him. After losing heavily at cards on one occasion, he commented wryly upon both his predicament and those who would render him near-infallible. 'Am I not as good a king as King David?' he declared, 'As holy a king as King David? As just a king as King David? And why should I then be crossed?' Likewise, he wasted no time in denying the time-honoured claim of English monarchs that they could treat the disease of scrofula merely by touching the affected parts. The age of miracles, he said, was past and he shrank from the ritual whereby the king would place his hands upon the ulcerous sores of those brought before him – a practice, James felt, that savoured far too much of Roman superstition. On one occasion, indeed – 'finding the strength of the imagination a more powerful agent in the cure' – he was actually prepared to belittle the ceremony publicly. When entreated by a foreign ambassador to perform the cure upon his son, the king, it seems, 'laughed heartily, and as the young fellow came near him he stroked him with his hand, first on one side and then on the other, marry without Pistle or Gospel'.

Yet when it came to his new kingdom, James experienced no such doubts about either his powers or his potential or, for that matter, his need to tread carefully, 'inasmuch', wrote one Englishman, 'as he imagined heaven and earth must give way to his will'. As one of his first measures, he did not hesitate, for instance, to install Lord Edward Bruce of Kinloss as Master of the Rolls for life, though the outcry was so great that no other Scot was ever again accorded such high judicial office. More embarrassingly still, even before he had reached London, James attempted unsuccessfully to appoint his old tutor, Peter Young, Dean of Lichfield, notwithstanding the fact that the post was not legally his to give. And these were not the only examples of how his glorious entry into England created what amounted to a curious euphoria that compromised his judgement and heralded the onset of unsettled times ahead. Though the Gowrie Plot was an event of minimal significance south of the Border, the anniversary of its failure, Tuesday 5 August, was nevertheless now set aside in England as well as

Scotland as a holy day of feasting and thanksgiving, while special 'Tuesday sermons', in which, among other things, the Almighty was urged to 'smite the king's enemies upon the cheekbone, break their teeth, frustrate their counsels and bring to naught all their devices' became a regular feature of the court's routine. There was, indeed, even an attempt – albeit unsuccessful – to foist these crude examples of royal propaganda upon both of the kingdom's universities.

Plainly, then, James's limited understanding of his new realm was exacerbated by the false impressions with which he was bombarded upon his arrival. Now, of course, he was free forever from the perpetual fear of kidnapping and assassination, from contending with clan feuds and the individual jealousies of Scottish noblemen, from the maddening pretensions of the Kirk, and the galling sense of unimportance in the great world of European politics that had been his lot hitherto. But far from entering the 'land of promise' – a land described by a Venetian nobleman in 1596 as 'the most lovely to be seen in the world, so opulent, fat and rich in all things, that you may say with truth poverty is banished' – James did not perceive the broader picture. From at least one perspective, of course, he cannot be wholly blamed for this, since England was not only in a state of latent tension, but also in the midst of a series of rapid and painful transitions. Unbeknown to any Italian visitor, it seems, 1596 was also a year of spiralling inflation, widespread agricultural distress, a crippling slump in trade and a heated dispute between Queen Elizabeth and the impoverished south coast ports over the levy of ship money. For even if England was from some perspectives a comparatively rich and splendid inheritance, the Crown itself was poor. Equally importantly, Elizabethan government was founded upon an intricate system of balances and compromises between ruler and ruled that could only be 'caught rather than taught'.

Yet James had neither the time nor, more importantly still, sufficient inclination to learn anew the subtleties of kingship. 'As the king is by nature of a mild disposition and has never really been happy in Scotland,' wrote the Venetian ambassador, 'he wishes now to enjoy the papacy, as we say, and so desires to have no bother with other people's affairs and little with his own. He would like to dedicate himself to his books and to the chase and to encourage the opinion that he is the real arbiter of peace.' But if James desired the Olympian status of a pope in his new kingdom, it would come at a cost, for, though his judgement was often sound, it was sometimes dangerously rash at critical moments. More importantly still, the personal style of government he unwaveringly pursued was only likely to succeed, insofar as the reigning monarch possessed the necessary charisma and majesty, and commanded the love of his or her subjects. Intelligence, high principles and good intentions were actually no more a guarantee of sound leadership at the start of the seventeenth century than they are today. And it was now – after the welcoming, the junketing and the initial friendly posturing were finally done – that James would have to set his stamp upon his restive realm.

11 ❧ The King, His Beagles, His Countrymen and His Court

'The English are for the most part little edified with the person or with the conduct of the king and declare openly enough that they were deceived in the opinion they were led to entertain of him.'

Christophe de Harlay, Comte de Beaumont, French ambassador to England
from April 1603 to November 1605

Though James knew little of England's laws and parliament, he was well equipped to grasp the elements of the struggle for power at Whitehall and the subtleties by which his predecessor had managed to maintain a fragile balance of forces around her council table. The enmity between Cecil and Raleigh, for example, was in any case certainly less noisy than the kind of knuckleduster fuming he had been forced to contend with in Scotland, and he had been kept closely informed of events by the letters of both Cecil and Henry Howard. Moreover, his opening moves on the broader front were wisely non-committal. On the one hand, he at once provisionally confirmed the existing council in office, while choosing to release Lord Southampton and Sir Henry Neville from the Tower, where they had been languishing in the aftermath of the Essex rebellion. As a further gesture towards healing old wounds and offering new beginnings, he also announced his intention of bringing up Essex's heir in his own household – restored in blood and title, and reared in the companionship of Prince Henry. And those who had in any way supported his mother's cause were to be brought back to favour and thus bound to the new dynasty alongside their former enemies.

In the meantime, the immediate shape of the new king's government had been decided on 3 May at Theobalds when he stopped at the home of Sir Robert Cecil on the final leg of his journey from Edinburgh to London. It was there that he had withdrawn with Cecil to a 'labyrinth-like garden, compact of bays, rosemary and the like' for an hour's intimate conversation to confirm the latter's primacy and seal, in the process, the rather more disconcerting triumph of Henry Howard – soon to become Earl of Northampton – and his sailor nephew, Thomas, who was swiftly promoted to the earldom of Suffolk. Charles Howard, too, who had commanded the English fleet against the Spanish Armada as Lord Howard of Effingham, duly retained the office of Lord Steward of the Household under his new title of Earl of Nottingham. In James's view, it would have been the ultimate folly to discard those very men who had so strikingly demonstrated their level-headed competence in securing his succession, and who appeared to embody so strikingly all that typified Elizabethan wisdom and prestige. It was only natural, too, that five of his loyal Scottish lieutenants – Lennox, Mar, Home, Elphinstone and Edward Bruce, Lord Kinloss – should join the reconstituted council, since the court at Edinburgh had effectively ceased to exist, though for Sir Walter Raleigh and his allies, against whom Cecil and Howard had been so successfully poisoning the king's mind, there was to be no crumb of comfort. Indeed, on 15 April James dismissed Raleigh as captain of his Guard, without financial compensation, and ordered him to leave Durham House in the Strand, which had been provided by the former queen for his private use over twenty years.

Dark, saturnine and colossally proud, the 50-year-old Raleigh possessed a swagger that, in spite of his undoubted brilliance, could never endear him to one such as James, who regarded him purely as a reckless old pirate, opposed at any price to peace with Spain. To others he was a 'Macchiavellian' and an 'atheist', but if such terms bore no relation to his actual views, he was certainly no judge of character – and nowhere more so than in the case of the new king. To present James so early on with *A Discourse Touching a War with Spain and of the Protecting of the Netherlands* merely confirmed Elizabeth I's conviction that her favourite was no statesman, and the king lost little time in attempting to put the upstart in his place. When Raleigh presented himself before James at Burghley House, for example, he was merely treated to the kind of clumsy putdown that was the king's stock in trade. 'Rawly, Rawly,' James declared upon their meeting, 'and rawly ha'e heard of thee, mon'. Before long, moreover, the former royal favourite had lost not only the captaincy of the royal guard but the governorship of Jersey, the lord wardenship of the Stanaries and his monopoly on the sale of sweet wines. All in all, it may well have been no more than Raleigh's presumption merited, but it was far more than one such as he could be expected to settle for passively. And, surely enough, this particularly glittering star of a bygone Elizabethan age would neither forgive nor forget.

Yet the flipside of Raleigh's eclipse was the triumph of an altogether more accomplished politician. 'The evidence of a king,' James himself observed, 'is chiefly seen in the election of his officers', and in Sir Robert Cecil, at least, he had acquitted himself most favourably, notwithstanding the fact that the two men had precious little in common. Wholly unlike his new master, the principal Secretary of State stood, in fact, for calculated dignity and restrained decorum. And though he would be able occasionally to share a recondite joke with the king, the rest of their relationship would be largely artificial as his grave and careful judgement was brought to bear upon even the lightest or most minute details. If James wished to tease him clumsily on his puny figure and address him as his 'little beagle', this was a small price to pay for maintaining the reality of power in his own hands, and he was usually more than capable of enduring the king's badinage under an umbrella of urbanity and stoical self-assurance. For there was a gravity and air of civilisation about Cecil that placed even a long-serving king in awe of him – especially a King of Scotland whose provinciality was inclined to surface so frequently. Perhaps, indeed, the very banter that James directed Cecil's way was itself a product of his own innate unease in the minister's presence. Over time, however, the king's awe and sense of debt would turn to frustration against the man who strove so doggedly to curb his impulsiveness and extravagance. Certainly, Cecil's death in 1612 would be a source of considerable relief and emancipation for James – though for the time being that prospect seemed as distant as the notion that the king could somehow cope without him.

As Principal Secretary, Master of the Wards and later Lord Treasurer, the diminutive minister remained until his death the pivot around which the entire machinery of government revolved, controlling all foreign affairs, directing Parliament, and managing every aspect of finance. Within weeks of James's accession, moreover, he had been created Lord Cecil of Essendon before becoming Viscount Cranborne in 1604 and Earl of Salisbury a year later. No living king, James openly acknowledged, 'shall more confidently and constantly rely upon the advice of a councillor and trusty servant than I shall ever do upon yours'. 'Before God,' the king declared, 'I count you the best servant that ever I had – albeit you be but a little beagle.' Such high praise could not, it seems, be delivered by James without a final tweak at Cecil's dignity. But the other key members of the council, which included the courtier earls of Shrewsbury and Worcester, the buccaneer-courtier Cumberland, Mountjoy, who returned from Ireland to become Earl of Devonshire, and the Earl of Northumberland, to whom the king gave credit for the good behaviour of the English Catholics, all accepted Cecil's primacy without question. The same was true for the new Scottish additions and, more importantly still, the ubiquitous Howards, Henry and Thomas, who, along with Worcester, a devout but utterly loyal Catholic, soon formed an inner circle of four on the council with Cecil himself.

But in dominating all areas of government and attempting to bridle the king's impulsiveness as best he could, the secretary would also stretch his physical resources to the limit by almost ceaseless work. As month after month of confusion and uncertainty followed the change in dynasty, Cecil would bemoan to his friend, Sir John Harington, the passing of the former queen. 'I wish I waited now in her Presence Chamber,' he wrote, 'with ease at my food and rest in my bed. I am pushed from the shore of my comfort and know not where the winds of the court will bear me.' 'I know it bringeth little comfort on earth …' he added, before appending his signature 'in trouble, hurrying, feigning, suing and such-like matters'. It was small wonder, then, that Shrewsbury was soon warning Cecil that he would 'blear out his eyes' and 'quite overthrow' his body without some form of respite. For although the king's letters to his principal secretary demonstrate his shrewdness and ability, as well as his capacity to grasp a situation readily and reach a swift decision, he was also disinclined to master details and prone to lapses of concentration – especially when his devotion to hunting and recreation took priority over all else. 'He seems to have forgotten that he is a king,' wrote the Venetian ambassador, 'except in his kingly pursuit of stags, to which he is quite foolishly devoted.'

The room where Mary Queen of Scots gave birth to the future James I of England in 1566. During his only return visit to his homeland in 1617, James ordered that the room be preserved and much of what is now seen is decoration dating from his reign. *(Dave and Margie Hill)*

At the age of 7, James's features bore a close resemblance to those of his father, as this portrait by Arnold van Bronckhorst clearly shows. In particular, the young king's wide-set eyes leave little doubt of his parentage, while his passion for hunting (which lasted throughout his life) is also emphasised by the bird of prey upon his left hand.

Portrayed here by Arnold van Bronckhorst shortly before his death at the age of 76, the tutor to the future James I enjoyed an outstanding reputation, both as a humanist scholar and historian of his native Scotland. Buchanan's rigorous methods would leave lasting imprints upon his most famous pupil's intellect and personality.

The last of the four regents of Scotland during the minority of King James VI, the Earl of Morton was arguably more successful than any of his predecessors, since he concluded the civil war that had been dragging on with the supporters of the exiled Mary, Queen of Scots. Yet his authoritarian rule earned him many enemies and an untimely end when he was beheaded by means of the 'Maiden', a primitive guillotine, which he himself is said to have introduced to Scotland.

IACOBVS · 6 · D · G · R ·
SCOTORVM
ÆTA · 29 ·
1595 ·

In 1584 Adrian Vanson succeeded Arnold van Bronckhorst as official painter to the Scottish Court. Aside from overseeing every aspect of royal painting, including banners used for the coronation of Anne as Queen of Scotland in 1590, Vanson and his studio would have been responsible for the production of the king's official likeness, such as the present portrait, either for prominent supporters, or for foreign courts.

The king's ongoing interest in witchcraft assumed a new intensity in the early 1590s after evidence had appeared to connect Francis Stewart, 5th Earl of Bothwell, with a diabolical attempt upon his life. Here the North Berwick witches, who had allegedly been enlisted by Stewart, meet the Devil in their local kirkyard.

This portrait from 1612 by Marcus Gheeraerts the Younger depicts James I's wife in mourning for her eldest son Henry Frederick, Prince of Wales, who had died from typhoid fever earlier that year.

Potentially the most able of the Stuart line, Prince Henry would not live to succeed to the throne. 'His body was so faire and strong,' declared his chaplain after the young prince's death at the age of 18, 'that a soule might have been pleased to live an age in it.'

Above: Between 20 May and 16 July 1604, eighteen conference sessions were held at Somerset House, leading to the Treaty of London, which was signed on 16 August and concluded almost twenty years of warfare between England and Spain. On the left are the members of the Hispano-Flemish delegation, on the right, the English commissioners, which, reading from the far end, included the Earl of Dorset, the Earl of Nottingham, Lord Mountjoy, the Earl of Northampton and Robert Cecil.

Robert Carr was a Scottish noble who met James in 1607 and very quickly rose to a position of considerable authority at court. As the premier royal favourite, Carr received a steady flow of gifts in the form of cash, land and titles, until petulance, jealousy and a scandalous marriage to Frances Howard eventually soured his relationship with the king.

King James's personal relationships are much debated, with George Villiers the last in a succession of handsome young favourites who were lavished with affection and patronage. In 1617, John Oglander wrote that he 'never yet saw any fond husband make so much or so great dalliance over his beautiful spouse as I have seen King James over his favourites, especially the Duke of Buckingham'. Edward Peyton, meanwhile, would note how 'the king sold his affections to Sir George Villiers, whom he would tumble and kiss as a mistress'.

Left: On 31 January 1606 Robert Keyes, Ambrose Rookwood, Thomas Wintour and Guy Fawkes were taken to the Old Palace Yard in Westminster to be hanged, drawn and quartered. Rookwood and Wintour were the first to ascend to the gallows. Grim-faced, Keyes went 'stoutly' up the ladder, but with the halter around his neck he threw himself off, presumably hoping for a quick death. The halter broke, however, and he was taken to the block to suffer the remainder of his sentence.

By his mid-50s, James had become increasingly sickly and careworn. A 'cradle king' from the age of 1, he had at various times encountered danger and disrespect, and now in his twilight years he was left to endure progressive physical decline and disillusionment.

Certainly, James's dislike of London, 'that filthy town', and Whitehall made it easy enough to abandon the seat of government at every opportunity – convenient or otherwise. Indeed, he would spend only about a third of the year in London, with predictable consequences. 'This is the cause of indescribable ill-humour among the king's subjects,' wrote the Venetian Molin, 'who in their needs and troubles find themselves cut off from their natural sovereign and forced to go before the council, which is full of rivalry and discord and frequently is guided more by personal interests than by justice and duty.' By 1 December 1604, indeed, Molin was reporting that posters had been fixed up in various locations around the capital, complaining that the king attended to nothing but his pleasures and left all to his ministers. Nor were such accusations by any means entirely groundless. Within two months of his accession James had issued a proclamation against illegal hunting in the royal forests and, with not a little sophistry, was soon attempting to justify his frequent absences. 'The king [...] finds such felicity in that hunting life,' wrote Chamberlain in January 1605, 'that he hath written to the council that it is the only means to maintain his health (which being the health and welfare of us all) he desires them to undertake the charge and burden of affairs.' In accordance with the king's wishes, the Privy Council issued orders prohibiting anyone other than members of the royal family from hunting with hounds within four miles of London, and ambassadors were rarely received at Royston in the way they had formerly been at Falkland during Elizabeth's time, since her successor did not like to be distracted while taking his leisure. 'He hath erected a new office and made Sir Richard Wigmore marshall of the field, who is to take order that he be not attended by any but his own followers, nor interrupted and hindered in his sports, by strangers and idle lookers on,' Chamberlain would report in 1609. And James's neglect of government was not the only cause for concern, since Lord Treasurer Buckhurst was soon uneasy, predictably, about excessive allowances for the royal buckhounds.

There was, moreover, much about James's actual hunting practice that made even contemporaries uneasy – his vindictive fury in pursuing and slaughtering the game, his dabbling in the dead animals' blood once the kill had been made, his rage when the quarry escaped, his low company and bad manners at the chase. 'Running hounds', as the king called them, would bring down and kill the stag, after which the king would dismount, cut the stag's throat and open its belly, thrusting his hands (and sometimes his feet) into the stag's entrails and daubing the faces of his courtiers. This, however, was the least offensive aspect of James's behaviour to local farmers and villagers who found themselves tormented by the indiscriminate rampaging of the king and his courtiers. 'As one that honoureth and loveth his most excellent Majesty with all my heart,' wrote the Archbishop of York to Cecil during December 1604, 'I wish less wastening of the treasure of this realm, and more moderation in the lawful exercise of hunting, both that poor men's corn be less spoiled, and other his Majesty's subjects be more spared.'

But James's delight in the 'sporting' destruction of animals was not an obsession he was willing to limit. Hawking, cockfighting, bull- and bear-baiting were all passions, and the bear-garden at Southwark, known as Paris Garden, which also housed lynxes and tigers, was owned by him personally. The Earl of Dorset, in fact, was 'brought into great grace and favour with the king', because of his love of cock-fighting. In addition, James kept cormorants to dive for fish and by 1605 had developed, according to Chamberlain, 'a great humour of catching larks'. A lion-baiting pit was also constructed at the Tower, and on one occasion, accompanied by young Prince Henry and several lords, he 'caused the lustiest lion to be separated from his mate, and put into the lion's den, one dog alone, who presently flew to the face of the lion, but the lion suddenly shook him off and grasped fast by the neck, drawing the dog upstairs and downstairs'. This, however, was not the end of proceedings, since the king 'now perceiving the lion greatly to exceed the dog in strength, but nothing in noble heart and courage, caused another dog to be put into the den, who proved as hot and lusty as his fellow and took the lion by his face'. And though this dog died, too, another one later recovered from its wounds, encouraging Prince Henry to order his servant Alleyne to look after the beast well, saying that since he had 'fought with the king of beasts', he 'should never after fight with any inferior animal'.

Not all such staged encounters were so predictable, however, since lions, it emerged, were generally unwilling to fight for entertainment purposes. Indeed, after a bear had killed a child and James arranged for the offending creature to be baited by a lion, the result was an embarrassing anti-climax in which the king of beasts chose to withdraw from the encounter without so much as a bared tooth or exposed claw. Nor, for that matter, were all the king's involvements with animals so violent. He was a keen patron of horse-racing, for instance, making it a royal sport after swift-footed

Spanish horses had been thrown ashore on the coasts of Galloway at the time of the wreck of the Armada, and establishing several race tracks, the most important of which was located at Newmarket. He also appears to have indulged a particular fascination for more exotic creatures, including Indian antelope and a flying squirrel from Virginia, as well as two young crocodiles, which were presented to him by Captain Christopher Newport after his journey to Hispaniola. The Prince of Orange sent him a tiger, while the Duke of Savoy presented him with another, as well as a lioness and a lynx – all of which died in transit. In 1623, meanwhile, King Philip of Spain would give James five camels and an elephant. At first, the camels were left to graze in St James's Park until stables were constructed for them at Theobalds, and though the elephant was for some reason kept from public view, its captivity was enlivened by a gallon of wine daily from September to April – a period during which its keepers considered it unable to drink water.

The chase, his 'sport', his curious pets, his love of country life were all, plainly, welcome distractions from the more tedious routines of everyday government. But even if the king's frequent excursions really were good for his health and thus the health of his kingdom too, the burden imposed on others – and not only Cecil – was now considerable. 'This tumultuary and uncertain attendance upon the king's sports affords me little time to write,' confided one official, while George Home, Earl of Dunbar, bemoaned the fact that he and his colleagues 'are all become wild men wandering in a forest from the morning till the evening'. But it was the Earl of Worcester, perhaps, who best encapsulated the problem. 'Since my departure from London,' he noted, 'I think I have not had two hours of twenty-four of rest but Sundays, for in the morning we are on horseback by eight and so continue in full career from the death of one hare to another until four at night; then for the most part we are five miles from home. By that time I find at my lodging sometimes one, most commonly two packets of letters, all of which must be answered before I sleep, for here is none of the council but myself, no, not a clerk of the council nor Privy Signet.'

Such packets of letters came down from the councillors in London daily and Salisbury sometimes sent messengers to talk with the king and report his wishes. But the dispatches from the capital might well be answered by any ranking official at hand, and it frequently fell to Sir Thomas Lake, who was in constant attendance upon James, to set down his master's thoughts and instructions after snatched consultations in the limited time available. Most often the king could be found at one of three houses – Royston, which he bought in 1604, Theobalds, which he acquired from Cecil in 1604 in exchange for Hatfield, and Newmarket – all of which were linked to London by private roads that he maintained for the purpose. But the council's business would often have to make its way to Thetford, Hinchingbrooke, Ware and Woking, too, rather than Windsor and Hampton Court, the two principal country palaces at the time of James's accession. And the expense as well as the inconvenience mounted further through the duplication of stables, deer parks, offices and living quarters, as even local farmers began to complain increasingly about the excessive burden imposed by the king's purveyors. When Jowler, one of James's favourite hounds, was lost near Royston in 1604, it was returned next day with a letter round its neck. 'Good Mr Jowler,' it read, 'we pray you speak to the king (for he hears you every day, and so doth he not us) that it will please his Majesty to go back to London, for else the country will be undone; all our provision is spent already and we are not able to entertain him longer.'

Meanwhile, the broader disruption caused by James's inattention to state affairs during the short periods he spent at Whitehall may well be imagined. Still inclined to rush in the way that George Buchanan had noticed so many years earlier, he could often exasperate those who had his best interests at heart. In 1603, for instance, Wilbraham noted that when Cecil presented James with patents for eight barons and two earls, 'the king signed them all at one time confusedly, not respecting who should have antiquity'. There were times, too, when haste could turn to outright flippancy – especially, it seems, when it came to the practice of dubbing knights, which, in his case, became such a common chore. On one occasion, Wilbraham tells us, he did not catch the long Celtic name of a Scot who was kneeling before him to receive his honour. 'Prithee,' James is said to have declared, 'rise up and call thyself Sir What Thou Wilt.'

Predictably, too, there was great irregularity in James's availability for more general business, with the result that suitors 'swarmed about his Majesty at every back gate and privy door, to his great offence'. Indeed, it was precisely because of the first Stuart's constant irritation at his loss of privacy, that Charles I soon decreed after his accession that suitors 'must never approach him by indirect means, by back stairs or private doors leading to his apartments, nor by means of retainers or grooms of the chambers, as was done in the lifetime of his father'. Rather than taking steps to deal with the problem himself, however, James had merely railed against his predicament, so that by the end of the reign he was still bedevilled by the same problem that his own informality had done so much to spawn. 'The king is not as her Majesty is,' Thomas Fowler had written upon a visit to James while Queen Elizabeth was still alive, 'any of his subjects being gentle or noble may speak his mind frankly to him'. And his inability to project a truly kingly aura now left all and sundry to pester him as they pleased. 'The king is much disgusted with it,' wrote a courtier in 1623, 'but knows not how to help it.' While he protested in private, moreover, he continued to think that no man was sincerely bound to him unless by a gift, which merely served to swell the throng – even confiding to Cecil on one occasion that he had been so prodigal in rewarding persons who had no claim upon him that he could not justly deny those who had.

And when Robert Cecil was not bailing his master out, he would continue to find himself bearing the tiresome burden of his master's deprecating familiarity for his trouble. In the king's own words, the tireless earl remained the little 'beagle' that 'lies at home by the fire when all the good hounds are daily running on the fields'. On another occasion, James wished that 'my little beagle had been stolen here in the likeness of a mouse, as he is not much bigger, to have been partaker of the sport which I had this day at hawking'. Even when weightier matters were involved, the tireless theme was maintained. In planning an embassy to France, for example, the king could not forego the opportunity to tell Cecil of his intention to dispatch a kennel of little beagles across the Channel and to ask him 'if ye mind to be of that number'. Rarely did the secretary bridle at either his workload or his nickname, though he certainly regretted the latter in particular. 'I see nothing that I can do,' he complained to Sir Thomas Lake, 'can procure me so much favour as to be sure one whole day what title I shall have. For from Essendon to Cranborne, from Salisbury to Beagle, from Beagle to Thom Derry, from Thom Derry to Parrot, which I hate most, I have been walked as I think by that I come to Theobalds I shall be called Tare or Sophie.'

Certainly, it is hard to escape the conclusion that there was a distinct element of unseemliness, if not outright spite, at the heart of much of James's playfulness, which extended to other confidants as well as Cecil. In 1605, on the eve of a visit to Greenwich, the king issued an apparently friendly warning to his most trusted councillors. 'If I find not at my coming to Greenwich,' he declared, 'that the big Chamberlain [Thomas Howard] have ordered well all my lodging, that the little saucy Constable [Cecil] have made the house sweet and built a cockpit, and that the fast-walking keeper of the park [Henry Howard] have the park in good order and the does all with fawn, although he has never been a good breeder himself, then I shall make the fat Chamberlain to puff, the little cankered beagle to whine, and the tall black and cat-faced keeper to glower.' Elsewhere, James pretended to be suspicious of their relations with his wife. 'I know Suffolk is married,' he writes, 'but for your part, master 10 [Cecil], who is wanton and wifeless, I cannot but be jealous of your greatness with my wife.' As for Northampton, meanwhile, 'who is so lately fallen into acquaintance with my wife … his part is foul in this, that never having taken a wife to himself in his youth, he cannot now be content with his grey hairs to forebear another man's wife'.

There were times, of course, when James acknowledged his servants' efforts. 'My little beagle,' he wrote on one occasion, 'although I be now in my paradise of pleasure, yet will I not be forgetful of you and your fellows that are frying in the pains of purgatory in my service.' 'Your zeal and diligence are so great,' he observed, 'as I will cheer myself in your faithfulness and assure myself that God hath ordained to make me happy in sending me so good servants, and the beagle in special.' But he was also quick to point out to the Archbishop of York that the absences so necessary for the maintenance of his health took up no more time than other kings spent upon feasting and visiting their whores. Besides which, such fair-weather praise as James sometimes deigned to offer his servants carried little substance when mixed with sneers and tantrums. 'Ye sit at your ease and direct all,' he would tell his ministers, while 'the king's own resolutions depend upon your posting dispatches, and when ye list, ye can (sitting on your bedsides) with one call or whistling in your fist make him to post night and day till he comes to your presence'. To such unthinking outbursts, the only sensible response was perhaps Cecil's, who indulged his master by flattery, begging James to send him copies of his writings or telling him how a kind word from the royal pen had cured a recent illness.

The court, meanwhile, was soon increasing in lavishness and cost while degenerating rapidly in orderliness and tone. According to the Venetian ambassador, it was soon fashionable for even the lesser nobles and councillors to appear in public with forty or fifty horsemen and sometimes with 200 to 300, so that 'the drain on private purses is enormous'. Vulgar ostentation became the order of the day, in fact, as great ladies sported ever more costly jewels at state functions and even the wives of ambitious civil servants would think it worthwhile to spend £50 a yard on the trimming of a dress. The value of presents became a subject for calculation and haggling too, it seems, for when de Beamont, the French ambassador, was recalled to his homeland in 1605, he complained bitterly that his parting present of plate weighed only 2,000 ounces. Quoting precedents and whingeing continually, he eventually received 500 ounces more. And when perquisites and commissions of this kind were the norm and even minor offices were for sale, the opportunities for corruption became legion – so much so that open peculation ran throughout the king's own household and, much worse still, every department of state.

The newly prevailing atmosphere of expenditure for expenditure's sake would, however, be epitomised most strikingly by the excesses of Sir James Hay who had arrived from Scotland with James at the time of the succession to be rapidly installed as a 'prime favourite' and gentleman of the bedchamber. A man of accommodating temper and good sense in most things, Hay was not without some diplomatic ability. But his extravagance and lavish expenditure, his costly entertainments and so-called 'ante-suppers' – at which banqueting tables were laden with splendid food that was then discarded without being consumed before the main, even more dazzling, dishes were brought in - became the theme of satirists and wonder of society, as his debts spiralled to more than £80,000. He left behind him, said the Earl of Clarendon, 'the reputation of a very fine gentleman and a most accomplished courtier, and after having spent, in a very jovial life, above £400,000, which upon a strict computation he received from the Crown, he left not a house or acre of land to be remembered by'. He had, wrote Clarendon, 'no bowels in the point of running in debt, or borrowing all he could' and 'was surely a man of the greatest expense in his person of any in the age he lived'.

Nevertheless, it was the personal extravagance of the king that fed as well as reflected this culture of brash display and conspicuous consumption. The number of gentlemen of the bedchamber, of gentlemen, ushers and grooms of the privy chamber and of the presence chamber, of carvers, cupbearers and sewers, of clerks of the closet and esquires of the body, of harbingers, yeomen, pages and messengers increased in line with the king's desire to advertise his exalted status. The gentlemen of the privy chamber, for instance, rose in number from eighteen to forty-eight, each with a fee of £50 a year, and before long there were 200 gentlemen extraordinary. Wardrobe costs, on the other hand, which averaged approximately £9,500 per annum in the last four years of Elizabeth's reign leapt to over £36,000 per annum in the first five years of James's. According to the records of the treasurer of the chamber, meanwhile, the cost of court ceremonial rose from £14,000 under Elizabeth to £20,000 under her successor. No man, it was soon being said, ate at court without costing the king £60 a year, while even the charge for one of the seamstresses or laundresses that teemed around the court was estimated at £86. And both the king and his queen spent extraordinary sums on jewels: James expending some £92,000 in the first four years of his reign alone, while Anne would run up a bill of £40,000 over ten years with the jeweller George Heriot. Only one year into the new reign, therefore, a royal commission had been appointed in the vain hope of curtailing household expenses.

In particular, the king's generosity to his favourites became a matter of widespread concern. 'I hear,' Chamberlain would write to Carleton in February 1607, at a time when all the City knew that money was low in the Exchequer, 'the king hath undertaken the debts of the Lord Hay, the Viscount Haddington and the Earl of Montgomery to the value of four and forty thousand pounds, saying that he will this once set them free, and then let them shift for themselves. In the meantime his own debts are stalled to be paid the one half in May come two years, the residue in May following.' Haddington was the same John Ramsay to whom James believed he owed his life on the day of Gowrie's conspiracy and therefore, arguably, had a special claim upon the king's generosity. But even in his case, let alone Hay's and Montgomery's, the merchants and tradesmen who had been left to wait over two years for money already long owing could well feel aggrieved – especially when James would go on, within twelve months, to mark Haddington's marriage with even more largesse. For along with the gold cup in which the king had drunk her health, the bride was also given not only 'a basin and ewer, two livery pots and three standing cups all very fair and massy, of silver and gilt' but a joint annuity of £600 out of the Exchequer to enjoy with her husband. Five years later, in the midst of an even worse financial crisis, James would give the Countess of Somerset £10,000 worth of jewels as a wedding present. And by 1610, a little over £220,000 had been given away in hard cash, with pensions granted by the king amounting to a further £30,000 a year. In other words, presents accounted for more than a quarter of James's total indebtedness, while annuities swallowed around 6 per cent of his yearly expenditure. The fact, moreover, that so many of his gifts had been lavished upon Scotsmen when the Scottish court itself had boasted only a 'small, unkingly household' merely added fuel to the fire.

For Englishmen, indeed, the transformation of the court into a hybrid entity, heavily and undesirably infested with barbaric foreigners, had become a cause of rancour and suspicion from the very moment of James's succession. The king, of course, had appointed his countrymen to bedchamber posts, paid their debts and proceeded to surround himself with them, and though he did so for good reason from some perspectives, there was little appreciation in the kingdom at large of either his motives or his predicament. It was only natural, of course, that he should want his friends around him, in court and elsewhere, and his friends in the first instance were inevitably Scots. Much more importantly still, however, there was now only one royal court, where before there had been two. In such circumstances, a hybrid court, accommodating both Scots and English was inescapable. But the former were swiftly branded greedy and uncivilised thugs, and the king would not help the situation by declaring to his first Westminster Parliament that Scotland, unlike England, had never been conquered by any outsider.

A key issue, predictably, was access to the king which appeared initially to be dominated by the newcomers. 'No Englishman, be his rank what it may, can enter the Presence Chamber without being summoned,' wrote the Venetian ambassador in May 1603, 'whereas the Scottish Lords have free entrée of the privy chamber.' But the greatest resentment continued to spring from the general perception that the Scots had a virtual monopoly on the royal bounty. In the parliamentary debate on purveyance in 1606, one speaker would describe the treasury as 'a royal cistern, wherein his Majesty's largesse to the Scots caused a continual and remediless leak'. And such hostility was ongoing. 'The Earl of Dunbar,' wrote Sir Dudley Carleton in 1608, 'is returned out of Scotland with a new legion of Scots worse than the former,' while in 1610 their influence upon James was once again being blamed for the kingdom's financial problems – this time in Parliament. 'The court is the cause of all,' declared Sir John Holles, 'for by the reception of the other nation that head is too heavy for this small body of England … The Scottish monopolise his princely person, standing like mountains betwixt the beams of his grace and us.'

Even Cecil, for that matter, now found his operations complicated by the king's involvement with his countrymen. 'It fareth not with me now as it did in the queen's time,' he confided to Sir Henry Yelverton who had been forced to seek help from the Earl of Dunfermline and Dunbar after offending James, '... for then I could have done as great a matter as this without other help than myself; she heard but few, and of them I may say myself the chief; the king heareth many, yea, of all kinds.' Nor would James's attempts to amalgamate the Scottish and English upper classes by marriage always prove successful. When Sir John Kennedy did not get along with his wife, a daughter of Lord Chandos, she took up with Sir William Paddy, the king's physician, and triggered an explosive response. 'You have heard, I am sure,' wrote Dudley Carleton to John Chamberlain in 1609, 'of a great danger Sir William Paddy lately escaped at Barn Elms, where the house was assaulted by Sir John Kennedy by night with a band of furious Scots, who besides their warlike weapons came furnished ... with certain snippers and searing irons, purposing to have used him worse than a Jew, with much more ceremony than circumcision.'

As early as February 1604, James had made a desultory attempt to bar Scottish officials and noblemen from venturing south, on the grounds that the administration of Scotland would suffer by their flocking to London. In 1607, moreover, he went on to make an outright apology to Parliament for his excessive largesse to his countrymen. 'My first three years were to me as a Christmas. I could not then be miserable,' he pleaded. 'Should I have been over-sparing to them, they might have thought that Joseph had forgotten his brethren.' More significantly still, however, the hanging of Lord Sanquhar for the murder of an English fencing-master who had accidentally put out his eye finally convinced many that James was determined to be even-handed. And though hatred of the Scots did not diminish in the country as a whole, at court at least there was a gradual acceptance that, while Scots were a permanent fixture in office around the king, there was no unwritten Scottish monopoly as such. However obnoxious to English courtiers, the Scottish link had not, therefore, reached truly critical dimensions, and the arrival of the new king had at least brought one enticing consolation for any red-blooded man of his court: the emergence of a new gaiety and hedonism.

Now, indeed, that the restraining hands of Andrew Melville and his ilk had been removed, James could spread his wings in other ways, too, for whatever Whitgift, Bancroft and other leading members of the English episcopacy might think in private about their master's lifestyle, they would never take to the pulpit to compare him with Jeroboam. Court festivities therefore became not only more numerous and extravagant but sometimes more disorderly as well. Of the more innocuous entertainments on offer, however, James particularly enjoyed the spectacle of the elaborate masques, which, with their hugely ornate floats, costumes and scenery, so delighted his wife. In the process, no expense was spared on these elaborate entertainments, which came to occupy a place of special symbolic significance at the Jacobean court. *The Masque of Blackness*, which Ben Jonson and Inigo Jones staged for the queen in January 1605 to celebrate the creation of Prince Charles as Duke of York cost more than £3,000, for example, and typified the new atmosphere. The court, wrote Arthur Wilson, whose history of James's life and reign was published in 1653, became nothing less than 'a continued masquerade, where the queen and her ladies, like so many sea-nymphs or Nereids, appeared often in various dresses to the ravishment of the beholders, the king himself being not a little delighted with such fluent elegancies as made the night more glorious than the day'. At times, it is true, he appeared mildly distracted and uninterested in proceedings, but, on the whole, wherever there was revelry, especially the kind which involved any hint of immodesty in females – in whom he remained more interested than is often suggested – James could be guaranteed to respond with elevated spirits.

The king's attitude to women had never, in fact, been chivalrous or gentlemanly, and though the Scottish court had been an informal, masculine place where little attention was paid to etiquette in any case, there is much about his outlook that remains regrettable. Certainly, if his *A Satire against Woemen* is taken at face value, there seems little doubt that he regarded them as inherently flawed. 'Dames of worthie fame,' he believed, 'are to be congratulated for triumphing over their evil natures, since women of all kinds were inherently vain, ambitious, greedy, and untruthful.' And if his attitude did not actually worsen in England, it nevertheless seems to have provoked more of a reaction. 'He piques himself,' observed the French ambassador, de Beaumont, 'on great contempt for women. They are obliged to kneel before him when they are presented, he exhorts them openly to virtue and scoffs with great levity at men who pay them honour. You may easily conceive that the English ladies do not spare him but hold him in abhorrence and tear him to pieces with their tongues, each according to her humour.'

Yet for all his faults, it was at feasts and banquets that James nevertheless came into his own, rarely missing the opportunity to address the revellers, embrace the gentlemen, kiss the ladies and raise his glass in numerous toasts. In Scotland, the Venetian ambassador observed, the king had 'lived hardly like a private gentleman, let alone a sovereign, making many people sit down with him at table, waited on by rough servants who did not even remove their hats'. Now, however, he dined 'in great pomp' and entertained his guests with 'extraordinary bravery'. His first Christmas in England, for example, was celebrated at Hampton Court where there were feasts in honour of the ambassadors from France, Spain and Poland, involving many plays and 'dances with swords' and a number of masques, in one of which the queen and eleven of her ladies appeared as goddesses bringing gifts to the king. The costumes in each masque, thought Roger Wilbraham, must have cost from £2–3,000, and the jewels £20,000, while those worn by the queen he judged to be worth £100,000. A year later, Sir Dudley Carleton, the courtier and future diplomat described the celebrations at Whitehall when the king's favourite, the Earl of Montgomery, married Lady Susan Vere. 'There was no small loss that night of chains and jewels and many great ladies were made shorter by the skirts,' wrote Carleton. 'There was gaming for high stakes, too, and another grand masque for which the queen and three other ladies were seated in a shell upon a great float carrying figures of sea-horses and other large fish ridden by Moors.' The 'night's work' was then concluded, we hear, with a banquet in the great chamber 'which was so furiously assaulted that down went table and trusses before one bit was touched'.

But by far the most notorious example of overindulgence and debauchery came in the summer of 1606 with the visit of Christian IV of Denmark whose concept of happiness, like that of all his countrymen, began and ended, it seems, with the contents of a bottle. According to Sir John Harington, who provided a vivid description of what transpired for William Barlow, Dean of Chester, 'the sports began each day in such manner as persuaded me of Mahomet's paradise'. 'We had women and indeed wine too of such plenty,' he declared, 'as would have established each sober beholder,' adding that 'the ladies abandon their sobriety and roll about in intoxication'. It was at the performance of the *Masque of Solomon and Sheba*, however, that the boundaries were well and truly crossed. Following a magnificent banquet at which both James and Christian and all their retinues had far too much to drink, things rapidly spiralled out of control.

For the Queen of Sheba fell over the steps as she sought to offer the Danish king a present and deluged him in wine, cream jelly, cakes and spices. And when Christian, having been roughly cleaned up 'with cloths and napkins', then tried to dance with her, both fell down and had to be carried out and put to bed.

James, meanwhile, chose to sit through the rest of the spectacle as things went from bad to worse. Most of the other performers, Harington tells us, 'went backward or fell down, wine did so occupy their upper chambers', while those representing Hope and Faith fared worse still. Hope, it seems, 'did essay to speak, but wine rendered her endeavours so feeble that she withdrew', whereupon Faith, having been abandoned by her partner, 'left the court in a staggering condition'. Nor, it seems, did the more sober efforts of Charity entirely rescue matters, for she returned to the two other virtues, only to find them 'sick and spewing in the lower hall'. 'After much lamentable utterance', the young lady playing Victory was also 'led away like a silly captive and laid to sleep in the outer steps of the ante-chamber', while Peace, 'much contrary to her semblance', appears to have 'rudely made war' against those of her attendants who had attempted to prevent her getting 'foremost to the king'. Using her olive branch, it seems, she 'laid on the pates of those who did oppose her coming'.

Even allowing for Harington's flare for a witty tale and recognising the fact that he owed James a grudge for patronising him insufferably, this was hardly the sort of evening to cause anything but scandal among sober City merchants and taxpayers and in such remote manor houses – of which there was no small number – who might boast a London correspondent to keep them in touch with the gossip of St Paul's. The House of Commons, moreover, had only just voted the king the tidy sum of £400,000 and Harington is unlikely to have been the only man to point the obvious moral that Parliament 'in good soothe', had not stinted in providing the king 'so seasonably with money'. Not only would such stories undermine Robert Cecil's subsequent negotiations with MPs to rescue the king's finances, they would also have a more pernicious broader and longer-term affect. For they marked the beginning of the rift between the Jacobean court and the country at large, which was to be James's worst legacy to his descendants – a legacy which would arguably influence the entire character of politics throughout the century ahead.

And though the excesses witnessed in 1606 may not be considered typical, the junketing continued throughout the reign – with no expense spared. On 8 January 1608, for instance, John Chamberlain, described the kind of gambling session that became a commonplace of court life. 'On Twelfth eve there was great golden play at court, no gamester admitted that brought not £300 at least,' he wrote. 'Montgomerie played the king's money and won him £750, which he had for his labour.' Five years later, the marriage of James's daughter, Elizabeth, to Frederick V Count Palatine of the Rhine was a wonder of ceremonial magnificence even for that exceptionally extravagant age, costing £50,000 and almost bankrupting the Crown in the process. 'This extreme cost and riches,' remarked Chamberlain after describing what the princess wore at her wedding, 'makes us all poor'. And the cost to the government was mirrored in the expenditure of those around the court as clothes became richer – and more revealing – and gentlemen competed in vain against Sir James Hay's unimpeachable reputation as the great spender of his age. On Twelfth Night 1621, according to Chamberlain, the carefree Scotsman organised a feast for the entire court that employed 100 cooks over eight days in the creation of 1,600 dishes, costing over £3,300. It seemed likely, thought Chamberlain, that 'this excessive spoil will make a dearth of the choicest dainties, when this one supper consumed twelve score pheasants, baked, boiled and roasted'. Nor should it be forgotten, of course, that Hay's considerable fortune had come in the first place from the royal bounty – a fact, which made the largesse of a once-beggarly Scot all the more galling in some quarters.

This is not to say, of course, that the king's own 'generosity' was without a wider political purpose. Cecil himself would observe in Parliament in 1610 that 'for a king not to be bountiful were a fault', and such generosity not only tied important men to his cause but coincided with and confirmed notions of the godlike nature of the king. Nor did the Jacobean court lack an altogether more refined aspect, just as one might expect with such a learned occupant of the throne. It was, for instance, a place at which literary activity in particular was heartily encouraged. The king 'doth wondrously covet learned discourse', wrote Thomas Howard to Harington, and while Jacobean censorship may well have been tighter than that of Elizabeth – as Ben Jonson discovered when he found himself in hot water for mocking Scotsmen in *Eastward Ho!* – it was hardly oppressive. Lancelot Andrewes, bishop and scholar, became a particular celebrity at James's court, while Inigo Jones received rich patronage and John Donne was virtually coerced into the clerical career that eventually afforded him such distinction.

And though the king's interest in serious drama was so limited that even the genius of Shakespeare appears to have largely bypassed him; he was nevertheless prepared to provide official encouragement when able. As early as 19 May 1603, for instance, letters patent were issued altering the name of 'Lord Chamberlain's Men' – the theatre troupe of William Shakespeare and Richard Burbage – to the 'King's Men', and allowing them to perform 'as well for the recreation of our loving subjects, as for our solace and pleasure when we shall think it good to see them … within their now usual house called The Globe, as well as all other boroughs and towns within the kingdom'. In the case of music, moreover, James was prepared not only to offer encouragement but to foot the bill. In 1596 the musicians of the chapel royal had petitioned the old queen for an increase in their stipend and were rebuffed. But what they lacked under Elizabeth, they gained under James and duly received an increase in their annual income from £30 to £40. Ultimately, the number of musicians on the payroll would more than double under James, as did the cost of the musical establishment in general, from £3,000 to £7,000 per annum.

Yet if the arts would flourish in James's time, the king's role was always primarily confined to largely passive recognition of established facts. And while James might easily have made his court so much more of an asset to his rule in England, it is no mere coincidence, perhaps, that the traditional picture of the Jacobean court took root so tenaciously: an endless stream of expenditure on a limitless parade of worthless people; a kaleidoscope of drunken maids of honour and effeminate young men produced by a complacent absentee king relentlessly pursuing deer. Greed, conspicuous consumption and sexual misbehaviour were all familiar features of the Whitehall scene before 1603, of course, and it was not for nothing that moral decay became a prominent theme of Elizabethan as well as Jacobean verse. However, the public face that Henry VIII and Elizabeth succeeded in projecting concealed a great deal of the baser behaviour which permeated their world, in much the same way that their personal gravitas would compensate for their own broader deficiencies. And while they, through careful stage-management and personal charisma, came to represent an ideal, James, for his part, remained an uncomfortable travesty of those very qualities he sought so desperately to embody. He had, of course, been brought up a king of Scots and ultimately his character and qualities had played out well enough upon the Scottish stage. But more than a border divided Scotland from England as James would soon discover. Curiously, therefore, his greatest fault as ruler of England would lie not in his laziness, his prodigality, his political theories or his unworthy favourites, but in something altogether more intangible and all the more irremediable: his plain, straightforward and frequently glaring lack of majesty.

12 ✦ Religion, Peace and Lucifer

'I could wish from my heart that it would please God to make me one of the members of such a general Christian union in religion, as laying wilfulness aside on both hands, we might meet in the middest, which is the centre and perfection of all things.'

From James I's address to his first English Parliament,
19 March 1604

B y the time that James I entered London for the first time on 7 May 1603, amid teeming crowds and lofty expectations, there were already two actively disappointed groups in the country: the long-suffering Catholic community and the motley crew of ambitious men on the fringe of official life who found themselves excluded from office by the triumph of the Cecil–Howard administration in which the king had placed his faith. For the former, in particular, James had seemed to offer fresh hope. Pursuing his dream of healing Europe's religious feuds, the new king had already resumed diplomatic relations with the papacy and drawn a careful distinction between those Catholics who accepted their duty of allegiance to the Crown and those that did not. To the loyal, at least, he was prepared to allow the free exercise of their religion in private, so long as they made no effort to increase their numbers. But even so eminently enlightened an approach to such an intractable problem was already inadequate, since in seeking Catholic support for his succession, James had encouraged still higher hopes that could now be neither satisfied nor extinguished. In 1599, the Scottish Jesuit, Robert Tempest, had boasted how he could produce evidence 'in the king's own hand' that he was a Catholic, and the pope's last informal communication to James before he left Scotland had been an inquiry whether Prince Henry might not be brought up in the faith of Rome. Penal laws and recusancy fines, or so it was widely believed, would soon be a thing of the past, while in Ireland, in particular, the old religion was making a new and strident show of confidence. 'Jesuits, seminaries and friars now come abroad in open show,' wrote one contemporary chronicler, 'bringing forth old rotten stocks and stones of images.'

It was hardly surprising, therefore, that frustrated Catholics would soon be indulging the penchant for conspiracy and intrigue that had already led to a number of spectacular incidents during the reign of Elizabeth – though the first attempt at subversion during James's rule would prove more farcical than threatening. Indeed, the so-called 'Bye Plot' revealed more about divisions within the Catholic priesthood between Jesuits on the one hand and 'secular' priests, who wished to remain loyal to the Crown, than about any mortal threat to the king. In fact, the plotters, led by the secular priest William Watson wished only for recusancy fines to be lifted and for Catholics to be accorded some posts in government – objectives which fell far short of the wishes of the leading English Jesuits, George Blackwell, John Gerard and Henry Garnet, who desired the complete restoration of the old religion and had only acquiesced in James's succession in the first place, since the King of Spain was not at that moment prepared to support opposition with armed force. When Watson laid plans for a Scottish-style kidnapping, therefore, the Jesuit leadership readily betrayed the plot to the authorities, with the intention of striking a telling blow against those 'loyal' Catholics who might interfere with their own more radical intentions. The result was a would-be attempt to 'take away the king and all his cubs' on St John's Day (24 June) 1603, which never materialised, and the subsequent execution of Watson and some of his confederates.

In the course of extinguishing this altogether pallid escapade, however, the government also exposed another, marginally more sinister conspiracy known as the Main Plot, which had apparently overlapped with Watson's intended venture at various points. The motives in this case, insofar as they can be gauged at all, were predominantly political, as men who found themselves frustrated by the continuance in office of Cecil and his friends decided to act. Lord Cobham, Warden of the Cinque Ports, had already attempted to intercept James on his journey south in a vain attempt to forestall the triumph of the Cecil–Howard grouping, and now – with the aid of a number of disaffected individuals including Sir Griffin Markham, a Catholic who already had links with the Bye Plot, and Lord Grey of Wilton, a leading Puritan – he attempted to persuade Count d'Aremberg, the ambassador of the Spanish Netherlands, to finance the landing of a Spanish force in Britain. The intention was to murder the king and his advisers, and to place Lady Arbella Stuart on the throne, after which she would be married in accordance with the wishes of the Catholic rulers of Spain and Austria.

The daughter of James's uncle, Lord Charles Stuart, Arbella had been left parentless early in life and was raised by her grandmother in the grandeur and seclusion of Hardwick Hall. She was a classical scholar whose learning was reputed to extend even to acquaintance with Hebrew and stood in high favour with the king. 'Nature enforces me,' James had written, 'to love her as the creature living nearest kin to me, next to my own children.' But, as a potential replacement for the king, she remained a painfully poor choice of candidate, for not only was she fundamentally loyal to his cause, she was also a Protestant. Under such circumstances, the Main Plot had no effect whatsoever other than to saddle its adherents with a clear-cut charge of treason. Almost incredibly, moreover, one of those implicated in this pro-Spanish daydream was none other than Sir Walter Raleigh whose career had been heroically anti-Spanish throughout the previous reign. Though despised by Cobham, who was the brother of Cecil's long-dead wife, Raleigh was nevertheless Cobham's cousin – and now would pay a heavy price for that connection.

Hitherto, only the personal favour of the former queen had kept Raleigh in office in the teeth of the enmity of the Cecils, both father and son. But the new king was known to favour peace with Spain, and two years earlier, Robert Cecil had informed James that Cobham, who was his own father-in-law, and Raleigh, 'in their prodigal dissensions would not stick to confess daily how contrary it is to their nature to resolve to be under your sovereignty'. Deprived of the captaincy of the royal guard and excluded from court, Raleigh is quite likely, moreover, to have played into his enemies' hands by bemoaning his mistreatment to Cobham, though the latter's evidence against him was later retracted and only delivered in any case at a moment when he had completely broken down. At the same time, Raleigh's passionate denials at his trial in the court room of Wolvesey Castle at Winchester in November 1603 continue to have a decided ring of truth about them.

The main charges were that he had conspired with Cobham 'to deprive the king of his government and advance the Lady Arbella Stuart to the throne', and set out to 'bring in the Roman superstition, and to procure foreign enemies to invade the kingdom' – all of which Raleigh vehemently and convincingly denied. But his protests were vain and his trial a carefully orchestrated sham, which proceeded with all the venom and virulence of a latter-day show trial. Prosecuted remorselessly by Sir Edward Coke, the great champion and exponent of the English Common Law, and denounced as 'a monster' and 'the greatest Lucifer that ever lived', Raleigh remained unwavering. 'Oh barbarous! …' he declared, 'I was never any plotter with them against my country, I was never false to the Crown of England.' But when he denounced his accusers as 'hellish spiders', Coke's response encapsulated the obvious injustice of the proceedings. 'Thou hast an English face but a Spanish heart,' he retorted, 'and thyself art a spider of hell. For thou confesses the king to be a most sweet and gracious prince, and yet thou hast conspired against him.'

The guilty verdict delivered by Lord Chief Justice Popham that inevitably followed convinced nobody and guaranteed, ironically, a wave of sympathy for Raleigh that would hardly have been forthcoming otherwise. Indeed, it remains questionable whether most of the others implicated in the Main Plot, including Cobham and Grey, also needed to have been treated in quite the way that they were. Characteristically, James dissected the moral niceties involved with an intensity that ultimately cut common sense – and common decency – to pieces. It was to Englishmen one of the most surprising things about their new ruler that, in his overwhelming urge to demonstrate both his intellect and zeal for justice, he would go to such tangled lengths to unravel the truth – and think out loud in doing so. In this case, predictably, he was torn between his duty to make an example of traitors and his urge to be merciful. 'To execute Grey, who was a noble young spirited fellow,' he reasoned, 'and save Cobham, who was base and unworthy, were a matter of injustice.' However, 'to save Grey, who was of a proud insolent nature, and execute Cobham, who had showed great tokens of humility and repentance were as great a solecism.' Crucially, however, even when James eventually opted for clemency, he did so in a manner that not only robbed the act of much of its virtue but demonstrated a degree of spite that sat ill with the principles of justice he claimed to personify. For Grey and Cobham, along with Sir Griffin Markham were each brought to the scaffold twice before their reprieve was finally read to them – a decision, in Cecil's words, to which James had 'made no soul living privy, the messenger excepted'.

In Raleigh's case, meanwhile, the king's callousness was altogether more pronounced. Raleigh remained, of course, an intolerably proud, quick-tempered and violent man of action whom his Elizabethan colleagues had found no more tolerable than James now did, and the policies of war and piracy he stood for were in any case precisely those that the king had made it his mission in life to reverse. But to commute his execution, which had been fixed for 13 December only to consign him subsequently to the Tower and leave him there for thirteen years with a suspended death sentence hanging over him was to show a meanness of spirit which even James's own son found himself unable to condone. None but his father, Prince Henry was to say, would have found a cage for such a bird. And when peace with Spain quickly followed in August 1604, it fell as a further hammer blow to the prisoner who could now look forward, in his own words, only to the 'bribeless judgement hall' of Heaven, where Christ alone would be 'the king's attorney'.

If, however, the conclusion of hostilities with Spain represented the cruellest of cuts for Sir Walter Raleigh, it marked for James merely the first step in realising his most cherished vision of himself as a wise and benevolent mediator-king who, after uniting Scotland and England, would then bring peace to the warring nations of Europe and thereafter seal his illustrious place in history by reconciling that continent's conflicting faiths. Now, after all, he was ruler of Europe's most powerful Protestant state, strengthened by union with Scotland, and he enjoyed a number of advantages derived from his experience to date. His prestige was high, for instance, in Scandinavia and northern Germany, and he was also on good terms with the Catholic states opposed to Spain. To English friendship with France he could add the old tradition of Franco-Scottish alliance, and he had also cultivated Tuscany and Venice. But if he had maintained peace with foreign countries as ruler of Scotland, it was due in no small measure to the remoteness and insignificance of his kingdom. And if he had hitherto dabbled promiscuously across the religious divide with both Catholic and Protestant powers, he would not be able to do so with such impunity in England. Indeed, James's hope from this point onwards that he could be both a champion of Protestantism and friend of Spain would prove not only a cardinal error but a classic demonstration of his belief that he could square circles by force of intellect and goodwill alone.

As early as 1590, in fact, James had sent ambassadors to the German princes to organise a joint threat of economic boycott to force Spain to come to terms. But until the Spanish had finally lost hope of conquering Ireland, and their rebellious Dutch provinces were capable of resistance without foreign aid, all hope of an end to fighting was vain. And these conditions were only to be fulfilled at the very end of Elizabeth's life, leaving her successor, by sheer good luck, the chance to wield the olive branch successfully. One of James's first actions as King of England, therefore, was to recall the letters of marque that had enabled English privateers to prey so greedily upon Spanish commerce under his predecessor, and to order the cessation of all hostilities with Spain on the grounds that since he, personally, had never been at war with that country, he could not become so by inheriting the English Crown. It was specious reasoning of precisely the kind that James specialised in when determined to achieve his own ends. But the Spaniards, too, were ready for peace, and by the end of September a Spanish ambassador, Don Juan de Tassis, was presenting his credentials at Winchester with a view to opening preliminary negotiations.

Since the war had reached a state of utter deadlock, the best that either side could now hope for was merely a cessation of hostilities, and there was little need for prolonged negotiation. Yet there were endless delays, largely on account of what Sir Henry Wotton called 'Spanish gravity sake' and it was not until August 1604 that the Constable of Castile finally crossed the Channel with full powers to sign what would become known as the Treaty of London. In the meantime, however, James's previously friendly attitude to the Dutch now became lofty and condescending. Holding the so-called 'Cautionary Towns' of Flushing, Brille and Rammekens as security for the large sums of money advanced by Elizabeth, the king's unfamiliar status as creditor seems to have gone to his head. He believed, said the Venetian ambassador, 'that at a single nod of his the Dutch would yield him all the dominion that they had gained', and he also talked foolishly of their revolt from Spain as though it were a crime. When told that Ostend might fall if English aid were withheld, his answer was characteristically insensitive. 'What of it?' he declared, 'Was not Ostend originally the King of Spain's and therefore now the Archduke's?' And when Johan van Oldenbarnevelt,

Land's Advocate of Holland, was dispatched to plead the Dutch cause, he was unable to obtain audience with James until smuggled into a gallery where the king was about to walk.

James, it is true, stood his ground against the Spanish stalwartly, correctly judging that they were in greater need of peace than his own kingdom. But what is often construed as the one great triumph of James's statesmanship was not a definitive solution to the long-standing tension between the two countries. Above all, Spain remained at war with the Dutch, and while Spain, unlike her rebellious enemy, was denied facilities to raise money and volunteers in England, suspicion and mistrust was bound to remain. Nor was the Treaty of London, signed at Somerset House, a source of unalloyed relief for Englishmen as a whole. For while the king resolutely refused to denounce the Dutch rebels outright, maintaining that while they and the Spanish continued to fight he 'was resolved always to carry an even hand betwixt them both', and Cecil successfully defended English trading rights with both sides, there remained a bitter taste for many who felt the treaty a betrayal not only of their valiant co-religionists but of their own great past. Indeed, fanned by invective from Puritan pulpits and darkening storm clouds in Germany where the Counter-Reformation was already stoking the fires of what would become the Thirty Years' War, anti-Spanish and anti-Catholic feeling would continue, in spite of James's usual good intentions, to remain a prominent feature of his English kingdom for the next twenty years.

Yet the king would not lightly forsake the selfsame good intentions in religion either, which now became the next arena for his mediating efforts. To the end of his life, in fact, James could never rid himself of the illusion that it was possible to 'win all men's hearts' by reason, logic and purely intellectual persuasion. But when the truth was at issue he could only construe it as his to determine, and when resistance persisted, he could only perceive it as wilfulness. 'It should become you,' he would write to Archbishop Abbot some years later, when they had differed over a point of theology, 'to have a kind of faith implicit in my judgement, as well in respect of some skill I have in divinity, as also that I hope no honest man doubts of the uprightness of my conscience; and the best thankfulness that you, that are so far my creature, can use towards me, is to reverence and follow my judgement, except where you may demonstrate unto me that I am mistaken or wrong-informed.' Even archbishops, then, might expect to defer to the king in matters of religion and the same was true for Catholics, Calvinists and anyone else who found themselves at odds with his views. For it was one of many curious ironies that a ruler who saw himself as a mediator in all things was so rarely prepared to compromise on his own ideas.

Without doubt, the Church of England that greeted James upon his arrival in 1603 was an institution much to his taste. Moderate, placid, hierarchical and deferential, administered by upper clergy who, though sometimes worldly and arrogant, were learned scholars and able administrators, it was a far cry from the more notorious elements of the Kirk he had left behind in Scotland. Whitgift, the Archbishop of Canterbury at the time of Elizabeth's death, and Bancroft, the Bishop of London who replaced him in 1604, could not have contrasted more starkly with the likes of Andrew Melville and John Durie who had plagued him previously. And there were others, too, just as willing, it seemed, to underpin their 'Anglicanism' with 'High Church' principles and the so-called 'Erastian' conviction that the state should enjoy unqualified primacy in all ecclesiastical affairs. William Barlow, Dean of Chester, Thomas Bilson, the learned Bishop of Winchester, and John King, Bishop of London (whom James dubbed the king of preachers) were only some of the divines who now, often literally, surrounded the throne. In due course, too, he would find in George Abbot, the Master of University College, a man whose zest for the Early Fathers and mild Calvinism, tempered by careful study of St Augustine, exactly matched his own. But it was in the presence of Lancelot Andrewes especially that James's raucous mirth was most respectfully suppressed. Dean of Westmister at the opening of the reign before being elevated successively to the bishoprics of Chester, Ely and Winchester, Andrewes possessed all the qualities guaranteed to endear him to the king, combining learning with wit, piety with adroitness, and austerity with the ready tongue of the courtier. And, as always, when James was won over he was won over unreservedly, speaking of Andrewes' sermons as a voice from heaven and asking the bishop on one occasion whether his sermon notes might be laid at night beneath the royal pillow.

Yet if James revered his Anglican divines as men and scholars, it was the Church they represented that he valued above all. Episcopal in structure and Calvinist in doctrine, the Church of England represented, indeed, an ideal model from the king's perspective, and in Richard Hooker, whose *Of the Lawes of Ecclesiasticall Politie* was published in 1593, it had found, it seems, its ultimate apologist. For Hooker's book treated the Church of Rome as merely one part of the visible Church – like those of Jerusalem, Antioch and Alexandra – and skilfully contended that the unreformed Church had fallen into error, becoming unsound in doctrine and corrupt in its behaviour. By contrast, Hooker argued, the Church of England had returned to original truths and godly practices, while retaining its apostolic links by virtue of its emergence from its Roman predecessor. Most important of all, however, Hooker was convinced like his king that state and society were so intimately and integrally connected that there could be no question of ecclesiastical independence from secular authority. So it was hardly surprising, perhaps, that according to Hooker's biographer, Isaak Walton, James considered the *Lawes* such 'a grave, comprehensive, clear manifestation of reason, and that backed with the authority of the Scriptures, the fathers and schoolmen, and with all law both sacred and civil'.

If James loved the Church of England quite literally as his own, however, it is altogether more doubtful whether he ever fully understood it. Addressing his first parliament in 1604, he distinguished three religious elements within his new kingdom. On the one hand, there was the religion 'publicly allowed and by the law maintained', as opposed to what were 'falsely called Catholics, but truly papists', whom in spite of the Bye and Main Plots, he still proposed to conciliate by toleration. The third group 'lurking within the bowels of this nation' was, he maintained, 'a private sect', consisting of 'Puritans and Novelists, who do not so far differ from us in points of religion as in their confused form of polity and parity, being ever discontented with the present government and impatient to suffer any superiority, which maketh their sect unable to be suffered in any well governed commonwealth'. For James, these Puritans were a distinct and largely monolithic body, mirroring their radical counterparts north of the Border – men espousing a democratic theory of ecclesiastical government, and intent like their Scottish counterparts upon relegating him to the status of 'God's sillie vassal'.

But such a neat categorisation of what the king termed 'Purinisme' involved a considerable and costly oversimplification, which dogged his efforts to understand the religious status quo in England and swiftly dashed his attempts to foster unity. For in reality the very word 'Puritan' had gained currency as a catch-all term of derision, which obscured more than it enlightened and encompassed a wide spectrum of opinion ranging from those wishing to bring about minor modifications to the Church's everyday practice to those outright 'separatists' who sought the complete 'independency' of each congregation from the stranglehold of state authority. Those who broadly accepted the Church of England, as constituted by Elizabeth I's religious settlement, also varied considerably in matters of detail. Some desired a compromise with Presbyterianism which would combine a Council of Elders with the bishop in the administration of diocesan discipline. Others wanted the use of ceremonial and vestments to be left to the discretion of the incumbent in each parish, and there was debate, too, over the positioning of the altar. Some decried 'Romish' practices, such as bowing at the name of Jesus and there were objections in some cases to the use of the sign of the cross in baptism, to the ring in marriage, and the rite of confirmation.

For James, who found himself well satisfied with the Church of England's existing rituals and practices, such matters were of little significance in their own right. Writing, for instance, upon the subject of clerical dress, he made it clear that division over such an issue merely 'gives advantage and entry to the papists'. 'No,' he declared, 'I am so far from being contentious in these things (which for my own part I ever esteemed as indifferent), as I do equally love and honour the learned and graved men of either of these opinions.' But in downplaying the need for dispute, James was also determined to stress the need for obedience on the grounds that 'in things indifferent, they are seditious which obey not the magistrate'. 'There is no man half so dangerous,' he contended, 'as he that repugns against order.' In emphasising the necessity of obedience over non-essentials, moreover, he also sowed further confusion in more significant areas by straddling conflicting positions, particularly over matters of doctrine, and balancing contending groups against each other. Above all, while Queen Elizabeth had sensibly discouraged religious debate, James not only leapt in head first, but consciously chose the deep end for doing so. This, after all, was a king who was never happier than when exchanging essays with Lancelot Andrewes or Hugo Grotius over the issue of final damnation, notwithstanding his condemnation of 'vain, proud Puritans', who believed that they ruled the Deity 'upon their fingers'. And this, too, was a ruler who believed himself capable of determining at a stroke the precise worth of those ceremonies and rituals unsupported by Scriptural injunction – the key bone of contention between 'Puritans' and his own episcopacy.

By 1603, ironically, the clamour for a drastic revision of the Prayer Book and for the abolition of bishops in favour of some more democratic model of ecclesiastical government had largely died down. Furthermore, an overwhelming majority of Englishmen still acknowledged the mystical authority of the monarchy and accepted the inseparability of Church and

State. All agreed that pluralism should be abolished and that a 'preaching, Godly ministry' must somehow be established. All agreed, too, that stipends must be increased. In 1585, Archbishop Whitgift had estimated that more than half the beneficed clergy of England had meagre incomes between £8 and £10 a year, while less than half could be licensed to preach for lack of university degrees. But by the end of Elizabeth's reign little had changed, and it was no special surprise that when two of his ex-pupils went to see him at Drayton Beauchamp, even Lancelot Andrewes was found 'tending his small allotment of sheep in a common field' while reading the *Odes of Horace*. Had James confined his activities to remedying such ills, he might well have made genuine progress. Had he avoided the summits of theological debate and the pitfalls of dabbling so wilfully in ceremonial niceties, he might also have saved both himself and his kingdom a good deal of acrimony and frustration.

Yet keen intellect and high principles did not, in James's case, always sit well with common sense and sound man management. Even as he was travelling down from Scotland for the first time, a selection of prominent Puritan clergy had respectfully presented him with the famous Millenary Petition – a skilfully drafted and studiously moderate document, wholly acceptable in terms of content to the majority of English bishops. The petitioners were not, they emphasised, factious men like the Presbyterians, nor schismatics like the so-called 'Brownists', but loyal subjects of the king, whose Christian judgement they now sought. They desired the discontinuance of the use of the sign of the cross in baptism, of the ring in marriage, and of the terms 'priest' and 'absolution'. They requested, too, that the rite of confirmation be abolished, the wearing of the surplice made optional, and the employment of music in church moderated. The ministry, on the other hand, was to be recruited from more able and learned men, while non-residence and pluralism were to be ended, the ecclesiastical courts reformed, and the Sabbath more strictly observed. All in all, there was little, ostensibly, to offend or threaten, and the graciousness of James's initial response was enough to warm Puritan hearts. The petition's suggestion of a conference between Puritans and Anglicans accorded closely, moreover, with the king's much-advertised love of intellectual inquiry and rational discourse.

What the king did not grasp, however, was that such a conference, whatever its outcome, would give Puritans a recognition they had never been granted by his predecessor and raise hopes that he could never realistically fulfil – hopes that were soon leading to disturbances of the peace in Suffolk. Equally importantly, the proposed conference represented a direct challenge to the Anglican bishops in whom James placed so much faith and who were soon launching a counter-offensive which would mould his conceptions of Puritanism for the rest of his reign. Oxford had answered the Millenary Petition by branding its authors seditious and identifying them with the Presbyterian ministers of Scotland that the king so loathed – men whose aim, it was said, was 'the utter overthrow of the present church government and instead thereof the setting up of a presbytery in every parish'. In July, moreover, James held long and earnest conference with Bishop Bancroft, the self-avowed arch-enemy of Puritan innovation, at his palace in Fulham, with the result that by October a proclamation had been issued, prohibiting petitions concerning religion and asserting that the existing constitution and doctrine of the Church of England were agreeable to God's Word and in conformity with the condition of primitive Christianity. All men, he told Whitgift subsequently, must 'conform to that which we have by open declaration published', while any clergyman employing unauthorised forms of service was to be punished severely.

Yet when Bishop Bilson urged James to abandon plans for the conference, the response was predictable. 'Content yourself, my lord,' the king informed him, 'we know better than you what belongeth to these matters.' And so it was that, as soon as the festivities of James's first Christmas in England were over – while peace negotiations with Spain were still dragging on, and before he had even met his first parliament – a representative Puritan delegation from Oxford and Cambridge was commanded to meet a selection of bishops and clergy under his chairmanship at Hampton Court on 14 January 1604. Although now wrongly convinced of the nature of the Puritan 'threat', he remained equally convinced nevertheless that it could be banished once and for all by the cleansing effect of his superior intellect and solemn judgement. For it was clear to him, at least, that Puritan leaders like Dr John Rainolds, the President of Corpus Christi, Oxford, or John Knewstubs of St John's College, Cambridge, would never be able to demonstrate that he was 'mistaken or wrong informed'. 'I did ever hold persecution as one of the infallible notes of a false Church,' James had once told Cecil, adding that he would 'never agree that any should die for error in faith'. And now he would have the chance to exercise his healing influence as what he himself described as a 'good physician' on a suitably imposing stage.

With a more accommodating and less outspoken approach on the king's part the Hampton Court Conference might well have achieved much. Puritan demands were, after all, more moderate than they had been for the past twenty years and, most significantly of all, far more moderate than they would ever be again. Most of those protesting at this time were, it should be remembered, demonstrably the best educated, most zealous and conscientious of the parish clergy, the majority of whom had hitherto loyally accepted regulations of which they disapproved in the interests of Church unity as a whole. To have conciliated them, therefore, before they became irreparably embittered with the episcopacy was not only the obvious priority but a distinct possibility at this critical juncture. 'Religion is the soul of a kingdom,' James would assure his audience at the very outset of proceedings, 'and unity, the life of religion.' Yet it was no coincidence that the Puritan representatives were quite conspicuously excluded on the first day while the king addressed his bishops. And although his preliminary speech, which lasted some five hours, committed him to 'examine and try' complaints about the Church 'and fully to remove the occasions thereof, if scandalous', it also made clear that, unlike his predecessors, who 'were fain to alter all things they found established', he saw no reason 'so much to alter and change anything as to confirm what he found well settled already'. The religious status quo was therefore to remain intact in all fundamentals, while the conference was to serve, it seems, as a show case for the king's skill in divinity before a suitably submissive and amenable gathering of awestruck admirers who, when apprised of their errors, 'must yield to him'.

With these priorities fixed in advance, it was clear, of course, that the four Puritan leaders, led by Dr Rainolds, who faced the nine Anglican divines, eight deans of the Church and lords of the Privy Council ranged against them were unlikely to enjoy a truly impartial hearing when admitted to the conference on the second day. And if eye-witness William Barlow's account of proceedings, *The Summe and Substance of the Conference*, may well have exaggerated the abrasiveness of James's attitude towards the Puritans, it remains hard nevertheless to deny that the king was inclined to lapse on occasion into the kind of sharp-tongued pedantry and dismissiveness that has so often been associated with him. The four Puritan leaders had been hand-picked, in fact, by the Privy Council and were far from being the 'brainsick and heady preachers' that the king both feared and despised. In addition, to Rainolds and Knewstubs, there was Laurence Chaderton, whom even Bancroft considered a good friend, and Thomas Spark, a comparatively innocuous lecturer in divinity at Oxford. Yet when all four entered the king's presence on the second day, looking as if they wore 'cloaks and nightcaps', they would be facing an uphill struggle.

It was not without some justification, indeed, that Barlow referred to them as 'plaintiffs', and while Spark said little, Chaderton was 'mute as any fish'. Knewstubs, it is true, condemned the use of the cross in worship, only to be roundly quashed by Lancelot Andrewes, and Rainolds, too, was given short shrift over infant baptism, the use of the ring in marriage rites and, above all, the use of the phrase 'with my body I thee worship' in the Anglican wedding ceremony. Nor could the king, knowing full well that Rainolds was a confirmed bachelor, resist a jarringly patronising jibe in response to his pronouncements on the union of men and women. 'Many a man,' said James, smiling at his hapless target, 'speaks of Robin Hood who never shot his bow.' 'If you had a good wife yourself,' he continued, 'you would think all the honour and worship you could do for her well bestowed.' And if the famous aphorism of 'No bishop, no king', with which James concluded the later discussion on the ordination of bishops, was from his point of view little more than an emphatic statement of undeniable fact, it remained nonetheless another case of the type of cudgel phraseology, which ill accorded with what was supposedly the avowed intention of the whole conference. Where James did offer genial agreement, moreover – on the need for producing a revised catechism, raising stipends, recovering lost Church revenues, providing a better 'teaching ministry', discouraging pluralism and enforcing proper observance of the Sabbath – he repeatedly undermined any resulting goodwill by spasmodic outbursts of needless condescension. 'And surely,' he declared at one point, 'if these be the greatest matters you be grieved with, I need not have been troubled with such importunities and complaints as have been made unto me; some other more private course might have been taken for your satisfaction.' Whereupon, we are told, 'looking upon the lords, he shook his head smiling'.

It was not, however, until the subject of ecclesiastical discipline was raised that James's swagger and volubility turned to outright anger and provocation. Until this point, at least, the king had made some effort to leaven his jibes with attempts to play the honest broker. When, for instance, Bishop Bancroft interrupted Rainolds on the grounds that 'schismatics are not to be listened to against bishops', he had been put firmly in his place on the grounds that there could be no 'effectual issue of disputation, if each party be not suffered, without chopping, to speak at large'. Likewise, when Bancroft objected to the Puritan proposal for a new translation of the Bible, James appeared equally fair-minded. 'If every man's humour might be followed,' the bishop had protested, 'there would be no end of translating.' To which the king replied that he had 'never yet' seen a Bible 'well translated in English', before urging the creation of what would become the 'Authorised' or 'King James' version, which has been justly characterised as the great glory of his reign. Yet the harmony of these exchanges was undermined all at once when Rainolds suggested to his cost that episcopal synods, 'where the bishop with his presbytery should determine all such points as before could not be decided', would be less obnoxious than the existing system of archdeacons' courts.

The connotations of the very word 'presbytery', linked as it was so inextricably with the ecclesiastical polity of the Presbyterian Kirk of Scotland, made it intolerably offensive to James, and the use of it was, to say the least, ill-advised. But the innocence of Rainolds' intention could not have been clearer from the broader content of his proposal, and what followed demonstrated all too aptly how the king was unable to bridle his emotions when delicate negotiation was involved. No less importantly, it proved conclusively that a hectoring tone, particularly when resulting from an apparently inexplicable misapprehension, was unlikely to win converts even to the most valid cause. At this point, according to Barlow at least, 'his Majesty was somewhat stirred, yet, which is admirable in him, without passion or show thereof'. But Barlow had his eye on promotion and was shortly to be rewarded with the bishopric of Lincoln for his sympathetic account of the entire conference. The reality, therefore – as recorded in all the variously reported versions of James's words – could not have been more starkly different.

Plainly mistaking Rainolds' meaning, the king proceeded to tell him, in fact, how a 'Scottish' presbytery 'as well agreeth with a monarchy as God and the Devil'. 'Should such a body ever be permitted within the Church of England', he continued, 'then Jack and Tom and Will and Dick shall meet, and at their pleasure censure me and my council and all our proceedings … When I mean to live under a presbytery I will go into Scotland again, but while I am in England I will have bishops to govern the Church'. And then, it seems, as a final flourish he turned to his Puritan audience and declared stridently that 'if this is all they have to say, I will make them conform themselves or I will harry them out of this land or else do worse'. So with all the insensitivity of a man utterly convinced of the transparency of his good intentions and correctness – as well as the unalloyed love of his subjects, which, he believed, entitled him to impunity even when making the most provocative statements – James demonstrated his failure to appreciate the fundamental principle that had underpinned his predecessor's whole system of government in Church and State. This principle rested on a series of delicate balances which could work in practice only so long as they were never subjected to any harsh dialectic and definition – or undermined by injudicious and needless threats. On this occasion as on others, James would eventually moderate his position and behave in practice altogether more pragmatically when his irrational blaze of anger had burnt itself out. But such unedifying outbursts were inevitably costly, not only because of the anger they provoked in turn, but far more importantly because of their impact upon the credibility of James's leadership and authority.

In this case, at least, the more damaging effects of the king's indiscretion were by no means immediately apparent. Indeed, the conference closed on the following day in an atmosphere of outward goodwill, with the Anglican divines heaping praise upon James, in spite of their misgivings that any concessions had been granted at all, and the king himself convinced that, since 'obedience and humility were the marks of honest and good men', the Puritans would thereafter toe the line. Archbishop Whitgift, it seems, was convinced that 'his Majesty spake by the special assistance of God's spirit', while Bancroft acknowledged 'unto Almighty God the singular mercy we have received at His hands in giving us such a king as since Christ his time the like he thought had not been'. In the meantime, Rainolds and his counterparts concealed their undoubted frustration with a humble plea that their brethren 'who were grave men and obedient unto the laws' might simply be given some time to determine whether they would conform to the new and more rigid enforcement of the Prayer Book ceremonies and the Thirty-Nine Articles.

But the fact remained that the underlying tone of Elizabethan government, however authoritarian in practice, had been altogether less abrasive. Lord Burghley, for instance, had considered it his duty to lessen the impact of Whitgift's ecclesiastical courts upon 'poor ministers' whom, he believed, were being made 'subject to condemnation before they be taught their error'. James, however, was the controversialist, thirsting for wordy and sardonic victory. 'The king,' wrote Sir John Harington, 'talked much Latin and disputed with Dr Rainolds at Hampton, but he rather used upbraidings than arguments', adding that if, as his bishops claimed, he had spoken 'by the power of inspiration', then 'I wist not what they meant, but the spirit was rather foul-mouthed'. And if Harington's or any other account should be doubted, there remain of course James's own comments to consider. 'We have kept such a revel with the Puritans here these two days as we never heard the like,' he informed the Earl of Northampton the day after the Hampton Court Conference closed. 'They fled me so from argument to argument without ever answering me directly, *ut est eorum mos*, as I was forced at last to say unto them that if any of them had been in a college disputing with their scholars, if any of their disciples had answered them in that sort, they would have fetched him up in place of a reply, and so should the rod have plied upon the poor boy's buttocks'. Thus, in the happy belief that he had 'peppered them soundly', James brought to an end the first part of his attempt to achieve a 'general Christian union in religion'.

James's indiscretions were capable, in fact, of wounding even his own avowed allies. The bishops, for instance, were less likely to have been assured of the divinity of the king's words when, not long after the Hampton Court Conference, he told Parliament that the Devil, sparing neither labour nor pains, was a busy bishop. But his sympathies remained unwavering. Only one month after the conference, moreover, Whitgift died and Bancroft was duly installed as Archbishop of Canterbury. And though the new archbishop's anti-Puritan sympathies have sometimes been exaggerated, he would nevertheless quietly choose to forget most of James's agreed concessions, as would the vast majority of his episcopal colleagues. Nor was the king's subsequent attention to his intended reforms ever sufficient to persuade Bancroft to do otherwise. Even if it was true, therefore, that only ninety of the Church of England's 9,000 incumbents eventually resigned in response to the Canons of 1604, this was mainly due to the fact that, in spite of their underlying hostility to reform, many bishops nevertheless proved reluctant to force so many of their best clergy into taking the ultimate step of defiance. 'The bishops themselves,' wrote Chamberlain, 'are loath to proceed too rigorously in casting out and depriving so many well reputed of for life and learning.' 'Only the king,' he added significantly, 'is constant to have all come to conformity,' while even an outspoken high churchman like James Montagu, Bishop of Bath and Wells and later Winchester, urged that recalcitrant ministers should be called to account gradually 'rather than all without difference be cut down at once' on the grounds that those who lost their places would gain more from pity than they would from their piety.

Yet, in spite of his detestation of Puritanism, James's good intentions for the Church as a whole were often evident. 'I have daily more and more cause to hate and abhor all that sect, enemies to all kings,' he informed Cecil in November after he had been presented with a Puritan petition while hunting near Royston. On the broader front, however he resented criticism of the Church in whatever form it came, supporting the ecclesiastical courts in their struggle with the courts of common law and defending his bishops when they came under fire from Parliament. Nor was he prepared to deepen ecclesiastical poverty by cynical alienations of property, and though simony was rife at court, he resisted it in clerical appointments. Indeed, he rejected with scorn a cynical scheme to reassess the evaluation of benefices in order to obtain large sums in first fruits, and on the other hand supported church leaders in their highly unpopular efforts to obtain enhanced revenues from tithes. In 1608, moreover, he was struck by the disgraceful condition of St Paul's Cathedral, and though he offered no money himself, nevertheless encouraged the Bishop of London to finance repairs.

James's appointments to the episcopacy were not, it is true, always judicious. Certainly, large numbers of royal chaplains who, like Robert Abbot, had won the king's favour for no especially compelling reason found themselves promoted. 'Abbot,' James informed this particular beneficiary of royal goodwill, 'I have had much to do to make thee a bishop; but I know no reason for it, unless it were because thou hast written a book against a popish prelate.' When, moreover, Lancelot Andrewes was passed over as Archbishop of Canterbury in 1611, amid general astonishment, the king explained his decision in terms that can only be described as eccentric. The successful candidate, George Abbot, a university man who had little experience of ecclesiastical administration, was told by the king that his appointment did not spring from his learning, wisdom or sincerity (though the king did not doubt that he possessed these qualities) but out of respect for the recently deceased Earl of Dunbar, who had recommended him. Yet, in other respects, James's ecclesiastical record was not without its merits. In this particular case, for instance, Abbot's appointment was undoubtedly less provocative to Puritan opinion than the elevation of Andrewes might have been and appears to have represented an incipient willingness on James's part to send signals of compromise. Much more important by far, however, was the ringing success of the publication of the 'Authorised Version' of the Bible, for which the king must be accorded all due praise.

If, as James himself acknowledged, the Hampton Court Conference had been intended 'to cast a sop into Cerberus's mouth that he bark no more', the upshot had clearly been less than wholly satisfactory. In 1610, indeed, the Commons' Petition on Religion, presented by the Puritan gentry in Parliament, plainly demonstrated the discontent of significant sections of the laity, and grumbling would only begin to abate at last with Bancroft's replacement in 1611. But John Rainold's proposal for a new English Bible on the conference's second day, which appeared at the time as an almost casual interjection, not only captured the king's imagination but brought out the best in him and, in doing so, prompted what was arguably one of his most significant achievements. Together with Bancroft and Cecil, he would engage the finest of Greek and Hebrew scholars to produce 'one uniform translation ... ratified by royal authority', which, if successful, was to represent both the lynchpin and crowning glory of James's quest for religious unity. Equally importantly, it would affirm in the process his own exalted conception of kingship, since the Geneva Bible, which was the version used by the majority of his common subjects, contained anti-monarchical margin notes which were, in his view, 'very partial, untrue, seditious and savouring too much of dangerous conceits'. If it could be superseded, along with the existing official Bible of the Church of England, the so-called 'Bishops' Bible', the slate could at last be wiped clean of contention and misapprehension. 'You will scarcely conceive how earnest his Majesty is to have this work begun,' Bancroft informed a colleague in June 1604 – and, as events would demonstrate, he did not exaggerate.

Bancroft himself had, of course, objected vehemently when a new translation was first mooted, only to change his tune completely upon realising the extent of the king's commitment. At Hampton Court, moreover, James's passion for sketching programmes and drafting directives had borne immediate fruit. The translation, he decided, should be made by the most learned linguists at Oxford and Cambridge, and thereafter reviewed by the bishops and other learned churchmen before being presented to the Privy Council and then 'authorised' ultimately by royal consent. Such, meanwhile, was Bancroft's sudden enthusiasm for the project that he was appointed general co-ordinator of the process of translation and by March, on the king's initiative, had asked Lancelot Andrewes to be one of the regional supervisors for three translation teams – the two others being Edward Lively and John Harding, both professors of Hebrew at the two universities. Fifty-four translators in all, each working separately within six groups would eventually confer with their group members before submitting their final translation to the scrutiny of the other groups. Ultimately, six men, two selected from each group, would review the work as a whole in London, after which Bishop Bilson and Miles Smith would give a last revision to the completed text.

Significantly, the translators were selected primarily for their linguistic expertise rather than their religious views, and while one Puritan, Hugh Broughton, was excluded for his radical opinions, Dr John Rainolds, who had been buffeted by the king at Hampton Court Conference, was nevertheless invited to contribute. James too, it seems, contributed directly by undertaking the translation of the Psalms in conjunction with Sir William Alexander, his friend and literary crony, who would nevertheless complain of the difficulty of working with the king, since 'he prefers his own to all else'. By the time of his death James had completed about thirty; at which point, as Bishop Williams remarked, he was called to sing psalms with the angels. Similarly, while James commanded that the Bishops' Bible be followed as far as possible, with words like 'church' retained in preference to 'congregation', he was responsible for making sure that the new version should be readily comprehensible even to the most humble of his subjects. The language of the Bishops' Bible had, after all, been not only inaccurate at times, but overly literal and in consequence lumpy, dense and difficult to navigate. Ecclesiastes 1:11, which was eventually rendered 'Cast thy bread upon the waters' in the King James Bible had, for instance, been presented in the earlier version as 'Lay thy bread upon wet faces'. Ultimately, indeed, although the Bishops' Bible was to be treated at the outset as what might be termed the 'default' version and left untouched if adequate, it would comprise only 8 per cent of the final Authorised Version.

To James's considerable credit, then, the bible which eventually saw the light of day in 1611 was, without any real question, the most significant and successful that had been produced to date. And though it was essentially a patchwork quilt, incorporating the finest elements of former translations, it would stand the test of time for good reason, since, as James seems to have appreciated, Jacobean culture was a culture of the word, and above all a listening culture, which gave the book both its clarity and poetic force. The bible was intended, after all, to be 'read in churches', and it was no coincidence therefore that the king had demanded that the words be 'set forth gorgeously'. Nor was it any coincidence that one of the last steps of the translation process was a 'hearing'. The result was a grand harmony, stateliness and splendour that in spite of its nature as a committee product and notwithstanding its high Anglican tone, largely superseded factional or sectarian divides. As such, the King James Bible was in many respects the embodiment of the highest and noblest of all his religious aims: the reconciliation of contending parties under the benevolent guidance of a wise, all-knowing and all-governing king.

It was not without some irony, therefore, that James remained in many respects more tolerant of English Roman Catholics than their Puritan counterparts. He harboured, it is true, a deep suspicion of Catholic priests and an outright abhorrence and terror of Jesuits, but he distinguished sharply between them and the Catholic laity. Indeed, before he left Scotland he had told Salisbury that he intended to seek a golden mean in dealing with English Catholics, on the one hand preventing them from rebellion and increasing their numbers until they were 'able to practise their old principles upon us', but asking at the same time for no more than outward conformity to the law by attendance at Church of England services. Even after the Main and Bye Plots, therefore, the Catholics were relieved of recusancy fines, though these had been collected in May 1603, primarily because the king was already stretched for money. The ideal of Christian unity was still, after all, far from dead at this time, and if Pope Clement VIII might somehow be persuaded to summon an ecumenical council of the kind that was still considered possible in some quarters, there remained hope that a middle ground could be established, so long as the Holy Father renounced temporal sovereignty and the political subversion of the Jesuits.

Certainly, James's own words speak eloquently enough of his intentions. 'We have always wished,' he wrote, 'that some good course might be taken by a general council, lawfully called, whereby it might once for all be made manifest which is the doctrine of antiquity nearest succeeding to the primitive Church.' He was, moreover, a declared 'Catholic' Christian, a member of the Ancient, Catholic and Apostolic Church, as constituted in the first five centuries of its existence. If, therefore, the papacy could be persuaded to purge itself of the unbiblical accretions that had emerged since that time, James was willing to accord Rome a high place in any newly united Church that might then arise. 'I would with all my heart,' he declared, 'give my consent that the Bishop of Rome should have the first seat. And for his temporal principality over the seignory of Rome, I do not quarrel it either. Let him in God's name be *Primus Episcopus inter omnes Episcopos*, and *Princeps Episcoporum*, so it be no otherwise but as Peter was *Princeps Apostolarum*.' James's only other requirement was that the pope should 'quit his godhead and usurping over kings'. 'I acknowledge,' he added for good measure, 'the Roman Church to be our mother church.'

It was typically dizzy oratory, fuelled in part by the kind of undiscriminating adulation which James was always unable to resist. 'We have a Constantine among us,' trilled George Marcelline, 'capable to preside as the other did in the Nicene assemblies, the presence of whom is able to dispose of differences, to soften the sharpest, to restore and place peace and concord among all good fathers, and to make them happily to finish such a design.' But Pope Clement was thinking along entirely different lines and by 1605 his hopes of James's conversion had reached their short-lived peak. Though he wished English Catholics to remain quiescent, he took few practical steps to lessen the threat from plots, and the queen's decision to urge a Catholic marriage for Prince Henry, coupled to her efforts to obtain office for her co-religionists, only served to undermine James's efforts further. Employing Sir Anthony Standen, the English ambassador in Italy, as her private agent in Rome, the queen also wrote to the Spanish infanta, imploring her to send two friars to Jerusalem to pray for herself and her husband. And by the time that James began to claw back the situation, the inevitable Protestant reaction had already outstripped him. Imprisoning Standen when he brought back sacred objects from the pope and commanding Anne's chamberlain, Lord Sidney, to exercise great care in the selection of her household would do little to quell the indignation of even moderate Anglicans that he himself had provoked by his attempts at reconciliation.

'It is hardly credible in what jollity they now live,' wrote one contemporary English Protestant of his Catholic counterparts. 'They make no question to obtain at least a toleration if not an alteration of religion, in hope whereof many who before did dutifully frequent the Church are of late become recusants.' Cecil, too, expressed concerns about the king's excessive clemency, which alienated the Anglican clergy and resulted in Catholic priests openly plying their trade in the country at large. And predictably there were the obvious comparisons drawn between the leniency extended to papists and the harsh treatment of Puritans. Indeed, even the Archbishop of York, Matthew Hutton, made this very point, while adding how Catholics 'have grown mightily in number, favour and influence'. Plainly, then, the king's irenic impulses found little sympathy with his councillors and bishops when it came to the Church of Rome. Nor did they impress his judges who continued to enforce the anti-Catholic laws wherever they could, for England as a whole, with its long tradition of hostility to the pope, was not ready for the toleration he proposed. On the contrary, the immediate results proved that the deep anti-Catholic prejudices of Englishmen, however irrational from some perspectives, were a sounder basis for policy than the theoretically high-minded sentiments of the king.

The revelation of the real numbers of Catholics in the country when they were allowed to disappear without penalty from the back benches of their Anglican parish churches, and the large numbers now attending Mass, startled even James. Previously, the returns which had been collected from every diocese of those who officially stayed away from church had led the government to estimate the total number of Catholics at about 8,500. When toleration allowed them into the open, however, it seemed that the papal claim to more than 100,000 was nearer to the mark – something which James believed, quite wrongly, could only be explained by widespread, rapid conversion resulting from his own policy of toleration. And it was increasingly clear, too, that while the majority of English Catholics were both loyal and peaceable, their leaders were inclined to think otherwise. The Jesuit Robert Persons, whom Sir Henry Wotton characterised with good reason as 'malicious and virulent', retained a place at the heart of papal policy in England and remained committed to the forcible restoration of Catholicism, even, if the need arose, at the price of assassinating a heretic ruler. Indeed, plans were already in hand for the imposition of censorship and the installation of an English Inquisition, which made nonsense of James's hopes that wounds could be healed and deals done.

Ironically, then, the admirable intentions of the 'British Solomon' were soon being replaced by growing irritation and impatience with those whom he sought to assist but could not help as a result of their own ignorance and fractiousness. Upon ascending the throne, he had suspended recusancy fines, allowed Catholics to worship in private as they pleased and turned a blind eye to the influx of Catholic priests. Now, however, only nine months after this first reversal of policy, a second was to occur. And at a meeting of the council in February 1605, he found himself venting his spleen against both Puritans and Catholics. As to the latter, he declared, he was so far from favouring their superstitious religion that if he thought his son would tolerate them after his death, he would wish him buried before his eyes. The only answer now, it seemed, was a restoration of the old Elizabethan measures and a rigorous execution of the laws against 'both the said extremes'. A proclamation duly ordered all Jesuits and priests to quit the country, and several were hanged in February, albeit without direct instructions from the government. Indeed, when the king learned of the hangings in Devon, he explicitly ordered that no executions should be carried out merely on grounds of religion.

From James's perspective, however, his first moves in favour of toleration had been foiled both wilfully and ungratefully by those who lacked his wisdom and vision, and the saboteurs would now have to reap the consequences. The fact that he had played with fire and, in doing so, exacerbated an already delicate situation seems to have escaped him – though, having excited Catholic expectations, the king too would now have a price to pay. For if Puritans wrote petitions when frustrated, there were those among the Catholic community who would express their discontent altogether more forcefully when no longer fed a diet of fair promises.

13 ⚘ Parliament, Union, Gunpowder

'We came out of Scotland with an unsullied reputation and without any grudge in the people's hearts but for want of us. Wherein we have misbehaved ourself here we know not, nor we can never yet learn ... To be short, this Lower House by their behaviour have periled and annoyed our health, wounded our reputation, emboldened all ill-natured people, encroached upon many of our privileges and plagued our purse with their delays.'

James I's complaint to his Privy Council,
7 December 1610

'Their Parliaments hold but three days, their statutes are but three lines.' So wrote Sir Anthony Weldon, that most caustic critic of the Scots, who on this occasion as on others both simplified and distorted broader realities north of the Border. The irony, however, was that Weldon's dismissive perception of the Scottish Parliament or 'Estates' as a submissive and ineffectual institution was propagated most effectively of all by the very King of Scotland who had now come to occupy the English throne. Some while before he headed for London, indeed, James VI, as he then was, had portrayed the Scottish Estates as little more than the chief court of the king and his vassals, and it was this institution - displaying, he suggested, no rash desires for liberty or innovation – that James I subsequently presented to his English subjects as the ideal parliamentary model. By 1603 his terminology had changed slightly, for he was now calling Parliament 'nothing else but the king's great council'. Yet his thinking was very largely unaltered. Parliament was assembled, or so he suggested, for the exclusive purpose of ratifying laws and punishing notorious offenders. And in holding up the Scottish Estates as an example to Westminster, he consciously chose to expound its operation in a way that suggested total subservience to the whim of the monarch. No member of that body, James told English MPs when the first parliament of the new reign assembled in March 1604, was allowed to speak without his chancellor's explicit permission, and any proposed new laws were automatically submitted to the monarch's scrutiny some twenty days beforehand, whereupon 'if there be anything that I dislike, they raise it out before'.

Yet the Scottish Estates had a long and often proud record of independent activity, which plainly contradicted the more obvious caricatures and suggested an altogether more subtle relationship with the monarchy than James saw fit to depict. Its origins dated back, in fact, to at least 1286 with the first use of the term 'the community of the realm', although William the Lion was recorded as having held a full parliament over a century earlier. Moreover, the notion that Scottish history was subsequently marred by a malign combination of supine parliaments, arbitrary rule and self-interested and remote noblemen is a simplification and misrepresentation firmly founded in Enlightenment historiography. By the early fourteenth century, the attendance of knights and freeholders had already become important, and from 1326 burgh commissioners also attended. Consisting of the three 'estates' of clerics, lay tenants-in-chief and burgh commissioners sitting in a single chamber, the Scottish Parliament thereafter acquired significant powers over particular issues. Most obviously it was needed to sanction taxation, and although taxes were raised only irregularly in Scotland during the medieval period, it also had a strong influence over justice, foreign policy and the conduct of war, as well as enacting a wide range of legislation on political, ecclesiastical, social and economic matters.

In reality, then, the underlying rationale of Scottish government had always been collaborative and inclusive, with the king-in-parliament at its apex, held in place by subtle checks and balances in a manner that seemed rare within a contemporary European context. Furthermore, this whole system actually reached its apogee in the 1590s under none other than James VI himself, which, in light of his modernising aspirations in other areas, was not as surprising as hindsight might appear to suggest. It was he, after all, who had encouraged the mapping of his country, the revamping of its weights and measures and the listing of its landowners and their estates by the Privy Council. And it was he, ironically, who appeared for so much of his reign to accept the theory and practice of the 'community of the realm' so readily. Indeed, whenever James convened the Estates, its physical layout could not have represented more tangibly the whole nature of the Scottish polity, with the king enthroned at the centre, the lesser barons and lairds in front of him, the nobility, barons and their guests, all appropriately ranked on his left, and, to his right, the burgh and shire commissioners, alongside the clergy.

Ultimately, moreover, the king could avoid calling Scotland's Parliament only if he had no need of money, was making no constitutional or religious changes, had no treaties to approve, no embassies to send or receive, no marriage to negotiate, no high-ranking miscreant to punish, and no need to finance or plan military expeditions. And though in the latter years of James IV, for instance, Parliament met rarely after the king had the comfort of a Tudor dowry, most monarchs in this relatively unwealthy country usually required both money and the parliaments to provide it. The Estates existed, in fact, precisely because Scottish monarchs were not absolute, and the very term 'community of the realm' implied not only that the realm was distinct from the ruler, but that Parliament was the guardian of the status of the kingdom and its people. By the end of the fifteenth century, it was accepted, indeed, that Parliament could directly restrain tyrannical monarchs, and by the time John Mair wrote his *Historia Majoris Britanniae* in 1521, he was able to assert that it could even frame laws of its own that were binding upon the monarch.

The question arises, therefore, just how far James's increasingly authoritarian views in the years directly before 1603 were actually encouraged by his impending succession to the English throne. Ironically, during the last decade or so before he became King of England, the Scottish Estates had enjoyed possibly its most effective period, undertaking in the 1590s its busiest and most wide-ranging legislative programme. Indeed, petitions to it had become so numerous that a vetting committee was proposed in 1594, though this did not prevent the overall explosion of law-making during the same period, as legislation poured forth on a broad spectrum of topics from consanguinity and divorce, through to property protection, legal guardianship, and the education of nobles abroad. Yet by 1600, James had nevertheless published *The Trew Lawe of Free Monarchies* and *Basilikon Doron* in which he clearly appeared to be advocating a move towards what can only be construed as some form of absolute monarchy.

There was no denying, of course, that the parliaments of the 1590s had been fractious, or that the king's imprisonment by a religious mob during a meeting of the Privy Council in Edinburgh's Tolbooth in 1596 prompted a desire on his part to redefine the theoretical authority of the monarch, as evidenced by his literary output thereafter. But it is equally likely that his transfer to London further stimulated his budding absolutism, for there was no developed notion of the monarch as *primus inter pares* south of the Border, where the nobles in particular were effectively on their knees before their ruler. More importantly still, there appeared no shortage of cash when compared to Scotland, permitting the king to indulge his absolutist fantasies in a way that could never have been possible otherwise. And when full account is taken of the recalcitrance of many MPs at Westminster under his predecessor, it becomes clearer than ever, perhaps, why James unwisely decided to assume the constitutional offensive in his new realm.

To all outward appearances, of course, England's Parliament had been growing steadily in status throughout the sixteenth century, and the reign of Elizabeth, above all, had certainly witnessed a number of spectacular incidents in which Crown and Parliament clashed over a variety of issues including free speech, her marriage, the succession and, of course, James's own mother, Mary Queen of Scots. In 1597, indeed, Elizabeth had been forced to accept that although she had formerly been 'exceeding unwilling and opposite' to all manner of innovations in ecclesiastical matters, there was now no choice but to give 'leave and liberty to the House of Commons to treat thereof'. More strikingly still, in 1601 there had been a vigorous and successful attack on her grants of trading monopolies, in the course of which one MP had dared to raise the whole issue of the balance between the authority of Parliament and the royal prerogative itself. 'To what purpose is it to do anything by Act of Parliament,' declared Francis Moore, 'when the queen will undo the same by her prerogative.' And by the time of the opening of her last Parliament, it was even being noticed that fewer voices than ever were being raised in the customary cry of 'God save your Majesty' as she passed among members.

James's task in managing his new English Parliament was therefore sure to be a delicate one. But in overestimating the scale of potential opposition and opting to assert his authority more vocally than his predecessor, he would actually instigate the kind of response that he had feared in the first place. In reality, the free speech debates of 1566, 1576 and 1571, the rancour over the queen's marriage and the succession, as well as the struggle over Mary Queen of Scots were actually far from typical, and insofar as real Crown–Parliament conflict occurred at all, it happened only once – over monopolies. On those occasions, moreover, when sections of the House of Commons had pressed a case against Elizabeth, the Crown was almost invariably victorious. In spite of religious controversy and attempts to establish a full-blown Presbyterian system in 1587, for example, the Elizabethan religious settlement stood fully intact in 1603, while the earlier free speech debates achieved nothing. Overall, indeed, harmony and co-operation had been the predominant feature of Parliament's relationship with Elizabeth, as no less than twelve out of a total of thirteen parliamentary sessions readily granted supply to the queen. Even more importantly, there had been little intrinsic interest in the general nature of the constitutional balance between monarch and subject until James himself raised it in arguably the most provocative manner possible. For although James's practice would frequently prove rather more subtle and accommodating than his rhetoric, his outspokenness on the question of his prerogative was almost invariably as jarring as it was unnecessary.

The catalogue of the king's indiscretions is, in fact, almost limitless. 'Hold no Parliament', he had informed his son in *Basilikon Doron*, 'but for necessity of new laws, which would be but seldom', and to force home the point he added later that any man desiring a new law should come to Parliament with a halter round his neck, so that if the law proved unacceptable he could be hanged forthwith. Fortified by Bancroft's flatteries in the wake of the Hampton Court Conference and secure in the knowledge of his own success in Scotland, he would also blandly inform his first Westminster Parliament of 'the blessings which God hath in my person bestowed upon you all', while in exalting his own status, he necessarily appeared to minimise Parliament's own. 'The state of monarchy,' James would tell the House of Commons, 'is the supremest thing upon earth. For kings are not only God's lieutenants upon earth and sit upon God's throne, but even by God Himself they are called gods.' Like God 'they make and unmake their subjects', he continued, having the power 'to exalt low things and abase high things and make of their subjects like men at chess, a pawn to take a bishop or a knight, for to emperors or kings their subjects' bodies and goods are due for their defence or maintenance'.

In truth, of course, such sentiments were neither new nor inherently offensive in their own right, and there is little doubt that many of James's more provocative utterances were delivered with all sincerity at times when he genuinely considered the royal prerogative to be under unjust threat from innovating MPs. But in spite of good intentions and a genuine wish to act in his subjects' best interests as a benevolent and paternal ruler, there remains little doubt that James's policy of employing attack as the best form of defence was often counter-productive. Above all, he simply talked too much. His predecessor's appearances in Parliament had, by contrast, been rare, judiciously timed and invariably regal in tone and execution. Confining herself to brief statements of policy at the start of a session, and the occasional rebuke or engaging appeal, which were all part of her armoury of 'love-tricks', Elizabeth I was able to obtain most of what she wanted without sacrificing those essential principles on which she knew she must stand firm. But she very rarely delivered substantial orations, such as that of 1601 in which she brilliantly covered her retreat over the issue of monopolies, while James, by contrast, was temperamentally unable, it seems, to curb his desire for publicity: to declaim at great length and in minute detail not only upon immediate policy but upon far-reaching philosophical issues encompassing Church and State. The result, in the opinion of one MP, was 'long oration that did inherit but wind'. Much more damagingly still, however, was discussion of matters best left alone and an extremity of expression in the heat of debate that led MPs, in turn, to deliver increasingly strident affirmations of their own rights and grievances.

Any successor to Elizabeth faced, then, an especially testing time, precisely because she had circumvented so much by saying so little. But if James inherited a challenging hand, there remains little doubt that he might have played it more skilfully at times, particularly with regard to matters of everyday procedure. During the last years of Elizabeth's reign, it was Robert Cecil who had managed the government's business in Parliament and he would continue to do so in the new reign, notwithstanding his promotion to the peerage. Yet the minister found himself increasingly frustrated not only by the king's meddling but by his tantrums, complaints and frequently misguided instructions. Royal messages, interruptions to debates and attempts by the monarch to dictate their course, which had been infrequent and weighty occurrences in the previous reign, now, in fact, became routine and an increasing disruption to royal business. Later, indeed, there would be outright complaints concerning the 'many intervenient messages' issuing from the throne that culminated in 1621 with a formal attempt to 'move the king that there be not so many interpositions'.

Likewise, James's passion for definitions often provoked dangerous counter-definitions from MPs, while his inability to resist poring over abstract technicalities at every opportunity could have only one outcome in an institution packed with common lawyers. And though these same lawyers continued almost without exception to reverence the lolling, ungainly figure in front of them, with his heavily padded clothes and thick Scottish accent, his general lack of majesty and charisma did nothing to enhance his cause or make his pedantry any more tolerable. Nor, for that matter, did his favouritism, his extravagance and his apparent inconsistency when it came to hard work. For any ruler so inclined to assert his own God-given authority as the Lord's Anointed could only hope for a truly amenable audience, if he seemed more obviously to personify it in his everyday habits and demeanour.

All in all, then, it was only inevitable, perhaps, that James found himself opposed in Parliament. Much more surprising, however, and much less forgivable was his bewilderment at this and his subsequent exasperation, which frequently manifested itself in either self-pity or pique. In 1604 he assured the Commons of his belief that their intentions were not seditious, before informing them nevertheless that they were rash, over-inquisitive and apparently distrustful. 'In my government bypast in Scotland, where I ruled among men not of the best temper,' he declared, 'I was heard not only as a king but, suppose I say it, as a counsellor.' Here, however, there was 'nothing but curiosity from morning to evening to find fault with my propositions'. All things, James concluded, were now 'suspected', and his bitterness and sense of hurt were even more intense six years later when he once again professed himself 'sorry of our ill fortune in this country', where his 'fame and actions' had been 'tossed like tennis balls' and 'all that spite and malice might do to disgrace and infame us hath been used'. Since he was a pious king, the father of his people and so manifestly willing to take such pains in redressing wrongs, the implication was clear. Only ill-intentioned men, bent upon perilous innovation could air 'grievances' against his government, established institutions such as the Court of High Commission, and above all the royal prerogative. And in taking such a firm stand against change of any kind, all appeals for alteration of existing practice became subsumed in James's mind under the same pernicious heading. 'All novelties are dangerous,' he asserted in 1610, 'and therefore I would be loath to be quarrelled in my ancient rights and possessions, for that were to judge me unworthy of that which my predecessors left me.' The fact that the Commons would ask for the same things over and over only convinced James further of their ill will.

But it was the new king's careless intervention in a matter he did not fully understand that prompted the first serious squabble in the reign, and one that would set the tone for a good deal of what was to follow. In a not altogether unprecedented attempt to influence the course of the forthcoming elections for the Parliament of March 1604, a proclamation had been issued to encourage sheriffs and electors 'to avoid the choice of any persons either noted for their superstitious blindness or for their turbulent humours other ways'. This attempt to categorise Catholics and Puritans as 'disorderly and unquiet spirits' and exclude them from election was not, however, the main bone of contention. Instead, it was the stipulation that election returns be made, not direct to the House of Commons, but to the Court of Chancery – a blatant reversal of the Elizabethan practice by which the House was the sole judge of cases involving disputed elections. In reality, the Crown's legal advisers were merely attempting to recover an item of Chancery's lost jurisdiction. Yet it was the sort of point on which MPs had already learned to be peculiarly sensitive, and the kind of issue, moreover, that required no direct intervention from the king, since, as the Commons respectfully indicated at the outset, it was 'an unusual controversy between courts about their pre-eminences and privileges' and therefore best treated as a matter 'between the Court of Chancery and our Court'.

When, however, the Commons seized upon a disputed election in Buckinghamshire involving a certain Sir Francis Goodwin, who had been chosen in preference to Sir John Fortescue, a councillor enjoying the backing of the government, the king swiftly plunged into the fray, treating the matter in effect as a test case for the status of royal proclamations as a whole. Chancery had, in fact, excluded Goodwin on grounds of outlawry, only to find after two days of debate that its decision had been nullified by the Commons, and this was enough, it seems, to provoke the full weight of royal displeasure. Informing MPs that their privileges depended on his goodwill, James also compared their complaints to the murmurings of the people of Israel and ordered them 'as an absolute king' to consult the judges on the legality of their proceedings. And though the response, according to Sir Henry Yelverton, the Attorney General, was merely 'amazement and silence', there remained little doubt that the king had overreacted. 'The prince's command is like a thunderbolt,' declared

Yelverton, 'his command upon our allegiance like the roaring of a lion. To his command there is no contradiction.'

There followed three weeks of deadlock, as the Commons reinforced their case with a selection of curious precedents, including one case of 1581 in which an election, voided on the grounds that the candidate had died, had eventually been declared valid by the House when the supposedly defunct MP finally appeared to claim his seat. The debate, it is true, was conducted respectfully and with its fair share of honeyed words. Sir Francis Bacon, representing the Commons at the conference called to resolve the matter, remarked, for instance, that he found James's voice the voice of God in man, and confirmed that his colleagues were ready to reconsider their position, something they had not done for any previous ruler. James, meanwhile, played his part in smoothing the waters by declaring that he would allow free rein to his kindly nature and decline to press his prerogative against his subjects' privileges. Yet it was only on 13 April that the Goodwin case was finally settled by a compromise of sorts which entailed the annulment of all previous proceedings and the calling of a fresh election. And when, thereafter, the House swiftly proceeded to decide two further cases without reference to either himself or Chancery, James was left with little choice other than to avoid unnecessary acrimony, as he should have done in the first place, since he had now not only lost but visibly lost.

There was little doubt, of course, that Parliament's intransigence reflected a sensitivity and assertiveness that, from the king's perspective, only served to justify his own dogmatism. Nor was it entirely his fault that a minor dispute with the warden of the Fleet Prison was subsequently dragged out by MPs for three weeks on the grounds that their 'privileges were so shaken before and so extremely vilified'. Certainly, if he had been better advised in January when the offending proclamation that had sparked the Goodwin dispute was first issued, the whole question of parliamentary privilege might never have exploded in the first place. But James had not only chosen the wrong battlefield, he had also failed in advance to prepare the chosen ground sufficiently carefully. For, while Elizabeth had achieved much of her success by cultivating the closest links between her Privy Council and Parliament, and by carefully managing parliamentary debates, the new king found himself personally defending his government's policy in a way that his predecessor would only deign to do in a position of crisis. And this situation, too, was the result of decisions whose consequences he had failed to foresee.

Above all, James had seriously weakened his influence in the House of Commons by the removal of key figures. His promotion of Robert Cecil to the earldom of Salisbury, for example, meant that Cecil could no longer exercise the same direct influence in the Commons that he had previously done, and the same applied to Sir Thomas Egerton, another wise and experienced supporter of the Crown, who became Lord Ellesmere at the start of the new reign. Indeed, in 1604 only two privy councillors, Sir John Herbert and Sir John Stanhope, were on hand in the Commons, though neither possessed much influence. Herbert, the Second Secretary of State was widely known, indeed, as 'Mr Secondary Herbert', and the existence of a significant body of support for the Crown in the shape of individuals like Sir Roger Aston, Sir Richard Levison and Sir Edward Hoby, not to mention the cadets of great courtly families such as the Howards and Sackvilles, would not make good the deficiency. For not only had the presence of talented councillors allowed Elizabeth to exert influence upon the Commons, it had also enabled her to gauge their mood. Herbert, however, had not even risen on the first day of the recent session to ask for the customary subsidy, and in the vacuum that this left, it was hardly surprising, perhaps, that MPs would ultimately find their own leaders and organise their business independently.

By the end of the session, in fact, an alarmed committee of the Commons had put together a document known as 'The Form of Apology and Satisfaction to be Presented to His Majesty', which amounted, in spite of its self-consciously respectful tone, to a bold lecture to a foreign king upon the constitution of his new country. Laden with cumbersome statements of love and loyalty, and never actually presented to the king because it was never accepted by the Commons as a whole, the 'Apology' nonetheless represents an interesting insight into at least one significant element of parliamentary opinion. Certainly, everything James had said in the previous session and every implication of the language he had used was seized upon, while each of the claims he had advanced was opposed by counter claims which, in the main, were every bit as sweeping, provocative and unhistorical as his own. Not only was the king told that he had been misinformed on several important points but he also heard how these 'misinformations' had been 'the chief and almost the sole cause of all the discontentful and troublous proceedings so much blamed in this Parliament'. Above all, it was suggested, James had threatened the Commons' privileges, as a result of which 'the liberties and stability of the whole kingdom' had been 'more seriously and dangerously impugned than ever (as we suppose) since the beginnings of Parliament'.

This, then, was strong stuff. Yet the 'Apology' did not stop here, for its authors went on to point out that MPs' privileges were not a matter of the king's grace, but a 'right and due inheritance' no less than lands or goods, and that the Speaker's formal request to the Crown at the beginning of each session was 'an act only of manners'. They reiterated, moreover, the same claim to complete freedom of speech which had stirred such coals in the previous reign, and famously complained how 'the prerogatives of princes may easily and do daily grow' while 'the privileges of the subject are for the most part at an everlasting stand'. Worse still, James's habit of making sweeping statements on fundamental aspects of constitutional theory broadened the authors' agenda into a summary of a further range of unremedied grievances – matters which, they said, they had previously refrained from pressing upon Elizabeth 'in regard of her sex and age'. They noted, for instance, the exasperation caused by the excesses of royal purveyors and complained bitterly of the burdens placed on landowners by the activities of the Court of Wards. More importantly still, they reminded James that Kings of England had no 'absolute power in themselves either to alter religion (which God defend should be in the power of any mortal man whatsoever), or to make any laws concerning the same otherwise than as in temporal causes, by consent of Parliament'. And while they agreed with the king and his bishops on the need for uniformity and obedience, they nevertheless requested that some of the points in dispute – the sign of the cross in baptism, the use of the surplice and of the ring in marriage – should be made optional, while any persecution of dissenters should be in the hands of Parliament rather than Convocation.

Nor did the fact that the 'Apology' was never ultimately presented to James prevent him from seeing a copy and reacting with predictable irritation. Ultimately, indeed, the flourish of loyal and affectionate assertions with which the document ended, would do nothing to temper the king's suspicions about its authors' overall intentions. 'The voice of the people,' they had asserted, 'in the things of their knowledge is said to be as the voice of God.' And when James returned to prorogue the session after he had gone off to hunt at Royston at the end of April, in order to gain some respite from his 'fashious and froward' opponents in the Commons, his final speech could not have been more forthright. He was sure, he said, that there were many dutiful subjects in Parliament, but the pertness and boldness of some idle heads had cried down honest men, and he would not give thanks where no thanks were due, since it was neither Christian nor kingly to do so. 'I cannot enough wonder,' he declared, 'that in three days after the beginning of Parliament, men should go contrary to their oaths of supremacy,' and in making this point he confirmed his preoccupation with Puritan opponents. 'I did not think the Puritans had been so great, so proud, or so dominant in your House,' he declared, though he ended, sensibly enough, with appeals and admonitions rather than threats. Acknowledging that he had seen no evidence of disloyalty, he told MPs nevertheless that they had done 'many things rashly'. He was, after all, 'a king as well born as any of my progenitors' who required respect and expected MPs to use their liberty 'with more modesty in time to come'.

However, the main business of James's first Parliament, apart from obtaining funds, had actually been the matter of the formal union of his two kingdoms, and here, too, he was roundly frustrated. The cold disdain of Englishmen for their Scottish counterparts had not, in fact, been extended to James personally, but fears that Scotland might, in effect, take over her southern neighbour as a result of his accession were common enough. The Scots, wrote one contemporary, 'were suffered like locusts to devour this kingdom, from whence they became so rich and insolent, as nothing with any moderation could either be given or denied them'. And Ben Jonson's *Eastward, Ho!* only confirmed the prejudice that James's ultimate objective, however nobly and sincerely held, would have to overcome. When one of the play's characters, a mariner described Captain Seagull, refers in Act III to the Scots residing in Virginia – 'a land so rich that even the chamber pots are made of gold' – he is quick to add a biting quip that would swiftly run the playwright into trouble with the king. 'I would a hundred thousand of them were there,' the captain continued, 'for we are one countrymen now, ye know, and we should find ten times more comfort by them there than we do here.' The result was a brief jail sentence for both Jonson and his co-authors George Chapman and John Marston.

Yet James, predictably enough, remained undeterred by all complaints concerning not only 'the effluxion of people from the northern parts' but the proposed union itself. From his perspective, after all, the case for amalgamation was eminently reasonable and therefore infinitely persuasive. 'Hath not God first united these two kingdoms both in language, religion and similitude of manners?' James suggested in his introductory speech to the Commons. 'Yea, hath He not made us all one island encompassed with one sea, and of itself by nature so indivisible as almost those that were borderers themselves on the late Borders, cannot distinguish, nor know, or discern their own limits?' Then came a reminder that previous trouble between the two realms had been 'the greatest hindrance and let that ever my predecessors of this nation gat in disturbing them from their many famous and glorious conquests abroad'. After which, James rounded off his appeal with a selection of Scriptural references, spiced with the kind of heavy humour and egocentricity that was unlikely to appeal to MPs far more preoccupied with the legal, constitutional and financial consequences of the king's proposal. 'I am the husband, and the whole island is my wife,' he told them after a brief historical survey of the development of the English monarchy. 'I am the head and it is my body; I am the shepherd and it is my flock,' he continued, and on this basis he therefore hoped that 'no man will be so unreasonable as to think that I, that am a Christian king under the Gospel, should be a polygamist and husband to two wives; that I, being the head, should have a divided and monstrous body; or that being the shepherd of so fair a flock (whose fold hath no wall to hedge it but the four seas) should have my flock parted in two.'

Any hope that MPs would countenance such a project proved wholly unrealistic, however. They gave way enough in the first session, it is true, to set up an Anglo-Scottish commission intended to consider how to 'make perfect that mutual love and uniformity of manners and customs' necessary to 'accomplish that real and effective union already inherent in his Majesty's royal blood and person'. But when in April 1604 the king announced his wish to assume the title of King of Great Britain and alter the name of England, a line in the sand was quickly drawn. It was a line, moreover, that the Commons, notwithstanding James's own talents in debate, had little difficulty in defending. Would not a change in the name of the kingdom, it was suggested, abrogate existing laws and necessitate their re-enactment? This, after all, was something that the judges, too, had suggested in spite of considerable pressure from the king. And should a change of name not, in any case, occur until union had actually been realised? A commission had been agreed – albeit it one that would never give the king what he wanted – and this commission should be allowed to submit its conclusions in due course.

Parliament, therefore, had defeated the king in his most favoured and revered preserve – the realm of abstract argument. But in spite of any apparent commitment to the rule of reason, James would still not give way.

He had presented the choice before Parliament with all the usual excess of vigour, telling its members how any rejection of his plans would be to 'spit and blaspheme' in God's face 'by preferring war to peace, trouble to quietness, hatred to love, weakness to strength, and division to union'. And when defeat followed, he would not retreat gracefully. 'I am not ashamed of my project,' he told MPs at the end of the session, 'neither have I deferred it out of a liking to the judges' reasons or yours.' Accordingly, in spite of a pledge that he would not for the time being alter his title, he duly began to style himself King of Great Britain by royal proclamation in October 1604 on the grounds that God had given this title to the island, and on the advice, it seems, of Sir Francis Bacon alone, since the council appear to have regarded the gesture as provocative. The king was determined, wrote the Venetian ambassador, 'to call himself King of Great Britain and like that famous and ancient King Arthur to embrace under one name the whole circuit' of the island. And, as Bacon suggested, by proceeding through proclamation rather than statute, he could now use the new style in letters, treaties, dedications, further proclamations and upon coins. The result, however, was a largely empty victory and one achieved, ironically, not only at the cost of offending Parliament but of jeopardising all further serious dialogue about the goal of union itself.

Nor would James's subsequent pressure prove any more fruitful. The English Parliament, for instance, continued to employ the old terminology and though the Scottish Estates were forced to adopt it, Scots themselves were, if anything, even more resentful. Councillors were also asked to consider the feasibility of reducing the laws of the two kingdoms to a single system and to consider the possible benefits that might accrue from free trade, while the king toyed, too, with the notion of making Archbishop Bancroft primate of Great Britain, though obstacles on all three counts proved insurmountable. The conference of English and Scottish commissioners, which assembled in London in October 1604, did not, for instance, even consider the creation of a single parliament, and English merchants, fearing competition, roundly rejected any prospect of free trade, as did English ship owners who protested that while a Scots sailor could live on nothing more than oysters, his English counterpart required beer and roast beef. Ultimately, the pacification of the Borders would continue steadily and there was eventually some progress towards a common currency. But while the College of Arms managed to devise a new flag by imposing the cross of St George upon that of St Andrew, James was still complaining in 1607 of the 'crossings, long disputations, strange questions, and nothing done' that had dogged proceedings.

Indeed, the only topic even to receive a full airing at the London conference was the intricate issue of whether the Scots might be naturalised as English subjects. The commissioners, following the English judges, had made a distinction between those Scotsmen born before James's accession to the throne of England (the so-called 'ante-nati') and those born afterwards (the 'post-nati'). The former, it was suggested, should be naturalised by statute, while the latter should be automatically naturalised by virtue of common law. Only the post-nati, however, were to be deemed capable of holding office – a distinction which James was prepared to accept, so long as it was recognised that his prerogative remained wholly intact. And if this additional proviso made bad reading for the House of Commons, MPs too gave no quarter on the claim that the post-nati were naturalised by common law. Common law precedents, it was suggested, were established in ancient times when nationalism was weak. In any case, argued Sir Edwin Sandys, 'unions of kingdoms are not made by law but by act express', and naturalisation should not be conferred so easily by the chance results of royal marriages.

As the debate unfolded, moreover, long-established prejudices against the Scots were swift to resurface. England was depicted as a rich pasture about to be overrun by herds of lean and hungry cattle, while Sir Christopher Piggott, despite royal rage, poured forth a torrent of abuse, deriding Scotsmen as proud beggarly, quarrelsome and untrustworthy. Even the post-nati, for that matter, were to be barred from holding office, and neither category of Scotsmen should be granted the full rights of English citizens. How, it was suggested, could the Scots be subservient to English law and held to the payment of English taxes without the establishment of a single parliament, which, in spite of the king's wishes, was not a practical option at this stage? And how could Scottish laws be prevented from diverging without one chancellor and one Great Seal. The only practical solution, the Commons suggested, was 'perfect union', which was itself impractical at this time, as even the king had come to recognise. Once again, it seems, James had been foiled by the very techniques upon which he himself set so much store, though this did not prevent him from telling MPs that those who now spoke up in favour of perfect union did so only with their lips rather than their hearts.

On almost all counts, then, the first Parliament of the new reign had been little more than an exercise in frustration – and a largely unnecessary one at that. But it was not only the royal prerogative and England's relationship with Scotland that raised hackles and conjured frowns of frustration. Nor was it only the authors of the 'Form of Apology and Satisfaction' who found themselves stirring. For in spite of James's early guarantees that he would 'never allow in my conscience that the blood of any man shall be shed for diversity of opinions in religion', the session also delivered ominous signs of a less tolerant approach to English Catholics. Hitherto, the king had suggested that he was disinclined to 'persecute any that will be quiet and give an outward obedience to the law', and where he had hinted at action at all, he had actually tended to suggest that exile might be a preferable solution to capital punishment. 'I would be glad,' he declared at one point, 'to have both their heads and their bodies separated from this whole island and transported beyond seas.' Likewise, while James made it clear in his opening speech to Parliament on 19 March that Catholics were not to 'increase their number and strength in this Kingdom', so that 'they might be in hope to erect their Religion again', he also spoke of a Christian union and reiterated his desire to avoid religious persecution, declaring his readiness 'to meet them in the midway, so that all novelties might be renounced on either side'.

Just one month earlier, however, on 19 February, shortly after he discovered that his wife had been sent a rosary from the pope via one of his own agents, Sir Anthony Standen, James had ordered all Jesuits and Catholic priests to leave the country and reimposed the collection of recusancy fines. Only a week after James's address to Parliament, moreover, Lord Sheffield informed him that over 900 recusants had been brought before the Assizes in Normanby in Yorkshire, and by 24 April a Bill was introduced in Parliament which threatened to outlaw all English followers of the Catholic Church. The very few Catholics of great wealth who refused to attend services at their parish church were fined £20 per month, while middle-class recusants were fined 1s a week and those of more modest means found themselves liable for a sum totalling two-thirds of their annual rental income. In the atmosphere of increased stringency that followed, the fact that James allowed his Scottish nobles to collect English recusancy fines proved doubly provocative, and 5,560 convictions for refusal to pay followed in 1605 alone. Nor did the otherwise haphazard and negligent collection of all these fines serve to lessen their predictable impact upon

Catholic opinion. To Father John Gerard, the king's speech was almost certainly responsible for the heightened levels of persecution the members of his faith now suffered, while for the priest Oswald Tesimond it was a clear rebuttal of the early claims that James had made – claims upon which the papists had built such confident hopes. More importantly still, however, James's decision to reimpose the collection of recusancy fines was the fuse that led directly to the gunpowder deposited 'under his Palace of Parliament House' in November 1605.

The monstrous simplicity of the Gunpowder Plot was, in fact, the secret of its potential success. For zealots like Robert Catesby and Sir Thomas Percy there was no hope for a triumphant *coup d'etat* unless some altogether extraordinary disaster should temporarily paralyse the governing class, and the destruction of king, queen, Prince Henry, bishops, lords and Commons in a single, devastating explosion was precisely the sort of event in a society so closely bound to ties of tradition and territorial loyalty at every level that might well ensure the necessary upheaval – at least long enough for the arrival of foreign aid. Certainly, the moral considerations that made the majority of Catholics shudder at such mass murder do not appear to have bothered the plotters themselves. When James eventually asked Guy Fawkes, for instance, if he did not regret his involvement, the answer was succinct and clinical. The only cause for sorrow was the plot's failure, he retorted. 'A dangerous disease requires a desperate remedy' was Fawkes's sole additional comment. And in expressing himself thus, he spoke no doubt for the whole gang who had employed him to plant and fire the thirty-six barrels of gunpowder that were intended to raise the English Catholic gentry to arms and install James's daughter, the Princess Elizabeth, upon the throne as the puppet of a Catholic government.

According to latest estimates, Fawkes had more than double the powder he needed and even accounting for deterioration of the explosive in storage, no one inside Westminster Palace – or outside to a distance of 100 metres – is likely to have survived. So long as the plot remained secret, moreover, the assassination plan, if not its intended after-effects, had a more than reasonable chance of success. The king's ministers, it should be remembered, had no complicated network of spies at their disposal of the kind that had allowed Walsingham to foil so comprehensively all the conspiracies centred round Mary Queen of Scots. And though Robert Cecil would eventually exploit the plot's occurrence with predictable opportunism, any notions that he somehow knew about the plot in advance remain wholly unsubstantiated. The habit of secrecy was, of course, deeply engrained in those Catholic households where a fugitive priest might lay hidden all day in a space behind a chimney, with his communion plate and vestments, and only dare to ride out to his humbler parishioners under cover of darkness. For their part, neither James nor Cecil had any reason to suspect an imminent plot and would in any case have had no real idea where to start looking for one, since Catesby and his fellow conspirators had set to work in May 1604 and slipped into the English countryside some six months before 5 November. Indeed, even at the time of the plot's accidental discovery, the other conspirators, with the exception of Percy, who was known to be Fawkes's employer, remained wholly unidentified.

Robert Catesby, moreover, was a particularly formidable figure in his own right. Born in or after 1572 at the family seat of Lapworth in Warwickshire, he was the son of a prominent recusant Catholic who had suffered years of imprisonment for his faith before being tried in the Star Chamber in 1581 alongside William Vaux, 3rd Baron Vaux of Harrowden, and his brother-in-law Sir Thomas Tresham, for harbouring the Jesuit Edmund Campion. Another relation, Sir Francis Throckmorton, had been executed in 1584 for his involvement in a plot to free Mary Queen of Scots. And if any confirmation of the younger Catesby's readiness to carry forward the family tradition of zealotry was required, it was furnished by his education. For in 1586, he entered Gloucester Hall in Oxford, a college noted for its Catholic intake, only to leave before taking his degree after refusing the Oath of Supremacy, an act which would have compromised Catesby's Catholic faith. Presumably to avoid this consequence, he may then have attended the seminary college of Douai in France.

But it was not until the death of his wife, Catherine, in 1598 and the death of his father earlier in the same year, that Catesby became fully radicalised, and reverted to a more fanatical Catholicism. In 1601, for example, he was involved in the Essex Rebellion. And although the Earl of Essex's purpose lay mainly in furthering his own interests rather than those of the Catholic Church, Catesby nevertheless hoped that if Essex succeeded, there might once more be a Catholic monarch. The rebellion was a failure, however, and the wounded Catesby was captured, imprisoned at the Wood Street Counter, and fined 4,000 marks by Elizabeth I. Thereafter, Sir Thomas Tresham helped pay a proportion of Catesby's fine, following which Catesby sold his estate at Chastleton. Yet his opinions did not moderate and as Elizabeth's health grew worse, he was probably among those 'principal papists' imprisoned by a government fearing open rebellion. Certainly, he funded the activities of some Jesuit priests, making occasional use of the alias Mr Roberts while visiting them, and in March 1603 he may also have sent Christopher Wright to Spain to see if Philip III would continue to support English Catholics after Elizabeth's death.

By the start of King James's reign, therefore, Catesby was already an experienced and devoted crusader for the Catholic cause who would not hesitate to use violence in support of his faith. More importantly still, however, he had not only the skills and tenacity but also the charisma to pose a real and substantial threat to the new monarch and his government. Writing after the events of 1604 to 1606, the Jesuit Father Tesimond's description of his friend was most favourable. 'His countenance,' wrote Tesimond, 'was exceedingly noble and expressive ... his conversation and manners were peculiarly attractive and imposing, and that by the dignity of his character he exercised an irresistible influence over the minds of those who associated with him.' Fellow conspirator Ambrose Rookwood, shortly before his own death, also declared that he 'loved and respected him [Catesby] as his own life', while Catesby's friend, Father John Gerard, claimed he was 'respected in all companies of such as are counted there swordsmen or men of action', and that 'few were in the opinions of most men preferred before him'. His frustration, meanwhile, at the failure of Essex's adventure actually seems to have sharpened an already well-honed monomania, which could only have served to increase the potency of any attempt on the king's life considerably.

However, as a result of lack of funds, the grinding physical labour of tunnelling and the wider objectives of the whole enterprise, the number of conspirators in the Gunpowder Plot became dangerously enlarged and led to their well-known betrayal by Francis Tresham, a wealthy Catholic gentleman who had been enlisted to gather stores of arms and prepare the West Country gentry for the impending insurrection. Distressed, it seems, by the prospect that the Catholic peers attending Parliament would almost certainly perish, Tresham opted to inform his brother-in-law, Lord Monteagle, and expose the conspiracy in a note delivered on the evening of 26 October, some eleven days prior to the opening of Parliament. 'I would advise you,' the note warned, 'as you tender your life, to devise some excuse to shift your attendance at this parliament, for God and man have concurred to punish the wickedness of this time.' But by instructing that the message be read aloud by his servant when it arrived during dinner, Monteagle attempted at one and the same time – as Tresham seems to have intended – to both thwart the plot and ensure that the conspirators were informed of their betrayal before the news was conveyed to Cecil, who decided to postpone a search until the last possible moment, partly, it seems, out of genuine incredulity, but more importantly in the hope that any conspiracy might thus be exposed more fully.

The king, meanwhile, who was away hunting was not shown the letter until two days before Parliament opened, and agreed that the note was likely to refer to an imminent attack. He remembered, he said, that his father had died by gunpowder, but it was not until three in the afternoon of 4 November that a search was first conducted of the cellar, and not until 11 p.m. that Guy Fawkes was finally arrested, still waiting with his 'blinde lanterne' and the watch a friend had bought for him specially, so that he might time his explosion accurately next morning. Knowing already of the warning letter to Monteagle and having encountered Lord Suffolk during an earlier search that afternoon, he had nevertheless pressed forward upon the slenderest hope that the government might not gauge his purpose in time. Yet his eventual discovery by Sir Thomas Knyvet sealed both his own and the plot's fate, as a few wild-eyed Catholic conspirators continued to gallop westward to raise a stillborn insurrection that even their supporters could see was now quite hopeless. Before long, indeed, John Chamberlain was already recording the lighting of 'as great store of bonfires as ever I thinke was seen', as the king's loyal subjects heard news of his deliverance and the first 'Guys' were burnt in celebration.

The king, meanwhile, had already retired for the night, but was awoken after Fawkes's arrest and promptly instructed that the prisoner be placed under close guard to prevent the possibility of suicide. Transformed, quite literally overnight, into something of a national hero, it was not long either before James was claiming full credit for single-handedly uncovering the plotters' designs. By early 1606, indeed, James had arranged for the publication of a short tract entitled *A Discourse of the Maner of the Discovery of the Late Intended Treason*, in which he was directly presented not only as the saviour of his own sacred person but as the deliverer of his kingdom as a whole and Parliament in particular. It was his 'fortunate judgement', it seems, that had been responsible for 'clearing and solving' the 'obscure riddles and doubtful mysteries' associated with the so-called 'Powder Treason', as it was known to contemporaries, and it was he, too, who had remained indifferent to the 'many desperate dangers' confronting him throughout. Appearing eventually in the king's collected works, the tract nevertheless makes clear in its preface that it was written by a court official under instruction from James himself, and leaves no doubt of James's perception of the entire episode's broader significance.

Since his Protestant faith had been so conclusively confirmed by Providence and he himself had been rescued by his own God-given perspicacity, the conclusions were indeed indisputable from the king's perspective, and he made them abundantly clear to Parliament only four days after the plot had been foiled. Comparing his escape to that of Noah from the flood and elaborating the parallel between the redemption of mankind and his own miraculous preservation, he reminded MPs that kings bore hallmarks of divinity and, like the tallest trees of the forest, were exposed to the greatest dangers. He had survived the Gowrie Plot, when his destruction would have brought immediate ruin to Scotland and deprived England of its future king, and now he had triumphed over an equally dastardly enterprise. When Tresham's letter to Monteagle had been presented to him, he had, he claimed, detected 'upon the instant' certain 'dark phrases therein', though the plot itself was not, he emphasised, the responsibility of English Catholics as a whole but of a few fanatics. Had the plot succeeded, he concluded, he would at least have perished in the noble execution of his regal duties, 'for Almighty God did not furnish so great matter to His Glory by creation of the world, as He did by redemption of the same ...'

No speech, in fact, could have captured more aptly the curious mix of egotism, good intentions and naivety that lay at the heart of James's kingship. At a time when his subjects were baying for retribution and sensing Jesuits – those 'reverend cheaters', 'prowling fathers' and 'caterpillars of Christianity' – behind every panel, he was prepared nevertheless to absolve the loyal majority of his Catholic subjects. But he remained almost obsessively preoccupied, too, with the plot's deep significance for him personally – something that manifested itself ultimately in a curious fascination with the trials and executions that followed as he framed specific questions for the prisoners, commanded the use of torture to extract information and pestered the government's prosecutor, Sir Edward Coke. At one time, indeed, he had thought to interview the captured plotters himself, though the idea, it seems, was ultimately too intimidating for him. Catesby, for his part, had been lucky enough to be shot dead while resisting arrest at Holbeach House, and Percy had died of his wounds soon afterwards.

Tresham, on the other hand, who had been in poor health before he joined the conspiracy, would die in the Tower on 22 December. But Guy Fawkes and the other surviving captives would incur no such good fortune before they were finally hanged, drawn and quartered on 27 January 1606.

Even so, neither James nor his subjects would be easily rid of the nagging anxiety and revulsion generated by the conspiracy. 'The king,' observed the Venetian ambassador, 'is in terror,' refusing to 'take his meals in public as usual' and living instead 'in the innermost rooms with only Scotsmen about him'. 'His Majesty on Sunday last', wrote the same Italian in early 1606, 'while at chapel and afterwards at dinner, appeared very subdued and melancholy; he did not speak at all, though those in attendance gave him occasion', which was 'unlike his usual manner'. And though he later 'broke out with great violence' against the 'cursed doctrine' by which some were 'permitted to plot against the lives of princes', declaring that 'they shall not think they can frighten me, for they shall taste of the agony first', he would confine his action ultimately to palliatives and pamphlets. The Oath of Allegiance, for instance, which was proclaimed law on 22 June 1606, required those who took it to affirm that the pope had neither 'any power or authority to depose the king … or to discharge any of his subjects of their allegiance…' and to acknowledge that no prince 'excommunicated or deprived by the pope may be deposed or murdered by their subjects …'. But when Paul V denounced the oath and forbade Catholics to comply, James merely plunged with characteristic relish into a protracted battle of print that was soon to spread to every corner of Europe.

'Hardly a day passes,' wrote the scholar Isaac Casaubon, 'on which some new pamphlet is not brought to him, mostly written by Jesuits,' and as James surrounded himself with his favourite coterie of 'ripe and weighty' Anglican divines, 'ever in chase after some disputable doubts which he would wind and turn about with the most stabbing objections that ever I heard', he became increasingly convinced, in his own words, that 'the state of religion through all Christendom, almost wholly, under God, rests now upon my shoulders'. One result was *Triplici nodo, triplex cuneus*, or an *Apologie for the Oath of Allegiance*, produced (or so it was claimed by the Bishop of Bath) over only six days and published in 1607, in which James did his level but laboured best to refute his Catholic critics. Such was the dreariness of the book's 112 pages that Boderie, the French ambassador, was adamant that James's principal councillors would have preferred if he had never published it 'or at least not acknowledged it as his own'. Reiterating time and again the familiar theme that Scripture, church councils and patristic authorities alike all advocated the primacy of secular authority, the king's last resort was a futile blast dismissing his arch-adversary, Cardinal Bellarmine, as a liar and a madman – an outburst rivalling an even more drastic loss of composure in debate four years later which led to the burning of the Protestant radicals, Edward Wightman and Bartholomew Legate, who became the last men to be executed for heresy in England.

Overall, of course, English Catholics continued to fare better than might have been expected. In the *Apologie for the Oath of Allegiance*, indeed, James was at pains to emphasise 'the truth of my behaviour towards the papists'. 'How many did I honour with knighthood of known and open recusants?' he asked. 'How indifferently [impartially] did I give audience, bestowing equally all favours and honours on both professions [religions]? And above all how frankly and freely did I free recusants of their ordinary payments [fines]?' He was even ready to add, for that matter, how 'strait order' had been 'given out of my own mouth to judges to spare the execution of all priests', and in a later edition of the *Apologie*, issued in 1609 under the title *A Premonition to all most Mighty Monarchs, Kings, Free Princes and States of Christendom*, he felt no compunction in describing himself as a 'Catholic Christian' and declaring that though 'I may well be a schismatic from Rome … I am sure I am no heretic'. For the time being, moreover, such professions would be indulged compliantly enough by the majority of James's Protestant subjects, for while the 'Powder Treason' had fuelled the anti-Catholic bile of most Englishmen to new heights, it had also placed them at one with their new ruler as never before or after. But if James VI of Scotland was now, by sheer good fortune, truly King of England in his subjects' eyes, he could only hope to prosper in the longer term by learning to govern his altogether less regal whims and inclinations.

14 ⚕ Finance, Favouritism and Foul Play

'... a Prince's court
Is like a common Fountaine, whence should flow
Pure silver-droppes in general; but if 't chance
Some curst example poyson't neere the head
Death and diseases through the whole land spread.'

John Webster, The Duchess of Malfi, *Act I, Scene i*

Some two years or so after James I ascended the throne of England, a royal commission reporting on the sorry state of the royal finances informed him, with all due delicacy, of the profligacy and greed that were sapping his resources and poisoning his court. 'The empty places of that glorious garland of your crown,' the king was told, '... cannot be repaired when the garden of your Majesties Treasure shall be made a common pasture for all that are in need or have unreasonable desires.' What the commissioners may have thought of the £15,593 lavished upon Queen Anne's childbed for the birth of Princess Mary on 8 April 1605, we can only guess. But it was the steady flow of gifts and pensions to a seemingly endless list of servants, associates, hangers-on and outright blackguards that emptied the royal coffers most remorselessly. A certain Jon Gibb, one of the king's lesser Scottish servants, had, for example, been gifted all of £3,000 that same year, while one of Queen Anne's favourites, listed in the accounts as 'Mrs Jane Drummond', had benefited to the tune of £2,000. And these, of course, were but droplets in a growing torrent of waste and excess. In 1603 'divers causes and rewards' accounted for £11,741, the next year £18,510, and the year following £35,239, while over the same period Exchequer spending on 'fees and annuities' rose giddily from £27,270 to £47,783.

In the meantime, like many incorrigible spendthrifts of his kind, James continued to salve his conscience by occasional half-hearted gestures of reform. On 17 July 1604, for example, he had signed a book of *Ordinances for the Governing and Ordering of the Kings Household*, which laid down, among other things, that only twenty-four dishes of meat should henceforth be served at the royal table instead of the customary thirty. The sergeant of the cellar, on the other hand, was to limit his issue of sack to twelve gallons a day and to offer it only to those noblemen and ladies who desired it 'for their better health'. Yet any notion that the financial crisis inherited from the previous reign and fuelled by James's broader improvidence could be remedied by savings from the royal larder were blatantly misconceived, particularly when soaring inflation was already drastically eroding income from the Crown's estates and undermining the rapidly dwindling yield from direct taxation. By the end of her reign, Elizabeth had accumulated a debt of some £430,000, though the disparity in value between the Scottish currency and its English equivalent may actually have served in part to lessen James's appreciation of the scale of his predicament. Scotland's pound, after all, was only one twelfth the worth of England's and when James reflected from the alternative perspective that the income of the Scottish Crown in 1599 had been merely £58,000 (Scots) as opposed to the £110,000 (English) available at the time of his accession, this too may well have exaggerated his impression of the new funds available to him.

James could, of course, comfort himself with the sounder assumption that some of the financial outlays dogging his predecessor's government no longer applied to his own. There was, for example, the cost of maintaining the expensive Border garrison at Berwick which had largely evaporated upon his accession, while the huge sums that Elizabeth found herself obliged to expend upon the Irish rebellion had also been curtailed by Lord Mountjoy's successful campaign at the very time that James was securing his new throne. During the financial year ending at Michaelmas 1602, the war in Ireland cost £342,074, only to fall after four years of the new reign to little more than a tenth of that figure. And when it is remembered that peace with Spain had been achieved in 1604, there were added grounds for cautious optimism about the Crown's potential solvency, so long as suitable economies could be sustained in other areas.

But moderation was, it seems, no less inimical to James's nature than humility and by 1607 he was already complaining bitterly of 'the eating canker of want, which,' he maintained, 'being removed, I could think myself as happy in all other respects as any other king or monarch that ever was since the birth of Christ.' Moreover, neither the expense of supporting a comparatively large royal family, nor the necessity of sustaining regal splendour by lavish gifts and patronage can remotely excuse the full measure of the king's wastefulness. 'My first three years were to me as a Christmas, I could not then be miserable,' James told Parliament at this time. But the ramifications of such generosity cannot be underestimated. On the one hand, as the wages of the king's servants, high and low, fell into arrears, graft and peculation infected every corner of his court. While royal bakers cooked lightweight loaves and misappropriated what they saved, and members of the king's boiling house interpreted their perquisite of the 'strippings' so freely as to leave little meat on the fowl served to 'the kings poor officers', Lord Treasurer Dorset – who would himself 'have spared a life to gain a bribe' – looked on largely impassively, borrowing heavily at interest rates of up to 10 per cent. And as Sir Julius Caesar, Chancellor of the Exchequer, entreated Sir Thomas Chaloner, governor of the Prince of Wales' household, to pay the wages of the boy's embroiderer, who 'is redy to perish for want of money', so the moral tone at court continued to decline in parallel.

Only a year before the meteoric rise to prominence of Robert Carr, it seemed that the king might have at last outgrown the need to lavish inordinate affection upon some handsome young man or other. James Hay had, of course, arrived from Scotland with the reputation of a favourite, and in the early months of his reign, England's new ruler had also fawned over Philp Herbert, Earl of Montgomery. But Hay's relationship with his master, though resented, was always seemly, while Montgomery always smelt far too strongly of the stables to appeal at any deeper level to the king's fancy. For James required manners and refinement as well as good looks from his ideal companion, and if gratitude, docility and a dash of vulnerability could be added to the mix, the king's devotion was assured. When Montgomery's wenching and drinking finally cooled the king's ardour for him, therefore, it was only to make space for Carr – an altogether more eligible competitor whom Sir John Harington described as 'straight-limbed, well-favoured, strong-shouldered and smooth faced', with fair hair and a pointed beard, and who, in the words of Sir Anthony Weldon, had 'had his breeding in France and was newly returned from foreign travel'.

The youngest son of Sir Thomas Ker of Ferniherst, who had served as Warden of the Middle March and been a faithful friend of Esmé Stuart, Robert Carr, as the surname became spelt in England, had been born around the time of his father's death in 1586, making him around 21 at the time that he was first dangled under the king's nose by none other than James Hay in an attempt both to undermine the Cecil–Howard stranglehold on power and advance once more the Scottish interest at court. Having served as a page who ran beside the royal coach in Scotland – a post from which he had been dismissed for clumsiness, according to Queen Anne – Carr seemed the perfect instrument for Hay's purpose. Athletic, personable and apparently guileless, he could be shaped to need, or so it seemed, and guaranteed to enliven the king's paternal instincts, which might grow with suitable prompting into something more compelling still. To all intents and purposes, the only requirement was a suitable setting to lay the bait, and such an opportunity was duly forthcoming on 'King's Day', 24 March 1607, when the annual jousting event to celebrate James's accession was held in the Whitehall tiltyard.

It was Hay, in fact, who made the first flamboyant entrance that day, attended by a number of gentlemen and pages adorned 'in their richest ornaments', one of whom, on a high-bred horse, had been appointed to carry the courtier's shield, and present it to the king. But the handsome young stranger's mount was 'full of fire and heat', we are told, and, after encouraging it to prance and curvet, he was thrown to the ground with such violence that his leg was broken. With the stricken rider lying prone before the royal stand, there could be, in fact, only one outcome. For the king, 'whose nature and disposition was very flowing in affection toward persons so adorned', was overcome with compassion, and 'mustering up his thoughts, fixed them upon this object of pity, giving special order to have him lodged in the court, and to have his own physicians and chirurgeons to use their best endeavours for his recovery'. Thereafter, it seems, James visited Hay's young gentleman not once but several times, captivated by his modesty and ingenuousness when questioned about the progress of his recovery. 'And though', Arthur Wilson tells us, the king 'found no great depth of literature or experience' in the patient, 'yet such a calm outside him made him think there might be good anchorage and a fit harbour for his most retired thoughts'.

So it was, then, that Robert Carr became firmly lodged in his sovereign's affections. Possessing, no doubt, a native shrewdness that enabled him quickly to gage the character of the man from whom he might hope all things, the young Scot seems, nevertheless, to have exhibited genuine charm and grace of manners, since even those who eventually came to hate his influence acknowledged his 'gentle mind and affable disposition'. Before long, James was personally teaching Carr 'the Latin tongue' and laying a foundation 'by his daily discourses with him, to improve him into a capability of his most endeared affections'. With no less care and trouble, the king also attended to his new favourite's appearance and bearing, equipping him with the finery in which he liked to see his courtiers 'make a brave show'. 'The young man,' wrote Sir John Harington in *Nugae Antiquae*, 'doth much study art and device: he hath changed his tailors and tiremen many times and all to please the Prince. The King teacheth him Latin every morning and I think some one should teach him English too, for he is a Scotch lad, and hath much need of better language'.

Harington makes clear, moreover, that James not only cared for Carr but smothered him with the kind of cloying attentiveness that was soon exceeding the bounds of strict propriety and plain common sense. 'The Prince,' the author informs us, 'leaneth on his arm, pinches his cheeks, smoothes his ruffled garments, and when he looketh at Carr, directeth discourse to divers others.' But this was not the limit of James's indiscretion, for in indulging his infatuation ever more ardently, the king's control of the young man became increasingly unwholesome. Robert Carr was to be, as James liked to phrase it, his 'creature'. 'Remember,' James wrote later, 'that all your being except your breathing and soul is from me.' Nor, from some perspectives, was this an exaggeration as the king's new favourite enjoyed the broader generosity of his master's patronage. In a letter from John Chamberlain to Dudley Carleton, dated 30 December 1607, we read that Robert Carr, 'a young Scot and new favourite', was appointed Gentleman of the Bedchamber. Then, on 6 December a royal warrant was made out 'To Robert Carr, Groom of the Bedchamber, for a yearly rent-charge of £600, to be paid to him for fifteen years by John Warner and three others, in consideration of a grant to them of certain arrears of rent due to the Crown'. And on 22 March 1608, there is a further warrant to pay £300 to Henryck von Hulfen 'for a tablet of gold set with diamonds and the King's picture, given by the King to Robert Carr, Gentleman of the Bedchamber'.

It was not until January 1609, however, that Carr was finally afforded a gift that placed his position far above that of any private gentleman. Since any advancement to higher honours necessitated a substantial endowment, the king opted in the worst possible way to employ Sir Walter Raleigh's estate at Sherborne for Carr's benefit. The only property saved for his family's benefit from the wreck of his fortunes, Sherborne was now lost to Raleigh as a result of a criminally careless flaw in the deed conveying the land to trustees. When so much Crown land was being sold to meet his most pressing debts, the king had therefore acted without compunction and in the teeth of widespread public hostility, which was shared by both Queen Anne and Prince Henry. 'I mun hae it for Carr,' James insisted, and, in accordance with his growing habit of flagrantly disregarding opposition to his immediate wishes and brazenly ignoring unpalatable facts, Sherborne was indeed acquired. Early in 1610, moreover, Carr was duly created Viscount Rochester, a Knight of the Garter and a Privy Councillor, before becoming Keeper of the Signet and, in effect, the king's private secretary in May 1611. Two years later he was to complete his ascent by becoming Earl of Somerset and Lord Chamberlain.

How far this remarkable advancement was linked to the emotional needs arising from the disintegration of the king's family life will naturally remain a matter for speculation. James had never, of course, been able to share any worthwhile intellectual activity with the queen, and her propensity for intrigue, gnawing intolerance to opposition, and widely broadcast flirtations with Rome had made it necessary, ultimately, to exclude her altogether from politics. Nor had she had ever been able to reciprocate the pent-up romanticism and desire for love and sympathy that her husband required of her. In spite of any residual friendship and tolerance they still shared, therefore, the death of the Princess Sophia within twenty-four hours of her birth in June 1606, followed the year after by that of the other baby daughter, Mary, seems to have damaged the couple's relationship irreparably. Still only 33, Anne remained pretty, if only blandly so, and, apart from the twinges of gout that she shared with her husband, continued to enjoy good health. But having borne James several children and endured a number of miscarriages along the way, the queen seems to have decided once and for all to escape the roundabout of pregnancy and bereavement she had ridden for too long and give herself over to more gratifying pursuits, such as the masques in which she caused such indignation by acting herself.

Nor, more importantly still, was the king able to fulfil his emotional needs by the kind of intensely devoted relationship that he might have been expected to enjoy with his eldest son. Indeed, as Prince Henry began to exhibit a cool, clear mind of his own around the age of 12, the gulf in personality and tastes between the two became increasingly evident. 'He was a prince,' wrote Sir Simonds D'Ewes, 'rather addicted to martial studies and exercises than to golf, tennis, or other boys' play; a true lover of the English nation, and a sound Protestant, abhorring not only the idolatry, superstitions and bloody persecutions of the Romish synagogue, but being free also from the Lutheran leaven.' Much more typically English than his father, then, Henry also preferred the company of 'learned and godly men' to that of 'buffoons and parasites, vain swearers and atheists'. But he was both insular and immovable in his prejudices, and while James had wished him to be all that he was not – athletic, self-confident and attractive – he was nevertheless hurt when the boy proved incapable of sharing his bookishness and open-hearted demonstrativeness. For Henry preferred action to dialectic and the tales of Elizabethan heroism to any talk of peace. By the age of 14, indeed, the prince found greater inspiration in the company of Phineas Pett, the Master Shipwright at Woolwich, than that of his father, acquiring far more knowledge about naval administration and dockyard construction, we are told, than king and council combined. That Prince Henry's greatest hero, however, should have been none other than Sir Walter Raleigh must surely have been his father's most galling disappointment of all.

Lonely and starved of affection as he was, therefore, it was not perhaps altogether surprising that James should have found in Robert Carr an emotional prop of sorts and a delectable object for his sweeter nature. But the naivety which led him to believe that he could turn his favourite into a statesman, and his blindness to the political consequences of his infatuation, were again indicative of that self-same lack of majesty that would always negate the king's more admirable qualities. Emotionally vulnerable – sometimes truly pathetic so – and stricken by insecurities that he was never ready to confront sufficiently earnestly, this was nevertheless a ruler who was incapable of doubting his own wisdom or the status of his divinely ordained office and believed that this was enough in itself to make him a leader of men. Such, then, was the potent combination of conflicting characteristics that had long infected James's kingship and would now threaten to poison the fibre of his entire court.

For the time being, however, it remained the king's financial position that troubled his ministers most pressingly. When Lord Treasurer Dorset dropped dead at a meeting of the Privy Council in April, 1608, his last 'accompt' showed debts totalling more than £700,000 and revealed, according to his successor, the Earl of Salisbury, that James's expenditure exceeded his ordinary revenue by some £80,000 a year. Wishing to consolidate all areas of policy under his sole control for an attempt at root and branch reform, and partly because there was nobody other than himself obviously qualified to assume the post, the Secretary of State therefore added the killing burden of the treasurership to his already overwhelming workload. For unless the Crown could secure adequate revenue to govern in times of peace without parliamentary grants, the king's independence from the tax-voting House of Commons, as Salisbury well knew, must surely be compromised. All hinged initially, however, upon clearing the mountain of government debt and the crippling burden of annual interest payments resulting from it.

In this last respect, at least, the new treasurer seems to have been surprisingly successful. Selling Crown property to the value of £400,000 and retrieving old debts amounting to a total of £200,000, Salisbury also revived various lapsed dues and fees and uncollected fines, and raised in the process a further £100,000. Yet the annual deficit continued to snap at the treasurer's heels and even his more drastic efforts to drive home the need for stringent economies proved unavailing with the king. James had made clear in *Basilikon Doron* that it was the duty of any prince to 'use true Liberality in rewarding the good, and bestowing frankly for your honour and weal'. The use of patronage was, after all, a tried and trusted method of guaranteeing loyalty, and even Salisbury observed to Parliament in 1610 that 'for a king not to be bountiful were a fault'. But James remained a long-term addict to excess: impulsive and compulsive at one and the same time, and driven by a heady need to satisfy his sentimental urges by giving. And just as Thomas Fowler had reported in 1588, the king's largesse still exceeded all sensible bounds of generosity as 'vain youths' and 'proud fools' continued to be lavished with royal gifts and favours. Nor had confession of his faults saved him from their consequences. 'I have offended the whole country, I grant, for prodigal giving from me,' he told Maitland in 1591.

So when Salisbury resorted to pleadings and shock tactics the outcome was hardly surprising. In 1610 a *Declaration of his Majesty's Royal Pleasure in the Matter of Bounty* committed James to 'expressly forbid all persons whatsoever, to presume to press us, for anything that may … turn to the diminution of our revenues and settled receipts …' Five years later, however, commentators were still bemoaning the throng of self-seekers besieging the throne. 'The King hath borrowed £30,000 of the aldermen of this city,' wrote John Chamberlain. 'But what,' he added, 'is that among so many who gape and starve after it?' Even more childlike lessons, for that matter, appear to have had no lasting effect. According to an anecdote related by Francis Osborne, Salisbury resorted on one occasion to piling up in front of James the £20,000 he had ordered the Exchequer to pay out as a gift, whereupon, we are told, 'the king fell into a passion, protesting he was abused, never intending any such gift: and casting himself upon the heap, scrabbled out the quantity of two or three hundred pounds', swearing that the intended recipient 'should have no more'.

Tall tale or not, the implication was nevertheless entirely borne out by the hard facts, which left the exasperated treasurer to resort to an altogether more painful course for the king's hard-pressed subjects. For if fire sales and savings were not the solution, then the yawning gap between expenditure and income could only next be bridged by raising import duties – an opportunity for which had conveniently presented itself as a result of the collapse, early in the reign, of the Levant Company. To compensate itself for the handsome yearly sum that the company had been paying for its monopoly of trade in the Eastern Mediterranean, the treasury subsequently imposed an extra duty on imported currants, and when a merchant named Thomas Bate refused to pay, the outcome was a lawsuit in the Exchequer Court which raised the whole issue of the Crown's right to 'impose' extra duties of this kind. Backed by sound Elizabethan precedents and the firm support of the judges, however, Salisbury prevailed and, after careful discussion with leading City merchants as to what the trade could reasonably stand, imposed in 1608 a new Book of Rates calculated to yield a further £70,000. In consequence, as the total value of the kingdom's trade continued to increase, the Crown's revenue rose from £264,000 in 1603 to £366,000 in the very same year that the new rates were implemented.

Sadly, however, and all too predictably, expenditure continued to rise even more rapidly over the same period – from £290,700 in 1603 to £509,524 in 1610, the year in which Salisbury finally called upon Parliament in the hope of agreeing a 'Great Contract' that might render the Crown solvent by surrendering the more provocative methods of raising revenue in return for a guaranteed grant of £200,000 lasting for the duration of the king's life. Yet the most promising financial reform of the reign was never to materialise. By July the bargain had actually been struck, though Parliament hesitated, it seems, 'to engage themselves in any offers or promises of contribution to the King, afore they were sure of some certain and sound retribution from him', and the final details were left until Parliament was reconvened in November. In the intervening period, moreover, MPs came to like the arrangement less and less until some bristled with resentment, while the king, possibly in consequence of statistics submitted to him by Sir Julius Caesar, Chancellor of the Exchequer, had decided that the agreed annual grant from Parliament was incommensurate with the monetary concessions he had granted. Poisoned too, it seems, by the influence of Robert Carr who was justifiably alarmed by the palpable hostility to Scots in general and himself in particular, James duly decided to abort his treasurer's plans by irritably dissolving Parliament in January 1611.

The prior behaviour of the Commons had demonstrated, however, just how far their confidence in the king's ability to manage his affairs was already compromised. Under the leadership of men like Edwin Sandys certain members had plainly adopted the principle that redress of grievances should be linked to financial co-operation, and proposed accordingly that the king's predicament should be used as a lever to wring wider concessions from him. They urged, therefore, that laws against recusants should be properly enforced and that all grants to courtiers should be cancelled: the first clear sign that Carr's rise to prominence was now a matter of open disapproval. 'Where your Majesty's expense groweth by the Commonwealth we are bound to maintain it: otherwise not', warned Sir Henry Neville, before demanding to know 'to what purpose is it for us to draw a silver stream out of the country into the royal cistern, if it shall daily run dry from private cocks'. But it was the member for Oxford City's last comment that carried with it the most wounding barb of all when he added how he would never 'consent to take money from a poor frieze jerkin to trap a courtier's horse withal'.

And as debate expanded to encompass 'impositions' and, in particular, the fear that James might soon see fit to raise far more than the sum laid down by the current Book of Rates, his only response was to visit the

House on 21 March and deliver the most outspoken defence of his royal prerogative to date. 'The state of Monarchy,' he declared in what has rightly become one of his best known speeches:

> is the supremest thing upon earth; for kings are not only God's lieutenants upon earth and sit upon God's throne, but even by God himself they are called gods ... In the Scriptures kings are called gods, and so their power after a certain relation compared to the Divine Power. Kings are also compared to the fathers of families, for a king is truly *parens patriae*, the politic father of his people ... Now a father may dispose of his inheritance to his children at his pleasure, yea, even disinherit the eldest upon just occasions and prefer the youngest, according to his liking; make them beggars or rich at his pleasure; restrain or banish them out of his presence, as he finds them give cause of offence, or restore them in favour again with the penitent sinner. So may the King deal with his subjects.

There followed, it is true, a reassurance from James that God would punish all kings who nevertheless failed to govern according to the laws. But this did not deter a minority of MPs from producing a solemn Petition of Right in defence of free speech or prevent calls for the reinstatement of 300 ejected clergy and criticism of the activities of the ecclesiastical courts. Nor was Salisbury spared the sting of the king's tongue when James finally called a halt to proceedings after discussion had turned to the scandals of Scottish favourites and the iniquities of court extravagance. 'Your greatest error,' James told him in the aftermath of his decision to prorogue Parliament, 'hath been that ye ever expected to draw honey out of gall, being a little blinded with the self-love of your own counsel in holding together of this Parliament, whereof all men were despaired, as I have oft told you, but yourself alone.' And just how little the king had learned throughout the last sorry year of ill-tempered debate was amply demonstrated by his prompt elevation of Carr to the House of Lords as Viscount Rochester and the scattering of another £34,000 in indiscriminate gifts, mostly to Scotsmen.

Thereafter, relations between the king and Salisbury appeared, superficially at least, to resume their former course. James returned to his rural delights, while his principal minister received the usual flow of instructions and admonitions, delivered more and more often now in the hand of Viscount Rochester to whom most royal correspondence was dictated. Many of James's letters dealt, in fact, with trivialities. He was irritated, for example, by the felling of trees in the Forest of Dean which disturbed the hawks, and concerned about the treatment of an albino hind. He wrote, too, about foreign affairs and the queen's illness of 1611, as well as the Oath of Allegiance and fines from those who refused it. On another occasion, he told Salisbury how he had heard from his pastoral retreat that deprived clergy still preached in the vicinity of Peterborough, and required the hard-pressed minister to admonish the bishop. But this did not stop him either from objecting to Salisbury's draft of a commission which, he believed, might be exploited to limit the royal prerogative.

Nor does the banality of much of James's correspondence conceal the fact that he continued to blame his minister for the failure of his first Parliament, and was intent upon quietly dropping him as his chief adviser. There were no more 'Little Beagle' letters, the old jocularity disappeared, and royal messages were uncharacteristically formal and business-like. Increasingly, too, Salisbury found himself relegated to routine matters, while the king took counsel with Northampton, who hated him, and Rochester who conspired against him at every turn. 'I have seen this parliament at an end,' the waning minister reflected, 'whereof the many vexations have so overtaken one another as I know not what to resemble them so well as to the plagues of Job.' To add to his woes, a scheme was hatched to seal an alliance with Spain by marrying Prince Henry to a Spanish princess and granting toleration to English Catholics – a project which only the uncompromising hostility of the prince himself ultimately thwarted.

Not altogether surprisingly, therefore, by February 1612 Salisbury was seriously ill. The king, meanwhile, as a friend informed the stricken minister, was 'careful exceedingly of your lordship's health', the more so, it seems, because he had continued in spite of his pain to attend to instructions about a royal paddock. There was a visit from the king, too, which appears to have consoled the patient further. 'This royal voice of visitation (like *visitatio beatifica*),' wrote Salisbury, 'has given new life to those spirits which are ready to expire for your benefit.' Yet within a few days James delivered a complaining letter. He did not like the manner in which Salisbury had dealt with a problem in London where many Englishmen were attending Mass in the chapels of ambassadors from Roman Catholic states. If he himself had not been absent, James reflected, the matter would have been better managed.

That April, as a last desperate remedy for the dropsy which was gaining on him, Salisbury resorted vainly to the healing waters at Bath before finally dying in the parsonage at Marlborough on 24 May during his return to Hatfield. Northampton, unable to conceal his malicious satisfaction, spoke heartlessly of 'the death of the little man for which so many rejoice and so few do so much as seem sorry'. And John Chamberlain, too, left little doubt that similar sentiments were circulating widely. 'I never knew so great a man so soon and so generally censured,' he wrote, 'for men's tongues walk very liberally and very freely, but how truly I cannot judge.' Yet it was Sir Francis Bacon, no friend, it must be said, to the late secretary and treasurer, who probably encapsulated most effectively his achievements and limitations. 'Your Majesty hath lost a great subject and a great servant,' he told the king on 31 May. 'I should say,' he added, 'that he was a fit man to keep things from growing worse but no very fit man to reduce things to be much better.'

For James, meanwhile, the news of his minister's demise appears to have represented nothing less than a blessed relief from a long-standing and irksome tutelage. Upon hearing of it at Whitehall, he delayed his intended departure for the country, according to Bishop Goodman's memorial of the reign, only until after dinner. Plainly, the obligation of gratitude and deference had become tedious to the king, and the restraints upon his conduct galling. No new Secretary of State was therefore chosen or any Lord Treasurer appointed to restrain and criticise the lavishness of his impulses. Instead, the king would receive his financial counsel henceforth from a commission, of which Northampton was the most influential member, and which soon ascertained that the debt so assiduously reduced by Salisbury to £300,000 in 1610 had risen once again by two thirds. In November 1612, moreover, Prince Henry also sickened and died, calling for his friend, David Murray, and his beloved sister, Elizabeth, and subsequently leaving his father freer than ever to administer his kingdom entirely as he pleased. All correspondence now was to be conducted through Carr, as Keeper of the Signet, or 'bedchamber men' who were, in any case, Carr's nominees. And with this, the transfer of effective power to the new favourite whom Salisbury had unobtrusively, but on the whole effectively resisted, became complete.

Though not promoted to any higher office, Viscount Rochester nevertheless became the mainspring on which the king's entire style of government now largely depended. Too dull of wit to offer effective counsel on matters of state, he was nevertheless faithful, obedient and ever watchful, and this, above all, made him a formidable guardian of his master's interests. 'I must confess,' wrote James, 'you have deserved more trust and confidence of me than ever man did, in secrecy above all flesh, in feeling and impartial respect ... And all this without respect either to kin or ally or your nearest and dearest friend whatsoever, nay, unmovable in one hair that might concern me against the whole world.' Nor was James's estimation of his favourite's better qualities by any means entirely unfounded. Bishop Goodman, for instance, would describe Robert Carr as 'a wise, discreet gentleman', and even Sir Anthony Weldon, crabbed and tainted witness that he was, acknowledged how the young Scotsman 'was observed to spend his time in serious studies, and did accompany himself with none but men of such eminences as by whom he might be bettered'. There was no denying, of course, that Carr took bribes, as did almost everyone else at court, but he was always ready to secure the king's approval in doing so. And though he was ready to benefit from others' misfortune, he did not in general deprive men of their posts and influence gratuitously.

Yet if Rochester was indeed discreet for the moment, shunning his Scottish compatriots and own kindred, he was inevitably under pressure to join one of the two factions into which the court was cleanly divided, and ultimately, like all favourites who have been pampered too long, he would become overweening, forgetful of his dependence upon the king and thereby invite disaster. Deprived of the Salisbury alliance on which their power had rested, the Howard grouping in particular, headed by the earls of Northampton and Suffolk, was bound to lose its primacy without the favourite's good offices. But while the Howards offered fawning blandishments, Rochester was also courted by his old friend, Sir Thomas Overbury, who sought to draw him to the anti-Spanish camp and the ranks of the 'parliamentary mutineers'. Holding aloof with good sense, the pig in the middle for some time made no move 'save where the king had his interest'. But love for the king was ultimately overwhelmed by ardour for another – the Earl of Suffolk's very own daughter. Thus, wrote Arthur Wilson, were Rochester's good and affable qualities finally swallowed up in a 'gulf of beauty'.

Already married to the young Earl of Essex, son of the former queen's own firebrand favourite, Lady Frances Howard was a bad lot – proud, headstrong and violent, and raised in an atmosphere of self-interest, self-indulgence and sexual and political intrigue that had left her capable of both flagrant immodesty and implacable hatred. Her marriage had occurred in January 1606, when she was still only 13 and her groom only a year older, and had resulted from a typically well-intentioned and misconceived attempt by the king to heal a long-standing feud dating back to the time that the Howards had helped deliver the young earl's father to the scaffold. James saw himself, after all, as *rex pacificus*, the bringer of peace and harmony to each and any situation, who had not only rescued his realm from war with Spain but had already engineered a marriage between Salisbury's son and a daughter of the Earl of Suffolk, and would now sow further concord by similar means. That the principals on this occasion were mere children was neither an obstacle nor a concern.

In the event, for two years after her nuptials the bride returned to her father's house while her husband left for the Continent to mature over two years of travel. But by 1609 the earl, a solid if humourless young man, was back in England and set in vain upon consummating his marriage in his country home at Chartley. Witness after witness, in fact, would later confirm that the two had repeatedly bedded together and the countess herself would testify how she had made every effort 'that she might be made a lawful mother'. Yet Essex, according to his own subsequent testimony, 'felt no motion or provocation, and therefore attempted nothing': a situation that persisted well beyond the compulsory period of 'triennial probation', after which a marriage could normally be nullified and the couple given their longed-for release. Whether, of course, the groom's impotence was natural or the consequence of drugs which, years later, it transpired his wife had secretly procured from quacks and ministered to him, will remain uncertain. But the countess's mounting aversion to her spouse was an open secret at court and by 1613 she had become the object of outright scandal, for it was widely rumoured that she was both angling for divorce and already Robert Carr's mistress. More salaciously still, it was also suggested that she had relieved Prince Henry of his virginity and that jealousy over her affection had been the real cause of his hostility towards the king's favourite.

The Howards, however, saw only opportunity in the countess's prospective marriage to Carr until, that is, they found themselves confronted by a formidable obstacle. For favourites have favourites of their own and Sir Thomas Overbury, poet, bosom friend and personal mentor to Robert Carr, would prove an implacable enemy to their designs. Clever, able and intolerably arrogant, Overbury had already made many enemies, but his ascendancy over the king's favourite made him a formidable entity at court. Enjoying the privilege of unsealing and reading reports from English ambassadors abroad before passing them on to Carr, complete with margin comments, it was said that Overbury knew more secrets of state than the Privy Council. And while a casual dalliance between his protégé, who would be created Earl of Somerset on 3 November 1613, and a Howard daughter might be borne, the prospect of their marriage was utterly unacceptable to him. 'Will you never leave that base woman?' Overbury is said to have asked his friend during a heated altercation at 1 a.m. upon Carr's return from a tryst with his loved one. After which, according to Henry Peyton who witnessed the exchange, 'they were never perfectly reconciled again'.

The king, meanwhile, who was always inquisitive in matters of sex and therefore particularly attracted by the more novel and tawdry aspects of this case, had immersed himself thoroughly in every detail of the wretched affair. In all likelihood, of course, he regretted his own part in encouraging the marriage initially, for at one point in the subsequent trial he inveighed against the risks of marrying too early. But he was surrounded, nevertheless, by men who favoured the countess's divorce and he was in no doubt either about the potential alliance between Carr and the Howards. The immediate result was the appointment in May 1613 of a commission to investigate the validity of the marriage, headed by the muddle-headed but scrupulously honest George Abbot who had succeeded Bancroft as Archbishop of Canterbury in 1611. Within a year, however, this same divorce case had assumed dimensions that the king could scarcely have imagined, as he waded thigh-deep into a stagnant pool of sexual scandal, intrigue, corruption, sorcery and, ultimately, poison.

'What a strange and fearful thing it was', wrote Abbot, '… that the judges should be dealt with beforehand, and, in a sort, directed what they should determine', and that the king should profess how he himself 'had set the matter in that course of judgement'. For James was utterly credulous from the outset to Frances Howard's lies and resolved that she should have her way. When, for instance, a jury of twelve matrons examined the countess and asserted her virginity, the king ignored that she had been allowed to wear a veil throughout the examination, and discarded claims that her cousin – a true virgin – or some other woman had impersonated her. As the case dragged on throughout the summer, moreover, James had tried to influence the commissioners' decision by inviting them to Windsor and browbeating them on theological issues relating to the case for more than three hours. Throughout, there had been much talk of witchcraft, though Abbot could find no mention in the Church Fathers of a link between '*maleficium*' and impotence in marriage.

Such, indeed, was Abbot's perplexity at the king's accusations of prejudice against the countess, 'which prejudice is the most dangerous thing that can fall in a judge for misleading of his mind', that the archbishop dropped at one point to his knees and tearfully implored the king to relieve him from his role as chairman. Completely oblivious to the irony of his own advice, however, James merely urged the dumbfounded cleric 'to have a kind of faith implicit in my judgement, as well in respect of some skill I have in divinity, as also that I hope no honest man doubts of the uprightness of my conscience'. Whereupon, after discovering that the vote of the commissioners would be tied he duly added two more members, Bishops Bilson and Buckeridge, with the result that on 25 September the divorce was finally granted by a vote of seven to five. That Bilson's son was thereafter created a knight, and Lancelot Andrewes, another in favour of a nullity verdict, soon became Bishop of London did not, of course, escape the notice of the cynics.

Even now, however, the sorry episode had still not run its course, for, after her eventual re-marriage on 26 December 1613, Carr's new wife showed no trace of forgiveness towards Overbury for opposing her divorce in the first place. Worse still, she not only hated him but feared he knew too much about her murky dealings with the quack doctor, Simon Forman, 'that fiend in human shape' as he was described by Richard Nichol, a contemporary poet. By now, in fact, Overbury had already fallen foul of a trap laid by Northampton in April, which had left him a close prisoner in the Tower. Using his daughter's hold on Carr and Carr's hold upon the king, the Howards' leader had arranged for his enemy to be offered a mission abroad while encouraging him to believe that he could count upon Carr's protection, should he refuse. Thereafter, when Overbury did indeed reject the offer for fear of losing influence at court, his insolence was punished accordingly, leaving him mortally exposed to the further intrigues of the woman who was soon to become Countess of Somerset.

Before that title was even hers, however, Robert Carr's bride had indeed seen off Overbury once and for all. Sending poison through a certain Richard Weston whom she had arranged to serve as Overbury's keeper, her first attempt at murder was foiled when Weston's design was discovered and prevented by Sir Gervase Helwys, Lieutenant of the Tower. But though Helwys suspected the main culprit he dared not accuse her and chose instead to keep the matter quiet, leaving her free to send further poisons, including arsenic and mercury introduced into tarts and jellies and a brace of partridges, some of which were sent by Carr himself, though there is evidence, mainly in the letters of Northampton who was certainly aware of his daughter's skulduggery, that the king's favourite had no direct knowledge of the plot. Ultimately, in any case, the lethal dose appears to have been delivered by an apothecary's boy whose handiwork resulted in Overbury's death the next day. And though a posthumous poem by Overbury entitled 'The Wife', which had been written, it seems, to discourage the marriage, would sell out five editions in less than a year, the nature of his death would remain, for the time being at least, a secret, as feasting and revelry marked the wedding and the new Countess of Somerset became the recipient of jewels worth £10,000 gifted to her by the king himself.

For the next year, indeed, Robert Carr enjoyed the high watermark of his fortunes, as James's confidence in him continued unbounded. He was, wrote Sir Geoffrey Fenton, the king's secretary in Ireland, 'more absolute than ever any that I have either heard or did see myself', while John Chamberlain observed how all matters were conducted between the king and his favourite 'within the shrine of the breast'. 'The Viscount Rochester at the Council table,' reported Gondomar, the Spanish ambassador, 'showeth much temper and modesty, without seeming to press and sway anything. But afterwards the King resolveth all business with him alone, both those that pass in the Council and many others wherewith he never maketh them acquainted'. With Northampton's death in June 1614, moreover, the duties of Lord Privy Seal and Warden of the Cinque Ports were, for the time being, entrusted to Carr who was also installed as Lord Chamberlain. He was even lucky enough, in the process, to be spared the poison chalice of the treasurership, which was passed instead to the Earl of Suffolk at a time when debt stood at £680,000 and £67,000 of the anticipated revenue for 1614 was already spent.

But Somerset lacked, it seems, the intuitive skill to handle his now increasingly complicated relationship with the king. During that summer James continued to indulge his peculiar delight in the domestic intimacies of his favourites and fussed over the countess almost as much as he did over her husband. When she fell ill after a wedding banquet in May, Chamberlain wrote that there had been 'much care and tender respect had of her, both by her Lord and the King'. Yet James's love was essentially possessive, and for all his gushing sentiments and lavish presents, the independence of his royal will and ego was what he had fought most passionately to establish and maintain throughout his life. Though he might happily become a slave to his own infatuation, therefore, he would never subject himself to the mercy of another's whim, and when Somerset now became rude and exacting, taking for granted what he had so far earned by chance, his many enemies made ready to strike in the most effective – and ironic – way possible. For it was in August 1614, on a hunting visit to Sir Anthony Mildmay's estate at Apethorpe that the king first encountered another young newcomer to the court, and by September Sir Geoffrey Fenton was observing how this same bright light, a youth named Villiers, 'begins to be in favour with his Majesty'.

15 ❧ Favourite of Favourites

'I, James, am neither a god nor an angel, but a man like any other. Therefore I act like a man and confess to loving those dear to me more than other men. You may be sure that I love the Earl of Buckingham more than anyone else, and more than you who are here assembled. I wish to speak in my own behalf and not to have it thought to be a defect, for Jesus Christ did the same and therefore I cannot be blamed. Christ had John, and I have George.'

Comment made by the King of England to his Privy Council in 1617

O n 5 April 1614, the king opened his second Parliament, expressing the hope that it might become a 'Parliament of Love'. By 7 June, however, the same assembly had been dissolved in general acrimony, to be dubbed by posterity the 'Addled Parliament'. And though James had displayed a studied moderation and respect for legality that belies his later reputation, the lack of trust and respect that dogged him was apparent throughout. 'Kings,' he had declared, 'that are not tyrants or perjured, will be glad to bind themselves within the limits of law ... For it is a great difference between a King's government in a settled state and what Kings in their original powers might do ...' Yet the Addled Parliament proved, it was said, 'more like a cockpit than a grave Council' as MPs refused to take Holy Communion in Westminster 'for fear of copes and wafer cakes' and a hot-headed Puritan minority railed against morris dances and games upon the Sabbath. 'The House of Commons,' James complained to the Spanish ambassador, 'is a body without a head' where 'nothing is heard but cries, shouts and confusion'. 'I am surprised,' he added, 'that that my ancestors should ever have permitted such an institution to come into existence.' And such, indeed, was the disorder leading to its dissolution without the desired grant of taxation that one of the House's members, Sir Thomas Roe, thought he had witnessed the end 'not of this, but of all parliaments'.

Henceforward, impositions would continue to be raised without parliamentary consent, and when James called for a 'benevolence' or free gift from his subjects in 1614 against the advice of his Lord Chief Justice, Sir Edward Coke, ripples of resistance were predictable. Though Archbishop Abbot had donated a selection of plate to the treasury and Coke himself had come forward with £200, humbler folk like Oliver St John of Marlborough, who was prosecuted in Star Chamber for his protests, were not so willing to comply. In the case of Edmund Peacham, meanwhile, the king became personally involved and ordered that the elderly Somerset rector be consigned to the Tower for daring to warn of the possibility of rebellion and his sovereign's death within eight days like Ananias and Nabal. When, moreover, James suggested to Sir Francis Bacon, his Attorney General, that the realm's leading judges might be consulted singly on the issue of whether Peacham had committed high treason, Chief Justice Coke again intervened to warn that 'such particular and auricular taking of opinion' was in breach of English common law. Even so – and in spite of Coke's overall conclusion that Peacham's outbursts, though scandalous, were not treasonable, since he had not impugned the king's title – a treason verdict was indeed delivered in Taunton by King's Serjeant Montagu and Chief Baron Tanfield of the Exchequer Court. In the event, only the foul air of the local jail, which quickly killed him, prevented the execution of Peacham's sentence.

Rober Carr, meanwhile, had become increasingly prone to what the king himself described in a letter as 'streams of unquietness, passion, fury and insolent pride, and a settled kind of induced obstinacy'. The same letter, addressed to the favourite personally in 1615, also details how he had raised complaints with his royal master at unseasonable hours, as if on purpose to vex him, and how the court had become increasingly conscious of their angry exchanges and the king's sadness thereafter. Why, James complained, was Carr now refusing to sleep in the royal bedchamber and continuing to trouble him with so many idle and unfounded concerns? 'Do not all courtesies and places come through your office as Chamberlain, and rewards through your father-in-law as Treasurer? Do not you two as it were hedge in all the court with a manner of necessity to depend upon you?' the letter continued. And the same tone of slighted affection and sincere sorrow was to climax in a profession that the king was writing 'from the infinite grief of a deeply wounded heart' that he can bear no longer.

Amid such utterances, however, there also lurked more ominous sentences of the deepest significance for Carr's future prospects. 'For the easing of my inward and consuming grief,' James appealed, 'all I crave is, that in all the words and actions of your life you make it appear that you never think to hold me but out of love, and not one hair by force.' As the letter unfolds, furthermore, there are threats as well as entreaties. 'I told you twice or thrice you might lead me by the heart and not by the nose', the favourite is reminded, and 'if ever I find you think to retain me by one sparkle of fear, all the violence of my love will in that moment be changed into as violent a hatred'. 'God is my judge,' the message concludes, 'my love hath been infinite towards you, and only the strength of my affection towards you hath made me to bear these things and bridle my passion ... Let me never apprehend that you disdain my person and undervalue my qualities; and let it never appear that your former affection is cold towards me. Hold me thus by the heart, and you may build upon my favour as upon a rock.'

Arguably, no words of James capture more aptly so many essential features of his personality: the potency of his passions, the underlying insecurity that made them such a political liability, and his residing need for both unreserved affection and utter control, which inclined him so often to treat criticism as disloyalty, and equate opposition with enmity. Such traits could both endear and enrage, and, as Robert Carr and George Villiers would now find, both sweep to prominence and wash away in the same flood tide. For the latter's emergence was 'so quick', as Clarendon later observed, 'that it seemed rather a flight than a growth'. By April 1615, George Abbot and other enemies of Carr, knowing the king's curious rule of seeking the queen's approval for his favourites, were soliciting her for Villiers' appointment as gentleman of the bedchamber. And though she temporised, noting with commendable foresight that the young cupbearer would soon prove a plague to 'you that labour for him', she nevertheless proved willing on St George's Day 1615 to visit the king's bedchamber with the most fateful of consequences. Telling James that she had a new candidate for the honour of knighthood worthy of St George himself, she then asked Prince Charles to hand her his father's sword unsheathed, and proceeded to compensate for the king's well attested fear of naked steel by guiding his hand as the blade was duly applied to Villiers' shoulders.

For some time already, the new gentleman of the bedchamber had been in constant attendance upon James as royal cup-bearer and had shown, on one occasion at least, a feistiness that equalled his grace and good lucks. For when one of Somerset's followers had previously spilt a bowl of soup onto his magnificent white suit, he had been stung to anger and struck the man in the king's presence: an offence which could have led in theory to the loss of his right hand. But James refused to take the matter further and was soon idolising his new favourite in the all too familiar fashion. In the same year of his knighthood, indeed, the young man who had started life as the younger son of a Leicestershire squire also became Viscount Villiers, and in 1617, Earl of Buckingham, while 1618 witnessed his promotion to marquis and appointment as Lord High Admiral. Five years later the king bestowed his highest accolade of all by creating him the only duke of non-royal blood in the kingdom.

'The Duke,' wrote Clarendon many years later, 'was indeed a very extraordinary person; and never any man, in any age, nor, I believe in any country or nation rose, in so short a time, to so much greatness of honour, fame and fortune, upon no other advantage or recommendation than of the beauty and gracefulness of his person.' The Puritan memoirist, Lucy Hutchinson, however, expressed an altogether earthier verdict on the same theme when she reflected how 'a knight's fourth son' had been raised 'to that pitch of glory … upon no merit but that of his beauty and his prostitution'. What Hutchinson meant by this may well be imagined, and the nature of the king's sexuality has, of course, been a residing source of speculation across the centuries. Writing in 1617, the politician John Oglander observed how he 'never yet saw any fond husband make so much or so great dalliance over his beautiful spouse as I have seen King James over his favourites, especially the Duke of Buckingham'. The MP Edward Peyton, moreover, was another who noted how 'the king sold his affections to Sir George Villiers, whom he would tumble and kiss as a mistress'. Nicknaming Villiers 'Steenie' after St Stephen who was said to possess the 'face of an angel', James would also end a now famous letter of 1623 by affirming their relationship in the most striking manner. 'God bless you, my sweet child and wife,' the king declared, 'and grant that ye may ever be a comfort to your dear father and husband.'

As the king's 'great dalliance' proceeded, moreover, Villiers reciprocated in kind. In reply to James, he confessed how 'I naturally so love your person, and adore all your other parts, which are more than ever one man had'. 'I desire only to live in the world for your sake,' he continued, and 'I will live and die a lover of you'. Writing many years later, Villiers also pondered if the king loved him now 'better than at the time which I shall never forget at Farnham, where the bed's head could not be found between the master and his dog'. Whether the incident at Farnham was, of course, an isolated incident or merely part of a short-lived phase in the relationship, as some commentators have suggested, can never be known for sure. James was, after all, in vigorous middle life at the age of 48 when the young Villiers was first presented to him, though his health would deteriorate steadily beyond the age of 50. In similar fashion, it has sometimes been argued that the ardent friendship between Villiers and Prince Charles might have been rendered impossible by any sexual relationship between the favourite and the prince's father. But Charles would always show a rare capacity for blinding himself to a situation he did not wish to face, and the discovery during restoration work at Apethorpe Hall in 2004–08 of a secret passage linking Villiers' bedchamber with the king's state apartment appears particularly compelling.

Nevertheless, during the earliest days of Villiers' ascent James still seemed anxious to reassure his other favourite. Indeed, he was at pains to guarantee that Robert Carr's position was in no way threatened by the new arrival, even hoping to engineer the rise of the newcomer under the earl's own mantle and protection, so that they could all three be happy and harmonious together. Sir Humphrey May, renowned for his tact, was therefore dispatched to Carr to convey that Villiers would be calling to offer his services, and according to Sir Anthony Weldon, Villiers presented himself precisely as required. 'My Lord,' Carr was told, 'I desire to be your servant, and your creature, and shall desire to take my Court preferment under your favour, and your Lordship shall find me as faithful a servant unto you as ever did serve you.' But the olive branch was brusquely rejected, it seems, as Carr gave vent to the wrath that was already undermining his status in the king's affection. 'I will have none of your service, and you shall have none of my favour,' he is reported to have raged. 'I will, if I can, break your neck, and of that be confident.'

These, however, were the rantings of a thoroughly beleaguered man. In November 1614, he had initially thwarted Villiers' appointment as a gentleman of the bedchamber by installing a bastard kinsman of his own. Yet by the end of that month, it was known that the king was once again ignoring the parlous state of his treasury by donating £1,500 towards the expenses of a Christmas masque, 'the principal motive whereof is thought to be gracing of young Villiers and to bring him on the stage'. As his enemies circled, moreover, Carr saw fit in July 1615 to inquire from Sir Robert Cotton whether a pardon might be issued under the Great Seal of England exonerating him from any and all offences he had committed in the past. In the meantime, while Sir Henry Yelverton, the Solicitor-General, and Lord Chancellor Ellesmere refused to sign the necessary documents, the pardon was actually supported during a heated debate in the Privy Council by none other than the king himself. 'And so, my Lord Chancellor,' James commanded, 'seal the pardon immediately, for that is my will.'

But in spite of a royal tantrum accompanied by a stormy exit from the council chamber and a subsequent flight to the country in search of peace of mind, the pardon was never sealed, as Ellesmere continued to demur. And as the king, in Gondomar's view, listened to further tales against him and courtiers openly cut him, Carr grew increasingly ripe for the final blow, which was duly delivered in September 1615 when further revelations about the death of Sir Thomas Overbury finally issued from a dying Englishman in Brussels, named William Reeve. Smitten by conscience, Reeve confessed to servants of William Trumbull, James's ambassador, that as a former apprentice to the London apothecary William de Lowbell, he had been charged to administer to Overbury an enema contaminated by a mercury sublimate, and that he had been paid a sum of £20 for the murder by Carr's own wife, the Countess of Somerset.

When Sir Ralph Winwood, no friend of the pro-Spanish Howards, was subsequently informed and the countess was further implicated by the suspicions of Sir Gervase Helwys, the ensuing scandal threatened to expose in one fell swoop the full scale of the moral depravity and corruption for which the royal court had long become a byword. Under such circumstances, the king made before his council, we are told, 'a great protestation before God of his desire to see justice done, and that neither his favourite, nor his son himself, nor anything else in the world should hinder him'. Appointing commissioners to determine 'whether my Lord of Somerset and my Lady were procurers of Overbury's death, or that this imputation hath been by some practised to cast an aspersion upon them', James issued instructions 'to use all lawful courses that the foulness of this fault be sounded to the depth, that for the discharge of our duty both to God and man, the innocent may be cleared, and the nocent may severely be punished'. But in doing so he plainly appreciated that any attempt at concealment carried far more danger still than thorough inquiry, as he would indeed tell Somerset later. If, he informed his desperate favourite, 'I should have stopped the course of justice against you in this case of Overbury, who was committed to the Tower and kept there a close prisoner by my commandment, and could not have been so murdered if he had not been kept close, I might have been thought to be the author of that murder and so be made odious to all posterity'.

Even so, James's conduct as the trial proceeded, notwithstanding his intense interest and constant interference, was generally creditable. The countess confessed her crime beforehand and some time after October 1615 she and her husband were arrested. And though Carr's direct responsibility for the murder remains uncertain, his destruction of Northampton's many letters to him and attempts to falsify the dates of Overbury's correspondence did little for his credibility. Seizing other letters in the possession of a certain Mrs Turner, the depraved woman from whom the countess had obtained charms and poisons, he even seems to have made a vain resort ultimately to blackmail the king himself. 'It is clear,' James wrote, 'that he would threaten me with laying an aspersion upon me of being in some sort accessory to his crime.' To his credit, however, James stood firm against Carr's 'scribbling and railing', informing him how he would never 'suffer a murder (if it be so) to be suppressed and plastered over' nor spare, 'I vow to God, one grain of vigour against the conspirators'.

At 9 a.m. on 24 May 1616, therefore, the Countess of Somerset was duly conveyed to Westminster Hall to face trial for murder, the headsman's axe – its blade turned away – preceding her as she entered. Though she had recently given birth to a daughter Anne and now stood – 'in black Tammel, a Cypress Chaperon, a cobweb lawn ruff and cuffs' – with downcast, gently weeping eyes, Sir Edward Coke would soon be defaming her as a whore, a bawd, a sorcerer, a witch, a felon, a devil and a murderer: the very incarnation, no less, than the seven deadly sins. Spectators, moreover, had paid dearly to behold the Lord Chief Justice at his trade. 'I know a lawyer', wrote John Chamberlain, 'who had agreed to give £10 for himself and his wife for two days', while another buyer 'gave £50 for a corner that could hardly contain a dozen'. For Coke's reputation preceded him: so powerfully indeed that when the elderly judge requested Somerset's presence in London, the accused vowed he would not go and, in doing so, called upon the king's support. But while James, in spite of all that had passed between them, still gushed sentiment for his fallen favourite and feared that he might 'never see his face more', the response was nevertheless unfaltering: 'Nay, man, if Coke sends for me, I must go.'

Meanwhile, in spite of the Lord Chief Justice's imprecations and a plea of guilty by Somerset's wife, which the countess acknowledged could not 'extenuate my fault', there was never any doubt that Lord Ellesmere's subsequent sentence of death against her would be overturned by the king's prerogative of mercy. One Italian observer, Eduardo Pallavicino, had been wholly overcome by the countess's nobility, grace and modesty, leaving him in no doubt that she had been led into crime by her husband. In Chamberlain's view, however, the accused had won pity both by her shows of tears and otherwise sober demeanour, 'which in my opinion was more curious and confident than was fit for a lady in such distress'. For her sins, moreover, she was spared the anguish of lengthy trial, since the entire process was over within no more than two hours. She had come, seen, sobbed and conquered, it seems – the beneficiary of the best possible legal solution from the king's own point of view: both clear-cut and bloodless, since confession and contrition were considered powerful mitigators of guilt, and proferring, under these most awkward circumstances, the best available hope of minimising public outrage.

Carr, for his part, had also been urged by the king to 'honour God and me' by confessing his guilt, after which the royal prerogative might likewise be employed to guarantee a pardon. In contrast to his wife, however, the embattled earl would face a trial at Westminster Hall on 25 May lasting from nine in the morning until ten at night, and one that did not run nearly so smoothly from his royal master's perspective. Wearing 'a plain black satin suit laid with satin laces in a seam' and 'a gown of uncut velvet', Carr obstinately refused, in fact, to confess his guilt. 'I am confident in mine own cause,' he declared, 'and am come hither to defend it.' On the other hand, his prosecutor, the Attorney General, Sir Francis Bacon, was unable and even a little unwilling, it seemed, to press home any truly convincing case that the accused had been a knowing accomplice to his wife. 'For the poisonment', he declared, 'I am sorry it should be heard of in our kingdom', since such a crime was not *nostri generis* but 'an Italian comfit for the Court of Rome'.

Defending himself, as Bacon observed, both 'modestly and wittily', Carr gave James, in fact, one of the most miserable days of his life as he watched the landing stage at Whitehall eagerly for any boat that might bring him news of the outcome. No courtier, it was said, had ever seen him 'so extreme sad and discontented' and his efforts to distract himself by discussing with Gondomar possible terms for a marriage treaty had proved wholly ineffective. That night, indeed, he would neither dine nor sup until he had learnt the result he most desired: a unanimous vote of guilty by the Lords that vindicated the king's justice and left him conveniently unentangled in the whole sorry episode. Hereafter, he could not only intervene once more to spare the fallen favourite's life but duly ensure that that life, as well as the life of the convicted countess, would be wholly worth living. For, even as the Somersets were promptly conveyed to the Tower under sentence of death, their long-term comfort and well-being was already assured.

In all, the couple would remain in the Tower for some six years, during which time, it seems, a 'great falling out' occurred between them, which continued for the rest of their days, leaving them, we are told, 'though in one house as strangers one to another'. The revulsion that Carr now felt towards the convicted murderess who had robbed him of his friend eventually became overwhelming, it seems, as the countess exploited her comparative liberty within the Tower's walls to conduct an affair with the so-called 'Wizard Earl' of Northumberland. But she would live a further sixteen years before finally meeting what appears to have been, if Arthur Wilson is to be believed, a particularly unwholesome end. 'Her death,' wrote Wilson, 'was infamous ... for that part of her body which had been the receptacle of her sin, grown rotten (though she never had but one child), the ligaments failing, it fell down and was cut away in flakes, with a most nauseous and putrid savour, which to augment, she would role herself in her own ordure in her bed [and] took delight in it.'

Before that time, however, both she and her husband had nevertheless been allowed to retire to Lord Knollys's house at Rotherfield Grays in Oxfordshire, a secluded country residence, on condition that they would confine their movements to within 3 miles of it. Still unable to cast off his sentimental attachment to his former favourite, the king had also ignored Carr's conviction and allowed him to remain a member of the Order of the Garter. The fallen favourite had saved his life in the first place with nothing more than a letter to his royal master requesting that he be hanged rather than beheaded and that his daughter might be maintained out of the income from his forfeited lands. And the king's goodwill did not end here, for on 7 October 1624, a little over five months before his death, a formal pardon was produced under the Great Seal, which allowed Carr to retain an income of £4,000 per annum until his own death in 1645.

In return, James would incur untold damage, both to his own reputation and that of his court, notwithstanding Archbishop Abbot's dutiful refrain that the king's life was 'so immaculate and unspotted from the world … that even malice itself could never find true blemish in it'. James's own relief that the emotional turmoil of Carr's downfall had been negotiated without major political disaster was palpable. But rumours of undisclosed facts persisted and moralists continued to complain that the king had appeared to condone such wickedness among those close to him. Indeed, the impression which Carr's rise had created among the country gentry and the nobility who did not frequent the court was as nothing compared with that created by the manner of his fall. Nor, it seems, were such misgivings confined to the more sober elements of Jacobean society, for John Chamberlain relates how Queen Anne and the Countess of Derby were mistaken, while driving in a coach, for the Countess of Somerset and her mother, and subjected to fierce abuse by a mob of Londoners.

As contempt and disillusionment bore in upon James, moreover, the effects upon his health and personality became increasingly marked. Arthritis, combined with gout, became chronic during the winter months from 1616 onwards and he found himself plagued, too, by abdominal colic, sleeplessness, frequent diarrhoea and, after a serious attack of jaundice in 1619, acute kidney pain resulting from nephritis – all of which depressed his spirits and rendered him either fractious or morose. 'He is of exquisite sensitiveness,' wrote Sir Theodore Turquet de Mayerne, his physician, 'and most impatient of pain; and while it tortures him with violent movements, his mind is tossed as well, thus augmenting the evil.' Passing urine 'red like Alicante wine' and refusing access to individuals like Sir Ralph Winwood, in order to avoid government business, the king turned increasingly to every available expedient to ease his anguish and relieve his symptoms. 'He demands relief from pain,' wrote de Mayerne, 'without considering the causes of his illness.'

In such circumstances, therefore, it was hardly surprising that James's dependence upon George Villiers, Earl, Marquis and later Duke of Buckingham, should now have increased to unprecedented levels. 'The king,' it was said, 'is not well without him, his company is his solace.' And Buckingham would indeed provide a powerful antidote for the misery and humiliation of Robert Carr's long-drawn-out ruin: a private haven of beauty, grace, sympathy and gaiety, in which the king could forget both his own ailments and the censure of the outside world. Tall, comely and handsome, with a fine forehead, clear blue eyes, dark chestnut hair and a pointed beard of golden brown, as well as long, slender legs which made him renowned for his elegance as a dancer, Buckingham exhibited an ideal combination of masculine strength and female delicacy to make him irresistible to the king. 'I saw everything in him full of delicacy and handsome features,' wrote Sir Simonds D'Ewes, the contemporary antiquarian, 'yea, his hands and face seemed to me especially effeminate and curious,' while another observer noted how 'from the nails of his fingers, nay from the sole of his foot to the crown of his head there was no blemish in him'. Yet he was manly in his tastes, excelling in sports and nurturing a roving eye for the opposite sex, for, as Arthur Wilson put it, 'if his eye cull'd a wanton beauty, he had his setter that could appoint a meeting'.

Nor, it seems, was Buckingham prone to the naivety or presumption that had finally put paid to his predecessor. On the contrary, the new favourite was altogether more formidable, because more able, than the old. 'No one dances better,' wrote Arthur Wilson, 'no man runs or jumps higher.' 'Indeed,' continued Wilson, 'he jumped higher than ever Englishman did in so short a time, from a private gentleman to a dukedom.' And the secret of this giddy ascent was his expert reading of the king's own needs and expectations. Pawed, petted, pampered and puppied, Buckingham pleased his royal master by diligent attendance at divine service and when James decided to produce a meditation on the Gospel of St Matthew, the favourite was quick to ask that he might act as amanuensis. 'How can I but write merrily when he is so I love best and beyond the world,' he told James in response to a request for merry letters, and after a gift from the king, his response was even more effusive. 'I am now,' he wrote, 'going to give my Redeemer thanks for my maker.' No hyperbole, indeed, was too much for Buckingham's pride or beyond his master's satisfaction: so much so that he was also capable of cultivating a witty, playful impudence that both enhanced and emphasised his hold upon the king. 'And so I kiss your dirty hands,' he wrote later.

But Buckingham was also prepared to be instructed. When, for example, James proffered a New Year's gift in 1619, dedicating *The Meditations upon the Lord's Prayer* to him, it was accompanied by a message declaring how 'I dayly take care to better your understanding to enable you the more for my service'. And it had not been long either before Queen Anne, always so hostile to Carr, was duly charmed by the handsome courtier's winning ways. Referring to him in several letters as 'my kind dog', she thanked him on one occasion for 'lugging the sow's ear' and urged him to remain 'always true' to her husband, in response to which Buckingham confirmed that in obedience to her desire, he had pulled the king's ear 'until it was as long as any sow's'.

And with the good offices of the royal family assured, Buckingham duly sought to employ his own relatives to bolster his position, fully aware, it seems, that Robert Carr's failure to do so had left him cruelly isolated when the moment of crisis arrived. Buckingham's brother John, for example, notwithstanding temporary bouts of insanity, was duly joined in marriage to the daughter of Sir Edward Coke and created Viscount Purbeck, while 'Kit', his other brother, who was widely regarded as little more than an amiable fool, would find himself created Earl of Anglesey in 1623. The favourite's sister Susan, meanwhile, was married to Sir William Fielding, who subsequently became Earl of Denbigh and the father of a daughter who was in her turn betrothed at the age of seven to the Marquis of Hamilton. Finally, as if to seal the happy nexus, Anne Brett, a cousin of the Villiers family, was married to Lionel Cranfield, the future Lord Treasurer and Earl of Middlesex.

But if Buckingham's grasping tribe of kinfolk caused ill-concealed murmurs in the country at large, it was the influence of his mother – an overweening and predatory old termagant - that evoked the most unremitting outrage. Descended from an impoverished branch of a great medieval family, she had been born Mary Beaumont and served as a waiting-gentlewoman to her cousin, Lady Beaumont of Coleorton, before attracting an offer of marriage from Sir George Villiers, a widowed Leicestershire knight of no exceptional means. Even after her husband's death, moreover, subsequent marriages, first to Sir Thomas Rayner and then Sir William Compton, an alcoholic nonentity, brought her little advantage. Yet if her choice in husbands belied her true ambition, the rise of her son was squeezed for every opportunity. Parading her 'numerous and beautiful kindred' before a string of wealthy husbands, she exploited what amounted to a vicious system of blackmail, in which the king frequently connived. It was she, it seems, who had set her mind upon Frances Coke as a bride for John Villiers in the spring of 1616, and it was her pressure for a generous marriage portion that ultimately sealed the Lord Chief Justice's dismissal for initially resisting the match. Such, indeed, was her reputation that even Buckingham himself discouraged her presence at court upon her elevation to the rank of countess in 1618.

Buckingham's own marriage in 1620, meanwhile, was arguably the final step in securing his status in English society. A Florentine observer living in England at the time considered it 'very dangerous for such a powerful courtier to marry at all', but the choice of Lady Katherine Manners, daughter of the Earl of Rutland, was an impeccable one, irrespective of the Catholicism of her family, and the union proved fruitful on all counts. Reputedly the richest heiress in England, her great wealth would provide Buckingham with precisely the independence he required, while her simplicity and devotion guaranteed that she would never become the kind of political liability that had finally undone Robert Carr. Indeed, her gentleness and womanly tenderness, devotion and purity of life, became conspicuous amid the almost universal corruption and immorality of the Court. 'There was never woman loved man as I do you,' she wrote her husband during one of his absences, and she doted equally tenderly upon the son and daughter that the marriage eventually produced.

But it was not only his choice of bride that distinguished the Duke of Buckingham so markedly from his predecessor. Above all, unlike Robert Carr, he wanted to enjoy the exercise of real political power and to employ it, wherever possible, in his royal master's interests. The former he certainly achieved on an extraordinary scale until he became, in the words of the Earl of Clarendon, 'the man by whom all things do and must pass' and '... entirely disposed of the wealth of the three kingdoms'. However, Clarendon's further claim that, in dispensing of patronage, Buckingham was guided 'more by the rules of appetite than of judgement ...' remains harsh. For, while no promotion was ever granted without financial sweeteners, the king's favourite was neither oblivious to the broader interest nor devoid of judgement in his choice of men. 'I never saw a young courtier,' James told Parliament in 1624, 'that was so careful for my profit without any respect as Buckingham was.'

Nowhere was this plainer, moreover, than in the appointment in 1614 of Lionel Cranfield as head of a commission to examine government expenditure in an effort to free the king from his perpetual bondage to debt. A thrusting man of business who had begun as a mere city apprentice before winning rapid success as a cloth merchant and member of the Mercers' Company, Cranfield had become a farmer of various royal revenues and eventually Surveyor General of the Customs in 1613. 'The first acquaintance I had with him,' James later recalled, 'was by the Lord of Northampton, who often brought him unto me as a private man before he was so much as my servant.' But it was Buckingham who 'fell in liking with him and brought him into my service' and Buckingham who 'backed him against great personages' and 'laid the ground and bare the envy'. One result was stringent savings: in the royal household, in the exchequer, in the wardrobe, in the navy, and in Ireland. The other was a mortal struggle between Buckingham and his vengeful Howard enemies who could neither forget his upstart origins nor forget how his rise had coincided with Robert Carr's disastrous ruin.

The corrupt practices of the treasury under the Earl of Suffolk's administration were, of course, a byword, and all, with the possible exception of the king himself, acknowledged that in order to gain payment for a bill or settle overdue expenses, a hard bargain must first be driven with Sir John Bingham, the sub-treasurer, and indeed Lady Suffolk. Only when these two expressed their satisfaction would the earl himself approve, and only when the whole unholy trio had been duly ripped from influence, therefore, was the king's financial predicament likely to amend. Possessing no administrative expertise, Suffolk's personal extravagance had led him to spend some £200,000 on his Audley End estate, and he had displayed the same insouciant disregard for economy in government. So now, as Buckingham's attitude switched from careless tolerance to hostility and stories of Lady Suffolk's transactions reached the ears of the king in June, the whole rotten tree of Howard influence, with all its branches, became ripe for cutting.

Within the month, in fact, Lady Katherine had been ordered from the capital, and by the end of July her husband's resignation was also demanded by the king. And though it would require a further eighteen months to complete the Star Chamber inquiry which culminated in imprisonment for both and a crippling fine of £30,000, the rout was comprehensive. Not without good reason, Sir Francis Bacon compared the countess to a woman who kept shop while her creature Sir John Bingley cried 'What d'ye lack?' And accordingly the Attorney General left no worm a hiding place. The Suffolks' two sons lost their court appointments and Lord Wallingford, as a son-in-law, his office as Master of the Wards. Sir Thomas Lake, meanwhile, who as Secretary of State had so far been able to fend off the more dangerous attacks upon his Howard cronies, now found himself tainted and doomed to resignation by a vicious and indefensible accusation of incest launched against the Countess of Exeter by his wife. The king himself, indeed, had exposed the perjury of a maid involved in the case by taking her to the room at Wimbledon and demonstrating that the arras, behind which she falsely claimed to have heard a compromising conversation, fell far short of the floor.

So it was, then, that by November 1619 a popular jest came to be in general circulation throughout the capital. For now, it was said, the entire Howard faction were at liberty to set up a Privy Council of their own within the Tower, with Suffolk as treasurer, Carr as chamberlain, Lake as secretary, Lord Wallingford as Master of the Wards, and the hapless Lord Howard Walden, who had also been sucked into the vortex, as Captain of Pensioners. Ultimately, indeed, only the senile Earl of Nottingham was left his freedom, though he too had been forced into resignation by the threat of an inquiry into Admiralty and Dockyard accounts. Perhaps because of his reputation as commander of the ships that defeated the Spanish Armada, he had been allowed to retire unmolested, though only to be replaced in February 1619 by Buckingham himself.

Now, however, there would be no new faction at the heart of government, since Buckingham, unsurprisingly, desired no near rivals. For replacements, he sought only talented and industrious servants who would neither seek to fashion policy nor aspire to control patronage. As secretaries, Sir Robert Naunton and George Calvert were ideal prototypes, since the king himself preferred 'conformable men with but ordinary parts', while Cranfield would be left to go about his business unimpeded, shaving Admiralty costs from £57,700 to £30,000, and reducing costs for the king's velvets, silks, saddle costs and other items from £28,000 to £20,000. For the time being, then, the wings of the great nobility, notwithstanding the wealth and territorial independence that had given them a certain independence from the Crown, were safely clipped – leaving only Buckingham and the ailing king himself to steer the ship of state.

16 ⇩ Faraway Realms

'Even such is Time, which takes in trust
Our youth, our joys, and all we have,
And pays us but with age and dust …'

*Sir Walter Raleigh's 'Epitaph', written in the Gatehouse at
Westminster Palace the night before his death*

The Castilian nobleman Don Diego Sarmiento de Acuña, better known as the Count of Gondomar, first cast eyes upon England as Spain's new ambassador in the spring of 1615, though he was to bring with him neither fresh new shoots of friendship nor even buds of compromise. On the contrary, conceiving his embassy as a sortie into enemy territory and taking for his motto the maxim *aventurar la vida y osar morir* – 'risk your life and dare to die' – he had brazenly refused to strike the colours of Spain upon his warships' entry into Portsmouth harbour, whereupon only an appeal to the king himself averted an exchange of cannon fire that was certain to have sunk the ambassador in his vessel. At the time, a marriage between Prince Charles and Christine of France, sister to Louis XIII, was already under negotiation and Gondomar had fostered little hope that an alternative bride in the shape of Philip III's daughter, the Spanish infanta Maria, could be plausibly presented to his English hosts. But the man whom Thomas Middleton characterised as the Black Night in his play *A Game at Chess* knew his craft and, more important still, the way to ply and prime the increasingly penniless king who now confronted him.

James chose for the intricate diplomacy in store a man of intelligence and exceptional honesty, Sir John Digby, who relayed from Madrid in

May 1615 what appeared to be wholly unrealistic Spanish demands. The children of any marriage were, on the one hand, to be baptised and educated as Catholics, and guaranteed the right to succession. In the meantime, moreover, the infanta was to be granted Catholic servants and a chapel which was to be a place of public worship for English Catholics, against whom all penal laws were to be rescinded. And while such terms were shocking by any standards, the bait of a Spanish dowry amounting to some £600,000 and James's fear that the King of Spain 'had many kingdoms and more subjects beyond comparison' proved sufficient to fix him in a dangerous scheme of deception. Though clearly unacceptable, as his margin comments upon the Spanish proposals make clear, James nevertheless refused to reject them out of hand, preferring instead to play the kind of double game at which he considered himself so skilled – all of which perplexed his subjects and undermined their confidence in his commitment to the Protestant cause. His hankerings for peace, dislike of rebels and republicans, and prejudice against the Dutch, not to mention his vanity, fears of assassination and growing indolence, were all, it seemed, eminently exploitable by one such as Gondomar, and when the wily Spaniard returned to his homeland in 1618, accompanied by 100 Catholic priests whom James had seen fit to release as a gesture of goodwill, the worst fears of many appeared confirmed.

Nor was James's dalliance with Spain the last eccentricity imposed upon him by financial necessity. Indeed, his decision to release Sir Water Raleigh from the Tower of London in March 1616 was not only equally astonishing in its way, but driven even more directly by a vain hope that his problems might somehow be solved at a stroke through bold action and a timely gust of good fortune. For some time, in fact, James had been under pressure from the anti-Spanish faction led by George Abbot, Sir Ralph Winwood and the earls of Southampton and Pembroke, to liberate Raleigh and permit him to make a return voyage to the Orinoco River that he had first visited in 1595. Such a strategy could be guaranteed to outrage the King of Spain and also proffered a vast store of gold, which, according to Raleigh himself, lay only a few inches below the ground 'in a broad slate, and not in small veins'. 'There was,' he claimed, 'never a mine of gold in the world promising so great abundance.' And though he was now over 60, grey, lame and malaria-ridden, he remained ready to enact his dreams of creating an English empire in Guiana, centred on the Orinoco delta, that might eventually destroy Spanish power in the Indies.

In *The Discoverie of the Large, Rich and Beautiful Empire of Guiana*, he told how he was still haunted by 'the strange thunder of the waters' and how he seemed to hear these same same huge waters – 'each as high over the other as a church tower' – while lying in his prison cell. And now he had a king to share his fantasies.

On 27 March 1616, therefore, John Chamberlain informed Dudley Carleton how 'Sir Water Raleigh was freed out of the Tower the last week and goes up and down seeing sights and places built or bettered since his imprisonment'. In the meantime, however, James had extracted the most solemn pledges from Raleigh that no Spanish subject should be molested without forfeit of his own life, and had also attempted to smother the Count of Gondomar's protestations with a series of further pledges of his own. The notorious sea-captain would be sent to Madrid bound hand and foot, he assured the ambassador, if a single Spaniard were harmed, and there were further assurances that Raleigh's release had involved no free pardon or any revocation of the death sentence imposed upon him in 1603. In effect, the great Elizabethan, who now trudged the streets of a capital made unfamiliar to him by years of incarceration, had therefore been granted a one-way ticket to disaster, though it was one he had both purchased and stamped with glowing confidence.

The king, in all fairness, may well have had some rightful grounds for sharing that confidence or at least wagering at reasonable odds upon a potential windfall of considerable proportions. Already, in 1604, Charles Leigh had established a settlement on the banks of the river Wiapoco, which lasted two years, while another party, encouraged by Prince Henry, had sailed soon afterwards under Robert Harcourt and survived until 1613. Likewise, a third expedition to Guiana – partly financed by Raleigh to the tune of £600 – had been led by Sir Thomas Roe in 1610. And there were grounds, however slender, for believing, too, that Raleigh's expedition of 1595 had established some kind of English claim in Guiana, notwithstanding the fact that the Spanish were firmly established upon the coast of modern-day Venezuela and at the very site of the mines of San Thomé that had captured James's imagination in the first place.

But if James was indeed making a genuine bid for treasure and for territory that might rightfully be his, and in the process granting Raleigh a chance to gain his freedom and achieve his dreams, the likelihood of success actually remained minimal. In the event, Raleigh's ship, *The Destiny*, would not leave Plymouth until June 1617 since the storms at sea were the worst since the sinking of the Spanish Armada almost thirty years earlier, and from the outset the expedition was dogged by misfortune. Initially compelled to land at Kinsale harbour in southern Ireland, Raleigh's seven warships and three pinnaces were subsequently forced to weigh anchor at Lanzarote in the Canary Islands, where Gondomar had little difficulty in persuading his government that the heavily armed vessels were planning to attack the Spanish fleet. Deaths among his leading officers from a strange sickness were then followed by the desertion of Cyrus Bailey, who ultimately returned to England to spread rumours that Raleigh was turning pirate. And though the coasts of Guiana were finally sighted in mid-November, the expedition's leader was by that time stricken by fever, cared for by his son Walter and nephew George.

The Indians who eventually greeted Raleigh's men were, however, friendly. 'To tell you that I might be here King of the Indians were a vanity,' he informed his wife in a letter, 'but my name hath still lived among them. Here they feed me with fresh meat and all that the country yields; all offer to obey me.' Yet Raleigh was unable to lead the subsequent search for gold and appointed Laurence Keymis, who, in spite of specific instructions not to provoke hostilities with the Spanish, nevertheless misjudged his landing spot and arrived too near the fortified village of San Thomé. While Raleigh himself was therefore waiting in Trinidad with other sickly members of his crew, hoping to trade with the Spaniards, Keymis found himself under a surprise attack, in which Raleigh's son was killed while leading a gallant stand at the head of a group of pikemen.

'God knows, I never knew what sorrow meant till now,' Raleigh wrote soon afterwards. But though he was heartbroken and infuriated with Keymis, who subsequently committed suicide, he nevertheless resolved upon one last attempt to reach the mines, which his captains refused to support. The result was a wretched return to England, where arrest by his kinsman Sir Lewis Stukeley, Vice-Admiral of Devon, awaited him soon after his arrival at Plymouth on 21 June 1618. He had been tempted to sail *The Destiny* to Brest and subsequently contemplated escape to France after being placed under house arrest. But he was betrayed and subsequently placed in the Tower, and when Roger North, one of his captains, denied the existence of any South American mine, Raleigh became the object of the king's cold, vindictive fury. Shortly after Bailey's return with tales of piracy, Sir Thomas Lake had noted how 'his Majesty is very disposed and determined against Raleigh and will join the King of Spain in ruining him'.

But now, considering himself the victim of a despicable hoax, and prey increasingly to Gondomar's taunts and goading, James determined to strike.

On 18 August, therefore, Raleigh was duly summoned before a commission to answer for his misdeeds. The king, much to his discredit, had already submitted to Gondomar's insolence in demanding that any sentence might be carried out in Spain, and in doing so had ridden roughshod over the opposition of his council, declaring that he could take what course he pleased 'without following the advice of fools and badly disposed persons'. He had also taken pains to guarantee that Raleigh should not be afforded the opportunity of a public hearing, since 'it would make him too popular, as was found by experience at the arraignment at Winchester [in 1603], when by his wit he turned the hatred of men into compassion for him'. Yet the commission itself, which included Archbishop Abbot and Sir Edward Coke, had the appearance at least of equity, even if no such gathering could have been unmindful of the king's express will. For Raleigh stood accused not only of disloyalty and deceit but of compromising the king's avowed policy of international peace. And though Prince Henry had admired him, and the queen would intercede on his behalf by means of her 'kind dog' Buckingham, the accused was by no means popular at court. Ultimately, therefore, Raleigh's death sentence, inevitable as it was, represented not so much the sacrifice of a national hero by a weak, embittered Scottish king as a calculated act of realpolitik. If, in the final analysis, an expendable liability might be offered up in the broader interests of peace and personal credibility, then James, as ever, was equal to his kingly obligations.

And the sentence, which at Philip III's behest was eventually carried out in England rather than Spain, duly resulted in a fitting addition to national folklore. 'He was the most fearless of death that ever was known,' wrote one observer, 'and the most resolute and confident, yet with reverence and conscience.' For on 28 October 1618, as he was about to be taken from the Tower to the Gatehouse at Westminster, where he was to pass the night before his execution, Raleigh encountered an old servant who noticed his untidy hair and tearfully offered him a comb. 'Let them kem it that are to have it', replied the condemned man in his broad West Country accent. 'Dost thou know, Peter,' he continued, 'of any plaster that will get a man's head on again when it is off?' And when delivered to the block itself the following day, there was similar bravado. Feeling the edge of the axe, Raleigh could not resist a remark to the presiding sheriff. 'This is a sharp medicine, but it is a physician for all diseases,' he quipped before laying his head on the block and uttering a final exhortation to the headsman: 'What dost thou fear? Strike, man, strike.'

The Americas, meanwhile, would remain for James a faraway and meagerly exploited realm. The first of the East India Company's voyages had set out in 1601 and returned under Sir James Lancaster a few months after James's accession, with cargoes yielding a 100 per cent profit. And though contemporary commentators condemned the trade for emptying the kingdom of gold bullion in exchange for goods, it was much too profitable to be suppressed entirely. There had therefore been another expedition in 1604, and from 1607 onwards similar excursions occurred annually. The richer peers, courtiers and politicians joined Sir Thomas Smith and his City colleagues as regular patrons of these ventures, and when, in 1609, the charter was renewed and the company reorganised, the earls of Salisbury and Nottingham, as well as the Earl of Worcester, all joined the board. In the meantime, as English interest in the Indian trade and Persian Gulf expanded, so Portuguese control of these same areas slackened, largely through lack of support from a Spanish government painfully overcommitted elsewhere.

But progress in establishing American settlements was altogether slower and less spectacular, and the Virginia Company, which received its first charter in 1606, proved a regrettably neglected enterprise which failed to realise its true potential before the King of England finally abandoned control of it in 1612. Raleigh and his half-brother Humphrey Gilbert, had dreamt of an overseas empire in strikingly modern and purely nationalist terms, and had used the hope of finding gold primarily as a lever to secure official support and financial backing. But this early imperialism had resulted in a series of costly failures at Roanoke, and King James, like most of his contemporaries, showed little imagination from 1603 onwards beyond treating American settlements as convenient repositories for the kingdom's surplus population. Moreover, the inexperience and jealousies of the pioneers and the hostility of the native Indians all but wrecked a second series of plantations in 1606, where only the adventuring genius of Captain John Smith and the friendship of Princess Pocahontas, daughter of the most important of the local chiefs, averted total disaster. Even in 1609, indeed, when James and Salisbury took a hand in the London Company's wholesale reorganisation, the results were limited. Though the Jamestown settlement on the Delaware River became secure, the colony succeeded ultimately for what all the backers considered at the time to be the wrong reason: tobacco. And while James, in particular, would rail against the spread of a filthy habit, which led to a rise in consumption from £20,000 in 1617 to £50,000 by the end of the reign, the windfall both to the government and the venture's backers remained comparatively paltry, and represented, like the rest of the king's colonial policies an uninspiring case of squandered possibilities.

Of more abiding interest to James, however, was another far-off realm – albeit one that was altogether more familiar to him personally and one that entailed no ocean-going perils to reach. By the end of 1616, as Raleigh pressed on with preparations for his impending voyage, the king had resolved, in fact, to make a long-deferred return to the homeland he had previously promised to visit every three years. Obeying a strong impulse, and taking advantage of an opportunity that he claimed to be the first, but sensed might be the last, he therefore informed the Scottish Privy Council on 15 December 1616, of his intended visit. 'We are not ashamed to confess,' he wrote, 'that we have had these many years a great and natural longing to see our native soil and place of our birth and breeding, and this salmon–like instinct of ours has restlessly, both when we were awake, and many times in our sleep, so stirred up our thoughts and bended our desires to make a journey thither that we can never rest satisfied till it shall please God we accomplish it.'

Yet the king's homing instincts were unpopular with his courtiers, none of whom relished a progress of unprecedented to a length to a land where only cold, discomfort and barbarism appeared to await them, and there were more pressing concerns, too, about the likely cost. Indeed, the whole council, including Buckingham in the first instance, had implored James not to go, though the favourite's opposition had melted soon enough for him to be granted his earldom once the journey was underway. Even the queen, for that matter, had balked at the prospect of accompanying her husband and was granted leave to stay at home. But no such indulgence was granted to the noblemen and clerics who sallied forth from Theobalds on 14 March 1617. Three English bishops – Andrewes of Ely, Neile of Durham and Montagu of Winchester, who had edited the king's *Collected Works* the year before – were all in James's entourage, along with a bevy of his Scottish kinsmen, such as the Duke of Lennox and the Marquis of Hamilton, and the English earls of Pembroke and Montgomery.

On the one hand, the leisurely journey along the Great North Road, which took him all of two months to complete, represented a nostalgic attempt to recapture his lost youth and experience anew the kind of euphoria that had greeted him on his journey to London in 1603. Attended by hundreds of gentlemen ushers, grooms and other officers, James enjoyed the hunting so much around Lincoln that he neglected to meet the county's sheriffs, who had gone to welcome him. But he nevertheless lapped up in full the state reception offered to him once more at York, where the kneeling Lord Mayor presented him with a cup of silver double gilt and a purse containing 100 double sovereigns. Neither the illness of the queen, whose physicians, according to John Chamberlain 'feared an ill habit of body', or the fever of Secretary Winwood, who also found himself 'much vexed with the perpetual visits of great folks' after being left in charge of English affairs, could dim the king's enthusiasm when he finally reached Berwick on 13 May and crossed the Border into the land of his birth.

Three days later, the royal entourage entered Edinburgh itself and it was here, on 19 June, that James celebrated his fifty-first birthday. The English, Chamberlain had informed Dudley Carleton just over a fortnight earlier, were 'much caressed' in Scotland, while the king himself continued to exhibit the kind of generosity that had been such a feature of his journey south over a decade earlier. 'So many knights are made,' wrote Chamberlain, 'that there is scarce a Yorkshire esquire left to uphold the race, and the order has even descended to the Earl of Montgomery's barber and the husband of the Queen's launderess.' Even so, many courtiers found their quarters along the Royal Mile inadequate and uncomfortable, and while James enjoyed his hunting enormously at Falkland and Kinaird, he was nevertheless more critical of his fellow Scots than previously, wishing that they might imitate their English counterparts more in their worthy habits than in drinking healths, 'tobacco takin' and 'glorie of apparel'.

There were darker memories, too, that James had plainly failed to displace. Left alone with a guide in a mineshaft at Culrose in Fifeshire, he suddenly suspected an assassination attempt and dissolved into cries of 'Treason', which were only calmed with considerable difficulty. It seems likely, too, that his visit to Stirling on 30 June was conducted with mixed emotions as he once again surveyed the site where his grandfather had met a violent end, and that his stay at Perth was also tinged by recollections of his narrow escape from death at the hands of the Gowries. Not dissimilarly, there were also echoes of a sullen Scottish Kirk, soaked in cynicism and suspicion regarding their king's religious plans. For James had already gone as far as he could in bringing Scotland candles and choristers, and when an organ from the Chapel Royal of Whitehall arrived for use at Holyroodhouse, the reaction was predictable. 'The organs are come before,' grumbled one Calvinist divine, 'and after comes the Mass.'

It was the restless Scottish Kirk, moreover, that had partly prompted James's visit in the first place. Still beguiled by dreams of unification, he hoped to enforce upon Scotland the notorious 'Five Articles of Perth' which required, amongst other things, kneeling at Holy Communion and the administration of Confirmation by bishops. Thus, or so he believed, might the Kirk's practices be brought into line with the Church of England. But though the Articles were indeed formally adopted by the General Assembly which met at Perth in 1618, James was nevertheless sufficiently attuned to the resulting opposition to realise that they could not be imposed as vigorously as he might have wished. And heady rhetoric of the sort produced by William Hay upon the king's visit to Glasgow belied a range of deeper realities. Eulogising James as 'that great peacemaker' and 'only Phoenix of the World' – the man who had achieved what others 'neither by wit, nor force, nor blood' had been able to accomplish – Hay not only proceeded to describe him as the king who had 'united two [of] the most warlike nations of the world' and 'made a yoke of lions' but entirely ignored the very insensitivity on James's part that exacerbated the gaping rifts that still remained. For when even the Scottish bishops objected to the gilded figurines of the apostles and patriarchs that had accompanied the king's organ to Holyrood, he could not resist a half-sneering letter in which he deplored the ignorance of the native clergy and suggested that his English doctors should give them instruction. Had he ordered figures of dragons and devils instead, he quipped, the Scots would have raised no objection.

And if James's own prejudices against his countrymen were not proof enough of the gulf between his kingdoms, the now notorious account attributed to Sir Anthony Weldon, who accompanied him on his northern odyssey, rammed the point home with all the cudgel-bluntness so characteristic of English commentators in general. 'For the country,' the author begins, 'I must confess it is too good for those that possess it, and too bad for others … There is great store of fowl – as foul houses and shirts, foul linen, foul dishes and pots, foul trenchers and napkins, with which sort we have been forced to fare …' But the tirade mounts in intensity as it unfolds. 'The country,' we hear, 'affords no monsters but women … To be chained in marriage with one of them were as to be tied to a dead carcase and cast into a stinking ditch; formosity or a dainty face are things they dream not of …' 'And therefore to conclude,' the account ends, 'the men of old did no more wonder that the great Messias should be born in so poor a town as Bethlem in Judea, as I do wonder that so brave a prince as King James should be born in so stinking a town as Edinburgh in lousy Scotland …'

So much, then, for any lofty expectations that a union of Crowns might really lead to unity of vision and purpose, and as the king's entourage rode southward again, leaving Carlisle in August and traversing once more 'that wild northern country, which no other English sovereign had passed for centuries', the relief was palpable – not least, it must be said, for many Scots themselves. For the official welcomes and pageants in every city, not to mention the cost of refurbishing seven royal palaces, and the mere expense of housing the English court for four months had taxed Scottish resources to the limit, though this, it seems, was of less than pressing concern to James himself as he continued on his way towards Preston and Hoghton Tower, home of Sir Richard de Hoghton, where on 17 August, at a feast given by the host, he would famously knight 'Sir Loin of Beef' for services to his palate. 'Swan roste, Quailes 6, Redd Deare Pye, Duckes boyld and Shoulder of Mutton roste' were also made available for the king's delectation, for, according to the Venetian diplomat Antonio Foscarini, he generally preferred meat to more exotic food, though fruit, and especially melons and cherries, had been specially transported from England during his Scottish stay. Such was Sir Richard's hospitality, moreover, that he eventually found himself consigned to the Fleet Prison for debt.

By the time that Hoghton Tower was behind him, however, the nagging realisation that his holiday idyll was almost over was doubtless weighing upon James increasingly heavily. On his journey south, he had revelled in the Lancashire countryside, hunting the stag and making a special visit to Hoghton's alum mines. Knowing of Sir Richard's involvement in the famous Pendle witch trial, he had also, it seems, encountered a group of witches, though he had gone on to insist that they should be kept beyond the outer walls. But his homeward journey through Coventry, Warwick and Compton Wyngates, and arrival at Windsor on 12 September offered little consolation for the ennui, sickness and vexation in store. According to the Venetian ambassador, Giovanni Batista Lionello, James was eventually met in London by 'five hundred of the leading burgesses on horseback and a countless number of people, who shouted for joy at his return'. But he was soon poorly with arthritis and gout and succeeded, it seems, in spraining his leg in bed. The queen, moreover, was now constantly ill and Christmas at Whitehall appears to have been particularly dull and dreary for the king, though he took some pleasure in a gift from the Czar of Russia, since it was richer than any given to Queen Elizabeth. 'I am sorry to hear,' wrote Chamberlain, 'that he grows every day more froward.'

Even the news of the birth of his second grandson in the Palatinate did not cheer James, and by May of 1618 altogether more ominous news from the same far-off land would plunge all Europe into crisis. The marriage of his daughter Elizabeth to Frederick V of the Palatinate on St Valentine's Day 1613, had in Robert Allyn's words seen England 'lend her richest gem, to enrich the Rhine', and the subsequent celebrations matched the significance of an event that would not only result in the creation of the Hanoverian dynasty a hundred years later but carry England into the very heart of European politics. Though the outstandingly extravagant Lords' Masque was considered 'long and tedious' by one observer, all else went so well, it seems, that public officials and ambassadors subsequently applying to the treasury for their 'Extraordinarys' were met with the not unfamiliar response that 'the King is now disfurnished of money'. Spectacular shows and fireworks, costing £9,000 had been staged along the Thames, while the Inns of Court excelled themselves in elaborate entertainments, and Lord Montague lavished £1,500 on frocks for his two daughters. And though the groom had been dismissed by some as 'a slight edifice on a small foundation' and was considered 'too young and small timbred' by Chamberlain, he was nevertheless a figure of considerable importance: the leader of the Evangelical Union of German Calvinist rulers and one of the so-called electoral princes of the Holy Roman Empire, whose privilege it was, along with the Princes of Saxony and Brandenburg, the King of Bohemia and the Archbishops of Mainz, Treves and Cologne, to elect the Holy Roman Emperor himself when that throne fell vacant.

By 1618, however, a marriage which had initially seemed to confirm James's credentials as what one contemporary tract termed the 'King of peace', was presenting him with the kind of challenge that few could have envisaged when his charming, vivacious, auburn-haired daughter – 'Th'eclipse and glory of her kind' – had taken her wedding vows. 'I have ever, I praise God, kept peace and amity with all,' James had told his first English parliament before informing MPs how of all 'the blessings which God hath in my person bestowed upon you', the first is peace. In flowing from James's dominions, moreover, peace was to become universal, it seems, as he boasted in 1617 that he had established harmony in all neighbouring lands. 'Come they not hither,' asks a tract entitled *The Peace-Maker, or Great*

Brittaines Blessing and written mainly by Lancelot Andrewes with small additions by the king himself, 'as to the fountain from whence peace springs? Here sits Solomon and hither come the tribes for judgement. O happy moderator, blessed Father, not father of thy country alone, but Father of all thy neighbour countries about thee.'

But the King of England's chosen self-image of '*rex pacificus*', like so many of his high-flown aspirations, conformed poorly with earthier realities. Friendly with all nations, allied with Protestant states, on peaceful terms with Spanish territories, the King of England intended to survey from on high an imposing vista of peace and concord on a European scale fashioned by his own hand. But no champion of Protestantism could realistically hope to flirt with Spain, and while James had succeeded with such diplomatic promiscuity in Scotland, he could not hope to do so in his southern realm, where both people and Parliament were hostile to a strategy that was never adequately explained, and where the impending convulsions on the Continent were beyond all hope of mediation. Rightly or otherwise, James was described by the country gentleman, Sir John Oglander, as 'the most cowardly man I knew', but the more general claim about his aversion to war as an instrument of policy remains indisputable. 'He could not,' wrote Oglander, 'endure a soldier or to see men drilled' and 'to hear of war was death to him'. But now, as Counter-Reformation Germany fractured into armed religious camps, hard-headed Dutchmen pursued their implacable enmity with Spain, and Spain herself assumed the offensive after the assassination of the French king, Henry IV, in 1610, war was not merely the best but the only policy available in the longer term. Indeed, having chosen '*Beati Pacifici*' – 'Blessed are the peacemakers' – as his personal motto, James would swiftly discover that peacemakers like himself were much more likely to feel themselves accursed rather than 'blessed', since the marriage alliances he had arranged with concord in mind had actually linked the English Crown to the very ruler who would now become one of the main protagonists in the outbreak of Thirty Years' War.

When the childless Holy Roman Emperor, Matthias, who also held the electoral throne of Bohemia, instructed in 1617 that his Catholic Habsburg cousin, Archduke Ferdinand of Styria, should be nominated as his successor to the Bohemian throne, the native Protestant lords were committed by May of the following year to rebellion. And when the King of England's son-in-law, Frederick of the Palatinate, pitched into the struggle with wild-eyed promises of support and hopes of wrecking Habsburg power throughout Germany, the blue touch paper was finally lit for the renewal of a general war of religion that had previously been abandoned in exhaustion in 1555. Since the Spanish Habsburgs were bound to come to the rescue of their cousins in Vienna, the danger was already critical, but when Frederick himself subsequently accepted the Crown of Bohemia from the rebels in October 1619, he not only unleashed a catastrophic conflict that had been looming for at least a decade, but at once plunged his father-in-law into the thick of a European maelstrom that he scarcely apprehended.

James's ignorance had not, however, prevented him from already leaping at a cynical suggestion made by Gondomar as a means of keeping England inactive for a few vital months, that he should mediate between the Bohemians and Ferdinand. 'The vanity of the present King of England is so great,' wrote Gondomar, 'that he will always think it of great importance that peace should be made by this means, so that his authority will be increased.' And with his mind thus clouded, James had duly dispatched a grandiose mission to Prague, headed by James Hay, who swiftly discovered that his king's mediation was considered wholly inappropriate not only by Ferdinand, whose military position had improved, but by the Bohemians too, who declared their preference for armed assistance rather than olive branches. And while Hay's 150 strong entourage vainly crossed and re-crossed Europe at a cost of £30,000, the election of Ferdinand as emperor and his deposition as King of Bohemia unfolded regardless.

Even so, James would be afforded an opportunity for more decisive action in August 1619 when Frederick sent Baron von Dohna to London to seek his advice on the offer of the Bohemian Crown – a prospect which rightly filled the English king with mortal dread. For not only would his personal honour now oblige him to intervene on behalf of his son-in-law, he would be hotly encouraged to do so by his own subjects. His daughter Elizabeth, after all, had already endeared herself to English men and women alike, and her marriage to a sound Calvinist was now a potential rallying call to all seeking firm action in defence of the Protestant cause in Europe. Only if swift action was forthcoming and war was somehow averted by Frederick's rejection of the Bohemian Crown might James therefore avoid the descent of his own kingdom into the abyss. But he remained, as he himself admitted, 'in a great strait, being drawn to one side by my children and grandchildren, my own flesh and blood, and to the other side by the truth and by my friendship to Philip [of Spain] and to the House of Austria'. And while James studied the niceties of the Bohemian constitution in quest of an answer, others drew their own conclusions. 'It seems to me,' wrote Tillières, the French ambassador, 'that the intelligence of this king has diminished. Not that he cannot act firmly and well at times and particularly when the peace of the kingdom is involved. But such efforts are not so continual as they once were. His mind uses its power for a short time, but in the long run he is cowardly. His timidity increases him day by day until old age carries him into apprehensions and vices diminish his intelligence.'

And by the time the King of England had finally made up his mind, it was, indeed, already too late. For in October 1619, while his father-in-law hesitated, Frederick duly arrived in Prague to claim his new throne, and in doing so committed what James had already admitted to Baron von Dohna would be an act of insupportable aggression. Since his subjects, James told Frederick's emissary, were as dear to him as children, he would not 'embark them in an unjust and needless quarrel'. But while James protested that the Bohemians had committed an outrageous act of rebellion against Ferdinand, their rightful king, and that any assistance to his son-in-law would both wreck his reputation as peacemaker and necessitate a summons of Parliament, he appeared to resort once more to the double game that came so naturally to him. Confiding to the Venetian ambassador his ongoing fear of Catholic plots, James declared how he could not even remain alive except by peace with Spain, and once more blamed Frederick as the usurper of a kingdom not his own. Yet on other occasions, it seems, he was inclined to express himself altogether differently. 'The king is taking great pains at present,' the ambassador informed the Venetian Senate on 22 November, 'to make everybody think so, showing displeasure at the election and at the Palatine's acceptance without his consent, but those who converse familiarly with him, tête à tête, easily perceive his delight at this new royal title for his son-in-law and daughter.'

Ultimately, James would neither directly discourage Frederick's acceptance of the Bohemian Crown nor actively support it – merely preferring to imply that he would acquiesce in the accomplished fact. And this was something that even his daughter's most earnest entreaties could do nothing to alter. Proclaimed upon her arrival by a wildly enthusiastic populace, Bohemia's 'Winter Queen' had given birth on 17 December 1619, to her third son, who was to be known to history as 'Rupert of the Rhine'. But by September of the following year, she was imploring her brother Charles to be 'most earnest' with their father about his 'slackness to assist us'. And after a year of playing cheerfully and incompetently at their roles as

King and Queen of Bohemia, both Elizabeth and her husband were indeed plunged into headlong flight amidst the remnants of their army which had been ripped to shreds by the troops of the Catholic League on 8 November 1620 at the Battle of the White Mountain. Bereft and beleaguered, and facing the imminent conquest of the Palatinate itself by Don Ambrosio Spinola Doria's Spanish troops, they were now no more than homeless pretenders to a Crown that would never be theirs again.

17 ❦ 'Baby Charles' and 'Steenie'

'What sudden change hath darked of late
The glory of the Arcadian state?
The fleecy flocks refuse to feed,
The lambs to play, the ewes to breed;
The altars smoke, the offerings burn,
Till Jack and Tom do safe return.'

From a pastoral poem written by James I in response to the
Prince of Wales' journey to Madrid in 1623

'The King,' wrote Sir Anthony Weldon, 'was ever best when furthest from his Queen.' And her death on 2 March 1619, appears to have been greeted with precisely the kind of broad equanimity that might have been anticipated in such circumstances. While Anne lay ill at Hampton Court with dropsy, James visited her dutifully twice a week, but it was Prince Charles rather than he who took up residence in an adjoining bedroom in an effort to provide some modicum of comfort and support. In the meantime, the king remained preoccupied with the issue of his wife's will, for fear that she might leave the majority of her jewels to her Danish maid Anna – a worry that would remain unfounded – though the gems, valued at £30,000, nevertheless found their way into the maid's possession illicitly with the help, it seems, of a Frenchman named Pierrot. Equally regrettably, before James left for a hunting trip at Newmarket in February, there had been angry words between the royal couple over the Catholic priests that hovered continually around the queen's sickbed. Ultimately, indeed, only Prince Charles and his sister Elizabeth, who wrote from Heidelberg on 31 May to express her inexpressible sorrow at 'so great a misfortune', appear to have been genuinely stricken by the queen's demise, and the verses that James later penned in her memory were largely coloured by more general reflections on the mortality of princes, 'who, though they run the race of men and die' were further ennobled by their passing, since 'death serves but to refine their majesty'. In the words of one observer, the king took his wife's death 'seemly', neither weeping publicly, nor managing, for that matter, to brave the illness that kept him from her funeral. Only later, arguably, as his own health collapsed and he reflected more broadly upon the transience of human affairs, would a deeper despondency descend upon him.

The malady that kept the king from Anne's obsequies at Westminster on 13 May was, however, real enough. It had begun with 'a shrewd fit of the stone' coupled with arthritis during his stay at Newmarket, and by the time of his arrival at Royston in mid-March his condition had deteriorated significantly. He was weak and faint, could neither eat nor sleep and was debilitated further, we are told, by a 'scouring vomit'. 'After the Queen's death,' wrote James's French physician, he suffered 'pain in the joints and nephritis with thick sand, continued fever, bilious diarrhoea, hiccoughs for several days, bitter humours boiling from his mouth so as to cause ulcers on his lips and chin, fainting, sighing, dread, incredible sadness, intermittent pulse'. At one point, indeed, there had been fears for his life, and though he had recovered sufficiently to be removed from Royston to Ware on 24 April, he was nevertheless carried part of the way in a Neapolitan chair provided for him by Lady Elizabeth Hatton, and the rest of the way in a litter. Even by the time of his midsummer hunting trip to Oatlands, Woking and Windsor, moreover, James was still seeking to strengthen his legs and feet by bathing them in the bellies of slain deer.

Upon his arrival in London on 1 June, however, it was already clear that any residual shadow cast by Queen Anne's death would not be long-lived. Riding through the city in a suit of pale blue satin, and sporting a hat of blue and white feathers, the king was received with such enthusiasm that the whole scene surprised and perplexed an embassy of condolence, sent by the Duke of Lorraine, which had arrived at the same time. The kingdom had thrown off mourning, it seems, to celebrate James's recovery to good health, though the twenty-four Frenchmen, clad in unrelieved black, remained less than impressed by the apparent lack of sensitivity. Convention, if nothing else, required more of the king than what had amounted, in effect, to a fleeting and partially self-centred fit of dolour. Nor could his own undoubted fears of death and dissolution justify his current wish to return to normality so rapidly, especially at a time when any outward play at celebration was marred so obviously by growing pressure both abroad and at home. For, as events in Europe continued to darken, the need for action on all fronts increased daily.

Above all, the marriage of the king's son was becoming a matter of particular urgency. Prince Charles, the sickly child who had never been expected to survive infancy and whose weakness of limb at the age of almost 5 made it necessary for the Earl of Nottingham to carry him at his investiture as Duke of York, had grown up shy, sensitive, obstinate, priggish and dull – mollycoddled and overawed by his father, and completely overshadowed his elder brother, who would often taunt him till he wept, 'telling him that he should be a bishop, a gown being fittest to hide his legs'. Yet with Henry's death in 1612, his own creation as Prince of Wales four years later, and the king's declining health, Charles had gradually emerged, for all his deficiencies, as a figure of increasing importance both at court and in the kingdom at large. And though in the opinion of the Venetian ambassador writing in 1617, he remained 'very grave', exhibiting 'no other aim than to second his father, to follow him and do his pleasure', he had nevertheless developed into a young man 'of good constitution so far as can be judged from his appearance', who enjoyed theatricals, rode excellently and delighted in hunting.

The prince's devotion to his father was, moreover, fully reciprocated by the king himself, though the glow of paternal pride and affection for his delicate, studious child was too often tainted by spiteful displays of annoyance. In consequence, the heir to the throne had come to harbour a particularly warm resentment towards the dazzling favourite whom all adored and who exercised such a hold over his father's affections. That Charles should have manifested such antagonism towards George Villiers was hardly surprising in view of the rivalry he posed, but it was magnified significantly by James's apparent partiality whenever the two fell out. In 1616, for instance, after Charles had tried on and mislaid one of Villiers' rings, the king is said to have called for his son and 'used such bitter language as caused his Highness to shed tears', before banishing the prince from his presence until the elusive ring was eventually found in his breeches by a valet. The heir to the throne would feel the sting of his father's anger, too, in a later incident that resulted from a childish prank where, by turning the pin of a fountain, he had caused water to spurt onto the favourite's splendid clothes. Witnessing the mischief, James this time not only spoke angry words but gave the prince two boxes on the ear, though this would not, it seems, prevent a more serious quarrel between the prince and Villiers over a game of tennis in 1618, when the latter, who was the prince's senior by eight years, is alleged to have raised his racket in anger. 'What, my lord,' said Charles with all the self-satisfied superiority of a young man enjoying an unfamiliar taste of victory, 'I think you intend to strike me!'

James, however, wished only for peace between his 'sweet babies', and the result was a characteristically lavish and honeyed attempt at reconciliation staged by the favourite after the king had called the two together and urged them, upon their allegiance to him, to love one another. In consequence, at a sumptuous banquet held in June 1618 to signal to the entire court the dawning of a new entente between the freshly created Earl of Buckingham and the Prince of Wales, the older of the two duly courted his young rival, and not only mended the rift but established himself at one and the same time as the prince's lasting idol. Held out of doors at Buckingham's new estate at Wanstead, the so-called 'Prince's Feast' was a triumph, in fact, for the host's grasp of political necessities and timing, and a testament to his intuitive grasp of Charles's underlying needs and inclinations. For their widely opposed temperaments, as Buckingham fully appreciated, could easily be turned to rich and permanent profit, if only the less prepossessing of the two could be offered the opportunity to share the glow of adulation in which he himself basked. Both, after all, were devoted to hunting, riding, poetry, music and painting, and for an introvert like the prince, who shared his father's emotional volatility, the gulf between antipathy and hero-worship might be easily bridged – as indeed it was.

By the time, therefore, that James had risen from his table at the end of the feast at Wanstead and made his way over to the place where Buckingham and his kin were seated, the man who had previously been firmly entrenched as rival, enemy and embodiment of all the virtues lacking in the prince himself had already been transformed into mentor, role model and oracle – a radiant being from whom a formerly delicate, awkward and taciturn individual could draw unfamiliar sources of confidence and allure. Drinking a toast to each of the Villiers family in turn, James then swore that both he and his descendants would 'advance that House above all others'. 'I live,' he declared, 'to that end.' And now, he added gratefully, he harboured no doubt that his heir would do the same. For Charles, too, would henceforth be turning to 'Steenie' for guidance and succour – writing to him as 'your true constant friend' and praying him 'to commend my most humble service to his Majestie'.

But while the best behaviour of the prince, whom Buckingham would soon dub 'Baby Charles', was now assured, the same was hardly true of the MPs that James was eventually compelled to summon for only the third time in his reign. In the aftermath of the Addled Parliament of 1614, the king had intended to cope for as long as possible by means of forced loans and benevolences, by the sale of honours and monopolies, and by the judicious levying of impositions. With the assistance of Cranfield as treasurer, moreover, such expedients had for some time proved adequate for his ordinary financial needs. But the Spanish invasion of the Palatinate in August 1620, which had driven his English subjects to fury, also jarred James's own sense of justice to such a degree that he was even prepared to vent his anger to Gondomar. He would never trust a Spanish minister again, the ambassador was told, amid angry tears, during an audience with James at Hampton Court in September. Nor, declared the king, would he permit either his children or his religion to perish. Instead, he would go in person to defend the Palatinate.

The outburst, it is true, was followed by misgivings and hesitation, as Gondomar presented the Spanish invasion as a pathway to long-term peace. Should Frederick renounce his claims in Bohemia, the ambassador contended, then the Palatinate could be duly restored to him. And such was Gondomar's persuasiveness that James was even prepared to dismiss Sir Robert Naunton, his secretary, from office. He remained uneasy, too, not only at the popular hatred of Spain but at the freedom with which it was expressed, as Puritan preachers found time, amid their personal attacks upon Buckingham, to fume at Spanish perfidy and the plight of Frederick and his English wife. Complaining that his subjects were becoming too republican, James therefore issued a proclamation forbidding contentious discussion of state affairs, while Buckingham did all he could to throw in his weight with Gondomar. 'The Puritans have rendered Buckingham Spanish,' wrote Tillières, the French ambassador, 'for seeing that they mean to attack him, he knows no way of securing protection against them except by the Spanish match.'

But however James handled the problem which faced him at Christmas 1620 he could not hope to do so unarmed and on an income barely sufficient even for his peacetime needs. For even if his role as mediator was to continue, as he always hoped, his efforts would carry little weight unless backed by at least the potential for military action. In the summer, therefore, when Spinola first threatened the Palatinate, James had permitted a force of 2,000 English volunteers under Sir Horace Vere to go to the defence of his son-in-law's hereditary lands. And their presence at once provided a convenient toe-hold, which could be used to provide leverage, should war become desirable or unavoidable. At the same time, since Vere's force was composed of volunteers, it could be disavowed or reinforced as advantage served. Under such circumstances, a summons of Parliament might prove a popular, comparatively low-risk strategy of precisely the kind that the king was so often inclined to favour.

The House of Commons that confronted James in January 1621, however, was soon threatening to prove even more truculent than its predecessor. Initially, there had been grounds for optimism. Both Crown and Parliament shared, after all, the same broad objective: the restoration of Frederick and his wife to at least their hereditary dominions in the Palatinate. Even Buckingham, for that matter, had temporarily joined the majority on the king's council that clamoured for war, and James's opening speech showed less of the customary cudgel bluntness and rather more humility than usual. He had been carried to the House in a portative chair and there were whispers that he might not walk again, but, in acknowledging the threat of war and his need for money, he appeared amenable and ready to curry sympathy. In speaking of his efforts to keep the peace, he also spoke graciously of his predecessor: 'I will not say that I have governed as well as she did, but I may say we have had as much peace in our time as in hers.' And his request for money was also couched in anything but strident tones. 'I have laboured as a woman in travail,' he declared, '... and I dare say I have been as sparing to trouble you not with monopolies or in subsidies as ever King before me, considering the greatness of my occasions and charges.'

It was the very issue of patents and monopolies, however, that soon dominated debate and led directly to criticism of those close to Buckingham. For, although the favourite had garnered little personal profit from the sale of exclusive marketing rights, he had nevertheless supported them for the benefit of his relations. Sir Giles Mompesson, one of the worst offenders, was connected to the Villiers nexus by his sister-in-law, while Buckingham's brother Kit and half-brother Edward had also benefited handsomely. Such, indeed, was the favourite's alarm that he initially sought the dissolution of

Parliament, only to be rebuffed by the king, before opting to turn tail and disown his corrupt kinsmen. In the process, he spared himself by posing as nothing less than the champion of reform, though Francis Bacon proved less fortunate. Pleading guilty to a charge of corruption on 3 May and describing himself as 'a broken reed', the Lord Chancellor was debarred from office, subjected to a fine of £40,000 and consigned to the Tower at the king's pleasure. 'Those who will strike at your Chancellor,' Bacon had warned James, 'it is much to be feared will strike at your crown.' But the king had insisted all the same upon an impartial hearing, before ultimately mitigating the sentence. Bacon had claimed, after all, that he had done no more than 'partake of the abuses of the time', and the king seems to have accepted as much. 'In giving penalties,' he declared, 'I do always suppose myself in the offender, and then judge how far the like occasion might have tempted me.'

Such admirable sentiments did not, however, prevent James from making a foolish and costly lapse into dishonesty of his own. Though the Parliament of 1621 had been summoned in response to the crisis on the Continent, the issue of foreign policy remained, in accordance with tradition, beyond its remit, and the king himself had touched on the European situation in only the vaguest terms. Assuring MPs that peace remained his objective, James nevertheless made clear that he must negotiate 'with a sword in his hand', and that, if necessary, he would spare no personal cost to recover the Palatinate. But in asking for funds, he concealed the real sum required – a sum that had been made clear to him by a report he had specifically requested from a council of war some months earlier. Advised at that time that an army of at least 30,000 men was required for intervention on the Continent and that such a force would necessitate a down payment of £250,000, followed by further payments of around £900,000 per year thereafter, James nevertheless chose to ask for £500,000. The result was an interim grant of only £145,000 from MPs made suspicious of their king's motives by his insistence on further negotiations with Spain rather than an immediate declaration of war.

When Parliament adjourned in June, therefore, the scope for optimism was limited. But when MPs reassembled in November, dissent was soon broadening ominously – not least because James had taken the remarkable decision to leave London for a Newmarket hunting trip before the new session began, leaving his ministers hopelessly exposed in their efforts to contain the situation. 'His Majesty seems to hope,' wrote the Venetian ambassador, 'that the Parliament will readily afford him every means of making war with little trouble on his part.' Yet before long, MPs were employing what they now declared to be their 'ancient and undoubted right to free speech' to encroach upon areas of policy that had always been closed to them. Some called for sea war with Spain rather than 'pottering and pelting in the Palatinate', as John Chamberlain put it, 'only to consume both our men and means'. Others called for broader action against Catholics at home, as enemies of the commonwealth. There were demands, too, that Prince Charles should be 'timely and happily married to one of our own religion'. And in the meantime James merely saw fit to dispatch from Newmarket an angry letter to the Speaker, which would pour oil from afar upon already troubled waters.

In suggesting that his absence – through what he termed an 'indisposition of health' – had emboldened certain 'fiery spirits' to debate matters 'far beyond their reach and capacity', James also complained how this had tended towards 'our high dishonour and breach of prerogative royal', and forbade that MPs should hereafter meddle in 'deep matters of state, nor deal with our dearest son's match with the daughter of Spain, nor touch the honour of that king'. But it was the threat accompanying the letter that forced the issue, for James also added 'that we think ourselves very free and able to punish any man's misdemeanours in Parliament as well during their sitting as after; which we mean not to spare hereafter upon any occasion of any man's insolent behaviour there that shall be ministered unto us'. Instead of sticking to the point at issue, on which he was certainly within his constitutional rights, James had therefore plunged knee deep into questions that had best been left unmentioned. Worse still, he had chosen his battleground poorly, for in lacking the natural gravitas and finesse of his predecessor, he had nevertheless resorted to intimidation and threats of force that he was ill-equipped to deliver. An assault on individual members was likely to leave him not only penniless and discredited but at the mercy of Spain, and the tone of his warning represented in any case a challenge that the more recalcitrant elements of the House of Commons were hardly able to ignore.

The result was a meeting at Newmarket between the king and a parliamentary delegation that demonstrated all too palpably the scale of the rift between the two sides. Though the MPs had arrived ostensibly with the intention of expressing their requests more moderately than before, James was not only unbending but brashly dismissive. Greeting the delegates with a patronising request that his servants 'bring stools for the ambassadors', he balked once more at the suggestion that freedom of speech was 'our undoubted right and an inheritance received from our ancestors'. 'We are an old and experienced king,' he objected, 'needing no such lessons.' He resented too, it seems, the petitioners' 'great complaints of the danger of religion within this kingdom, tacitly implying our ill-government on this point', and rejected what he deemed to be their desire to 'bring all kinds of causes within their compass and jurisdiction' like 'the Puritan ministers in Scotland' had supposedly done before them. Almost inevitably, moreover, he concluded with a further declaration that Parliament's privileges were solely 'derived from the grace and permission of our ancestors and us'.

By equating the present with his Scottish past and treating an opportunity for conciliation as a reckoning, James had therefore inflamed and exacerbated, and, in doing so, called forth a formal protestation from MPs on 18 December, since there was now no point in further debate. Instead, the privileges of the House of Commons would be set forth in writing, with neither hint of retreat nor trace of apology, leaving James to broil in the kind of frustration and fury that had marred his reign in Scotland. 'The plain truth is,' he wrote, 'we cannot with patience endure our subjects to use such anti-monarchical words concerning their liberties, except they had subjoined that they were granted unto them by the grace and favour of our predecessors.' And though councillors urged that he should not dissolve Parliament, Gondomar added counter-pressure of his own by suggesting that Spain could not negotiate while such a body remained in existence. Nor was the Spaniard alone, it seems, in his desire for dissolution, for he recorded gladly how 'the king was being valiantly urged on by the Marquis of Buckingham and other good friends'.

Finding that his bid for popularity by throwing his monopolist cronies to the wolves was unsuccessful, Buckingham had indeed returned to his former pro-Spanish course and predictably carried the heir to the throne with him. For now Charles too had begun to fancy himself as anxious for a Spanish match as his father. Cajoled, therefore, by those whose sympathy he most valued, and faced, apparently, with the intolerable prospect of surrendering to the House of Commons the very authority he had fought so strenuously to defend against the Scottish Kirk, James found diplomatic dependency upon Spain the only acceptable option. Nor, in doing so, could he temper his bile or resist the urge for a vacuously imperious gesture. Sending for the *Journal of the House of Commons*, he tore out, in the presence of his council, the very page on which the offending protestation had been recorded – an act which for Gondomar was 'the best thing that has happened in the interest of Spain and the Catholic religion since Luther began to preach heresy a hundred years ago'. 'It is certain,' he added, 'that the king will never summon another Parliament as long as he lives.' With no prospect of English intervention now at hand, moreover, the Emperor Ferdinand would duly confirm by the end of 1622 that the Palatinate was to be presented to his cousin Maximilian of Bavaria, leaving James to dangle on the end of a Spanish hook, baited with lukewarm prospects of a marriage that was, in any case, bitterest wormwood to all red-blooded Protestant Englishmen.

The interminable negotiations for Charles's union with a Spanish bride had already assumed a curious air of unreality since their initiation a decade earlier under the aegis of Carr and the Howards, when Gondomar had first arrived at the English court. Now, indeed, it was not only a different infanta, but a different prince: less passive, more influential, and, most significantly of all, altogether more passionate about the enterprise. For at the same time that Gondomar nursed dreams of the English royal family's conversion to Catholicism, and James held fast to the notion that a Spanish alliance might yet confirm his status as the 'peacemaker king', Charles harboured boyish visions of emulating the romantic feat of his father by bringing back his bride from over the sea. While professional diplomats like John Digby, Earl of Bristol, tediously trod water in Madrid, and his father offered unconvincing half-promises of relaxing the penal laws and allowing a Catholic upbringing for the infanta's children, the prince himself now dreamt of breaking the deadlock by direct action of the most effective kind. He would cross to France, incognito and without a formal pass, to win his bride in person. He would do so, moreover, in the sole company of his guide and mentor, Buckingham, who, seeing the opportunity for a spectacular personal victory, now encouraged the venture at every turn.

When Gondomar returned home in 1622, therefore, and while James and his council were seriously discussing a military expedition to recover Heidelberg, the prince and his hero were secretly writing to the absent ambassador of their intention. The Spaniard, indeed, had hatched the plan initially and, as negotiations flagged once more in February 1623, Charles and Buckingham mooted it with the king himself. As James well knew, the escapade would expose his son to the very real and largely unnecessary dangers of a journey halfway across Europe, unguarded and unattended. Equally recklessly, it would destroy at a stroke the delicate bargaining position built up by the Earl of Bristol and allow the Spaniards the opportunity to raise their terms as high as they pleased, while the king's English subjects seethed with indignation. But ill health, despondency and a doting fondness for his two 'sweet babies' seem to have sapped James's resolve until his consent was finally wrung from him during a surprise visit late one night. And though, according to Clarendon, he fell next morning 'into a great passion of tears, and told them he was undone, and that it would break his heart if they pursued their resolution', Charles and Buckingham were nevertheless allowed to prevail.

In consequence, on 18 February 1623 two heavily disguised young men using the names of Jack and Tom Smith crossed the Thames by ferry at Gravesend, leaving the King of England to brood and fret upon the dangers ahead of them. Wearing false beards, which in one case fell off inopportunely, they grossly overpaid the ferryman and further excited his suspicion by requesting that they be set ashore just outside Gravesend instead of at the usual landing place within the town. When, moreover, the local magistrates were subsequently informed of the likelihood that two suspicious travellers were slipping out of the country for the purpose of fighting a duel, an attempt was made to intercept them at Rochester, though they had left before they were apprehended. Escaping arrest, too, at the hands of Sir Henry Mainwaring, Lieutenant of Dover Castle, as well as the Mayor of Canterbury, the two would nevertheless reach Dover unscathed and arrive in Paris on 21 February after a wretchedly seasick crossing to Boulogne.

Just over a fortnight later, at 8 p.m. on 7 March, the Earl of Bristol was attending to important business at his embassy in Madrid when a mysterious Mr Smith demanded immediate access. The visitor, in fact, was Buckingham, and though Bristol disapproved of the venture, he had little option but to inform a jubilant Gondomar of the heir to the English throne's arrival. Hastening to his superior, the Count of Olivares, who conveyed the news in turn to King Philip, Gondomar had achieved, it seems, the ultimate diplomatic coup. For, while Philip chose to remain cool until the attitude of the Pope had been clarified, the bargaining position of his government had been enhanced immeasurably, since any return to England without the infanta in tow would involve such an intolerable loss of face for the two visitors. From Gondomar's perspective, meanwhile, the prince's arrival could only be explained by his imminent conversion to Catholicism – a belief that both Charles and Buckingham foolishly saw fit to encourage initially.

So far, however, at least James's worst fears for his son and Buckingham had not been realised. Though he had agonised over their safety, he had hailed them, nevertheless, as 'dear adventurous knights worthy to be put in a new romanso', and in spite of the Earl of Bristol's misgivings, the first signs appeared encouraging. 'I must confess ingenuously,' Bristol informed James, 'that if Your Majesty had been pleased to ask my advice concerning the prince his coming in this fashion, I should rather have dissuaded than given any such counsel, especially before the coming of the dispensation.' But though the papal dispensation sanctioning the marriage, to which the earl referred, was never likely to prove acceptable, the Spanish king, at least, had hidden his reservations admirably and made himself suitably agreeable, riding beside Charles as he escorted him to a suite in the royal palace. Nor was the prince disappointed upon meeting his 16-year-old inamorata for the first time. Fair haired with languorous eyes and full lips, the infanta Maria made such an impression, in fact, that Buckingham wrote home to James to tell how his son was 'so touched at the heart that he confesses all he ever yet saw is nothing to her'.

The initial meeting had been long delayed, however, as every conceivable device of the rigidly formal Spanish court was employed to keep the couple apart. And when at last an audience was granted, Charles was left in no doubt as to what he must wear and what he might say. Never allowed to speak to the infanta alone, he resorted ultimately to leaping the wall of her orchard – an act which not only breached the bounds of Spanish decorum but also succeeded in frightening his quarry uncontrollably. When permitted to see her at court theatricals, moreover, the prince found her impenetrably aloof as he watched from afar, 'half an hour together in thoughtful posture' and with an intense concentration that reminded Olivares of a cat watching a mouse. Convinced by her confessor of the eternal peril to her soul which would be entailed by each night sharing her bed with a heretic, the young girl was predictably repelled by the prospect of her sacrifice on the altar of marriage. And when Buckingham informed his wife of Charles's predicament, she responded, in all good faith it seems, with a characteristically ingenuous attempt at helpfulness that captured the underlying oddity of the situation. 'I have sent you some perspective glasses,' she told her husband, 'the best I could get. I am sorry the prince is kept at such a distance that he needs them to see her.'

In England, meanwhile, James was faced with increasing pressure as his councillors headed by the Earl of Arundel, the only Howard who now still held power, expressed consternation at the proposed marriage and dissatisfaction that the king had ever permitted the prince's journey in the first place. When pressed, the king was merely inclined to heap all blame upon both Buckingham and his son's high passion. 'The king,' wrote John Williams, Dean of Westminster, to the favourite, 'would seem sometimes, as I hear, to take it upon himself (as we have advised him to do by proclamation); yet he sticks at it and many times casts it upon you both.' And in sparing himself further opprobrium, James had clearly exposed Buckingham to the kind of hostility that he was less able than ever to ignore. 'Detestation of the Marquis', wrote the Venetian envoy Valaresso, 'has increased beyond all measure', while Dean Williams pulled no punches in informing the favourite how 'all the court and rabble of the people lay the voyage upon Your Lordship'. Such, indeed, was the outcry in London churches that James had no choice but to forbid all prayers for the prince's soul 'now that he was going into the House of Rimmon'.

In spite of James's misgivings about his predicament, however, the same flow of cloying correspondence to his two 'sweethearts' in Madrid continued unabated. 'God bless you, my sweet baby,' one letter ended, 'and send him good fortune in his wooing, to the comfort of his old father, who cannot be happy but in him. My ship is ready to make sail, and only stays a fair wind.' On another occasion, there were assurances to Buckingham that the king was wearing his picture 'in a blue ribbon under my wash-coat, next my heart'. And while he expressed concern on 25 March about an implication from Buckingham that he might lean further towards Rome, the king was nevertheless prepared to interpret the suggestion in the most positive light possible. 'I know not what ye mean,' he wrote, 'by my acknowledging the pope's spiritual supremacy ... but all that I can guess at your meaning is that it may be ye have an allusion to a passage in my book against Bellarmine, where I offer, if the pope would quit his godhead, and usurping over kings, to acknowledge him for the chief bishop, to which all appeals of churchmen ought to lie en dernier resort ... For I am not a monsieur that can shift his religion as easily as he can shift his shirt when he comes from tennis.'

There were paternal concerns, too, about the prince's welfare, as James begged his son not to exert himself in hot weather, 'for I fear my baby may take fever by it', and suggested that Charles and Buckingham should keep themselves fit by private dancing, 'though ye should whistle and sing to one another, like Jack and Tom, for fault of better music'. The prince's spending, it is true, continued to perplex the king, and after jewels valuing some

£80,000 were dispatched in what proved to be a fruitless effort to dazzle the Spaniards, Charles was urged to be 'as sparing as ye can', for 'God knows how my coffers are already drained'. But in other respects James's fussing and indulgence remained unstinting. Garter robes and insignia, for example, were specially dispatched, so that they could be worn on St George's Day, 'for it will be a goodly sight for the Spaniards to see my boys in them'. Nor, it seems, were Buckingham's relations neglected in James's thoughts at this trying time. He had written letters to the favourite's mother, consoling her during her son's absence, and kept a particularly close watch, it seems, upon his wife, believing that she might be pregnant. 'And, my sweet Steenie gossip,' the king wrote, 'I must tell thee that Kate was a little sick these four or five days of a headache, and the next morning, after a little casting, was well again. I hope it is a good sign that I shall shortly be a gossip over again, for I must be thy perpetual gossip.'

In spite of their futility, there were even arrangements for the prince's heroic homecoming with his bride. Eight great ships and two pinnaces were to sail, and planning was in hand for the infanta's magnificent cabin. A wing of St James's Palace was also enlarged and refurbished and specially equipped with an oratory for her use. And all the while, the prince remained as wide-eyed and artlessly optimistic as ever. 'I, your baby, have since this conclusion been with my mistress, and she sits publicly with me at the plays, and within this two or three days shall take place of the queen as Princess of England.' But it was now two years since the pope had first been asked to sanction the marriage and the condition that James should grant full liberty of worship to English Catholics seemed as implausible as ever. 'I have written a letter,' James had already told his two 'sweet boys', 'to the Conde de Olivares as both of you designed me, as full of thanks and kindness as can be devised as indeed he well deserves, but in the end of your letter ye put in in a cooling card anent the nuncio's averseness to this business.' 'The pope', James added ominously, 'will always be averse' unless the infanta be given 'free exercise of her religion here'.

But when the precise terms for the dispensation were finally brought from Madrid by Sir Francis Cottington in the late summer, they proved far more shocking still. Not only was the infanta to control the education of her children, she was also to be permitted to open her chapel in London for public worship, and retain a fully Catholic household, the members of which were to be personally selected by none other than her brother, Philip IV. The religious life of this household, moreover, was to be administered by a bishop at the head of twenty-four priests, all of whom, though resident in England, were not to be subject to English law. Worse still, it was stipulated that there must be complete freedom of worship for Catholics, and that the Oath of Allegiance should be altered to accommodate them. To cap all, James and his entire council were to agree on oath to all clauses of the dispensation, while the king was to swear additionally that he would obtain parliamentary agreement to these terms within a year. Even the date of the infanta's arrival remained doubtful, for that matter, since Spain remained reluctant to dispatch its princess until the year in question was finally over.

To suggest that Cottington's tidings fell as a hammer blow upon the King of England's pipe dreams would be an understatement. Vain hope gave way at once to despair, which dissolved soon after into hysteria, as James became convinced that his babes were now prisoners, and determined to recover them by signing anything that the Spanish government might now ask of him. The news that Cottington had brought him, he wrote to Buckingham and Charles on 14 June, 'hath stricken me dead. I feel it shall very much shorten my days, and I am the more perplexed that I know not how to satisfy the people's expectation here, neither know I what to say to the council …' And as the true scale of his essentially self-inflicted predicament dawned upon him, James's main concern remained personal: on the one hand, his own credibility, but above all the safety of the two individuals around whom his world centred. 'But as for my advice and directions that ye crave,' he wrote, 'in case they will not alter their decree, it is in a word, to come speedily away, and if ye can get leave, give over all treaty … alas, I now repent me sore that ever I suffered you to go away. I care not for match nor nothing, so I may once have you in my arms again. God grant it, God grant it, God grant it; amen, amen, amen!'

All, then, depended from James's perspective upon the swiftest possible conclusion of the marriage treaty, in the hope that something might be salvaged from the wreckage as a prelude to the return of his beloved boys. And accordingly, on 20 July, James formally ratified it in the Chapel Royal at Whitehall. For some time, in fact, the marriage had lost what little appeal in Spain it had ever had, but even the most outrageous Spanish demands, which had been raised largely with the intention of killing all negotiations once and for all, were now accepted without demur. The secret clauses, which had earlier reduced the King of England to a state of horrified incomprehension, were duly sworn by him in private before the Marquis of Inojosa, who had succeeded Gondomar as ambassador, and Don Carlos de Coloma, Philip IV's special envoy. But there was no reference to the £600,000 dowry, to which the Spaniards had already whittled the intended windfall that had been dazzling James's imagination for the past ten years, and without which, as he assured Buckingham, he must surely go bankrupt. Guarantees of Spanish help to bring about the restoration of Frederick and Elizabeth in the Palatinate also went unmentioned – leaving James to confess that he was 'marrying his son with a portion of his daughter's tears'. That same evening, however, in the new Banqueting House which Inigo Jones had built specifically for the wedding of the Prince of Wales, James and his Spanish ambassadors still dined in particular splendour from plates 'of pure and perfect gold'.

18 ⟱ Dotage, Docility and Demise

'All good sentiments are clearly dead in the king. He is too blinded in disordered self-love and in his wish for quiet and pleasure, too agitated by constant mistrust of everyone, tyrannised over by perpetual fear of his life, tenacious of his authority as against the Parliament and jealous of his son's obedience, all accidents and causes of his almost desperate infirmity of mind.'

From a report made by Alvise Vallaresso, Venetian ambassador to England, 1622–24

The last official portrait of Scotland's King of England dates to 1621. Painted by Daniel Mytens the Elder, it depicts him bare-headed and seated in a posture of limp repose, with a plumed hat on the table beside him, but no other symbol of regality beyond the Garter robes he wears and a Tudor rose woven into the tapestry behind his chair. His hands droop wearily over the arm of his chair. His tired eyes lie far back in their sockets beneath heavy lids. His lips are pursed in indifference and resignation. It is the face, in fact, of a deeply disillusioned man who has lost his vigour and abandoned all real desire to prevail against adversity. *Beati pacifici* – 'blessed are the peacemakers' – is there above the king's head, but hardly noticeable and only then, it seems, as a dutiful afterthought from an artist whose main intent was to capture an eloquent image of worn-out authority. Fit only to be cosseted by the ladies of the Villiers family and in particular Buckingham's mother, who according to Archbishop Mathew now 'fulfilled a double function as a middle-aged gossip and as a nurse', James, it seems, was already slipping into careworn lethargy, born of ill-health, the relentless passage of time and a world that had consistently refused to conform to his more noble aspirations.

There were, it is true, bright spots ahead for him, not the least of which was the much anticipated return of his beloved son. Towards the end of September, the prince and Buckingham embarked for England, sailing from the north-west coast of Spain and landing at Portsmouth on 5 October to a rapturous reception as bonfires blazed all along the Portsmouth road and hundreds of hogsheads of wine were emptied to fuel the ardour. At Cambridge, church bells rang out for two solid days, while at Blackheath the people were said to have been 'so mad with excess of joy that if they met with any cart laden with wood they would take out the horses and set cart and all on fire'. Not far from Tyburn, meanwhile, Prince Charles took time to reprieve a group of felons, and upon the heroes' arrival at Royston, the king clambered downstairs, in spite of crippling gout, to fall upon their necks in heartfelt thanks and affection. For some days, moreover, the high spirits continued. 'The prince and my lord of Buckingham,' wrote Sir Edward Conway, 'spend most of their hours with his Majesty, with the same freedom, liberty and kindness as they were wont.'

But the bonfires and bells in the country at large were at least partially deceptive, since they were not so much expressions of joy at the prince's safe return as of relief that he had returned both as a Protestant and without a Catholic bride in tow. And even as the Villiers ladies, whom the king had hastily summoned, were being regaled with rousing tales of romance and derring-do, an anthem from the 114th Psalm was being solemnly sung at St Paul's, which could not have reflected more eloquently the feelings of most Englishmen now that the 'house of Jacob', just like Israel before it, had been delivered from 'a people of strange language'. Even more perplexingly, perhaps, both the prince and his companion had now returned from Spain thoroughly disenchanted with the marriage and alliance they had hitherto striven so strenuously to forge. In particular, Buckingham's vanity seems to have played a crucial part in this curious transformation, for he had been created a duke by his adoring master to place him on an equal footing with the Spanish grandees confronting him, only to find that his hosts would neither defer to his affectations nor tolerate his sensitivity. In bridling at Spanish 'trickery and deceit', he was told directly by Olivares that negotiations would have been better left to a professional like the Earl of Bristol. And when Buckingham incurred displeasure by remaining hatted in Prince Charles's presence, and Charles's Protestant attendants were ejected from Madrid after Sir Edmund Verney had struck a priest, any grains of enthusiasm for a lasting treaty were swiftly dissipated.

Henceforth, indeed, nothing would satisfy Buckingham's wounded ego other than war itself. And war, of course, offered the added attraction of maintaining the gust of popularity he had so surprisingly experienced upon his return. To that end, therefore, the king would have to be either deceived or coerced: Parliament must be called at once and all doves on the council duly silenced or ruined. With the aid of the prince and the reliable offices of the Villiers ladies, moreover, James was to be effectively debarred from contact with any Spanish representative, and as Charles assumed more and more influence with the declining energy of his father, the last condition for the plan's success became a formality. For, while James had by no means entirely lost his native shrewdness and remained as averse to war as ever, he was unable to thwart the ongoing pressure for a postponement of the planned proxy marriage until an understanding had been reached with Spain concerning restitution of the Palatinate. Buckingham was now no longer the 'humble slave and dog' of former times, and travel had plainly broadened not only the princes's mind but his shoulders, too. 'The Prince,' wrote one courtier indeed, 'is now entering into command of affairs by reason of the King's absence and sickness, and all men address themselves unto him'. Accordingly, in January 1624 he felt sufficiently confident to inform his father categorically that he would not hear of either friendship or alliance with Spain.

And while the momentum of the newly resurgent war party gathered pace, a beleaguered and befuddled king duly wrecked his long-held dreams of peace by wearily insisting upon Spanish action in the Palatinate that could never be forthcoming, and by summoning a Parliament that was bent on conflict on all fronts. Telling his son that 'he would live to have his bellyful of Parliaments', James was now a largely broken reed, though when Buckingham eventually determined to organise the impeachment of Lionel Cranfield, Earl of Middlesex, for supporting the king's peace policy, the failing ruler was still capable of exercising a testy prescience. 'By God, Steenie,' came his retort, 'you are a fool and will shortly repent this folly and will find that in this fit of popularity you are making a rod with which you will be scourged yourself.' But, as so often, the king's resolve did not match his wisdom, and Cranfield would nevertheless fall to charges of financial corruption and find himself imprisoned in the Tower by the very Parliament which duly assembled on 19 February 1624.

Stricken, it seems, by a brooding conviction that those closest to him had, in effect, deserted him, James approached the session with minimal energy, mainly occupying himself beforehand with inconsequential matters like the importation of some Spanish asses from the Netherlands, 'making great estimation of those asses, since he finds himself so well served with the mules to his litter'. And as he engaged in any available displacement activity to avoid the looming realities surrounding him, he descended further into self-pity and listlessness. When he should have acted, he chose instead to delay or demur, and where he might have led he merely lamented. 'The king,' wrote the Venetian ambassador, 'seems practically lost … He now protests, now weeps but finally gives in.' And Tillières' observations were even more striking, as he described how James was descending 'deeper and deeper into folly every day, sometimes swearing and calling upon God, heaven and the angels, at other times weeping, then laughing, and finally pretending illness in order to play upon the pity of those who urge him to generous actions and to show them that sickness renders him incapable of deciding anything, demanding only repose and, indeed, the tomb'.

Under such circumstances, therefore, James's opening speech to the last Parliament of his reign proved uncharacteristically faint-hearted and defensive. Casting himself upon the compassion of his audience, he pleaded that he had worked consistently to preserve his people's love and was now to seek their advice on the very matter that he had hitherto barred from all discussion so tenaciously: the issue, namely, of war or peace. 'Never soldiers marching the deserts and dry sands of Arabia,' he claimed, '… could thirst more in hot weather for drink than I do now for a happy ending of this our meeting.' And so, it seems, the doors were suddenly to be opened wide to previously forbidden territory. 'The proper use of a parliament,' James continued, 'is … to confer with the king, as governor of the kingdom, and to give their advice in matters of greatest importance concerning the state and defence of the king, with the church and kingdom …' 'Consider of these,' came the king's remarkable concluding appeal, 'and upon all give me your advice … you that are the representative of this my kingdom' and 'my glasses to show me the hearts of my people.'

Still wishing in the first instance to stage a final rearguard defence of his peace policy by using Parliament's bellicosity to lever Spain into action over the Palatinate, the king's tired rhetoric was nevertheless outshone by Buckingham's, who now personified the nation's war fever and experienced little difficulty in swinging the House of Commons to his cause. When, moreover, Parliament did indeed call for an end to the marriage treaties with Spain and promised assistance in the event of war, the king reacted petulantly, retreating to Theobalds and refusing to see either Buckingham or Charles who, he claimed, had misrepresented his intentions. Thereafter, he sent secret instructions to his councillors in the Commons, intercepted a dispatch on its way to Spain to announce the ending of the marriage treaty and bemoaned the impeachment of Cranfield, which he proved powerless to prevent. And it was no small irony either that while three subsidies amounting to more than £400,000 were willingly delivered – 'the greatest aid which was ever granted in Parliament to be levied in so short a time' – the money was only proffered for a cause that ran directly counter to the king's wishes. The marriage treaties were dissolved and peace teetered in the balance. Nor, indeed, was any money to be disbursed on any authority other than that of a council of war nominated by the House of Commons.

In the meantime, Buckingham and Charles consolidated their niche as popular heroes, with all that had gone wrong in Madrid duly laid upon the Earl of Bristol's buckling shoulders. Throughout the spring and summer of 1624 they beavered at the task of forging a grand alliance against Spain and made extravagant commitments without the funds to enact them. £360,000 was promised to the King of Denmark and a further £240,000 to pay for the conscription of an English army of 12,000 men to fight under the notorious German mercenary Ernst von Mansfeld. Above all, however, Charles and Buckingham pursued agreement with France and in particular marriage to the French princess Henrietta Maria – a policy which caused additional embarrassment for James, since in spite of his promises to Parliament that no future marriage treaty would entail concessions to English Catholics, the French now proceeded to demand precisely that. For three days during September, in fact, the king resisted the pressure of his favourite who had made a confidant of the French ambassador, the Marquis d'Effiat. But his capitulation followed, and while the resulting treaty was presented innocuously enough to his subjects, James privately accepted the French formula and, in a letter, promised to fulfil it. The royal signature which was appended to the treaty with a stamp, since the king's arthritic fingers could no longer move a pen, effectively purchased nothing, for while France had entered the Thirty Years' War in resistance to Habsburg power, their interest did not extend to the restitution of the Palatinate to its rightful ruler. In consequence, England found itself at last at war, but for a cause that the king had never espoused and without prospect of achieving the only specific foreign policy objective that had encouraged him to engage in war talk initially.

As the reign drew to its end, however, at least no military action was underway, since the remnants of the English volunteer force in the Palatinate had by now ceased to exist and its leader, Sir Gerald Herbert, had been killed. Yet the absence of fighting was of little consolation to James as he fell ill once more during December 1624. Wholly pre-occupied with his dwindling pleasures, his ailments and his tantrums, he was further disheartened by the death in February of the old Marquis of Hamilton. Only the year before, James had lost his cousin Lennox – a fine figure of a man who had 'shared his pleasure with many ladies' before becoming the constant 'servant' of that imperious beauty, the Countess of Hereford. When her husband, a curious old eccentric, had died in 1621, Lennox had stepped into the breach and lost no time in marrying her. But after retiring to bed in perfect health one night, he had been found dead in the morning – the consequence, according to one court wag, of an overdose of aphrodisiac. Seeing his friends and contemporaries thus disappearing into the grave, James now told his courtiers how he would be next.

Nevertheless, he had recovered enough by July to gorge himself with melons and even to set out on a modified royal progress not long afterwards. But he failed to emerge from his chamber at Christmas, 'not coming once to the chapel, nor to any of the plays', and experienced a more serious decline in the New Year, as a result of his own stubbornness and indiscipline. The malaria, or so-called 'tertian ague' that attacked him in March 1625 was by general agreement 'without any manner of danger if he would suffer himself to be governed and ordered by physical rules'. He refused the advice of his doctors, however, and not only drank vast quantities of cold beer but opted resolutely for the remedies of the old Countess of Buckingham who fussed continually at his bedside.

Stricken by a series of painful convulsions and fainting fits, the king then succumbed, it seems, to a minor stroke which left him unable to control the muscles of his face and choking upon vast quantities of his own phlegm. Even at the time there was largely groundless talk of skulduggery, and rumours that poison may have been involved were soon fuelled by one of James's Scottish physicians, George Eglisham. In a pamphlet published in Latin at Frankfurt in 1626, Eglisham suggested that the Duke of Buckingham had administered a white powder to the king which made him very ill, after which his mother had applied a plaster, also unbeknown to the royal doctors. In a Jacobean court already tainted by the Overbury scandal, it could hardly have been otherwise, of course, and such scandalous gossip found ready propagators in the small handful of Robert Carr's former servants who still tended the king.

Certainly, on 14 March James is said to have drunk a posset prepared by a country doctor named Remington, who had been warmly recommended by Buckingham and his mother, whereupon the king's physicians reacted angrily, refusing to proceed until Remington's medicine and the countess's plasters were discontinued. According to Eglisham's account, indeed, there was an unsavoury scene at the king's bedside when some of his doctors declared outright that poison was involved and a furious Buckingham drove them at once from the bedchamber. When, moreover, the countess begged James to clear both her son's and her own name from such slanders, the king, it seems, fainted from shock at the very mention of the word 'poison'. Yet even disregarding the fact that James's condition had improved sufficiently within the week for him to request further remedies from the good countess, the evidence for foul play remains slender, to say the least. The potential profit for Buckingham from foul play was in any case minimal, for the king had effectively ceased to rule long before he ceased to live. And it was actually a violent attack of dysentery that delivered the killing blow, bringing the king's misery and degradation to a merciful close.

By that time James's malarial fits were lasting for up to ten hours, and shortly before the end finally arrived, he had called for Lancelot Andrewes, though his favourite bishop was now himself a sick man, and John Williams, Dean of Westminster and Bishop of Lincoln, was therefore summoned to deliver the last rites instead. Whenever conscious, the king's talk was of repentance, remission of sins and eternal life – a faint and fading echo of his lifelong interest in all things theological. But when Prince Charles arrived, his father was already beyond speech and unable to deliver the last message he had intended. Upon hearing of his imminent death, James had shown no sign of disquiet. In life, of course, he had been prey to every conceivable apprehension, but the king, whose fear of shadows had played such a part in shaping both the man and his rule, was stalwart, it seems, when the shadow of death itself finally descended. It did so shortly before noon on Sunday 27 March at Theobalds – far from his Scottish homeland. He was 58 years old, and for only one of those years, as a cradled infant, he had not borne the heavy burden of a royal crown.

19 ❦ Ruler of Three Kingdoms

'This I must say for Scotland. Here I sit and governe it with my Pen, I write and it is done, and by a Clearke of the Councell I governe Scotland now, which others could not do by the sword.'

James I to the English Parliament, 1607

Some twenty-six years before his death, when the Crowns of England and Ireland were still by no means guaranteed him, James had earnestly urged his heir 'once in three yeares to visit all your kingdomes', and in the early months after his succession to the English throne, this precept appears to have remained fixed in his thinking. In 1603, indeed, he had left his homeland amid farewells rather than goodbyes, and in August of the same year negotiated the purchase of the manor of Southwell from the Archbishop of York, making it clear that he required a half-way hunting and resting spot on his regular journeys north. Yet within a year of his accession, the postal service to Edinburgh had been greatly improved by proclamation, and thereafter some sixty royal letters a year, laden with directives, inquiries, exhortations and admonitions, were soon being diligently dispatched along the rugged Great North Road. Ruling a far-off land that was now inclined to peace did not, it seems, entail the king's personal presence in the way that he himself had envisaged, though the Scottish council register leaves no doubt of James's ongoing absorption in Scottish affairs. Even with the passing of the years, moreover, as his councillors became more and more adept at tempering or blunting his less judicious instructions, they continued to do so under close supervision and in their sovereign's best interest. For, as the Earl of Mar told James's successor in 1626, 'a hundred times your worthy father has sent down directions to us which we have stayed, and he has given us thanks for it when we have informed him of the truth'.

Certainly, upon his arrival in London in 1603, James had no intention of appointing a Lord Deputy for his native realm, though his need for worthy assistants remained paramount. At first, his right-hand man was Alexander Seton, Earl of Dunfermline, who had served as one of his cost-cutting 'Octavians' in 1596, though when faced with the revival of Presbyterian opposition in 1606, James duly opted for the firmer hand of George Home, Lord Treasurer of Scotland from 1601 and later Earl of Dunbar. By travelling between the English capital and Edinburgh at least once a year, and attending the king on his summer hunting expeditions, Home kept his master closely apprised of events north of the Border, regardless of the personal inconvenience and tedium that the royal passion for 'sport' imposed upon him. Ultimately, such distractions would be remedied by tireless effort and clarity of purpose, as the Scottish privy council became under his guidance a loyal, cohesive and potent instrument of centralised control. Indeed, until his death in 1611, Home remained the lynchpin of the king's avowed policy of maintaining an integral political connection between his two kingdoms. And the reinstatement of the Earl of Dunfermline thereafter did nothing to undermine the ongoing process of consolidation. On the contrary, James could not have been more fortunate in enjoying the services of two such talented and selfless assistants, as he demonstrated the art of absentee kingship with a degree of efficiency and finesse he would rarely achieve in England itself.

To its very great credit, the Scottish Privy Council, dominated as it was by a dedicated core of office holders, not only maintained but extended the ambit of royal control. On the one hand, laws imposing heavy penalties for 'the ungodly and barbarous and brutal custom of deadly feuds' were strikingly affirmed in 1613 by the execution of Lord John Maxwell after the murder of the Laird of Johnstone who had been slain by a gunshot to the back some five years earlier. Border raiding, too, declined as James strove 'utterlie to extinguishe as well the name as substance of the bordouris' in an effort to create a peaceful region of 'middle shires'. Dunbar's influence as a Borderer himself proved particularly invaluable in this respect, and in 1605 a joint Anglo-Scottish commission was established to stabilise the six Border counties, employing a small cavalry force which was ultimately dissolved in 1621 as a result of Cranfield's economies. Meanwhile, in an attempt to add teeth to his general policy of pacification, James also determined to introduce Justices of Peace on the English model, though by the time of his death they were still present in less than a quarter of Scottish territory.

As James governed from London, there were further efforts, too, to extend the sway of central authority in the Western Isles. In 1608 an expedition under the command of Lord Ochiltree, which had been dispatched to collect royal rents, resulted in the peaceful apprehension of a number of Highland chiefs, after which the Scottish council pursued a policy of co-operation encapsulated in the Statutes of Iona, whereby the chiefs' authority over their followers was recognised in return for an agreement that they would act as agents of royal jurisdiction within their domains. Restrictions on alcohol and the size of lords' households further undermined the time-honoured Gaelic pastime of fighting and feasting, and, most importantly of all for the longer term, the same lords were not only encouraged to abandon their residual Catholicism for the Protestant Kirk, but to educate their eldest sons in Lowland schools. The influx of Gaelic-speaking Protestant clergy, who made a reality of the parish system and turned it into a powerful agent of social order, was merely one more factor assisting the crucial process of Scottish state building, which had still been very much a work in progress when James first ventured south in 1603.

Only on Orkney, in fact, where sheer distance from Edinburgh allowed Earl Patrick, a distant royal cousin, to rule as a princeling, was there determined resistance to the Scottish privy council. After disregarding the Statutes of Iona, the earl was soon at odds, too, with Bishop James Law, a commissioner for the Northern Isles since 1610 who became a royal revenue collector in 1612. Ultimately, however, even 'Black Patie' would find himself bridled by the hangman's noose in 1615, after a brief attempt at rebellion, which was systematically crushed by the Earl of Caithness and followed by the earldom of Orkney's retention by the Crown. When, moreover, Caithness fell into debt and contemptuously disregarded the Edinburgh legal proceedings brought by his creditors, he too was driven into exile by the Scottish council in 1623.

Such victories were not, it is true, achieved without cost. Certainly, the last years of James's reign witnessed the onset of autocratic tendencies that boded ill for the future. In particular, the Five Articles of Perth, introduced in 1617 and forced through Parliament in 1621, were a direct affront to religious feeling in the king's homeland. 'I am ever for the medium in every thing', James had professed characteristically in 1607. 'Between foolish rashness and extreme length there is a middle way.' But the understanding of Scottish problems which had done so much to compensate for the potential difficulties of absentee rule was gradually deserting him in his declining years. As early as 1607, in fact, James was remarking of his countrymen north of the Border how 'I doe not already know the one halfe of them by face, most of the youth now being risen up to be men, who were but children when I was there'. And by 1621 a new political divide had emerged in the king's northern Parliament after the Earl of Rothes and Lord Balmerino, among others, found their complaints against the Five Articles and the effects of heavy taxation blocked by an unsympathetic phalanx of royal appointees.

In the third and most troubled of his kingdoms, meanwhile, James had neither personal links nor any trace of direct experience to guide him. At the time of his succession, Ireland lay stricken and seething, with links to Rome as strong as ever and any prospect of economic recovery rendered all the more unlikely by a grievous debasement of the currency that had fractured commerce and impoverished the populace. So when news of Elizabeth I's death reached Waterford, Cork and Clonmel, Ireland's principal towns, the resulting euphoria had been palpable. The books of Protestant clergymen were, one Irish Jesuit reported, summarily burned 'and the ministers themselves hunted away', whereupon 'masses and processions were celebrated as frequently and upon as grand a scale as in Rome itself'. In the wake of the queen's death, moreover, Irish men and women had continued to nurture exaggerated hopes of her prospective successor who was, of course, himself the son of a Catholic martyr and king of a land which during the 1560s and 1590s had supplied some 25,000 fearsome 'gallowglass' mercenaries to serve across the Irish Sea in the conflict against English expansionism.

By June 1605, in fact, fervent calls for freedom of worship had been roundly thwarted by a royal proclamation in which James made clear that he would never 'confirm the hopes of any creatures that they should ever have from him any toleration to exercise any religion than that which is agreeable to God's word and is established by the laws of the realm'. Yet James's other early actions remained laudable, since he knew full well that his orders for Catholic priests to leave his realms were nowhere more unenforceable than in Ireland where 'every town, hamlet and house was to them a sanctuary', and in practice gave scant encouragement to those elements in the Dublin government favouring wholesale repression. 'He would much rejoice,' he professed, 'if the Irish Catholics would conform themselves to his religion, yet he would not force them to forsake their own.' And in the meantime there was a broader attempt at Anglo-Irish reconciliation, delivered by Elizabeth's victorious general Lord Mountjoy who restored the rebel Earl of Tyrone to his lands and bestowed upon his ally, Rory O'Donnell, the earldom of Tyrconnell in September 1603. More importantly still, perhaps, James had promptly decided to override Cecil's worries about a silver shortage, to upgrade the Irish coinage in the same month. For the first time, therefore, a fixed rate of exchange was established, with the result that English coinage was soon circulating freely in former enemy territory and facilitating a marked improvement in both internal and external trade.

Once more, predictably, the king's success was by no means unalloyed. Sir Arthur Chichester, who became Lord Deputy in 1604, disagreed profoundly, for example, with Mountjoy's earlier moderation and opted instead for colonisation. Despising the Irish as 'beasts in the shape of men', he sought, it seems, to 'civilise' the land by demolishing the local power bases of Tyrone and Tyrconnell, and encouraging the plantation of Protestant settlers. The result was the so-called 'flight of the earls' in 1607, and the clumsy application of a policy of settlement that James had previously applied with limited success in his own Scottish Isles. Despite a substantial flow of English and, above all, Scottish tenant farmers into Ulster from 1609 onwards, in which James took a close personal interest, numbers were never sufficient to corral the native Irish into restricted areas which could be easily controlled, and the king's first practical project to push forward his ideal of a 'greater Britain' succeeded only in creating a hostile class of Catholic under-tenants who remained cheaper for the settlers to employ than further migrants. Thus were the seeds of a disastrous future conflict sown.

In the meantime, the central problem of Ireland, as far as the English government was concerned, remained finance. Between 1604 and 1619, the annual subsidy sent from England stood at over £47,000 and Cranfield's boast to Buckingham that he would make the land self-sufficient was never made good. On the contrary, the English Parliament of 1622 attacked corruption and royal prodigality in James's third kingdom, and when Viscount Falkland became Lord Deputy in 1622, and opted to enforce the recusancy laws as a means of raising money, the threat to internal stability, fuelled by declining relations with Spain, escalated ominously. 'Ireland is such,' wrote the Venetian ambassador in the year of Falkland's appointment, 'that it would be better for the king if it did not exist and the sea alone rolled there.' And a month before James's death, in spite of his personal intervention to curtail the Dublin government's escalation of religious persecution, John Chamberlain reflected London opinion all too aptly by describing Ireland as 'tickle and ready to revolt'.

Yet a commission appointed to assess the state of the country in 1622 still made clear the changes of James's reign. English law was steadily replacing Irish, English counties had been introduced as units of local government, and the merchant companies of the City of London were building new ports at Derry and Coleraine. And although the commission's report was never published, largely because of its criticisms of Buckingham's ravenously self-interested clients, there was other evidence, too, of a genuine Jacobean achievement in Ireland. 'The love of money,' observed Oliver St John, Chichester's replacement as Lord Deputy in 1615, 'will sooner effect civility than any other persuasion whatsoever.' And where famine had stalked the country during the 1590s, Irish towns now enjoyed greater prosperity than for centuries, as significant communities of artisans, merchants and moneylenders took root, and itinerant pedlars forged networks of internal trade between urban centres and the surrounding countryside. Through wardships and intermarriage, meanwhile, many leading families such as the Fitzgerald earls of Kildare acquired English educations and English wives, as well as links with Scottish noble families.

Overall, the administration of an imperial monarchy encompassing three kingdoms inevitably entailed considerable structural tensions at the heart of government. Resentment at the king's absence, problems over the disposal of offices and the sharing of war costs, conflicts over trade and colonies, foreign intervention and above all religion were all, in fact, ongoing problems for James to grapple with. Some, indeed, played no small part in triggering the civil war that ultimately consumed his heir and may yet, four centuries later, put paid to his unifying aspirations once and for all. For if conflicts of faith have thankfully receded, modern-day resentment at centralised control from long distance and antagonism over fiscal propriety now rankle with new vigour. Under such circumstances, James's absentee kingship of his Gaelic realms may well seem increasingly impressive across the centuries, though there is still, perhaps, no small irony in this, since it was precisely because he ruled his outlying kingdoms from afar that those personal indiscretions and inadequacies, frequently so damaging to his English dealings, were unable to compromise his nobler, wiser aspirations. If England, in truth, never consistently warmed to its resident Scottish king, his fellow countrymen and their Irish counterparts experienced no few benefits in his absence. And it remains one of the more curious features of British history that the descendants of 'the king's barbarians' – those savage Irish and brutish Highlanders whom he equally despised – would become, in the fullness of time, the most loyal supporters of his Catholic grandson and that grandson's ill-starred heirs.

Source Notes and Bibliographical Information

Contemporary, near-contemporary and later printed material

Though they must be treated with caution, the accounts of those contemporaries who boasted a personal knowledge of James VI and I remain the starting-point for any study of the man and ruler. *The Court and Character of King James: written and taken by Sir Anthony Weldon, being an eye and eare witnesse* which was published in 1650 and reprinted in 1651 under the title *Truth brought to Light*, is still the classic account and essential reading for any general student of the reign wishing to return to primary sources. It was answered in a work usually attributed to Thomas Sanderson, entitled *Aulicus Coquinariae*, and both the original book and Sanderson's response were reprinted in *The Secret History of the Court of King James* (Edinburgh, 1811, two vols), which was edited by Sir Walter Scott and went on to create what has become the traditional perspective on England's first Stuart monarch. Other famous accounts include M. de Fontenay's, which is to be found in *Calendar of State Papers relating to Scotland and Mary Queen of Scots, 1547–1603* (Edinburgh, 1913, vol. 7), ed. W. K. Boyd, and Arthur Wilson's *The History of Great Britain, being the Life and Reign of King James the First* (London, 1653). Nicolo Molin's description, meanwhile, which was presented to the Venetian government in 1607, is located in ed. H.F. Brown, *Calendar of State Papers and Manuscripts Relating to English Affairs, existing in the archives and collections of Venice, and in other libraries of Northern Italy*, vol. 10, (London, 1900), and there is also the well-known summary provided by Sir John Oglander in *A Royalist's Notebook: The Commonplace Book of Sir John Oglander of Nunwell, 1622–1652*, ed. F. M. Bamford (London, 1936).

The general reader wishing to broaden his or her understanding may also wish to consult the contemporary material available in: ed. G.P.V. Akrigg *The Letters of King James VI and I* (University of California Press, 1984);

ed. R. Ashton, *James I by his Contemporaries* (London, 1969); and ed. J.R. Tanner, *Constitutional Documents of the Reign of James I AD 1603–1625* with an historical commentary (Cambridge University Press, 1930).

Other relevant sources for the reign

Baker, L. M. ed., *The Letters of Elizabeth Queen of Bohemia* (London, 1953).

Bannatyne, R., *Journal of the Transactions in Scotland, during the contest between the Adherents of Queen Mary, and those of her son* (Edinburgh, 1806).

Bannatyne, R., *Memorials of Transactions in Scotland, AD MDLXIX – AD MLXXIII* (Bannatyne Club, Edinburgh, 1836).

Barlow, William, *The summe and substance of the conference, which it pleased his majestie to have with the lords, bishops and other clergie, at Hampton Court* (London, 1604).

Bell, R. ed., *Extract from the Despatches of M. Courcelles, French Ambassador at the Court of Scotland MDLXXXVI – MDLXXXVII* (Bannatyne Club, Edinburgh, 1828).

Bowes, Robert, *The Correspondence of Sir Robert Bowes, Esquire* (Surtees Society, 1842).

Bruce, J. ed., *Correspondence of King James VI of Scotland with Sir Robert Cecil and others in England* (Camden Society, 1856).

Bruce, J. ed., *Letters of Queen Elizabeth and King James VI of Scotland* (Camden Society, 1849) .

Buchanan, George, *Opera Omnia* ed. T. Ruddimann, 2 vols (Edinburgh, 1715).

Buchanan, George, *The Powers of the Crown in Scotland*, trans. C. F. Arrowood (University of Texas Press, 1949).

Calderwood, David, *A History of the Kirk of Scotland*, ed. T. Thomson (8 vols), (Edinburgh, 1842 (first published 1678)) .

Chamberlain, John, *The Letters of John Chamberlain*, ed. N. E. McClure, 2 vols (Memoirs of the American Philosphical Society, xii, Philadelphia, 1939).

D'Ewes, Simonds, *The Autobiography and Correspondence of Sir Simonds D'Ewes, Bart., during the reigns of James I and Charles I* (London, 1845).

Eglisham, George, *The Fore-runner of Revenge, Being Two Petitions: The one To the Kings most Excellent Majesty, the other to the most Honourable*

Houses of Parliament. Wherein is expressed divers actions of the late Earle of Buckingham; especially concerning the death of King James, and the Marquesse Hamelton, supposed by Poyson (London, 1642).

Ellis, H. ed., *Original Letters Illustrative of English History*, first series, 3 vols (London, 1825).

Ellis, H. ed., *Original Letters Illustrative of English History*, third series., 4 vols (London, 1846).

Foster, E. R. ed., *Proceedings in Parliament 1610* (Yale University Press, 1966).

Goodman, Godfrey, *The Court of King James*, ed. J. S. Brewer, 2 vols (London 1839).

Green, M. A. E. ed., *Calendar of State Papers, Domestic Series of the Reign of James I:* 1603–1610, 1611–1618, 1619–1623, 1623–1625 with Addenda 1603–1625 (London, 1857–1859).

Harington, John, *Nugae Antiquae: being a miscellaneous collection of original papers*, 2 vols, ed. T Park (London, 1804).

Historical Manuscripts Commission, *Calendar of the Manuscripts of the Most Honourable Marquess of Salisbury preserved at Hatfield House, Hertfordshire* (London, 1883–1965).

Hyde, Edward, Earl of Clarendon, *The History of the Rebellion and Civil Wars in England begun in the year 1641*, ed. W Dunn Macray, 6 vols (Oxford, 1888).

Laing, D. ed., *Original Letters relating to the Ecclesiastical Affairs of Scotland*, 2 vols (Ballatyne Club, Edinburgh, 1851).

Maidment, J. ed., *Letters and state papers during the reign of King James the Sixth, chiefly taken from manuscript collection of Sir James Balfour of Denmyln* (Edinburgh, 1838).

Mayerne, Theodore Turquet de, *Opera Medica* … ed. J. Brown (London, 1703).

Melvill, James, *The Autobiography and Diary of Mr James Melvill … with a Continuation of the Diary*, ed. Robert Pitcairn, 2 vols (Wodrow Society, Edinburgh, 1842).

Melville of Halhill, Sir James, *Memoirs of his Own Life*, ed. T. Thomson (Bannatyne Club, 1827).

Moysie, David, Memoirs of the Affairs of Scotland, 1577–1603, ed. J. Dennistoun, (Edinburgh, 1830).

Nau, Claude, *The History of Mary Stewart from the Murder of Riccio until her Flight into England*, ed. J. Stevenson (Edinburgh, 1883).

Nicholls, E., *Proceedings and Debates in the House of Commons in 1620 and 1621*, 2 vols (Oxford, 1776).

Nichols, J., *The Progresses, Processions and Magnificent Festivities of King James I*, 4 vols (London, 1828).

Normand, L. and Roberts, G. eds, *Witchcraft in Early Modern Scotland: James VI's Demonology and the North Berwick Witches* (University of Exeter, 2000).

Sawyer, E. ed., *Memorials of Affairs of State in the Reigns of Q. Elizabeth and K. James I. Collected (chiefly) from the original papers of the right honourable Sir Ralph Winwood*, 3 vols (London, 1725).

Spottiswoode, John, *The History of the Church and State of Scotland*, 4th ed. (London, 1677).

Stevenson, J, ed., *Correspondence of Robert Bowes, the ambassador of Queen Elizabeth in the court of Scotland*, Surtees Society (1842).

Strickland, A. ed., *Letters of Mary Queen of Scots* (London, 1844).

Thomson, T. ed., *A Diurnal of Remarkable Occurents that have passed within the Country of Scotland since the death of King James the Fourth till the year MDLXXV* (Bannatyne Club, Edinburgh, 1833).

Wilbraham, Roger, *The Journal of Sir Roger Wilbraham*, ed. H. S. Scott in *The Camden Society*, Volume the Tenth (London, 1902).

Wotton, Henry, *Letters of Sir Henry Wotton to Sir Edmund Bacon* (London, 1661).

Wotton, Henry, *The Life and Letters of Sir Henry Wotton*, ed. L. P. Smith, 2 vols (Oxford, 1907).

Modern biographies

The most recent full-length biographies are A. Stewart, *The Cradle King: A Life of James I* (London, 2003) and the more concise P. Croft, *King James* (Basingstoke, 2003). For a more thematic approach, there is also M. Lee, Jr, *Great Britain's Solomon: James VI and I in his Three Kingdoms* (University of Illinois Press, 1990) and R. Lockyer, *James VI and I* (Harlow, 1998). Three slightly older works by Caroline Bingham remain valuable: *James VI of Scotland* (London, 1979); *James I of England* (London, 1981); *The Making of a King: The Early Years of James VI and I* (London, 1968). Nor are two other biographies, which are now considered largely out-of-date, without interest: D.H. Willson, *King James VI and I* (London, 1956) and W. McElwee, *The*

Wisest Fool in Christendom: The Reign of James VI and I (New York, 1958). Mention should be made too of the following important article: J. Wormald, 'James VI and I: Two Kings or One', *History*, 68 (1983).

Modern works relating to the rule of James VI in Scotland, 1567–1603

Brown, K.M and MacDonald, A.R. eds, *The History of the Scottish Parliament, Volume 3: Parliament in Context: 1235–1707* (Edinburgh, 2010).

Brown, K.M. and Mann, A.J., eds, *The History of the Scottish Parliament, Volume 2: Parliament and Politics, 1567–1707*.

Brown, K.M. and Tanner, R.J., eds, *The History of the Scottish Parliament, Volume 1: Parliament and Politics, 1235–1560* (Edinburgh, 2004).

Brown, K.M., *Kingdom or Province? Scotland and the Regal Union 1603–1715* (Basingstoke, 1992) .

Brown, K.M., *Bloodfeud in Scotland, 1573–1625* (Edinburgh, 1986).

Burns, J.H., *The True Law of Kingship: Concepts of Monarchy in Early Modern Scotland* (Oxford, 1996).

Donaldson, G., *Scotland, James V to James VII* (Edinburgh, 1965).

Duncan, A.A.M 'The early parliaments of Scotland', *Scottish Historical Review*, 15 (1966).

Goodare, J., *The Government of Scotland, 1560–1625* (Oxford, 2004).

Hewitt, G.R., *Scotland Under Morton 1572–80* (Edinburgh, 1982).

Jones, C., ed., *The Scots and Parliament: Parliamentary History*, (Edinburgh, 1996).

Lang, A., *James VI and the Gowrie Mystery* (London, 1902).

Law, T.G., 'The Spanish Blanks and the Catholic Earls, 1592–1594', *Scottish Review* 22 (1893).

Lee, M., Jr, *Government by Pen: Scotland under James VI and I* (University of Illinois Press, 1980).

Lee, M., Jr, *John Maitland of Thirlestane and the Foundation of the Stewart Despotism in Scotland* (Princeton University Press, 1959).

Lynch, M., *Scotland: A New History* (Edinburgh, 1991).

MacDonald, A.R. 'Deliberative processes in the Scottish Parliament before 1639: multi-cameralism and the Lords of the Articles', *Scottish Historical Review*, 81 (2002).

MacDonald, A.R., *The Jacobean Kirk, 1567–1625: Sovereignty, Polity and Liturgy* (Aldershot, 1998).

Macinnes, A.I., *Union and Empire; The Making of the United Kingdom in 1707* (Cambridge University Press, 2007).

Mason, R.A., 'Rex Stoicus: George Buchanan, James VI and the Scottish Polity' in Dwyer, J., Mason, R.A. and Murdoch, A. eds, *New Perspectives on the Politics and Culture of Early Modern Scotland* (Edinburgh, 1982).

Mason, R.A., ed., *Scots and Britons: Scottish Political Thought and the Union of 1603* (Cambridge University Press, 1994).

Rait, R.S., *The Parliament of Scotland* (Glasgow, 1924), passim.

Riley, P.W.J., *The Union of Scotland and England* (Manchester, 1978).

Robertson, W., *The History of Scotland, during the Reigns of Queen Mary and James VI till his Accession to the Crown of England*, 2 vols, (London, 1759).

Stevenson, D., *Scotland's Last Royal Wedding: The Marriage of James VI and Anne of Denmark* (Edinburgh, 1997).

Tanner, R.J., *The Late Medieval Scottish Parliament* (East Linton, 2001).

Whatley, C.A., *The Scots and the Union* (Edinburgh, 2006).

Wormald, J., *Court, King and Community: Scotland, 1470–1625* (London, 1981).

Modern works relating to the rule of James I in England, 1603–1625

Akrigg, G.P.V., *Jacobean Pageant* (Harvard University Press, 1962).

Barrol, L., *Anna of Denmark, Queen of England: A Cultural Biography* (University of Philadelphia Press, 2001).

Bellany, A., *The Politics of Court Scandal in Early Modern England: News, Culture and the Overbury Affair, 1603–1660* (Cambridge University Press, 2001).

Bergeron, D., *King James and Letters of Homoerotic Desire* (University of Iowa Press, 1991).

Bingham, C., *Darnley: A Life of Henry Stuart, Lord Darnley Consort of Mary Queen of Scots* (London, 1995).

Birch T., *The Life of Henry Prince of Wales, Eldest Son of King James I* (London, 1760).

Borman, T., *Witches: James I and the English Witch Hunts* (London, 2014).

Bradshaw, B. and Morrill, J., eds, *The British Problem c.1534–1707: State Formation in the Atlantic Archipelago* (London, 1996).

Bradshaw, B. and Roberts, P., eds, *British Consciousness and Identity: The Making of Britain, 1533–1707* (Cambridge University Press, 1998).

Carter, C. H., 'Gondomar: Ambassador to James I', *Historical Journal* vol. 7 (1964), p.189–208.

Collinson, P., 'The Jacobean Religious Settlement: The Hampton Court Conference' in H. Tomlinson ed., *Before the English Civil War*.

Croft, P., 'Fresh Light on Bate's Case', *Historical Journal* vol. 34 (1991).

Croft, P., 'The Reputation of Robert Cecil: libels, political opinion and popular awareness in the early seventeenth century', *Transactions of the Royal Historical Society*, 6th ser., I (1991), p. 43–69.

Curtis, M., 'The Hampton Court Conference and its Aftermath', *History* vol. 46 (1961), p.1–16.

Cust, C. and Hughes, A., eds, *Conflict in Early Stuart England: Studies in Religion and Politics 1603–1642* (London, 1989).

Daiches, D., *The King James Version of the English Bible* (University of Chicago Press, 1941).

Durston, C., *James I* (London, 1993).

Ellis, S.G. and Barber, S., *Conquest and Union: Fashioning a British State, 1485–1725* (Harlow, 1995).

Fincham, K, *Prelate as Pastor: The Episcopate of James I* (Oxford, 1990).

Fincham, K. and Lake, P., 'The Ecclesiastical Policy of James I', *Journal of British Studies*, vol. 24 (1985).

Fischlin, D., Fortier, M. and Sharpe, K., eds, *Royal Subjects: The Writings of James VI and I* (Detroit, 2002).

Fraser, A, *The Gunpowder Plot: Terror and Faith in 1605* (London, 1996).

Galloway, B.R., and Levack, B.P., *The Jacobean Union: Six Tracts of 1604* (Edinburgh, 1985).

Galloway, B.R., *The Union of England and Scotland, 1603–1608* (Edinburgh, 1986).

Gibbs, P., *King's Favourite: The Love Story of Robert Carr and Lady Essex* (London, 1909).

Goodacre, G., and Lynch, M., eds, *The Reign of James VI* (East Linton, 2000).

Hammer, P.E.J., *The Polarisation of Elizabeth Politics: The Political Career of Robert Devereux, 2nd Earl of Essex, 1585–1597* (Cambridge University Press, 1999).

Harris, T., *Rebellion: Britain's First Stuart Kings, 1567–1642* (Oxford, 2013).

Haynes, A., *The Gunpowder Plot: Faith in Rebellion* (Stroud, 1994).

Jansson, M., *Proceedings in Parliament, 1614* (University of Philadelphia, 1988).

Larkin, J.F. and Hughes, P.L., *Stuart Royal Proclamations: Royal Proclamations of King James I, 1603–1625* (Oxford, 1973).

Larner, C., *Enemies of God: The Witch-Hunt in Scotland* (London, 1981).

Lindley, D., *The Trials of Frances Howard: Fact and Fiction at the Court of King James* (London, 1993).

Lindquist, E., 'The Failure of the Great Contract', *Journal of Modern History* vol. 57 (1985).

Loades, D., *The Cecils: Privilege and power behind the throne* (The National Archives, 2009)

Lockyer, R., Buckingham, *The Life and Political Career of George Villiers, First Duke of Buckingham 1592–1628* (London and New York, 1981).

Loomie, A.J., *Spain and the Early Stuarts, 1585–1655* (Aldershot, 1996).

McFarlane, I.D., *Buchanan* (London, 1981).

Moodie, T.W., Martin, F.-X. and Byrne, F.J., eds, *A New History of Ireland vol. 3: Early Modern Ireland 1534–1691* (Oxford, 1991).

Newton, D., *The Making of the Jacobean Regime: James VI and I and the Government of England, 1603–1605* (Woodbridge, 2005).

Nicholls, M. and Williams, P., *Sir Walter Raleigh: in Life and Legend* (London, 2011).

Nicholls, M., *Investigating Gunpowder Plot* (Manchester University Press, 1991).

Nicholson, N., *When God Spoke English: The Making of the King James Bible* (London, 2011).

Opfell, O., *The King James Bible Translators* (Jefferson, 1982).

Parry, G., *The Golden Age Restored: The Culture of the Jacobean Court* (Manchester, 1981).

Patterson, W.B., *King James and the Reunion of Christendom* (Cambridge University Press, 1997).

Pawlisch, H.S., *Sir John Davies and the Conquest of Ireland: A Study in Legal Imperialism* (Cambridge University Press, 1985).

Peck, L.L., ed., *The Mental World of the Jacobean Court* (Cambridge University Press, 1991).

Peck, L.L., *Court Patronage and Corruption in Early Stuart England* (Routledge, 1993).

Peck, L.L., *Northampton: Patronage and Policy at the Court of James I* (London, 1982).

Perceval-Maxwell, M., 'Ireland and the Monarchy in the Early Stuart Multiple Kingdom', *Historical Journal* vol. 34, 1991.

Perceval-Maxwell, M., *The Scottish Migration to Ulster in the Reign of James I* (London, 1993).

Prestwich, M., *Cranfield: Politics and Profits under the Early Stuarts* (Oxford, 1966).

Rait, R. S. and Cameron, A. I., *King James's Secret: Negotiations Between Elizabeth and James I. Relating to the Execution of Mary Queen of Scots, From the Warrender Papers* (London, 1927).

Rees, G. and Wakely, M., *Publishing, Politics and Culture: The King's Printers in the Reign of James I and VI* (Oxford, 2009).

Rhodes, N., Richards, J. and Marshall, J., *King James I/VI: Selected Writings* (Farnham, 2003).

Rickard, *Authorship and Authority: The Writings of James VI and I* (Manchester University Press, 2012).

Ruigh, R.E., *The Parliament of 1624: Politics and Foreign Policy* (Harvard University Press, 1971).

Russell, C., *King James VI/I and his English Parliaments*, eds Cust, R. and Thrush, E. (Oxford, 2011).

Russell, C., *Parliaments and English Politics, 1621–1629* (Oxford, 1979).

Seddon, P.R., 'Robert Carr, Earl of Somerset', *Renaissance and Modern Studies*, vol. 14 (1970), p. 48–68.

Sharpe, K., *Politics and Ideas in Early Stuart England: Essays and Studies* (New York, 1989).

Smith, A.G.R., *The Reign of James VI and I* (Basingstoke, 1973).

Somerset, A., *Unnatural Murder: Poison at the Court of James I* (London, 1998).

Sommerville, J.P., *King James VI and I: Political Writings* (Cambridge University Press, 1994).

Stewart, A., 'Boys' Buttocks Revisited: James VI and I and the Myth of the Sovereign Schoolmaster', in *Sodomy in Early Modern Europe*, ed. T. Betteridge (Manchester University Press, 2002).

Strong, R., *Henry, Prince of Wales and England's Lost Renaissance* (London, 1986).

Treadwell, V., *Buckingham and Ireland, 1616–1628* (Dublin, 1998).

Welsby, P., *George Abbot* (London, 1962).

Williams, E.C., *Anne of Denmark: Wife of James VI of Scotland: James I of England* (London, 1971).

Young, M.B., *James VI and the History of Homosexuality* (Basingstoke, 2000).

Zaller, R., *The Parliament of 1621: A Study in Constitutional Conflict* (University of California Press, 1971)

Author's Note

Biographers old and new, academic and otherwise, have been instrumental in shaping this book. Its earliest influences were David Harris Willson, George Philip Vernon Akrigg, William McElwee and Caroline Bingham. Later, as perspectives on its central character evolved, the book drew added inspiration from the work of a long list of others, but most notably Maurice Lee, Jr.

No writer is an island, and least of all this one. My thanks, therefore, are due to all those who have paved the way in their writings, as well as the smaller group of people who have supported me more personally in my efforts. In this latter respect, the help and encouragement of Mark Beynon, Juanita Hall and the team at The History Press has been unstinting, while Barbara, my wife, has continued throughout to hearten, uplift and cheer. To all concerned, I raise my glass.

Index

Index

Index